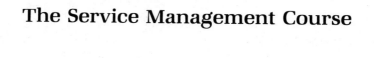

The Service Management Course

The Service Management Course

◆

Cases and Readings

W. EARL SASSER, JR.
CHRISTOPHER W. L. HART
JAMES L. HESKETT

HD
9980.5
.S27
1991

THE FREE PRESS
A Division of Macmillan, Inc.
NEW YORK
Maxwell Macmillan Canada
TORONTO
Maxwell Macmillan International
NEW YORK   OXFORD   SINGAPORE   SYDNEY

The Free Press
A Division of Macmillan, Inc.
866 Third Avenue, New York, N.Y. 10022

Maxwell Macmillan Canada, Inc.
1200 Eglinton Avenue East
Suite 200
Don Mills, Ontario M3C 3N1

Macmillan, Inc. is part of the Maxwell Communication Group of Companies.

Printed in the United States of America

printing number
1   2   3   4   5   6   7   8   9   10

Library of Congress Cataloging-in-Publication Data

Sasser, W. Earl.
    The service management course: cases and readings / W. Earl
Sasser, Jr., Christopher W. L. Hart, James L. Heskett.
        p.   cm.
    ISBN 0-02-914091-9
    1. Service industries—Management—Case studies.   I. Hart,
Christopher W. L.   II. Heskett, James L.   III. Title.
HD9980.5.S27   1991
658—dc20   91-6933
                                                                 CIP

Contents

Preface

In 1972, one of us took on the task of designing a graduate level course which would, two years later, be introduced as Management of Service Operations. At the time, there were few written materials suitable for use in such a course, particularly one which would make extensive use of problem case materials. Although it is hard to believe now, there were no relevant examples of courses with such an orientation at other schools. Many of the early materials were obtained from former students who were starting up service businesses. Fortunately, students electing the course sensed the excitement of the service industries and the great opportunities they represented. Within a short time, the course became one of the most popular of all electives in the Harvard Business School MBA program.

Later, a popular course in Services Marketing was also developed. It soon became clear, however, that the dividing line between service operations and marketing was a fine one indeed. It was impossible to discuss operating problems without directing attention to operating people who were also responsible for delivering the marketing promise, or to debate marketing alternatives without considering the implications for operations. And both courses spent significant amounts of time addressing the management of human resources.

In 1983, the two course offerings were merged into one, Service Management. Materials from both courses, by now reflecting extensive case development effort that had been carried out in some of the foremost service companies, were chosen for continued use. And new materials were prepared annually. The result is presented in this book.

Cases and readings are organized around the fourteen topics making up a companion volume, *Service Breakthroughs: Changing the Rules of the Game.* However, the material presented here is intended to stand alone, providing the basis for a course that can be organized in any number of ways. Each topic is introduced with comments and questions intended to suggest avenues for exploring the associated material.

ix

Of particular interest to service company executives may be the fact that a subset of four of these cases, the Paul Revere Insurance Company (A), (B), and (C) and the Malcolm Baldrige National Quality Award, have been used to introduce service-producing companies to the task of preparing for competition for the Award. The materials raise significant questions for everyone about the components of quality in services and how they are achieved.

We are indebted to several current and former colleagues who have written or supervised the preparation of some of the case materials in this book. They include Leonard Schlesinger, who supplied materials and ideas for the Au Bon Pain case and supervised the writing of The Oakland A's-1989, and the Ford Motor Company: Dealer Sales and Service cases. Walter J. Salmon supervised the development of the Nordstrom case. The OTISLINE case was prepared under the supervision of Warren McFarlan and the Mrs. Fields Cookies case was written under the supervision of James I. Cash. Rosabeth Moss Kanter supervised the preparation of the Banc One Corporation 1989 case. David Maister prepared the Rural/Metro Fire Department; Bradford Schools; and University Health Services: Walk-In Clinic cases. Christopher Lovelock supervised the preparation of the Southwest Airlines (A) case. Sandra Vandermerwe authored Scandinavian Airlines System SAS (A). And Therese Flaherty wrote the Goldome Realty Credit Corporation case.

Our work is a reflection of those who have taught with us since the initial course was first organized. They include the late D. Daryl Wyckoff, Paul Olsen, David Maister, Christopher Lovelock, William Fulmer, and Leonard Schlesinger. We thank all of them for their ideas and association.

Service Management has been fun to organize and teach as a course. Our students tell us that it has been equally fun to study, and even more fun to put into practice. That's the ultimate payoff and one for which this book is ultimately intended.

> W. Earl Sasser, Jr.
> Christopher W. L. Hart
> James L. Heskett

1

◆

Creating Breakthrough Services

In every industry, one or two organizations excel in relation to their competitors. This is true in services as well as manufacturing. We call them breakthrough services. Shouldice Hospital Limited doesn't fit our expectations of what hospitals are like. And Benihana of Tokyo influenced an entire generation of restaurants. In thinking about these companies, ask yourself questions that will: (1) enable you to understand them better in a general way and (2) help you in responding to specific demands being placed on managers in each situation. What makes these organizations different from their competitors? How successful are they? How, if at all, have they achieved this success? How do they achieve value in what they do for their customers? What do these organizations, different as their services may be, have in common? How likely are they to sustain their competitive advantage and overcome their shortcomings?

These questions are important for establishing a general understanding of service businesses in general and in setting the stage for addressing specific issues posed in each case. Given what you have just concluded about these organizations, how should Dr. Byrnes Shouldice go about expanding the capacity of his hospital? What are the strengths and weaknesses of each proposed alternative? If you were in his position, how would you implement the course of action you propose?

In comparing Benihana's cost profile with restaurants in general, as shown in the Benihana of Tokyo case, how do you explain the differences? Is the competitive advantage reflected here sustainable? As the company expands the number of its outlets, should it seriously consider franchising? Why? What trends would you suggest that Rocky Aoki track carefully in plotting the future strategy for his company?

Once you have addressed these specific questions, return once again to the more general questions posed in the first paragraph. Your responses may contain the seeds of your own breakthrough service concept.

Shouldice Hospital Limited

Two shadowy figures, enrobed and in slippers, walked slowly down the semi-darkened hall of the Shouldice Hospital. They didn't notice Alan O'Dell, the hospital administrator, and his guest, who had just emerged from the basement boiler room on a tour of the facility. Once they were out of earshot, O'Dell remarked good naturedly, "By the way they act, you'd think our patients own this place. And while they're here, in a way they do."

Following a visit to the five operating rooms, also located on the first of three levels, O'Dell and his visitor once again encountered the same pair of patients still engrossed in discussing their hernia operations, which had been performed the previous morning.

HISTORY

Born on a farm in Bruce County, Ontario, Dr. Earle Shouldice, who was to found the hospital bearing his name, first displayed his interest in medical research at the age of 12. He performed a postmortem on a calf that, he discovered, had died from an intestinal obstruction. After a year of following the wishes of his parents that he study for the ministry, Shouldice persuaded them to let him enroll in medicine at the University of Toronto.

An attractive brochure that was recently printed, although neither dated nor distributed to prospective patients, described Earle Shouldice as follows:

> While carrying on a private medical and surgical practice in the years between the two World Wars and holding a post as lecturer in anatomy at the University of Toronto, Dr. Shouldice continued to pursue his interest in research. He did pioneer work towards the cure of pernicious anemia, intestinal obstruction, hydrocephalic cases and other areas of advancing medical knowledge.
>
> His interest in early ambulation stemmed, in part, from an operation he performed in 1932 to remove the appendix from a seven-year-old girl and the girl's subsequent refusal to stay quietly in bed. In spite of her activity, no

Professor James L. Heskett prepared this case as a basis for class discussion rather than to illustrate either effective or ineffective handling of an administrative situation. Some of the data in this case are disguised. Copyright © 1983 by the President and Fellows of Harvard College; Harvard Business School case # 683-068 Rev. 6/89.

harm was done, and the experience recalled to the doctor the postoperative actions of animals upon which he had performed surgery. They had all moved about freely with no ill effects. Four years later he was reminded of the child when he allowed washroom privileges immediately following the operations to four men recovering from hernia repair. All had trouble-free recovery.

By the outset of the Second World War in 1940, Shouldice had given extensive thought to several factors that contributed to early ambulation following surgery. Among them were the use of a local anesthetic, the nature of the surgical procedure itself, the design of a facility to encourage movement without unnecessarily causing discomfort, and the postoperative regimen designed and communicated by the medical team. With all of these things in mind, he had begun to develop a surgical technique for repairing hernias[1] that was superior to others. He offered his services in correcting hernias for army inductees who otherwise would not qualify for service. Because hospital beds often were not available, sometimes the surgery took place in the emergency department of the Toronto General Hospital, and the patients were transported later in the day to a medical fraternity where they were cared for by medical students for two or three days.

By the war's end, word of the Shouldice technique had spread sufficiently that 200 civilians had contacted the doctor and were awaiting surgery upon his discharge from the army. Because of the scarcity of hospital beds, particularly for an operation that was considered elective and of relatively low priority, he started his own hospital. Dr. Shouldice's medical license permitted him to operate anywhere, even on a kitchen table, and consequently he received authorization from the provincial government to open his first hospital in a six-room nursing home in downtown Toronto in July 1945. As more and more patients requested operations, Dr. Shouldice extended his facilities by buying a rambling 130-acre estate with a 17,000-square-foot main house in the suburb of Thornhill, 15 miles north of downtown Toronto. Initially, a 36-bed capacity was created in Thornhill, but after some years of planning, a large wing was added to the house to provide a total capacity of 89 beds.

At the time of his death in 1965, Dr. Shouldice's long-time associate, Dr. Nicholas Obney, was named surgeon-in-chief and chairman of the board of

---

1. Most hernias, known as external abdominal hernias, were protrusions of some part of the abdominal contents through a hole or slit in the muscular layers of the abdominal wall which was supposed to contain them. Well over 90% of these hernias occurred in the groin area. Of these, by far the most common were inguinal hernias, many of which were caused by a slight weakness in the muscle layers brought about by the passage of the testicle in male babies through the groin area shortly before birth. Aging also caused inguinal hernias to develop. The other, much less common, external hernias were called "femoral," in which a protrusion appeared in the top inch or so of the thigh. Because of the cause of the affliction, 85% of all hernias occurred in males.

Shouldice Hospital Limited, the corporation formed to operate both the hospital and clinical facilities. Under Dr. Obney's leadership, the volume of activity continued to increase, reaching a total of 6,850 operations in the 1982 calendar year.

THE SHOULDICE METHOD

Only external types of abdominal hernias were repaired at Shouldice Hospital. Internal types, such as hiatus (or diaphragmatic) hernias, were not treated. As a result, most first-time repairs (called primaries) involved straightforward operating procedures that required about 45 minutes. Primaries represented approximately 82% of all operations performed at Shouldice in 1982. The remaining 18% involved patients suffering recurrences of hernias previously repaired elsewhere.[2]

In the Shouldice method, the muscles of the abdominal wall were arranged in three distinct layers, and the opening was repaired—each layer in turn—by overlapping its margins in much the same manner as the edges of a coat might be overlapped when buttoned. The end result was to reinforce the muscular wall of the abdomen with six rows of sutures (stitches) under the skin cover, which was then closed with clamps that were removed within 48 hours after the operation. (Other methods might not separate muscle layers, often involved fewer rows of sutures, and sometimes involved the insertion of screens or meshes under the skin.)

The typical first-time repair could be completed with the use of preoperative sedation (sleeping pill) and analgesic (pain killer) plus a local anesthetic, an injection of Novocain in the region of the incision. This allowed immediate patient ambulation and facilitated rapid recovery. Many of the recurrences and the very difficult hernia repairs, being more complex, could require up to 90 minutes and more. In some circumstances, a general anesthetic was administered.

THE PATIENTS' EXPERIENCE

It was thought that most potential Shouldice patients learned about the hospital and its methods from past patients who had already experienced them. Although

2. Based on a careful tracking of its patients over more than 30 years, it was estimated that the gross recurrence rate for all operations performed at Shouldice was 0.8%. Recurrence rates reported in the literature for these types of hernia varied greatly. However, one text published around that time stated, "In the United States the gross rate of recurrence for groin hernias approaches 10%."

over 1,000 doctors had referred patients, doctors were less likely to recommend Shouldice because of the generally regarded simplicity of the surgery, often considered a "bread and butter" operation. Typically, many patients had their problem diagnosed by a personal physician and then took the initiative to contact Shouldice. Many more made this diagnosis themselves and contacted the hospital directly.

The process experienced by Shouldice patients depended on whether or not they lived close enough to the hospital to visit the facility to obtain a diagnosis. Approximately 42% of all Shouldice patients came from the United States. Another 2% originated from provinces other than Ontario and from European countries. These out-of-town patients often were diagnosed by mail, using the Medical Information questionnarie shown in *Exhibit 1*.

Of every eight questionnaires sent, seven were returned to the hospital in completed form. Based on information in the questionnaire, a Shouldice surgeon would determine the type of hernia the respondent had and whether there were signs that some risk might be associated with surgery (for example, an overweight or heart condition, or a patient who had suffered a heart attack or a stroke in the past six months to a year, or whether a general or local anesthetic was required). At this point, a patient was given an operating date, the medical information was logged into a computerized data base, and the patient was sent a confirmation card; if necessary, a sheet outlining a weight-loss program prior to surgery and a brochure describing the hospital and the Shouldice method were also sent. A small proportion was refused treatment, either because they were too fat, represented an undue medical risk, or because it was determined that they did not have a hernia.

If confirmation cards were not returned by the patient three days or more prior to the scheduled operation, that patient was contacted by phone. Upon confirmation, the patient's folder was sent to the reception desk to await his or her arrival.[3]

Arriving at the clinic between 1:00 P.M. and 3:00 P.M. the day before the operation, a patient might join up with 30 to 34 other patients and their friends and families in the waiting room. After a typical wait of about 20 minutes—

---

3. Patients living within 50 miles from the hospital (about 40% of all patients) were encouraged to come to the clinic on a walk-in basis for an examination, usually requiring no more than 15 or 20 minutes for the physical and completion of an information questionnaire. If the doctor performing the examination diagnosed the problem as an external hernia, the individual could obtain immediately a future booking for the operation. On occasion, when a previously booked patient canceled at the last minute, a walk-in patient, or one selected from a special waiting list, could be scheduled for the next day. At the time of booking, the potential patient was given a specific date for the operation, a letter estimating the total cost of the operation (as required by the Ontario provincial government for all Ontario residents), and information supplied to out-of-province patients.

depending on the availability of surgeons—a patient was examined in one of six examination rooms staffed by surgeons who had completed their operating schedules for the day. This examination required no more than 12 to 20 minutes, unless the patient needed reassurance. (Patients typically exhibited a moderate level of anxiety until their operation was completed.) At this point it occasionally was discovered that a patient had not corrected his or her weight problem; others might be found not to have a hernia after all. In either case, the patient was sent home.

Following his or her examination, a patient might experience a wait of 5 to 15 minutes to see one of two admitting personnel in the accounting office. Here, health insurance coverage was checked, and various details were discussed in a procedure that usually lasted no more than 10 minutes. Patients sometimes exhibited their nervousness by asking many questions at this point, requiring more time of the receptionist.

Patients next were sent to one of two nurses' stations where, in 5 to 10 minutes and with little wait, their hemoglobin (blood) and urine were checked. At this point, about an hour after arriving at the hospital, a patient was directed to the room number shown on his or her wrist band. Throughout the process, patients were asked to keep their luggage (usually light and containing only a few items suggested by the hospital) with them.

All patient rooms at the hospital were semi-private, containing two beds. Patients with similar jobs, backgrounds, or interests were assigned to the same room to the extent possible. Upon reaching their rooms, patients busied themselves unpacking, getting acquainted with roommates, changing into pajamas, "prepping" themselves (shaving themselves in the area of the operation), and providing a urine sample.

At 5:00 P.M. a nurse's orientation provided the group of incoming patients with information about what to expect, the drugs to be administered, the need for exercise after the operation, the facility, and the daily routine. According to Alan O'Dell, "Half are so nervous they don't remember much from the orientation." Dinner was served from 5:30 to 6:00 P.M. in a 100-seat dining room on a first-come, first-served basis. Following further recreation, tea and cookies were served at 9:00 P.M. in the lounge area. Nurses emphasized the importance of attendance at that time because it provided an opportunity for preoperative patients to talk with those whose operations had been completed earlier that same day. Nearly all new patients were "tucked into bed" between 9:30 and 10:00 P.M. in preparation for an early awakening prior to their operations.

Patients to be operated on early in the day were awakened at 5:30 A.M. to be given preop sedation and to be dressed in an O.R. (operating room) gown. An attempt was made to schedule operations for roommates at approximately the same time. Patients were taken to the preoperating room where the circulating nurse administered Demerol, an analgesic, 45 minutes before surgery. A few minutes prior to the first operation at 7:30 A.M., the surgeon assigned to each patient administered Novocain, a local anesthetic. During the operation, it was the responsibility of the circulating nurse to monitor the patient's comfort, to note times at which the Novocain was administered and the operation begun, and to arrange for the administration of Demerol to the patient scheduled next on the operating table, depending on the progress of the surgery under way. This was in contrast to the typical hospital procedure in which patients were sedated in their rooms prior to being taken to the operating rooms.

Upon the completion of the operation, during which a few patients were "chatty" and fully aware of what was going on, patients were invited to get off the operating table and walk to the post-operating room with the help of their surgeons. According to Ursula Verstraete, director of nursing:

> Ninety-nine percent accept the surgeon's invitation. While we put them in wheelchairs to return them to their rooms, the walk from the operating table is for psychological as well as physiological [blood pressure, respiratory] reasons. Patients prove to themselves that they can do it, and they start their all-important exercise immediately.

Throughout the day after their operation, patients were encouraged to exercise by nurses and housekeepers alike. By 9:00 P.M. on the day of their operations, all patients were ready and able to walk down to the dining room for tea and cookies, even if it meant climbing stairs, to help indoctrinate the new "class" admitted that day.

Patients in their second or third day of recovery were awakened before 6:00 A.M. so they could loosen up for breakfast, which was served between 7:45 and 8:15 A.M. in the dining room. Good posture and exercise were thought to aid digestion and deter the buildup of gas that could prove painful. After breakfast on the first day after surgery, all of the skin clips (resembling staples) holding the skin together over the incision were loosened and some removed. The remainder were removed the next day. On the fourth morning, patients were ready for discharge.

During their stay, patients were encouraged to take advantage of the opportunity to explore the premises and make new friends. Some members of the staff felt that the patients and their attitudes were the most important element of the Shouldice program. According to Dr. Byrnes Shouldice, the 53-year-old son of the founder and vice president of the corporation, a surgeon on the staff and a 50% owner of the hospital:

> Patients sometimes ask to stay an extra day. Why? Well, think about it. They are basically well to begin with. But they arrive with a problem and a certain amount of nervousness, tension, and anxiety about their surgery. Their first morning here they're operated on and experience a sense of

relief from something that's been bothering them for a long time. They are immediately able to get around, and they've got a three-day holiday ahead of them with a perfectly good reason to be away from work with no sense of guilt. They share experiences with other patients, make friends easily, and have the run of the hospital. In summer, the most common after-effect from the surgery is sunburn. They kid with the staff and make this a positive experience for all of us.

The average patient stay for comparable operations at other hospitals was thought to be five to seven or eight days, but it had been declining because of a shortage of beds and the tendency to give elective surgery a low priority for beds. Shouldice patients with jobs involving light exercise could return to work within a week after their operations, but those involved in more strenuous work, whose benefits were insured, received four weeks of benefits and recuperation. All self-employed persons returned to work much earlier. In general, typical times for recuperation from similar operations at other hospitals were two weeks for those in jobs requiring light exercise and eight weeks for those in more strenuous jobs, due largely to long-established treatment regimens.

THE NURSES' EXPERIENCE

The nursing staff comprised 22 full-time and 18 part-time members. They were divided into four groups (as shown in *Exhibit 2)*, with supervisors for the hospital, operating room, laboratory, and central supply reporting to Ursula Verstraete, the director of nursing.

While the operating rooms were fully staffed from about 7 A.M. through the last operation ending in the mid- to late afternoon, the hospital was staffed with three shifts beginning at 7 A.M. , 3 P.M., and 11 P.M. Even so, minimal patient needs for physical assistance allowed Shouldice to operate with a much lower nurse-to-patient ratio than the typical hospital. Shouldice nurses spent an unusually large proportion of their time in counseling activities. As one supervisor commented, "We don't use bedpans." In a typical year, Verstraete estimated that she might experience a turnover of four nurses.

THE DOCTORS' EXPERIENCE

The hospital employed 12 full-time surgeons, 7 part-time assistant surgeons, and one anesthetist. Each operating team required a surgeon, an assistant surgeon, a scrub nurse, and a circulating nurse. The operating load varied from 30 to 36 operations per day. As a result, each surgeon typically performed three or four operations each day.

A typical surgeon's day started with a scrubbing shortly before the first scheduled operation at 7:30 A.M. If the first operation was routine, it usually was completed by 8:15 A.M. At its conclusion, the surgical team helped the patient walk from the room and summoned the next patient. While the patient was being prepared and awaiting the full effects of the Demerol to set in, the surgeon completed the previous patient's file by dictating five or so minutes of comments concerning the operation. Postoperative instructions were routine unless specific instructions were issued by the surgeon. After scrubbing, the surgeon could be ready to operate again at 8:30 A.M.

Surgeons were advised to take a coffee break after their second or third operation. Even so, a surgeon could complete three routine operations and a fourth involving a recurrence (a 60- to 90-minute procedure) and still be finished in time for a 12:30 P.M. lunch in the staff dining room.

Upon finishing lunch, as many as six of the surgeons not scheduled to operate in the afternoon moved upstairs to examine incoming patients between 1:00 and 3:00 P.M. A surgeon's day ended by 4:00 P.M. In addition, a surgeon could expect to be on call one weekday night in ten and one weekend in ten. Alan O'Dell commented that the position appealed to doctors who "want to watch their children grow up. A doctor on call is rarely called to the hospital and has regular hours."

According to Dr. Obney, chief surgeon:

When I interview prospective surgeons, I look for experience and a good education. I try to gain some insight into their domestic situation and personal interests and habits. Naturally, as in any field, we try to avoid anyone with a drinking or drug problem. Oftentimes these people can hide their illness very well and it can take a while before it is detected. Here, sometimes, recommendations can be of great help. I also try to find out why a surgeon wants to switch positions. And I try to determine if he's willing to perform the repair exactly as he's told. This is no place for prima donnas.

Dr. Shouldice added:

Our surgeons enjoy operating, but sometimes are less interested in the more mundane office routines that all vocations have. Traditionally a hernia is often the first operation that a junior resident in surgery performs. Hernia repair is regarded as a relatively simple operation compared to other major operations. This is quite wrong, as is borne out by the resulting high recurrence rate. It is a tricky anatomical area and occasionally very complicated, especially to the novice or those doing very few hernia repairs each year. But at Shouldice Hospital a surgeon learns the Shouldice technique over a period of several months. He learns when he can go fast and when he must go slow. He develops a pace and a touch. If he encounters something unusual, he is encouraged to consult immediately with other surgeons. We teach each other and try to encourage a group effort. And he learns not to take risks to achieve absolute perfection. Excellence is the enemy of good.

Dr. Obney assigned surgeons to an operating room on a daily basis by noon of the preceding day. This allowed surgeons to examine the specific patients that they were to operate on. Surgeons and assistants were rotated every few days. Scrub nurses and circulating nurses were assigned to a new operating room every two weeks and four weeks, respectively. Unless patients requested specific doctors, cases were assigned to give doctors a nonroutine operation (often involving a recurrence) several times a week. More complex procedures were assigned to more senior and experienced members of the staff, including Dr. Obney himself. Where possible, former Shouldice patients suffering recurrences were assigned to the doctor who performed the first operation "to allow the doctor to learn from his mistake."

As Dr. Obney commented:

> If something goes wrong, we want to make sure that we have an experienced surgeon in charge, and we don't like surgeons who work too fast. Experience is most important. The typical general surgeon may perform 25 to 50 hernia operations per year. Ours perform 600 or more.

The 12 full-time surgeons were paid a straight salary. A typical starting salary at that time for someone with 5 to 10 years of experience was $50,000. In addition, bonuses to doctors were voted by the board of directors twice a year, depending on profit and performance. The total bonus pool paid to the surgeons in a recent year was approximately $500,000. Assisting surgeons were part-time, and they received 51% of the $60 fee that was charged to patients who received their services.

The anesthetist was hired for $300 per day from a nearby partnership. Only one was required to be on duty on any given day and could supervise all five operating rooms in addition to administering an occasional general anesthetic to a patient with a complex case or to a child.

Training in the Shouldice technique was important because the procedure could not be varied. It was accomplished through direct supervision by one or more of the senior surgeons. The rotation of teams and frequent consultations allowed for an ongoing opportunity to appraise performance and take corrective action.

According to Dr. Obney:

We haven't had to let anyone go because they couldn't learn, or continue to adhere to, the method. However, a doctor must decide after several years whether he wants to do this for the rest of his life because, just as in other specialties—for example, radiology—he loses touch with other medical disciplines. If he stays for five years, he doesn't leave. Even among younger doctors, few elect to leave.

THE FACILITY

A tour of the facility with Alan O'Dell yielded some interesting information. The Shouldice Hospital comprised two basic facilities in one building—the hospital and the clinic.

On the first-level opening to grade at the back of the building, the hospital contained the kitchen and dining rooms as well as the office of the supervisor of housekeeping. The second level, also opening to grade but at the front of the building, contained a large, open lounge area, the admissions offices, patient rooms, and a spacious glass-covered Florida room. The third level had additional patient rooms, a large lounge, and a recreational area.

Throughout the tour, patients could be seen visiting in each others' rooms, walking up and down hallways, lounging in the sunroom, and making use of light recreational facilities ranging from a pool table to an exercycle.

Alan O'Dell pointed out some of the features of the hospital:

The rooms contain no telephones or television sets. If a patient needs to make a call or wants to watch television, he or she has to take a walk. The steps are designed specially with a small rise to allow patients recently operated on to negotiate the stairs without undue discomfort. Every square foot of the hospital is carpeted to reduce the hospital feeling and the possibility of a fall. Carpeting also gives the place a smell other than that of disinfectant.

This facility was designed by Dr. Byrnes Shouldice. He thought about it for years and made many changes in the plan before the first concrete was poured. A number of unique policies were also instituted. Because Dr. Shouldice started out to be a minister, ministers are treated gratis. And you see that mother and child in the next room? Parents accompanying children here for an operation stay free. You may wonder why we can do it, but we learned that we save more in nursing costs than we spend for the patient's room and board. Children may present difficulties in a hospital environment, but when accompanied by a parent, the parent is happier and so is the child.

While patients and staff were served food prepared in the same kitchen, the staff was required to pick up its food from a cafeteria line placed in the very center of the kitchen. This provided an opportunity for everyone to chat with the kitchen staff several times a day as they picked up a meal or stopped for coffee. Patients were served in the adjoining patient dining room.
According to O'Dell:

We use all fresh ingredients and prepare the food from scratch in the kitchen. Our kitchen staff of three prepares about 100 breakfasts, 200 lunches, and 100 dinners each day at an average raw food cost of $1.10 per meal.

Iona Rees, director of housekeeping, pointed out:

We do all of our own laundry in the building with two full-time employees. And I have only three on my housekeeping staff for the entire facility. One of the reasons for so few housekeepers is that we don't need to change linens during a patient's four-day stay. They are basically well, so there is no soiling of bed linens. Also, the medical staff doesn't want the patients in bed all day. They want the nurses to encourage the patients to be up socializing, comparing notes [for confidence], encouraging each other, and walking around, getting exercise.

Of course, we're in the rooms straightening up throughout the day. This gives the housekeepers a chance to josh with the patients and to encourage them to exercise.

The bottom level of the clinic housed five operating rooms, a laboratory, the patient-recovery room, and a central supply area where surgical instruments were cleaned and sterilized. This was the only area of the entire facility that was not carpeted, to prevent static electricity from forming in areas where potentially explosive anesthetics might be used. In total, the estimated cost to furnish an operating room was no more than $30,000. This was considerably less than for other hospitals requiring a bank of equipment with which to administer anesthetics for each room. At Shouldice, two mobile units were used by the anesthetist when needed. In addition, the complex had one "crash cart" per floor for use if a patient should suffer a heart attack or stroke during his or her hospital stay.

The first floor of the clinic contained admissions and accounting offices, a large waiting room with a capacity for as many as 50 people, and 6 examination rooms. On the second floor of the clinic, situated in much of what was the original house, was found the administrative offices. A third floor contained 14 additional hostel rooms where patients could be held overnight awaiting the assignment of a room and their operations. At such times when the hospital was particularly crowded, doctors were asked to identify those postoperative patients who could be released a day early. Often these were local residents or children.

ADMINISTRATION

Alan O'Dell, while he walked, described his job:

I'm responsible for a little of everything around here. We try to meet people's needs and make this as good a place to work as possible. My door is always open. And members of our staff will come in to seek advice about everything from medical to marital problems. There is a strong concern for employees here. Nobody is fired. [This was later reinforced by Dr. Shouldice, who described a situation involving two employees who confessed to theft in the hospital. They agreed to seek psychiatric help and were allowed to remain on the job.] As a result, turnover is low.

We don't have a union, but we try to maintain a pay scale higher than the union scale for comparable jobs in the area. For example, our nurses receive from $15,000 to $25,000 per year, depending on the number of years' experience. We have a profit-sharing plan that is separate from the doctors'. Last year the employees divided up $65,000.

If work needs to be done, people pitch in to help each other. A unique aspect of our administration is that I insist that each secretary is trained to do another's work and in an emergency is able to switch to another function immediately and enable the more vital workload to proceed uninterrupted. With the exception of the accounting staff, every secretary, regardless of her or his position in the hospital, is trained to handle the hospital switchboard and work at the reception desk. If necessary, I'll go downstairs and type billings if they're behind. We don't have an organization chart. A chart tends to make people think they're boxed into jobs.[4]

In addition to other activities, I try to stay here one night a week having dinner and listening to the patients to find out how things are really going around here.

4. The chart in *Exhibit 2* was prepared by the casewriter, based on conversations with hospital personnel.

Administrative Structure

The hospital was operated on a nonprofit basis and the clinic on a for-profit basis. Dr. Shouldice and Mrs. W. Urquhart, his sister, each owned 50% of each.

O'Dell, as administrator of the hospital, was responsible for all of its five departments: surgery, nursing, administration, maintenance, and housekeeping. Medical matters were the domain of Dr. Obney, the chief surgeon. Both Alan O'Dell and Dr. Obney reported directly to an executive committee composed of Drs. Shouldice and Obney, Alan O'Dell, Ursula Verstraete (director of nursing), and Mrs. Urquhart. The executive committee met as needed, usually twice a month, and in turn reported to an inside board (as shown in *Exhibit 2*). In addition to executive committee members (except Ursula Verstraete), the board included the spouses of Dr. Shouldice and Mrs. Urquhart, two former long-time employees, and Jack MacKay. The board met three times per year, or when necessary.

Operating Costs

It was estimated by the casewriter that the 1983 budgets for the hospital and clinic were close to $2.8 million and $2 million, respectively.[5]

THE MARKET

Hernia operations were among the most common performed on males. In 1979, for example, it was estimated that 600,000 such operations were performed in the United States alone. Only in the early 1980s had the hospital begun to organize information about either its client base of 140,000 "alumni" or the market in general.

According to Dr. Shouldice:

> When our backlog of scheduled operations gets too large, we begin to wonder how many people decide instead to have their local doctor perform the operation. Every time we have expanded our capacity, the backlog has declined briefly, only to climb once again. Right now, at 1,200, it is larger than it has ever been at this time of year [January].

The hospital relied entirely on word-of-mouth advertising, the importance of which was suggested by the results of a poll carried out by students of DePaul

5. The latter figure included the bonus pool for doctors.

University as part of a project (*Exhibit 3* shows a portion of these results). Although little systematic data about patients had been collected, Alan O'Dell remarked that "if we had to rely on wealthy patients only, our practice would be much smaller."

Patients were attracted to the hospital, in part, by its reasonable rates. For example, charges for a typical operation were four days of hospital stay at $111 per day, a $450 surgical fee for a primary inguinal (the most common hernia) operation, and a $60 fee for the assistant surgeon.[6] If a general anesthetic was required, an additional fee of $75 was assessed. These were the charges that compared with total costs of $2,000 to $4,000 for operations performed elsewhere.

Round-trip fares for travel to Toronto from various major cities on the North American continent ranged from roughly $200 to $600.

In addition to providing free services to the clergy and to parents of hospitalized children, the hospital also provided annual checkups to its alumni, free of charge. Many of them occurred at the time of the annual reunion. The most recent reunion, featuring dinner and a floor show, was held at a first-class hotel in downtown Toronto and was attended by 1,400 former patients, many of them from outside Canada.

The reunion was scheduled to coincide with the mid-January decline in activity at the hospital, when an average of only 145 operations per week were performed. This was comparable to a similar lull in late summer and contrasted with the peak of activity in September, when as many as 165 operations per week might be performed.

It was thought that patients from outside Canada were discouraged from coming to Toronto in midwinter by often misleading weather reports. Vacations interfered with plans in late summer. For many of the same reasons, the hospital closed for two weeks late in December each year. This allowed time for major maintenance work to be performed. Throughout the year, no operations were scheduled for Saturdays or Sundays, although patients whose operations were scheduled late in the week remained in the hospital over the weekend.

PROBLEMS AND PLANS

When asked about major questions confronting the management of the hospital, Dr. Shouldice cited a desire to seek ways of increasing the hospital's capacity while at the same time maintaining control over the quality of the service deliv-

6. At the time this case was written, a Canadian dollar was worth about 80% of an American dollar.

ered, the future role of government in the operations of the hospital, the use of
the Shouldice name by potential competitors, and the selection of the next chief
surgeon.

As Dr. Shouldice put it:

I'm a doctor first and an entrepreneur second. For example, we could refuse
permission to other doctors who want to visit the hospital. They may copy
our technique and misapply it or misinform their patients about the use of
it. This results in failure, and we are concerned that the technique will be
blamed for the recurrences. But we're doctors, and it is our obligation to
help other surgeons learn. On the other hand, it's quite clear that others
are trying to emulate us. Look at this ad. (The advertisement is shown in
Exhibit 4.)

  This makes me believe that we should add to our capacity, either here or
elsewhere. Here, for example, we could go to Saturday operations and
increase our capacity by 20% or, with an investment of perhaps $2 million
and permission from the provincial government, we could add another
floor of rooms to the hospital, expand our number of beds by 50%, and
schedule the operating rooms more heavily.

  On the other hand, with government regulation being what it is, do we
want to invest more money in Toronto? Or should we establish another hospital with similar design outside Canada? I have under consideration a couple
of sites in the United States where private hospital operations are more common. Then, too, there is the possibility that we could diversify at other
locations into other specialties offering similar opportunities such as eye surgery, varicose veins, or hemorrhoids.

  For now, I have my hands full thinking about the selection of someone
to succeed Dr. Obney when he retires. He's 65, you know. And for good
reason, he's resisted changing certain successful procedures that I think we
could improve on. We had quite a time changing the schedule for the
administration of Demerol to patients to increase their comfort level during
the operation. Dr. Obney has opposed a Saturday operating program on
the premise that he won't be here and won't be able to maintain proper
control.

Alan O'Dell added his own concerns:

How should we be marketing our services? Right now, we don't. We're
even afraid to send out this new brochure we've put together for fear it
will generate too much demand. We know that both patients and doctors
believe in what we do. Our records show that just under 1% of our patients
are medical doctors, a significantly high percentage. How should we capital-

ize on that? And should we try to control the misuse of the hospital's name by physicians who say they use our techniques but don't achieve good results? We know it's going on, because we get letters from patients of other doctors claiming that our method didn't work.

On the other hand, I'm concerned about this talk of Saturday operations. We are already getting good utilization of this facility. And if we expand further, it will be very difficult to maintain the same kind of working relationships and attitudes. Already there are rumors floating around among the staff about it. And the staff is not pleased.

We still have some improvements to make in our systems. With more extensive computerization, for example, we could improve our admitting procedures.

The matter of Saturday operations had been a topic of conversation among the doctors as well. Four of the older doctors were opposed to it. While most of the younger doctors were indifferent or supportive, at least two who had been at the hospital for some time were particularly concerned about the possibility that the issue would drive a wedge between the two groups. As one put it, "I'd hate to see the practice split over the issue."

SHOULDICE HOSPITAL LIMITED

Exhibit 1
Medical Information Questionnaire

FAMILY NAME (Last Name)	FIRST NAME	MIDDLE NAME

STREET & NUMBER (or Rural Route or P.O. Box) | Town/City | Province/State

County	Township	Zip or Postal Code	Birthdate: Month	Day	Year

Telephone
Home ....
Work .... If none, give neighbour's number ....

Married or Single | Religion

NEXT OF KIN: Name | Address | Telephone #

Date form completed

INSURANCE INFORMATION: Please give name of Insurance Company and Numbers.

HOSPITAL INSURANCE: (Please bring hospital certificates) | OTHER HOSPITAL INSURANCE
O.H.I.P. _____ BLUE CROSS | Company Name
Number _____ Number | Policy Number

SURGICAL INSURANCE:(Please bring insurance certificates) | OTHER SURGICAL INSURANCE
O.H.I.P. _____ BLUE SHIELD | Company Name
Number _____ Number | Policy Number

WORKMEN'S COMPENSATION BOARD | Approved | Social Insurance (Security) Number
| Yes | No

Claim No.

Occupation | Name of Business | Are you the Owner? Yes No | If Retired — Former Occupation

How did you hear about Shouldice Hospital? (If referred by a doctor, give name & address)

Are you a former patient of Shouldice Hospital? | Yes | No | Do you smoke? | Yes | No

Have you ever written to Shouldice Hospital in the past? | Yes | No
What is your preferred admission date? (Please give as much advance notice as possible)
No admissions Friday, Saturday or Sunday.

FOR OFFICE USE ONLY

Date Received	Type of Hernia	Weight Loss lbs.

Special Instructions | Approved

Consent to Operate ☐ ☐
Heart Report | Operation Date
Referring Doctor Notified

SHOULDICE HOSPITAL

7750 Bayview Avenue
Box 370, Thornhill, Ontario L3T 4A3 Canada
Phone (416) 889-1125

(Thornhill - One Mile North Metro Toronto)

MEDICAL
INFORMATION

Patients who live at a distance often prefer their examination, admission and operation to be arranged all on a single visit – to save making two lengthy journeys. The whole purpose of this questionnaire is to make such arrangements possible, although, of course, it cannot replace the examination in any way. Its completion and return will not put you under any obligation.

Please be sure to fill in both sides.

This information will be treated as confidential.

(continued on next page)

Exhibit 1
(Continued)

THIS CHART IS FOR EXPLANATION ONLY

Ordinary hernias are mostly either
at the navel ("belly-button") - or just above it

or down in the groin area on either side

An "incisional hernia" is one that bulges through
the scar of any other **surgical operation** that has
failed to hold - wherever it may be.

Right Groin   Left Groin

THIS IS YOUR CHART — PLEASE MARK IT!

(MARK THE POSITION OF EACH HERNIA
YOU WANT REPAIRED WITH AN "X")

Right Groin   Left Groin

APPROXIMATE SIZE . . .
Walnut (or less)   ☐   ☐
Hen's Egg or Lemon   ☐   ☐
Grapefruit (or more)   ☐   ☐

ESSENTIAL EXTRA INFORMATION

Use **only** the sections that apply to **your** hernias and put a √ in each
box that seems appropriate.

	Yes	No
NAVEL AREA (AND JUST ABOVE NAVEL) ONLY Is this navel (bellybutton) hernia your FIRST one?	☐	☐

If it's NOT your first, how many repair attempts so far? ☐

GROIN HERNIAS ONLY

	RIGHT GROIN		LEFT GROIN	
	Yes	No	Yes	No
Is this your FIRST GROIN HERNIA ON THIS SIDE?	☐	☐	☐	☐

How many **hernia** operations in this groin already? Right ☐   Left ☐

DATE OF LAST OPERATION [   ]

INCISIONAL HERNIAS ONLY (the ones bulging through previous operation scars)

Was the **original** operation for your Appendix? ☐ , or Gallbladder? ☐ ,
or Stomach? ☐ , or Prostate? ☐ , or Hysterectomy? ☐ , or Other? ....
....
How many attempts to repair the hernia have been made so far? ☐

Exhibit 1
(Continued)

PLEASE BE ACCURATE!: **Misleading figures, when checked on a admission day, could mean postponement of your operation till your weight is suitable.**

HEIGHT . ... ft......... ins.   **WEIGHT** ...... lbs. Nude   Recent gain? ...... lbs.
or just pyjamas   Recent loss? ...... lbs

Waist (muscles relaxed) .... ins.   **Chest** (not expanded) ....ins.

GENERAL HEALTH

Age .... years   Is your health now GOOD ☐ ,   FAIR ☐ ,   or POOR ☐

Please mention briefly any **severe past illness** – such as a
"heart attack" or a "stroke", for example, from which you
have now recovered (and its approximate date) ....
....

We need to know about other present conditions, even though your admission is
<u>NOT</u> likely to be refused because of them.

Please tick ☑ any condition
for which you are having **regular**
treatment:

Name of any prescribed
pills, tablets or **capsules** you
take regularly: –

Blood Pressure ☐

Excess body fluids ☐

Chest pain ("angina") ☐

Irregular Heartbeat ☐

Diabetes ☐

Asthma & Bronchitis ☐

Ulcers ☐

Anticoagulants ☐
(to delay blood-clotting
or to "thin the blood")

Other ....

**Did you remember to MARK AN "X" on your body chart to show us where
each of your hernias is located?**

SHOULDICE HOSPITAL LIMITED
Exhibit 2
Organization Chart

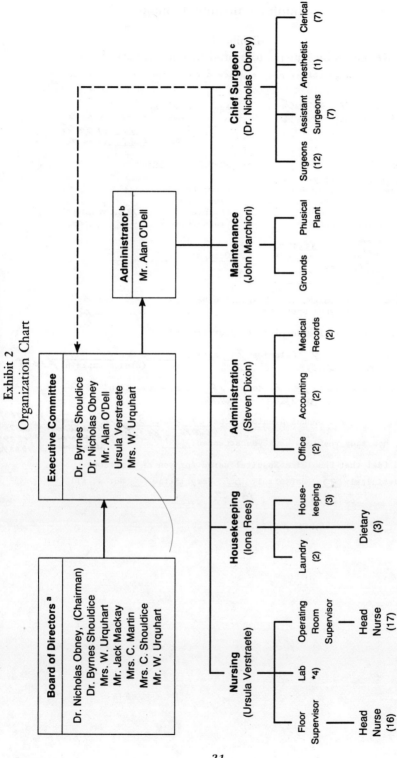

Board of Directors [a]

Dr. Nicholas Obney, (Chairman)
Dr. Byrnes Shouldice
Mrs. W. Urquhart
Mr. Jack Mackay
Mrs. C. Martin
Mrs. C. Shouldice
Mr. W. Urquhart

Executive Committee

Dr. Byrnes Shouldice
Dr. Nicholas Obney
Mr. Alan O'Dell
Ursula Verstraete
Mrs. W. Urquhart

Administrator [b]

Mr. Alan O'Dell

Chief Surgeon [c]
(Dr. Nicholas Obney)

Surgeons (12)
Assistant Surgeons (7)
Anesthetist (1)
Clerical (7)

Maintenance
(John Marchiori)

Grounds
Phusical Plant

Administration
(Steven Dixon)

Office (2)
Accounting (2)
Medical Records (2)

Housekeeping
(Iona Rees)

Laundry (2)
House-keeping (3)
Dietary (3)

Nursing
(Ursula Verstraete)

Floor Supervisor
Lab *4)
Operating Room Supervisor

Head Nurse (16)
Head Nurse (17)

[a] **Meets three times a year of as needed**
[b] **Meets as needed (usually twice a month)**
[c] **Informally to Executive Committee**

21

Exhibit 3
Responses by Patients to a Student Poll, January, 1983

Direction: For each question, please place a check mark as it applies to you.

1. Sex   Male _41_ _95.34%_   2. Age   20 or less ___
         Female _2_ _4.65%_   21-40   _4_ _9.30%_
                                       41-60   _17_ _39.54%_
                                       61 or more _22_ _51.16%_

3. Nationality   4. Education level

   Directions: Please place a
   check mark in nation you   Elementary   _5_ _11.63%_
   represent and please write in   High School _18_ _41.86%_
   your province, state or   College   _1330_ _30.23%_
   country where it applies.   Graduate work _7_ _16.28%_

   Canada _38_ Province _88.37%_
   America _5_ State _11.63%_   5. Occupation _____
   Europe ___ Country _____
   Other ___   _____

6. Have you been overnight in a hospital other than   Yes _31_
   Shouldice before your operation?   No _12_

7. What brought Shouldice Hospital to your attention?

   Friend _23_ Doctor _9_ Relative _7_ Article ___ Other _4_
          _53.49%_   _20.93%_   _16.28%_   (Please explain) _9.30 %_

8. Did you have a single _25_ or double _18_ hernia operation?
                         _58.14%_   _41.86%_

9. Is this your first Annual Reunion? Yes _20_ No _23_   ⎧ 2-5 reunions -11 47.83%
                                      _46.51%_ _53.49%_ ⎨ 6-10 reunions - 5 21.73%
   If no, how many reunions have you attended? ___   ⎩ 11-2 reunions - 4 17.39%
                                                           21-36 reunions - 3 13.05%

10. Do you feel that Shouldice Hospital cared for you as a person?
    Most definitely _37_ Definitely _6_ Very little ___ Not at all ___
                    _86.05%_   _13.95%_

Exhibit 3
(Continued)

11. What impressed you the most about your stay at Shouldice? Please check one answer for each of the following.

A. Fees charged for operation and hospital stay

Very Important _10_   Important _3_   Somewhat Important _6_   Not Important _24_

B. Operation Procedure

Very Important _33_   Important _9_   Somewhat Important _1_   Not Important ___
_76.74%_   _20.93%_   _2.33%_

C. Physician's Care

Very Important _31_   Important _12_   Somewhat Important _—_   Not Important _—_
_72.10%_   _27.90%_

D. Nursing Care

Very Important _28_   Important _14_   Somewhat Important _1_   Not Important ___
_65.12%_   _32.56%_   _2.33%_

E. Food Service

Very Important _23_   Important _11_   Somewhat Important _7_   Not Important _2_
_53.48%_   _25.59%_   _16.28%_   _4.65%_

F. Shortness of Hospital Stay

Very Important _17_   Important _15_   Somewhat Important _8_   Not Important _3_
_39.53%_   _34.88%_   _18.60%_   _6.98%_

G. Exercise; Recreational Activities

Very Important _17_   Important _14_   Somewhat Important _12_   Not Important _—_
_39.53%_   _32.56%_   _27.91%_

H. Friendships with Patients

Very Important _25_   Important _10_   Somewhat Important _5_   Not Important _3_
_58.15%_   _23.25%_   _11.63%_   _6.98%_

I. "Shouldice Hospital hardly seemed like a hospital at all."

Very Important _25_   Important _13_   Somewhat Important _5_   Not Important ___
_58.14%_   _30.23%_   _11.63%_

12. In a few words, give the MAIN REASON why you returned for this annual reunion.

_____

_____

_____

Exhibit 4
Advertisement by a Shouldice Competitor

The Canadian Hernia Clinic

Hernias (Ruptures) Repaired Under local anesthesia as by Canadian method.

No Overnight Hospital Stay.

Consultations Without Charge

**23061 St. Rd. 7
BOCA RATON, FLA. 33433
482-7755**

Benihana of Tokyo

"**S**ome restaurateurs like myself have more fun than others," says Hiroaki (Rocky) Aoki, youthful president of Benihana of Tokyo. Since 1964 he had gone from deficit net worth to becoming president of a chain of 15 restaurants that gross over $12 million per year. He sported a $4,000 sapphire ring, maintained a $250,000 home, and kept five cars including three Rolls-Royces. One wall of his office was completely covered with photographs of Rocky with famous personalities who had eaten at a Benihana. Rocky firmly believed: "In America money is always available if you work hard."

BACKGROUND

By 1972 Benihana was basically a steakhouse with a difference—the food was cooked in front of the customer by native chefs and the decor was that of an authentically detailed Japanese country inn. From a humble 40-seat unit opened in midtown Manhattan in 1964, Benihana had grown to a chain of 15 units across the country. Nine were company-owned locations: New York (3); San Francisco; Chicago; Encino and Marina del Rey, California; Portland, Oregon; and Honolulu. Five were franchised: Boston, Fort Lauderdale, Beverly Hills, Seattle, and Harrisburg, Pennsylvania. The last unit, Las Vegas, was operated as a joint venture with Hilton Hotels Corporation. Rocky, who was a former Olympic wrestler, described his success as follows:

> In 1959, I came to the United States on a tour with my university wrestling team. I was 20 at the time. When I reached New York, it was love at first sight! I was convinced that there were more opportunities for me in America than Japan. In fact, the minute I was able to forget that I was Japanese, my success began. I decided to enroll in the School of Restaurant Management at City College basically because I knew that in the restaurant business I'd

John Klug, Research Assistant, prepared this case under the direction of Assistant Professor W. Earl Sasser as the basis for class discussion rather than to illustrate either effective or ineffective handling of an administrative situation. This case was made possible by the cooperation of the Benihana Corporation and Russ Carpenter, Executive Editor of the magazine *Institutions/Volume Feeding*. Copyright © 1972 by the President and Fellows of Harvard College; Harvard Business School case 673-057 Rev. 3/82. Salaries and property values reflect the fact that this case was written in 1972. By 1990, the Consumer Price Index in the U.S. had risen to about 3 times 1972 levels.

never go hungry. I earned money those early years by washing dishes, driving an ice cream truck, and acting as a tour guide. Most importantly, I spent three years making a systematic analysis of the U.S. restaurant market. What I discovered is that Americans enjoy eating in exotic surroundings but are deeply mistrustful of exotic foods. Also I learned that people very much enjoy watching their food being prepared. So I took $10,000 I had saved by 1963 and borrowed $20,000 more to open my first unit on the West Side and tried to apply all that I had learned.

The origins of the Benihana of Tokyo actually date back to 1935. That was when Yunosuke Aoki (Rocky's father) opened the first of his chain of restaurants in Japan. He called it Benihana, after the small red flower that grew wild near the front door of the restaurant.

The elder Aoki ("Papasan"), like his son who was to follow in the family tradition, was a practical and resourceful restaurateur. In 1958, concerned about rising costs and increased competition, he first incorporated the hibachi table concept into his operations. Rocky borrowed this method of cooking from his father and commented as follows:

One of the things I learned in my analysis, for example, was that the number one problem of the restaurant industry in the United States is the shortage of skilled labor. By eliminating the need for a conventional kitchen with the hibachi table arrangement, the only "skilled" person I need is a chef. I can give an unusual amount of attentive service and still keep labor cost to 10–12% of gross sales (food and beverage) depending whether a unit is at full volume. In addition, I was able to turn practically the entire restaurant into productive dining space. Only about 22% of the total space of a unit is back of the house, including preparation areas, dry and refrigerated storage, employee dressing rooms, and office space. Normally a restaurant requires 30% of its total space as back of the house. [Operating statistics for a typical service restaurant are included in *Exhibit 1*.]

The other thing I discovered is that food storage and wastage contribute greatly to the overhead of the typical restaurant. By reducing my menu to only three simple "Middle American" entrees—steak, chicken, and shrimp—I have virtually no waste and can cut food costs to between 30% and 35% of food sales depending on the price of meat.

Finally, I insist on historical authenticity. The walls, ceilings, beams, artifacts, and decorative lights of a Benihana are all from Japan. The building materials are gathered from old houses there, carefully disassembled, and shipped in pieces to the United States where they are reassembled by one of my father's two crews of Japanese carpenters.

Rocky's first unit on the West Side was such a success that it paid for itself in six months. He then built in 1966 a second unit three blocks away on the East Side simply to cater to the overflow of the Benihana West. The Benihana East quickly developed a separate clientele and prospered. In 1967, Barron Hilton, who had eaten at a Benihana, approached Rocky concerning the possibility of locating a unit in the Marina Towers in Chicago. Rocky flew to Chicago, rented a car, and while driving to meet Mr. Hilton saw a vacant site. He immediately stopped, called the owner, and signed a lease the next day. Needless to say, a Benihana didn't go into the Marina Towers.

The number three unit in Chicago proved to be the company's largest money-maker. It was an instant success and grossed approximately $1.3 million per year. The food and beverage split was 70/30 and management was able to keep expense percentages at relatively low levels: food (30%), labor (10%), advertising (10%), and rent (5%).

The fourth unit was San Francisco and the fifth was a joint venture in Las Vegas in 1969. By this time literally hundreds of people were clamoring for franchises. Rocky sold a total of six until he decided in 1970 that it would be much more to his advantage to own his units rather than franchise them. Following are the franchises that were granted: Puerto Rico (not successful due to economic turndown), Harrisburg, Fort Lauderdale, Portland (company bought unit back), Seattle, Beverly Hills, Boston.

The decision to stop franchising was made because of a number of problems. First, all the franchises were bought by investors, none of whom had any restaurant experience. Second, it was difficult for the American investor to relate to a predominantly native Japanese staff. Finally, control was considerably more difficult to maintain with a franchisee than a company employee manager. During the period to 1970 several groups attempted to imitate the Benihana success. One even included a group with intimate knowledge of the Benihana operation who set up in very close proximity to one Benihana unit. They, however, folded within the year. Bolstered by the confidence that the Benihana success could not be easily replicated, management felt that one of the classic pressures to franchise was eliminated—i.e., to expand extremely rapidly to preempt competitors.

The amount of space devoted to the bar/lounge/holding area accurately indicates when the unit was built. When Rocky opened his first unit, he saw the business as primarily food-service sales. The Benihana West had a tiny bar that seated about eight and had no lounge area. Rocky quickly learned that this amount of bar space was insufficient, and at the second unit, Benihana East, he doubled the size of the bar/lounge area. But since the whole unit was larger, the ratio of space was not too different. A typical floor plan is included as *Exhibit 2.*

His third Manhattan operation, called Benihana Palace, opened in 1970. Here, the bar/lounge area was enormous, even in ratio to size. Figures from 1972 bear out the wisdom of the growth. At West, beverage sales represented about 18% of total sales. At East, they ran 20–22%. And at the Palace, they ran a handsome 30–33% of total sales. The beverage cost averaged 20% of beverage sales.

The heart of the "show biz" was in the dining area. The "teppanyaki" table was comprised of a steel griddle plate, with a 9½" wooden ledge bordering it to hold the ware. It was gas-fired. Above every table was an exhaust hood to remove cooking steam and odors and much of the heat from the griddle. Service was provided by a chef and waitress; each such team handled two regular tables.

The four food items—steak, filet mignon, chicken, and shrimp—could either be had as single entree items or in combinations. A full dinner had three, with the shrimp as appetizer. The accompaniments were unvaried: bean sprouts, zucchini, fresh mushrooms, onions, and rice.

Normally, a customer could come in, be seated, have dinner, and be on his or her way out in 45 minutes, if need be. The average turnover was an hour, and up to an hour and a half in slow periods.

The average check, including food and beverage, ran about $6 at lunch, about $10 at dinner. These figures included one drink (average price $1.50) at lunch, an average of one-plus at dinner.

The big purchase was meat. Only U.S.D.A. Prime Grade, tightly specified tenderloin and boneless strip loins were used. The steaks were further trimmed in house. Only a bit of fat at the tail was left, which was for effect only. When the chef began cooking the meat, he dramatically trimmed this part off and pushed it aside before cubing the remaining meat.

The hours of operation for the 15 units varied according to local requirements. All were open for lunch and dinner, though not necessarily every day for each. Lunch business was important; overall it accounted for about 30–40% of the total dollar volume despite a significantly lower check average. Essentially the same menu items were served for both meals; the lower menu price average at lunch reflected smaller portions and fewer combinations.

SITE SELECTION

Because of the importance of lunchtime business, Benihana had one basic criterion for site selection—high traffic. Management wanted to be sure that a lot of people were nearby or going by both at lunch and at dinner. Rent normally ran 5–7% of sales for 5,000–6,000 square feet of floor space. Most units were located in a predominantly business district, though some had easy access to residential areas. Shopping center locations were considered, but had not been accepted by 1972.

TRAINING

Because the chef was considered by Benihana to be a key to its success, all of them were very highly trained. All were young, single, native Japanese and all were "certified," which meant that they had completed a three-year formal apprenticeship. They were then given a three- to six-month course in Japan in the English language and American manner as well as the Benihana form of cooking, which was mostly showmanship. The chefs were brought to the United States under a "trade treaty" agreement.

Training the chefs within the United States was also a continuous process. In addition to the competition among the chefs to perfect their art in hopes of becoming the chief chef, there was also a traveling chef who inspected each unit periodically and was involved in the grand opening of new units.

While Benihana found it relatively difficult to attract chefs and other personnel from Japan due to the general level of prosperity there as well as competition from other restaurants bidding for their talents, once in the United States they were generally not anxious to leave. This was due to several factors. One was the rapidity with which they could rise in the American Benihana operation versus the rather rigid hierarchy based on class, age, and education they would face in Japan. A second and major factor was the paternal attitude that Benihana took toward all its employees. While personnel were well paid in a tangible sense, a large part of the compensation was intangible, based on job security and a total commitment of Benihana to the well-being of its employees. As a result, turnover of personnel within the United States was very low, although most did eventually return to Japan. To fully appreciate the Benihana success, the unique combination of Japanese paternalism in an American setting must be appreciated. Or, as Rocky puts it: "At Benihana we combine Japanese workers with American management techniques."

ORGANIZATION AND CONTROL

Each restaurant carried a simple management structure. It had a manager ($15,000/year), an assistant manager ($12,000/year), and two or three "front men" ($9,000/year), who might be likened to maitre d's. These front men were really potential managers in training. All managers reported to the manager of operations Allen Saito who, in turn, reported to Bill Susha, vice president in charge of operations and business development (see *Exhibit 3*).

Susha came to Benihana in 1971, following food and beverage experience with Hilton, Loew's, and the Flagship Hotel Division of American Airlines. He described his job as follows:

> I see management growth as a priority objective. My first step was to establish some sort of control system by introducing sales goals and budgets. At the most recent manager workshop meeting in New York—with managers from all over the country—I asked each to project his sales goal on an annual basis, then break it out by month, then by week, then by day. After I reached agreement with a manager on the individual quota figures, I instituted a bonus plan. Any unit that exceeds its quota on any basis—daily, weekly, monthly, yearly—will get a proportionate bonus, which will be prorated across the entire staff of the unit. I've also built up an accounting staff and controller to monitor our costs. It's been a slow but steady process. We have to be very careful to balance our need for control with the amount of overhead we can stand. We can justify extra "front men" standing around in the units. At the corporate level, however, we have to be very careful. In fact, at present the company is essentially being run by three people— Rocky, myself, and Allen Saito.

ADVERTISING POLICY

Rocky considered that a vitally important factor in Benihana's success was a substantial investment in creative advertising and public relations. The company invested 8–10% of its gross sales in reaching the public. Glen Simoes, the director of advertising and public relations, summed it up:

> We deliberately try to be different and original in our advertising approach. We never place advertisements on the entertainment pages of newspapers on the theory that they would be lost among the countless other restaurant advertisements.
>
> We have a visual product to sell. Therefore, Benihana utilizes outstanding visuals in its ads. The accompanying copy is contemporary, sometimes off-beat. A recent full-page advertisement which appeared in the *New York Times*, *Women's Wear Daily*, and *New York Magazine* did not contain the word "restaurant." We also conduct a considerable amount of market research to be sure we know who our customers really are.

Exhibit 4 shows the results of one market research survey. *Exhibit 5* is a further discussion of Benihana advertising policy. *Exhibits 6, 7, 8,* and *9* are examples of Benihana advertising copy.

FUTURE EXPANSION

Bill Susha summed up the problems of the future as he saw them:

I think the biggest problems facing us now are how to expand. We tried franchising and decided to discontinue the program for several reasons. Most of our franchisees were businessmen looking for investment opportunities who did not really know and understand the restaurant business—this was a problem. The Japanese staff we provided were our people and we have obligations to them that the franchisee could not or would not honor which at the time made us unhappy. The uniqueness of our operation in the hands of novices made control more difficult. Finally, we found it more profitable to own and operate the restaurants ourselves.

Presently, we are limited to opening only five units a year, because that is as fast as the two crews of Japanese carpenters we have can work. We are facing a decision and weighing the advantages and disadvantages of going into hotels with our type of restaurant. We are presently in two Hilton Hotels (Las Vegas and Honolulu) and have recently signed an agreement with Canadian Pacific Hotels. What we have done in these deals is to put "teeth" in the agreements, so that we are not at the mercy of the hotel company's management.

Further, one of our biggest constraints is staff. Each unit requires approximately 30 people who are all Oriental. Six to eight of them are highly trained chefs.

Finally, there is the cost factor. Each new unit costs us a minimum of $300,000. My feeling is that we should confine ourselves to the major cities like Atlanta, Dallas, St. Louis, etc., in the near future. Then we can use all these units to expand into the suburbs.

We've been highly tempted to try to grow too fast without really considering the full implications of the move. One example was the franchise thing, but we found it unsatisfactory. Another example is that a large international banking organization offered to make a major investment in us which would have allowed us to grow at a terrific rate. But when we looked at the amount of control and autonomy we'd have to give up, it just wasn't worth it, at least in my mind.

Another thing I'm considering is whether it's worth it to import every item used in construction from Japan to make a Benihana 100% "authentic." Does an American really appreciate it and is it worth the cost? We could use material available here and achieve substantially the same effect. Also, is it worth it to use Japanese carpenters and pay union carpenters to sit and watch? All these things could reduce our costs tremendously and allow us to expand much faster.

Rocky described his perception of where the firm should go:

I see three principal areas for growth: the United States, overseas, and Japan.

In the United States we need to expand into the primary marketing areas Bill talked about that do not have a Benihana. But I think through our franchises we also learned that secondary markets such as Harrisburg, Pennsylvania, and Portland, Oregon, also have potential. While their volume potential obviously will not match that of a primary market, these smaller units offer fewer headaches and generate nice profits. Secondary markets being considered include Cincinnati and Indianapolis.

The third principal area I see for growth is in suburbia. No sites have yet been set, but I think it holds a great potential. A fourth growth area, not given the importance of the others, is further penetration into existing markets. Saturation is not a problem as illustrated by the fact that New York and greater Los Angeles have three units each, all doing well.

We are also considering someday going public. In the meantime, we are moving into joint ventures in Mexico and overseas. Each joint venture is unique in itself. We negotiate each unit on the basis that will be most advantageous to the parties concerned, taking into account the contributions of each party in the form of services and cash. Once this is established, we agree on a formula for profits and away we go.

Four deals have now been consummated. Three are joint ventures out of the country. An agreement has already been reached to open a Benihana in the Royal York Hotel, Toronto, Canada. This will provide the vanguard for a march across Canada with units in or outside Canadian Pacific Hotels.

Second is a signed agreement for a new unit in Mexico City. From here, negotiations are under way on a new hotel to be built in Acapulco. Benihana stands ready to build and operate a unit in the hotel or, if possible, to take over management of the entire hotel. These units would form a base for expansion throughout Mexico.

The third extraterritorial arrangement was recently signed with David Paradine, Ltd., a British firm of investors headed by TV personality David Frost. Again, this is a joint venture with the Paradine group to supply technical assistance, public relations, advertising, and financing, and Benihana the management and know-how. This venture hopes ultimately to have Benihana restaurants, not only throughout Great Britain, but across the Continent.

Rocky also had a number of diversification plans:

We have entered into an agreement with a firm that is researching and contacting large food processors in an effort to interest them in producing a line of Japanese food products under the Benihana label for retail sale. There has been a great deal of interest and we are close to concluding a deal.

I worry a lot. Right now we cater to a middle-income audience, not the younger generation. That makes a difference. We charge more, serve better quality, have a better atmosphere, and more service. But we are in the planning stages for operations with appeal to the younger generation.

For instance, there is no Japanese quick service operation in this country. I think we should go into a combination Chinese-Japanese operation like this. The unit would also feature a dynamic cooking show exposed to the customers. Our initial projections show margins comparable to our present margins with Benihana of Tokyo. I see a check of about 99¢. We are negotiating with an oil company to put small units in gas stations. They could be located anywhere—on turnpikes or in the Bronx. I think we should do this very soon. We might call it the "Orient Express." I think I will get a small store in Manhattan and try it out. This is the best kind of market research in the United States. Market research works in other countries, but I don't believe in it here. We are also negotiating for a site on Guam and to take over a chain of beer halls in Japan.

The restaurant business is not my only business. I went into producing; I had two unsuccessful Broadway shows. The experience was very expensive, but I learned a great deal and learned it very fast. It's all up to the critics there. In the restaurant business, the critics don't write much about you if you're bad; but even if they do they can't kill you. On Broadway they can. They did.

I promoted a heavyweight boxing match in Japan. It was successful. I am going into promoting in the entertainment field in Japan. I am doing a Renoir exhibition in Japan with an auction over television. I am thinking about buying a Japanese movie series and bringing it here. I am also thinking of opening a model agency, probably specializing in Oriental models.

My philosophy of the restaurant business is simply to make people happy. We do it many ways in Benihana. As we start different types of operations, we will try to do it in other ways. I have no real worries about the future. The United States is the greatest country in the world to make money. Anybody can do it who wants to work hard and make people happy.

Russ Carpenter, a consultant and editor for *Institutions/Volume Feeding* magazine, summed up his perceptions as follows:

I basically see two main problems. What is Benihana really selling? Is it food,
atmosphere, hospitality, a "watering hole" or what? Is having entertainment in the lounge consistent with the overall image? All the advertising
emphasizes the chef and the food, but is that really what the public comes for?
I don't know. I'm only raising the questions. The other thing is how do you
hedge your bets? Is Benihana really on the forefront of a trend of the future
with their limited menu, cooking in front of you, and Oriental atmosphere,
or is it just a fad? This relates to whether the firm should emphasize restaurant operations only.

Exhibit 1
Operating Statistics for a Typical Service Restaurant

Sales	*Ranges (%)*
Food	70.0–80.0
Beverage	20.0–30.0
Total sales	100.0
Cost of sales	
Food cost (% of food sales)	38.0–48.0
Beverage cost (% of beverage sales)	25.0–30.0
Cost of total sales	35.0–45.0
Gross profit	55.0–65.0
Operating expenses	
Controllable expense	
Payroll	30.0–35.0
Employee benefits	3.0–5.0
Employee meals	0.1–2.0
Laundry, linen, uniforms	1.5–2.0
Replacements	0.5–1.0
Supplies (guest)	1.0–1.5
Menus and printing	0.25–0.5
Miscellaneous contract expense (cleaning, garbage, extermination, equipment rental)	1.0–2.0
Music and entertainment (where applicable)	0.5–1.0
Advertising and promotion	0.75–2.0
Utilities	1.0–2.0
Management salary	2.0–6.0
Administration expense (including legal and accounting)	0.75–2.0
Repairs and maintenance	1.0–2.0
Occupation expense	
Rent	4.5–9.0
Taxes (real estate and personal property)	0.5–1.5
Insurance	0.75–1.0
Interest	0.3–1.0
Depreciation	2.0–4.0
Franchise royalties (where applicable)	3.0–6.0
Total operating expenses	55.0–65.0
Net profit before income tax	0.5–9.0

SOURCE: Bank of America, *Small Business Reporter*, Vol. 8, No. 2, 1968

Exhibit 2

A typical
Benihana floor plan

Benihana West on West 56th Street in Manhattan, which replaced the original restaurant Rocky opened, is typical of the standardized 112- to 120-seat restaurant with a 55- to 60-seat cocktail lounge. The typical Benihana operation has 5,000 to 6,000 square feet.

2 Towel Washer by Hamilton
3 Work Table, custom
4 Work Table, custom
5 Three Compartment Sink, custom
6 Double Overshelf, custom
7 Double Slant Overshelf, custom
8 Rice Stocker, custom
9 Rice Cooker
10 Range With Oven by Vulcan Hart
11 Stock Pot Stove by Vulcan Hart
12 Swing Faucet
13 Exhaust Hood, custom
15 Reach-in Refrigerator by Traulsen
16 Scale by Howe Richardson
17 Combination Walk-in Cooler-Freezer by Bally
18 Adjustable Modular Shelving by Market Forge
19 Adjustable Modular Shelving by Market Forge
20 Shelf, custom
21 Dishwasher with electric booster by Champion
22 Soiled Dishtable with Pre-Rinse Sink, custom
23 Slant Overshelf, custom
24 Clean Dishtable, custom
25 Exhaust Hood, custom
26 Double Wallshelf, custom
27 Twin Soup Urn by Cecilware
28 Single Tea Urn by Cecilware
29 Towel Warmer
30 Water Station with Sink, custom
31 Rice Warmer
32 Utility Table, custom
33 Double Wallshelf, custom
34 Two Compartment Sink, custom

35 Overshelf custom
46 Work Table, custom
37 Open-Front Cold Cast with Adj. Shelves by Tyler
38 Double Overshelf, custom
39 Pre-Check Register by NCR
40 Utility Table with Dipperwell, custom
41 Double Overshelf, custom
42 Ice Cream Dipping Cabinet by Schaefer
43 Ice Cream Storage Cabinet by Schaefer
44 Double Wallshelf, custom
45 Reach-In Freezer by Traulsen
46 Ice Cube Maker by Kold Draft
47 Ice Crusher by Scotsman
48 Adjustable Modular Shelving by Market Forge
49 Pass-Through Refrigerator by Traulsen
50 Sake Warmer
51 Cash Register by NCR
52 Underbar Workboard by Perlick
54 Back Bar Refrigerator by Perlick
56 Underbar Bottle Cooler by Perlick
57 Remote Soda System Dispensing Station by Perlick
58 Remote Soda System Power Pak with Stand by Perlick
59 Pre-Check Register by NCR
60 Cash Register by NCR
61 Shelving, custom
62 Glasswasher by Dorex
63 Time Clock
64 Telephone Shelf Booth
65 Platform Truck by Roll A. Liss
66 Utility Table, custom

Exhibit 2
(Continued)

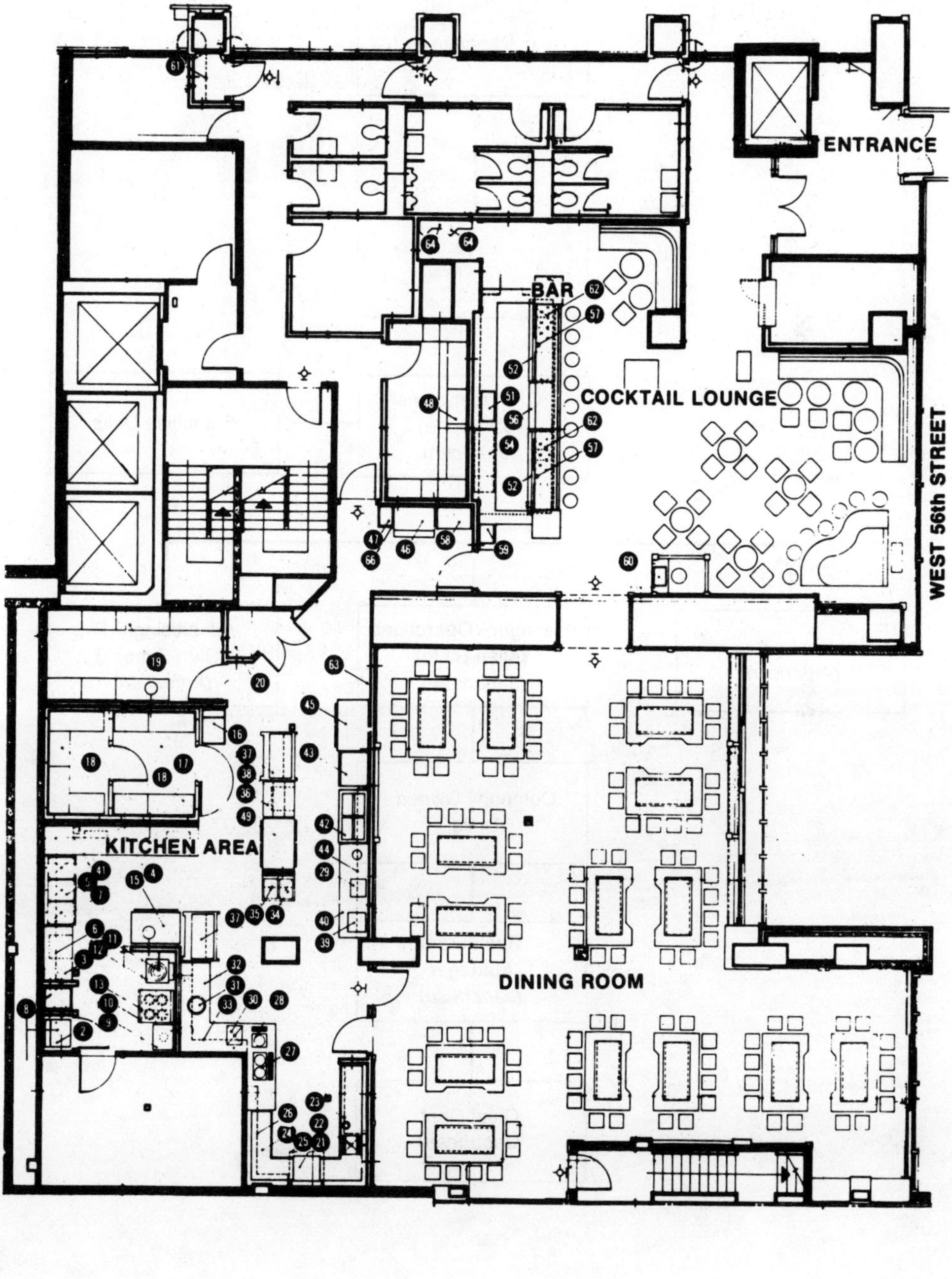

ENTRANCE

BAR

COCKTAIL LOUNGE

WEST 56th STREET

KITCHEN AREA

DINING ROOM

Exhibit 3
Benihana of Tokyo Organization

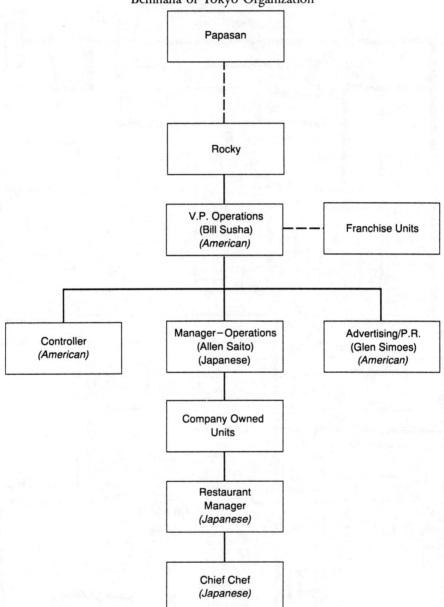

Exhibit 4
What the Customers Think

Every foodservice operator thinks he knows why customers come to his operation. Benihana, which has served two-and-a-quarter million customers in eight years, a high percentage of which were repeat business, thought it knew.

But when he joined as v-p of operations a year-and-a-half ago, Bill Susha wanted to be sure the hallowed presumptions were true.

He devised a questionnaire, and arranged that it be handed to departing customers. A remarkable number took the time to fill out and return the form.

The percentage figures shown here are averages of six stores. While there were many variations from unit to unit, the general thrust was constant, so the six-store figures have been averaged to save space.

The six units included the three in New York City, plus Chicago, Encino, Cal., and Portland Ore. The questions and averages are as follows:

Are you from out-of-town?

Yes	38.6%
No	61.4

Here on:

Business	38.7%
Pleasure	61.3

Do you live in the area?

Live	16.0%
Work	35.9
Both	45.1

Have you been to a Benihana in another city?

Yes	22.7%
No	77.3

How did you learn of us?

Newspaper	4.0%
Magazine	6.9
Radio	4.6
Recommended	67.0
TV show	1.0
Walk by	5.0
Other	11.5

Is this your first visit?

Yes	34.3%
No	65.7

What persuaded you to come?

Good food	46.7%
Service	8.2
Preparation	13.1
Atmosphere	13.3
Recommendation	5.7
Other	13.1

Food was:

Satisfactory	2.0%
Good	20.1
Excellent	77.9

Portions were:

Satisfactory	21.8%
Good	33.0
Excellent	45.4

Service was:

Satisfactory	9.8%
Good	21.6
Excellent	71.3

Atmosphere is:

Satisfactory	6.3%
Good	29.9
Excellent	63.2

(Continued)

Exhibit 4
(Continued)

Would you consider yourself a lunch or dinner customer.		**Sex:**	
		Male	71.4%
Lunch	17.3%	Female	28.6
Dinner	59.0		
Both	23.7	**Income:**	
		$ 7,500–$10,000	16.8%
Which aspect of our restaurant would		$10,000–$15,000	14.2
you highlight?		$15,000–$20,000	17.3
Food	38.2%	$20,000–$25,000	15.0
Atmosphere	13.0	$25,000–$40,000	17.9
Preparation	24.6	$40,000 and over	18.7
Service	16.3		
Different	2.2	**Occupation:**	
Friendly	2.4	Managerial	23.0%
Other	3.3	Professional	26.6
		White Collar	36.9
How frequently do you come		Student	6.9
to Benihana?		Housewife	5.0
Once a week or more	12.1%	Unskilled	1.1
Once a month or more	32.3		
Once a year or more	55.6		
Age:			
10–20	4.2%		
21–30	28.3		
31–40	32.0		
41–50	21.4		
51–60	10.1		
60 and over	4.0		

Exhibit 5
Summary of Benihana Marketing Philosophy

No icky, sticky, slimy stuff

"Part of what makes Benihana successful," Rocky Aoki believes, *"is our advertising and promotion. It's different, and it makes us seem different to people."*

Indeed it is, and does. Much of the credit belongs to Glen Simoes, the hip director of advertising and public relations for Benihana of Tokyo. With a background mostly in financial public relations, Simoes joined the chain a little over two years ago to help open the flagship Benihana Palace. Since then, he's created a somewhat novel, all-embracing public relations program that succeeds on many levels.

"My basic job," he explains, *"is guardian of the image. The image is that of a dynamic chain of Japanese restaurants with phenomenal growth."* Keeping the image bright means exposure. Part of the exposure is a brilliant advertising campaign; part is publicity.

Each has its own function. Advertising is handled by Kracauer and Marvin, an outside agency, under Simoes' supervision and guidance. Its function is to bring in new customers.

"Our ads," Simoes points out, *"are characterized by a bold headline statement and an illustration that make you want to read on. The copy itself is fairly clever and cute. If it works properly, it will keep you reading until you get the message—which is to persuade a stranger to come into Benihana.*

"The ads are designed to still fears about icky, sticky, slimy stuff," he adds. "We reassure folks that they will get wholesome, familiar food, with unusual, unique and delicious preparation, served in a fun atmosphere. We want to intrigue the people celebrating an anniversary or taking Aunt Sally out to dinner. A Japanese restaurant would normally never cross their minds. We're saying we're a fun place to try, and there's no slithery, fishy stuff.

"We have an impact philosophy. We go for full pages in national publications on a now-and-then basis, rather than a regular schedule of small ads. We want that impact to bring the stranger into Benihana for the first time. After that, the restaurant will bring him back again and again, and he will bring his friends.

"We do a good media mix," Simoes concludes. "We advertise in each of the cities in which we operate. Within each market we aim for two people: the resident, of course, but even more, the tourist-visitor. With them you know you're always talking to new people. We appear in city entertainment guides and work with convention and visitor bureaus to go after groups and conventions."

The second factor is publicity. Here, the intent is not the quantity of mentions or exposure, but the type. As Simoes sees it, "We are building. Each mention is a building block. Some are designed to bring customers into the store. Some are designed to bring us prospective financing, or suppliers, or friends, or whatever. We work many ways against the middle. And the middle is the company, the people, Rocky, the growth and all of it put together that makes the image."

Publicity takes many forms, it's media stories, and TV demonstrations. Simoes cites clipping and viewing services to prove that every day of the year, something about Benihana appears either in print or on radio or TV, a record he believes is unique. Publicity is department store demonstrations, catering to celebrities, hosting youth groups, sending matchboxes to conventions and chopsticks to ladies' clubs, scheduling Rocky for interviews and paying publicists to provide oneliners to columnists.

But no engine runs without fuel. And Rocky believes that advertising and promotion are a good investment. Believes so strongly, in fact, that he puts an almost unprecedented $1 million a year into advertising, and probably half that again into promotion, for a total expenditure of nearly 8% of gross sales in this area.

A few months back, Simoes, wholeheartedly pitching his company to a skeptical magazine writer, said heatedly there are "at least 25 reasons people come to Benihana." Challenged on the spot, he came back a few days later with a list of 31. They are:

1) the quality of the food; 2) the presentation of the food; 3) the preparation of the food; 4) the showmanship of the chef; 5) the taste of the food; 6) authenticity of construction; 7) authenticity of decor; 8) continuity of Japanese flavor throughout; 9) communal dining; 10) service—constant attention.

11) Youthfulness of staff; 12) frequent presence of celebrities; 13) excitement created by frequent promotions; 14) type of cuisine; 15) moderate price; 16) the uniqueness of appeal to the five senses; 17) the recent growth in popularity of things Japanese; 18) quick service; 19) unusual advertising concept; 20) publicity.

21) No stringent dress requirements; 22) recommendations from friends; 23) the basic meal is low-calorie; 24) banquet and party facilities; 25) the presence of Rocky Aoki, himself; 26) chance to meet people of the opposite sex; 27) the presence of many Japanese customers (about 20%); 28) locations in major cities giving a radiation effect; 29) acceptance of all major credit cards; 30) the informality of the dining experience; and 31) the use of the restaurant as a business tool.

Exhibit 6

Go forth now and cook amongst the Americans.

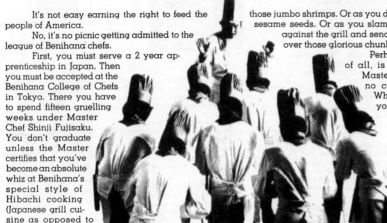

It's not easy earning the right to feed the people of America.

No, it's no picnic getting admitted to the league of Benihana chefs.

First, you must serve a 2 year apprenticeship in Japan. Then you must be accepted at the Benihana College of Chefs in Tokyo. There you have to spend fifteen gruelling weeks under Master Chef Shinji Fujisaku. You don't graduate unless the Master certifies that you've become an absolute whiz at Benihana's special style of Hibachi cooking (Japanese grill cuisine as opposed to classical Japanese cuisine.)

And what are some of the teachings of the Master?

Well, one of the first has to do with the cutting of the meat. "A Benihana chef is an artist, not a butcher," the Master says. So you must learn to wield a knife with dazzling grace, speed and precision. Your hands should move like Fred Astaire's feet.

You also learn that to a Benihana chef, Hibachi cooking is never solemn. As the Master says "It's an act of pure joy." So joy, really, is what you must bring to the Hibachi table. A joy that the people around you can see and feel. A joy they can catch as you sauté those jumbo shrimps. Or as you dust that chicken with sesame seeds. Or as you slam that pepper shaker against the grill and send the pepper swirling over those glorious chunks of steak.

Perhaps most important of all, is this saying of the Master's: "Benihana has no cooks. Only chefs." Which means that while you should be joyous, you must always strive for perfection. So you learn everything there is to learn about sauces and seasonings. You labor to make your shrimp the most succulent shrimp anyone's ever tasted. Your sirloin the most delicious and juicy. Your every mushroom and beansprout a song.

Over and over the Master drills you. Again and again you go through your paces. Fifteen exhausting, perfection-seeking weeks.

But the day comes when you're ready. Ready to bring what you've learned to the people of such faraway places as New York, Chicago and Los Angeles. It's a great moment.

"Sayonara, Honorable Teacher," you say.

"Knock 'em dead, Honorable Graduate," he replies.

BENIHANA of TOKYO

New York – Benihana Palace 15 W. 44 St . 682-7120 • Benihana East 120 E. 56 St.. 593-1627 • Benihana West 61 W. 56 St.. 581-0930
Boston. Harrisburg. Fort Lauderdale. Chicago. Seattle. Portland Ore.. San Francisco. Las Vegas. Encino. Marina Del Rey. Beverly Hills. Honolulu. Tokyo.

Exhibit 7

THEATER OF THE STOMACH

It's a little scary at first.

There you are sitting around this enormous table (which turns out to also be a grill) when suddenly he appears. A man dressed like a chef but with the unmistakable air of a samurai warrior.

He bows. Just to be on the safe side, you bow back.

Smiling inscrutably, he takes out a knife. You make a grab for your chopsticks.

He reaches into the cart he's wheeled in. From it he brings out rows of these really beautiful fresh whole shrimps.

Suddenly, the man turns into a kind of whirling dervish. Zip,

zip, zip...his knife flashes through the rows like lightning. The shrimps (now cut into bite-size morsels) seem to dance to the center of the grill. He presses on. With magnificent, sweeping gestures he adds freshly ground pepper to the shrimps. Then butter. Then soy sauce. The action never stops. He even spins around and throws sesame seeds out from over his shoulder.

At last comes the moment of truth. He flips a sizzling shrimp directly on your plate. You taste it. You have a small fit of ecstasy.

Naturally, that's just the first scene. The show goes on this

way...course after course after course. He performs. You eat. He performs again. You eat again. Steak. Chicken. Mouth-watering vegetables of every variety. You've never had such a feast, you've never seen such choreography.

Finally, it's over. He bows. You sigh. He thanks you. You thank <u>him</u>. He walks off.

If you weren't so full you'd get up and give him a standing ovation.

BENIHANA of TOKYO

New York—Benihana Palace 15 W. 44 St., 682-7120 • Benihana East 120 E. 56 St., 593-1627 • Benihana West 61 W. 56 St., 581-0930
Boston, Harrisburg, Fort Lauderdale, Chicago, Seattle, Portland Ore., San Francisco, Las Vegas, Encino, Beverly Hills, Honolulu, Tokyo.

Exhibit 8

Two philosophies of the steak.

The basic philosophy of the American restaurant.

The chef throws a slab of raw steak into the kitchen broiler.

It sits there until it's rare, medium or well-done.

The waiter brings it to your table.

You eat it.

The Benihana philosophy.

The chef comes right up to your hibachi table. (Why shouldn't you see the man who's actually creating your meal?)

He bows. (There's no reason why a chef can't be a gentleman.)

He sets the raw steak in front of you. (Isn't it nice to see for yourself that you're getting the very freshest, prime cuts?)

He asks you how you want it. (There's no luxury like the luxury of dealing directly with your chef.)

He cuts your steak into bite-size morsels. (Why should you have to perform any labor?)

His knife begins a snappy, rhythmic attack on the onions. (We believe there's as much drama in a dancing onion as in a dancing chorus girl.)

He slams the pepper shaker against the grill. (It's not good for a chef to suppress his excitement.)

As he cooks he adds all kinds of Japanese sauces and seasonings. (No, Worcester sauce is not part of our theory.)

At last he puts the sizzling steak directly on your plate. (The world's fastest waiter couldn't serve you better.)

You eat it. (Tell us. Has there ever been a more palatable philosophy?)

BENIHANA of TOKYO

New York – Benihana Palace 15 W. 44 St., 682-7120   •   Benihana East 120 E. 56 St., 593-1627   •   Benihana West 61 W. 56 St., 581-0930

Boston, Harrisburg, Fort Lauderdale, Chicago, Seattle, Portland Ore., San Francisco, Las Vegas, Encino, Marina Del Rey, Beverly Hills, Honolulu, Tokyo.

Exhibit 9

The Mission of Rocky Aoki

When Rocky Aoki, owner of Benihana, came to America about ten years ago, this was how a great many Americans felt about Japanese food:

(1) It wasn't as good as Chinese food.

(2) It was mostly sukiyaki and soup that tasted like hot brown water.

(3) If you ordered anything besides sukiyaki, you'd wind up with raw, slithery fishy things.

(4) OK, the food was very prettily arranged. But you walked out twice as hungry as when you walked in.

"My task is clear," said Rocky. "I'm going to change the way Americans think about Japanese food. I'm going to introduce hibachi cooking to America."

(Hibachi cooking or cooking on a grill, is nothing at all like the highly stylized classical Japanese cuisine.)

And so, in 1964, Rocky opened the first Benihana. It broke all the rules. You couldn't get sukiyaki there. Or raw fish. There wasn't even a conventional kitchen. You just sat around this big hibachi table—a combination grill and dining table—and waited for your chef to appear.

When he did, he came bearing a feast. Basket upon basket of beautiful fresh meat, poultry and vegetables. Then, right in front of you, he sprang into action. Slicing, seasoning and cooking, he prepared your meal with a speed and skill bordering on wizardry.

It was hard to believe. No exquisitely carved carrot slices. No wispy vegetables arranged in perfect flower patterns. Instead, solid food in abundance. Jumbo shrimps sauteed with lemon. Succulent chunks of steak. Young chicken dusted with sesame seeds. Mushrooms, scallions, beansprouts—served not together in some kind of mish-mash, but individually. It was enough to bring joy to the most jaded gourmet, bliss to the most ravenous appetite.

Well, the first New York Benihana was an enormous success. Within a year, Rocky had to open another one. That too became a smash. Soon Rocky was opening a Benihana in Chicago. And then one in San Francisco. And then another in Las Vegas. Today Rocky has Benihanas all over the United States.

When he opened his third New York Benihana—the Benihana Palace—Rocky Aoki declared: "I'll consider my mission accomplished when everyone in America has tried hibachi cooking at least once."

Come in and give a nice Japanese boy a break.

BENIHANA of TOKYO
No slithery, fishy things.

New York—Benihana Palace 15 W. 44 St., 682-7120 • Benihana East 120 E. 56th St., 593-1627 • Benihana West 47 W. 56th St., 581-0930

Atlanta. Boston. Fort Lauderdale. Harrisburg. Chicago. Denver. Bethesda Md.. Bala Cynwyd Pa.: Seattle. Portland. Ore.. San Francisco. Las Vegas. Encino. Beverly Hills. Marina Del Rey. Miami. Houston. Honolulu. Tokyo. Toronto.

2

◇

Developing a Vision
of the Business

Our general task here is to organize our thinking, both for Rural/Metro Fire Department and Scandinavian Airlines System (SAS), according to the framework provided by the strategic service vision set forth in the article, "Lessons in the Service Sector." In thinking about each venture, ask yourself: At whom is this service targeted? What's the service concept, stated in terms of results produced for customers? How is it being positioned in relation to customer needs and competitive offerings? What's the company's operating strategy, including such things as policies, organization, and human resource practices? How does it help management leverage value achieved for customers over the cost of providing the service (an important determinant of profit)? What are important features of the service delivery system, including facilities, locations, and the capacities they provide? To what extent are they supportive of (and integrated with) the operating strategy?

Now assume the position of the advisor to Chief Louis Witzeman at Rural/Metro Fire Department (RMFD). Can RMFD successfully be expanded on a multisite basis? What key management tasks would be involved in developing and operating branches, and what skills would be required? What short-term actions would you recommend to the new management team?

In addition to the general questions posed above, you might keep in mind the following as you read the Scandinavian Airlines System (A) case: What are the most important features of The First Wave? What has it achieved? What appear to be the most important challenges of The Second Wave? As an advisor to Jan Carlzon, what actions would you suggest he take to address them?

By now you may have concluded that some revisions in the strategic service vision framework and the questions it poses would be useful. This is a positive sign that you too are beginning to think differently and more thoughtfully about services with which you come into contact.

Lessons in the Service Sector
JAMES L. HESKETT

- A large food and lodging company creates and staffs more general management jobs than any ten manufacturers of comparable size. This company, like many others dispensing high customer-contact services, has eliminated functional lines of responsibility between operations and marketing. In its planning the company routinely combines operations and marketing with what I call a strategic service vision.

- The most profitable large American company assumes daily the task of managing a work force of window washers, cooks, and maintenance personnel. An almost single-minded concentration on people—their jobs, their equipment, their personal development—accounts for much of its success.

- The quality control process in a decentralized oil-field services business involves careful selection, development, assignment, and compensation of employees working under varying conditions and in widespread locations where close supervision is impossible. In this prosperous company, the process builds shared values and bonds people together.

- An international airline, by paying more attention to market economies than to production scale economies, reduces the average size of its aircraft and increases its net income.

- Products introduced since 1982 by a well-known financial service generated 10% of its revenues in 1985. The raw material for these products is data already existing in other forms in the company's vast data base.

These examples give a glimpse of forward-looking management practice. When examined closely, they offer insights into the ideas on which successful competitive strategies have been fashioned in the much-maligned and little-understood service sector.

It's no coincidence that dominant industries have cutting-edge management practices. Some U.S. railroads in the nineteenth century pioneered in divisional-

James Heskett is the 1907 Foundation Professor of Business Logistics at the Harvard Business School. Currently he teaches an MBA course, Service Management. This article is an outgrowth of his book, *Managing in the Service Economy* (Harvard Business School Press, 1986). Reprinted by permission of *Harvard Business Review.* "Lessons in the Service Sector" by James L. Heskett (March/April 1987). Copyright © 1987 by the President and Fellows of Harvard College; all rights reserved.

ized management of their far-flung systems and in good procurement procedures to support their sizable construction and operational needs. At the turn of the century, basic industries led the way in experimenting with scientific management. Then the rise of the large consumer goods manufacturer, epitomized by the auto industry, spawned concepts of decentralization and a full product line aimed at carefully segmented markets.

> *Whatever your business,*
> *services have*
> *something to teach.*

Today service industries have assumed the mantle of economic leadership. These industries, encompassing trade, communications, transportation, food and lodging, financial and medical services, education, government, and technical services to industry, account for about 70% of the national income and three-fourths of the nonfarm jobs in the United States. In generating 44 million new jobs in the past 30 years, they have absorbed most of the influx of women and minorities into the work force, softened the effects of every post-World War II recession, and fueled every recent economic recovery.

In view of this leadership role, now is a good time to look at the exemplars in the service sector for insights into ways of boosting productivity and altering competitive strategies. Despite their diversity, leading companies in many service industries display some common themes and practices. And they yield lessons for managers in any sector of business. Let's look first at the way the best service companies are structured.

INTEGRATED FUNCTIONS

Most goods-producing businesses follow the traditional organizational pattern of separate and equally important marketing and manufacturing functions, with coordinating authority at high levels. Some service businesses do the same thing, but the pattern is much less common in service companies where contact with customers is close, as in retailing, passenger transport, and food and lodging. In these businesses, service is marketed and produced at the same place and time, and often by the same person. Naturally, close coordination between marketing and operations management in these cases, regardless of reporting relationships, is essential.

Integration of marketing and operations is often found at very low levels in these organizations. In fact, more than 90% of all field managers in four multisite service companies surveyed in one study claimed responsibility for operations, personnel, and marketing, could not say which was most important, and paid great attention to each.[1]

Even where operations are buffered from marketing activities in organizations offering little customer-contact service, there are ways to break down the traditional functional barriers. Several years ago, the Chase Manhattan Bank launched an effort to upgrade its nonloan products, improve its external communications and customer service, and make its back-office (production) operations more market based. A weak spot was Chase's international business. In the highly visible "product" of international money transfer, differences of viewpoint between marketing—embodied in the account relations manager in the field—and the back office in New York had frustrated communication. Errors were frequent, a large backlog of inquiries about balances and transactions had piled up, and morale in the operations group was poor.

A study ordered by the executive put in charge showed that headquarters accounted for operational errors in only about one-third of all the inquiries and that the marketing people had little idea what operations could offer the bank's customers. The executive traced the backlogged errors to their sources, often a correspondent bank, and resolved them. He launched a campaign to improve operations staff morale around the theme "We make it happen" and formed a new group, the customer mobile unit, consisting of the bank's most experienced international operations people. The unit visited Chase customers at their businesses to help resolve problems and smooth operations. The executive brought the marketing and back-office people together to talk about ways to improve the flow of information. Perhaps most important, the bank revised reporting relationships so that operations units serving specific market segments reported to both the customer relationship manager and the head of operations—a move that improved functional coordination.[2]

The product manager's job was created in many manufacturing organizations to address the problem of coordinating manufacturing and marketing. But in most cases, product managers have had profit responsibility without the authority to coordinate. Assignment to these positions has been regarded as temporary, which encourages decisions with a short-term orientation.

Because of their importance, the high-contact service company makes a point of developing numbers of marketing-operations managers, often carrying the title of store or branch manager. At hand, therefore, is a large cadre of talent from which the company can draw senior managers already trained for administrative responsibilities.

STRATEGIC SERVICE VISION

The need of most service organizations to plan as well as direct marketing and operations as one function has led to the formation in leading companies of what I call a strategic service vision. Its elements consist of identification of a target market segment, development of a service concept to address targeted customers' needs, codification of an operating strategy to support the service concept, and design of a service delivery system to support the operating strategy. These basic elements are bordered by solid lines in *Exhibit I.*

A company naturally tries to position itself in relation to both the target market and the competition. The links between the service concept and the operating strategies are those policies and procedures by which the company seeks to maximize the difference between the value of the service to customers (the service concept) and the cost of providing it. This difference, of course, is a primary determinant of profit. And the link between the operating strategy and the service delivery system is the integration achieved in the design of both. These integrative links are bordered by broken lines in *Exhibit I.*

To see how the strategic service vision works, examine the Hartford Steam Boiler Inspection & Insurance Company. For many years, HSB has been in the business of insuring industrial and institutional equipment. Its market targets are organizations using boilers and related pieces of equipment with high operating risk. It offers the same risk reduction as many other insurance companies but positions itself against the competition by emphasizing cost reduction as well.

HSB concentrates on a few types of equipment and has built a large data base on their operating and performance characteristics. (Manufacturers of the equipment often turn to HSB to get wear and maintenance data.) The information furnishes the actuarial base on which HSB prices its insurance. The company's engineers, who inspect customers' equipment before and after it is insured, are also qualified to give advice on preventing problems and improving utilization rates, and through many years of association they often get very close to their customers. As a service manager of one HSB client told me, "If I tried to replace that insurance contract, my operating people in the plant would let me know about it."

This practice enhances the perceived value of the service to the customer at little extra cost to HSB. Of course, by reducing the risk to the customer HSB can improve its own loss ratio.

HSB has a larger cadre of engineers than any of its competitors. These engineers, in tandem with the big data base, make up a service delivery system that capitalizes on the knowledge of marketing and operating managers at all levels of the organization.

Exhibit I

Externally Oriented Strategic Service Vision

Target Market Segments
What are common characteristics of important market segments?
What dimensions can be used to segment the market?
Demographic?
Psychographic?
How important are various segments?
What needs does each have?
How well are these needs being served?
In what manner?
By whom?

Positioning
How does the service concept propose to meet customer needs?
How do competitors meet these needs?
How is the proposed service differentiated from competition?
How important are these differences?
What is good service?
Does the proposed service concept provide it?
What efforts are required to bring customer expectations and service capabilities into alignment?

Service Concept
What are important elements of the service to be provided, stated in terms of results produced for customers?
How are these elements supposed to be perceived by the target market segment? By the market in general? By employees as a whole?
How do customers perceive the service concept?
What efforts does this suggest in terms of the manner in which the service is:
Designed?
Delivered?
Marketed?

Value-Cost Leveraging
To what extent are differences between perceived value and cost of service maximized by:
Standardization of certain elements?
Customization of certain elements?
Emphasizing easily leveraged services?
Management of supply and demand?
Control of quality through—
Rewards?
Appeal to pride?
Visibility and supervision?
Peer group control?
Involving the customer?
Effective use of data?
To what extent does this effort create barriers to entry by potential competition?

Operating Strategy
What are important elements of the strategy?
Operations?
Financing?
Marketing?
Organization?
Human resources?
Control?
On which will the most effort be concentrated?
Where will investments be made?
How will quality and cost be controlled?
Measurements?
Incentives?
Rewards?
What results will be expected versus competition in terms of:
Quality of service?
Cost profile?
Productivity?
Morale and loyalty of servers?

Strategy-System Integration
To what extent are the strategy and delivery system internally consistent?
Can needs of the strategy be met by the delivery system?
If not, what changes must be made in:
The operating strategy?
The service delivery system?
To what extent does the coordination of operating strategy and service delivery system ensure:
High quality?
High productivity?
Low cost?
High morale and loyalty of servers?
To what extent does this integration provide barriers to entry by competition?

Service Delivery System
What are important features of the service delivery system, including:
The role of people?
Technology?
Equipment?
Layout?
Procedures?
What capacity does it provide?
Normally?
At peak levels?
To what extent does it:
Help ensure quality standards?
Differentiate the service from competition?
Provide barriers to entry by competitors?

☐ = Basic Elements   ⌐ ¬ = Integrative Elements

The net result is a strategic service vision (though HSB doesn't use the term) that is highly valued by its customers and very profitable for its provider. It addresses implementation issues as part of the strategic plan, and it requires agreement and coordination among marketing and operating managers throughout the organization.

INNER-DIRECTED VISION

High-performance service companies have gained their status in large measure by turning the strategic service vision inward, targeting important groups of employees as well as customers. In the head offices of these organizations, questions such as those listed in *Exhibit II* are heard often. The questions parallel those in *Exhibit I;* but in asking them about employees, management shows it's aware that the health of the enterprise depends on the degree to which core groups of employees subscribe to and share a common set of values and are served by the company's activities.

The basic elements, identified as in *Exhibit I*, start with the service concept designed with employees' needs in mind. The operating strategy is set to meet these needs in a superior fashion at the lowest cost, a result often achieved through the design of the service delivery system. The integrative elements in *Exhibit II* include positioning of a service concept, which it is hoped will lead to low turnover, low training costs, and the opportunity to develop shared goals and values. High-performance service organizations invariably have operating strategies designed to maximize differences between operating costs and value perceived by employees in their relations with the company. And delivery systems designed with the operating strategy in mind can form the foundation for remarkable gains in productivity.

A case in point is the ServiceMaster Company, based in Downers Grove, Illinois, which manages support services for hospitals, schools, and industrial companies. It supervises the employees of customers' organizations engaged in housekeeping, food service, and equipment maintenance. These are services that are peripheral to the customers' businesses and therefore get little management attention.

Many of the people whom ServiceMaster oversees are functionally illiterate. To them, as well as its own managers, ServiceMaster directs a service concept centered around the philosophy stated by its CEO, "Before asking someone to do something you have to help them be something." ServiceMaster provides educational and motivational programs to help these employees "be something."

To its own supervisors the company offers training leading to an ambitious

LESSONS IN THE SERVICE SECTOR

Exhibit II

Internally Oriented Strategic Service Vision

Target Employee Group	Positioning	Service Concept	Value-Cost Leveraging	Operating Strategy	Strategy-Systems Integration	Service Delivery System
What are common characteristics of important employee groups?	How does the service concept propose to meet employee needs?	**What are important elements of the service to be provided, stated in terms of results produced for employees and the company?**	To what extent are differences between returns to employees and the level of effort they put forth maximized by:	How important is direct human contact in the provision of the service?	To what extent are the strategy and the delivery system for serving important employee groups internally consistent?	What are important features of the service delivery system, including: The role of people? Technology? Equipment? Layout? Procedures?
What dimensions can be used to describe these employee groups? Demographic? Psychographic?	How do competitors meet such needs?	How are these elements supposed to be perceived by the targeted employee group?	The design of the service concept?	To what extent have employees been involved in the design of the service concept and operating strategy?	To what extent does the integration of operating strategy and service delivery system ensure: High quality? High productivity? Low cost?	What does it require of target employee groups? Normally? At peak periods of activity?
How important are each of these groups to the delivery of the service?	How are relationships with employees differentiated from those between competitors and their employees?	How are these elements perceived?	The design of the elements of the operating strategy?	How desirable is it to: Increase employee satisfaction? Increase employee productivity?	High morale and "bonding" of the target employee group?	To what extent does it help employees: Meet quality standards? Differentiate their service from competitors? Achieve expectations about the quality of their work life?
What needs does each group have?	How important are these differences?	What further efforts does this suggest in terms of the manner in which the service is: Designed? Delivered?	Job design?	What incentives are provided for: Quality? Productivity? Cost?		
How well are these needs being served?	What is "good service" to employees?		The leveraging of scarce skills with a support system?	How does the strategy address employee needs for: Selection? Assignment? Development? Evaluation? Compensation? Association?		
In what manner?	Does the proposed service concept provide it?		The management of supply and demand?			
By whom?	What efforts are required to bring employee expectations and service capabilities into alignment?		Control of quality through— Rewards? Appeal to pride? Visibility? Supervision? Peer group control?			
			Involving the customer in the delivery of the service?			
			Effective use of data?			

☐ = Basic element ⌐ ⌐ = Integrative element

54

"master's" program taught in part by the chief executive. New responsibilities and opportunities present themselves via the rapid growth of the company, approximating 20% per year, nearly all of it from expansion of existing operations rather than acquisition. Elaborate training aids and a laboratory for developing new equipment and materials enhance the employee-managers' "be something" feeling.

For customers' employees ServiceMaster tries to build the "be something" attitude and improve their productivity by redesigning their jobs and by developing equipment and pictorial, color-coded instructional material. In most cases it is the first time that anyone has paid attention to the service of which these employees are a part. ServiceMaster also holds weekly sessions to exchange ideas and offers educational programs to, among other things, develop literacy. ServiceMaster also recruits up to 20% of its own managers from the ranks in jobs it handles. The service concept clearly is improved self-respect, self-development, personal satisfaction, and upward mobility.

Another company slogan, repeated often, is "to help people grow." When a hospital served by the company decided to hire a deaf person, ServiceMaster's local head didn't object. Instead he authorized three of his supervisors to take a course in sign language.

It should be no surprise that the turnover rate among ServiceMaster's 7,000 employees is low. Further, the turnover rate in organizations it services is much lower than the averages for their industries. And when ServiceMaster takes a job, the productivity achieved by supervised support workers invariably rises dramatically.

Now a billion-dollar company, ServiceMaster had a return on equity from 1973 through 1985 that was the highest of all the largest service or industrial companies in the United States, averaging more than 30% after taxes. It oversees the support service employees for 15 hospitals in Japan, which probably makes it the largest exporter of managerial talent to Japan. According to one ServiceMaster executive, "The Japanese immediately recognize and identify with what we do and how we do it." This company turns its strategic service vision inward with dramatic results.

THE VISION APPLIED

In addition to building a strategic service vision, the best service companies apply it to customers and to those who deliver the service and oversee its delivery—in new or different ways. From my study of organizations like Hartford Steam Boiler and ServiceMaster, I've gathered a series of lessons useful for service providers to consider. These lessons can furnish goods producers food for thought too.

Rethink Quality Control

Executives whose careers have spanned service as well as manufacturing agree that reaching a consistently high quality level is tougher in services. In high-contact (so-called high-encounter) services, the interaction between two people or more varies with each transaction. In low-contact services, people many miles from the customer have to rely on their own judgment in handling orders and other transactions and in fielding complaints.

> ### The best companies integrate
> ### operations and marketing.

Those who have tried to solve the quality control problem by adding more supervision have found that it limits effectiveness. A service transaction cannot be halted, examined, and recycled like a product.

The most effective approaches to the problem have included restructuring of incentives to emphasize quality, designing jobs to give service providers higher visibility in dealing with customers, and building a peer group to foster teamwork and instill a sense of pride.

One incentive that is often effective in organizations ranging from rapid transit companies to hotels is the employee-of-the-month award—especially if based on customer feedback. Both monetary and nonmonetary incentives have been used successfully. What's more, the cost is low.

Making the person who delivers the service more visible is another technique. In England, at the Lex Service Group's luxury auto dealerships, the customer is encouraged to go directly to the mechanic working on the car. The Shouldice Hospital near Toronto, Canada, specializes in the repair of hernias using only a local anesthetic—a practice that allows the doctor to talk with the patient during the operation. Defective work is referred to the doctor responsible. The remission rate for hernias performed at Shouldice is less than one-tenth that of the average North American hospital. At Benihana, the U.S. chain of Japanese-style steak houses, the chef cooks at a grill in front of the restaurant guests. The chef's visibility and proximity to customers promote a consistently high quality of service and a consistently high level of tips.

Incentives and visibility may be insufficient for those tasks performed without supervision and out of view of the customer. In these cases, some companies rely on careful selection and thorough training of employees and the development of programs to build both a sense of pride in the service and a sense of identification with the company. This bonding process can be hard for rivals to emulate and can thereby contribute to competitive advantage.

Exhibit III
How Success Builds High-Contact Services

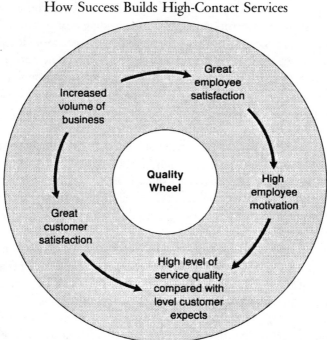

Schlumberger's wire-line service has roughly 2,000 geological engineers, each responsible for a mobile rig equipped with more than $1 million worth of computers and electronic gear that helps predict the outcome of petroleum producers' drilling efforts. Each year the company recruits those it considers the brightest of the crop of college engineering graduates, spends months teaching them how to use the equipment, and goes to great lengths to make them feel a part of a special tradition. As one engineer put it recently, "Indoctrination is just as important as technical training." This is all in preparation for an assignment to represent Schlumberger in the field, without direct supervision, often in a remote part of the world. Two measures of the success of this program are Schlumberger's dominant share of the world's wire-line business and the profit-to-sales ratios for this company, which consistently exceed others in its industry in good times and bad.

Often effective in achieving and maintaining quality is peer group control, supported by incentives, training, job design, and service delivery system design. In cases where professional standards have been established for a task, they reinforce peer group control.

In an architectural firm, the mere existence of a policy requiring partners' review of every piece of work can keep partners and associates on their toes. Surgeons are sometimes assigned in teams to foster the learning process and encourage peer group control. A partner of a leading real estate development company told me, "There are three things I'm most concerned about in my work. In this order, they are not to embarrass my colleagues, not to cast a bad light on the company by inadequately serving my clients, and making money." It's not surprising that this company has a strong sense of shared values, reinforced by a policy of encouraging partners to invest in the projects that they propose and carry out.

Recent research suggests that the internal strategic service vision, quality control, and success are connected, especially in those providers of high-encounter service requiring judgment in delivery. I show it as the "quality wheel" in *Exhibit III*. Studies directly link customer satisfaction and the resulting sales volume to the satisfaction derived by the person serving the customer.[3] Naturally, the more motivated the employee, the better the service.

The selection and development of employees, care in assignment, and the layout and equipment of the facility (in a high-contact environment) are all integral elements of the design of the service encounter, which in turn is based on the company's assessment of customer needs. Preconditioning of the customer may also be a part of the design of the service encounter. Review and redesign of the encounter go on continually as the organization assesses how well it is meeting those needs.

A part of the internal service vision is the design of policies and performance measures that further the fulfillment of customers' needs. For example, the server's well-being in the job apparently depends, at least in part, on the extent to which his or her superiors emphasize the solution of problems for customers rather than strict adherence to a set of policies and procedures.[4]

Driving the self-reinforcing elements of the wheel of quality takes a great deal of executive time and requires an honest interest in people across the organization. The senior vice president for finance of Delta Airlines, an organization well regarded for its service and its employee programs, remarked recently, "I would guess that 25% of the time of the finance department officers is spent listening to people problems."

For most service companies, people obviously are more important than machines in the control of quality. But even where the machines employed carry an unusually high value, as in Schlumberger and Delta, developing and building the dedication of people takes precedence.

Reassess the Effects of Scale

In service organizations, scale economies are often much more important at the company level than at the operating unit level. This is particularly true for companies that have many units over wide areas connected by a common identity. Such scale gives McDonald's and Hertz great purchasing clout and General Cinema the advantage of selling soft drinks of its own manufacture.

Large scale at the company level is important for exploiting network effects, a phenomenon much more important in the service than in the manufacturing sector. To a point, the addition of new network links augments volume for those parts already in place, thus building average network capacity utilization. The addition of service to Las Vegas from its Memphis hub gave Federal Express more volume on the Memphis-New York link. When Visa adds a large retailer to its network of card-accepting establishments, it increases the attractiveness of its credit card to present and potential cardholders and the potential volume to be realized by retailers already accepting the card.

> **Effective service requires**
> **people who**
> **understand the idea.**

Bigger is not better in those service industries in which the factory must be taken into the marketplace to sell a more accessible, visible, and convenient product that meets customers' needs. Factories operated by the Hyatt and Marriott organizations (called hotels) have not, on average, grown in size for years. These companies have settled on a range of hotel dimensions that can be designed, located, and operated effectively to achieve the capacity utilization, quality of service, and financial performance they want. The range describes sizes at which diseconomies resulting from poor supervision and inflexibility tend to outweigh advantages of larger scale. In the design and siting of hotels, Hyatt and Marriott give the less quantifiable advantages of market flexibility weight equal to operating economies of scale.

At the unit operating level, many service companies have found that the loss of flexibility and greater difficulty in supervising those delivering the service far outweigh any savings realized in operating costs as unit size grows. In the rush to cut costs per seat-mile, for example, many of the world's airlines bought large, wide-bodied aircraft like the Airbus 300 and McDonnell DC-10. While these planes performed admirably, their effective utilization required funneling large numbers of passengers into the airline's hub. Moreover, because business travelers, who represent the most attractive market segment, are prone to choose an airline on the basis of times and frequency of flights, the load and schedule consolidation necessary for effective employment of wide-bodied aircraft worked against the goal of building traffic.

When Jan Carlzon became CEO of Scandinavian Airlines System in 1980, wide-bodied aircraft were used extensively between the airline's hub at Copenhagen and major cities like London and Paris. With smaller DC–9s, SAS funneled travelers between the hub and other Scandinavian cities. To reclaim the business travelers SAS had lost, Carlzon relegated most of the wide-bodies to charter work and offered nonstop flights using DC–9s between Scandinavian and principal European cities.

A size question confronts nearly every power utility in the United States today. For years it was industry gospel that the more power-generating capacity concentrated in one place, the greater the economies of scale. This was the case until the 1970s, when ever-larger units began encountering reliability problems. Furthermore, construction schedule stretchouts, at times fomented by environmental groups' agitation against big plants, caused the expected power-generating economies to vanish. Finally, an improved capability for transmitting excess energy from one market to another made it possible to buy energy for less than the big units could afford to charge. So many utilities today are meeting the needs of smaller markets' fluctuating demands more economically through new means.

Replace and Create Assets with Information

For decades, manufacturers have sought ways of substituting information for assets. Foremost among these are forecasting and inventory control techniques. For many service operations, information offers creative new ways to substitute for assets.

Heating oil dealers, by maintaining data on the capacity of their customers' tanks, on habitual consumption rates, and on weather, program fuel oil deliveries to provide 100% availability while reducing delivery times and the number of trucks and drivers. These companies substitute information for assets.

The Rural/Metro Fire Department extends effective fire protection at a fraction of the cost of most municipally run fire departments. This Scottsdale, Arizona-based company analyzes data on past fires and uses much smaller, less expensive trucks staffed with smaller crews and equipped with a large-diameter hose that can shoot a lot of water on a fire very fast. On the way to a fire, a truck crew can learn the floor plan of the building to which it is going. While speeding through the streets, the crew examines a microfiche of the layout on a screen. Rural/Metro substitutes information for assets.

Many service industries are information driven, beginning with familiarity between the server and the served. In many (not all), assets have never been allowed to become dominant, perhaps because of limited capital. But with the development of new technologies for processing and communicating information, companies in these industries have advanced far beyond the use of information as a substitute for assets. They are instead using the information they have collected in one business as the basis for new services.

Companies servicing manufactured goods, for example, have built data bases on the types, wear rates, and failure rates of various parts of a furnace, appliance, or automobile. A company can use this information for sending timely service reminders to customers and also to manage parts inventories to reflect the age and condition of the particular machine serviced. In the process, the data have taken on great value for the producers of the goods—and they're willing to pay for the information.

A credit card service builds expenditure profiles for its customers; broken patterns may signal a problem like stolen cards. Theft is sometimes suspected when a large expenditure is made far from the cardholder's address. Instead of outright disallowance of a retailer's request for a big charge, one major travel card issuer tries to determine whether the cardholder indeed is traveling in the retailer's area. Information collected for this service yields person-specific data about travel patterns that often is valuable to airlines and hotel chains (to name two businesses). But the company limits the use of such information to ways that benefit its cardholders.

Dun & Bradstreet's $2.7 billion enterprise is centered on its data base, a file of credit information describing businesses in 30 countries. Through development and acquisition, the file steadily grows. D&B has consistently realized about 10% of its revenues from business that did not exist three years before. Nearly all of these services use the same data base but package the information in different ways. A potential competitor would have to spend an estimated $1 billion—nearly half D&B's net asset value—to duplicate the data base.

Though a data base may constitute a service provider's most important asset, it doesn't appear on the balance sheet and can't be depreciated. But the degree to which many such companies rely on an accumulation of knowledge as their chief competitive weapon and source of new business development suggests opportunities for their counterparts in the manufacturing sector.

Harlan Cleveland has pointed out that information, unlike most manufactured products, is often infinitely expandable (as it is used), compressible, substitutable (for capital, labor, or physical materials), transportable, diffusive (hard to keep secret), and sharable (as opposed to exchangeable).[5] If it is infinitely expandable, those who possess it are limited only by their imagination in creating new ideas, revenue sources, and job opportunities. As the demand for creative exploitation of information grows, so will job creation in the service sector.

THE SERVICE ECONOMY

Many successful service providers have strategies in common that offer lessons to other companies. Among these are:

Close coordination of the marketing-operations relationship.

A strategy built around elements of a strategic service vision.

An ability to redirect the strategic service inward to focus on vital employee groups.

A stress on the control of quality based on a set of shared values, peer group status, generous incentives, and, where possible, a close relationship with the customer.

A cool appraisal of the effects of scale on both efficiency and effectiveness.

The substitution of information for other assets.

The exploitation of information to generate new business.

Why these particular lessons among all I might cite? For one reason, they feature characteristics that distinguish many service industries from goods-producing industries. Notice the emphasis on people, ideas, and information instead of things. For another, they promise twin benefits as part of a business strategy. Each can further differentiation of the service product as well as lower costs.

These lessons have significance for the economy too. While the service economy has wrought a gigantic social restructuring of the United States, it has come in for unwarranted criticism for its low rate of productivity gains. Companies like those I have described, however, have created new jobs while raising productivity. If other companies learn these lessons, job opportunities in the service sector will continue to expand and productivity continue to rise. These developments will ease the pressures for the inflation of service prices, sharpen the already respected competitiveness abroad of U.S.-based services, and contribute to the partnership between services and manufacturing that is crucial to a healthy, balanced national business base.

NOTES

1. Christopher H. Lovelock, Eric Langeard, John E. G. Bateson, and Pierre Eiglier, "Some Organizational Problems Facing Marketing in the Service Sector," in *Marketing of Services,* ed. James H. Donnelly and William R. George (Chicago, Ill.: American Marketing Association, 1981), p. 168.
2. See James F. Loud, "Organizing for Customer Service," *The Bankers Magazine,* November—December 1980, p. 41.
3. Benjamin Schneider and David E. Bowen, "New Services Design, Development, and Implementation and the Employee," in *New Services,* ed. William R. George and Claudia Marshall (Chicago, Ill.: American Marketing Association, 1985), p. 82; and Eugene M. Johnson and Daniel T. Seymour, "The Impact of Cross Selling on

the Service Encounter in Retail Banking," in *The Service Encounter*, ed. John A. Czepiel, Michael R. Soloman, and Carol F. Surprenant (Lexington, Mass: D.C. Heath, 1985), p. 243.

4. This is the implication of John J. Parkington and Benjamin Schneider in "Some Correlates of Experienced Job Stress: A Boundary Role Study," *Academy of Management Journal*, June 1979, p. 270.

5. Harlan Cleveland, "Information as a Resource," *The Futurist*, December 1982, p. 37.

Rural/Metro Fire Department*

In the fall of 1980, Chief Louis A. Witzeman, founder, president, and owner of Rural/Metro Corporation, was preparing to retire from the largest privately owned and operated fire protection company in the United States. Since its formation in 1948, Rural/Metro had grown to provide fire protection to over 20% of Arizona's population, as well as communities in Tennessee and, until recently, Georgia. Several municipalities, such as Rural/Metro's home base of Scottsdale, Arizona, a Phoenix suburb, contracted for the company's services. In unincorporated areas, Rural/Metro operated on a subscription basis, providing fire protection to subscribers' homes for an annual fee.

Chief Witzeman may not have worn a white hat, but he did ride a white horse, as he liked to think of Rural/Metro. "I devoted my entire life to proving this white horse can gallop," he explained, "and I want it to keep galloping." So, in 1979, after rejecting several offers from outsiders to buy the company, Witzeman sold Rural/Metro to his employees through an Employee Stock Ownership Plan (ESOP). As part of the arrangement, Witzeman's equity of approximately $750,000 would be paid out of earnings over the next four to six years.

"I sold this company to my employees for less than I could have gotten otherwise, but that was a fair trade-off in my eyes," Witzeman said. "Nobody will ever know how much I love this outfit and the people who work here."

"Chief Witzeman planned to spend his retirement traveling, consulting, and lecturing on private management of public services. Before he retired, however, he wanted to ensure that a proper strategy had been chosen for Rural/Metro. Attempts to expand the company in other parts of the country had been fraught with difficulties, but there were many opportunities to increase the range of services offered. As James Bolin, Rural/Metro's controller, phrased it, the essential question facing management was: "Do we dance with the person we brought to the party or do we search around the dance floor for the one we really want to dance with?"

*All financial data in the text and exhibits of this case have been disguised, except where such data are a matter of public record.

This case was prepared by Assistant Professor David H. Maister, with the assistance of Research Assistant Rocco Pigneri, as the basis for classroom discussion rather than to illustrate either effective or ineffective handling of an administrative situation. Copyright ©1981 by the President and Fellows of Harvard College; Harvard Business School case # 681-082 Rev. 5/89.

COMPANY HISTORY

Rural/Metro got its start when twenty-two-year-old Lou Witzeman, then a reporter for the *Arizona Times*, watched a neighbor's house burn down because the area was beyond the Phoenix Fire Department's jurisdiction. Anxious about the safety of his own home, Witzeman tried to organize a tax-supported fire district in the neighborhood. When that didn't work, Witzeman asked his neighbors to pledge $10 per year to purchase, maintain, and operate a fire protection unit. At first this also was unsuccessful, but Witzeman expanded the proposed area of operation, contacted more residents, and eventually collected the $10,000 necessary to begin operations.

At its inception in 1948, Rural/Metro had a single pumper, four firefighters, and a makeshift $3,000 station. Additional equipment and personnel were acquired over the next three years as funds became available. When Scottsdale was incorporated in mid–1951, the new city administration contracted with Rural/Metro to provide fire service to the area.

By 1980 Rural/Metro was the oldest and most successful private fire protection firm in the United States. Approximately 12 other such firms were known to exist, but most were rural mom-and-pop operations covering very small areas. In contrast, Rural/Metro had expanded rapidly, along with the growth in population of Scottsdale and adjacent areas. It had also grown by expanding beyond the Phoenix area, and by increasing the range of services offered.

In fiscal 1980, company revenues exceeded $6 million from five operating units. The largest, accounting for the vast majority of revenues, was Rural/Metro Fire Department, Inc. (RMFD), which served Maricopa County, including Scottsdale (*Exhibit 1*). Apart from regular fire protection services, RMFD earned revenues from forest (brush fire) protection services during Arizona's dry season, and from various security services. A second operating unit, Aztec ambulance, provided ambulance services in Pinal County. In 1980 Aztec, on approximately $100,000 of revenues, lost approximately $20,000. A third unit, Yuma Rural/Metro Fire Department, provided fire protection to the suburbs of Yuma, 200 miles from Scottsdale in Arizona's southwest corner. In 1980, Yuma RMFD netted less than 6% of its (roughly) $200 thousand in revenues. Tennessee RMFD, a 50%-owned unconsolidated affiliate started in 1977, derived its revenues from subscription fire protection; Georgia RMFD operated fire protection services under contract to Hall County, Georgia.

Additional revenues came from consulting activities by Chief Witzeman and other members of Rural/Metro's management team. Because of its pioneering status and numerous firefighting innovations, Rural/Metro received many inquiries from across the United States and Canada about its activities, and performed fire department audits for municipalities.

Rural/Metro's contracts with municipalities—known as master accounts—*usually covered a 3- to 5-year period with annual adjustment clauses*, and were negotiated directly with municipal authorities.

In areas not served by a master account contract, homeowners or property owners paid, in advance, a yearly subscription fee based on the square footage of the structure or structures to be protected. This fee averaged $43 per property in 1980. The subscription business was regulated in Arizona by the Arizona Corporation Commission (ACC), a three-member elected utility commission that also regulated the state's water, gas, and electric utilities.

Rural/Metro did not own all of the property and equipment used in its business. In Hall County, Georgia, for example, the county owned the stations and equipment, and Rural/Metro had merely provided the service. In Scottsdale and Sun City, Rural/Metro owned about half of the equipment, whereas in some smaller communities it owned it all. In 1980, Rural/Metro had approximately 600 employees, about 300 of which were full time. Of the part-time employees, only about half received a paycheck in any one month. All employees were nonunion, although there was an attempt to unionize the company in the mid–1970s.

Rural/Metro doubled its revenues between 1976 and 1980, although its profitability was erratic. (See *Exhibits 2, 3.*) In 1978, a substantial amount of bad debts was expensed by Aztec ambulance, and an investment in an affiliate was written off, distorting 1978 results. A primary reason for the turnaround in 1980 was the recent rate increases granted by the ACC on subscription business. Other areas that produced improvements were forest-fire protection, which proved to be an excellent margin business, and a one-year rate increase of 17% in the master contract with Scottsdale.

ORGANIZATION

Along with Lou Witzeman, Rural/Metro's top management team (*Exhibit 4*) included Ron Butler, operations manager, who had been with the company since 1968. Before joining Rural/Metro, Butler spent eight years as a professional firefighter with the Glendale Arizona Fire Department, after several years' experience as a volunteer firefighter in Pennsylvania. Dan Giblin, sales director, managed the company's subscription sales efforts, while Jim Bolin, previously with a public accounting firm and a regional hotel development company, joined Rural/Metro in 1979 as controller. James Stenger oversaw the ambulance and security operations, and Bob Edwards, administrative battalion chief of Scottsdale, was in charge of RMFD's fire prevention activities.

RMFD, Rural/Metro's main operating arm, was organized into five battalions, each with a chief. As shown in *Exhibit 5*, these battalions operated 26 fire stations with 67 vehicles, covering 1,750 square miles. *Exhibit 6* presents operating statements for each of the battalions.

THE SCOTTSDALE CONTRACT

Rural/Metro's contract with the city of Scottsdale covered a five-year period before it came up for renegotiation. Payments to Rural/Metro were renegotiated every year, being $92,108 per month in 1979 and $97,526 per month in 1980. The contract also provided for increased payments to Rural/Metro to allow for rising payroll costs. These increments were based on the average compensation of firefighters in the five largest incorporated cities of Maricopa County, and on the U.S. Consumer Price Index. The contract specified that Rural/Metro was to provide 17 full-time positions. Although the contract called for staffing levels to be set so that each full-time position *could* be staffed 24 hours per day, Rural/Metro retained the right to schedule its work force during the day as it saw fit. In addition to these firefighter positions, Rural/Metro was expected to provide a chief, clerical and accounting personnel, and auxiliary firefighters at a proportion of two auxiliaries for each full-time position. Auxiliaries were to be recruited from among the employees of the city of Scottsdale, with all wages and costs being borne by the city.

Rural/Metro's obligations under the contract included annual reporting of fire statistics and annual inspections of industrial and mercantile establishments, fire hydrants, and other fire prevention equipment. It would make available to residents of the city "routine technical and fire protection advice such as is customarily offered by fire departments," and assist the city in the enforcement of its fire codes. Rural/Metro would "use its best efforts" to maintain the city's Insurance Services Office (ISO) grade and, in consultation with the city manager, choose a time to apply for upgrading.

The Insurance Services Office (ISO) assessed fire risk in communities throughout the United States, basing its assessment on a variety of factors, including the quality of fire protection services, building density, water availability, etc. It awarded "deficiency points" for each category and summarized its findings in a rating from 1 (outstanding) to 10 (very poor). This rating was used by insurance companies to set insurance levels.

When a fire alarm came in, Rural/Metro was obligated to dispatch at least one piece of fire equipment, unless it had actual knowledge that the alarm was false. For any structural fire, Rural/Metro had to respond with three fire trucks and 15 trained firefighters, except in multiple-alarm situations. For a fire of "conflagration proportions," Rural/Metro was required to dispatch all of its available equipment and, if necessary, to request aid from adjacent fire departments.

The contract explicitly recognized Rural/Metro's subscription activities in areas adjacent to Scottsdale, and acknowledged that the contract fees were based on the sharing of equipment costs across the contract and subscription services.

THE FIRE AUXILIARY SYSTEM

An important element of Rural/Metro's operation was its use of fire auxiliaries, or reserves. In Scottsdale, for example, 37 city employees, chosen primarily from the ranks of the public works and parks departments, were trained by Rural/Metro and used to supplement its full-time firefighting force. This allowed the company to maintain a full-time staffing level of only 0.49 employees per 1,000 population, compared with a national average of 1.67.

Applicants for auxiliary positions had to pass a physical and/or entry examination, and take the same basic training as full-time firefighters. The 94-hour auxiliary training program was a condensed version of the state-mandated 220-hour training course given to full-time firefighters. Auxiliaries were trained not only in the routine aspects of firefighting, but also for specialized tasks such as laying lines, nozzle work, and salvage and ladder work. Chief Witzeman estimated that auxiliaries became proficient at 50–66% of the tasks required in firefighting. He commented:

> The auxiliary is the G.I. Joe of firefighting. He is neither paid for being, nor expected to be, a line officer involved in critical decision making or the complexities of the more technical aspects of firefighting.

Auxiliaries were organized into four shifts. They were on call one week, and then off for three weeks. During their on-duty weeks, auxiliaries carried radio pagers and were assigned as firefighters, drivers, or officers of their assigned "companies." When an alarm was received, the auxiliaries responded directly to the fire or to the assigned fire apparatus.

An auxiliary's salary was paid by the city. A monthly retainer, ranging from $35 to $67.50 depending on rank and seniority, covered all responses during normal working hours. If summoned at other hours, the auxiliary was paid

$6.34 per hour with a minimum of one hour's pay. The average work time lost to the city through this system averaged one hour per man per month. Statistics revealed that fires occurred in Scottsdale pretty much according to a textbook curve, with a heavy incidence late in the day, and almost no activity during the very early morning hours. Two consistent peaks were indicated over the years, one around noon and the other in the early evening.

Chief Witzeman commented on the auxiliary system:

> The program is, at its most basic, an updating of the old volunteer system. That system began to fail in many areas as our way of living evolved into one in which it was routine for an individual to work miles away from home, as fire problems became more complicated, and for a number of other reasons that resulted in an inadequate level of discipline and training. Our program responds to these problems in the following ways. Our auxiliaries are full-time employees of the communities in which they serve. Consequently, they face the same problems if they fail in their part-time vocation of firefighting that they would if they failed to turn up for their regular job. Furthermore, the auxiliaries are always available because, as city employees, they live in or close to the city and work in the city.
>
> We have no problem recruiting auxiliaries. In fact, we don't have to do any recruiting at all since we have more applicants than we can use. For the auxiliary there is an excellent opportunity for job enrichment; the routine of day-to-day work is enlivened by excitement, a break from routine, a chance to serve the community. In many cases, the auxiliary's status as a firefighter exceeds that of his regular task. The enrichment works both ways. The firefighter responding to an alarm responds not only with his normal forces, but with engineers and other professional talent of the city who are in the auxiliary force. The city building inspector who has been a fire auxiliary turns a very sensitive ear to the needs of the fire department when he has not only inspected, but stood on the "safe side" of that fire wall the department fought for before the Board of Appeals!

In fiscal 1979, the auxiliary program cost the city of Scottsdale $85,600 in addition to Rural/Metro's fee of $930,000. Including hydrant rentals ($36,700), depreciation on buildings ($9,000), and other operating expense ($63,800), the total cost to the city for its fire protection was $12.50 per capita. This corresponded to a 1977 national average of $33.80 per capita for communities of Scottsdale's size. Per-capita fire loss was $8.49 during fiscal 1978, compared with a national average (including heavily industrialized and unprotected areas) of $13.00. Scottsdale's ISO rating provided another measure of Rural/Metro's effectiveness. In September 1980, the city's rating was upgraded from 5 to 4.

OPERATIONS

In master contract areas such as Scottsdale, fire stations were located so that
85% of the population was within five miles of a station and 95% was within
ten miles. When an alarm was received, the dispatcher obtained as much information as possible, including the type and severity of the emergency, the address,
and the phone number. Rural/Metro's dispatchers often encountered problems,
since many residents lived in Arizona for only a few months of the year and
were unfamiliar with addresses and locations.

When as much information as possible had been obtained (all telephone and
radio communications were taped and stored for one year for data collection,
management control, and legal reasons), firefighting equipment was rushed to
the scene. The amount and type of equipment dispatched depended on, among
other factors, the nature and severity of the reported fire, according to decision
rules pre-established by Rural/Metro management. While a conventional complement of firefighters and equipment would be dispatched to a structural fire,
for a relatively minor incident—such as a car fire—only an "attack truck" with
one firefighter would be dispatched.

The attack truck was one of Rural/Metro's most prominent innovations.
Painted lime green instead of the traditional red ("It looks like hell," noted Chief
Witzeman, "but the color doesn't wash out at night and we have drastically
reduced tail-end accidents"), most of Rural/Metro's equipment was built by the
company from old trucks it had salvaged, cannibalized, and reassembled. Rural/
Metro found that it could build trucks for a half to two-thirds of what it would
cost to buy new ones, and sometimes for even less. "There's no chrome on our
trucks," was one of Witzeman's favorite observations. Furthermore, from detailed analysis of fire data, Witzeman had discovered that close to 80% of all
fires were extinguished with less than 300 gallons of water. Accordingly, Rural/
Metro designed and built a specially equipped oversized pick-up truck with a
300-gallon water capacity. Dubbed the attack truck, this vehicle could be operated by a single firefighter. Chief Witzeman commented:

> The attack truck with one firefighter is always among the first pieces of
> equipment we send to a fire. If the fire is big, the additional firefighters
> and equipment also sent are there to do their job. But frequently, all but the
> attack truck can be returned.

Upon arrival, the senior officer at the scene (or the first to arrive) reported to
the dispatcher the severity and exact type of emergency. The fire station chief,
who overheard all communications, then determined whether additional equipment should be sent, and reported to the emergency himself to direct activity.
All on-duty reserves reported to all structural fires.

When there was an emergency that required more than the attack truck, trucks, firefighters, and auxiliaries from adjacent stations moved equipment to predetermined locations midway between the responding station and the adjacent station. This way, Rural/Metro's tightly staffed stations could respond quickly to multiple emergencies in the same district. These relocated, stand-by resources held their positions until all men and equipment returned to the responding station. Under this system, Rural/Metro units were generally en route to an emergency within 1.2 minutes of the alarm and at the scene within 5 minutes.

In subscription areas, much the same procedure was followed, except that reserves played a more active role, because full-time staffing was leaner. In fact, some subscription stations required no more than one full-time firefighter on duty at any time. In the event of a fire, some reserves reported to the station to obtain equipment while the rest reported to the fire, rather than all reserves reporting to the scene, as in a master contract area. *Exhibit* 7 presents a run report for a fire in a subscription area. (Run reports were completed after all alarms in all areas.)

Among Rural/Metro's fire suppression innovations was a special type of hose. Fire companies across the United States generally used two-and-a-half-inch diameter hose, but Rural/Metro believed that the European four-inch hose brought more water to the fire faster, while using less hose. Since American manufacturers did not produce the larger hose, Rural/Metro imported it from Europe. Bob Edwards, administrative battalion chief, noted:

> The tradition of the smaller hose dates back to the horse and manual pump days, when that was the maximum weight a firefighter could carry for long distances. Today, with synthetic materials, a four-inch plastic hose weighs half as much as that old two-and-a-half-inch hose. But the smaller size is still the mainstay of most fire departments.

Rural/Metro also helped to develop other special equipment, such as a remote-controlled fire hydrant opening device, and a remote-controlled tank-like "robot firefighter" that could advance 400 feet of hose to a fire too hot for firefighters. It also had experimented with a microfilm viewer mounted in fire trucks so that firefighters could study the floor plan, roads, and hydrant layout of a fire site while en route to the fire.

NONFIRE CALLS

Not all the calls Rural/Metro received were fire calls. In its subscription areas, Rural/Metro responded to 14,320 calls of all types in calendar 1978. Of these,

3,560 were fire calls, 6,437 were first-aid and rescue calls, and 4,223 represented all other categories combined. Often a householder would report a fire, only for Rural/Metro to discover burning toast, faulty domestic fire detectors, or the like. Whereas 23% of calls turned out to be fires, 41% were reported as such, and actual first-aid calls turned out to be 30% rather than the 35% reported.

First-aid calls were an important part of Rural/Metro's service, particularly in subscription areas. In these areas, which often did not have local ambulances and hospitals, Rural/Metro's fire stations were, by miles, the closest source of aid. Resuscitation equipment was kept in all stations, and all employees were given emergency medical training. In a survey conducted by the magazine *Arizona Weekly*, 43% of respondents said they would call their fire department if they needed emergency medical attention in their home (compared with 23% who would call a physician and 15% who would call an ambulance or hospital).

Chief Witzeman noted:

> We do a great deal more than putting out fires and that's appropriate. The firefighter is, and should be, the emergency odd-jobs man of the public.
> We have one station that kills more snakes than it puts out fires. Of course, we respond to community attitudes: in Fountain Hills, we kill the snakes; in Tucson, we turn them loose in the mountains! All of these community odd jobs can create a personnel problem; many of the guys don't like doing these sorts of things.

FIRE PREVENTION

Bob Edwards, administrative battalion chief, was in charge of Rural/Metro's fire prevention activities. His staff was very involved in city activities that affected fire protection—long-term city planning, building permits, occupancy permits, site plan review, fire drills and escape plans for hospitals and schools, hydrant installation, and other construction and development activities.

Rural/Metro's prevention activities were unique in that full-time firefighters comprised the "safety survey" staff. (Rural/Metro avoided the use of the terms "inspectors" and "inspection.") In this way, suppression and prevention were integrated rather than separated, as in conventional fire departments. One immediate outcome was a high arrest rate for arson. Because Edwards' staff was well equipped to identify and trace arsonous activities, 74 confirmed cases of arson led to 40 arrests, compared with a national average of 10 arrests per 100 arson fires.

Chief Edwards felt that maintaining good public relations was a vital part of his duties. He and his staff personally maintained ties with the media, city councils, mayors' offices, and the public in general. Every nonresidential building was inspected at least annually. Restaurants and hotels were checked every two to three months and hospitals were visited twice a week, with a major inspection every 90 days. Chief Edwards aimed for cooperative and amicable attitudes in safety surveys, with constructive suggestions given rather than fines or harsh orders.

In Rural/Metro's experience, the public's opinion of a fire department depended upon what the public encountered in the media. Therefore, Rural/Metro established many programs that allowed the public and the media to interact in a friendly, nonemergency setting, such as station open houses, free weekly blood pressure checks, and grade school lectures.

Rural/Metro's emphasis on cooperation was evident in 1980, when an ordinance requiring sprinkler systems in buildings that had not previously required them was proposed to the Scottsdale City Council. Rather than demanding the systems, and perhaps receiving bad press from the disgruntled owners, Chief Edwards' staff worked with manufacturers to design a sprinkler system that would pay for itself in six years through insurance premium savings.

In creating a safer Scottsdale through innovative and positive means, Rural/Metro was working with a city widely praised for its innovative civic management. For example, approximately one-third of its police force were civilians, performing clerical duties and relieving uniformed officers of "nonprofessional" tasks. It also had introduced mechanized garbage trucks with hydraulic arms, so that garbage workers could do their work without leaving the cab of their trucks.

SUBSCRIPTION SALES AND OPERATIONS

The sales department at Rural/Metro was responsible for sending out annual bills and increasing the subscriber base. Existing accounts were billed once a year, with follow-up reminders and letters sent to those failing to renew. When an account became delinquent by 30 days, it was given to a field representative for collection.

The responsibilities of the field representatives were to locate unsubscribed properties, to explain Rural/Metro's services, to collect firefighting information such as access, special hazards, and swimming pools, and, of course, to close the sale. In the majority of cases, homeowners reaped a financial benefit from subscribing, the drop in their insurance rates being as much as two to three times Rural/Metro's average $43 fee.

In 1979, 18,000 new accounts were generated by an average of 20 salespeople, who were compensated on a commission basis averaging $18,300 per year. Renewals ran at an average rate of 85% from year to year.

Rural/Metro had tried many methods of selling. Initially, it had used direct mail. In its existing service areas, however, over 80% of households were already signed up and it was felt that personal selling was required. Rural/Metro had also explored the possibility of having subscriptions collected along with house payments, and at one time had contacted every major mortgage company in Maricopa County, but had found little interest. In growing areas, such as Sun City, Rural/Metro worked with subdividers to ensure that they knew about the company, and that they told their buyers. Dan Giblin concluded:

> The fact remains that human nature is such that it expects some personal explanation of the service. People sign up and pay guarantees in advance for their telephone, gas, electricity, and water, because if they didn't the lack of these items would be immediately evident and they would be uncomfortable. If there is no fire protection, they don't think about it until disaster strikes or threatens.

In the year ended March 31, 1979, selling expenses at Rural/Metro totaled 25.6% of total subscription revenue and 77% of new-subscriber revenues. Of these expenses, 63% were sales commissions, and the remainder were sales-related costs and activities. In 1980, the ACC allowed Rural/Metro to charge a $20 initiation fee for first-time subscribers, of which the salesperson retained $9. No commission was paid on renewals.

Rural/Metro served subscribers both in areas adjacent to master contract stations (by agreement with the municipality) and in all-subscription areas. An example of all-subscription operations was the Yuma RMFD. Covering a sparsely populated area of 400 square miles, Yuma had one full-time firefighter position (staffed by two individuals who rotated shifts) and 30 auxiliaries. As in master contract areas, Rural/Metro had no difficulty attracting reserves, and did no advertising or other recruiting. Reserves were mainly young, blue-collar workers, many on night shifts. College students who lived free in the stations but were paid only for responses to alarms were also used. Yuma RMFD had three stations, but only one was manned. The other two, which housed only trucks, were operated by the reserves, who would report to the station when an alarm came in and collect the equipment. Because of the heavy use of reserves, inspection activities in remote all-subscription areas were somewhat curtailed. "Most people," commented Chief Witzeman, "don't believe a one-person station works. But one person, properly trained, is generally sufficient for the type of fires encountered in these areas."

Rural/Metro did not refuse service to nonsubscribers in a subscription area. If summoned, it would put out the fire, but charge 14 times its annual subscription fee plus a charge for labor and equipment hours. "We've never had any trouble collecting," noted Chief Witzeman, "and if we fail to put out the fire, we don't charge."

MANAGEMENT CONTROL

Witzeman received a regular series of reports on Rural/Metro's operations. Included among these were monthly battalion income statements, injury reports, vehicle accident reports, major customer complaints, and safety survey reports. Run reports were reviewed on an exception basis. Witzeman estimated that only 20% of all reports were worthy of detailed attention.

Ron Butler, operations manager, reviewed all battalion budgets monthly, and took care of significant equipment, customer, and operational problems. He traveled widely, making both scheduled and unannounced visits to fire stations, and screened information on water use, fire loss, number of calls, and elapsed times (between call-in, dispatch, and arrival) sent in monthly from each station. While Witzeman stayed mainly in Scottsdale, Butler took main responsibility for Rural/Metro's remote operations.

Witzeman noted that the information reporting system developed at Rural/Metro was very rare in the industry:

> Nobody has a system like ours. We are sitting on a gold mine of data that no other department has. Our concern for profitability has forced us to monitor and measure things that municipal departments never do.

In top management's view, the key to successful operations was the battalion chief. These individuals controlled their own budgets, set in agreement with headquarters. They were also responsible for personnel issues, particularly the selection and motivation of firefighters. According to Butler:

> The battalion chiefs have no real rules to follow. As long as they are effective and meet their budgets, I do not step in. I have no real daily contact with the battalions except for phone calls to ensure that all is going well and to solve minor problems.

All of Rural/Metro's current battalion chiefs had been promoted from within the company. "Our critical constraint is finding good battalion chiefs," noted Dan Giblin, marketing vice president. "All of the critical day-to-day decisions are theirs. We are not sure that we could bring in someone from a traditional municipal department to fill that role here; we would have to 'RURALize' them first."

Ron McManus, the battalion chief at Yuma, who was due to move to head-quarters to be Ron Butler's assistant, noted:

Being responsible for Yuma was like running my own business. I had all the responsibility, including good community relations, which is vital in this business. I was evaluated mainly on my subscription sales results, meeting my budgets, and, of course, on good service to my community.

A number of Rural/Metro's managers pointed to the important role played by Witzeman in the success of the company. Chief Edwards commented:

Working for Lou is different than working for the government. I have worked for municipal fire departments, but there was so much red tape that it was impossible to get anything done. Lou's great. If he agrees with a project, you're totally free to do it. Lou creates a spirit by complimenting you, especially when you least expect it. You'll be having lunch with some-body and Lou will tell that person about something you did six months ago that you thought passed by without his noticing. I have received terrific job offers, just as everyone else here has, but I refuse to leave.

Butler added:

There is a tremendous dedication in this firm. Most employees began work-ing for this company for nothing. Only recently has Rural/Metro been able to pay salaries at parity with other departments. Of course, our employ-ees get a lot of "strokes" from the community and from top management. We pass down compliments we receive from the public, comments and other good words. We go to fires, partially as a form of quality control, and so that the men don't feel that they are out there alone.

Chief Witzeman explained:

We have benefited from our underdog image. The underdog syndrome af-fects nearly everyone here, including clerical people and new firefighters. The feeling of "notoriety," that we are doing something different and worth-while, is a "kick" for all our personnel. We all have a feeling of pride as experts in our field, a feeling of belonging in our community. Also, our men are four or five times more qualified than the average municipal firefighter. The types of responsibility and decisions we require from one firefighter are shared by many people in a traditional fire department. Some of the things our firefighters are called upon to do only a battalion chief can do elsewhere. This responsibility breeds involvement and dedication.

TENNESSEE RMFD

In 1977, Rural/Metro bought out and consolidated three private firms offering subscription fire protection services in Tennessee. With these operations, Rural/Metro inherited a poor image, particularly from two of the three firms. "People felt that they had been ripped off so many times they would rather go without service than try again," commented Chief Witzeman. Compounding Rural/Metro's problems was the fact that it was hard in Tennessee for subscribers to lower their insurance premiums by buying Rural/Metro's services. Many areas were unprotected and rated 10 (very poor) by the ISO, and premiums could not be reduced until Rural/Metro had penetrated the market sufficiently and been operating long enough to justify an upgrading of the whole area.

Changes instituted by Rural/Metro included converting one 24-hour station into an 8-hours-per-day, 5-days-per-week station; bringing in a marketing supervisor; creating an operations manager; developing auxiliaries; expanding the maintenance program; and controlling the budget more tightly. In spite of these changes, Tennessee RMFD lost $80,000 in its first year, broke even in its second, and lost $57,000 in its third on revenues of $750,000. Butler concluded:

> We had some special problems in Tennessee. We inherited some equipment that was not up to our standards, and it took time to replace it. Given the low revenue base with which we started, we had a cash problem. The management and supervisory people we put in (or inherited) were not as strong as we would have liked, and because it was effectively a start-up, the pay scales were too low. If we had invested up front all the money we have subsequently spent, we would not have had the problems we did. But when you are opening up a subscription area, the economics sometimes prevent you from immediately putting in place the full level of staffing and equipment for which you are aiming.

GEORGIA RMFD

In November 1979, within a month of a report on Rural/Metro broadcast on the televised news program *60 Minutes*, Chief Witzeman was asked by Hall County, Georgia officials to audit their fire department operations. As a result of this audit, Rural/Metro made a proposal to Hall County to operate its fire department that was accepted, and the municipal department was closed down. Rural/Metro sold its management expertise and manpower to the county, which retained ownership of the buildings and equipment.

Soon thereafter, a referendum, led by the municipal fire department members, was held to recall the commissioners who had made this decision. The referendum was successful, and five new commissioners were elected. Rural/Metro continued to operate under its contract, eventually hiring approximately 60% of the original county firefighters.

One year later, as the time for contract renewal approached, the new commissioners decided to go to the people with a referendum asking whether private contract fire protection service should continue, or whether the county should revert to a county employee operation. Because Rural/Metro had provided a better level of fire *and* ambulance service for less than the cost of the prior fire protection alone, the people voted to retain private contract service.

When contract renewal time arrived, the commissioners put the contract up for bid. A new firm, whose directors were mainly local people, was formed and bid against Rural/Metro. The new firm's bid was $10,000 lower than Rural/Metro's (on a $1 million contract), and it was awarded the contract.

Georgia Rural/Metro had made a profit of approximately 3.5% of its revenues in its one year of operation. After it lost the contract, Rural/Metro heard reports that the service in Hall County had "returned to its previous lackadaisical level."

THE FUTURE

As they looked to the future, Rural/Metro's top management reflected on the difficulties of expanding fire protection services in other areas. Chief Witzeman commented:

> If there's one thing that hurts fire services, it's tradition. Changes have been too slow in coming, and too many people have paid heavy penalties for making them. Firefighters are like old mules. Years ago they were respected. Today they're grazing in the back pasture on dying grass. Heaven help those who mess with the image of big, red, chrome-burdened fire trucks, heroic firefighters, and the rest of the paraphernalia and tradition of the fire service. If the union doesn't get you for doing so, the voters will. Still, major change is inevitable. It will ultimately benefit all involved in the service tremendously.
>
> In providing fire service, the easy copout is to be content with the 1,250-gallon-per-minute pumper you have calculated that you need, pay from $100,000 to $125,000 apiece for brand-new, custom-made pumpers, schedule four or five full-time firefighters on duty around the clock for each pumper you have installed, be sure the pumping capacity is available

throughout your community at distances between one-and-a-half and three miles from every structure, and sit back and relax. Almost nobody will argue with your methods, because they will be quite conventional. Unfortunately, you will probably be spending at least twice as much money as you need to. Right now, a lot of firefighters spend 90% of their time playing ping-pong and polishing chrome.

One of the factors threatening the future growth of Rural/Metro's fire services was annexation of unincorporated areas (to which Rural/Metro provided subscription service) by adjacent cities. In Arizona, for example, cities such as Phoenix annexed new areas to increase population so that the annexing city would become eligible for more federal funding. This practice accelerated just before each national census. The high population growth rates of Maricopa County encouraged such annexation. A single annexation three years earlier caused Rural/Metro to lose $400,000 in subscription revenues.

James Bolin, controller, commented:

We are currently pursuing additional master accounts. They generally require less working capital than establishing a subscription service area. The costs of providing full service to a subscription area start on day one, while it can take years to develop the market penetration necessary to yield the subscription revenue needed. Both revenue and expense start simultaneously in a master account. Additionally, the larger master accounts generally provide some of the equipment for us, reducing the need for capital. In the long run, while there may be more profit potential in serving on a subscription basis, developing that business can put a significant fiscal strain on the company. It is a case of risk and return going hand-in-hand.

Because of its reputation in Scottsdale, Rural/Metro had many opportunities to expand its services locally (e.g., in forest-fire services and security). In fact, the company was considering contacting a cable TV installer to look into the feasibility of wiring home burglar alarms to the cable service and to Rural/Metro's alarm rooms. Additionally, forest-fire services could be expanded by forming a full-time crew of specially trained forest-fire fighters with mobile equipment who could follow the "brush-fire pattern," which moved annually from Arizona and New Mexico in early summer to central California in late summer.

Each year, Rural/Metro received 150–200 enquiries from municipalities that wished to learn more about its system. This formed the basis for a growing consulting business, accounting for up to 500 man-days in 1980. Butler explained:

We started out charging only $250 per day plus expenses to audit municipal fire departments and make recommendations, which we now realize was pretty cheap. More recently, we have been charging $600 per person per day (plus expenses), which means that an audit for a community of 20,000 people will cost $12,000 to $15,000. For a community of 50,000 to 100,000, the extra days required would raise the bill to over $20,000. It's hard for us to charge more. Within Rural/Metro, we have spent our careers looking for ways for municipalities to *save* money; it doesn't come easily to us to raise our consulting prices. Besides, we always hope that, as a result of our audits, the communities will ask us to come in and run their systems for them. Unfortunately, our ability to expand our consulting activities is limited. There are only a few people within Rural/Metro who can be spared, or who have the full range of expertise, to engage in it.

Other ideas for additional services included initiation of care and feeding of the elderly, and medical warning systems. Jim Bolin maintained:

Even though we run as lean as we can, there is dead time for full-time positions that could be put to use, especially at night. For example, our contract in Sun City calls for more manpower and equipment than may be necessary. Because Sun City is mainly comprised of elderly residents who are more helpless in a fire or emergency, they insisted on more resources than we recommended. We probably could find some way to put this idle capacity to use. For example, we could offer Sun City residents a beeper, wired into our alarm room, to summon help when they are in need of medical assistance.

Giblin reflected:

We have a good data base on our customers. We know they are concerned about fire safety, and we make it a point to know the number of residents, the type and size of structure they own, whether they have a swimming pool or not, and so on. Since we have such good demographics for approximately 70,000 households in Arizona, we could try to sell merchandise such as fire insurance.

With all of these options facing them, in addition to an offer to provide fire protection services at 17 Saudi Arabian airports, Rural/Metro's top managers had to decide "who they were going to dance with."

Exhibit 1
Schematic Maps of Arizona and Maricopa County

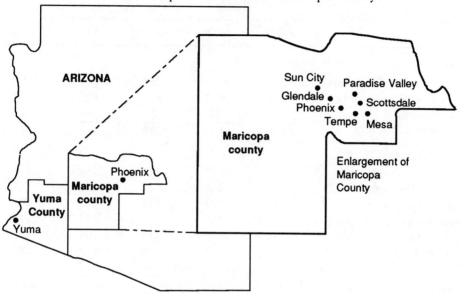

Exhibit 2
Corporation Income Statements, 1976–1980
($000)

	1980	1979	1978	1977	1976
Revenues					
Fire Fees and Subscriptions	5538	4634	3758	3021	2540
Ambulance & Security Fees	584	453	235	392	512
Miscellaneous	70	33	26	99	83
TOTAL	6192	5120	4019	3512	3135
Costs and Expenses					
Payroll & Payroll Taxes	4254	3679	2875	2486	2144
Rent and Utilities	272	246	187	155	145
Maintenance	246	175	127	122	104
Insurance	232	220	151	124	119
Gas and Oil	193	146	113	104	97
Depr. & Amort.	223	215	190	212	188
Other	581	445	372	219	249
TOTAL	6001	5126	4015	3422	3046
Operating Income	191	(6)	4	90	89
Adjustments[a]	7	2	(69)	—	—
Interest	(84)	(82)	(78)	(108)	(88)
Income before Taxes	114	(86)	(143)	(18)	1
Income Taxes	39	—	—	—	0.15
Net Income	75	(86)	(143)	(18)	0.85

[a]Gains on sales of fixed assets and equity in loss of affiliate.

Exhibit 3
Corporation Balance Sheets, 1976–1980
($000)

	1980	*1979*	*1978*	*1977*	*1976*
Assets					
Cash	196	96	28	48	39
Subscription Receivables	282	138	70	164	154
Prepaid Subscription Sales Expense	203	262	279	157	167
Other Current	184	174	140	128	48
Total Current	866	671	517	487	408
Land	98	102	101	172	165
Buildings and Improvements	185	214	209	254	172
Trucks and Automobiles	939	746	576	566	593
Equipment	923	873	751	653	562
Leased Equipment	643	462	527	461	426
Accumulated Depreciation	(1213)	(1020)	(851)	(736)	(594)
Net Property, Plant and Equipment	1575	1376	1313	1369	1323
Other Assets	214	203	205	173	214
Total Assets	2655	2251	2035	2029	1946
Liabilities					
Accounts Payable	205	396	251	169	234
Prepaid Subscriptions	1365	1140	1013	877	748
Current Position, LTD	175	158	161	197	187
Other Current	335	124	99	72	73
Total Current	2080	1817	1523	1315	1242
Notes Payable	592	567	559	613	582
Deferred Taxes	—	—	—	—	—
Common Stock	125	126	124	126	126
Retained Earnings	(143)	(258)	(172)	(10)	10
Treasury Stock	–	—	—	—	(15)
Total Stockholders' Equity	(17)	(133)	(48)	102	122
Total Liabilities and Equity	2655	2251	2035	2029	1946

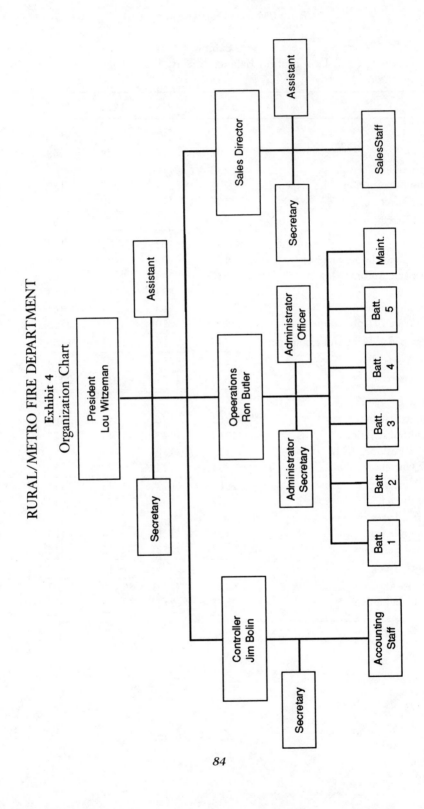

RURAL/METRO FIRE DEPARTMENT

Exhibit 4

Organization Chart

President
Lou Witzeman

Assistant

Secretary

Sales Director

Assistant

Secretary

SalesStaff

Opeerations
Ron Butler

Administrator
Officer

Administrator
Secretary

Maint.

Batt. 5

Batt. 4

Batt. 3

Batt. 2

Batt. 1

Controller
Jim Bolin

Secretary

Accounting
Staff

RURAL/METRO FIRE DEPARTMENT
Exhibit 5
Battalion Profiles

Battalion #	1	2	3	4	5
Location:	Scottsdale	Mesa	Sun City	Tucson	Green Valley
# Stations	7	5	6	7	1
# Vehicles	20	9	15	16	7
# Full-time positions*	25	7	15.5	10	3.5
# Reserves	20	30	25	50	15
Population Protected ('000)					
Subscription	14	99	96	110	10
Master	109	0	56	19	10
Area in Sq. Miles					
Subscription	450	300	500	400	100
Master	180	0	17	76	15
1978 Responses					
Structural fire	307	105	234	208	54
Nonstructural fire	1081	507	840	1423	78
First aid	3069	1136	1936	3419	487
Other	2946	824	1608	1558	235
Total	7403	2572	4618	6608	854
Master/Subscription	5673/1730	25/2547	1248/3370	147/6461	642/212

*Approximately 2.5 people are needed to man each position on 24-hour basis.

Exhibit 6
Battalion Income Statements, 1980
($000)

Battalion #	1	2	3	4	5
Location:	Scottsdale	Mesa	Sun City	Tucson	Green Valley
Revenues:					
Master-fire	1302	—	833	79	192
Subscription	497	522	400	1229	39
Fire Fees	21	3	10	16	—
Ambulance Sub.	26	—	—	7	—
Ambulance Fees	17	—	—	—	47
Bad Debts	(4)	—	—	—	(2)
Alarm Room	3	—	1	—	—
Other	13	—	8	49	—
TOTAL	1875	525	1252	1380	276
Expenses:					
Payroll	1222	166	676	362	133
Utilities	30	9	28	17	8
Insurance	73	12	34	29	10
Maintenance	74	38	64	47	10
Payroll Tax	188	26	107	59	22
Supplies	19	6	13	11	4
Other	178	82	128	137	40
TOTAL	1784	338	1050	662	227
Profit/Loss	91	188	202	718	49

Exhibit 7

RURAL/METRO FIRE DEPARTMENT

RURAL FIRE PROTECTION CO.
– RUN REPORT –

Date: 6/29/80 .... Run No. 7-80-340

ALARM CLASSIFICATION DISPATCHED
RESIDENTIAL ☐ COMMERCIAL ☐■
STILL ☐ FIRST AID ☐
SPECIAL DUTY ☐

Type fire: Trailer/Haystack from: YC30 ... S: .... Area: Yuma .... Dist: Four .... Insured? .... Insurance Co. .... Loss: $40,000.00

Address: Highway 95 & County 19th Owner: Howard Daniels .... Occupant: Howard Daniel .... Potential: $150,000.00 Loss est. by: YRMFD

Potential est. by: YRMFD .... Extent Ins. Coverage: .... Officer in charge: Owens .... Nearest Co. Sta. 17 ... mi. Sq. ft. of fire bldg. 729

Percentage of building involved at arrival: 100% .... Percentage of building involved after control: .... Alarm Time: 1423

TRUCK No.	STA. No.	MANPOWER	GALLONAGE FROM BOOSTER TANKS	1½" LAY	2½" LAY	4" LAY	HP or BOOSTER LINES USED	ALARM RESPONSE 1	2	3	OUT	97	IN
R-70	70	Ford SUBSCRIBER ⊗ NON-SUBSCRIBER	250				HP	*			1426	1446	1748
P-70	70	Babb	1,000	200'				*			1433	1450	1930
T-70	70	Scala	2,000	100'				*			1440	1510	1930
E-81		Somerton Firefighters	500				HL	*			1431	1434	1841
E71	71	Littlefield, Comer		Somerton Stand-by				*			1434		1906
B-70	72	Warner		Stand-by Station 70				*			1451	1508	1841
E7	1042	Owens						*			1433	1451	2015
E7a	1042	Hartsfield						*			1433	1500	2020
TOTALS			3,750							Total all water:	18,000		

WATER USE from other source than tank: Source: East Main Canal 14,000 Stand Pipe San Luis 250 .... Gallons: .... Manpower to fire but not sent on trucks: ....

Injuries: ∮ .... None

Manpower of stations: Daniels, Foster, Ritter, Winterhaven F.D. Unit #21 .... Cause: Unknown .... is cause definite.

with two firefighters.

DESCRIPTION OF OPERATION: R-70, P-70, T-70, Somerton E-1 responded to a commercial assignment reported as a trailer fire at Howard Daniel pellet mill (DBA Big D Feeds). Upon arrival R-70 found a mobile home fully involved, with exposures to the east and north. Somerton E-1 began an attack from the north protecting exposures, and upon the arrival of P-70 two 1½ lines were pulled and began attacking the fire was the east and south. The fire in the mobile home was quickly knocked down.

CONT...

SIGNED .... OK by Chief ....

Office Copy

At approximately this point a double haystack to the east and north of the fire ignited and rapidly spread. At this point efforts were concentrated on the haystack to prevent fire spreading into the mill area adjacent to the haystack. The haystack was allowed to burn down, while exposures to the mill and equipment were protected. After the fire was no longer a threat to the mill, and mop up was completed, all units returned to quarters.

MILITARY TIME

* Detail closely under "Description section
∮ On all injuries list cause, name, age, address, sex, doctor called, ambulance called, exact treatment given by department and who gave it

87

Scandinavian Airlines System SAS (A)
The First Wave

In its corporate heart every airline knows that its essential
product, an airline seat, is no different from any other's, give or
take a couple of inches of width or height or a bit of extra
padding.

SURVEY AIRLINES
The Economist

Our business is not flying airplanes, it's serving the travel needs
of our public. If we can do better than the other companies,
we'll get the business. If we can't, we won't get the business and
we don't deserve to.

JAN CARLZON
Scandinavian Airlines

In 1981 Scandinavian Airlines System, SAS as it is known in the industry, was struggling with a severe downturn in business and an accumulated two-year deficit of $30 (Skr 150) million after 17 consecutive profitable years. The worldwide recession had cut deeply into the airline industry and the multinational board of directors of SAS was understandably concerned.

The company president Knut Hagrup had resigned in 1978 and had been replaced by Carl-Olov Munkberg. Munkberg resorted to drastic cost cutting, including the elimination of 1,300 jobs through attrition. Expenditure dropped, but so did SAS's reputation. Then Curt Nicolin, an SAS director and chairman of ASEA, Sweden's huge electrical equipment manufacturer, persuaded the board to bring in Jan Carlzon. Young and energetic, Carlzon had a flair for marketing which had made him a public figure in Scandinavia, where his views on business and government financing had been sought by press and television.

His philosophy that the public would respond to creatively positive solutions and less bureaucracy had struck a popular chord and he had two success stories behind him to prove it. In his first year as head of Vigressor, a wholly owned tourist subsidiary of SAS, Carlzon had turned the company's results from deficit to profit. During the four years of his tenure, he expanded retail outlets through Sweden and Norway, added a hotel division and created holiday areas in 20 countries.

In 1978 Carlzon became president of Linjeflyg, the Swedish domestic airline that owned 50% of SAS. Within a year he restored the airline to profitability by launching price differentiation, low fare innovation, and boosting schedules to double passenger traffic. This he did despite stiff opposition from his management, which he later replaced. Nicolin had calmed the SAS board's fears that Carlzon was too much of a publicity hound and late in 1980 they placed Carlzon in charge of the airline division, retaining Munkberg as president. The arrangement caused conflict and confusion and Nicolin lobbied to put an end to the situation. By mid–1981 Carlzon replaced Munkberg.

COMPANY AND INDUSTRY BACKGROUND

SAS is the national carrier of Denmark, Norway and Sweden. Born in 1946 when the owners of the three flag carriers merged their fleets into a single airline, it comprises a consortium of three companies, Danish Airlines (DDL), with 2/7 ownership, Norwegian Airlines (DNL) with 2/7 ownership, and Swedish Airlines (ABA) with 3/7 ownership. Each parent airline is a limited company owned 50% by its government. The remaining 50% is held by more than 4,000 private and industrial investors. The SAS group includes this consortium of companies plus some 20 subsidiary and affiliated ones in transport-related sectors: catering, restaurants, and hotels, travel agencies and tour operators, domestic and charter airlines, cargo forwarders and insurance. The airline accounts for about 80% of the group's business both in turnover and profit.

SAS is in a unique situation compared with its European counterparts in that it has three domestic markets—Norway, Sweden and Denmark. Competing airlines tend to have a simple star-like routing system from one central airport, but SAS has the same star-like structure with a triangle in the center, representing the three airports of Kastrup (Copenhagen), Arlanda (Stockholm) and Fornebu (Oslo).

The Scandinavian market is small, geographically dispersed and is somewhat on the periphery of the mainstream of airline traffic. The cost level, the rate of inflation, and government user charges are generally high in Scandinavia and labor unions are strong.

The company's three basic route networks operate in totally different competitive environments: *domestic* which runs the five most important local routes and has access to the major slice of the market; *European and inter-Scandinavia,* where joint agreements and regulations imply that SAS should have a 50% share of any routes it operates; and *intercontinental* where its market share of world traffic is low and competitive.

Being a tri-country airline creates some built-in inefficiencies. For example, although Sweden dominates the consortium, a balance in numbers has to be kept on all levels, from management to crew in flight. Certain complementary head-office functions are split. The large main computer frames are located in Copenhagen, whereas the data division is in Stockholm. SAS has to retain three crew bases, one in each of the major cities and often crews have to be moved around as passengers in order to pick up a flight from another airport. A large proportion of the flights, particularly in Denmark, cover very short distances. There are also more maintenance bases than is justified by traffic volume.

Most nations have their own national carriers. Ownership varies from full government control to entirely private ownership. International aviation is governed by more than 2,000 bilateral agreements among the nations involved. These agreements determine capacity that may be offered and the destinations which may be served. They also prescribe that fares and rates be approved by the authorities in the countries involved.

Until about 1975 when the first oil crisis made its impact on the airline business, the industry had been stable and growing. After 1975 the picture changed dramatically. The world market was stagnating. Oil prices rose fast. President Carter introduced deregulation policies in America. England followed. Then the Common Market came out in favor of more liberal aviation. Newly licensed airlines began to compete on price, and the accelerating rate of growth in "package deals" exploded. The airlines continued to share the market with pool agreements and other arrangements. This new competition didn't, however, affect the final customer (in Europe). Rather, travel agents, forwarders and other middlemen benefited.

During this time and up to 1981, SAS had all the negative traits associated with deficits: declining productivity, overcapacity, poor punctuality and a bad service image on the ground. Kastrup, the main hub in the SAS system, was not looked upon, especially by Swedish and Norwegian customers, as a good airport. In fact, these passengers tried actively to avoid landing there.

But as far as most of the staff were concerned, the fact that SAS had lost Skr 150 million didn't seem to concern them. As one executive recalls "Life went on quite normally. People who join an airline business tend to stay forever. Most people had been here 10, 15 even 20 years. They couldn't have cared less whether we were in the black or red. . . ."

THE CARLZON PHILOSOPHY

Carlzon believed that SAS had become an "introverted" organization which had lost its fix on the customers' needs. He felt that management had been putting almost all its attention on the mundane aspects of flying airplanes and not enough on the quality of the customers' experience.

In contrast to the conservative and stately Scandinavian tradition, he wanted to change the airline from a technical- and production-oriented company to a market-focused one, by making all personnel obsessively aware of customer service. He believed he could force attitudinal and structural changes in SAS that would bring the delivery system into harmony with their customers' needs. This, he reasoned, would get the market to recognize a significant difference between SAS and all other airline choices.

A service company, he argued, needed a different approach to the customer from that of other manufacturers. SAS, he pointed out, is not the airline, or head office, or an overhaul station, it's the contact between one customer in the market and one SAS employee in the front line. He demonstrated this by an idea which he called "the moment of truth," an episode in which a customer comes into contact with any aspect of the company, however remote, and thereby has an opportunity to form an impression. "SAS," he declared, "had 50,000 moments of truth out in the market every day."

The marketing concept was new to SAS. The international airline had been shaped by a strong heritage of engineering. The former president, Knut Hagrup, an aeronautical engineer, was reputed once to have said to an executive, "I know all about airplanes. I have good people on finance. I don't know anything about marketing. . . ."

Executives had regarded the buying of even larger and faster airplanes as their most important responsibility. Said Carlzon, "We used to think our biggest assets were aircraft, overhaul stations and technical resources. But we have only one real asset, and that is a satisfied customer prepared to come back to SAS and pay for our costs once more. That's why the assets in our balance sheet should show the number of satisfied customers who flew SAS during the year, and not the number of airplanes which are not worth one single cent as long as there is no second-hand market in the world for used aircraft, and nobody wants to pay for a flight in those airplanes. So it's really fooling the banks to use these as the assets."

THE PROJECT TEAM APPROACH

Carlzon's immediate priority early in 1981 was to find a way to change the SAS situation in the shortest possible time. He took a different approach from his days at Linjeflyg. There he had planned and executed the turnaround within the existing line organization. This time, he decided to arrange the process of change from outside the formal SAS culture and structure, creating for a 5-month period a parallel management system.

He delegated total responsibility for operating the airline from day-to-day to one of his existing managers, Helge Lindberg, leaving himself free to head up a small project team of hand-picked people, a few trusted executives and new recruits, who would become key players once implementation began, and a group of individuals from an outside consulting company and advertising agency.

The project team's task was to analyze the historical background outside and inside the company, the organizational climate and functioning of SAS. It took a week for them to isolate the major characteristics of the business and its main weaknesses and come up with the direction the change should take. Then they defined the goals and formal strategies. This lasted from December 1, 1980, to March 2, 1981, followed by a few months of discussion and refining, before the full plan was presented to the board in June 1981.

"In the beginning" recalls Carlzon, "we had to decide what part of the market SAS should do business with, so that all our services could be designed to meet that specific market need and no other. This included reducing costs for which this market was not prepared to pay and eliminating them eventually so that every resource of expense was a profitable one. In the past we had hurt ourselves a little more every year by cutting away at services customers were prepared to pay for. And we got stuck with administration overheads where they were unprepared to pay."

The plan for the project team was that it would eventually spearhead the execution of the various tasks. Executives would either create new departments or take over old ones in the new mode, as strategies came on-stream in a kind of feeder system. Carlzon felt that the new concept would require radical redirection in thinking and energy, and that if handled in the traditional way would take too long to diffuse down the organization. He and his task force personally, therefore, spread the word to all levels of management in an intensive campaign he referred to as "visible management."

THE SAS STRATEGY

The goal set by the project team was: "To be profitable in flight operations even in a zero growth market." This formed the basis for a medium-term plan, aimed to solve both the revenue and cost problem (see *Exhibit 1* for operating cost/revenue relationships).

The Main Marketing Strategy

The main strategy was aimed at boosting revenues by luring more passengers to SAS, particularly business travelers at full economy fares as opposed to heavily discounted tourist fares. This was to be achieved by increasing service levels (see *Exhibit 2*). First Class was abolished within Europe and replaced with EuroClass at no extra cost to the full-fare business traveller. This was followed by the introduction of First Business Class on long-haul flights, where First Class was retained.

By positioning SAS as the Businessman's Airline, Carlzon hoped to steal passengers from the other carriers like Air France and British Airways, who were upgrading their service but charging for it. Air France, which was selling "classe d'affaires" at a 17% surcharge, demanded that SAS change its strategy and do likewise. When Carlzon refused it retaliated and stopped sales of SAS tickets through its travel agents. Finally the conflict had to be resolved at a government level and Air France matched the SAS price.

On the basis of research conducted to establish what businessmen regarded as the important parts of a travel experience both before and during flying (see *Exhibits 3A–3D*), the plan for a Businessman's Airline was put into action.

The new concept was communicated and distributed to the new profit units. Carlzon had made it clear that he wanted SAS to be better in a hundred details, rather than 100% better in only one detail. He asked management to find ideas for new services for business travelers. They came back and recommended 150 projects to implement the new concept, with an estimated investment cost of about $40 million and an extra $10 million needed annually in operating costs.

What followed was the development and introduction of a series of new services in rapid succession. While competitors were cutting back on new product development and promotions, SAS invested heavily in the Businessman's Airline Program (see *Exhibit 4*).

Some of the first features were separate check-in counters for full-fare passengers, who were guaranteed that they would wait not longer than six minutes. Full-fare passengers were segregated from economy travelers and given special seat assignments. Airport lounges were improved with relaxation areas, refreshments, newspapers and magazines, T.V., reservation assistance, work and meeting areas, telephone and telex facilities. Service on-board improvements included hot meal menus, new tray settings, free newspapers, increased cabin attendants, fewer seats for more legroom, improved seat pitch, and flexible cabin dividers.

Arriving on time was found to be the business traveler's most important consideration. Carlzon, therefore, instituted a punctuality drive which he largely supervised himself. In his office he had installed a viewing screen, which gave him details of all flights, their departure and arrival times and delays. Sometimes on a late flight he would phone through to the pilot to find out what had gone wrong. A special function was established in Copenhagen to monitor and analyze the punctuality performance of flights worldwide.

In the rush to reduce costs per seat mile, many of the world's airlines acquired large, wide-bodied aircraft. These Boeing 747s, Airbusses, and the McDonnell DC–10s performed well but airlines found that if seats could not be filled, their costs per passenger seat mile often produced higher than expected expenses. Since business travelers, who dominated the world's air traffic, demanded proper departure times and frequent flights, using these wide-bodied airplanes effectively worked against the strategy of increasing traffic.

Carlzon reckoned that SAS would sell even more seats if it ceased straining to fly the unsuitable aircraft which got in the way of giving more nonstop flights. The DC–9s were stopping at the airline's hub in Copenhagen just to funnel passengers onto the large wide-bodied aircraft. These planes were, therefore, grounded or relegated to charter work.

Other Markets and Marginal Strategy

Marginal sales were also regarded as significant to the airline since the businessman's travel pattern with its seasonal variations and preferences on departure times and days was expected to lead to excess aircraft capacity and crews at other times.

A marginal strategy was designed, therefore, to sell to the leisure travel market whatever capacity the business traveler could not use. As one executive put it, "We in services cannot build up stock as other manufacturers do and then sell it—once the aircraft has left, our production is gone forever."

The major thrust of this effort was geared to low-fare tickets on scheduled services departing at times not favored by businessmen. SAS wanted, however, to avoid marginal sales reaching a level where it needed an increase in resources or where low-fare tickets would compete with full-fare sales.

The business traveler and the leisure traveler are often the same person in different guises, and depending on their role at the time, their demands and expectations vary. Also, the pattern of leisure travel is different. Business travel usually follows general economic trends. During recession, the frequency of travel declines and price sensitivity increases. For business travelers, travel is frequently part of the job. Their travel is the best way to create and maintain contacts, survey new markets, pick up new business ideas, and carry out and finalize deals. Trips are an investment in present and future business.

For the leisure traveler, travel is nearly always associated with recreation and escape from everyday life—a chance to see new places and make new acquaint-ances. In contrast to business trips, vacations are planned far in advance and are seldom changed. For the tourist, the price is a very important factor. The trip itself is part of the pleasure. The pattern of leisure travel is somewhat different, too.

Demand often rises during recessions, possibly because households reduce in-vestments in capital goods and spend their money instead on leisure pursuits. Business and tourist travel patterns show wide seasonal variations by month, week and day. The businessman prefers to travel between Monday and Friday, while tourists plan their excursions for weekends and holiday periods. Destina-tions also vary by customer category.

The cargo market is very sensitive to general economic developments and usually reflects overall industrial trends. Cargo services are a part of the custom-er's production resources in the field of logistics. The customer makes a precise estimate of the cost of materials handling, inventories and capital in the purchas-ing process. Speed gives air cargo a competitive edge.

Three other complementary strategies formed part of the marginal strategy:

- Concentration—a traffic program focusing on destinations where SAS was strong, eliminating unprofitable or unpromising routes.
- Selective marketing—promoting vigorously in selected markets domestically and internationally. Budget directed at the business traveler.
- Trading—trading services with other airlines on a cooperative basis to offer a product bigger and better than SAS could with their own resources.
- Cargo—using research to emulate the passenger-service approach.

TRIM 82 COST REDUCTION PROGRAM

Part of the new venture was a cost-cutting campaign called Trim 82. Its goals were to reduce administration costs by $30 million a year, primarily in overhead functions. Carlzon refused to engage in a general centralized cost-cutting exercise, pointing out that this would only become a pointless exercise if departments would have the same percentage of costs taken out of them irrespective of their importance to the new business strategy.

Therefore, rather than simply hand down an across-the-board instruction call-ing for a percentage cut in budgets, the implementation team launched a search for opportunities to do more with less. Overheads were cut mainly in administra-tion. Redundant staff either left, were given an opportunity to retire early, or filled newly created jobs on the front line.

As part of the trim exercise, 10 aircraft were leased or sold; three 747s, three DC–8s, and four A300 airbuses. This was coupled with a reduction in pilots, "the surplus list," as it was referred to, amounting to "enough people to man an entire minor carrier fleet."

THE CULTURE REVOLUTION

Carlzon's "little red book," as it came to be known, was the first step in involving all employees within the company in the new wave of thinking. He wanted to find a way to communicate to all levels in the organization that SAS was in a serious crisis, fighting for its life, and get them to understand what he wanted to do about it.

The strategic plan was handed over to the advertising agency to put in more creative terms, and what came out was a booklet in cartoon form called "Let's Get In There and Fight" that detailed the airline's financial condition, the vision for the future, and the plan for delegating responsibility to front-line employees.

People were somewhat surprised in the beginning at the unusual form of the communication but in time they got used to it and came to expect it. Resistance was mainly on the technical side of the operation,especially from the older pilots. Expectations were lifted and morale improved. And this internal PR was reinforced by interest in the project taken up by the mass media.

Carlzon and his team personally visited front-liners all over the SAS system. A training company was hired to put 20,000 managers and employees through a two-day training program designed to give them a sense of the organization's purpose and their role in the new concept.

It became clear quite early on, that culturally for many Scandinavians the service idea was not regarded as professional. The concept of differentiating service for different customers was particularly foreign to their "jamlikhet" feelings of egalitarianism.

Before launching the mass training phase, Carlzon had hosted an intensive 3-week gathering of his top 120 executives and 30 of the senior union representatives. Training for middle managers proceeded more or less in tandem with the front-liner program, with supervisors joining performance-level people at large sessions of 100 people or more.

In the organization structure introduced in August 1981 (see *Exhibits 5–7*), Carlzon erased the pyramid and redrew his concept of the new organization as a kind of wheel with the CEO at the hub and operating departments revolving around him. Front-line workers with the most customer contact had formally been at the bottom of the chart. Carlzon put them on top. It became everyone else's responsibility, including his, to "serve" those who directly served the customer.

Strong emphasis was given in the new organization to delegating responsibility down the line where Carlzon believed competent result-oriented managers should be well-informed personnel who could work without supervision. In his own words he wanted to put workers in charge and management to serve as consultant to the organization. An internal consulting group was set up and asked to work directly with management all over the company to help overcome obstacles and move ahead the various projects.

The company was divided into various profit centers, varying in size from the airline division down to the particular route. A route manager was regarded as an entrepreneur who was free to decide the time and number of flights between two cities, contingent on the approval of the governments involved, and who could lease the airplanes and flight crews from other divisions.

Carlzon actively tried to encourage initiative on the part of staff. For example, as one of the stories goes, he applauded a pilot, whose plane was grounded by a sit-down strike on the Copenhagen runway, who responded by opening the bar, taking the passengers on a guided tour of the airport perimeter and pointing out interesting sights.

"Instructions" he said, "only succeed in providing employees with knowledge of their own limitation. Information, on the other hand, provides them with a knowledge of their opportunities and possibilities. . . . To free someone from rigorous control by instructions, policies and orders, and to give that person freedom to take responsibility for his ideas, decisions and actions, is to release hidden resources which would otherwise remain inaccessible to both the individual and the company. . . . A person who has information cannot avoid taking responsibility."

Carlzon, reputed to be strongly influenced by what he had read in Peters and Waterman's *In Search of Excellence*, sometime during 1983, started to think about the need to formalize a new corporate culture for SAS. Remarks one executive: "He had introduced lots of projects to change results but he knew it wouldn't last forever. He wanted something more to cement the program. But the culture had already changed the attitudes to service and the customer in particular. It was too theoretical. We didn't want to be professors of philosophy and the culture program finally petered out."

NEW CORPORATE IDENTITY PROGRAM

In April 1983, the New Corporate Identity Program was launched at Oslo's Fornebu airport with a presentation of a DC–9 in the carrier's new livery. A proposal to change the name to "Royal Scandinavia," emphasizing the monarchical element of the three nations rather than the socialist, had been rejected by the SAS board, but the dragon that had been on the side of the SAS aircraft since 1946 had vanished. Likewise, the Viking image SAS had nurtured for years had been put to rest as it was felt that too many people outside Scandinavia associated Vikings with violence.

Consultants were called in to help formulate and design the new image. Calvin Klein, known for his universal appeal, was asked to come up with a sophisticated restyling for uniforms that business passengers would find attractive.

The old familiar logotype was essentially retained because it was so well-known, but bold shapes in colors of the three nations' flags were added. Airplanes were painted white "to make them look larger than life and bigger than the competition." All execution elements of the exercise were coordinated in a corporate identity manual, from logo to baggage labels, seating to ticket offices, to standardize SAS's visual expression worldwide. Management announced that the exercise was more than a graphic facelift. There was also, they reasoned, a good economic reason for the physical changes in the SAS image since the exercise had saved the company many millions of kroner by extending the working life of its DC–9 fleet into the 1990s.

NEW MARKETING PROJECTS

To compete more vigorously, new ways of expanding its range of products through more extensive coordination among the various units of the SAS Group were developed. In addition, SAS emphasized the need for ongoing and new approaches to the products and services the company should market.

Total Travel Package

The focus on the business target market during 1982 led to a new idea—the extension of the concept to include a total travel package of all services needed by business travelers from point A to point B. The object was to cater not only to the customers' needs on the air journey itself but also on the trip to and from the airport, at the airport while waiting for the flight and on the journey to the hotel at the other end: "an unbroken chain of services."

In 1983 when the first airline check-in in a hotel was tested in the Hotel Scandinavia in Copenhagen, consumers responded with enthusiasm. Then the concept was formally introduced to management. Either SAS owned or else appointed hotels to be involved in the scheme. A limousine service was introduced to and from airports.

Distribution

A distribution program was begun in 1985. The main objective was to allocate resources to ensure that SAS could keep up technologically with what was starting to take place in the market. This meant finding ways to control the distribution network either via travel agents, SAS's own ticket offices or home and office computer terminals.

In Search of a New Aircraft

Carlzon announced in mid–1983 in Los Angeles that his company and American Airlines were negotiating with McDonnell-Douglas, Boeing, and Airbus Industrie of Europe to design a 120-passenger jetliner to carry business travelers in the early 1990s.

Carlzon's vision was a craft which he called a "Passenger Pleasing Plane" of an unorthodox design, with 75%–80% of the interior volume of the fuselage allocated to passenger comfort and in-cabin baggage storage, compared to the 35% allocated then. He said: "For the 1990s our starting point is that we need an aircraft which the passenger wants. Then we can add on engines and the cockpit, not the other way around."

In a news conference prior to an address to Scandinavian businessmen, Carlzon picked up a model of a narrow-bodied plane, turned it on its side and said: "This is what I see. The floor is lower; the roof higher. Seating would be no more than two seats abreast with an aisle. Belly space for the baggage would be reduced because there would be wardrobes for the traveler. Businessmen don't want to wait for luggage." He said he was looking beyond what was being built and what was on the drawing board for the business traveler. Unconcerned about the age of his fleet, his view was that when SAS was ready to introduce new planes the competition would have to go on using their old ones, because planes must last for at least 10 years.

RESULTS

By the end of the 1982 year SAS presented an almost unrecognizable picture (see *Exhibits 8–13*). The airline had become the most punctual in Europe, as well as the number one choice for Scandinavian businessmen. Its full-fare passengers had increased by 8% in Europe and 16% in the zero growth intercontinental market.

In the process, corporate overheads had been reduced by 25%. This resulted in a before-tax turnaround of $80 million, from a $10 million loss to a $70 million profit. With allowances made for extraordinary capital gain in 1982 from the sale of surplus aircraft, profits for 1982–1983 increased by 65%.

At that point SAS was flying between Scandinavia and 30 destinations in European capitals, a market worth 8–10 million passengers annually. Its share was just over 50%. The total passenger revenue had risen by 31% compared to 1981–1982, and the European network accounted for 40% of the airline's total traffic revenue. Intercontinental accounted for 27% of the revenue and domestic passengers 16% of overall revenue. Share of the intercontinental market amounted to 50%.

Fortune magazine in the summer of 1983 (see *Exhibit 14*) tested all the airlines in the world with business class and rated SAS highest. A few months later, SAS won the Airline of the Year award at a special ceremony in New York. The award was made by *Air Transport World*, the international trade and consumer magazine, for SAS's "overall excellence" and its "outstanding service to the traveling public." The magazine stressed SAS's marketing innovations "and its quest for dominance in business travel markets" as well as its financial and technical management.

Exhibit 1
Airline Revenues and Operating Expenses 1980/81

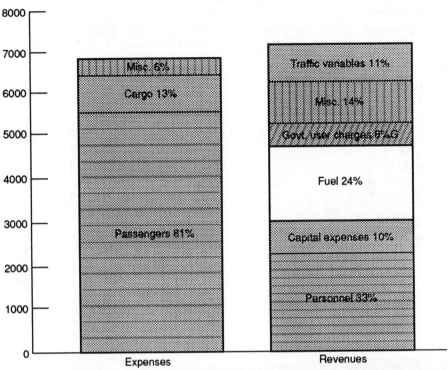

Exhibit 2
Upgraded Service Levels

A. Intercontinental

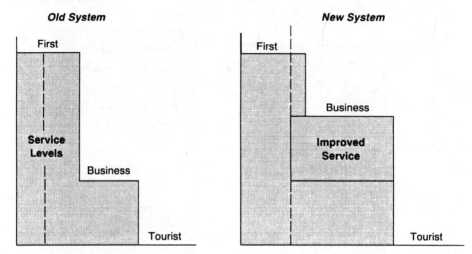

B. Europe

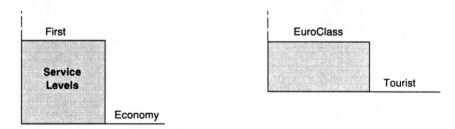

Elimination of first class travel (Europe only). EuroClass is not equivalent to the old first class.

Exhibit 3A
Results of Survey of Passengers at Time of Reservation:
Ranking of Reasons for Choosing Flight

	Very Important	Important	Less Important	Not Important	No Answer
Nonstop	67	31	1	0	2
Time of departure/arrival	73	23	2	0	3
Seat reservation	12	13	39	23	15
Aircraft type	3	19	46	17	16

Exhibit 3B
Ranking of Services at the Airport

	Very Important	Important	Less Important	Not Important	No Answer
Punctuality	88	11	0	0	2
Time at check-in	45	46	5	0	5
Separate check-in	31	38	21	4	8
Separate lounge	14	19	42	14	13

Exhibit 3C
Ranking of Services on Board

	Very Important	Important	Less Important	Not Important	No Answer
Seating comfort	63	34	2	0	3
Cabin attendants	34	57	5	0	3
Separate cabin	34	38	18	5	7
Working possibilities	27	45	17	3	10
Meals	17	57	14	3	10
Choice of meals	5	11	54	15	17
Newspapers	12	35	28	13	13
China and cutlery	4	33	32	18	14
Free drinks	3	11	42	28	18
Professional magazines	1	6	43	32	18

Exhibit 3D
Ranking of Cargo Services

	Most Important
Contact Service	
• Information feedback	63%
• Acceptance and delivery of shipments	42
• Fast documentation	31
• Cooperation ability	31
• Telephone service	24
• Confirmed booking	22
• Handling time of claims	21
Regularity, Safety	
• Reliable delivery times	40%
• Speedy terminal handling	25
• Frequent departures	20

Exhibit 4
Task and Timing Map

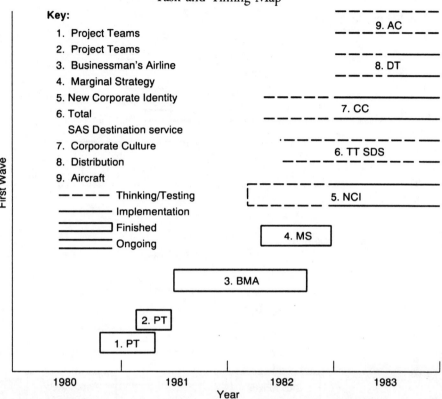

Exhibit 5
SAS Group Organization Structures

1. Prior to November 1980

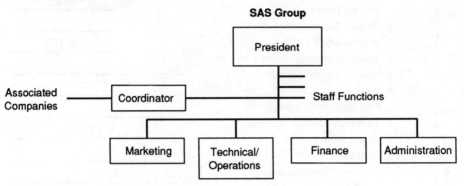

2. November 1, 1980–March 31, 1981

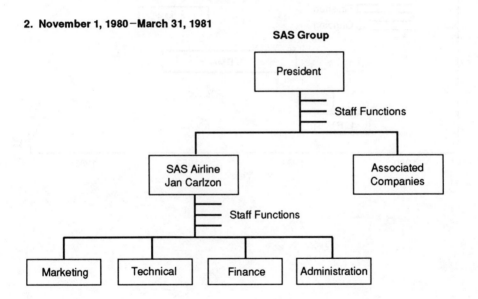

Exhibit 6
SAS Group Organization Structures

3. April 1, 1981   July 31, 1981

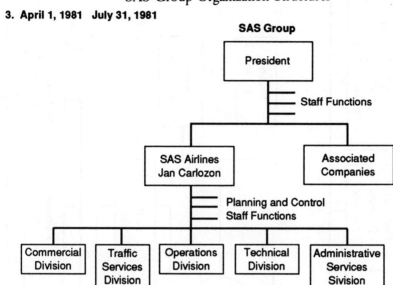

SAS Group

President

Staff Functions

SAS Airlines
Jan Carlozon

Associated
Companies

Planning and Control
Staff Functions

| Commercial Division | Traffic Services Division | Operations Division | Technical Division | Administrative Services Sivision |

4. August 1, 1981

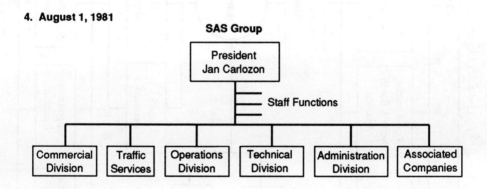

SAS Group

President
Jan Carlozon

Staff Functions

| Commercial Division | Traffic Services | Operations Division | Technical Division | Administration Division | Associated Companies |

SCANDINAVIAN AIRLINES SYSTEM SAS (A)
Exhibit 7
The SAS Organization—August 1981

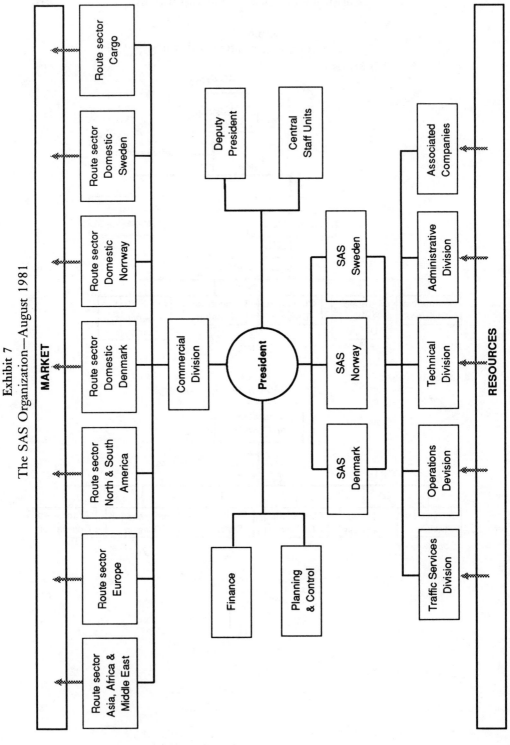

108

Exhibit 8
Profit and Loss Statements—October 1 to September 30
(in Skr millions)

	1982–1983	*1981–1982*	*1980–1981*
Traffic Revenue	10463.1	8442.3	6823.0
Other Revenue	2137.3	1559.7	1181.0
Operating Revenue	12600.4	10002.0	8004.0
Operating Expenses	11583.7	−9277.2	−7618.7
Operating Result before Depreciation	1016.7	724.8	385.3
Depreciation	−398.8	−408.6	−370.2
Operating Result after Depreciation	617.9	316.2	15.1
Dividends from Subsidiaries	21.6	7.4	6.7
Other Dividends Received	1.0	0.7	0.6
Other Financial Income	247.3	231.2	135.7
Financial Expenses	−426.9	−362.8	−267.3
Profit/Loss after Financial Income and Expenses	460.9	192.7	−109.2
Gain on Sale & Retirement of Equipment, etc.	11.2	59.8[b]	12.8
Extraordinary Income	—	95.8[c]	103.9[a]
Extraordinary Expenses	−10.3	−12.3	−12.9
Extraordinary Depreciation	—	—	−103.6[a]
Profit/Loss before Allocations and Taxes	461.8	336.0	−109.0

[a] The extraordinary income includes Skr 103.9 million for unredeemed tickets. Simultaneously Skr 103.6 million was depreciated on surplus flight equipment due to excess capacity and the difficult market for used aircraft.

[b] This included half the profit made on the sale of a Boeing 747B aircraft in January 1982. The aircraft was based back for 5 years. At the time of sale Skr 53.3 million was credited; the balance of Skr 49.6 million was deferred to be credited to income over the lease period.

[c] A pension bonus of Skr 98.8 million was received in Denmark. This was a refund for the 5-year period, 1977–1981.

Exhibit 9
Airline Results
(in Skr millions)

MSEK	1980–1981	1981–1982	1982–1983
Total revenue	8004	10002	12600
Result after financial income and expenses	− 109	+ 193	+ 461
Sale of equipment and extraordinary items	0	+ 143	+ 1
Result before allocations and taxes	− 109	+ 336	+ 462

Exhibit 10
Result—Punctuality

● **SAS is Europe's most punctual airline!**

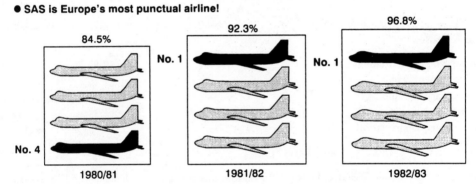

●**Fornebu, Arlanda and Kastrup: the most punctual airports in Europe, month after month.**

Exhibit 11
Traffic Handled by European Carriers, 1980–1983

Change (% of Last Year)	1980–1981	1981–1982	1982–1983
Total European Market	+ 4	0	− 3
SAS	+ 1	0	+ 5
SAS (EuroClass)	− 3	+ 7	+ 5
SAS (Tourist Class)	+ 5	− 5	+ 5

Exhibit 12
Intercontinental Passengers

	Percent Change from Previous Year Total Number Passenger Miles	Share of Total SAS Passengers	
	1982–1983	*1981–1982*	*1982–1983*
First Class	−18	3%	3%
"First Business Class"	+11	24	27
Discounted Fares	−3	73	70

Exhibit 13
Production, Traffic, Cabin Factor

		1982–1983 Production	vs.	1981–1982 Passenger Traffic	Cabin Factor[b]	
					1981–1982	*1982–1983*
Europe	AEA[a]	−0.9%		−1.4%	57.5%	57.2%
	SAS	0		+5.8	56.9	59.8
Intercontinental	AEA[a]	+0.1		−0.5	64.7	64.4
	SAS	−3.2		−0.5	66.6	68.4

[a]AEA = Association of European Airlines.

[b]Cabin factor = the percentage of seats occupied.

SCANDINAVIAN AIRLINES SYSTEM SAS (A)

Exhibit 14

Results of 1983 Fortune Magazine Survey of Airlines' Business Class Service

| | In-Flight Amenities | | | On-Ground Amenities | | | | | | Charge[a] |
Airline	Seat Width	Distance between Seats	Choice of Entrees	Separate Check-in	Special Baggage Handling	Lounge	Open Bar	Copying Machine	Work Area	Over or (Under) Economy
North American Flights										
Air Canada	17–18"	34"	o	o	o					0
Air One	25"	36–37"	o	N/A	N/A					0
American	18"	35–37"	o	o	o					$30
Midway Metrolink	22"	34"	o	o	N/A		o	o	o	($116)
Pan American	18½"	37–38"	o	o	o	o	o			7%–18%
Republic	20"	36"	o	o	o	o				$10
TWA	20¼"	38"	o	o	o	o	o			$10–$30
United	21"	36–38"	o		o					40%
Intercontinental Flights										
Aer Lingus	18"	39"	o	o	o					31%
Air Canada	20½"	39"	o	o	o	o	o			8%–18%
Air France	18"	34"	o	o	o	o	o			13%
Alitalia	19½"	35"	o	o	o	o	o			20%
American	18"	35–37"	o	o	o	o	o			42%

Airline	Seat width	Seat pitch							Charge
British Airways	24"	35"	○				○	○	117%
Japan Air Lines	20½–24"	34–37"	○				○	○	12½%
KLM	18"	37"	○				○	○	14%
Lufthansa	18"	37"	○				○	○	6%
Northwest Orient	19–21½"	34–56"	○				○	○	10%
Pan American	18½"	34–37"	○			○	○	○	12%–26%
Qantas	22"	38"	○		○	○	○	○	13%
SAS	19"	38"	○	○	○	○	○	○	0
Singapore	19½"	36"	○			○	○	○	10%
Thai	23"	42"	○			○	○	○	12½%
TWA	21"	38"	○			○	○	○	22%–50%
United	19"	36–38"	○			○	○	○	10%–12%
Varig	18"	38"	○			○	○	○	7%–12%

SOURCE: *Fortune*, August 22, 1983.

N/A = Not Applicable.

○ = An amenity included in the service.

What You Pay, What You Get

[a]Midway Metrolink charges less than competitors do for econo-class. On intercontinential flights, the charges listed for U.S. carriers and Canada are for frequently traveled routes. Other airlines' intercontinental fares are for flights between the United States and prinicpal cities in their home countries. British Airways' 117% surcharge is for the New York-to-London route, where economy fares are so low that all airlines tack on a large extra charge for business class. Seat widths vary a lot; by comparison, coach seats are typically 18 inches wide. The measurement between seats is from seat back to seat back, an indication of leg room.

3

◆

Building Customer Loyalty

Existing customers cost less to serve and are generally more profitable than new ones. Loyalty to a service results from meeting or exceeding customers' expectations. It pays, although few organizations measure its value. A few outstanding service organizations not only measure it but go to extraordinary lengths to build and preserve customer loyalty. This requires asking what a targeted customer is worth, measured in terms of the contribution from the stream of purchases the customer may make over time. Given this determination, an organization can develop appropriate responses to the following questions: Who are our most profitable customers, expressed both in demographic (age, income, etc.) and psychographic (life-style, perceived risks, etc.) dimensions? What are their needs, expressed in terms of results they seek? How do they evaluate competing service (based in part on the degree to which a service can be judged before or even after use)? How has the service been differentiated in ways important to customers, both in terms of substance and style? What can be done to develop better customers? To what degree are customer experiences being measured and managed? How are customers being taught to be enlightened customers, often less costly to serve? How are their costs to switch to a competing service being raised? How are they being made better at what they do in ways attributed to the service?

Southwest Airlines, in the case describing it, is faced with a decision requiring an assessment of the loyalty of its customers. This is critical to any decision about a response to Braniff International Airways' "half-price sale" to Southwest's primary market. In order to understand better what might be done, it is useful to ask: Who are Southwest's primary customers? How well has Southwest met their needs? By what means? What is Braniff up to in cutting prices? What are the likely outcomes of various pricing responses on Southwest's part? Are there non-pricing options open to Southwest for preserving customer loyalty?

Moving to Bradford Schools, ask yourself what makes a good secretary. What is good service in secretarial training? How can Bradford measure, monitor, communicate, and raise its service level? In view of changing social trends, does a service like this have a future? If so, with what targeted groups is it important that Bradford build loyalty? What would you suggest the management of Bradford Schools do to insure such loyalty?

These are the kinds of questions that breakthrough as opposed to merely good service managers ask themselves.

Southwest Airlines (A)

"**Y**'all buckle that seat belt," said the hostess over the public address system, "because we're fixin' to take off right now. Soon as we get up in the air, we want you to kick off your shoes, loosen your tie, an' let Southwest put a little love in your life on our way from Big D to Houston." The passengers settled back comfortably in their seats as the brightly-colored Boeing 737 taxied toward the takeoff point at Dallas' Love Field airport. Moments later, it was accelerating down the runway and then climbing steeply into the Texas sky on the 240-mile flight to Houston.

On the other side of Love Field across from the airport terminal, Southwest Airlines executives ignored the departing aircraft's noise, clearly audible in the company's modest but comfortable second-floor offices next to the North American–Rockwell hangar. They were about to begin an important meeting with representatives from their advertising agency to discuss alternative strategies in response to an announcement by their chief competitor, Braniff International Airways, that it was introducing a 60-day, half-price sale on Southwest's major route effective that same day, February 1, 1973.

COMPANY BACKGROUND

Southwest Airlines Co., a Texas corporation, was organized in March 1967. The founder, Rollin W. King, had graduated from the Harvard Business School in 1962 and was previously an investment counselor with a San Antonio firm. Since 1964, King, who held an airline transport pilot's license, had also been president of an air taxi service operating from San Antonio to various smaller south Texas communities.

During the mid-1960s, King and his associates became increasingly convinced that a need existed for improved air service between Houston, Dallas–Fort Worth, and San Antonio. These four cities were among the fastest growing in the nation. By 1968 Houston's standard metropolitan statistical area had a population of 1,867,000. Dallas's population was 1,459,000, San Antonio's

Assistant Professor Christopher H. Lovelock prepared this case as a basis for class discussion and not to illustrate either effective or ineffective handling of an administrative situation. Copyright © 1975 by the President and Fellows of Harvard College; Harvard Business School case 575-060 Rev. 2/85.

850,000, and Fort Worth's 680,000. Located 30 miles apart in northeastern Texas, Dallas and Fort Worth were frequently thought of as a single market area. Although each had its own airport—with Dallas's Love Field the busier of the two and the only one served by the airlines—construction had recently begun on the huge, new Dallas–Fort Worth Regional Airport, located midway between the two cities and intended to serve both.

Braniff International Airways and Texas International Airlines (TI) provided most of the air service between these markets. In 1967 Braniff operated a fleet of 69 jet and turboprop aircraft on an extensive route network, with a predominantly north-south emphasis, serving major U.S. cities, Mexico, and South America. Total Braniff revenues that year were $256 million, and the airline carried 5.6 million passengers. Texas International Airlines (then known as Trans-Texas Airways) was a regional carrier, serving southern and southwestern states and Mexico. In 1967 it operated a fleet of 45 jet, turboprop, and piston-engined aircraft on mostly short-haul routes, carrying 1.5 million passengers and generating total revenues of $32 million. Both Braniff and TI were headquartered in Texas.

Service by these two carriers within Texas represented legs of much longer, interstate flights; travelers flying from Dallas to San Antonio, for example, might find themselves boarding a Braniff flight that had just arrived from New York and was calling at Dallas on its way to San Antonio. In 1967 local travel between Dallas and Houston (the most important route) averaged 483 passengers daily in each direction, with Braniff holding 86% of this traffic (see *Exhibit 1*).[1] Looking back at the factors that had first stimulated his interest in developing a new airline to serve these markets, King recalled:

> The more we talked to people, the more we looked at figures of how big the market was and the more we realized the degree of consumer dissatisfaction with the services of existing carriers, the more apparent the opportunities became to us. We thought that these were substantial markets, and while they weren't nearly as large as the Los Angeles–San Francisco market, they had a lot in common with it. We knew the history of what PSA [Pacific Southwest Airlines] had been able to do in California with the same kind of service we were contemplating.[2]

On February 20, 1968, the Texas Aeronautics Commission granted a Certificate of Public Convenience and Necessity to Southwest, permitting it to provide

1. Local travel figures excluded passengers traveling between these cities as part of a longer journey.

2. PSA had built up a substantial market share on the lucrative Los Angeles–San Francisco route, as well as on other operations within California. Southwest executives subsequently carefully studied PSA when designing their operations.

intrastate air service between Dallas—Fort Worth, Houston, and San Antonio, a triangular route with each leg ranging in length from roughly 190 to 250 miles (see *Figure A*). Since the new airline proposed to confine its operations to Texas, its executives maintained that it did not need certification from the federal Civil Aeronautics Board (CAB).[3]

The next day, Braniff and TI asked the Texas courts to enjoin issuance of the Texas certificate. These two airlines already served the proposed routes and considered market demand insufficient to support another airline. The resulting litigation proved costly and time consuming, eventually reaching the U.S. Supreme Court. However, the suit was finally decided in Southwest's favor.

During the summer of 1970 M. Lamar Muse, an independent financial consultant, approached King. Muse had resigned the previous fall as president of Universal Airlines—a Detroit-based supplemental carrier—over a disagreement with the major stockholders on their planned purchase of Boeing 747 jumbo jets. Muse had read of Southwest's legal battles and told King and his fellow directors that he would like to help them transform the company from a piece of paper into an operating airline.

The wealth of experience that Muse could bring to the new airline was quickly recognized. Before assuming the presidency of Universal in September 1967, he had served for three years as president of Central Airlines, a Dallas-based regional carrier. Before 1965 he had been secretary-treasurer of Trans-Texas Airways, assistant vice president-corporate planning of American Airlines, and vice president-finance of Southern Airways. After working informally with Southwest for a couple of months, Muse became a company employee in October 1970 and was elected president, treasurer, and a director on January 26, 1971. King was simultaneously named executive vice president of operations.

Muse explained one reason why he was attracted to Southwest:

> I felt the interstate carriers just weren't doing the job in this market. Every one of their flights was completely full—it was very difficult to get reservations. There were a lot of canceled flights; Dallas being Braniff's base and Houston TI's base, every time they had a mechanical problem it seemed like they always took it out on the Dallas-Houston service. From Dallas south to San Antonio and Houston is the tag end of Braniff's system, everything was turning around and going back north to Chicago or New York or wherever. There was so much interline traffic that most of the seats were occupied by those people. While Braniff had hourly service, there really

---

3. The Civil Aeronautics Board regulated all interstate airlines in matters such as fares and routes, but had no authority over airlines operating exclusively within a single state. (The CAB should not be confused with the Federal Aviation Administration [FAA], which regulated safety procedures and flight operations for all passenger airlines, including intrastate carriers.)

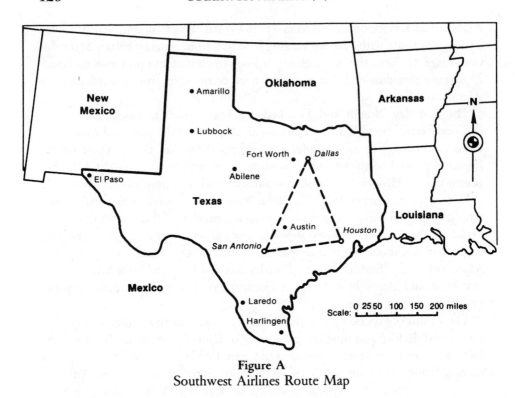

Figure A
Southwest Airlines Route Map

weren't many seats available for local passengers. People just avoided flying in this market—they only went when they had to.

Muse added that Braniff's reputation for punctuality was so poor that many travelers popularly referred to it as the "World's Largest Unscheduled Airline."

Optimistic over the outcome of Southwest's legal battles, Muse and King spent many weeks on the West Coast in late 1970 and early 1971, prospecting for new aircraft. The airline industry was then in a recession, and aircraft purchasers were courted assiduously. Southwest initiated high-pressure negotiations with McDonnell-Douglas, Boeing, and several other airlines for the purchase of new or used jets.

Finally, the Boeing Company, having overproduced its Boeing 737 twin jet (in a speculative assessment of future orders that had failed to materialize), offered both a substantial price reduction and favorable financing. In March 1971 Southwest signed a contract for three Boeing 737–200 aircraft, some months later increasing the order to four. The total purchase price for the four 737s was $16.2 million, compared with a previous asking price of approximately $4.6 million each.

Muse and King regarded the 737 as a better aircraft for their purposes than the McDonnell-Douglas DC–9s operated by TI or the larger, trijet Boeing 727s, which required a larger crew and were flown by Braniff on its Texas routes.

PREPARING FOR TAKEOFF

Back in Texas, Muse and King faced some urgent problems and an extremely tight deadline. Scheduled operations had been tentatively set to begin on June 18, slightly over four months away. During this time, Southwest had to raise additional capital to finance both startup expenses and what might prove to be a prolonged period of deficit operations. The existing skeleton management team had to be expanded by recruiting several specialist executives. Personnel had to be hired and trained for both flight and ground operations. Meantime, numerous marketing problems had to be resolved and an introductory advertising campaign developed to launch the new airline. Finally, Braniff and TI were pressing their legal battles to stifle Southwest.

The company's lawyers handled the legal matters while the Southwest executives moved quickly to confront financial, personnel, and marketing problems. The airline's financial position demanded immediate attention, since at year's end 1970 the company had a mere $183 in its bank account (see *Exhibit 2*). Between March and June 1971, Southwest raised almost $8 million selling convertible promissory notes and common stock.

Four executives with many years' airline experience soon filled vacancies on the management team. Three had previously worked for either Braniff or TI and had recently been fired by those carriers—a fact that Muse considered one of their strongest recommendations for employment with Southwest.

Decisions on route structure and schedules had already been made. Initially, two of the three Boeing 737s would be placed in service on the busy Dallas-Houston run, and the third would fly between Dallas and San Antonio. Meanwhile, Southwest did not plan to exercise its rights to operate service on the third leg of the triangle between Houston and San Antonio.

Flight frequency depended on aircraft availability. Allowing time for turning around the aircraft at each end, management concluded that flights could be offered in each direction between Dallas and Houston at 75-minute intervals, and between Dallas and San Antonio at 2½-hour intervals. Both services were scheduled for 50 minutes. The Monday-Friday schedule called for 12 daily round trips between Dallas and Houston and six daily round trips between Dallas and San Antonio. Saturday and Sunday schedules were more limited, reflecting both the lower travel demand on weekends and the need for downtime to service the aircraft.

The pricing decision, meantime, had been arrived at following talks with PSA executives in California. King recalled:

What Andy Andrews [president of PSA] said to Lamar and me one day was the key to our initial pricing decision. Andy told us that the way you ought to figure your price is not on how much you can get or what the other carriers were charging. He said, "Pick a price at which you can break even with a reasonable load factor, and a load factor that you have a reasonable expectation of being able to get within a given period of time, and that ought to be your price. It ought to be as low as you can get it without leading yourself down the primrose path and running out of money."

After estimating the money required for preoperating expenses and then carefully assessing both operating costs and market potential, Muse and King settled on a $20 fare for both routes, with a break-even point of 39 passengers per flight. In comparison, Braniff and TI coach fares were $27 on the Dallas-Houston run and $28 on the Dallas–San Antonio service. The two executives believed that an average of 39 passengers per flight was a reasonable expectation considering the market's growth potential and the frequency of flights Southwest planned to offer, although they projected a period of deficit operations before this break-even point was reached. They anticipated that while Braniff and TI might eventually reduce their fares, Southwest could expect an initial price advantage.

Early in 1971 Muse met with the vice president of marketing, Dick Elliott, to select an advertising agency. (The airline already employed a public relations agency to handle publicity.) The Bloom Agency, a large regional advertising agency conveniently headquartered in Dallas, was awarded the account. The assignment was to come up with a complete communications program—other than publicity—within four months. "We've got no hostesses and no uniforms and no airplanes and no design and no money," Muse told the agency people, "but we're going to have an airline flying in 120 days!"

Bloom approached Southwest Airlines "as though it were a packaged goods account." The first task was to evaluate the characteristics of all U.S. carriers competing in the Texas markets. To simplify comparisons, a two-dimensional positioning diagram was prepared, rating each airline's image on conservative-fun and obvious-subtle scales (see *Figure B*). These judgments were based primarily on an analysis of recent airline advertising, to determine each carrier's image.

TI was immediately dismissed as dull and conservative, with a bland image. (*Exhibit 3* shows typical TI advertisements at that time.) Braniff's advertising, however, presented an interesting stylistic contrast. From 1965 to 1968 Braniff had employed Wells, Rich, Greene, a New York agency that had developed an innovative marketing and advertising strategy for its client, with a budget exceeding $10 million in 1967. Braniff's aircraft were painted in various brilliant colors

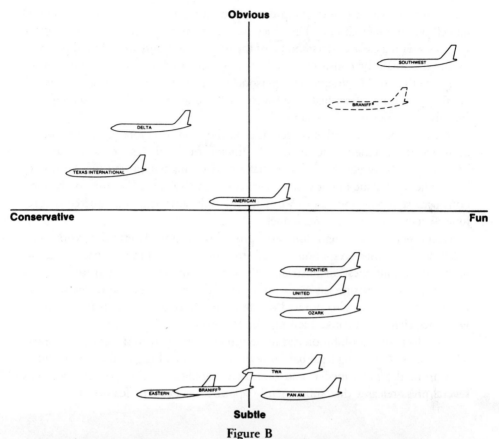

Figure B

Positioning Diagram of U.S. Airlines Advertising and Competing in Texas

SOURCE: The Bloom Agency (February 11, 1971)

a. Former advertising by Wells, Rich, Greene ("The End of the Plain Plane," "The Air Strip").

b. Clinton E. Frank advertising, 1971.

covering the entire fuselage and tailfin. Hostesses wore couture costumes created by an Italian fashion designer, and the advertising sought to make flying with Braniff seem glamorous and exciting. This approach proved extremely successful and was believed by many observers to have prompted Braniff's rapid growth during the second half of the 1960s. Bloom's executives, however, concluded that by 1971 Braniff's image was changing from a fun image to a subtler, more conservative style (see *Exhibit 4*), with an advertising budget reduced to approximately $4 million. This left a vacuum for Southwest Airlines to fill. So the agency decided to position Southwest beyond the fun-obvious side of the old Braniff image.

Accordingly, the account group developed "an entire personality description model" for the new airline. The objective was to provide the agency's creative specialists with a clear understanding of the image that Southwest should project, so that this might be consistently reflected in every facet of the communications campaign they had to design. This personality statement, also used as a guideline in staff recruiting, described Southwest as "young and vital . . . exciting . . . friendly . . . efficient . . . dynamic."

One constraint on marketing activities in the months before passenger operations was the planned issue of over $6 million of Southwest stock on June 8. The company's lawyers had advised that a media campaign promoting the airline before the stock issue might violate Securities and Exchange Commission regulations against promoting stock. Virtually the only advertising conducted before June 8, therefore, was for personnel.

Recruitment advertising in one area proved outstandingly effective, with over 1,200 young women responding to advertisements placed in national media for positions as Southwest air hostesses. Forty applicants were selected for training and although airline officials made no secret of the attractive looks of the successful candidates, it was also pointed out that their average scores on the required FAA proficiency test ranked among the highest of all U.S. carriers.

The advertising prohibition did not entirely keep Southwest out of the news. The airline's continuing legal battles with Braniff and TI received extensive publicity from the mass media, and Southwest's public relations agency put out several press releases that subsequently appeared as news or feature stories.

SERVICE BEGINS: THE FIRST SIX MONTHS

On June 10, 1971, The Bloom Agency's advertising campaign for Southwest finally broke. It began modestly with small teaser ads in the newspapers, containing provocative headlines such as "The 48-Minute Love Affair," "At Last a $20 Ticket You Won't Mind Getting," "Love Can Change Your Ways," and "A Fare to Remember." The unsigned ads contained a telephone number for the reader to call. On phoning, a caller in Dallas would hear a taped message:

> Hi. It's us. Southwest Airlines. Us with our brand-new, candy-colored, rainbow-powered Boeing 737 jets. The most reliable plane flying today. And we start flying June 18, to Houston or San Antonio. You choose—only 45 minutes nonstop. In that time, we'll be sharing a lot of big little things with you that mean a lot. Like love potions, a lot of attention and a new low fare. Just $20. Join us June 18. Southwest Airlines. The somebody else up there who loves you.

Approximately 25,000 telephone calls resulted from these ads.

Table A
Southwest Advertising and Promotional Expenditures, 1971 and 1972

| | *1971* | | | *1972* |
	Preoperating	*Operating*	*Total*	*(budgeted)*
Advertising				
Newspaper	$139,831	$131,675	$271,506	$60,518
Television	36,340	761	37,101	127,005
Radio	5,021	60,080	65,101	95,758
Billboards	26,537	11,670	38,207	90,376
Other publications	710	20,446	21,156	28,139
Production costs	52,484	43,483	95,967	83,272
Other promotion and publicity	29,694	27,200	56,894	48,366
	$290,617	$295,315	$585,932	$533,434

SOURCE: Company records

On Sunday, June 13, all newspapers in the three market areas ran a four-color double-truck[4] ad for Southwest (see illustration, next page). Daily, full-page newspaper ads appeared for the next two weeks in all markets highlighting the advantages Southwest Airlines offered the traveler—new aircraft, attractive hostesses, low fares, fast ticketing, and inexpensive, exotically-named drinks. TV advertising was also heavy and included 30-second spots featuring the Boeing 737, the hostesses, and what was referred to as the "Love Machine" (see *Exhibit 5*). Whereas the competition used traditional, handwritten airline tickets, Southwest counter staff shortened ticket purchases, using a machine to print out tickets and a pedal-operated tape recorder to enter names on the passenger list as they checked in—both ideas were copied from PSA. Rounding out the advertising campaign were prominently displayed billboards at entrances to all three airports served by Southwest. Nearly half the year's promotional budget was spent in the first month of operations (see *Table A*).

Scheduled revenue operations were inaugurated in a blaze of publicity on Friday, June 18, but evidently the competition was not about to take matters lying down. In half-truck and full-page newspaper ads, Braniff and TI announced $20 fares on both routes. The CAB had disclaimed authority over intrastate fares and Texas law barred jurisdiction by TAC over carriers holding Federal Certificates of Public Convenience and Necessity; thus, the CAB carriers could charge any fare they wanted. Braniff's advertising stressed frequent, convenient service "every hour on the hour," hot and cold towels "to freshen up with," beverage

---

4. "Double-truck" is a printer's term that describes material printed across two full pages. A "half-truck" ad is printed across two half pages.

At last, there's somebody e

The planes are new. The pilots are not. We've talked to, tested, and evaluated very good, reputable, reliable pilots that any major airline would hire. Out of them all we've selected a group — maybe an elite — of the very best in the business, with an average of 15,200 hours in the air.

Our ground crew is no small potatoes, either. They're well-trained in dozens of skills that insure your comfort aboard Southwest Airlines.

It's us, Southwest Airlines.

Us, with our brand new Boeing 737's.

We fly to Dallas/Ft. Worth, Houston and San Antonio. Your choice, all flights non-stop.

In that time you're going to feel there really is somebody else up there who loves you.

By sharing a lot of little things with you. Big, little things that mean a lot to travelers.

Three years ago the Boeing 737 was introduced to the public all over the world. Today — as of this morning — the Boeing 737's have accumulated 1,000,000 flight hours, carrying nearly 70 million passengers approximately 430 million miles. The Boeing 737 is the super reliable jet specially designed for short haul traffic. Obviously, it is more than just a beautiful body. No other airlines will be flying 737's on these routes. And Southwest Airlines won't be flying anything else.

And we give trading stamps. Not the ordinary kind. Ours are Love Stamps. You get one from our hostess if for any reason she finds you uphappy in any way with our service. The basic idea is that we want you to trade in your bad feelings for good ones. The Love Stamp hopefully will make amends—with a free drink or something, and then you'll feel better about us right away. And want to ride our airplanes again, and again.

JUNE 18

LOVE STAMP
GOOD FOR ONE FREE LOVE POTION ON YOUR NEXT FLIGHT

Dallas/Ft. Worth to Houston (and back)
Dallas/Ft. Worth to San Antonio (and back)
All flights non-stop.

Dallas/Ft. Worth to Houston		Houston to Dallas/Ft. Worth	
Depart	Arrive	Depart	Arrive
7:30 a*	8:18 a	7:30 a*	8:18 a
8:45 a*	9:33 a	8:45 a	9:33 a
10:00 a	10:48 a	10:00 a*	10:48 a
11:15 a*	12:03 p	11:15 a	12:03 p
12:30 p	1:18 p	12:30 p*	1:18 p
1:45 p**	2:33 p	1:45 p	2:33 p
3:00 p	3:48 p	3:00 p**	3:48 p
4:15 p**	5:03 p	4:15 p	5:03 p
5:30 p	6:18 p	5:30 p**	6:18 p
6:45 p**	7:33 p	6:45 p	7:33 p
8:00 p	8:48 p	8:00 p**	8:48 p
9:15 p**	10:03 p	9:15 p**	10:03 p

Dallas/Ft. Worth to San Antonio		San Antonio to Dallas/Ft. Worth	
Depart	Arrive	Depart	Arrive
7:00 a*	7:50 a	8:15 a*	9:05 a
9:30 a	10:20 a	10:45 a	11:35 a
12:00 n	12:50 p	1:15 p	2:05 p
2:30 p	3:20 p	3:45 p	4:35 p
5:00 p	5:50 p	6:15 p	7:05 p
7:30 p**	8:20 p	8:45 p**	9:35 p

*Except Sunday
**Except Saturday

Double-Truck Introductory Ad

else up there who loves you.

By paying attention to you, giving efficient service, and getting you there on time.

And, if for some reason, you don't get all the love we've got to give, we'll make it up by giving you a Love Stamp. Why are we doing all this? Because we need your love, too. And we know we won't get it unless we give it.

She will not plee-aze you. Plee-aze is stiff, formal and very affected English for please. It is usually accompanied by a gleaming toothpaste smile. People who say plee-aze are trying very, very hard to be nice to you. Too hard. And it isn't real. It's like plastic flowers vs. real flowers. You can feel the difference. That's why in our hostess school we haven't taught our girls how to be nice to you. We figure if they didn't already know, they weren't for us. In our school we teach other things. Mostly how to take care of you. Then we dress them in our exciting new hot pants designed for Southwest Airlines by Lorch of Dallas. That really ought to please you.

$20

Save from $14 to $16 per round trip. Eventually, the other airlines may meet our price, but remember, you can't buy love.

Love Potions for the very weary. Order by numbers 1-10, and they're only $1.00 each, not $1.50. That's what happens when you have somebody else up there who loves you.

A love machine which issues you tickets in under 10 seconds. Another way we prove our love: love machines in two great locations — at the ticket counter and at the departure gate, take your pick. Then you give your $20 (or any one of five charge cards) to our people stationed behind the love machines and you're on your way.

DALLAS 826-8840 • HOUSTON 228-8791
SAN ANTONIO 224-2011 • FORT WORTH 283-4661

This is another Southwest Airlines exclusive — our phone number. Keep it on file in your head or elsewhere because it's not in the phone book yet! Use this number to call ahead for reservations if you want to. If you don't want to, that's o.k. too. You don't need reservations to board the plane. Just come, plunk down $20 and out pops your ticket from our Love Machine. We plan to make waiting in line a thing of the past.

SOUTHWEST AIRLINES
The somebody else up there who loves you.

127

discount coupons and "peace of mind" phone calls at the boarding gate; it also announced increased service between Dallas and San Antonio, effective July 1 (see *Exhibit 6*). TI, meantime, announced that on July 1 hourly service would begin on the Dallas–Houston route, leaving Dallas at 30 minutes past each hour. TI also introduced extras such as free beer, free newspapers, and $1 drinks on routes competing with Southwest (see *Exhibit 7*). Southwest countered with advertising headlined "The Other Airlines May Have Met Our Price But You Can't Buy Love."

Advertising and promotion continued regularly both on television and with frequent publicity events, usually featuring Southwest hostesses. A direct-mail campaign targeted 36,000 influential business executives in Southwest's service areas. Each received a personalized letter from Muse describing Southwest's service and enclosing a voucher worth half the cost of a round-trip ticket; about 1,700 vouchers were redeemed.

Surveys of Southwest's passengers departing from Houston revealed that a substantial percentage would have preferred using the William P. Hobby Airport, 12 miles southeast of downtown Houston, rather than the new Houston Intercontinental Airport, 26 miles north of the city. Accordingly, in mid-November, 7 of Southwest's 14 round-trip flights between Dallas and Houston were transferred to Hobby Airport, thus reopening this old airport to scheduled commercial passenger traffic. Additional schedule revisions made simultaneously included a reduction to four round-trips each weekday of the Dallas–San Antonio flights, inauguration of three daily round-trips on the third leg of the route triangle between Houston (Hobby) and San Antonio, and elimination of the extremely unprofitable Saturday flights on all routes. These actions contributed to increased transportation revenues in the final quarter of 1971 over those of the third quarter, but Southwest's operating losses in the fourth quarter fell only slightly, from $1,006,000 to $921,000 (see *Exhibit 8*). At year's end 1971, Southwest's accumulated deficit stood at $3.75 million (see *Exhibit 2*).

THE SECOND SIX MONTHS

In February 1972, Southwest initiated a second phase of the advertising campaign, hired a new vice president of marketing, and scrapped its public relations agency. Meanwhile, the company recruited the agency's publicity director to fill a newly created position as public relations director at Southwest.

The objective was to sustain Southwest's presence in the marketplace after eight months of service. Frequent advertising, with a wide variety of messages, was directed at the regular business commuter. Surveys had shown that such travelers represented 89% of Southwest's traffic. The campaign made extensive use of TV advertising, featuring many of Southwest's hostesses.

Dick Elliott, whom the president described as having performed a herculean task in getting Southwest off the ground, had resigned to join a national advertising agency. The new vice president of marketing, Jess R. Coker, had spent 10 years in the outdoor advertising business after graduating from the University of Texas. His assignment before joining the airline had been as vice president of Southern Outdoor Markets, a company representing 85% of all outdoor advertising in the 14 southern and southeastern states. Coker assumed responsibility for all marketing functions of the airline, including advertising, sales, and public relations (see *Figure C*). He often met weekly with the account executive from The Bloom Agency to discuss not only media advertising but also numerous other details handled by the agency, including the preparation and execution of pocket timetables, point-of-sale materials for travel agents, and promotional brochures.

Although the majority of tickets were sold over the counter at the airport, sales were also made to travel agents and corporate accounts. Travel agents received a 7% commission on credit card sales and 10% on cash sales. Corporate accounts—companies whose personnel regularly used Southwest—received no discount, but benefited from the conveniences of a private supply of ticket stock that they issued themselves and a single monthly billing. Coker commanded a force of six sales representatives, whose job was to develop and service both travel agents and corporate accounts, encouraging maximum use of Southwest through distribution of point-of-sale materials, development of package arrangements, distribution of pocket timetables, and so forth. Sales representatives also promoted Southwest's air freight business, which featured a special rush delivery service for packages. Each representative, as well as most company officers, drove an AMC Gremlin car, strikingly painted in the color scheme of Southwest's aircraft.

Southwest's new public relations director, Camille Keith, also reported to Coker. Keith was a former publicity director of Read-Poland, Inc., the public relations agency that had previously handled the airline's account. Keith's responsibilities focused on obtaining media coverage for the airline, and also included publication of Southwest's in-flight magazine and joint development of certain promotions with the advertising agency.

Between October 1971 and April 1972, average passenger loads systemwide increased from 18.4 passengers per flight to 26.7 passengers, still below the number necessary to cover the rising total costs per trip. The volume of traffic during the late morning and early afternoon could not support flights at hourly intervals. Conforming to Houston passenger preference, Southwest gradually shifted its operations to Hobby Airport and abandoned Houston Intercontinental.

On May 14, a new schedule reduced daily flights between Dallas and Houston from 29 to 22, primarily by curtailing service between 9:30 A.M. and 3:30 P.M. from once an hour to once every two hours. Eleven daily flights were still offered on the Dallas–San Antonio route and six between San Antonio and Houston, with some minor schedule changes. Hobby Airport was to be used exclusively for all flights to and from Houston. Braniff quickly retaliated by introducing service from Dallas to Hobby and undertaking an extensive publicity program promoting this move.

Financially, the new schedule allowed the company to sell its fourth Boeing 737. Experience had shown that the 737s could be turned around (i.e., loaded and unloaded) at the gate within 10 minutes. This meant that an hourly schedule on the Dallas-Houston run could be maintained with only two aircraft, instead of three. With the slack provided by the reduced midday frequencies and a schedule that involved periodically flying an aircraft around all three legs of the triangular routes, management concluded that three aircraft would suffice. By mid-1972, the airline industry had recovered from its 1970–1971 slump, and

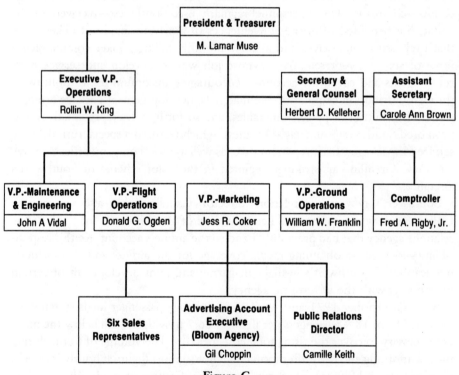

Figure C
Southwest Partial Organization Chart, 1972–1973

aircraft manufacturers had waiting lists for the popular models. Southwest found a ready buyer for its surplus 737 and made a profit of $533,000 on the sale. With this capital gain, lower operating costs, and a continued increase in revenues, net loss fell from $805,000 to $131,000 between the first and second quarters of 1972 (see *Exhibit 8*).

For some months Southwest had been experimenting with a $10 fare on Friday flights after 9:00 P.M. In May this reduced fare was extended to post–9:00 P.M. daily flights. These discount flights attracted more business than the standard-priced flights (see *Exhibit 9*).

In June 1972 Southwest Airlines celebrated its first birthday, giving Camille Keith an opportunity for more of the publicity stunts for which the airline was already famous. Posters were hung inside the aircraft and in the waiting lounges, the aircraft cabins were decorated, and an on-board party was held every day for a week, with birthday cake for the passengers and balloons for the children. This hoopla, promoted by newspaper advertising, generated considerable publicity for the airline and, in management's view, reinforced Southwest's image as the plucky, friendly little underdog that had survived an entire year against powerful, entrenched competition.

Not all public relations was just hoopla, Keith stressed, mentioning that she worked closely with the advertising agency to coordinate the airline's mass communication plan.

One example of a specialized promotional campaign involving inputs from both Keith and The Bloom Agency was the Southwest Sweetheart's Club. Using a mailing list, a direct-mail piece was sent to executive secretaries in Southwest's market area, offering them membership in this club. For each reservation on Southwest made for the boss, the secretary received a "sweetheart stamp," and for each 15 stamps, obtained a free ride on Southwest. Other bonuses for members included a twice-yearly drawing for a Mexico City vacation.

INTRODUCTION OF NEW PRICING POLICIES

After operating a year, Southwest management decided to scrutinize the fare structure and its relationship to costs and revenues. They concluded that the airline could no longer afford a $20 fare on daytime flights. New tariffs were therefore filed with the Texas Aeronautics Commission, effective July 9, 1972; these raised Southwest's basic one-way fare from $20 to $26, established a round-trip fare of $50, and offered a $225 Commuter Club Card, providing unlimited transportation on all routes for 30 days.

One problem was how to break the news of the increased fares to the public.

Talking with representatives of The Bloom Agency, Keith suggested that Southwest announce a new Executive Class service on full-fare flights, offering passengers new amenities. The idea was quickly refined: two rows of seats would be removed from the aircraft, reducing capacity from 112 to 104 seats but increasing legroom; also, passengers would be offered free drinks. (The hostesses would probably not have time to serve more than two drinks per passenger on such short flights.) Full-page newspaper ads appeared proclaiming Southwest Airlines' new Executive Class service, with first-class legroom and free cocktails. The $26 fare also provided free security check charges that had been introduced the previous month.

The key consideration was the competition's reaction. "For a few days," admitted Coker, "we were really sweating." Braniff initially added another aircraft to its Dallas-Hobby Airport flights on July 11, thus offering on-the-hour service most of the business day. However, on July 17, TI increased its fares to match Southwest's; then on July 21 Braniff met all aspects of the fare and on-board service charges, also adding a $10 "Sundowner" flight to Hobby at 7:30 P.M. Braniff's increased service and the higher fares, as well as cutbacks in the number of Southwest flights, caused Southwest's July passenger count to fall on all three routes (see *Exhibit 10*). Overall, Southwest's patronage fell 2% in the third quarter of 1972, compared with the second quarter, but transportation revenues increased.

During September a third phase of the advertising campaign was launched, based on the slogan "Remember What It Was Like Before Southwest Airlines?" The agency considered this a war cry to rally consumers. The principal media used were television (see *Exhibit 11*) and billboards.

At the end of October another major pricing change occurred. The $10 discount fares, which had never been advertised, were replaced by half-fare flights ($13 one-way, $25 round-trip) in both directions on the two major routes each weekday after 8 P.M. Saturday flights were reintroduced and *all* weekend flights were offered at half-fare. A three-week advertising blitz accompanied the new schedule and prices, using one-minute radio commercials on such stations as country and western, and Top 40.[5] The response was immediate: November 1972 traffic levels were 12% higher than those in October—historically the best month in Southwest's commuter markets.

In the new year management turned its attention to the remaining problem. The company was actually making money on its Dallas-Houston flights, but incurring substantial losses in the Dallas-San Antonio market, where passenger volume was much lower (see *Exhibit 10).* Southwest offered only 8 flights a day on this route, versus 33 by its major competitor, and was averaging a mere 17

---

5. A "Top 40" station plays currently popular rock music recordings.

passengers on each full-fare flight. Southwest management concluded that unless patronage dramatically improved, this route would be discontinued. In a last attempt to obtain the needed increase, Southwest announced on January 22, 1973, a "60-Day-Half-Price-Sale" on *all* flights between Dallas and San Antonio. This sale was advertised on television and radio (see *Exhibit 12*). If successful, Muse intended to make this reduced fare permanent, but he believed that announcing it as a limited time offer would stimulate consumer interest more effectively and reduce the likelihood of competitive response.

The impact of these half-price fares was faster and more dramatic than the results of the evening and weekend half-price fares introduced the previous fall. As the first week ended, average loads on Southwest's Dallas–San Antonio service rose to 48 passengers per flight and continued to rise sharply as the next week began.

On Thursday, February 1, however, Braniff employed full-page newspaper ads to announce a half-price "Get Acquainted Sale" between Dallas and Hobby on all flights, until April 1 (see *Exhibit 13*).[6]

Muse called an urgent meeting of the management team, including King, the marketing vice president, the public relations director, the company's attorneys, and the account people from The Bloom Agency. Southwest had to decide how to respond to Braniff's move.

---

6. Braniff flights to Houston Intercontinental continued at the higher fare.

SOUTHWEST AIRLINES (A)

Exhibit 1

Southwest Airlines and Competitors: Average Daily Local Passengers Carried in Each Direction, Dallas–Houston Market

	Braniff[a]		TI[a]		Southwest		Total Market—
	Passengers	% of Market	Passengers	% of Market	Passengers	% of Market	Passengers
1967	416	86.1%	67	13.9%	—	—	483
1968	381	70.2	162	29.8	—	—	543
1969	427	75.4	139	24.6	—	—	566
1970							
1st half	449	79.0	119	21.0	—	—	568
2nd half	380	76.0	120	24.0	—	—	500
Year	414	77.5	120	22.5	—	—	534
1971							
1st half	402	74.7	126	23.4	10	1.9%	538
2nd half	338	50.7	120	18.0	209	31.3	667
Year	370	61.4	123	20.4	110	18.2	603

1972

January	341	48.3	105	14.9	260	36.8	706
February	343	47.6	100	13.9	277	38.5	720
March	357	47.5	100	13.3	295	39.2	752
April	367	48.3	97	12.8	296	38.9	760
May	362	48.5	84	11.3	300	40.2	746
June	362	46.8	81	10.5	330	42.7	773
1st half	356	48.0	93	12.5	293	39.5	742
July	332	48.1	74	10.7	284	41.2	690
August	432	53.7	56	6.9	317	39.4	805
September	422	54.9	55	7.2	291	37.9	768
October	443	53.1	56	6.7	335	40.2	834
November	439	50.6	55	6.3	374	43.1	868
December	396	52.1	56	7.4	308	40.5	760
2nd half	411	52.1	59	7.5	318	40.4	788
Year	384	50.1	77	10.0	306	39.9	767

1973

January[b]	443	51.5	62	7.3	354	41.2	859

SOURCE: Company records

NOTE: Passenger figures should be doubled to yield market statistics for travel in both directions.

[a] These figures were calculated by Muse from passenger data that Braniff and TI were required to supply to the Civil Aeronautics Board. He multiplied the original figures by a correction factor to eliminate interline traffic and arrive at net totals for local traffic.

[b] Projected figures from terminal counts by Southwest personnel.

Exhibit 2
Southwest Airlines: Balance Sheet at December 31, 1972, 1971, and 1970

	1972	*1971*	*1970*
Assets			
Current assets			
Cash	$133,839	$231,520	$183
Certificates of deposit	1,250,000	2,850,000	—
Accounts receivable			
Trade	397,644	300,545	—
Interest	14,691	35,013	—
Other	67,086	32,569	100
Total accounts receivable	479,441	368,127	100
Less allowance for doubtful accounts	86,363	30,283	—
	393,078	337,844	100
Inventories of parts and supplies, at cost	154,121	171,665	—
Prepaid insurance and other	75,625	156,494	31
Total current assets	2,006,663	3,747,533	314
Property and equipment, at cost			
Boeing 737–200 jet aircraft	12,409,772	16,263,250	—
Support flight equipment	2,423,480	2,378,581	—
Ground equipment	346,377	313,072	9,249
	15,179,629	18,954,903	9,249
Less accumulated depreciation and overhaul allowance	2,521,646	1,096,177	—
	12,657,983	17,858,726	9,249
Deferred certification costs less amortization	371,095	477,122	530,136
Total assets	$15,035,741	$22,083,381	$539,699

Exhibit 2
(Continued)

	1972	1971	1970
Liabilities and Stockholders' Equity			
Current liabilities			
Notes payable to banks (secured)	$950,000	—	—
Accounts payable	124,890	$355,539	$30,819
Accrued salaries and wages	55,293	54,713	79,000
Other accrued liabilities	136,437	301,244	—
Long-term debt due within one year	1,226,457	1,500,000	—
Total current liabilities	2,493,077	2,211,496	109,819
Long-term debt due after one year			
7% convertible promissory notes	—	1,250,000	—
Conditional purchase agreements—			
Boeing Financial Corporation			
(1½% over prime rate)	11,942,056	16,803,645	—
	11,942,056	18,053,645	—
Less amounts due within one year	1,226,457	1,500,000	—
	10,715,599	16,553,645	—
Contingencies			
Stockholders' equity			
Common stock, $1.00 par value,			
2,000,000 shares authorized,			
1,108,758 issued (1,058,758 at 12/31/71)	1,108,758	1,058,758	372,404
Capital in excess of par value	6,062,105	6,012,105	57,476
Deficit	(5,343,798)	(3,752,623)	—
	1,827,065	3,318,240	429,880
Total liabilities	$15,035,741	$22,083,381	$539,699

SOURCE: Southwest Airlines Co. annual reports 1971, 1972

NOTE: Notes to financial statement not shown here.

Exhibit 3
Examples of TI Newspaper Advertising, 1970–1971

if we listed all the 66
cities in the 9 states
and mexico that we jet to
it would take up this
entire costly page. we'd
rather spend the money
getting you there on time.

Texas International
We run an intelligent airline.

**we don't run
big expensive ads,**

we run big expensive jets instead.

serving 9 states and mexico
Texas International
We run an intelligent airline.

NOTE: Reproductions same size as originals

Exhibit 4
Example of Clinton E. Frank Press Advertising for Braniff International, 1970

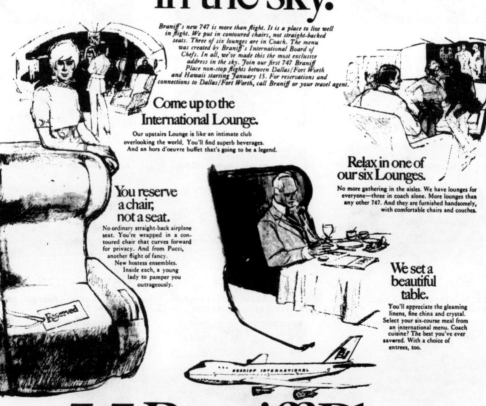

Welcome to "747 Braniff Place." The most exclusive address in the sky.

Braniff's new 747 is more than flight. It is a place to live well in flight. We put in contoured chairs, not straight-backed seats. Three of six lounges are in Coach. The menu was created by Braniff's International Board of Chefs. In all, we've made this the most exclusive address in the sky. Join our first 747 Braniff Place non-stop flights between Dallas/Fort Worth and Hawaii starting January 15. For reservations and connections to Dallas/Fort Worth, call Braniff or your travel agent.

Come up to the International Lounge.

Our upstairs Lounge is like an intimate club overlooking the world. You'll find superb beverages. And an hors d'oeuvre buffet that's going to be a legend.

Relax in one of our six Lounges.

No more gathering in the aisles. We have lounges for everyone—three in coach alone. More lounges than any other 747. And they are furnished handsomely, with comfortable chairs and couches.

You reserve a chair, not a seat.

No ordinary straight-back airplane seat. You're wrapped in a contoured chair that curves forward for privacy. And from Pucci, another flight of fancy. New hostess ensembles. Inside each, a young lady to pamper you outrageously.

We set a beautiful table.

You'll appreciate the gleaming linens, fine china and crystal. Select your six-course meal from an international menu. Coach cuisine? The best you've ever savored. With a choice of entrees, too.

747 Braniff Place

The most exclusive address in the sky.

BRANIFF INTERNATIONAL

Exhibit 5
Southwest Airlines' Introductory TV Advertising, June 1971

SOUTHWEST AIRLINES

CODE NO: SWA-3-30-71
TITLE: "TV Love Machine"

TELEVISION STORYBOARD
THE BLOOM AGENCY

1. (Natural sfx, people talking up and under)...

2. ...

3. ...

4. ...

5. (Wm Anncr VO) If you're standing in line...

6. ...you're not flying...

7. ...Southwest Airlines.

8. Because our Love Machine gives you a ticket...

9. ...in under ten seconds.

10. HOSTESS: Have a nice flight.

11. (Sfx: music and jet engine) 12 flights each day to Houston...

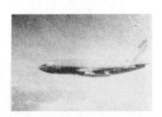

12. ...6 to San Antonio, for a loveable $20...

13. ...on Southwest Airlines.

14. "The somebody else up there...

15. ...who loves you."

SOURCE: Company records

140

Prepared by: Clinton E. Frank, Inc.

NOTE: The original of this advertisement extended across the bottom half of two full newspaper pages.

NOTE: The original advertisement covered a full-sized newspaper page.

SOUTHWEST AIRLINES (A)
Exhibit 8
Southwest Airlines: Quarterly Income Statements

	1971		1972			
Income Statements ($000s)	Q3	Q4	Q1	Q2	Q3	Q4
Transportation revenues[a]	$887	$1,138	$1,273	$1,401	$1,493	$1,745
Operating expenses						
Operations and maintenance[b]	1,211	1,280	1,192	1,145	1,153	1,156
Marketing and general administration	371	368	334	366	313	351
Depreciation and amortization	311	411	333	334	335	335
Total	1,893	2,059	1,859	1,845	1,801	1,842
Operating profit (loss)	(1,006)	(921)	(586)	(444)	(308)	(97)
Net interest revenues (costs)	(254)	(253)	(218)	(220)	(194)	(204)
Net income (loss) before extraordinary items	(1,260)	(1,174)	(804)	(664)	(502)	(301)
Extraordinary items	(571)[c]	(469)[c]	—	533[d]	—	—
Net income (loss)	$(1,831)	$(1,643)	$(804)	$(131)	$(502)	$(301)

SOURCE: Company records

[a] Included both passenger and freight business.

[b] Incremental costs per flight were $226 during the second half of 1971, $231 in the first half of 1972, and $244 in the second half of 1972. Management estimated that variable costs per passenger carried amounted to $2.53 during the first half of 1972 and to $2.80 during the second half of the year. These variable costs per passenger included $.13 for passenger beverages and suppliers in the first half and $.43 in the second half of 1972.

[c] Write-off of preoperating costs.

[d] Capital gain on sale of one aircraft.

Exhibit 9
Southwest: Discount vs. Regular Fare Flights

	All Routes				
	Regular Flights		*Discount Flights[a]*		
Month	*Passengers*	*Flights*	*Passengers*	*Flights*	*Price Changes*
1971					
June[b]	5,530	424	—	—	
July	15,459	988	—	—	
August	16,121	1,026	—	—	
September	16,440	939	—	—	
October	21,044	1,146	—	—	
November	19,042	963	73	3	$10 fares on some evening weekend flights
December	20,178	981	198	5	
1971 total	113,814	6,467	271	8	
1972					
January	20,694	899	170	4	
February	20,696	912	216	4	
March	24,656	1,014	702	10	
April	24,077	916	573	8	
May	23,112	869	2,189	51	$10 fare on all flights after 9 P.M.
June	22,972	784	4,636	78	
July	18,994	740	5,720	78	Basic fare raised to $26
August	21,257	819	5,739	81	
September	19,020	717	5,358	83	
October	21,894	786	6,599	98	
November	19,825	648	12,141	197	Half-price fares weekdays after 8 P.M. and on all weekend flights
December	17,142	604	10,617	176	
1972 total	254,339	9,708	54,660	868	
1973					
January[c]	18,893	599	13,635	239	Half-price fares on all Dallas–San Antonio flights

SOURCE: Company records

[a] Included flights on which gifts were offered.

[b] Part-month only.

[c] Estimated figures.

Exhibit 10
Southwest: Number of Flights and Passengers on Each Route

Month	Dallas–Houston		Dallas–San Antonio		San Antonio–Houston	
	Passengers	*Flights*	*Passengers*	*Flights*	*Passengers*	*Flights*
1971						
June[a]	3,620	276	1,910	148	—	—
July	10,301	642	5,158	346	—	—
August	11,316	672	4,805	354	—	—
September	11,674	612	4,766	327	—	—
October	14,552	764	6,492	382	—	—
November	14,060	654	4,167	240	888	72
December	14,665	687	4,004	165	1,707	134
1971 total	80,188	4,307	31,302	1,962	2,595	206
1972						
January	16,122	634	2,788	141	1,954	128
February	16,069	640	2,755	142	2,088	134
March	18,285	669	4,270	209	2,803	146
April	17,732	605	4,617	189	2,301	130
May	18,856	584	4,254	198	2,461	138
June	19,782	521	5,198	201	2,628	140
July	17,596	494	5,011	193	2,107	131
August	19,620	546	4,978	208	2,398	146
September	17,472	489	4,734	184	2,172	127
October	20,776	545	5,197	200	2,520	139
November	22,461	507	6,640	199	2,865	139
December	19,080	468	6,211	186	2,468	126
1972 total	223,581	6,702	56,653	2,250	28,765	1,624
1973						
January[b]	21,948	505	7,710	197	2,870	136

SOURCE: Company records

[a] Part-time only.

[b] Estimated figures.

Exhibit 11
"Remember What It Was Like Before Southwest Airlines," TV Advertising, September 1972

SOUTHWEST AIRLINES

CODE NO: SWA-34-30-72
TITLE: "Executive Class"

**TELEVISION STORYBOARD
THE BLOOM AGENCY**

1. HOSTESS: Remember what it was like...

2. ...before there was somebody else up there who loved you?

3. There was no such thing as executive class service to Dallas, Houston and San Antonio.

4. With first class leg room, free cocktails for everyone,...

5. ...and a schedule you could depend on.

6. (Sfx: jet taking off)...

7. ...

8. ...

9. Remember?

10. (Natural sfx up and out)

Exhibit 12
Southwest: Radio Advertising for Half-Fare Flights
All San Antonio Flights, January 1973

Number: 118–23—2   **Length:** 60 seconds   **Date:** 12/21/72, revised 12/29/72

Music: *Clinky piano*

Announcer: It's time for Captain Moneysaver, the man who knows how to save your dough!

Captain Moneysaver: Hello, moneysavers! Since Southwest Airlines introduced its half-price sale on all flights every day between Dallas and San Antonio, many listeners have asked that age-old question: Can I get there cheaper?
Cheaper than $13? Sure!
You can strap 5,000 pigeons to your arms and fly yourself. Or propel your body with a giant rubber band. Put a small motor on a ten-speed bike . . .

Music: *Light, happy*

Hostess: Southwest Airlines announces the 60-day half-price sale between Dallas and San Antonio. It's good on all flights every day. Just $13 one way. 25 round trip. So what are you waiting for?

Cowboy: You mean I kin fly between San Antonio and Dallas on a real jet airplane fer only $13?

Announcer: That's right! On any Southwest Airlines flight, every day.

Cowboy: They still gonna have them pretty girls and all?

Announcer: Same Southwest Airlines love service. And it's cheaper than the best bus service.

Cowboy: Howzit compare to my pickup?

Music: *Light, happy*

Hostess: Fly now while it's half fare on every Southwest Airlines flight every day between Dallas and San Antonio. All our love at half the price.

Voice: Half price? Can they do that?

Second voice: They did it!

Prepared by: The Bloom Agency

SOURCE: Dallas newspapers

Bradford Schools, Inc.

Bradford Schools, Inc., founded in 1969, was a Pittsburgh-based organization that owned and operated schools offering post-secondary business training in the fields of secretarial science, accounting and retailing. As stated in a student handbook, the purposes of the schools were to "provide training which will enable a student to achieve high levels of skill and competency in a chosen business vocation or profession; to assist students in becoming socially competent members of their communities, to the extent that each can appreciate and successfully cope with the human relations problems that will be encountered; and to provide a background in business administration subjects that is broad enough to bring students a fuller realization of economic facts of life, to the end that each is capable of achieving a satisfactory and rewarding career."

As of October 1980, Bradford owned 9 schools in Pittsburgh, Houston, Boston, St. Louis, Fort Wayne, Charlotte (N.C.), Dallas, Philadelphia and New York. With 1980 revenues of $10.7 million (*Exhibit 1*), the company had ambitious growth plans. Its corporate long-term plan called for 20% annual compound growth in tuition revenues, with a target of net profit after taxes at a level that would return 6% on sales and a 20% return on equity. (*Exhibits 1* and *2* contain current financial information.) To achieve this, the company planned to develop and/or acquire schools in 8 new cities by 1990, with multiple schools per city.

Joe Calihan, Bradford's president, reflected on his company's achievements to date and the challenges posed for the future:

> I think we are well poised for future growth. Our management controls are good and, because of all the attention we have given it, we have strongly committed people. The time has therefore come to think about what we do. We are in the business of training people to increase their value to an employer. To date, we have aimed primarily at the female high school market, but the post–World War II "baby boom" is coming to a close and all forecasts point to declining high school enrollments. In addition, the high schools are increasingly teaching business-related subjects. This means we need to give attention to two main items. First, should we consider different types

This case was prepared by Assistant Professor David H. Maister as a basis for class discussion rather than to illustrate either effective or ineffective handling of an administrative situation. Copyright © 1980 by the President and Fellows of Harvard College; Harvard Business School case 681-049 Rev. 6/88.

of programs apart from secretarial, accounting and retailing? If so, how do we select which fields? What should our criteria be? Second, in the fields that we already compete in, how do we ensure our future success? The quality of our programs is judged not only by our students but also by the employers that hire them. As I look to the future of this company, it is clearly important that we address the issue of what is meant by value. What is the perceived value of our service? What do our customers want or need? We need some way to measure our schools so that we can prove the value of our services and demonstrate the success of our commitment to quality education. But what *is* a "quality education" and what do we have to do to provide it?

THE PROPRIETARY BUSINESS SCHOOL INDUSTRY

In 1980 there were 512 schools accredited as post-secondary business schools by the Association of Independent Colleges and Schools (AICS), with approximately 350,000 students enrolled. Ninety-five percent of accredited schools offered secretarial programs. It was estimated that there were an additional 600 unaccredited post-secondary business schools, most of which were very small institutions. Statistics on job openings are given in *Exhibit 3*.

The AICS defined a business school as "a non-collegiate post-high school institution predominantly organized for vocational training of students for career patterns in business." Business schools usually stated their objectives in terms of vocational competence, set skill goals for completion of courses, and emphasized placement as the educational objective. Curricula tended to be relatively short and intensive, leading to one or a number of closely related occupational objectives. The programs of such institutions rarely exceeded one year in length.

The major competition for proprietary business schools came from junior and senior colleges of business, many of which were also proprietary institutions. A junior college of business offered a two-year program devoted substantially, but not exclusively, to business subjects. According to AICS, a junior college placed greater emphasis on achievement beyond the purely vocational. Frequently, objectives required courses of considerable breadth, including general education, citizenship, research, etc. For accreditation by the AICS, a junior college's program needed to include work in most or all of the following fields: communication arts, fine and practical arts, languages, literature, mathematics, psychology and social science. Junior colleges awarded diplomas or degrees, or prepared students for state-conferred designations or licenses upon examination. Senior colleges ran four-year programs leading to degrees. Programs at publicly owned community colleges, whose tuition fees were significantly lower than proprietary schools, could be of two- or four-year length. About 85–90% of all proprietary school students completed their programs, compared to 25–35% of community college students.

Ownership of proprietary business schools was widespread, with only a few multischool companies in the industry. Among the most prominent of these was Katharine Gibbs, which in 1980 had 4,000 students in 7 schools, mainly in the Northeast. Now owned by Macmillan, Inc., a publisher of educational materials, the company had been founded in 1911 at Providence, R.I., by its namesake, a wealthy society matron. Over the years Katharine Gibbs had acquired a prestigious and "upper-class" image. However, it was likely that Katharine Gibbs would undergo some changes. In January 1980, Lynn Salvage (a 34-year-old Harvard MBA who had previously managed the First Women's Bank in New York) was appointed president of the Gibbs school. In a newspaper interview she was quoted as saying "Here at Gibbs, we aim to be the leader in developing the staff that will manage the office of the future. We are shedding our white gloves and progressing beyond our typewriters and steno pads to enter the area of the table-top computer and word processor." She spoke of her "crusade" to transform the managerial attitude toward the executive secretary, to professionalize the corporate support staff, to establish close ties with the vendors of office technology, to expand the school's role as a mechanism for women re-entering the work force, and to establish the school throughout the nation and perhaps abroad.

Another corporation participating in this market was I.T.T. which owned a mixture of over 20 technical and business schools, offering programs ranging from auto mechanics to secretarial science. However, the vast majority of schools were "mom-and-pop" institutions. "The level of sophistication," noted Mr. Calihan, "is not high in this industry, either in course content or management. There are still schools around that teach penmanship and how to make a stencil. The overall reputation of the industry is not high. A number of newspapers have written exposés about rip-offs and conmen operating at the fringes with hard sells and wild misrepresentations. One computer school 'operator' enrolled a full class and then took off with all the money. Others promise jobs but train people for careers where there are no openings. This industry has a poor image."

BRADFORD SCHOOLS

Joe Calihan joined Bradford Schools in 1970, as its financial officer. After a turbulent period when some of the company's original owners and founders departed, taking one of the schools with them, Mr. Calihan became the major stockholder in 1977. Two other schools were closed, leaving Bradford with a core of five schools in 1977 (Pittsburgh, Boston, St. Louis, Fort Wayne and Charlotte). In 1980, each of these was profitable (*Exhibit 4*), and Bradford expanded by acquiring schools in Houston and New York and opening new schools in Dallas and Philadelphia.

Mr. Calihan noted:

Our strategy has a number of elements. The mainstay of our success has been our admissions process. We developed a presentation on secretarial careers which we make in a large number of high schools in our areas. The presentation is not a hard sell; we have tried to make it a service which gives career advice and informs high school students of the options open to them, the skills and requirements they will need in the job market. As such, we are welcomed into the schools by the careers advisory teachers. However, it serves us well because we naturally get many inquiries as a result of these presentations. We then have the opportunity to try and convert these leads into "sits" (students enrolled in a course). A few other business schools have adopted this practice, but we are the only ones who rely on it exclusively. We have developed our procedures very well, and we get into 90% of the schools we want to. Other schools have tried different forms of recruitment, like newspaper and late-night T.V. advertising, but we don't think the quality of applicants generated these ways is very high. The quality of our students is illustrated by the following statistics for one of our schools: 21% of the incoming class graduated in the top fifth of their high school class, 55% in the top two-fifths and 84% in the top three-fifths.

We have a number of advantages that we stress in our recruiting. We occupy downtown locations and modern facilities, which we believe acclimatizes students to the type of environment in which they will work. Compared to the junior colleges, our programs are short and do not include irrelevant topics like world history. Relative to Katie Gibbs, our students tend to come from blue-collar homes. In many cases they are the first person in the family to receive any form of education after high school.

We try to preserve our professional, quality image. We are not cut-rate hustlers, of which there are a few in this industry. We are ethical and do our best to communicate this. Our fees are usually close to the highest in the cities in which we compete, but we give pro-rata refunds to any student that leaves before the end of the course. We are proud of our placement services and record. Of those of our graduates who wanted to be placed, 99.7% have been. We also make our placement services available to our alumnae: they can use our service anywhere in our system, no matter from which school they graduated. We also allow our alumnae to return for refresher courses, free of charge, at any time. A good high school student with business training could get a job starting at $670 or so per month. But if she attended our school she could increase that by $70 or $100.

PROGRAMS

Although most of the schools offered 10-month courses in accounting and retailing (each with 1,100 classroom hours), the core of Bradford's business was in secretarial programs, accounting for approximately 75% of its students company-wide. Three programs were offered at most schools: (1) a 24-week program (600 class hours) aimed at high school graduates with 2 years of high school classes in typing and shorthand; (2) a 40-week program (1,000 class hours) aimed at high school graduates with less than 2 years' typing and shorthand; and (3) a 48-week "cooperative" program for advanced students who worked alternate weeks for an employer while attending classes. Bradford normally arranged for two students to be paired in the cooperative program, so that the employer had the year-round services of a student-secretary. Students in cooperative programs arranged the compensation with their employer, but this was normally at an "entrance rate" which covered approximately 85% of their tuition.

Within each of the secretarial programs, students were given the opportunity to specialize in legal or medical secretarial programs, requiring 6 additional weeks of study and an extra tuition fee of $350. Although variations existed between schools, separate program commencement dates were offered. At the Bradford School in Pittsburgh, the 6-month program was offered starting in July or September, the 10-month in February, July or September. All cooperative secretarial students began in July.

The structure of the 10-month secretarial program is given in *Exhibit 5*, with brief course content descriptions in *Exhibit 6*.

ORGANIZATION AND CONTROL

Each school was headed by a president, who bore full profit-and-loss responsibility for his or her school's operations. Four main departments existed beneath the president: admissions, education, placement and staff services. Except where a school had not yet reached maturity, each of these departments was headed by a director who reported to the president.

Initially, each school president reported directly to Joe Calihan. However, in preparation for the planned growth, Mr. Calihan had appointed three senior vice presidents (all from within the organization) whose function was to supervise the schools in their area (*Exhibit 7*).

In the past, Bradford schools had experienced high turnover in the position of school presidents.

It used to be that the primary task of the president was in sales and marketing. The emphasis was on new admissions. However, they were not necessarily good managers. Four or five years ago I created a financial model for how a school should work. It specified in some detail target cost and productivity levels for each major function. It never worked, and we thought our presidents were failing. We had different levels of costs per student in different areas. We faced the choice of scrapping the whole idea of models or developing models that people had commitment to.

We made a number of changes in 1979. We set the goal of having directors for each of the four functions at each school. We had always had education and placement directors, but not always directors of admissions and staff services. This meant that the directors could look after day-to-day matters, allowing the presidents to focus on intermediate-term planning.

Next, we decided to try to win commitment from the organization as a whole. When I became president in 1973, I spent 4 years trying to convince people that we cared about what we were doing. We had two things working against us. We had a very mixed-up ownership structure: three people with very different stakes, which kept the organization from moving forward. We eventually sorted that out in 1977. Second, I didn't really understand the concept of how to get people committed to certain goals.

The solution was to involve people in the process of determining the goals. We applied this across the board. We involved every one of our managerial people in a training program called the Managerial Grid, and formed numerous teams to establish our targets and discuss how we were going to achieve them. We now have an Admissions Planning Team, an Educational Planning Team, and a Placement Planning Team, each of which meets 3 or 4 times a year. The teams are made up of all the directors from each school in addition to myself and occasionally others from our corporate staff. We use these teams, among other purposes, to develop new financial and operations models, which are essential elements in our control system.

The company model established target cost and productivity levels for each major function at a school, at both an aggregate and detailed level. The aggregate financial model for schools of various sizes is shown in *Exhibit 8*. The detailed model is illustrated by a description of the admissions process.

ADMISSIONS

Through the Admissions Planning Team, Bradford had established a target of enrolling 2.7% of the female high school population within a radius of 30 miles, and 1.7% of that population in the 30- to 60-mile radius.

The admissions process had five main stages. First, "territory managers" reporting to the director of admissions visited high schools to win permission to make presentations to the students. For schools which Bradford had visited before, this often was just a matter of confirming a prior "booking." At new schools, more effort was involved. At the Boston school, there were four territory managers each covering a different geographical area. Presenters, trained during July and August, gave their career talks during September through December to seniors—with "second talks" scheduled in December through March. In some schools, presentations were also made to the junior class. From those presentations came contacts: potential students who inquired about Bradford's program. A staff of appointment secretaries telephoned these students to establish a degree of interest and to schedule interviews. Applicants were then interviewed (preferably together with their parents, in order to discuss financial arrangements). Finally, a decision was made on acceptance or rejection.

Specific targets were established, based on experience at all Bradford schools, for each of these stages. For example, targets were established for the number of presentations to be made by each presenter, for the number of leads to be generated, for the percent successfully contacted, the percent that came in for interviews, the percent converted to applications, the percent accepted, and the percent of these that actually enrolled. While these target percentages were based on systemwide historical experience, they were discussed and agreed to by the employees responsible at the beginning of each year. Thus each employee had a well-defined target to aim at and be appraised by (for example, percent of leads contacted and percent of contacts scheduled for interview by the appointment secretaries). For an example of specific targets, see *Exhibit 9*.

Mimi Ohlinger, the director of admissions at the Boston school, explained the interview and selection process:

> The interviewers' main role is to convert the student into an applicant, and they are judged by their success at this. However, they also attempt to observe the student's speech, appearance, attention and interest, and any domestic or personal situations that might affect the student's ability to complete the course successfully and pursue a business career. Based upon these factors, the student's grade point average, rank in class, recommendation of the high school counsellor, the reputation of the high school, previous business-related courses of high school, a decision is taken by the Accept-

ance Committee. This is composed of the directors of admissions, placement and education, as well as the person responsible for financial aid. However, few applicants are rejected by the committee. At one, not untypical school, the rejection rate was 2.9%. "The phrase we use around here," commented one school president, "is that we can't play God. If we cannot say that the student will fail for sure, then we accept. There are some people in the company that want us to accept *all* applicants, and weed out the bad ones through attrition or dismissal."

An important component of the interview and selection process was the discussion of financial aid. Fees for Bradford's programs were set by each school president, usually in consultation with Mr. Calihan as part of the budgeting process. An application fee of $25 was payable with all applications, and a (refundable) deposit of $200 payable upon receipt of the letter of acceptance. This deposit was applied against tuition. For students entering the Boston school, tuition for the 6-month secretarial program was $3,100, and $3,700 for the 10-month program. Textbooks and supplies (sold by the school bookstore) cost approximately $250.

THE EDUCATION DEPARTMENT

Each school's educational activities were managed by the director of education, who was responsible for curricula, scheduling of programs, admissions acceptances and management of the educational budget. Each educational program was headed by a program administrator (PA) (reporting to the educational director) whose role was to supervise students, faculty and staff in order to coordinate all activities relating to the specific program. At the St. Louis school, for example, there were 5 PAs: one for each of the cooperative secretarial, retailing and accounting programs, one that supervised both the February and July 10-month programs, and one that supervised the September 10-month and the July 6-month programs.

Approximately 10% of Bradford's faculty were new business teachers. Approximately 80% had been trained in business education and had been teaching elsewhere when they came to Bradford. The remainder, including many of the technical instructors in areas such as accounting, had no prior teaching experience before joining the company. No companywide policies existed on teacher recruitment or training. One director of education commented:

I tend to go with new teachers because I want to train them my own way. Faculty that come to us with a public sector background sometimes find it hard to adjust to our environment. For example, they are used to teaching classes of 15 or so, whereas our class size is 32 to 36 students. We have had a lot of discussion and research optimum class sizes, and you cannot demonstrate any relationship between learning and class size: it's totally dependent on the teacher. So, when I recruit I look for energy, warmth, flexibility. We'd rather have enthusiasm than a master's degree. Faculty from public sector backgrounds also have difficulty with our fast pace and performance standards. In the public sector teachers are given a group of students and can do what they want: no one is held accountable. Here we have program administrators overseeing the faculty, paying close attention to student comments.

Faculty worked full 7½-hour days, and were required to teach 25 hours per week. The average monthly salary was $1,200, and faculty were employed an average of 10 months per year. Systemwide, 25% of the faculty held master's degrees, although this varied from 56% in one school to zero at another. The median length of service at Bradford varied by school, but averaged 2.5 years, with the average (median) number of years' teaching experience being 6.0. No companywide policies existed on teacher training. At one school, each faculty member was required to attend at least 2 seminars each year on Progressive Methods in Business Education. Secretarial faculty had to spend at least one month each four years in business. At other schools no such programs or proce-dures existed. "It would be incredibly beneficial," said one school president, "to find some way to keep our faculty current with hands-on office experience. The students love the anecdotes that such teachers bring to class and it helps the learning experience. But how can we accomplish it? It would clearly be uneco-nomic for us to have experienced faculty disappearing, even if we could find them temporary jobs commensurate with their experience."

Turnover among faculty was very low. "People like to stay with us," com-mented Mr. Calihan, "and we haven't done a very good job at weeding out our weak faculty. In part this is due to the lack of measurement system." Most schools employed some form of student evaluation of teachers (an example is given in *Exhibit 10*), although the way in which this was done, the frequency, and the use of the results varied from school to school. At most schools the results of such questionnaires, as well as those of classroom observation of the instructor by the program administrator, were discussed privately with the in-structor. At only one school were results of the questionnaires distributed to all faculty.

"At my school," commented Mary Pisani, president in St. Louis, "teacher evaluation is informal, but easy to keep track of. Our students become very good consumers, and let the program administrators know if anything is going wrong. In addition, the Typing III instructor will soon find out if the Typing II instructor hasn't done her job. The quality of our instruction has really gone up since we introduced program administrators and the concept of faculty teams. As far as possible I try to assign teachers to be involved with only one program, so that together with the PA they form a team which is responsible for that group of students. Since we did this, the level of commitment has really gone up. I find that faculty are now more willing to put in extra tutoring and run special clinics, even though there is no extra pay involved. This has been very helpful, because there is little room for slippage in our programs. Except in shorthand, each student must move along with the rest of the class; when Typing II finishes at the end of the 16th week, the student has to be ready for Typing III."

It was not always possible to dedicate each teacher to a single program. While most teachers were required to teach more than one subject (for example, typing, shorthand and business communications), schedule conflicts and the desire to keep faculty fully utilized often meant that individual faculty taught in more than one program. "I try to limit teacher preparation to no more than 2 courses per 8-week period," noted Ms. Pisani, "which also tends to force teachers to work across programs sometimes."

In a single program there would usually be more than one section. For example, in the 1980 July 10-month program at St. Louis, there were 120 students, divided into 4 sections. Sections were formed as the result of a typing-speed test given to all incoming students, with the novices put in one class and others grouped by speed level. The sections thus formed stayed together for all of their subject courses throughout the program. "This can be a problem," noted Ms. Pisani "because the lowest group soon comes to call themselves the 'dumb group,' feeling they can't achieve as much as the others. Yet there is only one set graduation standard for all to aim at. Naturally, the teachers prefer to work with the other classes."

Outside of the classroom, Bradford had a number of companywide policies that distinguished it from many schools. Attendance at classes was mandatory, and attendance records become a permanent part of the students' graduation transcript. A strict dress code was enforced, and punctuality emphasized. Though the particulars varied by school, there was also a faculty dress code. Classes were scheduled during business hours (8:30 to 4:30). While students who attended classes 5 hours per day might leave early, "we try to schedule their first weeks here so that they have a first hour and an eighth-hour class so they get used to business hours." "We pride ourselves," said Mr. Calihan, "on helping our students mature by keeping to a business-like atmosphere ourselves. We don't dismiss classes early, we don't close for snow except in extreme cases. If offices are open, we are open."

PLACEMENT

Placement activities at each school were managed by a placement director. The main activities of the placement department were interviewing students to discover where they wanted to work and what type of jobs they wanted; contacting companies to solicit job opportunities; scheduling appointments for students with these companies and counselling of students. At some schools, placement counsellors also taught the Professional Development course in the schools' programs.

There was no companywide policy on charging employees placement fees. "We are not an employment agency," commented one placement director, "and since we don't take a fee we avoid feeling responsibility to the employer and keep it focused on the student's needs." However, other Bradford schools did charge fees. "Our graduates are much in demand," noted the president of the Pittsburgh school. "In 1978 we produced 20% of the newly trained secretaries from post-secondary institutions, $2\frac{1}{2}$ times the next largest producer. Our graduates are appreciated because they know how to behave in an office, how to dress, how to speak. The employers around here say you know what you're getting when you hire a Bradford grad."

When contacting companies, placement departments attempted to discover facts about the job environment so that these could be matched with the student's strengths. Included among these factors would be the extent of dealing with the public, whether the job was as a personal secretary or in a pool, the amount of deadline pressure and so on.

At some schools, little effort had to be placed on obtaining job orders. "There is a tremendous scarcity of good secretaries today," said Margaret Howard, the Boston placement director; "and we are well known in our community. We receive about 200 to 300 job orders per month." However, at other schools greater efforts were needed. "Most of our students want to work locally," noted one officer, "which sometimes takes work.

"We try to keep a close watch on our placements," continued Ms. Howard. "We print and distribute to our students a monthly 'News from the Job Market' which lists jobs obtained by our graduating students. We also publish once a year a listing of jobs obtained arranged by the high school from which each girl graduated. This is a very effective motivating tool, and is extremely useful in recruiting. We bring back alumnae to share their job experiences in our career development course." One school had also polled its alumnae about their Bradford experience (*Exhibit 11*).

THE "ADDED VALUE" PROBLEM

In February 1980, the Education Planning Team met to discuss the company's educational objectives. Four targets were set: (1) increase productivity (reduction in dollars expended on a per student basis to produce a given level of results); (2) added value that justifies the amount of tuition paid by the students; (3) be among the top 5% of business training schools so that the marketplace will "perceive our excellence and uniqueness"; (4) establish a "system" of education that enables accomplishment of all objectives specified above while providing an economic return that enables growth to occur as specified in the corporate long-range plan.

In looking at the objective for their secretarial programs, the team agreed that the minimum graduation requirements should be set so as to assure employability. This, in turn, implied the identification of "specific competencies." Standards were set for shorthand and typing skills, and specific competencies established for the areas of written communications (functional grammar, punctuation and spelling), oral communication (telephone skills, dealing with office visitors) and standard secretarial procedures (filing, business arithmetic, use of office machines, and knowledge of such areas as petty cash, and accounting terminology). The team also brainstormed a list of other competencies desired:

Goal-setting

Maturity

Self-confidence

Pride in profession

Dealing with conflict

Ethics

Problem-solving

Decision-making

Assertiveness

Professional appearance

Inquisitiveness

Initiative

Punctuality

Loyalty

Ability to differentiate standards

Team member

Flexibility

Cooperativeness

Social responsibility

Continuance of viewing school as resource

Understanding of productivity

Accountability

Understanding of relationship between freedom and responsibility

Understanding of free enterprise system

Open-mindedness

Continued willingness to learn

Orientation toward high standards

Self-evaluation

Attitude

Effective interviewing

Effective time management

Etiquette; manners

Identification of problems

Social awareness

Willingness to do small/menial tasks

Ability to cope with personal life problems

The team noted that this list included both "skills" and "behaviors," and expressed a commitment that Bradford Schools should offer its students educational experiences that would lead to improvement in these areas. The challenge, they felt, was first, how to do this, and secondly, how they could measure and communicate the results.

Exhibit 1
Income Statements
($000)

	1980	1979
Revenues		
Tuition and fees	$8597	$6867
Dormitory and food service	1200	940
Books and supplies	461	421
Interest	155	19
Other	295	126
Total revenues	$10709	$8373
Costs and Other Deductions		
Salaries and employee benefits	$4449	$3287
Other operating costs	1787	1324
Facilities	2011	1402
Books and supplies	365	338
Interest	29	51
Depreciation and amortization	353	226
Total costs	$8995	$6628
Operating income	$1714	$1744
Other (Income) and Expense		
Management training	$160	$ 233
Other	(260)*	167
Total	$(100)	$ 400
Income before taxes	$1814	$1344
Taxes	800	649
Net income after tax	$1014	$ 696

*Gain on sale of assets.

Exhibit 2
Balance Sheet
($000)

	1980	1979
Assets		
Cash and commercial paper	$1141	$ 237
Receivables	1149	683
Prepaid admission costs	2206	2145
Other current	617	231
Total current	5114	3296
Fixed assets, less depreciation	1296	1016
Other	422	262
Total Assets	$6831	$4574
Liabilities		
Total current	$1629	$ 959
Deferred income	1990	1865
Long-term debt due after one year	283	385
Deferred income taxes	1150	600
Common stock, at par	88	88
Capital in excess of par	72	72
Retained earnings	1619	604
Total Liabilities	$6831	$4574

Exhibit 3
U.S. Department of Labor
Occupational Projections and Training Data for Selected Occupations
According to the U.S. Department of Labor Statistics, less than 20% of all jobs by 1980 will require a degree. But most of the remaining 80% will require training beyond high school.

Occupation	*Average Annual Openings through 1985*	*Annual Training Completions through 1985*	*Expected Annual Shortage or (Oversupply) of Trained Personnel through 1985*
Secretaries and Stenographers	439,000	187,629	251,371
Retail Occupations	190,000	69,460	120,540
Accounting and Bookkeeping	166,000	94,088	71,912
Social Service and Psychology Related	49,850	142,285	(92,435)
Art, Design, Graphics, etc.	15,500	56,027	(40,527)
Kindergarten, Elementary, and Secondary Education	131,500	251,870	(120,370)

"Occupational Projects and Training Data," Bulletin 1918, 1976, Appendix B, table B-1, Appendix C, tables C-1, C-2, C-4, C-5, C-7. Annual projections through 1985.

Exhibit 4
1980 Income Statements by School
($000)

	Pittsburgh	Boston	St. Louis	Ft. Wayne	Charlotte
Revenues					
Tuition and Fees	2096	2424	1322	896	903
Dormitory and Food Service[a]	375	0	145	87	403
Books and Supplies	93	94	89	49	57
Other	26	19	9	61	13
	2590	2537	1566	1092	1376
Expenses					
Education	453	422	279	140	198
Administrative	257	260	176	137	118
Placement	68	66	44	16	33
Admissions Amortization	451	391	285	246	264
Continuing Education	5	44	19	70	10
Special Program[b]	17	374	0	0	0
Occupancy	198	281	128	87	97
Residence and Food	384	0	117	155	367
Books and Supplies	79	73	77	38	41
	1912	1911	1125	888	1129
Operating Income	678	626	441	204	247
Corporate Allocation	153	122	110	61	67
Income before Taxes	525	504	331	143	180
Taxes (State and Federal)	271	258	161	75	88
Net Income	254	246	170	68	91
Enrollment					
Class: 7/79	438	281	363	128	249
: 9/79	291	350	95	105	45
: 2/80	97	44	56	15	17
Total	826	675	514	248	311

[a] Because of a shortage of student housing in some cities, Bradford had decided to operate its own dormitories. Corporate plans called for expansion of these activities.

[b] Primarily CETA programs, government-funded training programs for the unemployed. While CETA revenues and expenses are included in the financial information given in this exhibit, enrollment statistics do not include CETA students.

Exhibit 5
Structure of 10-Month Secretarial Program

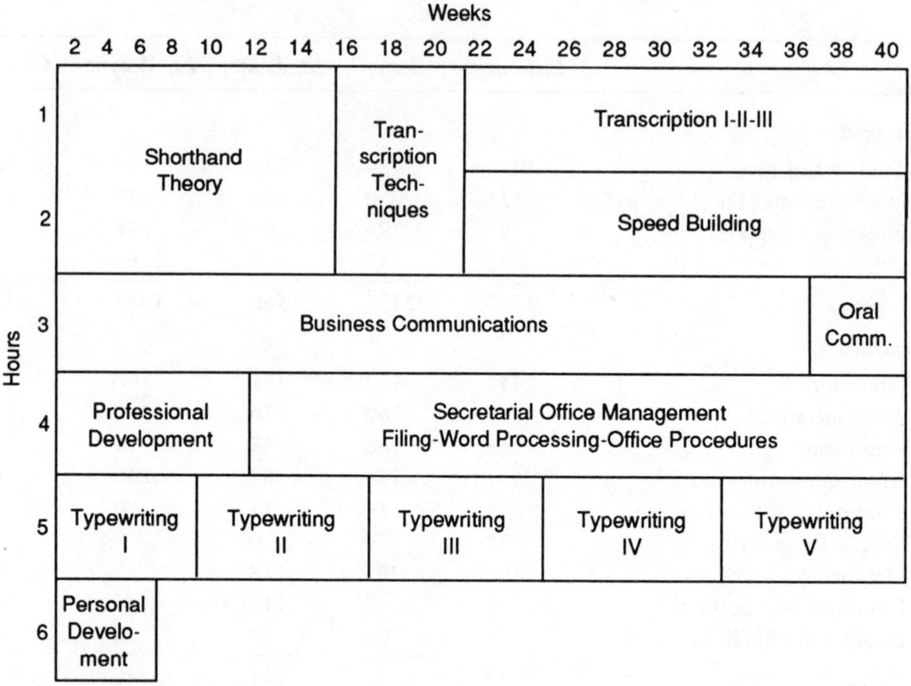
Weeks
2 4 6 8 10 12 14 16 18 20 22 24 26 28 30 32 34 36 38 40
Hours
1
2
3
4
5
6
Shorthand Theory
Tran-scription Tech-niques
Transcription I-II-III
Speed Building
Business Communications
Oral Comm.
Professional Development
Secretarial Office Management
Filing-Word Processing-Office Procedures
Typewriting I
Typewriting II
Typewriting III
Typewriting IV
Typewriting V
Personal Develo-ment

Medical or Legal Option 6 Additional Weeks

Exhibit 6
10-Month Secretarial Curriculum

INTRODUCTION SHORTHAND

An introduction to the principles of Gregg Shorthand. Included is the development of rapid reading and writing techniques. Emphasis is placed upon the mastery of brief forms, phrases, a basic business vocabulary, the formation of good language skills, business letter dictation and the introduction to pre-transcription techniques.

ADVANCED SHORTHAND

The two key areas of skill development are separated and each student is placed in a speed building section and a transcription section. During the secretarial program, every student spends two hours daily in the development of shorthand skill.

Exhibit 6
(Continued)

Speed Building

Concentration in this class is on assisting the student to develop the ability to accomplish faster, more accurate dictation skills. Speed building may start at a level as low as 50 wpm. Each individual is encouraged to progress through the speed building levels at her own rate of progress. If an individual can meet the requirements established for any given speed level, she may progress to the next level within a minimum time period of two weeks. Expert students may progress to levels of dictation offered at 160 wpm or more.

Transcription

The ultimate goal of the transcription course is to have each student reach a highly employable level of ability. This is accomplished by establishing specific goals throughout the program. Each course places increasingly more importance on degree of accuracy. Accuracy in transcription is built by exposing the student to the following topics in part:

1. English skill—punctuation, spelling, sentence structure, proper word usage, vocabulary
2. Proofreading
3. Letter styles
4. Transcription of material
5. Erasures
6. Carbon copies

These are some of the areas covered which will help the student achieve 100% mailability of transcribed material.

INTRODUCTORY TYPEWRITING

A beginner's course for students who have not had previous training in typewriting or who need a complete keyboard review. Correct posture, mastery of the keyboard, operating techniques, a knowledge of the parts of the typewriter, centering, and basic letter writing are taught.

ADVANCED TYPEWRITING

Each student is scheduled for one typewriting class period daily throughout the secretarial program. Students in advanced classes progress through increasingly more demanding presentations of letter styles, business forms, erasing, carbon copies, and other typing techniques.

(Continued)

Exhibit 6
(Continued)

As the student reaches the closing portion of the course, special emphasis is placed on production typewriting. Additionally, the student is introduced to and trained on the transcriber equipment.

Specific attention is given to the individual's speed and accuracy. An analysis of each student's specific need for improvement is part of the ongoing course content.

BUSINESS COMMUNICATIONS

All students must have an in-depth knowledge of English grammar, punctuation, and sentence structure. This information is then applied to composing and typing perfect data sheets and business letters. Some specific types of letters are application letters, order letters, acknowledgement letters, and credit letters.

SECRETARIAL OFFICE MANAGEMENT

This is a comprehensive finishing course that ties together the various secretarial skills the student has studied and introduces her to additional aspects of secretarial work, such as filing, the use of business machines, and processing mail. Ten-month secretarial students also receive a review of business math. Additionally, the concept of word processing is presented. Students become familiarized with the terminology and varied job responsibilities of a word processing operator, including such tasks as working from rough draft material and text editing. Several weeks are also set aside for in-basket problems done in an office-type situation. The course is structured so that all previously learned skills are utilized as an integral part of the program.

ORAL COMMUNICATIONS

This course is specifically designed to develop the individual's skills on the telephone. Emphasis is placed on proper telephone etiquette.

CAREER DEVELOPMENT

This is a two-segment course designed to help students analyze themselves, their abilities, and their needs and through this process move more easily from student to employee. One segment includes units in personal success: communication, job selection, interviewing, money, and finally on "the job." The other segment, related to grooming and personal development, includes units on makeup, hair care, wardrobe, diet and exercise, and visual poise.

The methods of presentation will include lectures by instructors from the placement office, guest speakers, both internal and external, and class discussion as well as assignment of outside research projects.

BRADFORD SCHOOLS, INC.
Exhibit 7
Key Management Positions

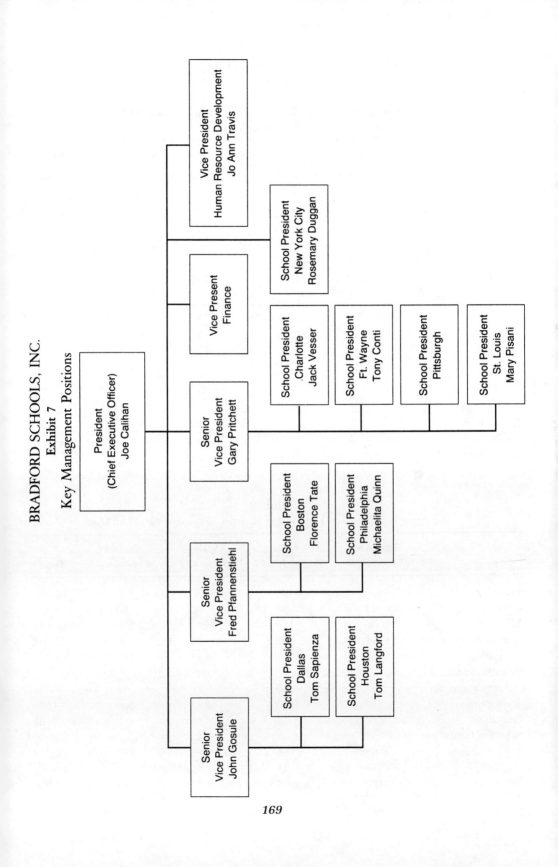

Exhibit 8
Summary of Ideal Financial Model for Schools of Various Sizes (1981 Dollars)
Developed

Enrollment	400	500	600	700	800	900	1000
Net Tuition ($2714/Student)	1086	1357	1628	1900	2171	2443	2714
Expenses							
Admissions	346	349	405	455	487	540	600
Education	367	450	524	606	694	765	850
Placement	59	61	71	79	88	99	110
Staff Services	189	213	256	295	322	360	400
Corporate Allocation	76	95	114	133	152	171	190
TOTAL	1037	1168	1370	1568	1743	1935	2150
Application Fees	19	19	22	26	30	33	37
Bookstore	15	19	22	26	30	33	37
Other	12	15	18	21	24	27	30
Net from Operations	95	242	320	405	512	601	668
Less: Taxes (50%)	48	121	160	203	256	301	334
Net after Taxes	47	121	160	202	256	300	334

Capital Expenditures are equal to depreciation charges.

Exhibit 9
Admissions Planning Targets for Boston School, 1980–1981

	Summer 5/1–9/20	*Fall* 9/21–12/31	*Spring* 1/1–4/1	*Remainder* 4/1——	*Total*
Leads	8800	4800	2200	250	16,050
Contact %	91	93	90	80	91%
ISC	8000	4464	1980	200	14,645
Interviews %	19	33	25	93	25.4%
Interviews	1560	1475	495	186	3,720
Conversion to Applications %	33	40	57	86	43%
Applications	515	590	282	160	1600
Rejections	20	24	11	7	62
Adjusted Gross Applications	495	566	271	153	1,538
Sit Rate	58	56	65	91	60.5%
Enrollments	290	315	175	135	900

Exhibit 10
Student Evaluation Form Questions*

Name of Course _____ Class Period _____

1. The instructor presents a neat, professional appearance.
2. The instructor is on time for classes.
3. The instructor demonstrates knowledge of subject matter.
4. The instructor has needed materials ready at the start of class.
5. The instructor motivates the students.
6. The instructor maintains order in the classroom.
7. The instructor provides individual help for students as needed.
8. The instructor gives clear, purposeful instructions for assignments.
9. The instructor distributes tests that are accurate, well organized, and clearly printed.
10. The instructor scores tests and assignments accurately and returns them promptly.
11. The instructor informs the students of course requirements and standards to be used in grading.
12. The instructor provides clear and complete instructions before tests and monitors the tests.
13. Does the instructor explain clearly?
14. Is the instructor available for pre-planned appointments?
15. Does the instructor relate course material to current trends in business?
16. Does the course challenge you?
17. Does the instructor establish student relationships which encourage learning?
18. The instructor has distracting mannerisms and repetitious expressions.
19. Make an *Overall Evaluation* of this instructor.

Comments: (Please use the reverse side)

*Students were asked to indicate strength of agreement or disagreement.

Exhibit 11
Selected Comments from Alumnae Questionnaire, Boston School

Would you recommend Bradford to someone entering the business field?

1. "Yes, has an excellent curriculum, necessary courses and excellent placement department."
2. "Acquainted me with the real world of business."
3. "Young, understanding teachers, good courses and placement services."
4. "Oftentimes too grinding; need a break. Six straight months was too much."
5. "You get good training, but I think in a 2-year program you could learn more."
6. "Without Bradford, I wouldn't be working; high school wasn't enough."
7. "It has a good reputation when you are looking for a job."
8. "Hard work that paid off."
9. "Prepares you for a fussy and particular boss."
10. "Helps you grow up."
11. "If you only want accounting and not liberal arts, Bradford is an excellent school."
12. "While I was there, I felt the strict manner was unnecessary but now I can apply the strictness to my day-to-day work situation."
13. "Few teachers showed a personal interest in students, classes were over-crowded, high tuition."
14. "Bradford made me a professional and polished secretary."
15. "It's like going to work everyday."
16. "Bradford gives you confidence in your abilities."
17. "They prepare you to take responsibility."
18. "I'd recommend it to anyone interested in becoming a career woman."
19. "I feel Bradford is able to professionalize a person's world. You are trained to handle pressure."

The Oakland A's—1989

INTRODUCTION

Some people thought that I was crazy to leave Madison Square Garden Sports for the A's. MSG sports was one of the best run and most respected sports management companies in the country; the A's were one of the worst run and least well respected. In 1980 the A's were a minor league club; they were a cadaver.

So said Andy Dolich, the A's vice president of Business Operations, as he thought back to his decision to join the Oakland Athletics (A's) in 1980, soon after the team was purchased by the Haas family, owners of the Levi Strauss company.

Dolich continued:

But I was lucky. I had marketed a sport most people knew little about: professional soccer. I also had worked in a sport that no one knew anything about: professional box lacrosse. I was lucky because I had to work hard to promote those sports. I had learned the hard way about how to market sports and I thought that this experience would be useful in marketing the A's.

In the ensuing nine years, the A's achieved a total turnaround. Not only did the team go to the World Series twice (winning it in 1989), but season ticket sales dollars had increased an astounding 6000% from 1979 to 1989 and overall yearly attendance rose nearly 900%. Consequently, the team's finances went from large losses to small gains. And, in keeping with the Haas family's corporate philosophy, the A's organization also became a strong positive force in service to the community.

In 1989, the A's no longer found themselves in the difficult position of 1979. Instead, the club faced more pleasant but no less important or complex challenges. The A's ownership had been investing in the team for ten years and

Research Associate Mark Pelofsky prepared this case under the supervision of Professors Leonard A. Schlesinger and W. Earl Sasser, Jr., as the basis for class discussion rather than to illustrate either effective or ineffective handling of an administration. Copyright © 1990 by the President and Fellows of Harvard College; Harvard Business School case 9-690-088 (Rev. 5/21/90). To order copies, call (617)495-6117 or write the Publishing Division, Harvard Business School, Boston, MA 02163. No part of this publication may be reproduced, stored in a retrieval system, or transmitted in any form or by any means—electronic, mechanical, photocopying, recording, or otherwise—without the permission of the Harvard Business School.

wanted to reap the rewards of this investment without destroying the organization's carefully cultivated image and goodwill.

MAJOR LEAGUE BASEBALL

In 1989 there were 26 professional baseball teams in the "Major Leagues." The teams represented cities or states in the United States and Canada (see *Exhibit 1* for a list of the teams). The Major Leagues were divided into the National and the American Leagues; each league was subdivided into a West and East division. The American League had 14 teams and the National had 12. Each team had a network of at least four affiliated "minor league" teams, usually independently owned, that developed players not yet ready for the "big leagues."

The teams played a 162-game regular season—81 at home—commencing in April and concluding in early October of each year. At the end of the regular season, each league had a League Championship Series (LCS) between the champions of its two divisions to determine which team would represent the league in the World Series. The World Series pitted the champion of the American League against the champion of the National League. The first team to win four games became the "World Champions."

Baseball teams were usually owned by individuals or partnerships. Most of the owners had amassed fortunes in other businesses before getting involved with the ownership of a Major League team. There were a limited number of exceptions to this ownership pattern; for example, the Chicago Cubs were owned by The Chicago Tribune Co. The owners of all the teams formed the board of directors of Major League Baseball. This board decided many key issues including who would be selected the Commissioner of Baseball, the person responsible for the overall administration of Major League Baseball.

THE ECONOMICS OF BASEBALL

The economic return from ownership of a Major League Baseball team was a hotly debated topic. Agents for players argued that the owners were making large profits which should be shared with them. The owners claimed that they were losing money and couldn't afford big salary increases.

Because most teams were privately owned, very little financial information was available to the public. In addition, some team owners often had financial interests in the stadium, a television station or other related business, making the clear delineation of profits difficult.[1]

In addition, there was a certain resistance from baseball fans and journalists concerning the concept of earning large profits from baseball. Roy Eisenhardt, the president of the A's from 1980 to 1986, explained:

> The fans don't articulate it, yet I don't believe they expect the owner to make a profit from their baseball team. . . . Baseball is perceived almost as a public utility that has been granted a monopoly and is obligated to deliver quality services, so a team isn't looked on with favor when it makes a lot of money. . . . We really are the curators of this game. It's a public asset, and we are the guardians of that asset.[2]

In keeping with the idea of baseball as a "public asset," Major League Baseball enjoyed an exclusion from antitrust laws. There were three "institutional arrangements" that would violate antitrust laws if they were found in other industries: "1) the control over entry of new franchises into the league; 2) the territorial exclusivity that goes with a league franchise; and 3) player-control arrangements (the reserve system)."[3] Government had allowed Major League Baseball to exist as a "legal cartel" because traditionally it was considered more a sporting than a business venture.[4]

Baseball team owners derived revenue from several sources: individual and season ticket sales, television and radio broadcast rights fees, food sales at the park, souvenir sales, and stadium parking fees. Teams also licensed their name and logo for use on clothing and other products sold outside of the baseball stadium. See *Exhibit 2* for a graphic depiction of a team's revenue and cost streams and *Exhibit 3* for a team-by-team comparison of pricing.

Ticket Sales

Between 1947 and 1987 the annual growth rate for average club attendance was 1.1% in the American League and 1.5% in the National League. In the immediate postwar era, team attendance averaged approximately 1.25 million per year

1. Gerald W. Scully, *The Business of Major League Baseball* (Chicago: The University of Chicago Press, 1989), p. 129. Facts not otherwise documented in this section are from this source.

2. Roger Angell, *Season Ticket* (New York: Ballantine Books, 1988), p. 119.

3. Jesse W. Markham and Paul V. Teplitz, *Baseball Economics and Public Policy* (Lexington, Mass.: D.C. Heath, 1981), p. 12.

4. Scully, op. cit., p. 8.

in both leagues. By 1987, the National League clubs averaged over 2 million per year and the American League average was not far behind.

Meanwhile, real ticket prices rose more slowly than attendance. Nominal average ticket prices were $1.00 in 1920, $2.05 in 1960, and $6.70 in 1986. Using 1967 dollars to eliminate the effects of inflation, those nominal ticket prices converted to $1.66, $2.31, and $1.98 for those years, respectively.

Revenue from concessions and parking was closely tied to attendance. Gerald W. Scully, a professor of management at the University of Texas at Dallas and author of *The Business of Major League Baseball*, estimated that these categories generated revenue equal to approximately 17% of the revenue from ticket sales.

Television/Cable/Radio

In 1989, each team in the Major Leagues received approximately $7 million from league-negotiated national television and radio contracts. In addition, each team was free to negotiate deals with local television, radio, and cable stations to broadcast the games locally. (See *Exhibit 1* for a list of each team's local broadcast fees.)

Broadcast fees had grown more rapidly than gate receipts. In 1970, teams received an average of $1.3 million per year for both national and local broadcast rights. By 1980, that number rose to $3.1 million and exceeded $13 million in 1987. (See *Exhibit 4* for the trends in broadcast fees.) Because some of the teams were owned in common with broadcasting companies, these broadcast fee amounts probably understated their actual value.

A new national television broadcast package was negotiated for the 1990–1993 seasons which called for CBS to pay nearly $1.1 billion over four years. A cable network, ESPN, won the first-ever cable package to broadcast baseball, agreeing to pay $100 million per year for the 1990–1993 seasons. The combination of these two packages increased baseball's broadcast revenues for 1990 by 46% over 1989.[5]

Player Salaries

Player salaries also rose throughout the 1970s and 1980s, offsetting the growing broadcast fees from television and cable. Driving much of that salary increase

5. John Helyar and Meg Cox, "ESPN Wins Contract to Carry Baseball." *The Wall Street Journal*, January 6, 1989, p. B3.

was the advent of "free agency," the right awarded in 1975 to players with six or more years' experience to play out their contracts and sign a new contract with the highest bidder.

Another development that added to the volatility of player salary levels was the initiation of job actions by the Major League Players Association. In 1980, the players went on strike for one week during the exhibition season. The following season, the players struck on June 12 and a settlement was not reached until August 8. The players held another mid-season strike in 1984, which lasted only a few days. In early 1990, the owners "locked-out" the players from spring training until a new basic agreement was signed in March.

In 1974, the average cost of player salaries for a whole team was $1.1 million. By 1988 the average salary of a single player had reached $449,826 or $8.3 million for an entire team. Between 1979 and 1984, salaries rose approximately 25% per year while club revenues rose approximately 15% per year. Over the next five years, salary growth slowed to about 8% per year while club revenues rose 15%–20%.

In response to the slowing of the free agency market, the Players Association filed a grievance charging the owners with colluding to boycott free agents during the 1985–1987 seasons. The Players Association won the grievances covering 1985 and 1986. By early 1990, the disposition of the 1987 grievance had not yet been decided.

At the end of the 1989 season, possibly in an attempt to avoid the appearance of collusion, the owners again began paying rapidly increasing salaries. In 1990, several players received contracts paying more than $3 million per year. Observers estimated the average player salary was about $600,000 going into the 1990 season.

The Value of Winning

A winning team usually generated more attendance and, therefore, more revenue than a losing team. Winning teams often could negotiate larger contracts for local television and radio broadcasts, and received additional national broadcast money if they were involved in the League Championship Series or the World Series.

Winning, alone, was not enough to guarantee profitability. And factors such as market size could produce profits for teams that were losing on the field. For example, the San Francisco Giants had a financial loss in 1982 despite finishing with a .537 record (winning 53.7% of their games). Conversely, the New York Mets earned a profit while playing only .401 baseball in that same year.

Market Size

One of the factors for a team's success unrelated to its winning percentage was its geographic location. Teams located in larger cities could generate more revenue through broadcast rights simply by having a larger potential viewing or listening audience. In addition, these teams needed a smaller share of the market to fill up the ballpark. Offsetting some of the advantage of market size, several large cities (New York, Chicago, Los Angeles, and San Francisco/Oakland) had two Major League teams competing for the same audience.

Profitability

Economist Roger G. Noll of Stanford University reported that in 1983, according to team records, the average team lost approximately $3.1 million on revenues of just over $20 million. A typical team income statement from 1983 is reproduced as *Exhibit 5*.

  Gerald W. Scully restated the owners' figures by eliminating depreciation of player contracts (a deduction uniquely available to professional sports teams) and reducing higher-than-market expenses incurred by teams in non-arms-length transactions. After making these adjustments, Scully concluded that 15 clubs made money while 11 lost in 1982, one of the worst years for baseball in recent history. These adjustments transformed the reported losses of just over $4 million per team into an average profit of $427,000.

Capital Appreciation

Even if an owner made little or no money in operating the team, historically, most owners made a healthy profit when they eventually sold the franchise. Scully estimated that the compound growth rate of the value of baseball teams had been between 9 and 15 percent in the 1980s, based on the sale price of teams in the latter part of the 1980s (New York Mets for $100 million in 1986, Baltimore Orioles for $70 million in 1988,[6] and 53% of the Texas Rangers for $45 million in 1989[7]), by 1989 observers believed that many teams were worth at least $85 million with some worth over $100 million. Buyers generally could write up the player contracts asset to about 50% of the purchase price and

6. "Jacobs-Led Investor Group Buys the Baltimore Orioles," *The Wall Street Journal*, December 7, 1988, p. A4.

7. "Bush Group to Buy 53% of Rangers from Chiles," *The Wall Street Journal*, March 20, 1989, p. A4. Note that the agreement included Arlington Stadium and the land surrounding it.

depreciate it over five years, creating a substantial non-cash loss that could be written off against profits from other common-owner businesses.

THE OAKLAND A'S—1968 THROUGH 1980

Charles O. Finley, a Chicago resident and former insurance salesman, bought the Kansas City A's in 1961 for a total outlay of about $4 million.[8] After a rocky tenure in Kansas City, Finley decided to imitate the success of several other teams and move the team to California in 1968. Oakland provided Finley with a clean slate and a larger stadium (48,000 compared to only 34,000 in Kansas City).

In Oakland, Finley managed to create a winning team in hopes of filling the larger capacity of Oakland's Alameda County Coliseum. In fact, the Oakland A's became one of the most successful teams in baseball history, winning three straight world championships in 1972, 1973, and 1974, and winning their divisional crown in 1971 and 1975. The combined record over these five years was 476 wins against 326 losses for a winning percentage of .594. However, even during the three World Series years, the A's drew one million fans in only one season, 1973.

Despite this on-field success, Finley was perhaps better known for creating controversy and turmoil. Baseball writer Roger Angell wrote:

> Charlie Finley ran a different sort of show: a one-man band. A self-made millionaire insurance man, he ruled the club in absentia—by telephone from Chicago, for the most part. (Sometimes he listened to broadcasts of entire games over the long-distance phone.) He got rid of sixteen managers in twenty years, wrangled with players and commissioners. . . . [9]

When free agency came into baseball in 1975, Finley decided not to get involved in the bidding wars for players. Instead, Finley sold many of his top players for cash, and would have sold even more of them if the then Commissioner of Baseball hadn't disallowed a players-for-cash transaction that he felt was not in the interests of baseball. From 1976 through 1980, the A's finished with a combined 356 wins and 452 losses, a winning percentage of only .441. Finley also reduced the A's administrative staff to only four people including his nephew, Carl Finley.

Given Charlie Finley's unwillingness to spend money for players, marketing, or customer service, the A's attendance dropped from 1,000,000 in the early

8. *Oakland Tribune*, Sunday, August 24, 1980, page c-12, by Ron Bergman and Jack Rux.
9. Scully, op. cit., p. 101.

part of the decade to 300,000 in 1979, the lowest attendance figure in the Major Leagues, and lower than some minor league teams. In 1980 there were only 74 season ticket holders who held a total of 328 season tickets. The only good news regarding ticket sales was Finley's appointment, in 1980, of Billy Martin, a controversial and outspoken manager. Martin led the team to its first .500-plus season since 1976 and attendance picked up to 842,000 in 1980.

THE HAAS FAMILY

During the late 1970s observers in Oakland predicted that the A's would soon be sold to oil and entertainment tycoon Marvin Davis and moved to Denver. City officials and civic-minded people in Oakland believed that keeping the team in Oakland would be important for the city's image and efforts to revitalize Oakland and the rest of the "East Bay" community. So Bay Area business people began to put together a coalition to buy the team from Finley to keep it in Oakland.

After the collapse of this coalition, the Haas family, owners of Levi Strauss, decided to buy the A's at a price of $12.7 million. The ownership team included Walter A. Haas, Jr., his son Walter J. (Wally) Haas, and Roy Eisenhardt (husband of Walter's daughter Elizabeth).

Wally Haas described the philosophy of the family:

When Finley owned the team, the fans felt that it was "Charlie's team." We wanted to return the team to the community. Though we wanted to use sound business principles in the operation of the team, we also wanted to make sure that we ran the business in a very socially responsible way. We felt it was the right thing to do.

Buying a baseball team gave us the opportunity to use the family philosophy in a powerful way. Even though my father was the owner of one of the largest clothing manufacturers in the U.S., it was not until we bought the team that he became really well-known.

Andy Dolich related Roy Eisenhardt's importance in forming the direction of the organization:

Roy Eisenhardt was a visionary. He thought of the team as an experimental franchise. He said that the owners planned to operate the team in a manner that was consistent with the family philosophy of corporate good citizenship. No one really knew how the community would react nor the results that could be achieved from this approach to baseball management.

The combination of a nearly complete lack of staff and the excellent reputation of Levi's attracted an avalanche of resumes to the A's. Many of the people hired to work in the A's management had little or no sports management experience, contributing to the atmosphere of excitement and uncertainty.

THE OAKLAND A'S 1980–1989

Andy Dolich described the state of the A's when the new owners took over in 1980:

> It was like a quonset hut here. There was one dusty telephone in the reception room, and nobody in sight, and when you picked it up nothing happened. Inside, we found some old trophies jammed together to hold a lot of loose files, and when we took them down we found that they were the club's World Championship trophies from 1972, 1973 and 1974. . . . [W]e discovered that only nineteen percent of the incoming phone calls were ever answered. So we had a job to do.[10]

However, Finley's neglect of the team also created a great opportunity for the new ownership. Andy Dolich said, "That contrast in reputations was a public relations *dream.*"[11]

Looking around professional sports, the A's management drew an example of operational excellence from the Los Angeles Dodgers baseball team. Tom Cordova explained, "The Dodgers were in control of their product. They even tried to gain control over the quality of their future players by developing the best farm system [minor league affiliates] around. Even if the team didn't win, the Dodgers were in the position to make money. "

Attendance

A confluence of several events gave the new owners a relatively dramatic improvement soon after the team changed hands. The new owners launched a marketing campaign, the team began to win, and manager Billy Martin instituted a more exciting brand of baseball. The fans responded with their feet and wallets: the team exceeded one million fans in the strike-shortened 1981 season. The

---

10. Scully, op. cit., p. 99.
11. Angell, op. cit., p. 102.

total attendance of 1.3 million for 55 games was more than 50% greater than the 840,000 that attended 81 home games in 1980. Although attendance did not grow every year, it never again fell below one million during the 1980s.

In 1988, the A's drew over two million fans for the first time in the history of the franchise. In 1989, the number topped 2.6 million. Season tickets similarly rose from just over 300 in 1980 to over 13,000 in 1989.

Success on the Field

On the field, the A's won the divisional crown in 1981 but tumbled to the bottom half of the division in the seasons from 1982 to 1985. The team began rebuilding in 1985 and hired Tony La Russa to be the manager in 1986. By 1988 the team went to the World Series where it lost to the Los Angeles Dodgers despite being considered the favorites. The following year the team swept its cross-town rivals, the San Francisco Giants, in the World Series to become world champions for the first time since 1974. (See *Exhibit 6* for attendance records and on-field results.)

The baseball operations were separate from the business operations, but the two flourished for some of the same reasons. Sandy Alderson, the vice president for baseball operations, commented:

> The same philosophy underlies both sides of the operation. We have a multi-faceted product of which baseball is probably the most important element. But there are important environmental issues. Fans come out because of the team or a specific game but find out the Coliseum is a nice place to take the family. Like the business side, we have a long term view and use some of the same principles of motivation that the business uses.
>
> The baseball operation is motivated by profit but not always as much as the business side. Winning tends to override budgetary considerations from time to time. There is a lot of "psychic profit" from pride and winning.

Financial Performance

By the late 1980s, the A's were earning financial as well as psychic profits. However, in the first half of the decade, the Haas family had spent significantly to rebuild the operations and attempt to create Roy Eisenhardt's vision of a "championship" caliber organization. The A's reported losses of close to $60 million in the first seven years of the Haas ownership, according to the vice president, finance, Kathleen McCracken. Not all of the loss was cash; some of it was due to depreciation of the player contracts and some of it represented interest paid to the owners. However, in 1988 and 1989 the A's earned a small profit.

Organization

Wally Haas credited much of the turnaround in the organization to the recruitment of high quality people to the A's organization. "We had to build the organization quickly so we focused on recruiting quality people. We hired Andy Dolich to help us create the type of organization we wanted."

Baseball writer Roger Angell believed that the success of the A's was embodied in the business staff:

> The telling ingredient in the club's management-side effort may be beyond precis, for it lies, one senses, in the looks of that staff and in its demeanor, which is youthful, laid back, and fully engaged. There are a great many women and blacks on the roster—hardly commonplace in big-league offices— and very few people you pass in the hall appear to be immediately threatened by the arrival of a serious birthday.[12]

Staff members sensed that there were other differences between the A's and other baseball teams. "The people I work with are more than just 'co-workers,'" explained Kathy De Lima, who, by 1989, had been with the club for eight years. Kathy began working for the A's in a secretarial position and had been promoted to the position of Advertising and Broadcasting sales manager. "This place is 'home' for many people. It is nice to be affiliated with a successful venture. Some of the salaries here might be lower than at other organizations but people here don't leave because no other job will compare with working for the A's."

The sentiments of the staff did not develop by accident; the A's worked at creating high morale among employees. In the late 1980s, management established an employee committee that met regularly to discuss a wide range of issues. Another employee committee, called the "Esprit de Corps" committee, initiated social activities for the organization. In addition, staff members received benefits such as season tickets and trips with the team.

By 1989 there were approximately 59 full-time staff working in the business side of the operation. In addition, there was a seasonal sales staff who bolstered the selling effort during the peak times of the year.

The A's also accomplished a number of other administrative improvements that played a major role in the organization's transformation. First, the team spent millions in promotion, including the creation of a series of television advertisements to promote "Billyball," the wide-open style of play instituted by then-manager Billy Martin. In addition, the team added computer systems to automate ticket sales information, player statistics, and many other previously manual operations. Finally, Kathleen McCracken created a budget and control system

12. Angell, op. cit., p. 100.

that provided significantly more information for the owners, and a greatly enhanced ability for the A's management to manage the organization's finances.

The team's success on the field doubtlessly played a major role in the increased attendance and resultant financial improvements. However, at least two other categories of improvements helped transform the A's into a major success story: customer service and community service.

CUSTOMER SERVICE

Under Charlie Finley, the A's customer service was virtually non-existent. Wally Haas stated that one of the reasons the A's sold so few tickets in the late 1970s and 1980 was that there simply weren't enough people to answer the phones. In contrast, the Haas philosophy of running the team focused on providing outstanding customer service. Wally Haas believed that Disney provided the proper model of family entertainment that the A's should follow. Commenting on another outstanding example of customer service, Wally Haas stated, "Some people call us the Nordstrom of baseball. Maybe someday people will say that Nordstrom is the A's of retailing."

One of the major objectives of the various customer service efforts was to create an enjoyable and economical entertainment package so that, when the fortunes of the team declined on the field, they might hold up at the box office. Teams inevitably went through cycles on the field and the A's hoped that their extra efforts would help them draw attendance even when the team was losing.

Many baseball experts felt that attending an A's game had some distinct advantages over attending a San Francisco Giants game. Author Bob Wood, in his book *Dodger Dogs to Fenway Franks*, reviewed the experience of attending a game at each of the 26 Major League ballparks. He ranked a game at the Oakland Coliseum seventh overall. (See the *Appendix* for a narrative on attending an A's game.)

To gauge their performance from the fan's point of view, the A's performed surveys and held focus groups. These mechanisms provided feedback on customer service for the A's management.

Food

The A's Oakland Alameda County Coliseum provided far more menu items and many more high-quality food choices than the typical major league park. The food was provided by an outside vendor who worked with the Coliseum management and the A's in deciding the menu for the A's games. Some of the more unusual items served at the Coliseum included pizza, fajitas, and baked potatoes.

Security

Ushers and security guards helped the A's provide a safe family environment. These security services were also provided by an outside vendor through the Coliseum management.

These security personnel often had to perform the difficult duty of helping fans enjoy the game while simultaneously enforcing rules, including the occasional ejection of a customer from the premises. Ushers also had to tread the fine line between enforcement of rules and providing good service.

The Stadium

An important part of the service experience for the fans lay in the physical characteristics of the Coliseum. The County owned the stadium and contracted out the management of the facility to a non-profit management company. This management company, in turn, contracted out the food and parking concessions. Therefore, any improvements the A's wanted had to be implemented cooperatively with the management of the facility. Kevin Kahn, director of Stadium Operations for the A's, commented:

> In 1981 the relationship between the A's and the County was somewhat adversarial, perhaps as a result of Charlie Finley's absentee ownership. I think the Coliseum people from the County were a little shocked when we started focusing our attention and money on improving customer service.

Bill DiCarlo, assistant general manager of the Coliseum management company, explained the nature of the working relationship with the A's:

> I speak with the A's on a daily basis and our event services department probably is on the phone to the team three or more times per day. We have an occasional formal meeting but we primarily work together on an informal and frequent basis.
>
> Both the A's and our organization want people to come back to the Coliseum and to have a good time whether the team wins or not. So we take the long-run view when making management decisions. For example, we had some problems with fans drinking too much. In response, we limited purchases of beer to two per person, sold smaller cups, and cut off sales in the 7th inning. This policy took money out of our pockets by reducing beer sales but we and the A's believe it will produce a better environment to watch a game and therefore be worthwhile in the long-run.

The A's and the Coliseum management made several physical enhancements to the Coliseum to improve the fans' enjoyment of the game. One of the most significant additions was the two scoreboards. The Coliseum installed a new high-tech "Diamondvision" scoreboard, essentially a 30-by-40 foot television screen that showed instant replays, close-ups of the players, and television-style advertisements (although the A's insisted that all ads had to be without dialogue and could contain only video and music). In contrast, the A's also installed a manually operated scoreboard that kept track of all of the day's action from around Major League Baseball.

Television sets were added to the concession stands so that fans waiting in line would not miss any of the game. Similarly, the A's added the radio feed of the game into the bathrooms. Both the men's and the women's bathrooms were equipped with baby changing tables and supplied with free Pampers by their manufacturer, Procter & Gamble.

The A's converted some of their Mezzanine Loge seating (between the second and third deck) to luxury "skyboxes," adding another new feature to the Coliseum. According to Tom Cordova, this addition to the Coliseum created great demand at the high end for seating in a location which previously was not necessarily desirable. Constructing the skyboxes involved taking 40 seats and turning them into two boxes, one with 12 seats and one with 18. In 1989, the cost of building a skybox was approximately $50,000 to $65,000, and the A's charged $39,000 per year for the 12-seat box and $48,000 for the 18-seat box. In addition, the A's catered food for these boxes, which resulted in higher per capita expenditures for food for people sitting in these boxes. In 1989, there were 35 skyboxes (including the owner's box and other special boxes), containing a total of 566 seats.

To enhance safety, in addition to the alcohol policies outlined by Bill DiCarlo above, beer was not served in the stands; fans wanting beer would have to navigate their way to the counter (or get someone to do it for them). In addition, the ushers and other stadium staff were trained under the TEAM (Techniques for Effective Alcohol Management) program.

The A's worked with BART (Bay Area Rapid Transit—the subway system) and the highway patrol to help improve the traffic flow into and home from the Coliseum. In its promotions, the A's often publicized the use of the subway system, which provided a very convenient way for fans in Oakland and San Francisco to get to and from the Coliseum.

Sponsored Activities

Another significant change to the Coliseum was the institution of the Procter & Gamble "Clean Team." Tom Cordova, the director of sales, explained:

Most often we approach potential sponsors, ask questions and from there generate ideas. This time we approached Procter & Gamble with a specific idea of how to get involved. The concept centered on the idea of making the Coliseum, and especially the bathrooms, as clean as people's homes. We wanted fans to think of the Coliseum as a clean place and Procter & Gamble, manufacturer of leading household brands, was the obvious first choice. Over a period of five months we negotiated a successful partnership. Procter & Gamble receives a high degree of visibility in the ballpark, signs in the bathrooms, merchandising for the retail trade and a substantial amount of media exposure. In fact to introduce the program we held a press conference in one of the ladies bathrooms and even served lunch. To accommodate the families with young children, diaper changing tables were built in men's and women's bathrooms and free Pampers diapers were provided.

Fans could also participate in a number of baseball-related activities at an A's game. High above the action, fans could become radio or television broadcasters in the A's "Fantasy Play-By-Play" booth. For a fee, a fan would sit in the announcer's booth and call an inning of baseball while the game was actually being played. The fan got a choice between bringing home the audio tape or the video tape of the inning. Sponsors paid to get their advertisements dubbed in to the tape. The A's contributed the space in the stadium in return for a share of the profits and an attraction for fans. On the lower levels, fans could have the speed of their fastball pitches clocked by a radar gun or, for the more sedate, have their picture taken with cardboard likenesses of the A's players. The profits from these activities were donated to the A's Community Fund.

The A's involved many local and national companies in baseball by making these organizations "sponsors." A sponsor could buy a wide range of custom-designed promotional packages with the team. Some sponsors were basically advertisers on the A's broadcasts and in the Coliseum billboards. Others sponsored special "value-added" premium giveaway days at the park such as A's cap day and special events such as fireworks and music concerts. Tom Cordova explained that, traditionally, teams used these special days to attract fans to normally slow nights. The A's, in contrast, scheduled these attractions on "power days," already popular dates, to give the sponsors the most exposure for the money. "We don't believe in discounting," Cordova explained. "We believe in providing value added for the same amount of money." (See *Exhibit* 7 for a list of special events.)

One promotion dreamed up by Andy Dolich was the Safeway Saturday Barbecues. Six times a year, the A's would treat the first 10,000 fans to a free full barbecue lunch. Safeway Supermarkets was the "title" sponsor, and the A's also solicited individual food companies to provide free food and a rights fee to the A's in exchange for publicity.

Cordova explained the promotion:

The sponsors get positive publicity and sampling opportunity for their products for relatively little cost. The A's get goodwill from their fans as well as an additional attraction to the game. And the fans get good quality food free. It is a win-win-win situation.

One of our most important goals is making the team accessible. We practice Johnny Appleseed marketing, growing fans from children through adulthood. By having these Safeway Saturdays a parent or parents can take the family to the game and feed them for the price of the tickets. A family of four seated in the bleachers could have a whole day of entertainment plus lunch for $14. We even give them a free $1 BART card (subway ticket) so they can get home from the game for free. We hope the kids that come to these special days with their families will bring their own families some day.

Dave Preuss, the owner of a restaurant chain in Oakland, commented on his involvement with the A's:

I have been a sponsor with the A's for three years. The first year the team was horrible, the second year it went to the World Series and the third year it won the World Series. The price of my package didn't go up or did only slightly. The A's want their sponsors for the long run.

It is hard to believe how nice and cooperative the A's are to work with. For example, when I opened a new restaurant, I went to the game and the A's put a congratulations message on the scoreboard announcing the opening. I never have to ask for the extras; Tom Cordova always thinks of them.

Preuss explained that the A's provided other benefits for their sponsors as well. For example, the team took approximately 150 sponsors down the coast to an A's game against the California Angels in Anaheim. In addition, sponsors often had access to hard-to-get tickets. Finally, Preuss got to "throw out the first ball" for the game on his 40th birthday.

Ticket Policies

The A's ticket pricing policies displayed the character of Johnny Appleseed marketing discussed by Tom Cordova. Because the A's were focused on giving parents the opportunity to be heroes in their own homes, tickets were priced with the family in mind.

Seven Monday night games during 1989 were designated as half-price dates. All tickets in the Coliseum were half-price except bleacher seats, which were always $3.50. Ticket prices and number of seats in each section were:

	Price	*Number of Seats*
Mezzanine Loge Box	$10	600
Field Level (1st Deck)	10	17,000
Plaza Level (2nd Deck)	9	11,000
Upper Reserved (3rd Deck)	7	14,000
Bleachers	3.50	5,000

In addition to the half-price Mondays, tickets in all sections except the field level and bleachers were half-price always for fans 14 and under, 65 and older, in the active military, or in a wheelchair.

Individuals or businesses could also purchase season tickets in any one of a number of packages. There were numerous packages available such as full season tickets (a ticket to every game) and weekend-only tickets. In addition, the A's could create a customized package tailored to a customer's personal preferences.

Season ticket holders received many benefits including access to League Championship Series and World Series tickets. The A's also had an unusual return policy for their season ticket holders. Any ticket unused *after* the game could be exchanged for one of several "dead-ticket" dates, usually a week-night game later in the season. This policy protected an individual's or business's entertainment investment. "A business is not going to renew its season tickets if the owner opens his desk drawer at the end of the season and finds forty unused tickets," Tom Cordova explained.

Most season tickets were sold to businesses or groups. In 1989, approximately 13,000 full-season equivalent packages were sold through a combination of renewals from the previous season and the work of 12 salespeople. Some of these salespeople were paid on commission while others were salaried marketing representatives.

COMMUNITY SERVICE

According to the owners' plan, the A's became well-known for their keen interest in getting involved with the community. The A's used the attraction of Major League Baseball and the philanthropy of the Haas family to generate numerous community service activities.

Dave Perron, a former teacher, was brought to the A's to be the director of Community Affairs. Unlike others who share that title in other organizations, Perron held significant responsibility with the A's and, signifying this responsibility, shared the executive suite with Wally Haas.

An innovative fund called the "A's Community Fund" was established to help the A's support community activities. The A's raised money for this fund which in turn supported many of the team's community service activities. Perron estimated that the team gave away approximately 100,000 tickets in 1989 through the A's Community Fund. Excerpts from the A's Community Affairs brochure are reproduced as *Exhibit 8.*

The example set by the owners spread throughout the organization. The A's players and personnel also became involved in community service activities. For example, in honor of Walter Haas, the employee committee initiated the personal contribution of eight hours of community service time from each of 80 members of the organization.

A'S ECONOMICS

The A's reported a loss in 1982 of over $10 million. However, after removing depreciation expense and other unusual costs, Scully estimated that the club's actual cash loss in 1982 was about $5.5 million. Compared to the San Francisco Giants, the A's had marginally higher revenues but significantly higher expenses. The A's lost a total of 2.4 times as much as the Giants in 1982 and 1983.[13]

By 1984, the A's loss grew to $15.2 million, far and away more than any other team that year. The next biggest loss that year was the $9.4 lost by the Yankees.[14] Much of the A's loss was attributed to the costs of a significantly increased marketing effort and the development of minor league affiliates.

Finances improved with the team through the last half of the 1980s. In 1989, the year the A's won the World Series, the team received $7.33 average revenue per fan in attendance, comprised of the following:

Net ticket revenue	$5.48[a]
Food/beverage	1.20
Parking	0.24
Magazine/novelties	0.41
Total	$7.33

[a] The A's had to pay 20% of gross ticket sales to the opposing team and 3% to the American League.

13. Scully, op. cit., p. 138.

14. Scully, op. cit., p. 121.

These revenue figures were net of product costs and the portion taken by the vendor and the Coliseum. The gross spending per fan totaled approximately $15. However, the A's rent for the Coliseum was keyed to attendance. All Coliseum expenses paid by the A's, including rent, in 1989 amounted to $1.60 per ticket sold.

In 1989 the A's garnered over $5 million from selling their own local broadcast rights. The local television station broadcasted 53 A's games and the network of affiliated radio stations covered all games. The organization also had a relatively unusual approach to its radio broadcasts. Instead of selling the rights to a local radio station to broadcast the games, the A's bought the entire time period from the radio station and resold part of the air time for ads. Through this arrangement, the A's gained control of the airwaves beginning 25 minutes before the game and ending 25 minutes afterwards and greatly increased their revenue from radio.

Total attendance for the 1989 season was 2,667,225. Season ticket sales produced revenue of $8.6 million, more than half of the nearly $15 million produced from the sale of all tickets for home games. Estimated operating profits in 1989 were approximately $4 million including income from the post season. From these profits, approximately $1.5 million would be deducted for depreciation, interest expense, and loss from termination of player contracts. See *Exhibit 9* for an indexed Income Statement for 1989.

CHALLENGES AHEAD

By 1989 the A's organization was a stark contrast to the one inherited by the Haas family in 1980. Nevertheless, the club faced some significant challenges for the future.

Setting ticket prices for 1990 presented an example of a specific problem which was representative of larger issues. With attendance at record levels in 1989 and the A's near the bottom of the league in ticket prices, the team could easily raise ticket prices across the board for 1990. In addition, the A's could convert more of the Loge into luxury skyboxes. However, team management wanted to continue to make A's baseball accessible.

The same dilemma surrounded the decision concerning the type of broadcast contracts to pursue. Specifically, management had to consider whether or not to initiate pay cable or pay-per-view broadcasting to increase broadcast revenues.

The season ticket return policy also needed to be examined. Previously, the team had adopted a very liberal policy, allowing holders of any of the various plans to return unused tickets even after the game date and get new ones in exchange. However, the team was considering tightening up the policy to reduce the number of tickets given away that it might otherwise be able to sell.

In addition, the team gave away more than 100,000 tickets to charities and community groups in 1989. Although no plans existed to reduce the number of giveaways, management knew that with increasing paid attendance they had to be careful which tickets they gave away.

All of these decisions had to be considered within the context of the seemingly imminent return to Oakland of the Raiders, the professional football team that had moved from Oakland to Los Angeles in 1981. Given that there were a limited number of corporations and individuals that would buy tickets for professional sports, the return of the Raiders created yet another competitive use for a fixed pool of disposable income.

Wally Haas commented on the road ahead for the A's:

> It is difficult to take things away. We need to tighten up our policies so that we reward the high-end customers. But because we have been generous in the past, we have faced resistance from those who no longer qualify for some of the benefits they used to receive.
>
> We need to be careful about being smug. We also have to face the reality of budgets and trying to make a profit. We still want to be accessible and still want to contribute to the community. Our challenge for the future will be balancing all of these objectives.

Exhibit 1
The Major League Baseball Teams
Local Broadcasts Rights
(*$ millions*)

	Local Broadcast Fees, 1987[a]
The American League (AL)	
The AL West	
The Oakland A's	3.0
The Kansas City Royals	3.1
The Texas Rangers	6.0
The Minnesota Twins	4.0
The Seattle Mariners	2.2
The California Angels	4.2
The Chicago White Sox	9.3
The AL East	
The Boston Red Sox	6.5
The New York Yankees	17.5
The Milwaukee Brewers	3.6
The Toronto Blue Jays	7.8
The Detroit Tigers	5.0
The Cleveland Indians	3.0
The Baltimore Orioles	6.3
The National League (NL)	
The NL West	
The Los Angeles Dodgers	5.0
The Cincinnati Reds	6.8
The San Diego Padres	4.2
The Houston Astros	3.6
The Atlanta Braves	4.0
The San Francisco Giants	2.9
The NL East	
The Philadelphia Phillies	9.5
The New York Mets	16.5
The Pittsburgh Pirates	4.0
The Chicago Cubs	4.3
The Montreal Expos	7.0
The St. Louis Cardinals	5.1

[a]From Gerald W. Scully, *The Business of Major League Baseball* (Chicago: The University of Chicago Press, 1989), p. 109; based on information in *Broadcasting*, 2 March 1987.

THE OAKLAND A's—1989
Exhibit 2
Revenue and Expense Flows for a Typical Major League Team

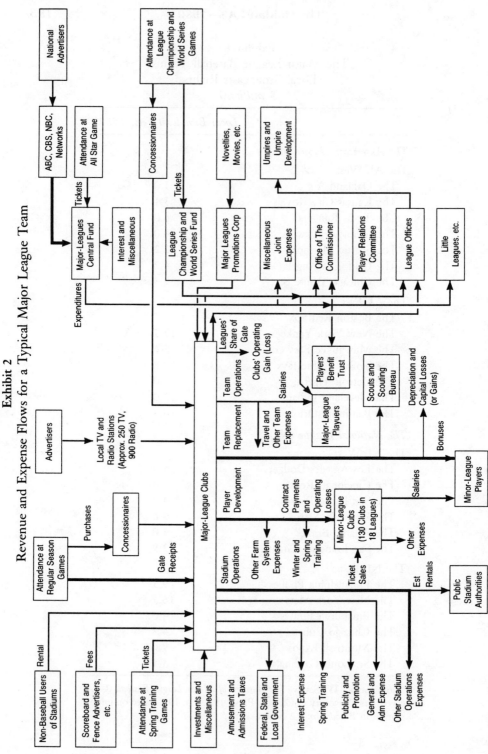

SOURCE: Jesse W. Markham and Paul V. Teplitz, *Baseball Economics and Public Policy* (Lexington, Mass.: D.C. Heath, 1981). Reprinted with permission.

THE OAKLAND A'S—1989
Exhibit 3
Team by Team Comparison of Pricing

Team	Ticket Price Range		Parking	Snacks						Pennant	Novelties			A Day at the Park[a]
				Popcorn	Pretzel	Peanuts	Hot Dog	Soda	Beer		Cap	T-Shirt	Program	
National League														
New York Mets	$6.00 to	$11.00	$3.50	$1.10	$0.95	$0.80	$1.60	$1.15	$2.25	$3.00	$7.50	$10.00	$1.25	$85.30
Chicago Cubs	4.00 to	10.50	7.00	1.25	1.25	1.00	1.50	0.85	2.00	2.50	5.00	10.00	2.00	83.70
San Francisco Giants	2.50 to	10.00	3.00	1.00	1.25	0.75	1.25	1.00	2.00	2.50	10.00	12.00	2.00	83.50
Philadelphia Phillies	4.00 to	9.00	3.75	2.00	1.25	1.25	1.25	1.25	2.50	3.00	8.00	12.00	1.00	80.75
Houston Astros	4.00 to	10.00	3.00	1.15	1.35	1.00	1.55	1.10	1.75	2.00	7.00	12.00	1.25	80.65
St. Louis Cardinals	4.00 to	10.50	3.50	1.00	1.25	0.80	1.10	0.80	1.45	2.50	8.00	11.00	1.25	80.20
Atlanta Braves	4.00 to	9.50	3.00	0.75	1.00	1.25	1.25	1.00	2.25	2.50	6.50	12.00	1.50	78.00
Pittsburgh Pirates	3.00 to	9.50	1.50	1.25	1.25	1.25	1.25	1.00	2.25	2.00	7.00	10.00	1.00	74.75
San Diego Padres	3.50 to	8.50	3.00	1.00	1.25	1.00	1.25	0.75	1.75	2.50	7.00	12.00	2.00	73.75
Montreal Expos	3.16 to	9.48	3.16	0.51	1.19	0.51	0.95	0.75	1.78	2.17	5.53	9.88	1.98	71.71
Cincinnati Reds	3.50 to	8.50	2.75	0.75	1.00	0.75	1.00	1.00	2.50	2.00	6.00	10.00	3.00	71.25
Los Angeles Dodgers	4.00 to	7.00	2.00	0.75	NA	0.50	1.75	0.75	2.25	3.00	6.00	11.00	1.50	65.75

(Continued)

THE OAKLAND A'S—1989
Exhibit 3
(Continued)

Team	Ticket Price Range	Parking	Snacks						Novelties			Program	A Day at the Park[a]
			Popcorn	Pretzel	Peanuts	Hot Dog	Soda	Beer	Pennant	Cap	T-Shirt		
American League													
Boston Red Sox	$5.00 to $12.00	$5.00	$1.00	$1.30	$0.85	$1.50	$1.15	$2.25	$2.50	$6.00	$11.00	$1.50	$89.95
Detroit Tigers	4.00 to 10.50	5.00	1.00	1.25	1.00	1.50	1.15	2.25	3.00	7.00	15.00	1.50	89.55
New York Yankees	4.50 to 11.00	4.00	1.25	1.00	0.85	1.50	1.00	2.00	2.75	7.50	10.00	1.25	84.60
Chicago White Sox	4.00 to 10.50	5.50	1.25	1.25	1.00	1.50	1.00	2.25	2.00	6.00	9.00	2.00	82.50
Texas Rangers	4.00 to 10.00	3.00	1.50	1.25	1.00	1.25	1.00	1.75	2.00	6.00	14.00	1.50	80.75
Minnesota Twins	3.00 to 10.00	4.00	1.00	1.50	1.00	1.50	0.95	2.00	2.00	7.00	10.00	2.00	80.40
Toronto Blue Jays	3.16 to 11.85	3.95	0.79	1.19	0.79	0.99	0.79	1.90	1.98	5.14	6.32	1.98	78.88
Cleveland Indians	4.50 to 9.50	4.00	1.00	1.35	0.90	1.40	0.90	2.25	2.50	7.00	10.00	1.75	78.40
Milwaukee Brewers	4.00 to 10.50	3.00	0.85	1.50	0.90	1.30	1.00	1.75	2.00	6.00	10.00	1.25	78.20
Seattle Mariners	3.50 to 9.50	4.00	1.00	1.50	1.00	1.50	0.80	2.00	2.00	7.00	10.00	2.00	78.10
Oakland A's	3.00 to 9.00	4.00	1.00	1.25	0.80	1.75	1.00	2.20	2.50	7.50	7.50	2.50	76.45
Baltimore Orioles	4.75 to 9.50	3.00	1.25	1.25	1.25	1.00	1.00	1.50	2.00	6.50	12.00	1.50	75.75
California Angels	3.00 to 8.00	3.00	0.75	1.50	1.00	1.50	0.75	2.25	2.50	7.00	12.00	1.50	73.25
Kansas City Royals	3.00 to 9.00	3.00	0.80	1.25	0.80	1.25	0.75	1.25	2.00	6.25	10.00	0.50	69.60

SOURCE: *Money*, April 1988, p. 44. This table is reprinted from *Money* Magazine by special permission; copyright 1988 The Time Inc. Magazine Company.

NOTES: Tickets and parking are based on 1988 prices. Except for the Chicago Cubs, Houston Astros, Boston Red Sox, and California Angels, the latest figures available for snacks and novelties are for 1987; some items are expected to increase slightly when the new season begins.

NA = (not available)

[a] Four of the highest-priced tickets plus one of each snack and novelty.

Exhibit 4
Television and Radio Broadcast Revenues[a]
($000)

Year	Local Rights	National Rights	Average Revenue per Club
1950	3,365	——	210
1960	9,355	3,174	783
1970	21,850	9,600	1,310
1980	38,650	41,575	3,088
1985	116,900	161,000	10,688
1987	153,350	196,500	13,456
1990	Not Available	275,000	Not Available

[a]From Gerald W. Scully, *The Business of Major League Baseball* (Chicago: The University of Chicago Press, 1989), p. 108.

Exhibit 5
Typical Income Statement for a Major League Team, 1983[a]

	($000)	% of Revenue
Revenues:		
Game receipts	$10,370	52%
Broadcast fees	6,267	31
Concessions and other	3,426	17
Total revenue	$20,064	100%
Costs:		
Team—Nonsalary	2,409	12
—Player salaries	8,256	41
Player development	2,180	11
Team replacement	2,334	12
Stadium operations	2,668	13
Sales	1,724	9
General and administrative	2,449	12
Spring training	414	2
Miscellaneous	192	1
Total costs	$22,625	113%
Profit (loss) from operations	(2,562)	(13)
Other income (expense)	(624)	(3)
Total profit (loss) before taxes	(3,186)	(16)

NOTE: Team Replacement is depreciation of player contracts expense; most of other expense is interest expense net of interest revenue.

[a]From Gerald W. Scully. *The Business of Major League Baseball* (Chicago: The University of Chicago Press, 1989), p. 118.

Exhibit 6
Attendance Figures, 1980–1989

Year	Attendance	Team Performance
1980	842,259	2nd place
1981	1,311,761	1st place, lost League Championship Series
1982	1,735,489	5th place
1983	1,294,941	4th place
1984	1,353,231	4th place
1985	1,334,609	4th place
1986	1,314,646	3rd place
1987	1,678,921	3rd place
1988	2,287,335	1st place, lost World Series
1989	2,667,225	1st place, won World Series

Exhibit 7
Special Events and Promotions During the 1989 Season

Giveaway	Sponsor
Activity books	Wells Fargo Bank
Pins	Unocal
Mitts	Carefree
Wallets	Leaf
Autographed balls	California Egg Commission
Flashlights	Eveready/Anheuser-Busch
Roll-up caps	Bank of America
Visors	Lipton
Beach towels	Planters
Wallet watches	Gatorade
Painter caps	U.S. Forest Service
Player cards	Mother's Cookies
Bats	Coca-Cola
T-shirts	Ortega
Binders	PG&E
Posters	Kodak

Other Promotions	Sponsor
Safeway BBQ's	Safeway
	Nalley's
	Elgaaen-Booth
	Bradshaws
	KC BBQ Sauce
Family Night	Alameda Newspapers
Oldtimer's Game	Equitable
Youth Baseball Camp	Shappell
Superheroes Day	Kaiser
Dot Racing	SF Newspaper
Fireworks	Anheuser-Busch
Fantasy Play-by-Play	Anheuser-Busch
All-Star Ballot	Gannett
Picnic Plaza	Kingsford
Newspaper Toss	San Jose Mercury News
Lucky Fields	Lucky's
A's Credit Card	Mastercard
Clean Team and Other	Procter & Gamble

Exhibit 8
A's Community Affairs Summary of Programs

Speed Pitch—Fans test the speed of their fastest pitch for a $1 contribution to the A's Community Fund.

United Way Charities—For each home run hit by Jose Canseco, corporate sponsors contribute to the United Way. There is also a special "United Way Day with the A's" at which the United Way's services are honored by the A's.

Oakland A's/BASHOF Scholarship—A scholarship was established by the A's and the Bay Area Hall of Fame (BASHOF) recognizing an outstanding male and female citizen/athlete for community, academic, and athletic achievement.

Lucky's/A's Youth Fields—Lucky Stores and the A's provide the cost of rehabilitation or construction of a community baseball facility each year.

M.S. Read-a-Thon—School-aged children in the community receive A's tickets and other A's prizes for reading a certain number of books. In addition, corporate sponsors contribute to the M.S. Society for each book read by the kids.

Big Brother/Big Sister Program—Volunteers and their matches are guests of the A's at a game each year.

IBM Student Pennant Race—Students in 5th and 6th grades exhibiting outstanding academic achievement are made guests of the A's at a picnic and baseball game.

Hispanic Advisory Committee—A committee of leaders in the Northern Californian Hispanic community serve as a liaison between the community and the A's front office.

The Mammal Project—The A's and the Marin Airporter fund Oakland Public School field trips to the Marine Mammal Center.

Name in Lights—Fans can send messages over the A's scoreboard for a donation to the A's Community fund.

Los Atleticos—The A's publish a Spanish/English newsletter informing the community of activities, scholarship opportunities, A's games, and more.

A's Advisory Board—A group of community leaders advise the A's on community programs and needs within the area.

Fire-fighters Appreciation Night—Fire-fighters of Northern California enjoy pre-game activities and an A's game as guests of the team.

Community Fund Golf Tournament—A's players team up with fans at a golf tournament that benefits the A's Community Fund.

CPR Saturday—500 participants receive CPR training at the Coliseum and get a free ticket to the game as well.

Senior Appreciation Day—Low income seniors from around the Bay Area attend an A's game as guests of the team.

Project Excel—Campbell's Soup and the A's give a free ticket to every student in grades 4 through 12 who earn a 3.5 gpa or better. In 1988 over 85,000 tickets were distributed.

Exhibit 8
(Continued)

Shappell Industries/Oakland A's Youth Baseball Camp—Approximately 400 high school students receive a free week of baseball instruction, cap, T-shirt, and baseball glove.

Community Fund Baseball Card and Memorabilia Show—A's players sign autographs at this annual sports show the revenues from which go to the A's Community Fund.

Box 1—This section of the Coliseum is specially designed for blind and visually impaired fans to enjoy the game. Members of the A's Team (described below) help these fans with special needs.

PG&E Power Days—Inner city youth attend baseball clinics and the following A's game as guests of the team and Pacific Gas & Electric. If an A's player hits a home run that day, all of the participants get to come to another game.

Kids for Kids Toy Drive—Twenty area schools collect toys around the holiday season. These toys are given to the A's who redistribute them to less fortunate kids who are invited to a party thrown by the A's.

Black Adoption Night—The Black Adoption Placement and Research Center of Oakland gains greater awareness of the needs of black and special needs children through publicity at an A's game.

Adopt-a-School—Members of the A's organization present special seminars at local schools.

Chrysler/Plymouth Community Home Run Fund—Chrysler/Plymouth dealers donate $100 for every home run to the A's Community Fund.

Family Service—See's Candy sponsors publicity for the Family Service Agencies of Northern California at an A's game.

Cops Corner—Police distribute free A's tickets to deserving members of the community in recognition of community service activity.

Book and Food Drives—Fans are asked to bring either books or cans of food to the ballpark. Books are donated to the Oakland Library which sells them to buy new equipment. Food is donated to the Salvation Army. Fans who donate are given tickets to a future A's game.

Walter A. Haas Jr. Community Achievement Award—Presented annually to the A's player who best demonstrates the organization's concern for social responsibility. The winner gets $1,000 donated to the charity of his choice.

Summer Reading Program—The A's offer free tickets to kids who read their quota of books by the end of the summer.

Coaches Passport—The A's and Nabisco give away free tickets to area high school baseball and softball coaches.

(Continued)

Exhibit 8
(Continued)

A's Team—This special service squad, dressed in yellow and green uniforms, helps the fans with special needs navigate to and around the Coliseum.

Community Fund Minority Graduate Scholarships—The A's donate $1,000 to a minority student pursuing a graduate degree in sports administration, sports journalism, or sports medicine.

Holiday Party—Over 600 children and 400 seniors are invited to a party as guests of the A's.

64 Roses—This program has several components, each of which raises funds for the fight against cystic fibrosis.

Hot Shots Booth—Fans donate $3 to the A's Community Fund for a picture with life-sized cardboard cut-outs of A's players.

SPONSORS: Wareham Property Group, Wells Fargo, Northern California Chrysler Dealers, Nissan, Grand Auto, Oscar Mayer, Clorox Corp., McKesson Corp., KICU-36, PG&E, Oakland-Alameda Coliseum, Police Officer Associations of Northern California, Marin Airporter, Campbell's Soups, Double Rainbow Ice-Cream, Nabisco, Lucky Stores, Nalley's, Shapell Industries of Northern California, KPIX-5, Festival Cinemas, the J. M. Smucker Co., Levi Strauss & Co.

Exhibit 9
A's Pro Forma

	1989 *(% of Revenues)*	*Projected 1990* *(% of 1989 Revenues)*
Operating Revenues		
Gate receipts, net	42.4%	
Skybox revenue	2.1	
Television and radio	25.5[a]	
Novelty and coliseum revenue	14.2	
Advertising	7.6	
Publications	0.6	
Sponsorships	2.7	
Royalties	2.9	
Miscellaneous	2.1	
Total operating revenues	100.0%	
Operating Expenses		
Major league	43.6%[b]	54.2%[b]
Minor and instructional league	7.8	7.9
Scouting	3.1	4.7
Business operations	13.0	13.0
Administration	14.2	13.5
Coliseum expenses	9.1	9.0
Central fund expenses (league expenses)	4.3	6.8[c]
Total operating expenses	95.1%	109.3%
Operating income before post season	4.9%	
Post-season operating income	3.5%	

SOURCE: The Oakland A's.

[a] This figure is net of a partial payment against the eventual collusion settlement against Major League Baseball. This partial payment reduced the A's television and radio revenue by 19%.

[b] Includes player salaries.

[c] The new contract called for a much larger contribution to the central fund for the players' retirement fund.

APPENDIX

TAKE ME OUT TO THE BALLPARK
(A Trip to an A's Game)

The casewriter arrived at the stadium several hours before the start of the game on a Monday night in late September, 1989. The ride from San Francisco on the subway had taken about 30 minutes and, as Roger Angell wrote, had seemed shorter.

The walk from the subway to the Coliseum took about three minutes, and the walkway led to a gap in the wall that looked over the rightfield bleachers. Down on the field the visiting Texas Rangers took batting practice. The crack of the bat echoed eerily, the hard cement and empty seats bouncing the sound around instead of absorbing it. Between batters the only sound was the hum of the lawnmowers manicuring the field for that evening's game.

A man with a lunchbox and wearing an A's cap approached from the subway walkway and stopped a few feet from the fence. He reached up into a small box on a beam which supported the A's manual scoreboard and seemed to turn a key. A few moments later a plank from the bottom of the scoreboard began to lower from one end. After the plank came closer to the ground it became clear that this was a staircase into the scoreboard, reminiscent of stairways many houses have into the attic that unfold from the ceiling of a closet.

"We have the scores from all of the games, not just the American League," the man responded when asked about the differences between his scoreboard and the one imbedded in Boston's famous left-field wall, better known as the Green Monster. "And we change the scores much more frequently because we have our own wire in there," he continued with obvious pride. "There are only two of us working in there and, especially on weekends, we have to work pretty hard to keep track of as many as 13 games."

"I have to go to work," he said, almost annoyed at the detour that this conversation had created. Any longer and he might not be able to get everything ready in time for the game, he seemed to be thinking. The man climbed the stairs and the staircase slowly closed behind him. Later, watching the scoreboard, it was easier to appreciate the man's pride in his work as the manual scoreboard seemed to change non-stop for three hours. Especially with the season ending and the A's in contention, many fans took great interest in the results from other games.

Being a Monday, all tickets were half price except the bleachers, which were always $3.50. Entering the stadium, the effect of half-price night manifested itself in the number of families and sheer volume of fans coming through the turnstiles.

By game time, almost 33,000 fans had turned out for a Monday night game against a mediocre team. In addition, there was a lack of interest in the outcome of the game because the A's could not clinch the division title that night but were so far ahead that there was little doubt about the ultimate outcome of the pennant race.

The casewriter's seats were in the reserved section on the first-base side of the Coliseum. Fans wore light sweaters or jackets on this perfect fall evening.

As the game began, attention turned to the field but a flurry of activity persisted in the aisles and the concourses behind the seats. Food and drink were served in an abundance of volume and variety. More curious than hungry, the casewriter's group bought a sausage pizza from a vendor in the aisle. The 10-inch pizza was served in a square pizza box and was cut into eight slices. The pizza was reasonably good but great in comparison to food at most ballparks. As the group was to find from sampling the other menu items, the food at the Coliseum ranged from good to excellent. The chicken breast sandwich was the group's favorite.

Watching a game at the Coliseum was enjoyable for several reasons. First, the stadium seemed smaller than it was, creating an atmosphere more intimate than the 33,000 attendance figure would indicate. Second, the A's seemed to have deftly chosen elements from both the past and the present to give the fans high-tech entertainment mixed with the great traditions of baseball. The A's two scoreboards provide a perfect example of this combination. Behind the center-field bleachers, the A's installed Diamondvision, the giant television-like scoreboard and, a few hundred feet away, a manually operated scoreboard that kept track of all of the activity from around the Major Leagues. Finally, the A's chose modern over traditional in their choice of music; the once ubiquitous organ had been replaced by a stereo system that played popular music during any break in the action on the field.

Behind the scenes, the Clean Team, the innovative joint venture between Procter and Gamble and the A's, was in evidence sweeping and picking up trash. The result was concourse areas free from litter and the feeling that cleanliness was a priority for the A's. The bathrooms were fairly clean (though still no place to have lunch in). The baby changing table in the men's room, located in a wall recess near the exit, consisted of a metal table and a cardboard box holding a few individually wrapped Pampers decorated with cartoon characters.

Probably the most surprisingly good element of the experience of attending an A's game was the work of the ushers and security personnel. At the top of each aisle, ushers kept a plastic chain across the aisle, allowing only people with tickets in the section to pass. This procedure kept fans who paid top dollar for tickets from being annoyed by people trying to move down from the less expensive seats. It seemed like the usher memorized every face that came through so that he never asked anyone twice to show their ticket, an especially important consideration to people returning to their seats with food.

A woman asked the usher where she could find a hamburger, an item not sold at all of the concession stands. The usher reached into a box and pulled out a small map of the Coliseum. Then, like a tour guide, the usher traced the path from where they were standing to the proper concession stand and gave her the map. All of this was done not just politely but with enthusiasm. Like the manual-scoreboard operator, the usher seemed to understand the importance of doing every job well.

Finally, after a slow game in which the A's normally explosive bats were quiet, a fan in the casewriter's section began to get a little rowdy, shouting insults and throwing something at one of the ushers. Even though this happened in the ninth inning, late enough to let it slide in most ballparks, the usher radioed for security and the fan was removed from the park.

The A's lost 3–2 but the fans were not overly disappointed because the A's had all but locked up the divisional championship anyway. Many people talked about the playoffs and the opportunity to avenge last year's loss in the World Series to a Los Angeles Dodgers team that, on paper, was outclassed by the A's but on the field dominated them, needing only five games to win four.

After attending an A's game, several observations lead one to the conclusion that there is something different about this organization. The A's understand that their product is baseball, that baseball has a nearly magical quality for many people—adults and children—and that no team can win forever. The A's want families to think of a baseball game as the perfect outing: relatively inexpensive, fun, safe, and accessible.

Many other organizations have reached some of the same conclusions. A trip to a game just across the Bay to Candlestick Park reveals some of the same features (baby changing areas, videos of Giants games in which the fan's picture is edited into the action, etc.). The difference with the A's seems to be their ability to motivate everyone from the scoreboard operator to the ushers to the food vendors to understand the mission of the team: providing family entertainment. Their ability to instill the mission is especially remarkable given the fact that many of the direct service workers don't work for the A's, or even the Coliseum, but for a third-party vendor.

4

◆

Focusing and Positioning
the Service

S ome of the most successful service enterprises are carried out with single-minded purpose or method or both. We call this focus. It can be achieved by targeting a particular type of customer and meeting a set of related needs experienced by that customer. Or it can be achieved by offering a clearly defined service, often restricted in its scope, extraordinarily well. Focus allows a service provider to concentrate on a highly valued set of customers as well as those things that are absolutely critical to superior ways of serving them. It requires that we ask: What is the source of focus in this business? The customer? Operations? How does the focus in operations reflect customer needs?

Positioning follows from a determination of focus. It may start with considerations about how a business may want customers to think about it and what "position" it wants to achieve in their minds. But it goes far beyond this. It raises questions such as: How does (or should) this business distinguish itself from competition in customers' minds? Has it determined what is important to them? How does it meet these needs relative to competition? What are its competitive strengths and weaknesses? How do its policies and practices (its operating strategy) and the "place and plant" (its service delivery system) by which it is delivered reflect its positioning strategy? Given needs that are not being met, are there opportunities for positioning the service in non-traditional ways? What, if anything, does this suggest should be changed?

Lynn Shostack's article, "Service Positioning through Structural Change," emphasizes the need to reflect a service's focus in its positioning strategy, carrying the latter to the individual steps in the service delivery process. Does she carry the idea too far? Can her suggestions be implemented in practice? To what extent do some local services with which you are familiar succeed or fail by her criteria?

As you read about The Hartford Steam Boiler Inspection and Insurance Company, a venerable service organization, ask yourself which of the issues mentioned here might be relevant to Donald Wilson's task of correcting service-level problems facing HSB. What is this company's business? Who are this company's targeted customers? Has it identified them properly? Are their needs reflected in its service? Why are policy lead times so long? What can be done to deal with this concern?

The CompuServe (A) case presents a company variously described as being in from two to five businesses. What, if any, are the sources of focus in this company? Can it sustain all of the services it offers? One of the most important influences on strategic direction is the way in which available funds are allocated for alternative efforts. To which of the expressed needs would you allocate funds in this case if you were in Jeff Wilkins's place? Why? What does your decision say about the focus and position that you feel are best for CompuServe?

Responses to these questions are at the very heart of a company's strategy. Once they have been determined, we can next turn to ways of implementing the strategy and achieving desired goals.

Service Positioning
Through Structural Change
G. Lynn Shostack

The basis of any service positioning strategy is the service itself, but marketing offers little guidance on how to craft service processes for positioning purposes. A new approach suggests that within service systems, structural process design can be used to "engineer" services on a more scientific, rational basis.

When a firm or provider establishes and maintains a distinctive place for itself and its offerings in the market, it is said to be successfully positioned. In the increasingly competitive service sector, effective positioning is one of marketing's most critical tasks.

For some marketers (e.g., Ries and Trout 1981), positioning is strictly a communications issue. The product or service is a given and the objective is to manipulate consumer perceptions of reality. As Lovelock (1984) rightly points out, however, positioning is more than just advertising and promotion. Market position can be affected by pricing, distribution and, of course, the product itself, which is the core around which all positioning strategies revolve.

Apart from promotion, pricing, and distribution, the product is indeed a critical, manageable factor in positioning. Products often are engineered explicitly to reach certain markets, as the original Mustang was designed to reach the youth market and light beer was created to tap the calorie-conscious consumer. Sometimes products are invented first and positioned afterward. The Xerox copier and the Polaroid camera are examples of products that were first created, then positioned to various markets. Finally, an existing product may be changed in order to change its market position, as the Jeep was altered physically from a military vehicle to a vehicle for the family market.

Services are not things, however. McLuhan (1964) perhaps put it best and most succinctly more than 20 years ago when he declared that the *process* is the

G. Lynn Shostack is Managing Director, The Coveport Group, Inc. Reprinted from *Journal of Marketing*, Vol. 51, January 1987, pp. 34–43. Published by the American Marketing Association, Chicago, IL 60606.

product. We say "airline" when we mean "air transportation." We say "movie," but mean "entertainment services." We say "hotel" when we mean "lodging rental." The use of nouns obscures the fundamental nature of services, which are processes, not objects.

As processes, services have many intriguing characteristics. Judd (1964), Rathmell (1974), Shostack (1977), Bateson (1977), and Sasser, Olsen, and Wyckoff (1978) were among the first to ponder the implications of service intangibility, service perishability, production/consumption simultaneity, and consumer participation in service processes. They found that traditional marketing, with its goods-bound approaches, was not helpful in process design, process modification, or process control.

If processes are the service equivalent of a product's "raw materials," can processes be designed, managed, and changed for positioning purposes the way physical goods are? The purpose of this article is to take a closer look at processes as structural elements and suggest some ways in which they can be "engineered" for strategic service positioning purposes.

PROCESS CHARACTERISTICS

Processes have been studied for some time in disciplines other than marketing. Systematic, quantified methods for describing processes have been developed in industrial engineering (Deming 1982), computer programming (Fox 1982), decision theory (Holloway 1979), and operations management (Schroeder 1981), to name a few examples and well-known authors in each field. Though their techniques and nomenclatures may differ, process-oriented disciplines share certain basic concepts. First, each of them provides a way of breaking any process down into logical steps and sequences to facilitate its control and analysis. Second, each includes ways to accommodate more variable processes in which outcomes may differ because of the effects of judgment, chance, or choice on a sequence. Finally, each system includes the concept of deviation or tolerance standards in recognition that processes are "real time" phenomena that do not conform perfectly to any model or description, but rather function within a band or "norm" of some sort.

Little process description can be found in marketing literature. However, several writers on services have drawn upon manufacturing sources in using the words "standardized" and "customized" to define the poles of a process continuum (see Levitt 1976; Lovelock 1984). "Standardized" usually implies a nonvarying sequential process, similar to the mass production of goods, in which each step is laid out in order and all outcomes are uniform. "Customized" usually refers to some level of adaptation or tailoring of the process to the individual consumer. The concept of deviation usually is treated as a quality issue, in reference to services that do not perform as they should.

COMPLEXITY AND DIVERGENCE

Extracting from various approaches, we can suggest two ways to describe processes. One way is according to the steps and sequences that constitute the process; the other is according to the executional latitude or variability of those steps and sequences. Let us call the first factor the complexity of the process and the second its divergence. Deviation, a real-time operating factor, can then be thought of as an inadvertent departure from whatever process model and standards have been established for the first two factors.

We can define a service's complexity by analyzing the number and intricacy of the steps required to perform it. Accounting, for example, is more complex than bookkeeping because accounting is a more elaborate process, involving more functions and more steps. Architecture is more complex than plumbing. Plumbing is more complex than lawn mowing.

Apart from complexity, however, some processes include a high level of executional latitude and others do not. The degree of freedom allowed or inherent in a process step or sequence can be thought of as its divergence. A highly divergent service thus would be one in which virtually every performance of the process is unique. A service of low divergence would be one that is largely standardized.

Every service can be analyzed according to its overall complexity and divergence. A physician's services, for example, are highly complex. They are also highly divergent. As the service is being performed, a doctor constantly alters and shapes it by assimilating new data, weighing probabilities, reaching conclusions, and then taking action. Every case may be handled differently, yet all performances may be satisfactory from the consumer point of view. Architecture, law, consulting, and most other "professional" services have similarly high divergence (as well as high complexity), because they involve a considerable amount of judgment, discretion, and situational adaptation.

However, a process can be high in complexity and low in divergence. Hotel services, for example, are a complex aggregation of processes, but hotels standardize these processes through documentation and establishment of executional rules for every sequence from room cleaning to checkout. Telephone services are also highly complex, yet telephone companies have standardized and automated them to ensure uniformity and achieve economies of scale.

Services also can be low in complexity but high in divergence. In process terms, a singer renders the service of entertainment in one step: sing. This service is infinitely divergent, however, because each execution is unique and unlike that of any other provider. A painter "merely" paints, a teacher simply "transmits knowledge," a minister "spreads the gospel." These services do not consist of orderly, mechanical procedures, but of unique performances. Services that involve interpretative skills, artistic crafting, or highly individualized execution often appear simple in process terms, yet are highly divergent in operation. In fact, for such services, defining "what" is done in process terms is often easier than describing "how" it is done.

BLUEPRINTING COMPLEXITY AND DIVERGENCE IN SERVICE SYSTEMS

Though processes can be reduced to steps and sequences, services must be viewed as interdependent, interactive systems, not as disconnected pieces and parts. One approach for visualizing service systems is a mapping technique called "blueprinting" (Shostack 1984a,b). Blueprinting is a holistic method of seeing in snapshot form what is essentially a dynamic, living phenomenon.

For process design purposes, a blueprint should document all process steps and points of divergence in a specific service. This documentation must be carried to whatever level of detail is needed to distinguish between any two competing services. In other words, specific blueprints of real services are more productive than generic or generalized visualizations in working out position strategies based on process.

Figure 1 shows how one Park Avenue florist's service appears in blueprint form. The "fan" is borrowed from decision theory (see Holloway 1979) in which a fan attached to a circle is used to show a range of potential events that may occur, whereas a fan attached to a square denotes a range of potential actions that may be taken. This is a useful symbol for divergence and is used throughout the following illustrations. The florist provides a service of low complexity that is highly divergent. Though the process steps are few, the fans indicate broad executional latitude stemming from the judgment and decisions of the individual performing the service.

For comparison, *Figure 2* illustrates a complex but standardized service—consumer installment lending at a large commercial bank. Here, the process has many more specific steps, but the steps are executed in a strict and unvarying manner. As Levitt would say, the service has been "industrialized" (1976). There is one and only one permissible manner and order in which the service is provided. Parts of the process have been automated for further conformity, and the bank's design for this service does not allow employees who are part of the service system to modify or change the service in any way. Such a service may not function perfectly at all times. However, as noted before, such quality failures

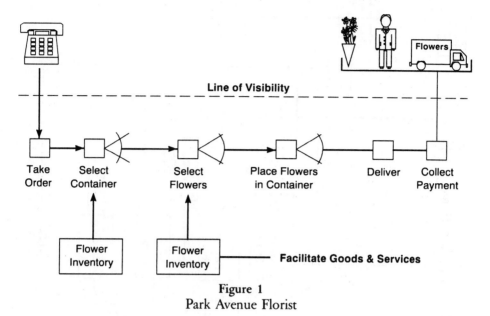

Figure 1
Park Avenue Florist

represent deviation from a design standard, whereas true divergence is an integral part of the process.

Figure 3 shows yet another structure—the highly complex and highly divergent service of a general medical practitioner. Here, not only is the process complex, but virtually every step involves variable execution.

Blueprints as a Tool in Consumer Research

It may be noted that this analytical approach is a useful and natural companion to market research. Lovelock (1984) noted the difficulty of researching service "attributes" for positioning purposes, which is caused at least partly by the inherent ambiguity and subjectivity of verbal descriptions. Blueprints provide visible portraits to which consumers can react, and which can facilitate exploration of more parts of the service system than just its processes. Blueprints can be used to educate consumers, focus their evaluative input on various aspects of the service system, elicit comparative or competitive assessments, and generate specific responses to contemplated changes or new service concepts. As Schneider and Bowen (1984) pointed out, regardless of whether consumers are privy to or even aware of all parts of the process, their awareness of its results and evidence makes them potentially valuable participants in the design of the entire system, not just those parts they see.

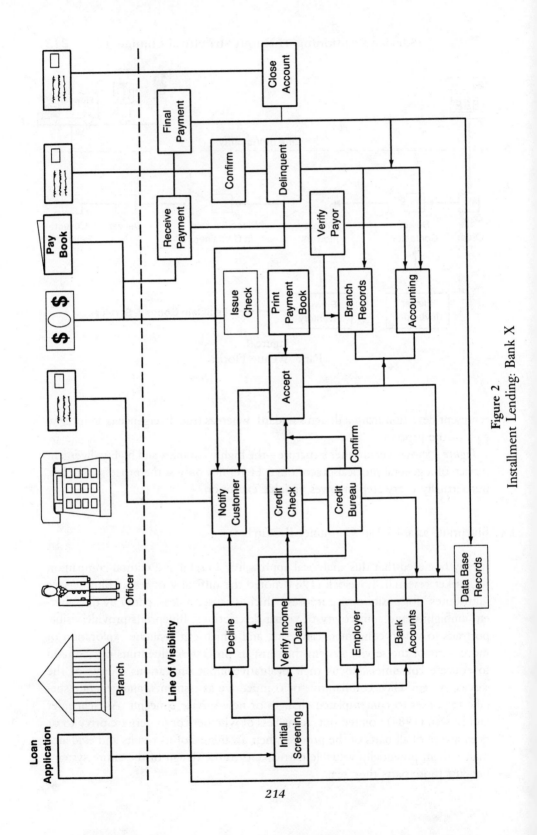

Figure 2
Installment Lending: Bank X

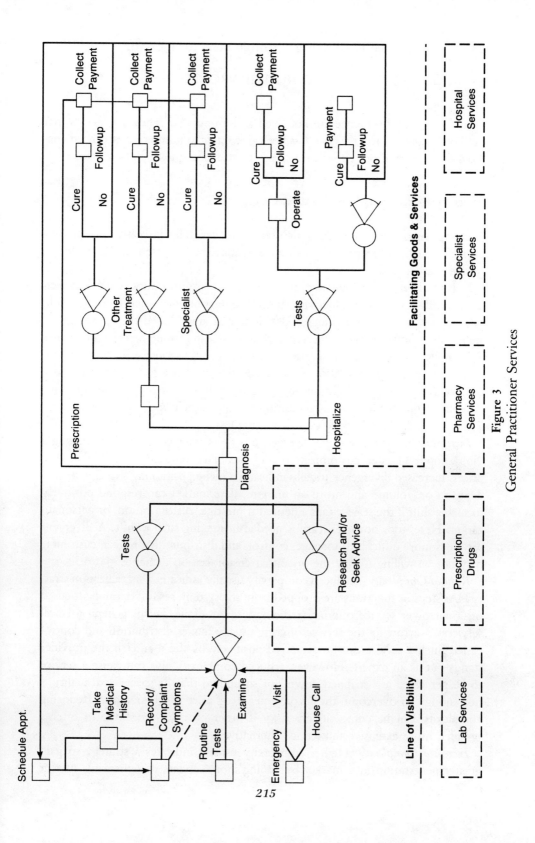

Figure 3
General Practitioner Services

215

CHANGING THE PROCESS

Complexity and divergence are not fixed and immutable. They are factors that can be changed. Once a service has been documented accurately, it can be analyzed for opportunities either to increase or decrease one or both variables.

Alternative Directions for Structural Change

A change in overall complexity or divergence generally indicates one of four overall strategic directions. Each one has management consequences as well as certain market risks.

Reduced Divergence. Reducing divergence leads to uniformity which tends to reduce costs, improve productivity, and make distribution easier. It usually indicates a shift to a volume-oriented positioning strategy based on economies of scale. The positive market effects of such a move can include perceived increases in reliability—more uniform service quality and greater service availability. However, reducing divergence also can have negative market effects. It dictates conformity as well as inflexibility in operating procedures. Customers may perceive the shift as one that lowers customization and limits their options, and may reject a highly standardized service even if it costs less.

Increased Divergence. Raising divergence is the service equivalent of creating a "job shop." Greater customization and flexibility tend to command higher prices. Increased divergence usually indicates a niche positioning strategy, dependent less on volume and more on margins. The market can respond positively to such a shift if the service taps a desire for prestige, customization, or personalization. Here, too, however, care is needed in making such a shift. A divergent service is more difficult to manage, control, and distribute. Moreover, customers may not be willing to pay the price that customization demands.

Reduced Complexity. Reduced complexity usually indicates a specialization strategy. As steps or functions are dropped from the system, resources can be focused on a narrower service offering (radiology, for example, versus general medical services). Narrowing the service offering usually makes distribution and control easier. Such a service can be perceived positively by the market if the provider stands out as an expert. However, reduced complexity also can cause a service to be perceived as "stripped down" or so limited that its specialized quality is not enough to overcome the inconvenience or price of obtaining it. Reducing complexity can be competitively risky if other providers continue to offer a broader, more extensive full-service alternative.

Increased Complexity. Higher complexity usually indicates a strategy to gain greater penetration in a market by adding more services or enhancing current ones. Supermarkets, banks, and retailers have expanded their service lines with this strategic goal in mind. Increasing complexity can increase efficiency by maximizing the revenue generated from each customer. In contrast, too much complexity can be confusing to customers and can cause overall service quality to fall. Thus, a highly complex service system may be vulnerable to inroads by competitors who specialize.

MARKETING STRATEGY AND STRUCTURAL CHANGE

Service industries offer numerous examples of changes in complexity and divergence and how they affect market position. Barbering, for example, is a relatively simple service, but beginning in the 1970s some providers began to reposition it. They added processes borrowed from women's beauty salons, such as tinting, body perms, and backcombing, redefined their mission, and transformed "hair cutting" into "hair styling"—a more complex, divergent service structure. Hair styling tapped or created a new market segment of men willing to pay substantially higher prices for a more elaborate process and carved a niche in the market through structural differentiation.

In retailing, there are many examples of adding to the complexity of service systems. Supermarkets began as specialty food stores and have added banking services, pharmacist services, flowers, books and magazines, and even food preparation to their basic food retailing structure. In the fast-food industry, what were once simple hamburger outlets have become providers of breakfast, dining room services, and even entertainment. Retailing also affords many examples of reducing complexity, as evidenced by the emergence of businesses specializing only in pasta, only in cookies, and only in ice cream.

For examples of lowered divergence, we need only to look at professional services. Legal services, for instance, have historically had both high complexity and high divergence. A consumer needing legal assistance first had to seek out and select an attorney, and was then dependent upon the variable performance of that individual. Over the past few years, however, this service has been repositioned through the actions of business-minded entrepreneurs who perceived a market need for less complex, less divergent alternatives. The result has been the creation of legal "clinics" and chains that offer a limited menu of services executed uniformly at published rates. This repositioning not only has opened a new market for legal services, but also has had and will continue to have a profound effect on the positioning strategies of traditional law firms.

A similar downshifting and repositioning of traditional personal accountant services was effected by the innovations of H&R Block, which tapped a vast market of consumers who did not require the variable and costly services of a personal accountant, but who were willing to pay someone else to prepare their tax returns.

Most of these examples are based on entrepreneurial response to the perception of an unmet market need. What is perhaps less clearly recognized is that such changes need not be intuitive or accidental. They can be made deliberately to support explicit positioning or competitive strategies.

IMPLICATIONS OF SERVICE SYSTEM CHANGES

Let us assume that *Figure 1* is an accurate representation of a specific florist's service. Assume further that in an analysis of competitors, very similar structures were found. One strategic option to reposition and differentiate the service would be to re-engineer it as a less divergent system. *Figure 4* illustrates a redesigned blueprint that accomplishes this objective. The number of container choices has been limited to two; there are only two groups of flowers and only two choices of arrangement for each group. Thus, only eight combinations are possible.

Obviously, the new design has implications for inventory management as well as productivity. Inventory can be ordered in larger, more economic quantities. More arrangements can be produced by the florist because the process is more standardized. These two effects will lower prices and potentially allow the service to be repositioned to a broader market. The new structure also will allow wider service distribution, because simpler blueprints are easier to replicate. FTD (Florists' Transworld Delivery) arrived at a similar conclusion and expanded florist services from a local craft into a national service industry.

However, if all the florists in a particular market had structures similar to *Figure 4*, a logical positioning strategy might be to move toward the design shown in *Figure 1*—a highly artistic, high-priced structure. Alternatively, a marketer might choose to increase complexity alone, through retailing a selection of plants and supplies, or to increase both complexity and divergence by offering flower arranging classes.

Identifying and Evaluating Strategic Choices

Services can be structurally evaluated on a stand-alone basis and also as members of service families. Within a service family, a marketer can consider positioning strategies based on structural complementarity, structural diversity, and overall developmental direction.

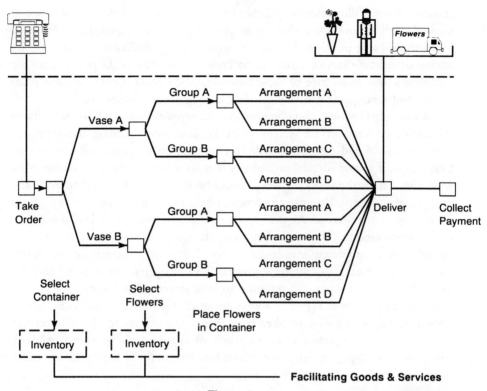

Figure 4
Florist Services: Alternative Design

In *Figure 2*, a bank's consumer installment lending service is diagrammed. This service, of course, is only one of a constellation of services that constitute consumer banking. Though consumer banking, in its totality, is an extraordinarily complex service system, most blueprints of its component services would show low divergence stemming from 20 years of effort to standardize and automate the service system.

One strategy for a bank with this structure is to continue increasing complexity by adding more subservices while continuing to minimize divergence through standardization and automation. For a competitor, an equally valid strategy would be to adopt the counterposition, which would call for increasing the customization of services. The latter strategy is evident in banks offering "private" banking, an integrated package of services for the upscale market that includes such divergent services as customized lending, portfolio management, and financial planning.

The general practitioner previously described also has numerous strategic choices. *Figure 5* illustrates the relative structural positions held by a number of medical service providers, including the general practitioner analyzed in *Figure 3*. From the present position, he/she can move in any direction on the scale by adding or deleting service functions to create a new family. Depending on the complexity and divergence of these functions, the overall service system's complexity and divergence will change, thus altering its relative position.

For example (*Figure 6*), retailing orthopedic supplies would add complexity to the doctor's overall service system, but little divergence. Adding counseling, in contrast, would add considerable divergence, but little operational complexity. Conversely, if minor surgical procedures that have been performed in the office were eliminated, the service system would be reduced in both complexity and divergence and move closer to the position held by diagnosticians, who perform no treatment themselves. At the extreme position, complexity and divergence could be lowered to the point where only the simple service, such as X-rays, is provided in a completely standardized way. Consumer research can be instrumental in facilitating this strategic process, and blueprints are a useful tool for focusing consumer input and response to new structural concepts.

In simplified terms, *Figure 7* shows some changes that a midpriced family restaurant might consider to alter complexity and divergence for competitive purposes. Any prospective change or mix of changes can be compared with competitors' offerings to determine which mix is most likely to provide the maximum competitive differentiation.

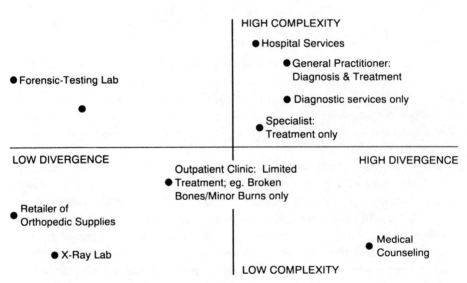

Figure 5
Relative Positions Based on Structural Analysis

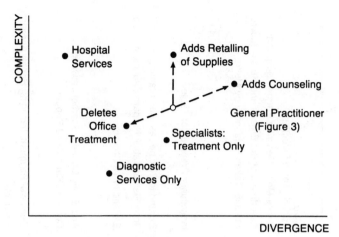

Figure 6
Positional Shifts through Structural Change

Positioning charts are a useful tool for market analysts wishing to compare the perceived performance of competing services on two or three attributes simultaneously. Examples of such charts (also known as perceptual maps) are given by Tybout and Hauser (1981) and Lovelock (1984). Blueprinting works well in tandem with this technique by serving as a focal point for determining which parts of the service system or process components are important to the market, and in evaluating change across many elements of the system.

IMPLEMENTING CHANGE

Though processes are intangible, the means by which services are rendered are very real. There are only two, people (both providers and consumers) and facilitating goods. Any shift in overall complexity or divergence, or the introduction of any new process design, must be implemented with a clear understanding of the potential impact on these "producers" of the process.

Role of Service Employees and Customers

Considerable attention has been paid to people in the service system. Whether they are providers or consumers, the management and control of human behavior is a critical factor in process design, change, and operating quality. Mills (1985) suggests that management controls over service employees should depend

LOWER COMPLEXITY/DIVERGENCE	CURRENT PROCESS	HIGHER COMPLEXITY/DIVERGENCE
No Reservations	TAKE RESERVATION	Specific Table Selection
Self-seating. Menu on Blackboard	SEAT GUESTS, GIVE MENUS	Recite Menu: Describe Entrees & Specials
Eliminate	SERVE WATER AND BREAD	Assortment of Hot Breads and Hors d'oeuvres
Customer Fills Out Form	TAKE ORDERS	At table. Taken Personally by Maitre d'
	PREPARE ORDERS	
Pre-prepared: No Choice	Salad (4 Choices)	Individually Prepared at Table
Limit to Four Choices	Entree (15 Choices	Expand to 20 Choices: Add Flaming Dishes; Bone Fish at Table; Prepare Sauces at Table
Sundae Bar: Self-service	Dessert (6 Choices	Expand to 12 Choices
Coffee, Tea, Milk only	Beverage (6 Choices	Add Exotic Coffees; Sherbet between Courses; Hand Grind Pepper
Serve Salad & Entree Together: Bill and Beverage Together	SERVE ORDERS	
Cash Only: Pay When Leaving	COLLECT PAYMENT	Choice of Payment. Including House Accounts: Serve Mints

Figure 7
Structural Alternatives

on the structure of the service system. For low-contact, standardized services, behavior can be controlled through mechanistic means, such as rules and regulations. However, for high-contact, divergent services, Mills suggests that employee self-management and peer-reference techniques are more effective. Smith and Houston (1983), in contrast, propose that a script-based approach to managing customer and employee behavior can help to control expectations as well as process compliance. Bowen and Schneider (1985) speak of "boundary spanners," that is, employees with high customer interaction, as a valuable source of design information and as change agents whose acceptance and commitment are critical to success in altering any process. Schneider and Bowen (1984) as well as others (Berry 1983; Heskett 1986) stress that employee involvement and "internal" marketing to employees are important factors in ensuring successful service operations. Deming (1982), however, argues that both behavior and motivation are controlled by the design of the process itself and that if the process is properly designed, high motivation and effectiveness will be the natural results.

In terms of consumer participation, Lovelock and Young (1979), Chase (1978), Bateson (1985), and others have discussed whether and how to involve consumers in the service process, and the management of their involvement. Chase argues that consumer participation should be kept to a minimum in the interests of greater process efficiency. However, as we have seen, process design offers many routes to market success. A service (self-service gasoline stations, for example) can be designed for maximum consumer participation and still be profitable. In fact, Bateson's (1985) work suggests that consumers can be segmented on the basis of control needs, resulting in services that are designed to capitalize profitably on the consumer's own desire for participation.

These brief descriptions illustrate the richness and diversity of current thought about the human side of service systems. Our purpose here is not to choose one approach over another, but to underscore the fact that people are just as important as structural design. If people issues are not addressed effectively, even the best design will fail.

Role of Facilitating Goods

Facilitating goods are also important in structural planning. Educational services, for example, can be rendered by a human being who lectures in a traditional classroom setting. Education also can be rendered via videotape, television, computer, and book, to name just a few alternative facilitating goods. For the designer of a new or different educational service, any of these choices will yield a different service structure. These structures will differ in complexity and divergence, as well as in cost dynamics, distribution constraints, and market position.

Sometimes facilitating goods are used as a replacement for human performance to reduce divergence. Computers are the prime example of a good that has been used in this way to standardize service systems. However, simplification is not the only use for technology. Technology also can be used to increase complexity and divergence. When bank automated teller machines first were introduced, for example, they could deliver only simple cash dispensing and deposit services. Now, technology has allowed the addition of funds transfer and investment services to the system, increasing its overall complexity. Tomorrow, what are called "smart" cards will make possible the delivery of a wide range of credit, payment, and information services. Ultimately, technology may even make possible a degree of customization (i.e., divergence) that only human providers can now deliver.

For all these reasons, the consideration of changes to any service structure demands an appreciation of the interrelatedness and intricacy of service systems. Unlike a product, a service cannot be engineered and then made in a factory. "Producing" a service is a dynamic, continuous event. .

CONCLUSION

Though our discussion focuses on process design, other elements of the service system can and do affect market position. Advertising and promotion are, of course, powerful forces in the positioning process. American Express, for example, has repositioned its credit services to women solely through advertising.

Distribution channels also affect market position. Marketing stock brokerage through Sears stores is one example of positioning a service to a new, broader consumer base through a change in distribution channels. Moreover, as Shostack (1985), Blackman (1985), and others have noted, various forms of physical service evidence, from the environment in which a service is rendered to the correspondence, brochures, signage, and even people to which a customer is exposed, can affect position. Facilitating goods also can affect position, even without process change. A provider who substitutes limousines for taxicabs, for example, may succeed in charging higher prices and tapping a different market for exactly the same transportation service.

In short, the issues involved in service positioning are numerous, and this discussion by no means encompasses all of the subjects relevant to the positioning process. In a structural sense, however, processes themselves appear to have characteristics that not only affect market position, but also can be deliberately and strategically managed for positioning purposes. By manipulating complexity and divergence, a service marketer can approximate some of the product analysis and design functions that are traditional in product marketing. Moreover, the use of blueprints provides a mechanism through which services can be "engineered" at the drawing board, as well as a tool for identifying gaps, analyzing competitors, aiding in market research, and controlling implementation.

The marketplace affords evidence that both complexity and divergence are concepts that are understood and employed in service industries. Though the practice is not formalized, it works. How much more powerful the result might be if marketers brought a professional discipline, capable of crafting service systems on a rational basis, to bear on the service positioning task!

For managers in service industries, taking a structural approach can help increase their control over some of the most critical elements of service system management. For marketers, process design may be a tool that can substantially increase their impact and role in the service sector and help service marketing come of age.

REFERENCES

Bateson, John E. G. (1977), "Do We Need Service Marketing?" *Marketing Consumer Services: New Insights*, Report # 77–115. Cambridge, MA: Marketing Science Institute.

—— (1985), "Perceived Control and the Service Encounter," in *The Service Encounter*, John Czepiel et al., eds. Lexington, MA: Lexington Books.

Berry, Leonard L. (1983), "Relationship Marketing," in *Emerging Perspectives on Services Marketing*, Leonard L. Berry et al., eds. Chicago: American Marketing Association, 25–8.

Blackman, Barry A. (1985), "Making a Service More Tangible Can Make It More Manageable," in *The Service Encounter*, John Czepiel et al., eds. Lexington MA: Lexington Books.

Bowen, David E. and Benjamin Schneider (1985), "Boundary-Spanning-Role Employees and the Service Encounter," in *The Service Encounter*, John Czepiel et al., eds. Lexington, MA: Lexington Books, 124–47.

Chase, Richard B. (1978), "Where Does the Consumer Fit in a Service Operation?" *Harvard Business Review*, 56 (November–December), 137–42.

Deming, W. Edwards (1982), *Quality, Productivity and Competitive Position*. Cambridge, MA: Massachusetts Institute of Technology, Center for Advanced Engineering Study.

Fox, Joseph M. (1982), *Software and Its Development*. Englewood Cliffs, NJ: Prentice-Hall, Inc.

Heskett, James L. (1986), *Managing in the Service Economy*. Boston: Harvard Business School Press, 45–74, 117–34.

Holloway, Charles A. (1979), *Decision Making under Uncertainty: Models and Choices*. Englewood Cliffs, NJ: Prentice-Hall, Inc.

Judd, Robert C. (1964), "The Case for Redefining Services," *Journal of Marketing*, 28 (January), 58–9.

Levitt, Theodore (1976), "The Industrialization of Service," *Harvard Business Review*, 54 (September–October), 63–74.

Lovelock, Christopher H. (1984), *Services Marketing, Text, Cases, & Readings.* Englewood Cliffs, NJ: Prentice-Hall, Inc., 55–6, 133–9.

Lovelock, Christopher H. and Robert F. Young (1979), "Look to Consumers to Increase Productivity," *Harvard Business Review,* 57 (May–June), 168–78.

McLuhan, Marshall (1964), *Understanding Media.* New York: McGraw-Hill Book Company.

Mills, Peter K. (1985), "The Control Mechanisms of Employees at the Encounter of Service Organizations," in *The Service Encounter,* John Czepiel et al., eds. Lexington, MA: Lexington Books.

Rathmell, John M. (1974), *Marketing in the Service Sector.* Cambridge, MA: Winthrop Publishers, Inc.

Ries, Al and Jack Trout (1981), *Positioning.* New York: McGraw-Hill Book Company.

Sasser, W. Earl, Jr., R. Paul Olsen, and D. Daryl Wyckoff (1978), *Management of Service Operations: Text, Cases, and Readings.* Boston: Allyn & Bacon.

Schneider, Benjamin and David E. Bowen (1984), "New Service Design, Development and Implementation," in *Developing New Services,* William R. George and Claudia Marshall, eds. Chicago: American Marketing Association, Proceedings Series, 82–102.

Schroeder, Roger G. (1981), *Operations Management.* New York: McGraw-Hill Book Company.

Shostack, G. Lynn (1977), "Breaking Free from Product Marketing," *Journal of Marketing,* 41 (April), 73–80.

—— (1984a), "A Framework for Service Marketing," in *Marketing Theory, Distinguished Contributions.* Stephen W. Brown and Raymond P. Fisk, eds. New York: John Wiley & Sons, Inc., 250.

—— (1984b), "Designing Services That Deliver," *Harvard Business Review,* 62 (January–February), 133–9.

—— (1985), "Planning the Service Encounter," in *The Service Encounter,* John Czepiel et al., eds. Lexington, MA: Lexington Books, 243–53.

Smith, Ruth A. and Michael J. Houston (1983), "Script-Based Evaluation of Satisfaction with Services," in *Emerging Perspectives on Services Marketing,* Leonard Berry et al., eds. Chicago: American Marketing Association.

Tybout, Alice M. and John R. Hauser (1981), "A Marketing Audit Using a Conceptual Model of Consumer Behavior: Application and Evaluation," *Journal of Marketing,* 45 (Summer), 82–101.

The Hartford Steam Boiler Inspection and Insurance Company
Inspection Is Our Middle Name

The Hartford Steam Boiler Inspection and Insurance Company (HSB) had been the number one company in the $160 million boiler and machinery insurance industry since it was founded in 1866. Working through its nationwide network of 20 branches, HSB inspected and insured many types of industrial equipment ranging from small compressed air tanks and apartment building furnace boilers to 5,000 horsepower chemical plant compressors, electric utility steam turbines and huge nuclear reactor pressure vessels.

During early 1974, HSB President Wilson Wilde and several other top-level HSB officers had begun to wonder whether increases in the quality of service being offered to the company's customers had been keeping pace with changing market demands. One symptom of the quality problem was higher than desired turnover in several areas of the company; another symptom seemed to be an increasing amount of time needed to deliver policies. The time required to deliver a completed policy after an agreement to insure had been signed had been recently averaging between 50 and 70 days in some branches, and in a few instances delivery had taken as long as three years, the typical duration of an HSB policy. During this time period, the customer was insured under a loosely structured agreement known as a "binder" rather than under a specific and detailed policy. Competitors that did not inspect could sometimes deliver policies in less than one week.

COMPANY HISTORY

After more than a century of operations, HSB in 1968 grossed $35.8 million in earned premiums and netted $1.94 a share in earnings; by 1973 the company had grown to $62 million in annual premiums and had earned $3.94 per share. Late in the summer of 1974, HSB stock had been trading over the counter for $25 a share. (See *Exhibit 1* for financial summary.)

As of mid-1974, HSB insured more than one million separate objects in 200,000 different locations. The coverage normally provided by the company included provisions for actual dollar losses arising from accidental damage to and due to the equipment in question, various forms of liability coverage, and a provision for business interruption losses which indemnified the insured against the loss of profits due to machinery failure. HSB's accounts varied in terms of size of premiums, size of risk exposure to the company, number and location of objects and many other factors. A summary comparison of these characteristics is presented in *Exhibit 2*.

As of the end of 1973, five companies controlled approximately 80% of the business; the remainder was shared by nine other firms. For four out of the last five years, Hartford had experienced lower losses per dollar earned premium than any of the top four companies, and during that period the company had grown at a considerably faster rate than the industry average. (See market share data, *Exhibit 3*.)

In the past few years, the company had made several moves to modernize and streamline operations. In 1970, HSB installed an IBM 370/135 to ease its tremendous data handling task and to assist the company in developing management information systems and more efficient operational methods. In 1972 the company also initiated a formalized budgeting system, and by 1974 the system was being utilized in most areas of the company's operations.

HSB had also begun providing a Special Inspection Service (SIS) in 1971 to supplement its regular activities. SIS was offered to manufacturing firms on a fee basis and consisted of an HSB inspector inspecting a boiler or pressure vessel as it was being constructed. This service was often performed on a third-party basis (at the request of either an equipment purchaser or the government) to monitor a vendor. In addition, HSB was often consulted by manufacturers, industry associations and governmental authorities on the development and advancement of design and construction codes. In mid-1974, SIS involved approximately 80 full-time and 70 part-time HSB inspectors and was contributing to revenues at a $5 million annual rate.

As a result of offering its extensive and comprehensive inspection service combined with coverages tailored to individual insured clients, HSB was able to command a higher price in the market than most of its competitors while still maintaining market dominance. According to Mr. Wilde, HSB's prices averaged about 10% higher than those of its major rivals.

INDUSTRY TRENDS

There were several industry trends and characteristics that affected HSB's operations. The property and casualty industry, of which boiler and machinery was a small segment, had generally approached selling of insurance in two ways. One way was to deal directly with the insured customer through a salesman who was a full-time employee of the company; All-State, State Farm and others who used this method were called "direct writers." The second way was to sell through independent agents. The agent was employed on a commission basis and the insurance companies using this method—called agency companies—employed few or no salesmen themselves. HSB had traditionally been an agency company and still used agents for all of its transactions. Even if HSB sold a policy on a direct basis, an agent was paid a commission, though often a reduced one since the agent performed little or no work to earn it. "The agent will always be a part of our distribution channel," explained Mr. Donald K. Wilson, Vice President for Agency, "even though we are moving towards more direct selling."

According to Mr. Wilde, there had been a trend over the last 10 to 15 years for direct writing companies to use agents more frequently and, conversely, a trend for agency companies to do more direct writing of policies.

It used to be that there was a spread of about 20% between the cost to a customer of direct-written policies and ones sold through agents. Most of that 20% was agents' commissions. Now there is a more competitive marketplace; the spread has been shrinking and over the next few years it will continue to shrink.

Hartford Steam Boiler used both local and national agents, though it wrote much of its business with the larger insurance brokers such as Marsh & McLennan, Inc. and Johnson & Higgins, Inc. Mr. Wilde felt that there had been an increasing trend towards consolidation among agents; essentially the larger ones had been buying out smaller ones.

There had also been a move towards more "packaging" of insurance policies, that is, combining on a wide range of risks. "If we don't deliver the policy in a reasonable period of time," noted Philadelphia branch manager William B. Mount, "then the agent can't wrap it up with his other coverages, so we're holding up his premium cash flow of, say, $100,000 even though we're taking only $5,000."

Additionally, there had been a trend towards self-insurance, especially in light of increasing insurance costs. "Sometimes a guy will gasp at the idea of $300,000 for boiler insurance in a big corporation," explained Mr. Zindel, "and will ask, 'what do we need that for?' Then the company might drop its insurance and effectively become self-insured."

Still, HSB was not as worried as some companies in its industry. "No matter what," noted Mr. Wilson, "we can always sell loss prevention service. Consumerism and OSHA [the 1971 Occupational Safety and Health Act] are both putting more pressure on a corporation's risk manager to do a better job. Our service is not always sold with an insurance policy."

Besides these trends, HSB, along with other insurance companies, faced certain inherent characteristics of the business. One was the industry's historical cyclicality—after a few years of prosperity the companies start underselling each other and inevitably industry profits become leaner. "The last two years have been a disastrous period," noted Mr. Wilde. "Lots of price cutting in the fire and casualty industry—the industry as a whole lost money in 1973. That is, companies netted a profit by making money on their investments, but they lost on insurance."

Part of HSB's competitive problem was that for most insurance firms, boiler machinery insurance was but a tiny part of the parent company's business, whereas it was Hartford's only business. "Some of our competitors go in to a broker and look at our bid on a policy and simply undercut it 6%," explained Earl Kemmler, Vice President for Engineering. "Now that's a hell of a competitive situation, though they can get burned real bad. When losses get to a point where everyone notices, they will tell their salesmen to stop cutting prices willy-nilly."

Inflation had recently proven a burden for HSB. Since the company operated normally with a three-year contract, the income HSB earned from a particular risk was fixed at the amount of the premium. However, the cost of repairing damage or compensating business losses was not fixed.

ORGANIZATION AND PERSONNEL

The HSB organization consisted of five major functional areas reporting to President Wilde: agency (sales, marketing and branch office operations); engineering (inspection); underwriting; finance and legal (see organization chart, *Exhibit 4*). Underwriting, finance and legal divisions operated from the home office, while the two other areas were primarily represented in branch offices. The company's 20 branch office managers (who were mainly responsible for sales and office administration) reported directly to Mr. Donald K. Wilson. The branch manager did not directly supervise the engineering functions; the chief inspector reported instead directly to Engineering Vice President Earl Kemmler. Branch managers, through office managers, supervised the branch underwriting operation, a generally routine clerical function. The home office underwriting staff, headed by Vice President Robert Wolf, provided the branch manager with (1) quality control evaluation for the clerical function and (2) active advice and participation on significant or specialized risks. Despite these reporting relationships, the branch managers retained profit and loss responsibility for all activities in the branch.

Normally, if conflicts arose at the branch level as to the advisability of taking on a risk, the problem was resolved at the branch office level. Unresolved disputes were sent to the home office for a decision; if the vice presidents could not agree, there was provision for the dispute to be placed before the Underwriting Committee, composed of five senior officers, for final resolution. This procedure was used only in isolated cases and on very large risks; indeed, disputes sent to the home office generally emanated only from a few branches.

INSPECTION

Hartford Steam Boiler's distinctive competence was embodied in its inspection service. "We offer an inspection service like no one else," commented President Wilde. "There are really only two companies with a great interest in loss prevention, as opposed to just loss insurance. The other one is our competitor of 75 years, the Factory Mutual Companies. But whereas we have more than 825 inspectors and engineers, including 70 at the home office, Factory only has about 200 inspectors total." HSB prided itself on its customer response time; it claimed that if an accident occurred, an HSB inspector could be on the site in less than one hour, depending on location. "If somebody's boiler goes off," explained Mr. Wilde, "he wants us there in a hurry, and we are. This is one of the strengths of the branch office system. Our inspectors are in virtually every major community in the country."

The 755 inspectors deployed throughout the branch office system were almost entirely "practical" engineers; that is, they were trained to be able to diagnose and repair, rather than design, heavy machinery. In almost every state inspectors were required to pass a uniform ASME exam to become licensed boiler machinery inspectors. Inspectors had traditionally been recruited from navy and merchant marine ranks, many having retired from the service while in their late thirties after 20 years of service. Often the inspectors had been engineering officers on vessels, and most tended to be "jacks-of-all-trades" rather than specialists. "Our inspectors, by the time they reach a certain level, are expected to be able to inspect anything that we insure," noted Mr. Kemmler, "from simple air tanks to complex four-color rotogravure presses or 5,000 horsepower ammonia compressors."

The company generally did not hire college graduate engineers as inspectors. Explained Mr. Kemmler:

> Graduate engineers don't like to get their hands dirty, and sometimes we do things that aren't very pleasant. For instance, we insure most of Swift and Company's equipment—storehouses, blood driers and those awful rendering tanks. In order to make sure there are no defects, an inspector has to climb in the blood driers and chip away the dried blood. It's hot in there, you're sweating, and when the dried blood hits you, you come out looking like someone got you with a cleaver. And of course the smell is just horrible. We haven't been too successful with graduate engineers.

The inspector's four main duties were ranked according to priorities. The first priority was responding to accidents. If a boiler went down and an entire plant was shut down, it was crucial to both the insured and to Hartford that the plant become operational in the shortest period of time. The second inspection priority was completion of First Inspection Orders (FIOs). These were the inspections required when a company was put on binder. They must be completed prior to formal policy issuance; an inspector must get into an insured's premises quickly and determine whether the risks are indeed insurable ones. The third priority was inspections required by law (inspections in many cases fulfilled state and legal requirements); the fourth was the routine inspections done as part of the loss prevention service. (Required frequency of inspection varied depending on the equipment involved.) These priorities created some conflicts. For example, if there was an accident, an inspector had to cancel other appointments or find substitute inspectors in the branch to assist him.

To minimize business interruption claims, the engineering department offered repair expediting capabilities. "Our people know who's who in the many big companies that supply heavy machinery and we can get those things moving in a hurry," explained Mr. Wilde. "Once when a 4,000 horse-power motor failed in a chemical plant, we knew where another firm had one sitting idle and we shipped it in about four days. It would have taken eight months to get a new one."

Inspectors' salaries began at approximately $8,400 per year. The company provided a car of the inspector's choice and paid the operating costs of the vehicle. HSB estimated that these additions increased the "real" salary to nearly $9,300, plus all normal fringes. HSB estimated that it required approximately one year and $8,000–$10,000 to train an inspector in HSB's methods. Salary experts had assured HSB that its salary scale was competitive within the insurance industry. However, the company experienced a high turnover among its inspectors, averaging about 17% in 1973. Mr. Kemmler explained:

> HSB has a problem similar to that of IBM. It serves as a training ground. Inspectors are in demand by other companies—construction, architectural and such—and many of them are either working on a cost-plus basis or can simply afford to pay more for inspectors.

Moonlighting was an accepted fact of life for most inspectors. Various company employees estimated that between 50% and 75% of the company's inspectors held down some form of part-time job. Mr. Kemmler did not feel that this was detrimental to HSB operations.

> We have no objection to it as long as it does not interfere with normal activities and does not provide a conflict of interest with the company. As long as an inspector is available for an emergency at 2 a.m. we don't care if he drives a taxi or raises chickens on the side.

INSPECTOR DUTIES AND RESPONSIBILITIES

Each branch had one chief inspector who was in charge of the branch's inspection activities. Reporting to him were between two and nine supervising inspectors and to them, approximately eight field inspectors per supervisor. The chief inspector was responsible for all inspection activities, accident investigation and claim adjustments. Inspectors normally submitted all inspection reports to supervising inspectors for review. It was felt by the engineering department that this added an extra measure of experience and expertise to each inspection.

If a branch were required to inspect objects with which it had little inspection experience, the inspectors could contact the home office engineering staff for assistance. This staff of 70 engineers comprised a corps of specialists who assisted the branches with inspections, surveys, accident investigations and administrative functions.

Inspection territories varied depending primarily on the geographical location of the branch. An inspector in the New York branch, for instance, might have a territory a few square miles in size while his counterpart in the Denver branch might cover an area 300 by 400 miles. Travelling time ranged up to 30% of an inspector's total time, though a typical figure was 15%. In addition, Mr. Kemmler estimated that an inspector spent 15% of his day writing reports. According to Mr. Kemmler, an inspector was completely responsible for scheduling his workday, though he did have certain required inspections in a given time period. In most branches, inspectors rarely came into the branch, conducting most company business by mail and telephone from their homes. Mr. Kemmler felt that this certain degree of freedom to plan one's own time was an attractive fringe benefit for a prospective inspector.

Time required for inspections ranged from three minutes for standard risks such as an air tank to more than several weeks for examination of a large complex turbine or compressor. A chief inspector familiar with the types and number of objects in his territory "works up what he feels is a proper workload for each of his inspectors," explained Mr. Kemmler. "This is done by hand, but by people who know the territory and who know what has to be done." Typically, an inspector averaged between 5 and 20 inspections per day for standard equipment and between 1 and 20 per week on complex machinery. Approximately 10% of HSB's insured objects were considered to be "complex" objects requiring more inspection time, and these objects were generally distributed evenly throughout the branch system.

While the chief inspector was portrayed as slightly lower on the organization chart than the branch manager, the inspector maintained veto power over risks to be insured. If a risk did not meet the company standards, the inspector could prevent it from being insured, though if the client was large and the reason for rejection small or correctable, the risk could be insured for "agency reasons" at the discretion of the home office. Not all HSB employees felt that this veto power was an optimal situation. Said one HSB employee: "The *de facto* social system is that the chief inspector runs the branch manager's life. That creates an enormous problem. The engineers see themselves as the saviors of the company, the technicians who keep the lunatic salesmen and underwriters honest."

UNDERWRITING

Underwriters at HSB appraised objects to be insured and determined what premiums, deductibles and other financial conditions—if any—would make the object an acceptable risk for HSB. The home office staff included a Vice President, Mr. Robert Wolf, his Assistant Vice President, Mr. William Zindel, and three regional underwriters who had overall responsibility for the underwriting activities of between six and seven branches each. Additionally, an underwriting services staff of seven at the home office, which performed research and rating services for the regional managers, collected and analyzed data on the performance of the branch underwriting departments.

Each branch employed between 5 and 30 underwriters (an average branch had 15) who performed the largely clerical function of "rating," that is, formally evaluating the data necessary to make an underwriting decision according to prescribed rules and procedures established by the home office. Since there was no true underwriting involved in the jobs, the branch office underwriters were generally referred to as "raters."

According to Mr. Zindel, an underwriter faced five alternative choices with regard to a policy. He or she could: (1) take the risk in question; (2) reject it; (3) adjust the premium and/or deductible amounts to compensate for unusual risk exposure; (4) adjust the coverages applicable to certain objects to be covered; or (5) have the objects physically modified with the help of the engineering department to ensure conformity with regulations. This last option was exercised more frequently at HSB than was the case in most other insurance companies.

Administratively, branch office underwriters reported to the branch managers and, ultimately, to the agency department. From a functional standpoint, the underwriters received guidance from the home office underwriting department.

Branch underwriters handled the less hazardous risks, while larger risks were evaluated by the home office staff for a final decision. The branch underwriters did not normally accompany the agents or the inspectors in the field to see the smaller risk standardized items. The rates on such standard items were taken directly from a rate sheet.

On larger risks, the home office underwriters did go out into the field with the engineering staff to inspect risks. "You can gain a far better insight into just what it is you're insuring if you go out and see the damn thing instead of sitting here listening to someone else's description," explained Mr. Zindel. The price on larger risks was usually negotiated between HSB and the insured. The underwriting department wanted special agents to become more "underwriting oriented" to reduce the number of underwriting rejections of salesmen quotes.

Mr. Zindel was especially concerned about the motivation and morale of the underwriters in the branches and the resulting high turnover (greater than 20% per year). He felt that not only was the job frustrating without decision-making responsibility, but also that it was generally believed that there was no career path in underwriting.

SALES

The sales function was the branch manager's primary responsibility. Each branch employed "special agents" who were HSB's sales personnel and whose main task was to call on independent insurance agents of agency companies and induce them to sell HSB coverage rather than that of its competitors. A typical branch employed seven or eight special agents, though the number varied depending on the number of accounts and the amount of premium volume the branch generated.

The special agent had several responsibilities. One was to attract new accounts;

a second was to ensure renewal of policies in force. In addition, the special agents were usually conduits for any policy changes that the customer might initiate. The salesmen dealt with a wide range of risk and premium sizes, though the bulk of the special agents' business was in the smaller risk area. On the smaller risk policies, according to Hartford branch manager James G. Miller, the independent insurance agents were the company's "salesmen"; on these, HSB often made no contact with the insured and special agents rarely visited the insured's place of business.

HSB employees disagreed as to who the HSB customer was. According to one branch manager, the independent agent was the only true customer. "On small policies, since we rarely send special agents (HSB salespersons) out to the insured, the independent agent is the only real customer. On larger accounts, the boiler insurance may only be a small part of the total premium, so the insured isn't too concerned about who writes it. Either way, the independent agent controls the account." Mr. Wilson, the Agency Vice President, disagreed. "Some people say we have two customers, the independent agents and the ultimate purchaser of the policy," he explained. "I don't see it that way. The independent agents are just our marketing arm. We don't have direct solicitors or a high-powered sales force because we are paying 16% or 17% out to our producers (independent agents); our customer is the insured."

HSB's special agents spent a lot of time "beating the bushes" due to the relative unimportance of boiler insurance compared to other types of insurance and due to the fact that HSB's competitors often wrote other types of insurance. Generally, a special agent was expected to see or telephone as few as 3 or 4 to as many as 35 agents in one day.

There had been an increased interest on the part of the home office in generating more "major" accounts, accounts which contributed large annual premiums. Historically, major accounts were handled by the branches in the same manner as small ones, though the branch manager often visited major accounts with the selling agent. Recently Mr. Michael Moran was transferred from HSB's Canadian subsidiary to take charge of the home office major account marketing thrust. The Canadian subsidiary had traditionally done all major account marketing directly through its home office, not through branches, and Mr. Moran had been in charge of that effort.

There had been some concern about the major account marketing effort in certain quarters of the company. One branch manager was worried that, if an agent wrote the policy in Hartford directly from the home office, the agent would be the only person who could assist an insured who had a problem, even though a locally based branch manager might be much closer to the insured. Another questioned the economics of the decision: "We are probably making a heck of a lot more money on the $500 accounts than on the major ones if you look at the loss ratios. There's no reason to believe that we make more money on a large account."[1]

ADMINISTRATION

Administration, along with sales and marketing responsibilities, fell under the jurisdiction of the agency vice president, his assistants, and the branch managers. Administrative responsibilities included branch accounting, physical production of the policies, accountability for all customer service interfaces, staffing, salary and other personnel-related issues (not including engineering personnel).

In 1970 HSB began using its computer to store policy data, calculate premiums and actually print completed policies. As of the end of 1973, approximately 65% of the company's policies had been produced by computer. It was generally believed that 85% or more of the company's policies would one day be produced by computer.

While the branch manager held overall responsibility for the branch, his primary concern was sales, and approximately 70% of his time was devoted to some aspect of that responsibility. Reporting to the branch manager was an office manager who was the person directly in charge of the branch's policy production process.

FROM REQUEST TO DELIVERY

Typical workflow for the production of a new policy from request to delivery was as diagrammed in *Exhibit 6*. When a request for insurance was presented by or solicited from an independent agent (producer), the special agent assigned to that account performed a cursory inspection (survey), the insured filled out an application for insurance and the company issued a binder covering the insured until his completed policy was delivered and the insured could be billed. When a binder was issued, the special agent requested the inspection department in his branch to do the inspection required prior to policy issue by submitting a First Inspection Order (FIO) to the supervising inspector. When the FIO was completed by the field inspector and was approved by the supervising inspector, the company then proceeded to write the policy. If irregularities were discovered

---

1. Loss data by premium amount was not available, though the company expected to compile this data by early 1975. The casewriter developed estimates which are included in *Exhibit 5*. Also included are the estimates of inspection and sales commission expense ratios.

during the course of inspection, the special agent was notified as to the nature of and remedy for the fault.

With FIOs and approval completed, the branch office production machinery geared up. If the policy involved a fairly straightforward risk, the information on the application form was translated into machine language by "coders" using a data processing manual to guide their efforts. The data were then transferred to off-line terminals which connected with the home office computer twice daily for the transmission and reception of data on a batch basis.

Usually within 24 to 48 hours the computer transmitted policy information to the branch and a completed policy was then assembled and sent out to the agent and the insured. Any errors made in policy preparation were reported to the branch office when the batch transmission arrived from the home office; the errors were then corrected and the policy was retransmitted as a new one at the earliest possible time.

If the policy was rated and prepared manually, then the application and inspection data was handed to the branch office underwriters, who determined the appropriate premium rates, deductibles, and other parameters, using the rate manual and the underwriting handbooks. The policy was then typed on Magnetic Tape Selectric Typewriter (MTST) machines, checked, assembled and mailed. When the policy was sent out to the producer and the insured, both the policy data and the inspection data were given to the inspection records department where the required inspection slips were prepared. The slips were entered into the field inspectors' bibles—the slip books—which indicated when objects required inspections.

The focal point of the branch office inspection function was the slip desk where the thousands of inspection records and requirements were stored for easy access. A typical office with between 75,000 and 150,000 objects under its jurisdiction possessed about 200 4-inch thick looseleaf slip books; each contained approximately 200 pages. A slip was issued for an individual policy, not for an individual object, so the number of objects per slip could range from 1 to several hundred.

Inspection territories for field inspectors were assigned geographically, a situation which one office manager felt was less than optimal: "There is little flexibility or planning in the engineering area. No coordination. If in one day 50 FIOs—high-priority items—came in, they could all conceivably go to two inspectors. The other inspectors would continue to perform routine work." Each inspector possessed his own set of slip books corresponding to objects insured in his territory and worked primarily from that set of books.

The branch office managers generally felt they faced three related problems. One was that the home office had set a goal of 21 days for policy delivery; this goal was being met only on the simplest policies at some branches. The second was that inspections were often completed later than originally scheduled. This was the responsibility of the chief inspector but was a prime cause of slow policy delivery. A medium-sized branch might average 29 days for a First Inspection Order to be completed in the field, 11 days for the supervisory inspector to approve the FIO once completed, 10 days to underwrite the risk after the supervisory inspector's approval, and 10 days for filing, recording data and other miscellaneous tasks. The third problem was that interpersonal conflicts often arose between the branch managers and chief inspectors. According to most branch managers, if the chief inspector "went by the book" on all risks, big or small, the likelihood of conflict was great.

DEVELOPMENT OF COMPANY PLANS

As Wilson Wilde and other members of management had debated ways to cope with HSB's immediate problems of getting policies delivered more quickly and making sure those were profitable, several longer-term issues had been raised. These focused largely on the implications of major trends for HSB's business in the future and the need to clearly define the firm's products, markets and operations to compete effectively. Mr. Wilde hoped that appropriate plans could be developed that would fit both the company and its environment.

Exhibit 1
Comparative Income Statement*
(Dollar amounts in millions)

	6 Months 1974**	1973	1972	1971
Underwriting Income				
Premiums Written	$33.2	$62.4	$61.0	$55.8
Change in Unearned Premiums	(2.9)	(0.3)	(2.7)	(1.3)
Premiums Earned	30.3	62.1	58.3	54.5
Underwriting Expenses				
Losses & Loss Adjustment Exp.	12.2	21.5	18.1	13.7
Taxes (excl. Fed. Inc.)	1.4	2.5	2.2	2.1
Commissions	5.0	10.1	9.5	8.9
Inspection	6.4	12.4	11.2	10.7
General	6.5	12.4	11.0	10.5
Total Underwriting Expense	31.5	58.9	52.1	45.9
Underwriting Gain (Loss)	(1.2)	3.2	6.2	8.6
Net Investment Income	3.0	5.2	4.7	4.4
Net Income—Canadian Subsidiary	(0.2)	0.5	0.7	0.6
Income before Federal Income Taxes	1.6	9.0	11.5	13.6
Federal Income Taxes				
Current	(0.6)	1.8	2.6	4.6
Deferred	0.2	0.1	0.9	—
Total Federal Income Taxes	(0.4)	1.9	3.5	4.6
NET INCOME	2.0	7.1	8.0	8.9
NET INCOME PER SHARE ($)	$1.13	$3.94	$4.47	$4.99
(1.8 million shares outstanding)				

*Fiscal Year Ends December 31.

**Unaudited.

Exhibit 2
Analysis of Policies
Chart #1: Premium Size (by policy)

Premium Size ($000)	Number of Policies	Percent of Total Policies	Percent of Total Premium
0–0.1	3,077	3.7%	0.3
0.1–0.5	56,477	67.5	22.6
0.5–1	11,953	14.3	12.2
1–2	6,504	7.8	13.3
2–3	2,204	2.6	7.8
3–5	1,753	2.1	9.4
5–10	1,113	1.3	9.6
10–25	489	0.6	8.2
25–50	85	0.1	3.1
50–100	25	—	1.8
Over 100	29	—	11.6
Totals	83,709	100.0	99.9

Chart # 2: Location of Objects

Number of Object Locations for Policy	Number of Policies	Percent of Policies
1	71,486	85.4%
2	6,223	7.4
3	2,183	2.6
4	1,106	1.3
5	649	0.8
6–9	1,194	1.4
10–49	785	0.9
50–99	54	—
100–499	25	—
500–999	1	—
999 +	3	—
Total	83,709	99.8%

Chart # 3: Number of Objects

Number of Objects Insured	Number of Policies	Percent of Policies
1	20,687	24.7%
2	17,404	20.8
3	11,344	13.6
4	7,206	8.6
5	4,637	5.5
6–9	9,426	11.3
10–24	7,445	8.9
25–49	3,683	4.4
50–99	1,327	1.6
100–499	513	0.6
500–999	10	—
999 +	27	—
Total	83,709	100.0%

THE HARTFORD STEAM BOILER INSPECTION AND INSURANCE COMPANY

Exhibit 3

Boiler and Machinery Ins. Earned Prem. and Losses—Major Co's.

(000's Omitted)

	Earned Premium					Incurred Losses					Loss Ratio				
	'69	'70	'71	'72	'73	'69	'70	'71	'72	'73	'69	'70	'71	'72	'73
HSB	40,193	45,487	53,620	56,931	60,167	10,384	13,900	12,341	16,463	19,044	26%	31%	23%	29%	31.7%
Factory Mutual Cos.	19,329	23,534	28,789	31,961	34,547	8,342	9,284	9,236	13,310	24,081	43%	39%	32%	42%	69.7%
Kemper Group	10,925	12,012	13,641	14,771	15,580	5,643	6,348	5,005	6,112	7,189	52%	53%	37%	43%	46.1%
Employer's Comm. Union	7,892	8,794	10,098	9,455	10,315	2,378	3,551	3,049	2,332	3,695	30%	40%	30%	25%	35.8%
Continental Ins. Co.	6,236	7,405	8,001	8,194	8,008	2,128	2,428	2,616	2,203	1,825	34%	33%	33%	27%	22.8%
Travelers Group	6,870	7,068	8,253	6,973	7,101	2,144	416	1,880	2,070	760	31%	6%	23%	36%	10.7%
Zurich American Grp.	3,905	4,392	5,266	5,566	5,908	2,119	977	2,096	1,537	3,452	54%	22%	40%	28%	58.4%
Royal-Globe Ins. Co. Grp.	5,176	5,693	5,025	3,137	4,698	3,874	3,137	2,017	2,060	1,334	75%	55%	40%	56%	28.4%
Home Group (Ins.)	2,833	3,298	3,488	3,361	3,689	1,098	1,313	1,706	1,089	1,296	39%	40%	49%	32%	35.1%
Maryland Casualty	6,678	8,232	3,856	3,605	3,116	1,959	4,112	1,837	1,130	717	29%	50%	48%	31%	22.6%
Chubb (Inc. P.I.)	1,456	1,721	2,231	2,295	2,236	379	360	340	1,366	629	26%	21%	15%	60%	28.1%
Crum & Forster Grp.	514	705	922	1,111	1,106	228	106	319	501	84	44%	15%	35%	45%	7.6%
Continental Nat'l. Am.	990	1,162	1,309	1,147	1,069	83	413	285	118	270	8%	36%	22%	9%	25.2%
New Hampshire Grp.	345	488	602	552	633	149	131	301	174	92	43%	27%	50%	32%	14.6%
Total	113,445	129,991	145,101	149,059	158,223	40,908	46,476	43,028	50,465	64,468	36%	36%	30%	34%	40.7%

HSB as % of Earned Premium: 1969—35.4%; 1970—35.0%; 1971—37.0%; 1972—38.2%; 1973—38.0%.
HSB as % of All Losses: 1969—25.4%; 1970—30.0%; 1971—28.7%; 1972—32.6%; 1973—29.5%.

Industry Five-Year Growth: 28%.
HSB Five-Year Growth: 33%.
Industry Five-Year Growth excluding HSB: 25%.

THE HARTFORD STEAM BOILER INSPECTION AND INSURANCE COMPANY

Exhibit 4

Domestic Organization Chart*

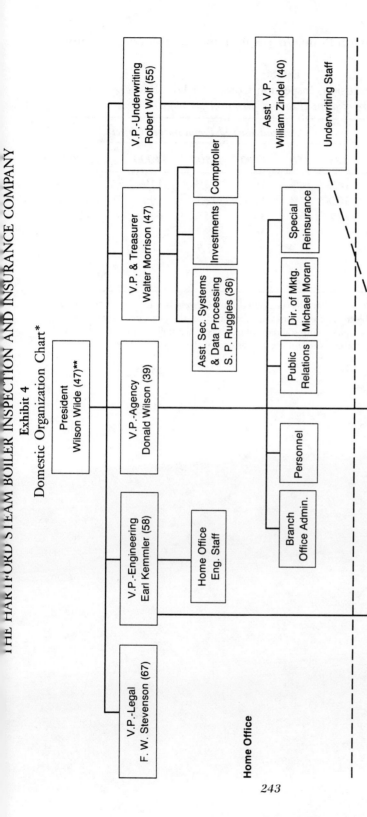

Home Office

President
Wilson Wilde (47)**

V.P.-Legal
F. W. Stevenson (67)

V.P.-Engineering
Earl Kemmler (58)

Home Office
Eng. Staff

V.P.-Agency
Donald Wilson (39)

V.P. & Treasurer
Walter Morrison (47)

V.P.-Underwriting
Robert Wolf (55)

Asst. Sec. Systems
& Data Processing
S. P. Ruggles (36)

Investments

Comptroller

Branch
Office Admin.

Personnel

Public
Relations

Dir. of Mktg.
Michael Moran

Special
Reinsurance

Asst. V.P.
William Zindel (40)

Underwriting Staff

Branch Office

Branch
Managers

20

Office
Managers

20

Special
Agents

Branch
Underwriters

Office Clerical
Employees

Chief
Inspectors

20

Field
Inspectors

730

*Total employees: 1,850. Home office employees: 350.

**Numbers in parentheses indicate age.

243

Exhibit 5
Sales Commission, Inspection Costs, and Loss Ratio
(By size of annual earned premium per object)

	Annual Earned Premium per Object [1]					
	$25	*$50*	*$100*	*$500*	*$1000*	*$10,000*
Sales Commission	18%	16%	16%	13%	11%	7%
Inspection Costs	30%	22%	19%	16%	10%	4%
Loss Ratio	25%	33%	35%	35%	42%	52%
Total Dollars (000,000 of Annual Earned Premium, based on policies in force as of August 15, 1974)	8.8	21.4	22.7	7.9	3.8	3.0

[1] The case writer divided the 1 million objects insured into 6 categories by size of the annual earned premium for each object. The categories are identified by the estimated average earned premium per category. The simpler, more standard objects were, naturally, on the lower end of the scale; the more complex objects were on the higher end of the scale.

Exhibit 6
Typical Branch Office Workflow

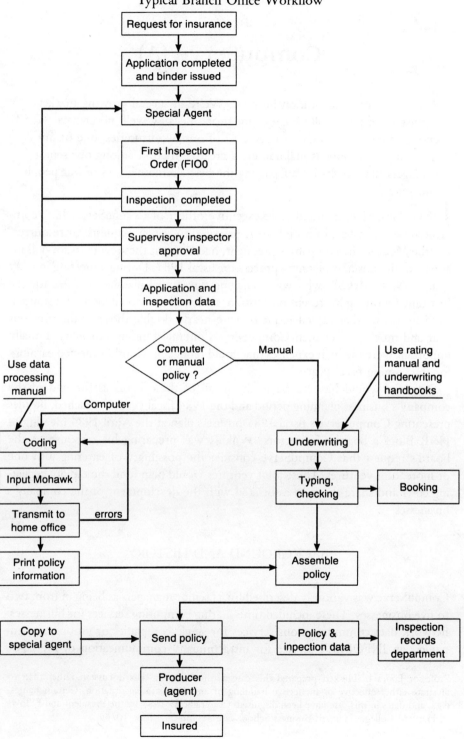

CompuServe (A)

This is a resource allocation business. We're in several growing markets against some potentially huge competitors. Because we'll never have enough time and money to pursue all of our opportunities, one of my most important jobs is maintaining a creative friction among our senior managers that results in our picking the best alternative uses of our people and funds.

Jeff Wilkins, chairman and chief executive officer of CompuServe, Inc., commented on one aspect of his job as he prepared to review requests for resources. Charlie McCall, the company's president, had brought these requests to Wilkins as part of the business planning process for fiscal 1985. During a meeting in early March 1984, McCall, who was managing the annual planning process for the first time following his recent promotion, reviewed individual items and summarized by saying that capital requests were nearly double those of the previous year and much greater than CompuServe's internal funding capability. Equally important were the high expenses that could reduce previously expected earnings for the coming fiscal year.

Decisions would have to be made on all of these items as the end of the company's business planning period and the 1984 fiscal year approached. Besides presenting CompuServe's fiscal 1985 business plan at the April 1984 meeting of H&R Block's board of directors, Wilkins was preparing his response to the board's request that CompuServe consider the possibility of entering into one or more joint ventures. These joint ventures would help fund the rapidly escalating costs and share the risks associated with the development of the company's businesses.

BACKGROUND AND HISTORY

CompuServe was variously described by its senior managers as being in from two to five businesses. These included time-sharing computing services for businesses; network data communications services for single companies or groups of companies; an INFOPLEX service for intracompany communication of messages,

Professor James L. Heskett prepared this case as the basis for class discussion rather than to illustrate either effective or ineffective handling of an administrative situation. Certain names, data, and dates in this case have been disguised. Copyright © 1985 by the President and Fellows of Harvard College; Harvard Business School case #9-386-067 Rev. 10/89.

data, and information; and two related types of videotex services, called Executive Information Service (EIS) and Consumer Information Service (CIS), each supplying a wide range of information and communicating capability to users of personal computers who connected themselves to the CompuServe network by telephone modems.

The company was established in 1969 in Columbus, Ohio, as a subsidiary of the ILEX Corporation. CompuServe provided in-house computer processing support to another ILEX subsidiary, Golden United Life Insurance Company, and developed its own markets outside ILEX for time-shared and batch-processed computer services.[1]

Among those recruited to manage the new company was Jeffrey Wilkins, the son-in-law of Harry Gard, president of ILEX. Wilkins was running a burglar alarm company that he had founded in Arizona and had recently completed a master's degree in electrical engineering at the University of Arizona. To Wilkins, CompuServe represented the opportunity that he and a classmate, Alexander (Sandy) Trevor, had said they would take advantage of together when they graduated. But there were questions to be resolved, according to Wilkins:

> I realized I had a need for independence. If I were to come back to Columbus, it was important for me to have a clear understanding with my father-in-law that I would have to be able to run the show. When I put it to him, all he said was, "All I ask for is a plan." When I had put it together and it showed that we would need $500,000 before we reached a break-even cash flow, I thought he would never buy it. It seemed like a lot of money to me. After all, my wife and I would have to borrow $1,000 just to be able to make the move back to Columbus without any family help. But once he saw the plan, he approved it immediately; it was my first important lesson about the power of carefully prepared business plans, particularly for those who don't understand your business well. It was to come in handy later.

With the rapid growth of both CompuServe and Golden United, ILEX directors decided it would be in CompuServe's best interests to become a separate company. It was spun off to ILEX shareholders in 1975, with Gard and Wilkins assuming the positions of chairperson and president, respectively. Barely 30 years old, Wilkins doubled his efforts to shape the company as an aggressive upstart by seeking new customers for existing services and by offering new services that reflected the rapidly changing computing and communications capabilities and needs of existing and potential customers.

The introduction of minicomputers that might replace time-sharing services

1. Some of the background information is based on the case "CompuServe (A)," S-BP-195A (Stanford University Graduate School of Business, 1979).

spurred CompuServe's management to develop new avenues of growth. One such avenue was provided by alternative uses of an expanded communications network employed by CompuServe in its basic business. Also, the introduction of personal computers in 1978 presaged a new era in computing, one in which Wilkins wanted his company to participate.

To capitalize on the opportunities that CompuServe's management envisioned, investments in network, hardware, software, and people would be needed. CompuServe could not fund these investments. According to Wilkins:

> Our Executive Committee, at the time, concluded that in order to compete in this industry, we would have to be a big player. This meant one of several things: 50% growth per year, which we knew we couldn't sustain; acquisitions (we had made one and lost all the people in the acquired company); or getting acquired. Concluding that it might have to be the latter, we formed some criteria, deciding that our parent (1) should have a lot of cash, (2) should not be in our business, and (3) should have a mature management team, offering upward mobility for CompuServe's managers. In 1979, we were getting an offer a week. In November, I contacted H&R Block [the world's largest preparers of individual income tax returns], went to Kansas City, and immediately liked what I saw and heard. It was clear that they didn't know our business and would let us run it. They met the other criteria as well.[2] An important matter that I insisted on was that I had to have a seat on H&R Block's board in order to learn more about the company and manage our relationship more intelligently.

In May 1980, H&R Block acquired CompuServe for $10.3 million in cash and 510,615 shares of H&R Block stock valued at about $12.5 million. CompuServe's shares were held by 12,000 stockholders, nearly all owners of Golden United insurance policies. Gard (with 7% of the shares), Wilkins (5%), and McCall, then a CompuServe vice president (2%), were the largest beneficiaries of the sale.

After the sale, Wilkins's assumptions about H&R Block proved to be correct. By the end of the 1984 fiscal year, CompuServe's annual revenues were projected to reach $51.7 million, yielding income to its parent of $5 million before tax. H&R Block was planning to report in its 1984 annual report that "With [CompuServe's] strategic directions firmly established, and initial technological and market development outlays made in fiscal 1982 and 1983 to support those directions substantially behind them, financial results advanced in line with objec-

---

2. In the fiscal year that ended on April 30, 1980, H&R Block had earned more than $32 million after taxes on revenues of roughly $229,600,000. At the time, it had a current ratio of 3.5 to 1, only about $1 million in long-term debt, and stockholders' equity of $133 million.

tives and long-term plans." (See *Exhibits 1* and *2* for CompuServe's internal financial statements for fiscal years 1981 through 1984.)

LINES OF BUSINESS

During the first 14 years of its existence, CompuServe was unique in its industry because it consistently earned a profit. In part, this was due to the sequential development of its businesses, starting with computer services centered around traditional data processing.

Computer Services

CompuServe was founded to maintain a service bureau relationship, primarily with Golden United Insurance and then with other clients. An early manager of the company's technical development was Sandy Trevor. Wilkins described Trevor as "a first-rate technical guy, but also good philosophically and someone with a broad perspective."

Computer services generally encompassed three categories: data services, facilities management, and software and support services. Initially, computer service companies sold computer time and processing services to companies that could not afford their own. As a customer's needs grew and justified its owning or leasing a computer, it often purchased facilities management from its former data-processing supplier. Originally, the equipment manufacturer developed the computer programs. As the users' needs increasingly diversified, however, computer service companies produced these programs. CompuServe rapidly acquired capabilities in all three areas. It concentrated on services with value-added content and built long-term client relationships that allowed CompuServe to develop custom-designed hardware and software, through Trevor's group, that not only added value but also reduced costs. This gave CompuServe an advantage over its competitors. In 1976, the company established a research and development center in Tucson, Arizona to develop state-of-the-art hardware (particularly devices peripheral to a mainframe computer) and software.

By the late 1970s, five trends were cited as responsible for significant changes occurring in the industry:

1. The development of minicomputers encouraged former customers to take some data-processing functions in-house.
2. Software offerings were becoming more sophisticated and more competitive. As equipment costs decreased and the use of custom-designed soft-

ware increased, the computer services industry became labor intensive, focusing on people.

3. There was a move toward both hardware and software compatibility.
4. A new group of competitors was entering the market.
5. Increasing market consolidation through acquisitions had begun, as larger computer service companies sought to enter new markets, acquire desirable products, and add to their existing customer base and pool of professional talent.

Some computer service companies saw this as a threat to traditional processing and time-sharing services. Other companies viewed it as an opportunity to offer new data-management services. At the time, CompuServe developed a program in which a client, in effect, could buy a piece of a machine. When the client's needs grew, CompuServe would sell an entire machine and manage it.

Industry consolidation began as service companies focused on specific industries and tailored software development and marketing efforts to them in an attempt to sell high value-added services. Acquisitions became commonplace. Automated Data Processing alone bought 13 smaller service companies between January 1976 and December 1978. Tymshare Inc. had made 12 acquisitions since 1971. And 2 of the top 10 companies in the industry had been bought. National CSS by Dun & Bradstreet and On-Line Systems by United Telecommunications. In fact, the convergence of computers and communications brought potential competition into the industry.

In the summer of 1978, American Telephone and Telegraph Co. (AT&T) introduced a proposed service to the Federal Communications Commission called Advanced Communications Service (ACS), which would allow equipment from different manufacturers that used different computer languages to communicate compatibly over telephone lines. IBM, Comsat, and Aetna Insurance also formed a joint venture, Satellite Business Systems (SBS) in 1977. SBS's purpose was to build and operate a domestic satellite communications network to provide customers with integrated voice, data, and video capability. This network employed all-digital transmission without using any telephone company equipment.

By 1978, CompuServe's revenues of $15.7 million placed it in the top 10 computer services companies, albeit near the bottom of that list. These 10 companies realized nearly $900 million in revenues in 1978. Automated Data Processing headed the list with $300 million, closely followed by Computer Services Co. Tymshare Inc. was the only other company with over $50 million in revenue.

Concerned about confining itself to a maturing computer services business with large and more numerous potential competitors, CompuServe's management turned to communications as a natural means of product diversification.

Electronic Mail

Upon request in 1975 from an important customer who was experiencing information delay among his plants, CompuServe developed an intracompany communications system that was easy to use and inexpensive to operate. After three years of successful operation, CompuServe's management decided to market the service in 1978 under the name INFOPLEX.

A year after its introduction, with five customers using the service, revenues from sales of INFOPLEX were below expectations. Nevertheless, following a successful six-month pilot project for the Owens-Corning Fiberglas Corporation of Toledo, INFOPLEX sales began to pick up. A team, headed by George Minot, marketed INFOPLEX. Clark Woodford, later to be named vice president of telecommunications services, was on the team along with six sales representatives and two technical support people.

Among the competitors beginning to develop the electronic mail business were Telenet, Dial-Com, and General Electric Information Services Company (GEISCO). The latter, in 1984, claimed to be the largest in the industry. As soon as smaller competitors had provided early market development, companies such as AT&T and IBM were expected to become more aggressive players. Although the advent of personal computers rejuvenated the business in the early 1980s, industry sales were estimated to be about $100 million in 1984, with modest growth projected to 1990. By fiscal 1984, CompuServe reported about $6 million in revenues from INFOPLEX.

Network Services

The computer service business required that CompuServe maintain a network of leased lines to allow time-sharing on its host computers and for data communication with its customers. This network could be leased to firms that desired communications links with customers or suppliers.

By mid-1984, intercompany network services were growing much more rapidly than intracompany networks. Developed in 1980 by CompuServe and managed, along with INFOPLEX, by Woodford, intercompany communications services had blossomed into an industry with $320 million in sales in 1984, projected to be $2 billion by 1990.

CompuServe's competitive advantages in network services were its ability to build a network with operating costs and customer charges significantly lower than AT&T's Wide Area Telephone Service (WATS). Because, according to Woodford, "Users have to be able to get at information they need," it was important to understand a customer and tailor a network to his needs in developing network services. For example, CompuServe's network services included a system called Plastivision. It linked customers with Borg-Warner Chemical's ABS Plastics Division and provided the latest information available on the materials, specifications, and design capabilities of its products.

Telenet and Tymnet, both with annual revenues approximating $140 million, were considered the leaders in network services. In contrast, CompuServe's goal for fiscal 1985 was a market share of about 2%. It appeared likely that the goal would be met when CompuServe announced a new contract with VISA for a credit authorization network to be used by VISA's retail customers. At the outset, this single account was expected to yield $250,000 per month in revenue, with a volume of three million transactions per month. VISA's natural growth and the possibility of 100% credit authorization (that is, verifying transactions below $50) meant that the system could be processing as many as 90 million transactions per month by 1990. Tymnet was developing a similar system for MasterCard.

The VISA contract pointed up the next constraint on the growth of network services. This was network capacity. According to Woodford, only 160 cities were connected to the network; more were needed. This required significant additional investment and management time. As Woodford stated:

> Each new network node requires that we research the coverage of each telephone exchange in the city to determine the one that will give our customers the lowest cost coverage. Then we look to see whether we can place our network switch in an H&R Block office, where we have better access and can get more effective service than in other rented facilities. The only problem is that Block offices are moved, or their telephone numbers are changed, and we aren't notified.

Network customers paid an access charge as well as a charge per transaction. According to Woodford, "As long as you prove that you're reasonable in both, then service is the difference." CompuServe's service was considered equal to or better than that of its competitors. One reason for this was that the company manufactured its own switches. Trevor pointed out that this allowed the company to build greater reliability and serviceability into its switches than those used by competitors:

> When you know that you're not going to sell them to others, you don't have to make the switches pretty. For example, we put in an extra large fan designed to reduce operating temperatures and associated service costs. And we design the switches to give us just the amount of power we need. But most important, we build in a microprocessor that can be accessed by telephone directly from Columbus. This enables us to perform much of our service by remote control.

Woodford estimated that Telenet employed 300 people to service its 1,200 nodes. Thirty-five people serviced CompuServe's 700 nodes in 160 cities. Ninety percent of CompuServe's problems were fixed without sending anyone to the site. CompuServe's manufacturing facility could produce about 25 switches per month in the spring of 1984.

Network services were sold along with other CompuServe products through the company's 29 branches, staffed with 120 sales representatives, account representatives, account executives, and branch managers. These branches were under the direction of Bob Massey, vice president of direct sales. In addition, five specialists who worked with the branches to sell network services, eight network technical specialists who were troubleshooters, and one person who designed educational seminars for electronic-mail users reported to Woodford. The sales process for a new network account was complex, requiring design consultation and a presale relationship that often extended over many months.

Consumer Information Services

With the development and likely popularization of the personal computer, a small group of CompuServe's managers, led by Wilkins, decided that the company should develop and offer an information service to personal computer owners. They could access the company's network by telephone modems connected to their computers. At first, the primary market was envisioned as limited to computer owners who could afford the equipment, including managers in large or small businesses.

The new service would utilize the videotex technology that CompuServe employed in its intracompany network service. Sales for home use would increase usage of CompuServe's nearly idle capacity during nonbusiness hours and provide low-cost entry into the consumer information service business.

Among the original services in the package offered to individuals were (1) third-party software, for which CompuServe paid royalties to the software's producers based on volume of sales; (2) historical stock market quotations; (3) single- or multi-player electronic games; (4) a "Bulletin Board" listing of ads and messages; and (5) nonprime raw time for computer access.

According to John Meier, vice president of market development and services, who was one of the few early supporters of the new service:

In August 1979, we offered a not-very-friendly service to computer hobbyists. We were a month behind a service called The Source getting into the market. We called our service MicroNet and thought it was just a hell of a name. To show you just how naive we were, we chose for our test group the Midwest Affiliated Computer Clubs, whose members could build an electronic circuit out of a bucket of sand. But we lucked out. They promptly suggested a service that has become one of the most popular with our customers, the Special Interest Group (SIG), which allows owners of a particular brand of computer, for example, to exchange information. Of course, the idea works for any other group with special interests as well.

McCall pointed out that some of the company's most successful products had received little research. He recalled how one of CompuServe's most popular consumer services was introduced:

Sandy Trevor had bought and was playing with the consumer service offered by The Source. It included something called CHAT that allowed their users to talk to each other. One day, Sandy came to our Executive Committee meeting and suggested we offer something like it. No one paid much attention to him, and we went on to the next item on the agenda. So Sandy went home that weekend, programmed a service he called CB, and put it on the menu without discussing it any further. It allows groups of people, each with a "handle," to communicate, just like citizens band radio. But if two people want to get more personal, they can lock out everyone else. That service now logs more time than any other in CIS except Special Interest Groups.

Four significant developments put CompuServe much more seriously into consumer information services during the summer of 1980. First, CompuServe entered into a Newspaper Information Provider experiment with the Associated Press and 11 major newspapers to provide news to computer users. The modestly successful experiment yielded considerable consumer data that CompuServe could not have obtained otherwise. Second, an improved videotex core technology called DISPLAY was built. Third, an agreement was reached in which Tandy would distribute starter kits for the consumer service through its Radio Shack retail outlets. Finally, the name MicroNet was changed to Consumer Information Service (CIS).

Meier felt that CIS had several important effects on the company:

We've been able to survive by hedging our bets and staying light on our feet. And we didn't overreact when it looked like our computer services business was going down the drain. But there is a very strong industrial culture that we ran up against when CIS was proposed. At first, those who had little interest in it humored us along because CIS represented a possible use of off-peak capacity. But then, when we asked for an advertising budget, I was the only one in the management group with a consumer product background. When we proposed it and H&R Block bought the idea, the reaction among several of our team was, "They've lost their heads." But even more important, making computers accessible and user-friendly has taken its toll on some of the people who've built the company. It has been difficult for them to get used to the idea of hiding the technology for a vast audience as opposed to making the technology more explicit for a small audience. And it has retarded our development of the consumer services business.

The introduction and marketing of CIS gave CompuServe visibility among its industrial customers and the management at H&R Block. One CompuServe executive said that until then "the people at Block were worried that they never saw our name in print alongside the major players. That increased their perception of the risks involved in our competitive strategies."

By the end of fiscal 1984, CIS had 120,000 subscribers and was signing on 7,000 new ones each month. Although the number of subscribers might be misleading, because there was no incentive for a user to discontinue the service (as in The Source), it suggested that CompuServe was the leader in consumer information services.

The product had been enhanced greatly since its introduction. Nearly any service that met a threshold level of relevance was added to CIS. The assumption was that the fixed cost was low and the total product would benefit from the availability of the widest possible range of services. Thus, as of early 1984, subscribers could choose from over 800 different services, generally grouped around core products that offered communication, entertainment, information, education, or social interaction benefits. Efforts were being made to improve certain services. For example, TWA's PARS reservation system was available to users in the fall of 1984 to supplement CIS's complete listings of the *Official Airline Guide*. With these two services, a user could access flight information; make a reservation; pay for the ticket by designating a credit card number; and arrange for tickets to be issued by a travel agency, through the mail, or by a participating airline ticket office.

CompuServe had conducted home banking experiments with Huntington National Bank, based in Columbus, Ohio. Paul Ayres, director of electronic delivery of banking services for Huntington, was quoted as saying:

> There are not great masses of people beating down our doors for this service. . . . Having the services available through CompuServe is a big plus because the customer can get a variety of services. You are not just limited to banking.[3]

3. Tim Miller, "It's a Matter of Small Steps—Not Giant Leaps," *Business First Magazine Columbus*, March 18, 1985, p. 6.

CIS was about to expand its retail offerings to include what was described in the 1984 H&R Block Annual Report as "potentially the most important . . . [new feature], the Electronic Mall, in a joint venture with L. M. Berry, a leading Yellow Pages publisher based in Dayton. The Mall, open and on-line 24 hours a day, offers subscribers the ability to order goods and services from national retailers (including firms such as Sears, Bloomingdale's, Waldenbooks, and Record World) . . . from their homes." The Mall sold goods at retail by presenting advertising and display material from each of the more than 20 stores represented as well as other advertisers. This supplemented CIS's offering of Comp-U-Card's shopping service and offered at deep-price discounts a wide range of durable goods not associated with any one retailer. CompuServe planned to license the Electronic Mall service to other on-line services such as The Source and Dow Jones News Service.

CompuServe had committed substantial investments for the marketing of CIS throughout its short history. For example, when revenues were barely $2 million, $1.6 million was committed for advertising in the following year. The proposed fiscal 1985 advertising budget for CIS was $3.7 million, and included nearly $1 million for the production and use of the company's first television advertising.

CompuServe's marketing research indicated that 96% of CIS subscribers were male, 51% were married, 54% had one graduate degree or more, and 45% had an income of $45,000 or more. Research also indicated that children were heavy users of certain services such as games, CB, and Special Interest Groups.

CIS was marketed through three channels. These included a network of about 8,200 retailers of computer-related products who sold "starter kits" that included instructions, an application form for a CIS account, and five hours of free time on the service for a suggested retail price of $39.95. Starter kits also were distributed by computer manufacturers as part of their product offering, the cost being absorbed by the manufacturer. CompuServe began to rely on direct mail and advertising that featured direct-response coupons to reach the many potential users who did not subscribe when they purchased their personal computers. Direct-marketing efforts increasingly were creating friction between CompuServe and its retailers.

In the spring of 1984, CompuServe's management closely followed the development of three competing services: the Dow Jones News Service, The Source (purchased when The Reader's Digest Association experienced financial difficulty), and Viewtron, a subsidiary of Knight-Ridder, one of the largest newspaper publishing chains. Comparative profiles of the strategies of CompuServe's competitors for the consumer information services market were prepared by a study team composed of CompuServe associates and appear in *Exhibit 3*.

All of these ventures were well financed through their parent companies. For example, it was widely reported that Viewtron would cost Knight-Ridder a $17 million charge against earnings before taxes in 1984. In addition, IBM, Sears, and CBS announced a joint venture called Trintex to provide a news, information, and transactions service to homes in 1986. J.C. Penney, RCA, and Citicorp were also thought to be discussing a similar venture.

Executive Information Service

One CompuServe executive described the Executive Information Service (EIS) as a "case in itself. Nobody knows what to do with it. We got into it when Jeff just said 'we want to do EIS.' There is a question whether it is a separate product or a consumer product adapted for the business market."

The EIS offered individuals various business-oriented services, including CompuServe's complete line of financial services; tools to process the information, including spreadsheet analysis capabilities; INFOPLEX electronic mail services; electronic conferencing; as well as the full range of news, travel, and shopping features of CIS.

Average per-hour revenues to CompuServe for the EIS were $15 compared with $6.50 for CIS. In addition, the starter kit cost $100 as opposed to prices as low as $19.95 for CIS. Consequently, it was important that CompuServe seek out information providers (IPs) such as Lotus and Printing Industries of America to obtain products with broad appeal to the EIS market.

It appeared that EIS's closest competitor was the Dow Jones News Service, although according to one internal report, it was difficult to explain differences in the needs that EIS, Dow Jones, or The Source filled. Rather, the emphasis was on repackaging existing products with a business appeal and adding products necessary to be in the business in order to identify products that satisfied needs within particular industry niches.

There was not universal agreement about CompuServe's product strategy. Dissenting comments were voiced by several senior managers, including the following: "CIS and EIS were strictly gorilla projects; Lord help the person who would have stepped in front of either of them." "We make a clear decision to go, then 'muddle,' à la electronic mail, a missed opportunity." "We have trouble killing a product around here."

OPERATING STRATEGY

Besides its product-oriented marketing and operating groups, throughout its history CompuServe sought to achieve competitive advantage on cost and quality of service through its operations. It was one of the largest users of DEC equipment, employing 35 KI10 and KL10 host computers in its two facilities located several miles apart near Columbus, Ohio. The company leased a network of long-lines from AT&T for use in its network services and from GTE's Telenet and Tymshare's Tymnet for use in its consumer services. CompuServe designed and manufactured switching and other devices in its own plant and developed software to manage the system. By 1984, all capabilities on the system were interactive as opposed to an earlier emphasis on batch processing.

With each new piece of business, a circuit was built to connect the customer to the appropriate host computer. Most software and data were available on all hosts, but with the expansion of business, it was possible to program less of a mix of business per host, allowing a custom-tuning of the operating system. This produced increased capacity on some hosts by as much as 30% in memory and up to 50% in processing. The company also developed its own disc controller, buying a basic unit from Telefile, building a channel interface, and developing special programs that increased the disc transfer rate by as much as 50%. In sum, these efforts allowed CompuServe to accommodate as many as 10,000 simultaneous users (the overall measure of capacity) on its host computers, more than twice the capacity quoted by DEC in its sales literature. Because of the extensive alterations that were made in hardware, CompuServe performed its own maintenance of DEC and other equipment.

The group that was responsible for managing the central computing units also helped to price the products. The group's manager, Trevor, said:

> I'm the chief technical officer, so why would I price a product? But I do. I obviously want to cover costs, whatever they are [smile].[4] That's sometimes hard to determine, given the high proportion of shared facilities and operations. For example, only about 10% of network activity is directly attributable to the network services business. Facility sharing has given us both a competitive advantage and a cushion for learning how to price new products. For example, with consumer services, we were pricing a product that required no additional computer mainframe capability, given the fact that most of this usage was in off-peak evening hours. In contrast, experiments like Viewtron don't have that kind of cushion.

Basic prices for unsurcharged consumer services, for example, were $6.25 per hour for connect time between 5 P.M. and 8 A.M. and $12.50 per hour for daytime usage for 300 baud (a measure of communication speed) capability. Services that required more capacity per user, such as the *Official Airline Guide*

---

4. Because of the high proportion of joint costs that were incurred in the production of CompuServe's products, analyses of product profitability were thought to have limited relevance for decision-making purposes.

file, were assessed a surcharge. Given the growth of CIS, it appeared that soon the peak usage time would be early evening hours on week nights.

Senior managers occasionally voiced concerns about CompuServe's operating philosophy: "There definitely is a not-invented-here syndrome in this company." "If the question is build or buy, there is a bias to build." A particular concern was that management, with its industrial service orientation, had a bias for providing the same high level of service to all customers. As one manager stated, "We can't provide the same high level of service to consumers that we provide to our large commercial customers. Do we have the ability to design service levels for two distinct markets?"

ORGANIZATION AND CULTURE

Every member of CompuServe's top management joined the company between 1970 and 1977. In addition to Sandy Trevor, Charlie McCall was hired from Control Data, where he had been affiliated with the Service Bureau Corporation before IBM had been forced to sell it in an earlier antitrust consent decree. Although Jeff Wilkins would later rate McCall's ability to manage operations very highly as well, McCall took over responsibilities for marketing.

Shortly afterward, Bob Massey and Maury Cox were hired from the same company, and Clark Woodford was hired from IBM. Barry Berkov joined the company in 1977 from Xerox. He was preceded by John Meier, who became corporate commercial director in 1976 after consulting for CompuServe while serving as a marketing consultant with an industrial-design firm.

Judy Schenk, who by 1984 was vice president of human resources, joined the company in 1974 at the suggestion of a friend who was an assistant to Wilkins. At the time, she was an accounting clerk in a local firm. According to Schenk:

> Looking back, those were very exciting and sometimes scary times. I was brought into accounting. At the time, I told Jeff that I didn't know a lot about accounting. But he told me that with a friend of his, Dave Swaddling, joining the firm to manage finance, someone with the professional business experience I had could get by all right. A year later, the need for a personnel function became apparent. Jeff asked me to head that up, in spite of the fact that I told him I hadn't worked in personnel. I guess the most important qualification for any job was whether you were a CompuServe "type," whether you had a diverse set of experiences (especially with "whole" jobs) and interests, a "can-do, will-do" attitude, decision-making ability, receptiveness to change and an openness to new ideas, and an ability to work in small groups. There was a lot of emphasis on fitting jobs to people. When

Jeff hired George Minot [director of government marketing in 1984], I had to find him a job. We found out what George could do and tailored a job to his capabilities.

The final member of the 1984 senior management team, Dave Swaddling, joined the firm in 1975. Wilkins hired him from a Big Eight public accounting firm after meeting him at a private school. Wilkins was treasurer of the school and realized that Swaddling's background qualified him to take over that position.

Swaddling's associates described him as having a combination of numerical capability with a "big-picture view" of the company, as being entrepreneurial in his financial role, and as "definitely having Wilkins's ear." (After the sale of the company to H&R Block, Swaddling's job changed to what was variously described as helping Wilkins prepare for his meetings with H&R Block's management; concentration on the mentoring of younger people; and managing the design and construction of CompuServe's plush new office facilities, which would replace the small, spartan offices that all CompuServe executives occupied. Swaddling also was responsible for developing and maintaining a model of the firm that translated sales goals and capacity plans into headcount estimates, financial operating plans, and capital investments. (The model suggested that CompuServe's operating performance was much more sensitive to headcount increases than to additional capital expenditures.) Associates concurred with Wilkins's opinion that in selecting senior associates, except perhaps for Swaddling, he attempted to find people whose skills complemented his.

A recently hired manager of human resources, Chriss Douds, described her impression of the company:

Jeff Wilkins persuaded me to come with CompuServe about a year ago. At the time, I was managing human resources for [a local bank].

Here I found what I would call an achievement culture. You're respected for the job you do, not who you are or the number of degrees you have. Everyone is on a first-name basis. People are all called associates, and there is a heavy emphasis on self-direction.

As for facilities, as you can see, there isn't much fuss about offices. They are now spread through five separate buildings, and this has posed something of a problem. But people wander around a lot and visit each other's offices. And we make a lot of use of our own INFOPLEX (computerized communication) system. How do you reconcile this with the social orientation of our management? I suppose it's the high-tech, high-touch phenomenon. Interestingly, though, among our training programs for our employees, we have none that are computer based.

Overall, we try to be above average in compensation, but absolutely tops in fringe benefits. Emphasis is placed on enjoying what we are doing. As Jeff puts it, "We work hard; we might as well have fun." We have a heavily subsidized dining room. It was someone's idea to call it the Oak Room, so that has stuck. And have you seen our fitness center? It was one of Jeff's high-priority projects. Nearly everyone uses it. It works out very well with the flex-time arrangement we have for all of our employees. I'm an afternoon person, so I usually hit the fitness center for an hour or so before I come to the office.

You may not believe this, but we don't have a retirement plan. The average age of the people here is about 30. The exempts may be closer to 40, but there is no one over 50. In spite of the age level, you'll notice that people here dress for business. Jeff and the others have always dressed well, and I suppose that sets the tone for everyone else.

There is at least one function each year involving all members of the families of employees. We have it in the winter and call it the "gala." It gives everybody a chance to dress up and show off. This is in addition to our informal and formal recognition events that almost always include spouses. [Several associates commented that this and other company policies reflected in part Jeff Wilkins's strong dedication to his family.]

Since the sale of CompuServe to H&R Block, Wilkins had occupied both the positions of chairperson and president. In February 1984, he resolved the uncertainty about who would be the number two associate in the company by naming McCall to the position of president and chief operating officer. CompuServe's 1984 organization chart appears in *Exhibit 4*.

BUSINESS PLANNING

The business planning cycle was geared to produce a final plan by the end of each fiscal year (April 30). The process that McCall oversaw in the winter and spring of 1984 was typical. It began with the preparation of estimates of the business volumes for the coming year by Massey for business services, Woodford for network services, and Meier for consumer services. These estimates were based on what was described as a combination of formal projections and a "feel" for each market. The estimates were adjusted for increases in marketing efforts.

Once the director of operations knew the anticipated business volume, his group prepared estimates of the amount of capacity required for both mainframe and network operations and the additional capital investment required for each. Of much greater importance were the resulting estimates of increases in headcount that were required to support the anticipated level of business. For example, the investment in more software usually involved hiring people. Headcount figures from 1980 to 1984 appear in *Exhibit 5*.

After the initial plan was prepared, planned revenues and costs were compared to the minimum growth target set forth in the executive compensation plan. This plan called for a 20% growth in earnings before tax in each of the six years following the sale of CompuServe to H&R Block.

Goal Setting and the Executive Compensation Plan

The executive compensation plan, developed in lieu of stock options or other incentives when H&R Block acquired CompuServe, originally included 11 of the 14 CompuServe officers at the time. The reward these officers received was based on an amount determined each year by the H&R Block Board Compensation Committee in discussion with Wilkins. The pool of money designated for this purpose ranged from $650,000 in fiscal 1981 to $982,000 in fiscal 1984. The actual amounts earned under the plan varied according to the increase in operating income achieved each year, as follows:

Increase in Operating Income	Proportion of "Pool" Awarded
12%	30%
13	40
14	50
15	60
16	70
17	80
18	90
19	95
20	100

The starting base for computing operating income increases was $2,378,000 in 1979. The agreement stated that if operating income fell short in any one year, as long as maximum operating income targets were met over the entire six years of the plan, all incentives would be paid. The plan specified that for 6 years the original chairperson (Harry Gard) was to receive 20% of the amount awarded, the CEO (Jeff Wilkins) was to receive 40%, and the remaining 40% was to be distributed on a basis determined each year by Wilkins to the other nine participants.

In addition, an annual pool for the nine senior associates (excluding Gard and Wilkins) was available under an MBO (Management by Objectives) program, in which individuals identified important annual goals and performance measures and negotiated them with Wilkins. The amounts available under this plan ranged from $80,000 in fiscal 1981 to $155,000 in fiscal 1984. In total, it was estimated that the amounts available to the nine senior participants, other than Gard and Wilkins, under both of these incentive plans approximated 40% of their total compensation each year.

Discrepancies between the preliminary budget and the amount of operating income needed to achieve 100% of the compensation plan pool then became the basis for negotiation. A team comprising McCall, Swaddling, and two members of their staff negotiated with each operating manager in a 4 on 1 meeting. As one member of the team said, "We negotiate until we're in balance with our minimum growth target plus a small cushion, then we know we're done. We don't have any trouble spending extra operating income that might accrue during the year." According to McCall, Wilkins's usual role in the business planning process focused on negotiating the amount of cushion needed in addition to the minimum operating income growth target.

"Earning Hits"

The executive compensation plan was revised twice to accommodate one-year earnings hits caused by unusual annual expenditures of importance to the long-term health of the company. In 1982, for example, because of the first large advertising expenditure for the Consumer Information Service (CIS), Compu-Serve fell about $1 million short of meeting its 20% operating income increase goal. In agreement with the H&R Block compensation committee, this amount was set aside and would be paid back the next year. Similarly, in 1983, when expenditures for the expanded network staffing represented a $1.3 million "one-time earnings hit," it was agreed that 20% would be paid back the following year and the remaining 80% in fiscal 1985. (See *footnote c* of *Exhibit 1* for an explanation of the procedure for accounting for exclusions from and paybacks to operating income.)

The Fiscal 1985 Plan

Before conducting his final round of negotiations with individual CompuServe operating managers, McCall met with Wilkins in early March 1984 to establish the direction of these negotiations. In particular, McCall was concerned about the responses to be made to the managers of CompuServe's two fastest-growing businesses and to Trevor, the manager of CompuServe's Computer Resources Group.

In preparation for the discussion, McCall left Wilkins with projections of the effects of initial capital and operating budget requests on the company's fiscal 1985 financial performance. These documents, presented in *Exhibits 6* and 7, indicated that capital budget requests totaled $18.5 million. Although depreciation would yield $4.7 million and projected earnings $3.2 million, the difference would have to be borrowed from Block, thus exceeding the amount the company had borrowed from its parent during the first four years of their relationship.

Projected earnings of $3.2 million were far below the $7.1 million called for by the executive compensation plan and expected by H&R Block. The difference resulted from larger-than-expected requests for expenditures for data line services and CIS advertising.

Woodford's Request. Woodford had been particularly emphatic in support of his request to McCall's planning team for a $6 million expansion of the communications network and the addition of 27 technicians to his staff of 35 that was assigned to monitor and repair the company's communications network. This would increase the payroll for that function by $1.35 million. He had pointed to the rapid growth of the business, the difficulties of competing with much larger firms, and the need for a critical mass of markets connected to the network. According to Woodford, it was necessary to have nodes in 300 to 400 cities "to be a player." This contrasted with CompuServe's network, which connected 160 cities. Further, he argued that the quality of service was critical to maintaining the customer base since CompuServe had proven its competitiveness in price.

McCall's planning team observed several uncertainties concerning the network services business. Because the business relied on the old Bell System, from which network lines were leased, doubling the number of service people and investing the roughly $6 million needed to bring the network up to a fully competitive level involved risk. Higher network access charges that AT&T might assess local telephone companies could reduce point-of-sale credit authorization activities, for example. Similarly, if AT&T's charges to WATS users were reduced drastically, much of the demand for CompuServe's network could evaporate. Because CompuServe charged for each message on a basis reflecting the actual time used as opposed to AT&T's charges based on a 60-second minimum, if AT&T were to cut its minimum time increment to, perhaps, five seconds, it could eliminate an important source of cost saving by the CompuServe system. AT&T was rumored to be considering reducing its minimum message charge increment to 30 seconds.

Finally, AT&T's method of charging for leased lines had favored point-to-point networks, in which two points might have to communicate through a third point, such as CompuServe's. This put competitors' multi-drop systems, in which each node could access every other node directly, at a cost disadvantage. If AT&T were to alter its pricing method, it could eliminate a source of advantage for CompuServe.

But Woodford was philosophical about this and said to the team:

Can you afford not to take the risk and make the investment? We'll need the coverage anyway for our other businesses. You know, we don't do anything that we can't leverage through use by several businesses.

Meier's Recommendation. Meier, vice president of market development and services, recommended a significant increase in advertising expenditures for the CIS. He pointed out that his plan was necessary to defend CIS's large market share and to prepare for a new era of competition that would include large, well-financed competitors growing out of services planned by previously announced joint ventures. With a large and rapidly growing base of personal computer owners with modems, he felt that CompuServe should consolidate its leadership image by engaging for the first time in television advertising. Of the 70% increase that he had requested in advertising, nearly $1 million would be devoted to the production and showing of a CIS television ad.

Both Woodford and Meier had alluded to the importance of their groups making their numbers for sales increases during the coming year. It was one of the measures on which their MBO bonuses would be based.

Trevor's Plan. Trevor, in contrast, used the level of services provided by the central computing facilities as one of his important measures. In his discussions with McCall's team, he reminded his associates of the basic company policy to expand capacity ahead of demand in order to avoid possible service degradation, which could lead to a loss of customers for all of CompuServe's businesses. Using other estimates of business increases, he indicated that $6.5 million would be required for central computing equipment during 1985. Trevor's group had always received the funds it felt were needed to maintain service standards.

New Office Building. The final major capital budget item of $6 million resulted from Wilkins's decision to build a badly needed office building that would also house the company dining room, training facilities, and reception area. Swaddling was responsible for managing this project and had presented the plans to his colleagues on the planning team.

RELATIONSHIP WITH H&R BLOCK

As CompuServe's needs for capital grew, the relationship with its parent, H&R Block, had become, in the words of Wilkins, "more complex." Immediately after the sale of CompuServe to Block, Wilkins assumed responsibility for managing the relationship on CompuServe's behalf. He quickly realized that basic differences between the two companies' lines of business and management policies would warrant careful liaison efforts.

H&R Block was founded in 1955 by Henry W. Bloch, the president and chief executive officer, and his brother. They borrowed $5,000 from a great aunt to fund their venture. At the time, Bloch was working as a stockbroker. By 1962, the company was doing well enough in tax consulting to go public, and by 1984, nearly one out of ten income tax returns filed in the United States was prepared by H&R Block in its nearly 7,800 offices. In addition, the company operated another 1,200 offices in other countries.

Over the years, Henry Bloch had found it difficult to find other businesses that could provide a return comparable to that earned by his company. Acquisitions of a door-to-door distribution company and a Bermuda-based insurance company were sold after the two companies gave disappointing performances. In 1978, H&R Block acquired Personnel Pool of America, which generated most of its revenues by providing supplementary nursing and ancillary personnel for both hospitals and home care.

In June 1980, H&R Block completed its other and latest business development effort. It entered into an agreement whereby a new majority-owned subsidiary, Block Management Company, would provide a broad range of marketing and administrative services to Hyatt Legal Clinics. This firm was founded by Joel Hyatt, a young entrepreneur. It provided, through a chain of store-front facilities, legal services in the general area of domestic relations, wills, bankruptcy, probate, and other legal services that people frequently needed. In spite of its efforts to diversify, only 10% of H&R Block's earnings before taxes in 1984 were expected to come from the operations of its subsidiaries. (See *Exhibit 8* for a summary of selected financial data for H&R Block.)

As a condition of selling CompuServe, Wilkins was elected to Block's board and allowed to retain CompuServe's outside directors as members of the new subsidiary's board. All of the latter were Wilkins's personal acquaintances and highly regarded members of the central Ohio business community.

Instead of joining CompuServe's board himself, Henry Bloch asked Robert Davidson, his executive vice president and chief operating officer, to join. (Bloch had been increasing the amount of time he devoted to outside activities.) Although Wilkins thought that Davidson had limited understanding of the needs of a growing technology-based company, he did have solid general business acumen. The two men developed an effective working relationship.

Although Wilkins's decision to serve as a buffer between the two companies had minimized H&R Block's involvement in the management of CompuServe, it presented problems as time passed. Wilkins described these as follows:

I guess I'm more concerned than my associates about whether we have the resources to compete in these developing businesses. Many of them assume that the shots are being called in Columbus. Because we finance our operations through loans from Block, on which we pay the prime rate of interest (11% in early 1984), it's generally believed in the company that capital budgets totally are within CompuServe management's prerogative. In addition, I keep hearing our associates say, "Block first put up the money for the promotional budgets we needed for the CIS and then for the network expansion. They will continue to finance us." While they know that Block approves extraordinary expenditures as long as they are paid back within specified time periods, I'm not sure they fully realize that there is probably a limit to the amount of and number of such "earnings hits." We have to make our annual numbers.

On the other hand, the people at Block don't understand the need for continuing increases in capacity. If you guess wrong in this business, you want to guess wrong on the high side of demand in order to avoid customer degradation. And while we are hiring a lot of people into the organization at lower levels, we haven't had much luck hiring senior people. We tried bringing in a vice president of marketing in 1975 from the Service Bureau Corporation. He had great analytic skills but an abrasive manner. He lasted about a year. Much the same happened with a vice president of sales that we hired in 1979. This put additional pressure on us to develop and promote people from within, especially in our consumer business, where we are really thin.

Differences in management outlook and policies at Block and CompuServe were thought to be marked. Senior managers at Block were somewhat older than those at CompuServe, and none of them had engineering backgrounds. They ran a company that had produced increased earnings in all but one of its 29 years without extensive use of debt. Block's managers proudly pointed out that they all flew coach class on company business. In contrast, much of Wilkins's company travel was by first class. If necessary to make the trip to Block's board meetings in one day to avoid being away from his family, Wilkins chartered an aircraft. As Wilkins stated, "I'm the type that says, 'Give me the numbers and I'll make them, but don't ask me how I do it.'"

Recognizing this, Wilkins, with Swaddling's help, carefully prepared each of his presentations to Block's management to explain CompuServe's business and the reasons why it had continuing capital needs. He assiduously tried to avoid surprising Block's management with unexpected capital requests or earnings adjustments. Nevertheless, as it became increasingly apparent to Block's management and board that CompuServe's current lines of business would require significant new investment, Block's board suggested that CompuServe explore the possibility of joint venture alternatives.

Because CompuServe had met its adjusted financial goals during the first four years of its relationship with H&R Block, executive compensation had been generous. It had reached the height of absurdity, in Wilkins's opinion, when a Kansas City newspaper article, in which he had mistakenly been assumed to be a resident of that city, listed him as the highest-paid executive, with a salary of $650,000. Henry Bloch appeared on the same list and ranked third.

STRATEGIC PLANNING

Strategic planning was carried out at CompuServe for some years by a small group of senior managers under the leadership of Wilkins and Thomas Dennis, a director and business school professor. But as the business opportunities along with the demands they placed on the company increased, it was decided that a more extensive procedure was needed. According to Wilkins:

> The people at Block were reading in the *Wall Street Journal* about these $50 million joint ventures to offer just one of the consumer information services that we were including in our CIS. They couldn't figure out how we were going to compete. As a result, their board asked us to determine if we thought we needed some kind of joint venture to finance our future expansion of the CIS. In order to respond, it looked like we needed a full-scale version of the planning exercises we had been holding for some years. Because Block often employed consultants themselves, I made sure I included not one but two in the exercise.

The planning exercise in the late spring of 1984 had several phases. First, teams of managers were organized to prepare written statements as background for presentations and discussions to be held in the full group. These statements were organized around a common set of headings, suggested by Dennis, and designed to describe the company's current strategy, which included the following: marketing strategy (product, pricing, promotion, distribution); production strategy (facilities, integration, capacity, technology, operations planning and control, work force management); and research and development strategy (basic and applied research, product innovation, process innovation, leader/follower strategy).

Following the presentations, a small group gathered to map future strategic directions. Included in this group were Wilkins, McCall, Swaddling, Meier, Trevor, two of CompuServe's "outside" directors (Davidson from H&R Block and Dennis), and representatives from two internationally known management consulting firms. Excerpts from the minutes of the meeting are presented in *Exhibit 9*.

With the rapidly escalating demands for capital to support CompuServe's growing businesses and with the parent organization becoming increasingly restive about supplying all the capital needed, Wilkins once again entertained the possibility of a joint venture as he sat down to begin working through the preliminary 1985 planning figures with McCall.

Exhibit 1
CompuServe Consolidated Income Statements, Fiscal Years 1981–1984
(*$ in thousands*)

	1984[a]	*1983*	*1982*	*1981*
Revenue—net of credits				
Commercial services	$35,596	na[a]	na[a]	na[a]
Network services	2,508	676	36	—
Information services[b]	13,138	4,490	2,158	749
Executive services	463	—	—	—
Other	46	120	93	426
Branches	na[a]	26,164	25,271	20,220
Government	na[a]	4,741	4,603	5,229
National accounts	na[a]	3,223	970	882
Total revenue	$51,751	$39,414	$33,131	$27,506
Less direct contract costs	1,547	775	549	615
Less royalty expense	3,647	2,599	2,141	1,663
Net revenue	$46,557	$36,040	$30,441	$25,228

NOTE: For fiscal years ending April 30 of each year. Certain of these data are disguised.

[a] The basis for recording revenues was changed in fiscal 1984. Revenues attributed in previous years to branches, government, and national accounts are roughly comparable to commercial services.

[b] Consumer information services.

Exhibit 1
(Continued)

	1984[a]	*1983*	*1982*	*1981*
Expenses				
Salaries and benefits	15,976	14,681	12,664	10,257
Depreciation	3,874	3,242	2,963	2,191
Interest	1,149	1,039	1,255	883
Other property costs	4,610	1,576	1,607	1,515
Data lines	4,242	3,023	2,282	1,324
Other personnel costs	2,912	2,020	1,830	1,920
Advertising	3,307	2,947	1,560	926
Other expenses	4,262	2,580	2,170	2,720
Total expenses	$40,332	$31,108	$26,331	$21,736
Operating income	6,222	4,931	4,109	3,492
Plus operating income	—	36	25	112
Less other exclusions:[c]				
Branch expansion	650	489	395	302
CIS advertising	(132)	(873)	1,005	—
Merger expense	71	20	66	81
Network expansion	(299)	1,311	28	27
ComLink expenses	—	—	146	—
Compensation plan	982	903	815	746
Income before taxes	$ 4,950	$ 3,117	$ 1,679	$ 2,448

[c]This figure is a net of several items not included in the computation of operating income for purposes of determining executive bonuses under the executive compensation plan. Negative figures indicate amounts "paid back" that were charged in earlier years, also by prior agreement between CompuServe and H&R Block management. These items were also charged as other expenses before calculating operating income in the years in which the expenses occurred.

Exhibit 2
CompuServe Consolidated Balance Sheets, Fiscal Years 1981–1984 ($ in thousands)

	1984	1983	1982	1981
Assets				
Current assets				
Cash and marketable securities	$21	$504	$95	$492
Receivables	10,518	8,065	6,085	5,308
Other current assets	2,289	1,304	951	888
Total current assets	$12,828	$9,873	$7,131	$6,688
Other assets				
Hardware	35,301	28,700	24,515	20,719
Land and buildings	11,002	7,431	7,399	5,557
Other assets	6,154	5,943	4,888	3,620
Less depreciation allowances	(19,852)	(16,782)	(13,616)	(11,061)
Total other assets	$32,605	$25,292	$23,186	$18,835
Total assets	$45,433	$35,165	$30,317	$25,523
Liabilities and Equity				
Current liabilities				
Accounts payable—trade	2,423	1,208	968	892
Taxes payable	1,747	1,610	1,624	1,436
Term debt—current	236	239	1,012	800
Block current[a]	3,480	2,386	1,405	387
Other current liabilities	1,807	1,611	1,334	1,159
Total current liabilities	$9,693	$7,054	$6,343	$4,674
Long-term liabilities				
Term debt	3,032	1,701	1,878	2,997
Deferred credits and liabilities	—	1,568	1,568	1,568
Other	—	—	15	23
Total long-term liabilities	$3,032	$3,269	$3,461	$4,588
Block advances	10,900	7,950	5,650	4,150
Total liabilities	$23,625	$18,273	$15,454	$13,412
Equity				
Capital stock	1	1	1	577
Additional paid-in capital	10,601	10,601	10,601	3,188
Retained earnings—price	6,206	4,178	1,578	6,828
Current earnings	5,000	2,112	2,683	1,518
Total equity	$21,808	$16,892	$14,863	$12,111
Total liabilities and equity	$45,433	$35,165	$30,317	$25,523

NOTE: Selected data have been disguised. Figures for year-end 1984 are estimates.

[a] This item represents accumulated unpaid interest on amounts borrowed from H&R Block.

Exhibit 3

Excerpts from an Assessment of Competitive Strategies for the Consumer Information Services Market, June 1984

	CompuServe	Dow Jones	The Source	Viewtron
Target market	Primarily domestic/residential user	Business computer users	Consumers; home users	Consumers; home users
Current subscription base and rate growth	120,000 (adding 7,000 per month)	140,000 (adding 7,000 per month)	65,000 (adding 5,000 per month)	1,500 (adding 200 per month)
Product	High-quality mass communications medium	Business information to make job easier	Wide variety of home management services	Wide variety of local and regional services; high-quality graphics
Equipment required	PC plus modem	PC plus modem	PC plus modem	Special sceptre terminal
Subscription fee	$19.95	$49.95	$100 plus $10 per month minimum	$40 per month, including terminal rental
Pricing: Basic evenings	$6.25 per hour	$9.00 per hour	$7.75 per hour	
Basic weekday	$12.50 per hour	$72.00 per hour	$20.75 per hour	
Promotion	Advertising in business and computer magazines; magazine to subscribers	Strong: advertise in *Wall Street Journal* and business and computer magazines; magazine to subscribers	Advertising primarily in computer magazines	Strong public relations; advertising regionally; magazine to subscribers
Distribution	Starter kits through retail stores and OEMs; direct sales by mail	Strong OEM program; retail; direct telephone sales	Retailers; OEMs; direct mail; telephone sales	Computer retail stores; AT&T phone centers; mass merchandisers
Quality of service	Acceptable customer service; good response time; thorough documentation; easiest to use; high level of reliability	Good customer service; good response time; frequently updated data bases; documentation is thorough; commands are complex	Good customer service; good response time; menu tricky to operate	Complicated paging system; having problems maintaining information providers on the system

COMPUSERVE (A)
Exhibit 4
CompuServe Organization, April 1984

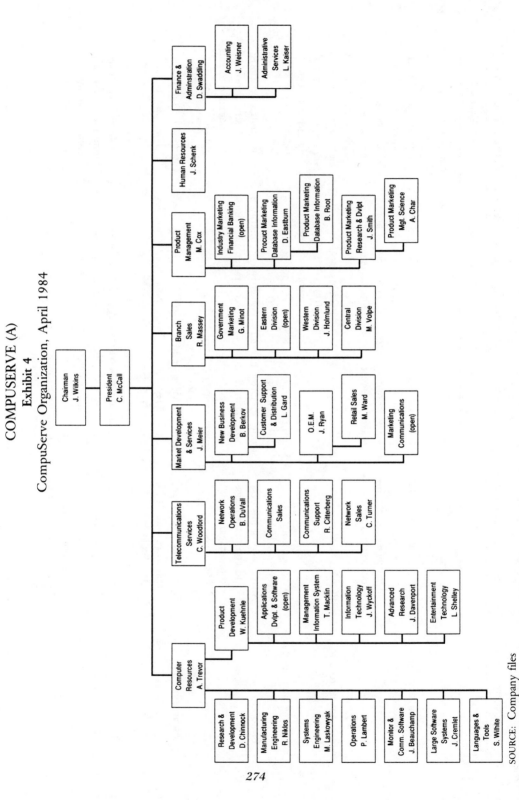

SOURCE: Company files

Exhibit 5
CompuServe Headcount Totals at End of Fiscal Years
1980–1984

	1980	1981	1982	1983	1984
Function					
Marketing and product development	72	92	64	113	105
Sales (including branch personnel)	116	142	167	184	177
Computer technologies	103	127	186	177	156
Administration	42	38	42	56	149[a]
Total	333	399	459	530	587

[a] Much of this increase over 1983 is due to a reallocation of other costs to administration.

Exhibit 6
CompuServe's Preliminary Operating Plan, 1985
($ in thousands)

Revenue	
Commercial services	$38,350
Network services	6,550
Consumer services	19,420
Executive services	750
Total	$65,070
Less direct contract costs	3,150
Less royalty expense	4,970
Net revenue	$56,950
Expenses	
Salaries and benefits	$19,380
Depreciation	4,700
Interest[a]	2,820
Other property costs	5,340
Data lines	6,360
Other personnel costs	3,440
Advertisement	5,610
Other expenses	5,030
Total	$52,680
Operating Income	
Plus other income	—
Less other exclusions	—
Less compensation plans[b]	1,050
	$ 3,220

NOTE: Assuming all remaining requests for major operating funds were approved.

[a]Assuming a prime rate of 10% and an increase in the loan of money from H&R Block of $12 million in addition to the $14.4 million already outstanding.

[b]Assuming 100% of the executive compensation plan bonus would be distributed.

Exhibit 7
CompuServe's Preliminary Sources and Uses Statement
for Fiscal 1985 ($ in thousands)

Sources

Operating income	$ 3,220
Depreciation	4,700
Payables and accrued expenses	1,530
Addition to loan from H&R Block	11,000
	$20,450

Uses

Receivables	$ 1500
Prepaids and inventory	450
New building	6,000
New hardware	6,500
New network facilities	6,000
	$20,450

NOTE: Assuming all remaining requests for major operating funds and capital were approved.

COMPUSERVE (A)
Exhibit 8
H&R Block, Inc., Selected Financial Data, Fiscal Years 1979–1984 ($ in millions)

	1984[a]	1983	1982	1981	1980	1979
Revenues						
Tax return preparation fees	$282.8	$244.0	$187.7	$169.7	$149.1	$132.1
Other	132.8	97.5	131.0	118.1	80.5	66.0
Total	$415.6	$341.5	$318.7	$287.8	$229.6	$198.1
Operating expenses	327.5	268.2	348.3	217.8	169.0	142.9
Earnings before tax	88.1	73.3	70.5	70.0	60.6	55.2
Taxes on income	40.1	32.5	32.2	32.3	28.5	25.8
Net earnings	$48.0	$40.8	$38.3	$37.7	$32.1	$29.4
Earnings per average share (in dollars)	$3.88	$3.34	$3.17	$3.14	$2.85	$2.62
Assets						
Current assets						
Cash and marketable securities	$151.8	$110.2	$119.4	$106.8	$ 99.0	$ 90.4
Other current assets	83.3	46.2	24.9	25.0	12.9	10.1
Total current assets	$235.1	$156.4	$144.3	$131.8	$111.9	$100.5
Investments and other assets	97.4	80.9	76.6	70.0	63.5	61.0
Property and equipment	58.6	49.0	45.7	34.6	11.4	9.5
Total assets	$391.1[b]	$286.3[b]	$266.6	$236.4	$186.8	$171.0

Liabilities and Equity

Current liabilities						
Taxes on income	52.5	41.3	43.7	36.9	34.4	34.0
Other current liabilities	94.9	34.9	30.9	29.9	18.5	19.1
Total current liabilities	$147.4	$76.2	$74.6	$66.8	$52.9	$53.1
Long-term debt	6.2	6.6	7.3	3.9	1.1	1.7
Stockholders' equity	237.4	203.4	184.7	165.7	132.8	116.2
Total liabilities and equity	$391.0[b]	$286.2[b]	$266.6	$236.4	$186.8	$171.0
Price per share of common stock						
High	44¾	43¾	39½	36	27¼	25⅞
Low	36¼	25¼	28¾	22⅝	21½	19⅛
Percentage of earnings from tax return preparation and net investment income[c]	90%	93.7%	89%	83.3%	90%	92.4%

[a] All fiscal years ending April 30. Figures for 1984 are estimates.

[b] Assets and liabilities may vary due to rounding.

[c] These percentages are after the deduction of all unallocated corporate and administrative expenses from these figures.

Exhibit 9
Exerpts from Minutes of a Strategic Planning Meeting, Winter 1984

Attendees: Jeff Wilkins, Charlie McCall, Dave Swaddling, John Meier, Sandy Trevor, all of CompuServe; Robert Davidson, director of both H&R Block and CompuServe; Thomas Dennis, business school professor and CompuServe director; Philip Burnham, outside consultant; and John Tyson, outside consultant.

Wilkins: The goal today is to evaluate, discuss, modify, and come up with a strategy for our information services. . . . We have two outside resources, representing competing consulting firms, both of whom are very experienced in videotex and computer communications. . . . If we discover this session isn't working quite right, we will, recess and reconvene in some other fashion. . . . Bob [Davidson] asked me if this group was willing to go "no holds barred," and I told him that they were a very strong group of people and able to shed any biases. . . . Today we will be focusing on information services with CIS as the dominant part. We will focus on the home market. . . . I would like to give you . . . the conclusion I have reached as a model and ask you for your reactions.

First, we perceive Dow Jones as a major competitor in the business market who is trying to get into the home market. When Dow Jones was at 90,000 subscribers, their number of active users. . . . who used it during a given week was 3%. At this point, Knight-Ridder is struggling desperately and is now trying to go after the PC [personal computer] market. No one has focused on the economics of the business. They all believe the technology curve is going to do it for them, and they should not be worried about how to do it. Second, even after all our past and present successes . . . no one really knows for sure if there is a real market. There is a high probability. Some significant bets are (1) Prestel, (2) The Source, (3) AT&T, (4) Viewtron, and (5) Trintex (CBS, Sears, and IBM). Everyone is thinking and demonstrating that the consumers are willing to pay for information services. Nobody is making money at it, but each bet gets bigger and each set of players better. . . . We recognized very early that we had to have a critical mass of services; this brings people to our door.

Dennis: There are two basic models around which a strategy can be formed. One is to substitute new ways of delivering services that are provided now, services such as home banking and home shopping, something we've called substitute services. That's what Viewtron and Trintex are trying to do. The other model is to provide new services based on capabilities made possible by the personal computer that weren't there before, the so-called value-added strategy. Examples of this are electronic mail and Consumer Information Service's special interest groups.

That's what The Source and we are doing now. . . . Because there is value-added, it helps explain why people are more willing to pay for it; but it's not clear if they are willing to pay enough to make it economic. If modems are integrated into PCs, there will be a tremendous opportunity for growth of information services of both kinds.

Burnham: The downside of moving strongly into value-added services is that someone could take away the existing business. There is a risk to us if someone bets heavy, the

Exhibit 9
(Continued)

market increases rapidly, and a competitor increases its penetration. There are 1.5 million modems in homes and .5 million modems in use in business.

Dennis: The potential market is not defined by whether I have a modem now. It's defined by whether you [CompuServe] have something I need. Is it better to concentrate on a value-added strategy and let the base build?

Burnham: I doubt if the people substituting one service for another will buy a modem.

Dennis: That won't make any difference when they start to build them into the computer.

Wilkins: What do we mean by a large market? And what do we mean by a large market share?

Tyson: The definition of a large market will vary depending on which industry you want to impact. Pick advertising.

Advertisers become interested when penetration of a market reaches 15% to 20% of households.

Dennis: None of the forecasts for PCs gets you into 20% soon; probably five years plus. . . . But by that time we must be thinking of what AT&T will do to put some sort of terminal in the home.

Burnham: As for CompuServe, a quarter of a million subscribers will be the turning point. Then there will be a tremendous change in the perception of CompuServe. . . . We believe there is a total market for substitution services of up to 30 million households . . . and the consumers will be very diverse.

Dennis: How valid is the market research on something they don't conceptually understand?

Wilkins: I hear you saying that value-added services is an important place to stay for the near term, that it is protectable, and that we should do everything possible to increase our penetration of it. . . . But what about substitute services? Is there a particular organization that we ought to be working with that can supply us with the consumer market expertise that would help us move up the curve faster? If it's going to require $50 million over the next five years, for example, CompuServe could only provide half of this, even if its sales hit $250 to $300 million.

Trevor: I'm still concerned that other companies don't need us. They can buy technology.

McCall: A lot of companies have proved to us that they want to do a joint venture with us.

Swaddling: Why would they put big money in a company they don't control?

Trevor: A joint venture partner will want total control somewhere down the road.

Wilkins: I don't think that is the way they see it. Based on those we're doing business with now, they see it as additional business generated.

(Continued)

Exhibit 9
(Continued)

Burnham: It is not necessary to dilute CompuServe equity to achieve what we want. We need other people to do certain complementary things, but I'm not certain we need to give them equity.

Tyson: I need more time to think about whether to dilute equity. When you entertain getting a partner is when you have things you want to do but can't do them yourselves. Otherwise, you won't be good negotiators.

Wilkins: We have said we want promotion dollars, we want to get a market share, and we want to get help in market expertise. The limitation has always been taking losses. It is unacceptable that we not make money. Block will not fund this big a venture. . . . We want $50 million to go hire good people that we need badly for this business, and we want someone else's money.

Dennis: We should make a list, go to potential partners, tell one they are our first choice and that we want to make a deal. Would it hurt to pick an area and try this? Do three, one in each area. Go to Citicorp, Sears, American Express.

5

◆

Determining the True Costs and Benefits of Service Quality

Poor quality fosters many costs, few of which are measured. Perhaps the most obvious of these is the loss of customer loyalty and the sales and profit stream that accompany it. Even less likely to be measured are customer costs associated with lost time, expense, and aggravation suffered in correcting problems of poor service. Rarely taken into consideration too are the costs resulting from server dissatisfaction which are evidenced in increased employee turnover, training, and yet further service deterioration. These costs suggest the value of good service and help in establishing guidelines for amounts that a service provider might spend for the appraisal of service performance and various preventative measures that might be instituted, including service recovery (righting wrongs), prior to the loss of a customer.

The Goldome Realty Credit Corporation and Club Med (A) cases give us a chance to put some of these concepts to work. At Goldome, for example: What is the company's business? How is money made or lost in this business? What does "good service" mean here? How is Goldome doing? What's the revenue loss here from the loss of loyalty of mortgagees? How likely it is to happen? How does this compare to the costs of the proposals for change you would support? What is your opinion of the PID team's report? As Mollie Higgins, what would be your reaction to the PID team's analysis and recommendations? As Peter Ross, what decision would you make concerning the PID team's recommendations?

Now put yourself in Jacques Giraud's shoes at Club Med. How do you feel about the future of the company, nervous or confident? What is the Club Med "magic"? What are the keys to this business? How easy would it be for a competitor to replicate the Club Med service concept? Is this the greatest threat to the business? As an advisor to Jacques Giraud, what, if anything, would you suggest he do? Could you calculate the amount of money the company could afford to spend on your recommendations?

Determining the true value and cost of quality sheds an entirely new light on corrective actions that might be taken and the willingness of management to take them. It is perhaps the best application in service management of the maxim, what gets measured is what gets managed.

Goldome Realty Credit Corporation

Peter M. Ross, senior vice president in charge of servicing at Goldome Realty Credit Corp. (GRCC), the eleventh largest U.S. mortgage bank, had called an all-day meeting of the Customer Service telephone area management team for Friday, December 13, 1985. The purpose of the meeting was to discuss and make decisions on the recommendations submitted by the Profitability Improvement Division (PID) after a study of Customer Service.

The PID team estimated that, by following its recommendations, Customer Service managers could reduce annual expenses in the telephone area by $265,000, or over a quarter of the 1986 budget, without impairing service quality. The recommendations were broad in scope, ranging from improving telephone answering workstations to reassigning tasks from the telephone area to other departments within GRCC.

THE RETAIL FINANCIAL SERVICES INDUSTRY

Until the late 1970s, most commercial and residential mortgages in the United States were funded by savings banks through their mortgage departments. Most savings banks used funds from savings accounts, for which they paid a legally imposed maximum annual interest rate (e.g., 5.5%) to finance mortgages earning a higher rate (e.g., 8.5% or 8%). An interest-rate spread of 2% to 2.5% had sustained a stable and profitable thrift industry for over 150 years. With the rise in interest and inflation rates during the 1970s, however, consumers began to demand financial instruments that would preserve the value of their assets better than 5.5% savings accounts. At the same time, technology helped make it possible to develop new financial products to meet this demand.

In 1978, the Federal Reserve Board decontrolled the rate of interest on savings deposits, beginning a period of deregulation and drastic change for savings banks and other financial institutions in the United States. An abundance of new financial products was offered to retail and commercial customers. Some brokerage houses, such as Merrill Lynch, expanded into a wide range of financial services. Some banks, such as Citibank, expanded their business considerably beyond the

This case was prepared by Associate Professor Marie Therese Flaherty as the basis for class discussion rather than to illustrate either effective or ineffective handling of an administrative situation. Copyright© 1986 by the President and Fellows of Harvard College; Harvard Business School case #9-687-015 Rev. 11/88.

traditional, regulated confines of banking. Even Sears, Roebuck entered the competition with a broad range of retail financial services, ranging from real-estate brokerage to individual financial planning.

In this new, more competitive environment, banks began to finance an increasing proportion of the residential mortgages in the United States. These mortgage banks, rather than using their own funds, obtained financing by selling groups of mortgages to government-sponsored financial intermediaries such as the Government National Mortgage Association (Ginnie Mae), the Federal National Mortgage Association (Fannie Mae), and the Federal Home Loan Mortgage Corporation (Freddie Mac). Those intermediaries, which had been established by the federal government to create a secondary market in mortgages and thus expand the pool of capital available to finance home ownership, resold groups of mortgages to the public, either in their original form or in the form of guaranteed securities. The mortgage banks retained responsibility for servicing the mortgage, i.e., collecting mortgage and tax payments, paying the real estate taxes, administering foreclosure proceedings in the event of default, paying the investing institutions, and reporting to them on the status of their investments—as long as the service was satisfactory to the intermediary.

Although some mortgage companies were independent, others were subsidiaries of other corporations or of commercial banks. A mortgage subsidiary offered a bank several advantages. It was not restricted to the bank's geographic area, it did not have to sell the mortgages it granted to the parent bank, and because it sold the mortgages quickly, it was exposed to limited interest-rate risk.

There was considerable instability in the mortgage industry during the mid-1980s. For example, GMAC (number 2 in 1985) entered the mortgage industry in 1985 by acquiring most of Norwest (number 2 in 1984) after Norwest had incurred very large losses in hedging new mortgages during the period before they were sold to institutional investors. Like many companies in the industry, Norwest was wholly owned by another company that required a steady flow of cash from it.

Citicorp Homeowners grew from number 20 in 1984 to number 6 in 1985 by increasing its portfolio serviced from $5 billion to $8.7 billion. This subsidiary did not include Citicorp's mortgage operations in the Northeast, which themselves had originated over $4 billion in new mortgages in 1985. This growth had been possible in part because Citicorp had bypassed the institutional investors and sold securities based on its mortgages directly in the financial markets. (This business often was not identified separately because it was part of the bank's operations.) If the two Citicorp mortgage banking operations were consolidated, they would rival the largest firm in the industry.

By mid-1985, Dallas-based Lomas & Nettleton Financial Corp., the largest servicer of mortgages, serviced 678,000 mortgages with a dollar value of $20.2 billion.

GOLDOME AND THE DEVELOPMENT OF GRCC

In 1980, Ross Kenzie who had had a successful 22-year career at Merrill Lynch, became chief executive of the $3 billion Buffalo Savings Bank (in Buffalo, New York). At the time the bank had $3 billion in assets. In 1982 Kenzie changed the bank's name to the Goldome FSB (federal savings bank) and, by 1985 he had transformed it into the largest mutual savings bank in the United States. By 1985 Kenzie was head of Goldome, a nationwide financial service holding company with assets of $13 billion and more than 30 subsidiaries, including Goldome FSB and Goldome Realty Credit Corp.

GRCC grew out of the Buffalo Savings Bank's mortgage department. In late 1980 the mortgage department sold its first two $1-million pools of mortgages to Ginnie Mae. This relieved the bank of the financial risk of speculating in long-term interest rates and of its dependence on internal financing. But it also necessitated tightening the mortgage department's operating procedures to meet Ginnie Mae's requirements.

During 1981 the Buffalo Savings Bank mortgage department introduced the industry standard software to its operations, reorganized, and implemented controls to ensure that new mortgages conformed to the detailed requirements of the secondary market. For example, the practice of many lawyers of crossing out words in a mortgage agreement that they did not approve of would make a mortgage unsuitable for sale to the government-sponsored institutional investors.

Then, during the first three months of 1982, the Buffalo Savings Bank acquired several troubled banks. As a result, it grew from $3 billion in assets and 40,000 mortgages serviced in Buffalo to about $9 billion in assets and 94,000 mortgages in a multistate service portfolio. This put added strain on the nascent mortgage bank, since it had to maintain its low delinquency rate, pay its investors monthly, and pay residential taxes from funds it held in escrow between the mortgagors' monthly payment date and the tax payment date. Ross said, "This growth was difficult and required long hours of detailed work by all of our people. During it we all worked together day and night. We also hired several experienced managers from other mortgage banks."

GRCC AND RESIDENTIAL MORTGAGE BANKING

In August 1983, several managers, including Peter Ross (current senior vice president of Loan Administration) in Goldome FSB's mortgage department wrote the strategic plan for Goldome's new mortgage banking subsidiary GRCC. The business concept was that GRCC would service a large portfolio of mortgages on residential and commercial property located throughout the United States.

Additions to the servicing portfolio were to come in part from the holdings of the troubled banks Goldome FSB acquired. But in the long term, additions to the servicing portfolio were to come mainly from new mortgages originated by GRCC. Residential mortgages accounted for over 70 percent of GRCC's business. *Exhibit 1* presents an organization chart for GRCC and part of Goldome. *Exhibits 2* and *3* present GRCC's balance sheet and income statement as of November 1985. *Exhibit 4* shows the ratio comparisons presented to GRCC managers at Goldome with the financial statements.

GRCC originated residential mortgages in regional offices located in growing housing markets throughout the country. The number of origination offices changed often because new offices were typically founded whenever Goldome FSB established a banking presence in a new location or a promising origination market was found. In addition, although origination employees were very well paid, largely through commissions, many were laid off during cyclical downturns in the housing market. GRCC's chief financial officer estimated that in 1985 GRCC spent approximately 60 basis points (b.p.), or 0.6%, of the principal in originating the typical residential mortgage.

In Buffalo, GRCC grouped the mortgages issued nationwide into pools of around $5 to $10 million each for sale to institutional investors. To minimize the period during which it was vulnerable to interest-rate fluctuations, GRCC matched mortgages with investor financing quickly and hedged unmatched holdings in the financial markets.

After a mortgage was originated or acquired from another bank, servicing it was Peter Ross's responsibility. First it was recorded in the central computer, then the mortgage file was stored in the vault. Subsequently, the mortgage was serviced according to the process diagram depicted in *Exhibit 5*.

SERVICE FOR RESIDENTIAL MORTGAGES

GRCC was required by contract with the institutional investors to provide four general types of service for each mortgage. (1) Each month either each mortgagee's required payment was either received and recorded, or the delinquency operation was asked to initiate collection proceedings and, if payment was not ultimately received, foreclosure proceedings were begun. (2) For each mortgage for each year, related tax and insurance payments were recomputed, several bills were sent out, and funds were held in escrow and periodically disbursed to the appropriate agency. (3) Each month the institutional investors whose mortgages were serviced by GRCC were sent payments for mortgages and reports on delinquencies in the portfolio. (4) GRCC was also required by certain regulatory agencies to answer questions and resolve problems related to the servicing of their mortgages. For example, the Federal Housing Administration (FHA) required that all its mortgagees be able to reach its servicing agencies by an 800 or local telephone number.

It was critical to perform the servicing function well to maintain a steady cash flow. A high delinquency rate meant that the mortgage bank would have to borrow the cash to pay its investors at the proper time and that foreclosures—on which mortgage banks generally lost considerable money—would increase. Similarly, late tax payments would result in a 1% to 2% penalty from the local taxing authorities. In addition, the late payment would require someone in the tax department to process the paperwork by hand.

GRCC charged on average the industry standard fees for servicing residential mortgages: 38 b.p. of the principal. The average size of the principal in GRCC's portfolio was $35,000; the size of the typical new mortgage in 1985 was $70,000. The average life of the mortgages in GRCC's portfolio was 12 years.

The average servicing cost did not vary with the size of the mortgage, but servicing costs increased dramatically for mortgages for which monthly payments were frequently delinquent (especially those that were ultimately foreclosed). In part to defray and prevent delinquency costs, GRCC and its competitors routinely imposed penalty fees on their mortgagees whose monthly payments were late. Ross believed that there was little cost advantage in servicing a portfolio larger than $2 billion.

Ross believed that GRCC's average cost of servicing a mortgage was about $2 higher than that of the largest mortgage companies. In December 1985 he estimated that it cost GRCC an average of $77 to service a residential mortgage. *Exhibit 6* shows how this cost was distributed among the servicing-related operations.

Ross noted:

During our rapid-growth period, it was incredibly difficult to keep our operations under control. And we were not always on top of all the details. There were months when we did not pay all tax bills due, and we incurred penalty charges. Even in late 1984 our delinquency rate was as high as 12%, while the U.S. average was close to 6%. Since then we have improved. Our average delinquency rate reached the U.S. average last October.

We always kept the most critical functions under control. As a last resort we would throw people at the problems, thus ensuring the most essential tasks were completed. As a result, in 1984 our costs were probably somewhat heavy in the personnel areas for the industry. Now that our operation is in control, our strategy is to cut the costs of servicing a mortgage to the bare minimum. We have already improved productivity in Escrow and Investor Reporting. In 1983 we serviced 100,000 loans with 124 people in those departments, but now we service 140,000 loans with only 88 people in those departments.

PROFITABILITY IMPROVEMENT DIVISION

PID was established in late 1984 by Paul Ruch, Goldome's chief operating officer. PID's mission, according to Ruch, was "to objectively assess all areas in which meaningful and lasting contributions to profit can be made via reduction in direct operating expense through the improved utilization of technology and/ or better defined and standardized systems and procedures." PID was given responsibility to approve all replacements or additions to personnel throughout Goldome, including GRCC but excluding the other subsidiaries. In late 1985 the 25 professionals in PID (industrial engineers, MBAs, business analysts) were grouped in four project teams located in the banking subsidiaries in Buffalo, Florida and New York City, in addition to GRCC.

Jay Kutler, vice president of PID, had, since the 1981–82 acquisition of two New York City banks, directed the Downstate Information Services Department, including a methods and procedures group. He noted that his teams used the same techniques in several areas of Goldome (such as branch banks and data processing), working mainly with nonexempt job categories. Kutler said:

> PID's programs and services were designed to assist and support department and branch management in the development of information to improve productivity and profitability. Further, the programs and services involved supervisory and management personnel in the use of analytical "tools" to enhance operational effectiveness, efficiency and eliminate duplication. PID project teams utilize various methodologies to develop task and activity standards, including predetermined time systems, work sampling, self-logging, and in some cases a stopwatch, to test and validate the data obtained using the other methods. Also, project teams, regardless of their location, follow prescribed standards regarding the project phases that must be accomplished for each study.
>
> Since PID's primary mission is to assist management in improving operational and service efficiency and effectiveness, at lower costs, we must not only develop accurate and timely procedures and standards, but we must also provide meaningful workflow enhancements through the development of recommendations. The publication of a department's or branch's monthly performance (or staffing) model is to provide an ongoing report of how well that group is performing against standards, as well as how and where performance can be improved. Since a standard is a measure of how

long a task or activity should take to accomplish by an average well-trained employee, it is important that management continually evaluate performance, so that they can anticipate potential operational and/or service problems. The performance model must be used by the managers in justifying replacement or additional employees. We begin by agreeing to 75% of standard with the operation's management and then try to move toward 100%. Since my people approve those requests before they go to the human resources department, I can ensure that everyone uses the performance models.

PID had identified $5 million of calculated cost savings since the program was started in April 1985: $1 million came from declining requests for personnel, $2.4 million from implementation of the staffing model in various departments (e.g., demonstrating to managers how they could provide better service with fewer people), and $1.6 million from improving work methods.

George Huyler headed PID operations for western New York. He said that he was trying to

> . . . increase the value of PID to our customers within Goldome. I have tried to make our client consulting relations less adversarial and more concerned with the quality of work life for all employees, as well as with the effectiveness of the work systems. I think the reason we have done so well is that we remain basically reasonable. . . . GRCC is a particularly important site for us within Goldome because the company is dynamic and willing to experiment.

During 1985, Huyler received 1,808 requests for new and replacement staff in western New York. In almost all cases PID teams worked with the managers to either prepare a good business case for the request or to determine a way to run the operation that made the person requested unnecessary. Only 56 requests were denied.

WORK MANAGEMENT PROJECT

Peter Ross had invited a PID team to work in GRCC to analyze the operations of the telephone area in Customer Service. In October 1985 a three-member PID team led by Susan Wojnowski arrived to spend three months studying the Customer Service operation.

Earlier in the fall both Ross and GRCC President Kevin O'Neil had personally visited the Customer Service telephone area to ask the Customer Service representatives (CSRs) to cooperate with the PID team. The CSRs had worked enthusiastically to provide information to the team.

The PID team spent two months full time working with the CSRs to learn about the operation, understand the CSRs' perceptions, and identify possible areas for improvement. First, they studied the CSRs' current activities using a stopwatch and a Master Clerical Data (MCD) standard, designed by Serfe A. Birn Co. At the same time, they met with a volunteer group of CSRs in a series of roundtable discussions. These meetings focused on the CSRs' interest in improving the communications between Customer Service area and the Tax and Escrow departments. The PID team used the CSRs as a sounding board for many of its potential recommendations. The team also used information on standards and volumes as the basis for a staffing model. Finally, it provided a report with recommendations for improving the Customer Service area's operation.

CUSTOMER SERVICE—TELEPHONES

Fourteen full-time and the equivalent of 1.5 part-time CSRs answered mortgagors' questions about all aspects of GRCC's activities and received all telephone complaints. Mollie Higgins, the manager of the telephone area, had a three-foot-square sign on her wall proclaiming "The Victim of Circumstance Department." *Exhibit 7* shows the telephone area's expenses for October 1985.

The department had 28 workstations, each with a telephone line and a computer terminal with access to basic information in the central database on the current status of each mortgagor's account. In a normal period some of the workstations were not occupied. Twelve telephone lines were local, eight were WATS band 5 (unrestricted national area), and eight were WATS band 0 (restricted to western New York). In January all 16 WATS lines were going to become band 5. WATS prices at the time for band 5 were: for one access line $36.80; for the first 15 hours each business day, an additional $36.80 an hour; for the next 25 hours, $21.09 an hour; for the next 40 hours, $19.24 an hour; and for all time over 80 hours, $16.92 an hour.

For the Work Management Project the PID team studied the activities of a typical CSR (paid an average of $8.71 an hour, including benefits) during October. Standard times for typical tasks were computed by observing average CSRs with a stopwatch and by using the MCD standard for clerical tasks. The frequency of tasks was arrived at by the CSRs themselves; they kept logs of their tasks as they performed them. Higgins agreed that the information from that study shown in *Exhibit 8* provides a good profile of the CSRs' tasks.

Part of each CSR's day was spent at a workstation answering the telephone. The telephone calls the representatives received fell into four general categories. (1) Simple *inquiries* could generally be answered quickly by referring to the mortgagor's file in the central database. The file made it clear, for example, whether the loan could be *assumed* when the house was resold, whether a new *coupon book* had been sent to the mortgagor to accompany payments, what the mortgagor's *credit rating* was, what the current *mailing address* record was, how much *insurance* the mortgagor carried through GRCC, and the current *principal balance*. Most simple inquiries required the CSR to explain a bill that the customer had just received. (2) *Referrals* took slightly longer, since the CSR had to determine the correct GRCC office to refer the caller to. (3) *Explanatory* calls could take quite a long time, as CSRs, referring to computer records, explained to callers their current adjustable-rate mortgage (ARM) rate, the method of escrow *analysis*, why *late charges* were levied, and so on. (4) *Research* calls required CSRs to make inquiries off the phone to check payments made to or by GRCC or to answer miscellaneous homeowner questions. (The italicized words refer to categories in *Exhibit 8.*)

Higgins noted that the volume of calls varied over the year according to the season and to activities in other parts of GRCC. At escrow analysis time and when GRCC serviced a new portfolio of mortgages, there were many questions. Higgins estimated that in the course of a year six months would have a call volume of around 15,000; during two months volume would be as high as 22,000 calls; and during four months it could be as low as 10,000 calls.

When the calls came in heavily, Higgins and the group's two supervisors walked through the area, calling for everyone to get on the phones. At those times they, as well as several employees from the nearby Research Department, also took phone duty.

Call volume and content was also varied in response to routine servicing activities. Each morning the CSRs met with their supervisors. At the meeting the supervisors warned the CSRs of the kinds of calls to expect that day. Many of the calls concerned problems homeowners were having with GRCC. And on a given day, many callers had similar problems. For example, if the Tax Department had not received the tax bills for a particular county in Florida (because the company that assembled them for GRCC was remiss), then all GRCC customers in the county would have received dunning notices, and many of them would call Customer Service. Similarly, soon after escrow analyses were mailed to homeowners in a particular geographic area, many would call Customer Service to ask how their new payment had been calculated. If another GRCC department had a problem (such as a backlog), its managers ideally let the Customer Service supervisors know about it so the CSRs could be prepared for homeowners' questions. But at times the CSRs were the first GRCC employees to realize that a department had a problem.

Part of each CSR's day was spent working at or near the workstations on tasks designated in *Exhibit 8* as worktime tasks. Some of the most time-consuming were: writing *general work orders* for the nearby Research Department to follow up on, studying an *escrow analysis*, and *composing special letters* to mortgagors. CSRs also requested and studied the *physical mortgage files* when the computer-based files were not adequate to answer a mortgagor's question. CSRs had a personal commitment to answer the mortgagee's questions and solve their problems promptly. One CSR commented.

> I could send any request to the Research Department as a work order. But it will take a week or two for them to process it. And they may not understand what I write on the work order, so they will have to call me back to see if I remember. Even then, the mortgagor will only get a letter response to what may not even be their question.

October 1985, when the PID study was begun, had been a high-volume calling month, because GRCC had taken on a new portfolio of 13,000 mortgages to service. The average hold time per call had been 6.69 minutes, more than double the 3 minutes Ross had established as the standard (and that the group had usually maintained), and the phone bill had been $34,683.

Higgins said:

> CSRs typically remain in the area for less than a year. Then they move on to other departments in GRCC; they know the whole company, so they are useful everywhere. In this department they take personal responsibility for resolving the customer question. Many of the questions are simple. But they also hear about all the problems people have with their mortgages and try to get the problems resolved. I am always on the phone complaining to other departments.
>
> For example, in some parts of the country the taxing authorities put much more severe penalties on people who are late in paying than they do in New York. We feel sorry for the old lady from Florida whose name is published in the paper because she has not paid her local taxes even though she has paid us and we have not paid her taxes; we try to get the Tax people to pay her bill immediately. I understand that the Tax Department pays 300,000 tax bills a year and only makes mistakes on a few, and that they do not want to interrupt their regular work to process these problems. . . . And they should tell us if a computer problem made a large group of bills wrong. . . . In the last few years things have improved enormously. If they did their job better, we could do ours better.

PID RECOMMENDATIONS

Susan Wojnowski explained that her team's approach was to analyze the operation for all possible sources of cost and performance improvement, not to make choices for managers. She also noted that the telephone area of Customer Service had been particularly efficient. The productivity measurements she and her team had taken in other parts of Goldome usually revealed productivity to be about 55–60%. But the telephone area's measured productivity in October was 73% (standard hours/paid hours from *Exhibit 8*). The CSRs worked through lunch to get answers for their telephone clients.

PID's recommendations fell into the following categories:

	Estimated Annual Savings
Workstation design and layout	$20,563.97
Training	—
Computer system enhancements	—
Roundtable discussion suggestions	22,356.67
Work flows and unit tasks	88,963.13
Coupon book design and distribution	32,762.20
Staff scheduling	97,191.90

The December Work Management report included 50 specific recommendations. Each consisted of a finding (based on detailed observations), a problem definition (diagnosing the reasons that there was room for improvement), recommendations (detailing actions to be taken in response to the findings and the problem), and in many but not all cases, estimated annual savings. All but three of the recommendations accounted for estimated savings of less than $4,000 each. They included such items as buying squeeze bottles (so that reps could avoid licking envelopes) and publishing the mortgage assumption group's telephone number in coupon books (to avoid the need to answer some calls destined for another group and to avoid paying the WATS charge while calls to the wrong group were waiting for Customer Service lines).

REACTIONS TO THE PID TEAM'S RECOMMENDATIONS

The case writer spoke with Nancy Strup and Mollie Higgins on December 12. They were ready to implement all but two of the recommendations. About these two they had serious misgivings. These were two with large estimated savings.

First, under work flows and unit tasks, redefining the CSRs' tasks so as to have CSRs do less research, resolve fewer questions, and answer the phones more, should save about $89,000 a year. Strup and Higgins supported many of PID's recommendations to reduce the CSRs' workload. For example, PID suggested that CSRs no longer tell phone callers to send payments to them for personal processing. This resulted in a short list of tasks that would disappear or decrease substantially. PID also recommended having CSRs refer questions that required research to the Research Department, rather than resolving them and getting back to the mortgagor. This would decrease the duration and frequency of the CSR work time tasks enumerated in *Exhibit 8*. In particular, the PID team recommended reassignment of work time tasks as follows:

Tasks to be Retained by CSRs	*Tasks to Disappear or Decrease Substantially*	*Tasks Reassigned to Research*
— Request payment administration work order — Send form letters — Data change input in computer record — Sign off/on computer system — Send assumption card — Sign off/on phones — Amortization schedule analysis	— Process a late payment — Photocopy — Payoff statement request — Mortgage file request — General work order — Credit rating — Compose special letter — Filing	— Coupon books — Exception cards — Examine escrow analysis — Request reanalysis — Collect escrow in advance

Second, under staff scheduling, changing the staffing pattern to have phone-answering capacity more closely match the patterns of incoming calls was recommended. The main thrust of the recommendations in this area was to increase the proportion of part-time workers to full-time workers and to change part-time workers' hours daily to reflect demand fluctuations. (Part-timers then worked from 10 a.m. to 2 p.m.) The PID team had been particularly thorough in this aspect of its recommendations. It had used a queuing model, simulated on the computer to estimate the call frequency and likely capacity utilization. Furthermore, it had presented the managers with a range of staffing patterns that could be used to get different waiting times. This was the staffing model PID would use in the future to evaluate staff requests from the telephone group. The model assumed that the changes recommended by PID would be made. In particular, with current staffing levels the model predicted that the CSRs could achieve a three-minute wait time—if the job restructuring recommendations were implemented.

The staffing model proposed the following requirements for staff in relation to wait time:

	Current Staff Pattern Full Time Equivalent		Proposed Staff Pattern Full Time Equivalent		
		Average Wait Time			
	3 min.	1 min.	2 min.	3 min.	4 min.
Full-Time	14.0	7.0	7.0	7.0	7.0
Part-Time	1.6	5.4	3.9	3.5	3.4
Est. Annual Salary					
Expense:	$264,958.20	$194,910.30	$174,552.30	$169,123.50	$167,766.30
Est. Annual Salary					
Savings:		$ 70,047.90	$ 90,405.90	$ 95,834.70	$ 97,191.90

Mollie Higgins noted that the log the PID team compiled would be useful to her in documenting the number and types of problems her group was encountering on the phones. "Then the particular department managers will know it's a real problem and not —'just my nature'"

Nancy Strup, assistant vice president of GRCC, managed the three Customer Service areas, including the telephone area. She had joined GRCC in 1983 after earning an MBA while working for five years for another mortgage bank in the Midwest. She commented cautiously on the PID recommendations:

Most of the particular recommendations are very reasonable and useful. They went into great detail and even suggested that we get squeeze bottles for the CSRs so that they will not have to lick envelopes with their tongues.

But there are a few which cause us some concern. The biggest question in my mind is whether we should remove from the CSRs the responsibility to answer questions and do some research. In October, when they did the study, we got 15,000 calls. Now only one in 22 results in a work order because the CSRs know how to answer all the others. The CSRs have all learned about GRCC and the answers to particular questions by doing the research required to answer the questions of customers. If we remove that research responsibility, will we generate many more work orders? The PID people have not worked with the research section yet, so they cannot know how much money we will have to spend there in order to do the extra research.

Also the PID staffing model recommends that we hire many more part-time people and that we reduce our full-time hires. And the schedules they suggest for the part-timers vary every day: some would work four days and different times each day. All the schedules require work after 4 p.m. one day a week. I don't know whether we could even find good people to do that. But most of our part-timers come from teller jobs in the bank, and many have young children in school. They like our 10–2 hours. Finally, our CSRs are concerned about their career paths within GRCC.

All these changes would drastically change the nature of the CSR's job. We would probably have to train CSRs extensively; whereas now they train on the job. I think we would have to get a different type of person to be a CSR if the job were all phone answering. This all raises questions about what kind of service we want the CSRs to deliver.

Fran Randall and Margaret Smith, the two telephone supervisors, had worked for GRCC since the summer of 1984.

Our priority is to give the best service to customers that we can. Now our staff takes pride in answering questions and in helping people with problems with other departments. If they remove our research, they will remove the knowledge the CSRs need to do a good job in answering questions. Besides, people in this country are oriented to pick up the phone and they want an answer, especially for something as important as their insurance or mortgage. If Research answers the questions by mail, they will keep down the minutes per call because we won't answer customer questions and it will take weeks for customers to get answers in writing. . . . Besides, if we wanted to be telephone operators . . .

Why can't the Tax Department pay taxes right away when we discover a person whose tax has not been paid? Before the tax sale takes place? Peter Ross and upper management should deal with the problem, not just Customer Service. Other departments have to change their opinion of the priorities here.

Both Higgins and Strup were enthusiastic about a PID recommendation to increase the training program for the CSRs.

Kutler said in a phone conversation:

PID teams knew that dedicating workers to phones had worked well in many other Goldome departments. GRCC managers will learn that too. We have made similar changes in telephone answering departments in other parts of Goldome. Always, both service and productivity increase. These CSRs enjoy solving problems, but repeatedly getting the same problem is frustrating. And their research tasks are detailed, boring, and not very creative. They send out coupon books for mortgage payments, or process an escrow payment, or go through nitty-gritty details in the archives to see if someone put a mistaken number into the computer. When these CSRs do both "research" and phone answering, they are very hard to manage productively. They have too many interruptions.

Ross reflected on the issues of productivity and service in the telephone area.

We will use the studies of the PID team to help us reduce our operating costs and use technology better. I have no good estimate of how much we should be able to save until PID studies an area. But when the managers of my departments are using the standards to manage, then I will know that PID has been a real success and the cost savings will follow.

The team's first assignment was the telephone area in Customer Service. I expect that they will also find major savings possibilities in Hazard Insurance, Tax Paying, and New Loan Setup. I am less certain that there are big savings to be found in Delinquency, but I will definitely send the PID team there after the other studies are done.

We now have the recommendations. I and my managers disagree on their applicability. The critical question is whether I have the managers and supervisors that have the ability and willingness to implement the PID theories.

In addition, last week when I presented our 1986 plan to Ross Kenzie, has only comment was, "In 1986, you *will* improve Customer Service."

GOLDOME REALTY CREDIT CORPORATION

Exhibit 1

Organization Chart, December 1, 1985

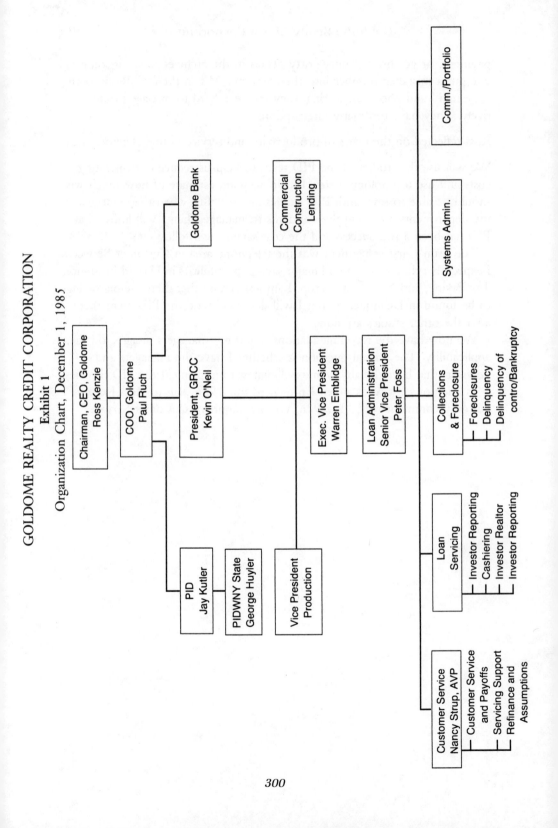

GOLDOME REALTY CREDIT CORPORATION
Exhibit 2
Balance Sheet, November 1985

Assets		Liabilities and Stockholders' Equity	
Cash	$ 1,125,185	Goldome Short-term Borrowings	$228,840,445
Short-term Investments	0	External Short-term Borrowings	23,086,781
Mortgage Loans	249,721,944	Bank Overdraft	0
Construction Loans	106,106	Accrued Interest Payable	1,931,679
Accrued Interest Receivable	1,543,123	Accounts Payable and Accrued Expenses	7,896,148
Advances and Other Accounts Receivable	21,172,067	Mortgage Escrow and Other Deposits	0
Prepaid Commitment Fees	1,675,061	Due to Affiliates	0
Prepaid Expenses and Other Assets	1,968,572	Unearned Commitments and Other Liabilities	6,672,338
Due from Affiliates	(1,068,573)		
Total Current Assets	$275,101,143	Total Current Liabilities	$268,427,391
		Goldome Long-term Borrowings	$ 9,975,000
		External Long-term Borrowings	0
		Deferred Credits	0
FHMA Common Stock	$ 55,203	Total Liabilities	$278,402,391
		Stockholders' Equity	
Property and Equipment	3,502,569	Preferred Stock	$ 625,000
Costs of Purchased Servicing	$ 31,445,616	Common Stock	16,000
Deferred Servicing Premium on Sales of Mortgage Loans	9,932,240	Paid-in Capital	30,188,442
Real Estate Owned	808,661	Retained Earnings	14,377,725
Unamortized Goodwill	2,764,125		
Total Assets	$323,609,557	Total Liabilities and Stockholders' Equity	$323,609,557

GOLDOME REALTY CREDIT CORPORATION
Exhibit 3
Functional Income Statements for the Period Ending November 30, 1985
(in thousands)

	Residential	Commercial	Servicing	Administration	Total YTD	% of Budget	Budget
Operating Income:							
Loan Origination Fees	$ 5,051.3	$2,493.6	$ 269.4	$ 0.0	$ 7,814.3	57.6%	$13,558.5
Transfer/Assumption Fees	26.2	0.0	549.7	0.0	575.9	73.2	787.0
Service Fees	10.5	2,089.9	14,526.1	0.0	16,625.5	108.2	15,366.7
Marketing Gains/(Losses)	1,277.9	0.0	0.0	0.0	1,277.9	371.7	543.8
Net Interest Margin	112.0	0.0	0.0	7,678.1	7,790.2	195.4	3,987.0
Late Charges	0.0	37.7	1,859.8	0.0	1,897.6	152.2	1,247.0
Other Interest Income	0.0	0.0	0.0	115.0	115.0	82.5	139.4
Other Income	520.1	387.1	1,880.9	1.6	2,789.7	95.9	2,909.9
TOTAL OPERATING INCOME	$ 6,998.0	$5,008.3	$19,086.0	$7,794.7	$38,886.0	101.4%	$38,339.1

Operating Expense:

Salaries and Commissions	$ 7,444.0	$1,327.8	$ 4,117.9	$1,596.7	$14,486.4	88.5%	$16,369.2
Benefits	1,117.8	155.0	797.0	265.6	2,335.3	76.3	3,061.6
Furniture, Equipment, and Occupancy	3,513.3	478.2	2,463.4	924.0	7,378.9	113.1	6,524.5
Data Processing	782.3	23.0	1,560.9	26.4	2,392.6	88.7	2,698.0
Other Interest Expense	0.0	0.0	0.0	1,765.4	1,765.4	1,277.9	138.2
Other Expenses	1,097.0	289.3	2,200.8	1,591.8	5,178.9	114.7	4,513.4
TOTAL OPERATING EXPENSE	$13,954.3	$2,273.3	$11,139.9	$6,169.9	$33,537.5	100.7%	$33,304.8
NET INCOME BEFORE INCOME TAX	(6,956.4)	2,734.0	7,946.1	1,624.8	5,348.5	106.2	5,034.3
INCOME TAX				534.9	534.9	106.2	503.4
NET INCOME AFTER TAX (NIAT)	($6,956.4)	$2,734.0	$ 7,946.1	$1,089.9	$ 4,813.7	106.2%	$ 4,530.8
FUNCTIONAL BUDGET NIAT	($4,309.4)	$2,858.1	$ 6,167.7	$ (185.7)	$ 4,530.8		
NIAT BUDGET VARIANCE	($2,647.0)	($124.1)	$ 1,778.4	$1,275.6	282.8		

Exhibit 4
Profitability Performance Measures for the Period Ending
November 30, 1985

	Current Month	*1985 YTD*	*1985 Financial Plan*	*1983 Largest Servicers*
Return on Average Assets (Annualized)	1.02%	1.69%	NA	2.60%
Return on Average Equity (Annualized)	7.03	11.65	12.50	22.40
Net Operating Income/ Total Income	5.6	11.3	9.7	19.8
Total Interest Income/ Total Income	49.0	34.1	33.1	42.5
Loan Servicing Income/ Total Income	30.4	35.2	32.6	30.4
Loan Origination Income/ Total Income	16.2	16.6	29.1	22.7
Personnel Expense/ Total Expense	33.1	40.2	46.1	34.7
Nonpersonnel Expense/ Total Expense	66.9	59.8	53.9	65.3
Interest Expense/ Total Expense	31.8	19.8	22.0	34.4

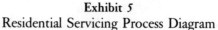

Exhibit 5
Residential Servicing Process Diagram

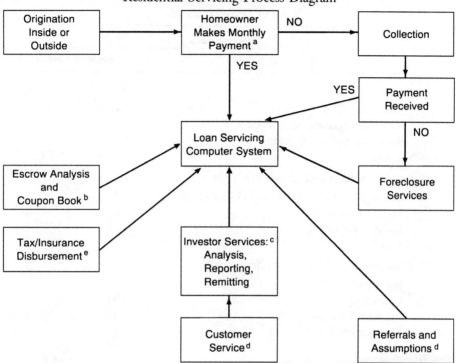

[a]Done once per month.

[b]Done once per year.

[c]According to contract with investor.

[d]Customer initiated.

[e]Done according to schedule of local taxing authority or insurance company.

NOTE: Arrows indicate changes routinely made in the central computer system.

Exhibit 6
Estimated Annual Cost of Adding One Residential Loan
(as of December 1985)

Variable Costs	
Operation	*Incremental Cost*
Customer Service	
Telephone Area	$ 5.31
Vault Management and Support	0.18
Refinance and Assumptions	1.29
Subtotal	6.78
Investors Services and Escrow Processing	
Tax and Escrow Analysis and Disbursement	3.53
Hazard Insurance	2.22
Investor Reporting	3.92
Subtotal	9.67
Delinquency and Foreclosure Services	
Foreclosure	1.76
Collection	2.47
Payment Processing	.43
Computer Services	9.00
Other	2.26
Subtotal	15.92
Total Incremental Annual Cost/Loan	32.37
Total Incremental Fixed Costs	
Occupancy	12.00
Managerial Salaries	10.00
Parent Charges	7.00
Foreclosure Losses	10.00
Computer Support	6.00
Subtotal	45.00
Total Costs	$77.37

NOTE: These numbers have been changed to protect the competitive interests of GRCC.

Exhibit 7

Customer Service Telephone Area Expenses for October 1985

Salaries (including clerk/typist and 2 supervisors)	$21,203
Use and Occupancy	5,217
Communication	34,683
Office Supplies and Postage	1,616
Data Processing[a]	2,158
Travel and Entertainment	159
Other Expenses	955
Total Expenses	$65,991

[a] Includes only equipment and maintenance.

GOLDOME REALTY CREDIT CORPORATION
Exhibit 8
Standards for Staffing Model Based on Month of October 1985

Work Time Tasks	Standard Minutes Per Task	October 1985 Volume	Telephone Calls	Standard Minutes Per Task	October 1985 Volume
			Inquiry (Avg. = 2.51 min.)		
Request Payment Administration			Assumption	2.39	468
Work Order	4.30	422	Coupon Book	2.91	788
Process a Late Payment	2.67	112	Credit Rating	2.48	752
Photocopies	4.33	76	Mailing Address	2.47	1,124
Send Form Letters	4.14	504	Optional Insurance	2.61	258
Coupon Books	0.51	386	Principal Balance	2.19	947
Payoff Statement Request	2.11	300	*Referral (Avg. = 2.78 min.)*		
Exception Cards	0.86	91	Delinquency	2.56	761
Mortgage File Requests	2.70	97	Discharge	3.98	1,100
General Work Order	12.65	1,076	Foreclosure	3.19	202
Data Change Input in			Originations	2.34	248
Computer Record	1.06	1,344	Search and Survey	1.83	146
Sign On/Off Computer System	0.46	1,140	*Explanatory (Avg. = 3.07 min.)*		
Obtain Credit Ratings	0.98	2,121	ARM Schedule	2.67	69

Task	Rate	Volume
Send Assumption Cards to Mortgagors	2.29	207
Examine Escrow Analysis	10.59	2
Request Reanalysis of Mortgagor's Escrow	1.76	192
Compose Special Letter	9.52	112
Filing	0.56	4,725
Collect Escrow in Advance	2.24	3
Sign On/Off Phones	0.76	380
Amortization Schedule Analysis	4.83	100

Task	Rate	Volume
Analysis	6.63	682
ARM	6.09	239
Late Charge	2.07	1,392
Paid	2.05	240
Release of Escrow	1.00	33
Release of Liability	1.00	10
Research		
Conversion	3.34	387
Homeowners	2.87	1,874
Payment	3.07	2,308
Tax	4.03	1,216
Year End	5.68	104

Total Standard Hours Required	1,268.73
Absenteeism and Vacation (10%)	126.87
Clerical Support (37.5 hour/week)	150.00
Total Standard Hours	1,545.60
Total Paid Hours	2,158.75
Staff Required at 100% Performance	13.08
Actual Staff	15.5
Authorized Staff	13.00

Club Med (A)

In January 1987, Jacques Giraud, president and chief executive officer of Club Med, Inc., was reflecting upon his first year at the company's helm. He was pleased with the company's financial performance in 1986, and he was excited about its prospects for future growth. His optimism was tempered, however, by the knowledge that competition was growing. Until now, Club Med had faced only a handful of competitors throughout the world and almost no direct competition in what was referred to as the "American Zone." In recent years, however, several organizations had attempted to duplicate the Club Med experience, among them SuperClubs, Jack Tar Villages, Sandals, and Eden II resorts, all based in the Caribbean. In Germany, Robinson's had captured an estimated 75% to 80% of the German market for all-inclusive vacation packages.

Giraud swiveled his chair and turned to gaze out over Central Park. He mused:

> We have done well so far in the North American Market—our success seems virtually assured. But are we really as competition-proof as some people think? Or are we going to wake up one day to a big surprise—like the U.S. auto companies did? Has the lack of competition until now inflated our egos, fattened our bellies, and blinded us to internal weaknesses? We have been successful for so long, and have taken so many things for granted, that I wonder what our strengths really are. And where our problems lie. As Molière said, "It is not only what we do, but also what we do not do, for which we are accountable."

COMPANY BACKGROUND AND HISTORY

Often referred to as "the Club," Club Méditerranée was the ninth-largest hotel company in the world in 1986. It had been founded by a group of friends in 1950 as a nonprofit sports association. The group was led by Gerard Blitz, a Belgian diamond cutter and water-polo champion, who, like the others in the group, was on a tight budget and had an affinity for sports and vacations in scenic seaside locations. Members of the association slept in sleeping bags and

This case was prepared by Assistant Professor Christopher W. L. Hart, with the research assistance of Dan Arczynski, Dan Maher, and Lucy N. Lytle, as the basis for class discussion rather than to illustrate either effective or ineffective handling of an administrative situation. Copyright© 1986 by the President and Fellows of Harvard College; Harvard Business School case #9-687-046 Rev. 10/88.

took turns cooking meals and washing dishes. As the association grew, running it as an informal, loosely organized group became increasingly difficult.

In 1954, Blitz invited his close friend, Gilbert Trigano—an active association member whose family business had been supplying the group with U.S. Army-surplus tents—to join the association on a full-time basis. Trigano, who saw commercial potential in the concept, became managing director and set out to transform the association into a business. In 1985, Club Méditerranée S.A., a publicly owned company traded on the Paris Stock Exchange, had 108 resort villages throughout the world and hosted 820,000 vacationers annually. *Exhibit 1* shows the locations of the company's villages.

Throughout this growth, the "family spirit" endured among the Club's managers, and was a significant part of the company's culture. All of the top managers at Paris headquarters had formerly worked in the villages, many in the position of general manager ("village chief" in the Club's parlance).

In 1972, Club Med, Inc. was formed as a U.S. subsidiary of Club Méditerranée. Gilbert Trigano's son Serge, 39, who had worked his way up in the firm, became president and chief executive officer of Club Med, Inc., in 1982. The subsidiary sold the company's vacation packages and operated its resorts in North America, the Caribbean, South America, Asia, and the South Pacific. *Exhibits 2, 3,* and *4* show selected operating data for Club Med, Inc.

In 1984, about 25% of the subsidiary's shares were sold in a public offering on the New York Stock Exchange. They sold at a hefty price-earnings multiple of 16, which many people thought was too high. The stock became a favorite of several influential Wall Street analysts, however, who realized that Club Med had several operational features that differed significantly from traditional hotel chains. First, the company earned $3 million per year just in interest from customers' prepaid vacation deposits. Second, capacity was measured as the number of beds in a village, not the number of rooms. (Singles were assigned roommates.) Third, a respected analyst, who specialized in the gaming and lodging industries, projected strong sales growth for the U.S. subsidiary, based on a historical analysis of the Club's market penetration in other countries. (See *Exhibit 5.*)

In 1985, Jacques Giraud, who had been *directeur général* of Club Méditerranée, moved from Paris to New York to take over as president and chief executive officer of Club Med, Inc. from Serge Trigano, who moved back to Paris to head the parent firm.

INDUSTRY STRUCTURE

Club Med was in a strong position with respect to buyers, suppliers, and labor. (See *Exhibit 6.*) Buyers, for example, could buy the "true formula" only from the Club. According to company management, it would cost a consumer 50% to 100% more to attempt to replicate the Club Med experience through other vacation options. The price of a week's vacation during the winter season at Club Med's Caribbean villages, including round-trip airfare from New York, ran from 1,000 to $1,400 per person.

Second, the company enjoyed a strong bargaining position with its suppliers. Commercial airlines jumped at the opportunity to sell seats to Club Med at volume discounts, which Club Med sold as part of vacation packages at a substantial profit. Because the Club's villages created jobs and tourism revenue, economically depressed countries in exotic locations competed fiercely to become the sites of new Club Med villages. The benefit packages they offered often included low-cost financing, foreign-worker agreements, tax breaks, and, in some cases, direct equity investment.

Club Med also possessed considerable leverage with labor. A surprisingly large number of young and talented people were eager to work as Club Med "GOs."[1] In 1984, the company received 35,000 GO applications for 2,000 positions worldwide. Turnover was high, however—nearly 46% among newly recruited American GOs in their first season, and 27.6% overall. Additionally, the company enjoyed a strong bargaining position in negotiating the wages of local village workers.

Exhibit 7 gives comparative performance data for Club Med and the two industries in which it operates: lodging and air transport.

DISTRIBUTION NETWORK

Club Med bundled the ground portion of its vacation package (i.e., lodging, meals, sports activities, ground transportation) with air transportation and sold the complete packages either through travel agents or directly to consumers. Direct sales were made through its reservations center in Scottsdale, Arizona, or through "vacation stores" it had established in several large North American cities.

Club Med management recognized that the number of travel agencies had increased enormously during the 1970s and early 1980s, jumping from approximately 6,700 in the United States in 1970 to over 24,000 by 1983. This growth

---

1. The term "GO" (pronounced "gee-oh") stands for "gentils organisateurs" in French, "congenial hosts" in English. Each Club Med village employs a team of about 80 GOs who handle all jobs other than housekeeping and maintenance. GOs organize the activities in a Club Med village and mingle freely with guests (called "GMs": "gentils membres" in French, "congenial members" in English).

was largely due to airline deregulation. The end result was that an average of 80 travel agencies opened or went out of business each day, travel increased, and travel-agent commissions went up as competing airlines tried to capture a larger share of the travel-agency market. It appeared that the travel-agency business would become increasingly concentrated; a protracted market shakeout was expected, and would lead to the demise of many small, undercapitalized operations. Conversely, large firms with scale economies (i.e., American Express, Thomas Cook) were expected to capture an increasing share of the travel market.

Club Med vacation packages were widely distributed, with 12,000 agencies booking 115,000 customers in 1982. However, approximately 50% of the Club's nondirect sales were booked by only 2,000 agencies. Unfortunately, turnover among these top-sellers was high—half of the top 2,000 agencies in 1982 were not among the top agencies in the previous year.

In 1983, Club Med's strategy for dealing with the fast-changing distribution network was to increase the loyalty to Club Med of top-selling travel agencies by:

- educating their travel agents about the Club Med vacation package;
- designating top-selling chains as "Club Med experts" and have Club Med's sales representatives direct most of their attention to these chains;
- tying in Club Med's promotional efforts exclusively with the "expert" agencies;
- rotating a "flying team" of GOs who hold informational seminars throughout North American cities;
- creating travel-agent schools and placing the graduates with "expert" agencies.

COMPETITION

By 1986, Club Med was no longer the only successful chain of all-inclusive, club-style resorts. Other companies in the western hemisphere had entered the all-inclusive resort market. Moreover, new competitors were appearing on the scene at an alarming rate. The advertisement of one competitor is featured in *Exhibit 8*.

Nonetheless, over the years many companies that had tried to compete with Club Med had failed. This led to much speculation throughout the lodging industry: Why was the record of would-be competitors so dismal? No known analysis of this topic had yet been published.

As opposed to pay-as-you-go traditional hotels, all-inclusive (AI) resorts offered lodging, all meals, recreational activities, and airport transfers for one preset price.

Airfare was usually offered as an option, at charter rates. Except for a few optional activities (i.e., deep-sea fishing, day excursions), guests usually did not need to make any purchases while staying at the resort. Most AI resorts offered a wide range of recreational activities, with specially selected staff members acting as activity directors, organizing games and teaching sports like windsurfing and scuba diving.

The Jamaica-based Jack Tar Village company operated AI resorts in Grand Bahama, Montego Bay, Runaway Bay, Puerto Playa, and Saint Kitts. Its village in Grand Bahama featured 12 tennis courts, 27 holes of golf, a shopping arcade, and "the largest swimming pool in the western hemisphere." The hotel facilities in Saint Kitts included a movie theater, a beauty salon, and a casino featuring blackjack, roulette, and slot machines. A new 250-room hotel, featuring a duty-free shopping zone and an aquarium, was scheduled to be built in Frigate Bay in the fall of 1986.

Jack Tar's glossy color advertisements, implicitly criticizing Club Med's spartan rooms and its methods of operation, promised that their all-inclusive price "covers virtually everything, including unlimited wine, beer and cocktails . . . You'll get a nicer room with full size beds, air-conditioning, and other first-class hotel amenities rarely found at other 'all-inclusive' resorts . . . You won't have to carry cash to the beach, sign vouchers, or keep up with drink tokens or beads." (At Club Med, GMs purchased plastic "bar beads" which were exchanged at the bar for drinks.)

This advertisement prompted one executive at Club Med to remark:

> So what if Jack Tar Villages includes the price of cigarettes and drinks at the bar in their package? [At Club Med these items were not included in the all-inclusive price.] A customer who would choose them over Club Med for that reason is what we would consider an undesirable customer. Our clientele generally doesn't include people whose aim is to drink a lot of free booze. We serve free wine at dinner because that is the European way.

Another competitor was the SuperClubs organization, which operated four AI resorts in Jamaica: Couples I; Hedonism II; Jamaica, Jamaica; and Boscobel Beach. Couples I, located in Ocho Rios, was the first couples-only resort in the Caribbean when it opened in 1978. After a slow start (occupancy dipped as low as 10% the first year), the resort gained acceptance among travel agents and, by June 1982, management reported its 50th consecutive week of 100% occupancy, at least 18% of which was repeat business. Couples I boasted the highest year-round occupancy of any hotel in Jamaica—95%.

Hedonism II, a 20-acre, 280-room resort located in Negril Bay on the west coast of Jamaica, appealed to a slightly different market. It opened in 1974, and, according to its management, enjoyed 90% occupancy during the winter season, dropping to 60% in the off-peak seasons. With its beach equally divided between nude bathing and normal beachwear, and a windowed bar looking into a pool where nude swimming was allowed late at night, Hedonism II had a reputation as Jamaica's most uninhibited and sex-oriented resort. The available activities included tennis, basketball, exercise rooms, jet skiing, and parasailing (the latter two available off-site for an extra charge).

Two major operational distinctions between Club Med and SuperClubs were drinks and staff. First, whereas Club Med required guests to purchase drinks at the bar (with "bar beads"), SuperClubs included all drinks in its AI price. Second, the staff at Club Med villages was composed primarily of its GO team, the members of which rotated to different villages every 6 months, forming entirely new teams. The SuperClubs operations had a much smaller number of GOs—called "activity directors." Ordinarily they were individuals recruited from the local area; they did not rotate among SuperClubs' properties on a scheduled basis.

Another major distinction between Club Med and SuperClubs was packaging and distribution. As mentioned previously, Club Med bundled the ground portion of the vacation package with air transportation and sold the complete packages either through travel agents or directly to consumers. SuperClubs, on the other hand, bundled complete ground packages and sold them through large tour wholesalers—operations that combined the ground packages with airline seats purchased in bulk—and then sold the complete vacation packages through travel-agency chains. SuperClubs paid a 20% commission for this service.

When a Club Med executive was asked about the Club's strategy for dealing with such competitors as Jack Tar and SuperClubs, he explained that Club Med was "currently discussing how to deal with this issue." He added:

> This much is certain: Traditionally, Club Med's strength has been that our customers recommend us to their friends. Word-of-mouth business is very important to us. Where we risk losing business is with people who have never visited a Club Med, and who don't have any friends who've come here. That's the kind of people our competition might attract.
>
> Granted, the Club Med concept no longer is unique. Our competitors have copied the key ingredient—an all-inclusive price and an enthusiastic, pampering staff. *The difference is that they generally operate within a traditional hotel context.*

THE CLUB MED SERVICE CONCEPT, OPERATING STRATEGY, AND SERVICE DELIVERY SYSTEM

Club Med's rapid growth and dominance in the resort-vacation business was the product of its unique vacation concept. The Club Med concept has been de-

scribed as the process of transforming a group of uptight, urban professionals—
who start out as total strangers—into a fun-loving, relaxed group of friends and
acquaintances, "converts" who assist the GOs in welcoming the next group of
uptight, urban professionals into the village.

Club Med GMs (guests) truly were "members" in the sense that they paid a
$25 initiation fee and annual dues of $40. Members received newsletters and
high-quality catalogs featuring the Club's villages, and were given the opportunity to purchase such ancillary services as travel insurance.

Club Med villages were designed and operated to create an atmosphere in
which the GMs had nothing to worry about except relaxing and enjoying themselves. One female GM, reclining in a poolside chaise longue, observed, "I figured I was a workaholic because I could never forget about my job when I went
on vacation. I always felt kind of uneasy. But I've only been here for two days
and I've completely *forgotten* about work!" She sat up and called out to a group
of men and women playing water volleyball: "Hey honey, do you remember
what company I work for?" Multiple responses from the pool indicated that the
question was irrelevant and not to be repeated. The case writer admitted to
himself that he was having trouble remembering why he came to Club Med. "I
guess I won't need my calculator," he mused.

Each Club Med village was organized along similar lines. The chief of the
village had overall responsibility for village operations. Reporting to the village
chief were seven chiefs of service, each of whom was in charge of a different
functional area. The 80 or so GOs in a village reported to their respective chiefs
of service.

The GOs received a salary of about $400 a month, and were given room and
board which was estimated to cost Club Med an additional $250 per month.
GO-related expenses were considered to be a fixed cost, since the company's
policy was to keep the number of GOs in any village fixed, regardless of occupancy percentage.

Club Med village sites were selected for their natural beauty, good weather,
and recreational potential. Each facility typically had 150 to 300 rooms laid out
around a central core of facilities that included a large pool, an outdoor bar, a
theater, a main dining room, shops, and offices. The architectural design was
intended to facilitate interaction among GMs and GOs. Villages were built on
properties of 40 acres or so to provide plenty of space for such sporting activities
as windsurfing, sailing, waterskiing, snorkeling, archery, soccer, basketball, volleyball, tennis, and, in some villages, scuba diving. Additionally, each village had
landscaped areas with walkways to give GMs plenty of room to roam without
having to forego the village's safety and ambiance.

The rooms in Club Med villages were spartan, but clean. They lacked such
traditional conveniences as clocks, TVs, radios, telephones, postcards, and writ-

ing paper, the intent being to separate GMs as much as possible from the demands of civilization. One GM, an investment banker, cracked, "Three days ago, I was having telephone withdrawal symptoms. . . . I *craved* a phone! Today, I wish the damn things had never been invented. It must have been great in the old days when you made a decision, mailed a letter, and headed for the links." To promote a sense of trust in the village, there were no room keys (although rooms could be locked from inside). Unfortunately, theft was not unknown, especially in certain villages.

Everything in a village was organized to promote social intercourse. Meals were buffet style, and the buffet tables were elaborately laid out to convey a sense of variety and abundance. GMs and GOs were randomly seated together in groups of six or eight, again to promote interaction, and they could fill up on a wide variety of cheeses, fruits, breads, salads, vegetables, entrees, and desserts. Conversations among those seated at a table were spontaneous, especially after a few glasses of beer or wine (which were available in unlimited quantities at lunch and dinner). One GM commented, "I felt uncomfortable at first, being seated with people I didn't know. It's not a problem, though. A lot of the people I've met have turned out to be really nice. And, if you don't like certain people, it's easy to get away from them at the end of the meal." To give GMs the option of enjoying a quiet meal away from the crowd, most villages had at least one separate specialty restaurant where reservations were required.

Each village was equipped with a state-of-the-art sound system. An expert sound engineer kept music playing throughout the day and evening in the core area around the pool and bar. The music, which was selected by the sound engineer with the approval of the village chief, varied from village to village. Classical music was not the norm (although each village had an area where taped classical music was played while the sun set).

Club Med promoted social interaction not only in the public areas but also in the rooms, assigning roommates to unaccompanied singles (always of the same sex). This concept was foreign to many GMs, but most did not find it to be a serious problem. Few would have *preferred* roommates, but it was generally recognized that "doubling up" held down the price of a Club Med vacation. An impromptu focus group assembled at the bar generated the consensus opinion that Club Med vacations were indeed inexpensive in comparison to the price of vacations at traditional Caribbean resorts (i.e., pay-as-you-go).

The Club's vacation concept was designed to eliminate the need for GMs to make any financial decisions during their stays. Except for bar drinks and items purchased in village shops (e.g., suntan lotion, clothing), the entire vacation was paid for in advance. GMs charged extras to their rooms and settled their accounts at the end of the week, when they picked up their passports and airline tickets at the village "bank" (where all valuables were to be stored, to minimize the possibility of theft). Drinks were purchased with colored-plastic pop beads that could be strung together or worn around the neck (except that the beads often did not hold together). A scotch and soda cost ten 40-cent orange beads; a Coke went for four orange beads. According to Club Med management, the beads were a popular symbol of the Club and an effective way to keep GMs' thoughts off monetary concerns.

GMs could choose from many individual and group recreational activities scheduled during the day. The Club was famous for sports, but it also offered such activities as arts and crafts, cards, and, in some villages, computer work-shops. At designated times, lessons taught by professionally qualified GOs were available for all major sports. Group activities included volleyball, softball, aerobics, bicycling, basketball, and picnics. Many GMs enthusiastically participated in as many of these activities as possible; others preferred to engage in individual pursuits (e.g., reading a book by the pool). In general, GMs settled into vacation routines that met their individual preferences after two or three days of investigating their options.

While the flexible daily schedule was always changing, nighttime activities usually followed a single pattern. Every evening started with the GMs congregating around the bar for a happy hour of pre-dinner drinks and semi-organized group games (e.g., Trivial Pursuit). Drinks were liberally awarded as prizes. Dinner started at 7:30 or 8:00, depending on the village. After dinner, GMs and GOs reconvened around the bar for a half hour or so of after-dinner drinks and dancing in a large patio area bordered by the bar, pool, and theater. Next came a Club tradition: the GO show. Each night, the GO team (all amateurs) put on a stage show, typically involving dancing, lip synch, and slapstick comedy. The shows were of varying length and quality, and GMs' reactions were mixed.

One new GM, Edward Robinson from New York, was delighted with the shows. "To see those kids putting out that kind of energy and enthusiasm, especially after doing a full day's work, makes *me* feel like a kid again. I think these GOs are fantastic."

At the end of each show, another Club ritual began: the "crazy-signs dance." All the GOs took to the stage and led the GMs in a set of animated hand motions performed to French songs. Most GMs joined in enthusiastically, although many found the hand motions difficult to master. One GM, Mike O'Brien from New Jersey, commented sourly: "I've been to three Club Meds and still can't get the crazy signs down. I feel stupid screwing up in front of the other guests. Most of them screw up too, though."

In general, however, the crazy-signs dance generated an up-tempo mood. Those who wished to continue dancing would next trek over to the disco, which opened shortly after the "show" ended. The disco was usually isolated at one end of the village to reduce the noise level for those GMs who preferred to go to bed.

The disco GO, a sound engineer, played taped music of current hit songs, occasionally broken up with an "oldies review." There was also a bar, plenty of seats, and easy access to the beach. The disco was open until the last GM left, which could be around dawn. Then the daily routine started again, with a tempting breakfast buffet set up in the dining room.

This set of activities was predictable—unlike the environmental and political conditions Club Med had to contend with in its far-flung destinations. Some of the local airports' facilities were barely adequate to handle a full load of vacationers. Some villages had physical problems, making them harder to manage than other villages with better design and facilities. Additionally, if Club Med struck a deal with a host government in a joint venture, with the local government agreeing to maintain the facility, and for some reason such upkeep became impossible to provide (i.e., a severe economic downturn, as in Mexico), the Club occasionally had difficulty keeping its facilities in top condition.

Mother Nature didn't always cooperate with the Club, either. One GM, Eddie Lewis from Boston, arriving at the village in Cancun, was miserable as a result of a long flight and transfer delays. His frustration was compounded when he saw that it was raining and learned it was expected to rain his whole vacation week. Yet, by the end of that time, he said, "I just had a great vacation—one of the best ever. I didn't even matter that I couldn't go windsurfing. I had a wonderful time anyway. Those Club Med people—and especially Sylvio de Bortoli, the village chief—sure know what they're doing.

"In fact," he continued, "I heard a story this week about the tradition the Club has when its time to turn over the village to a new chief. One particularly creative village chief, Michel Simon, decided it would be fun to play a practical joke on his replacement, who was coming in that evening from Tahiti. Michel gathered the entire village, all the GOs and GMs—we're talking several hundred people here—and took them across the bay in Playa Blanca, Mexico—to an empty hotel!

"He had everyone pretend this was the *real* Club Med village. When the unsuspecting new chief arrived, he was treated to a sumptuous dinner, a wonderful show, and, of course, a few glasses of wine. Everyone played along until the new chief went to bed, whereupon the group returned, en masse, to the real Club on the other side of the bay. Boy, was that guy surprised when he woke up in a *deserted* hotel!"

CUSTOMER PROFILE

A market survey exploring the profile of a typical Club Med GM was completed in September 1986. The results were based on responses to an eight-page self-administered questionnaire mailed to 50,000 GMs who had visited a Club Med village in the past year (i.e., in the summer of 1985 or in the winter of 1985–86). The questionnaire covered a range of topics, including demographics, lifestyle, experience with Club Med, and Club Med imagery. The response rate was in excess of 40%.

Club Med had worked hard to change the swinging-singles, sex-oriented image it had acquired in the 1970s. Ongoing market research showed the success of their efforts. Demographic data on Club Med's clientele revealed the average age to be 37, with a median income of $39,000 and an average income of $54,000. More than 70% were aged 25 to 44. Half were married, and 40% had children. More than 75% were college graduates and 28% held advanced degrees. For selected results of a 1986 GM survey, see *Exhibit 9*.

CUSTOMER SATISFACTION

Club Med's most important marketing tool was satisfied GMs. An industry rule-of-thumb was that people returning from vacation would tell an average of ten others about their experiences, either pro or con. The importance of word-of-mouth to Club Med was evidenced by the 65% of first-time GMs who decided to go primarily on the basis of recommendations from friends and acquaintances. These first-time GMs accounted for 60% of all GMs. During the past several years, approximately 25% of all new GMs had become repeat customers. Repeat GMs took an average of four additional Club Med vacations. The Club estimated its contribution margin at 60%.

To monitor GM satisfaction, each GM received a mail questionnaire immediately after returning home. (*Exhibit 10* shows the questionnaire.) Roughly 50% of the questionnaires were returned to Club Med headquarters, where the data were entered into a computer and summarized on a weekly basis, by village. (The average response rate for guest surveys in the lodging industry, by contrast, was 2% to 4%.) These statistical summaries were taken very seriously. Examples of guest-satisfaction ratings are shown in *Exhibit 11*. *Exhibit 12* shows a compilation of qualitative comments written on the questionnaires used to generate these ratings.

BACK IN NEW YORK

"It's that Club Med 'magic,'" Jacques Giraud laughed, when told of the GM in Cancun who had a great vacation despite flight problems and horrible weather. "In fact, there was a lot of magic in Cancun *that* season when Sylvio was the village chief. The physical circumstances were unusually difficult, yet he managed to boost the GM satisfaction ratings fifteen points higher than they were the year before. But I would like to know exactly *what* the Club Med magic is. I recently held an informal brainstorming session with my managers, including all the village chiefs in the American zone. They came up with some interesting observations about our strengths and weaknesses." (For a summary of these points, see *Exhibits 13* and *14*.) Winking, he suggested to the case writer, "Maybe we should have your students visit a Club Med village for a week, to give them a better sense of what the Club is about. Yes . . . a field study!" Giraud turned back to the panoramic view of Central Park. "Then *they* could clarify and resolve the issues that I face."

CLUB MED (A)

Exhibit 1

Locations of Club Méditerranée Villages, Worldwide

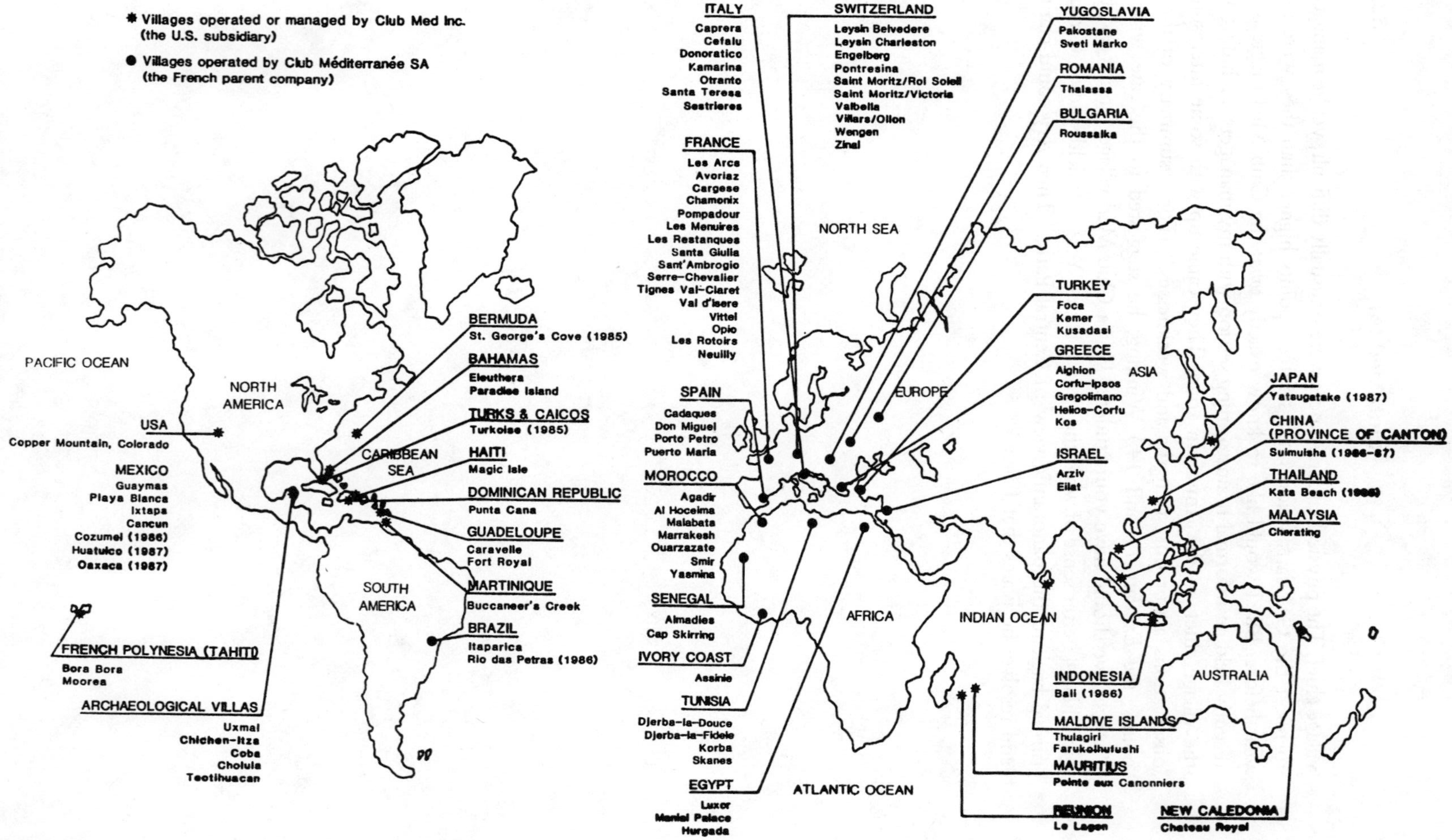

Exhibit 2a
Club Med, Inc. Operating Data
(U.S. dollars)

	1981	*1982*	*1983*	*1984*	*1985*	*1986*
Sales Revenue (millions)	$180	$207	$212	$235	$280	$337
Net Income (millions)	7.9	7.1	9.7	12.0	15.6	18.0
Guests (000)	169	196	208	238	282	332
Net Income/ Sales	4.4%	3.4%	4.6%	5.1%	5.6%	5.3%
Sales/Guest	$1,065	$1,056	$1,019	$987	$993	$1,015
Net Income/ Guest	47	36	47	50	55	54

Selected Financial Performance Results of U.S. Lodging Firms

	*Return on Sales**			*Return on Equity*		
	1984	*1985*	*1986*	*1984*	*1985*	*1986*
Marriott	—	—	—	22.1%	22.1	20.6
Ramada	1.5%	3.0	1.5	3.6	6.7	3.6
Hilton	16.6	14.1	13.2	18.6	16.1	14.4
LaQuinta	—	—	—	7.9	4.9	3.5
Four Seasons	—	—	—	—	—	22.2

*NOTE: 1984 sales in the U.S. resort-lodging industry were approximately US$10 billion.

Club Med (A)

Exhibit 2b
Occupancy and Capacity

	1984	1985	1986
North America			
Number of Beds:			
All Areas	9,602	11,052	12,384
North America	470	470	470
Mexico/Caribbean	7,332	8,632	9,364
Total	7,802	9,102	9,834
Occupancy:	64.2%	62.2%	60.9%
North America	72.7%	63.5%	65.4%
Mexico/Caribbean	63.4	64.2	64.4
Asia			
Number of Beds	1,800	1,950	2,550
Occupancy	65.5%	52.9%	47.3%
Total	63.6%	64.2%	64.4%

NOTE: Club Med reports occupancy in terms of *beds* available for guests. This method is significantly different from that generally used in the hotel industry, which expresses occupancy in terms of *rooms* available for guests.

Exhibit 3
Consolidated Income Statement for Club Med, Inc.
Year ended October 31, 1986
($000)

REVENUES	$336,950
Cost of revenues[a]	221,613
Gross profit	$115,337
Sales, general & administrative expenses	83,989
Depreciation and amortization	11,544
OPERATING INCOME	$ 19,804
Interest income (expense)	418
Foreign currency exchange gains (losses), net	(1,135)
Income before taxes and extraordinary items	$ 19,087
Provision for taxes[b]	(1,714)
Income before extraordinary items	$ 17,373
Extraordinary items	682
NET INCOME	$ 18,055
	= 11.6% ROI

SOURCE: 1986 Annual Report, p. 23.

[a] Cost of revenues includes wages.

[b] Club Med operates in a number of countries and consequently is taxed according to rules of various jurisdictions, some of which do not impose an income tax. The company's effective tax rate in 1986 was 5.4%.

Exhibit 4
Consolidated Balance Sheet for Club Med, Inc.
Year Ended October 31, 1986
($000)

Assets		
Current Assets:		
Cash and Marketable Securities	$ 53,621	17.1%
Accounts Receivable	15,358	4.9
Inventories	8,292	2.6
Other	13,808	4.4
Total Current Assets	$ 91,079	29.0%
Property and Equipment:		
Villages	$214,193	68.3%
Other	7,596	2.4
Construction in Progress	27,638	8.8
	$249,427	79.5%
Less Depreciation and Amortization	(47,274)	−15.1
Net Property and Equipment	$202,153	64.4%
Other Assets	20,591	6.6
TOTAL ASSETS	$313,823	100.0%
Liabilities and Shareholders' Equity		
Current Liabilities:		
Accounts Payable	$ 12,061	3.8%
Amounts Received for Future Vacations	22,470	7.2
Current Maturities of Long-Term Debt	1,695	0.5
Accrued Expenses	14,842	4.7
Other	9,086	2.9
	$60,154	19.2%
Long-term Debt[a]	$ 91,151	29.0%
Minority Interest and Other	3,506	1.1
Shareholders' Equity	159,012	50.7
TOTAL LIABILITIES	$313,823	100.0%

SOURCE: 1986 Annual Report, p. 24.

[a] $39.6 million is at or below the London Inter-Bank Offering Rate (LIBOR, the rate at which banks lend money to each other), and $26 million is at LIBOR plus 1/2% to 5/8%.

Exhibit 5
Potential Size of Markets in Various Countries

	Approximate Current Number of GMs	*Estimated Potential*	*Esimated % Growth Potential*	*Approximate Growth as a % of Total Growth Potential*
Europe/Middle East				
France	356,000	356,000[a]	0%	0.0%
Israel	19,000	19,000	0	0.0
Belgium	38,000	39,600	4	0.1
Switzerland	20,800	25,200	21	0.3
Italy	106,000	114,200	8	0.6
Austria	7,500	19,000	153	0.8
West Germany	35,000	215,250	515	12.6
Great Britain	7,500	123,400	1,545	8.1
Scandinavia	11,400[a]	68,400	500	3.9
Netherlands	7,200[a]	43,200	500	2.5
Spain	9,600[a]	57,600	500	3.4
Ireland	900[a]	5,400	500	0.3
Total Europe/ Middle East	620,600	1,087,150	75%	32.7%
North America				
U.S.A./Canada	179,800	780,050	334%	42.1%
Asia/South Africa				
Japan	12,000	229,250	1,810%	20.1%
Australia	18,000	38,750	115	1.5
New Zealand	4,000	6,600	65	0.2
Hong Kong	1,600	5,400	237	0.3
Taiwan	3,700[a]	9,400	154	0.4
Malaysia	4,600[a]	4,600	0	0.0
Singapore	4,100	4,100	0	0.0
South Africa	5,000	12,300	146	0.5
Total Asia/ South Africa	53,000	380,400	618%	23.0%
All Other	46,600	78,300	68	2.2
Club Med, Inc. Region	279,400	1,238,750	343	67.3
Entire World	900,000	2,325,900	158	100.0

SOURCE: Drexel, Burnham, Lambert, Inc.

[a]Based on propensities to vacation at Club Med (x.x people/1,000). Propensity of French citizens to vacation at Club Med divided in half to generate demand estimates for other nations.

Exhibit 6
Structural Analysis Model: Club Med

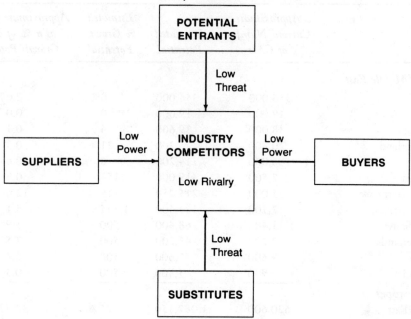

BARRIERS TO POTENTIAL ENTRANTS

Economies of Scale
- Volume discounts
  - Air travel
  - Food

- Advertising

- Semitransferable demand among numerous villages

Experience-Curve Effects
- 30 years, experience

"Proprietary" Process
- Recipe for Club Med "magic"

- Village chiefs

Brand Identity
- Club Med name
  65% new business through word-of- mouth

- Fantasy and romance

High Capital Requirements
- $20 to $25 million per 600-bed club

- Need several clubs to gain scale economies

Favored Political Status
- Tax incentives
- Joint ventures with host governments

DETERMINANTS OF SUPPLIER POWER

- Many price-competitive airlines

- Airline seats cannot be inventoried

- Many price-competitive food companies

- Host governments want hard foreign currency

- Strong demand to work for Club Med at low wages

- Minimal threat of forward integration by suppliers

DETERMINANTS OF BUYER POWER

- Purchasers are private individuals

- Price of similar vacation 50—100% higher if buyers self-package

- High perceived risk of wrong vacation choice

- Buyers cannot integrate backward (except for buying a second home or timesharing)

INTRA-INDUSTRY RIVALRY

- Few rival firms

- Most based in Jamaica (Club Med has no Jamaican villages)

— — — — — — — — — — —

DETERMINANTS OF SUBSTITUTE THREAT

Buyers Face High Switching Costs
- High opportunity cost of leisure time

- Reasonable Club Med price

- Risk averse buyers

- Substitutes few and dissimilar:
  – cruise ships traditional resorts

- Price of equivalent alternative vacations

SOURCE: Dan Arczynski, "Club Méditerranée: A Competitive Analysis." Competitive Analysis Course, Harvard Business School, May 5, 1986.

Exhibit 7
Comparative Cost Data: Club Med and Industry Averages

	Club Med	Industry Average
Lodging Industry		
Sales[a]	100%)	100%
Cost of goods sold	(48)	(40)
Labor	(27)	(36)
Sales, general and administrative	(9)	(5)
Advertising	(5)	(3)
Interest	(3)	(7)
Depreciation	(4)	(6)
Profit before taxes	4%	3%
Air Transport Industry		
Sales[b]	100%	100%
Cost of goods sold	(89)	(98)
Profit before taxes	11%	2%

[a] Club Med's revenue from land packages and village operations was $227.6 million in 1986 (68% of total revenue).

[b] Club Med's revenue from air transportation was $92.6 million in 1986 (27% of total revenue).

Club Med's other revenue came primarily from membership, management, and cancellation fees.

SOURCE: *The New York Times*, February 1, 1987.

Exhibit 9
Selected Market Research Results

Sex of Respondent			
	Total	*Summer*	*Winter*
Base-Total Sample	(19,527)	(8,408)	(11,119)
• Male	47%	48%	46%
• Female	53	52	54

Age of Respondent			
	Total	*Summer*	*Winter*
Base-Total Sample	(19,527)	(8,408)	(11,119)
• 18 to 24	8%	8%	8%
• 25 to 29	22	23	21
• 30 to 34	22	22	22
• 35 to 39	18	19	18
• 40 to 44	13	12	14
• 45 to 49	7	6	8
• 50 to 54	5	4	5
• 55+	5	5	5

Marital Status			
	Total	*Summer*	*Winter*
Base-Total Sample	(19,527)	(8,408)	(11,119)
• Married	48%	48%	48%
• Single	36	37	36
• Divorced	11	11	10
• Other	5	4	6
• Have children	40%	38%	42%

Exhibit 9
(Continued)

Geographic/Sales Region, U.S. Market			
	Total	*Summer*	*Winter*
Base-Total Sample	(19,527)	(8,408)	(11,119)
• Northeast	34%	28%	38%
• Pacific	23	28	19
• New York	20	19	21
• Midwest	10	9	12
• Southeast	5	7	4
• Southwest	4	6	3
• Mountain	4	4	3

Likelihood of Vacationing at Club Med in Future			
	Total	*Summer*	*Winter*
Base-Total Sample	(19,527)	(8,408)	(11,119)
• Extremely/Very	74%	77%	72%
—Extremely	48	53	44
—Very	26	24	28
• Somewhat	18	16	19
• Not Too/Not at All	8	7	9
—Not Too	6	6	7
—Not at All	2	1	2

CLUB MED (A)

Exhibit 10

GM Questionnaire

G.M. Questionnaire

Club Med Village: _____

Dates of your stay: From: _____ to: _____
                        Month/Day/Year   Month/Day/Year

Name: _____ Member # _____

Address: _____

City: _____ State: _____ Zip: _____

	OVERALL IMPRESSION	ORGANIZATION	TEAM OF C.O.'s	FOOD	BAR	SPORTS	DAYTIME AMBIANCE	EVENING ENTERTAINMENT	MUSIC AND DANCE	MINI CLUB	EXCURSIONS	ACCOMMODATIONS	CLUB FLIGHTS AND TRANSFERS	CLEANLINESS
EXCELLENT	6	6	6	6	6	6	6	6	6	6	6	6	6	6
VERY GOOD	5	5	5	5	5	5	5	5	5	5	5	5	5	5
GOOD	4	4	4	4	4	4	4	4	4	4	4	4	4	4
FAIR	3	3	3	3	3	3	3	3	3	3	3	3	3	3
POOR	2	2	2	2	2	2	2	2	2	2	2	2	2	2
VERY POOR	1	1	1	1	1	1	1	1	1	1	1	1	1	1

1. Did Club Med meet your expectations?
   ☐ Far below expectations ☐ Surpassed expectations
   ☐ Fell short of expectations ☐ Far surpassed expectations
   ☐ Met expectations

2. If this was not your first Club Med, how many other times have you been to a Club Med village? _____

3. How did you make your Club Med reservations?
   ☐ Through a travel agent ☐ Through Club Med Reservations

4. Quality of your reservations handling (pre-travel information):
   ☐ Very Poor ☐ Poor ☐ Fair ☐ Good ☐ Excellent

5. Which one factor was most important in your choosing Club Med for your vacation?
   ☐ Previous stay with us ☐ Advertisement ☐ Editorial Article
   ☐ Travel Agent Recommendation ☐ Friend/Relative Recommendation

6. Kindly indicate your age bracket:
   ☐ Under 25 ☐ 25-34 ☐ 35-44 ☐ 45-54 ☐ 55 or over

7. Kindly indicate your marital status: ☐ Married ☐ Single

8. Would you vacation with Club Med again? ☐ Yes ☐ No

9. If you answered yes to question 8, where would you like to go on your next Club Med vacation?
   ☐ U.S.A. ☐ Mexico ☐ French West Indies ☐ Caribbean
   ☐ Europe ☐ Other: _____

Your Comments: _____
_____

150M 1/84 PRINTED IN U.S.A.

Exhibit 11
Guest Satisfaction Ratings:
Ixtapa, Cancun, and Paradise Island Villages[a]

	Ixtapa, Mexico (n = 654)	Cancun, Mexico (n = 856)	Paradise Island, Bahamas (n = 512)
Overall Impression	95.7%	92.3%	81.4%
Organization	92.8	90.7	80.1
Team of GOs	94.1	93.3	79.0
Food	80.8	65.8	82.6
Bar	74.4	70.6	72.5
Sports	97.2	95.6	93.8
Daytime Ambiance	96.3	93.2	91.1
Evening Entertainment	89.4	83.3	70.9
Music and Dance	85.1	80.9	77.5
Rooms	87.4	61.5	78.0
Flights and Transfers	75.5	56.7	61.7
Cleanliness	94.5	77.3	78.5

NOTES:

1. Data disguised; from one season.

2. During this season in Cancun: weather was terrible; tennis courts in bad need of repair; major renovation of facility under way.

[a] Percentages of respondents who checked "excellent," "very good," and "good" on questionnaire in Exhibit 10.

Exhibit 12
Summary of Qualitative Comments from Questionnaires:
Ixtapa, Cancun, and Paradise Island Villages

	Ixtapa, Mexico (n=654)	Cancun, Mexico (n=856)	Paradise Island, Bahamas (n=512)
Overall Vacation Rating			
Excellent/Good	125	174	77
Disappointing/Poor	10	15	20
GO Team			
Friendly/Good	182	215	83
Rude/Unhelpful	24	32	65
Village Chief "Great"	8	105	3
Miscellaneous			
Air Charter Poor	10	151	27
Transfers Poor	4	30	5
Need Room Keys	6	5	43
Reported Theft	7	11	23
Rooms Uncomfortable	32	154	52
Food Average/Poor	42	118	30
Bar Drinks Overpriced/Weak	42	49	20
Bar Beads a Hassle	12	12	7

NOTE: Many questionnaires were returned without comments, and many were returned with multiple responses. In other words, of the 856 questionnaires returned by GMs who visited Cancun, many had no qualitative comments on them, while others had multiple comments.

Exhibit 13
Summary of Main Points Listed by Club Med Managers

Strengths

- GOs
- Company spirit; a "family"
- Understanding customer needs
- Innovator
- All-inclusive concept
- "Float" (i.e., customer pays before taking the vacation)
- Marketing and distribution strategy
- Size (economies of scale)
- Wide choice of destinations
- Excellent locations
- Low capital-intensity (due to funding from host governments, etc.)
- Ability to manage in diverse international settings
- Service concept appeals to broad market
- Experience
- Open communication throughout company
- Leadership

Weaknesses

- Subject to political problems in countries where villages located (e.g., Haiti)
- Subject to foreign-exchange fluctuations
- GO turnover
- Cultural differences between management and employees (e.g., European managers and American GOs).
- Remoteness of villages (communication difficult)
- Singles-oriented image
- Broad market appeal could allow competition to specialize
- Spartan accommodations

Exhibit 14
Comments from Club Med Managers Concerning Company Strengths
and Weaknesses

Strengths

- "Club Med understands the needs of its customers, which translates into satisfied customers. And satisfied customers are particularly important for a company, like ours, that depends on repeat business."
- "Our services are constantly evolving. For example, as various sports gain popularity, we start offering them at Club Med."
- "The Club is an innovator."
- "Our policy of nomadism (i.e., rotating the GOs every six months) leads to flexibility, variety, and it insures that the villages have an international flavor."
- "There is a high level of commitment among Club Med employees. It is like family—and *is* the family for many employees."
- "We have an adaptable management style. We can operate the Club in many diverse international settings."
- "Our service concept appeals to a very broad market. Club Med is for everybody, not just for a specific kind of customer."

Weaknesses

- "The company has been criticized for having a strong French-orientation."
- "Having such a broad market appeal might leave other companies room to specialize. They could go after niches in the market."
- "If I were working for a competitor of Club Med, I might recommend that my company be *completely* all-inclusive. No charge for cigarettes or drinks at the bar."
- "Club Med's accommodations are very spartan. And we don't offer double beds for couples, or single rooms for singles."
- "If Club Med doesn't continue to change and adapt to the demands of the market we would hurt ourselves more than any of our competitors ever could."

6

◆

Developing Devices
for Achieving Total
Customer Satisfaction

Two of the most important devices for achieving total customer satisfaction are service guarantees and service recovery initiatives. Both assume, however, that effective practices described elsewhere in this book already are in place. Service guarantees are at least as important for revealing and controlling service failures as they are for marketing a service. Questions of importance in appraising the effectiveness of a service guarantee include: Is it unconditional (containing no requirements), focused on important customer needs, easy to understand and communicate, and substantial in payoff to the customer and in penalty to the provider? Is it easy to invoke and credible? Is it stated in ways that represent a declaration of trust? Is the service of the organization in which it is being considered already good enough to support the credibility of the guarantee? Are service personnel already good enough at what they do to regard the guarantee as a challenge rather than a demoralizing experience? Can enough of the factors affecting quality be controlled, or service recovery be employed, to enable servers to deliver on the guarantee?

Effective service recovery involves recognizing that a service failure has occurred and doing something to correct it. Questions asked repeatedly in firms that have established a climate for successful service recovery include: Have service failure points (including those involving complex scheduling, complex service processes, new service introductions, high employee turnover, chronic inadequate training of servers, or difficult-to-control external factors) been identified? Have appropriate responses been implemented? To what degree is this programmed? To what degree are servers empowered to effect immediate recovery when failure occurs?

Many questions regarding service guarantees are addressed in Christopher

Hart's article, "The Power of Unconditional Service Guarantees." In reading it, ask yourself how one or more service guarantees with which you are familiar measure up to the criteria set forth by Hart. For what types of businesses is an unconditional service guarantee most feasible? Most advisable? Why?

At "Bugs" Burger Bug Killers, described in the article, "Getting the Bugs Out," what are means by which this company is able to justify prices that are several times those of its competitors? Can it possibly sustain this position in the industry? What are the limits to which Al Burger can grow a business with this kind of strategic service vision? Depending on your response and assuming that he has great ambitions for the company, what advice would you give him?

The short case, Federal Express: The Money Back Guarantee (A), offers an opportunity both to appraise the effectiveness of this company's implicit guarantee of overnight delivery (as its advertisements state, "when it absolutely, positively has to be there") and to design an unconditional service guarantee for the company, if you think it is advisable. In reading the case, ask yourself: What should Federal Express do for this customer? In your view, what should Federal Express's general policy be for similar service mishaps? What do you think actually happened?

In the case, The Customer Complaint (A), how would you evaluate Gail Pearson's letter as an example of service recovery? What changes would you make in it? Why?

Total customer satisfaction does not mean service perfection. But through the vehicles of unconditional service guarantees and effective recovery efforts, imperfect service can nevertheless be remedied in ways that lead to total satisfaction and customer loyalty.

The Power of Unconditional Service Guarantees

CHRISTOPHER W. L. HART

When you buy a car, a camera, or a toaster oven, you receive a warranty, a guarantee that the product will work. How often do you receive a warranty for auto repair, wedding photography, or a catered dinner? Virtually never. Yet it is here, in buying services, that the assurance of a guarantee would presumably count most.

Many business executives believe that, by definition, services simply can't be guaranteed. Services are generally delivered by human beings, who are known to be less predictable than machines, and they are usually produced at the same time they are consumed. It is one thing to guarantee a camera, which can be inspected before a customer sets eyes on it and which can be returned to the factory for repairs. But how can you preinspect a car tune-up or send an unsuccessful legal argument or bad haircut back for repair? Obviously you can't.

But that doesn't mean customer satisfaction can't be guaranteed. Consider the guarantee offered by "Bugs" Burger Bug Killers (BBBK), a Miami-based pest-extermination company that is owned by S. C. Johnson & Son.

Most of BBBK's competitors claim that they will reduce pests to "acceptable levels"; BBBK promises to eliminate them entirely. Its service guarantee to hotel and restaurant clients promises:

- You don't owe one penny until all pests on your premises have been eradicated.

- If you are ever dissatisfied with BBBK's service, you will receive a refund for up to 12 months of the company's services—plus fees for another exterminator of your choice for the next year.

- If a guest spots a pest on your premises, BBBK will pay for the guest's meal or room, send a letter of apology, and pay for a future meal or stay.

Christopher W. L. Hart wishes to thank Dan Maher for assistance in researching and writing this article. Reprinted by permission of *Harvard Business Review.* "The Power of Unconditional Service Guarantees" by Christopher W. L. Hart (July/August 1988). Copyright © 1988 by the President and Fellows of Harvard College; all rights reserved.

- If your facility is closed down due to the presence of roaches or rodents, BBBK will pay any fines, as well as all lost profits, *plus* $5,000.

In short, BBBK says, "If we don't satisfy you 100%, we don't take your money."

How successful is this guarantee? The company, which operates throughout the United States, charges up to ten times more than its competitors and yet has a disproportionately high market share in its operating areas. Its service quality is so outstanding that the company rarely needs to make good on its guarantee (in 1986 it paid out only $120,000 on sales of $33 million—just enough to prove that its promises aren't empty ones).

A main reason that the "Bugs" Burger guarantee is a strong model for the service industry is that its founder, Al Burger, began with the concept of the unconditional guarantee and worked backward, designing his entire organization to support the no-pests guarantee—in short, he started with a vision of error-free service. In this case, I will explain why the service guarantee can help your organization institutionalize superlative performance.

WHAT A GOOD SERVICE GUARANTEE IS

Would you be willing to offer a guarantee of 100% customer satisfaction—to pay your dissatisfied customer to use a competitor's service, for example? Or do you believe that promising error-free service is a crazy idea?

Not only is it not crazy, but *committing* to error-free service can help force a company to *provide* it. It's a little like skiing. You've got to lean over your skis as you go down the hill, as if willing yourself to fall. But if you edge properly, you don't fall or plunge wildly; you gain control while you pick up speed.

Similarly, a strong service guarantee that puts the customer first doesn't necessarily lead to chaos and failure. If designed and implemented properly, it enables you to get control over your organization—with clear goals and an information network that gives you the data you need to improve performance. BBBK and other service companies show that a service guarantee is not only possible—it's a boon to performance and profits and can be a vehicle to market dominance.

Most existing service guarantees don't really do the job: they are limited in scope and difficult to use. Lufthansa guarantees that its customers will make their connecting flights *if* there are no delays due to weather or air-traffic control problems. Yet these two factors cause fully 95% of all flight delays. Bank of America will refund up to six months of checking account fees if a customer is dissatisfied with any aspect of its checking-account service. However, the customer must close the account to collect the modest $5 or 6 per month fee. This guarantee won't win any prizes for fostering repeat business—a primary objective of a good guarantee.

A service guarantee loses power in direct proportion to the number of conditions it contains. How effective is a restaurant's guarantee of prompt service *except* when it's busy? A housing inspector's guarantee to identify all potential problems in a house *except for* those not readily apparent? Squaw Valley in California guarantees "your money back" to any skier who has to wait more than ten minutes in a lift line. But it's not that easy: the skier must first pay $1 and register at the lodge as a beginner, intermediate, or expert; the guarantee is operative only if *all* lifts at the skier's skill level exceed the ten minutes in any half-hour period; and skiers must check with a "ski hostess" at the end of the day to "win" a refund. A Squaw Valley spokesperson said the resort had made just one payout under the guarantee in a year and a half. No wonder!

What is a good service guarantee? It is (1) unconditional, (2) easy to understand and communicate, (3) meaningful, (4) easy (and painless) to invoke, and (5) easy and quick to collect on.

Unconditional

The best service guarantee promises customer satisfaction unconditionally, without exceptions. Like that of L.L. Bean, the Freeport, Maine retail store and mail-order house: "100% satisfaction in every way. . . ." An L.L. Bean customer can return a product at any time and get, at his or her option, a replacement, a refund, or a credit. Reputedly, if a customer returns a pair of L.L. Bean boots after ten years, the company will replace them with new boots and no questions. Talk about customer assurance! Customers shouldn't need a lawyer to explain the "ifs, ands, and buts" of a guarantee—because ideally there shouldn't be any conditions; a customer is either satisfied or not.

If a company cannot guarantee all elements of its service unconditionally, it should unconditionally guarantee the elements that it can control. Lufthansa cannot promise on-time arrival, for example, but it could guarantee that passengers will be satisfied with its airport waiting areas, its service on the ground and in the air, and its food quality—or simply guarantee overall satisfaction.

Easy to Understand and Communicate

A guarantee should be written in simple, concise language that pinpoints the promise. Customers then know precisely what they can expect and employees know precisely what's expected of them. "Five-minute" lunch service, rather than "prompt" service, creates clear expectations, as does "no pests," rather than "pest control."

Meaningful

A good service guarantee is meaningful in two respects. First, it guarantees those aspects of your service that are important to your customers. It may be speedy delivery. Bennigan's, a restaurant chain, promises 15-minute service (or you get a free meal) at lunch, when many customers are in a hurry to get back to the office, but not at dinner, when fast service is not considered a priority to most patrons.

In other cases, price may be the most important element, especially with relatively undifferentiated commodities like rental cars or commercial air travel. By promising the lowest prices in town, stereo shops assuage customers' fears that if they don't go to every outlet in the area they'll pay more than they ought to.

Second, a good guarantee is meaningful financially; it calls for a significant payout when the promise is not kept. What should it be—a full refund? An offer of free service the next time? A trip to Monte Carlo? The answer depends on factors like the cost of the service, the seriousness of the failure, and customers' perception of what's fair. A money-back payout should be large enough to give customers an incentive to invoke the guarantee if dissatisfied. The adage "Let the punishment fit the crime" is an appropriate guide. At one point, Domino's Pizza (which is based in Ann Arbor, Michigan, but operates worldwide) promised "delivery within 30 minutes or the pizza is free." Management found that customers considered this too generous; they felt uncomfortable accepting a free pizza for a mere 5- or 15-minute delay and didn't always take advantage of the guarantee. Consequently, Domino's adjusted its guarantee to "delivery within 30 minutes or $3 off," and customers appear to consider this commitment reasonable.

Easy to Invoke

A customer who is already dissatisfied should not have to jump through hoops to invoke a guarantee; the dissatisfaction is only exacerbated when the customer has to talk to three different people, fill out five forms, go to a different location, make two telephone calls, send in written proof of purchase with a full description of the events, wait for a written reply, go somewhere else to see someone to verify all the preceding facts, and so on.

Traveler's Advantage—a division of CUC International—has, in principle, a great idea: to guarantee the lowest price on the accommodations it books. But to invoke the guarantee customers must prove the lower competing price by booking with another agency. That's unpleasant work. Cititravel, a subsidiary of Citicorp, has a better approach. A customer who knows of a lower price can call a toll-free number and speak with an agent, as I did recently. The agent told me that if I didn't have proof of the lower fare, she'd check competing airfares on her computer screen. If the lower fare was there, I'd get that price. If not, she would call the competing airline. If the price was confirmed, she said, "We'll refund your money so fast, you won't believe it—because we want you to be our customer." That's the right attitude if you're offering a guarantee.

Similarly, customers should not be made to feel guilty about invoking the guarantee—no questioning, no raised eyebrows, or "Why me, Lord?" looks. A company should encourage unhappy customers to invoke its guarantee, not put up roadblocks to keep them from speaking up.

Easy to Collect

Customers shouldn't have to work hard to collect a payout, either. The procedure should be easy and, equally important, quick—on the spot, if possible. Dissatisfaction with a Manpower temporary worker, for instance, results in an immediate credit to your bill.

What you should *not* do in your guarantee: don't promise something your customers already expect; don't shroud a guarantee in so many conditions that it loses its point; and don't offer a guarantee so mild that it is never invoked. A guarantee that is essentially risk free to the company will be of little or no value to your customers—and may be a joke to your employees.

WHY A SERVICE GUARANTEE WORKS

A guarantee is a powerful tool—both for marketing service quality and for achieving it—for five reasons.

First, it pushes the entire company to focus on customers' definition of good service—not on executives' assumptions. Second, it sets clear performance standards, which boost employee performance and morale. Third, it generates reliable data (through payouts) when performance is poor. Fourth, it forces an organization to examine its entire service-delivery system for possible failure points. Last, it builds customer loyalty, sales, and market share.

A Guarantee Forces You to Focus on Customers

Knowing what customers want is the sine qua non in offering a service guarantee. A company has to identify its target customers' expectations about the elements of the service and the importance they attach to each. Lacking this knowledge of customer needs, a company that wants to guarantee its service may very well guarantee the wrong things.

British Airways conducted a market study and found that its passengers judge its customer services on four dimensions:[1]

1. Care and concern (employees' friendliness, courtesy, and warmth).

2. Initiative (employees' ability and willingness to jockey the system on the customer's behalf).

3. Problem solving (figuring out solutions to customer problems, whether unusual or routine—like multiflight airline tickets).

4. Recovery (going the extra yard, when things go wrong, to handle a particular problem—which includes the simple but often overlooked step of delivering an apology).

British Airways managers confessed that they hadn't even thought about the second and fourth categories. Worse, they realized that if *they* hadn't understood these important dimensions of customer service, how much thought could their employees be giving to them?

A Guarantee Sets Clear Standards

A specific, unambiguous service guarantee sets standards for your organization. It tells employees what the company stands for. BBBK stands for pest elimination, not pest control; Federal Express stands for "absolutely, positively by 10:30 A.M.," not "sometime tomorrow, probably." And it forces the company to define each employee's role and responsibilities in delivering the service. Salespeople, for example, know precisely what their companies can deliver and can represent that accurately—the opposite of the common situation in which salespeople promise the moon and customers get only dirt.

This clarity and sense of identity have added advantage of creating employee team spirit and pride. Mitchell Fromstein, president and CEO of Manpower, says, "At one point, we wondered what the marketing impact would be if we dropped our guarantee. We figured that our accounts were well aware of the guarantee and that it might not have much marketing power anymore. Our

---

1. See British Airways study cited in Karl Albrecht and Ron Zemke, *Service America!* (Homewood, Ill.: Dow Jones-Irwin, 1985), pp. 33–34.

employees' reaction was fierce—and it had a lot less to do with marketing than with the pride they take in their work. They said, 'The guarantee is proof that we're a great company. We're willing to tell our customers that if they don't like our service for any reason, it's our fault, not theirs, and we'll make it right.' I realized then that the guarantee is far more than a simple piece of paper that puts customers at ease. It really sets the tone, externally and, perhaps more important, internally, for our commitment to our customers and workers."

A payout that creates financial pain when errors occur is also a powerful statement, to employees and customers alike, that management demands customer satisfaction. A significant payout ensures that both middle and upper management will take the service guarantee seriously; it provides a strong incentive to take every step necessary to deliver. A manager who must bear the full cost of mistakes has ample incentive to figure out how to prevent them from happening.

A Guarantee Generates Feedback

A guarantee creates the goal; it defines what you must do to satisfy your customers. Next, you need to know when you go wrong. A guarantee forces you to create a system for discovering errors—which the Japanese call "golden nuggets" because they're opportunities to learn.

Arguably the greatest ailment afflicting service companies is a lack of decent systems for generating and acting on customer data. Dissatisfied service customers have little incentive to complain on their own, far less so than unhappy product owners do. Many elements of a service are intangible, so consumers who receive poor service are often left with no evidence to support their complaints. (The customer believes the waiter was rude; perhaps the waiter will deny it.) Second, without the equivalent of a product warranty, customers don't know their rights. (Is 15 minutes too long to wait for a restaurant meal? 30 minutes?) Third, there is often no one to complain to—at least no one who looks capable of solving the problem. Often, complaining directly to the person who is rendering poor service will only make things worse.

> ***Without a guarantee,***
> ***customers won't complain.***
> ***Or come back.***

Customer comment cards have traditionally been the most common method of gathering customer feedback on a company's operations, but they, too, are inadequate for collecting valid, reliable error data. In the first place, they are an impersonal form of communication and are usually short (to maximize the response rate). Why bother, people think, to cram the details of a bad experience onto a printed survey form with a handful of "excellent—good—fair" check-off boxes? Few aggrieved customers believe that completing a comment card will resolve their problems. Therefore, only a few customers—usually the most satisfied and dissatisfied—provide feedback through such forms, and fewer still provide meaningful feedback. As a broad gauge of customer sentiment, cards and surveys are useful, but for specific information about customer problems and operational weaknesses, they simply don't fill the bill.

Service companies thus have a hard time collecting error data. Less information on mistakes means fewer opportunities to improve, ultimately resulting in more service errors and more customer dissatisfaction—a cycle that management is often unaware of. A guarantee attacks this malady by giving consumers an incentive and a vehicle for bringing their grievances to management's attention.

Manpower uses its guarantee to glean error data in addition to allaying customer worries about using an unknown quantity (the temporary worker). Every customer who employs a Manpower temporary worker is called the first day of a one-day assignment or the second day of a longer assignment to check on the worker's performance. A dissatisfied customer doesn't pay—period. [Manpower pays the worker, however; it assumes complete responsibility for the quality of its service.) The company uses its error data to improve both its work force and its proprietary skills-testing software and skills data base—major elements in its ability to match worker skills to customer requirements. The information Manpower obtains before and after hiring enables it to offer its guarantee with confidence.

A Guarantee Forces You to Understand Why You Fail

In developing a guarantee, managers must ask questions like these: What failure points exist in the system? If failure points can be identified, can their origins be traced—and overcome? A company that wants to promise timely service delivery, for example, must first understand its operation's capability and the factors limiting that capability. Many service executives, lacking understanding of such basic issues as system throughput time, capacity, and process flow, tend to blame workers, customers, or anything *but* the service-delivery process.

Even if workers *are* a problem, managers can do several things to "fix" the organization so that it can support a guarantee—such as design better recruiting, hiring, and training processes. The pest-control industry has historically suffered from unmotivated personnel and high turnover. Al Burger overcame the status quo by offering higher than average pay (attracting a higher caliber of job candidate), using a vigorous screening program (making those hired feel like members of a select group), training all workers for six months, and keeping them motivated by giving them a great deal of autonomy and lots of recognition.

Some managers may be unwilling to pay for an internal service-delivery capability that is above the industry average. Fine. They will never have better than average organizations, either, and they will therefore never be able to develop the kind of competitive advantage that flows from a good service guarantee.

A Guarantee Builds Marketing Muscle

Perhaps the most obvious reason for offering a strong service guarantee is its ability to boost marketing: it encourages consumers to buy a service by reducing the risk of the purchase decision, and it generates more sales to existing customers by enhancing loyalty. In the last ten years, Manpower's revenues have mushroomed from $400 million to $4 billion. That's marketing impact.

Keeping most of your customers and getting positive word of mouth, though desirable in any business, are particularly important for service companies. The net present value of sales foregone from lost customers—in other words, the cost of customer dissatisfaction—is enormous. In this respect, it's fair to say that many service companies' biggest competitors are themselves. They frequently spend huge amounts of money to attract new customers without ever figuring out how to provide the consistent service they promise to their existing customers. If customers aren't satisfied, the marketing money has been poured down the drain and may even engender further ill will. (See the insert, "Maximizing Marketing Impact.")

A guarantee will only work, of course, if you start with commitment to the customer. If your aim is to minimize the guarantee's impact on your organization but to maximize its marketing punch, you won't succeed. In the long run, you will nullify the guarantee's potential impact on customers, and your marketing dollars will go down the drain.

Phil Bressler, owner of 18 Domino's Pizza franchises in the Baltimore, Maryland area, demonstrates the right commitment to customers. He got upset the time his company recorded its highest monthly earnings ever because, he correctly figured, the profits had come from money that should have been paid out on the Domino's guarantee of "delivery within 30 minutes or $3 off." Bressler's unit managers, who have bottom-line responsibility, had pumped up their short-term profits by failing to honor the guarantee consistently. Bressler is convinced that money spent on guarantees is an investment in customer satisfaction and loyalty. He also recognizes that the guarantee is the best way to identify weak operations, and that guarantees not acted on are data not collected.

Compare Bressler's attitude with that of an owner of several nationally franchised motels. *His* guarantee promises that the company will do "everything possible" to remedy a customer's problem; if the problem cannot be resolved, the customer stays for free. He brags that he's paid, on average, refunds for only two room guarantees per motel per year—a minuscule percentage of room sales. "If my managers are doing their jobs, I don't have to pay out for the guarantee," he says. "If I do have to pay out, my managers are not doing their jobs, and I get rid of them."

Clearly, more than two guests of *any* hotel are likely to be dissatisfied over the course of a year. By seeking to limit payouts rather than hear complaints, this owner is undoubtedly blowing countless opportunities to create loyal customers out of disgruntled ones. He is also losing rich information about which of his motels need improvement and why, information that can most easily be obtained from customer complaints. You have to wonder why he offers a guarantee at all, since he completely misses the point.

WHY YOU MAY NEED A GUARANTEE
EVEN IF YOU DON'T THINK SO

Of course, guarantees may not be effective or practicable for all service firms. Four Seasons Hotels, for example, could probably not get much marketing or operational mileage from a guarantee. With its strong internal vision of absolute customer satisfaction, the company has developed an outstanding service-delivery system and a reputation to match. Thus it already has an implicit guarantee. To advertise the obvious would produce little gain and might actually be perceived as incongruent with the company's prestigious image.

A crucial element in Four Season's service strategy is instilling in all employees a mission of absolute customer satisfaction and empowering them to do whatever is necessary if customer problems do occur. For example, Four Seasons' Washington hotel was once asked by the State Department to make room for a foreign dignitary. Already booked to capacity, Four Seasons had to tell four other customers with reservations that they could not be accommodated. However, the hotel immediately found rooms for them at another first-class hotel, while assuring them they would remain registered at the Four Seasons (so that any messages they received would be taken and sent to the other hotel). When rooms became available, the customers were driven back to the Four Seasons by limousine. Four Seasons also paid for their rooms at the other hotel. It was the equivalent of a full money-back guarantee, and more.

Does this mean that every company that performs at the level of a Four Seasons need not offer a service guarantee? Could Federal Express, for example,

Maximizing Marketing Impact

The odds of gaining powerful marketing impact from a service guarantee are in your favor when one or more of the following conditions exist:

The price of the service is high. *A bad shoe shine? No big deal. A botched $1,000 car repair is a different story; a guarantee is more effective here.*

The customer's ego is on the line. *Who wants to be seen after getting a bad haircut?*

The customer's expertise with the service is low. *When in doubt about a service, a customer will choose one that's covered by a guarantee over those that are not.*

The negative consequences of service failure are high. *As consumers' expected aggravation, expense, and time lost due to service failure increase, a guarantee gains power. Your computer went down? A computer-repair service with guaranteed response and repair times would be the most logical company to call.*

The industry has a bad image for service quality—*like pest-control services, security guards, or home repair. A guard company that guarantees to have its posts filled by qualified people would automatically rank high on a list of prospective vendors.*

The company depends on frequent customer repurchases. *Can it exist on a never-ending stream of new triers (like small service businesses in large markets), or does it have to deal with a finite market? If the market is finite, how close is market saturation? The smaller the size of the potential market of new triers, the more attention management should pay to increasing the loyalty and repurchase rate of existing customers—objectives that a good service guarantee will serve.*

The company's business is affected deeply by word of mouth *(both positive and negative). Consultants, stockbrokers, restaurants, and resorts are all good examples of services where there are strong incentives to minimize the extent of customer dissatisfaction—and hence, negative word of mouth.*

drop its "absolutely, positively" assurance with little or no effect? Probably not. Its guarantee is such a part of its image that dropping the guarantee would hurt it.

In general, organizations that meet the following tests probably have little to gain by offering a service guarantee: the company is perceived by the market to be the quality leader in its industry; every employee is inculcated with the "absolute customer satisfaction" philosophy; employees are empowered to take whatever corrective action is necessary to handle complaints; errors are few; and a stated guarantee would be at odds with the company's image.

It is probably unnecessary to point out that few service companies meet these tests.

External Variables

Service guarantees may also be impractical where customer satisfaction is influenced strongly by external forces the service provider can't control. While everybody thinks their businesses are in this fix, most are wrong.

How many variables are truly beyond management's control? Not the work force. Not equipment problems. Not vendor quality. And even businesses subject to "acts of God" (like weather) can control a great deal of their service quality.

BBBK is an example of how one company turned the situation around by analyzing the elements of the service-delivery process. By asking, "What obstacles stand in the way of our guaranteeing pest elimination?" Al Burger discovered that clients' poor cleaning and storage practices were one such obstacle. So the company requires customers to maintain sanitary practices and in some cases even make physical changes to their property (like putting in walls). By changing the process, the company could guarantee the outcome.

There may well be uncontrollable factors that create problems. As I noted earlier, such things as flight controllers, airport capacity, and weather limit the extent to which even the finest airline can consistently deliver on-time service. But how employees respond to such externally imposed problems strongly influences customer satisfaction, as British Airways executives learned from their market survey. When things go wrong, will employees go the extra yard to handle the problem? Why couldn't an airline that has refined its problem-handling skills to a science ensure absolute customer satisfaction—uncontrollable variables be damned? How many customers would invoke a guarantee if they understood that the reasons for a problem were completely out of the airline's control—if they were treated with warmth, compassion, and a sense of humor, and if the airline's staff communicated with them honestly?

Cheating

Fear of customer cheating is another big hurdle for most service managers considering offering guarantees. When asked why Lufthansa's guarantee required customers to present written proof of purchase, a manager at the airline's U.S. headquarters told me, "If we didn't ask for written proof, our customers would cheat us blind."

> *A guarantee can generate breakthrough service and change an industry.*

But experience teaches a different lesson. Sure, there will be cheats—the handful of customers who take advantage of a guarantee to get something for nothing. What they cost the company amounts to very little compared to the benefits derived from a strong guarantee. Says Michael Leven, a hotel industry executive, "Too often management spends its time worrying about the 1% of people who might cheat the company instead of the 99% who don't."

Phil Bressler of Domino's argues that customers cheat only when *they* feel cheated: "If we charge $8 for a pizza our customers expect $8 worth of product and service. If we started giving them $7.50 worth of produce and service, then they'd start looking for ways to get back that extra 50 cents. Companies create the incentive to cheat, in almost all cases, by cutting costs and not providing value."

Where the potential for false claims is high, a no-questions-asked guarantee may appear to be fool-hardy. When Domino's first offered its "delivery within 30 minutes or the pizza is free" guarantee, some college students telephoned orders from hard-to-find locations. The result was free pizza for the students and lost revenue for Domino's. In this environment, the guarantee was problematic because some students perceived it as a game against Domino's. But Bressler takes the view that the revenue thus lost was an investment in the future. "They'll be Domino's customers for life, those kids," he says.

High Costs

Managers are likely to worry about the costs of a service-guarantee program, but for the wrong reasons. Quality "guru" Philip Crosby coined the phrase "quality is free" (in his 1979 book, *Quality Is Free*) to indicate *not* that quality-improvement efforts cost nothing but that the benefits of quality improvement—fewer errors, higher productivity, more repeat business—outweigh the costs over the long term.

Clearly, a company whose operations are slipshod (or out of control) should not consider offering an unconditional guarantee; the outcome would be either bankruptcy from staggering payouts or an employee revolt stemming from demands to meet standards that are beyond the organization's capability. If your company is like most, however, it's not in that shape; you will probably only need to buttress operations somewhat. To be sure, an investment of financial and human resources to shore up weak points in the delivery system will likely cause a quick, sharp rise in expenditures.

How sharp an increase depends on several factors: your company's weaknesses (how far does it have to go to become good?), the nature of the industry, and the strength of your competition, for example. A small restaurant might simply spend more on employee recruiting and training, and perhaps on sponsoring quality circles; a large utility company might need to restructure its entire organization to overcome years of bad habits if it is to deliver on a guarantee.

Even though a guarantee carries costs, bear in mind that, as Crosby asserts, a badly performed service also incurs costs—failure costs, which come in many forms, including lost business from disgruntled consumers. In a guarantee program, you shift from spending to mop up failures to spending on preventing failures. And many of those costs are incurred in most organizations anyway (like outlays for staff time spent in planning meetings). It's just that they're spent more productively.

BREAKTHROUGH SERVICE

One great potential of a service guarantee is its ability to change an industry's rules of the game by changing the service-delivery process as competitors conceive it.

BBBK and Federal Express both redefined the meaning of service in their industries, performing at levels that other companies have so far been unable to match. (According to the owner of a competing pest-control company, BBBK "is number one. There is no number two.") By offering breakthrough service, these companies altered the basis of competition in their businesses and put their competitors at a severe disadvantage.

What are the possibilities for replicating their success in other service businesses? Skeptics might claim that BBBK's and Federal Express's success is not widely applicable because they target price-insensitive customers willing to pay for superior service—in short, that these companies are pursuing differentiation strategies.

It is true that BBBK's complex preparation, cleaning, and checkup procedures are much more time-consuming than those of typical pest-control operators, that the company spends more on pesticides than competitors do, and that its employees are well compensated. And many restaurants and hotels are willing to pay BBBK's higher prices because to them it's ultimately cheaper: the cost of "errors" (guests' spotting roaches or ants) is higher than the cost of error prevention.

But, because of the "quality is free" dictum, breakthrough service does not mean you must become the high-cost producer. Manpower's procedures are not radically more expensive than its competitors'; they're simply better. The company's skills-testing methods and customer-needs diagnoses surely cost less in the long run than a sloppy system. A company that inadequately screens and trains temporary-worker recruits, establishes no detailed customer specifications, and fails to check worker performance loses customers.

Manpower spends heavily on ways to reduce errors further, seeing this spending as an investment that will (a) protect its market position; (b) reduce time-consuming service errors; and (c) reinforce the company's values to employees. Here is the "absolute customer satisfaction" philosophy at work, and whatever cost increase Manpower incurs it makes up in sales volume.

Organizations that figure out how to offer—and deliver—guaranteed, breakthrough service will have tapped into a powerful source of competitive advantage. Doing so is no mean feat, of course, which is precisely why the opportunity to build a competitive advantage exists. Though the task is difficult, it is clearly not impossible, and the service guarantee can play a fundamental role in the process.

Getting The Bugs Out
Tom Richman

> *In the extermination business, there is Al Burger and there is everybody else.*
> *What does he know that the others don't?*

Howard Roth, born and reared in the Bronx, had to work late one evening at the cheap North Miami Beach, Fla., steak house where he was, temporarily and not by choice, the night manager. A new exterminator was coming to attack the resident cockroaches. Roth let the crew in, went for a drink, and came back later to see how things were going. He opened the door and couldn't believe what he saw. "It was the middle of the night, and here were these five guys, filthy dirty, crawling under and into everything, just doing a super job. Jesus Christ, I said to myself. After a while one guy got up off the floor and we started talking. I didn't know it at first, but he was the boss."

Roth switched jobs.

He hired himself, says the boss, Alvin Burger (rhymes with merger). "We're talking and Roth says, 'I'm gonna go to work for you. Anybody who can motivate people to do this kind of work, I want to be associated with him.'"

That was 17 years ago. Today, Miami-based "Bugs" Burger Bug Killers Inc. services nearly 12,000 restaurant and hotel accounts spread over 43 states, and the boss doesn't personally supervise every job anymore. No matter. The work gets done just as it would if he were there.

Al Burger has no MBA and little patience for the financial and administrative details of business. But he has overcome the biggest hurdle facing any small, growth-oriented company whose sole competitive advantage is quality of service. The more than 400 service specialists working for "Bugs" Burger (the company) today are just as motivated, and get just as dirty, as the original crew 17 years ago. Al Burger (the man) couldn't do a better job himself.

Says who?

The competition, to begin with. "'Bugs' Burger," says Jim Gillis, owner of All Boston Exterminators, "is number one. There is no number two."

And customers. "Let me put it this way," says Bob Crooks, manager of Gallagher's Restaurant, in Garland, Tex. "You have 'Bugs' Burger, and then you have to go waaay down to get to the second best."

And employees. "I left 'Bugs' Burger and worked for another company," says Alan Rosenberg, a service specialist in Boston who was recently promoted to district manager. "It was a step backward. They had no standards. So I came back. This is the only company I ever saw where the owner and the people on the job all think the same way."

With anticipated 1984 sales of $25 million, "Bugs" Burger is not the largest company in the national pest-control market, estimated at close to $2 billion annually. Orkin Exterminating Co. and Terminix International, both corporate subsidiaries with branch operations or franchises in about 40 states, rack up greater sales: $213 million for Orkin and $160 million for Terminix in 1983. Most of the rest of the industry consists of small, local operators. Indianapolis alone has about 75 pest-control companies. The competition is cut-throat, and the service, according to people with years of experience in the industry, is about the same way everywhere: minimal. Most customers assume they will get the same results no matter who they hire, so they hire on price. "Bugs" Burger doesn't operate in that market. "It's like he's a Mercedes," says Gillis, "and you've got a whole lot of Chevettes driving around out there."

"Bugs" Burger's marketing hook is its audacious guarantee—an unconditional promise to eliminate all roach and rodent breeding and nesting areas on the clients' premises, with no payment due until the pests are eliminated. If the company fails, the guarantee says, "Bugs" Burger will refund the customer's last 12 monthly payments and will pay for one year's service by another exterminator of the customer's choice.

The company doesn't promise that a restaurant diner or a hotel guest will never see another roach, but it does promise that if one shows up, it won't be native-born. Should an immigrant bug ride in with the groceries and stroll across a diner's table, "Bugs" Burger pays for the meal and sends the offended gourmet a letter of apology as well as a gift certificate for yet another free meal. "Customers feel like they've hit the state lottery," says the manager of one client restaurant. "They come in the next time and look for the little things." Hotel guests experiencing a similarly close encounter also get their night's lodging free, an apology, and an invitation to return—on the house. To help the company make good on its promises, "Bugs" Burger customers agree in writing to prepare their premises for monthly servicing and are fined if they don't.

Although the company says it has only once had to honor its full guarantee to a customer, it does spend about $2,000 a month reimbursing diners and room guests for reported pest sightings.

The professors and consultants would say that Al Burger has segmented the market and claimed the upscale commercial customers, those who will pay a premium price for superior service, as his niche. His company's monthly fees run four to six times those of its nominal competitors, sometimes more, and an initial "clean-out" charge alone can run four times the regular monthly fee. But Al Burger has not only created a new price structure, he has also taken a business with about as much prestige as, say, garbage collection, and given it respectability among both customers—". . . 'Bugs' Burger, one of my favorite subjects," responded Boston restauranteur Roger Berkowitz when he was asked about Burger—and employees. "In this company, the serviceman is number one," says Roger Gillen, a "Bugs" Burger employee in the Ft. Lauderdale office.

Al Burger's dad ran a not-very-profitable pest-control business in Albany, N.Y. His older brother bought another marginal operation in Miami. In 1954, after high school, two years in the Army, and a spell of selling vacuum cleaners door-to-door, Al Burger moved south to work for his sibling. He lasted five and a half ("miserable") years, quit, went to work for a competitor, and resigned. Immediately, he and Sandee, his wife of two years, formed their own partnership. Al was the marketing and service department, Sandee was the administration. They had, at first, no customers. "Most buys," says Al, "stole them. They planned their moves [to their own companies] so they could take a percentage of their accounts with them. I started from ground zero. I had to live with myself."

Al Burger has always been hobbled by a conscience. Owning his own company had never been a dream, but six years of working for other people had frustrated him. Employers in the pest-control industry, by and large, paid poor wages, provided no training, and were inured to high annual employee turnover rates. Further, in his experience, the service most companies provided their customers was unforgivably poor. The industry, he says, had convinced its customers that the best they could do was keep the critters—roaches and rodents—under control. Burger knew that with a little more time and effort they could be eliminated.

That conviction became the underpinning not just of "Bugs" Burger's exterminating techniques, but of the company's marketing and personnel management philosophies as well. Unlike the rest of the industry, which talks about "controlling" pests and holding them to an "acceptable" level, Al Burger sets a standard for his people that is unambiguous and requires no interpretation. While an employee might be uncertain about how many roaches is *some* roaches, *no* roaches is pretty easy to understand.

Moreover, it is an unvarying standard. To guarantee "customer satisfaction," as many companies do, is only to say, "We'll do as little as you let us get by with and only as much as you demand." The customer may be happy, but the serviceman on the route is confronted with working to a standard that varies from one customer to another, which is no standard at all. There is nothing to hold him accountable to, expect the whim of client complaints.

Companies frequently answer this dilemma by avoiding the issue of quality standards altogether, instructing employees instead to follow a prescribed routine. In the case of pest extermination, that could mean applying the indicated type and quantity of chemicals to a list of likely breeding areas. Follow the routine, the employee is told, and you can't be criticized—whether the rates and roaches are killed or not. After all, the company has promised to do only the best it can, and who is to say what that is?

"Bugs" Burger's quality-control system, an integral part of the company's operations, is extraordinary in itself. But the system exists only to ensure compliance with the unambiguous standard. Take away the standard, or fuzz it up, and the organization, like a basketball team with no hoop to shoot for, loses its purpose.

"I started my business," Al Burger says, "because I thought it was unethical to take money for poor-quality performance. I thought there should be standards and ethics in the industry." When he said so before a meeting of the Florida Pest Control Association in 1960, suggesting to his colleagues and competitors that they could upgrade their service by paying more attention, and more money, to the people they hired, he was hooted off the stage. "I almost cried. I went to the door," Burger says, "and I told 'em I quit."

To this day, Al Burger and the industry he is nominally a part of maintain an unusual relationship. Burger is unforgiving in his criticism. Most owners in the industry, he says, "are former routemen who are thieves and lazy to boot. That's what you've got—a lack of scruples. And why should *their* routemen care? They've probably got their own businesses on the side."

Spokesmen for the industry he reviles don't refute him. "So long as the larger firms demand that their routemen service 18 to 20 accounts a day," says Lee Truman of Indianapolis, a former president of the National Pest Control Association and an industry consultant, "there's no way you can do a professional job. They get by, the customers accept it, and that's pretty much the industry standard. . . . Burger doesn't do anything but use the same techniques all of us could use, and he gets rid of the roaches. . . . We talk professionalism a lot, but we don't practice it."

"In this company," as Roger Gillen, a routeman for 10½ years, says, "the serviceman is number one." Scott Hebenton and Philip Hargrove in Boston, each with less than one year's experience on a route, say much the same. Michelle Kolodny, manager of the company's central office in Miami, says, without prompting, "It's the service specialists that pay my salary." "Nobody is a big shot in this company," says Frank Perez, now the vice president in charge of service but 17 years ago one of the four employees Howard Roth saw working with Al Burger in that greasy steak house. (Roth himself is now executive vice president.) "Our service people," Perez adds, "are the privileged class."

And so it goes. No matter who you talk to in the company, before long he or she pays homage to the men and women (about 7% of the service specialists are female) in the field. It could be just lip service, but it isn't.

On paper, the "Bugs" Burger service organization looks unremarkable. It separates the country into four divisions, each division into regions, and regions into districts headed by managers supervising a dozen or so service specialists each. But superimposed on this ordinary structure is a quality-control system of thoroughly frightening proportions.

Service specialists work unsupervised, at night, on schedules they set for themselves. After each routine monthly service call on every account, however, the routeman files a report in which, if he wants to remain a routeman with "Bugs" Burger, he spills everything. Were there any problems with the customer's sanitation practices? Did the routeman have access to all the premises? Did the customer do the necessary preparation? Did the routeman see a roach or a rodent, or evidence of roaches or rodents? Did he kill any roaches or rodents? Does he need any help with the account? As the routeman is told from the time he first interviews for a job with the company, honesty pays. At "Bugs" Burger, mistakes are forgiven; liars are not.

The information filed by the routeman is checked, not once but several times, by managers at various levels. District managers call each customer a day or two after every monthly service. District managers, regional directors, and divisional vice presidents spend much of their time visiting customers' premises, armed when they arrive with a computer printout of the routeman's reports. The computer printout also includes customer complaints received in Miami. (When customers call "Bugs" Burger from any city in the country except Honolulu, using either the local or toll-free number listed in the phone book, the telephone rings at the Miami corporate headquarters, not at the routeman's home or the local office.) And just to keep all of *those* managers honest, a full-time, two-person quality-control team headed by Al Burger's daughter Susan hopscotches the country calling on customers and filing their own reports. Routemen don't know when or how frequently their clients will be called on by someone from management. The only certainty is that they will be called on, and that if there are complaints, Miami will hear about them first.

Naturally, company managers insist that all this checking up is really done for the routeman's benefit. "Our job," says Tom Schafer, vice president of technical services, which includes quality control, "is to support the service department." Routemen "appreciate" the help these reports and visits give them, assures Perez.

That is exactly the sort of thing you would expect to hear from management. What is surprising, however, is that you get the same story from the field.

"Yeah, it's pressure," says Scott Hebenton in Boston, "but it helps you keep up your standards."

"It gives us that little extra motivation," says Alan Rosenberg. "It would be easy to slack off one night, make it up the next month. But when you think, well, they might call this account *this* month."

Don't they resent it?

"I don't," says Hebenton. "Without it I guess we'd be just like any other company."

An employee-turnover rate of less than 3% last year suggests that most people at "Bugs" Burger feel much the way Hebenton does. Something about this system of management and quality control builds pride instead of resentment among the people whose performance is constantly monitored.

Jack Kaplan, the company's vice president for human resources, thinks it is a "mentality . . . that says, 'You are critical to the success of this company, and I'm going to make you feel that way from day one.' Most people coming here from different backgrounds aren't used to hearing words like that."

Employees first encounter this attitude during the hiring process, which involves two rounds of interviews, elaborate personality and aptitude testing, a polygraph examination, and thorough explanations of the job and the company—all conducted by officials from Miami headquarters, who eventually turn over the names of qualified applicants (2% or 3% of those who answer the ads) to local service managers for the final decision. The people hired already feel part of an elite group just from having survived what they know is an exhaustive selection process. Further, it is a process that doesn't automatically select the young. "I appreciate it," says Hebenton, hired last year at age 37, "because an older guy has just as good a chance." Kaplan recalls interviewing a 45-year-old woman in Roanoke, Va., who asked, he says, "Would you hire an old broad like me?" They did. "Her district manager says she's fantastic," he adds.

New hires undergo a 5-month training program. "It's like boot camp in the Army," says Kaplan, "only it's three times as long and twice as tough." Recently hired service specialists confirm Kaplan's analogy. During the program, they are not assistants, helping someone else. They do real work under the full-time instruction of a field manager. After about three months, new recruits attend a two-week school in Miami, where, one says, "there is no fooling around. You go to class from eight o'clock until six or seven o'clock, then you do your homework and show up again the next morning. It's pretty intense." (Letting no opportunity to exercise a little quality control slip by, company officials test the recruits in Miami, not just to see what they have learned, but also to check the techniques they had been taught by field managers against the company's standards. What public school administrators can't get away with, "Bugs" Burger can.)

Finally, in the sixth month, the new service specialist gets a route. In one sense he is on his own, because the responsibility of keeping customers' premises clear of nesting and breeding pests is ultimately his. Says serviceman Phil Hargrove, "It's like your own little business."

Not quite, but neither are Hargrove and his peers just employees hired to do a high-quality job.

Burger's routemen occupy a unique middle ground. They control the upside of their working lives—their own schedules, their incomes, and, to a large extent, their career paths within the company. What they don't have, in contrast to most workers and all independent business owners, is any downside risk. They can't lose, and that is why they will accept whatever performance standard the company wants them to meet. Once hired and trained at "Bugs" Burger, the only way you can fail is to lie. Cover up a mistake, slack off and don't report it, or ignore a problem, and you are in trouble. But ask for help, and you have it.

Routemen can talk to their district managers on the telephone or ask them to come to the job site, anytime. Regional directors and divisional vice presidents always travel with a working uniform in their bags. "They never look at it as a negative," says Scott Hebenton, "if you ask for help." Recently, the company flew eight out-of-state service specialists to Boston to get their Massachusetts licenses so that they would be available to augment the local forces if a job suddenly demanded a larger army. "They spare no expense," says Hargrove, slightly amazed. "Any serviceman knows," says Jack Kaplan, "that if he wants to talk to Mr. Burger, all he has to do is pick up the phone."

Nor does a "Bugs" Burger service specialist worry about losses from conditions beyond his control:

- If a major customer decides to drop the service at the end of his contract, the company subsidizes the routeman's compensation until a replacement is signed on.

- When a salesman badly underestimates the hours required to service a new account, the company subsidizes the routeman for the time he puts in, because it won't allow him to shortcut the service.

- Customers that won't cooperate with a routeman by maintaining sanitary conditions or by preparing the premises for treatment are dropped. The serviceman, again, is subsidized until a new client is found to fill out his route.

- Promotions from service specialist to district manager—and all other promotions within the company—are made on a three-month, or longer, trial basis, with the salary differential held in escrow during the trial. If a supervisor or, as is more frequently the case, the former routeman decides the promotion isn't working, he gets either his old route back, or a better one. Roger Gillen, an 11-year "Bugs" Burger veteran, tried a management job and left it. "I'm not a management type of person, and you just can't replace a good serviceman." There is no shame at "Bugs" Burger in staying with the job you do well—and for which you are paid well. Servicemen receive $1,200 a month in salary plus 20% of all the monthly gross billings on their routes in excess of $5,100. The average routeman makes $24,000, but $32,000 or more isn't unheard of, according to company sources.

Benefits are impressive, too: full health insurance; disability insurance that pays full salary for three months and 60% thereafter; a pension plan; profit sharing; cost of living adjustments; performance bonuses; and, coming soon, employee equity in an affiliated company selling janitorial supplies.

"An old lady," Al Burger recalls, "told me that if you give without thinking about what you might get back, eventually you'll get back 100 times what you gave. That was Mrs. Lummus. When I was 21, working for my brother, she called. She had a terrible roach problem in Miami Beach, but no money. So I got rid of her roaches, and she made me tea and cookies. I remember that she told me. It's a good thing to carry with you."

High-minded thoughts, of course, do not by themselves ensure business success. While they can inform and influence a management organization, they can't take its place, and Al Burger, he will admit today, is no organizer. In 1978, sales were nearly $6 million, but the business was foundering. Burger realized, with a little help from Howard Roth, that he had reached the limits of his managerial capabilities. "I was panicking, beginning to make mistakes. I was disoriented. I actually had heart palpitations. Too many things were happening that I couldn't cope with. . . . Howard Roth—a guy with a ninth-grade education who really understands people—he sat me down and said, 'Here's a guy that you're going to hire.'"

The guy was Art Graham, who, as president of Pizza Hut Canada Ltd., had just turned the company around. He had worked for "Bugs" Burger briefly in the early '70s, but hadn't appreciated the growth opportunities in the business. In 1978, while Graham was in Miami for the Super Bowl game, Roth persuaded him to come back. Graham built a management structure where none had existed before and pulled the profit margin to 12% of sales within six months, up from 1%. He wrote the company's first business plan and constructed its first annual operating budget.

Al Burger, meanwhile, concentrates on what he does best: marketing and firing up the troops. "Basically," says district director Scott Hebenton, "what Al Burger is, is a service specialist . . . and when he talks to you it's like he's right inside your head. He knows exactly what you're thinking out there on the route. 'Oh, I'm tired. Why not just cut this short and go home.' He's a good motivator."

Both management and motivation remain important. On the marketing front, for example, some of the competition is beginning to catch on to Burger's gimmick—the elimination guarantee—and while they have raised their prices accordingly, "Bugs" Burger is still the premium-price service. The company loses $2 million or more annually in unrenewed contracts as existing customers switch to lower-cost exterminators.

"Bugs" Burger's response to the competition has been to develop some productivity-enhancing equipment for routemen to use, and to map out some innovative, but still confidential, pricing options. The one thing Burger won't allow is cuts in service. "The minute we start doing that," he says, "our standard falls apart. You can't tell a service specialist not to do a good job on one account and then expect him not to do a bad job on the others. People will strive for that elusive level of perfection. All they need is the right attitude, and that all depends on the goals and standards you set for them."

Al Burger, in short, is still a man with a mission. He won't rejoin the national trade association until it changes its name from pest control to pest elimination. "He was a voice in the wilderness," says Lee Truman of Indianapolis, "but now an awful lot of people think he's been right all along."

And despite the competition, he remains cool and self-confident. The owner of one of Honolulu's most expensive restaurants didn't hide his condescending skepticism when Burger first stopped by on a sales call. But Burger had already toured the dining rooms, kitchens, and work areas. He had seen the thumb-size roaches scampering over the glassware, gone unerringly to where the egg cases were hidden, noted that rats had walked across the floured surface of the pie-crust machine leaving paw prints and their distinctive calling cards.

Condescending or not, here was a man, Al Burger knew, who needed and eventually would pay for "Bugs" Burger's kind of service.

Federal Express:
The Money Back Guarantee (A)

Date: Thursday, March 31, 1988
Time: 10:00 a.m.
Place: Amelia Island Plantation Resort, Florida
Setting: An executive education seminar

Sylvia Cooper, a business school professor, was delivering an executive education seminar for 30 senior managers of a *Fortune 500* company. On the night before her big presentation, she showed participants a Tom Peters video, *A Passion for Customers*, that included a complimentary segment on Federal Express. On the morning of her presentation, she had reason to feel remorse about showing that segment.

Reason: The day before, Cooper's secretary had used Federal Express to send her a videotape and some other material she needed for her Thursday presentation. (The videotape had just been completed by the audiovisual department at her school.) A front-desk clerk had told Cooper that Federal Express deliveries usually arrived by 10:00 a.m. By that time on Thursday, the daily delivery had indeed been made, but Cooper's package was not there. Her presentation was scheduled for 2:00 p.m.

When Cooper learned that her package had not arrived, she asked whether it could have been overlooked, and suggested that perhaps it was on a delivery truck elsewhere at the resort. The front-desk manager agreed to send someone to check the parcels on all the delivery trucks. When Cooper called the front desk back at 10:30, she was told that a complete search had not turned up her package.

Cooper then called her secretary, Alice, to make sure she had sent the package. Alice said she had, and offered to check the university mailroom to see if a mistake had been made there. "Call me back in 10 minutes," she told Cooper. When Cooper called back, Alice explained that the mailroom had sent the package, and that everything appeared to be in order at her end. Knowing that Federal Express employed a sophisticated tracking system, Cooper asked Alice to

Professor Christopher W. L. Hart prepared this case as the basis for class discussion rather than to illustrate either effective or ineffective handling of an administrative situation. Copyright © 1989 by the President and Fellows of Harvard College; Harvard Business School case # 9-690-004.

call Federal Express to locate the package. To do so, Alice went back to the mailroom to obtain the airbill number.

When she called Alice back at 11:00, Cooper learned that her package had been a "missort." According to the tracking system, it was sitting at the Federal Express terminal in Savannah, Georgia. The resort was about a three-hour drive from Savannah.

Cooper often cited Federal Express in classes and seminars she taught as an example of service excellence; therefore, she decided to see what she could learn by calling the company herself. She was interested in finding out how Federal Express would "make things right" for her and save her 2:00 p.m. presentation.

On the first ring—just as shown in the Tom Peters video—a customer service representative answered.

Cooper: I have a serious problem. Yesterday, my secretary sent a package that should have reached me at Amelia Island this morning. Apparently it was missorted, and it's sitting in Savannah. I need the material in that package by 2:00 this afternoon. What can you do for me?

Federal Express: I will need some information, ma'am. What is your airbill number?

C: 619732942.

FE: Thank you. Please hold while I check its status.

C: No, I *know* the status—(Pause).

FE: Ma'am, your package is a missort. It ended up in Savannah, Georgia.

C: That part I know. What I need to know now is what are you going to do about it?

FE: It's our policy that we'll get the parcel to you just as soon as possible. And we won't charge you for it. [For Federal Express's money-back guarantee, see *Exhibits 1* and *2*.]

C: That doesn't do me any good. I need to know when it will be delivered.

FE: Well, ma'am, we send missorted parcels ASAP. You should have it tomorrow morning.

C: That's too late—I need the material at 2:00 *today*. And I won't even be here tomorrow, I'll be back at home.

FE: That's no problem, ma'am. We'll send it to your home address. What is the address?

C: The address is on the airbill, but that's not the point. I've got to have that material today. Can you get it to me some other way—put it on one of your trucks, or put it in a cab, or in a *helicopter*, for heaven's sake!

FE: (Silence at the end of the line.)

What should Federal Express do for this customer?

In your view, what should Federal Express's general policy be for similar service mishaps?

What do you think actually happened?

Federal Express handles roughly 875,000 packages each day. What would you guess its error rate to be?

Exhibit 1
Federal Express Money-Back Guarantee—Short Form

Two Money-Back Guarantees

Federal Express backs its dependability with *two* money-back guarantees.

First, we guarantee that if we fail to deliver your package by 10:30 A.M. we'll give you your money back. Even if delivery is only 60 seconds late.

Second, our technologically advanced system allows us to tell you the exact status of your package within 30 minutes of your call. If we can't, you'll get your money back.

Exhibit 2
Federal Express Money-Back Guarantee—Long Form

MONEY-BACK GUARANTEE POLICY

Federal Express offers two money-back guarantees:

1. *Service Failure* At our option, we will either refund or credit your shipping charges upon request if we deliver your shipment 60 seconds or more after our published delivery commitment.

In order to qualify for refund or credit the following conditions apply:

- For invoiced shipments and for shipments by customers using our automated systems, you must notify us in writing or by telephone of a service failure within 15 calendar days from the invoice date.

- For shipments not invoiced by Federal Express (paid by cash, check or credit card) you must notify us in writing or by telephone of a service failure within 15 calendar days from the date of shipment.

- A service failure will not be deemed to have occurred if within 30 calendar days after you notify us we provide you with:

  (a) proof of timely delivery, consisting of the date and time of delivery and name of the person who signed for the shipment; or

  (b) service exception information reflecting that the failure to timely deliver resulted from an exception described under "Liabilities Not Assumed."

- At the time you notify us, you must provide the account number, if any, the airbill or package tracking number, the date of shipment, and the recipient's name, address and Zip Code®.

- Only one refund or credit is permitted per package. In the case of multiple package shipments, this money-back guarantee will apply to every package in the shipment. If a service failure occurs for any package within the shipment a refund or credit will be given for the portion of the shipment charges applicable to that package.

- Package Consolidators are not eligible for this money-back guarantee (see "Package Consolidators" section).

- A refund or credit will not be given for shipments delayed due to incorrect addresses or Zip Codes® or to the unavailability or refusal of a person to accept delivery or sign for the package or due to any of the causes described under "Liabilities Not Assumed." In addition, for shipments to and from Puerto Rico and to international destinations, refund or credit will not be given if failure to deliver is the result of Tax Authority or customs delays arising from inspection requirements or from omissions in documentation.

- This money-back guarantee does not apply to shipments destined outside our primary service areas.

- This money-back guarantee does not apply to requests for invoice adjustment based on overcharges (see "Billing").

Exhibit 2
(Continued)

- Effective April 1, 1988, for invoiced shipments and for shipments by customers using our automated systems, you must notify us in writing or by telephone of a service failure within 15 calendar days from the invoice date and must within the same 15 calendar days pay for all shipments on the invoice as to which timely delivery occurred based on our records. You must furnish with your payment the invoice numbers to which your payment applies. If an invoice is not paid in full, the reason for each unpaid charge must be noted with its airbill or package tracking number.

2. *Package Status* At our option, we will either refund or credit your shipping charges upon request if we cannot report the status of your package within 30 minutes of inquiry.

Package status is defined as the most recent electronically-scanned location of your package as reflected in our COSMOS computer system.

In order to qualify for refund or credit, the following conditions apply:

- You must telephone us and make your request wihtin 15 calendar days after the date of shipment. Written requests will not be accepted.
- The response period under this money-back guarantee is 30 minutes per package. Where more than one package status inquiry is made in a call, we will respond within 30 minutes of receiving all package related information.
- You must provide your account number, if any, the airbill or package tracking number, date of shipment, pieces and weight and the recipient's name, address and Zip Code® on the first call.
- Only one refund or credit is permitted per package. In the case of multiple package shipments, this money-back guarantee will apply to each package in the shipment.
- This money-back guarantee does not apply to shipments destined outside our primary service areas.
- Package Consolidators are not eligible for this money-back guarantee (see "Package Consolidators" section).
- Due to time zone differences, the package status money-back guarantee does not apply to international shipments.

LIABILITIES NOT ASSUMED

FEDERAL EXPRESS SHALL NOT BE LIABLE, IN ANY EVENT, FOR ANY DAMAGES, WHETHER DIRECT, INCIDENTAL, SPECIAL OR CONSEQUENTIAL IN EXCESS OF THE DECLARED VALUE OF A SHIPMENT ARISING FROM TRANSPORTATION SUBJECT TO THE SERVICE CONDITIONS CONTAINED IN THIS GUIDE, WHETHER OR NOT FEDERAL EXPRESS HAD KNOWL-
(Continued)

Exhibit 2
(Continued)

EDGE THAT SUCH DAMAGES MIGHT BE INCURRED, INCLUDING, BUT NOT LIMITED TO, LOSS OF INCOME OR PROFITS.

Federal Express shall not be liable for, nor shall any adjustment, refund or credit of any kind be made as a result of any loss, damage, delay, mis-delivery or non-delivery except such as may result from our sole negligence and the liability for which shall not exceed the declared value of a shipment, including, but not limited to, any such loss, damage, delay, mis-delivery or non-delivery caused by:

(a) The act, default or omission of the shipper, recipient or any other party who claims an interest in the shipment.

(b) The nature of the shipment or any defect, characteristic or inherent vice of the shipment.

(c) Violation by the shipper or recipient of any of the terms and conditions contained in our Service Guide, as amended from time to time including, but not limited to, improper or insufficient packing, securing, marking or addressing, or failure to observe any of the Service Conditions relating to shipments.

(d) Acts of God, perils of the air, public enemies, public authorities acting with actual or apparent authority on the premises, authority of law, acts or omissions of customs or quarantine officials, riots, strikes or other local disputes, civil commotions, hazards incident to a state of war or weather conditions, national or local disruptions in air or ground transportation networks due to events beyond our control, such as weather phenomena, strikes by government or employees of such organizations or natural disasters.

(e) Acts or omissions of any person or entity other than Federal Express, including our compliance with verbal or written delivery instructions from the shipper or recipient.

(f) Loss of articles loaded and sealed in packages by the shipper, provided the seal is unbroken at the time of delivery and the package retains its basic integrity.

Upon the occurrence of any of the events described in (d) above, we commit to servicing all customers by making all reasonable efforts to transport and deliver packages to their designated recipient as quickly as practicable under the circumstances.

THE CUSTOMER
COMPLAINT LETTER (A)

Following are two actual pieces of correspondence with only names and places changed. They provide an example of how the proprietor of a restaurant dealt with a justifiably angry and disappointed customer.

THE COMPLAINT LETTER

October 13, 1986

123 Main Street
Boston, Massachusetts

Gail and Harvey Pearson
The Retreat House on Foliage Pond
Vacationland, New Hampshire

Dear Mr. and Mrs. Pearson:

This is the first time that I have ever written a letter like this, but my wife and I are so upset by the treatment afforded by your staff, that we felt compelled to let you know what happened to us. We had dinner reservations at the Retreat House for a party of four under my wife's name, Dr. Elaine Loflin, for Saturday evening, October 11. We were hosting my wife's brother and his wife, visiting from Atlanta, Georgia.

We were seated at 7:00 p.m. in the dining room to the left of the front desk. There were at least four empty tables in the room when we were seated. We were immediately given menus, a wine list, ice-water, dinner rolls and butter. Then we sat for 15 minutes until the cocktail waitress asked us for our drink orders. My sister-in-law said after being asked what she would like, "I'll have a vodka martini straight-up with an olive." The cocktail waitress responded immediately, "I'm not a stenographer." My sister-in-law repeated her drink order.

This article was originally authored by Professor Martin R. Moser and published in the May 1987 issue of *The Cornell Hotel and Restaurant Administration Quarterly,* and is reprinted here with the permission of the Cornell University School of Hotel Administration. © 1987.

Soon after our waiter arrived, informing us of the specials of the evening. I don't remember his name, but he had dark hair, wore glasses, was a little stocky, and had his sleeves rolled up. He returned about 10 minutes later, our drinks still not having arrived. We had not decided upon our entrees, but requested appetizers, at which time he informed us that we could not order appetizers without ordering our entrees at the same time. We decided not to order appetizers.

Our drinks arrived and the waiter returned. We ordered our entrees at 7:30. When the waiter asked my wife for her order, he addressed her as "young lady." When he served her the meal, he called her "dear."

At ten minutes of eight we requested that our salads be brought to us as soon as possible. I then asked the waiter's assistant to bring us more rolls (each of us had been served one when we were seated). Her response was, "Who wants a roll?", upon which, caught off guard, we went round the table saying yes or no so she would know exactly how many "extra" rolls to bring to our table.

Our salads were served at five minutes of eight. At twenty-five minutes past the hour we requested our entrees. They were served at 8:30, one and one-half hours after we were seated in a restaurant which was one-third empty. Let me also add that we had to make constant requests for water refills, butter replacement and the like.

In fairness to the chef, the food was excellent, and as you already realize, the atmosphere delightful. Despite this, the dinner was a disaster. We were extremely upset and very insulted by the experience. Your staff is not well trained. They were overtly rude, and displayed little etiquette or social grace. This was compounded by the atmosphere you are trying to present and the prices you charge in your dining room.

Perhaps we should have made our feelings known at the time, but our foremost desire was to leave as soon as possible. We had been looking forward to dining at the Retreat House for quite some time as part of our vacation weekend in New Hampshire.

We will be hard-pressed to return to your establishment. Please be sure to know that we will share our experience at the Retreat House with our family, friends and business associates.

Sincerely,

Dr. William E. Loflin

THE RESPONSE

November 15, 1986

The Retreat House on
Foliage Pond
Vacationland, New Hampshire

Dr. William E. Loflin
123 Main Street
Boston, Massachusetts

Dear Dr. Loflin:

My husband and I are naturally distressed by such a negative reaction to our restaurant, but very much appreciate your taking the time and trouble to apprise us recently after dining here. I perfectly understand and sympathize with your feelings, and would like to tell you a little about the circumstances involved.

The Lakes Region for the past 4-5 years has been notorious for its extremely low unemployment rate and resulting deplorable labor pool. This year local businesses found that the situation had deteriorated to a really alarming nadir. It has been virtually impossible to get adequate help, competent or otherwise! We tried to overhire at the beginning of the season, anticipating the problems we knew would arise, but were unsuccessful. Employees in the area know the situation very well and use it to their advantage, knowing that they can get a job anywhere at any time without references, and knowing they won't be fired for incompetency because there is no one to replace them. You can imagine the prevailing attitude among workers and the frustration it causes employers, particularly those of us who try hard to maintain high standards. Unhappily we cannot be selective about employees as we would wish, and the turnover is high. Proper training is not a luxury, but an impossibility at such times.

Unfortunately, the night you dined at The Retreat House, October 11, is traditionally one of the busiest nights of the year, and though there may have been empty tables at the time you sat down, I can assure you that we served 150 people that night, despite the fact that no fewer than four members of the restaurant staff did not show up for work at the last minute, and did not notify us. Had they had the courtesy to call, we could have limited reservations, thereby mitigating the damage at least to a degree, but as it was we, our guests and the employees who were trying to make up the slack all had to suffer delays in service far beyond the norm!

As to the treatment you received from the waitress and waiter who attended you—neither of them is any longer in our employ, and never would have been had the labor situation not been so desperate! It would have indeed been helpful to us had you spoken up at the time—it makes a more lasting impression on the employees involved than does our discussing it with them after the fact. Now that we are in a relatively quiet period, we have the time to properly train a new and hopefully better waitstaff.

Please know that we feel as strongly as you do that the service you received that night was unacceptable, and certainly not up to our normal standards.

We hope to be able to prevent such problems from arising in the future, but realistically must acknowledge that bad nights do happen, even in the finest restaurants. Believe me, it is not because we do not care or are not paying attention!

You mentioned our prices. Let me just say that were you to make a comparative survey, you would find that our prices are about one half of what you would expect to pay in most cities and resort areas for commensurate cuisine and ambience. We set our prices in order to be competitive with other restaurants in this particular local area, in spite of the fact that most of them do not offer the same quality of food and atmosphere and certainly do not have our overhead!

I hope that this explanation (which should not be misconstrued as an excuse) has shed some light, and that you will accept our deep regrets and apologies for any unpleasantness you and your party suffered. We should be very glad if someday you would pay us a return visit so that we may provide you with the happy and enjoyable dining experience that many others have come to appreciate at The Retreat House.

Sincerely,

Gail Pearson

7

◆

Managing for Quality
and Productivity Gains

M anagers who have made the transition from product- to service-producing
firms often cite the greater difficulty of managing quality in services as
the biggest difference in managing in the two sectors. The one thing that is not
different is that improvements in quality generally are accompanied by productivity improvement and vice versa. Service quality is the difference between what
is delivered and what was expected by customers, requiring a clear understanding
of both. This leads directly to the development of service standards for reliability,
timeliness, assurance, empathy, and tangible evidence that are sometimes cited
as the basic dimensions of service quality. Steps necessary to achieve them may
require a complete reevaluation of such things as facilities, technology, information systems, people, and incentives and controls.

Productivity is the relationship between output (results) and inputs (effort).
Productivity improvements may be achieved through methods ranging from engineered work study to worker self-determination. Either of these (or others)
may be effective, but should reflect such things as the culture of the organization,
the complexity of the task under study, and the objectivity with which output
can be measured.

In addition to asking whether methods for obtaining quality and productivity
improvement fit the job, the need, and the culture of the firm, it is important
to ask: Who and how many people should the initiative involve? To what extent
are ideas for improvement coming from the bottom up? How are they measured?
Is there appropriate follow-up to suggested improvements? Are people adequately
recognized for their effort and accomplishments? What indications are there that
progress is being made?

The cases that follow, The Paul Revere Insurance Company (A) and (B) and
Florida Power & Light's Quality-Improvement Program, illustrate two different
approaches to the task of managing for quality and productivity gains. In looking

over The Paul Revere's initiative described in the (A) case, which of its elements do you feel are most important? To what extent have the objectives of the Quality Has Value (QHV) process been achieved? What are the strengths and weaknesses of the process? Would larger incentives lead to more significant results in this program? Why? What could account for the problems The Paul Revere is having with QHV in its field offices? What would you suggest be done about it? Can this process be packaged for use by other Textron divisions?

Turning to The Paul Revere Insurance Company (B) case, ask yourself: Was it a good idea to take a two-pronged approach involving quality teams on the one hand and a value analysis effort on the other? Why? What impact, if any, did this decision have on the value analysis effort? Is, as suggested by several consultants, The Paul Revere taking on too much at one time by proceeding with both the quality teams and value analysis? What did you like about the process used for implementing and carrying out value analysis at The Paul Revere? What would you have done differently? As Mike Koopersmith, how would you respond to Bob Jeffrey's "feeler"?

In comparing the Florida Power & Light approach with Paul Revere's, what are the similarities and differences between them? What factors are responsible for the success of each company's quality-improvement process? Which is likely to have the greatest favorable impact on productivity as well? Why? What drawbacks do you see to either of these processes? Where would each work best? Why might an organization prefer one approach over another?

The third item under this topic is a description of the recently initiated Malcolm Baldrige National Quality Award by the U.S. government. The interesting tie between these three documents is that John Hudiburg, then Chairman of Florida Power & Light, served as the president of the foundation created to provide support for the Malcolm Baldrige Awards competition. And The Paul Revere Insurance Company was among the first service firms to compete for the award. How would you rate The Paul Revere, based on what you know from the case, using criteria set forth in the description of the Malcolm Baldrige Award? What changes in criteria or weightings would you recommend to the designers of the Baldridge Award? Why? How much impact would you expect the Award to have on the quality of services delivered by U.S. firms? Why?

The Paul Revere
Insurance Company (A)

> *A decision to institute a quality team process is, if you will,*
> *a decision to allow a revolution. Revolutions come from*
> *the bottom up. If there is to be a new, American revolu-*
> *tion—a service industrial revolution—all the troops must*
> *be enlisted.*[1]

This is how Patrick Townsend, director of Quality Team Central, described the Quality Has Value (QHV) program adopted in January 1984 by The Paul Revere Insurance Company. In its first two-and-a-half years, this program accounted for more than $13 million in annualized savings. During the same period, first-year premium sales increased 50%, while staff increased only 4%.

By September 1986, the company's QHV process seemed firmly established. Moreover, Townsend perceived that the program was entering a phase of consolidation and assessment. He was scheduled to give a presentation to the Quality Steering Committee the following week concerning the future of QHV. He knew he would be expected to discuss the elements that made the process successful, identify the areas still in need of improvement, and predict whether QHV could be packaged for use by The Paul Revere's fellow Textron subsidiaries and perhaps sold to other companies.

Townsend wondered whether QHV would continue to work as well in the future as it had so far. There were no ready answers, but he knew that his ability to predict the program's future needs depended largely on his understanding of its past. Would a different approach be required at some point? If so, how could changes be phased in without sacrificing employee support and enthusiasm for the system?

---

1. Patrick L. Townsend, *Commit to Quality* (New York: John Wiley and Sons, 1986), p. 75.

Lucy N. Lytle prepared this case under the supervision of Assistant Professor Christopher W. L. Hart as the basis for class discussion rather than to illustrate either effective or ineffective handling of an administrative situation. Copyright © 1986 by the President and Fellows of Harvard College; Harvard Business School case #9-687-013 (*Rev.8/89*).

COMPANY HISTORY

The Paul Revere Insurance Company originated as the Masonic Protective Association, an organization established in Worcester, Massachusetts, in 1895, to write accident and sickness insurance for members of the Masonic fraternity. Francis Harrington, one of the company's founders and its first president, began his career as a livery stable operator and later became a three-term mayor of Worcester and a state senator.

In 1922, the company was renamed the Massachusetts Protective Association; Harrington's eldest son, Charles, was named his successor. Eight years later, The Paul Revere Insurance Company was established to serve the general public.

An undergraduate thesis described the historical culture of The Paul Revere Insurance Company:

> From its beginning in 1895 . . . The Paul Revere was a family-run paternalistic company. Its officers were all Harrington men, a prominent Worcester family who preferred to keep the business within the family. [Although the company paid relatively low] salaries to employees, it also provided job security for those who were willing to trade off one benefit for the other. . . . People were told when they could take breaks, use the rest rooms, and smoke. . . . The last option was for men only. Women were not allowed to smoke nor were they allowed to travel for the company.[2]

In 1967, The Paul Revere was purchased by AVCO, a diversified company. AVCO, in turn, was acquired by Textron, a large conglomerate, in 1984.

The Paul Revere's core business was selling individual and group disability insurance policies through independent insurance-brokerage firms, which were serviced by The Paul Revere's field sales offices. In 1986, the company insured 850,000 people, with a home office staff of 1,220, and 1,250 field agents, brokers, and clerical workers. Paul Revere employees were non-union. (For financial information, see *Exhibits 1* and *2;* an organization chart is presented in *Exhibit 12.*)

ORIGINS OF QUALITY IMPROVEMENT

By 1983, The Paul Revere had lost its long-established position as the nation's leading disability insurance underwriter to The Provident Insurance Company. This loss was due, at least in part, to a decision made by top management in the

2. Judy Bleemer, quoted by Patrick L. Townsend, *Commit to Quality,* pp. 20–21.

late 1970s to expand into other types of insurance, diverting attention and resources from the disability field. Although The Paul Revere continued to be a consistent moneymaker, its president, Aubrey Reid, was determined to regain the number one spot. Charles Soule, executive vice president of insurance operations, had read Philip Crosby's book, *Quality Is Free*, and predicted that in the near future The Paul Revere's customers would demand higher-quality service. Soule recalled:

> I first read Crosby's book in 1981. Excited by his ideas, I helped to put together a proposal suggesting ways to improve quality at The Paul Revere. At that time, people here were not particularly enthusiastic about the idea, so the proposal died a quiet death. Then, in the spring of 1983, I raised the issue again. At approximately the same time, the chairman of the board of AVCO, then the parent company of The Paul Revere, sent a directive to all AVCO companies instructing them to institute quality-improvement programs. The prevailing attitude quickly changed from "Let's not make too big a deal about quality improvement" to "Are we doing enough?"

In a letter sent to all employees on August 17, 1983, Reid stressed the permanent nature of the company's burgeoning quality-improvement efforts:

> This is not a quick-fix program. . . . Quality performance and quality measures will become an integral part of each employee's job, including individual job standards and performance appraisals.

DEVELOPING A PROGRAM

A Two-Pronged Approach

At Reid's direction, in the spring of 1983, an eight-member Quality Steering Committee (QSC) was formed, chaired by Soule and William Pearson, vice president of human resources. The committee comprised the number one or number two executive from every division and major department in the company.

Initially, the QSC met once a week for one to four hours. As the meetings progressed, it became apparent that the group was divided into two camps. Soule explained:

> On one side we had the "humanists," the people who maintained that if the company made a large initial investment in quality it would pay off later. They believed that if the secretaries said they could do a better job with antiglare screens for their computer terminals, then we should buy them without delay. On the other side were the "bean-counters," the people who

relentlessly calculated the cost of quality-improvement meetings in terms of labor hours lost.

It was a difficult situation. We didn't want to stifle creativity and individual initiative, nor did we want to take an unstructured approach where ideas could fly around without control. In the end, we developed a two-pronged approach involving quality teams and value analysis proceeding simultaneously.

To symbolize the two-pronged approach, the overall program was named Quality Has Value.

Quality in Fact and Quality in Perception

One of the first tasks facing the QSC was to define quality. During discussions, two definitions of quality emerged—"Quality in Fact" and "Quality in Perception"—and the committee agreed that QHV would incorporate both aspects. Quality in Fact emphasized conformance to specifications, while Quality in Perception involved improving the customer's perception of the quality of a particular product or service.

Measurement

Even after a two-pronged approach was agreed upon, the question of how to measure quality continued to stimulate considerable discussion. According to one member, the committee eventually decided that:

When people at The Paul Revere talk about quality, we mean conformance to specifications and that it is always cheaper to do it right the first time. We measure the cost of quality in dollars, and a key part of our program is determining the cost of quality and setting improvement goals.

The QSC modeled its system on Philip Crosby's "cost of quality evaluation" scheme.[3] Whereas Crosby defined three categories (prevention costs, appraisal costs, and failure costs), the committee used four:

- Prevention: training in new procedures, systems testing
- Detection: reviews of work balance, control
- Correction: redoing work that includes errors, computer reruns

---

3. Philip B. Crosby, *Quality Is Free* (New York: The New American Library, Inc., 1979), pp. 105–7.

- Failure: not being on time, nonconformance that requires corrective action, rework, and/or special explanation, when, in addition, the particular item has been received by the final customer

In a 1983 census, each department at The Paul Revere was asked to list the amount of time it devoted to each quality category in an average week. (See *Exhibit 3*.) The numbers were not precise, but were best estimates. The final number gave an indication of the magnitude of existing problems.

The employees estimated that, of the time spent on quality, 45% went to prevention, 25% to detection, 18% to correction, and 12% to failure. An overall figure of 44% of work time spent on quality was consistent among the divisions, and Townsend believed this confirmed his theory that a series of good-faith best estimates added up to a valid number, with the high and low estimates balancing out one another.

A separate cost-of-quality estimate was done at AVCO's request. In 1983, two Paul Revere executives set the company's cost of quality at approximately $9.65 million. In 1984, by converting time into wages and adding material costs, the quality teams estimated that the actual cost was closer to $16 million. The 1985 figures were calculated using the same method. That year, the cost-of-quality figure dropped to $14 million, the estimated percentage of total time allotted to quality decreased from 44% to 41%, and the time devoted to each category of quality effort shifted. There was a 5% increase in prevention and a 5% reduction in the time spent on correction and failure.

Corporate Culture Change

A major aim in the development of QHV, in addition to measuring the cost of quality and setting goals for improvement, was to stimulate change in the corporate culture. This change was both a specific goal of QHV and an expected, evolutionary result of the process. The Steering Committee members felt that, historically, upwardly mobile American managers had been taught that the way to get ahead was to "listen up and proclaim down" the corporate ladder. They wanted the QHV process to teach people to "listen down" and accomplish change within the organization at a grass-roots level.

Hiring Patrick Townsend

In October 1983, Patrick Townsend was hired to oversee The Paul Revere's emerging QHV program. After graduating from college with degrees in math and computer science, Townsend served in the U.S. Marine Corps for 20 years, attaining the rank of major. He fought in Vietnam, commanded a refugee camp, and was awarded the Marine Corps Bronze Star for outstanding performance in combat. Most recently, he had worked as a public affairs and recruitment advertising officer. Pearson recalled, "We thought Pat had all kinds of talents, but we didn't know exactly what we'd put him in charge of."

Townsend described his self-styled role as QHV's "mechanic":

> Somebody has to consider the quality process the most important business of the company. The mechanic's job is to be the central spokesman, the champion, if you will, of quality. The mechanic also oversees the day-to-day functioning of the quality-improvement program. Those responsibilities include running Quality Team Central, coordinating all the activities of the quality teams, participating in the recognition process, acting as a liaison between top management and lower-level quality teams, and promoting QHV both within the company and in the business world.

To explain the QHV process in detail, Townsend wrote a book, *Commit to Quality*, as well as several articles for newspapers and magazines.

QUALITY TEAMS

Quality Circles—With a Difference

In developing a system of quality teams for The Paul Revere, the QSC members used a modified quality-circle approach. Japanese quality circles generally involved only about 15% of the people in an organization. But because the QSC wanted to change The Paul Revere's corporate culture, it organized a series of quality teams that included everyone in the company, from the president to the maintenance staff.

The committee also decided to omit the presentations to management traditionally required before ideas developed by quality circles could be implemented. Employees were allowed to begin implementing their ideas immediately.

Quality teams included all members of a particular department, employees with similar responsibilities, or employees with a cross-section of roles and responsibilities. The department head, or the highest-level manager on a team, was designated team leader. Each team leader was required to be a member of a quality team at the next level up the corporate ladder as well, often the team led by his or her boss. In this way, quality-improvement suggestions moved up through the company. Originally, the home office had 127 teams of approximately 10 people each.

To foster a spirit of fun and friendly competition, the quality teams were encouraged to choose names. Paula Revere and the Raiders, the Dinner Belles, and the Lawful Awfuls were some of the names selected.

One of the chief tenets of the quality-team program was that no employee would be fired as part of a quality-improvement idea that led to staff reductions. "The result was that people weren't afraid to say, 'I don't think you need to have me doing this particular task anymore,'" one employee recalled. One nine-member department actually eliminated itself, and the people were offered jobs elsewhere in the company.

Quality Team Tracking Program

Each team met weekly to discuss quality-improvement ideas and to calculate the estimated savings associated with their implementation. The teams logged these suggestions and the estimated cost savings onto a computerized Quality Team Tracking Program (QTTP). (See *Exhibit 4*.) Each suggestion was given a rating: "1" indicated an area for possible work; "2" that the idea was pending; "3" that the idea had been scrapped; "4" that the idea had been implemented; and "5" that the idea had been certified (as explained below).

Quality team members could chart the progress of other teams by reviewing the ideas they had logged on QTTP. The entire QTTP file was available through any of the more than 150 computer terminals scattered throughout headquarters.

Quality Team Central

At the end of each week, Quality Team Central (QTC), composed of Townsend, four productivity analysts, and a secretary, received a computer printout of all status 4 ideas. QTC analysts then scheduled meetings with individual team leaders to discuss their ideas and the actions taken and to review any cost savings the teams had calculated. If the idea was acceptable, Quality Team Central certified the project and upgraded its status to a 5 on the computer. Once an idea was certified, it counted toward a series of awards.

One benefit of this system, according to Townsend, was that the four productivity analysts, who had been responsible in the past for conducting work-analysis studies and work-measurement programs, were "transformed from the 'bad guys,' whose presence in an area previously aroused apprehension and resentment, to the 'good guys,' who helped to certify ideas and propel a team toward rewards."

Training

A dozen promising employees were designated as team-leader instructors. These instructors took part in a 40-hour program, "Group Action," designed by Zenger-Miller consultants, that trained them to conduct meetings in a participative manner, drawing out ideas and using problem-solving techniques. The Paul Revere instructors, in turn, taught these techniques to the team leaders. Classical techniques of statistical process control (e.g., Pareto analysis, fishbone diagrams, and scatter diagrams) received little attention; instead the discussions emphasized the less sophisticated, but still effective, technique of brainstorming.

New employees received a brochure and a packet of materials describing the QHV process shortly before they began their jobs. They also participated in a half-day class on quality improvement. (See *Exhibit 5.*)

VALUE ANALYSIS WORKSHOPS

The second major component of The Paul Revere's QHV program was value analysis (VA) workshops. These workshops brought together all managers of a work unit or department over a period of six to eight weeks to analyze the functions of their unit and to either eliminate those functions or reorganize them to best allow the unit to fulfill its essential purpose (i.e., the reason for the unit's existence). Key questions were, What work do we do?, How do we do it?, Why do we do it this way?, and How can we do it better? This emphasis complemented that of the quality teams; while the quality teams asked, Are we doing things right?, value analysis asked, Are we doing the right things?

Despite this complementarity, several consultants warned the QSC that it would fail if it ran quality teams and tackled value analysis concurrently. Undaunted, the committee insisted on running the two programs simultaneously, provided that both served a common quality goal. Eventually, one consulting firm (the Robert E. Nolan Company) agreed that concurrent programs were feasible and tailored its VA workshops to fit QHV objectives. Nolan's VA facilitators usually asked workshop participants to set dollar targets, but Soule emphasized that he "wanted any dollar targets to be secondary." Accordingly, the consulting firm sent a vice president to attend several QSC meetings in order to understand the aims of the QHV process. The Nolan Company was also willing to phase itself out once it had trained in-house employees to facilitate the VA workshops.

Each workshop began with an information-gathering phase, during which the workshop members gathered facts about the operation of their unit and described the unit's functions using a verb-noun phrase such as "process applications" or "investigate claims." Then, in the analysis phase, the group identified its essential purpose and rated the department's functions in terms of their importance, reliability, and cost. (These ratings were the workshop participants' "best guess" estimates; the entire rating process took approximately one hour.) Next came the creative phase, during which the group brainstormed ideas for improving department performance. Typical ideas included work simplification, elimination, combination, rearrangement (including shifting tasks to other departments), and standardization. Later, these ideas were analyzed in depth; those that were deemed appropriate and feasible were incorporated in a summary report presented to upper management for approval.

Participation in the value-analysis process was mandatory; every department was expected to spend several weeks dissecting its work. Unlike the ongoing quality teams, the VA workshops were temporary—although they generated suggestions for lasting changes. Approximately two VA workshops took place at any one time, and the departments were analyzed on a piecemeal basis. Although every employee was a member of a quality team, only managers (about 300 of the home office's complement of 1,250 to 1,300) participated in the VA workshops. The managers' dual membership linked the two programs and facilitated a two-way flow of ideas. Most managers felt that this dual membership minimized conflict between the quality teams and the value-analysis program.

The first 42 VA workshops, conducted during the 1984–1986 period, resulted in recommendations that, when fully implemented, brought an estimated net benefit to The Paul Revere of $6 million–$8 million.[4]

SURVEYS

In 1983, at the direction of the QSC, The Paul Revere's market research department prepared and conducted a series of surveys. One survey polled home office employees, another targeted field employees, and a third was sent to policyholders. The surveys probed respondents' perceptions of the courtesy, accuracy, and promptness of various departments. The information gathered was used to highlight areas in need of quality improvement (e.g., a clerk who spent an hour each week alphabetizing data cards learned that the supervisor who received them threw them out without looking at them). They also served as a benchmark against which to compare the results of future surveys and to measure changes in quality. For the most part, however, the anticipated follow-up surveys were never conducted because no one assumed responsibility for the project.

4. For an in-depth consideration of the value-analysis workshops, see *The Paul Revere Insurance Company (B)*, HBS Case No. 9-687-033.

One survey that was followed up, the Life Office Management (LOMA) survey, was first conducted in September 1984. LOMA was an employee-attitude survey developed for the life insurance industry. The Paul Revere's results were compared with the national averages for the industry and, on the basis of this comparison, areas in need of improvement at The Paul Revere were identified (e.g., benefits, training, and child care). Action teams of volunteers were formed to devise suggestions for improving these areas. The teams publicly presented recommendations to Reid, then disbanded. There were plans to conduct a follow-up LOMA survey in March 1987.

REWARD SYSTEMS

To remind the quality teams that work could be a source of pleasure, enjoyment, and fun, the company deliberately made the idea of celebration a part of the QHV program. The emphasis was on gratitude and finding ways to say thank you to the employees for their help in improving the quality of the organization. The program was multifaceted because the QSC believed that different people heard "thank you" in different ways.

One committee member explained:

> For some people, public acknowledgment or recognition of their value to the company is the primary motivator. For others, material awards are the primary source of inspiration. The point is—who cares? If Larry Bird sinks two free throws with one second left on the clock and wins the National Basketball Association Championship, does anyone really care why he did it? What counts is that the Celtics won. The team is better for his efforts.

The recognition program cost The Paul Revere $80,000 in 1984.

Going for the Gold

QHV's primary reward system was based on either the number of ideas generated *or* on savings (i.e., ideas did not necessarily have to entail cost savings), and it was modeled on the Olympics. The first year, generating 10 ideas or $10,000 in annual savings won each member of the team a bronze pin, presented by a QSC chairman. Twenty-five ideas or $25,000 in savings garnered a silver pin and the choice of a $20 gift from a gift catalog. Fifty ideas or $50,000 in savings earned a gold pin, presented by the president of the company, and the choice of a $50 gift. (See *Exhibit 6.*) Each fiscal year, after attaining the gold level once, a team had to come up with another 50 ideas or $50,000 in savings to get another pin and gift, as well as an invitation to a special luncheon or dinner with top management. In 1985, the gift catalogs were replaced by gift certificates redeemable at local stores and restaurants.

Townsend reflected:

> The average quality circle in the United States implements six ideas a year. In Japan, it's even lower—closer to four or five. Fortunately, this was not discovered until after we decided on goals of 10, 25, and 50. Had it been known earlier, we would have set our sights considerably lower.

Of the 127 quality teams, 126 reached the bronze level by the end of 1984. Of these, 101 also attained silver, and 72 were awarded gold. In fact, 10 teams made double gold, and one even attained the triple-gold level. Ironically, the one team that did not reach the bronze level during the first year was led by a member of the QSC. According to Townsend, this team leader "got hung up on the philosophical aspect of quality, and he didn't want to give credit for things he felt the people should have been doing all along." In 1985, the highest level reached by any team was seventh-level gold. The winners, Tech Services, made a computer software adjustment that made the purchase of a $162,000 piece of hardware unnecessary.

Suggestions ranged from something as basic as moving a file cabinet closer to the desk of the employee who used it most often to reissuing and resoliciting a revised group insurance policy, which garnered $365,000 in additional revenue. In another change, maintenance workers quickly paid for a trash compactor in time and expense saved by eliminating extra trips to the dump yard. In the Financial Services Division, a new clerk realized that the company's policy of maintaining minimum balances in its checking accounts across the country was costing about $3,000 a year. The vice president who led the team estimated the cost at closer to $5,000, and the policy was changed immediately. (Quality teams composed of higher-level managers focused on communication issues, and members made presentations to lower-level quality teams dealing with various issues concerning quality improvement.)

In 1986, the QSC decided to base award levels on self-assessment because of complaints that "bean-counting" (coming up with the twenty-fifth idea) was pushing teams toward focusing on small changes. Instead of having a certain number of ideas certified, teams listed goals for themselves. During quarterly progress checks by Quality Team Central, each team indicated the level (bronze, silver, or gold) it felt it had attained. By and large, the teams' self-assessments matched those of Quality Team Central. (*Exhibit 7* presents the self-assessment form.)

Each December, Most Valuable Team (MVT) and Most Valuable People (MVP) awards were distributed at a Quality Celebration for all employees held at Mechanics Hall, a magnificently restored nineteenth-century music hall near the home office. To stress the importance of team efforts, the MVT awards were presented last, and the winners walked onto the stage to the theme music from the motion picture *Chariots of Fire*. After the ceremony, employees were told that they had the rest of the day off and received a ham or a turkey for Christmas. A costumed Minuteman distributed balloons with a logo promoting quality at The Paul Revere.

Lapel Pins

When the idea of rewarding employees with bronze, silver, and gold lapel pins was first proposed, a member of the Quality Steering Committee objected that no one would wear them. Townsend reminded him that he had just spent 20 years in the Marines—an organization where people "risked their lives for little pieces of ribbon." The committee concluded that people would wear decorations that had meaning and value attached to them, and the lapel pins were approved.

To encourage employees to wear their pins, a Lunch-for-a-Pin program was started. Once a week, a member of Quality Team Central picked 10 names out of a hat. If those people were wearing their pins, they received a free lunch pass.

When it was discovered in 1985 that many women were not wearing the pins because they did not like sticking the tie tack through their clothing, the pins were altered so they could be worn as charms hung from a necklace or bracelet.

In 1986, the casewriter accompanied Pearson and Townsend on a tour of the home office. As they presented gift certificates to, and chatted with, bronze- and silver-level teams, the team members appeared to be genuinely flattered by the attention. Only one employee in 25 had his pin with him, however, and he quietly lifted it out of his desk when he saw the group approaching.

Program for Ensuring that Everybody's Thanked

Based on the concept of "management by wandering around," PEET—the Program for Ensuring that Everybody's Thanked—required top managers to get to know team leaders informally. Each month, 18 executives were given the names of two team leaders and asked to visit their work areas and talk with them about their quality-improvement ideas.

The program met with some resistance at first. One employee recalled:

> For the first year, more than one executive just threw out the "PEET Sheets"
> because no one was keeping track of the process. Aubrey Reid got wind
> of this and quietly made some phone calls. Now it's a regular part of QHV.

Quality Coins

In addition to their PEET responsibilities, the company's top 20 executives were expected to hand out five quality coins each month. The coins were a way of offering a tangible thank you to individuals for noteworthy things they had done. Although the coins could be exchanged for a free meal in the company cafeteria, according to one employee, approximately 80% of the recipients opted to keep them as "a reminder of one of the few times they had actually been thanked for something they had done."

To provide monthly updates on quality-team activity and to create enthusiasm for and understanding of the process, an employee newsletter, *Quality News,* was started. In addition, Quality Is Good News bulletin boards were set up to display thank-you letters employees received.

One of the effects of the recognition program, Townsend noted, was a change in the way employees related to one another:

> When QHV began, most people's first question was "What can you do for me?" After a while, what attitude changed to "What can I do for me?" Now, we're at the stage where people are finally beginning to ask, "What can I do for you?"

RESISTANCE TO QHV

The Field

An obvious lack of enthusiasm for QHV in the field offices presented a significant problem, since slightly more than half of The Paul Revere's 2,470 employees worked in 130 field offices of varying sizes, with an average of 10 people per office.

According to several employees, an antagonistic relationship between headquarters and the field offices was considered almost inevitable. The thinking in the field seemed to be, "If those jerks in the home office had any understanding at all of what our jobs entail, if they were willing to bend just a little in our direction for once, there wouldn't be any problems." In contrast, the attitude at headquarters was, "If those prima donnas in the field would just read their mail and follow a few simple rules, everyone would be better off."

A chronic lack of communication between the two areas intensified the antagonism. Townsend explained:

> The sales force has seen many short-term, high-pressure, home-office–generated programs come and go. Convincing them that the concern about qual-

ity will become part of a new corporate culture isn't easy. We do our best to transmit information and enthusiasm via announcements, newsletters, phone calls, and videotapes. But even the implementation process is complicated because many of the ideas generated in the field require the cooperation of people in the home office to carry them out.

By the end of 1984, 557 ideas had been submitted from the field, with 140 of those certified (by regional vice presidents) and 76 implemented and certified in the home office.

In general, field ideas tended to be smaller in scale than those generated in the home office. One suggestion was to replace a male office manager's voice on a telephone answering machine with a female recording delivering a more enthusiastic and friendly message. Another office switched to number nine envelopes for return mailings because these fit within number ten envelopes without folding, saving both time and energy. Townsend maintained, however, that the field offices were often the catalyst for larger improvement ideas in the home office.

Middle Management

Another pocket of resistance emerged among some middle managers in the home office. Townsend noted:

> I think they're hoping to outwait it. They assure themselves it's just another "program of the month," they grouse to each other, and they try, consciously or not, to slow the progress of those beneath them. There haven't been any specific acts of resistance, just a general malaise.
>
> I'm not sure what to do to gain their acceptance of the program. Would more education about the benefits of quality help? Should top management take a harder line and warn them that managers who choose to ignore the input received from their subordinates, particularly in an organization that is actively soliciting such input, are acting in a professionally suicidal manner? Should I ignore them, hoping their resistance will weaken with time?

RESULTS

Between January 13, 1984, when QHV was officially launched, and November 30, 1984, the end of The Paul Revere's fiscal year, 7,109 ideas were logged onto the QTTP. Of these, 4,115 were implemented and certified for a combined annualized savings of $3.25 million. This figure combined the estimated savings from both "hard" and "soft" dollars. Hard dollar savings indicated budgeted money that now would not be spent or additional income that otherwise would not have been generated. Soft dollars involved time or capacity savings. The hard 1984 realized savings were $1.035 million. In its first two-and-a-half years, QHV chalked up total annualized savings (i.e., in hard and soft dollars) of more than $13 million. (See *exhibits 8, 9,* and *10.*)

These savings were compared with those generated by The Paul Revere's long-standing suggestion program, which was replaced by QHV in 1984. In 1983, 216 ideas had been submitted, of which 86 were implemented, for annualized savings of $41,000. These results were considered standard for such a program.

Between 1984 and 1986, first-year premium sales increased 50%. Soule attributed 25% of this increase to quality-improvement changes and the remainder to long-term strategic-planning changes (i.e., rate changes and the development of more customer-focused products) that had gone into effect during that period.

In December 1985, The Paul Revere's QHV process was honored as "the best quality process in the Textron network" by Rear Admiral Frank C. Collins, Jr., U.S. Navy (retired), now vice president of Quality Operations, Textron, Inc. *Exhibit 11* presents a list of the quality competition criteria. *Exhibit 13* contains employee comments about QHV.

Pearson recalled:

When The Paul Revere first applied to enter the annual AVCO/Textron Quality Excellence Competition, the reaction of many of our fellow subsidiaries, the majority of whom do defense-related work and operate under the strictest Department of Defense quality standards, ranged from amusement to scorn. Before he came to The Paul Revere to inspect QHV, even Collins himself was highly skeptical that a quality program devised by a small New England insurance company could even compare to, much less best, those of AVCO's other subsidiaries. Once he saw QHV's results, however, his response changed to shock, then to grudging admiration. Improbable as it seemed two-and-a-half years ago, today the AVCO/Textron quality flag waves proudly on the roof of The Paul Revere.

In 1986, The Paul Revere regained the number one position in its bread-and-butter field of individual noncancellable disability insurance.

After reviewing the development of QHV, Townsend noted:

The Paul Revere has undergone sweeping changes in the past two-and-a-half years and, as a result, I believe the quality of the company has increased dramatically. The challenge now is to keep the momentum going and to define the directions in which the process should grow in the future.

In retrospect, I realize that we made a few mistakes along the way and that there are still some areas in need of attention. At the same time, however, there's a lot that we did right, and we need to identify those elements as well—to make sure we keep them up in the future. Before the talk of packaging QHV, and possibly selling it, can become anything more than an idle scheme, we have to understand what makes the process work. I think I do—and I believe that quality improvement is the wave of the future for service organizations like The Paul Revere.

Exhibit 1
Balance Sheet

Assets

	Dec. 31, 1985
Total bonds	$673,121,432
Total preferred stocks	13,746,845
Total common stocks	43,213,832
Mortgage loans	212,924,723
Real estate	9,829,072
Policy loans	52,830,704
Cash	15,526,042
Short-term investments	3,354,359
Life 7 annuity premiums due	10,968,887
Accident & health premiums due	17,102,732
Due from ceding company	76,584,652
Accrued investment income	20,206,446
Other assets	30,256,098
Admitted Assets	$1,179,665,824

Liabilities

Net policy reserves	$805,574,068
Policy claims	44,346,316
Commissions, taxes, expenses	13,910,106
Unallocated items	12,635,057
Securities val. reserve	679,084
Additional benefit fund	117,639,942
Deposit admin. fund	47,931,648
Other liabilities	31,422,958
Total Liabilities	$1,074,139,179
Common stock ($5 par)	9,800,000
Paid in & contrib. surplus	15,000,000
Unassigned surplus	80,726,645
Total	$1,179,665,824

Exhibit 2
Selected Financial Information
(in thousands of dollars)

Year	Assets	Capital Surplus Funds	Conditional Reserve Funds	Net Premiums Written	Total Insurance Issued	Total Insurance in Force
1980	$ 814,948	$ 92,284	$19,058	$197,674	$ 979,484	$5,476,235
1981	814,841	55,545	14,248	199,567	553,058	5,721,773
1982	871,892	63,893	18,430	202,285	608,942	5,626,825
1983	939,635	77,431	21,228	218,555	1,455,990	6,160,618
1984	1,090,134	105,032	6,186	305,765	588,493	6,201,672
1985	1,179,666	105,527	679	332,211	3,220,500	8,885,339

Exhibit 3
The Four Categories of Quality (%)

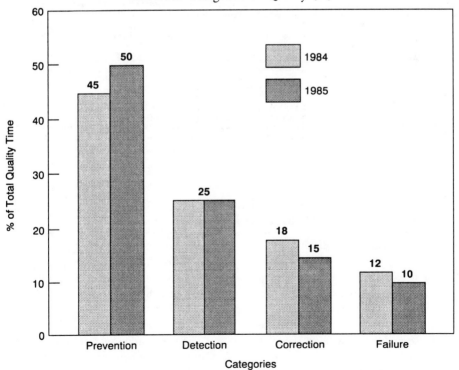

Exhibit 4

Blank QTTP Screen

```
                    Edit SAS data set: QUALITY.MASTER          | Screen  1
Command ===)                                                   |----------
                                                               | New    14
--------------------------------------------------------------------------
                         OUR POLICY IS QUALITY
Team Leader: _ _ _____  Cost Center: ___ Route ♦ _____  Team No: ___
Team Name: _____      Meeting Date: _____  No. of Attendees: __
Item  Prty       Descriptions of Actions Considered or Taken
No.   No.
----  ---   --------------------------------------------------------------------
            --------------------------------------------------------------------
            --------------------------------------------------------------------
            -----------------------------------  --Status--   Referred by
Effective Date  Next Action Date  Team   Other    Team No.    Est Annual Value
---------       ---------         _ *    _ **      ---         --------
       * Team Status    active=1,  pending=2,  deleted=3, implemented=4
       ** Other Status  higher=7,  lower=8,    other=9
****************************************************************************
PF01 = Add    PF06 = Duplicate   PF07 = back 1  PF08 = Forward 1   PF12 = Exit
```

Completed QTTP Screen

```
                    Edit SAS data set: QUALITY.MASTER          | Screen  1
Command ===)                                                   |----------
                                                               | Obs    13
--------------------------------------------------------------------------
                         OUR POLICY IS QUALITY
Team Leader: J _ Ferguson       Cost Center: 77 Route ♦ 105-02  Team No:  70
Team Name: The Grinches         Meeting Date: 11/12/85  No. of Attendees:  7
Item  Prty       Descriptions of Actions Considered or Taken
No.   No.
 67   ___    PROFS audit to be sure all ID's are in conformance with
             standards, all links are correct.
            --------------------------------------------------------------------
            -----------------------------------  --Status--   Referred by
Effective Date  Next Action Date  Team   Other    Team No.    Est Annual Value
---------       ---------         2 *    _ **      ---         --------
       * Team Status    active=1,  pending=2,  deleted=3, implemented=4
       ** Other Status  higher=7,  lower=8,    other=9
****************************************************************************
PF01 = Add    PF06 = Duplicate   PF07 = back 1  PF08 = Forward 1   PF12 = Exit
```

Exhibit 5

QHV Brochure for New Employees

THE QUALITY PROCESS

Upon joining The Paul Revere you will find yourself soon being assigned to a Quality Team and you will hear many things about "Quality." It's all because of Paul Revere's Quality Has Value Process.

The first thing to understand is that it is a *process*, not a program. This is not something that will be completed next month or at the end of the fiscal year. It is an integral part of The Paul Revere way of doing things. It is part of our culture.

The most important feature of The Quality Has Value process is that the managers and supervisors at every level

Exhibit 5
QHV Brochure for New Employees

look to their subordinates for ideas. Information, recommendations and ideas flow both ways.

This, or course, means added responsibility for everyone. If a Paul Revere employee sees a way to improve The Quality of his or her job—or to improve the way their departments operate, they are expected to say so. And to be ready to help implement the improvement.

THE QUALITY TEAM

The structure established to enable this process to unfold is anchored on The Quality Team. A Quality Team normally has about 10 members and, where possible, they work together in the same department or unit. The Team Leader has received special training in conducting meetings and helping a group solve problems. Quality teams usually meet for a half hour every week.

A Quality Team's primary aim is to improve the Quality—both in fact and in the eyes of the customer—of the things the members work on from day to day. The Quality meeting may only be a half hour, but concern about Quality is a continuous activity.

If a Quality Team determines that a particular improvement will not only increase the Quality of the work they do but will also impact other work areas, it is up to them to coordinate with the other people. Coordination is kept as simple as possible. Helping in this coordination is one of the responsibilties of Quality Team Central. (More about them later.)

If, however, a Quality Team has an idea which, if implemented, would involve a significant portion of the company, then there is another approach. Virtually all team leaders are also members of another Quality Team at a higher level of supervision or management. This "chain" can be used to move ideas up to the level capable of implementing them.

THE CHALLENGE TO YOU

Being a member of a Quality Team will be an exciting and challenging part of your new position here at The Paul Revere. We know of no other company of our size that looks to every employee in the organization to be constantly on the lookout for ways to improve its Quality. We believe that the procedures we have established make it possible for everyone to contribute as much as they are capable of. And just as all employees contribute to the idea bank . . . all employees will share in the benefits as we become the very best company in our business.

QUALITY TEAM CENTRAL

To help the process along, there is an organization called the Quality Team Central. They are responsible for answering questions and offering help to Quality Teams. They also keep track of progress by teams so that they can be recognized and thanked as appropriate. As the name Quality Team Central implies, this group provides the centralized coordination for all aspects of our ongoing Quality process.

Welcome to The Paul Revere and to the Quality Process.

Exhibit 6
Quality Pins 1984

Here's how the Quality Recognition Program works . . .
BRONZE AWARD

When a team meets the qualification criteria for the Bronze Award, each team member receives a Bronze cloisonné lapel pin which recongizes each team member's contributions to "Paul Revere Quality"

SILVER AWARD

When a Quality Team reaches the Silver Award level, each team member receives a Silver-plated lapelpin to show off his or her pride in Paul Revere Quality. In addition, each Silver Award qualifier receives the opportunity to select a merchandise award from an attractive selection of items from the Quality Awards Catalog J.

GOLD AWARD

When a Quality Team reaches the Gold Award level, each team member receives a Gold-plated lapel pin . . . Paul Revere Quality at its best! In addition, each team member can select a merchandise award from the Quality Award Catalog F, which features a beautiful array of appealing items.

Exhibit 7
Quality Has Value '86—Self-Assessment Form

Date: _July 23, 1986_

Quality Team Name: _Bar Belles_

Team Leader Name: _Joan Gay_   Ext. # _5565_

Department(s) Represented: _Law_

Rating for just-ending three-month period (circle one):

         PASS   BRONZE   SILVER   GOLD

Reasons for rating (please be as specific as possible; reference to Team Quality Goals is urged):

GOALS: (FOR THE ENTIRE YEAR)

1. Invite 2 "customers" each quarter to get input as to what we can do to improve our communications with them.

    Ann Marie from the Mail Department spoke to us and gave us many helpful ideas. A question-and-answer period followed.
    Joe Rogers from the Research Institute of America spoke to us regarding the RIA sets of books in our law library. (See certified idea #51.)

2. Develop chart for Agents/Brokers to use in preparing applications (beneficiary and assignment, etc.). Nila Allen is working on this.

3. Certify 5 ideas each quarter.

    (#47)   1.   A & S Collateral Assignment Forms sent out from Supply Department. Notify Field in Agents Bulletin.
    (#48)   2.   Learn how to use "red books" in law library.
    (#49)   3.   Learn how to close a suit and file in vault.
    (#50)   4.   1986 Library Management Book.
    (#52)   5.   Flesching software package.

DATE ASSESSMENT DUE TO QUALITY TEAM CENTRAL: _July 23, 1986_

4. Improve communications within department.

    a. Ordered Bulletin Board—will have every person's name in department, plus spaces for indication if person is out sick, on vacation, etc., and date of return to office.

    b. Quality Meeting Minutes—distributed to all members of team (particularly helpful to those who missed meeting—also helpful to remember what was said).

    c. Colleen Schenck (our supervisor) speaks to us at beginning of our meetings when she feels it is necessary.
    —as our supervisor—it is a quick way to communicate with us as a group because we are all assembled.
    —as liaison with the "Bar"—to relay any information from that team.

    d. Notices (quick blurb) on bright colored paper posted above mail slots re: lost papers, file, book, pen, etc.
    —very effective—with immediate response.
    —saves time—the person who misplaced the item does not have to go around to each person in the department and inquire if he/she has seen the lost item.

5. Examine, redefine, and reorganize filing procedures for all lines and types of filings.

    So far, the life filing chart has been updated.
    More work will be done on this goal during the next two quarters.
    (Procedures need to be written down, and the Life and A & S books need to be cleaned out.)

(continued on next page)

Exhibit 7
(Continued)

6. Train secretaries so there is at least one backup for each function—every secretary to be responsible for teaching her functions to a logical partner.

    Sixteen functions listed and all have been taught. (See attached list.)

7. Bring policy forms/records/books up to date.

    These books have not been updated since 1982. Since they are used by other departments also, we plan to make copies of the finished project to distribute to the other departments. We have gathered all the D.I. forms to be put into separate books for policies, riders, amendments, and applications, ready to go to the Printing Department for copying.

THESE 2 NEW GOALS HAVE BEEN ADDED:

8. In response to Aubrey Reid's April 30, 1986, letter to Quality Team Leaders regarding the appearance, accuracy, and clarity of our communications, please see the attached copy of our May 22, 1986, memo to him regarding the steps we took to address the problem, and also see the attached copy of his reply to us.

9. Compile a LAW DEPARTMENT HANDBOOK/MANUAL.

    We did not have such a manual in the Law Department, and felt that there was a definite need for one with the various changes in personnel in our department recently, and because many of our procedures have changed in recent years due to computer technology, etc. With this manual, we will have a source of uniform instructions available for all Law Department procedures.

    This manual is about halfway finished so far.

We feel we are GOLD because this is the halfway mark for the year, and we have accomplished more than half the work toward our goals.

    Goals #1 and #23 are complete for this quarter.
    Goals #4 and #6 are complete.
    Added Goal #8 is complete.

Work that remains for the next two quarters is: Goals #1 and #3 each quarter, and completing Goals #2, #5, #7, and added Goal #9.

NOTE: PLEASE INCLUDE AWARD FOR WINNIE KWIATKOWSKI (EVEN THOUGH SHE RETIRED A FEW WEEKS AGO) BECAUSE SHE WORKED ON SEVERAL OF THESE GOALS.

Exhibit 8-A
Implemented/Certified Ideas, Fiscal 1984

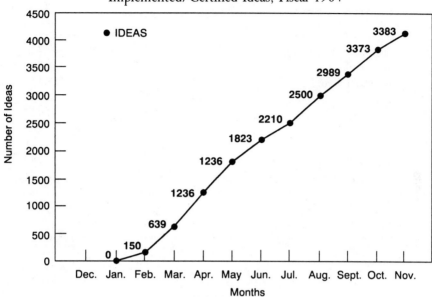

Exhibit 8-B
Implemented/Certified Ideas, Fiscal 1985

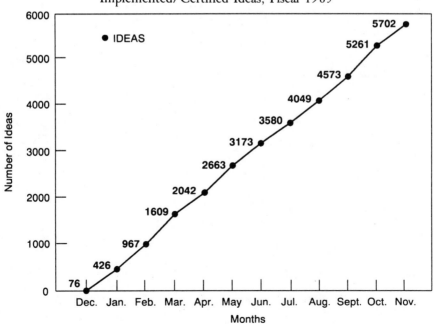

Exhibit 9
Quality Team Results

	1984	*1985*
Ideas logged on the QTTP	7,135	9,250
Ideas certified	4,115	5,702
Annualized savings	$3,250,000	$7,459,531
Bronze teams	127 of 128	123 of 125
Silver teams	101	117
Gold teams	72	104
Double gold teams	10	48
Triple gold teams	1	12
Quadruple gold teams	0	4
Quintuple gold teams	0	4
Sextuple gold teams	0	1
Septuple gold teams	0	1

Exhibit 10
Team Awards, Fiscal 1984

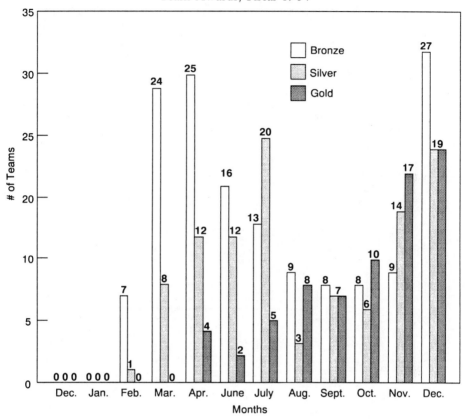

Exhibit 11
Quality Competition Criteria

Decisions were based on the existence and effectiveness of a company's:

- quality policy
- quality organization
- quality program
- customer feedback mechanism
- cost of nonconformance
- quality teams
- formal quality-training programs

THE PAUL REVERE INSURANCE COMPANY (A)

Exhibit 12

Organization Chart

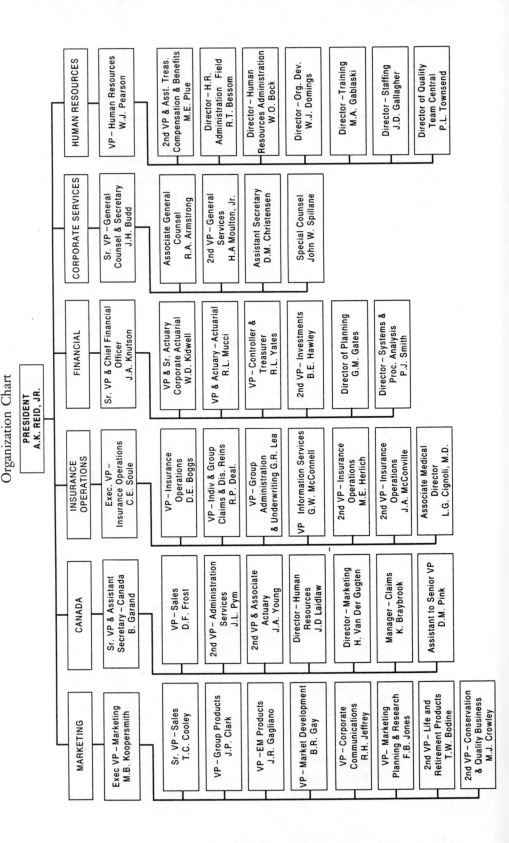

PRESIDENT
A.K. REID, JR.

MARKETING
- Exec VP – Marketing M.B. Koopersmith
  - Sr. VP – Sales T.C. Cooley
  - VP – Group Products J.P. Clark
  - VP – EM Products J.R. Gagliano
  - VP – Market Development B.R. Gay
  - VP – Corporate Communications R.H. Jeffrey
  - VP – Marketing Planning & Research F.B. Jones
  - 2nd VP – Life and Retirement Products T.W. Bodine
  - 2nd VP – Conservation & Quality Business M.J. Crowley

CANADA
- Sr. VP & Assistant Secretary – Canada B. Garand
  - VP – Sales D.F. Frost
  - 2nd VP – Administration Services J.L. Pym
  - 2nd VP & Associate Actuary J.A. Young
  - Director – Human Resources J.D Laidlaw
  - Director – Marketing H. Van Der Gugten
  - Manager – Claims K. Braybrook
  - Assistant to Senior VP D.M. Pink

INSURANCE OPERATIONS
- Exec. VP – Insurance Operations C.E. Soule
  - VP – Insurance Operations D.E. Boggs
  - VP – Indiv & Group Claims & Dis. Reins R.P. Deal.
  - VP – Group Administration & Underwriting G.R. Lea
  - VP Information Services G.W. McConnell
  - 2nd VP – Insurance Operations M.E. Herlich
  - 2nd VP – Insurance Operations J.A. McConville
  - Associate Medical Director L.G. Cignoli, M.D.

FINANCIAL
- Sr. VP & Chief Financial Officer J.A. Knutson
  - VP & Sr. Actuary Corporate Actuarial W.D. Kidwell
  - VP & Actuary – Actuarial R.L. Mucci
  - VP – Controller & Treasurer R.L. Yates
  - 2nd VP – Investments B.E. Hawley
  - Director of Planning G.M. Gates
  - Director – Systems & Proc. Analysis P.J. Smith

CORPORATE SERVICES
- Sr. VP – General Counsel & Secretary J.H. Budd
  - Associate General Counsel R.A. Armstrong
  - 2nd VP – General Services H.A Moulton, Jr.
  - Assistant Secretary D.M. Christensen
  - Special Counsel John W. Spillane

HUMAN RESOURCES
- VP – Human Resources W.J. Pearson
  - 2nd VP & Asst. Treas. Compensation & Benefits M.E. Plue
  - Director – H.R. Administration Field R.T. Bessom
  - Director – Human Resources Administration W.O. Bock
  - Director – Org. Dev. W.J. Domings
  - Director – Training M.A. Gablaski
  - Director – Staffing J.D. Gallagher
  - Director of Quality Team Central P.L. Townsend

THE PAUL REVERE INSURANCE COMPANY (A)

Exhibit 13

Employee Comments about QHV

Employee Praise for the QHV Process

- "The QHV process has created a 'danger-free' atmosphere where people feel comfortable suggesting ways to improve their jobs. Before this program started, you hesitated to put forward your ideas because chances were that no one would listen to you."

- "QHV has facilitated the flow of information throughout the company, both up and down (between employees and supervisors) and laterally between departments."

- "Quality team activities have opened doors between upper management and lower-level employees. In the old days, when you saw a supervisor walking down the hall you kept your mouth shut and looked away. Now you're more likely to say hello and address one another on a first name basis."

Employee Criticism of the QHV Process

- "Some people complain that management is pounding us over the head with quality. They feel that they have enough to do just to keep up with the demands of their jobs—going to quality team meetings, etc., is one more drain on their time."

- "There is the potential for abuse in this system. I know, for example, of a couple of cases where people tried to circumvent internal control points by suggesting that they'd have more time to do quality work if they didn't have to fill out various forms. The problem is that many of those forms serve a purpose and doing away with them creates chaos and blurs the chain of command."

- "I have some questions about the way the cost savings are calculated—the line between 'hard' and 'soft' dollars doesn't seem very clear."

(Continued)

THE PAUL REVERE INSURANCE COMPANY (A)
Exhibit 13
(Continued)

Employee Praise for the QHV Process	Employee Criticism of the QHV Process
• "When QHV was launched, I was one of the people who griped, 'Here they go cramming another quality program down our throats,' and I predicted it would last six months. Well, I was wrong. QHV has really changed this company for the better—now I consider it one of the company's benefits."	• "The employees who have worked at The Paul Revere the longest tend to be the most cynical about QHV. Some of them don't want to change the way thigns have been done for years, and some of them are bitter because every year for 25 years they made suggestions and were ignored. Now, someone that has been with the company two weeks can have the same idea and suddenly it's heralded as a wonderful suggestion."
• "Changing the quality team leaders after the program's first year made a big difference. I was asked to replace my boss as the leader of our team, and the change made people more willing to speak their minds. They no longer felt intimidated by the 'big-wigs.'"	
• "If you liken QHV to a car, then QTC is the steering wheel—but it's the quality teams that power the engine."	
• "The other day I heard someone from another department complaining about a fellow employee, saying 'I don't understand what's wrong with Fred, he just wants to do his job.'"	

The Paul Revere
Insurance Company (B)

"**Y**ou want to eliminate your own job? No one has ever proposed that one to me!" Mike Koopersmith, executive vice president for marketing at The Paul Revere Insurance Company, could hardly believe his ears. Bob Jeffrey, second vice president of corporate communications, was proposing that the functions in his department be parceled out to other departments and his own job abolished. Jeffrey, who was rather excited about the idea, explained:

> I think the diversity and complexity of the functions in my department are beyond the scope of one senior manager to direct. I believe most of our functions fit as well or better under other departments. If we moved our functions and people out, my position would be redundant.

> As you know, my department has been involved in a value analysis workshop for quite a few months now. It's pointing up organizational issues as being at the root of some of our difficulties. So I began thinking that one way to deal with those issues would be to disperse our functions to areas that made sense; advertising and sales promotion, for example, fits with product/market management. I didn't want to bring it up in our workshop, though, unless you first accepted it as a real possibility.

Koopersmith glanced over at Bill Domings, value analysis director: "Well, Bill, it looks like this group has really taken value analysis to heart. I need a little time to digest this."

VALUE ANALYSIS

Value analysis (VA) was a customer-oriented discipline developed to create an optimal ratio of user utility to cost. Developed and applied primarily in manufacturing settings (where it was called value engineering), this technique encouraged thinking about a component or product in terms of its functions rather than its

This case was prepared by Dr. Artemis March, with the research assistance of Dan Maher, under the supervision of Assistant Professor Christopher W. L. Hart, as the basis for class discussion rather than to illustrate either effective or ineffective handling of an administrative situation. It was revised by Research Associate Lucy N. Lytle. Copyright © 1987 by the President and Fellows of Harvard College; Harvard Business School case #9-687-033 (Rev. 1/88).

physical aspects. Employee teams identified and analyzed each function of the component or product in terms of its current specifications, costs, and value to the customer. This functional perspective opened up new avenues for rethinking how products were designed, what materials they used, the specifications they called for, how they were produced, and so on. Concentrating on particularly critical or costly components, the team worked to develop alternate ways to design and produce a product so that it met customer needs at lower cost. (The origins and generic methodology of value analysis are described in "A Note on Value Analysis: Its History and Methodology," HBS Case Services, case 0-687-066.)

When applied to a service setting, value analysis used a work unit or department as its unit of study, analyzed its functions, and rearranged them in the way that best allowed the unit to meet its "essential purpose." Team members defined their unit's essential purpose in the simplest of terms, using one verb and one noun. The food services department at The Paul Revere, for example, defined its purpose as "feed people," and the individual underwriting department settled on "assess risks." After ripping apart their unit's current functions and tasks, team members eliminated or rearranged them in a hierarchy that became the basis for redesigning the unit. Whereas in manufacturing settings a cross-functional team usually conducted the analysis and redesign, in service settings managers within the unit comprised the team, on the premise that they were the people most likely to understand the unit's functions and activities.

MARRIAGE OF VALUE ANALYSIS
AND THE "QUALITY HAS VALUE" PROGRAM

During the 1983–84 period, senior managers at The Paul Revere decided to launch a companywide quality effort. (See the previous case in this volume, "The Paul Revere Insurance Company (A)," for an account of the quality program.) Although Charles Soule, executive vice president of insurance operations, had proposed a quality program in 1981, he found a more receptive climate two years later when AVCO, the company's parent, directed all of its subsidiaries to inaugurate quality efforts. Aubrey Reid, president of The Paul Revere, then gave Soule the nod to improve quality. An eight-member Quality Steering Committee (QSC) was formed. Co-chaired by Soule and William Pearson, vice president of human resources, it comprised the number one or number two executive from each major department in the company. Early meetings "messed around with the idea of quality," and revealed the presence of two camps: those who believed that quality was an investment that would yield long-term payoffs, and those who were concerned about the labor hours lost in quality meetings.

Separate from and prior to these early quality discussions, another stream of internal questioning was taking place. Pearson recalled:

> We were asking ourselves a lot of questions: Are we organized the right way? Are we staffed appropriately? What should our span of control be? Do we have too many layers of management? I talked with my organization development manager, Al Materas, about how to get a grip on these issues. We thought maybe we should look into a process that cut across the entire company. We were anxious to get on with an organizational analysis, but we knew AVCO wouldn't let us postpone our quality effort.

Materas was familiar with one such process from his days working with the Robert E. Nolan Company, a consulting firm that ran value analysis workshops.

Pearson and Soule wondered if they could launch a quality program and value analysis concurrently. They solicited the advise of several consultants, all but one of whom assured them that such a dual effort was bound to fail. There would be conflict between the two programs, too much change at once, and the result would be chaos. Preferably, some consultants said, the company should first concentrate on "doing the right things" (value analysis) and then concentrate on "doing things right" (quality). Soule and Pearson concluded, however, that it made no sense to do the right things badly or the wrong things well, and that the company ought to undertake both programs simultaneously. This dual approach also satisfied both camps with the QSC. The program was named Quality Has Value (QHV) to symbolize the marriage of the two approaches.

PROGRAM PLANNING AND STRUCTURE

The decision to launch both programs entailed, according to Pearson, "a tremendous need for planning and coordination." Quality teams required leader training and weekly team meetings, and value analysis required facilitator training and a time commitment from managers of about 40 hours during the six- to eight-week period of the average workshop. Decisions had to be made about how to coordinate and schedule these activities.

In addition to the decision to launch quality improvement efforts and value analysis concurrently, the committee made another decision that would affect the outcome: both programs were made mandatory. Every employee became a member of a quality team, and every manager would, sooner or later, be part of a value analysis workshop. However, the link between the two programs was not, in Soule's words, "tied down too tightly." The Steering Committee provided guidelines, rather than rules, for program interaction. The committee also established a policy that no one would be forced out of a job as a result of workshop or team recommendations.

The two programs differed, however, in their approval and implementation processes. Quality teams would immediately implement, on a continuing and usually piecemeal basis, whatever they could do themselves. In contrast, each value analysis workshop would tie its recommendations together in a single package. Decisions about whether to accept or reject each recommendation would be made by the superior of the senior manager in the workshop. Responsibility for implementation was given to the units, most of which developed their own review processes. Although value analysis facilitators updated computerized records on what had been done and the savings that had been effected, they did not, like Quality Team Central, certify the group's actions.

Bill Domings pointed up some of the other differences between the two programs:

> In my view, quality teams focus on day-to-day improvements made primarily by nonmanagement employees. It is a very visible, ongoing process. It needs lots of PR and shots of adrenaline to keep the juices flowing. Value analysis is a one-time, top-down process that looks at where work belongs rather than how it is done. It is a behind-the-scenes approach that doesn't require fanfare. It is not different from management; it simply creates the time-space for examining work functions and organization—something managers would do by themselves if they had more time.

CONSULTANT'S ROLE

Although the QSC decided to develop the quality effort internally, it wanted outside expertise in running the value analysis workshops. Of the consultants interviewed, "only Nolan," according to Patrick Townsend, who had been hired to coordinate the quality team portion of QHV, "thought we could handle both and that we had an interesting approach."

The Connecticut-based consulting firm had extensive experience working with insurance companies as well as considerable expertise in conducting value analysis workshops. Never before, however, had Nolan run such workshops in conjunction with a quality program. Neither were its usual value analysis objectives compatible with QHV. Soule elaborated:

> Their approach normally started at a point I was uncomfortable with. At the beginning of a workshop, they wanted each group to set dollar goals as their target. So I sat down with Bob Nolan and told him that we wanted

to do the workshops—*but* as *part* of the QHV program. So he sent his number two guy to our Steering Committee meetings to understand where our QHV process was headed and to tailor their approach accordingly.

Not only was Nolan willing to customize its approach, it was also willing to phase out its consultants after they had trained Revere employees to run the workshops.

During 1984, Nolan consultants conducted value analysis workshops while training six Paul Revere employees to assume the facilitator role. Following orientation lectures, facilitators-to-be observed a Nolan consultant conduct a workshop, shared the conduct of the next workshop, and then reversed roles and facilitated on their own while the consultant observed. Every session in each phase was followed by a debriefing. After that, the company facilitators were on their own. During early 1985, Nolan largely phased itself out of the program.

IN-HOUSE FACILITATORS

After wrestling with whether or not it wanted in-house facilitators, the QSC chose this route because of the continuity it might provide. Pearson described what was sought:

> Facilitators drive the process, so we talked a great deal about who we should have. We looked for people who could get the job done, who were good at communications, who had credibility within the company, and who were available.

The six chosen initially were middle managers, some from training or human resources, who retained a half-time commitment to their old jobs and facilitated on a half-time basis.

Of this initial group trained by Nolan, only one, Bill Domings, remained in the program. The best returned to their other duties after a few months. Pearson acknowledged removing Townsend as a facilitator because "he was too much a Marine," and Soule acknowledged that "we did better choosing people the second time around." Palma O'Keefe, who joined the program as a full-time facilitator in 1985, assessed what had happened:

> Most of those in the first group tried to follow very set pieces, but in value analysis, you have no script. Instead, you must listen intently, and go with the flow. Some people didn't have the sensitivity, and most were uncomfortable dealing with the touchy stuff. Nolan doesn't deal with the human side at all in their training.

Soule added, "A facilitator has to be able to listen and not be too pressed to answer. They failed if they couldn't do that, if they couldn't let the group wrestle with it."

Domings attributed the loss of several facilitators to the part-time nature of the assignments, noting that "we learned that you need to be full time in this role." Domings began on a part-time basis, but four months later he assumed directorship of the program. In his full-time capacity, Domings both facilitated workshops and coordinated the overall effort. During the 1984–86 period, he assisted in or ran about half of the workshops; Nolan personnel ran some, and O'Keefe and another in-house facilitator ran the rest. Both Domings and O'Keefe felt that two workshops per week (each of which met twice, and called for extensive work between meetings) was the maximum a facilitator could handle effectively. Facilitators were also responsible for writing reports and seeing them through the approval process.

VA METHODOLOGY AT PAUL REVERE

Before the workshops began, members were selected, three-hour meetings were scheduled, and members were oriented to the process. During the information phase of the workshops, facts about the operations of the unit were gathered, and each function was described using a unique verb-noun phrase. During the analysis phase, the group identified its essential purpose (i.e., the reason the unit existed) in a two-word phrase. It then separated its many functions into two major groups: basic and support functions. Basic functions were those necessary for performing the unit's essential purpose, whereas support functions enhanced the unit's performance, but were not necessary for meeting its essential purpose. Each set of functions encompassed both primary and secondary activities. The major tool the groups used to sort out their functions and activities was a functional analysis specification technique (FAST) diagram. (See *Exhibit 1*.) Moving from left to right on the diagram (i.e., from function to primary and then secondary activities) answered the question, "How?" while moving from right to left answered, "Why?" Current activities that did not meet the function's needs were eliminated or set aside for later consideration.

Using scales ranging from 0 to 10, the group then evaluated the relative importance to the user, and the reliability of, each activity. These estimates were based on workshop members' experience with their customers—who, in many cases, were the field offices or other departments rather than policyholders. Next, members estimated the time spent on each activity and its cost. Cost figures were developed by assigning salary cost based on hours spent on the activity, adding expenses specific to that activity, and allocating other expenses in proportion to time spent.

During the creative phase, groups brainstormed alternative ideas for how to perform their functions. Later, they evaluated these ideas, and made recommendations.

VA PROGRAM IMPLEMENTATION

The Steering Committee made certain that it chose units that were likely to have successful workshops to go through value analysis first. During the 1984–86 period, over 40 workshops were conducted, and most departments and divisions went through value analysis. During 1986, field office managers began to participate in workshops geared to field office administration.

Resistance to outside consultants and concern about position cuts were anticipated, and did materialize in some groups; they tended to diminish, however, as the grapevine spread the word about positive workshop experiences. As promised, the company did not fire anyone as a result of a workshop's recommendations. Pearson explained, "We moved some people out of the departments they had been in, outplaced others, and encouraged early retirements, but we dealt with people humanely rather than in a cut-throat way."

Quality teams and value workshops were rarely competitive, and offered little resistance to ideas that originated with the other. According to several managers, a two-day flow took place routinely, with the dual membership of many managers serving as the key link. Quality teams were encouraged to implement their ideas at the lowest level possible, but also to move up as high as necessary to get them executed. They were also encouraged to provide information and ideas to workshops, and to pass along their ideas about organizational issues. In turn, workshops were encouraged to pass along implementation details to the quality teams.

Domings took most of his policy guidance from Soule, with whom he met weekly. Once the workshops were up and running, Soule saw his role as threefold: to keep on top of how things were going through weekly meetings, to discuss the unit with the facilitator before its workshop started in order to "point out some of the opportunities that existed," and to see that implementation was occurring. Domings sought Soule's assistance on difficult issues, but Soule rarely got personally involved in a workshop.

During the evolution of the program, Domings believed that the scope of the issues which groups were willing to tackle became broader. He felt that this shift occurred partly because he had become less tentative about dealing with sensitive issues as he gained experience and comfort with the process. At first, he reported:

We dealt with the functions, but not the organization of those functions. So their recommended reorganizations took place within a set piece; they did not yet question the organizational framework itself. But a function can be done poorly because of its organization. We started the workshops in January 1984. After we were about nine months into it, organization was more of an issue and it seemed we had to deal with it.

When asked whether he or the workshop members had pushed hardest for the change, Domings replied:

Before the workshops, organization was something the boss did. People viewed structures as cast in concrete; we had had very few organizational changes in the past, so they implicitly saw this as untouchable. But as these issues began to come up in the workshops, they got more comfortable talking about them—particularly since we talked about roles and functions rather than persons. During this same period, as I participated in discussions about how to improve various functions, I could see that sometimes the "right answer" was to change the organization. As I became more confident about what they needed to look at, I was more comfortable with pushing them to get outside their narrow mindsets.

Domings' favorite tool for teaching people "to get outside their boxes" was an exercise which asked the person to connect 9 dots, arranged three by three, with four lines; a line must go through each dot once and only once. Most people struggled for a long time to connect the dots with lines that ran within the implicit square that framed the dots. Although they were never told that they could not go outside the frame, most failed to do so, even though it was the only way to connect the dots with four lines. When the answer was given, it inevitably triggered a discussion about self-limiting perceptions, and the need to go outside boundaries in order to think creatively about a subject.

RESULTS

About 80% of all workshop recommendations were accepted as workable by the decision makers. Of these, approximately 60% were implemented. Those ideas that died did so for a number of reasons, including costing too much, not being such good ideas on second thought, lacking the systems or people to implement, or becoming irrelevant.

Although there was no clear audit trail that transferred VA savings to the corporate bottom line, the workshops identified savings that, when aggregated, totaled $8 million for the entire three-year period. About half of these savings were considered "hard": budgeted expenses that would not have to be spent; best estimates were that about $3 million of these hard-savings recommendations had been implemented. The other half were "soft" dollars: capacity or person-hour increases resulting from spending less time on an activity (i.e., spending fewer hours on X left more time to do Y and Z). These two types of savings had to be weighed against increased costs, because some recommendations required additional outlays. The result was the net savings to a department and to the company.

Among the most successful changes generated by the VA process was the reorganization of the Group Administration Department, which was responsible for administering approximately 2,400 policies held by organizations whose members were collectively covered. Carter Harris, director of group administration, explained:

> Responsiveness to customers' needs was an increasingly important factor affecting The Paul Revere's competitiveness, and I was determined to use our VA workshop to make two important changes: first, customers should have direct access to whoever handled their policies; second, operators should have a sense of ownership of policies.

The final VA recommendations presented at the end of 1984 called for replacing the department's multi-unit organization with a more streamlined system composed of Customer Service Representative (CSR) teams and General Service units (e.g., accounting, mail sort). (*Exhibit 2* shows the department's organization prior to and after value analysis.) Customers were given the name and direct-dial number of the CSR handling their policy. The CSRs, in turn, were equipped with personal computers for on-line access to records for answering customer questions and making changes to records. All policy changes were consolidated automatically by the computer.

At the same time, the administration set an internal standard of solving customer's problems within 24 hours or, if a solution was not immediately possible, to call the customer and explain the reason for the delay. The administration also announced that if the department received information affecting premiums by the tenth day of the month, those changes would be reflected accurately on bills mailed on the fifteenth.

Harris contrasted the department's earlier organization with its VA-generated system:

> Previously, inaccurate monthly bills were almost guaranteed for most of our larger customers, who added or lost some employees each month, because premium changes were recorded more slowly than the billing cycle. Customers complained that their bills were wrong but, by the time the problems

were cleared up, it was often too late to enter these changes on the next monthly bill, which led to more confusion and bad-feeling.

In comparison, our new system gives us greater flexibility, improved customer contacts, a broader scope of jobs, lower interdependence among the various units, and the capability to quickly update our information.

CORPORATE COMMUNICATIONS WORKSHOP

In the summer of 1984, just six months after the VA workshops had started, Bob Jeffrey asked that the Corporate Communications Department be scheduled for value analysis earlier than originally planned. Beginning in the fall of 1984, and running through late winter, this workshop proved to be one of the company's longest. It also raised some important questions about the VA process.

The Department

Over the years, the Corporate Communications Department had gained several functions and managers. By 1984, its activities included planning conferences and meetings, handling corporate travel, developing advertising and publicity, managing media and industry relations, implementing corporate identity programs, producing product-support materials, developing sales contests and promotions, producing in-house publications, and developing and administering recognition programs for sales and sales management. These activities were organized into five staff functions, each of which reported to Jeffrey. In addition, Lauren Knapik reported to Jeffrey. She supervised support staff; coordinated promotions, contests, and awards; prepared reports; and prepared and maintained materials pertaining to the budget and other administrative matters. (See *Exhibit 3.*)

When he advanced from sales promotion director to second vice president in 1981, Jeffrey inherited what was then termed the Advertising and Sales Promotion Department. A conference planner was added in 1982 to relieve Jeffrey and his sales promotion director of that task. That same year, a corporate communications consultant was added to direct the external agency that developed national advertising; to develop local advertising; and to handle direct mail, the annual report, and public relations. Jeffrey described the situation:

> The diversity of our functions made my span of control too broad. And if one of my staff members was out or left, I was the only one who knew how to do the job, so I had to pitch in. I was often more involved in operations rather than in managing.

Department Problems

Although a company survey had rated the department very highly on the quality of its work, the group experienced internal problems. Jeffrey explained:

> Our people had capability, but they lacked depth of experience. They had not done the work before, so they needed training. Planning meetings, for example, is very detail-oriented—from the selection of sites to running meetings. It requires a lot of communication and coordination. So I led them through it step by step. I was coach, editor, travel agent, and wore about six other hats. Of course, the fact that I'm a nitpicker who demands perfection didn't make the situation any easier.

Because support staff reported to a supervisor rather than to the people for whom they performed work, various strains and frictions regularly occurred. Although each support person tended to work more for one particular manager than for others, each worked on projects for all the departments' managers. This created a problem when staff who shared the same support person had peaks of work at the same time. Lack of direct reporting increased communication needs and frustrated managers who could not insist that their work get done.

The Workshop

The workshop was attended by six managers, all from inside the department, including Jeffrey and Knapik. Sorting out the department's functions and identifying its essential purpose took an uncommonly long time because the members felt they had more than one essential purpose. Jeffrey recalled:

> We couldn't, for the life of us, boil down those five functions into one essential purpose. First and foremost in our minds was "support sales." The second, I think, was "support corporate."

Once the participants began to develop their FAST diagram and got used to the verb-noun format, things moved relatively smoothly—indeed, more so than in many of the groups. (See *Exhibit 1.*) The group rated the importance of each function and the reliability with which it was performed, estimated the total amount of department time given to that function, and attached a cost to its performance. (See *Exhibit 4.*)

The group generated 450 ideas for improving the performance of its functions. (See *Exhibit 5.*) A two-stage evaluation process first rejected many of the ideas, and then subjected the rest to in-depth analysis. Rejection criteria included the idea's being impractical, illegal, already under study by others, the concern of another department, counterproductive to the needs of the function, or requiring resources that could not be made available. The final list of recommendations and their estimated savings are shown in *Exhibit 6.*

The result, in Jeffrey's view, was "many fine suggestions, but they were not earthshaking." He found this disappointing because he felt that "we had a group of the most creative people in the company." He believed that staff vacancies (the sales promotion services manager left during the process) and his own presence may have reduced the workshop's effectiveness. He admitted:

> My style is authoritative and directive, and was even more so then. The folks that worked for me at the time of the workshop were not as likely to challenge me as my current staff. They had the correct impression that unless they were able to really sell me on a change, they might just as well not even suggest it. I wanted to know up front what the benefits of a proposed change would be, and I did not and do not have a reputation for being particularly tolerant of failure. I am inclined to say, "That would never work," or "We tried that once." Consequently, I think that the workshop discussions, when I was part of them, were probably not open and free-flowing enough to be conducive to an understanding VA discussion. As a result, Bill Domings and I talked, and we decided they should have some sessions alone with him.

During one such session, Domings asked the group to vote on whether to have Jeffrey present; the group declined to vote, arguing that if a decision needed to be made, Domings should be the one to make it.

The Reorganization Options

During the course of the workshop, Jeffrey began considering two organizational choices. The first was to decentralize the department's multiple functions and eliminate his own position. Advertising and sales promotion, for example, could fit with product/market management; conferences and meetings with sales management; publications with human resources; and public relations with either human resources or corporate affairs. Believing that the other workshop members would reject this possibility, and concerned that they might be unduly alarmed about its implications for their own situations, he discussed it only with Domings and with his boss, Mike Koopersmith.

Jeffrey's second option was to add a layer of management between himself and the staff. This tier would have two managers, each of whom would direct and integrate a cluster of functions. Jeffrey was not absolutely set on what those clusters would be. He had, however, long felt the need for a closer link between sales training (selling new products), sales promotion, and meetings (most of which were for sales agents and managers). (The possibility of moving sales training to corporate communications was under consideration at the time.) Jeffrey was concerned, however, that adding a layer of management might run counter to a span-of-control study that had been authorized by top management and was being conducted with the assistance of Nolan consultants.

Workshop Reorganization Recommendations

Although the option of dismantling the department had not been broached with workshop participants, the idea of moving corporate communications (the lesser of the department's two essential purposes) out of the department was discussed. According to Domings, it made sense to the participants, but they did not choose to recommend it. What they did choose was to reorganize all of their current functions by clarifying the responsibilities of old roles, identifying dispersed tasks that could be grouped into new roles, redefining the managerial and administrative needs of the department, and modifying some reporting relationships.

Analysis of the department's functions and activities led to the development of clearer job descriptions for existing roles. It also made visible the amount of task dispersion in some areas, particularly sales awards. This work included developing and maintaining numerous vendor relationships concerned with the design, purchase, and engraving of awards and plaques, as well as a considerable amount of administration and coordination of award activities. The group decided the bits and pieces were better consolidated and performed by one person—the work was a full-time job. They recommended, therefore, that the new position of recognition administrator be created. Recommendations for two other new positions emerged from awareness that the managers had too much work because they lacked appropriate people to delegate some of it to. One such need was for a copywriter who could draft speeches and write ad copy, promotions, and newsletter material, and thus serve the entire department. Second, making travel arrangements consumed much too much of the conference planner's time, and had grown to become a full-time job in itself. (See *Exhibit 7.*)

At the same time, the department members desired some modification of existing reporting relationships. They wanted direct reporting relationships for the two staff specialists who would work exclusively for a particular manager—a travel coordinator for the conference planner, and a direct mail coordinator for the advertising/public relations manager. By contrast, the copywriter and recognition administrator would serve the entire department, and report to the new manager of communications services position.

Analysis of the department's administrative and managerial needs suggested that Jeffrey needed someone to assume a higher level of responsibility than a supervisor could. The members decided to upgrade the supervisory position to the management level. The new position, called manager of communication services, would include directing the allocation of staff support, preparing the budget, overseeing the implementation of value analysis recommendations, and managing the implementation of office automation. One observer described how the existing and prospective positions differed:

> Knapik had reluctantly added supervision to her many other responsibilities. Although she supervised staff people and handled their hiring, firing, and evaluations, she was not responsible for creating career paths for them. She got budget materials ready for Bob, but didn't actually prepare the budget. You can apply this same kind of distinction to most of the other activities involved.

In short, the workshop called for three main changes: 1) adding three new positions (recognition administrator, travel coordinator, and copywriter); 2) upgrading the supervisory position to communication services manager; and 3) direct reporting to staff managers by some staff specialists.

These proposed changes, along with many smaller changes, were tied together in a report that went to Jeffrey and then to Koopersmith. The three new positions were accepted, as was the change to manager, but Jeffrey rejected the request for direct reporting. A week later, Jeffrey and Domings were in Koopersmith's office, with Jeffrey explaining his conclusion that the department should be eliminated.

THE DECISION

Koopersmith listened intently to Jeffrey's account of the value analysis workshop and its recommendations, asked for clarification on a few points, and promised to inform him of his decision the following Monday morning. "Now what do I do?" he wondered, as he looked at the department's VA report on his desk. "I think I'd better start by figuring out how this situation came to pass. The Nolan consultants never said anything about this happening as a result of value analysis workshops!"

Exhibit 1
FAST Diagram—Corporate Communications

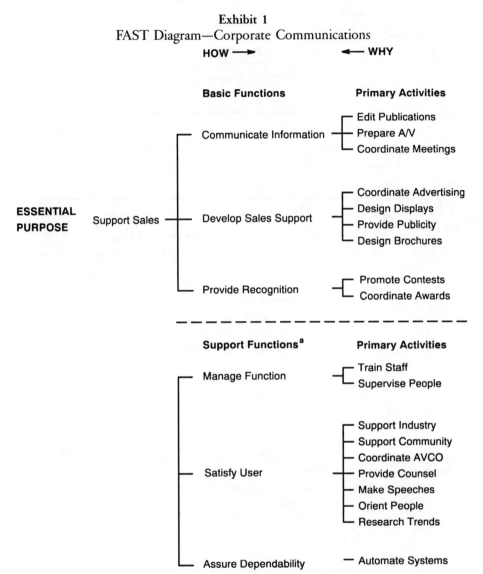

^aEach unit chose from a list of five support functions those that fit its situation; Corporate Communications chose these three. Each workshop made up its own primary support activities and chose the function with which to associate them.

Exhibit 2
Group Administration Department Organization Charts

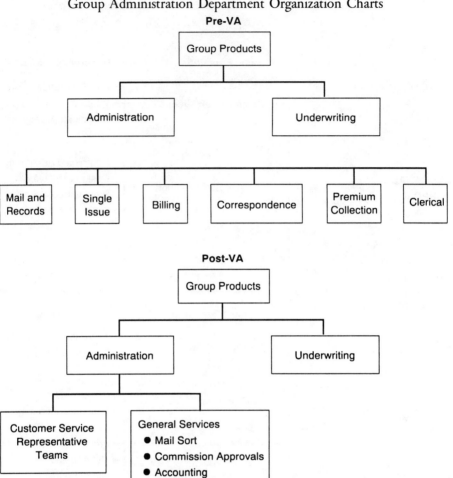

Exhibit 3
Corporate Communications Department, 1984

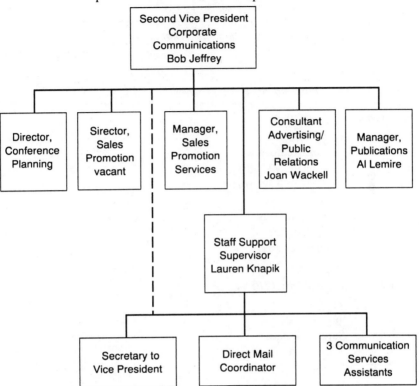

Second Vice President
Corporate
Commuinications
Bob Jeffrey

Director,
Conference
Planning

Sirector,
Sales
Promotion
vacant

Manager,
Sales
Promotion
Services

Consultant
Advertising/
Public
Relations
Joan Wackell

Manager,
Publications
Al Lemire

Staff Support
Supervisor
Lauren Knapik

Secretary to
Vice President

Direct Mail
Coordinator

3 Communication
Services
Assistants

Department complement: 12.

Exhibit 4
Value Analysis Costed Functions
(April 8, 1985)

		Department: Corporate Communications				
			Totals: Ratings		100.0% % of	$901,000
F#	I#	Function Area	IMP	REL	Time	$(000)
Basic Functions (1 thru 50)						
1		Edit Publications	7	4	14.1%	$127.1
2		Prepare Audio/Visual	7	8	4.2	37.9
3		Coordinate Meetings	8	8	19.5	175.4
4		Coordinate Advertising	7	5	6.0	53.6
5		Design Displays	6	6	3.3	29.8
6		Provide Publicity	8	6	4.8	43.1
7		Design Brochures	9	7	6.5	58.8
8		Promote Contests	8	6	5.6	50.6
9		Coordinate Awards	9	7	4.9	44.4
Support Functions (100 thru 150)						
101		Train Staff	8	5	3.9	35.1
102		Supervise People	8	5	5.5	49.8
103		Support Industry	5	5	2.5	22.6
104		Support Community	5	4	2.0	18.2
105		Coordinate AVCO	5	6	4.0	35.7
106		Provide Counsel	9	8	5.6	50.6
107		Make Speeches	7	7	0.9	7.9
108		Orient People	7	7	1.8	16.1
111		Support QHV	7	7	4.8	44.3

Importance Scale

10—Mandated, i.e., required by law rather than just the boss

8—Important, both in the eyes of the department's customers and in order to meet the essential purpose

6—Contributes value

4—Nice to have

2—Limited value

0—No value

Reliability Scale

10—Perfect, a rare score

8—Well done

6—Acceptable; occasional problems

4—Some persistent problems

2—Unreliable

0—Awful

THE PAUL REVERE INSURANCE COMPANY (B)

Exhibit 5

Abridged List of Corporate Communications Workshop Suggestions[a]

F#	I#	Function Idea	Totals Ratings		100.0% % of Time	$901,000 $(000)
			IMP	REL		
1		*Edit Publications*	7	4	14.1%	$127.01
		Basic Functions (1 thru 50)				
	2	Eliminate Paste-up				
	3	• Have Printing do it				
	4	• Automate it				
	5	• Have lower-level person do it				
	6	• Have same level do it				
	7	Improve Coordination of Report Producers				
	11	Improve Time Service				
	12	Establish Better Priorities				
	13	Reduce Number of Approvals				
	14	Better Train People to Work Independently/Effectively				
	15	Get Someone Else to do Photos				
	16	Have People Write Own Articles				
	19	Have Someone Else Keyboard				
	20	Have all Publications under Central Control				
	23	Improve Lists of Titles, etc.				
	24	Do Not Use Titles/Designations—Put in Route List				
	25	Don't Repeat Bulletin Board Notices				
	26	Combine Lantern and Marketing Update				
	27	Eliminate Management News				
	28	Put Management News on PROFS/Video				
	30	Have Someone Else Proof Earlier				

(Continued)

THE PAUL REVERE INSURANCE COMPANY (B)

Exhibit 5
(Continued)

F#	I#	Function Idea	Totals Ratings IMP	REL	100.0% % of of Time	$901,000 $(000)
		Basic Functions (1 tbru 50)				
2		*Prepare Audio/Visual*	7	8	4.2%	$37.9
	1	____ Do More Slide Typesetting Internally				
	3	____ Have One A/V Coordinator for Paul Revere				
	4	____ Use More Computer Graphics				
3		*Coordinate Meetings*	8	8	19.5%	$175.4
	1	____ Do More Cross Training				
	6	____ Improve Supplier Coordination and Use				
	7	____ Establish Electronic Communication with Hotels				
4		*Coordinate Advertising*	7	5	6.0%	$53.6
	1	____ Set Guidelines to Avoid Rushes				
	2	____ Set Guidelines for Who Needs to be Involved				
	4	____ Let H.O. People Know What We're Doing				
5		*Design Displays*	6	6	3.3%	$29.8
	1	____ Modernize Display Areas				
	2	____ Relocate Sales Spotlight				
	3	____ Isolate Space in the Cafeteria				

[a]These suggestions can be alternatives or complementary.

Exhibit 6
Savings Summary
Corporate Communications

Section		Recommendation	Expense	Capacity Savings	Other
B. Utilize Technology	1.	In-house Typesetting for A/V	$15,000		
	2.	In-house Travel Agency Terminal		$ 5,000	
	4.	Modernize Displays		5,000	
	5.	Implement Software Systems		15,000	
C. Coordinate Incentive Program	2.	Redesign Sales Contest Kit	3,000		
	3.	Simplify/Streamline Contest Procedures	8,000	2,000	
	6.	Consolidate Awards Administration		5,000	
	7.	Transfer Handling of Merchandise Returns		3,500	
D. Provide Recognition	1a.	Registration Kits		1,825	
	1b.	Reuse Badges	200	1,525	
	1e.	HO People in Meetings	(2,000)		
	1f.	Communication of Results	(1,000)		
	1g.	Use Rental Cars	958		
	1i.	Permanent Displays and Signs	1,500	1,525	
	3.	Main Lobby Display	(500)		
	4.	Delegate Canadian Award Administration to Canada		6,000	
E. Promotion	4.	Training	(3,000)		
F. Produce Publications	2.	Replace Management News with Newsletter		500	
	2.	Organize and Consolidate Storage Space	1,000	3,050	
	3.	Sell Surplus Items	500		
	4.	Survey Responsibility		1,525	
	5.	Increase Local Community Program Involvement	(11,000)		
	6.	Reduce Number of Bulletin Boards		1,000	
	TOTALS		$12,658	$52,450	0
	GRAND TOTAL		$65,108		

NOTE: Figures in parentheses represent costs.

Exhibit 7
Corporate Communications Organization, 1985

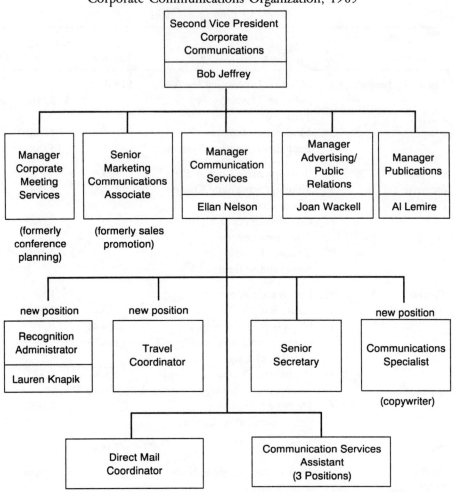

Department complement: 14.

Florida Power & Light's
Quality-Improvement Program

John Hudiburg, chairman of the board and chief executive officer of Florida Power & Light Company (FPL), watched through the windows of his office as FPL's employees returned to work after the New Year's holiday in January 1987. This past year had given them all good cause to celebrate, he thought.

Ten years ago, like many other U.S. utility companies, FPL was in a state of near-crisis. A new oil shortage had hit, and energy prices were skyrocketing. Customer dissatisfaction with FPL was rising even faster than energy prices and general inflation. FPL's return on investment had fallen significantly below the ceiling established by the state's Public Service Commission. Having committed to several significant capital expenditures, the company would be forced to ask for yet another rate increase from already unhappy—and already pinched—customers. And FPL's long-term survival might well depend on making even heavier expenditures to reduce the company's dependence on oil. But FPL seemed hamstrung not only in planning for the future but simply in coping with its current problems. For the first time, FPL executives realized how bureaucratic and inflexible their company had become during "good times."

But today, due primarily to the implementation of a companywide Quality-Improvement Program (QIP), the future looked far brighter for FPL. Once again the utility was winning high approval ratings from customers, regulators, and industry leaders. The most gratifying recognition had come in June 1986, when FPL was honored for its Quality Improvement Program with the Edison Award—the "Oscar" of the utility industry—by its peers.

From worst case to best case in ten years, Hudiburg thought. Actually, six years: QIP had started only in 1981. How much better could FPL become?

OVERVIEW OF FPL OPERATIONS

Florida Power & Light, founded in 1925 and based in Miami, was Florida's largest utility. Its five regional divisions, nine fossil-fuel plants, and four nuclear

This case was prepared by Joan S. Livingston, under the supervision of Assistant Professor Christopher W. L. Hart, as the basis for class discussion rather than to illustrate either effective or ineffective handling of an administrative situation. Copyright © 1987 by the President and Fellows of Harvard College; Harvard Business School case #9-688-043 (Rev. 3/89).

units supplied electricity to 2.8 million customers, or about two-thirds of the nation's fifth-largest state. In 1986, the company had posted a net income of $365 million on total operating revenues of about $4 billion.

The company recently had begun to diversify from its core energy business. A holding company called FPL Group was formed in 1984; FPL, and newly acquired companies in technical services, financial services, and real estate, were subsidiaries of Group. Among these was Colonial Penn Insurance, whose acquisition FPL Group completed in 1986. That same year, FPL Group became the first U.S. electric utility company to have its stock listed on the Tokyo Stock Exchange.

FPL employed 14,500 workers, approximately 40% of whom were members of a bargaining unit. Even through the tough years, employee turnover was low, relative to that in other industries; in 1987, turnover from all causes, including retirement and death, hovered around 5%.

ORIGINS OF QUALITY IMPROVEMENT AT FPL

Although quality improvement did not become a formal, companywide program at the utility until 1981, FPL first experimented with quality principles in the 1970s, when it began making plans for building its St. Lucie II nuclear power plant, near Ft. Pierce, Florida. FPL executives had been frustrated during earlier construction projects by poor performance on the part of contractors and associated costs and delays. For the St. Lucie II unit, to begin construction in 1977, the company established explicit quality standards up front—rather than applying traditional "quality control" checks after construction—and brought most of the functions previously performed by contractors in-house. It also opened up lines of communication between departments to trouble-shoot and "debug" the project in an all-out attempt to prevent the problems it had encountered during earlier projects. Other utilities were skeptical, but FPL's results were dramatic.

Despite delays occasioned by acts of God (including Hurricane David) and of man (new government regulations, enacted after the Three Mile Island accident), the St. Lucie II plant was built, licensed, and operating in six years, versus an industry standard of 9 to 12 years; it cost $1.4 billion, versus the average $4 billion; and its "energy availability" was 90%, fully 30 points over the industry average. The plant was rated as one of the best-performing, lowest-cost units in the U.S. by *Nucleonics Week*, the Utility Data Institute, and the Nuclear Regulatory Commission. In granting the plant its operating license, one Nuclear Regulatory Commissioner said, "This is a utility that does things right."

The utility that did things right at St. Lucie had not done so consistently in its other endeavors, as the crisis of the '70s made clear. As late as 1981, FPL was in "a hostile environment, and for the first time, in a survival mode," according to then FPL chairman (now FPL Group president and CEO) Marshall McDonald.

That was the year that FPL "declared an all-out war on anything less than total quality," McDonald recalled. "I made the observation that we had been looking at the horse from the wrong end, and it was not a pretty sight. We had been concerned with keeping rejects down, instead of quality up. We had been busy keeping imperfection under control, rather than trying for perfection. We had sometimes burnt the toast and then scraped it clean, instead of fixing the toaster. Some of us had even learned to like burnt toast."

At St. Lucie, FPL had seen what the results of even a small-scale, relatively unstructured quality-management program could be: lower costs, faster turnaround, higher quality. It wanted to—it needed to—tap these benefits across the board in its other operations. "We knew we had a tiger by the tail here," FPL president Robert Tallon remarked. "The trick was to get the tiger in the tank."

As a result, McDonald announced in 1981 the establishment of the QIP, whose goals included the following:

- To trim down inflexibility and excess procedures, organization, and people.
- To make the organization more resilient, better able to react to change.
- To shift management's thinking from supply orientation to market orientation.

McDonald and then other company executives embarked on an in-depth study of quality concepts. This familiarization began simply—McDonald sent copies of Phil Crosby's *Quality Is Free* to FPL's top 30 executives—but soon encompassed frequent "study missions" to Japan. In particular, FPL executives visited Kansai Electric, whose quality program—begun in 1981—won it the coveted Deming Prize in 1984, and attended seminars with such quality "gurus" as W. Edwards Deming, Joseph Juran, and Al Gunneson; the company also had ongoing consultations with several Japanese quality counselors (including Asaka, Nayatani, Macabe, Kondo, and Kano).

FPL's QI program grew a step at a time as this investigation proceeded. Initially it consisted only of *Quality Improvement Teams*; it expanded in 1984 with the introduction of *Policy Deployment*, a formal means of linking corporate strategic goals with individual departments' priorities, and the program grew again in 1986, when the company introduced a concept called *Quality in Daily Work*. (These three phases of QIP are explained in detail below and summarized in *Exhibit 1*.) Had anyone questioned whether FPL's new-found commitment to quality was purely lip service—and some in the company had—that doubt was erased in 1986, when "Contribution to QIP" became an item on every FPL performance-appraisal form and hence an explicit factor in pay raises.

Guiding QIP was the Quality-Improvement Department, established in 1981 and headed by Kent Sterett. The department was designed to support the quality process—not to lead it, which was seen as the responsibility of top management and the line organization.

By 1987, the fact that QIP had permeated the organization was evident both at the Miami headquarters and at a second corporate office in Juno Beach. Posters depicting FPL's Edison Award were on display in reception areas and many offices. Large exhibits depicting the progress of various quality efforts were taped and tacked to walls throughout FPL facilities. Hudiburg's long-term goal for the company—"During the next decade, we want to become the best-managed electric utility in the United States and an excellent company overall, and to be recognized as such"—seemed to be posted everywhere.

McDonald had called for "a permanent change of attitude, a radical cultural change," in 1981. If the signs in corridors and offices were any indication, he'd gotten what he'd asked for.

PHASE I: THE QUALITY IMPROVEMENT TEAMS

FPL started QIP with only a handful of quality-improvement teams, patterned after Japanese quality circles. Based on the advice of the company's consultants, these pilot efforts were "engineered" to succeed; team members and projects were carefully selected, the goal being to generate widespread enthusiasm for quality teams and to prompt other employees to say, "I've got a problem I want to work on, too."

After the pilot teams had, predictably, succeeded at their tasks, the company invited employees to form other teams. (Team participation was then, and still is, voluntary—although one executive acknowledged, "The higher up in the organization you go, the less voluntary it is.") Twenty-five percent of FPL's workers volunteered at this first stage. Within a few years, more than 50% were on one or more quality-improvement teams (QITs), and the number of teams had grown accordingly:

1981— 10 (pilots)	1984— 600
1982—100 teams	1985—1,200
1983—300	1986—1,400

Teams generally comprised 5 to 7 members, and met for one hour per week (although some, with management authorization, met for two hours semiweekly). There were four types of team: *functional teams,* composed of workers representing only one area or department; *cross-functional teams* of workers from two or more different areas, charged with working on problems that cut across functional boundaries; *task teams,* whose members were selected by management for their expertise to work on specific problems identified by management; and *lead teams.* A central component of the QIP, the lead teams consisted of top managers of a department or location, who were responsible for the success of the teams under their direction. Groups made regular presentations on their progress to the lead teams, which made sure the QITs stayed on track and on schedule.

Team projects covered all aspects of the company's operations from mundane to mammoth: reducing both billing errors and radiation-exposure accidents, improving turnaround time on both customer inquiries and on plant refueling. Known formally by names like the Fort Lauderdale Collections Team and the Steam Generator Blowdown Team, the groups often came up with more colorful descriptors, like the Jellybusters.

Whatever its nature, every team had to follow the same basic steps (spoken of, almost religiously, as "The Process"):

1. Reason for improvement	To identify a theme (problem area) and the reason for working on it (i.e., "Why are we working on this?")
2. Current situation	To select a problem and set a target for improvement, i.e., narrow the focus to: "What are we going to work on and what are we going to get to?"
3. Analysis	To identify and verify the root causes of the problem.
4. Countermeasures	To plan and implement countermeasures that will correct the root cause(s) of the problem. In America, these would be called "solutions." However, FPL's Japanese mentors make a distinction here. They assert that no solutions exist—you can reduce the seriousness of the problem, but it will never "go away."
5. Results	To confirm that the problem and its root cause(s) have been decreased and the target for improvement has been met.
6. Standardization	To prevent the problem and its root causes from recurring.
7. Future plans	To plan what is to be done about any remaining problems, *and to evaluate the team's effectiveness.*

When the first teams were formed, there were no formal guidelines outlining this process. As a result, many teams got stalled, working on poorly defined problems or failing to analyze root causes properly. The result, often, was frustration. FPL had recently adopted a technique from Komatsu in Japan, a storyboard format (see *Exhibit 2*) summarizing the steps above—the teams filled in the blanks as their work progressed. In addition, a "QI Story Review and Feedback Form" was used by lead teams and managers evaluating the QI teams' progress and final presentations. The QI Story review and feedback form lays out in detail what is expected at each step of the process and helps to ensure the story has been told clearly. Specifically, it provides:

1. A systematic process for reviewing and critiquing a QI Story.
2. A structure for reinforcing and enhancing QI Story skills.
3. A means of giving specific feedback to the originator(s).

In a company survey, employees reported that these forms had been very helpful, clarifying where their teams stood at any given point and what they were expected to do next. Some of the early teams had taken two years to reach completion on their projects (and some had quit trying); by 1987, 70% of the groups that had finished their projects had done so within a year, and FPL had set a goal to bring that figure up to 90% by the end of 1987.

Management by Fact

Quantitative analysis—also known as "management by fact"—was a cornerstone of the FPL approach. (A sign outside Sterett's office read, "In God we trust; all others must bring data.") Team members were expected to analyze not just the frequency of problems and possible solutions but also to produce data proving that a problem actually existed.

The importance of objective analysis was underscored by the experience of one team that attempted to skip the root-cause analysis. It had decided to work on reducing the amount of mail returned as "undeliverable," which was averaging 350 pieces per month, by attacking what their "gut feel" told them the root cause was: incorrect postage. When that turned out to not be the root cause—the postage was correct in almost all cases—the team theorized that the root cause was the ineptitude of the local Post Office.

A member of the lead team supervising the work in progress asked the team where its data were: how did they know that the Post Office was, in fact, the source of the problem? "It's a gut fact," one of the team members replied. "We've all been here long enough that when we know something, it's not gut feel, it's gut fact."

The team members were instructed to collect the other kind of fact, and were surprised to learn that the primary cause of undeliverable mail was FPL's faulty initial recording of customer data. The problem turned out to be that when new customers applied for service, they were asked for their addresses. Many didn't know their zip codes, so they gave their "best guess." Additionally, FPL personnel made keypunch errors that were never corrected.

Supervision. To avoid similar misdirection and keep the QI teams on track, trained facilitators were assigned to work with each group, and lead teams directed and supervised the teams' efforts. In the early stages, members of the QI department also sat in on some team meetings, coaching employees on everything from redefining a problem to making charts easier to read.

Although the teams exercised a good deal of discretion over the projects they selected for analysis, it was management's job to approve or disapprove a team's action plan. (On average about 95% of the team recommendations were approved.) After devising their plan—and after a series of practice sessions with their lead team—each team made a formal presentation to the appropriate level of management (depending on the project), describing the group's work from A to Z.

FPL felt that this system capitalized on the skills of its workers and led to better decision making. The employees closest to a problem were directly involved in its resolution, and benefited from their interaction with management; management benefited because employees did all the homework, leaving managers only to make a go/no-go decision. The process also forced managers to stay current on all the details of day-to-day operations in their areas, since they were expected to play an active role in the presentations—asking questions, evaluating a team's work on the feedback forms, and so forth.

Recognition. Teams were formed not only to solve company problems but also to give employees a sense of participation, the feeling that management wanted to hear what they had to say. Formal recognition for team efforts was therefore deemed critical. McDonald said, "I've always been convinced that people want to do good work, and even more than that, they want to be recognized for doing good work. An important part of our QIP is recognition for excellence."

FPL had experimented with various rewards for successful projects and now offered such gifts as baseball caps and lamps made from electric meters, but the major reward for the very best teams in the company—besides seeing their ideas implemented—was to go to a banquet with all of FPL's top executives. For 1987, FPL upped the ante by offering to send the members of the best team in the company to Japan.

A team's work was evaluated not on the basis of productivity gains, cost savings, or some other measure, but entirely on how well the team used the process. At one awards banquet, for example, a team that had saved FPL $28 million was honored right along with a team of clerical workers whose action plan had produced a $12,000 saving.

Refining the Team Concept

Although FPL had not formally analyzed the total costs and benefits of its quality efforts, in 1987 Hudiburg asserted that the teams were saving the company millions of dollars each year. They had also boosted company performance in scores of areas. Accordingly, customer approval rose from 63.8% to 71.2% between 1985 and 1986, complaints had dropped 61% in five years, and reliability at the customer meters had improved over 30%.

It had taken some time before these benefits were achieved. It is axiomatic that a quality effort cannot succeed without top management commitment. FPL had that, but McDonald's commitment was not initially shared by everyone in the organization.

As noted earlier, many early teams encountered difficulties. Some found the process slow going and decided, out of frustration, to abandon their projects. The frustration stemmed from several causes: unfamiliarity with the process, misdirection, and lack of a formal structure to support the teams' efforts.

These were some of the problems that beset employees trying to *contribute* to the QIP. In addition, a majority of FPL's employees—75% of them—did *not* volunteer to participate in a team when first offered the opportunity, presumably because they harbored doubts about the program's objectives. (In other companies, so-called quality programs often amounted to nothing more than productivity-enhancement strategies: ways of getting employees to take on more work, or of "downsizing" the organization.) "In the beginning, employee trust was not a 'given,'" Kent Sterett said.

FPL executives now talked of "win-win" situations and "employee buy-in," referring to the need to communicate management's intention to support workers' quality efforts and what workers stood to gain from the process. They said that the workers themselves would have "ownership" of the quality program, that no jobs would be eliminated as a result of quality-related productivity gains, and that the quality program was meant as a carrot rather than as a stick—a way of enriching employees' jobs and improving their quality of work life.

More and more employees ultimately "bought in." But middle managers were slower to come on-line. FPL had given employees a forum and a vehicle for change in the QITs, but had not thought through how the employee teams would affect the employees' supervisors. In fact, at the inception of QIP, middle managers were told, "Stay away from the teams—you'll just stifle people." As a result, there was initially considerable resistance to the QIP on the part of mid-level supervisors; the program worked around them instead of with them or through them, while at the same time it was identifying problems in their areas of responsibility.

FPL belatedly realized that "buy-in" was necessary at more than the top and the bottom of the company. Middle managers had to play a role in the QIP if it was to be effective, and they needed training in how to supervise and use the program. "Before you tell someone to do a job, it's only common sense that you give that person the tools they need to do a good job," McDonald said. "In this case, that meant training." FPL now had a total of more than a dozen in-house training programs, including team-member training, facilitator training, and three (mandatory) courses specifically for managers. Perceiving training as an ongoing, continual need, the firm also offered a variety of refresher courses and, in 1987, enrolled 100 managers in a five-week course in advanced statistical process control as well.

In addition to giving managers tools to cope with the company's new program, FPL soon furnished them with an incentive to do so. Some had postponed the required training courses, apparently in the hope that QIP would pass if they just waited it out. McDonald and Hudiburg elicited a higher participation rate by noting that anyone interested in a *career* with the company would jump aboard the quality bandwagon.

Even then, in the 1981–83 time period, the program was not working as well as hoped. When McDonald "announced" the attitude change, in 1981, the company had no formal structure or support for the quality effort; having found few model programs relevant to a service business, it was learning by trial and error. The first wave of QITs in the early 1980s produced so many recommendations that management was unable to process them promptly, for example, and there were too few facilitators spread over too many teams, with the result that many teams got stalled for a few sessions.

The answer to the facilitator shortfall was straightforward: train and deploy more people. In 1987 FPL had 100 full-time and 75 part-time facilitators drawn from throughout the company. (Full-time facilitators left their regular positions for 18-month periods; pay was comparable to what they had been making previously.) The lack of structure was solved a step at a time through the development of formal organizational systems to support the QI process. Sterett recalled, "In the beginning, we never set out to build a pyramid—we set out to lay some bricks. We didn't even know what a [quality] pyramid looked like."

In 1984, the pyramid included a QI organizational chart (*Exhibit 3*), guidebooks and videos, and training materials (and later expanded to include practical tools like the Quality Improvement Story format). The organizational chart was topped by the *Quality Council*, comprising McDonald, Hudiburg, and FPL's other 15 top executives, who met once every two months to discuss quality issues exclusively; it also included the four kinds of QI teams, overseen by each *Vice President's Lead Team.*

To process the recommendations emanating from the teams, FPL also created *"Information Central,"* a database maintained by the company with information on the status of all previous and current company QI projects. Sterett's department also provided support by issuing guidelines, helping with QI evaluations, and facilitating communication among teams and executive groups.

Finally, in 1984, most of the people and the processes were in place: the QITs knew what to do and how to do it. But FPL's management was still not entirely satisfied. They felt the teams were "chasing too many rabbits": working willy-nilly on two many projects without reference to overall corporate objectives. Thus was the second phase of QIP—Policy Deployment—begun.

PHASE II: POLICY DEPLOYMENT

In the words of Wayne Brunetti, group vice president, "We want to go for the brass ring, but we can't afford to go around in circles. Policy Deployment will keep FPL on the straight and narrow."

The phrase "Policy Deployment" was borrowed from FPL's sister company in Japan, Kansai Electric. It was conceived as a means of linking corporate goals to individual actions and thereby forcing departments to concentrate on those actions with the biggest payoffs (looking for "breakthroughs," in McDonald's words). A broad concept, PD encompassed such traditional management functions as strategic planning, budgeting, and management by objectives. (In fact, just as the company's executive committee now met under the name of the Quality Council, FPL's budgeting committee was renamed the Policy Deployment Committee.)

The PD process entailed setting short-term, mid-term, and long-term objectives, through consensus, at every level in the organization. Like the QI teams, this process took time to refine. Initially, participants set forth as many plans and objectives as they wanted—still too many rabbits. By 1987, managers were allowed to select only a few areas for emphasis in the PD process. These areas were identified through a two-pronged research effort. Customer surveys were conducted by an outside market-research firm. Additionally, in-house surveys were administered to employees to ascertain their thoughts about the company's needs. Once this information was collected and tabulated, top management used it as a major source of input for setting the company's mid-term strategic agenda.

Departments were expected to develop their QIP projects based on the PD objectives. The company's mid-term plan of achieving customer satisfaction, for example, would be supported by a short-term plan to improve reliability and supported at the department level by projects designed to reduce power outages.

Policy Deployment began each year with a "problem diagnosis," based on a new program of regular Executive Visitations to all areas of the company, a Presidential Review, ideas for improvement submitted by each manager (but developed through consensus among the manager's employees), and consumer surveys.

The PD Committee and the Executive Committee then drafted mid-term and short-term plans and presented them for review at a biannual Situation Conference ("Sitcon"), attended by all managers and executives. After these goals were formalized, each department and division was asked to develop an action plan (the short-term plans and their associated projects), spelling out what it would do to support the plans. This process too was based on "management by fact": comprehensive data collection, proposed performance improvements (including performance measures to be used), and schedules.

Hudiburg described Policy Deployment as simultaneously a bottom-up approach and a top-down approach. Ideas for improvement came from the trenches (and customers); financial and other support for the ideas came from the executive suite.

Brunetti summarized it this way: "With this corporate roadmap in every hand, we now fully expect to arrive at our corporate goals as quickly and efficiently as possible. . . . This is a no-nonsense way for us to be the best there is."

PHASE III: QUALITY IN DAILY WORK

One of McDonald's goals for the Florida Power & Light quality program was "to create dissatisfaction with the status quo, to recognize that there is always a better way of doing things. This means we must encourage continuous improvement in every job." Whereas the QI teams worked on improving department or interdepartment operations and Policy Deployment was geared toward companywide improvements, the third phase of FPL's program—"Quality in Daily Work"—emphasized improving each individual worker's performance.

QIT and PD efforts most often dealt with improving service to external customers—the ratepayers. The Quality in Daily Work concept explicitly recognized the need to improve service to internal customers. A secretary's customer, for example, might be a division manager, while the drafting department's customer might be the engineering department.

Quality in Daily Work (QIDW) was established to "institutionalize" the use of QI techniques by all employees at all their tasks. Employees were encouraged to apply a customer orientation and analytical quality techniques to their daily work, including better communication with their internal customers and with people in other departments. But again, it would not suffice simply to exhort employees to improve. "We learned the hard way," said James Walden, vice president of power resources. He recalled, "that to permanently change the way employees thought about and worked with other employees, we needed a formal process." (A flowchart depicting this process appears in *Exhibit 4*.)

Some QIDW projects were ambitious, aimed at improving cooperation between departments that had historically blamed each other for problems—getting them to agree on each other's accountabilities and set standards for each other's performance. Other projects were simpler. One secretary, for example, followed the process in analyzing her job. It was easy to identify her customer—her boss—and her top-priority job, which was typing his letters accurately. She tracked and graphed her error rate in typing documents, and identified the root causes of the errors (documents that had to be retyped). One of these was her boss's poor handwriting. By identifying this problem and conveying it to her "customer," she cut her error rate significantly. Another QIDW effort occurred in the company's mailroom, where workers decided to take action on the problem of misaddressed company mail. By taking a few simple steps to communicate with people throughout FPL about the extent of the problem and how to solve it, they reduced the incidence of misaddressed mail by 98% in two months.

When this third phase of the QIP was introduced, FPL executives emphasized that quality improvement was not something employees were expected to do in *addition* to their regular work; it was the *way* they were to do their work. It was also the way the executives were to do their work.

Asked how many days he had spent on the QIP in 1986, Hudiburg answered, "Fifty-five days. And frankly, I'm embarrassed that I'm able to answer that question. Next year, I expect that I won't be able to—that I won't be able to distinguish quality efforts from my other work. It shouldn't be that I spend 55 days on quality and the rest of my time on 'normal' operations. What we call quality is a totally comprehensive management system; it's the way we manage our business."

CURRENT CHALLENGES AND FUTURE PLANS

The way FPL managed its business had brought it recognition from hundreds of other companies large and small. But Hudiburg was still not completely content. "We're only really just getting started," he said. "It will be at least two more years before I'm satisfied."

He mentioned problems that still hindered the quality program, as well as the firm's plans to expand the scope of the QIP in the future. "One problem is that our leaders still don't fully understand quality, and that includes me. There are also a few mossbacks around who've seen fads come and go, and who aren't supporting the process as well as others. There are big gaps between our best areas and our worst."

A vice president made a similar point: "Not all of our managers have equal enthusiasm about what we're trying to do. We still get numerous complaints—from managers and employees—about new terminology and new concepts. Some get frustrated, and that's a real barrier to implementing the concepts."

Indeed, some employees complained about the continual introduction of new programs and new buzzwords. One of FPL's key concepts was "PDCA," for "Plan, Do, Check, Act"; this meant that every action should be followed up with analysis to determine whether the desired results were achieved, and to revamp the action if they were not. Some employees had taken to saying that PDCA should stand for "Please Don't Change Again."

Certain employees felt that the team process, including the extensive data analysis, was burdensome, requiring too much work and too much time for the results achieved. In particular, managers accustomed to making fast, unilateral decisions were sometimes unhappy about the teams' structured, participative decision-making mechanism.

One operations manager close to retirement said that he was ambivalent about the QIP: "On one hand, I'm now getting credit for the things I've been doing all along. I made plenty of decisions that saved the company millions of dollars, and no one knew about it before except me. Now, with the reports and presentations and charts all over the walls, everybody knows about it. But I don't always like having to go through a long, drawn-out analysis—and sometimes I don't. It's a pain in the butt."

"I've got a desk that's this high with reports pertaining to the quality program about things where, before, I would have just said, 'Do this,'" he continued. "And I've got to read every last one. Sometimes I think people are spending too much time just making their damn charts look pretty, instead of getting something done."

A foreman expressed some similar feelings. "We like it that the company is interested in hearing what we have to say, and QIP has produced some excellent results," he said, "but I think the process is wasting a helluva lot of time and money. We often joke that they should QIP the QIP! It's interesting that we've never been asked what we think about QIP."

In fact, QIP made provision for "small" problems within a department's control that could be easily solved. A quality team simply had to fill out and submit a "Q memo," detailing the problem and what they did about it. There were no formal accounting Q-memo results, nor were teams recognized for this kind of activity.

In addition to responding to this kind of concern, Hudiburg felt that the quality effort needed more refinement before it would produce optimum results. FPL's performance, though better than that of most U.S. utilities, still lagged well behind Kansai's. One current FPL project was to reduce the incidence of "scrams": the number of times a nuclear plant had to be taken out of service, usually due to false equipment readings. During one year, FPL's four nuclear units had experienced an average of seven scrams each; the company had set a target of five scrams each for 1987, or a total of 20 scrams for the year.

Hudiburg asked his Japanese counterparts how many scrams Kansai had had in 1986 in its nine nuclear plants. "They said none. I thought at first there was a translation problem." Five years earlier, Hudiburg added, "Kansai's record was no better than ours and maybe worse. They've just shown steady improvement year after year, and that's what we've got to do."

Sterett said that the company's plans for the future included systematic work on refining the three phases of the QIP. The company had also decided to apply quality techniques to its quality process, establishing a Quality Assurance System to monitor and enhance the QIP's effectiveness and to put more effort into identifying and meeting customer needs.

"Although we've come a long way," McDonald observed, "survival is still an issue. Customer expectations are continually rising, and like many service organizations we face the possibility of deregulation and more competition. If we get into a situation where we have to be competitive, we want the company to have been so good that customers say, —I like Florida Power & Light, I'm proud of it, and that's who I want to do business with.'"

One facet of QIP just getting under way had to do with the companies FPL did business with: its new, formal Vendor Quality Improvement Program to improve the quality of goods and services provided by FPL's vendors and contractors. The company had rolled out a specialized QIP orientation program just for vendors.

It was also rolling out its QIP philosophy to the subsidiaries of FPL Group. In 1986, for example, it helped Philadelphia-based Colonial Penn Insurance launch a quality program called Commitment to Excellence. There was little question in the minds of most FPL managers that the quality-improvement process they had developed could be transferred successfully to other organizations. Hudiburg was optimistic about the prospect of helping Colonial Penn, Telesat Cablevision, Alandco Inc. (a real-estate firm), and the group's other holdings to initiate their own quality efforts. "In Florida Power & Light we have a model that's so successful that transferability shouldn't be a problem," he said.

Exhibit 1
Statements of Purpose, Three-Phase Quality Effort

Overall Purpose

The Quality Improvement Program in Florida Power & Light consists of three major components:

- Quality Improvement Teams
- Policy Deployment
- Quality in Daily Work

Taken together, these components will provide an integrated set of procedures and attitudes that promote continuous improvement in every aspect of work throughout the company.

The QIP is based on (1) respect for people, (2) customer satisfaction, (3) management by fact, and (4) PDCA [Plan, Do, Check, Act].

[In addition to PDCA, another widely used FPL abbreviation was "COCO": for Clarity in problem definition, Objectivity in considering ideas, Commitment to the effort, and employee Ownership of the process.]

QUALITY IMPROVEMENT TEAMS provide a structured environment for employees to work together toward the goals of:

- Improving the quality of the products and services the company provides.
- Developing the skills and abilities of all employees.
- Promoting communication and teamwork.
- Enhancing the quality of work life.

POLICY DEPLOYMENT targets the achievement of breakthroughs by the concentration of company efforts and resources on a few priority issues. The goals are:

- An increased level of performance in areas selected for breakthrough.
- Improved communication of company and department direction.
- Improved horizontal coordination within the company.
- Broad company participation in the development and maintenance of a corporate vision, fundamental objectives, and tactical agenda items.

QUALITY IN DAILY WORK is the application of PDCA to all activities necessary to meet customer needs and reasonable expectations on a daily basis. The goals are:

- Maintain the gains achieved through improvement projects.
- Consistency in operations and results.
- Clarification of individual contributions toward the achievement of customer satisfaction.
- Incrementally improve daily operations.

FLORIDA POWER & LIGHT'S QUALITY-IMPROVEMENT PROGRAM

Exhibit 2

Storyboard Format for Quality Teams

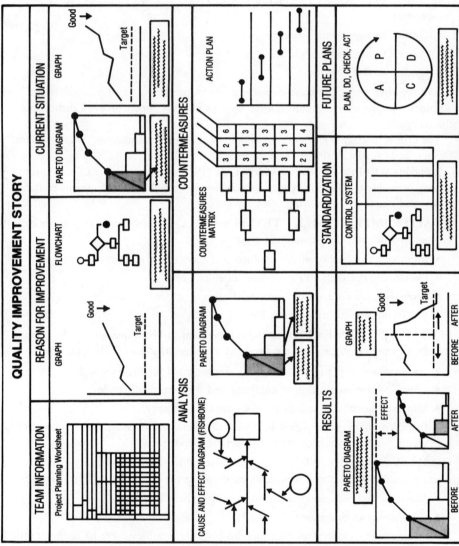

Source: Adapted from the concept of the QC story, originally named by Mr. Nogawa, president of Komatsu, for the purpose of reporting improvement activities. Professor Ikezawa and others expanded the procedure to include its use as a guide for solving a problem.

Exhibit 3
Quality Organizational Chart

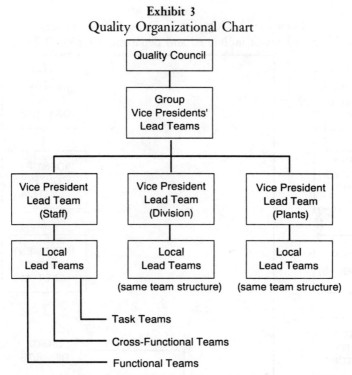

NOTE: The major point of this chart is that the QIP organization is exactly the same as the corporate organization.

Exhibit 4
Flowchart of "Quality in Daily Work" Process
(for analysis of individual and department responsibilities)

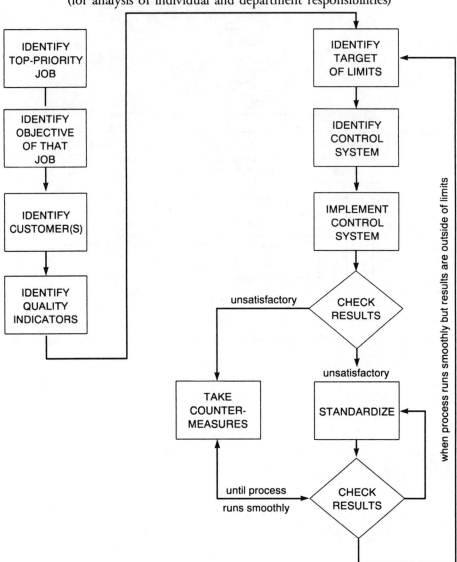

The Malcolm Baldrige
National Quality Award

The [Baldrige] Award salutes companies that improve the
quality of their goods and services, thus enhancing productivity,
lowering costs, and increasing profitability. Just as important, it
offers a vehicle for companies, large and small, in
manufacturing and in services, to examine their own
approaches to quality. It offers companies a standard with
which to compare their own progress to that of the country's
very best.

—President Ronald Reagan
March 31, 1988

BACKGROUND

On August 20, 1987, President Reagan affixed his signature to Public Law
100–107. This ground-breaking piece of legislation, known commonly as the
Malcolm Baldrige National Quality Improvement Act, established the nation's
first annual award to recognize total quality management in American industry.
The Malcolm Baldrige National Quality Award represents the United States
government's endorsement of quality as an essential part of successful business
strategy in the 1990s.

The legislation and the award were the work of an American Congress that
had become increasingly concerned about the eroding competitiveness of many
U.S. firms in the world marketplace. After investigating the issues of world quality and productivity, the members of the One Hundredth Congress found that
"the leadership of the United States in product and process quality has been
challenged strongly (and sometimes successfully) by foreign competition, and our
Nation's productivity growth has improved less than our competitors' over the
last two decades."

By establishing a national quality improvement act, the Congress sought to
encourage and incite greater U.S. competitiveness through the recognition and
commendation of exceptional quality in American business. (See *Exhibit 1*.) As

Christopher Bogan and Lee Harper prepared this case under the supervision of Professor Christopher W. L. Hart as the basis for class discussion rather than to illustrate either effective or
ineffective handling of an administrative situation. Copyright © 1989 by the President and Fellows of Harvard College; Harvard Business School case # 9-690-001.

an instrument of government, the Baldrige Award seeks to improve quality and productivity by:

1. helping to stimulate American companies to improve quality and productivity for the pride of recognition while obtaining a competitive edge through decreased costs and increased profits;

2. establishing guidelines and criteria that can be used by business, industrial, governmental and other organizations in evaluating their quality improvement efforts;

3. recognizing the achievements of those companies which improve the quality of their goods and services and thereby provide an example to others; and

4. providing specific guidance for other American organizations that wish to learn how to manage for high quality by making available detailed information on how winning organizations were able to change their cultures and achieve quality eminence.

Already the Baldrige Award and its comprehensive criteria for evaluating total quality in an organization have had considerable impact.

"The [Baldrige quality assessment] guidelines are outstanding. They're more than outstanding; they are really to me inspirational," said James Houghton, chairman of Corning Glass. "I know that in Corning we have passed out the guidelines for our divisions and just said, 'if you want to really know what quality is all about, take a look at this.'"

Some observers have begun referring to the award as the "Nobel Prize" for business. In the award's first two years, the National Institute of Standards and Technology (NIST), which administers the award, sent out approximately 60,000 application forms, each containing the 192-point Baldrige criteria for assessing overall organizational quality.

"The effort to improve U.S. products is considered key to battling foreign competition and changing the perception of many consumers who associate higher quality with foreign-made goods," noted a recent front-page *Washington Post* business story about those companies applying for the Baldrige Award.

Indeed, quality has become a business imperative for a growing number of American corporations. Market competition, from auto and semiconductor sales to package delivery and financial services, is increasingly taking place in a world arena. Confronted by foreign competitors that often enjoy lower labor costs and their home government's active policy support, American firms are turning to companywide total quality management as a strategy to reduce their costs, improve productivity and increase customer satisfaction and customer loyalty—all of which things tend to translate into increased market share, higher profits and greater overall competitiveness. "Quality," observed a senior vice president at

Federal Express, "is to economic success as the nuclear reaction process is to energy production: the output is wildly disproportionate to the input once it builds to a chain reaction."

Though many of the analytical techniques most commonly associated with quality control were developed in the United States, it is the Japanese that transformed quality from arcane statistical analysis, used primarily to control variability in manufacturing processes, to a system of values that has broad-reaching implications for nearly all business activities. Quality was a linchpin in Japan's post–World War II reconstruction strategy. Doggedly pursuing this strategy, a tiny island nation has risen phoenix-like from economic ruin to what sometimes seems to be near hegemony in many industries.

For nearly 40 years Japan has recognized its corporate quality leaders by bestowing on them the prestigious Deming Prize, named after the American statistician, Dr. W. Edwards Deming, who championed many of the analytical techniques employed in formal quality control. The Deming Prize has become so esteemed in Japan that each year, much like America's Academy Awards, millions of Japanese watch the Deming Prize ceremony aired live on television.

The success of Japan and other countries pursuing quality-based competitive strategies has chastened many in Congress and American industry. "In our cellular (telephone) operation, I can tell you why we improved our quality: we met the devil," says Edward F. Staiano, an executive at Motorola, Inc. "In 1984 we had to sit down . . . and we had to make a decision as to whether we were going to stay in the business or whether we were going to get put out of the business by the Japanese." For its part, Congress established the Baldrige Award. Motorola, in turn, launched an ongoing companywide quality improvement initiative. That initiative so powerfully and positively transformed the organization that Motorola was honored as one of the first three American corporations to receive a Baldrige Award in 1988. The other two winners were the Commercial Nuclear Fuel Division (CNFD) of the Westinghouse Electric Corporation and Globe Metallurgical, Inc., a small feroalloys maker based in Ohio. In 1989, Milliken & Co., a privately owned textile maker based in South Carolina, and Xerox Corp. were the nation's Baldrige winners.

THE BALDRIGE QUALITY-ASSESSMENT CRITERIA

Named after Malcolm Baldrige, who served as the United States Secretary of Commerce from 1981 until his death in July of 1987, the Baldrige National Quality Award focused on an organization's total quality management system and the improvements that system generates. In order to evaluate and recognize effective quality systems, Baldrige administrators at the NIST created comprehensive quality-assessment criteria based upon the comments and observations of more than 200 quality experts from throughout the country. The Baldrige criteria consequently reflect the combined experience and wisdom of many people. As a set of principles, they are "nondenominational" in the sense that they do not favor any one system or dogma. Instead, the Baldrige criteria are designed to be flexible, evaluating quality on three broad dimensions: (1) the soundness of the approach or systems; (2) the deployment or integration of those systems throughout the entire organization; and (3) the results generated by those systems. (See *Exhibit 2*.)

The Baldrige quality criteria focus on seven broad topical areas, shown in *Exhibit 4*, that are integrally and dynamically related in a manner suggested in *Exhibit 3*. Leadership is the starting point and a key measure of an organization's total quality program. Leadership drives the entire quality system, which in the Baldrige vernacular consists of four areas, including Information and Analysis, Planning, Human Resource Utilization and Quality Assurance. Actual quantitative and anecdotal results tracked over time provide a way to measure progress and to judge the effectiveness of the system. Customer Satisfaction is the ultimate goal or touchstone of an organization's combined quality programs.

In short, the Baldrige criteria create an integrated set of indicators of excellence and continuity that together describe total quality. In the Baldrige view, total quality is a value system. It is a way of life, an approach to doing business that affects every corporate decision and permeates the entire organization.

When a company applies for the Baldrige Award or uses the Baldrige quality-assessment criteria internally to evaluate its quality program, the organization must address 44 subcategories and 192 individual items that fall under the seven broad topical areas. Each topical area and subcategory is weighted according to general importance. (See *Exhibit 4*.)

For evaluation purposes, a maximum 1,000 points are allocated to the seven Baldrige quality categories. Just as the Japanese stress the importance of both the means and the ends when considering quality, the Baldrige criteria tie approximately half their points to the quality process (methods and means) and half to the results (ends and trends). The means or process is a leading indicator of the ends that will be attained. In turn, the results verify that the appropriate process is in place and being used effectively.

Leadership, to which 12% of the assessment's total score is assigned, examines how senior executives create and sustain clear and visible quality values in the organization. This section also focuses on top management's involvement in and commitment to creating and championing quality both inside and outside the company.

At the heart of the Baldrige criteria is the belief that quality permeates every nook and cranny, including the executive suite, of preeminent companies. In these organizations, senior management plays a constant, direct and active role in quality improvement. "I will tell you that today, as an operating general manager, one of the highest priorities I have every day is quality," observes Motorola's Staiano. "It governs every single decision I make. I never ask a question about how much did we ship; I only ask the question of how much improvement did we get in quality."

From Leadership the Baldrige criteria direct their focus at Information and Analysis, which accounts for 6% of the overall assessment score. This section examines the scope, validity and use of the data underlying a company's total quality system. Next comes Planning for Quality, which accounts for 8% of the Baldrige assessment score. This section examines how a company integrates quality planning into its overall business planning and then explores strategies for achieving and retaining short-term and long-term quality leadership. In its efforts to internalize quality, for instance, Globe Metallurgical, Inc., has created a five-year quality plan that is tied directly to its five-year strategic plan. The company's long-term quality plan covers 96 items in 20 pages, including projects, goals, responsibility assignments and target dates. Moreover, employees throughout the company keep a two-year "quality calendar" on their walls with dates and deadlines for all-important quality assignments.

Human Resource Utilization, which represents 15% of the overall Baldrige assessment score, examines an organization's effectiveness in developing and using the full potential of its work force for quality improvement. Worker participation, education and training, recognition of achievements and workplace environment are a few of the areas covered.

How important is human resource development in quality-driven companies? At an organization like Westinghouse's CNFD, nearly 90% of the work force have received quality-related training in the past three years. Indeed, Motorola spends more than $45 million annually to support one million hours of training of which at least 40% "is devoted to quality improvement processes, principles, technology and objectives."

The Quality Assurance of Products and Services, to which 14% of the assessment's total score is assigned, scrutinizes a company's overall quality control systems. First it closely examines the ways an organization attempts to design quality into its goods and services, and then it evaluates the manner in which the company integrates quality control with continuous quality improvement. The Baldrige criteria view quality assurance in far-reaching terms, asking companies to demonstrate that their control systems actively involve suppliers, dealers, distributors and all other external providers of the organization's goods and services.

The Baldrige criteria's sixth area of focus is Quality Results. Curt Reimann, director of the Malcolm Baldrige National Quality Award, explains the importance of this category, which accounts for 15% of the assessment's total score, by observing that "if it doesn't get measured, it doesn't get improved." Quantitative results, tracked over time, provide verification that appropriate quality control systems are in place and functioning well. This sixth category evaluates current quality levels and improvement trends over a three- to five-year time horizon. Both product and process quality trends are examined, comparing an organization's results to industry averages and to the performance of competitors. This concept of "benchmarking" an organization's performance against its own historical performance and the performance of other companies is central to the Baldrige criteria. By tracking its own performance and competitors' performance over time, an organization becomes involved in continuous evaluation in order to effect continuous improvement and learning. It's not surprising that all five Baldrige winners excel in collecting, analyzing, and using their results to drive continuous quality improvement. Globe Metallurgical, for example, calculates daily cost of nonconformance figures for its operations. Motorola states that the organization has saved $250 million from quality improvements over the past two years. Richard Buetow, Motorola's director of quality, estimates his company has received a 20 to 1 return for every dollar invested in its quality improvement programs. It is this kind of quantification and continual improvement that has helped Globe and Motorola set new world standards for their products.

Customer Satisfaction is the last Baldrige category and the final arbiter of the merit and effectiveness of an organization's quality system. In the Baldrige view, customer satisfaction *is* the ultimate goal of quality; accordingly this section accounts for 30% of the assessment's total score. Companies are asked to examine extensively their knowledge of their customers, their customer service systems and their ability to meet their customers' requirements.

All three Baldrige winners carry to extremes their commitment to customer satisfaction. Motorola managers, for instance, wear pagers so that customers can reach them any time, any place. Globe responds to all customer queries and complaints—no matter from where the complaint emanates—within 24 hours, and CNFD, which has had 100% on-time delivery for the past three years and a product reliability record that approaches perfection, creates quality teams comprised of CNFD employees and customers.

APPLICATIONS OF THE BALDRIGE
QUALITY-ASSESSMENT CRITERIA

For companies using them, the Baldrige criteria serve many purposes. Indeed, part of the Baldrige criteria's power lies in the fact that they can be applied in many different ways to organizations whose quality-improvement programs are of all different maturities.

As a practical tool for assessing operations, the Baldrige guidelines can be used:

1. to help define and design a total quality system;
2. to evaluate ongoing internal relationships among departments, divisions and functional units within an organization;
3. to assess and assist outside suppliers of goods and services to a company; and
4. to assess customer satisfaction.

Early-stage companies can literally use the Baldrige guidelines as a checklist or blueprint to help them design their overall quality programs. Middle-stage companies can use them as a road map to guide them down the road to continued quality improvement, and advanced-stage companies can use them as an evaluative tool to help fine-tune their quality programs and benchmark them against other industry and world leaders.

"The (Baldrige) feedback has shaken us awake," admits Bob Lea, a vice president of human resources at The Paul Revere Insurance Company, one of two service firms to receive final site visits by senior award examiners during the 1988 Baldrige competition. "We see we still have a long way to go." Though The Paul Revere did not formally apply for the 1989 Baldrige Award, the company continues to focus on the Baldrige quality criteria. "If you want greater market share, more new business and more repeat business, then you do what it takes in quality to get the Baldrige Award," says Jane Gallagher, Paul Revere's quality manager. "These things go hand in hand."

The Baldrige guidelines also provide a common language for discussing quality across companies, functional areas, industries and disciplines. The field of quality traditionally has been a Babel of ideas, jargon and philosophy, much of which does not translate easily from one setting to another. By providing a broad, flexible approach to assessing total quality, the Baldrige system fosters improved information sharing and overall communications. These activities in turn lead employees and management to develop a shared meaning of total quality that can be built into the organization's goals and policies. From such shared meaning develops an organizational value system that is customer-focused, quality-driven and central to the culture of the company. So deeply does Motorola believe in the value of total quality control that the company has ordered *all* 10,000 of its suppliers to begin preparing themselves to apply for the Baldrige Award, as tangible evidence of their commitment to total quality management, or lose Motorola's business.

The role of the Baldrige Award as an instructor of quality is also rapidly growing. The application process compels management and employees:

1. to recognize the far-reaching importance of quality;
2. to examine the organization's total quality progress and current standing; and
3. to exchange information between departments, divisions and organizational levels.

One service company, for instance, has designated seven-person teams for each of its 11 divisions to prepare individual Baldrige applications. A companywide application is then consolidated from the group efforts. Through this process, the company exposes many employees to the Baldrige criteria. Moreover, as these divisional teams discover weaknesses within their operating areas, they red flag these weaknesses for immediate corrective action.

Assimilating the Baldrige view of total quality can also lead to actions with profound long-term consequences. At Globe, Motorola and Westinghouse's CNFD, quality planning has been elevated to the same level as strategic planning and integrated with it. Indeed, all these organizations have wrought significant cultural and organizational changes in order to support companywide total quality.

AWARD PROCESS

Thousands of companies have requested the Baldrige guidelines for internal use. However, a much smaller number of companies actually submit the 50- to 75-page written applications in May formally seeking the award. In 1988, the Baldrige Award's first year, 66 companies applied, and in 1989, 40 companies applied. Ultimately, no more than two companies in each of three categories—manufacturing, service and small business—will be named Baldrige winners. Although service companies applied in both years, none received an award. The Baldrige judges were sending out a signal: only the absolute best companies will receive Baldrige Awards. Being good is not enough. It wasn't until 1990 that the Federal Express Corporation became the first service company to win the award.

The Baldrige applications are scored by quality experts from business, consulting and academia. Of the 1,000 points that can possibly be awarded on the overall application, only 11 of 66 applicants received more than 751 points in 1988. A "good company" usually falls in the 500 range on the Baldrige scoring. (See *Exhibit 5.*)

Only about 10% of the applicants will become Baldrige "finalists" and receive site visits from a team of examiners. From this group of finalists, the Baldrige winners are chosen. All companies applying for the award receive from the examiners a written feedback report summarizing the examiners' findings of the company's organizational strengths and weaknesses.

Many companies speculate about the best way to prepare a winning application. But in fact there is no one right approach. One *Fortune* 500 company acknowledged that over several weeks, it deployed more than 80 people and spent more than $250,000 in its unsuccessful efforts to write, edit and professionally publish a winning application in 1988. In contrast, one person wrote Globe Metallurgical's application over a three-day weekend.

For those companies that actually win a Baldrige Award, sudden celebrity is assured. The three 1988 winners report receiving between 10 to 15 calls daily from organizations wishing to learn about their winning strategies. Even a small company like Globe, which employs about 200 people, has seen inquiries come pouring in from throughout the world, including invitations to speak on quality in Moscow, Beijing and London.

SUMMARY

When former Secretary of Commerce C. William Verity inaugurated the first Malcolm Baldrige National Quality Award, his words probably sounded a bit overwrought to some. ". . . This Award encourages American businesses at every level to practice effective total quality control of goods and services," enthused Secretary Verity. "It recognizes companies that have achieved superior quality performance. Those Award winners will be the true standard-bearers for a full-fledged national quality movement that is now gaining momentum. . . ."

Three years after the establishment of the Malcolm Baldrige National Quality Award, the award's vital signs were strong. In that time, it had grown from a fragile infant into a healthy baby. Will the Baldrige Award incite the broad-based revolution in American productivity and competitiveness that the members of Congress hoped to foment when drafting the Malcolm Baldrige National Quality Improvement Act of 1987? That remains to be seen.

The initial response to the Baldrige criteria for evaluating total quality has been overwhelmingly positive. The Baldrige guidelines are proving to be useful and inspirational to scores of companies at all different stages of developing and deploying total quality systems. Moreover, the award itself has brought international attention and prestige to a handful of American companies that have clearly demonstrated their preeminent leadership in the area of total quality management.

The experience of the award's first five winners suggests that companies throughout the country—indeed, around the world—are deeply interested in and concerned about quality. The Baldrige Award and quality guidelines consequently have the potential of becoming much more than a mere prize and grading system. They have the capacity to become the global standard by which organizational quality is judged.

Exhibit 1
H.R. 812

ONE HUNDREDTH CONGRESS
OF THE UNITED STATES OF AMERICA
AT THE FIRST SESSION

Begun and held at the City of Washington on Tuesday,
the sixth day of January, one thousand nine hundred and eighty-seven

An Act

To amend the Stevenson-Wydler Technology Innovation Act of 1980 to establish the Malcolm Baldrige National Quality Award, with the objective of encouraging American business and other organizations to practice effective quality control in the provision of their goods and services.

Be it enacted by the Senate and House of Representatives
of the United States of America in Congress assembled,

SECTION 1. SHORT TITLE.

This Act may be cited as the "Malcolm Baldrige National Quality Improvement Act of 1987."

SECTION 2. FINDINGS AND PURPOSES.

(a) FINDINGS.—The Congress finds and declares that—

(1) the leadership of the United States in product and process quality has been challenged strongly (and sometimes successfully) by foreign competition, and our Nation's productivity growth has improved less than our competitors' over the last two decades;

Exhibit 1
(Continued)

(2) American business and industry are beginning to understand that poor quality costs companies as much as 20% of sales revenues nationally, and that improved quality of goods and services goes hand in hand with improved productivity, lower costs, and increased profitability;

(3) strategic planning for quality and quality improvement programs, through a commitment to excellence in manufacturing and services, are becoming more and more essential to the well-being of our Nation's economy and our ability to compete effectively in the global marketplace;

(4) improved management understanding of the factory floor, worker involvement in quality, and greater emphasis on statistical process control can lead to dramatic improvements in the cost and quality of manufactured products;

(5) the concept of quality improvement is directly applicable to small companies as well as large, to service industries as well as manufacturing, and to the public sector as well as private enterprise;

(6) in order to be successful, quality improvement programs must be management-led and customer-oriented and this may require fundamental changes in the way companies and agencies do business;

(7) several major industrial nations have successfully coupled rigorous private sector quality audits with national awards giving special recognition to those enterprises the audits identify as the very best; and

(8) a national quality award program of this kind in the United States would help improve quality and productivity by—

   (A) helping to stimulate American companies to improve quality and productivity for the pride of recognition while obtaining a competitive edge through increased profits.

   (B) recognizing the achievements of those companies which improve the quality of their goods and services and providing an example to others.

   (C) establishing guidelines and criteria that can be used by business, industrial, governmental, and other organizations in evaluating their own quality improvement efforts, and

   (D) providing specific guidance for other American organizations that wish to learn how to manage for high quality by making available detailed information on how winning organizations were able to change their cultures and achieve eminence.

(b) PURPOSE.—It is the purpose of this Act to provide for the establishment and conduct of a national quality improvement program under which (1) awards are given to selected companies and other organizations in the United States that practice effective quality management and as a result make significant improvements in the quality of their goods and services, and (2) information is disseminated about the successful strategies and programs.

THE MALCOLM BALDRIGE NATIONAL QUALITY AWARD
Exhibit 2
Baldrige Criteria—Scoring Guidelines

Score	Approach	Deployment	Results
0%	• no system evident	• limited to examples	• anecdotal
10–40%	• beginnings of sound, systematic, prevention-based approach	• early stages of deployment	• some examples of progress with evidence that results are caused by approach
50%	• sound, systematic, prevention-based approach • fair integration	• major areas • extension plans	• positive trends in major areas with evidence that results are caused by approach
60–90%	• sound, systematic, effective, prevention-based system • good integration	• major area plus many support areas	• good to excellent results with evidence that results are caused by approach
100%	• sound, systematic, effective, approach refined through evaluation/improvement cycles • world-class approach • excellent integration	• full deployment • excellent integration	• excellent (world-class) results in major areas • good to excellent results in support areas • sustained results • results clearly caused by approach

Exhibit 3
Baldrige Categories
Dynamic Relationships

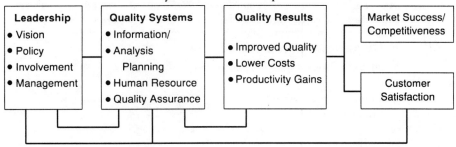

Exhibit 4
Malcolm Baldrige National Quality Award
Examination Categories, Subcategories and Point Values

1989 Examination Categories/Subcategories	Maximum Points	Percent of Total
1.0 Leadership	*120*	*12*
1.1 Senior Management	30	
1.2 Quality Values	20	
1.3 Management System	50	
1.4 Public Responsibility	20	
2.0 Information and Analysis	*60*	*6*
2.1 Scope of Data and Information	25	
2.2 Data Management	15	
2.3 Analysis and Use of Data for Decision Making	20	
3.0 Planning for Quality	*80*	*8*
3.1 Planning Process	30	
3.2 Plans for Quality Leadership	50	
4.0 Human Resource Utilization	*150*	*15*
4.1 Management	25	
4.2 Employee Involvement	40	
4.3 Quality Education and Training	30	
4.4 Employee Recognition	20	
4.5 Quality of Worklife	35	

(Continued)

Exhibit 4
(Continued)

1989 Examination Categories/Subcategories	Maximum Points	Percent of Total
5.0 Quality Assurance of Products and Services	*140*	*14*
5.1 Design and Introduction of Products and Services	25	
5.2 Operation of Processes	20	
5.3 Measurements and Standards	15	
5.4 Audit	20	
5.5 Documentation	10	
5.6 Quality Assurance of Operations and Business Processes	25	
5.7 Quality Assurance of External Providers of Goods and Services	25	
6.0 Quality Results	*150*	*15*
6.1 Quality of Products and Services	70	
6.2 Operational and Business Process Quality Improvement	60	
6.3 Quality Improvement Applications	20	
7.0 Customer Satisfaction	*300*	*30*
7.1 Knowledge of Customer Requirements and Expectations	40	
7.2 Customer Relationship Management	125	
7.3 Customer Satisfaction Methods of Measurement and Results	135	
TOTAL POINTS	**1,000**	

Scoring Criteria

Introduction

The system for scoring examination items is based upon three evaluation dimensions: (1) approach; (2) deployment; and (3) results. All examination items require applicants to furnish information relating to one or more of these dimensions. Specific criteria associated with the evaluation dimensions are described below.

Approach

Approach refers to the methods the company uses to achieve the purposes addressed in the examination items. The scoring criteria used to evaluate approaches include one or more of the following:

Exhibit 4
(Continued)

Scoring Criteria

- the degree to which the approach is prevention based
- the appropriateness of the tools, techniques, and methods to the application
- the effectiveness of the use of tools, techniques, and methods
- the degree to which the approach is systematic, integrated, and consistent
- the degree to which the approach embodies effective self-evaluation, feedback, and adaptation cycles to sustain continuous improvement
- the degree to which the approach is based upon quantitative information that is objective and reliable
- the indicators of unique and innovative approaches, including significant and effective new adaptations of tools and techniques used in other applications or types of businesses

Deployment

Deployment refers to the extent to which the approaches are applied to all relevant areas and activities addressed and implied in the examination items. The scoring criteria used to evaluate deployment include one or more of the following:

- the appropriate and effective application to all transactions and interactions with customers, providers of goods and services, and the public
- the appropriate and effective application to all internal processes, activities, facilities, and employees
- the appropriate and effective application to all product and service characteristics

Results

Results refers to outcomes and effects in achieving the purposes addressed and implied in the examination items. The scoring criteria used to evaluate results include one or more of the following:

- the quality levels demonstrated
- the contributions of the outcomes and effects to quality improvement
- the quality improvement gains
- the demonstration of sustained gains
- the breadth of quality improvement gains
- the significance of gains in terms of their importance to the company's business
- the comparison with industry and world leaders
- the company's ability to account for gains in terms of specific quality improvement actions

---

Exhibit 5
1988 Malcolm Baldrige National Quality Award
Distribution of Written Application Scores

Range of Scores	Range Number	Applicants in Range	Comments
0–125	1	0	No evidence of effort in any category. Virtually no attention to quality.
126–250	2	0	Only slight evidence of effort in any category. Quality issues of low priority.
251–400	3	1.6	Some evidence of effort in a few categories, but not outstanding in any. Poor integration of efforts. Largely based on reaction to problems, with little preventive efforts.
401–600	4	47.5	Evidence of effective efforts in many categories, and outstanding in some. A good prevention-based process. Many areas lack maturity. Further deployment and results needed to demonstrate continuity.
601–750	5	34.4	Evidence of effective efforts in most categories, and outstanding in several. Deployment and results show strength, but some efforts may lack maturity. Clear areas for further attention.
751–875	6	16.4	Effective efforts in all categories, and outstanding in many. Good integration and good to excellent results in all areas. Full deployment. Many industry leaders.
876–1,000	7	0	Outstanding effort and results in all categories. Effective integration and sustained results. National and world leaders.

8

◆

Managing Demand
and Supply

Conventional approaches to managing services concentrate on calibrating capacity (whether expressed in terms of people, finances, or facilities) to expected demand. Service leaders manage both demand and supply by developing ways of influencing customer behavior and even buying patterns. In addition, they create devices for achieving flexibility in their capacity. Successfully managing both demand and supply requires that the following general questions be posed: What is the amount, speed of change, and predictability of change in demand patterns in this business? What are the costs of failing to meet peak demands? What are the costs of overstaffing at times of weak demand? By what amount, if any, do costs of overstaffing exceed costs of various ways by which flexible capacity might be achieved? To what extent can patterns of demand be influenced by pricing incentives (and disincentives), advertising, and the design of the service itself?

Perhaps the most concrete example of demand and supply management in services is embodied in the waiting line, the source of frustration for many customers being "inventoried" in such lines. And yet, some organizations are masters of minimizing the aggravation of waiting. This raises additional questions: To what extent can demand be inventoried through waiting lines and other devices? What devices, such as accurate progress reporting, useful diversions, and outright entertainment, can be used to minimize the aggravation of waiting? Conversely, by what means can service supply be inventoried? Through the use of part-time employees or rental equipment? Through the cross-training of employees? Through arrangements to share capacity? Through the involvement of customers in the service delivery process itself? Or through superhuman effort by mere mortals?

Many of these ways of managing demand and supply are described in more detail in the article by Earl Sasser, "Match Supply and Demand in Service Industries." As you read it, ask yourself what basic characteristics might be typical of businesses able to make the most effective use of each device suggested. What service businesses, in addition to those mentioned in the article, might benefit most from his suggestions?

The management of demand and supply is critical to the success of both FBO, Inc. and the University Health Services, described in the following cases. In reading and analyzing the FBO, Inc. case, you might usefully keep in mind the following questions: How well is FBO's existing scheduling system for refueling operations working at Metro Airport? What are ways to improve the existing pooling concept? Based on your evaluation of alternatives under consideration, as described in the case, what recommendations would you make to Mr. Reiling? (Note: In order to focus your analysis, you may wish to do such things as construct an income statement for FBO, develop a schedule for the time period 6:30 a.m. to 12 noon, and estimate the utilization of available manpower and equipment.) List and consider the "rules of thumb" by which FBO appears to be managed. Do you agree with them? Are there others that would better assist operations planning and control?

Another kind of waiting line awaits us at the University Health Service. How would you evaluate the performance of the Walk-In Clinic? Are waiting times now acceptable? Why are "walk-in appointments" a problem? What should Kathryn Angell do about them, if anything? What other actions, if any, would you recommend to Angell?

By now it should be apparent, contrary to popular belief, that there are ways of inventorying services. The outstanding service is designed and managed in ways that insure that it is not powerless to accommodate fluctuating demand patterns.

Match Supply and Demand
in Service Industries
W. Earl Sasser

The literature on capacity management focuses on goods and manufacturing, and many writers assume that services are merely goods with a few odd characteristics. Unfortunately, these researchers never fully explore the implications of these strange traits:

1. Services are direct; they cannot be inventoried. The perishability of services leaves the manager without an important buffer that is available to manufacturing managers.

2. There is a high degree of producer-consumer interaction in the production of service, which is a mixed blessing; on the one hand, consumers are a source of productive capacity, but on the other, the consumer's role creates uncertainty for managers about the process's time, the product's quality, and the facility's accommodation of the consumer's needs.

3. Because a service cannot be transported, the consumer must be brought to the service delivery system or the system to the consumer.

4. Because of the intangible nature of a service's output, establishing and measuring capacity levels for a service operation are often highly subjective and qualitative tasks.

Whereas the consumption of goods can be delayed, as a general rule services are produced and consumed almost simultaneously. Given this distinction, it seems clear that there are characteristics of a service delivery system that do not apply to a manufacturing one and that the service manager has to consider a different set of factors from those that would be considered by his or her counterpart in manufacturing. And if one looks at service industries, it is quite apparent that successful service executives are *managing* the capacity of their operations and that the unsuccessful are not. So, the "odd characteristics" often make all the difference between prosperity and failure.

Consider the following service managers' actions, which resulted in fiascos:

Increasing the wrong kind of capacity—In studying the battle statistics in the war for market share among airlines, competitors observed that an air carrier in a minority position on a particular route would often get a smaller proportion of the total passengers flown on the route than the share of seats flown.[1] Conversely, the dominant airline would carry a disproportionately larger share of the total passengers flown. The conclusion was obvious: Fly the seats, and you get the passengers.

In an effort to fly more seats, the airlines lined up to purchase jumbo jets. However, when competitors began flying smaller planes more frequently on the same routes and reaping a good number of passengers, it became painfully apparent to many airlines that frequency (and, to some extent, timing) of departures is the key to market share. Consequently, the airlines "mothballed" many of the jumbos or sold them if they could.

Not increasing all-around capacity—A resort operator decided to increase the number of rooms in a lodging facility and not to expand the central services required to support the additional guests. The fact that room rentals contribute up to 90% of total revenue and that tennis courts, swimming pools, meeting rooms, parking areas, and so on contribute next to nothing, or nothing, convinced the operator to create an imbalance in favor of revenue-producing activities. However, the number of guests adjusted itself to the level of occupancy that the central services could support, not to the level of room capacity. The room capacity beyond the level supported by the central services was wasted.

Not considering the competitive reaction—The Orlando, Florida, lodging industry's response to the announcement of Disney World's opening is a classic example of this type of service management fiasco. Disney executives had learned well the lessons of Orange County, California, and Disneyland, where revenue is limited to on-site entertainment, food, and souvenir dollars. However, businesses besides Disney have made large profits in lodging, restaurant, and recreational facilities. Correctly perceiving that the same thing would happen in Florida, Disney purchased 200,000 acres south of Orlando, eight times the number owned in Anaheim.

When news broke that Disney would build in central Florida, however, everybody with a hotel or motel in his or her portfolio began plans for Orlando units, even through Disney had preempted all the land within two miles of the Magic Kingdom. The subsequent overbuilding has been well documented. More than

---

1. See William E. Fruhan, Jr., *The Fight for Competitive Advantage: A Study of the United States Domestic Trunk Air Carrier* (Boston: Division of Research, Harvard Business School, 1972).

Exhibit 1
Comparison of Chase Demand and Level Capacity Strategies
for the XYZ Brokerage Firm

	Chase Demand	*Level Capacity*
Labor-skill level required	Low	High
Job discretion	Low	High
Compensation rate	Low	High
Working conditions	Sweatshop	Pleasant
Training required per employee	Low	High
Labor turnover	High	Low
Hire-fire costs	High	Low
Error rate	High	Low
Amount of supervision required	High	Low
Type of budgeting and forecasting required	Short-run	Long-run

30,000 rooms were built to service a market estimated to need only 19,000. As an Orlando lender moaned, "We had a great little 200-room property there, the only one at the intersection. In less than a year, there were 5,000 rooms either built, under construction, or planned within a quarter mile of that intersection. We had to foreclose, and our occupancy has been running at only 35%."

Undercutting one's own service—A new entrant in the overnight air freight transportation industry discovered that attempts to capture market share by adding to the existing number of planes and branch offices increased costs faster than revenues. Still looking for market share, the company then offered lower rates for second- and third-day deliveries. Because it had excess capacity, however, the company always delivered packages on the next day. As consumers discovered this fact, the mix of business shifted dramatically to the lower-priced services. So although there was an increase in volume, the resulting lower margins pushed the break-even volume even higher.

These pitfalls are not inevitable. Successful service executives do avoid them, and there are enough examples of well-managed service businesses from which to glean some wisdom on how to match demand for services with capacity to supply them. There are two basic capacity-management strategies available to most companies and a number of ways open to executives to manage both the demand and supply sides of their businesses. I will discuss the strategies and choices in turn.

TWO BASIC STRATEGIES

Consider the national operations group of the XYZ brokerage firm. The group, housed in an office building located in the Wall Street area, handles the transactions generated by registered representatives in more than 100 branch offices throughout the United States. As with all firms in the brokerage industry, XYZ's transactions must be settled within five trading days. This five-day period allows operations managers to smooth out the daily volume fluctuations.

But fundamental shifts in the stock market's volume and mix can occur overnight, and the operations manager must be prepared to handle extremely wide swings in volume. For example, on the strength of an "international peace" rumor, the number of transactions for XYZ rose from 5,600 one day to 12,200 the next.

However, managers of XYZ, not unlike their counterparts in other firms, have trouble predicting volume. In fact, a random number generator can predict volume a month or even a week into the future almost as well as the managers can.

How do the operations managers in XYZ manage capacity when there are such wide swings? The answer differs according to the tasks and constraints facing each manager. Here's what two managers in the same firm might say:

- Manager A—"The capacity in our operation is currently 12,000 transactions per day. Of course, what we should gear up for is always a problem. For example, our volume this year ranged from 4,000 to 15,000 transactions per day. It's a good thing we have a turnover rate, because in periods of low volume it helps us reduce our personnel without the morale problems caused by layoffs." (The labor turnover rate in this department is over 100% per year.)
- Manager B—"For any valid budgeting procedure, one needs to estimate volume within 15%. Correlations between actual and expected volume in the brokerage industry have been so poor that I question the value of budgeting at all. I maintain our capacity at a level of 17,000 transactions per day."

Why the big difference in capacity management in the same firm? Manager A is in charge of the cashiering operation—the handling of certificates, checks, and cash. The personnel in cashiering are messengers, clerks, and supervisors. The equipment—file cabinets, vaults, calculators—is uncomplicated.

Manager B, however, is in charge of handling orders, an information-processing function. The personnel are key-punch operators, EDP specialists, and systems analysts. The equipment is complex—cathode ray tubes, key-punch machines, computers, and communication devices that link national operations with the branches. The employees under B's control had performed their tasks manually until increased volume and a standardization of the information needs made it worthwhile to install computers.

Because the lead times required to increase the capacity of the information-processing operation are long, however, and the incremental cost of the capacity to handle the last 5,000 transactions is low (only some extra peripheral equipment is needed), Manager B maintains the capacity to handle 17,000 transactions per day. He holds to this level even though the average number of daily transactions for any month has never been higher than 11,000 and the number of transactions for any one day has never been higher than 16,000.

Because a great deal of uncertainty about the future status of the stock certificate exists, the situation is completely different in cashiering. Attempts to automate the cashiering function to the degree reached by the order-processing group have been thwarted because the risk of selecting a system not compatible with the future format of the stock certificate is so high.

In other words, Manager A is tied to the "chase demand" strategy, and his counterpart, Manager B, in the adjacent office, is locked into the "level capacity" strategy. However, each desires to incorporate more of the other's strategy into his own. A is developing a computerized system to handle the information-processing requirements of cashiering; B is searching for some variable costs in the order-processing operation that can be deleted in periods of low volume.

The characteristics of these two vastly different strategies are outlined in *Exhibit 1*.

Service managers using the chase strategy are usually responsible for unskilled employees performing jobs with little or no discretion for low pay in a relatively unattractive environment. Managers use the level strategy most often where more highly skilled people perform jobs for high pay, with some or a lot of discretion in a relatively pleasant environment.

Because the skill-level requirement for "chase" is lower than that for "level," the training cost per employee will also be lower for "chase." However, the annual training costs in a department using the chase strategy could be much higher than for one using the level strategy. The chase strategy requires more employees, and those employees exhibit a higher rate of turnover because of the job characteristics just described.

The chase strategy is usually more costly than the level strategy for other reasons as well. The high turnover rate and the use of unskilled employees both contribute to a high error rate, which means that more supervisors are needed to ensure that jobs are performed according to specifications.

For the chase strategy, the lead times required to attract and train new employees in periods of increased volume and to reduce the work force in periods of contraction are so short that forecasting and budgeting is needed only for the short run. However, because managers using a level strategy need a longer lead time to acquire or dispose of equipment and trained personnel, for them, forecasting and budgeting is a long-run process.

Although the chase demand strategy has many negative connotations for enlightened managers, there are some service delivery systems, such as amusement parks and resort hotels with highly seasonal or random fluctuations in demand, that survive only as a result of its successful application.

MANAGING DEMAND AND SUPPLY

Besides electing to adopt one of the strategies just described, the service executive may select one or another additional way to cope with a fluctuating demand schedule. To understand how one business did it, see the boxed insert "Finding a Creative Solution," pages 471–472.

Altering Demand

The manager can attempt to affect demand by developing off-peak pricing schemes, nonpeak promotions, complementary services, and reservation systems. Let's look at each of these demand-leveling options in turn:

Pricing. One method managers use to shift demand from peak periods to nonpeak ones is to employ a differential pricing scheme, which might also increase primary demand for the nonpeak periods. Examples of such schemes are numerous. They include matinee prices for movies, happy hours at bars, family nights at the ball park on week nights, weekend and night rates for long-distance calls, peak-load pricing by utility companies, and two-for-one coupons at restaurants on Tuesday nights.

Developing Nonpeak Demand. Most service managers wrestle constantly with ideas to increase volume during periods of low demand, especially in those facilities with a high-fixed, low-variable cost structure. The impact of those incremental revenue dollars on the profitability of the business is tremendous. Examples of attempts to develop nonpeak demand are not hard to find. Hamburger chains add breakfast items to their menus, and coffee shops add dinners to theirs. Urban hotels, which cater to the business traveler during the week, develop weekend "minivacation" packages for the suburban population in their geographic areas, while resort hotels, jammed with pleasure travelers during school vacations, develop special packages for business groups during off-seasons.

However, caution must be used in developing plans to increase demand for the underused periods of the service facility. Many companies have made costly mistakes by introducing such schemes and not seeing the impact they would have on existing operations. As Wickham Skinner has noted, for manufacturing companies, there are some real costs associated with "unfocusing" the service delivery system, which is exactly what market-expanding activities have a tendency to do.[2] New concepts often require equipment and skills not currently found in a service delivery system. The addition of these skills and equipment may require a new type of labor force, a new layout, or more supervision.

Even if the new concept succeeds in creating demand in nonpeak periods, the effects are not always positive. Managers often use slack time productively as a time to train new employees, do maintenance on the equipment, clean the premises, prepare for the next peak, and give the workers some relief from the frantic pace of the peak periods. A new concept, therefore, may have a tendency to reduce the efficiency of the present system at best, or, at worst, to destroy the delicate balance found in most service delivery systems.

Developing Complementary Services. Another method managers use to shift demand away from peak periods is to develop complementary services, which either attract consumers away from bottleneck operations at peak times or provide them with an alternative service while they are in the queue for the capacity-restricted operations. For example, restaurant owners have discovered that on busy nights most patrons complain less when sitting in a lounge with cocktails than when standing in line as they wait for tables in the dining area. Also, the profitability of restaurants with bars can more than double.

A diversion can also relieve waiting time. A hotel manager installed mirrors on each floor's central lobby so that customers could check their appearance while they waited for the elevator. Banking by mail or by automated tellers are other ways to cut down customer waiting time.

Creating Reservation Systems. Service executives can effectively manage demand by employing a reservation system, which in essence presells the productive capacity of the service delivery system. When certain time periods are booked at a particular service facility, managers can often deflect excess demand to other time slots at the same facility or to other facilities at the same company and thereby reduce waiting time substantially and, in some cases, guarantee the customer service.

For instance, if a motel chain has a national reservation system, the clerk can usually find a customer a room in another motel of the chain in a fairly close proximity to his or her desired location if the first-choice motel is full.

In a similar manner, airlines are often able to deflect demand from booked flights to those with excess capacity or from coach demand to first class, especially

2. See Wickham Skinner, "The Focused Factory," *Harvard Business Review,* May–June 1974, p. 113.

if their competitors do not have seats available at the consumers' desired flight time.

However, reservation systems are not without their problems, the major one being "no-shows." Consumers often make reservations they do not use, and, in many cases, the consumer is not financially responsible for the failure to honor the reservation. To account for no-shows, some service companies oversell their capacity and run the risk of incurring the wrath of customers like Ralph Nader, who do show. Many service companies have made it a policy to bill for capacity reserved but not used if the reservation is not cancelled prior to a designated time.

Controlling Supply

The service manager has more direct influence on the supply aspects of capacity planning than he or she does on the demand side. There are several things a service manager can do to adjust capacity to fluctuating demand.

Using Part-time Employees. Many service companies have found that it is more efficient to handle demand whenever it occurs than it is to attempt to smooth out the peaks. The peaks vary by type of business—during certain hours of the day (restaurant), during certain days of the week (hair styling), during certain weeks of the month (banking), and during certain months of the year (income tax services). These service businesses usually maintain a base of full-time employees who operate the facility during nonrush periods but who need help during peak periods. One of the best-known resources is part-time labor pools, especially high school and college students, parents who desire work during hours when their children are in school, and moonlighters who desire to supplement their primary source of income.

Maximizing Efficiency. Many service managers analyze their processes to discover ways to get the most out of their service delivery systems during peak demand periods. In effect, such analyses enable the service company to increase its peak capacity for little additional cost.

For example, during rush periods employees perform only the tasks that are essential to delivering the service. If possible, managers use slack periods for doing supporting tasks, which in essence they are inventorying for peak periods.

To maximize efficiency, managers examine even peak-time tasks to discover if certain skills are lacking or are inefficiently used. If these skills can be made more productive, the effective capacity of the system can be increased. For example, paramedics and paralegals have significantly increased the productive time of doctors and lawyers. Even rearranging the layout of the service delivery system can have a major impact on the productivity of the providers of the service.

Another way to attack the peak capacity constraint is by cross-training. The

Finding a Creative Solution

A southeastern U.S. resort had a problem: in all probability, the demand for its tennis facilities would be very high in July and August, higher than it had the capacity to serve. Management knew it could build extra courts, at a cost of $12,000 each, but since those courts would only be used during the vacation months, they would cause a net loss to the company.

The managers agreed that each guest who wanted to play tennis should get the chance to play at least once a day for an hour. Agreeing on a service level established a base line for the number of court hours needed. The resort estimated that twice the number of courts it had was needed, and because there was no more room for the additional courts at the existing location, decided to build a new tennis clubhouse and a shop at a new site, all of which would be costly.

When balanced against the costs associated with not having enough courts for guests at a resort that had heavily promoted its tennis facilities in the national media, however, the projected costs seemed small. Management saw the prospect of losing contributions if guests did not return in the future because of inadequate tennis facilities as a real cost, and the prospect of losing a real estate deal as a catastrophe. To cope with its capacity problem, management made several new moves.

To manage the demand, the resort managers made sure that all promotional literature carried a warning to prospective guests that the courts would be crowded in July and August. A reservation system to allocate court time made it possible to steer demand to times when the courts were often not in use. Changing the court fees increased the attractiveness of doubles play (four could play for the same price as two.) Recognizing that the real deterrent to doubles was not money but available partners, the resort set up tennis mixers and round robins. These were held at the beginning of each week to enable the new group of vacationers to meet and size up each other's tennis game. Finally, by promoting activities that were not filled to capacity, such as surfing, sailing, and nature walks, manage-

> *ment reduced the tennis demand and shifted some of it from peak hours.*
>
> *The resort was just as innovative in managing capacity. First, it added lights to a number of courts so that tennis play could continue after dusk. Second, the resort opened the courts at 6 A.M., two hours earlier than before, and provided complimentary coffee and doughnuts to the "early birds." Finally, management built a few new courts but neither a clubhouse nor a tennis shop at the new site. Instead, a tent was set up to house someone to check reservations, collect fees, and sell balls. The original shop and clubhouse served the other needs. The overflow tennis area was opened only in the peak months and was staffed mainly with college students on summer vacation.*
>
> *The combined effect of these moves was that the total investment in the new courts and facilities turned out to be much less than the original estimate. In fact, the moves helped make tennis a profitable operation.*

service delivery system is composed of various components. When the system is delivering one service at full capacity, some sections of the system are likely to be underused. If the employees in these sections are able to deliver the peak service, they add capacity at the bottleneck. When the demand shifts and creates a bottleneck in other components of the system, the employees can shift back again.

Increasing Consumer Participation. The more the consumer does, the lower the labor requirements of the producer. Bag-'em-yourself groceries, salad bars at restaurants, self-service gas pumps, customer-filled-out insurance information forms, and cook-it-yourself restaurants are all examples of increased consumer participation in the production of services.

There are, of course, some risks to increasing consumer input: consumers might reject the idea of doing the work and paying for it too; the manager's control over delivery of the service is reduced; and such a move can create competition for the service itself. A cook-it-yourself restaurant customer might just stay at home.

Sharing Capacity. The delivery of a service often requires the service business to invest in expensive equipment and labor skills that are necessary to perform the service but that are not used at full capacity. In such cases, the service manager might consider sharing capacity with another business to use required, expensive, but underused resources jointly.

For example, a group of hospitals in a large urban area might agree that it is unnecessary for each to purchase expensive medical equipment for every ailment and that they ought to share capacity. One would buy cardiac equipment, another gynecological and obstetrical equipment, another kidney machines. Participating doctors would have admitting privileges at all hospitals. By sharing equipment, hospitals would not only better use expensive resources, but as groups of trained and experienced specialists developed at each facility, hospitals would also deliver better medical care.

The shared-capacity concept is possible in the airline industry in several forms. Several airlines with infrequent flights in and out of a particular airport share gates, ramps, baggage-handling equipment, and ground personnel. In fact, some domestic airlines flying different routes with different seasonal demands exchange aircraft when one's dip in demand coincides with another's peak.

Investing in the Expansion Ante. Wise service managers often invest in an "expansion ante." When growth occurs, it sometimes becomes clear that some of the new development could have been done when the facility was originally constructed for much less cost and disruption. A careful analysis before the facility is built will show what these items are. For instance, for a small investment, a restaurateur can build his kitchen with extra space in order to service more diners later on. Contractors can run wiring, plumbing, and air conditioning ducts to the edge of the building where the expansion will take place. The manager can inventory enough land for the expansion and additional parking requirements. These actions will allow the restaurant manager to increase capacity without having to renovate the kitchen, redo the wiring, plumbing, and air conditioning systems, or purchase adjacent land at much higher prices.

SEEKING THE BEST FIT

Managing demand and supply is a key task of the service manager. Although there are two basic strategies for capacity management, the enlightened service manager will, in almost all cases, deviate from these two extremes.

The challenge to the service manager is to find the best fit between demand and capacity. In order to manage the shifting balance that characterizes service industries, managers need to plan rather than react. For example, managers should try to make forecasts of demand for the time periods under question. Then he or she should break the service delivery system down into its component parts, calculate the present capacity of each component, and arrive at a reasonable estimate of what the use of each component will be, given the demand forecast.

Because each system cannot handle infinite demands, the manager needs to question how much of the peak demand the system must handle. Just what is the appropriate level of service for the delivery system to provide? Once the manager can approximate the answer to these questions and has decided which of the basic strategies to employ, he or she is ready to experiment with the different options to alter demand and capacity. Each plan and option a manager arrives at can be costed, and the best fit for the particular service selected.

Ultimately, of course, on the demand side, a manager's true aim is to increase revenues through an existing service delivery system of given capacity. Once the true variable costs are subtracted out, all revenues flow to the bottom line. On the supply side, the manager aims to minimize costs needed to increase or decrease capacity.

When facing increased demand, the business raises its revenues with minimal investment. In times of capital rationing, small investments are often the only ones available to the company. When facing contracting demand, the manager needs to select the best way to adjust the system's capacity to a lower volume.

In following the ideas outlined in this article, service managers need to think creatively about new ways to manage demand and supply. The most important thing to recognize is that they both can be managed efficiently and that the key to doing so lies in planning.

FBO, Inc.

It was a beautiful day in July. John Reiling, general manager of FBO, Inc., sat at his desk and thought through, once again, the contract refueling operations for the commercial airline flights that FBO serviced at Metro Airport. Reiling felt that the present refueling operations were inefficient. Although the scheduling of contract refueling operations had been problematic for a long time, Reiling was particularly concerned now because costs had increased while revenues had remained level. As a result, profit margins had begun to drop.

To complicate matters, FBO employees at Metro were unionized and they were satisfied with the present refueling operations. Since FBO had experienced union problems concerning work changes in the past, Reiling felt that the union and the individual employees might resist changes in the refueling operations. However, he felt certain that improved scheduling in the refueling operations would result in considerable cost savings. Reiling summarized his opinion: "Since the union is pleased with the present mode of operations, there must be a better way to do things."

BACKGROUND

Services. FBO was licensed by the Metropolis Airport Commission to operate at Metro Airport under the terms of a 15-year permit that would expire in three years. Commercial airlines contracted with FBO to provide refueling services for commercial flights. FBO's retail operation provided numerous services to private and corporate aircraft. Typical retail services included fueling, baggage handling, vehicle maintenance, hangar/aircraft storage, maintenance and avionics services, office cleaning, and collection of aircraft parking fees.

Competition. FBO and its single competitor, Acme Aviation, were the only aviation services licensed to operate at Metro Airport. Corporate and private aircraft used the services of either FBO or Acme, as did commercial airlines electing not to provide their own refueling services. FBO serviced nine of the eighteen commercial airlines; Acme serviced six. Three commercial airlines self-serviced.

Financial Performance. The commercial operations accounted for approximately 40% of FBO's revenue at Metro. Retail operations accounted for the remaining 60%. Total revenues had been steady for the past few years, approximately $3.2 million per year.

Facilities. FBO operated from three locations at the airport: Hanger 6, Hangar 8, and the Central Terminal Building.

Hangar 6 contained FBO's own administrative offices and its corporate/private aircraft services lobby, as well as the dispatch counter and pilots' lounge, aircraft hangar/storage space, maintenance, and avionics services. Hangar 8 housed FBO's fleet of aircraft refueling vehicles as well as other automotive ground handling equipment. The Central Terminal Building housed FBO's small line shack, which served as a ready room for its commercial airline refueling staff.

Employees. FBO employed 82 people at Metro, including nine managers. Seventy-three were union employees, of which 23 worked in the contract refueling operation. The age range of employees was 20–60 years. Duration of employment ranged from 2 to 25 years; average length of employment was approximately 8.5 years.

UNION-MANAGEMENT RELATIONS

FBO's employees were represented by the International Brotherhood of Teamsters, Chauffeurs, Warehousemen and Helpers of America, Local #999. The union contract was renegotiated every two years. FBO management felt the contract was cumbersome and expensive because of specific work rules and restrictive employee classifications, but especially because of the rules for awarding overtime.

Seniority played an important role at FBO. When new shift schedules were made, they were given to employees for bidding. The most senior employees within each classification had first choice of shifts. Overtime was also offered by seniority. However, junior employees were required to accept overtime assignments that were rejected by more senior employees. *Exhibit 1* presents excerpts from the union contract regarding hours of work and overtime.

The union had organized FBO sixteen years ago. Since that time, FBO's relations with the union had not been cordial. The company had suffered strikes during two of the last three contract negotiations. During the negotiations that took place five years ago, at issue was the number of refuelers that should be used to service a plane. Previously, this task had required two refuelers. Management felt that only one person was necessary. A nine-week strike ensued before this issue was granted to management. During the contract negotiations that took place three years before, employee classifications was a major issue. The company wanted to eliminate all group classifications that were unrelated to hangar activities. Elimination of refueler, tower, and ramp classifications meant that an employee could perform all three tasks. The union was opposed to such changes. After a two-week strike, management withdrew its demand and signed a contract. There had been no strike one year earlier when a settlement was reached which included a 7% wage increase.

CONTRACT REFUELING—COMMERCIAL SERVICES

Contract Arrangements. The airlines serviced by FBO arranged contracts with both FBO and an oil company. The oil company supplied the fuel at an agreed-upon price while FBO acted as a mediator, collecting fuel from the oil company and dispensing it to the planes. FBO's contract with an airline included total gallons to be dispensed during a year as well as a fixed, per gallon pumping fee. The pumping fee was, on average , 2.56¢ per gallon. This year, FBO had contracted to deliver approximately 50 million gallons.

Equipment. FBO utilized 11 fuel trucks in the commercial refueling operations. The trucks were leased at a cost of $1,200 per truck per month and had capacities of 7,800 gallons each. Operating and maintenance costs amounted to about $5,000 per year. This cost included fuel and oil for operating the trucks, as well as parts and labor for maintenance, but it did not include the refuelers' salaries.

Fuel Requirements. While the total number of gallons to be pumped during the year was contracted, the specific amount of fuel to be pumped into a plane was decided daily by the airlines. The quantity of fuel required depended on the type of plane, its destination, its passenger load, and weather conditions.

Airline personnel usually waited until a few hours before departure to determine the exact amount of fuel needed for each flight in order to take advantage of the most current information about the weather and passenger loads. Occasionally, fuel requests were changed even as passengers were boarding the plane. When airline personnel determined the amount of fuel needed, the quantity was recorded on a card that was held by the airline dispatchers[1] for pickup by FBO. A refueler could not service a plane until he or she had the proper card, which was prepared in triplicate: one copy was left with the dispatcher; a second copy was retained by FBO; a third copy was left with gate personnel. *Exhibit 2* shows

---

1. Although FBO serviced nine airlines, only four dispatch counters were available because some of the larger airlines handled dispatching, arrival, and departure information for smaller airlines.

the various types of planes that FBO refueled and the quantities of fuel each type required.

Flight Schedules. In the contract refueling operation, FBO serviced 98 commercial flights per day, Monday through Friday; 81 flights on Saturday and 85 flights on Sunday. Two large boards, coinciding with FBO's two daily shifts, were maintained at the pool (a small line shack located in the airport terminal) with a complete schedule of the estimated time of arrival (ETA) and estimated time of departure (ETD) for all flights serviced by FBO. Airline schedules changed about two or three times a year. The Monday–Friday schedule of airline arrivals and departures for the summer, including aircraft type, appears in *Exhibit 3.*

Several planes serviced by FBO were grounded overnight. However, because of safety concerns, these planes could not be refueled until morning. The refueling cards were usually available at 6:00 A.M. and refuelers generally began refueling at about 7:00 A.M.

Performance Criteria. Essential performance criteria for refueling operations were on-time, courteous service; safety; and quality fuel.

1. *On-time service.* FBO met each plane as it arrived at the gate and completed refueling operations as quickly as possible. If necessary, however, FBO could service a plane up until just before the plane was ready to pull away from the gate, without causing a delay. Management ideally wanted refueling to be completed at least five minutes before departure time.

2. *Safety.* Refuelers maneuvered trucks carefully to avoid collisions with planes. Refuelers backing into or out of fueling positions were required to have assistance. However, refuelers pulling away from a plane in a forward direction were permitted to do so unassisted.

3. *Quality fuel.* Refuelers made sure that the proper fuel was dispensed to the plane and that the fuel contained no contaminants. Fuel trucks were emptied every morning to remove water that might have condensed inside the tanks overnight.

4. *Courteous service.* FBO management insisted that their employees deliver their services courteously.

Organization of Refueling Operations. Contract refueling operations utilized a pooling concept. Employees and trucks were assigned to a pool. A small 8' x 18' line shack located in the airport terminal served as the refueler's pool. About 700 yards from the pool, near the taxi-ways, were parking spaces for the fuel trucks. FBO had been unable to secure permission from the Airport Commission to move these parking spaces closer to the terminals. However, drivers could park momentarily outside the line shack to ascertain whether they were immediately needed. In addition, one or two parking spaces about 50 yards from the pool were allocated to drivers whose services were required within two or three minutes.

Refueling operations required the services of one lead refueler, one floater, and several regular refuelers. The lead refueler was responsible for distributing assignments to the refuelers. (When necessary, the lead would refuel planes, but would never top trucks because topping would require the lead to be away from the pool for too long a time period.) The work had to be coordinated so that planes were serviced without delay and fuel trucks were refilled (topped) when necessary.

The floater was responsible for driving a station wagon throughout a shift, collecting fueling cards from the dispatchers, driving refuelers to and from fuel trucks, and helping refuelers back up their trucks.

Regular refuelers reported to the pool and waited for assignments. A refueler might be assigned to refuel a plane or top a truck too low on fuel to be used in another refueling. The lead frequently gave a refueler two or three assignments at one time. A lead refueler earned approximately $7.50 an hour; a refueler earned $6.50 an hour. In addition, fringe benefits represented about 25% of straight-time pay.

Communications with the Airlines. Refuelers had no contact with the control tower and no formal communication with individual airlines and therefore did not know in advance whether a given plane would arrive on time. FBO had not tapped into the closed-circuit television communication system. To tap into the system would require the installation of four separate channels. Management considered the estimated cost of about $4,000 to $5,000 per installation to be an excessive expense. In addition, the television information was not updated quickly enough to be useful, and important airplane landing information was not provided.

Despite this absence of communication, FBO personnel generally knew that a plane was on the ground before a refueler was dispatched. Airline personnel often (but not always) phoned the lead refueler in the ready room if planes were behind schedule. In addition, dispatchers usually knew which planes would arrive late and informed the FBO floater. This information reduced the number of unnecessary trips to the gate.

Communication among the Refuelers. The floater informed the lead refueler by walkie-talkie which flights had fuel cards, how much fuel each plane required, and whether an assigned plane would arrive on schedule. The lead then issued assignments without waiting for fuel cards. By driving around the airport, the floater could determine when a refueling truck needed assistance in backing up, and when to drive a refueler from the truck parking area to the ready room. The floater also informed the lead when refueling assignments were completed.

The floater, upon request from the lead, then drove refuelers to their trucks or issued new assignments to refuelers.

FBO management had considered installing radios in fuel trucks to improve efficiency of refueling operations, but Reiling had objected. In his words, "You put radios in those trucks and the employees will steal them faster than you can say FBO."

In order to determine when to dispatch refuelers, the lead utilized the airline schedule, information from the floater, and information telephoned in by airline personnel. The lead utilized fueling cards as well as information obtained directly from the refuelers and the floater. The lead did not always know how much fuel was in each truck, especially during peak periods or when a refueler had been given several assignments at one time.

Refueling Process. Upon receiving an assignment, the refueler checked to see if a truck was available at or near the pool. If not, the floater, upon request from the lead, drove the refueler to the regular truck parking area. The refueler picked up the necessary fuel card from the lead or the floater.

The refueler then drove to the gate to meet the assigned plane. If the plane had not yet arrived, the refueler checked with gate personnel. If the expected arrival time was within five minutes, the refueler would wait. Otherwise, the refueler drove back to the pool in case another plane needed immediate refueling. Trucks not needed within two or three minutes were parked near the pool if space was available. Otherwise, the truck was returned to the regular parking area, usually after the refueler requested personal transport.

A refueler might, unknown to the lead, be using a fuel truck with insufficient fuel to complete an assignment. Under those circumstances, the refueler would start pumping fuel into the plane and then phone the load to request a backup truck. Occasionally, however, the refueler did not check the fuel supply in advance, and ran out of fuel before completing an assignment. Such an occurrence might create a departure delay.

Often the lead, knowing a truck had insufficient fuel to complete an assignment, assigned the truck along with a backup truck. This procedure was designed to reduce the number of fuel tank refills.

Topping Trucks. The lead recorded the amount of fuel in each truck, and presumably knew if a refill was needed after an assignment was completed. If a truck needed refilling, the lead requested to have the truck topped immediately at the fuel farm.[2] If the lead was unaware that a truck needed refilling, the refueler returned to the pool and informed the lead. If enough fuel remained,

---

2. The fuel farm, located on the far side of the airport, was maintained by the oil companies, and consisted of several large fuel pumps that supplied various kinds of aviation fuel.

the refueler—under direction of the lead—completed another assignment, returned to the pool, or drove to the regular parking area.

Time Requirements. The following list describes each aspect of the fueling process and time required for completion:

1. Driving from the pool to the regular parking area—two to three minutes.
2. Driving to the gate from the pool—two to three minutes.
3. Refueling the plane—15–20 minutes.
4. Driving from the gate to the truck parking area—two-to-three minutes.
5. Driving to the fuel farm—10 minutes.
6. Topping off the truck—20 minutes.
7. Driving back from the fuel farm—10 minutes.

Staffing and Shift Schedule. Contract refueling operations employed 23 refuelers, each of whom worked five shifts per week. Each shift was 8-1/3 hours (8 paid hours). Employees were permitted to take two 10-minute breaks. Employees also had a 10-minute cleanup period at the end of the shift. The union contract required that the half-hour meal break be given between the third and one-half and fifth and one-half hours of each shift. Breaks were not formally scheduled. The aggregate shift schedule appears in *Exhibit 4*. The schedule for the individual shifts appears in *Exhibit 5*.

Overtime. FBO shifts did not exceed 8 1/3 hours, but the company's budget allowed for overtime wages at about 10% of straight-time wages paid during the year. FBO attributed overtime to three main factors: (1) Airline schedules were disrupted by bad weather as well as pilot and flight controller slowdowns, which caused late arrivals and schedule delays of several hours. As a result, refuelers remained at the airport to service delayed flights. Flight schedules were disrupted by bad weather and slowdowns approximately 36 days a year. (2) Each year there were 11 paid holidays, during which overtime was paid at 2 1/2 times the straight-time rate. (3) Additional overtime was incurred to cover unscheduled absences of refuelers. In fact, the absenteeism rate, currently about 8%, had increased in recent years and was a major contributor to excessive overtime wages, currently about 14% of straight-time wages.

ALTERNATIVES UNDER CONSIDERATION

Reiling focused on improving the scheduling of fueling operations. He considered assigning refuelers to specific trucks, to specific airlines, to top fuel trucks only, or a combination of these alternatives. Reiling's goal was to achieve maximum utilization of manpower and to improve cost control. He hoped he could reduce the number of trucks and associated maintenance costs, as well as reduce person-nel requirements. In the event that fewer people were needed, FBO would not lay off employees but would allow its work force to shrink through attrition.

By assigning employees to specific trucks, Reiling believed drivers would take better care of their vehicles because of a feeling of ownership and pride. In the event of damage to a vehicle, management would have greater control since the driver would be known. He believed this plan would reduce truck maintenance costs by 5% to 10%. By assigning specific people to particular airlines, he hoped to provide better service to the airlines and have refuelers develop relationships with airline personnel. In addition, refuelers would become familiar with the flight schedules of their designated planes.

Reiling realized that there were risks in these alternatives. Flexibility would be reduced. Workers might refuse, even in emergencies, to refuel planes that were not affiliated with their designated airlines. Reiling wondered if he should simply utilize the pool concept more efficiently.

Reiling was convinced he could do *something* to improve the refueling opera-tions significantly. During the last strike, FBO managers did all of the servicing. These managers, who had previously done strike work together, worked 12-hour shifts, seven days a week. During this time the commercial refueling opera-tions were not organized under the pool concept. Instead, teams were assigned to specific airlines. Management felt that under this system they were able to provide more efficient service to the airlines. During the strike 14 managers handled the commercial refueling operations normally handled by 23 union em-ployees.

IMPLEMENTATION

The implementation of any new plan worried Reiling. The transition would be very difficult. Should changes be made on a piecemeal basis or all at once? He favored piecemeal changes because he could experiment and then select the best system. He could also present the problem and solutions to the union and the employees and solicit their support. If they had the opportunity to influence a final decision, they might be more tolerant of change. They might also contribute some good ideas. On the other hand, the union always believed that management was trying to lay off people. Perhaps the union would not be willing to coop-erate.

Nevertheless, new schedules were coming up for bids in September, and a decision had to be made. In addition, Reiling wanted to make changes in the summer because delays were much less serious in the summer. Employees might slow down operations if they opposed a new strategy. If enough delays were caused during the winter, the airlines could petition the Airport Commission, who could give FBO 30 days' notice to vacate the airport.

Pondering all these issues, Reiling gazed out at the clear summer sky, trying to formulate a strategy for operations and an implementation plan.

Exhibit 1
Excerpts from the Most Recent Union Agreement

HOURS OF WORK AND OVERTIME

A. Eight (8) consecutive hours in the twenty-four- (24-) hour period following the time an employee starts a scheduled shift, exclusive of an unpaid lunch period, will constitute a regular work day.

B. Forty (40) hours consisting of five (5) days of eight (8) hours each, worked within seven (7) consecutive days will constitute a regular work week for an employee.

C. Overtime at the rate of time and one-half shall be paid for all hours worked in excess of eight (8) in a work day.

D. Overtime at the rate of time and one-half shall be paid for all hours worked in excess of forty (40) in an employee's scheduled work week, and for all hours worked on a regularly scheduled first day off and overtime at the rate of double time for all hours worked on a regularly scheduled second day off, if the employee also works on the scheduled first day off. . . .

F. Lunch periods shall be completed between three and one-half ($3\frac{1}{2}$) and five and one-half ($5\frac{1}{2}$) hours on each shift. If the Employer requires an employee to work through such lunch period, the employee will be paid at the rate of time and one-half for time worked during such lunch period and, in addition, will be given fifteen (15) minutes for lunch at least two (2) hours before quitting time. . . .

H. An employee called back to perform work after completion of scheduled hours on a work day and after leaving the Employer's premises shall be paid the applicable overtime rate for not less than four (4) hours.

An employee who reports for work as scheduled without having been notified in advance by the Employer not to report shall receive not less than eight (8) hours of pay at this regular straight-time rate, unless the employee initiates the failure to complete the scheduled hours, is sent home for just cause, is excused from such hours at the employee's request, or no work is available as a result of work stoppage or interference with operations in connection with a labor dispute. . . .

Q. An employee who works overtime will be allowed eight (8) hours off duty between the time of completion of the overtime assignment and the start of the next scheduled shift, and will not suffer a loss of regular pay for reporting late for such next shift as a result of this allowance.

Exhibit 2
Contract Airline Refueling

Fuel Gallonage Uplifts

Airline	Type of Aircraft	Uplift Gallonage Range
Alpha	DC-9	1000–1500
	CONV-580	300–500
Beta	DC-9	1500–2400
	B727	2500–4500
	DC-10	2000–3000
Gamma	B727	2500–3500
	L-1011	3500–5000
Delta	B737	1000–1300
Epsilon	B727	1600–2000
Zeta	B727	3000–3500
Eta	DC-9	1500–2200
Theta	DC-9	1000
Iota	DC-9	1000

FBO, INC.
Exhibit 3
Summer Monday–Friday Arrival and Departure Schedule

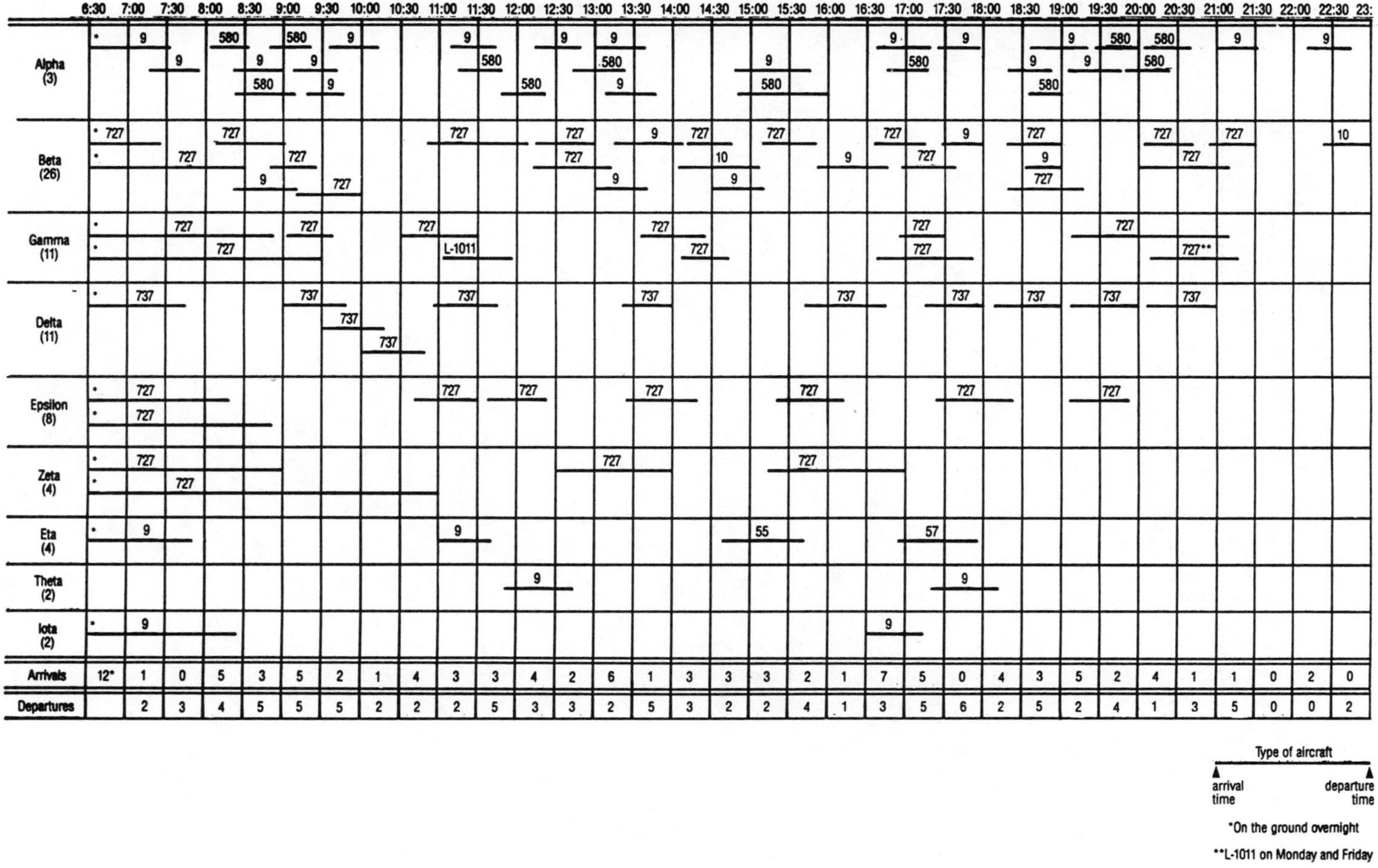

Type of aircraft

▲ departure time
▲ arrival time

*On the ground overnight
**L-1011 on Monday and Friday

485

Exhibit 4
Aggregate Staffing Schedule—Commercial Refueling

Shift	Number of Refuelers per Shift						
	Mon	Tues	Wed	Thur	Fri	Sat	Sun
A_1 (6:30–14:50)	7	7	7	7	7	8	7
A_2 (7:30–15:50)	2	2	2	2	2	—	—
B_1 (14:30–22:50)	6	6	6	6	6	5	6
B_2 (15:30–23:50)	2	2	2	2	2	2	2

Exhibit 5
Individual Shift Schedule—Commercial Refueling

Title	M	T	W	Th	F	Sa	Su
A₁ Shift—6:30–14:50							
1. Lead Refueler	A_1	A_1	A_1	A_1			A_1
2. Refueler	A_1	A_1	A_1			A_1	A_1
3. Refueler		A_1	A_1	A_1	A_1	A_1	
4. Refueler			A_1	A_1	A_1	A_1	A_1
5. Refueler	A_1	A_1			A_1	A_1	A_1
6. Refueler	A_1			A_1	A_1	A_1	A_1
7. Refueler			A_1	A_1	A_1	A_1	[a]
8. Refueler	A_1	A_1	A_1	A_1	A_1		
9. Refueler	A_1	A_1	A_1			A_1	A_1
A₂ Shift—7:30–15:50							
10. Refueler	A_2	A_2	A_2	A_2	A_2		
11. Refueler	A_2	A_2	A_2	A_2	A_2		
B₁ Shift—14:30–22:50							
12. Lead Refueler		B_1	B_1	B_1	B_1	B_1	
13. Refueler	A_1	A_1	B_1	B_1			A_1
14. Refueler			B_1	B_1	B_1	B_1	B_1
15. Refueler	B_1	B_1			B_1	B_1	B_1
16. Refueler	B_1	B_1	B_1	B_1			B_1
17. Refueler	B_1	B_1	B_1	B_1	B_1		
18. Refueler	B_1	B_1			B_1	B_1	B_1
19. Refueler			B_1	B_1	B_1	B_1	B_1
B₂ Shift—15:30–23:50							
20. Refueler	B_1	B_2	B_2	B_2	B_2		
21. Refueler	B_2			B_2	B_2	B_2	B_2
22. Refueler	B_2	B_2	B_2			B_2	B_2
23. Alternate Lead	B_1	B_1			A_1	A_1	B_1
Refueler	[a]			A_1	[a]	[a]	[a]

[a]Works shift on the retail side of the field.

University Health Services: Walk-In Clinic

K athryn Angell stared out her office window at Holyoke Center in July 1980, oblivious to the bustle on Mount Auburn Street. In July 1979, shortly after receiving her master's degree in health policy and management from the Harvard School of Public Health, Angell had been hired as assistant director for ambulatory care at Harvard's University Health Services. A major objective of this new position was to reorganize the Walk-In Clinic—the topic of Angell's thesis.

Angell was the chief administrator of the clinic, responsible for its daily functioning, the organization of medical and support services, and overall planning. She was charged with improving the delivery of medical care through better coordination of services and implementation of new programs. Soon after assuming her duties, Angell implemented a triage system in the Walk-In Clinic, whereby arriving patients were screened by a triage coordinator to determine whether they should be treated by a nurse practitioner or a physician. A year later, Angell was ready to evaluate the clinic's performance.

UNIVERSITY HEALTH SERVICES

University Health Services (UHS) offered medical care to Harvard University students, staff, faculty, and their dependents who elected health care plans that included UHS services. Because the system was prepaid for over 90% of the potential users, UHS operated primarily as a health maintenance organization.

The medical services offered included surgical and 24-hour emergency facilities, an inpatient infirmary, four outpatient clinics (including the Walk-In and three primary care clinics associated with specific Harvard professional schools), mental health services, laboratory and X-ray facilities, and a variety of other specialized services. Patients could choose a personal physician, who could be seen by appointment in the physician's office and who would, if necessary, refer

Shauna Doyle and Rocco Pigneri prepared this case under the direction of Professor David H. Maister, as the basis for class discussion rather than to illustrate either effective or ineffective handling of an administrative situation. It was revised by Professor Christopher W. L. Hart and Lucy N. Lytle. Copyright © 1981 by the President and Fellows of Harvard College; Harvard Business School case #9-681-061 (Rev. 2/89).

the patient to a specialist. The outpatient clinics treated acute ailments and emergencies.

UHS was budgeted approximately $10 million to meet its total health care expenses for the 1979–1980 fiscal year (*Exhibit 1*). Of the total, the Walk-In Clinic accounted for approximately 20%, including its share of professional and clerical labor, overhead, and supplies. Salaries for primary care physicians ranged from $35,000 to $55,000. Nurses were paid $16,000 to $26,000, depending on their experience. UHS incurred additional costs of 18.5% of salary in benefits for both physicians and nurses.

Physicians worked 40 hours a week for 46 weeks per year. Of the 40 hours, approximately 12 were spent in the Walk-In Clinic, 16 in meeting patients by appointment in the physician's office, 5 on duty at the UHS infirmary, and 7 on administrative and other matters. By well-established precedent, all UHS primary care physicians (general practitioners) were required to undertake duty in the Walk-In Clinic. Doctors who worked part-time were usually allocated a proportionate share of their time in the clinic. Included in the time for appointments (which were usually scheduled by the physician's secretary in half-hour intervals) were two half-hour periods per week known as "reserve time." These were periods when the doctor might ask patients to see her or him in the office, perhaps to check on the progress of treatment; only the physician could schedule appointments for reserve time. The physician could sometimes see up to four patients in one half-hour of reserve time. Most doctors preferred seeing patients in their office to Walk-In Clinic duty, partly because of the hectic pace of the Walk-In Clinic, but also because they preferred treating patients with whom they were familiar.

THE WALK-IN CLINIC

The Walk-In Clinic at Holyoke Center provided the most comprehensive ambulatory care of the four UHS walk-in clinics. Patients with acute medical and surgical problems were served on a first-come, first-served basis Monday through Friday, 8 A.M. to 5:30 P.M. The clinic was also open on Saturdays from 8 A.M. to 12:45 P.M. Emergencies (of which there were few) were, of course, treated immediately. The clinic had 12 treatment rooms, four for nurses and eight for doctors. However, three of the doctors' rooms were permanently assigned to physicians as their UHS offices, and were available for Walk-In Clinic use only when those physicians were scheduled for clinic duty.

In 1979, over 37,400 patients visited the Walk-In Clinic for treatment of problems ranging from colds, nausea, and respiratory illnesses to acute appendicitis and chest pains. Of the patients who visited the clinic, 67% were students,

23% were staff, and 10% were dependents and Medex and Medicare subscribers. One UHS study conducted over a three-week period in 1980 showed that an average of 143 patients were seen per day (*Exhibits 2* and *3*).

The Walk-In Clinic was staffed on the basis of past experience with peak periods of patient visits, which typically occurred between 10 A.M. and 4 P.M. (*Exhibit 4*). No criteria existed for establishing staffing levels; minor adjustments were made each year to increase coverage in busy periods. Kathryn Angell scheduled 22 physicians for specific times throughout the week, usually in blocks of three to four hours. Because of part-timers, administrative duties, and other factors, there were on average only 150 physician-hours available per week to the Walk-In Clinic. The clinic was also staffed by two registered nurses and by 11 nurse practitioners (registered nurses with additional medical training who could treat minor ailments without consulting a physician). A few nurse practitioners also treated patients by appointment. Nurses and nurse practitioners worked eight-hour shifts, including one hour for lunch. Nurse practitioners staffed the UHS emergency room at night and on weekends; they also performed a variety of semi-administrative duties, such as receiving test results over the phone. Approximately 45% of nurse practitioners' hours were available to treat patients in the Walk-In Clinic.

PRE-TRIAGE ORGANIZATION

Before the triage system, a typical Walk-In Clinic patient provided basic identification information on a sequentially numbered sheet at the front desk, then took a seat in the waiting area. The receptionist next requested the patient's record from the Medical Records Department; retrieving it and sending it to the clinic took eight or nine minutes. The receptionist then brought the record to the medical desk, where a clerk checked to ensure that all recent lab reports were present and that the patient's address and phone number were current. When checking was completed, in about five minutes, the clerk placed the record and the numbered sheet in a pile ordered according to the arrival of patients. When a patient's record reached the top of the pile, he or she was seen by the first available nurse. If the problem was minor, the nurse provided the necessary treatment. If the patient still needed to see a doctor after 10 minutes of "diagnosis" with the nurse, he or she returned to the waiting area and the nurse put the medical record in a pile for the physicians, again according to the order of arrival. The patient was then seen by the first available physician.

Dissatisfaction with the Walk-In Clinic was widespread. The major complaint was the waiting time between sign-in and treatment. This period averaged 23 minutes, but as many as 22% of all patients had to wait more than 35 minutes for their first contact with a nurse. A November 1978 study of the clinic found that patients who requested specific physicians at sign-in waited an average of 40 minutes before seeing the desired staff member (these patients were not seen first by a nurse); this group accounted for approximately 19% of all patients. If a nurse had to refer a patient to a doctor, an average of 10 minutes elapsed between the end of the nurse visit and the meeting with the doctor. Some patients complained that the length of their wait was not related to the nature of the visit (such as a 55-minute wait for a prescription renewal). Other patients reportedly avoided visits to the clinic because of the expected wait. Patients viewed the Walk-In Clinic as cold, inefficient, and impersonal.

Members of the UHS administrative and medical staff also thought the clinic could function better. Sholem Postel, MD, deputy director and chief of professional services (physicians and nurses) at UHS, commented on the pre-triage system's problems:

All the nurses were involved in seeing all the patients initially. This created a bottleneck as each nurse independently decided the extent of care for a patient and then provided as much of that care as possible before, if necessary, having the patient wait to be seen by a physician. This led to inconsistency and too much variation in treatment, given the different skills and experience levels of individual nurses.

Furthermore, though nurses saw all the patients who did not request a particular doctor, they treated only 40% of all patients definitively. The result: duplicated efforts (time, questions, and examinations) for those patients who were subsequently sent to an MD.

THE TRIAGE SYSTEM

A triage system was introduced in September 1979 to overcome these problems. The system was defined as "the preliminary evaluation and referral of patients to the necessary health resource, based on decisions about the nature of the patients' problems and knowledge of the priorities and capabilities of the available health care resources." (*Exhibit 5* compares the total processing times under the pre-triage and triage systems. *Exhibit 6* presents the percentage of patients treated by the system's various providers.)

Under the triage system, the arriving patient filled out an Ambulatory Visit Form (AVF), which requested the reason for the visit as well as identification information (*Exhibit 7*). If the patient checked "emergency care," the receptionist immediately notified a physician, nurse practitioner, or triage coordinator, who then assessed the patient's condition. In most cases, however, the receptionist simply reviewed the AVF for completeness and requested the patient's record from Medical Records. A clerk matched the record with the AVF, ensured that all personal information and prior tests were properly filed and updated in the record, and then placed the record chronologically in a "triage pile."

One of two triage coordinators (highly experienced registered nurses) called for the patient initially. The triage coordinator visited briefly with the patient in a private room and then summarized the patient's problem. If the coordinator decided the ailment warranted more immediate care, she put the patient ahead of others waiting to see a physician.

As one triage coordinator explained:

My duties are to determine the chief complaint of the patient and to triage him or her to a physician or nurse practitioner. I'll spend three or four minutes per patient in an average encounter, and I rarely have to deviate from this—only when people are unable to clearly describe their symptoms or when they overestimate the severity of their illness. However, there is no time constraint in determining the status of a patient.

The triage coordinator did not treat the patient but determined, according to guidelines and her discretion, whether the patient needed to see a nurse practitioner or a physician in the Walk-In Clinic, or whether the problem could be better handled by an appointment or referral to another UHS service. Patients were triaged to a nurse practitioner if their ailments fell under one of 13 categories (*Exhibit 8*). All ailments outside these categories required the attention of a physician, unless the triage nurse felt a nurse practitioner could treat the problem. If a nurse practitioner treated a problem that was not included in the 13 categories, however, a physician's authorization was required. This meant the nurse had to find a doctor who would sign the medical record. In some cases, the doctor chose to meet with or examine the patient before signing the medical record. Other doctors would sign without further examination. Expanding the guidelines beyond the 13 ailments would, by state law, require detailed treatment guides so that a nurse practitioner could treat the patient without consulting a physician. UHS planned such expansion in the near future, though it was not known how many patients this might affect.

After the visit with the triage coordinator, the patient returned to the waiting area while his or her record was placed chronologically in the nurse practitioner or the physician pile, unless more immediate care was deemed necessary. Physicians saw an average of 3.1 patients per hour, and nurse practitioners, about 1.8 patients per hour, though the numbers varied widely.

When the triage system was instituted, UHS administrators expected that the waiting time to see a triage coordinator would be about 15 minutes and that waiting time to see a nurse practitioner or a physician would be less than 10 minutes. A 1980 UHS study reported, however, that patients actually waited a mean of 19.7 minutes to see the coordinator and a mean of 18.6 minutes from the start of the visit with the coordinator to the start of the visit with a nurse practitioner or a physician. The average total waiting time was 37.5 minutes, including triage time (*Exhibit 9*). Angell commented:

> When we introduced the triage system, we thought the nurse practitioners would accept more of the patient load and leave the physicians more time per patient. Unfortunately, it has not worked out that way. Among the reasons may be that the triage coordinators are sometimes classifying patients as MD/NP (physician/nurse practitioner) to maintain the flow when they feel the practitioners are backed up. The physicians' share of patients thus gets increased in overload situations. We did not want to have MD/NP as a classification and have asked the triage coordinators to stop using it. When in doubt, they are to triage the patient to a nurse practitioner.

About 5% of the patients seen by a nurse practitioner were referred to a physician. If the additional treatment was expected to be brief, the patient remained in the nurse practitioner's room until the doctor arrived. If longer treatment by the physician was anticipated, the patient joined the MD waiting line, according to his or her AVF number. Thus, any other patient in the MD queue who had arrived before the referred patient would still be seen first. Although the mean times to be triaged to a doctor or nurse practitioner were about the same (approximately 19 minutes), the mean waiting time to see a physician was much longer (25.2 minutes) than was the mean waiting time to see a nurse practitioner (6.7 minutes).

One reason for this time difference may have been the percentage of patients who asked to see a specific doctor or nurse. After the triage system was instituted, this proportion increased to 24% of all patients, up from 19% previously. These patients still had to see a triage nurse first, who might try to dissuade them from waiting for a specific provider. If the patient chose to wait, however, he or she did not receive priority over patients who had arrived earlier. For almost one-third of the physicians, more than 40% of their clinic patients requested them (*Exhibit 10*).

Although the waiting time for triage was the same for the patients who asked for a specific provider and for those who did not, the former waited an average of 8.6 minutes longer to see a provider. But as Mary Dineen, nurse practitioner and supervisor of outpatient nursing, commented:

> It seems doctors are allowed "walk-in appointments" with their own regular patients. Patients whose doctors have heavily booked appointment schedules become aware of the doctor's walk-in schedule and come to the Walk-

In Clinic at prearranged times to meet. This may be a necessary evil to some degree, but today, for example, two of the five doctors on duty are 100% occupied with "walk-in appointments." This decreases are available MD resources by 40% for true walk-in patients today and fills up our waiting room.

Peter Zuromskis, a physician in the Walk-In Clinic, also suggested reasons for the misuse of the walk-in operation:

My evaluation of the dissatisfaction our patients have sometimes expressed with this system is that it represents an approach to acute ambulatory care quite different from that they have previously experienced. Patients understandably find appealing the nostalgic image of the general practitioner who knows his patients well and is able to provide advice and treatment of minor illnesses in his office with an apparent minimum of clerical encumbrances. This is clearly impossible in a clinic that provides the volume and variety of medical care services UHS offers to a large and heterogeneous population with a wide variety of diseases, from relatively minor complaints to major medical emergencies. Our aim is not and should not be to provide an atmosphere reminiscent of the country doctor's office, but rather to provide the best possible care to all our patients, particularly those whose medical needs are most urgent.

Although the new system had been receiving unsolicited praise, Angell knew it still had problems. She worried that by focusing on the "mechanics" of the problem she would overlook other dimensions. Some patient complaints still noted "excessive" waiting times and misunderstanding of the triage system, illustrated by the following opinion submitted to the UHS Patient Advocate:

In order to see a doctor about a very simple problem (a mild sore throat), I have seen a triage nurse (who stamped my form and passed me on) and a nurse practitioner (who looked, felt, and probed, but dared not offer an opinion). I am now 30 minutes into my visit, much handled, but not within sight of a doctor.

However, the medical, clerical, and administrative staff within the Walk-In Clinic felt the triage system was an improvement, though the clinic still wasn't as efficient as they would like it to be. As Warren Wacker, MD, the director of UHS, commented:

Right now, I'm satisfied with the results of the triage system, and I expect the system to be operating very well in another year. Of course, we'll have to resolve some sticky issues in the meantime. For instance, we need to expand the 13 nurse practitioner guidelines and further define the roles of nurse practitioner and physician within the Walk-In Clinic. Another item is, how do we educate students in the Walk-In Clinic concept? Expectations of traditional medicine don't fit with the walk-in concept.

ANGELL'S DILEMMA

Angell now had the task of sorting through a year's data, the concerns raised by several groups associated with the clinic, and her own observations. What changes needed to be made, if any? Were waiting times now acceptable? Angell knew that work was in progress to expand the 13 nurse practitioner guidelines, but would this be enough to solve any remaining problems? She wondered to what degree waiting time in a service facility affected one's perception of the quality of service provided.

Among her biggest concerns were the "walk-in appointments." She commented:

In the past, we have asked the doctors to refrain from encouraging their patients to meet them in the Walk-In Clinic. However, the practice continues. Some of the doctors feel that they want their patients to see only them. Part of this is for medical reasons (the doctors wish to check on their patients' progress) and part of it is a general philosophy that medical care involves more than just treatment and that personal relationships add to both the quality of health care and the patient's perception of good service. Many patients, perhaps appropriately, have the attitude of wanting to see "my doctor." Apart from the fact that you can never dictate to doctors, the UHS has always had a philosophy of not trying to tell physicians how to practice medicine.

Part of the problem is the general availability of appointment time. All our patients have the freedom to select their own "personal physician" from among any of our doctors. However, this often means that some are overloaded. Our overall staffing level at UHS is set approximately to provide one physician per 2,000 people covered by our various health plans. At the moment, the only way we try to limit the number of patients "assigned" to any given doctor is by pointing out to the potential patient the difficulty of getting an appointment with an overloaded physician, and this is generally only done if the patient asks about it. We do not know how many patients each doctor is seeing as the patients' personal physician, since this is an arrangement made by the doctor and the patient and not a formal assignment.

There are a number of potential alternatives for dealing with this problem.

We could try to educate our patient public on the separate purposes and missions of doctor appointments and the Walk-In Clinic—try to get them to use each appropriately. We could ask the triage coordinators to be a little more aggressive in asking patients who request a specific physician whether they really need to see that person and suggest alternatives. Ultimately, we could establish a firm policy of not accepting specific physician requests in the Walk-In Clinic.

Angell had these questions and more to consider over the next two weeks. She would then share her findings and proposals with Ms. Dineen and Dr. Postel, who would have to agree on any necessary changes and help implement them.

Exhibit 1
Income and Expense Statistics for UHS Operations

	1979–1980	*1978–1979*	*1979–1980*
Income			
Student health fee	$3,390,023	38.2%	34.4%
Student insurance	1,636,925	17.3	16.6
Harvard University			
Group Health Program	900,212	7.0	9.1
Payroll assessment	1,589,487	16.9	16.1
Care for Medicare	252,074	1.6	2.5
Radiation protection	435,603	3.8	4.4
Other services	1,628,448	15.2	16.9
Total	$9,832,772	100.0%	100.0%
Expenses			
Salaries, wages, and benefits	$5,223,685	53.5%	53.7%
Student insurance	1,636,925	17.2	16.8
Building operations and			
maintenance	388,870	4.3	4.0
Medical/dental supplies	278,987	2.3	2.8
Outside laboratories	176,309	2.2	1.8
Malpractice insurance	49,048	1.1	.5
All other	1,967,436	19.4	20.5
Total	$9,721,260	100.0%	100.0%

Exhibit 2
Patient Visits per Day/Arrivals per Hour

Daily Average of Patient Visits

Monday	163
Tuesday	151
Wednesday	136
Thursday	137
Friday	128
Average	143

Average Number of Patient Arrivals per Hour

8–9 a.m.	18.2
9–10 a.m.	17.6
10–11 a.m.	16.8
11–12 a.m.	15.2
12–1 p.m.	11.8
1–2 p.m.	16.9
2–3 p.m.	16.2
3–4 p.m.	15.9
4–5 p.m.	11.6
5–6 p.m.	2.8

Exhibit 3
Patient Distribution by Reason for Visit

Reason[a]	% of Total
Emergency	1.4%
Medical: initial visit[b]	41.3
Medical: return visit	11.3
Medical: specific provider	24.0
Surgical: initial visit[b]	0.1
Surgical: return visit	0.8
Lab result	2.0
Premarital test	0.4
Blood pressure	2.2
Prescription: confirmed diagnosis	0.8
Prescription refill	2.0
Administrative	1.0
Other	1.7
Unspecified	11.0
	100.0%

[a] As indicated by the patient.

[b] Initial visit for the specific complaint, not patient's first visit *ever* to the Walk-In Clinic.

Exhibit 4
Medical Professional Scheduling: Walk-In Clinic

	Monday		Tuesday		Wednesday		Thursday		Friday	
	# MDs	# NPs	# MDs	# NPs	# MDs	# NPs	# MDs	# NPs	# MDs	# NPs
8–9 a.m.	2	2	2	2	2	2	2	2	2	2
9–10 a.m.	2.5	4	3	4	2.5	4	2	4	2.5	4
10–11 a.m.	5	4	4	4	5	4	5	4	5	4
11–12 noon	3	4	3	4	3	4	3	4	4	4
12–1 p.m.	3	2.5	2	2.5	2.5	2.5	3	2.5	2.5	2.5
1–2 p.m.	3	2.5	3	2.5	3	2.5	2	2.5	3	2.5
2–3 p.m.	3	4	4	4	3	4	3	4	4	4
3–4 p.m.	4	4	4	4	4	4	4	4	4	4
4–5 p.m.	3	2.5	2	2.5	2	2.5	3.5	2.5	3	2.5
5–6 p.m.[a]	1	2	1	2	1	2	1	2	1	2

NOTE: MD = medical doctor. NP = nurse practitioner (statistics do not include triage nurses).

[a] The clinic admitted its last patient at 5:30 p.m. Staff were required to stay until 6 p.m.

Exhibit 5
Comparison of Total Processing Times, Pre-Triage and Triage (minutes)

	Pre-Triage	*Triage*
I. Initial Processing		
• Sign-in/AVF form	2	2
• Record retrieval	8.5	8.5
• Record check	5	5
• Wait for triage	NA	4.2
• Triage	NA	3.5
II. Patients Treated by Nurse Practitioner		
• Wait for NP	7.5–19.5	6.7
• Treatment by NP	32.8	32.8
III. Patients Treated by Physician		
• Wait for NP	7.5–19.5	NA
• Evaluation by NP	32.8	NA
• Wait for MD	10	25.2
• Treatment by MD	19.4	19.4
IV. Patients Treated by Specific Provider		
• Wait for specific MD or NP	24.5	33.8
• Treatment by specific MD or NP	19.4, 32.8	19.4, 32.8

NOTE: NA = not applicable

Exhibit 6
Percentage of Patients Treated by Various Providers

	Pre-Triage	*Triage*
Patients treated by nurse practitioner	40%	28%
Patients treated by physician	41%	48%
Patients treated by specifically requested physician or nurse practitioner	19%	24%

Exhibit 7
Ambulatory Visit Form

UNIVERSITY HEALTH SERVICES : WALK-IN CLINIC

AMBULATORY VISIT FORM

N° 82336

FOR PATIENT USE: PLEASE FILL OUT THIS SECTION COMPLETELY

TIME & DATE _____

UHS/ HARVARD I.D. NO. _____

NAME: PLEASE PRINT _____
First   Middle   Last

BIRTHDATE ___ Mo. ___ Day ___ Yr.   MALE ☐   FEMALE ☐

LOCAL ADDRESS _____

PHONE DURING THE DAY _____

LOCATION OF VISIT:
☐ Holyoke Center   ☐ Law School   ☐ Medical Area
☐ Business School

IS THIS YOUR FIRST VISIT TO A UHS FACILITY? YES ☐

IF YOUR MEDICAL RECORD IS KEPT AT A UHS FACILITY OTHER THAN
HOLYOKE CENTER, PLEASE CHECK HERE: BUSINESS ☐ LAW ☐ MEDICAL AREA ☐

STATUS
☐ H/R UNDERGRAD., CLASS _____
☐ GRAD. SCHOOL (Name) _____
☐ LESLEY COLLEGE
☐ EPISCOPAL DIVINITY SCHOOL
☐ STAFF WITH HARVARD BC/BS
☐ STAFF WITH HARVARD UNIVERSITY GROUP HEALTH PROGRAM (HUGHP)
☐ STAFF WITH NO HARVARD INSURANCE
☐ HARVARD MEDEX
☐ MEDICARE (ONLY)

☐ STUDENT DEPENDENT WITH UHS COVERAGE
☐ STUDENT DEPENDENT WITH UHS COVERAGE — UNDER 14 YEARS OLD
☐ HUGHP DEPENDENT
☐ HUGHP DEPENDENT–UNDER 14 YEARS OLD
☐ MEDEX DEPENDENT
☐ SUMMER SCHOOL: STUDENT _____
    FACULTY _____ FAC. DEPENDENT _____
☐ NON-MEMBER OF HARVARD UNIVERSITY
☐ OTHER _____

FOR WALK-IN PATIENTS ONLY

The following information is designed to help us treat you promptly and efficiently. All information will be kept confidential. If you do not wish to complete the rest of the form, please check "personal" and you will be seen in turn.

WHAT IS THE REASON FOR YOUR VISIT? PLEASE CHECK:

☐ I NEED EMERGENCY CARE.   ☐ BLOOD PRESSURE CHECK ONLY

GENERAL MEDICAL PROBLEM
☐ FIRST VISIT FOR THIS PROBLEM
☐ RETURN (REPEAT) VISIT FOR THIS PROBLEM
☐ TOLD TO SEE:
    NURSE OR DOCTOR

PRESCRIPTION(S) ONLY
☐ DIAGNOSIS CONFIRMED; INSTRUCTED TO OBTAIN PRESCRIPTION
☐ PRESCRIPTION REFILL: UHS _____ OTHER _____

GENERAL SURGICAL PROBLEM
☐ FIRST VISIT FOR THIS PROBLEM
☐ RETURN (REPEAT) VISIT FOR THIS PROBLEM
☐ TOLD TO SEE:
    NURSE OR DOCTOR

ADMINISTRATIVE PROBLEM
☐ SPORTS CLEARANCE
☐ MEDICAL EXCUSE FOR EXAM
☐ MEDICAL FORMS TO BE COMPLETED
☐ PERSONAL
☐ OTHER _____

LABORATORY PROCEDURES ONLY
☐ LAB RESULTS DESIRED
☐ PREMARITAL TESTS DESIRED
☐ PREGNANCY TEST REQUISITION

FOR UHS USE ONLY

TRIAGE TIME _____   TIME PT. SEEN _____   TIME SEEN _____

TYPE OF CONTACT
☐ WALK-IN
☐ APPOINTMENT
☐ BROKEN APPOINTMENT
☐ CANCELLED BY UHS
☐ CANCELLED BY PATIENT
☐ LEFT BEFORE BEING SEEN
☐ RESERVE
☐ OTHER

PROVIDER 1 NUMBER _____   NAME _____
PROVIDER 2 NUMBER _____   NAME _____

SERVICE
☐ MEDICAL
☐ SURGICAL
☐ EMERGENCY
☐ ALLERGY
☐ DENTAL
☐ DERMATOLOGY
☐ EAR, NOSE, & THROAT
☐ EYE
☐ GASTROENTEROLOGY
☐ GYNECOLOGY
☐ IMMUNIZATION
☐ MENTAL HEALTH
☐ NEUROLOGY
☐ NUTRITION
☐ OBSTETRICS
☐ ORTHOPEDICS
☐ PEDIATRICS
☐ PHYSICAL THERAPY
☐ UROLOGY
☐ OTHER

☐ INITIAL VISIT FOR THIS PROBLEM
☐ RETURN VISIT

HEMATOLOGY
PROVIDER NO.: 1   2
☐ ☐ COULTER CBC
☐ ☐ DIFFERENTIAL
☐ ☐ OCCULT BLOOD (GUAIAC)
☐ ☐ PLATELET COUNT
☐ ☐ PROTHROMBIN TIME
☐ ☐ RETICULOCYTE COUNT
☐ ☐ SEDIMENTATION RATE
☐ ☐ OTHER

Please circle as many lab test boxes as apply.

CHEMISTRY
PROVIDER NO.: 1   2
☐ ☐ BILIRUBIN
☐ ☐ BLOOD GLUCOSE
☐ ☐ BLOOD UREA NITROGEN (BUN)
☐ ☐ CHOLESTEROL
☐ ☐ CREATININE
☐ ☐ ELECTROLYTES
☐ ☐ SGOT
☐ ☐ SMA 12/60
☐ ☐ T4
☐ ☐ T3 UPTAKE
☐ ☐ TRIGLYCERIDES
☐ ☐ URIC ACID
☐ ☐ OTHER

SEROLOGY
PROVIDER NO.: 1   2
☐ ☐ HETEROPHILE
☐ ☐ RPR
☐ ☐ RUBELLA
☐ ☐ OTHER

BACTERIOLOGY
PROVIDER NO.: 1   2
☐ ☐ CERVICAL/URETHRAL CULTURE & GRAM STAIN
☐ ☐ STOOL FOR CULTURE
☐ ☐ STOOL FOR OVA & PARASITES
☐ ☐ THROAT CULTURE
☐ ☐ URINE CULTURE
☐ ☐ OTHER

MISCELLANEOUS
PROVIDER NO.: 1   2
☐ ☐ BLOOD TYPE & RH
☐ ☐ ELECTROCARDIOGRAM
☐ ☐ MONILIA
☐ ☐ PAP SMEAR
☐ ☐ PATHOLOGY
☐ ☐ PREGNANCY TEST
☐ ☐ PULMONARY FUNCTION
☐ ☐ TRICHOMONAS (WET PREP)
☐ ☐ URINALYSIS
☐ ☐ OTHER

Exhibit 8
Categories Treatable by Nurse Practitioners

1. Acute viral respiratory illness (primarily colds)
2. Amenorrhea (missed menstruation)
3. Cerumen (wax in ears)
4. Enterobiasis (pinworms)
5. Lower urinary tract infection (females)
6. Mononucleosis
7. Nausea, vomiting, diarrhea
8. Pediculosis capitus (lice)
9. Pediculosis publis (lice)
10. Pharyngitis (sore throat)
11. Rubella (German measles)
12. Seasonal rhinitis (hay fever)
13. Vaginitis (vaginal infection)

Exhibit 9
Percentage of Patients Waiting, by Time Waited

Interval (minutes)	Waiting Time to be triaged[a]	Waiting Time to be seen[b]	Total Waiting Time
0–4	1%	24%	0%
5–9	8	14	3
10–14	24	12	7
15–19	25	11	10
20–24	19	9	10
25–29	11	8	14
30–34	6	8	11
35–39	2	5	10
40–44	1	4	8
45–49	1	3	6
50–54	1	2	7
55 +	1	0	14
	100%	100%	100%
Average	19.7	18.6	37.5

[a] Measured from time patient was handed the AVF form to complete.

[b] Measured from the time triaging begins to time patient meets MD or NP.

Exhibit 10

Summary of Patients Seen and Waiting Time to First Available Appointment, by Physician[a]

Physician[b]	Total # of Patients Seen	# of Patients Who Asked to See Specific MD (%)	Total # of Hours	# of Patients Seen per Hour	Calendar Days To First Available Appointment
Zuromskis	113	33 (29.2)	36	3.14	9
Bogota	50	23 (46.0)	17	2.94	24
Wellington	89	— —	18	4.94	5
Byrd	76	26 (34.2)	33	2.30	15
Recife	78	48 (61.5)	24	3.25	25
Brunei	113	45 (39.8)	36	3.14	17
Lobito	28	10 (35.7)	6	4.67	21
Santiago	91	43 (47.3)	29	3.14	3
Hobart	59	27 (45.8)	24	2.46	28
Seoul	90	34 (37.8)	28	3.21	5
Kingston	113	26 (23.0)	25	4.52	7
Java	78	16 (20.5)	27	2.89	13
Rome	74	32 (43.2)	19	3.89	7
Ottawa	82	31 (37.8)	26	3.15	5
Caracus	53	17 (32.1)	18	2.94	7
Manila	25	18 (72)	9	2.78	23
Durban	48	41 (85.4)	18	2.67	29
Luanda	61	5 (8.2)	21	2.90	8
Papua	34	— —	9	3.78	—
Glasgow	35	2 —	9	3.89	12
Cristobal	33	3 (9.1)	19.5	1.69	2
Aukland	16	1 (6.3)	12.5	1.28	—
	1439	481 (33.4)	464	3.10	12

[a]Statistics in this exhibit are taken from a 3-week study.

[b]Some names in this exhibit have been disguised.

9

$\diamond$

Managing Networks

Services are particularly dependent on networks. Such networks take many forms. In addition to the commonly recognized transportation and telecommunications networks we use every day, less visible networks of personal relationships form the backbone of many financial and other services. In addition, less personal institutional networks enable us to make use, for example, of credit cards and other financial instruments. Multiunit services form an implicit network by displaying the same sign on their outlets, thus linking units to one another by reputation. One of the more interesting properties of networks is that they often become more valuable to individual users as they are expanded. But at least in their early stages of development, the costs of expansion may be much greater than the additional revenues networks produce.

Service managers for which networks are critical are faced with a number of questions. Among them are: How, if at all, can the often high investment required to build a network be reduced, shared, or deferred? In building a network, is the ultimate goal to minimize network distances, maximize user accessibility to all points connected by the network, reach the maximum number of targeted users, make network usage as convenient as possible, or minimize investment in the network itself? What kinds of competitive advantage are gained by achieving each of these objectives? Can network capacity be shared by customers, competitors, or businesses encountering peak loads at different times of the day, week, month, or year? Have appropriate steps been taken to manage quality in networks relying heavily on the linkage of network users by name? To what extent are mutual needs for timely response or shared trust (in networks of relationships) recognized and fostered in the design of procedures and controls?

In the Medibus case, describing a transportation service linking retirement home patrons and the sites they regularly patronize, questions of managing this transportation network include the following: How well is Medibus's operation designed to meet the needs of its target market? How could its network be designed to better meet these needs? What are the economics of this operation (assuming an average speed of 30 miles per hour while in transit)? How are they affected by your recommendations for network improvement? What other changes, if any, would you recommend in Medibus's operation? Why?

Turning to the case, Caruso's Pizza, we find two contrasting alternative delivery systems, "express" and "hot shot." The first question that might be asked is, Why isn't Caruso's express delivery operation profitable? What are the strengths and weaknesses of each delivery system described in the case? What will it take to make either work really well? As an advisor to Jim Caruso, what would you suggest he do? Why?

MediBus, Inc.

Our first two months (January and February 1975) of operations have been much better than projected. Sales have been about double our budgeted figures. We have ordered another ambulette which will be delivered in April. We are well on our way to develop a profitable enterprise and should be a $2 million firm in 2–3 years. My biggest concern is charting the course which will take us there.

RICHARD GABRIELE, President (age 39)

THE SERVICE

Medibus, Inc., a transportation service exclusively for disabled, handicapped, and elderly persons, had begun pilot operations on January 1, 1975. From headquarters in Smithtown, N.Y., on Long Island, ramp-equipped vehicles were dispatched with uniformed drivers trained in first aid. The air-conditioned vehicles, called "ambulettes," were specifically designed to carry a maximum of four wheelchair and five ambulatory passengers at one time (see *Exhibit 1*). As Dick Gabriele, MediBus founder and president explained:

> MediBus is not an emergency or ambulance service and does not charge rates required by those services. It will carry anyone in a wheelchair, on crutches, using a walker, or able to walk into the MediBus. Because of its unique approach and equipment, MediBus opens up many possibilities for persons who are unable to use conventional taxi or bus service to visit their doctor, dentist, therapist, or recreational facility.
>
> Modest rates are charged for each trip with special rates for group, Medicare, and Medicaid clients. For those institutions which utilize MediBus for the medical transportation needs of their clients, MediBus will transport their clients on both recreational and social trips. These trips are billed directly to the institution. [See *Exhibit 2* for a rate schedule.] In addition, MediBus, as of March 3, provides health care equipment and sick room supplies on either a rental or sales basis.

This case was prepared by Professor W. Earl Sasser as a basis for class discussion rather than to illustrate either effective or ineffective handling of an administrative situation. Copyright © 1975 by the President and Fellows of Harvard College; Harvard Business School case #9-675-177 (Rev. 11/87).

BACKGROUND

The MediBus concept had been developed by Richard Gabriele during the fall of 1974 while he was serving as a consultant to Ecologic Instrument Corporation, a company he had founded in 1971 and of which he had served as president until October 1974.[1] Ecologic manufactured analytical instruments and pollution control equipment and had annual sales of approximately $1.5 million. In January 1974, Ecologic had been sold to United States Filter Corporation, and Mr. Gabriele had been retained under management contracts as operating head of the subsidiary. However, he had stepped down from this position in October 1974 as a result of a disagreement with U.S. Filter management over whether Ecologic should concentrate on short- or long-term profits. Mr. Gabriele had explained his view of the situation:

> U.S. Filter wanted Ecologic to reduce all development efforts and concentrate our efforts selling the existing line. I disagreed. We were close to some major development breakthroughs. If our competitors hit the market with the new products, our existing line would be obsolete in a year. Therefore, I thought U.S. Filter's approach was short-sighted although their payon scheme to me placed a heavy weight on short-term profits. As a result of our disagreement, U.S. Filter negotiated with me on the remaining term of my management contract. I left officially on December 31, 1974, which gave me time between October and December to plan a new business.

During the month of October, Mr. Gabriele had screened many business opportunities. After a couple of weeks, he had decided to focus on the health care field, which he had gotten to know so well in his 11 years of selling to the health care industry. Promising areas had included medical supplies (especially disposables), clinical laboratories, and rental of health-related equipment. One day he noticed an ad in *The Wall Street Journal* offering franchises for a medical transportation service. The firm, MediCab, Inc., based in Westchester County, New York, had been an outgrowth of a taxi company which had begun catering to the transportation needs of non-acutely ill, nonambulatory persons. Mr. Gabriele had explained his encounter with MediCab:

---

1. Prior to the founding of Ecologic Instrument Corporation, Mr. Gabriele had been a cofounder (1969) of Automated Environmental Systems, Inc., a company engaged in the manufacture of pollution control instrumentation. As vice president of marketing, he guided AES's marketing efforts for three years until AES was merged with Textfiber, a double-knit fiber manufacturer. For 11 years prior to the founding of AES, Mr. Gabriele had been involved in sales and sales management in the hospital supply and equipment business.

I visited their headquarters in response to the ad with the thought of acquiring a franchise. They were providing exactly the same kind of transportation service in Westchester County that we are providing today in Suffolk County. We just capitalized on their ideas.

A couple of days later, I called together Sam[2] and Julie[3] for a meeting. At that meeting we put together the idea for a total medical service company to provide not only the transportation service of MediCab but to provide, in addition, nursing care, equipment rental, and eventually part-time physician services.

A business plan had been developed during the last two weeks of November 1974. Included as *Exhibit 3* is a pro forma profit and loss statement for the pilot operations center with 3 to 8 MediBuses. The founders' thinking had been shaped in part by the material contained in a *Long Island Business Review* article. The pertinent sections of that article are included as *Exhibit 4*.

MARKETING STRATEGY

Because of competitive conditions (discussed below) and the fact that Messrs. Gabriele and Richman were residents, Suffolk County had been selected as the primary market during the start-up phase. A map of Long Island is included as *Exhibit 5*. In January 1975, the key personnel who had decision-making authority in the choice of medical transportation in each nursing home in Suffolk County had been visited by either Mr. Gabriele or Mr. Richman and given a verbal presentation of the MediBus service. The title of the decision makers varied from nursing home to nursing home depending upon the size and organization of the institution. In larger institutions, the nursing director was usually the key decision maker; in smaller ones, it was often an administrator's secretary. The decision makers had been given promotional literature designed to answer questions for both customers and clients. Several weeks later, a letter which reiterated the earlier delivered "message" had been sent to each key decision maker. On each sales visit, an effort had been made to stick a MediBus label, which featured the MediBus phone number, on as many phones as possible at

---

2. Sam Goldstein (age 57) ran a small industrial advertising firm which specialized in advertising and promotion for smaller firms. He often took an equity interest for services rendered. Mr. Goldstein had met Mr. Gabriele when Ecologic Instrument was founded in 1971.

3. Julius Richman (age 42) was formerly director of marketing and sales of Ecologic Instrument Corporation. He had worked with Mr. Gabriele for over ten years.

locations from which a possible call for the service might be made. Mr. Richman explained the overall strategy:

> We usually call on the recreation director first. [Each nursing home to qualify for Medicaid was required to have a recreational director.] We explain to the director our recreational/social package. He/she usually gets very excited because many of the nonambulatory residents are restricted to in-house activities because adequate transportation is not available for trips away from the institution.
>
> Next, we locate the person who makes decisions about the medical transportation needs of the institution's residents. We tell him/her we have spoken to the recreational director and that we cannot provide the recreational/social transportation service on a regular basis unless we can participate in providing for the institution's normal medical transportation needs. We try, if at all possible, to get the person to inspect our vehicle, which usually impresses him/her and sells itself.

In addition, a direct mail campaign had been targeted to the medical profession in Suffolk County. The promotional pieces explained how the physician's patients could receive medical transportation to and from the physician's office.

CLIENTS AND CUSTOMERS

Only 10% of business came from private sources; the other 90% of MediBus's business came from third parties such as nursing homes, hospitals, outpatient clinics, and charitable organizations. A breakdown of these institutional trips for the period, February 24–28, is given in *Exhibit 6*. MediBus referred to these third parties as *customers*. The persons actually transported were called *clients*. Most clients had a disability, but many did not think of themselves as being sick.

The customers called the MediBus office and made appointments for clients. MediBus appointments were usually made at the same time that appointments were made with doctors, dentists, optometrists, etc. Approximately 90% of the appointments were made at least three days before the day of the trip. Only 2–3% of the appointments were made for travel on the same day.

Payments for over 90% of the transportation services rendered by MediBus were made by Medicare and/or Medicaid. Some clients were regular clients, scheduled for weekly or even daily trips. For example, one client was transported to a methadone clinic six days each week for medication. A random sample of Medicaid invoices for the month of February is included as *Exhibit 7*.

A typical client response was provided by a 74-year-old widow who was confined to a wheelchair:

I have been living in this nursing home for over a year. I must visit my doctor for an examination quarterly. I never did like to ride in an ambulance to the doctor's office. Several weeks ago I rode in a MediBus; the driver was courteous and talked to me all the way there and back. Now, I will request MediBus whenever I go.

A physician explained his first contact with MediBus:

I received a call late one afternoon from a company for which I serve as company physician that a minor accident had occurred and that a person who was hurt, but not seriously, needed to see me. The quickest an ambulance company could get the patient to me was 2½ hours. They are always slow. Because one of the MediBus stickers was on one of our phones, I asked my nurse to see if they could transport him. They could. In fact, he was in my office in less than 45 minutes. I was so impressed that I introduced the driver to about eight other physicians in the building. We have used them since, and they have not let us down.

A nursing home administrator explained why MediBus was being used by his facility:

We use MediBus because our residents like MediBus's vehicles and drivers. In the past, we had been indifferent about who transported our clients because, in most cases, the payment was covered by Medicaid. However, our residents have a fear of ambulances and the MediBus has a cheerful, clean appearance.

We plan to use MediBus for a recreational trip or two this summer, but not many because we have to pay for those trips. We can only allocate 50¢ per day per resident for recreational/social purposes.

COMPETITION

In Suffolk County, medical transportation services were provided by three major ambulance companies. In Nassau County the situation was quite different, as Richard Gabriele explained:

In Nassau, we have a problem. The private ambulance association, consisting of 8 ambulance companies, convinced the Nassau County Medicaid office to enter into an exclusive contract for transporting Medicaid clients. As a result, only members of the association can provide our type of transportation services in Nassau County, and we are presently not members of the association.

The association's contract is renewed monthly. We hear rumblings that the Medicaid officials in Nassau County are not pleased with the present level of service. We also hear that officers of the association are giving preferential treatment to the officer's firms to the disgust of other members of the association. We have made overtures to the Commissioner of Health in Nassau County that there has been a restraint of trade because the contract was not awarded on a competitive bid basis.

Mr. Gabriele next explained the competitive advantage of MediBus over ambulances:

In the past, customers called ambulance companies for their clients. The ambulance companies use this type of business to "fill in" between their emergency calls. They use the same vehicles for both emergency and non-emergency service. Our main advantage is that clients have an intense fear of travelling in an ambulance. Many of their former friends were last seen entering an ambulance. After their first trip with MediBus, clients request our vehicles. Word of mouth has been terrific.

Ambulance companies are not actively seeking our business. They have concentrated on stretcher patients, local emergencies not filled by fire departments, and transportation of patients to major medical centers. In fact, we are not hurting the ambulance companies. Nursing homes are sending out more clients as they use our service and their confidence factor increases—not only more, but more frequently! We are generating a market that really wasn't there before. This fact is confirmed by Medicaid officials.

MediBus claimed another competitive advantage with regard to private clients. Their rates were about 50% less than ambulance charges for private clients. Ambulance companies charged more because their operating costs were higher. Ambulances were required by New York State to have two trained medical attendants in the vehicles at all times. Such emergency medical technicians were paid substantially more than MediBus drivers.

According to Richard Gabriele:

The response to MediBus by our ambulance competitors has been limited. One competitor circulated a rumor that we are not licensed by New York State, but we are. Other competitors have pointed out that we are not licensed to handle emergency cases and that we are not open seven days a week, twenty-four hours a day (which are true).

PRICING

Each county Medicaid office in New York had a department of transportation which monitored the rates and funds for health-related trips. Each county set its rates independently of other counties. In Suffolk the rate for nonemergency trips was $10 one way, $10 for each hour of waiting time over the first hour, and $0.50 per mile for all over 40. Medicaid permitted MediBus to deposit its clients with doctors, and return for pick up when notified by the doctors' offices. Dick Gabriele explained, "Medicaid allows us to keep our vehicles moving during wait time because they have not increased their allowable transportation charges since 1970." If more than one person, such as an aide, spouse, or child, was carried at the same time in the same vehicle, there was an additional charge of $2.50 per person. The maximum charge for a Medicaid-paid round trip was $20.00.

Each new client of MediBus required certification from the Medicaid office that he or she was eligible for transportation benefits. Each month, MediBus submitted its list of clients to the local Medicaid office for recertification. There was no limit to the number of medically related trips a client might take. (A price schedule is given in *Exhibit 2*.).

EQUIPMENT RENTALS

In early March, 1975, MediBus began offering a rental service for health-related equipment and supplies such as wheelchairs, hospital beds, walkers, crutches, etc. To minimize investment in equipment, MediBus structured an arrangement with a local surgical supply company to serve as one of the supply company's marketing arms, for which MediBus received a 30% commission on all rental income it generated. Mr. Richman commented, "Every transportation client is a potential renter! Every driver is a potential salesman of health-related equipment!" These rentals were covered by Medicaid in most instances.

OPERATIONS

In March of 1975, MediBus's facilities consisted of one small office in a professional building, which housed all of the officers of the company. With only three vehicles, MediBus's management felt that the operations function of the MediBus concept was rather uncomplicated. The ambulettes were operated by three drivers, all of whom were members of volunteer fire departments. In addition, there was a part-time driver on call and, if necessary, both Mr. Gabriele and Mr. Richman served as drivers. According to Mr. Gabriele:

> The drivers make or break the business. They are up front. How they treat the passengers and how they maintain the appearance of their vehicles determines whether or not the passenger is satisfied enough with our service to request us on their next trip.

The activity of the MediBus office centered around Ms. Marilyn Hartmann,[4] who was responsible for receiving requests for services, scheduling the drivers, keeping records of trips, billing, and general administrative requirements. A trip was normally initiated by a phone call to Ms. Hartmann from one of the nursing homes or a private individual. These requests were usually made three days to one week in advance. Upon receiving a request, Ms. Hartmann checked her log book to see if the requested time was available. If time was available, the order was recorded with the particulars as to destinations, points of origin, and expected time of wait. If time was not available, Ms. Hartmann first tried to get the customer to reschedule the appointment to a time when a MediBus was available. If this could not be done, then she explained that the MediBus could not provide the service at that time. Ms. Hartmann noted that the hours from 10 a.m. to 12 noon and from 2 p.m. to 4 p.m. were popular times because these hours coincided with most doctors' office hours. Approximately 70% of all pickups were scheduled in these two time periods for the month of February. Ms. Hartmann explained, "During the last two weeks, I have been forced, on occasion, to decline additional trips during these periods. I try to switch the requests to less hectic times, but often the appointment for medical services cannot be changed."

Ms. Hartmann emphasized the importance of on-time pick-ups and getting the clients to the physician's office on schedule. However, she did note that the timing of the client's return to the nursing home was not as critical:

> Most of our elderly clients have nothing to rush back to. They don't object to waiting a few extra minutes in the doctor's office or taking a long way back to the nursing home if we want to take two clients in the same vehicle. If we can transport two clients who are headed for the same area at the same time, we can still bill for two trips. However, this only happens a couple of times a week.

At the end of each business day, Ms. Hartmann calculated the charges for

---

4. Ms. Hartmann, who had been employed by Mr. Gabriele for the past seven years, was a stockholder in MediBus, Inc.

each trip made during the day and entered the total on the bottom of the day's page in the log book. (February daily statistics, compiled from the log book, are included in *Exhibit 8*.) She then turned the page to the next day's schedule and assigned the requests to the three vehicles to ascertain if there were any potential problems. A definite schedule was impossible to develop because it was difficult to forecast, with any accuracy, client delays, traffic delays, and/or physician delays.

The next morning, Ms. Hartmann distributed a schedule to each driver and went over each assignment to ensure the daily schedule was clear. During the day the drivers checked in with Ms. Hartmann by phone[5] when they arrived at their destinations. If a long wait was anticipated, an additional trip was normally scheduled during the waiting time. If no additional trip was scheduled, the driver remained available at the destination for unscheduled requests. If the driver did not wait with the client at the destination, Ms. Hartmann periodically checked with the doctor's office (or wherever the destination might be) to ensure that the client would be ready for return at the specified time or to find out if the client was finished early and waiting for the return of the MediBus. This, according to Ms. Hartmann, was her biggest problem:

> Nurses and receptionists underestimate how long a patient will be there. They usually say it will be 15 to 30 minutes and it usually turns out to be longer than an hour and a half. Since the driver remains with the client when a short wait is expected, this deception often ties up a vehicle for an extended period of time.

In order to minimize driving time, and to utilize ambulettes during wait times for unscheduled requests, Ms. Hartmann tried to assign the vehicles to particular areas. It was often possible to assign vehicles to certain areas such as the "South Shore" because most "South Shore" clients went to "South Shore" destinations. This had a beneficial side effect in that the drivers got to know both their passengers and the personnel in the physicians' offices and nursing homes very well; it was felt that this personal relationship facilitated the drivers' ability to provide good service.

Mr. Gabriele recognized the key role which Hartmann played in the company's operations:

> Marilyn is excellent in dealing with people. She is friendly with all the drivers and has developed a rapport with a number of the administrators in the nursing homes who call to schedule trips.

---

5. Two-way radios for the vehicles were on order and were expected to be operational in late March.

FINANCIAL STRATEGY

The basic financial strategy of MediBus had been to keep capital outlays at a minimum level. Most of the equipment had been leased: vehicles, office furniture, two-way radios. Even initial promotional expenses had required little capital outlay, since the fees[6] for these services had been paid by Sam Goldstein as the contribution for his share of the equity. In the first two months of operation, Gabriele and Richman had received no salaries.[7] Regarding the future sources of financing, Gabriele said, "We have the personal resources to back the company so we don't have to worry about bankers or venture capitalists."

MediBus closely watched the inflow of funds. Because of Medicaid's reputation for slow payment (New York City Medicaid was reputed to take over six months to pay its bills), MediBus billed Medicaid weekly. Although it had been expected to be on a 75-day collection cycle, the first payment was received 45 days after the date of billing; the second took only 40 days. Gabriele or Richman visited the county Medicaid office weekly to ensure requirements for submitting good invoices were being met. According to Dick Gabriele, "MediBus has quickly obtained a reputation for submitting good invoices." Billings to private clients were due upon presentation and were being collected within 10 days.

FRANCHISING

During 1976, MediBus planned to embark upon a national franchising program throughout the United States and Canada utilizing the Suffolk/Nassau County pilot operation as a model for franchise success. Under this franchise program, MediBus planned to lease to franchisees all equipment and vehicles[8] plus supply a training program for new operations managers. In addition, the company planned, on an ongoing basis, to guide and assist each franchisee in marketing, promotion, financial controls, scheduling, and training. In return, MediBus would receive from qualified franchisees an initial franchise fee of from $10,000 to $15,000 plus 6% of revenues on a continuing basis.

Gabriele explained his rationale for franchising:

> We have an edge. Our operation will be different from one such as Medi-
> Cab. We plan on working more with the franchisee. We will handle all

6. These totalled $1,650 for January and February combined.

7. Beginning in April, Messrs. Gabriele and Richman would draw annual salaries of $25,000 and $20,000, respectively.

8. It was estimated that, annually, the company would earn $250 per vehicle leased.

their billing, most of their initial selling, factoring of their receivables and most of their administrative functions. We will be providing a total package of several health-related businesses to the franchisee. Our initial plans are to franchise outside the New York, New Jersey, Connecticut area. We will definitely operate Suffolk and Nassau counties as company-owned operations because we have a competitive advantage since we know the area so well.

We are not naive. We know it will be harder to penetrate markets further away from here. We hope to overcome this problem by selecting franchisees who are local personalities with good connections.

THE FUTURE

Dick Gabriele summed up his feelings about the future:

I am very optimistic about our present position. The profit and loss statement for our first two months of operation must be a rarity for a start-up situation. Our balance sheet (*Exhibit 9*) is solid. We are beating our quarterly projections (*Exhibit 10*) by a wide margin.

However, he expressed concerns about several areas:

Operations—As we add vehicles to increase our capacity, it will be easier to schedule and provide better service. But will we get enough business to support the overload of vehicles?

And as we expand the number of vehicles, I am not sure our present methods of operation will be adequate. What should I be planning for later this year when I have seven vans in operation?

Marketing—I believe that third-party endorsements of our services are key to the generation of volume because they give us the credibility which is so desperately needed by a small firm. How can we get that third-party support?

We haven't made a dent in the private market for our services. Marketing in this segment will have to be done by newspaper and yellow page advertising.

We cannot afford to sell on a personal basis to individual private clients.

We have only made a couple of recreation trips in our first two months of operation. How can we better market our off-peak capacity?

Compensation—How should we compensate our drivers? We need to stimulate them, not only to provide courteous, on-time service, but to sell our rental service as well.

Franchising—I am confident that in twelve months we will have a good handle on the operations here on Long Island. We want to expand quickly to prevent competition from getting a foothold in other areas. MediCab already has several franchise operations, including MediCab of Mass Bay which services the metropolitan Boston area.

We cannot get the name MediBus registered as a federal trademark because it too closely resembles other registered names. We need to have this problem resolved by the time we begin offering franchises.

Unknowns—What really bothers me is that there must be some things that I haven't even thought about. Those are the things that can destroy the fragile existence of a firm such as MediBus.

Exhibit 1
MediBus Ambulette

Exhibit 2
Rate Summary

| | One-Way Trip | Round Trip | Extra Time[b] | Extra Mileage | Additional | |
					Fee	Charges
Medicare/ Medicaid	$10	$20[a]	$10/hr.	$0.50/mile—each mile over first 40	$2.50/ person[c]	
Private	$18 (10 free miles)	$30 (20 free miles)	$15/hr.	$1.30/mile—each mile over free miles allowed	$20/hr.[d]	
Recreational/ Social	$15/hr./ vehicle (10 free miles) (up to 9 passengers per vehicle)	—	$10/hr.	$0.75/mile—each mile over first 10	—	

[a] Minimum fee for round trip.

[b] Over the first hour; first hour is included in price of round trip. Extra time is all travel and passenger wait time after first free hour. Additional wait time is subject to this charge, even when the MediBus is utilized for other trips during the wait time.

[c] Nonclient passengers, such as nurses, aides, or family members accompanying the client.

[d] Additional charge for nonscheduled hours, such as weekends and holidays.

MEDIBUS, INC.
Exhibit 3
Pro Forma P&L
For Different Numbers of Vehicles, December 1974

	3 Medibuses	4 Medibuses	5 Medibuses	6 Medibuses	7 Medibuses	8 Medibuses
Income						
255 Average No. Work Days at $100/day/vehicle	$76,500	$102,000	$127,500	$153,000	$178,500	$204,000
Expenses						
Vehicle Lease	9,180	12,240	15,300	18,360	21,420	24,480
Insurance	2,400	3,200	4,000	4,800	5,600	6,400
Gas and Oil	3,900	5,200	6,500	7,800	9,100	10,400
Maintenance	750	1,000	1,250	1,500	1,750	2,000
Miscellaneous	750	1,000	1,250	1,500	1,750	2,000
Payroll Drivers[a]	21,060	28,080	35,100	42,120	49,140	56,100
Office Payroll	7,370	7,370	7,370	7,370	7,370	7,370
Payroll Taxes[b]	2,843	3,545	4,247	4,949	5,651	6,353

Office and Furniture					
Rent	3,180	3,180	3,180	3,180	3,180	3,180
Telephone[c]	1,500	1,500	1,500	1,500	1,500	1,500
Office Supplies	240	240	240	240	240	240
Postage	600	600	600	600	600	600
Legal & Accounting	1,200	1,200	1,200	1,200	1,200	1,200
Deposits & Security	680	680	680	680	680	680
Advertising, Promotion	750	750	750	750	750	750
Printing & Duplicating	100	100	100	100	100	100
Total Expenses	56,503	69,885	83,267	96,649	110,031	123,413
Net Income	19,997	32,115	44,233	56,351	68,469	80,587
	26%	31%	35%	37%	38%	40%

[a] Average $135/week/driver.

[b] 10% of payroll for drivers plus office payroll.

[c] $125/month—average.

Exhibit 4
Facilities, Patients, and Payments

LONG ISLAND FACILITIES[a]

There are at present some 7,040 nursing home beds serving a combined Nassau-Suffolk population estimated at 2,705,172, eight percent of whom are over 65. Health-related facilities [HRFs] now provide space for 2,462 patients. In Nassau and Suffolk the number of HRF beds are almost equal—1,418 and 1,044 respectively. In Nassau, however, where the population is somewhat older and larger, there are far more nursing home beds than in Suffolk. For every three beds in Suffolk there are four in Nassau. The actual numbers are 2,901 against 4,139.

Almost all of the 56 nursing homes and 20 health-related facilities on the Island are proprietary. In each county there is one public institution.

PATIENT PROFILE

In 1972, the Suffolk County Department of Health's Division of Hospital Affairs, the bureau responsible for the supervision of local facilities, released its most recent annual report. From its statistical findings, a thumbnail sketch of the typical nursing home patient emerges. The average patient is female and between the ages of 75 and 84. Women, who are known to outlive men generally, outnumbered them in Suffolk nursing homes three to one. Only a small portion of the patients—slightly more than eight percent—were less than 64 years old. People 75 to 84 years old were the most prevalent, averaging 43.3%. The next largest breakdown was the 85-and-over age group with 28.2%. The remaining 20.1% were between the ages of 65 and 74. It is of tangential interest to learn that according to the Suffolk figures the nursing home population is growing older. In the past three years, the post-75 group has increased noticeably at the expense of the younger people.

The greatest number of patients—over 40%—were bedridden. The rest were almost evenly divided between ambulant and semi-ambulant. Few stayed longer than a year—the average being 275 days. Thirty-four percent were discharged and either went home or to other facilities. Twenty-seven percent were transferred to hospitals for more intensive care. Thirty-nine percent died. Predominantly, they were county residents, indigent and on Medicaid.

PAYING THE BILLS

Since legislation was passed in 1966, children of aged parents are no longer responsible for their parents' medical bills. Only the assets of the sick person can be tapped for medical expenses. When these funds are totally exhausted, people over the age of 65 become eligible for Medicaid.

Medicaid will pay for nursing home or health-related facility care. Concomitant costs, such as physicians', dentists', optometrists', podiatrists' and chiropractors' fees and drugs

Exhibit 4
(Continued)

---

and therapy are also covered. Persons with an annual income of less than $2,000 and less than $1,600 in allowable reserves, in which the cash value of any life insurance policy is figured, qualify. Those with assets above these figures must wait until their funds are depleted to these levels to become eligible.

Under Medicaid, all personal income like Social Security and pension checks goes automatically to defray the costs of medical care. Only a $500 burial fund is allowed. Medicaid will pick up whatever part of the total bill the elderly person cannot pay. In addition, it will furnish the indigent person with a $24 a month stipend for his personal needs.

Medicaid is an assistance program enacted under Title 19 of the Social Security Act to furnish medical care to low-income and needy people. It is funded by federal, state and local taxes. In New York State, 50 percent comes from federal resources, 25 percent from the state and 25 percent from local revenues. Medicare, on the other hand, is an insurance program. All people over the age of 65 are automatically eligible—regardless of their financial assets—if they have paid into Social Security. As with Social Security, Medicare covers dependent husbands and wives.

Medicare can help pay part of the costs of short-term nursing home care. Medicare certification is not extended to health-related facilities. It is less comprehensive than Medicaid and its applicability is more limited. To be covered, an elderly person must be admitted to a skilled nursing facility within two weeks of a hospital discharge. The original hospital stay must be a minimum of three days. As with Medicaid, admission to the nursing home must be undertaken on the determination of a physician. The patient must require round-the-clock care for recuperation or rehabilitation of the ailment for which he was hospitalized. Unlike Medicaid, Medicare will only pay for the first 100 days of a nursing home stay.

In addition to the cost of the facility, Medicare Medical Insurance will pay for 80% of all doctors' bills, tests, X-rays, medical equipment and devices, injections and ambulance transportation after the patient pays the first $60.

Application for Medicare is routine and made through the local Social Security Office. Applications for Medicaid required two investigations to determine financial and medical needs. The latter is usually done through the individual's physician or hospital. The former is lengthy and requires a good deal of documentation.

Because of the high cost of nursing care, Long Island's Department of Health estimates that 70% of Suffolk's nursing home and HRF bills and perhaps 80–85% of those in Nassau are paid by Medicaid. Medicaid pays the homes their cost and, in the case of private facilities, a return on equity now set at 10 percent. The nursing home reimbursement rates paid by Medicaid now range from $25.53 to $42.35 a day in Nassau and from $25.54 to $46.14 in Suffolk. Some rates include the cost of prescription drugs and therapy.

---

[a] The three sections of this exhibit (Long Island Facilities, Patient Profile, and Paying the Bills) were extracted from a Marine Midland Bank survey of nursing homes published in the October 2–8, 1974, issue of the *Long Island Business Review*.

MEDIBUS, INC.
Exhibit 5
New York Section 4

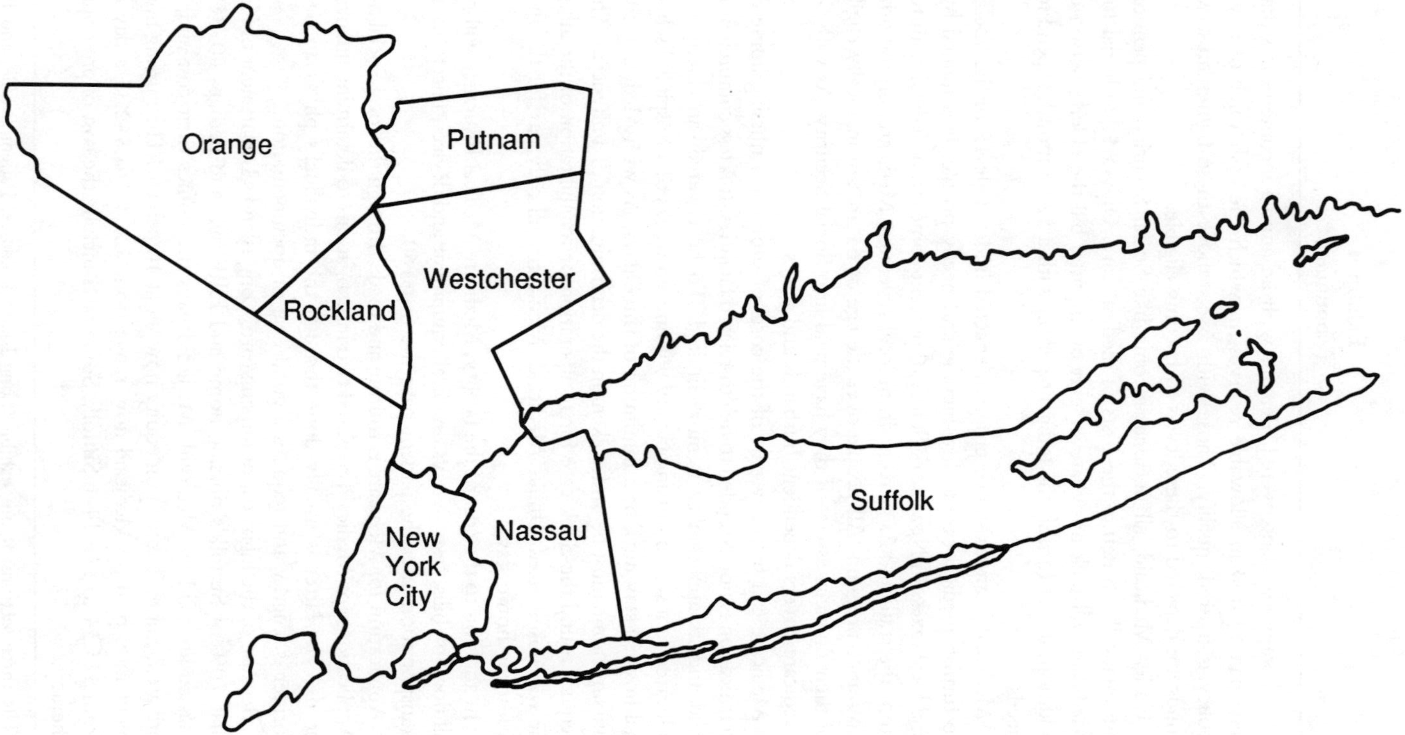

Orange

Putnam

Rockland

Westchester

New
York
City

Nassau

Suffolk

Exhibit 6
Trips from Institutions
February 24–28, 1975

Name	Type of Institution	Number of Trips
Broad Lawn Manor	Nursing Home	2
Brunswick Hospital	Hospital	1
Huntington Clinic	Out-patient Clinic	7
Lakehurst	Nursing Home	1
Mather Hospital	Hospital	2
Oak Hollow	Nursing Home	15
Saint Charles Hospital	Hospital	1
Saint James Nursing Home	Nursing Home	4
Saint James Plaza	Nursing Home	6
Sayville	Nursing Home	2
Smithtown General Hospital	Hospital	3
Smithtown Nursing Home	Nursing Home	1
Smithtown Rehabilitation Center	Out-patient Clinic	8
South County Nursing Home	Nursing Home	2
Woodhaven	Nursing Home	8
	TOTAL	63[a]

[a] In addition, there were four private clients during the period, February 24–28.

Exhibit 7
Random Samples of Invoices to
Medicaid of Suffolk County, N.Y.

Job #	Round Trip Mileage	Trip Time (Hours)	Total Fee[a]
1	6	3	$43.00
2	35	2	32.75
3	20	3	40.00
4	15	2.5	35.00
5	16	3	40.00
6	20	3	50.00
7	45	2	47.75
8	16	3	42.50
9	35	2	32.75
10	8	2	30.00
11	15	3	40.00
12	41	2	37.25
13	35	2	32.75
14	24	4	50.00
15	24	2.5	37.50
16	166	3.5	108.00
17	20	2.5	45.00
18	34	2	34.50
19	19	2.5	37.50
20	69	2	58.25
21	53	2.5	50.00
22	20	2	32.50
23	21	3	50.00
24	12	2	30.00
25	34	2	34.50
Average	32.1	2.5	42.86

[a]The actual fees varied from the price list in many cases due to technicalities of the Medicaid system.

Exhibit 8
Daily Statistics, February 1975

Day	Date	Round Trips Taken	Trips Cancelled[a]	Total Revenue
M	3	13	0	$ 424
T	4	10	1	338
W	5	11	1	663
TH	6	12	0	536
F	7	20	2	672
S	8	1	0	65
		67	4	$2,698
M	10	13	2	$ 482
T	11	10	1	450
W	12 (snow)	3	7	147
TH	13	13	0	527
F	14	8	0	273
S	15	1	0	35
		48	10	$1,914
M	17	16	2	$ 583
T	18	11	2	462
W	19	7	2	232
TH	20	15	0	603
F	21	13	1	484
S	22	2	0	90
		64	7	$2,454
M	24	10	1	$ 412
T	25	21	5	890
W	26	12	3	514
TH	27	16	1	634
F	28	8	2	311
		67	12	$2,761

[a]Cancelled by customers and clients.

Exhibit 9
Balance Sheet, February 1975

Assets

  Current Assets

Cash	$ 865.94	
Accounts Receivable	$14,863.80	
Prepaid Income Taxes	$ 183.54	
Other	$ 4,088.14	
Total Current Assets		$20,001.42

  Property & Equipment

Vehicles	----------------	
Furniture & Fixtures	$ 167.43	
Leasehold Improvements	$ 109.10	
Less Accum. Depreciation	----------------	
Total Property and Equipment		$ 276.53

  Other

Deposits & Miscellaneous		$ 2,328.00
Total Assets		$22,605.95

Liabilities

  Current Liabilities

Accounts Payable	$ 3,359.99	
Income Tax (NYS)	$ 33.50	
Notes Payable (Stockholder)	$ 322.00	
Total Current Liabilities		$ 3,715.49
Net Worth		$22,605.95

Common Stock—200 Shares, No Par

Total Liabilities and Net Worth		$22,605.95

MEDIBUS, INC.
Exhibit 10
First Quarter Projections

Number of Vehicles	January 2		February 3		March 3	Quarter
	Budget	Actual	Budget	Actual	March Budget	Quarter Budget
Sales	$3,450	$6,423	$4,000	$9,174	$8,000	$15,450
Cash Receipts		469		1,231		
Cash Disbursements						
Vehicle leases	780	812	780	987	780	2,340
Communication leases	—	—	—	—	275	275
Insurance	—	61	—	—	1,100	1,100
Gas and oil	220	114	200	381	200	620
Maintenance	—	42	—	411	75	75
Misc. fees	200	100	—	—	100	300
Payroll-drivers[a]	1,400	368	1,400	831	1,400	4,200
Payroll-admin.	1,500	1,610	1,300	1,288	1,306	4,100
Payroll taxes	168	75	168	184	168	504
Rent	265	265	265	265	265	795
Office equipment	—	29	35	167	35	70
Telephone	200	197	200	266	200	600
Postage	110	71	100	96	100	310
Office supplies	50	153	50	42	50	150
Advertising	100	—	50	—	25	175
Legal and accounting	175	360	75	—	75	325
Printing	30	30	20	140	25	75
Interest and loans	—	—	—	35	75	75
Other	50	777	300	—	—	350
Total	$5,248	$5,064	$4,943	$5,093	$6,248	$16,439

[a] Drivers were paid $2.75 an hour. Messrs. Gabriele and Richman drove a great deal in January and February. Only one driver was hired in January, one more was added in February, and a third in early March.

527

Caruso's Pizza

Jim Caruso reflected as he finished reading a 1984 *Forbes* article about Tom Monaghan, owner and chief executive officer of Domino's Pizza.[1] In 1960, Monaghan and his brother borrowed less than $1,000 to start a pizzeria in Ypsilanti, Michigan, 30 miles west of Detroit. Today, Tom Monaghan owned 94% of Domino's Pizza, a billion-dollar company and the food service industry's most rapidly growing restaurant chain. Perhaps his luckiest catch, however, was his 1983 purchase of the Detroit Tigers baseball team. In 1984, the Tigers won the World Series. Caruso smiled as he thought to himself, "If I can build *my* pizza business into a billion-dollar company, I'm going to buy a lot more than a baseball team."

BACKGROUND

Caruso, a restaurateur of twelve years, owned and operated seven pizza restaurants bearing his name in Columbus, Ohio (pop. 600,000; total metropolitan area: 1,000,000). He had been experimenting for more than a year with a system he saw as a breakthrough in pizza delivery.

Whereas most delivery operations prepared and delivered pizzas individually to order, Caruso's system involved producing pizzas in batches and storing them in delivery truck holding ovens. As orders were received over the telephone, a dispatcher notified the truck closest to the customer via two-way radio. When a truck ran out of inventory, it returned to its base to restock.

Sales using the new system had been strong, but profitability had been less than Caruso had hoped for. Moreover, there had been constant bickering among restaurant employees since the experiment began. Despite these problems, Caruso felt pressure to expand the concept. "Competition in pizza delivery is really heating up. If I don't go for it, my competitors will shut me out of the market—and I'll never know if the new delivery concept can work."

This is a condensed and combined version of the cases, Caruso's Pizza (A) and (B), prepared by Assistant Professor Christopher Hart and Mark Delfino, The Boston Consulting Group, with the research assistance of Lucy N. Lytle, as the basis for class discussion rather than to illustrate either effective or ineffective handling of an administrative situation. Names and locations have been disguised. Copyright © 1987 by the President and Fellows of Harvard College; Harvard Business School case #9-687-071 (Rev. 12/87).

1. Richard Behar, "Domino Theories," *Forbes*, February 13, 1984, pp. 124, 128.

He suspected that the key to making the express delivery system work was heavy order volume. To achieve this, he was considering leasing a computerized telephone order-entry system. He explained:

> Order-taking is a lot more professional, and the data can be used for production planning, route scheduling, direct mailings, market research, locations for new stores—all kinds of things. The system can even be set up to operate off *one* phone number for *all* the units. If Caruso's has a special phone number and we give it plenty of advertising and promotion, when people get hungry for pizza, who are they gonna call? "Domino-Busters," that's who—Caruso's pizza.

THE FOOD SERVICE INDUSTRY

In 1954, food service sales (coming mainly from restaurants and cafeterias) represented 25% of America's food dollar. By 1985, this percentage had risen to 42%. By the year 2000, the food service industry's share of the eating and drinking market was expected to grow to 50%.

The fastest-growing food service segment was fast food. Fast-food operations (which included pizza parlors and pizza delivery operations) recorded 1985 sales of $44.9 billion. *Exhibit 1* shows sales figures for fast-food industry segments.

TRENDS IN THE PIZZA BUSINESS

As shown in *Exhibit 2*, the pizza industry was highly fragmented. Pizzas sold in restaurants for nonrestaurant consumption, carryout, or delivery accounted for the lion's share of the market, with 1986 sales of $5.1 billion. Revenues from frozen and packaged pizza, purchased primarily in grocery stores and delicatessens, amounted to $1.8 billion that year. Although packaged pizzas were less than half the price of those purchased in restaurants (or delivered), they were losing market share steadily. As a whole, the pizza market was expected to grow at 8% to 10% annually through 1990. Estimated 1986 sales for the four pizza industry segments are shown in *Exhibit 3*.

To obtain a larger slice of the food service pie, pizza restaurants had been focusing their competitive efforts in two areas: (1) new products, and (2) pizza delivery. Single-serving pizzas were introduced in the early 1980s to attract convenience-oriented lunch customers. Thicker crust "pan pizza" was also introduced and widely advertised during this period. By 1985, pan pizzas accounted for over half the pizzas consumed in restaurants.

Competition in the fast-growing pizza-delivery business was intensifying. Domino's, a delivery-only chain, opened 850 units in 1985 for a total of over 2,900 units in early 1986. After experimenting with 100 delivery-only units for two years, the Pizza Hut restaurant chain announced in 1985 that it would open 1,300 of them in the next few years. By 1986 it had begun delivery operations in four major U.S. cities where the restaurant units were company-owned. The company decided to separate its restaurant and delivery operations because franchisees feared that delivery units would cannibalize their restaurants' carryout sales. "I don't want to be constantly worrying about whether my carryout business is getting screwed by company-owned delivery units," said one franchisee. Indeed, at least one national operator, Shakey's Pizza, announced to its franchisees that it had no intention of entering the delivery segment—mainly to allay possible franchisee concerns.

In addition to Domino's and Pizza Hut's expanding operations, some strong local and regional chains (e.g., Mr. Gatti's and Pantera's) were moving into new cities and opening combination restaurant/delivery operations. Many small, local pizza restaurateurs, fearful of losing their traditional carryout business to large national and regional operators, responded by starting their own delivery services. By 1985, articles about food delivery were blanketing the trade press; the pizza-delivery rush was on.

PIZZA PRODUCTION

Although pizza could be differentiated by the type, quality, and quantity of dough and ingredients, pizza production was a simple process that varied little from one operation to the next. Each morning, dough was made by mixing flour, yeast, and water. Once the dough had risen, it was rolled into balls of various weights (e.g., a single-serving pizza required a 5-ounce ball) and refrigerated. When a pizza order was received, a dough ball of the appropriate size was removed from the refrigerator and rolled through a machine that turned it into a round pie shell. (This machine made the traditional technique of tossing the pizza dough into the air obsolete.) Next, the shell was placed in a pie tin called a round. Topping ingredients (e.g., cheese, sauce, meats, vegetables) were measured and added in a sequence that varied from one restaurant to the next.

Finally, the pizza was baked. Increasingly, pizza operators were using conveyor-style ovens because they required less supervision. Two to 4 minutes were needed to prepare a pizza for baking. Baking time varied from 4 to 6 minutes for a thin-crust pizza, and from 8 to 12 minutes for the average pan pizza. (At an extreme, many of the famous Chicago-style stuffed pizzas took more than 20 minutes to cook.) Pizza Hut worked with an oven manufacturer to develop a special oven that could cook its pan pizzas in 6 minutes. Domino's thin-crust pizza, in contrast, took only 2 minutes to prepare and 5 minutes to cook.

PIZZA DELIVERY: THE "HOTSHOT" METHOD

Pizza delivery also was a simple process with which any restaurant could experiment. Since most pizza restaurants' ovens operated at less than 100% capacity, many operators perceived delivery as requiring no additional capital investment. One local operator who decided to expand into pizza delivery said, "I already have the overhead bills to pay. All I have to do is add a couple more phone lines and make sure I can get the pizzas to my customers. No problem." Usually, orders were taken over the phone by employees already on the staff. For peak periods—Friday and Saturday nights—one or two extra employees were sometimes hired to handle the increased number of phone orders. (Indeed, as many new entrants into pizza delivery soon realized, delivery orders and restaurant traffic usually peaked at the same time.)

Once a pizza was baked, it was usually boxed, stored in an insulated bag, and delivered by the next available delivery person. If possible, a driver would deliver multiple orders before returning to the restaurant, provided that the orders could be baked and delivered within minutes of each other. In reality, this was uncommon. The system of driving back and forth from the pizza production operation to customers—standard practice in the pizza delivery business—was known as hotshot delivery.

Hotshot delivery drivers were usually independent contractors. They were responsible for providing their own vehicles and paying their transportation costs (e.g., gasoline, insurance, maintenance, repairs). Most drivers considered their only "real" transportation costs to be gasoline and oil, however. A typical driver stated: "I only count my out-of-pocket expenses. I have to lay out dough for insurance, maintenance, and repairs anyway, so it doesn't matter. What I care about is the money that ends up in my pocket." (Some drivers kept track of their mileage for tax purposes. The IRS allowed transportation costs of $.21 per mile.) The average pizza delivery totaled two miles: one mile to the customer and one mile back to the store.

Operators supplied drivers with insulated delivery bags and signs that could be illuminated and affixed to the top of delivery vehicles. Compared with delivery labor costs, the cost of these items was negligible.

A delivery-*only* operator (like Domino's) purchased the same type of production equipment as a restaurant operator, but needed neither the space nor the equipment to accommodate in-store traffic (e.g., tables, chairs, dishes, dishwashing machine). Staffing plans were based on forecast order volume. Delivery personnel, who averaged two or three deliveries per hour, were paid the minimum wage of $3.35 per hour, plus an average of $.50 per delivery. Drivers also earned tips, ranging from 0% to 10%, depending on the type of customer. (College students, for example, were notoriously low tippers.) The average tip income equalled 3% to 4% of sales.

DOMINO'S PIZZA DELIVERY SYSTEM

Domino's was an adherent of the well-known KISS philosophy: "Keep it simple, stupid." Its product line was limited to two sizes of thin-crust pizza, 12" and 16", with a variety of toppings. Cola was the only beverage offered. Domino's had differentiated and positioned itself as a consistently fast deliverer of thin-crust pizza.

In fact, Domino's set the delivery standard for the industry, promising delivery in "less than 30 minutes or your money back." In actual practice, however, most Domino's locations offered late-delivery discounts of 25% to 35%—not 100%. In a 1985 interview, Domino's chairman, Tom Monaghan, said, "About 10% of our pizzas are late." Delivery time averaged 24.8 minutes systemwide.

To maintain its product quality and delivery-time standards, Domino's store usually served customers only within a two-mile radius. A Domino's store rarely accepted an order from a customer more than two miles away, and would never promise a delivery farther than three miles. Domino's believed a store needed a population base of at least 10,000 and preferably 20,000 to be profitable. Most Domino's units served population bases of roughly 40,000.

A typical Domino's unit opened at 4:00 p.m. Monday through Friday, and at noon on Saturday and Sunday. Closing was between midnight and 1:00 a.m. Sunday through Thursday, and at 2:00 a.m. on Friday and Saturday. Most units did not take orders during the day, but because many consumers wanted less expensive, single-service pizzas for lunch, some Domino's units were experimenting with lunchtime delivery.

Domino's advertised on national television, but most of its advertising was done locally, using radio and newspaper. A Domino's regional marketing staff coordinated cooperative marketing programs for the franchisees in a given ADI.[2] Radio spots promoted Domino's name and its pizza-delivery service, while print advertising listed the locations and phone numbers of all participating Domino's locations. At the local level, franchisees supplemented these promotional efforts

2. Area of dominant influence. An ADI was the area in and around a particular city served by the city's primary services and media: television, radio, and newspaper.

with coupons, handbills, university advertising, and the like. Domino's required each franchise to spend at least 3% of sales on advertising. Additionally, each franchisee paid a royalty fee of 5.5% of gross sales.

Although financial information about privately held Domino's was unavailable, *Exhibit 4* shows the estimated operating performance of a typical Domino's unit. The profitability compared favorably to that of a typical pizza restaurant grossing slightly more sales; a Domino's unit required only one-third the capital investment, however.

THE EXPRESS DELIVERY TRUCK CONCEPT

In 1984, Jim Caruso attended a seminar at a national pizza operators' convention that changed the way he thought about the pizza business. The speaker, Ron Roderick, had developed a patented temperature- and humidity-controlled oven and a production/delivery process that allowed an operator to prepare batches of pan pizzas and store them for up to two hours in holding ovens without any degradation in quality. (Each oven held up to 40 pizzas.)

Roderick was succinct in stating the advantages of his system: "Operators can forecast demand and offer pizzas with standard ingredient combinations the same way McDonald's estimates demand and produces standard products in advance of orders. My delivery system gives you more efficient use of labor—which translates into lower overall delivery costs. And the holding ovens allow you to deliver a better pizza." When a member of the audience pointed out that accurate demand forecasts were crucial to minimizing waste, Roderick replied, "You can do a sophisticated forecast with a computer or you can rely on best guess!"

As shown in *Exhibit 5*, the new system used a small Ford or Chevy truck with a specially designed bed. The bed had three doors: one to an area holding one or more coolers for storing cold items such as soda and salad; one to the holding oven; and one to the propane tanks that fueled the oven. Movable oven racks enabled an operator to stack products of virtually any size, so that the trucks could stock single-serving pizzas at lunch.

Each truck could be loaded with up to 40 large pizzas. When a delivery order was received at a unit, an order taker relayed the information to the dispatch operator, who checked the inventory of the truck nearest the caller's location. If the order could be handled by that truck, the dispatch operator gave the order taker an estimated delivery time, based on how long the dispatch operator estimated it would take the truck to reach the customer. The order taker then told the customer the expected delivery time, and the dispatch operator communicated the order to the truck driver over a two-way walkie-talkie radio. Closing the loop, the dispatch operator subtracted the delivered products from the truck's recorded inventory.

If a customer placed an order that could not be accommodated by the truck's unsold inventory, the order taker had three options: (1) try to persuade the customer to change the order to one that *could* be filled out of the truck's inventory; (2) determine whether a truck working an adjacent territory could fill the order within the delivery-time requirement; or (3) explain to the customer that the order could be filled, but the delivery time would be much longer, because the truck would have to return to its base. The dispatch operator was responsible for production scheduling—determining the inventory required to restock the trucks and passing this information along to food production personnel.

In a traditional hotshot operation, all pizzas were made and delivered in response to phone orders. With delivery trucks equipped with holding ovens, on the other hand, products were made in advance of being ordered and were carried in inventory. Orders could be placed by phone or drivers could sell pizzas directly off their trucks. Ron Roderick recommended that drivers be paid a sales commission to encourage off-truck sales. "You give the drivers a piece of the action and you'll see sales jump."

Roderick's presentation indicated that operators who were using the express delivery system had developed innovative merchandising methods. Some operators strategically positioned their trucks near schools and factories to intercept potential customers at the end of the school day or workday. Many drivers developed a regular lunch delivery route, and let office workers know when trucks would stop outside of particular buildings. The trucks' large storage capacity also made it possible to cater social events and club meetings.

The express delivery system enabled an operator to offer a product superior to that offered by competitors using hotshot delivery. Hotshot delivery, coupled with a promise of quick delivery, required a production system that minimized preparation time. Accordingly, the vast majority of delivery operators offered thin-crust pizza only. Moreover, to save time, these operators boxed pizzas directly from the oven, and immediately put them into insulated delivery bags. As the pizza cooled, steam was released, creating a soggy pizza. Consequently, consumers perceived the quality of delivery pizza to be mediocre. According to Roderick, "I hated delivery pizza when I was growing up, and always wondered why they didn't deliver the good pizza I got at the restaurant. Now I know— and the death of soggy pizza is coming."

Since the express delivery system allowed an operator to produce pizzas in advance of orders, production time was not crucial. A thick-crust pan pizza, for example, could be cooked in a conveyor oven and, when finished, placed on a metal rack for two to three minutes to cool to a uniform temperature of 180 to 200 degrees. Then it was boxed in a time-stamped container and put in one of the holding ovens (which had been patented by Roderick). Pizza were transferred to truck holding ovens as needed. The truck ovens also operated at 180 degrees and a constant flow of air controlled the humidity. The stability of the pizzas' temperature allowed them to be held for roughly two hours without any release of steam or deterioration of product quality. In his seminar, Ron Roderick mentioned that lasagna and hot sandwiches also kept well in the holding ovens.

Despite these advantages, the delivery truck system entailed several drawbacks. First, the operator had to buy the trucks and pay all transportation costs. Second, accurate communication between the dispatcher and drivers was essential. A customer could be promised 10-minute delivery for a pizza that the dispatch operator's records showed as being in unsold inventory, but that had, in fact, been sold off-truck. Miscommunication of orders, names, and addresses produced similar problems.

THE EXPERIMENT

After numerous conversations with Roderick, Caruso purchased four delivery trucks and installed a dispatch system in his highest-volume store. The delivery area included 20,000 Columbus residents and the nearly 40,000 students at Ohio State University.

Caruso decided to offer a limited selection of pan pizza from the chain's regular menu, and to supplement this "menu core" with a daily special (e.g., meatball sub or lasagna). Delivery was free, but delivery items were priced 10% above restaurant prices. Although margins were comparable to Domino's, Caruso's prices represented a 23% premium over the price of equivalent-sized Domino's pizzas. Delivery was available from 11:00 a.m. until midnight on most days, and until 2:00 a.m. on Friday and Saturday nights.

After one year, delivery sales in the one operation had generated nearly $500,000 in sales, exceeding the average sales of a Domino's unit. Moreover, this volume was achieved with only limited advertising. Caruso was certain that he had tapped into a strong market, which tempted him to launch express delivery immediately in the rest of his units. But his enthusiasm was tempered by the performance figures given to him by his accountant. (See *Exhibits 6* and 7.) "Maybe the numbers are screwed up," he mused. "At half a mill in sales, this thing has got to be profitable. The biggest problem I see is bickering between the regular kitchen staff and the express delivery staff—order takers, dispatchers, and drivers. Maybe I should bring in a consultant who does team-building, to get everyone pulling their oars in the same direction."

To develop the express delivery operation fully throughout the Columbus market, Caruso figured he would need to build five more restaurants. "I've got 50% of the ADI covered with my existing seven units. With five more, I'll cover another 30%. The other 20% I'm not worried about. Domino's, by the way, needs 20 units to cover the same area. Finding investment funds isn't a problem. I've got a real estate syndicator who will set up and sell limited partnerships for the new units. I would lease them back."

THE ONE-PHONE-NUMBER SYSTEM

Although Caruso was confident that he could get the capital to build the delivery-only units he needed to cover the Columbus market, he was nervous about "jumping in too quickly." He had recently learned, however, of a new computerized telephone order-entry system which might be able to generate the heavy order volume he felt was necessary to insure the success of his express delivery concept.

Traditionally, every pizza operation, whether independent or chain, took and delivered its own orders. Once an order was placed and filled, little (if any) customer information was retained. Few consumers knew which operators delivered in their areas and only the most loyal customers memorized the phone number of their favorite pizza delivery operation.

In recent years, however, a few pizza operators had blanketed large metropolitan markets with units and then installed a computerized, one-phone-number system to handle orders from all of the units. A regional chain, Mr. Gatti's, had recently installed such a system in Austin, Texas, and claimed a 60% increase in delivery business.

With this computerized system, an operator advertised one phone number in a given market. Calls were received at a central order-processing facility, where orders were taken randomly by one of a staff of order-takers, each of whom was equipped with a computer terminal.

Upon receiving a call, the order-taker entered the customer's phone number into the computer. The computer indicated whether the customer had placed another order (or orders) recently. If not, the customer's name, address, order, and any special delivery instructions were keyed into the computer. After reading the order back to the customer and receiving confirmation, the order-taker gave the customer an expected delivery time. Once order processing was complete, the information was sent via phone line to a printer located at the appropriate unit. The computer automatically selected the unit by matching the customer's address to unit territories. The entire process took two to three minutes.

If the customer *had* ordered within the past year, the computer displayed the customer's name, address, information on previous orders, and any special delivery instructions. After verifying the name and address date, the order-taker might ask the customer, "Do you want your usual pizza with pepperoni and mushrooms?" If the customer answered "Yes," the order-taker could press a button to enter the order and then finish the conversation by promising a delivery time. This type of order took a minute or less to process.

The computer system could aggregate orders by product, ingredient, and time taken. The information could be used to assist stores with future purchasing, production planning, and personnel scheduling. If orders were received from areas not presently served by the operation, the data could be compiled and used to determine where new units should be located.

OTHER OPERATORS' EXPERIENCE

Caruso talked with several operators who had installed one-phone-number systems. Two examples illustrated the system's strengths and weaknesses.

Pizza Pizza, located in Toronto, had successfully implemented a computerized one-phone-number order-handling system. Pizza Pizza's 85 stores covered approximately 85% of the 3 million people in the Toronto ADI. The company advertised its phone number extensively on radio spots, and it ran promotions with jeans and video stores, theaters, and practically any other organization that sold to individuals in its target market. Orders were processed by a $1 million computer system that required an average of 48 seconds to take an order. The phone number was so popular that Canadian customs officials at Toronto International Airport frequently required arriving passengers who claimed to be Toronto residents, but who lacked proper identification, to recite Pizza Pizza's number. In 1984, Pizza Pizza's sales topped $40 million and its aggressive competitive posture had kept competitors at bay. This performance was remarkable, considering that Pizza Pizza's thin-crust pizza was rated only average.

Learning of Pizza Pizza's success, Frank Allen, CEO of Pantera's Pizza in St. Louis, figured that he could take the St. Louis market by storm. Unlike Pizza Pizza, which limited its operations to carryout and delivery, Pantera's was an eat-in restaurant chain, with 48 units serving the St. Louis ADI of 2.9 million. Thirty of the stores were located in Missouri; the other 18 were located in Illinois, across the Mississippi River. Pantera's installed a one-phone-number system, modeled after Pizza Pizza's, for use with its hotshot delivery business. After 18 months, performance was not what Allen had envisioned. Unfortunately, the telephone company could not tie Pantera's stores on each side of the Mississippi into one phone number. At the end of 1985, Pantera's had tied all 30 of its Missouri stores into its one-phone-number system, but none of the 18 stores located in Illinois.

Pantera's charged its franchised stores $.35 per order processed. By March 1986, the system was generating about 40,000 orders per month—only about half of the computer's capacity. Equipment and manpower costs were running $18,000 per month, roughly $.45 per order.

The telephone problem was not the only cause of Pantera's subpar results. Unlike Pizza Pizza, neither Pantera's name nor its phone number had become household words in St. Louis. Allen attributed this to inadequate advertising and a phone number that lacked a catchy ring. In addition, Pantera's offered a thicker, better-quality pizza, one that took longer to cook. Because the company used hotshot delivery, it often could not provide delivery within 30 minutes. Since the restaurants had not been designed to handle the extra volume from delivery orders, it became very difficult to operate effectively at peak-demand periods.

The Columbus telephone company told Jim Caruso it would agree in writing that all of Caruso's units could be tied into one phone number.

CARUSO'S DECISION

"If you want to find Mr. Caruso, you'll have to go to the restaurant—with the express delivery trucks. I don't think he'll be in the office until later today," his secretary said.

Accordingly, the case writer went to the restaurant and found Caruso there in the parking lot, chatting and laughing with his drivers, who had just returned from the lunch rush. Spotting the case writer, Caruso gestured at the workers surrounding him and said, "See what a great manager I am, Mr. Business Theory? Management by wandering around—I'm up on all the latest stuff, huh?"

Caruso grabbed a pizza from the nearest truck and carved off a piece. "Here . . . you were wondering how the pizza tastes after it's been in the holding oven for a while. This one is two hours old. Try a slice."

"Not bad," the case writer admitted, taking pleasure in managing to gobble most of the cheese and toppings with one bit of crust. "A little crunchy, but not bad with a little Coke."

Caruso was obviously relishing the opportunity to perform in front of his drivers, who were responding enthusiastically. "You know, if we decide to go with this one-phone-number system, we're gonna need a really unique phone number. One that's catchy and also gives people an idea of what our pizza is like—like GR-PIZZA. Or maybe 'Want a time that's really rousin? Just grab the phone and dial 831-eight thousand!' 'For a pizza that's great, call 8888 . . . '"

Later that day, Caruso sat down to plot his strategy. For starters, he decided to compare the economics of a one-phone-number system with a Domino's system—advertising multiple stores, each with a separate phone number. Although no one had combined a one-phone number system with express delivery, a leading computer vendor indicated that the necessary software modifications could be made for $50,000.

Caruso felt that a full-scale express delivery operation could generate annual sales of $4 million. For his calculations, he decided to use the average sales volume for a typical Domino's unit—$400,000 per year. Without central order processing, each unit would need five telephone lines. With a one-phone-number system, only two would be required: one for the printer to handle orders from the central computer, the other for regular business operations. For every 40,000 incoming orders per year, one phone line at the central order-taking facility would be needed. Additionally, one phone line for every 80,000 orders was needed to transmit orders from the computer to the units. Costs for computer equipment with capacity of 600,000 orders per year would be roughly $5,000 per month. Caruso assumed that the order-processing facility would need one supervisor at $2,500 per month, and overhead costs would amount to roughly $65,000 annually. He put the information together into the table shown in *Exhibit 8*.

Staring down at the paper before him, Caruso wondered about the future:

> If I *don't* go with a one-phone-number system, I leave the door open for competitors like Domino's. Maybe that's what's bothering me—Domino's. Suppose I get my ten express delivery units out there and all of a sudden Monaghan decides Columbus is the ideal market to try express delivery—*and* a one-phone-number system. WHAM! Could I tangle with the elephant and win? I've built a nice profitable business with my seven restaurant units. Maybe I should be thinking about counting my money instead of expanding.

Exhibit 1
The Fast-Food Industry
(all figures in billions)

Fast-Food Segment	Projected 1986 Food and Beverage Sales		
	Large Chains	Small & Independent	Total
Hamburgers	$18.3	$3.5	$21.8
(McDonald's, Wendy's)			
Chicken	5.4	2.2	7.6
(Kentucky Fried Chicken)			
Pizza	3.8	3.4	7.2
(Pizza Hut, Domino's)			
Sandwiches	3.0	1.7	4.7
(Rax, Arby's)			
Ice Cream/Doughnuts	2.9	1.4	4.3
(Dairy Queen, Dunkin Donuts)			
Mexican	1.6	0.8	2.4
(Taco Bell)			
Seafood	1.0	0.2	1.2
(Long John Silver's)			

SOURCE: *Restaurants & Institutions*, January 8, 1986.

NOTE: No alcoholic beverage sales are included.
    Large chains = *Restaurants & Institutions* top 400 companies.

Exhibit 2
The Pizza Industry—Major Competitors

Name	# of Units	Average Unit Volume	Estimated 1985 Sales (millions)[a]
Pizza Hut	4,332	$450,000	$1,949
Domino's	2,300	416,000	957
Godfather's	900	450,000	405
Pizza Inn	720	415,000	291
Little Caesar's	600	383,000	229
Shakey's	318	520,000	165
Round Table	430	440,000	189
Mr. Gatti's	350	450,000	158

SOURCE: *Restaurant Business*, September 20, 1985.

[a] Estimated by *Restaurant Business*.

Exhibit 3
The Pizza Industry—Market Segments

Segment	1986 Sales (billions)	1986 Share	1983 Share
In-restaurant	$2.8	30%	30%
Carryout	2.3	25	30
Delivery	2.3	25	16
Frozen & Packaged	1.8	20	24
Total	$9.2	100%	100%

Exhibit 4
Economics of Typical Pizza Restaurant and Domino's Delivery-Only Operation

	Typical Dine-In		Domino's Delivery-Only	
Sales	507,000	113%	415,000[a]	109%
Coupons & Discounts	(37,000)	(8)	(20,000)	(5)
Empl. Meals/Waste	(20,000)	(4)	(15,000)	(4)
Net Sales	450,000	100	380,000	100
Cost of Food	(126,000)	(28)	(100,000)	(26)
Gross Margin	324,000	72	280,000	74
Wages—Mgmt.	(22,500)	(5)	(20,000)	(5)
Wages—Production	(45,000)	(10)	(30,000)	(8)
Wages—Servers	(31,500)	(7)	—	—
Wages—Delivery	—	—	(70,000)	(18)
Wages—Order Taking	—	—	(8,000)	(2)
Wages—Other	(9,000)	(2)	(8,000)	(2)
Other Delivery Expense	—	—	(4,000)	(1)
Store Overhead Expense	(27,000)	(6)	(15,000)	(4)
Operating Margin	189,000	42	125,000	33
Advertising	(18,000)	(4)	(12,000)	(3)
Rent	(27,000)	(6)	(9,000)	(2)
Other (including interest, depreciation)	(45,000)	(10)	(25,000)	(7)
Profit before Taxes	99,000	22	79,000	21
Franchise Royalty	(18,000)	(4)	(19,000)	(5)
Profit before Taxes	81,000	18%	60,000	16%
Capital Investment	350,000	100%	120,000	100
Amount Financed	210,000	60	72,000	60
Cash Outlay	140,000	40	48,000	40

[a] Average price per pizza = $10.00.

Continental Body Corp.

MANUFACTURERS OF MOBILE FOOD SERVICE EQUIPMENT

HOT PIZZA DELIVERY

- Each compartment separately heated with automatic controls for adjusting temperature

- Double oven with separate compartments (Stainless steel–39" wide x 21" high x 34" deep)
- Removable chrome rack for easy loading and routing

- Stainless steel cold food compartment and shelf

- Toll free order placing just call 1-800-344-5800

  Residents of Illinois call collect 312-379-5800

- All doors lock
- Each compartment has separate locks

- Hinge-up door self-opening by driver

- Entire frame undercoated

TONY'S
PIZZA EXPRESS
426-8800

542

Exhibit 5
(Continued)

Capital Investment

Truck—Ford Ranger or Chevy S-10	$ 8,000	5 years
Patented holding oven	1,500	5 years
Truck cab with painting and preparation	4,900	5 years
Two-way radio	800	5 years
Other equipment: 3 coolers, clipboards	200	5 years
TOTAL INVESTMENT	$15,400	

Annual Operating Costs

	Average	Range
Insurance	$ 800	$400–1,200 (Location and age of truck)
Maintenance	600	400– 800 (Age and care of truck)
Repairs	1,000	500–1,500 (Age and care of truck)

Exhibit 6
One-Year Financial Results: Restaurant and Delivery Operations

	Restaurant Sales		Delivery Sales	
Sales	718,031	114	486,101	113%
Coupons & Discounts	(72,543)	(12)	(16,333)	(4)
Employee Meals/Waste	(17,159)	(3)	(38,209)	(9)
Net Sales	628,329	100	431,558	100
Cost of Food	(172,832)	(28)	(127,554)	(30)
Gross Margin	455,498	72	304,004	70
Wages—Mgmt.	(20,031)	(3)	(18,431)	(4)
Wages—Production	(62,734)	(10)	(43,156)	(10)
Wages—Servers	(43,913)	(7)	—	—
Wages—Delivery	—	—	(64,734)	(15)
Wages—Dispatch	—	—	(17,262)	(4)
Wages—Order Taking	—	—	(21,578)	(5)
Wages—Other	(18,642)	(3)	(8,631)	(2)
Delivery Expense (gas, repair, maintenance)	—	—	(21,194)	(5)
Store Overhead	(44,568)	(7)	(28,254)	(7)
Operating Margin	265,610	42	82,803	19
Advertising	(32,661)	(5)	(21,796)	(5)
Rent	(37,435)	(6)	(1,050)	(0)
Other (including interest depreciation)	(93,145)	(15)	(49,811)	(12)
Profit before Taxes	102,409	16%	10,147	2%

Exhibit 7
Express Delivery Truck Economics

	Lunch	*Dinner/Late Night*
Sales Volume per Delivery	$ 6.00	$ 10.00
Deliveries per Day	20	24
Daily Sales Volume	$120.00 per truck	$240.00 per truck
Hours per Day	4	8
Delivery Days per Year	250	350
Miles per Delivery	1.3	2.4
Miles per Gallon	8	12
Delivery Wages	15% of sales	15% of sales
Number of Trucks	4	4

Other Assumptions:

1. One dispatch operator manages four trucks at a wage of $5.00 per hour (for each hour of delivery operation).
2. Gas and oil expense: $1.00 per gallon gasoline used.
3. No anticipated residual value for delivery trucks.

Exhibit 8
Economics of a One-Phone-Number System

	No System	*Phone System*
Annual unit volume	$400,000	$400,000
Number of units	10	10
Columbus-wide sales	$4,000,000	$4,000,000
Sales volume per order	$10.00	$10.00
Operating margin per order (Domino's)	$3.30	$3.30
Orders per year	400,000	400,000
Central lines in	0	10
Central lines out	0	5
Nonsystem lines per unit	5	2
Total phone lines	50	25
Annual lease cost/line	$420	$420
Orders taken per hour	20	30
Order-taker hours	20,000	13,333
Hourly order-taking wage	$4.00	$4.00

10

◆

Managing Information Technologies

The "holy trinity" of technology comprises methods, materials, and information. Information is of special interest here because it provides the means of operation for many service firms, the end product for many others, and both means and ends for yet others. Little wonder that 70% of information technology sold in the United States is purchased by service firms. Internal information systems have for years been used in all types of firms for planning and control purposes. But outstanding service providers increasingly are developing externally oriented information systems to track and predict customer (or supplier) behavior as well as the most effective practices in serving customers. These "experiential" systems result in data bases of accumulated experience that become important sources of competitive advantage over time in services ranging from the practice of medicine to airline transportation.

General questions that are useful to bear in mind in appraising the management of technology include: To what extent can basic methods, materials, and information technologies be combined for maximum advantage? Does the implementation of one or another of these technologies meet real needs of customers and employees? Can this be communicated effectively to them? Is the purpose for new technology primarily empowerment or control? Does the proposed technology empower customers, employees, or both? To what extent will it displace people? What are the relative roles of technology and people in the delivery of the service? What is the relationship between expenditures for technology and the training of people to use it? In developing and introducing new technology: Should the organization make or buy it? Should it adapt the technology to a service concept or vice versa (in cases where the technology is very powerful, for example)? Should it utilize portions of the technology during development? Should it test results on a localized basis? Has adequate provision been made for participation in the development process and for training and communication to reduce anxiety during introduction?

As you read the OTISLINE case, it may be helpful to keep the following questions in mind: Who are Otis Elevator's targeted customers? What do they value in selecting an elevator? What role does after-sales service play in delivering what they expect? How has OTISLINE changed the work carried out by the North American service operation? What, if any, impact has the system had on Otis's competitive position? What advice would you give Otis's management regarding future concerns and directions?

At Mrs. Fields Cookies, how is the information system described in that case used? To what extent does it empower store managers? Headquarters management? Are there limits on the number of typical Mrs. Fields Cookie stores that can be managed with this system? Can the existing system be implemented without change in La Petite Boulangerie stores? Why? What changes, if any, should be made in the system to reflect the new demands that are likely to be placed on it? How would you compare the information system at Mrs. Fields Cookies with OTISLINE? Which is best adapted to the needs of its respective service concept? Why?

You may well conclude after studying this material that technology that is primarily hardware-oriented rarely provides sustainable competitive advantage. If so, you will probably agree with leading service managers that advantage more often comes from the experiential data that a firm collects, the software it uses for its processing, and the people who are responsible for managing information technology and the information it produces.

OTISLINE

When elevators are running really well, people do not notice
them. . . . Our objective is to go unnoticed.

BOB SMITH
Executive Vice President
Chief Operating Officer
Otis Elevator

In late November 1985, John Miller, director of information systems for Otis
Elevator North American Operations, contemplated the future of OTISLINE,*
a computer application developed to improve Otis Elevator's responsiveness to
its service customers. The nationwide implementation of OTISLINE was under
way, and the company was considering several other applications that could use
the system's infrastructure.

COMPANY OVERVIEW

Otis Elevator, a subsidiary of United Technologies Corporation, was the world
leader in elevator sales and service (i.e., maintenance). Its 1984 revenue of $2
billion represented 13% of United Technologies' total revenue.[1] Otis Elevator
was organized into four geographic divisions: North American Operations, Latin
American Operations, Pacific Area Operations, and European Transcontinental
Operations.

Otis Elevator, named for the company's founder, Elisha Graves Otis, described
its business as the design, manufacture, installation, and service of elevators and
related products, including escalators and moving sidewalks. By the end of the
nineteenth century, Otis's name was known worldwide and had become synonymous with one of the most useful and dramatic inventions of the century, the
passenger elevator.[2] *Exhibit 1*, an excerpt from the company history, *Going Up*,
describes the events leading up to the installation of the first passenger elevator.

Research Assistant Donna Stoddard prepared this case under the supervision of Professor Warren
McFarlan as the basis for class discussion rather than to illustrate either effective or ineffective
handling of an administrative situation. The names of Otis Elevator employees have been disguised. Copyright © 1986 by the President and Fellows of Harvard College; Harvard Business
School case #9-186-304 (Rev. 1/88).

*"OTISLINE" is a registered servicemark of Otis Elevator Company.

1. *1984 Annual Report*, United Technologies Corporation.

2. Jean Gavois, *Going Up* (Hartford, Conn.: 1983), p. 74.

The Otis name connoted technological leadership, reliability, and quality. Since Otis Elevator was perceived to be the best, customers were willing to pay a premium for its products. The company marketed three elevator lines: Otis Hydraulics for low-rise buildings (up to 6 stories), Otis Geared for mid-rise buildings (up to 24 stories), and Otis Gearless for high-rise buildings. Otis had been most successful in selling elevators for projects that were large, that required customized elevators (atrium elevators, for example), or that required state-of-the-art elevator technology. Otis Elevator's large, highly regarded service organization often led customers to prefer an Otis elevator over another manufacturer's product.

In the late 1970s, microprocessor technology transformed the design of elevators, replacing the outdated mechanical elevator control systems. Otis Elevator's Elevonic 401, with three microcomputer-based control units, was one of the most advanced elevator systems at this time.[3] *Exhibit 2* gives a description of the Elevonic 401. Microcomputer technology enabled Otis Elevator North American Operations (NAO) to increase its market share significantly between 1980 and 1984. Management believed that microcomputer technology would also help shape the future of the service business.

ELEVATOR INDUSTRY OVERVIEW

By 1985, new equipment sales and service of elevators in North America represented approximately $1 billion and $2 billion markets, respectively. The industry was very competitive, with Otis, Westinghouse, Dover, Montgomery, Schindler, U.S. Elevator, and Fujitec the major manufacturers. Otis, however, was the leader in both sales and service. Because elevator sales were directly correlated to the building cycle, they were cyclical, but the elevator service market was very stable. Elevator manufacturers often accepted a low margin on the sale of an elevator in order to obtain the service contract since service accounted for a significantly higher portion of profits.

The service market attracted many participants because of its steady demand and high profitability. Consequently, thousands of elevator service companies existed, including both elevator manufacturers and many small companies devoted exclusively to elevator service. These companies could service elevators from almost any manufacturer since all elevators made prior to the introduction of microprocessor-based elevator control systems used similar electromechanical technology.

---

3. *Elevonic* is a registered trademark of Otis Elevator.

For a small building project, the elevator manufacturer was selected by the contractor, architect, or building owner. Larger projects often involved all three parties in the decision-making process. They selected a manufacturer on the basis of ability to satisfy the elevator performance specifications and architectural requirements, price, and reputation.

An elevator service company was selected on the basis of reponsiveness, quality, and price. An elevator manufacturer was typically awarded 60% to 80% of the service contracts for its newly installed elevators. As a building aged and competition for tenants increased, the cost of service often became the major consideration, and the lowest bidder received the service contract. Since servicing elevators with microprocessor-based control systems often required the use of proprietary maintenance devices, the manufacturer was more likely to keep these service contracts. Many elevator manufacturers offered discounts for long-term service contracts in an effort to attract and maintain service customers.

NORTH AMERICAN OPERATIONS OVERVIEW

North American Operations, with 8,000 employees at the end of 1985, was the second-largest division of Otis Elevator. The scope of its business necessitated a large, geographically dispersed field organization. *Exhibit 3* shows the NAO organization chart.

Branch offices and smaller field offices reported to district offices, which bore profit and loss responsibility. (Hereafter, district, branch, and smaller field offices will be referred to as "field" offices.) Field offices handled both sales and service and ranged in size from one or two people in outlying areas to as many as 100 people in large metropolitan areas. NAO's customer base was equally diverse; Otis installed elevators in buildings ranging from 2 stories to the 110-story World Trade Center in New York City.

NAO Information Services

NAO installed its first computer, an IBM 1401, in 1965 to automate maintenance billing. From 1965 until 1978, the computer was used for production control and accounting. From 1978 to 1981, on-line capabilities expanded its uses to include data entry and inquiry for inventory control and accounting.

In 1981, Otis implemented a companywide cost-reduction drive to improve NAO's profitability. Bob Smith, then president of NAO, asked John Miller to suspend all efforts in new systems development until a clear course of applications could be charted. Smith was concerned that the company was spending its applications development resources to automate old manual procedures rather than to establish new, helpful systems. Sixty percent of the programmers were laid off, no hardware upgrades were allowed, and no new applications were implemented. The work load was cut back as much as possible since the system in place (an IBM 370/158) was often running at 100%.

The year 1982 was one of transition for NAO's information services area. With the cost-reduction program completed, management began to assess the ability of information services to improve the quality of its maintenance service.

In late 1981, NAO had begun to investigate the feasibility of using information technology to establish a centralized customer service department (on either a regional or a divisionwide basis) to accept customer requests for elevator maintenance during nonworking hours, that is, non-prime-time callbacks. (A callback is a customer request for elevator maintenance.) Otis and other elevator service companies were then using commercial answering services for non-prime-time callbacks. Otis supplied the answering service with a duty roster from which it selected a service mechanic to dispatch to the customer. In small cities, the same answering service was commonly used by several elevator service companies. During prime time (regular working hours), the customer called the local NAO field office, where an Otis employee accepted the call and dispatched the appropriate service mechanic.

Customers assess the quality of an elevator company's service offerings mainly by its responsiveness to callbacks. The callback response time is the time it takes a service mechanic to arrive on site after the customer reaches Otis Elevator (or its answering service). Although Otis received assurances from the local answering services that it would be promptly notified of a customer callback, the quality of the answering services varied greatly. In a videotape that described the need for the centralized customer service department, Bob Smith stated, "A commercial answering service does not have the same interest that we have to get service to the customer as fast as possible."

By August 1982, a centralized customer service system had been successfully piloted in a major eastern market, and Otis management decided to create a North American customer service center to dispatch service mechanics, in response to callbacks, 24 hours a day. A project team composed of individuals from many functional areas, including information services, was selected to implement this concept, which was called OTISLINE.

An IBM 3083 was installed in early 1983 to replace the IBM 370/158, and by 1985 extensive peripheral equipment, including state-of-the-art direct access storage devices, tape drives, and telecommunications equipment, had been installed. These additional resources were acquired to support the OTISLINE customer service center. The 1985 NAO information services budget was more than twice as large as the 1982 budget.

Most of the 2,300 service mechanics employed by NAO in 1985 had assigned routes and were responsible both for callbacks and for preventive maintenance for specific elevator customers. NAO calculated that reducing callbacks for each installed elevator by one a year would save Otis $5 million annually. Out-of-service elevators not only irritated customers and handicapped their businesses, but also affected their opinion of the quality of an Otis elevator.

OTISLINE OVERVIEW

Brad Robertson, director of service operations, was the leader of the OTISLINE development team and was responsible for the implementation and management of the OTISLINE customer service center. During the development of OTIS-LINE, Robertson reported to the vice president of finance; after an August 1985 reorganization, he reported to the vice president of marketing.

In describing OTISLINE, Robertson stated:

OTISLINE improved the visibility of our service business and helps management and local office personnel to provide quality service to our customers more effectively. Our responsiveness to customer callback requests has been greatly enhanced. OTISLINE's reporting functions provided district, regional, and NAO headquarters management with a significant amount of information on the quality of service rendered to our customers. Prior to OTISLINE, management became aware of many service problems only if there was a customer complaint. OTISLINE has allowed us to produce "excess" callback reports for various levels of management. For example, elevators receiving three or more callbacks in a month are reported to the district manager; those receiving eight or more in 90 days are reported to the regional vice president. Critical situations are reported to the president.

The excess callback reports highlight problem installations and have enhanced our ability to quickly diagnose problems that may be due to a specific component malfunction. With this information, local office management (or engineering management if the problem is with a component malfunction) can focus resources on key problem areas.

The success of OTISLINE is attributable to the top management support of the project, which fostered cooperation among functional areas and provided the resources and motivation required to "make it happen."

OTISLINE not only improved the quality of NAO's customer service; it also changed the way NAO does business. The OTISLINE system affected almost all of NAO's business functions, including information services, customer service, service mechanic dispatching and control, and service marketing and engineering. In addition, its infrastructure has been used to support applications that enhance the productivity of elevator sales representatives and service mechanics. In the future, OTISLINE may interface directly with installed elevators by means of remote diagnostic technology.

Following is a description of OTISLINE's impact on specific business activities.

Information Services

The OTISLINE application is a part of NAO's Service Management System (SMS), an integrated data base management system (*Exhibit 4*). Prior to OTIS-LINE, the SMS data base contained the customer master file (customer name, building location, contract information) and other information that was used to monitor and control the service business, such as route information and service price estimating data. With OTISLINE, the SMS was expanded to include *all* maintenance activity for elevators under a service contract. Some applications, such as service price estimating, were improved, and new applications such as billing will be added. The SMS data base is accessed and updated by an OTIS-LINE dispatcher through a display attached to the IBM 3083 host computer. Designed in the late 1970s, the SMS data base significantly shortened the time required to develop OTISLINE. According to Tim Clark, manager of systems development, the development of the OTISLINE application would have taken four to five years if the SMS data base had not already been in place.

The OTISLINE application was designed to enable the OTISLINE dispatcher to respond to a customer in less than a second by giving the dispatcher a local display and by engineering short data base paths to the necessary information. Subsecond response time was an important design element because experience had shown that when more than 2% of transactions had longer than a five-second response time, the time taken to handle customer service requests was unacceptable.

Because of the strategic nature of the OTISLINE application, a large portion of the information services budget was earmarked for its support. The data center operations budget was also increased significantly to support OTISLINE's stringent response-time and performance requirements. New methodologies of systems development were being introduced as a direct result of OTISLINE. By the end of 1985, 37 local terminals had been installed at the OTISLINE Service Center; future plans called for the installation of 150 personal computers in the field offices with OTISLINE inquiry capability.

Customer Service

The OTISLINE Service Center was staffed by highly skilled dispatchers. About half of them had college degrees, and many spoke two languages. New hires received from four to six weeks of in-house training, covering

- The OTISLINE software (the dispatching system)
- The IBM display
- Operation of the phone system
- Appropriate telephone salutations and courtesies
- Listening and customer satisfaction skills
- Overview of Otis Elevator organization structure
- Elevator terminology and possible system problems

The objective of the training was to ensure the dispatcher's ability to handle customer calls in an efficient and effective manner. The company held periodic seminars to update the dispatchers on system changes, to review sample dialogues for situations that were likely to be encountered (for example, an irritated customer or a trapped-in-an-elevator scenario), and to discuss the criteria used to assess dispatcher performance.

OTISLINE dispatchers were trained to be courteous, sensitive, and efficient and to speak clearly. They were taught to update the data base with information obtained during a call, thus allowing quicker identification of both the building and the elevator during subsequent calls from the same customer. Periodically, a supervisor or manager listened in as a dispatcher handled a call and then completed a dispatcher evaluation form and reviewed it with the dispatcher.

Customers accessed OTISLINE by calling a toll-free number connecting them to the North American customer service center. Incoming calls were distributed either to the next available dispatcher or to a specific dispatcher (calls from a French-speaking province in Canada, for example, would be routed to a French-speaking dispatcher). Calls coming in on designated critically important lines were moved automatically to the head of the queue.

The telephone system produced a variety of statistics. Reports showed the amount of time each dispatcher was available to accept calls during the shift, thus enabling Otis to measure dispatcher performance against department standards and averages. The system also produced statistics on how long customers had to wait for an available dispatcher. This information helped management determine when to employ additional staff in order to maintain a high level of responsiveness.

The OTISLINE application display screens were designed to lead the dispatcher and the customer quickly through a series of questions to identify the building and elevator needing service. When a customer call was received, the OTISLINE dispatcher filled in the display screen shown in *Exhibit 5*. OTISLINE could recognize a building and elevator in four different ways: (1) the building identification number; (2) the telephone number; (3) the building name, city, and state; or (4) the building address, city, and state. A "no hit" situation was encountered if the building and elevator needing service could not be identified using one of these criteria. The dispatcher then was expected to assure the customer that a service mechanic would be dispatched, end the call, and use alternate procedures to find the information on the building and elevator. If a "hit," or identification, was made, the dispatcher verified the building address and elevator identification number, ended the call, and logged the service request. Another dispatcher then paged the appropriate mechanic.

The OTISLINE Service Center was organized to promote dispatcher efficiency. During a shift, each dispatcher was usually assigned one function: to accept calls, to page service mechanics, or to handle new equipment sales (described later). Thus one callback request often involved four OTISLINE dispatchers: one to log the service request, one to page the service mechanic, one to receive the call from the service mechanic, and one to log the situation resolution data from the service mechanic's "closing" call.

By the end of 1985, 11 of the 47 NAO districts were using OTISLINE for 24-hour dispatch of service mechanics. The service center received 4,300 calls on an average weekday. However, the center would be expected to handle 10,000 incoming calls per day as soon as the system was implemented for all of the districts. Customer calls accounted for one-third of the total calls, 75% of which were service requests. The majority of the calls were from service mechanics who had been paged or had just closed a callback.

Dispatching and Control of Service Mechanics

Prior to OTISLINE, each field office handled the dispatching of service mechanics during normal working hours and used answering services after hours and on weekends and holidays. Service mechanics were required to complete a written report for each callback. These reports provided the data for a callback and repair history log that the field office's service desk representative maintained. This log was used by the local office to support daily operations and by the engineering department to flag problems and establish preventive maintenance procedures. Since these logs were maintained manually, the preparation of summary reports was very time consuming. Thus callback data were reported to district, region, or NAO headquarters only upon request.

With OTISLINE, instead of filing a written report for each callback, the service mechanics called OTISLINE, described the situation when they arrived at the building, and reported the steps taken to repair the elevator. The service mechanics carried a pocket notebook in which they recorded information on each service call. The notebook also listed the questions they would need to answer for the OTISLINE dispatcher when completing the callback report.

One measure of performance in field offices was the number of callbacks received. Prior to OTISLINE, the accuracy and consistency of callback reports varied from office to office. Identifying chronically malfunctioning components and other recurring problems was difficult because detailed information was not yet stored in a central data base.

With OTISLINE, the quality and timeliness of information available to district, region, and NAO management increased significantly. All customers (including large installations with onsite service mechanics) now called OTISLINE to request service. The OTISLINE dispatcher then paged the service mechanic to request service on a particular elevator. All data about service calls were stored in a central computer (see *Exhibit 6*), so the local offices no longer needed to keep manual elevator maintenance history logs.

Initially, some field office managers were skeptical of the OTISLINE concept. They felt that the system would decrease their control over the dispatching of service mechanics for callbacks and that therefore they would not know the location of their service mechanics throughout the day. OTISLINE is being improved to address these concerns. Personal computers with OTISLINE inquiry capability will be installed in field offices to enable local management to track callback activity in their territories.

Bob Smith noted that although centralizing service mechanic dispatching seemed contrary to NAO's decentralized organization, the quality and reliability of Otis products provided Otis's edge over its competitors. With OTISLINE, service and engineering managers had the information they needed to continue to boost the quality and reliability of Otis products.

Marketing—New Equipment Sales

The company also used OTISLINE to support elevator sales. New equipment sales representatives could access the New Equipment Sales (NES) application by calling OTISLINE. NES was an integrated data base management system designed to automate the production of status reports on elevator sales prospects. It had three primary components: negotiation, estimation, and disposition.

Negotiation allowed the new equipment sales representatives to organize data about new equipment projects and to communicate the status of those projects to the appropriate managers.

Estimation provided cost estimates and configurations for certain new products that could be used by the new equipment sales representative and local office to determine the elevator sales price.

Disposition provided the mechanism to record the outcome of a negotiation as a customer decision to purchase an elevator from Otis, as a competitive loss, or as an abandoned effort.

NES made data about competitive losses and performance of new equipment sales representatives easily accessible to management. In the future, when a negotiation becomes a sale, the NES information will be used to establish a record in SMS.

Marketing—Service

A brochure published in 1984 to describe OTISLINE to the NAO service mechanics listed six components of Otis Elevator's philosophy of service: responsiveness, reliability, innovation, communication, teamwork, and customer satisfaction. OTISLINE addressed all of these elements.

Responsiveness. OTISLINE dramatically improved NAO's responsiveness to customer maintenance requests. The system kept track of the status of the response to customers' calls. If the service mechanic assigned to a route was unable to take a call, either an alternate service mechanic or the service supervisor was paged. Response time was especially critical for certain customers such as hospitals and buildings with only one elevator. Backed by OTISLINE, the company began to offer a guaranteed response time to these customers. The system also produced reports of response-time statistics that could be reviewed with customers.

Reliability. OTISLINE dispatchers updated the SMS to maintain data on actions that had been necessary to repair out-of-service elevators. This data could be used by management to allocate resources to locations with recurring problems and by engineering to spot trends that indicated elevator design problems.

Innovation. As the leader in the industry, Otis was expected to deliver more than its competitors. NAO was the first to offer a professionally staffed customer service center.

Communication. OTISLINE improved communication between Otis customers and the service and sales departments. It also provided a more effective way for service and sales departments to submit reports to management.

Teamwork. The OTISLINE dispatcher was one of many members of the team concerned with providing a high level of service to Otis customers.

Customer Satisfaction. Customer satisfaction, as measured by a reduction in both the volume of complaints and service calls, improved as a result of the implementation of OTISLINE.

The United Technologies 1985 *Annual Report* noted that Otis strengthened its number one share of the service market in North America. OTISLINE contributed to NAO's ability to improve service quality and to compete successfully with lower-priced independent service companies.

FUTURE APPLICATIONS

Bob Smith felt sure that information technology could be used in many ways to further enhance Otis Elevator's marketing of service.

Remote Elevator Monitoring (REM). Otis Elevator had been testing REM, an application by which a microprocessor-based elevator could monitor its control system and log performance statistics directly onto a distant computer. In the pilot installations, elevators communicated problems to a personal computer at NAO headquarters. The personal computer then analyzed the problems and produced trouble reports used to dispatch service mechanics before the elevator went out of service.

Further development of REM would enable an elevator to communicate with a central computer that would determine the cause of the problems, transmit a message to the OTISLINE system, and dispatch a service mechanic.

The great advantage of REM was its ability to identify problems before an elevator was out of service. The service mechanics could adjust running elevators to keep them operating at maximum performance levels, and NAO could handle specific problems before customers were even aware of them.

In-Car Phones. The most sensitive kind of callback occurred when passengers were trapped in an elevator. Many Otis elevators were equipped with a telephone with which the passenger could automatically reach the OTISLINE dispatcher to notify the service department of the situation. The OTISLINE phone system recognized calls coming in on these lines and moved such calls to the head of the queue. The OTISLINE dispatcher was then alerted via a message on the telephone display or an audible beep that an emergency call had been received. The dispatcher could then work with the passenger to identify the location of the elevator and dispatch a service mechanic immediately.

Replacement of Service Mechanic Pagers with Hand-Held Terminals. Field service mechanics were contacted using pagers. Eventually these pagers could be replaced with hand-held terminals through which the OTISLINE dispatcher could send a message directly to the service mechanic, thus eliminating the need for service mechanics to call in for messages. The service mechanic could also use the hand-held terminal to complete callback reports and to order parts for out-of-service elevators.

New Equipment Ordering. NES could be expanded to include files for new equipment orders. When the new equipment sales representative called in to report that a project had resulted in a sale, he or she could also place the order for the elevator. This information could be transmitted directly to the plant, thereby shortening the lead time for manufacturing the elevator. Moreover, by reducing the amount of time taken to notify the plant of an order, NES could improve management of the plant's raw material inventory.

Contract Management. After Otis made a sale, its ability to monitor and abide by the customer's installation schedule was extremely important. Slippages in the installation schedule could be caused by building contractor delays, by technical problems encountered by the Otis superintendent at the construction site, or by elevator manufacturing delays. Both Otis and building management had to be aware of these problems. A personal computer could be installed at the construction site so the construction superintendent could document slippages in the schedule. This information could be communicated to the factory and to others involved in the installation and could be used to keep both Otis management and the building owner aware of the reasons for changes in the installation schedule.

Telemarketing of Service. The SMS data base contains information on all installed Otis elevators in North America. The OTISLINE facility could be used to contact those customers whose service contract was not with Otis. The OTISLINE dispatcher could find out when the current elevator maintenance contracts would expire and could produce a prospect list to be distributed monthly to the service sales representatives.

In a 1985 NAO management newsletter, Bob Smith stated:

> The real significance of OTISLINE is its ability to collapse both distance and time, resulting in faster responses to customer problems, better maintenance procedures, and, ultimately more reliable elevators. . . . This can translate into real competitive advantage. We're confident that it will, and we are investing accordingly.

Exhibit 1
The First Elevators

31128

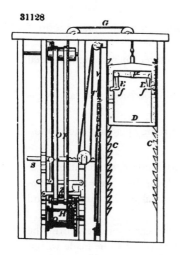

The story of Elisha Graves Otis is a textbook tale of
inventiveness, opportunity and enterprise. Along with
other folk heroes of Victorian America, Otis took his place
in books of precept and example. Imagine the scene:
a small factory in Yonkers, making cheap iron bedsteads.
The young Elisha Otis, master mechanic and inventor of
a system for raising and lowering beds, contemplates the
arid prospect of his future. Then in comes Mr. Newhouse
from Hudson Street, New York, to ask if Mr. Otis could
adapt his safety elevator to the problem of shifting
merchandise. Could he, in fact, build him two elevators
for hauling goods rather than lifting bedsteads. Two years
later there were 27 Otis elevators in service in New York,
and the foundations had been laid for enduring fame
and fortune. Otis demonstrated his safety elevator in
characteristically dramatic fashion at the New York
Crystal Palace exhibition in 1853. He had himself hoisted
up on the elevator platform, in full view of alarmed
spectators and delighted journalists, and promptly cut
the suspension cord. Nothing happened; the rack and
pinion safety lock ensured that he was *All safe, Gentlemen!*
The first passenger elevator was installed in
E. V. Haughwout and Co.'s store on Broadway in 1857;
it was the talk, and envy, of the town, attracting
thousands of visitors.
Otis Collection.

BROADWAY: THE STORE OF MESSRS. E. V. HAUGHWOUT AND CO.

Reprinted with permission of Otis Elevator.

Exhibit 2
Description of Elevonic 401

SYSTEM HARDWARE

The advent of microprocessor technology has enabled Otis to reassign elevator control strategies from hardware to microcomputer software.

Elevonic 401 control hardware is an integrated network of three microcomputer-based control units; a

Group Controller (in the machine room) to make dispatching decisions and call assignments; a

Car Controller (one per car in the machine room) to govern the operation and motion of the car; and a

Cab Controller (mounted behind the car operating panel) to interface with control hardware on the car, communicate cab data (e.g. passenger load, car calls) with the car controller, and control car-operating panel speech synthesis, visual display functions and coded secure entry.

Transducers, the sensors of the system, together with the car controller, form the closed loop structure that provides feedback that enables corrections to be made within milliseconds.

The group and car controllers employ the latest microprocessor technology. They differ in the number of cards in their card files and in the resident software. Although control hardware is standard for all Otis high-rise duties, and designed to suit practically all building specifications, custom software is added to personalize the controllers for each building's specific requirements.

The cab controller serves as a bi-directional information link between the cab mounted devices (car call buttons, load weighing transducers, speech synthesizer, secure entry modules) and the car controller. Multiplexing (transmitting hundreds of signals back and forth over a single pair of wires) between controllers significantly reduces the number of wires required for communication between controllers and peripheral devices. For example, while previous systems required an average of three traveling cables, the new Elevonic 401 system utilizes just one.

System hardware determines the quantity and quality of input received by the control system permitting control decisions and corrective actions to be made and implemented within milliseconds. Digital measurement yields such benefits as the precise control knowledge of car velocity, acceleration and position.

Transducer feedback, obtained as digital numbers, is compared by the controller with the prescribed specifications. The difference, or error, is driven toward zero to enforce the specified flight pattern programmed in the computer.

The hardware components of the new Elevonic 401 system permit placing total operating authority under software control. Minimum physical or mechanical adjustments are required to maintain control. Changes in strategy and performance requirements are implemented in the software. The result is more precise, more efficient control, with the capacity to control a greater number of functions with much greater flexibility—making instantaneous decisions based on real time conditions.

Exhibit 3
NAO Organization Chart

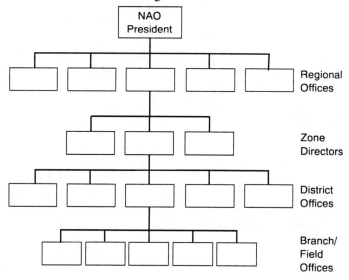

Exhibit 4
NAO Service Management System

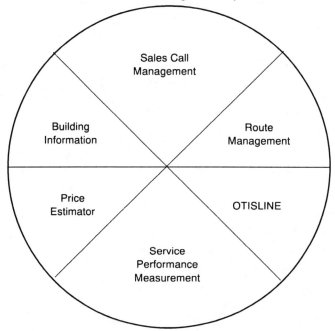

Reprinted with permission of Otis Elevator.

Exhibit 5
Customer Call Recording

    Type:

    Phone:

    Name of Caller:

    Building ID:

Request

    Building Name:

    Address:

    City:

    State:

If Message, Phone Number Customer Called: Next Function:

Reprinted with permission of Otis Elevator.

Exhibit 6
Callback Data Stored Online

Elevator identification

Date/time service requested

Requestor of service

Time service mechanic notified

Time service mechanic arrived on site

Condition of elevator on arrival

Time elevator back in service

Repair action taken

Service mechanic responding to request

Maintenance supervisor

Cause of malfunction or problem

Reprinted with permission of Otis Elevator.

Mrs. Fields Cookies

Creating something new, given the old and familiar, is an art rather than a science. The late, latter-day da Vinci, Buckminster Fuller, has been credited with this ability. "Part of Fuller's genius," wrote Tom Richman,[1] "was his capacity to transform a technology from the merely new to the truly useful by creating a new form to take advantage of its characteristics." What Fuller's geodesic designs had done for plastic, observed Richman, the administrative management processes Debbi and Randy Fields developed for Mrs. Fields Cookies did for information technology.

Fuller, who once suggested that a particularly awkward application of a new technology to an old process would be "like putting an outboard motor on a skyscraper," would very likely have approved of the Fields' creation—"*a* shape if not *the* shape, of business organizations to come," according to Richman.

> It gives top management a dimension of personal control over dispersed operations that small companies otherwise find impossible to achieve. It projects a founder's vision into parts of a company that have long ago outgrown his or her ability to reach in person.
>
> In the [Fields'] structure . . . computers don't just speed up old administrative processes. They alter the process. Management . . . becomes less administration and more inspiration. The management hierarchy of the company *feels* almost flat.

Debbi Fields had created the business. Randy had devised a corporate structure fit to be wed to an information system. Theirs was a case of putting an outboard motor, not on a skyscraper, but on a boat.

THE COMPANY

In 1988, Debbi Sivyer Fields, as president of Mrs. Fields Inc. and Mrs. Fields Cookies, had dominion over 416 Mrs. Fields cookie outlets, 122 La Petite Bou-

Keri Ostrofsky prepared this case under the supervision of Professor James I. Cash as the basis for class discussion rather than to illustrate either effective or ineffective handling of an administrative situation. Copyright © 1989 by the President and Fellows of Harvard College; Harvard Business School case #9-189-056 (Rev. 7/29/89).

1. Tom Richman, "Mrs. Fields' Secret Ingredient," *Inc.* (October 1987): 67–72.

langerie stores, 129 Jessica's Cookies and Famous Chocolate units, 2 Jenessa's retail gift stores, Jenny's Swingset (a children's casual clothing store in Park City), Mrs. Fields Dessert Store (a Los Angeles store that sold ice cream, cookies, cakes, and pies), Mrs. Fields Candy Factory (in Park City), Mrs. Fields Cookie College (for training store managers and assistant managers), and a macadamia nut processing plant in Hawaii. Mrs. Fields Cookies operated 370 cookie stores in the United States, 10 in Canada, 6 in Hong Kong (through 50% ownership of Mrs. Fields Cookies Far East Ltd., a joint venture with a local company, Dairy Farm Ltd.), 7 in Japan, 6 in the United Kingdom, and 17 in Australia. The company employed 8,000 people, 140 in staff positions at the Park City corporate offices.

Mrs. Fields Cookies, like many of Buckminster Fuller's designs, achieved elegance of function by marrying what might at first seem to be incongruous elements. Customers knew Mrs. Fields Cookies as the upscale brown, red, and white retail outlets that dispensed hot, fresh, chewy cookies like grandmother used to bake. Few were aware that by 6:00 a.m. Utah time, a computer in Park City, high in the Uinta Mountains, would know of their purchase and every other purchase made at the more than 500 Mrs. Fields Cookie stores in 25 states and five countries on four continents.

The cookies, of course, came first. Debbi Sivyer began baking cookies as a teenager. "Chocolate chip cookies were an easy project . . . just the thing to keep you busy on a rainy afternoon. . . . The Sivyer clan was always delighted to discover a plateful of chocolate chip cookies, and they weren't expensive to make."[2] Debbi perfected her recipe while a teenager, working first for the Oakland A's baseball club (retrieving foul balls on the third base line) and later for a local department store. These experiences fueled her enthusiasm and drive, and were a source of the fundamental philosophies she would later bring to the management of Mrs. Fields Cookies.

At 19, Debbi married economist and Stanford University graduate Randy Fields, then 29. Finding her expertise in demand by her husband's clients, who often asked that she bake for their visits, Debbi convinced Randy that she should go into the cookie business. The couple borrowed $50,000 and, in August 1977, within a year of being married, Debbi opened her first store, Mrs. Fields Chocolate Chippery, in Palo Alto, California. Debbi sold $50 worth of cookies on her first day in business, and $75 worth on her second day, thereby winning a friendly bet made between Debbi and Randy regarding the total sales she would make each day.

More than a year passed before Debbi opened a second store in a high-traffic tourist area of San Francisco. "With the first store, I had what I wanted," Debbi

2. Several quotations in this case are taken from Debbi Fields, *One Smart Cookie* (New York: Simon and Schuster, 1987).

recalled. "As Randy had his thing to do every day, I had mine. When the people at Pier 39 shopping mall called and asked me to open a store there, I was immensely flattered . . . thanked the leasing agent profusely, and turned him down. . . . What I saw as a store, he perceived as a business—a business that could grow. The point wasn't to make money, the point was to bake great cookies, and we sacrificed for that principle." Her employees' desire for growth and greater opportunity finally convinced Debbi to open the second store.

Explosive Growth

The San Francisco store was followed by several others in northern California and, in 1980, by an outlet in Honolulu, Hawaii. Mrs. Fields next expanded east to Salt Lake City, Utah. By 1981, the company had 14 stores. Seeking further opportunities for expansion, the Fields tried to attract shopping mall managers at a 1982 trade show in Las Vegas, but drew a lukewarm response. At the same trade show a year later, Debbi handed out cookie samples to conventioneers from a booth arranged as a working prototype of a store, complete with oven and mixer. This brought her to the attention of the landlords, some of whom not only let Mrs. Fields' into their existing malls, but asked that stores be opened in future locations, as well. The cookie company's East Coast debut also came in 1983—Bloomingdale's invitation to open a Mrs. Fields store in its New York location was considered a major milestone by Debbi and Randy.

International Expansion

In 1982, Chuck Borash, a vice president at Mrs. Fields, suggested that international expansion be the next project. The challenge was irresistible and, after some preliminary research, the company formed Mrs. Fields International and targeted Japan, Hong Kong, and Australia.

The Fields searched for a Japanese partner, which they were told was a prerequisite to doing business in Japan. Prospective partners warned Debbi and Randy that the cookies would have to be changed to appeal to the Japanese palate, specifically, that the spices and physical scale of the cookies were wrong. When Debbi, Randy, and several other executives visited a potential partner in Japan, Debbi brought along ingredients to make cookies according to her recipe, a company trade secret. "Agreement was universal that these cookies were all wrong for the Japanese taste," Debbi recalled, "and yet in less than a minute, there wasn't a crumb to be seen." Although that was the end of the partnership, the actions of these executives convinced the Fields that they could sell cookies in Japan, and they opened several stores without a partner.

Adjustments were necessary in some countries, however. For example, it was decided that the practice of encouraging sampling when business was slow should be continued in the international stores. The store manager in Hong Kong, however, was unable to interest people in sampling cookies. When Debbi visited the store and tried offering samples herself, she encountered the same reaction. Observing that neighboring store window displays were very neatly organized, in contrast to her piled samples, Debbi rearranged the tray so that people could take one piece without touching the others, and the passersby became willing to sample. Overall, Mrs. Fields International looked to be a promising avenue for expansion.

Products and Competition

Mrs. Fields' cookies came in 14 varieties. An early move into brownies and muffins was followed, in 1988, by expansion into candies and ice cream. All baked products were made on premises in the individual stores and were to be sold within a specified time. Cookies not sold within two hours, for example, were discarded (usually given to the local Red Cross or another charity).

Mrs. Fields Cookies was part of the sweet snack industry, which included the packaged snacks segment (e.g., Frito Lay's Grandma's Cookies; Nabisco's Fig Newtons, Vanilla Wafers, Chips Ahoy, and Oreos; and Keebler's Soft Batch). Competitors for impulse snack dollars included New York's David's Cookies, Atlanta's Original Great American Chocolate Chip Cookie Company, and the Nestlé Company's Original Cookie Co.

Specialty stores selling chocolates, ice cream, cinnamon rolls, and croissants constituted another segment of the sweet snack food industry. Shopping malls represented the largest source of spontaneous business for specialty stores, and some 80% of Mrs. Fields' outlets were in malls. Competition for the most favorable mall locations, which were typically next to large apparel stores rather than in areas with other food stores, was fierce. "Customers," noted one industry observer, "are too busy filling up on traditional 'main meal' fare to think seriously about . . . any edible specialty items. Even if they decide afterward to have them as a dessert, they won't have the patience to stand in line once again."[3] As most malls had few such locations, developers were selective about the stores they allowed outside the "food courts." Said one New York leasing director, "We can only accept operations with some sort of proven production record."[4]

3. *Chain Store Age Executive,* September 1986, p. 66.

4. Ibid., p. 62.

MANAGEMENT PHILOSOPHY

The second Mrs. Fields store raised a host of new issues for Debbi, who recognized that she could not be in two places at one time, yet historically had resisted delegating authority.

> Management theory claims that it is wrong not to delegate authority to those who work for you. Okay, I'm wrong, but in my own defense, I have to say that my error came from caring too much. If that's a sin, it's surely a small one. Eventually, I was forced, kicking and screaming, to delegate authority because that was the only way the business could grow.

Debbi Fields had no formal business school training. She attributed her success to learning by doing, and imparted her standards to her employees through example. Whenever possible, she visited her stores and sold cookies behind the counter. On a visit to one store in early 1988, she and a data processing employee with no retail experience generated an additional $600 in sales.

Debbi believed in having fun. "We combine intense work with spontaneous wackiness that keeps everybody loose and relaxed in the middle of tension," she observed. She also believed in treating employees as though they were customers. "For all the things we say to be effective, the people in the stores have to believe in what they're doing. . . . If we can sell them on quality and caring, they will sell the customers. . . . If we make them understand how important they are—by deeds, not just words—they will make their customers feel important in turn."

Store designs were closely controlled. Each store was made to look as inviting and accessible as possible, with products displayed so customers could see exactly what was available. Most stores had their ovens directly behind the sales counter so the aroma of baking cookies would fill the store. Each of the store elements was designed to impart to customers a "feel good" feeling.

The Fields had consistently refused to franchise their stores. The notion went against their ideals, as expressed by Debbi.

> This business—every business—works in its own quirky ways, and Mrs. Fields Cookies was not created specifically to make a profit. I can't imagine a franchisee buying into it for any other reason. And once the profit motive worked its way to a dominant position, it would be downhill. It's a feel good product. It has to be sold in a feel good way.

Franchisors typically controlled standards by specifying actions and quantifying details for the franchisees to follow. Because Debbi regarded each outlet as an extension of her original Palo Alto store, where each sale reflected her own personal philosophy of making the customer happy, she viewed franchising as a loss of control over the end product and loss of touch with the customer.

Even in partly owned stores, such as those in Hong Kong, Debbi and Randy played a major role. For example, Mrs. Fields provided product and technical knowledge for the Hong Kong stores, for which Dairy Farms Ltd. provided real estate and on-site management.

Financing Strategy

Although the Fields had always managed to find bank financing when they needed it, each experience had been more unpleasant than the last. Consequently, when expansion pressed them to find additional capital, Debbi and Randy decided to go public, pay off the banks, and use the rest of the money to finance growth. Their initial offering, made on the London Exchange in 1986, was not very successful. English institutional buyers did not know the company (there was only one store in London), and doubted that growth could be sustained without franchising. The stock settled, and then began to rise slowly. In 1987, Randy announced that future growth would be funded by cash flow and debt, not by further public offerings.

Accounting was straightforward. Expenses incurred in a store were charged to the store. Conversely, no corporate expenses were allocated to stores. "When you do that," explained Randy, "you lose track of what corporate is doing." Each store operated as a profit center, with average store revenue of $250,000 per year.

In 1987, Mrs. Fields Inc. had after-tax profits of $17.6 million on revenue of $113.9 million, a 34% increase from 1986 revenue, and a 9.6% increase from 1986 net income (see *Exhibit 1*). In 1988, a write-off of $19.9 million on revenues of $133.1 million for store and plant closings left Mrs. Fields' with an after-tax loss of $18.5 million.

Organization

The Fields believed that "the less hierarchy, the better . . . that with hierarchy, the larger an organization, the more managers turn to managing people and less to managing key business processes." Thus, employees had titles and job responsibilities, but there was no official organization chart. Communication took place between people as needed, regardless of title or position.

Staff. Field sales staff included store clerks, store management, and district and regional managers. At year end 1987, 105 district sales managers (DSM) reported to 17 regional directors of operations (RDO), who reported to four senior regional directors.

One regional director described her job and the company's management philosophy as follows:

> I manage six district managers, each of whom manages six stores. I also manage a store myself, so I know what my district managers need to know. To do this, I print out about 300 pages of reports a day. My district managers get about 50 pages a day. Daily, I work with my controller in Park City to discuss any accounting differences in my stores.
>
> My store managers are on average 20 to 25 years old and have one to two years of college education. I believe we are split 50/50 between males and females. The turnover of store managers is about 100% per year, although many work in that job 12 to 14 months. When they leave, they usually return to college. I think our turnover is above average for this kind of business, however.
>
> My store managers are compensated in two ways. First, they receive a salary which is competitive with other retail food store managers in this area. Second, they are eligible for a monthly bonus if they meet their sales forecasts. They receive 1.25% of sales, and if they exceed their quota, they receive 10% of all revenue above the goal. The company does not limit the amount of bonus, in fact, one store manager made an additional 90% of his salary, I believe.

Quotas, which determined the amount of bonus a store manager could make, were set by the district sales manager. They were based on year-to-year trends. The DSM considered each store separately, looking at past trends, the maturity of the market served by the store, and future projections of how the store could grow. The DSM then forecast how much or how little additional sales could be made at that store and set the quota. Quotas were set on volumes.

Mrs. Fields' "promote from within" policy reflected the high value the company placed on loyalty. Rewarding loyalty extended even to suppliers. In 1987, Mrs. Fields' purchased approximately $6.6 million worth of chocolate from the same supplier it had used on its first day of business, when a company salesman had treated Debbi as if she were his only customer.

The financial side of the stores' business was handled at headquarters. Local marketing decisions were made by the regional and district managers. The average number of stores under the supervision of a DSM decreased from 5.3 to 4.2 in 1987.

Corporate. At corporate headquarters, responsibility for store management fell to store controllers, who reported to Debbi through a vice president of operations. The controllers, each of whom managed between 35 and 75 stores, reviewed daily computer reports summarizing sales overall and by product type for each store; monitored unusual conditions, problems, and trends, as well as cash underages and overages; and contacted field managers for explanations. Within 24 hours of the store controllers' review, Debbi saw the same reports at an aggregate level.

MIS (Management Information Systems). The objective of being able to run each store essentially as Debbi ran the original Palo Alto store guided the implementation of information technology at Mrs. Fields. The strategic goal of the MIS area, according to Randy Fields, was "to put as much decision making and intelligence into the store level PC as is necessary to free the manager to do those things that uniquely people do." Randy believed that it was "demeaning for people to do what machines can do." Store managers, he felt, had better things to do than paperwork—such as selling cookies.

Director of MIS Paul Quinn reported directly to Randy Fields and was responsible for implementing his vision. Quinn's 11-person organization was responsible for development, support, and operations for the store personal computers and financial and sales systems, and for managing the firm's telecommunications equipment, a Rolm Private Branch Exchange (PBX), and a voice-mail system. The MIS organization chart is shown in *Exhibit 2.*

With respect to systems development at Mrs. Fields, Quinn explained:

Anyone can come to me or any of my people and ask for anything. We do an ad-hoc cost/benefit analysis and justify a system on one of three criteria:

- Potential payback (will it cut costs and/or save money)?
- Drive sales (will it generate new sales)?
- Strategic importance (will it put the company in a position to take advantage of something it could not otherwise do, like the interview system)?

"Strategic" in our industry means promoting sales and controlling labor and food costs. If you can do that you will be successful. I am in an enviable position as the MIS director here, because this company has more information than people can act upon. When someone wants a new report, I have usually already collected the information; it's just a matter of massaging and formatting.

Randy believed that keeping the staff small kept employees solving business problems rather than managing layers of people. He believed this kept jobs interesting and, moreover, that smaller groups of people made decisions faster and better. Randy felt that in order to avoid large groups, a company had to either limit business growth or leverage its people.

Randy saw information systems as a way to accommodate growth without expanding staff. He consistently encouraged the people working with the technology to think up new, creative applications. "Suppose you could not have any people working for you," he would say. "What must the computer do for you then? Don't be limited by what you think the computer can do." An accounts payable clerk, who routinely paid invoices that were regular and consistent, had wondered whether this redundant activity might be automated. This employee's initiative gave rise to the development of an expert system, which was designed to not only automate the routine elements of the activity, but also learn how to respond to exceptions by prompting the manager for input each time an exception was encountered. As the system learned, the exceptions became routine, and the system was able to respond to them automatically without further input from the manager.

COOKIE STORE OPERATIONS

Mrs. Fields' cookie stores were typically divided into two areas (see *Exhibit 3*). The ovens faced the retail area, fronted by an island of counter space used to fill and unload cookie sheets. Customers were drawn into the store by the openness of the design, and by the aroma of hot cookies fresh from the ovens plainly in view under the lucite-covered display. The back room contained the mixers, a workspace, a small office area with a personal computer, and sufficient storage space for ingredients. This was Mrs. Fields at the level of the friendly, inviting retail outlets located in high-density shopping areas around the world.

But there was another level to Mrs. Fields—the level of the sophisticated management information system that tracked the financial performance of each company-owned outlet and provided comprehensive scheduling of activities within stores, including marketing support, hourly sales projections, and even candidate interviewing for prospective employees.

Each store's personal computer accessed a sophisticated store management system designed by Randy and the MIS organization (see *Appendix A*). Menu-driven applications included day planning, time clocks, store accounting and inventory, interview scheduling, skills testing, and electronic mail (see *Appendix B*). One application dialed the headquarters' computer, deposited the day's transactions, and retrieved any mail for store employees.

A store manager's day began in the back room at the personal computer. After entering workday characteristics, such as day of the week, school day or holiday, weather conditions, etc., the manager answered a series of questions that caused the system to access a specific mathematical model for computing the day's schedule. The manager was subsequently advised how many cookies to bake per hour and what the projected sales per hour were. The manager would enter the types of cookies to be made that day and the system would respond with the number of batches to mix and when to mix them. For example, the following mixing information

When to mix	Length of time	# of batches to mix
8 a.m.	10 a.m.–3 p.m.	31
1 p.m.	3 p.m.–6 p.m.	7

would tell the manager: "At 8 a.m. mix 31 batches of cookies. Use the dough from 10 a.m. to 3 p.m. At that time the dough is no longer up to our standards, so discard any remaining dough. At 1 p.m. mix 7 batches of dough for use from 3 p.m. to 6 p.m."

As store sales were periodically entered throughout the day, either manually by the manager or by an automated cash register, the system would revise its projections and offer recommendations. For example, if the customer count was down, the system might suggest doing some sampling. If, on the other hand, the customer count was acceptable, but average sales were down, the system might recommend that more suggestive selling be done. Store managers could follow or disregard these suggestions.

From sales and inventory information stored in the computer, the information system computed projections, and prepared and (after being checked by the store manager) generated orders for supplies. A single corporate data base tracked sales in each store and produced reports that were reviewed daily. Headquarters thus learned immediately when a store was not meeting its objectives and was able to respond quickly. *Exhibit 4* shows a schematic diagram of the overall information system.

The information system had been explicitly designed to reflect the manager's perspective in order to foster the kind of symbiotic relationship described above, according to Debbi. "Asking store managers making salaries of $20,000 to $25,000 annually to meet an annual quota of a half-million dollars," she explained,

> is like asking them to fly to the moon. They cannot really relate to those big numbers. But if you break it down to $50 or $60 an hour, the quotas become easy goals. Even if an hourly quota is missed by $5 or $6, our employees feel they can easily make it up the next hour.

The most efficient way for managers to communicate was via electronic mail, but they also daily called their phone mailbox in Park City for audio messages. Debbi, who had from the outset promised to respond within 48 hours to electronic and voice mail directed to her, sent messages through this network several times a week. Thus, the manager did not simply read memos from the president, but often personally heard her voice.

The information system helped Debbi maintain a degree of personal involvement with each store manager. "Even when she isn't there, she's there," wrote Richman, "in the standards built into the scheduling program, in the hourly goals, in the sampling and suggestive selling, on the phone. The technology has 'leveraged' Debbi's ability to project her influence into more stores than she could ever reach effectively without it."[5]

The information system also helped the manager make hiring decisions. After conducting initial interviews, the manager entered information from the handwritten applications into the computer, which compared it with stored information on previous applicants who had been hired. The system thus helped the manager to narrow the field to applicants who were "Mrs. Fields' kind of people," people who possessed attributes the company valued highly—e.g., honesty, values, punctuality, availability, education, experience, salesmanship, knowledge, and attitude—and hence would fit into the corporate culture. Promising applicants were recalled for an interview conducted interactively with the computer. The applicants' answers were compared with those of existing employees and became part of the personnel data base. The manager could override the system's final recommendation on hiring by going to the personnel department. The manager could do this, or go anywhere else within Mrs. Fields for that matter, electronically.

DIVERSIFICATION

In April 1987, Mrs. Fields Holdings Inc. acquired from PepsiCo a 119-store French bakery/sandwich chain, La Petite Boulangerie (LPB). In the month following the acquisition, Randy reduced the subsidiary's administrative staff from 53 to three, explaining: "We absorbed many of the overhead functions into our existing organization including accounting, finance, personnel, human resources, training, and development. We left two people in operations and one in R&D."

This was not Mrs. Fields' first acquisition. The company had acquired another retail cookie chain, the Famous Chocolate Chip Company, in 1984. The forerunner of Mrs. Fields' current MIS system had been designed to incorporate that chain's cookie stores into the Mrs. Fields fold. But the LPB acquisition was different, primarily due to the size of the company, which Randy estimated would add $45 million in revenue in 1987. LPB stores baked (from frozen

5. "Mrs. Fields' Secret Ingredient," p. 67.

dough) and served croissants, breads, and other baked goods as well as hot soups and sandwiches. "It was," according to Randy, "a logical extension for the bakery aspect of Mrs. Fields Cookies."

The focus of the company's "expanded store" strategy was Mrs. Fields Bakeries. "These," explained Randy, "are destination outlets combining full lines of both cookies and bakery products." La Petite Boulangerie provided the real estate and Mrs. Fields the "feel good" element, for these upscale, sit-down cafes. This was not mere expansion; this was a new concept for Mrs. Fields. Debbi was involved with designing the new combination stores, and planned to have existing senior managers work in them for a month or two in order to become familiar with their operation.

Randy was excited about the combination store approach. It presented an opportunity to carve out a niche in a highly fractionalized market, and the size of the operation constituted an investment barrier to competition. The Mrs. Fields name was demographically well established, and Randy believed whatever they put it on would sell. Furthermore, a recent market analysis had suggested that enormous, demographically driven growth in the popularity of quality baked goods would not be significantly affected by fluctuations in the economy.

Randy wanted to pay for future expansion with profits, and he was convinced that the greater profits generated by the combination stores would enable them to open more new stores.

> As you will see from the financial results, our strategy required a comprehensive rationalization of our real estate portfolio, including consolidating and closing a number of stores that either did not complement the bakery store concept or were performing poorly. This necessitated a real estate writedown of $19.9 million, which we consider R&D expense related to opening our new combination stores. This program is now completed, with the cost fully provided for the 1988 accounts. This has enabled us to establish both a broader and more solid base with greatly enhanced potential for generating future profits.

Corporate direction was clear. "Our bakery strategy," Randy explained,

> is long-term, and is based on our operational experience and extensive market and consumer research. But it will take some time for the company to reach its full potential due to the significant expenditures inherent in the bakery store program and the sheer size of the market we intend to dominate.

These changes caught the attention of the financial press, which suggested that Mrs. Fields faced the characteristic management dilemmas of a growing business. Its expansion, both domestically and abroad, had precipitated changes in organizational and financial structure. The company was in a state of flux. It was attempting to diversify, some claimed belatedly, into combination stores. Earlier it had begun to sell its proprietary information system. Finally, what Randy viewed as record revenues were reported by the press as record losses in 1988 (see *Exhibit 1*).

FUTURE GROWTH

What was a cookie company to do? Just a year earlier, explaining what he meant by "having a consistent vision," Randy Fields had said

> that he could have described as far back as 1978, when he first began to create it, the system that exists today. But he doesn't mean the machines or how they're wired together. MIS in this company, he says, "has always had to serve two masters. First, control. Rapid growth without control equals disaster. We needed to keep improving control over our stores. And second, information that leads to control also leads to better decision making. To the extent that the information is then provided to the stores and field management level, the decisions that are made there are better, and they are more easily made."[6]

Had Mrs. Fields lost control? Just a year earlier, the MIS director had remarked that he had more information available than people could act upon. Was the information system still that cornucopia? The Fields had accommodated past expansion by modifying their information system. Was that what was needed now? Randy Fields wondered as he walked purposefully through corporate headquarters, one floor below the Main Street shopping mall in Park City.

6. Ibid., p. 72.

Exhibit 1
Financial Information
(U.S. $000)

	1988	1987	1986	1985
Statement of Operations				
Revenues	$133,143	$113,908	$84,751	$72,562
Cost of goods sold	42,049	32,739	19,961	19,165
Selling, general and administrative costs	74,525	50,643	39,442	38,477
Depreciation and amortization	9,133	5,903	4,505	3,498
(Losses) from closed stores	(19,900)	(5,397)	(1,375)	(577)
Income (loss) before interest and taxation	$ (12,464)	$ 19,226	$19,468	$10,845
Net Interest	6,039	1,540	2,333	4,088
Taxation	0	0	1,000	347
Net income (loss)	$ (18,503)	$ 17,686	$16,135	$ 6,410
Dividends paid	0	10,453	4,500	0
Earnings (net loss) retained by company	$ (18,503)	$ 7,233	$11,635	$ 6,410
Consolidated Balance Sheet				
ASSETS				
Property and equipment at cost less depreciation	82,827	82,033	51,496	37,838
Leasehold developments at cost less depreciation	10,672	11,429	5,529	2,809
Other[a]	1,273	863		
Current Assets:				
Inventories	6,640	7,779	4,406	3,198
Accounts receivable	3,816	3,585	3,222	1,522
Prepaid expenses and miscellaneous	8,937	9,363	4,761	2,105
Due from affiliates	5,000	0	740	0
Cash	3,971	6,059	1,543	2,257
	$123,136	$121,111	$71,697	$49,729
LIABILITIES AND SHAREHOLDERS' EQUITY				
Current Liabilities:				
Accounts payable, due to affiliates and accrued expenses	18,762	24,963	11,295	7,006
Income taxes	550	184	514	63
Long-term debt	69,732	42,734	13,187	20,100
Shareholders' equity and retained earnings	34,092	53,230	46,701	22,560
	$123,136	$121,111	$71,697	$49,729

[a] Other assets include costs of developing computer software for sale or license to third parties.

Exhibit 2
MIS Organization

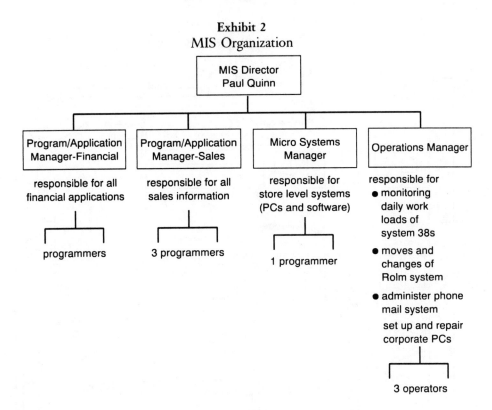

Exhibit 3
Typical Mrs. Fields Store Floorplan*

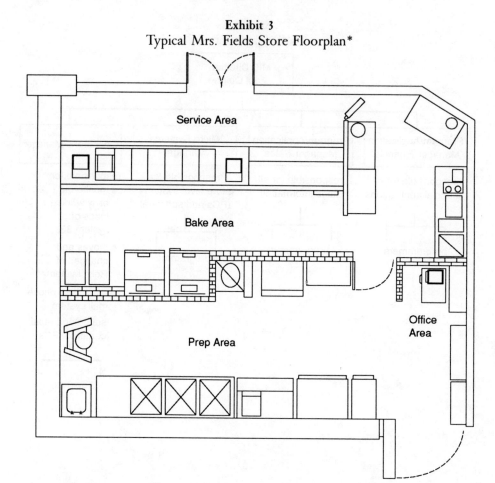

Service Area

Bake Area

Prep Area

Office
Area

*NOTE: This floorplan is approximately 600 sq. ft. Stores ranged from 400 sq. ft. to 1250 sq. ft.

Exhibit 4
Mrs. Fields' Information Systems Diagram

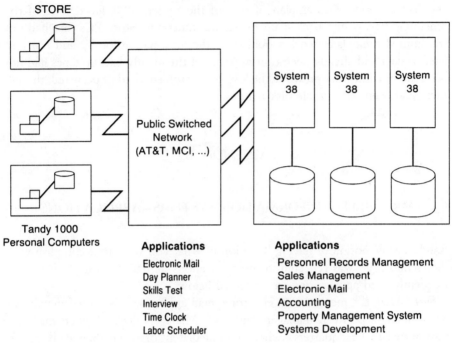

STORE

Tandy 1000
Personal Computers

Public Switched
Network
(AT&T, MCI, ...)

System 38   System 38   System 38

Applications

Electronic Mail
Day Planner
Skills Test
Interview
Time Clock
Labor Scheduler

Applications

Personnel Records Management
Sales Management
Electronic Mail
Accounting
Property Management System
Systems Development

APPENDIX A

MRS. FIELDS' INFORMATION SYSTEMS—HARDWARE

Mrs. Fields' standard personal computer configuration was a Tandy 1000 (an MS-DOS system with 8086-based CPU) with one floppy disk drive, a 20 megabyte hard disk, and an internal 1200 bps modem used for communication with the Utah data center. Tandy computers were chosen because of a favorable service arrangement. Mrs. Fields maintained a 24-hour service contract with Tandy, but most managers simply contacted the nearest Radio Shack if they had problems.

Software was the responsibility of the Micro Systems manager in Park City. The data center in Park City utilized three IBM Systems 38s, each equipped with six 9335 hard disks. Chosen for their data base strengths, the System 38s were dedicated, one to sales systems, one to financial systems, and one to applications development.

With all significant corporate data residing in one data base, disaster planning was of critical importance. The company had experienced several system failures, and had a simple disaster plan: if one of the Systems 38s failed, one of the remaining two would back it up for critical functions. Store PCs that had not transmitted their daily work would store the information locally and transmit later. If data had already been transmitted, but the nightly backup tapes had not been run, the information would be lost. Such problems hadn't occurred, though there had been recoverable disk failures.

APPENDIX B

MRS. FIELDS' INFORMATION SYSTEMS—APPLICATIONS

Randy Fields' notion of having "a vision of what you want to accomplish with the technology" was reflected in the applications he had developed. The most frequently used applications are described below.

Form Mail, the menu-driven electronic mail application, was used mainly for brief messages between managers and staff. Managers decided when mail was transmitted to headquarters—whether immediately or when their daily paperwork was sent.

Day Planner was the first application a store manager used each morning. It produced a schedule for the day based on the minimum sales target (in dollars), the day of the week, and type of day (holiday, school day, etc.). This schedule was updated every time hourly sales information was entered into the system. (Manual entry by the manager was to be eliminated by cash registers custom designed to automatically feed the hourly sales into the personal computer.)

Labor Scheduler was an expert system that, given requirements for a specific day, scheduled staff to run a store.

Skills Tests was a set of computer-based multiple choice tests any employee could take to be considered for raises and promotions. The system indicated how many questions were answered correctly and provided tutorial sessions for questions answered incorrectly. Scores were sent to the personnel data base when other information was transmitted to the corporate offices.

Interview helped store managers make hiring decisions. Managers entered information from applications filled out by candidates into the program, which made recommendations based on the historical demographics of people who had previously interviewed and worked for Mrs. Fields. Prospective employees were called back to the store for an interactive interview with the program, which made a final recommendation for hiring.

Time Clock was a planned application that would enable employees to punch in and out via the Tandy computers. The automatic time card maintained by the system would facilitate the payroll process.

11

◆

Mobilizing People

Successful service managers often have a preoccupation with becoming the employer of choice, devoting untold effort to developing and retaining good people, making sure that the best people retain jobs in close contact with customers (particularly in consumer services), and empowering front-line managers while maintaining adequate control. A lack of good managers and employees often represents a major constraint on growth, particularly for a multisite service. This sometimes leads to a decision to foster growth both through owned and franchised operations. The best service firms seek to make their employees feel as if they've been enfranchised, their franchisees act like employees, or both. They try to build unusual levels of loyalty in both employees and franchisees, recognizing that high turnover in either can be costly after some period of introduction to the job and the company.

Questions of importance in appraising human resource programs can be structured around the employee life cycle of recruitment, selection, development, and reward. Responses to these questions depend on the type of service being offered and the role of people in its service delivery system. Included among them are: At which stage of the life cycle should the most effort be concentrated? Are the desired people found through recruitment and selection or through a "weeding out" process that takes place in development? Should pay be based on performance? If so, are steps taken that insure that incentives tie the best people to the organization? Has the amount and type of supervision been calibrated to the qualities sought and developed in employees, the degree to which they are empowered, and the way in which they are rewarded?

Outstanding service performers seek to become the employer of choice for managers as well as entry-level personnel by breaking out of what the management of Au Bon Pain, according to one of the cases that follows, has termed the "cycle of failure." This cycle involves: (1) low pay, (2) jobs with little responsibility, (3) chronic turnover, (4) a shortage of talent, (5) inadequate motivation among managers, and (6) continued low pay. This often involves broadening job responsibilities, reducing personnel, and raising compensation to uncommon levels through well-designed pay-for-performance systems. The end result frequently is a "new look" organization with fewer levels and shorter lines of communication. In some cases it has resulted in turning the organization upside down, essentially putting all managers in the service and support of front-line service personnel with direct contact with customers.

Clearly, Au Bon Pain has established a pay-for-performance system in its Partner/Manager Program experiment. How successful has it been? What problems might you expect with it? Will it provide enough control to Au Bon Pain's management? Would you recommend that management adopt it? Why? If so, should it be extended to all units and managers? What adjustments, if any, would you recommend be made in it? What impact will it have on Au Bon Pain's middle managers? On the firm's organization?

Fairfield Inn's management has designed a pay-for-performance system, too. How well is it adapted to the objectives that Fairfield Inn's management has set for its inns? How would you compare this pay-for-performance system with Au Bon Pain's? How easily can this concept be franchised? What part of it should be most carefully protected in any franchise agreement? Which, if any, of the alternative franchise approaches described in the case would you recommend that Mike Ruffer adopt? Why?

Turning to the Banc One Corporation case, you might ask yourself how important pay-for-performance is in this company. How do you account for the performance of the bank in recent years? What is so unusual about the "uncommon partnership"? What role does the CEO, John McCoy, play in preserving the "partnership"? What could go wrong here? Based on your analysis of the case, what should be on McCoy's agenda for action?

After you have considered the readings, Mickey Mouse Marketing and More Mickey Mouse Marketing, which describe practices for mobilizing people at Walt Disney World, how would you compare the approaches used at Walt Disney World to those employed either at Au Bon Pain or Fairfield Inn? How do you explain the differences? The readings make the Disney approach sound easily transferable to banks (they were written for a banker's magazine). What do you think of its transferability to other industries? Is it more transferable to some businesses than others? Why?

In the United Parcel Service (A) case, we find a successful company confronted with the problem of integrating "outsiders" into an organization with a strong culture and the need for people with new skill specialties. Questions you may want to keep in mind while reviewing this case include: How is the introduction of new systems programmers into the organization going so far? Why? What would you suggest UPS do differently in the future concerning this challenge?

Will this same approach work with pilots? How would you suggest they be integrated into the company?

These organizations are seeking to mobilize people, both employees and franchisees. The cases describing them are intended to stimulate imaginative thinking about what is possible and appropriate for other types of services.

Au Bon Pain:
The Partner/Manager Program

Au Bon Pain has tried every progressive human-resource strategy or policy available—we've had them all. Quite honestly, I don't believe that any incremental strategies work long term in the multi-site service business, particularly in a labor market—like Boston—that is characterized by low unemployment levels. I'm convinced that developing *new* solutions for human resource management at the unit level is the basis of competitive advantage. Instituting our Partner/Manager Program throughout the company now could give us an important edge. This is our chance to blow the company out, or to blow ourselves up.

This is how Len Schlesinger, executive vice president and treasurer of the Au Bon Pain (ABP) Company, described the situation he and company president Ron Shaich faced in January 1987. Six months earlier, in July 1986, 2 of the 24 company-owned stores had embarked on an experiment that could lead to a revolutionary change in the company's store manager compensation system. The Partner/Manager Program Experiment ran for six periods of four weeks each (the first period of the experiment, period 8, ran from July 13 through August 9). The experiment concluded on December 20, 1986. Now, Schlesinger and Shaich had to decide whether to roll out the program in all of the company's stores, run it on a trial basis involving only some of the stores, withdraw it to make needed improvements, or abandon it.

HISTORY

Au Bon Pain, a chain of upscale French bakeries/sandwich cafes, opened its first store in Boston's Faneuil Hall in 1977. This store was originally developed

This case was prepared by Research Assistant Lucy N. Lytle, under the supervision of Professor W. Earl Sasser, as the basis for class discussion rather than to illustrate either effective or ineffective handling of an administrative situation. Copyright © 1987 by the President and Fellows of Harvard College; Harvard Business School case #9-687-063 (Rev. 2/89).

as a marketing vehicle for Pavallier, a French manufacturer of ovens and other bakery equipment. In 1978, Louis Kane, an experienced venture capitalist, bought the store and the rights to the concept. Two years later, Kane teamed up with Ron Shaich, a Harvard MBA who had worked as the director of operations for the Original Cookie Company, a national chain of over 80 retail cookie stores, and who had just opened The Cookie Jar, a cookie store in a high-traffic location in downtown Boston. The two agreed to merge their businesses, enabling Kane to utilize his extensive real estate skills while Shaich handled the operational end of the business.

ABP quickly became known both for the high quality of its croissants and baguettes and for its prime locations. Although the company was based in Boston, Massachusetts, the chain expanded rapidly during the next six years to include stores in New York, New Jersey, Maine, Pennsylvania, Connecticut, and New Hampshire. By 1986, there were 24 company-owned units in the ABP chain. (For a complete list of ABP store locations and sizes, see *Exhibit 1*.)

Originally, each of the ABP units operated as a self-contained production bakery in the back, with a retail store and seating area in the front. A bakery chef was assigned to each store to handle the demanding process of rolling out croissants and baking breads in the classic French style. In addition to croissants and breads, sandwiches, coffee, and beverages were also sold. Some test stores offered soups, salads, omelettes, cookies, and sorbets as well. Generally, 65% of a unit's business was take-out.

In 1980, Shaich and Kane decided to centralize production, and they fired 15 of the company's 18 bakers. They transferred the remaining three to the Prudential Center store, where the dough was prepared, frozen, and then shipped to the other units. This change eliminated the need for a highly trained chef in each unit, improved inventory control, increased product consistency, and reduced the size of each unit's production area. Three years later, production was moved to ABP headquarters in South Boston. Frozen dough, which had a shelf life of eight weeks, continued to be shipped to all the units on a weekly, or semi-weekly basis.

Len Schlesinger, formerly an associate professor in organizational behavior at the Harvard Business School, joined the company as its executive vice president and treasurer in early 1985. He was charged with the task of systematizing efforts to increase sales and improve quality throughout ABP by increasing employee ownership—both financial and psychological—in the organization.

ABP's major competitors included Vie de France, PepsiCo's La Petite Boulangerie, and Sara Lee's Michelle's Baguette and French Bakery. By 1986, however, all three were suffering from a combination of low profitability and decreased sales.

"THE CYCLE OF FAILURE"

According to Schlesinger and Shaich, in 1985 ABP's retail operations confronted for the first time a set of human resource problems endemic to the fast-food industry. These problems included a continuing crew labor shortage, a chronic shortage of associate managers, an inability to attract and select high-quality management candidates, an inadequately trained management staff, and what Schlesinger referred to as the tendency of many district managers to play "super GM" (general manager)—meaning that they focused obsessively on following up day-to-day activities (a GM's responsibility) at the expense of defining clearly the district manager's role. Labeled by Shaich as "the cycle of failure," the problems interrelated systematically to induce a pattern of poor performance at the store level.

Shaich noted:

> Our lack of attention to these issues had created problems at the crew level that remained unsolved. These, in turn, magnified managerial problems, and vice versa. It created a vicious cycle—the cycle of failure—and led to a significant degradation of the customer experience. Len and I concluded that if Au Bon Pain was to achieve its objectives of delivering a high-quality customer experience which resulted in sales and profitability, we had to break out of this cycle once and for all.

Schlesinger added:

> It was clear, especially in the Boston market, that the labor crisis had engendered a serious decline in the quality of the crew candidates we attracted and ultimately hired. In the past, we had focused on simply staffing our stores rather than on attracting desirable candidates. All of our energies were devoted to the short-term operational needs of the business in this area.
>
> At the same time, training for the crew was practically nonexistent and, where it did exist, poorly executed. Development, too, tended to follow a Darwinian "survival of the fittest" approach. The problem was compounded by the fact that we were committed to a promote-from-within policy which precluded the opportunity to acquire skilled talent from outside.
>
> Beyond that, considerable work remained to be done to develop our reward system into a long-term compensation system which more directly tied the managers into the success of their stores.

EXISTING COMPENSATION SYSTEM IN 1986

Our existing compensation system, which we devised in 1985, goes a long way toward addressing the problems contributing to the cycle of failure. It's a simple system under which managers are paid according to their level of responsibility and the sales activity of their stores.

Shaich made this observation as he outlined the two basic components of ABP's existing compensation system (i.e., the system in place prior to the development of the Partner/Manager Program): base pay and a volume adjustment. Under the plan, general managers earned a base salary of $375 a week. Salaries rose as weekly sales volumes increased, up to $633.75 a week at the highest-volume store.

Base Pay

A manager's base pay was determined by his or her level in the organization: general manager, senior associate manager, first associate manager, or second associate manager (which included manager trainees). In July 1985, the base pay levels were as follows:

Level	Weekly Pay	Annual Pay
General Manager	$375.00	$19,500
Senior Associate Manager	350.00	18,200
First Associate Manager	341.54	17,760
Second Associate Manager	336.54	17,500

Volume Adjustment

In addition to base pay, a volume adjustment was calculated each week for first associate, senior associate, and general managers. (Second associate managers were not eligible for a volume adjustment.) Because ABP had a wide range of store volumes with varying managerial responsibilities and workloads, it established three categories of stores:

Store Volume	Weekly Sales
Low	$ 4,000–10,000
Medium	$10,000–20,000
High	over $20,000

The formulae for determining salaries for general, senior associate, and first associate managers (i.e., base pay plus volume adjustment) are presented in *Exhibit 2*.

THE DEVELOPMENT OF THE PARTNER/MANAGER PROGRAM

In the spring of 1986, Schlesinger and Shaich developed a draft of a new compensation/incentive system—the Partner/Manager Program—for the managers of ABP's stores. Shaich explained:

> Len and I had identified the problems inherent in the cycle of failure. The next step was to figure out how to pay people more. Since 1985, under our existing compensation system, we had tried to develop a pay system which allowed the managers to make more money than they had before while still tying them to the success of their stores and the company.

In brief, the Partner/Manager Program would reclassify general managers as "partner/managers" and provide them with a base salary of $500 per week. Each partner/manager could choose an associate manager, who would be paid $400 per week. The partner/manager would be entitled to a 35% share of the unit's incremental profits under the new system; the associate manager would receive 15%; and ABP would receive the remaining 50%.

A store-lease payment would be deducted monthly from the store controllable profits to cover unit-level fixed expenses, corporate overhead, and reasonable profit expectations. The amount of the store-lease payment would be guaranteed for 13 periods (i.e., one year), with the following exceptions, which would require an adjustment. First, the addition of fixed assets would trigger an increase in the store-lease payment of 25% of the total fixed asset cost divided across 13 periods. Second, additional sales, which triggered a percentage rent clause in the real estate lease, would increase the store-lease payment by the percentage specified in the real estate lease.

Incremental profits would be equal to a unit's net controllable profits minus its store-lease payment. These profits would be distributed to the managers at the close of each period (i.e., every four weeks). ABP would hold in reserve $7,500 for the partner/manager and $2,500 for the associate manager until the end of their contracts, which could last one, two, or three years.[1]

---

1. During the Partner/Manager Program Experiment, which is described in detail later in this case, Schlesinger and Shaich opted to distribute the managers' share of the incremental profits in a lump sum at the end of the six-month trial period.

The managers would be required to work a minimum of 50 hours per week, and the partner/manager and/or the associate manager would have to be on duty in the store during 90% of its operating hours. The quality of each store would be monitored through "mystery-shopping" reports, "white-glove" inspections, and 100% customer satisfaction "moment-of-truth" indicators. A violation of any of the listed rules could result in the dismissal of either or both of the managers if the problem was not corrected within a specified amount of time. (See *Appendix A* for a working draft of the Partner/Manager Program.)

GOALS OF THE PARTNER/MANAGER PROGRAM

Product of Research

The Partner/Manager Program was the result of research and careful thought, according to Schlesinger:

> It's not something that we developed overnight. We looked into the compensation systems of a number of fast-food chains, including Sambo's, Chick-Fil-A, Golden Corral, and Kentucky Fried Chicken. The Partner/ Manager Program is a customized imitation of the processes we studied. In some ways, it is revolutionary—but it is not without precedent in this industry.
>
> Under this system, we would manage our partner/managers with loose controls and less overhead, hold them tightly accountable to outputs (i.e., customer satisfaction as determined by mystery shopping) rather than inputs, and require them to invest themselves in their stores. Hopefully, through their efforts, the good managers would earn considerably more than they do now.

Shaich added:

> We want to hire people who really care . . . the kind of person you'd want on your side when you go into a street fight. A person who does a good job for the people beneath him, not to impress somebody higher up. This is an organization that has rewarded trying for years. Now it's time to reward results.
>
> One of the aims of this program would be to employ fewer managers, who would work harder, and make more money than their predecessors. We want people willing to pay the price to earn big bucks.
>
> Personally, I believe that people earning less than $30,000 per year should

be managed through individually based incentive/compensation plans.[2]
People higher up in an organization, with a longer time horizon and broader
responsibilities, should have a low salary and stock options, like at People
Express. The problem at People was that while stock ownership is meaningful, it's money that gets results.[3]

The Role of the District Manager

Not only would the Partner/Manager Program change ABP's compensation
system, but it also would alter the ways in which the individual units were
supervised. Schlesinger explained:

> Under this program, the district managers would function as coaches, rather
> than as policemen—and they would supervise 8 to 10 stores rather than
> the traditional 3 or 4. The district managers would serve as consultants by
> generating ideas for sales building and cost reduction, and as support people
> by helping out during busy seasons and assisting with the training of new
> associate managers. They would earn perhaps 5% of the incremental profits
> generated by each of the units they supervise. Of course, we haven't worked
> out all the details yet.

One of the factors necessitating the change in the district managers' role was
what Shaich termed the "Stockholm effect" (psychological phenomenon that
occurs when, over time, hostage victims develop sympathetic feelings toward
their captors). He noted:

> In the past, the district managers, like the general managers, became excuse-
> givers. Instead of holding the general managers accountable to Au Bon
> Pain's standards—as customers do—the district managers began to sympa-
> thize with the managers' excuses. They became agents of the status quo
> rather than agents of change.
>
> Now it's clear that the partner/managers would be primarily responsible
> for handling any problems that arise. I expect that 90% of the problems we
> used to deal with at headquarters, the managers would now figure out on
> their own.

2. For an example of such a company, see Harvard Business School case #9-376-028, *The Lincoln
Electric Company.*

3. For further information, see Harvard Business School case #9-483-103, *People Express (A).*

Increased Stability

One of the goals of the Partner/Manager Program would be to increase stability at the unit level by reducing turnover and by encouraging managers to commit themselves to working at a specific unit for at least one year. Shaich discussed this idea:

> The program would require each manager to have a real financial commitment to his or her store in the form of his or her share of the incremental profits—some of which would be held back by Au Bon Pain until the end of the contract. We expect that after working in the same unit for at least a year, a manager would have the chance to become very familiar with the store's cycle—what its sales volume is like, when its peak periods are, and so on. In the long run, this knowledge would increase the quality of each store's operations.
>
> At the same time, the managers would get to know their customers and crew on a personal basis. Significantly, consulting psychologists have found that the most important single variable that keeps a customer coming back to a store is whether or not someone in the store knows that customer's name. There are employees at Golden Corral, for example, who know the names of 2,700 customers. This "retention quotient" has major implications for a company like Au Bon Pain as our research indicates that some of our customers—the ones we refer to as the "Au Bon Pain Club"—visit our stores up to 108 times per year.

QUALITY CONTROL

Although the Partner/Manager Program would reduce the degree of corporate supervision of the individual stores, quality control measures remained in place. For example, units were mystery shopped at least once a week. Mystery shopping involved having a professional shopper hired from outside ABP evaluate the store from a customer's perspective. The mystery shopper judged a store on the basis of "moment-of-truth" indicators, generated in customer focus groups, which were aimed at achieving 100% customer satisfaction. Although they were subject to change, one set of indicators is shown in *Exhibit 3*. Mystery shoppers encountering "perfect service" carefully noted the names of those responsible and reported their experiences back to headquarters. According to Len Schlesinger, this was happening about once per month, and when it did "it set off all kinds of bells, awards, and recognition." Stickers were frequently attached to cash registers reminding employees that their next customer could be the mystery shopper.

In addition, white-glove inspections, using a 140-item checklist covering all phases of store operations, were conducted by an Au Bon Pain auditor every accounting period. The inspections lasted eight hours, and the days when they occurred were not announced in advance.

Decreased Recruiting Budget

Schlesinger expected a dramatic decrease in ABP's recruiting budget as a result of the publicity surrounding the news that it would be changing its compensation system. He predicted:

> If we go public with this program, the resulting newspaper and trade journal articles would help us to attract and stockpile a new group of managerial candidates. We could cut our annual recruiting budget from $230,000 to $60,000 by substituting press for want ads.

POTENTIAL PROBLEMS

Burning Out

Shaich and Schlesinger both raised the issue of managers burning out during the program. They agreed that being a partner/manager or an associate manager under the new program would be a potentially stressful experience—sufficiently stressful that it could cause some managers to drop out before their contract ended. Schlesinger, however, was philosophic about it:

> Burning out managers would be one concern. But the way I see it, we're all adults entering into a business contract. We understand the benefits and the risks.

Physical Limitations

At least three physical factors limited productivity and sales: (1) each unit's proofing capacity (i.e., the capacity of the machines in which the dough rose for approximately two hours), (2) each unit's freezer capacity, and (3) the limitations of Au Bon Pain's product line.

Schlesinger predicted:

If Au Bon Pain adopts the Partner/Manager Program, people will claim that we have come up with a new way to con people—but that wouldn't be true. The program would establish a clear, tangible link between the results the managers achieved and the money they would make.

We wouldn't hold up goals that aren't attainable, because we would need to create a base of heroes. Under the Partner/Manager Program most people would make about $40,000 a year. The heroes would make between $60,000 and $100,000, and they would set an example for which everyone would strive.

THE PARTNER/MANAGER PROGRAM EXPERIMENT

Eager to discover if the program would be successful in a real-life situation, Schlesinger and Shaich invited the general and associate managers of two stores to participate in a six-month trial run of the Partner/Manager Program. Gary Aronson, the general manager of ABP's Burlington Mall store (20 miles west of Boston), and Frank Ciampa, his associate manager, agreed to give it a try. So did Brian McEvoy, the general manager of the CityPlace store in Hartford, Connecticut (100 miles south of Boston), and his associate manager, Stephen Dunn.

The managers did not feel that they were coerced into participating in the experiment. "We were able to choose whether or not we wanted to participate," McEvoy said. Before the experiment began, both Aronson and McEvoy met with Schlesinger and Shaich to discuss a rough draft of the program. "We gave them our input, and they incorporated our suggestions into a revised version," Aronson explained. Later, all four managers met with Schlesinger and Shaich to review the changes and discuss any questions about the program.

Aronson explained why he agreed to participate in the experiment:

> Frank and I decided that our number one priority was to show that a program like this could work. We wanted to convince people that this was something revolutionary, and that it would not only turn around this company, but that it has the potential to change the whole industry. The way I see it, this program is going to turn us all into a bunch of professionals.

McEvoy was motivated both by the "financial incentives of the program" and by his perception that it was an alternative to following the traditional career path—which would have involved moving to Boston and trying to get promoted to the position of district manager. He noted, "First of all, my wife and I didn't really want to relocate because it would have upset her career. At the same time, even if we did move, there wouldn't have been any guarantees that I would have been able to move up in the company."

Managers' Backgrounds

> What initially attracted me to Au Bon Pain was that they allowed their managers more mobility and more access to upper-level management than most fast-food chains. They also let their managers have an input into the decision process.
>
> I believe that the only way you can grow as a manager is to work in a less structured environment. At Au Bon Pain, you can't run on buzzers and bells like you can at McDonald's or Burger King; you have to be able to think.

This is how Stephen Dunn, associate manager of the CityPlace store in Hartford, recalled his first impression of ABP. Dunn graduated from the University of Massachusetts in 1981 with a business degree in hotel/restaurant/travel administration, and he had experience working in full-service, fast-food, catering, and banquet situations. In 1985, he was recruited by a headhunter retained by ABP and accepted a position as the associate manager of the CityPlace store.

Ironically, Brian McEvoy, Dunn's partner and the general manager of the CityPlace store, never intended to work for ABP. After graduating from the University of Massachusetts in 1980 with a degree in history, followed by two years of teaching experience and a brief stint in the Navy, he viewed his original meeting with Shaich as a "practice interview." Later, impressed with the company, he took an entry-level job as an associate manager. At the start of the Partner/Manager Program Experiment, he had been with the company for three years.

Gary Aronson, the general manager of the Burlington Mall store, dropped out of college after one semester, and worked for Kentucky Fried Chicken for eight years before joining ABP in 1983 as an associate manager. He explained, "I switched jobs because I saw a lot of opportunity for me at a place like this. I didn't feel that the management team I was training with was that experienced, and I knew I'd find a way to shine real quickly."

Aronson's associate manager, Frank Ciampa, graduated from Bentley College in 1984 with a bachelor's degree in marketing management and an associate's degree in accounting. He joined ABP in 1985 as a manager trainee—in the hope that he could use this position as a stepping stone to a job in the corporate side of the business. He admitted:

> If you'd asked me a year ago what I wanted to be after working here for several months, it sure wasn't to be a partner/manager. But since I've been working with Gary under the Partner/Manager Program, my whole mentality has changed. Now, I'm in no hurry to work in the office—I enjoy being a manager.

Managers' Activities during the Experiment

"Len tells people that I run the place like a family deli, and I suppose that could be true," Aronson admitted. Both his wife and Ciampa's mother worked in the store, and Ciampa's father, a manufacturing equipment mechanic, helped with maintenance.

Originally, Aronson employed two associate managers. When the experiment began, however, he took the opportunity to have one of the two transferred to another unit. He explained that, according to the program, he didn't need three managers to run the store. "It means that Frank and I have to work longer hours," he conceded, "but it's worth it." The Burlington Mall store was open from 9:00 a.m. until 10:00 p.m. Monday through Saturday, and 11:00 a.m. through 6:00 p.m. on Sunday.

During the experiment, Aronson took on a number of wholesale accounts, noting;

> The store doesn't open until 9:00 a.m., but Frank and I get here by 4:30 or 5:00 most mornings to prepare our wholesale products. We've even begun to do a little catering. If we can keep the four or five accounts we've got right now, I bet we could make about $40,000 worth of sales next year just on the wholesale line.

Aronson and Ciampa also took advantage of the increased managerial responsibility called for in the program and initiated some money-saving repairs. Ciampa recalled:

> During the first week of the experiment, we decided to knock out a platform built against one wall in order to make room for eight more seats in the cafe area. Of course, making this change wasn't high on the list of priorities for the company's construction department, so Au Bon Pain estimated it would cost $10,000. We found a guy who'd do it for only $3,000, and we did it right away.
>
>   Similarly, when it was time to repaint the store, headquarters estimated it would cost $1,200 to paint one wall. We had the whole store painted ourselves for about $800.

At the same time, Aronson began calculating food cost on a monthly, rather than daily, basis. "It drives the people at headquarters crazy," he grinned, "but I'm running the best food cost of any of the stores. As long as I'm alert, and trust the people I'm working with, I've never had a problem with stealing or cheating." He added that the turnover rate in his store was close to 0%.

The CityPlace store was open from 6:30 a.m. until 6:00 p.m. Monday through Friday. It was closed on the weekends. McEvoy admitted, "I don't want to work 80 hours a week the way Gary does now. I'm starting to like having my weekends off." He alternated shifts among himself, Dunn, and Barbara Jones, his shift supervisor. Dunn observed:

Au Bon Pain provides us with a labor grid to guide us in making decisions about how many people to schedule to work at different times during the day. We generally employ more people than the grid specifies. For example, they say that in the morning we should be able to run the store with four people. We always try to schedule six in an attempt to decrease the amount of time it takes to fill a customer's order.

McEvoy added:

In order to schedule extra crew members to work during peak hours, we had to pay them more because they were only working a two-hour-long shift. However, having the extra workers allowed us to improve our service and decrease the time customers had to wait for their order, so it paid off in increased sales.

Approximately three months into the experiment, McEvoy and Dunn began a telephone express service. Under the new system, office workers called in orders of $25 or more, which they picked up a little while later. "It's a lot quicker than having to stand in line and wait while the order is filled, and it helps us to serve all our customers more efficiently," McEvoy explained. The telephone express service was currently available to only the office workers in the CityPlace building, but McEvoy was considering expanding it to other areas.

Managers' Evaluation of the Partner/Manager Program

All four managers agreed that one of the program's benefits was less corporate supervision of the units. This change was most apparent in the new role assumed by the district managers. Schlesinger acted as the district manager for both stores, and Ciampa noted that he had visited the Burlington Mall store no more than three or four times in as many months, although he kept in contact over the telephone.

McEvoy predicted, "The district managers will become less like policemen and more like advisors and coaches. Instead of being told 'You must do this,' managers will hear comments like 'How can we build sales?' and 'How can we improve the store?'"

Aronson added:

Some managers love to have the district manager come around so that he or she can admire how clean the floor is. Frank and I don't need that. We know exactly what to do. Having someone else around actually brought down the quality of our work because we were busy explaining everything.

Aronson and Ciampa believed that the program had the potential to reduce the tendency of many managers in the fast-food industry to move from one job to another, starting at the ground level each time and slowly working their way up. Aronson explained:

In most professions, if you're good at what you do, when you change jobs you start out making more money than you did before. The fast-food industry's mentality is different. For example, when I left International Food Services, I was the highest-paid manager there and I was working in the highest-volume store. But when I decided to join Au Bon Pain, I had to start at the ground floor again and work my way up. It's the same story every-where. I had to take a $135/week cut in pay in addition to going through the emotional upheaval of moving from one job to another. The prevailing attitude seemed to be "Well, maybe you're a whiz with fried chicken, but you don't know anything about croissants."

Now Ron and Len have realized that they can't operate the way the Wendys and the Burger Kings deal with people. To be successful in the future, this company will have to bring in established people who've shown that they can do the job. A manager with five or six years' experience in the fast-food industry has to be worth a lot more than someone just out of school. If we start paying people what they're worth, I believe we can pick up some prime-time players and make this a really interesting company.

Aronson felt that, in the past, some of the instability generated by managers moving from store to store was the result of decisions made at the company headquarters. He asserted:

Once a manager had a store running smoothly, BINGO! They suddenly wanted to transfer you to a problem store. The better a manager you were, the more problems you had to take care of. After a while you began to ask, "What am I? A clean-up crew?"

Dunn believed that holding back part of the managers' share of the incremental profits until the end of their contract would reduce the desire to store-hop. He said, "Now, I'm a lot less company-oriented, and a lot more store-oriented. I'm less willing to leave the unit where I'm working and move to another store." McEvoy pointed out, however, that "the way for an ambitious person to make even more money would be to move to a higher-volume store. Personally, I'm not interested in relocating right now, but the temptation is always there."

Despite the decreased corporate supervision of the units under the program, the managers still perceived a continuing corporate overemphasis on details and paperwork. Aronson complained:

> There's too much emphasis on the detail end, not enough on the meat-and-potatoes end. The majority of my customers want good food, quality service, and they want it fast. But every time we've been mystery shopped during the experiment, we've received the same basic criticism. Although our overall score is quite high, the mystery shopper generally objects that the floor hasn't been swept. Frankly, during lunchtime this place is a zoo. If we tried to sweep then, we'd get complaints from the customers about the dust flying in their food.

McEvoy generally agreed with Aronson's point, but admitted that he was more concerned that he was close to reaching maximum output on much of his equipment.

Dunn brought up another issue:

> Under this new program, an associate manager's greatest fear will be that everything that he or she can make or lose hinges on the partner/manager they're working with. The partner/manager calls the shots, that's the bottom line, even though you've got your money tied into this thing too.

The managers also discussed the length of their workweek. Aronson reported that he and Ciampa were each working an average of 80 hours per week—25 hours more per week than they had been working before.

Aronson recalled:

> I knew that during the experiment I wouldn't have much time left over for anything else, and that was a real consideration. I finally told my family to put up with it for six months, and in the end I would make it worth their while. In the first 16 weeks, we had two days off. I've worked some days from 4:30 in the morning until 11:00 at night.

McEvoy and Dunn each worked 50 to 55 hours a week. McEvoy explained, "The amount of hours we're working hasn't really changed that much." Dunn added: "We work as long as it takes to get the job done. Whenever we've worked extra hours, it has been because we were understaffed, not because we decided to work long hours because of the experiment."

Dunn summarized his evaluation of the experiment:

> To be blunt, parts of the program are good, and parts are bad. Burnout, particularly in this industry, is high. If someone is going to be locked into this thing, and they're going to have the added pressure of knowing that their money—a large part of their share of the bonus—is tied up in whether

or not they can last out their contract, well, in my opinion, that kind of stress could actually cause a person not to perform as well as they could. I'm not trying to be negative, but they've got to be careful who they choose to be managers and how they monitor them.

There are also the shift supervisors to deal with. A lot of them act like managers in every degree but in the paperwork, including sales building. In fact, when we began this experiment, Brian decided to pay our shift supervisor 2% of our half of the incremental profits. When other shift supervisors hear about the phenomenal amounts of money being made by the managers, how will that effect their motivation?

Finally, even if this program dramatically improves the quality of our applicants for managerial positions, what are we going to do about the turnover rate for lower-level employees? It's close to 400% a year in this store. High turnover is an industry norm. How does that effect the quality of the customer experience?

Results

During the experiment, sales in the Burlington Mall and CityPlace stores increased dramatically. The operating statements for both units during periods 1–7 and during the experiment (periods 8–13) are shown in *Exhibit 4. Exhibit 5* summarizes the stores' performance against the company's plan and compares it to their 1985 performance. While both McEvoy's and Aronson's base salaries remained at $500 per week, their actual, annual earnings were closer to $50,000 and $70,000, respectively.[4] A memo outlining the final distribution of profits is presented in *Exhibit 6.*

THE DECISION

Shaich considered the experiment a resounding success, and suggested that:

The problems don't lie in the concept, which I'm convinced is basically sound. The challenges will be in its execution. There are a lot of implementation issues we still have to deal with—that's one of the costs of being in

---

4. Art Veves, Burger King's regional director of Human Resources in Boston, reported in a telephone conversation that the average Burger King manager earned between $24,000 and $30,000 annually, plus a bonus of approximately $2,500. The salary expectations for a McDonald's manager were roughly equivalent to these figures.

the vanguard on an issue like this—but I think the potential gain is worth the risks.

The key to success will be for us to get out of the way once this thing starts. We've developed the concept, and now we have to stand back and let the managers operate it. In time, I believe we'll witness startling results. In my opinion, at least 25% more sales can be made. Len puts the figure closer to 50%, and Louis Kane thinks it's even higher. I'd love to flip the switch tomorrow and set the program in motion.

Schlesinger added, "In time, this plan will be broadly applicable to any multi-unit service concept on the face of the earth."

Aronson was more guarded, asserting:

With the right people, this program can work. But to suddenly turn it over to all the stores—personally, I think that would be a big mistake. There are some people who would try and squeeze it dry. In the short term they could show fantastic results, food and labor costs down, etc., but in the long term you wind up with underportioning and dirty stores.

McEvoy agreed:

I don't think they should roll out this program to every store right away, especially if they're hiring a lot of new managers. It takes a while for a person to settle in. The strict deadlines for solving problems set out in the Partner/Manager document would put too much pressure on new managers who aren't used to handling everything by themselves. Holding them accountable could blow them right out of the water.

Ciampa added:

Even under the best of circumstances, the company will be lucky if 50% of the people working for them now make it under the new program. People are used to getting a lot of supervision. It used to be that the louder you cried, the more attention you got.

Dunn added a final caution:

During the experiment, we've had phenomenal sales growth. But, and I've said this to Len and Ron, 85% of that growth would have occurred in any case because of the type of individuals Brian and I are. It just happened that the experiment began when we were starting to get things together. Specifically, at that point, Brian and I had been working together for nine months. We were comfortable with each other and we knew our customers. It was the middle of the summer and we were fully staffed because a lot of high school kids wanted summer jobs. Our equipment was functioning correctly for the first time in a long time, and we had just converted from an inefficient cafeteria-style system to one in which the person working the cash register automatically keyed in the sandwich order to the kitchen.

When asked if they planned to sign up for the long-term deal, Aronson, Ciampa, and McEvoy indicated they would if certain conditions were met (e.g., Aronson would sign up for only a one-year deal). Dunn replied, "No comment."

After a meeting in early January, during which he reviewed both his own and Shaich's comments and the reactions of the managers involved in the experiment, Schlesinger concluded:

From an MBA viewpoint, it's an interesting situation. We've got two hand-picked managers and six months of data on which to base a decision whether or not to shake up this whole company. Are we foolish if we grab at this opportunity?

Exhibit 1
Company-Owned Stores

Location	City	State	Year Opened	Square Footage	Number of Managers
Faneuil Hall Marketplace	Boston	MA	1977	1,400	4
Burlington Mall	Burlington	MA	1978	1,400	2
Logan Airport	Boston	MA	1981	800	4
Cherry Hill Mall	Cherry Hill	NJ	1984	1,000	2
Harvard Square	Cambridge	MA	1983	2,500	4
Park Plaza	Boston	MA	1984	1,000	4
Arsenal Mall	Watertown	MA	1984	2,300	3
CityPlace	Hartford	CT	1984	2,400	2
2 Penn Center	Philadelphia	PA	1985	2,700	2
Riverside Square	Hackensack	NJ	1984	1,800	3
Crossgates Mall	Albany	NY	1984	1,400	1
Cape Cod Mall	Hyannis	MA	1985	1,000	3
Crystal Mall	Waterford	CT	1984	600	2
Rockefeller Center	New York	NY	1985	2,500	5
Prudential Center	Boston	MA	1985	3,000	4
Filene's	Boston	MA	1984	800	3
Filene's (Franklin St.)	Boston	MA	1985	150 ⎫	4
Filene's (Basement)	Boston	MA	1984	600 ⎭	
Copley Place	Boston	MA	1984	2,500	4
Copley Place (Stuart St.)	Boston	MA	1985	1,000	2
Maine Mall	South Portland	ME	1983	500	1
Cookie Jar	Boston	MA	1980	700	2
Newington	Newington	NH	1984	800	2
Kendall Square	Cambridge	MA	1986	2,600	3
Dewey Square	Boston	MA	1986	2,400	2

AU BON PAIN: THE PARTNER/MANAGER PROGRAM

Exhibit 2

Weekly Manager Salaries for Given Weekly Sales Volumes
(compensation system prior to the Partner/Manager Program)

Volume/Week	General Manager (Base = $375) Volume Adjustment	Weekly Total	Senior Associate Manager (Base = $350) Volume Adjustment	Weekly Total	First Associate Manager (Base = $341.54) Volume Adjustment	Weekly Total
$1–4,000	$ 0.00	$375.00	$ 0.00	$350.00	$ 0.00	$341.54
5,000	13.12	388.12	5.25	355.25	2.53	344.07
10,000	78.75	453.75	31.50	381.50	15.21	356.75
15,000	118.00	493.00	47.25	397.25	22.81	364.35
20,000	157.50	532.50	63.00	413.00	30.42	371.96
25,000	174.38	549.38	69.75	419.75	33.67	375.21
30,000	191.25	566.25	76.50	426.50	36.93	378.47
35,000	208.13	583.13	83.25	433.25	40.19	381.73
40,000	225.00	600.00	90.00	440.00	43.46	385.00
45,000	241.88	616.88	96.75	446.75	46.71	388.25
50,000	258.75	633.75	103.50	453.50	49.97	391.51

(Continued)

AU BON PAIN: THE PARTNER/MANAGER PROGRAM

Exhibit 2

(Continued)

To compute the weekly salary for general managers, the following formulae were used:

low-volume store: base pay + .013125 (volume − $4,000)
medium-volume store: base pay + $78.75 + .00785 (volume − $10,000)
high-volume store: base pay + $157.50 + .003375 (volume − $20,000)

For senior associate managers, the formulae were:

low-volume store: base pay + .00525 (volume − $4,000)
medium-volume store: base pay + $31.50 + .00315 (volume − $10,000)
high-volume store: base pay + $63.00 + .00135 (volume − $20,000)

For first associate managers, the formulae were:

low-volume store: base pay + .002535 (volume − $4,000)
medium-volume store: base pay + $15.21 + .001521 (volume − 10,000)
high-volume store: base pay + $30.42 + .000652 (volume − $20,000)

Exhibit 3
PEGS (Product, Environment, Great Service)

STORE NAME: _____ # _____ COMPLETED BY: _____

DAY: s m t w th f s   DATE: _____/_____/_____   SHIFT MANAGER: _____

TIME: _____:_____ am / pm   MGR. SIGNATURE: _____

PRODUCT	Yes	No

I.   ALL PRODUCTS AVAILABLE ALL DAY. SIGN SPECIFIES SOUPS/SANDWICHES AS OF 10:00 A.M. (Especially watch for fresh O.J., all croissants including almonds, big breads, and petit pain/hearth rolls.)

II. ALL ITEMS MUST BE FRESH AND PREPARED TO ABP SPECIFICATIONS. NO BAKED GOODS OUT OF THE OVEN MORE THAN SIX HOURS (COOKIES AND MUFFINS EIGHT HOURS.) NO WARM CROISSANT IN OR ON THE WARMER FOR MORE THAN 4 HOURS. (Check times on trays and talk with customers about the quality of food when completing # VI. Sample different items.)

III. TEMPERATURES: SOUPS 155-165°, WARM CROISSANT MINIMUM OF 145°, COLD BEVERAGES 36-42°, HOT BEVERAGES 185°. (Must be checked with a thermometer.)

ENVIRONMENT

I.   NOTHING ON FLOORS OR CARPET MORE THAN FIVE MINUTES. BOTH FLOORS AND CARPET MUST BE CLEAN. (Identify a specific piece of trash and note the time...recheck after five minutes.)

II. DISPLAY PRODUCTS: ALL ITEMS PROPER SIZE, COLOR, CLEAN AND ORGANIZED. (All items properly identified with product description cards, observe.)

III. NO CONDIMENTS STATIONS OUT OF STOCK. (Salt, pepper, sugar, sweet & low, stirrers, napkins, creamers with ice or icepack, comment cards, menus, water, cups, straws.)

IV. ALL UNOCCUPIED SEATS/TABLES CLEANED WITHIN TWO MINUTES. ALL TABLES BALANCED PROPERLY SO THEY DON'T TILT WHEN FOOD IS PLACED ON THEM. (Identify a specific table and note the time...recheck after two minutes. Actually check five tables to make sure they don't tilt.)

V.   BATHROOMS CLEANED AND STOCKED ALL DAY. (Toilet paper, soap, towel.)

GREAT SERVICE

I.   NO MORE THAN THREE MINUTES IN LINE. (Identify, by description, a minimum of five customers. List their entry time, counter departure time, and when appropriate, the time they leave the sandwich pick-up area. Calculate the difference for total wait time.)

II. PLEASANT GREETING AND EYE CONTACT IN THREE SECONDS OR LESS WHEN A CUSTOMER HAS REACHED THE COUNTER. REGISTER CLOSED SIGNS CLEAN AND IN USE. (Observe a transaction at each register.)

III. WHAT THE CUSTOMER ORDERED IS WHAT THEY RECEIVE. CORRECT CHANGE GIVEN FOR THEIR PURCHASE. (Talk with at least five customers. Sandwich expediter calls out ticket number and reads off entire sandwich order. Observe.)

IV. BOTH CSR / MGR EXHIBIT A "WANT TO SERVE" ATTITUDE. (All register people must be able to speak and understand English. Talk with at least five customers.)

SCORE THE NUMBER OF ACTUAL "YES" OUT OF TWELVE

/12

customer description	enter line	leave line	leave sand. bar	sand. bar wait	total line time

GENERAL COMMENTS: _____
_____
_____
_____

Exhibit 4A
Store Operating Statement, Burlington Mall
(pre-experiment)
Percentage of Net Sales (numbers have been disguised)

	Periods						
	1	*2*	*3*	*4*	*5*	*6*	*7*
Regular Sales	100.0	98.5	98.9	100.0	100.0	100.0	100.0
Wholesale	0.0	0.0	0.0	0.0	0.0	0.0	0.0
Promotions	0.0	1.5	1.1	0.0	0.0	0.0	0.0
Net Sales	100.0	100.0	100.0	100.0	100.0	100.0	100.0
Discounts	0.4	0.4	0.6	0.7	1.0	0.9	0.5
Net Net Sales	99.6	99.6	99.4	99.3	99.0	99.1	99.5
Management	9.1	9.8	11.7	11.4	7.8	9.0	8.9
Shift Supervisor	0.0	0.0	0.0	0.0	0.0	1.2	1.1
Crew	15.1	14.3	14.9	13.8	14.1	13.2	13.9
Benefits	2.6	3.0	2.9	4.1	3.1	1.6	3.1
Total Labor	26.8	27.1	29.5	29.3	25.0	25.0	27.0
Food Cost	29.4	30.1	31.1	30.0	30.5	30.2	32.0
Paper Cost	1.8	1.2	1.4	1.2	2.0	1.4	1.8
Controllables	1.5	1.4	1.1	2.0	2.1	1.8	2.3
Utilities	1.9	2.8	2.3	2.3	1.8	2.1	2.2
Controllable Profit	38.2	37.0	34.0	34.5	37.6	38.6	34.2
Fixed Expenses	3.4	3.6	3.5	3.4	3.0	3.1	3.3
Occupancy	9.3	9.5	9.6	9.5	12.3	10.3	10.4
Store Profit	25.5	23.9	20.9	21.6	22.3	25.2	20.5

Exhibit 4B
Store Operating Statement, Burlington Mall
(*experiment*)
Percentage of Net Sales (numbers have been disguised)

	Periods					
	8	*9*	*10*	*11*	*12*	*13*
Regular Sales	97.0	97.1	96.0	95.2	93.9	95.8
Wholesale	3.0	2.9	4.0	4.8	6.1	4.2
Promotions	0.0	0.0	0.0	0.0	0.0	0.0
Net Sales	100.0	100.0	100.0	100.0	100.0	100.0
Discounts	0.4	0.3	0.2	0.2	0.2	0.2
Net Net Sales	99.6	99.7	99.8	99.8	99.8	99.8
Management	6.4	5.6	5.7	5.4	4.9	3.7
Shift Supervisor	1.8	0.8	0.1	1.3	2.4	2.3
Crew	13.0	12.9	12.9	12.5	11.9	11.3
Benefits	2.0	1.7	1.7	1.6	1.6	1.0
Total Labor	23.2	21.0	20.4	20.8	20.8	18.3
Food Cost	28.7	29.1	29.7	29.4	29.4	28.6
Paper Cost	1.7	1.5	2.0	1.6	1.9	1.7
Controllables	1.3	0.8	1.1	0.9	1.1	1.5
Utilities	3.4	2.7	2.8	2.2	1.3	0.4
Controllable Profit	41.3	44.6	43.8	44.9	45.3	49.3
Fixed Expenses	3.0	2.9	2.8	2.8	2.4	2.0
Occupancy	11.8	9.2	9.5	9.5	11.2	9.2
Store Profit	26.5	32.5	31.5	32.6	31.7	38.1

Exhibit 4C
Store Operating Statement, CityPlace
(pre-experiment)
Percentage of Net Sales (numbers have been disguised)

	Periods						
	1	*2*	*3*	*4*	*5*	*6*	*7*
Regular Sales	100.0	96.5	97.8	100.0	100.0	100.0	100.0
Wholesale	0.0	0.0	0.0	0.0	0.0	0.0	0.0
Promotions	0.0	3.5	2.2	0.0	0.0	0.0	0.0
Net Sales	100.0	100.0	100.0	100.0	100.0	100.0	100.0
Discounts	0.3	0.3	0.4	0.4	0.3	0.3	0.4
Net Net Sales	99.7	99.7	99.6	99.6	99.7	99.7	99.6
Management	7.0	6.8	7.3	6.5	7.1	7.1	6.8
Shift Supervisor	1.8	2.0	1.9	2.1	2.3	2.0	1.5
Crew	12.2	13.1	13.6	13.2	12.4	13.2	14.6
Benefits	2.3	2.9	2.1	2.9	2.3	2.3	2.8
Total Labor	23.3	24.8	24.9	24.7	24.1	24.6	25.7
Food Costs	28.0	29.1	29.9	31.2	27.5	29.1	30.9
Paper Cost	2.4	2.7	2.8	2.8	3.1	3.2	3.2
Controllables	1.3	1.5	1.9	3.8	2.0	4.7	1.8
Utilities	1.6	1.5	2.1	1.6	1.8	1.7	1.7
Controllable Profit	43.1	40.1	38.0	35.5	41.2	36.4	36.3
Fixed Expenses	8.5	8.9	9.9	8.3	8.8	9.1	7.8
Occupancy	12.4	12.9	12.4	12.2	12.1	12.1	11.7
Store Profit	22.2	18.3	15.7	15.0	20.3	15.2	16.8

Exhibit 4D
Store Operating Statement, CityPlace
(*experiment*)
Percentage of Net Sales (numbers have been disguised)

	Periods					
	8	*9*	*10*	*11*	*12*	*13*
Regular Sales	100.0	100.0	100.0	100.0	98.6	98.1
Wholesale	0.0	0.0	0.0	0.0	1.4	1.9
Promotions	0.0	0.0	0.0	0.0	0.0	0.0
Net Sales	100.0	100.0	100.0	100.0	100.0	100.0
Discounts	0.3	0.3	0.3	0.4	0.5	0.3
Net Net Sales	99.7	99.7	99.7	99.6	99.5	99.7
Management	6.0	5.8	6.2	5.0	5.7	5.7
Shift Supervisor	1.9	2.0	2.0	1.7	1.9	1.8
Crew	14.6	14.6	13.4	15.0	13.9	14.3
Benefits	2.2	3.0	2.1	3.0	2.1	2.0
Total Labor	24.7	25.4	23.7	24.7	23.6	23.8
Food Cost	27.6	29.6	29.6	29.9	31.0	30.6
Paper Cost	2.8	3.1	2.9	2.9	3.0	3.1
Controllables	2.6	2.3	1.6	2.1	1.7	1.6
Utilities	1.2	1.7	9.6	0.6	9.7	3.8
Controllable Profit	40.8	37.6	32.3	39.4	30.5	36.8
Fixed Expenses	6.9	7.6	11.3	7.2	5.9	7.4
Occupancy	9.6	10.3	9.7	9.2	13.0	8.9
Store Profit	24.3	19.7	11.3	23.0	11.6	20.5

Exhibit 5
Performance Against Plan and Prior Year
(current dollars)

		Periods 1–7	Periods 8–13
Sales vs. Plan	Burlington	(11,695)	56,719
	CityPlace	12,903	69,311
	Total	1,208	126,030
Sales vs. Last Year	Burlington	(1,600)	70,478
	CityPlace	33,512	93,558
	Total	31,912	164,036
Controllable Profits vs. Plan	Burlington	(3,844)	53,562
	CityPlace	4,613	18,580
	Total	769	72,142
Controllable Profits vs. Last Year	Burlington	(2)	57,449
	CityPlace	2,706	29,741
	Total	2,704	87,190

Exhibit 6
Partner/Manager Profit Distributions

Memorandum		

TO: Gary Aronson, Frank Ciampa, Steve Dunn, Brian McEvoy
FROM: Len Schlesinger
DATE: January 15, 1987
RE: Partner/Manager Profit Distributions
cc: Ron Shaich
       Louis Kane

	Burlington	*CityPlace*
Store-Lease Payment	$127,526.25	$103,619.50
Fixed Asset Additions	110.62	45.49
Percentage Rent	3,556.48	0.00
TOTAL DUE ABP	131,193.35	103,664.99
Credits		
Period 8	23,225.00	23,680.65
Period 9	28,740.00	20,218.65
Period 10	27,705.00	23,444.46
Period 11	29,445.00	23,809.65
Period 12	33,172.00	24,071.65
Period 13	45,122.00	23,024.65
TOTAL CREDITS	187,409.00	138,249.71
LESS TOTAL DUE ABP	131,193.35	103,664.99
PROFIT POOL	56,215.65	34,584.72
ABP Share	28,107.82	17,292.36
P/M Share	19,675.48	12,104.65
Assoc. P/M Share	8,432.35	5,187.71
P/M Weekly Wage		
Salary	500.00	500.00
Share	819.81	504.36
TOTAL	1,319.81	1,004.36
ANNUALIZED	68,630.12	52,226.72
Assoc. P/M Weekly Wage		
Salary	400.00	400.00
Share	351.35	216.15
TOTAL	751.35	616.15
ANNUALIZED	39,070.20	32,039.80

APPENDIX A

AN INTRODUCTION TO THE PARTNER/MANAGER PROGRAM

Drafted: Spring 1986 by Len Schlesinger and Ron Shaich.
Abridged by Research Assistant Lucy N. Lytle, under the supervision of Professor W. Earl Sasser, January 1987.

I. Company Objectives

As Au Bon Pain moves into the future, we must develop for our bakery/cafe managers a compensation/incentive system that is second to none in our industry segment. The foundation of ABP's success is talented people who achieve results and, in turn, share in the financial rewards of their efforts. The Partner/Manager Program provides the opportunity for a select group of managers to be in business for themselves, but not by themselves. The company provides support by monitoring the quality standards, which will be vigorously enforced, and by refining and expanding our retail concept and system. Our ability to attract talented and enthusiastic people who thrive in our environment is nothing less than the prime ingredient necessary to achieve all the goals that we have set.

Au Bon Pain believes fundamentally that the individual bakery/cafe units' sales and profitability are strongly influenced by their retail operations' quality. Furthermore, we believe that the retail operations' quality is directly affected by the presence of:

- A management team that truly cares about the quality of the customer experience
- A management team that has experience and is committed to working at a specific unit for an extended period of time
- A management team that is committed to the Au Bon Pain operating system but that is flexible enough to make some of its own decisions and adaptations to build sales in its market
- A crew with strong interrelationships and a commitment to the management team, and thus to the customer
- An explicit focus on managing outputs (service, sales, food costs, controllable costs, labor costs) vs. inputs
- A store-manager/company "you win-we win" approach

Developing these traits has been very difficult, however, due to Au Bon Pain's internal structure and to the following dynamics of the fast-food labor market, specifically:

- A managerial labor pool that forces us to take more "chances" in hiring entry-level talent, in addition to significant turnover at the associate manager level
- A centralized, system-wide orientation toward the operations and marketing functions in our bakery/cafes which currently stifles our ability to exercise initiative at the store level
- Excessive crew turnover and sloppy hiring, which severely degrade the quality of the customer experience and exacerbate the day-to-day problems of the management team

To address these problems and to move toward reaching an idealized version of our retail operations, we are proposing a radically reconceptualized framework for managing human resources in Au Bon Pain bakery/cafe units. It is titled the Partner/Manager Program.

II.   Objectives of the Partner/Manager Program
- To develop a management compensation system that enhances dramatically our ability to attract and retain the finest managers in the industry
- To shift our organizational focus from being promoted to district manager as the desired carrer path to achieving partner/manager status (a terminal general manager's position)
- To increase dramatically a store management team's tenure and thus its feelings of "local ownership"
- To lessen our top-down management approach to retail operations by:
    1) increasing local unit responsibilities for decision making and execution, with an accompanying reward system that increases management commitment to unit results
    2) encouraging partner/managers to "push" the corporate office to respond to local needs
- To reduce dramatically district manager supervision of retail stores and to shift the district manager's role from a police officer/checker to a business/sales consultant
- To provide a human-resource mechanism that frees ABP to grow at an accelerated rate without great pain ("hyperphased growth")
- To maximize simultaneously store-level profits, ABP return on investment, and management salaries
- To provide the opportunity for our partner/managers to build financial "nest eggs"
- To provide job security to those people who perform for ABP and for themselves

III. Management of the Partner/Manager Experiment

The experiment will run for six periods, from July 13 until December 20, 1986. Len Schlesinger will assume direct responsibility as the district manager for the two stores selected to participate.

Experimentation at a Burlington Mall store will test our abilities to revive a mature shopping mall location and to tap into area offices as a growth vehicle in the face of increased competition. The CityPlace experiment will provide us with considerable data on how best to leverage an office building location to its fullest potential.

IV. The Economics of the Partner/Manager Program

A. Each store's general manager will be reclassified as a partner/manager at a base salary of $500 per week. Each will be authorized to hire/retain one associate manager at a base salary of $400 per week. Any additional management support can be added at a partner/manager's discretion. All managers must, however, take their bonus (i.e., their 50% share of the store's incremental profits) from a fixed pool.

B. Au Bon Pain will determine a "store-lease" payment required to support a unit's fixed expenses, corporate overhead, and reasonable profit expectations. During the experiment, this payment will be $127,526 for the Burlington Mall unit, and $103,619 for the CityPlace unit.

C. The store-lease payment will be guaranteed for the period of the experiment, with the following exceptions, which will require adjustments:

   1) The addition of fixed assets will trigger an increase in the store-lease payment of: .25 × total fixed asset cost.

      EXAMPLE: A new counter is added to Hartford at a cost of $10,000. On an annual basis, this addition would increase the store-lease payment by $2,500.

   2) Additional sales, which trigger a percentage rent clause in the real estate lease, will increase the store-lease payment by the percentage specified in the real estate lease.

      EXAMPLE: The rent for the Burlington unit assumes that the store will achieve the 1986 plan. All sales over this plan will increase the store-lease payment to Au Bon Pain by 8% of the incremental sales dollars.

D. Profits will be distributed to the partner/manager and associate manager as follows: actual store controllable profits − store-lease payment = incremental profits or losses.

   incremental profits × .50 = ABP share

incremental profits $\times$ .35 = partner/manager share

incremental profits $\times$ .15 = associate manager share

E. The partner/manager's and associate manager's share of the incremental profits will be distributed at the close of each period. Au Bon Pain will hold in reserve $7,500 for the partner/manager and $2,500 for the associate manager until the end of their contracts.

F. For the Partner/Manager Program Experiment, profit distributions will occur after the final review of the experiment is completed (approximately February 1, 1987).

V. Supervising and Managing the Partner/Manager Experiment

A. The two stores will be "mystery shopped" at least once a week, and the mystery-shopping reports will serve as critical indicators of store-level quality standards.

B. The two stores will be subjected to three "white-glove" inspections. These will be conducted by an independent ABP auditor who is not connected with the experiment. The inspections will cover all phases of store operations and will be a major input to the overall evaluation of the experiment.

C. The two stores will be expected to comply with the 100% customer satisfaction "moment of truth" indicators and will be evaluated against them.

D. The partner/manager, associate manager, or a certified ABP shift supervisor must be on duty in the store during all store hours. The partner/ manager and associate manager must each work in the store a minimum of 50 hours a week, and the partner/manager and/or the associate manager must be on duty in the store during 90% of its operating hours.

E. Au Bon Pain reserves the right to discharge, remove, or replace the partner/manager or associate manager at any time. All store managers, crew, and shift supervisors will remain employees of Au Bon Pain.

VI. The "Rules"

Violation of the following conditions will engender a default and/or the termination of the partner/manager's and/or associate manager's experiment.

A. The partner/manager shall use the Au Bon Pain bakery/cafe premises solely for the operation of the business, keep the business open and in normal operation for such minimum hours and days as ABP may from time to time prescribe, and refrain from using and suffering the use of the premises for any other purpose or activity at any time.

B. The partner/manager shall maintain the bakery/cafe in the highest degree of sanitation, repair, and condition. In connection therewith, he or she shall make such additions, alterations, repairs, and replacements thereto as ABP may require, including without limitation, periodically repainting the premises; repairing impaired equipment, furniture, and fixtures; and replacing obsolete signs.

C. The partner/manager further understands, acknowledges, and agrees that—to ensure that all products produced and sold by the bakery/cafe meet ABP's high standards of taste, texture, appearance, and freshness, and to protect ABP's goodwill and proprietary marks—all products shall be prepared by only properly trained personnel in strict accordance with the Retail Baker's Training Program.

D. The partner/manager shall meet and maintain the highest health standards and ratings applicable to the bakery/cafe operation.

E. The partner/manager shall operate the bakery/cafe in conformity with such uniform methods, standards, and specifications and ABP may from time to time prescribe to ensure that the highest degree of quality and service is uniformly maintained.

F. Unless transferred at Au Bon Pain's request, the partner/manager and/or associate manager will not be eligible for the profit-sharing disbursements unless he or she completes the full time-period of the experiment. If transferred, the affected manager will receive a pro-rated share based on the percentage of total controllable profit contributed while he or she was employed in the store.

The partner/manager agrees:

1) To maintain in sufficient supply, and use at all times, only such products, materials, ingredients, supplies, and paper goods as conform with ABP's standards and specifications. The partner/manager shall not deviate from these standards by using nonconforming items.

2) To employ a sufficient number of employees to meet the standards of service and quality that ABP may prescribe.

3) To comply with all applicable federal, state, and local laws, rules, and regulations with respect to ABP employees.

4) To permit ABP or its agents or representatives to enter the premises at any time for the purpose of conducting inspections; to cooperate fully with ABP's agents or representatives in such inspections by rendering such assistance as they may reasonably request; and, upon

notice from ABP or its agents or representatives, to take such steps as may be necessary to correct immediately any deficiencies detected during such inspections.

The partner/manager agrees further that failure to comply with the requirements of this paragraph will cause ABP irreparable injury and will result in the subject termination of his or her employment and the loss of any incremental profit funds held in reserve.

In addition, the partner/manager shall be deemed to be in default and ABP may, at its option, terminate this agreement without affording him or her any opportunity to cure the default, upon the occurrence of any of the following events:

A. The operation of the bakery/cafe results in a threat or danger to public health or safety that is not corrected by the partner/manager within one week of notice.

B. The partner/manager is convicted of a felony or any other crime or offense that is reasonably likely, in the sole opinion of ABP, to affect adversely the ABP system or goodwill associated therewith.

C. The partner/manager fails to comply with the covenants in A–E above provided, however, that for any correctable failure he or she has 30 days after notice from ABP to correct the failure.

D. The partner/manager, after correcting any default, engages in the same activity, giving rise to the same default, whether or not the deficiency is corrected after notice.

E. The partner/manager repeatedly is in default of or fails to comply substantially with any of the requirements imposed by this agreement, whether or not the deficiencies are corrected after notice.

Fairfield Inn

Mike Ruffer, the vice president and general manager of Fairfield Inn, Marriott's new entry into the economy, limited-service motel industry, summarized the dilemma facing Fairfield Inn's top executives in 1989:

> How does a new chain with limited ad dollars take on competitors like Days Inn, Hampton Inn and Red Roof Inn—each with more than 200 units already operating? When we started Fairfield Inn, we knew that it was going to be a distribution game, but now in the face of rapid room supply increases and greater competition, the established players are making it a marketing and ad spending game as well.

Ruffer paused and looked out of his window at Marriott's corporate headquarters located about a half mile away in a Bethesda, Maryland, office park. He continued:

> The dynamics of the business have changed considerably in the past 2 1/2 years. Our original recommendation called for a portion of our unit growth to come from franchising. Yet, when Bill Marriott nixed the idea because of his desire to have full control over the operations, we were still confident that we could successfully establish a meaningful presence and achieve good unit distribution.
>
> Since then, however, the economy category has experienced annual, double-digit growth in room supply—most of it occurring in the chains that are predominantly franchise focused. Good sites which have typically been scarce and costly are becoming more so. And due to the rapid growth of other chains, we not only run the risk of being preempted from entering markets, but the growth of these other competitors greatly increases the size of their marketing "war chest" in the battle for the customer.
>
> Our preference in Marriott has historically been to manage our own operations rather than employ a franchising strategy. Yet, if we aren't able to in-

crease our rollout rate, the true unit potential of this new business may never be fully realized.

COMPANY BACKGROUND

Fairfield Inn, with 25 properties open in March 1989, was the newest concept in Marriott's lodging and food services empire. In 1988, the Marriott Corporation had sales of over $7.3 billion, an operating income of $398 million, and a net income of $232 million. (In the past year, Marriott stock had traded in a range of $26 to $35, and there were 108.7 million shares outstanding.)

Marriott Corporation traced its roots back to the peak of the Great Depression. On May 20, 1927, Charles Lindbergh took off in the Spirit of St. Louis on his historic transatlantic flight, Babe Ruth was in the midst of his 60-home-run year, and J. Willard Marriott and his wife Alice opened a nine-stool root beer stand named The Hot Shoppe in Washington, D.C.

By 1989, the Marriott Corporation had over 230,000 employees, was serving more than 5 million meals daily, and was developing over $1 billion of real estate every year as one of the ten largest real estate developers in the United States. The corporation was divided into three major divisions: Contract Services, Restaurants, and Lodging.

Contract Services

Marriott's Contract Services provided 44% of the company sales and 32% of its operating income in 1988. The best known of these services was probably Marriott's In-Flite Services, the company's airline catering operations. Marriott pioneered this business in 1939 and by 1989 provided food and other services to over 140 airlines at 92 flight kitchens located in 70 airports throughout the world. Marriott's Contract Services also included Education Services that provided food services to 585 colleges and high schools. Health Care Services handled food services at over 400 hospitals and retirement centers.

Restaurants

J. Willard and Alice Marriott's single Hot Shoppe had been expanded to a restaurant operation encompassing over 1,000 owned and franchised popularly priced restaurants that included Bob's Big Boy, Roy Rogers, Hot Shoppes, and Travel

Plazas by Marriott. In 1988, this division delivered 13% of Marriott's sales and 16% of its operating income.

Lodging

Marriott's Lodging Group encompassed 451 hotels with over 118,000 rooms. Marriott was America's leading operator (as opposed to franchisor) of hotel rooms. Lodging operations represented 43% of sales and 52% of operating income in 1988. The lodging group, including Fairfield Inn, was subdivided into five distinct segments.

Marriott Hotels and Resorts were full-service hotels in the luxury/quality segment. In 1988, the system included 192 hotels in 38 states and 13 countries and totaled over 83,000 rooms. The cost of a room ranged between $75 and $195 a night.

The first Marriott Suites hotel opened in early 1987 in Atlanta. This full-service chain provided guests with their choice of one- and two-bedroom suites, a restaurant, a lounge and several meeting rooms. Three more Marriott Suite hotels opened in 1988, and the company planned to have a total of 40 open by 1993. Room rates typically ranged from $85 to $125.

Residence Inn by Marriott was America's leading moderate-price extended-stay suite concept and was acquired by Marriott in July 1987. The typical Residence Inn guest stayed for five or more consecutive nights. Guests were usually corporate employees who were in the process of being relocated to a new city, on some sort of temporary project assignment, or working in some kind of consulting capacity. At the end of 1988, there were 130 Residence Inns in 37 states with nearly 15,000 suites. Room rates ranged between $65 and $90.

Courtyard by Marriott was a lodging concept that was only six years old and focused on the moderate-price segment of the hotel industry. A property normally had 150 rooms, a restaurant, a lounge and several meeting rooms. In 1988, Courtyard had 111 properties with 16,000 rooms in 27 states. Rates ranged from $50 to $88 each night.

THE FAIRFIELD INN DECISION

The decision to venture into the economy/limited-service (ELS) segment (below $45 a night) was not an easy one and raised several questions for Marriott's senior management. They included the following:

1. Could Marriott compete as a late entry into a market segment already crowded with Red Roof Inn, Holiday Corporation's Hampton Inn, Days Inn, La Quinta, Comfort Inn, and over 45 other regional or state chains?
2. Would Marriott be jeopardizing its Courtyard clientele or cannibalizing some of its existing business by selling guests down to an economy-priced product?
3. Could Marriott design a product and property that was attractive enough to build a thriving business, yet cost effective enough to meet Marriott's corporate net present value goals and its 12% target internal rate of return (IRR) for new development projects?

Mark Pacala, Fairfield's vice president of operations, was one of the strategists with Marriott's Corporate Planning Department who first looked at the ELS segment in 1985 as a possible growth opportunity for Marriott. According to him:

Going ahead with Fairfield Inn was a very tough decision. The market was growing rapidly and established competitors had already built strong brand names with a consistent product. We knew we'd be walking into the middle of a share grab game.

The no-go position was that we didn't know anything about this market segment, Marriott was too quality-oriented, we might tend to overinvest (hence, couldn't meet IRR goals because of high costs), and we would be entering too late into this market.

The go position was that it's the second biggest segment in the lodging industry and the fastest growing. It would allow us to diversify. There was no one dominant national player, so we could take a little bit of share from everybody. Lastly, if things didn't work out, we projected that we could recover our costs by selling out to one of the established chains.

Despite their initial reservations, Marriott's Corporate Finance Committee approved the Fairfield Inn planning group's original request for $10.0 million to develop two five-property ELS test markets. In December 1985 approval was given, and in October 1987 the first Fairfield Inn opened in Atlanta.

THE ECONOMY, LIMITED-SERVICE (ELS) HOTEL BUSINESS

The economy segment of the U.S. lodging industry accounted for as much as 28% of all available rooms in 1988. Economy properties' room rents normally fell in the $25 to $45 per-night range. Economy hotels typically did not have restaurants, luxurious lobbies, or extensive meeting facilities. One authority estimated that for these reasons, economy hotels could break even with occupancy rates between 52% and 55%, about 10 to 12 occupancy points below the level at which full-service properties tended to break even.

The top 50 ELS lodging chains had a combined total of 5,042 properties and 498,800 rooms at the end of 1987, a year in which occupancy rates for the entire ELS segment firmed up. Occupancies are shown in *Exhibit 1*.

The ELS segment was the fastest-growing part of the U.S. lodging industry. In 1987, the segment expanded with 606 properties and 67,800 rooms. This translated to growth rates of 13.7% and 15.6%, respectively, in number of properties and number of rooms. In 1988, market experts anticipated that just over 1,000 properties with 102,200 rooms would be added to the ELS segment. Projected growth rates for several of the leading chains in the segment are included in *Exhibit 2*.

The expansion of the segment paralleled corporate America's increased emphasis on controlling travel and entertainment (T&E) expenses. American Express's biennial Survey of Business Travel Management noted that "the number of chief executive officers and senior financial managers who rate rising T&E costs as a 'top concern' has risen from 45% to 55% in the past two years."

In 1990, industry experts estimated that American companies would spend at least $115 billion on T&E expenses, up from the $95 billion spent in 1988. While air travel costs were the largest single expenditure, responsible for 40% of every T&E dollar, lodging was next, accounting for 23% of every T&E dollar.

Established Competition

Days Inn of America, based in Atlanta, Georgia, with 84,800 rooms and 590 properties throughout America, was the largest ELS chain in 1988. It owned 12% of its hotels and franchised the rest. In 1988, Days Inn opened 163 new properties and added 22,000 rooms. Occupancy rates for the chain were between 63% and 68%. Although Days Inn room rates averaged between $35 and $40 dollars per night, published room rates varied from $18 to $109 a night depending on the location of the property. Days Inn accounted for 17% of all rooms in the ELS segment in 1987.

Motel 6's 48,800 rooms and 431 properties ranked it as the second-largest economy chain in the U.S. in 1988. All of the properties were owned and operated by Motel 6. Occupancies ranged from 70% to 75%, and its published room rates ranged from $17.95 to $28.95. In 1987, Motel 6 initiated a major radio advertising campaign that had spokesperson Tom Bodette telling travelers that "We'll leave a light on for you." Bodette's folksy voice and inviting manner increased the awareness levels of Motel 6 within its target market.

Comfort Inn, headquartered in Silver Spring, Maryland, was the third-largest ELS chain in the U.S. with 375 properties and 33,700 rooms in 1988. Comfort Inns were 100% franchised. Its unit's occupancies varied between 65% and 70%, and published room rates were from $30 to $50 per night.

Red Roof Inn was founded in Ohio in 1964 and opened its 200th property in Orlando in 1989. All Red Roof Inns were owned by the company. New Red Roof Inns had been opened at the rate of about 15 a year for the past three years. Its occupancies ranged from 77% to 82%, and room rates averaged between $35 to $40 a night.

Holiday Corporation's Hampton Inn had the most ambitious growth plans of all ELS chains. By 1988, Hampton Inn had 152 properties and more than 19,000 rooms. Holiday Corp. retained direct ownership of 12% of the properties and franchised 88% of the chain. Room rates ranged from $29 to $68 a night.

In a 1986 meeting of the Holiday Corp.'s limited-service hotel division, Ray Schultz, Hampton Inn's president, told managers, owners, and operators in attendance that, "We're not the biggest yet, but we will be. . . . Don't get greedy. Stay away from raising rates. Operate lean and efficiently. And hire, train, and motivate good people."[1]

Michael Rose, chairman and CEO of Hampton's parent company, emphasized that, "In a survey of Hampton customers, 98% said they would use a Hampton Inn again. Two-thirds said they would actually go out of their way to stay at a Hampton Inn hotel. . . . Design has been an important factor, but in the long term, outstanding customer service is the key to success."[2]

According to Hampton's President Schultz:

> We basically are competing in the upper and middle ranges of the limited-service segment. We see our main competitor (as of 1986) as being the La Quintas, the Comforts, the Days Inns. . . . We're going into a "burst" mode of advertising, where periodically we'll attempt to make travelers aware of our product. We're aiming for national awareness. . . . We're finding that new inns are running in the high 50s or low 60s percentagewise (in occupancy). After about six months, they're in the middle 60s. After a year, occupancy rates are typically in the 70-percent range. . . . We made aggressive plans, and we're fulfilling them, so I'm not so surprised that we're growing so fast. The competitors around us are the ones who are surprised.[3]

1. Bill Gillette, "Hampton Plans to Rule Limited-Service Market," *Hotel & Motel Management*, June 30, 1986, p. 2.

2. Ibid.

3. Bill Gillette, "Schultz Leading Chain's Growth," *Hotel & Motel Management*, June 30, 1986, p. 38.

Market Analysis and Fairfield's Positioning

The size of the entire U.S. ELS segment was estimated at 285 million room nights annually in 1985. The market was broadly divided into business travelers who accounted for 178 million room nights and pleasure travelers who purchased 107 million room nights. Overall demand growth in the ELS segment was expected to range from 4 to 6 percent each year throughout the next decade. Fairfield Inn was designed for the transient market, business and pleasure travelers who were seeking clean, comfortable, and convenient lodging in the $30 to $40 price range. Its anticipated guest mix was 65% business transients and 35% pleasure transients.

Business travelers in the economy segment usually traveled by auto and followed regional drive patterns in the course of their business and sales calls. When deciding where to stay for the night, the most important attributes for these travelers were cleanliness; overall value for the money spent; secure feeling; friendly, efficient employees; and overall service. Traveler comments obtained from focus group interviews conducted for Fairfield Inn's management appear in *Exhibit 3*.

According to Marriott's in-house research, business travelers could be subdivided into two basic traveler segments, "functional travelers" and "stylish travelers." Fairfield Inn's strategy was to make the functional business traveler the primary customer group; in 1985, this segment was estimated to comprise 66% of business travelers purchasing 72% of room nights occupied by business travelers.

Functional and stylish travelers possessed different attitudes toward lodging and had different demographic and travel profiles. The functional business traveler wanted the basic amenities (clean room, good price/value, and consistency) but didn't need lots of extras. Functional travelers preferred motels like Fairfield Inn, Red Roof, and Knights Inn. Stylish travelers wanted the basics plus some food and beverage service, business services and meeting rooms, and recreational facilities. Stylish travelers tended to prefer motels like Hampton Inn, Signature Inn, and La Quinta Motor Inn.

Fairfield Inn targeted the functional traveler group because this group was composed of the most frequent travelers, was the largest economy consumer group, and generated the most potential new room nights. Market research indicated that the vast majority of travelers within this price segment were new Marriott customers and not established Courtyard clientele. Also, the weekend pleasure customers' lodging needs were quite similar to those of the functional business traveler, so Fairfield's product and price allowed Marriott's new brand to attract the weekend pleasure traveler.

Market analyses conducted by Fairfield Inn's management showed four key customer target groups among frequent automobile travelers who were current users of other economy price hotels:

1. Traveling salespeople or regional managers were travelers with an assigned territory to cover. They had fairly strict per diem allowances for travel and lodging. They desired a good clean room that was also conducive to working at night.

2. Government and military employees had a rigid per diem budget that they were allowed to spend on lodging. Economy hotels met their needs quite well.

3. Self-employed businesspeople tried to minimize expenses by staying in reasonably-priced lodging. Since all bills were paid out of their "own pockets," members of this group were rate-sensitive and didn't want to be charged for services not used.

4. Extended stayers were defined as guests staying more than a week. Typically, these people were relocating or part of a project team.

Additionally, Fairfield Inn's management wanted to set a price high enough to discourage truckers and construction crews as guests. They wanted to exude the image of being a businessperson's hotel during the week.

Guest tracking surveys conducted in 1988 confirmed that Marriott's first 15 ELS properties were reaching their target customers. Fairfield Inn's weekday guest was an over-the-road (as opposed to air traveling) salesperson who was about 40 years old, made 33 business trips a year, and had a personal income of $52,600.

Focus groups conducted with ELS hotel customers indicated that pleasure travelers wanted a well-run, secure, inexpensive place to spend the night while on the road to some other destination or to use as a "base-camp" for visiting friends or family within the local area.

The ELS pleasure traveler represented a broad segment of the U.S. population. Marriott researchers estimated that 25% of U.S. families stayed in economy lodging at least one night each year for pleasure travel. Broadly speaking, these customers lived within a 300-mile radius of the hotel and drove there with their family. Marriott's research showed that many travelers who stayed in higher-priced lodging while on business also preferred to stay in ELS lodging when traveling for pleasure. The typical weekend guest at Fairfield Inn was 40 years of age, but had a lower personal income than weekday guests.

THE FAIRFIELD INN CONCEPT

After completing the initial feasibility studies, the real challenge for Fairfield Inn's operating managers was in designing, producing, implementing, and operating a Fairfield Inn concept. Mike Ruffer clearly delineated the expectations for Fairfield Inn:

In any lodging segment that we or Marriott compete in our objective going in is not to be the biggest; we do however want to be best of the class. Our long-term success is more dependent upon how well we serve our guests time and again. Consistently. Superior hospitality and execution day-to-day will let us "win" over time.

The mission statement that was developed by Fairfield Inn's management team reflected a desire to be the best:

At Fairfield Inn, our team's mission is to

- Impress our guests
- Have committed employees pursuing excellence
- Recognize and reward excellent performance.

Mel Warriner, vice president of human resources, commented, "You'll notice we don't use the word satisfy. It's too mediocre. We are hanging our strategic hat on service. We want the guest to leave and say 'Wow, this was different.'"

Fairfield Inn's rooms rented for $36 per night, and each property had about 130 rooms. Fairfield Inn management anticipated that established properties would have an annual occupancy rate of 78%.

Fairfield Inn's amenities package was designed using surveys that asked experienced ELS customers what they wanted. According to Bob Ziegler, Fairfield's director of marketing communications: "We sampled more than 600 people. We screened them on several criteria, whether they took six or more business trips a year, expected to pay between $20 and $45 a night when they were paying for their own lodging, and stayed in competitive hotels during the past year."

Each Fairfield Inn offered guests king-size beds, free cable television, remote-control television, thick towels, free local phone calls, large comfortable chair, large work desk (45 × 28 inches), alarm clock, free coffee and tea in the lobby, swimming pool, inside or outside room entry, smoking or non-smoking rooms, long-cord telephones, separate full-length mirror, a meeting room just off the lobby, and vending machines with a variety of snacks, juices, and soft drinks.

Fairfield Inn's top management realized early on that if its concept was going to succeed in an already-crowded ELS segment, it would have to successfully combine an efficient, attractive property (see *Exhibit 4* for a picture of a Fairfield Inn) with a highly motivated staff. As Mel Warriner put it, "Too often employees are just marking time. At Fairfield, we are committing ourselves to reducing turnover in the housekeeping and lower staff levels dramatically below the industry's 150%–200% per year average. We hire people who like to make people smile. We have designed what we feel is an innovative pay-for-performance system that encourages the pursuit of excellence." Management called this the Scorecard System.

The Scorecard System

According to Robert J. McCarthy, Fairfield's vice president of marketing, "Scorecard is the single most unique thing we are doing. It's not a typical hotel amenity, but it may be our most powerful amenity."

Each Fairfield Inn check-out counter was equipped with two Scorecard computer monitors, as shown in *Exhibit 5*. When a guest checked out, it was the guest service representative's (or GSR, the equivalent of a front desk clerk at Fairfield) responsibility to cheerfully ask the customer to please rate the quality of his or her stay and the services he or she received by entering either excellent, average, or poor on the Scorecard monitor's keypad.

The complete Scorecard system involved six questions (listed in *Exhibit 6*), but customers only answered four questions during each check-out. The question about the cleanliness of the room was answered by every guest, while the software program rotated the remaining five questions in the other three Scorecard slots. These other questions queried the guest about the friendliness and efficiency of the clerk at arrival and check-out, an overall rating of this Fairfield Inn, value for the price paid, and an overall rating of cleanliness and staff hospitality.

In order to facilitate use of the Scorecard, each GSR and guest room attendant (GRA or housekeeper) was assigned a special employee code number. Scorecard's software system automatically matched each guest's rating for every question to the appropriate service personnel. In this way, the ratings produced a performance "scorecard" for the property and every employee on the property that regularly came in contact with guests, as shown in *Exhibit 6*.

The Scorecard ratings played a major role in the incentive compensation levels of each employee at the Inn. They were published monthly and posted in the break room at each Fairfield Inn. A GSR or GRA was able to earn a bonus of up to 10% of salary every quarter, with 50% of the bonus based on individual performance and 50% based on the entire staff's performance at each property. Fairfield Inn's base wages for each position ranked in the top quarter among salaries offered by local hotels and motels.

Joanne Eckhardt, a GSR in Detroit, commented:

> Scorecard gives corporate an immediate rating on a guest stay since we're all logged in. It gives credit where credit is due. You're not getting the same amount of pay as everyone else. It's very fair. With Holiday Inn (her previous employer) there was no incentive and no option to progress within the system. It was like you were expendable. Here at Fairfield Inn, I've seen

them promote front desk clerks into management, or if you're happy doing what you're doing, they recognize and reward you.

Linda Wilson, another GSR, said:

I love to see it when guests checking out push excellent. At Signature Inn, the only people who ever got a bonus check were the front desk crew and the manager. Housekeeping, maintenance, and laundry got absolutely nothing. They tried to keep bonuses really hush-hush. Back then, I was assistant supervisor of housecleaning and it really made me mad that the front desk got a bonus and we didn't. They said that front desk sells the hotel, but what do you think happens if the guest walks into a room that's dirty. At Fairfield, we're a team.

According to Deneige Teague, a guest linen attendant (laundry room):

The money is nice. No other hotel company offers it. My bonus is based on the Inn's overall rating. Here, we are very proud of what we do. It's our property. When someone walks in that room we all have the same idea—to make sure they get a great room and come back again.

Scorecard ratings seemed to serve as a focal point for some good-natured competition among each Inn's staff and across the various Fairfield locations. Joyce Smith, a GRA, said, "Every time the ratings get posted we all rush up to see how well we did. Everybody takes care of their own section of rooms and wants to have the cleanest rooms in the hotel."

Rob Munro, a guest room supervisor, added:

Scorecard is an incentive. We try and encourage the GRA's to take great pride in their work. Each day I will review two rooms (out of the 14 assigned daily to each GRA) with the person. I try to be really positive because we want to keep the person from getting discouraged. They are going to make a lot of mistakes initially—water spotted chrome, a stopper not in the tub, or dust on the chair legs. Fairfield is very particular. We don't have a lot of extras, so we want everything to be absolutely clean. Some of our high standards come from our hiring. We get people with good attitudes and good personalities. But it's up to the supervisors and managers to provide the right working environment.

Personnel Selection

The Scorecard system and Fairfield's focus on hospitality was based upon hiring good people from the start and developing a strong relationship among the entire staff during the pre-opening stages of a property.

Fairfield Inn managers made their employee selections after evaluating the potential candidates in a series of personal interviews (as many as three rounds) and on the basis of a personality skills profile test designed by Selection Research Institute.

"Generally, we like to hire people who enjoy pleasing other people. For GRA's, we try to identify people who like to clean and enjoy housework. Similarly, for our maintenance jobs we focus on finding people who enjoy fixing things. Part of the six-to-eight-week training program for Fairfield managers is a three-day seminar on how to interview job candidates and how to evaluate the personality skills test," commented Mark Pacala.

Sue Graves, Fairfield's Detroit area manager, who supervised six area properties, remembered opening up the airport property a year earlier: "When we opened that Detroit property we were running about two weeks behind (in construction and finishing) so that allowed me and the assistant managers to interview more people," she said. "We interviewed over 500 people to fill 19 positions at the first property, and in the last 90 days we haven't had any turnover."

Another way that Fairfield management had generated a tremendous amount of enthusiasm among the hourly employees at each hotel was through a team-building exercise in the pre-opening meeting where management and hourly employees had a round-table discussion of mutual expectations.

The team-building discussion began with employees and management generating a list of what they would want if they each were a guest at this Fairfield Inn. The next segment of the team-building exercise encouraged hourly employees to generate a list of expectations for each other. At the Warren property, a suburb of Detroit, the employee promises to each other were: dependability, teamwork, positivity, consideration, honesty, reliability, loyalty, integrity, encourage others, pats on the back, caring, understanding, jokes, a sense of humor, camaraderie, friendship, communication, light-heartedness, and to not sweat the small stuff.

Next, the hourly employees generated a list of their expectations from management. At Canton, these expectations included: sensitivity, respect, a second chance, empathy, fairness, friendship, protection, creativity, teach us, keep us informed, keep us a part of decisions, stand by us, listen to our ideas, money, sense of humor, understanding, support, and patience.

At each Fairfield Inn, the posters that had been generated in the team-building exercise were prominently displayed in the employee break room located next to the property manager's office.

Organization

Each Fairfield Inn had a staff of about 21 employees to run the property. The staff was composed of a manager, assistant manager, and 19 hourly employees:

four GSRs, 11 GRAs, one guest room supervisor, one maintenance chief, one custodial facility attendant, and one guest linen attendant.

The regional support group for each cluster of 10 to 12 Fairfield Inns was composed of a field marketing manager and an area manager. The area manager was directly responsible to headquarters for the performance of each Inn in his or her region.

Fairfield's decentralized organization was combined with a highly centralized operations system. Each Fairfield Inn was directly linked to a central computer at the Bethesda headquarters through an in-house system known as "The Coordinator." The resulting "flat" organization structure allowed each property manager to focus on "impressing the guest."

"The administrative load is really minimal. It's like night-and-day when compared to the inventory and labor reports I had to complete in another Marriott group. Not having tons of paperwork allows you to be out with your guests. Every morning, I try to be out at the front desk or lobby between 7:30 a.m. and 9:00 a.m. so I can personally greet and get to know our guests," commented Norm Bartlemay, the manager at Detroit's Canton property.

Guest and Employee Incentives

Another program developed by Fairfield Inn in 1988 was the creation of a discretionary promotions fund. The fund gave property managers the opportunity to provide special events and promotions for both their employees and guests. Each manager was allocated $175 every month to spend on employee incentives and $125 to use on guest incentives.

At the Detroit airport property, a "hospitality committee" composed of the maintenance chief, one guest room attendant, and an assistant manager determined how to allocate the money for guest incentives. In recent months, regular guests had been surprised with gift certificates to Bob Evans restaurants, green carnations on St. Patrick's Day, and Easter baskets full of jelly beans in their rooms.

For the employees, incentives usually took the form of cash bonuses and gift certificates. For example, in March 1989 at the Warren property, the winner of the month's "White Glove Award," the person scoring highest on daily room inspections, had his/her choice of $25 cash, a $25 dinner certificate for a local restaurant, or an equivalent amount of movie passes. Additionally, the winner's name was prominently displayed in the break room for the next month.

At the Madison Heights property, Manager Joan Susinskas handed out Easter baskets hand-stuffed with goodies to each of the team members when the employees came into her office to pick up their weekly paychecks. At the Warren property, people were talking about the employee Easter Egg hunt scheduled for the next day. Associate Manager Mary Von Koughnett had already generated a great deal of excitement by announcing that plastic eggs stuffed with various amounts of cash would be scattered throughout the property. After the "hunt," a coffee-and-donuts breakfast was scheduled for all employees. According to Koughnett, "With a staff of 15, it's real important to know how to deal with each one individually as well as in a group. You've got to make your employees feel like they are kings and queens. If someone calls in sick, we want to call back later in the day to see if anyone can bring over anything. We've become a really close group that cares about each other. At this property, our turnover has been almost nil. Last week, I had to hire the first new person since we opened last August" (eight months previously).

Fairfield Inn also had developed a unique paid leave program for its employees. The program was designed to reduce the industry's traditionally high absenteeism and high turnover rates among GRAs and GSRs.

Each employee was initially given a week of vacation per year. For every month with perfect attendance (not missing any scheduled work days or not failing to arrange for a substitute), the employee would "earn" a half day of paid leave. Perfect attendance for a quarter would earn the employee one full day of paid leave in addition to the three half days already earned for perfect attendance during each month of the quarter. Thus, an employee who had perfect attendance for a year would earn ten extra days of paid leave (4 quarters × 2.5 earned days), for a total of three weeks of vacation and paid leave.

Although the paid leave program had been in effect for less than a year in 1989, it appeared that Fairfield Inn had been successful in reducing its turnover versus the industry average. Mel Warriner reported, "Rough numbers from last quarter indicated that the annualized turnover of our hourly employees was about 91%, or approximately half the industry rate. Additionally, 85% to 90% of the eligible employees had earned some bonus leave during the last quarter. The turnover among our managers was four percent compared to the 15% management turnover rate that is normal in Marriott's full-service chains."

Another incentive designed to help Fairfield managers compensate for the inevitable GRA staffing problems was the Bonus Pay Program. Normally, GRAs were expected to clean 14 rooms during a seven-hour shift. However, GRAs were given the opportunity to clean additional rooms when unexpectedly high occupancies or a GRA's absence required that more rooms be cleaned per GRA. If the GRAs were able to complete cleaning the additional rooms during their shift, they would be compensated in cash at the end of the shift. The bonus was equal to one-half the employee's hourly rate for each room cleaned. Instead of the cash bonus, the employee could also choose to remain on the time clock for 30 minutes longer for each additional room assigned.

Economics

Occupancy rates, room rates, operating expenses, and investment costs were the major variables determining whether or not a Fairfield Inn property would be successful.

Fairfield Inn's development costs for a particular site were typically between $4.5 and $5.0 million. This included land (2.1 acres versus the 4 acres needed for a Courtyard), building and systems, FF&E (furniture, fixtures, and equipment), opening inventory, fees, and construction interest. Marriott usually funded 100% of the investment internally, then sold the entire property to outside investors (e.g., through a real estate syndication), and retained a management contract for operating the property. (Pro-forma operating statements for a typical Inn are shown in *Exhibits* 7 and 8).

OPTIONS FOR FUTURE GROWTH

In 1989, Mike Ruffer and the rest of the Fairfield Inn management team were faced with three basic questions regarding the growth of Marriott's newest hotel chain: (1) Do we follow the traditional Marriott strategy of operating but not owning facilities? (2) If we don't, should we use a "standard" franchising approach (like Hampton Inn), or do we use a "McDonald's approach" to franchising? (3) Is there some appropriate mix of these alternatives?

The decision to grow internally versus expanding through franchising would have a large effect on the ultimate size of the Fairfield Inn chain. In 1986, an internal Marriott group completed an intensive study of site opportunities for an ELS chain. The report concluded that Fairfield Inn could grow to 350 units in a company-managed scenario or to 500 units in a franchising scenario.

Franchising would give Fairfield Inn access to many good undeveloped locations that were owned by developers and individuals unwilling to sell, but who wanted to use their land as an equity stake in a commercial project. Fairfield Inn's projected roll-out schedules under each scenario are shown in *Exhibit 9*.

FRANCHISING OPTIONS

The Fairfield Inn concept seemed to be an ideal candidate for franchising. The product was relatively simple, a hotel without food and beverage operations where furniture, fixtures, and equipment could be controlled through a tightly-worded franchise agreement. Additionally, Marriott's history showed that the company was able to successfully manage "formula systems." Lastly, by linking the franchisee with ancillary support services (property management system, reservations network, group health insurance, etc.), Fairfield corporate would be able to maintain leverage with future franchisees and provide operations expertise.

Fairfield's ancillary services would create additional value for franchisees by providing them with benefits unavailable to an independent operator. Fairfield's management would in all likelihood price these services at a break-even level for Marriott. By pricing at its cost, Marriott could not be accused of "tying arrangements."[4] In fast-food restaurants, McDonald's had successfully used a similar strategy to increase the real and perceived value of the McDonald's system for its franchisees.

However, under a franchise system, Fairfield Inn would lose control over prices. Federal laws dictated that franchisees had to be able to set their own prices.[5] One challenge for management under franchising would be to influence pricing among franchisees so that their room rates were consistent with Fairfield's desired position in the ELS segment.

Franchising would also impact the revenues that Fairfield Inn would deliver to Marriott. Fairfield Inn's competitors offered a variety of franchise packages. This suggested that Mike Ruffer and his management team would have a tremendous amount of flexibility in structuring any franchise agreement if they elected to franchise. Under franchising, Fairfield Inn's management group estimated the net present value generated by each property was approximately $400,000 for Marriott in 1988 dollars while also delivering an 18.0% cash-on-cash return to the franchisee. (This compared with an estimated net present value for a Marriott-owned property of $450,000 in 1988 dollars.) Under franchising, Marriott's initial investment would be reduced significantly.

Two potential franchising approaches were known in-house as the "Standard" and the "McDonald's" franchising plans.

---

4. A tying arrangement is one in which the seller, with market power, conditions the sale of one product (the franchise) on the purchase from the seller (or a third party in which the seller has an interest) of a separate product, at a higher price than the buyer would have paid had both tying and tied products been purchased from other sources. Tying arrangements are violations of the antitrust laws and are not subject to economic justification.

5. As of 1989, establishment by a franchisor of the prices which franchisees charge for any product was a violation of Section 1 of the Sherman Act, regardless of whether the purpose of the arrangement was to raise, lower, or stabilize retail prices. A franchisor could suggest retail prices so long as it did not attempt to coerce franchisees to comply with its "suggestions."

The Standard Plan

The primary target under a "standard plan" would be management companies with in-house development and construction management abilities as well as lodging operations experience. Existing franchisees of other Marriott lodging concepts would provide a core of qualified franchisees who could finance, develop, construct, and staff their properties. The franchise terms would be a 20-year agreement with no renewal. Marriott would receive a 4% royalty on gross revenues and a $45,000 application fee.

Under the Standard plan, the overall number of projects developed would be increased because of sites brought in by franchisees. Only franchisees that were meeting operational performance criteria would be encouraged to build additional properties. The franchisee would manage construction, and Marriott would approve a general contractor. Marriott would control construction quality with a thorough design guide and with inspection visits to the construction site during key phases of development. The granting of the actual franchise would be contingent on the construction being completed satisfactorily.

A franchisee would need to arrange his or her own financing.

The "McDonald's" Plan

Under this plan, the primary target would be experienced hotel operators wanting to acquire their own property. These franchisees would have a demonstrated ability to meet Marriott operating standards. They would be required to personally participate in the business, thus most likely limiting them to one Inn each. The franchise agreement would be for 20 years with no renewal. Marriott would receive a 4% royalty of gross revenues plus lease payments for the land and building. A $45,000 fee would be payable with application for a franchise.

Marriott would handle virtually all development. This would include analyzing market potential, conducting feasibility studies, and site selection and the approval process. Additionally, Marriott would construct each Inn.

Marriott would retain title to the land and building while the property would be leased to the franchisee. Franchisees would finance the remainder of the investment on their own.

Syndication

Fairfield Inn's third option for future growth was to follow a frequently used Marriott strategy of syndicating the properties.

As Bill Marriott, Jr., explained in his 1988 letter to shareholders, "We extend our competitive advantage by using innovative financing techniques to minimize internal capital needs and access the lowest cost of capital available We have 'decapitalized' our lodging business by selling hotels while retaining operating control under long-term agreements. We earn development fees by designing and constructing hotels for sales to investors and management fees for operating the hotels successfully."

A simplified syndication process followed these steps:

1. Marriott buys the land and develops the sites.
2. Marriott builds a Fairfield Inn on each piece of land.
3. When properties are open, they are sold via a public or private syndication, in groups.
4. After the sale, a syndicate of investors has ownership of all properties in the block, while Marriott staffs the hotel with its own employees for a management fee of 4 to 5 percent of revenues and an incentive fee based on operating results.

Each syndication by Marriott was different, but it was becoming typical for Marriott to offer a guaranteed return for the first three years to the investors. If Fairfield was going to syndicate, investors would expect about a 9% cash-on-cash return after-tax according to Richard Palmer, Fairfield Inn's vice president of finance. In the case of a cash flow shortfall for the properties, Marriott's syndication agreement usually guaranteed covering the debt-service payments for the first three years in addition to the guaranteed return to investors.

In a syndication, Marriott would earn development fees ranging from 2 to 5 percent based on a $5 million investment for each property. However, the transaction costs of a syndication, which included investment banker fees, printing and distribution costs, and closing costs, were estimated by Palmer to be in the neighborhood of 5% of the value of the properties to be syndicated. The syndication option had virtually the same corporate overhead costs as the owned option. Franchising would require less overhead per property.

Under a syndication scenario, Fairfield Inn's internal growth would provide a working environment with numerous opportunities for employees at every level to move up. However, it would also stretch the organization to find, hire, and train enough people to staff each property. Lastly, under a rapid expansion strategy, whether syndicated or franchised, Fairfield Inn would be challenged to insure that standards of excellence for customer service were consistent across the chain at each new property.

Mark Pacala commented:

It seems that the most important issue facing Fairfield Inn is how committed the employees will be to guest service under each growth option. Right now, we've created a very special environment for employees. We're new, it's exciting, and we've only got 25 properties. There seem to be three components that are of critical importance to our future. First, can we require that franchisees use Scorecard? Second, can we insist that they compensate their people based on Scorecard performance? Third, can we get them to recruit based on the Fairfield Inn selection techniques that we use? The culture of Fairfield Inn will ultimately determine how successful we are in the ELS segment.

Exhibit 1

Occupancy Rates, Lodging Industry and Economy/
Limited-Service Segment, 1982–1987

Year	Entire Lodging Industry	Economy/Limited-Service Segment
1982	64.6%	65.6%
1983	65.2	65.3
1984	65.9	65.2
1985	64.4	64.0
1986	64.7	62.7
1987	65.6	63.5

Exhibit 2

Projected Economy Lodging Capacities

	Number of Rooms 1986[a]	Number of Rooms 1987	Number of Rooms 1988	Number of Rooms 1989[b]	Number of Rooms 1995[c]	Annual Growth Rate[d]
Days Inn	49,500	66,400	84,800	69,000	137,000	12%
Hampton Inn	11,600	13,400	19,100	23,000	85,000	25
La Quinta	24,100	23,500	25,200	25,700	85,000	15
Comfort Inn	18,200	23,800	33,100	44,500	64,000	15
Red Roof Inn	16,500	17,600	19,500	21,500	50,000	13
Fairfield Inn	—	NA	265	2,400	49,500	—

[a] As of January 1, based on annual information prepared by Laventhal and Horwath and published in *Hotel and Motel Management* magazine.

[b] The number of rooms for Days Inn was adjusted downward to reflect the amount of their room inventory that is effectively being sold at less than $45 per night, comparable to economy lodging.

[c] Estimates made in 1986.

[d] For three years prior to January 1, 1986.

Exhibit 3
Customer Comments Regarding Fairfield Inn from Business Travelers

About the importance of price. . . .

"The company sets the limit for us. They say 'Anything over $45 and you pay the difference.' "

"I often work on a per diem basis. You can go to a really nice hotel and eat at McDonald's or you can stay at a cheap place and eat steak."

"I don't have any limit, but I don't spend an extra $30 for something I don't think I need. I might find something better to spend it for."

"I'm on straight commission. I'm an indpendent contractor, so I set my own limit and I look for a fair price."

Selecting a place to stay. . . .

"I've been on the highways for 40 years, and it gets to where you can pretty well drive by them and tell which ones are good."

"I want to drive up to the room. I don't like all those places they're making now where you've got to walk through the lobby, drag all your junk with you and drag it all back out with you."

"I want the convenience of being able to carry my files in and being able to do my paperwork in the evening."

"Some places go out of their way to make you feel at home and you want to go after a place like that. That means a lot."

About the Competition. . . .

"I prefer Hampton over Red Roof. The rooms were much nicer—they were much prettier. I just like the way the rooms were done. They have more luxury than Red Roof. I don't think Hampton is considered a budget hotel."

"Knights Inn transcends tackiness—purple bed sheets . . . I won't go back."

"One thing I like about Knights Inn is you can pack right at your door."

"It's like a White Castle that jumps right out at you . . . that red roof. They have a good sign that catches your eye."

"Red Roofs are at good locations. They work the exits very well."

Choosing a place to stay. . . .

"It's all a matter of economics. When you're traveling to a location and not planning on spending the whole day at a motel, you drive till you sleep, sleep, then you get up and go again."

"My wife gives the final say on where we'll stay."

"I really like the little book with the little map that says 'here it is', you go down the street and there it is!"

"I look at billboards. As you're driving into town you're trying to spot something that might ring a bell in your mind—somewhere you've stayed before or something you've heard."

(Continued)

Exhibit 3
(Continued)

Customer Comments Regarding Fairfield Inn from Pleasure Travelers

"If the outside of the hotel is shabby looking, I always think the inside is going to be like that. I'm not talking real fancy. It can be just a neat appearance on the outside and all the lights are working. Normally, the inside will be neat also."

Some expectations. . . .

"Whether it's $29.95 or $49.94 or $95.99 a night, you want your motel to be as comfortable as home, if possible. That's what you're looking for. You don't want to get hassled when you complain about a drippy faucet. You want a place that's managed."

"Courteous people at the desk. If they have to pay those people a little more money, they're going to be nice to me—especially when there's a problem. That's one of my biggies."

"It doesn't matter if they're a clerk or a manager, they ought to be polite."

About the rooms. . . .

"As long as it's clean and it's tidy and it's sanitary, I have no problem."

"If I'm staying just a short while, all I really want is a good bed to sleep in and a clean bathroom to take care of business the next morning, and I don't need lots of space. Even with children you don't need lots of space."

"Once you close your eyes, all rooms are the same size anyway."

Exhibit 4
Photo of a Typical Fairfield Inn

Exhibit 5
Photo of the Scorecard Computer Monitor in Use

FAIRFIELD INN
Exhibit 6
Guest Scorecard Period Report

Report GSIRPT-04 Run on 01/09/89			Atlanta Report Period 13: Quarter 4				Fiscal Week 13-01-89 to 01-07-90	Page 1
			This Period				Previous	Quarter to
Question	# of Resp.	# of Excl.	# of Ave.	# of Poor	Average		Period Average	Date Average
Friendliness and efficiency of clerk at check-in	299	287	12	0	98.0		95.5	96.6
Friendliness and efficiency of clerk at check-out	308	300	7	1	98.5		96.8	97.6
Cleaniness of room	510	482	27	1	97.2		95.7	96.9
Overall rating of this Fairfield Inn	319	290	29	0	95.5		92.9	94.2
Value for the price paid	301	256	42	3	92.0		89.2	91.3
Overall Inn cleanliness and staff hospitality	286	272	14	0	97.6		95.9	96.8
Capture rate (responses/check-outs)					42.4%		26.7%	36.2%

Current period capture rate calculation = $\dfrac{1128 \text{ check-outs with responses}}{2660 \text{ total check-outs}}$

Exhibit 7
Fairfield Inn Investment Assumptions
(105-room inn)

	Fairfield Low	Fairfield High	Per Room Low	Per Room High
Land	$ 528,000	$1,410,000	$ 5,029	$13,429
Building and Systems	2,425,000	3,190,000	23,095	30,381
FF&E[a]	480,000	480,000	4,571	4,571
Fees	140,000	160,000	1,333	1,524
Construction Interest	140,000	270,000	1,333	2,571
Total	$3,713,000	$5,510,000	$35,361	$52,476
Pre-opening Expenses	135,000	135,000		
Working Capital	15,000	15,000		
Capitalized Development	56,000	56,000		
Total	$3,919,000	$5,716,000		

[a]Fixtures, Furniture, and Equipment.

Exhibit 8
Fairfield Inn Economics
(105-room inn)
(Percentage of total revenues—year 4 of stabilized operations)

Revenues

Rooms	96.0%
Telephone	3.0
Other	1.0
Total	100.0%

Department Profits[a]

Rooms	74.6
Telephone and other	32.1
Total (average of the two)	72.9%

Deductions

General and administration	7.3
Heat, light, and power	4.8
Repair and maintenance	3.6
Group insurance	1.6
Reservations	1.4
National marketing	2.5
Local marketing	3.3
Other	4.0
Total	28.5%
House profit	44.4%

• Owned:		• Syndicated:		• Franchised:	
House profit	44.4%	Management fee	4.0%	Royalties	4.0%
Depreciation	(10.8)	Chain services fee[b]	1.5	Franchising	
Property taxes	(4.4)	Incentive fee	4.5	overhead	(1.2)
Corporate and		Corporate and			
division overhead	(4.0)	division overhead	(4.0)		
Interest	(20.0)				
Total	5.2%		6.0%		2.8%

[a] After direct costs of labor, material, and commissions.

[b] The chain services fee is a "cost pass through" to cover costs of area managers and central accounting functions.

FAIRFIELD INN
Exhibit 9
Fairfield Inn Roll-Out Scenarios
(as projected in 1986)

	Year	1987	1988	1989	1990	1991	1992	1993	1994	1995	1996
Fully Owned											
Units Opened during Year	1	16	42	50	50	40	40	40	40	31	0
Cumulative	1	17	59	109	159	199	239	279	319	350	350
Fully Franchised											
Units Opened during Year	0	0	10	50	100	125	150	65	0	0	0
Cumulative	0	0	10	60	160	285	435	500	500	500	500

Mickey Mouse Marketing

N. W. (RED) POPE

The financial industry would do well to emulate the marketing acumen of Mickey Mouse.

The world's most famous character has become a respected and envied symbol of the very best there is in target marketing, salesmanship and customer relations. The leader which sets the standards that others in the attraction industry seek to match is the Disney Organization.

And in that marketing magic initially concocted by Walter Elias Disney over 50 years ago there are some very valuable lessons for the financial industry. For while the business of entertainment and the business of finance appear as far apart as an X-rated movie and a Disney G release, there is one obvious and necessary common denominator both share.

People.

People inside, and people outside. Customers and employees.

How Disney looks upon people, internally and externally, handles them, communicates with them, rewards them is, in my view, the basic foundation upon which its five decades of success stands. The banking and thrift industry, conversely, has appeared to put more emphasis on results, solutions, growth and problems than on the basic method for achieving results or growth or solving problems with solutions—i.e., people.

People. Inside and outside. Customers and employees.

Sitting as I do every day in the shadow of Cinderella's Castle (East), and exposed to the Pixie Dust which permeates the atmosphere hereabouts, I have come to observe closely and with reverence the theory and practice of selling satisfaction and serving millions of people on a daily basis successfully. It is what Disney does best. It is one of the things banking needs to improve on most.

If anyone better understood the direct relationship between employees and customers, I haven't heard about him or her. If ever there was an organization built on people interfacing with people, it is Disney.

For two articles I will relate to the financial industry some of the personnel policies and customer relations theories of the late Walt Disney and his successors in the theme park business, with the obvious hope that our customers will some-

N. W. (Red) Pope was Vice President-Marketing of Sun Bank, N. A., Orlando at the time this article was written. Reprinted by permission, *American Banker*, July 25, 1979. Copyright © 1979 by *American Banker*.

day be able to say what almost every person who has been to Disneyland or Walt Disney World has said: "It was everything I expected, it was worth every penny, and I was served to my satisfaction by people who were enthusiastic, knowledgeable and pleasant."

The articles will dwell on the internal side—the people on the theme park payroll—and the customers, those who pay. But to Disney the two are so intertwined it may be difficult to separate one from the other. As you follow the piece, always keep your bank's policies, theories, philosophies and methods in mind in relation to how Disney does it. Compare your way with the Disney way.

Put aside the fact the Disney organization has been at the entertainment business for more than 50 years and in the theme park business for almost 20 years.

And don't consider the fact Walt Disney Productions has an ample supply of cash and financial support to do some rather remarkable things now and again. In the early days the exact opposite was true. So the Disney strength of today grew out of some rather lean times of yesterday. My point has more to do with attitude, philosophy, direction and execution than cash or credit.

The beauty of it all is that the "Disney Way" has been in effect since Steamboat Willie changed his name to Mickey Mouse. Success did not prompt Walter Elias Disney to establish specific consumer and staff procedures and approaches. Rather, his innovative usual methods of people management brought about Disney's overall success as an organization.

There's little question about the fact that Disney is in the entertainment business. So it is natural that show business terms are employed. Instead of Personnel, there is Casting. That alone gets the average young man or woman in the right frame of mind when he or she goes in for a job. And that's important at Disney. The frame of mind is the difference between being an employee, or being a Cast Member (CM). Show biz, if you will.

At Disney if your job has you interfacing with the public in any way whatsoever, you're "onstage" when you do your thing. If your work is not public-interfacing, you're "backstage." One is not better than the other. That is emphasized. It takes both to "put on the show," as the Disney people say it, and they mean just that.

No little, insignificant jobs at all. That is emphasized. It takes many people, doing many types of jobs, to put on the show every day. No job is without its importance to the show. The first time a new Disney cast member goes to his or her job there is a feeling of being a part of the overall success.

The most obvious element at Casting is the professionalism. Those who interview and hire and place are pros in the personnel business. They know what they are doing, and how to do it. An interview at Disney is impressive to the thousands of people, most of them young, who apply for jobs. And there are up to 14,000 jobs at Walt Disney World in season. Be aware that first impressions on the potential employee are as important as those on the employer.

What kind of people are interviewing job applicants at your bank? Do they give the proper impression to applicants? Is your personnel function really professional?

The new Cast Member, once hired, is given written instructions as to the steps he/she will go through in preparation-to-work stages. Written information, not verbal. He is told when to report, where to report, what to wear to report, how long he will be in each training phase. He is provided a booklet that tells him, or her, what is expected in appearance, hair style and length, from makeup to jewelry, from clean fingernails to acceptable shoes. Regardless of age or sex or job to be performed, there is conformity to the code. Everything is in writing. No chance for misinformation, misinterpretation. Attention to detail.

Everyone must attend Disney University and "pass" Traditions 1 before going on to specialized or technical training. That's right, Disney U.—a multilevel educational institution run on Disney property by a full-time staff. In addition to several basic Disney philosophy courses there are evening classes in Spanish or accounting or drama or disco dancing. All Cast Members are eligible to attend and college credits are given for many courses.

Traditions 1 is an all-day experience wherein the new hire gets a constant offering of Disney philosophy and operational methodology. Every audiovisual and static presentation method is used. And no one is exempt from the course, from V.P. to entry-level part-timer. All must matriculate at Disney U. before any time is spent on a job, backstage or onstage.

Here is where banks so often fail to take advantage of a marvelous opportunity. We don't have our policies in writing. We tell the new people to "report on Monday." That's it. When they show up, we so often hand them benefits booklets that are out of date and expect them to decipher the material. If a briefing is given, it is boring, ill-produced, lacks imagination and is usually way over the heads of those forced to sit through it. Our principal method of indoctrinating a new hire resembles handing a new recruit a gun and showing him which end to hold, and then walking off, leaving the person to load, aim and fire the best he can.

Disney expects the new CM to know something about the company, its history and success, its management style before he actually goes to work. Every person is shown, during Traditions 1, how each division relates to other divisions, and how each division—Operations, Resorts, Food and Beverage, Marketing, Finance, Merchandising, Entertainment, etc.—relates to "the show." In other words, here's how all of us work together to make things happen. Here's your part in the big picture.

Are you listening?

The new CM shows up his first day at Disney U. He is ushered into a room with round tables, four to the table. Coffee and juice and a Danish are offered. It is 8:30 a.m. A name tag is given each person, but we'll get into that later. The "instructor" is with that group for the next eight hours.

Everyone is introduced—not by the instructor, or by himself. The four people at the table are asked to get to know each other and then all of them will introduce each other. Immediately you know three other people by name, face, where they came from and their future jobs. You are a part of a group now, not alone—one of the crowd.

All of you gather for a picture. You smile. When your Traditions 1 day is over at 4:30 p.m., you are given a copy of the weekly Disney newspaper for the theme park and there on the front page is your group photo, with your name in the caption! Impressed? Certainly.

For about half of your eight hours you're in a classroom setting, watching films or slides or listening to an enthusiastic young lady use magnetic elements to show how the company operates. The other four hours are spent on a guided tour of the park. Onstage, backstage—you are exposed to it all. And at lunchtime you are taken to one of the many company cafeterias and treated to as much lunch as you desire. Free. Impressed? You begin getting the idea this company wants you to be happy on the job, and knowledgeable.

How many banks take their new hires throughout the facility, explaining each department's function and how all relate to the business of the bank? Do we treat our new hires to a lunch? Take their picture, give them the company newspaper, explain the benefits properly?

Sure, your bank isn't Walt Disney World and you don't have the people, the money to do all that. Are you sure you don't? Have you tried?

Remember those name tags? Everyone at a Disney theme park wears one; every person who works for any Disney enterprise wears one. Everybody. From the chairman of the board of Walt Disney Productions to that guy sweeping cigarette butts off Main Street after the parade. The dishwasher few people see, the ticket taker at the entrance, the secretaries, security people—everyone wears a name tag.

With only the first name on it. That's it. President of Disney Productions, director of marketing, popcorn vendor, cook, first name only.

And the rule is that when addressing each other, only first names will be used. No Mr. or Mrs. or Miss or Ms. First names, please. It is part of the "family feeling" Disney advocates. It is part of the oneness, the unity, the "no one is better than anyone else" policy.

Can you imagine the average teller addressing the chairman of the board as "Charlie." Or the janitor calling the V.P./commercial loans by his first name? Perhaps banks need to be more formal than entertainment entities. It is probably expected that banks not be too familiar, too folksy, for money and credit is perceived as a more serious business than the attractions business.

Or is it? Have we structured ourselves so stiffly, are we so status-level-position conscious that communication doesn't properly occur? Do we have the feeling that sometimes it is "Them" and "Us"? Do we demand formality, aloofness?

After a day to learn what's what, get the Pixie Dust, the name tag and the photo, the new CM is dispatched to his/her job-training assignment. Very little OJT occurs at WDW—Walt Disney World. On-the-job observing, perhaps, but little training.

Example. My two kids, ages 18 and 16, average intelligence, reasonably quick, are accepted for casual temporary—summer, Christmas, Easter, etc., employment.

They are to take tickets, either at the main entrance or the Magic Kingdom entrance. Take tickets. That's it. How tough can that be?

Four eight-hour days of instruction are required before they can go "onstage"! They are paid to learn, but before a Disney CM interfaces with a Guest—Disney has no customers at theme parks, only Guests—the management must be absolutely certain that the CM can, and will, perform properly. After all, we are dealing with Guest Satisfaction, they say. Nothing is spared to assure Guest Satisfaction.

"Why," I inquired, "does it take four days to learn how to take tickets?" Waste of time, I thought.

My two Traditions 1 graduates, with his new haircut and her "a-little-lipstick-only" makeup, jump to the defense of 32 hours of education in the fine art of taking tickets.

I was informed there are x varieties of tickets, each having special meaning. What happens if someone wants to know where the restrooms are, when the parade starts, what bus to get back to the campgrounds, what the park's hours are, where do we eat inside, what happens if I lose my child, how many bricks in the castle? Questions ad infinitum.

"We need to know the answers or where to get the correct answers quickly," I am advised. "After all, Dad, we're onstage and help produce the show for our Guests. Our job, every minute, is to help the Guest enjoy the park."

Wow! Can you imagine one of our bookkeepers, a proof operator, a secretary, a collector rising to the defense of four days of intensive prejob training so they could better serve our customers? Well, why not?

After four days, they went on the line. First to observe, then to try it under careful supervision. After a few hours, they were put to the task. It is this way in every job throughout the park where some specific training is required and general knowledge demanded. Regardless of the time it takes or the instructional costs, no one interfaces with a Guest until he or she is proved ready to properly serve that Guest.

Stop and examine the average bank's teller training programs. The New Accounts person. Baptism under fire.

And so I said to my minimum-wage-to-start-with tycoons after the first day, "How does it feel to be ticket takers?"

Again I was berated.

"Ticket takers? Dad, we're WDW Hosts."

I had forgotten. Everyone onstage and backstage in the theme park area itself has a title with the word "host" in it. There is no Policeman. There is a Security Host. There is no monorail driver; there is a Transportation Host. There are no street cleaners; there are Custodial Hosts. No french fries server, but a Food and Beverage Host. Guests have hosts, don't they? Certainly, so everyone at Disney is a Host or Hostess.

And everyone who interfaces with a Guest in the park is "themed"—costumed to fit the job. The world's largest laundry does all those costumes and uniforms every day, or all night, as the case may be. Come to work in the morning and after clocking in go to Wardrobe. Show biz again.

Mike Mescon, the incredibly provocative Georgia State professor/lecturer, says if he headed a bank he would drop almost all bank titles and use instead the term, Salesperson. For, Mr. Mescon emphasizes, that's what it is all about. Selling. Low-key or hard-sell, salesmanship and customer service are two elements that separate banks from one another. The bank that can train its people properly, motivate its people, reward its people and has its people enthusiastically representing that bank on and off the job will win.

Walt Disney was a marketing magician, no doubt. But his keen insight into personnel and customer relations, separately and collectively, enabled him to create the world's most successful entertainment conglomerate by starting with a mouse he drew and named Steamboat Willie in 1928.

The next article, also keying on the Disney Way, will highlight Customer Relations and feature several marketing approaches banks might use to sell to their target groups.

More Mickey Mouse Marketing
N. W. (RED) POPE

Nothing I've had published in 30 years prompted more mail or phone calls than "Mickey Mouse Marketing," the first of two articles concentrating on customer and staff relations as practiced by the Walt Disney organizations.

While this could mean all my previous stuff was pretty bad, it might also mean this piece was particularly good. I don't think it was either. What I think prompted the cards and calls was that the gist of the article touched some of banking's exposed nerves.

A banker in New York wrote he had known for years how good Disney was at customer relations, and how bad his bank was at it, but he hadn't been able to get money to do much about the latter. The Denver banker said he knew his bank's training was horrible, but management hadn't given that priority billing. The Pennsylvania banker remarked that until bankers cared as much about how well the customer was served as how well the bank was served, banking would never change its customer relations.

An Ohio banker wrote me stating that odds were pretty long on bankers looking upon their personnel as high priorities. His way of stating that was "human resources inside our banks are yet to be ranked as important as computers, branch offices or, for that matter, the board of directors' annual retreat. In the main, staff morale is not all that big a need to too many bank managers."

The good part about the letters was that people apparently were moved to critical introspection upon reading the piece. The bad part was that almost without exception everyone admitted management apathy or lack of commitment.

Incidentally, Disney does not make its programs or methods or manuals or personnel available, as a rule, to outsiders on a "for sale" or consulting basis.

Now, back to Part Two in the continuing saga of how Walt Disney World, and other Disney entities, look upon their bread (staff) and butter (guests). Remember, please, as you read on, compare how your bank does things with the way Mickey Mouse and his associates do them.

Of the 100 million people who have passed through Walt Disney World's turnstiles since October 1971, a great many ask seemingly stupid questions about the place. Stupid to us, perhaps, but not to Disney. Like how many bricks are

N. W. (Red) Pope was Vice President-Marketing of Sun Bank, N. A., Orlando at the time this article was written. Reprinted by permission, *American Banker*, September 12, 1979. Copyright © 1979 by *American Banker*.

in the Castle, how many lights are there in the theme park, how many boats do you have here, how long did it take to build this place, how much did it cost, how many telephones are there in the whole place, how often do you have to paint the submarines, how many hot dogs do you sell here each year? Ad infinitum.

To many businesses this sort of barrage of trivia inquiry would lead to an abrupt, "How should I know, kid!" To Disney it is the sort of stuff dreams (and attendance) are built on. And if any employee (Host or Hostess) cannot give the answer to any question . . . that's right . . . any question, then there is a telephone exchange to call. Immediately. The minute the question is asked and the Disney staffer can't answer it, call that number, and ask!

Twenty-four hours a day a cadre of switchboard operators with factbooks to rival the largest phone books in America are standing by to answer those "very stupid" questions, on the spot. Like, the most meals served in a single day was 220,500 (12/31/75). And 13 million ketchup packets are given out annually and 24 tons of french fries are sold every week, and 3 1/2 million pounds of hot dogs were sold to the guests last year.

And if you add up all the boats and rafts and submarines and ferrys and canoes and other floating materiel throughout the 27,400 acres, you'd have the seventh-largest navy in the world, and that's a fact.

The bottom line is: serve the Guest. If someone cares about hot dogs, tell 'em the answer. Whatever the Guests want to know, get 'em the facts, now!

Sometime, stand in your lobby and watch your personnel attempt to answer basic, not stupid, questions. How much are your safe deposit boxes? What are your CD rates? How much can I get for a Canadian dollar? Does your bank have a branch office in the south part of town? What's your best rate on an auto loan? What hours are your drive-ins open?

Maybe the person asked doesn't have the answers, or perhaps shouldn't try to give out rates, but how does she, or he, respond? How does he, or she, serve the customer?

One fast rule at Disney theme parks is that no employee will be served before a guest. In fact, Disney provides cafeterias, breakrooms, snack bars and other facilities for its people "backstage." This includes special live and automated teller operations our Sun Bank runs for Disney employees so they can do their banking conveniently.

If you want a soft drink and you work at Disney, go backstage. If you want to buy a Minnie Mouse blouse, do it at the company store. Need a check cashed? Backstage. From toilets to parking, Disney makes sure its guests' needs are not slowed by staff use. While we in banks don't run theme parks, I'll have to admit I've seen our bank employees in teller lines ahead of customers.

Every week Walt Disney World's cast communications division of Disney

University produces an eight-page 8 1/2 × 11 newspaper called *Eyes and Ears*. One glance at its contents and you know it was prepared for Disney people. It is a people publication, featuring all sorts of activities, improved employment opportunities, special benefits, educational offerings and even a complete classified section. The stories are very short, newsy, punchy. Lots of pictures of cast members. A brief feature perhaps. And I've never, never seen a single photo in that newspaper in seven years that showed anyone not smiling. Contrived? Maybe, but it got to me, didn't it?

Banks produce some of the worst employee publications possible. Poor writing, story selection, not enough photos, and often those published are poor quality, and too much about the brass or the home office. And the reason is, I think, that we expect people in marketing or personnel or some other division to take on the paper as an additional job. We don't hire newspaper people to produce newspapers. We hire loan officers to make loans, and auditors to audit, and managers to manage, but we feel some obligation to assign the internal communications to someone as an afterthought, an extra job, assuming it is a simple, quick thing.

"Give it to the boss' nephew . . . he used to write for the high school newspaper."

One evening during a BMA (Bank Managers Association) conference when some of us were "learning from one another," the subject of company publications, house organs, arose. Most of us agreed poor quality was a standard. One member of the group admitted, blushingly, that his personnel director had decreed the bank would have some sort of newspaper to appease all the EEOC (Equal Employment Opportunity Commission) types, and to show some union that his bank "talked" with its people, regardless of content or quality. He said the bank president wanted to prove, if the need arose, that his bank had an ongoing communications vehicle, content notwithstanding.

Disney feels, on the other hand, that informed people are happier, less confused, more aware of benefits and opportunities, and more cognizant that management genuinely wants and strives to communicate. In addition to the weekly newspaper, Disney produces on a regular basis single-page bulletins for management, two-page "hot news" bulletins with promotions and transfers on a regular basis and, less frequently, an eight-page standard-size newspaper for all Cast Members.

The written word is most important to employees of any company. But it must be professionally done to properly communicate. A cheap, shoddy and poorly-constructed publication will be obvious to the intended readers. Perhaps they will take that to mean management isn't all that interested in doing any better. And that publication is an extension of the bank. How we are perceived by those that see it, inside or out, is cause for concern.

Disney also cares what its staff members think about the theme park as a place to work. When your reputation and continuation in business depends upon how well employees serve paying customers, then perhaps some attention should be given to the "care and feeding" of the employees. (Hear that, banks?)

There are several types of employees at a Disney theme park, from the permanent, year-'round types, to what Mickey terms "the casual temporary cast member." This means summers and holidays and maybe weekends, when the attendance is greatest and staff needs are highest. Like my two kids taking tickets during peak seasons. Disney is a master at being able to use part-timers, keeping the higher paid group at a minimum, a trick many banks are beginning to pick up, especially in the teller area.

As the summer ends, some 3,000 casual temporaries are returning to school, Disney asks each to complete a simple questionnaire, anonymously. My job was, my division or department was, my age is, my formal education is, I live _____ miles from the park, etc. I am a: man-woman. Notice it didn't say male, female. They find out some basics first.

Then they ask the respondent to check one of five applicable answers, from very good to poor, to these:

- I think the reputation Walt Disney World has with the public is. . . .
- Looking at Walt Disney World compared with other companies, I would say it is managed . . .
- How did you feel when you told people what company you worked for?
- How did you feel your wage (salary) compared with wages (salaries) paid for similar jobs outside Walt Disney World?
- Inside Walt Disney World?

Then there are questions about hiring practices and procedures, the orientation program, the initial training given. Did you feel satisfied with your job? How important did you feel it was? Was it interesting?

For eight pages and eighty-four questions the Disney management wants to know, from those in the less glamourous jobs all the way to the more outstanding positions, if its people are happy, treated fairly, trained properly and communicated with. Why? Because the basis for operating a theme park dedicated to the happiness of all sorts of people must be . . . happy people. Inside. People with pride, respect for the employer. And to get those kids back next summer, Disney knows it has to offer the best surroundings, training and opportunities.

Banks are beginning to pay some heed to what its employees think about working conditions and opportunities, too. Next to interest paid on time deposits, salaries and wages are the second-highest cost in most banks. The cost of turnover is exorbitant. Our training has been inadequate. We have not been competitive in the personnel marketplace. And, like Disney, a bank is a service business which requires people to interface with the customer in so many transactions.

When the energy crisis hit Florida, and California, and gasoline became as precious as glass slippers, Disney realized its large contingent of people, working literally around the clock, might be hard-pressed to get gas to come to work. Mobilization occurred. First, in all publications car pools were encouraged and, via computer, actually designed for everyone on the payroll. Large buses were contracted to run regular schedules from the largest neighborhood areas to the park, for 90 cents. And if eight or more cast members arranged a car pool and would agree to pay for gas, oil and maintenance, Disney would provide a van! Free! Finally, to assure some gas for work-oriented travel, Disney put in its own cast gas station!

Many banks have opted to reduce the lighting, raise the thermostat, or permit removal of jackets. But Disney, keying to employee needs, went further. It did the analysis, it made the decisions to lease vans, work out car pool schedules and set up bus routes before it asked for employee cooperation. Many banks I'm aware of asked every employee interested in a car pool to contact personnel.

The obvious happened. Both people contacted personnel. Perhaps had the banks leased vans, set up the routes, put the thing into service and said, "Okay, we've committed and set it up, now you take advantage of it," more people would have done just that. Waiting for enough volunteers to come forth will seldom provide sufficient personnel to fight the battle, much less win the war.

I hope all bank vice presidents (and above) are sitting down to read these next two items.

Annually all the "white-collar" types at Walt Disney World, the management if you will, undertake a week-long program called *cross-utilization*. In essence it means giving up the desk, the secretary and the white collar and donning a themed costume or an apron and heading for the frontline action. For a week the "bosses" sell tickets or popcorn, dish out ice cream or hot dogs, load and unload rides, park cars, drive the monorail or trains, or take on any of the 100 "onstage" jobs that make the park come alive to guests.

According to my sources at Disney, the cross-utilization concept is designed to give management a better "hands-on" view of how the guests need to be served and, at the same time, management gets a better understanding of what the Cast Member must go through to properly serve the guests. And assignments are made for cross-u, not selections offered. You take the job given you and head for Wardrobe, and a long eight hours on your feet with a smile on your face, ready or not.

Now, all the time you've been reading this you have been envisioning the V.P./installment credit in a drive-in teller cubicle, the V.P./trust holding down a collector's job, perhaps the V.P./marketing working in the proof department, the president of the bank handling the new accounts desk and all those dumb questions. There's the commercial loan V.P. operating the mailroom, and somehow our operations V.P. is in marketing trying to handle a newspaper reporter's persistent questions about why the "little man" is being charged so much interest while, at the same time, attempting to compute market share for 15 branch offices manually.

Kind of makes you smile, doesn't it?

Second, and I quote from a recent *Eyes and Ears:* "As many of you are aware, our vice presidents and directors (Note: a director at Disney is a level below a V.P., in a management function such as director of marketing, director of finance, director of food and beverage, etc.) have been scheduling themselves to visit the Magic Kingdom to increase their awareness of both the guest experience and the work experience of our cast members. So don't be surprised if you're stopped during your workday to chat with one of our V.P.s or directors. He's genuinely anxious to see your operation and what you do each day!"

Following that statement to the troops there is a schedule showing what day which V.P. or director will be in the park. Both day and night shifts are covered. And wouldn't you know . . . those V.P.s and directors are supposed to write a report on their findings!

What is all this mingling about? What is this orchestrated entry into the trenches with the folks doing the dirty jobs going to achieve? Well, for my money it is going to tell one heck'uva lot of hard-working people that "somebody up there cares."

How can you spend eight hours shoving out those fries, alongside a couple of sweatin' and smilin' kids making $3.20 an hour, and not be learning something positive about personnel relations, and management?

How can you stand there for eight hours, smiling and saying "Howdy" to 60,000 people, trying to answer their questions in Spanish, direct them to the nearest rest rooms, look at their faces of anticipation, and not learn something about the consumer public?

Perhaps periodically it would be most revealing, and educational, if the bank's brass, and some of our board members for that matter, came down to the lobby on a Monday morning. Or meandered out into the drive-in lanes on a Friday afternoon. Talked to the people in line. Or took the place of that person in the teller window. Chances are it wouldn't take many such trips for improved communications to come about, for some improved benefits to be put in, for some staff morale to improve and for productivity on both ends to get even better.

Mutual understanding for each other's needs and problems. Mutual respect for each other, as people, and as fellow bankers.

To all those who say they are too busy, whose schedules won't permit them to idle away a couple of hours doing such things, I'd suggest the demands upon senior executives at Walt Disney World at peak season are at least as compelling as those of most bankers. It is, I submit, a matter of priorities. He who sees the need, who wants to fill it, will. Case closed.

Disney has a private recreation area with lake, rec hall, picnic areas, boating and fishing and volleyball and family-outing opportunities ad infinitum for its Cast Members' exclusive use—professionally staffed.

There is a library, staffed, with everything from "How To Do It" books to the latest fiction best sellers, for the benefit of the Cast Members.

There is a division of Disney University called Cast Activities. Its sole purpose is to provide educational, recreational, entertainment and cost-saving opportunities to the employees.

Several women from Casting make the rounds of all work areas, offices, backstage and onstage, daily to check Cast Members' hair lengths, makeup, general appearance. Disney has rules about how to dress. You understand them when you report to work. You get one warning. The public sees fresh-faced, neatly-attired people serving them, but that didn't happen by accident.

There is no question that much of Disney's success with people, inside and out, stems from quite a bit of regimentation. Some say it is militaristic in fact. And, in spite of all those smiling faces out there in Fantasyland, there are more than a few sour attitudes behind the braces.

But in spite of the rules, the regulations, the demand that everyone do everything the Disney Way, there is no question the people who work there have a special feeling for that 50-year-old mouse. They know the management overtly works at employee relations. They are cognizant that if they want a lifetime career, or a summer's employment, there is a cornucopia of possibilities within the organization. They know all this because the company management puts employee relations just under guest relations as a top priority, and not far under.

And that is, of course, the real answer.

When a company's customers are happy with the service and the product, and find enthusiastic and knowledgeable personnel who are anxious to help, chances are that company will continue to enjoy the lucrative patronage of those customers for a long, long time.

When a company's employees know, and are continually reminded, that their employer is genuinely concerned with and has interest in their personal well-being, and undertakes meaningful programs to manifest that interest, chances are things are alive and well inside the shop.

Hark! Could that be your bank's employees whistling as they arrive for the day's toil? Listen . . .

"Hi ho, hi ho, it's off to work we go . . ."

Banc One Corporation 1989

It is said that a bank, or any business for that matter, cannot
continue to grow without making radical changes in its
philosophy of doing business. Something has to give. While
there is some value in that thinking, it is hardly an argument for
slower growth at Banc One or for revision of a decentralized
management strategy that has worked extremely well for us.[1]

JOHN B. MCCOY, 1986
Then-President, Banc One Corp.

My role is chief personnel officer. If I get the right people in the
right job, that's all I have to do.

JOHN B. MCCOY, 1989
Chairman & CEO, Banc One Corp.

John B. McCoy rose from his desk on the 16th floor of Banc One's Columbus
headquarters while the video crew gathered its equipment. He had just finished
taping this quarter's "Chairman's Corner" section of the company news video
program. Weeks earlier, on June 29, 1989, Banc One, the largest bank holding
company in Ohio and one of the U.S. banking industry's top financial performers, announced that it had beaten five other bidders to purchase 20 of M-
Corp.'s failed Texas banks. McCoy had just told employees in his taped message,
"Banking is people. The uncertainty is over for the people of MCorp. The great
spirit of Banc One will make a difference—we will win back customers and make
it work. Our goal is to be the biggest and best bank in the state!"

McCoy knew it would be a challenge to transfer Banc One's remarkable success to its largest acquisition, especially at a time when Banc One itself was
undergoing major change. With few exceptions, for two decades the company
had grown by acquiring small- to medium-sized midwestern banks with good
performance records in nondilutive, friendly deals. The Texas banks had assets
equal to one-half those of Banc One, they were located in the South, and they
were insolvent. Banc One's past success in integrating newly acquired banks derived from its abilities to nurture an "uncommon partnership" with the new
bank (called an "affiliate") and to induce better performance from its managers.

Paul S. Myers prepared this case under the supervision of Professor Rosabeth Moss Kanter as the
basis for class discussion rather than to illustrate either effective or ineffective handling of an
administrative situation. Copyright © 1989 by the President and Fellows of Harvard College;
Harvard Business School case #9-390-029.

1. John B. McCoy, "Commentary: Small-Guy Philosophy Drives Top Performance," *Financier*
(August 1988): 42–44.

The "uncommon partnership" balanced autonomous banking decisions based on knowledge of the community at the local level with a strong set of corporate values and operating principles.

Was Banc One entering a new phase that would test McCoy's skill as a general manager and his vision as a corporate leader?

BANC ONE: SUPER-REGIONAL SUPER BANK

In March 1989, before the MCorp purchase, Banc One had 56 affiliate banks with 566 offices, 5 nonbank affiliates (i.e., subsidiaries of Banc One), 18,000 employees, and $23.7 billion in assets. Net income had increased at a compound annual growth rate of 18.39% since 1978 (see *Exhibit 1*). In 1988 Banc One was the most profitable bank holding company as measured by return on average assets among the country's 50 largest banks. With few exceptions, earnings per share and stock price had risen steadily over the past decade (see *Exhibit 2*).

Banc One was primarily a retail bank which focused on offering loans and other financial services to individual consumers and to small-and medium-sized "middle market" firms. Its branches operated as "stores" concentrating on product sales to meet income targets. McCoy liked to describe Banc One as similar to McDonald's: "Our stores have a lot in common. We're not selling chicken in one place and steaks in another. We're selling the same thing everywhere." The company sought the high-margin business in the retail and middle market loans, industry diversity, and balanced growth. In 1987 the corporation's net interest margin of 5.8% compared to a U.S. regional bank average of 4.41%. Banc One ranked among the 10 largest U.S. banks in both credit card and student lending.

In the corporate segment, Banc One confined its commercial lending to middle market customers largely in the communities in which its affiliate banks operated. Other than commercial real estate loans at 6% of the total loan portfolio, no standard industrial classification of loans represented over 2.5% of the loan portfolio. Banc One avoided energy, agriculture, and LDC (less developed country) loans which all had been sources of serious problems for many U.S. banks. In late 1987 and early 1988 through sales and write-offs, Banc One eliminated its small $98 million portfolio of LDC loans, thereby strengthening its loan portfolio. Banc One's significant nonbank activities included trust, leasing, and mortgage operations and extensive data processing.

Overall, Banc One's goal was to deliver superior customer service while obtaining high financial returns. Member banks prided themselves on treating customers as individuals rather than mere account numbers. One affiliate president noted, "From the customers' point of view, if you're not delivering that quality personal service they're not going to stay with you." Banc One believed that its customers saw it as an innovative, fast-paced company always at the leading edge of new products and that customers thus expected to receive from Banc One banks the best products and prices. Advertising emphasized service delivery and specific product offerings equally. Banc One invested steadily in technology R&D to develop new retail products, to improve its competitive lead time, to lower costs, and to generate fee income by providing services to other financial institutions. It used a complex and detailed central financial control system for business planning and performance measurement.

History of Innovations[2]

Banc One could trace its heritage back 121 years to when it started in Columbus, Ohio, as City National Bank (CNB). Its modern history began when John G. McCoy assumed the presidency upon his father's death in 1958. McCoy made two fundamental decisions: (1) to run "a Tiffany bank rather than a Woolworth's"; and, (2) to achieve that goal, "to hire the best people and then delegate; there wasn't any use of putting you in if you were the finest in the world, and then telling you how to do it." For the second decision his father offered no model; he had made every decision in the bank himself.

John G.'s guiding principle was "to provide financial services to people," whom John G. believed chose a bank "because of one word: convenience." To help implement that principle in his first year, he hired John Fisher, a young radio ad man, as head of a newly-created advertising department. John G. commissioned him to "find out what the customer wants," and forbade him to learn how to open an account or make a loan. Soon in charge of marketing and public relations, Fisher created a new image for CNB with slogans like "the loaningest bank in town"; "the best all around bank all around town"; and "the good neighborhood bank," featured on a prize-winning billboard ad in 1961. In less than a decade, deposits grew from $140 million to over $400 million.

Fisher's creative vision went beyond ad pitches. Some industry observers credited him with revolutionizing banking by coupling technology with marketing. At John G.'s insistence, since the early 1960s the company had set aside approximately 3% of earnings each year for R&D in hopes of identifying ways that technology could improve efficiency and customer service. The company's innovations included introducing the forerunner of the automated teller machine (ATM) in 1969 and in 1972 becoming the first U.S. bank to install ATMs in

---

2. Portions of this section have been excerpted from the 1982 HBS case, Banc One Corporation and the Home Information Revolution, No. 682–091, originally prepared by Dr. Karen Freeze and Professor Richard Rosenbloom.

every branch office. Not all of its innovations took hold. It pioneered efforts, though unsuccessfully, to build a point-of-sale credit card network in 1977 and introduce at-home banking in 1979.

CNB became the first bank to offer credit cards outside of California by introducing the City National BankAmericard (now VISA) in 1966. This innovation not only provided the bank with profits and industry visibility, but it also helped start the charge card revolution which changed Americans' spending practices. The company gained additional national exposure in 1976 when Merrill Lynch picked it as the processing arm of its new Cash Management Account (CMA) venture. The CMA accounts permitted customers to use funds from their brokerage accounts via a debit card or checks provided by the bank. This pathbreaking alliance helped foment the burgeoning revolution in the U.S. financial services industry.

Driven by the success of its credit cards and its partnership with Merrill Lynch, in the 1970s the company expanded its operations by selling its credit- and debit-card processing expertise to other banks, credit unions, thrifts, finance companies, and brokers. By 1989 Banc One was regarded as a data processing powerhouse.[3] It handled its own 3.2 million cards, over 3.5 million cards for third parties (e.g., credit unions), and supplied the check clearing and back office operations for many other banks and financial service firms. In 1989, Banc One's Future Systems Group unveiled Phase I of a new system developed in partnership with Electronic Data Systems (EDS) and Norwest, a Minneapolis bank holding company, to attempt to meet the banking industry's data processing needs for the next 20 years.

At the retail level, Banc One experimented with store concept and design. In Kingsdale, Ohio, the company introduced a full-service banking facility called a "Financial Marketplace" with supermarket hours—open 72 hours a week including Sunday afternoons. The state-of-the-art merchandising system comprised boutiques offering home financing, travel services, trust services, business loan operations, a realtor, and investment services. Colorful neon lights identified each separate service area. Interactive (touch-screen) video displays answered customer questions, and drive-in windows made for quick and easy personal service. Four companies leased boutique space: Banc One Investment Services, Banc One Travel, Nationwide Insurance Corp., and HER realtors. Leasing offered Banc One the advantage of learning how to sell products which banks by law could not provide, while creating awareness of its own investment and travel subsidiaries. It also directly challenged companies like Sears and American Express which offered a portfolio of financial services. The success of the Kingsdale store led to

---

3. *Wall Street Journal,* June 13, 1988, p. B1.

a second "supermarket," and both were performing well beyond expectations by 1989.

To ensure continuing innovation, Banc One established a "Greenhouse Group" under John Fisher's leadership in June 1989 to create and nurture new ideas outside of the mainstream of the organization. Initial projects included a toll-free, 24-hour-a-day telephone service; interaffiliate check cashing and deposit service; and a home banking service.

Growth through Acquisitions

Limited in growth by Ohio law to one-county branching, City National Bank merged in 1968 with a smaller bank, Farmers Savings and Trust ($55.2 million in deposits) to form a bank holding company, the First Banc Group (FBG). Another Ohio law prohibiting nonbank institutions from including the designation "Bank" in their names dictated the new spelling, "Banc." FBG began acquiring small banks around Ohio. Between 1968 and 1980 it bought 22 banks, each under $100 million in assets.

A decade old in 1977 and still growing rapidly, First Banc Group had 16 members and $1.95 billion in aggregate assets. With FBG's next decade in mind, John G. and his colleagues—including FBG's new president (and John G.'s son) John B. McCoy—began to consider the implications of federal limits on the company's growth. With the entire banking industry in upheaval as it faced challenges from other financial institutions, McCoy and others expected revisions in the law against interstate banking. Anticipating that event, FBG sought a new name unique in the country. At John Fisher's suggestion, they selected "Banc One" and registered the name in every state. The name change took place in October 1979. Thereafter, the holding company would be known as *Banc* One, and each bank as *Bank* One, followed by its location. Thus City National Bank became Bank One of Columbus.

Between 1980 and 1983 Banc One began to purchase mid-sized banks in major markets. Previous acquisitions were in rural and semi-urban county seat-type markets. In short order, Banc One bought banks in Cleveland, Akron, Youngstown, and, in June 1983, the $1.6 billion Winters National Bank of Dayton. Winters held assets about one-third the size of those of Banc One.

In 1984 John G. McCoy retired and his son John B. became CEO in addition to his duties as president; in 1987 John B. became chairman and gave up the presidency. In the meantime, changes in state banking laws that allowed bank holding companies to bank in other states spurred a third phase of Banc One's acquisitions toward purchases of larger banks. Looking first to Indiana, Banc One made a purchase about every two weeks in the fall and winter of 1985 and gained six banks. After months of courtship, Banc One announced in May 1986, that it would purchase American Fletcher Bank of Indianapolis. Banc One increased its assets by more than a third overnight because American Fletcher held $4.5 billion in assets and was the second largest bank in Indiana. This move gave Banc One the largest market share in the state. Shortly after this, Banc One made acquisitions in Kentucky, Michigan, and Wisconsin.

Nonbank acquisitions, including a mortgage company and travel agencies, complemented Banc One's operations. Four specialty leasing companies (e.g., for photocopiers, telephone switchboards) balanced its retail strategy at the small end of the market. Nonbank holdings accounted for just 7% of earnings, not including the card processing business, which was considered part of the banking operation. This nonbank area, though, was seen as having the most growth potential, perhaps outpacing the rest of the business by 25%–50%.

Integration of New Affiliates

Banc One sought successful banks run by managers with proven track records. CEO John B. McCoy commented in 1986 that "the success [of our acquisitions] will be achieved through basically two things: a local management team that knows the market and a similarity between the two organizations' [Banc One's and the acquisition's] products and services." Of the deals that never went through, 80% failed because of Banc One's lack of confidence in a potential acquisition's current management. With rare exceptions, current officers remained in place after a Banc One acquisition. McCoy recounted an often-told story that had become part of the company folklore:

> When my dad was running the bank, the head of the largest bank in Cleveland called and said, "Why don't we take us and Cincinnati and form one bank—we'd be really strong." My dad thought that was a great idea, so the guy came for breakfast to discuss putting the three banks together. As breakfast was being served, Dad asked, "So, what will I do in the new bank?" He was told, "Oh, there wouldn't be any need for you!" That was that. Our issue [when we make acquisitions] is how to use current management, not to get rid of it.

Thus, assessment of people was central to acquisition decisions. For example, in the spring of 1989 during the due diligence period in Texas, a team of 20 Banc One analysts and executives from affiliate banks studied MCorp's operations. McCoy recalled:

> Our accounting guy said, "The controls aren't good, but I'm impressed by the people." Then the next guy said something similar. So we went back

to focus on the people: why they're here, who the boss is, why they haven't left. When we got comfortable with the people, we went ahead.

McCoy expected the incumbent bank managers to operate the new affiliate profitably and soundly. Banc One put significant pressure on new affiliates to attain higher earnings. It asked each to take a look at its costs, to improve its proficiency in technology, to expand its loan-making capability, and to professionalize its banking workplace. Banc One had an exceptional track record of improving the performance of its new affiliates. The average acquisition increased its return on assets 66%. For example, at the time of its acquisition, Winters' (Dayton) return on assets was approximately .7% and net income reached $7 million. Five years later, in 1988, ROA was 1.62% and earnings hit $32.4 million. American Fletcher had never scored an ROA greater than 1%; in just three years with Banc One, its ROA stood at 1.55%.

To spur performance improvements Banc One assigned a "mentor bank" of comparable asset size to share information and expertise with the new bank and to help it build competence in Banc One's products, systems, and operating procedures. Typically, the mentor bank president and various staff members spent at first two or three days each month visiting the new affiliate. New member banks also sent their personnel to the mentor affiliate, and to other banks, to learn about such functions as data processing and financial controls. One affiliate president remarked:

> The operating culture gets transmitted in part by sharing information between the one with the Banc One culture and the one without. It's easy to see when you have an ROA of .6% and the other bank has 1.5% that there are [better] ways of doing things that you can learn.

Early in the assimilation of new affiliates, Banc One imposed its powerful financial control system, the Management Information Control System (MICS), as an additional tool to help the banks set and meet performance targets. The MICS tracked all balance sheet and income statement data as well as productivity and loan quality ratios (see *Exhibit 3*). Affiliates received an inch-thick monthly computer report that included detailed performance results.

Financial discipline was an integral value in the system, and managers placed a strong emphasis on the MICS numbers. The system recorded the yearly business plan and financial forecasts for each affiliate. While the original budget stood as a commitment to achieving a stated earnings level, actual results led to revisions in monthly targets. One affiliate manager explained:

> The MICS printout becomes an operating tool for all managers. It doesn't go into a black binder and get hidden away in some drawer. Every month

we use it to update our forecasts for the rest of the year. It's the "Banc One Bible." The monthly printout is required reading for all officers and supervisors—those people who make the business forecasts.

MICS brought new affiliates a degree of financial sophistication not typically enjoyed by independent banks. In the words of one financial officer, "MICS helps an affiliate understand itself better. It tells you where you've been, who you are, and where you want to go."

McCoy also found MICS to be a powerful general management tool, because:

Everyone is on the same financial system and accounted for the same way. In accounting class at Stanford Business School, we'd look at two banks' [income] statements and they'd be totally different; that left an impression on me. Our practice is to measure everyone the same way. Our other rule is that everyone has access to everyone else's numbers. They can see who is the best, who is the worst. If you see you're the worst, you pick a better bank and see what's happening there. It's friendly peer competition, but not deadly competition. You're in the same company but not competing in the same market.

Our commercial loan delinquency rate is 2%, in the top quartile in the country. Most CEOs would look at that figure and go on to other things. We start there. We list every single bank. We find that some are at 7%, some at 1.5%. We don't have to call the president with the worst number; he knows the call is coming. If I say to him, "Your loan delinquencies are bad," he would roll his eyes and say, "McCoy, you don't understand my market." He's right; I don't understand his market. But the numbers are there; it's his decision how to learn from someone else with better numbers.

Bringing new affiliates on-line with MICS did not always go without a hitch. For Bank One, Dayton (the former Winters Bank), the conversion was difficult, time consuming, and it negatively affected customer service. One manager recalled:

We spent a lot of time that first year fighting change. Our systems were uprooted and managers viewed that as a big loss because they had spent so much time fighting for it. Lots of turf issues arose. We fought battles from the perspective that those systems were "mine"; we really felt they were trying to take something away from us for no reason. We spent most of our energies trying to maintain what was instead of what was going to be.

Despite facing the often frustrating human dilemmas of organizational change, Banc One for the most part smoothly integrated its new acquisitions. Many affiliates gave credit for this success to one element of their new Banc One relationship: the "uncommon partnership."

The Uncommon Partnership

The First Banc Group had adopted "the uncommon partnership" as its slogan, and it became the hallmark of Banc One's relationship with its affiliate banks. McCoy's principle was, "If it involves people, we do it at the local level; if it involves paper, we centralize it." Affiliate autonomy encompassed local lending decisions, pricing based on local market conditions, personnel policies and compensation, and responses to community needs. Such autonomy was "uncommon" in banking. Most holding companies and franchisers imposed a standardized set of rules and practices on their affiliates.

The "uncommon partnership" philosophy was a strong selling point. In one case Banc One's offer to acquire a bank was $6 per share less than a competitor's, but target company directors felt that Banc One's uncommon partnership would provide more long-term value to shareholders so they accepted the lower offer. Treasurer George Meiling explained:

> In the ideal M&A (merger and acquisition) discussion, we don't even talk dollars or price until about the third meeting. We want to get all the social issues and have them understand how it is going to operate. We tell them not to listen to Columbus because we are trying to sell them on the deal. We give them our phone book and have them pick a president of an affiliate they want to talk to. And a lot of banks do it. Our best salespeople are really our presidents.

Banc One tried to bring a number of benefits to newly affiliated banks. While responsibility for traditional banking activities remained with the affiliates, the corporate office in Columbus provided (for a fee) central services including legal, new product development, and marketing. Affiliation also allowed banks to offer a broad range of products not usually offered by small independent banks, such as leasing and commercial lending. The Banc One name itself had great value in attracting customers, since the company's reputation for quality service had brought it national recognition. Affiliates gained leverage from the operational and financial resources of a much larger bank. Banc One shared its enormous product R&D experience with affiliates. Affiliates could obtain data that helped them predict which products would be most successful in their local markets. Frank McKinney, chairman of Banc One Indiana, summarized the advantages of Banc One membership this way: "It's like you have a very nice six-cylinder car that gets 18 miles per gallon, and that's the best you can do. So you ask,

'What do we have to do to get 24?' That's why we affiliated."[4] An Ohio affiliate president concluded,

> The uncommon partnership offers our customers the best of both worlds: those local [lending] decisions as well as services not generally offered by a $100 million bank. Because of the uncommon partnership, we're allowed to spend more time with our customers. For example, I don't have my staff bogged down with tracking the changes in regulations. The corporate legal staff does that. We can instead focus on serving the customers.

Work Environment

Along with the uncommon partnership, other aspects of Banc One's work environment had always been determined at the top of the company in Columbus and then diffused throughout the various affiliates. Since the Columbus bank accounted for 50% of total company revenue before the 1983 Winters acquisition in Dayton, the operating practices of that bank easily influenced those of the smaller affiliates. But when Dayton became 25% of the company, and Columbus shrank to 30%, John Fisher, now senior vice president, saw the need for some unifying devices:

> I concluded that if this continues, every time we do a merger we'll begin to look a lot more like the new affiliates and less like ourselves. You can just see how if we replicate the mergers, down the road there would be no surviving Banc One operating philosophy or culture. We didn't have a lot of things to give them that would make them look like us. We did have our common name and could offer shared services in data processing. We needed to develop things we could transfer to new affiliates to glue us together as a single organization.

Coincidentally, John B. McCoy had just become CEO. Fisher sensed that McCoy was searching for a platform to call his own, a way to make a distinctive mark on the company that would separate him from his father. He presented to McCoy a "white paper" in October 1984, that proposed quality as that platform. Fisher wrote:

> [Our senior staff] meetings almost invariably, and virtually exclusively, deal with the financial results. Never do they begin by asking about the customer. That's not a criticism of our emphasis on financial performance. It's only a statement of fact about our focus. Our management style is so single-

4. "Banc One Eases Fears of Wholesale Changes," *Indianapolis Star*, June 12, 1988.

minded, so inward-oriented that we have become almost totally dependent on financials. We have no other refined management tool to give direction or provide decisions for our business.

To address this concern, Fisher proposed a plan that included establishing a corporate positioning theme, creating a training program for executives, and expanding intracorporate communications through a variety of vehicles.

McCoy acted on Fisher's suggestions. In 1985, Banc One selected as its positioning theme the phrase "Nine Thousand People Who Care," a statement of a goal as much as common identity. All employees were invited to Columbus to celebrate the announcement of the new slogan at a major rally televised on closed circuit around the state for employees who could not attend. By early 1989, after several acquisitions, the slogan stood at "Eighteen Thousand People Who Care."

The company song captured this theme. McCoy remembered once attending an IBM function with Fisher and hearing its company song. "I said, 'We'd never sing a song in our company.' John Fisher said, 'We will, and I'll have tears in your eyes.' A year later, we had a song." Banc One's broadcast advertising included the song, and employees sang it at various celebrations and company events. In the spring of 1988, McCoy challenged employees to form groups and record their performance of the company song; the winning performers would star in a "music video" produced for company-wide broadcast. Other songs played a part in the Banc One culture as well, as special company events would inspire employees to write a set of lyrics for the occasion. For example, a group of managers sang its own version of "Leaving on a Jet Plane" to Senior Vice President Bill Boardman while he was in the middle of negotiating the Texas acquisition (see *Exhibit 4*).

One of the most prominent and successful vehicles for transmitting Banc One's values and operating standards was Bank One College. The college was an internal training program originally designed to give senior managers experience working together and to be a catalyst for collaboration and idea exchange among affiliates. The college took participants from their geographically dispersed locations and immersed them in two weeks of intense day and evening experiences. Top executives, including McCoy and Fisher, presented the corporation's operating philosophy and plans. Other classes and presentations honed the managers' problem-solving skills. The college used role-playing and "Outward Bound"-type team-building activities to develop trust, sharing, unity, and cooperation.

College director Beth Luchsinger commented, "Our challenge is to continue fostering innovation while sustaining growth. We use the college as a vehicle to achieve that." While the college's emphasis was always on sharing information and promoting learning between affiliates, conversations with McCoy before each session produced an agenda of specific discussion themes based on current Banc One issues.

Although the semi-annual program had a long waiting list of participants, some potential candidates were skeptical about the college. A few considered it a form of brainwashing and refused to attend. On each of these occasions, McCoy contacted these executives and urged them to attend and then report their evaluation back to him. Three presidents resigned shortly after their two-week experience. Luchsinger reported that each had realized over the course of the college program that "this was not the company they wanted to work for. They didn't buy into the philosophy or the way of operating here."

One important by-product of the college was the expanded network of relationships formed by the participants. Annual reunions of all the graduates helped maintain these ties. Most who had attended the college praised this consequence of their experience. "It was a fantastic experience," extolled one college alumnus. "I have 24 great friends now that I'm in touch with all the time. I go to reunions, and the network of relationships just grows and grows, which means more and more information is available. You can't get too much information in this business—it just changes too quickly."

Information-sharing and idea-exchange were central to Banc One's operating philosophy. Management stressed face-to-face meetings, preferring personal interactions to electronic communications. One Banc One executive, who had spent most of his career with IBM, remarked, "The informality of the organization is unique in banks. I was surprised by the willingness to question procedures. That shows a commitment by the organization to encourage people to think and express their ideas." The annual corporatewide Presidents' Council meetings brought together all the bank presidents to discuss current issues with corporatewide relevance. In addition, the state holding companies held similar Presidents' Council meetings frequently throughout the year. McCoy and other top corporate executives attended these meetings when invited and participated in open discussion forums. One president remarked, "McCoy doesn't have a problem with dissent. He encourages it. People are not shrinking violets in this company."

Many affiliate officers reported calling their peers to inquire about how another achieved a particularly good performance or solved a problem. Karen Horn, CEO of Bank One, Cleveland, a highly experienced bank executive who came to Banc One from the presidency of the Federal Reserve Bank of Cleveland, saw value in this peer exchange:

When we are dealing with an issue, there are 59 other folks out there that are vaguely in the same business we are that might have good ideas about it. There are also some people in Columbus who might have good ideas about it, and they may be more or less forceful, depending on the situation, in trying to get their ideas implemented. The openness and interchange between the affiliates is one of the enormous strengths of Banc One.

Communication to employees was frequent and detailed. The monthly company newsletter, *The Wire*, reported the latest events, internal organizational changes, promotions, work anniversaries, and assorted items of employee interest. Beginning in 1986, Banc One broadcast systemwide a 30-minute, network news-style video magazine, *The Quarterly Report*. Local affiliates taped professional quality reports, and senior managers appeared to answer questions about the past quarter's results and current company issues.

The corporatewide quality program was another unifying force. Bill Bennett, chairman of Bank One, Dayton, had developed a formal quality program in response to lapses in quality caused by merging data systems shortly after its acquisition. His hands-on approach included walking around the various banks' facilities, monitoring quality, and encouraging employees to focus on improving customer service. The success of the program in Dayton led to a systemwide, participative quality program under John Fisher's leadership. Included were competitive rankings of affiliates' performance on quality ratings and annual Chairman's Awards for quality leaders. In 1988 some 488 quality teams were addressing issues ranging from the process of sending out a customer statement to the design of a proposed new account.

Awards were abundant. The Chairman's Award was given annually at the Corporate Quality Awards banquet. "We Care" awards were presented regularly to employees to recognize individual or group contributions to superior customer service; for example, two administrative assistants received "We Care" awards for volunteering to work until 2 a.m. to draw up a crucial buy/sell agreement by the deadline. In 1988, 210 employees earned this recognition. The most coveted award was the "Blue One" award, given to the banks scoring highest on profitability, credit quality, reserves and liquidity, and productivity. Names and photos of award recipients regularly appeared in *The Wire* (see *Exhibit 5*).

Other celebrations regularly took place. One particularly enthusiastic event welcomed the new Wisconsin affiliates in 1988. June 13 was declared "Name Change Day," the day when the acquired banks would be called Bank One. The day began with a pancake breakfast served by top executives to all Wisconsin employees. Each employee received a Bank One bag filled with "welcome aboard" gifts, including a T-shirt, cap, and balloons. CEO McCoy and other officials spoke at a rally later in the morning. The employee band played the "Bank One" song and, reading off mimeographed pages, everyone sang along and was officially initiated onto the Banc One team.

One of the more controversial aspects of Banc One's culture was its Code of

Ethics. Banc One defined ethics as its accountability and responsibility to its depositors and shareholders. When a new bank joined Banc One, each of its employees received a copy of the Code of Ethics that she/he must sign, attesting knowledge of and agreement with its contents. The code provided guidelines for behavior regarding conflict of interest, personal conduct, and financial affairs (see *Exhibit 6*). These latter personal issues raised concerns about violations of privacy and discomfort at the corporation's seeming imposition of a strict morality. Roman Gerber, corporate general counsel, remarked: "To be very frank, our code probably goes a bit further than some corporate codes go in trying to dictate or guide conduct."

The code also had strict disclosure requirements for officers and directors regarding personal financial obligations. Gerber reported, "This perhaps more than any other piece of the Code of Ethics has been resisted." Some affiliates believed that such disclosure went beyond what an employer was entitled to know. This component of the code was optional for the individual banks. Gerber commented that "rather than just jamming it down their throats, we would rather have them come to understand and come to accept it over time."

Leadership

McCoy described his role and activities this way:

> Besides chief personnel officer, my other job is Goodwill Ambassador. There are times I feel I'm running for office. On the first day in Texas I tried to walk around as many floors as I could, let people see who we are. We had dinners for all the officers; I talked about our philosophy.

McCoy held informal weekly staff meetings (no minutes); in 1989, they included Fisher, Don McWhorter (Chairman of Services Corp.), John Westman (CFO), Bill Boardman (SVP Acquisitions), and Gerber. Others were invited to discuss particular issues. He also held a monthly policy committee meeting that added the state company heads to the staff meeting group to examine events and results across the company. In addition to chairing meetings of the board of directors, McCoy attended the state Presidents' Council meetings when invited. But he noted that, "When things are running well, I don't have to go to a lot of meetings. Because of the strengths of our forecasts and financial systems, we don't do a lot of reviews—only if there is a problem." In fact, McCoy joked, "No one wants to take my phone calls, because they know that I only call with bad news."

McCoy relied on Fisher as a confidant and sounding board for a variety of business decisions. He regarded Fisher as the company's "idea man" and believed that Fisher's successful efforts over the years to make Banc One a marketing-driven company were the reason that human resource and quality programs often emanated from the Marketing area.

> He's a unique individual. He's always coming at you with ideas. John is a good observer of what's going on in the company. He's at the point in his career where he has nothing to lose if he says, "That guy in Dayton is in trouble," or, "There's a problem in Cleveland." I can talk to him. He'll say, "That's dumb. That's right."

Fisher attributed his influence to McCoy's vision and interest in innovations and fresh thought. "The thing that has helped make us unique is the creative flame he has helped nurture," he explained.

Most press accounts as well as investment analyst reports described Banc One as a superior company with talented and dynamic managers. McCoy personally selected people for the top corporate slots including the state holding company presidents, though he discussed candidates with his key managers individually. Each holding company chose its local bank presidents and officers, though there had not been too many selection decisions due to the usual retention of existing management after acquisitions. According to McCoy, successful managers at Banc One affiliates were entrepreneurial in their outlook toward opportunities, willing to share information and decision-making power with their peers and subordinates, and open to new ideas; they were good at turnarounds but also able to sustain growth by avoiding major mistakes.

McCoy set a high common standard for managerial performance. According to Fisher he used "a velvet glove" to motivate the affiliates. McCoy tried to create a work environment that reflected his belief that people are good, bright, and want to do the right things but don't always know what they are. "The affiliates have a sharing relationship," McCoy remarked. "It's not, 'Hey, you dumb guy.' I'd much rather have a friendly company than an unfriendly one."

Affiliate officers were evaluated on budgeted versus actual earnings (adjusted for events outside of affiliate control) and on ROA. Their bonuses varied as a percentage of total compensation, but were between 10% and 50%. To earn 100% of the bonus, managers had to meet their budget targets and earn a 1.4% ROA. There were payoff curves for other combinations of these two variables. Several senior managers acknowledged that while the monetary bonus played a distinct motivational role, it was not the most important factor. According to one affiliate president, friendly competition among the affiliates was the greatest incentive:

> No one wants to be on the bottom of the lists. Lots of [senior] people could have moved to different organizations and made more money. But once

you get the Banc One spirit in your blood you can't leave it. You want to win the Blue One award, the Chairman's Award.

Banc One held onto its best managers. One officer reported that while many of his peers frequently received calls from executive search firms, none had been stolen away by other companies. Low turnover meant high retention of experience and knowledge, and maintenance of the extensive networks of relationships among the various affiliates. But high standards meant that jobs were not sinecures. In the case of one affiliate bank president with 20 years' service whose job grew too big for him to handle, McCoy reported:

> I told him I'm convinced he can't do [the job], that I've given him a chance for the past year and I must make a change. I said he has two choices: we can get him an outplacement counselor to help him get an outside job or he can become the president of a smaller bank. He chose to take the outside job. It was announced in the company that he simply wanted that job. There was no embarrassment, no cutting him off at the knees. That's the style I want. If everyone feels the hammer is coming right at him, it's harder to get good performance. Of course, if someone breaks the law, they're out the next minute; that's happened.

McCoy believed that leaders came from every level in the company. One effort to emphasize this philosophy proved unworkable. McCoy tried to do away with the proliferation of officer titles at Banc One. Remarked McCoy, "We do a lot of team projects here. There was a junior analyst on the due diligence team in Texas, a great contributor. He was treated as an equal, not as a gofer. If we get a lot of good people on a team it doesn't matter what their titles are." Focus groups conducted with employees below the officer level agreed with the elimination of titles. Senior managers, however, resisted this change, and McCoy did not force the issue.

Organizational Dilemmas of Growth

In 1987, in response to the complexities of multistate and nonbanking operations, Banc One organized its affiliates into a state holding company structure, with corporate headquarters and staff offices in Columbus (see *Exhibit 7*). In January 1989, Banc One Ohio had 26 affiliates including banks in Ohio, Michigan, and Kentucky; Banc One Indiana, 11 affiliates; and Banc One Wisconsin, 19 affiliates. The state holding company structure allowed for future growth since it could be duplicated as new states were added; it encouraged development of local management talent; and it helped successfully integrate new affiliates.

Sandwiched between the centralized and decentralized features of the Banc

One system were some "centralized shared responsibilities," those activities with which central subsidiaries or offices assisted the local banks and holding companies by providing expertise, policy guidelines, and resources for particular products and services. For example, the corporate marketing department assisted affiliates in product development and promotion, and Banc One Services Corporation supplied the data processing/item processing services for all units. In addition, Banc One corporate offices in Columbus, in conjunction with the state holding companies and affiliates, performed financial analyses and forecasting. Mortgages, investment banking, insurance, and leasing were all shared with central nonbank subsidiaries. To add structure and some direction to these "centralized, shared responsibilities," Banc One created the Services Corporation in January 1988, to handle operations functions for all of the affiliate banks. These functions included data and credit-card processing as well as software and system development to support new products. A year later, in a move that further centralized some operations, the Services Corporation was restructured into five major groups to separate the data processing for information services from that for financial services.

For some affiliates, however, the existence of a more centralized Services organization created tension regarding locus of control. A particularly sore spot was the price affiliates were charged for central services. Mike Elvir, executive vice president of the Services Corporation, commented:

> This is a source of major irritation. They don't want us to be a profit center. They think it is unfair and makes it hard for them to compete. [The issue of pricing] is raised within the first 20 minutes of almost all dialogues I have with people. Currently our price is based on a market-based price; it is 90% of the composite price found. But affiliates still argue. They go out and find one supplier who will give it to them for less. They forget that same one supplier will not give them all the services they need at such a low price. A lot of energy is wasted on this issue as affiliates try to prove us wrong. McCoy believes the organization gains a lot by letting affiliates feel they can challenge our pricing. But McCoy and his minions put such a large pressure on increasing margins that the affiliates will never be happy with what we do. This is the cost we pay for the uncommon partnership—as aggravating as it is, I agree with it. The benefits gained from their operating like independent business people outweighs what we lose.

Elvir identified a second trouble spot Banc One had with its affiliates: meeting the needs of diverse entities.

> Regional banks all want autonomy but all require operational support. What is good for one bank is not good for another—a $4.5 million bank in

Indiana does not want the same thing as a $700 million bank in Wisconsin. The decisions made are meant to satisfy the majority. Systems need to be common.

This lack of similar needs extended throughout the corporation and raised some crucial questions. Some managers continued to express the concerns voiced by John Fisher in 1983 at the time of the Winters acquisition. How could Banc One maintain a single set of practices and values when the organization's "culture" continued to be diluted with new affiliates, each bringing its own systems, styles, and needs? Craig Kelley, vice president-director Affiliate Marketing, commented:

> We have created a monster. We have commonality in name, and we share a slogan and a corporate logo. But there are no common operating procedures—not even in how to open an account. For example, there is no common check cashing system. We have a great franchise system, but customers are not guaranteed that they can cash a check at various Bank One locations—it is up to the whim of local management.
>
> How can we maintain the sense of affiliate self-ownership and impose some commonality, some sense of sameness? So much is driven down to the bank level that there is not a feeling of family; there is not the sense of being a part of something larger. We must put the uncommon partnership aside and say who we are.

Moves away from local autonomy were particularly prominent in two other areas: product line and procurement. In the summer of 1988, Banc One announced a corporatewide uniform product line. After months of discussions involving participants from every Banc One affiliate, the corporate product uniformity committee reduced the number of financial products offered from 63 to 10. New guidelines standardized features, marketing approaches, and product terms and conditions. These changes would make pricing decisions easier, simplify marketing tasks, and streamline operations. For example, uniform products were expected to help solve the marketing problem of creating ads for affiliates that each had its own way of packaging and selling identical and/or similar services.

At the same time, Banc One extended to the entire organization a central office materials procurement program developed at Banc One, Wisconsin. Savings opportunities were estimated at around $5 million annually. Banc One hoped to use its leverage as a $24 billion company to obtain better prices than any individual local unit. McCoy respected the desire of local banks to buy from local suppliers with whom they had long-established relationships, so initially the program was optional. He hoped, however, that the participating banks' bottom-line results would provide incentives for others to join. On this point, one Michigan affiliate president acknowledged that he supported the move to centralized purchasing with one caveat: The group must serve him at least as well, if not better, than his in-house operations had. "I have the authority," he said assuredly, "to find my own suppliers if I'm not happy with the job Columbus is doing."

Some affiliate managers saw the movement toward increased centralization and standardization as part of a systematic plan to take away the power of local banks. A few were unconcerned—as long as Banc One continued to leave the banking functions of making loans and accepting deposits to local officials. Nevertheless, managers in Columbus, including John Fisher, saw corporate unity as the paramount concern. Commented Fisher:

> We're here saying, "Hey McCoy, the way to do this baby is to have more central programs. If you don't have central programs, then there is nothing here to help you steer." Yet, the other folks out in the field are saying, "You don't need that. We can do all that stuff out here. We don't need corporate ads. We don't need uniform products." McCoy is caught and his two ears are hearing different voices. One group calls for centralization and another wants more autonomy.

THE FUTURE CHALLENGE

In February 1989, *Financial World* magazine named Banc One one of 30 great companies for the 1990s, calling it "the cream of a pack of excellent super-regionals" and noting its "highly innovative products and services" and its skill at "digesting new technology and smaller banks." Despite such accolades, concern at the company over limited future growth of its existing customer base and pressure to maintain its record of superior financial performance had led to conservative actions, such as selling credit card receivables to investors and limiting consumer credit lines, and had intensified Banc One's willingness to make a major acquisition.

In June 1989, Banc One agreed to purchase MCorp's 20 banks for $375–510 million, depending on the banks' financial results, to be paid over five years. The banks' 65 branch offices across the state made up the Deposit Insurance Bridge Bank, which with $13.1 billion in assets was the third largest Texas bank. The FDIC offered an incentive by agreeing to indemnify all the Bridge Bank's identified and classified nonperforming loans, reducing the asset value of the acquisition by essentially cleaning the balance sheet and leaving only the good assets; it was the third costliest bailout in FDIC history. The biggest risk in entering Texas was the future uncertainty of the state's economy. The depressed oil and gas industry had hit the state hard. Even if the depression had bottomed out, any further weakness could hurt the bank's financial performance.

The Bridge Bank purchase was Banc One's first acquisition outside of the Midwest; it involved a large bank, not a small- or medium-sized one. Not only was Bridge Bank unsuccessful and unprofitable, but it was insolvent as well. Unlike all other Banc One acquisitions, Bridge Bank had little strength in the retail or middle market segments. Nor did Bridge Bank lease small ticket items or have a mortgage department. Its focus, and what had led to its downfall, was the commercial lending sector. McCoy commented that there was a major clash of cultures involved, not because of Texas and Ohio styles, but because of loan size: "Ours are $1 million loans, theirs are $50 million."

Banc One named its Chairman McCoy as chairman of Banc One Texas. Thomas Hoaglin, chairman and CEO of Bank One, Dayton, was named president and CEO of the new Texas entity. Under Hoaglin's leadership, Dayton was Banc One's top financial performer in 1988, and the bank won a special quality service award that year. While Banc One also planned to name several more senior executives, McCoy told the *Wall Street Journal*, "We found what appeared to us to be good management at the grassroots level, and that's one of the main things that kept our interest in the organization. . . . Believe me, those of us from Columbus don't know much about Texas, so we're going to rely on Texans to run our Texas bank."[5] At the time of purchase, the Bridge Bank had its central headquarters in Dallas directing all major decisions. Banc One was considering changing the organization to a state holding company-type structure along the lines of the rest of Banc One: separate banks, each with a president and the autonomy to make lending decisions, reporting to a Banc One, Texas headquarters.

Banc One received approval for the purchase on June 29, 1989. McCoy described the days following:

> We were told the Friday before the 4th of July we could go ahead. We sent 80 people selected by the Marketing department [down to Texas] on the 4th. On the 5th and 6th of July there were Banc One people in every office. We held training sessions with videos, we gave [our new employees] videos to take home, we had dinners. We told them how we operate. We sent people from Wisconsin and Indiana who told them, "We didn't believe it two years ago either, but this is how we operate. . . .

As McCoy thought about the future, he told a visitor,

---

5. *Wall Street Journal*, June 29, 1989, p. A6; June 30, 1989, p. A3.

The reason we are in Texas is we think there are really good people [in those banks]. We are buying a $10 billion bank with very capable people. They will question us hard about why we do things the way we do. It will just mean lots and lots of trips for them to our other banks. Success will not happen by my telling them why, but by their going to Indianapolis or Akron and seeing how those banks got their results.

But would Banc One's traditional methods for upgrading people and improving performance work fast enough and effectively enough in the new environment, especially in light of other challenges to the "uncommon partnership?" Should McCoy be considering any new ways for Banc One to meet the challenges ahead?

BANC ONE CORPORATION 1989
Exhibit 1
Selected Financial Data, 1978–1988

Income and Expenses $(millions)

Year	Total Income	Net Interest Income	Non Interest Income	Non Interest Expense	Income before Securities Transactions	Net Income
1988	$2,734.5	$1,142.0	$452.3	$902.6	$332.9	$340.2
1987	2,384.8	1,092.6	346.8	838.6	227.7	231.5
1986	2,260.6	1,005.2	306.8	757.7	216.0	236.5
1985	2,096.8	869.6	274.1	648.7	198.5	204.5
1984	1,889.2	715.8	227.7	552.3	161.4	162.7
1983	1,457.4	545.8	182.6	454.3	129.2	128.2
1982	1,355.7	460.1	142.3	380.6	101.5	96.6
1981	1,133.3	365.2	107.5	305.8	75.1	73.8
1980	883.9	332.8	87.6	259.0	73.4	73.2
1979	735.0	319.4	70.5	233.3	70.2	69.7
1978	586.4	283.9	60.8	202.6	62.4	62.9
Annual Growth:						
1988/87	14.67%	4.52%	30.42%	7.63%	46.20%	46.95%
Compound Growth:						
5 Years	13.41	15.91	19.89	14.72	20.84	21.55
10 Years	16.65	14.93	22.22	16.11	18.23	18.39

Balance Sheet $(millions)

	Yearly Average Balances			Year-End Balances		
Year	Total Assets	Common Equity	Earning Assets	Loans and Leases	Deposits	Primary Capital
1988	$23,484	$1,906	$21,054	$17,325	$19,502	$2,278
1987	21,854	1,650	19,479	15,629	18,176	2,028
1986	20,244	1,437	17,961	14,028	16,741	1,741
1985	17,662	1,223	15,485	12,399	15,480	1,537
1984	15,217	1,008	13,351	10,498	13,348	1,218
1983	12,689	830	11,122	8,346	11,510	1,017
1982	10,783	701	9,300	6,265	8,866	832
1981	8,887	572	7,566	5,371	7,463	683
1980	8,024	523	6,852	4,761	6,602	610
1979	7,410	477	6,354	4,635	6,242	549
1978	6,713	431	5,769	4,057	5,643	494
Annual Growth:						
1988/87	7.46%	15.52%	8.09%	10.85%	7.30%	12.33%
Compound Growth:						
5 Years	13.10	18.09	13.61	15.73	11.12	17.50
10 Years	13.34	16.03	13.82	15.62	13.20	16.52

(Continued)

BANC ONE CORPORATION 1989

Exhibit 1
(Continued)

Consolidated Condensed Balance Sheet

$(thousands)	December 31, 1988	December 31, 1987
Assets:		
Cash and equivalents	$ 2,191,511	$ 2,172,607
Securities (market value approximates $4,556,300 and $4,417,600 at December 31, 1988 and 1987)	4,624,612	4,453,264
Loans and leases:		
Comercial, financial and agricultural	6,992,281	6,337,308
Real estate, construction	765,504	729,408
Real estate, mortgage	2,802,756	2,434,652
Consumer, net	5,450,426	4,858,713
Tax exempt	635,796	726,050
Leases, net	678,024	542,850
Total loans and leases	17,324,787	15,628,981
Reserve for possible loan and lease losses	237,342	216,547
Net loans and leases	17,087,445	15,412,434
Other assets	1,370,086	1,114,978
Total assets	$25,273,654	$23,153,283
Liabilities:		
Deposits:		
Non-interest bearing	$ 3,363,214	$ 3,487,548
Interest bearing	16,138,542	14,688,528
Total deposits	19,501,756	18,176,076
Short-term borrowings	2,745,559	2,335,800
Long-term borrowings	378,874	327,710
Other liabilities	606,634	511,064
Total liabilities	23,232,823	21,350,650
Preferred stock	25,454	26,353
Common stockholders' equity	2,015,377	1,776,280
Total liabilities, preferred stock and common stockholders' equity	$25,273,654	$23,153,283

Consolidated Condensed Statement of Income
for the three years ended December 31, 1988

$(thousands, except per share amounts)	1988	1987	1986
Interest income:			
Interest and fees on loans and leases	$1,875,841	$1,651,697	$1,514,010
Interest and dividends on securities	367,831	344,225	332,644
Other interest income	27,806	38,691	73,762
Total interest income	2,271,478	2,034,613	1,920,416
Interest expense:			
Interest on deposits	1,013,102	873,128	920,497
Other borrowings	197,923	184,233	168,885
Total interest expense	1,211,025	1,057,361	1,089,382
Net interest income	1,060,453	977,252	831,034
Provision for loan and lease losses	183,422	206,974	146,746
Net interest income after provision for loan and lease losses	877,031	770,278	684,288
Other income	463,070	350,149	340,145
Other expenses	902,557	838,619	757,742
Income before income taxes	437,544	281,808	266,691
Income tax provision	97,356	50,312	30,160
Net income	$ 340,188	$ 231,496	$ 236,531
Per common share information (amounts reflect the 10% common stock dividend effective February 19, 1988)			
Net income per common share	$2.61	$1.82	$1.92
Weighted average common shares outstanding (000)	129,410	125,123	119,307

SOURCE: Banc One Corporation 1988 Annual Report

Exhibit 2
Earnings per Share and Stock Price, 1978–1988

Data per Common Share

Year	Net Income — Pooled	Net Income — As Originally Reported	Income Before Securities Transactions	Cash Dividends	Book Value	Stock Price
1988	$2.61	$2.61	$2.57	$.92	$15.59	$22.25
1987	1.82	1.98	1.82	.82	13.91	21.82
1986	1.92	1.94	1.81	.75	12.88	20.80
1985	1.74	1.83	1.75	.63	11.58	21.28
1984	1.48	1.58	1.53	.54	10.12	14.12
1983	1.29	1.41	1.35	.47	9.45	12.90
1982	1.10	1.21	1.17	.40	8.84	12.86
1981	.99	1.10	1.02	.36	8.40	7.89
1980	1.01	.94	1.01	.33	8.06	6.58
1979	.96	.86	.97	.30	7.44	5.05
1978	.88	.75	.87	.25	6.73	4.83

Annual Growth:

1988/87	43.41%	31.82%	41.21%	12.20%	12.08%	1.97%

Compound Growth:

5 Years	15.14	13.11	13.74	14.38	10.53	11.52
10 Years	11.48	13.28	11.44	13.92	8.76	16.50

Common Stock Data
(as originally reported)

Data per Common Share

Year	Average Shares Outstdg. (000)	Common Shares Traded (000)	Common Shareholders	Stock Splits & Dividends	Total Market Capital $(mil)	Year-End Price/ Earnings
1988	129,410	42,347	43,892	10%	$2,876	8.5x
1987	105,009	38,297	37,693		2,360	11.0
1986	100,238	21,457	36,855	10%	2,082	10.7
1985	68,254	8,270	24,748	3:2	1,491	11.6
1984	64,673	4,116	24,998	10%	929	8.9
1983	57,031	5,361	21,529	3:2	802	9.1
1982	47,785	2,919	12,974	3:2/10%	655	10.6
1981	34,988	1,466	10,564		301	7.2
1980	34,119	764	8,833	10%	222	7.0
1979	32,245	557	8,709		173	5.9
1978	34,245	535	8,535	10%	165	6.4

SOURCE: Banc One Corporation 1988 Annual Report

Exhibit 3
Management Information Control System (MICS)
"Major Highlights" Summary Data Sheet, February 1989

	FEB ACTUAL	B/(W) PR FCST	B/(W) BGT	FCST F-Y-F	B/(W) FR FCST	B/(W) BGT	PYR 4TH QTR	1ST QTR	2ND QTR	3RD QTR	4TH QTR
	-------	-------	-------	-------	-------	-------	-------	-------	-------	-------	-------

EARNINGS ANALYSIS

LOAN INT
LOAN FEES
INV INC
INT EXP
NIM
PROVISION
NET FUNDS FNCT
SERVICE CHGS
NON-INT INC
NON-INT EXP
PRETAX NET
NET TAX
NCE
NET SEC
NET INCOME

INCOME

LOAN YIELD %
INV YIELD %
E/A YIELD %
OVERALL RATE
NIM %
FUNDS FNCT %
RCA %
RCE %

LOAN QUALITY

RES RATIO EOM %
CHG-OFFS/LOANS %
NPL/LOANS %

BALANCE SHEET

LOAN GROWTH %
DEPOSIT GROWTH %
LOAN/DEPOSIT %
LG LIAB DEP %
EQUITY/ASSETS %

PRODUCTIVITY

FTE/MM ASSETS
DEP'S/OFFICE
N-I EXP/ASSETS %
N-I EXP/NOE %
N-I EXP/REV %

Exhibit 4
Songs

Bank One Song

(Advertising Campaign since 1985)

In our hometown we're proud to be
    The finest bankers there.
And one by one we do our best
    It's how we show we care.
So when you cross the heartland states
    You'll find us standing strong.
With all of us behind each one
    You'll hear us sing this song. . . .

We are Eighteen Thousand People
    Who Care
BANK ONE,
Yes, we're Eighteen Thousand People
    Who Care about our customers.
Eighteen Thousand People Who Care
    How well we serve.
We're a company,
    A winning team
Of Eighteen Thousand People Who Care.

Leaving on a Jet Plane

(Banc One version, Spring 1989)

All my bags are packed, I'm ready to go.
I'm standing here on the sixteenth floor,
I hate to return again without a deal.
But the dawn is breakin', it's early morn,
The plane is waitin', I'm ready to board.
I'm Texas bound and so
It's a hell of a steal.

There's no solution to dilution.
M Bank's pain is Banc One's gain . . .
Their customer will never be the same.
I'm leaving on a jet plane,
Don't know when I'll be back again.
Oh John, I love to go.

Exhibit *5*

Excerpts from *The Wire*, July 1989

We Care Awards

BANK ONE, FREMONT employees **Wendi Jay, Ann King** and **Mary Ann Woessner** assisted in the capture and arrest of a suspected felon to earn their We Care Awards.

In April, a local business contacted the bank and reported two stolen payroll checks. Later that morning a customer asked Wendi to cash a payroll check at the drive-through window.

Wendi recognized the check as one that was stolen and contacted her supervisor, Ann. Ann had the bank's security officer call the police and made note of which direction the customer went after leaving the bank. Meanwhile, Mary Ann, a commercial note teller, got a complete description of the car and its license number and turned this information over to the authorities. The police officer on the scene contacted a police cruiser in the area, and the suspect was apprehended.

We Care Recipients

ANTIGO
Diane Molle, Executive Secretary
Ethel Wenek, Bookkeeper
Sue Zupon, Bookkeeper
CRAWFORDSVILLE
Vicki Lutes, Cashier
Sandy Porter, Loan Clerk
DAYTON
Dan Johnson, Auditor
Carol Chester, Retail Banking
   Administration Specialist

DOVER
Wanda Prysi, Bookkeeping Clerk
Cheryl Morgan, Assistant Branch
   Manager
FREMONT
Wendi Jay, Teller
Ann King, Teller Supervisor
Mary Ann Woessner,
   Commercial Note Teller
INDIANAPOLIS
Peggy Jennings, Cash
   Management Specialist
LAFAYETTE
Cheryl Myers, Customer Service
   Representative
Elizabeth Derringer, Merchant
   Representative
LIMA
Brent Gibson, Branch Manager
Donna Martello, Assistant
   Branch Manager
SIDNEY
Mary Putnam, Teller
STURGIS
Lou Ann James, Teller
Susan Osmun, Teller

PROUD EMPLOYEES — Displaying their We Care Awards are (left to right) Mary Ann Woessner, Ann King and Wendi Jay of BANK ONE, FREMONT.

YOUNGSTOWN
Alice Bovo, Mortgage Loan
   Closer
Obadiah Hall, Credit Processor
Kevin Lamar, Vault Supervisor
SERVICES CORPORATION
Audrey Martin, Authorizations
   Supervisor
David Kocak, Authorizations
   Supervisor
Doug Kirby, Proof Operator
William Tredick, Clerk

New Code of Ethics To Be Distributed

A new BANC ONE CORPORATION Code of Ethics soon will be distributed to all BANK ONE employees.

The brochure has been rewritten to answer questions that have been raised about BANK ONE policies and to better explain certain legal provisions in those policies. The new edition is also written in a more understandable language style.

Because of the importance of the message in the Code of Ethics, all employees will be required to sign a statement acknowledging that they have received the brochure. The statement will be kept in each employee's personnel file.

Exhibit 6
Excerpts from *Banc One Code of Ethics*

I. INTRODUCTION

BANC ONE's success is directly related to customer and investor trust and confidence. We must recognize that our first duty to our customers and to our stockholders is to act in all matters in the manner that merits public trust and confidence. Basic to this obligation is the requirement that every director, officer, and employee conduct their business affairs in strict compliance with all applicable laws and regulations.

For this reason, this Code of Ethics is issued as standard for all directors, officers and employees of BANC ONE. Just as the policies in this Code are not all-inclusive, these policies must be followed in conjunction with good judgement and basic principles of sound banking.

II. CONFLICT OF INTEREST

The basic policy of BANC ONE is that no director, officer or employee should have any position of interest (either financial or otherwise), make or receive any payment, or engage in any activity which conflicts, or might reasonably conflict, with the proper performance of his or her duties and responsibilities to BANC ONE. . . . Each director, officer and employee must manage his or her personal and business affairs so as to avoid situations that might lead to conflict, or even the appearance of a conflict . . .

III. PERSONAL CONDUCT AND FINANCIAL AFFAIRS

A. Personal Conduct

Directors, officers and employees of BANC ONE are expected to conduct their personal and financial affairs on a sound, moral, ethical, and legal basis. They are expected to conduct their personal as well as their financial affairs in a manner which (1) is consistent with, and does not violate basic moral or ethical standards within the community, and (2) recognizes and respects the personal property rights of others. They are also expected to comply with applicable personnel policies of their BANC ONE employer, including those set forth in company personnel manuals, relating to the use, possession or sale of alcoholic beverages or illegal drugs, to personal appearance, to conduct in the performance of their employment, and to dealing with personnel, customers, and suppliers.

(1) Financial Affairs. Directors, officers and employees shall maintain their personal financial affairs in a manner which is prudent. Officers are required to complete and to submit at least annually to their CEO a questionnaire relative to their compliance with various provisions of the Code of Ethics and legal requirements applicable to them as BANC ONE officers . . .

Exhibit 7
Banc One State Holding Company Structure, June 1989

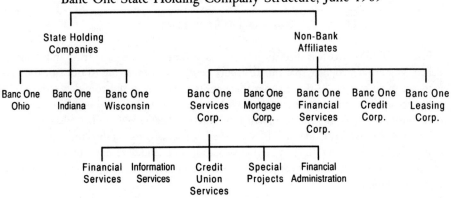

Banc One Corporate Organization, June 1989 (pre-Texas)
Banc One Corp Senior Executives

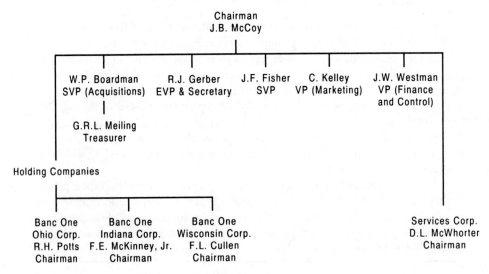

United Parcel Service (A)

The management committee at United Parcel Service (UPS) wrestled with the last item on the agenda. Frank Erbrick, head of the Information Services department, had been invited to make a presentation.

Responding to Erbrick's presentation, Jack Rogers, chief executive, inquired: "So you're convinced that we can't locate this talent internally or develop it in the smart computer-trained kids working in our districts?"

"Oh, I think we can groom some from the inside, but we also have to get a large number of the senior programmers and middle managers from the outside. The field has gotten very specialized," replied Frank.

Erbrick was interrupted by Operations Vice President Frank Middendorf: "Look Frank, we don't need people to *make* the computers, just *run* them."

Erbrick turned to Middendorf: "Come on Frank, these people aren't Martians, but there's been a revolution in technology. We can hardly keep up with the language they speak. You'd do the same damned thing if you had my job."

Middendorf put one heel up on an adjacent chair, looked back at the others, and growled. "Yeah, but thank God I don't have your job. Someone has to make the money you're spending."

A playful banter of heated debate came to an end. As with most management decisions at UPS, consensus would be reached after an open airing of differences, whereupon the debate would be over. Critics would then join the enthusiasts in support of whatever was decided concerning the staffing of Information Services. In considering this issue, Jack Rogers had asked for some discussion about the larger significance of assimilating new hires into the UPS culture.

A new plan for hiring outside talent for Information Services could represent a challenge to the company's long-established practice of equal pay across departments. Furthermore, management salaries were low and determined by hierarchical level. Senior managers, such as Rogers, earned at least one-third less in wages than did their counterparts in comparable positions. Instead of short-term wages, the company relied upon a long-term bonus plan based upon annual stock grants from the company to all of its 15,000 full-time managers. With only six levels of management, the pay differences were slight, but substantial wealth was accumulated by UPS managers through their stock appreciation and dividends over

Associate Professor Jeffrey Sonnenfeld and Research Assistant Meredith Lazo prepared this case as the basis for class discussion rather than to illustrate either effective or ineffective handling of an administrative situation. Copyright © 1987 by the President and Fellows of Harvard College; Harvard Business School case #9-488-016 (Rev. 3/89).

their long careers. The hiring of new specialized talent for assignments in key programming, financial, marketing, legal, engineering, and aviation positions at higher wages would challenge the strength of UPS's long, successful career system.

Rogers commented on this: "What do you guys think we need to anticipate about the impact of these kinds of moves? As you know, our business is changing more in our eightieth anniversary than it has in any previous year."

John Alden, the head of business development, commented: "With the onslaught of new competitors chipping away at all parts of the business, we have to meet marketing and technological challenges, and that means recruiting more specialized talent."

Vern Cormie, another operations vice president, asked, "But how much can this system take? Can these people be routed out of their specialties into the districts?"

Joe Moderow, the corporate counsel, responded: "Well, specialists can still drive package cars." (Moderow had joined UPS as a part-time clerk while earning a college economics degree. He had managed industrial engineering and operating departments during his graduate schooling and after earning his J.D.) He continued, "Engineers, analysts, programmers, and even attorneys can be broadened. I want my guys to have solid management skills, not just legal expertise."

Oz Nelson, executive vice president, countered this by stating, "Well, as much as Joe has enjoyed getting away from other attorneys to work with managers—and who can blame him—many of the specialists we're bringing in do not want to be generalists. They have trained for years to become experts in their specialties, and frankly, that's why we want them. Perhaps we can keep them more distinct from our operating culture."

Rogers responded, "Oz, I'm not certain that we can keep all such types hidden from the business. Some new acquisitions, for example, may hit us in the core. When outsiders are not in operations driving the business, I'm not as concerned."

Vice President of Personnel Don Layden—formerly a senior general manager—commented, "This is not the first time this company has attacked this sort of problem. We have moved into new nations, new industries, and new parts of the country. Each time, we have had to face the challenge of introducing new people to the UPS system, orienting them, training them, matching their expectations, and helping them grow. The challenge is to be aware of whatever psychological contract is implicitly set up with each set of new hires—whether they are young college kids or mid-career avionics engineers."

Rogers responded, "Don, I think you're right. We made some mistakes in our national expansions to some regions but we did it right in our roll-outs in other regions. We knew that internal expansions could not be built with anything less than highly skilled managers. Perhaps there are other such lessons here."

Ed Jacoby, the new chief financial officer, added: "Our consultants, bankers, and auditors tell us we need to hire new talent and shouldn't worry about them fitting. We have this need to make everyone a member of the family with substantial stock and decades of service. After 30 years, I myself question this. Maybe we'd be better served by a cadre of fresh technical support that comes and goes and keeps us current."

Layden again recalled UPS's past experience, saying, "I think that even if we look at Germany . . ."

Rogers interrupted at this point: "That's right, Don. You led the operations team that corrected the crisis in Germany. Maybe you see what hidden patterns are emerging here. Why not throw out some observations for the committee meeting next week. We need to focus on how we bring outsiders to UPS as well as the extent to which we should do it."

COMPANY BACKGROUND

Jim Casey, with help from his brother George, founded the United Parcel Service in 1907 under the name American Messenger Company. At that time messengers responded to telephone calls received at their headquarters; they ran errands and carried notes, hand-baggage, and trays of food from restaurants; they delivered packages by foot, streetcar, or bicycle.

As more advanced methods of communication became available to the public, the company placed a greater emphasis on services requiring package transportation. Only companies with a similar ground infrastructure could compete. With the introduction of the motorcycle, UPS now could offer a faster and better delivery service.

In 1913 the new company acquired its first delivery car, a Model T Ford, establishing its identity as offering a state-of-the-art package delivery service. Two years later, its management adopted its trademark—the pullman-brown color, which continued to identify it through the years.

In 1919 Jim Casey, realizing that labor unions were unavoidable in the near future, invited the International Brotherhood of Teamsters to represent the UPS drivers and part-time hourly employees. He explained to his co-workers, "I think it's possible to be a good UPS member and union member at the same time." Because of this early relationship, UPS was able to forge a flexible union-management partnership with such noteworthy features as variable start time, working as directed with minimum work rules, working across job classifications, combinations of inside and outside labor, part-time employment for half the work force, and mandatory overtime as needed. Through the years, the relationship between the company and the union had been reasonably good, although there had been occasional work stoppages.

In 1922 UPS took a major strategic step when it began an experimental intercity "common carrier" service in Southern California. By becoming a common carrier, it was legally required to serve any shipper who was willing to pay, no matter how small the shipment or how remote the location within the service territory. Its common carrier service pioneered the automatic daily pickup call, acceptance of checks made out to the shipper in payment of CODs, additional delivery attempts, automatic return of undeliverables, and streamlined documentation with weekly billing. This experiment was so successful that it grew to dictate the company policy and operating principles for service in future years.

At this time, other company operating features were established, such as uniformed drivers; painted, well-maintained vehicles; an emphasis on courtesy; and an insistence on meeting service commitments. Shortly thereafter, in 1929, *The Policy Book* was created to standardize these traits and other corporate ideals throughout all branches of the business. Although revised every few years by a special management committee, the book continued to serve as a template from which all new policy was made. (Excerpts from *The Policy Book* are presented in *Exhibit 1*.)

In spite of stringent regulatory restrictions on motor-carrier rates and routes in the United States, by participating in repeated legal battles to obtain certificates of "public convenience and necessity," UPS had expanded its service to all 50 states, covering them fully or in part, by 1980. With the passage of the Motor Carrier Act of 1980, which deregulated the entire trucking industry, geographical restrictions were lifted and UPS was able to provide service to any point throughout all 48 contiguous states. As regulatory barriers vanished, other natural barriers like economies of scale, infrastructure, service recognition, and specialized skills took their place.

By this time, UPS had embarked on a strategy of diversification. As competition intensified with deregulation, UPS allocated large amounts of capital to modernize an antiquated data processing department. Beginning in 1976, it planned an aggressive international expansion. In 1982 it introduced Next Day Air Service in the United States. By 1987 it owned 89 aircraft, leased 140, and had 13 Boeing 757 jets—the most cost-efficient package freighters on the market—under construction. By 1987 UPS offered service to Canada, 16 European countries, and Japan. Foreign freight carriers, initially used for transporting packages from the planes to final destination points in foreign countries, became "service partners," or jointly run companies set up to participate in a full package delivery service, in 1986.

By 1987 UPS was the largest transportation company and the largest air freight carrier in the world. Jim Casey, who continued to come to the office regularly until just before his death in 1981, lived to see this ambitious dream come true.

THE INDUSTRY AFTER DEREGULATION

Deregulation, the competition it spawned, and the rapid growth of the overnight package delivery service by air were important characteristics of the package freight and document transportation business in the early 1980s. The deregulation of the airline industry in 1978 had a significant impact on three major groups in the package delivery business: common carriers specializing in small package delivery on the ground, air freight forwarders, and existing air express carriers. Prior to deregulation, long-distance common carriers like UPS were unable to own or operate private aircraft without subjecting themselves to the profit and pricing controls by the Civil Aeronautics Board (CAB). Instead they used passenger and freighter aircraft (operated by carriers such as United Airlines and Flying Tigers) to satisfy their air transportation needs. The second group— air freight forwarders (such as Airborne Freight)—were companies that assumed responsibility for the local freight pickup and delivery of freight to be transported on either commercial or freighter aircraft owned by others. After deregulation, many common carriers and forwarders purchased their own fleets and became integrated air carriers, offering a complete solution to a customer's express delivery needs. Owning their aircraft allowed the companies better control over service and costs associated with air delivery—something one competitor, the Federal Express Corporation, had been doing for several years as the nation's only major air express carrier. Deregulation of freight transport by air brought about by legislation, sometimes referred to as the "Federal Express Bill," assisted Federal Express by enabling it to increase substantially its package volume and revenues. To avoid CAB controls on all aircraft with total weight of over 7,500 pounds, Federal had transported all of its freight on small, inefficient Dassault Falcons (converted executive jets) with cargo space of only 6,200 pounds. By 1976, the company was sending as many as six Falcons a night to one city and spending $25,000 a day more than it would with larger planes. With deregulation, it immediately purchased 10 second-hand Boeing 727s and increased its service to 300 cities. Accordingly, its daily package volume immediately increased by 34%.

Deregulation allowed UPS to service parcels up to 100 pounds. However, the company continued to restrict itself to a 70-pound limit. Because UPS had been run as an efficient operation during regulatory days, it was not underpriced by the influx of new entrants penetrating the market with lower operating costs and nonunion labor. However, with the threat of competition more apparent than in previous years, UPS began to fine-tune its operations, decreasing its costs and increasing its productivity. Management appropriated substantial funds for the Information Services department to develop new technologies that would enhance its customer service and keep the company in step with increased competition. Residential and business customers demanded that carriers have fast and reliable service, low rates, effective package-tracking capabilities, and computerized documentation and billing of letters and parcels. UPS, although deficient in some of these capabilities, remained the leading carrier on the ground, with the U.S. Postal Service posing the only major threat.

U.S. Postal Service

For years, UPS's major competitor had been the U.S. Postal Service's (USPS) fourth-class parcel post. On a number of occasions over the years, UPS executives had argued that income from the USPS's large ($20 billion in 1986) first-class (letter) service was used to subsidize the price of its parcel post service below true costs. Nevertheless, careful attention to service and cost-reducing ideas had enabled UPS to overtake slowly the USPS's parcel post in volume early in the 1970s. By 1986, USPS reported an average daily volume in its parcel post service of about 2.3 million packages per day, compared with UPS's 8.3 million packages per day.

The USPS also competed in the air with its Express Mail service. From a volume of 7.7 million pieces in 1978, this service had grown to 40 million pieces in 1986. Most of these consisted of documents or very small items that could fit into an envelope.

In the early 1980s, the USPS had implemented many changes in its marketing and operating strategy that threatened UPS's leadership in surface small-package shipments. In 1986 Preston Tisch took over as Postmaster. With a strong background in marketing, he aspired to change the USPS image by emphasizing customer service. The USPS also was making a concentrated effort to compete in the delivery of low-weight packages traveling short distances by offering reduced rates and expedited service. This service was also the fastest-growing segment of UPS's business.

Federal Express

Incorporated in 1971 by Frederick Smith, Jr., as an air freight business specializing in the overnight delivery of small packages, Federal Express nearly went bankrupt before making its first profit of $3.6 million in 1976. Emulating the UPS hub concept by creating one hub in Memphis to serve the entire United States, Fred Smith emphasized technology as an important element in his company's strategy. As a reflection of his interests, he was a member of the Advisory Committee to the National Academy of Engineering on technology in the service industries. In 1979 he created an Advanced Technology Center in Colorado Springs, Colorado, and by 1986 employed 95 information technology professionals in his organization.

This group had developed the COSMOS, ZODIAC, and DADS hardware and software systems for scheduling, tracking, and sorting packages and documents rapidly and accurately. The COSMOS system was used in receiving and scheduling pickup requests at regional offices where technology and staffing combined to produce adherence to standards such as answering customer calls on the first ring. Packages and documents were bar-coded for identification and tracking purposes. Individual Federal Express couriers were assigned trucks with DADS terminals. A driver, using a hand-held Supertracker optical reader, recorded pickup times and package numbers. The reader, when plugged into the DADS unit in the truck, communicated package status to a regional customer service facility. This information, combined with the ZODIAC system used in the hub for sorting by labels and positioning for reshipment to destination, provided comprehensive package tracking and control from the scheduling of a pickup to delivery. It was described by one senior manager in the company as "the absolute bedrock of this company's success." The company had not been consistently successful with new technology, taking a reported $190 million after-tax write-off late in 1986 with the discontinuance of its electronic ZAPMAIL service. However, in 1986, Federal Express was handling about 537,000 packages and documents per day, realizing revenues for the fiscal year of more than $2.6 billion. Net income was $132 million, a 74% increase from the previous year.

Other Competitors

Airborne Freight, Inc., a traditional freight forwarder, had made a total commitment to the domestic and international package express market. It owned 33 aircraft and leased 43. In 1986 its express service handled 105,000 pieces per day, had revenues of $542 million, earned a net income of $13 million, and was the country's fourth-largest express service. Its future plans included targeting the high-volume corporate user, expanding its sales force by 10% to 12%, and increasing the number of locations served with morning deliveries.

Emery Air Freight at one time had been the leading air freight forwarder in the United States. The company began its express service in 1978 with later pickup times and lower rates than Federal Express. However, by 1986, Emery lagged far behind Federal, UPS, Airborne, and Express Mail services. Its volume reached only 42,000 pieces per day.

Purolator's specialty was in ground package delivery. Purolator's volume of next-day letters and packages in 1986 of 68,000 pieces per day was slightly larger than Emery's. However, Purolator realized less revenue and a larger loss than Emery in 1986. In 1987 the two firms merged, gaining 12% of the total one-day air express market.

In March 1985, Roadway Package Systems (RPS) began operations in 18 midwest and northeast states, with terminals in 33 cities and hubs in 3 other locations. A subsidiary of Roadway Services, Inc. (RSI), which included one of the largest over-the-road trucking businesses in the United States, RPS had become a potential threat to UPS, with a goal of capturing 10% of the small-package market through business-to-business delivery service of small packages up to 100 pounds. Its parent company had a presence in 31 states, operating 83 terminals and 9 hubs. In 1986 RSI's revenues were $1.7 billion, and net income was $16 million. It was anticipated that by the end of 1987 RPS could have a volume of 257,000 packages per day.

One particularly attractive feature about RPS was its sophisticated billing and package tracking system. A shipper could call a toll-free number at any time to find out the location of a package. UPS did not yet offer this service. The immensity of the UPS ground network and the vast amount of computer memory needed to track the 2.3 billion packages it delivered in 1986 were given as reasons. Industry sources suggested that, despite its technological innovation, RPS's operations were marked by relatively high rates of damage, lost packages, and less efficient sorting. In 1986, however, UPS estimated that it lost several thousand packages per day to RPS. In 1987 industry sources predicted that RPS's daily volume would increase from about 3% of that of UPS to more than 7% by 1991.

In contrast to the fact that UPS was clearly a giant on the ground in the early 1980s, it was a mere fledgling in the air. It began its overnight service four years after most of the competition. This delay set UPS far behind in service and image, forcing its management into a catch-up game for the first few years of its express operations. Although UPS had developed a two-day air service, Blue Label, in 1952, with the exception of ground pickup and delivery, UPS had subcontracted the service to various air carriers. For many years, UPS did not consider overnight air service to be within its mission. However, with the annual growth rates for the air express package market averaging 15% to 20% in the late 1970s, and with the leader of small-package air freight transportation, Federal Express, doubling its profits and nearly tripling its revenues in the few years after deregulation, UPS management realized that air express was no longer a minor market niche.

To accommodate next-day service, UPS had developed a large hub in Louisville, which, by 1983, could accommodate not only the Next Day Air operation but the Second Day Air service as well. By 1985, UPS air service included next-day air letters and packages, second-day packages, and international shipments. Total air volume for 1986 amounted to 84 million packages.

Financial and employment data for major competitors in surface and air package delivery services in 1986 are shown in *Exhibit 2*.

UPS OPERATIONS

Over the years, UPS had pioneered the concept of daily pickup and delivery service to retail and commercial accounts with delivery to all locations, including homes. Because of its relatively low rates and dependable service, retailers and manufacturers alike had come to rely on it for small shipments.

One analysis of the company's operations offered the following conclusions:

> [Among] the main reasons for UPS's strength is its emphasis on building route density [number of packages per stop and customers per route mile], standardizing the job of the route driver to allow for comparison and control, and designing its sorting facilities and transport equipment to handle packages of no more than 108 inches in combined length, width, and height, and 70 pounds in weight. This single-minded approach to a service concept allows UPS to realize substantial profits while often charging its customers as little as half that of its competition.[1]

The core of the UPS service was provided by the package car, package center, feeder truck, and hub. The familiar chocolate brown package car and its driver represented the entire UPS operation to the public. Over the years, the standard car had been designed by the company and manufactured to its specifications.

---

1. James L. Heskett, *Managing in the Service Economy* (Boston: Harvard Business School Press, 1986), p. 71.

Package Car

Most drivers treasured the customer contact. A 45-year-old former marine commented on his feelings about driving a package car:

> I thought this job would be a perfect transition to civilian life but it's been so much fun and the money is so good, I've stayed on. My wife is vice president of an insurance company, but I've got more job security and interesting work than she does. She works with papers and pens and I work with packages and people. A lot of guys with seniority go for feeder driver jobs. It pays a little better and is less physical. But I just love the customers on my route. I would hate to let them go. They count on me and I know all about them. Plus, the physical activity gives me such a good workout, I don't have to join a gym. Those feeder guys gain 50 pounds in just a few months!

Drivers generally worked more autonomously than employees inside the hub. The daily challenge was both physical and mental. The average driver had to deliver or pick up 360 packages per day regardless of any unanticipated problems. Drivers were held strictly accountable for every package in their cars. They were given a complete instruction booklet on "Package Delivery and Pickup Methods" and five days of one-on-one training. The booklet contained 31 detailed instructions on how to best perform the job from start to finish. It included turning on the delivery car's engine at the start of the day, ways to greet the customers during the day, and the final check-in procedure at the end of the day. Drivers had to determine for themselves how to handle abnormalities such as late starts due to delayed package center operations, adverse weather conditions, flat tires, or accidents.

UPS maintained a precise and comprehensive system of measuring performance by route. For this reason, little personal supervision of car drivers was required once the initial training was completed.

Package Center

A package center was the basic unit of UPS's operations. Through package centers and a deliberate process of decentralization, UPS was able to maintain personal contact with every individual residing at an address anywhere across the United States and in many foreign countries.

At UPS's 1,200 package centers, packages were shifted from cars to feeder trucks for line-haul transport to one or more of the company's 120 hubs at U.S. and foreign locations.

Although centers varied in size according to the district in which they were located, their operations were the same. At each center, packages received from hubs in feeders were unloaded and loaded onto package cars at night, ready for delivery the following morning. When package cars returned from their routes to the centers in the evening, part-time hourly employees unloaded the packages, placed them on sort belts, and reloaded them onto feeders that transported them back to hubs and on to their final destination points.

Because of limited car-driver openings, only 10% to 15% of part-timers hired into the package center were eventually promoted into driving positions. To uphold its agreement with the Teamsters, for every three full-time driving positions, UPS filled two slots with people promoted from the hub and one with someone from outside the firm.

One could become a center manager usually only after he or she had driven a package car and held a full-time supervisor's position. Two full-time supervisors reported to a center manager, and three or four center managers reported to a division manager. In addition, delivery supervisors were employed at each center to perform "service checks" by accompanying drivers when they were delivering, observing and reinforcing safety guidelines, emphasizing techniques outlined by the prescribed job methods, and providing on-the-job training for all new drivers.

Full-time supervisors were considered first-level "partners" in the company, eligible for the management-incentive stock plan. By 1986, there were 15,600 such partners throughout the company supervising another 152,600 employees.

Hub

The hub operation, although based on a simple concept of central unload, sort, and load, required complex and sophisticated coordination. Depending on its size, the hub had either two or three sort shifts that took place at noon (12 noon to 3 P.M.), twilight (5 P.M. to 8 P.M.), and midnight (11 P.M. to 2 A.M.). The completion of each task during a sort and adherence to service standards depended on the successful completion of the prior sort. The hub facility embodied a fantastic maze of incoming and outgoing belts and chutes, all directing packages that were brought to the hub by large tractor-trailer trucks (feeders). Packages were manually unloaded from feeders and placed on various belts that led to outbound stations. The packages at each station were going to the same geographic area and were again loaded onto outbound feeders. The pace of work at a hub was furious during a sort. (Employment data and the volume of packages handled through each of three hubs on the UPS system are shown in *Exhibit 3*.)

New hires were interviewed and selected by the personnel department on criteria such as independence, flexibility, physical fitness, and reliability. Ninety-five percent were students, recruited from local colleges. The department tried to employ the same percentage of white males, females, and minorities that lived in the community. Most new hires started as part-timers inside the hub or as drivers. They were generally drawn to UPS for the supplementary income. Later, after recognizing the extensive opportunity to move into management or specialized areas like engineering or data programming, many decided to make UPS their career. (Lengths of service for UPS employees are shown in *Exhibit 4.*)

New hub operations were brought up to speed with the help of a team of visiting training managers and supervisors from various districts around the country. They typically stayed for 8 to 12 weeks to help the new hub and its management in its initial development. The program they provided offered both formal training and an informal process of role modeling in which the old (and most successful) demonstrated to the new the attitudes and standards that represented a common thread throughout the organization.

POLICIES AND ORGANIZATION

Policies concerning employee ownership, decentralization, communication, managerial development, the unpretentiousness of its facilities, and its emphasis on customer service were particularly representative of the UPS culture. They are set forth in *The Policy Book,* examples from which are presented in *Exhibit 1.*

Employee Ownership

UPS, a private company, offered no stock to the public. A unique profit-sharing and stock-ownership plan caused many UPS employees to consider their UPS employment a lifelong commitment. The plan was designed so that in profitable years all UPS employees shared in the company's profits, earning far more than they would from a normal salary. Jim Casey said in 1922 when 50 UPSers joined him in ownership:

> There is no bigger incentive than for someone to work for himself. . . . The basic principle which I believe has contributed to the building of our business as it exists today is the ownership of our company by the people employed in it.

Although people at the full-time supervisory level and in upper management were considered partners or owners of the company, everyone was entitled to participate in at least one of the employment benefit plans. There were three main profit-sharing plans at UPS: a Thrift Plan for all regular employees who had completed at least one year of service; the UPS Management Incentive Plan, for full-time managers only; and the Stock Option Plans for the roughly 1,200 employees holding positions equal to or above the division manager level.

UPS also offered a package of benefits designed to provide long-term financial security and immediate health care services for all employees. Both the retirement and health care plans were noncontributory for all employees who met minimum age and service requirements. The plans were designed to reflect the changes in the economy due to inflation. All employees, part- and full-time, were provided with health and retirement benefits. Dale Orred, the national benefits manager, commented about the UPS commitment to give its part-time employees the same medical benefits as full-timers: "We can't think of a better way to spend our money. We don't look upon it as an excess, nor should they [part-timers] see it as an entitlement. It is part of our management philosophy."

In a 1985 opinion survey given to a sample of 16,039 district employees, the majority of workers selected "good pay and benefits" as the most important job attribute at UPS. The president of Teamsters Local 804 in Long Island City, New York, was quoted as saying that "if UPS announced it had 1,000 openings for drivers tomorrow, there would be 100,000 applicants."[2]

Decentralization

UPS emphasized decentralization. The operating organization was divided into regions, districts, divisions, and operating areas.

The district was considered the basic unit of the delivery operation. A district could be part or all of a metropolitan area, state, or several states. The district manager and staff formed a complete operating group with full responsibility for service and cost within the district. In 1986 UPS operations were divided into 70 districts in the United States.

Regional management and staff provided services to all districts in their respective regions and arranged for an exchange of information among districts. Headquarters management performed a coordinating function on operational matters and provided certain services, such as finance and real estate, not available in the regions and districts themselves.

Charts of the UPS corporate and operations organizations are shown in *Exhibits 5* and *6*.

---

2. "Behind the UPS Mystique: Puritanism and Productivity," *Business Week*, June 6, 1983, p. 68.

Communication

In line with the partnership philosophy was an emphasis on corporatewide communication. Believing that every department was entitled to know the activities of the others, UPS's management designed tools to help build a network that would facilitate communication. A publication called *The Big Idea* was produced and distributed within every district to inform employees about national and local UPS news. Weekly Monday meetings were held at the company's headquarters in Greenwich, Connecticut, where representatives from each department gathered to meet with the top management committee. Each representative reported on his or her department's previous week's accomplishments and the following week's objectives. Issues like safety, employee recognition, new programs and policies, technology, customer priority, assignment changes, and training programs were reviewed. Minutes were taken during the meeting and then disseminated to the 15,600 managers at UPS. Each spring, a conference involving the top 200 managers in the company was held. Discussion about future strategic plans and present organizational accomplishments occurred during this annual conference. Managers from various regions and districts exchanged information, forged common objectives, and communicated best and worst performances and technological innovations. Upon returning to their districts and departments, the district managers presented a summary of the issues discussed at the conference to a more immediate group of managers in a modified, day-long presentation that usually included a lunch or dinner.

In addition to the interaction between departments and districts, significant emphasis was placed on communication within areas. Standard methods such as performance appraisals and opinion surveys were used to communicate opinions and performance levels in specified task areas. For verbal communication, districts held Pre-work Communication Meetings (PCMs). A PCM was a three-minute meeting held prior to the start of every work day in the hub or package center to discuss either specific questions about work tasks or larger issues involving competition and strategic direction. Either the immediate supervisor or a representative from a staff function such as customer service or safety would attend a driver or sort PCM and speak about a related issue concerning that operation. Customer service representatives alone gave over 50,000 PCMs a year. For more personal, one-on-one communication, a managerial tool called the "Talk, Listen, Act" (TLA) program was used to encourage closer coordination and interaction between managers, supervisors, package handlers, and drivers. A TLA was a scheduled meeting that gave employees protected time to express concerns, make suggestions, or simply establish more informal relationships with their managers. TLA meetings were required and monitored by the company for each employee and his or her immediate manager.

Internal Development of Employees

Through the dedication to its promotion-from-within policy, effective training schools, on-the-job training, and role modeling, the company had succeeded in preparing some of its most junior workers for top-level positions. However, because it had many more part-time employees than available full-time positions, it could promote only a small percentage of its part-time supervisors into full-time delivery jobs, the next step in the career track. Out of a total of 54,350 driving positions in 1986, 25% to 30% were filled by part-time promotions. Drivers then had the opportunity to move into full-time supervision and become eligible for ownership in the company. From the full-time supervisory level, an employee usually was transferred laterally for exposure to support roles and other functions of the company before moving up the vertical path. Paul Oberkotter, the former chief executive officer, commented on the benefits of internal development:

> It's an intangible sort of thing. Everything we do to develop managers is in support of it. Individuals learn to get along and manage through personal influence and credibility of experience rather than through title and coercion. For example, we tracked Jack Rogers through 50 different types of permanent assignments and short-term projects. We saw his strengths grow and the areas where he needed work. Over time he became known throughout the organization. No one was frightened when he was named chief executive officer. He could make substantial changes in this business without worrying people about their security or the continuation of the culture. He was not an untried personality. He had broad knowledge, experience, and UPS commitment.

Although UPS had always been a people-oriented company, the forceful management practices once common in many industries had often surfaced in first-line supervision. Top management had been explicitly working to close any lingering gaps between the long-held management philosophy of cooperation and actual supervisory practice. One training manager who had been with UPS 17 years commented:

> The management style of UPS has changed. The mystique of the organization has not. The mystique is the belief that everyone who makes it at UPS must give 100% effort. The management style and method for motivating employees is different now. We use people policies, based on integrity and fairness, not force. At times we used to inject brown blood with a two-by-four. Now we do it through osmosis. I personally try to understand every individual I supervise and know what makes that person tick.

As UPS reached out to a new generation of workers with different needs and multiple employment opportunities, this new approach became more important. Instilling the "people policies" became a challenge for the 1980s. Structure and accountability were emphasized but now were sweetened with recognition, reward, and daily encouragement for a job well done.

Humility: A Company Ethic

Certain other aspects about UPS, however, had not changed. Over an 80-year period, the organization had retained a humility that was perhaps best reflected in the physical appearance of its facilities and by the attitude of its top executives. The buildings were stark, contemporary, and simple. UPSers scrupulously emphasized cleanliness and also discouraged elaborate decor. Chairs and tables were functional. Walls, if not barren, displayed folksy, Norman Rockwell-type images of UPS package cars serving small communities. Carpets, where they existed, were thin and laid for the convenience of cleaning, not comfort. Offices were comparably sized. Parking spaces were available on strictly a first-come, first-served basis. The parking lot was filled with conservative, mid-sized cars. People who drove flashy sports cars were subject to peer teasing. No one at UPS had his or her own secretary, including the CEO. All executives answered their own telephones. Executives did their own photocopying, travel arrangements, and scheduling. Even the board of directors shared the same conference room used for managers' or supervisors' meetings. There was no executive dining room in the national, regional, or district headquarters. Instead, UPS provided a cheerful cafeteria where anyone from a clerk to a programmer to a senior manager could enjoy a morning or mid-day meal.

Customer Service

An entire section of *The Policy Book* was devoted to the company's service. It stressed such things as quality, low and uniform prices for all shippers (large and small alike), uniformity of service over wide geographical areas, and assistance to customers in improving their procedures.

Stories told at management gatherings often highlighted customer service. The following is typical:

> A few days before Christmas, a railroad official called the Chicago office of United Parcel Service and confessed that a flatcar carrying two UPS trailers had unaccountably been left on a siding in the middle of Illinois. UPS is no Santa Claus, but it tries its best to deliver Christmas packages on time. So

the regional manager paid for a high-speed diesel that whipped the flatcar into Chicago ahead of an Amtrak passenger train, and he ordered two of UPS's fleet of 24 Boeing 727s diverted to Chicago to get the contents of the trailers to their destinations in Florida and Louisiana in time for Christmas. In spite of the extraordinary expense, the manager neither asked permission nor even informed UPS headquarters in Greenwich, Connecticut, until weeks later.

"We applauded it when we heard about it," said Oz Nelson, then UPS vice president for customer service. "We give these guys complete authority to run their operations and do their jobs. We push decision making down to the lowest possible levels."[3]

INFORMATION SERVICES

The Information Services department, called Data Processing until 1985, was created in 1971 and operated out of the UPS facility on Forty-third Street in Manhattan for five years. It was made up of a small group of UPS mavericks. For many years, however, the high-spirited group was unable to exert influence over any function within the company other than accounting. With neither financial nor moral support from the national headquarters in Greenwich, Connecticut, the department suffered from what Jay Walsh, one of the original engineers in the group, called "a classic case of corporate neglect." The rest of UPS considered their data processing jobs "cushy," not understanding exactly what they entailed, but concluding that if it didn't require any physical exertion, it couldn't be that difficult. One driver in the Meadowlands commented, "No one has a cake job at UPS, except perhaps the people sitting behind those computers, pushing the keys or . . . doing whatever they do."

Data Processing was operating with poor equipment and providing poor service and was rapidly falling behind the competition in technological and data programming capabilities. The department remained quite small and reclusive until 1981, when the threat of technologically more advanced competition suddenly brought it into the spotlight.

With the onslaught of Federal Express and RPS, most UPSers realized that to remain the dominant carrier in the package delivery service they would have to join their competitors in the age of computer technology. Although UPS had the most extensive ground network, it had fallen behind in certain technological innovations such as package scanning, radio-dispatched pickups, package tracking, and data-acquisition devices.

3. Ibid., p. 66.

UPS could either go outside the company to fulfill its technological needs or it could develop a system internally. In keeping with the belief that if "given the proper tools, our people could do anything," it chose the latter. For the Data Processing department, it was like winning a lottery.

Funds were not the only thing that the group was given. The department was given organizational respect and the task of developing and implementing systems that would significantly affect the operations of every department within the company. Its collective mission was "to provide management with the information it needs to meet the company's goals in a responsive manner and at a reasonable cost." The department's name was changed to Information Services (IS).

In 1976 the department had moved into a larger building in Paramus, New Jersey. From 1976 to 1986, the IS capital expenditures grew tenfold. In 1987 its mainframe processed about 450,000 transactions per day and served almost every department. It had concentrated on designing operations-oriented systems, but plans were to begin work on more service-oriented projects in 1988. Some of the major projects completed by mid–1987 included a trailer- and package-tracking system, an automated customer service telephone center, a plant engineering maintenance system, electronic call tag, and on-line billing and invoicing.

Since 1985, the department had experienced particularly rapid growth. The number of on-line terminals directly connected to the central computer had grown from 685 to an expected 3,000 by the end of 1987, with 15,000 projected by the end of 1991. In 1985 UPS had 700 personal computers in operation. In 1986 that number jumped to 4,000, and the department completed 269 projects for specific district needs.

To immediately staff the entire operation with people who had grown up with UPS and understood its needs and priorities but who were also specialists in computer science was impossible. These people did not exist. The training that workers received in the hubs did not give them the technical skills necessary to "get the job done" in Paramus. Therefore, management had to make a choice. It could either hire people from within UPS, send them to a school to acquire the necessary skills, and delay service for a few years until these people were qualified, or it could hire people from outside organizations and try to mold them into UPSers.

Rino Bergonzi, the systems and operations manager who held one of the most senior positions ever given to an outside hire in the company's history, commented on the necessity of addressing this change:

> IS inside of UPS has been weak. Skills are lower than we need, and there is a tremendous need for recruiting. There has not been much specialization. We'd like our people to learn many different skills. Some are now overwhelmed. They didn't possess great technical expertise nor did they have

strong contacts even within UPS. We are going to continue a lot of recruiting, building, and training. . . . Turnover may go up as we grow.

Department managers within IS sent out notices to the districts, informing them of their staffing needs and asking them to have interested workers take an aptitude test in engineering. If these people did well, they would go to Paramus for an interview and would usually be hired. All transfers, starting in Paramus in an entry-level position, were immediately sent outside to the Chubb School in New Jersey for a 10-week training session—a slow and costly process. Even after they graduated from the school, they were qualified for only junior positions and still required substantial guidance.

Although the need to hire people from the outside was recognized as a necessity by most employees at UPS, it was not completely accepted. People in the district felt that because these "outsiders" had not been exposed to operations (hub and package centers), they could not understand or appreciate the UPS service. In fact, many UPSers from "the districts" viewed the entire Paramus facility as a "different" and certainly less desirable environment in which to work. One 35-year-old customer service area manager commented:

> I was over in Paramus on special assignment last year. It was very different. It's not like the districts at all. I don't think we are doing a very good job of making them a part of the rest of UPS. UPS is one of the most efficiently run companies around. Why should IS want to be any different?

Employees at Paramus received mixed signals about what would be expected of them, how "outsiders" fit in, and what to expect in the way of career development. A 24-year-old systems programmer, who was promoted from the district, said, "I am motivated by an opportunity to excel, to move into a higher level of management or a senior engineering position. Yet, no one is quite sure in IS what steps you must take to obtain those positions." Another programmer about the same age, coming from the South Ohio district where he was a part-time preloader while going to college, commented about the different cultures in Paramus and in the district, "The managers in Paramus don't define the tasks as clearly. They often set deadlines for projects that are unrealistic. It's frustrating because they often don't realize how much time the job requires."

The IS department had done some experimental hiring of people from outside directly into UPS. It had set up a curriculum of entry and development programs to aid the assimilation process of an IS employee. The agenda encompassed the recruitment, interviewing, and selection processes and included an orientation, a training program, and a special two-week "district experience" for those who had not worked in a hub or package center. For recruiting purposes the personnel department drew up a profile of a "most desirable candidate." Gary Lee, a manager for the personnel department, described that candidate: technically qualified, career-minded, mature, professional, hands-on, results-oriented, and adaptable to the culture.

Jim Segrue, another personnel manager for Paramus, explained how he selected people from outside UPS: "First, I take them on a short walk to see if they can 'maintain driver pace.' Then, when we begin talking, I note whether this person can hold eye contact. Is he or she healthy, intelligent, emotionally stable, and accustomed to working hard?" If the person was technically qualified and the first interview went well, the person was invited to return for a second interview. Over the course of both interviews, the person was informed about the standards, expectations, and benefits of working for UPS. Segrue further explained: "I tell them that we can offer lifetime employment and that we like to promote from within. Yet, I also inform them about our long hours, no-beard policy, and other standards we uphold as a company."

Some were scared off by the stringent policies, such as no coffee at desks, two 15-minute breaks during the working day, and no beards or long mustaches. Many also expressed concern about the necessity of working long hours and on Saturdays. One systems manager, recently hired from Western Union, commented about the coffee and break policy:

> They shouldn't try to run an IS environment like a hub. . . . We should absolutely be allowed to have coffee at our desks. Instead, every day at 3:30 P.M. this place looks like a factory on break! Everyone jumps up from their chairs and goes to the cafeteria to socialize and drink coffee.

Other employees, after hearing in their interviews and reading in the policy book that promotion-from-within was one of the most honored UPS policies, were confused and disappointed when they saw outside hires being placed in positions they thought they were being trained for. Some felt they had been misled. One entry-level programmer commented, "It's frustrating that management is not following the promotion-from-within policy. I understand that people with greater expertise are needed, but I wish they would have told us the real policy during orientation."

Many new hires from the outside were pleased with the culture. One of the first, who was hired in October 1985, commented:

> I came to UPS because I liked its values and the work ethic. When the people who interviewed me told me about the low turnover, I knew the company was doing something right. My impressions were right. There is an incredible amount of trust and cooperation among people. That's what I was looking for after the bad experience I had with my last job.

The orientation program for these outside hires had been different than the one for internal recruits. The new hire from the district usually attended a special school beforehand for 10 weeks of technical training. The outsider was usually hired with the expertise necessary to begin working right away. In place of technical training, the outside hire had a three-day orientation program and spent two weeks in a district with a driver. One programmer from the outside who had not yet participated in the district experience said, "I can't wait to see the guts and gore of this operation and finally understand what all of these old guys are really talking about. Yet, I would think you could only unload a truck for so long before you lose your mind!"

Valerie Monte, an employment manager at the Meadowlands hub, reflected upon her experience as an on-car supervisor and hostess for the visitors from Paramus: "At first we didn't like the idea of this district experience. We didn't feel like babysitting the technical part of the company during our peak season. But, much to our surprise, those people really dug in and helped us out. We gained a lot of respect for them and I know they respected us too. Later that month, we invited them all back and gave them awards for outstanding participation."

THE BIGGER QUESTION

Jack Rogers and other members of the top management group at UPS knew the issue of outside hires was not confined to Information Services. A rapidly growing air business confronted the company with a similar issue, although much of the growth had been accomplished to date by contracting air services from suppliers. If UPS were to acquire another firm, it would have to confront the issue of outsiders head-on. For several members of the group, the issue was not whether but how to approach the assimilation process.

Exhibit 1
Excerpts from the UPS Policy Book

When the words "we," "us," and "our" are used in this book, we should keep in mind that they are intended to include all the people in the company, as well as the company itself. This is true for the reason that the policies apply to all. . . .

Please note that neither the policy's summary statement nor its explanation spells out *how* a policy is to be carried out. This Policy Book is not a "how-to-do-it" manual. . . .

Our objectives are as follows:

- To fulfill a useful economic purpose—satisfying the need for prompt, dependable delivery of small packages, serving all shippers and receivers wherever they may be located within our service areas—with the best possible service at the lowest possible cost to the public.

- To maintain a strong, forward-looking, efficient, and cooperative organization which will be ever mindful of the well-being of our people and enable them to develop their individual capabilities.

- To keep the ownership and control of our company in the hands of its managers and supervisors—to build an organization of people who think and act as partners rather than as "hired hands."

- To maintain a financially strong company earning a reasonable profit—which is the only way we can provide security for the members of our organization, continue to provide quality service for our customers, and reward our shareowners with dividends and increases in value of the shares in which their money is invested.

- To develop additional profitable businesses which complement our efforts to maintain a financially strong company.

- To be alert to changing conditions and ready at all times to adjust our viewpoints and operations to meet them.

- To earn and preserve a reputation as a company whose well-being is in the public interest and whose people are respected for their performance, character, and integrity.

- To establish and maintain a high standard of excellence in everything we do.

POLICY GROUP I

Our Company and Organization
[*The following are two of twenty-five policies in this policy group.*]

We function as partners. Although we are organized in corporate form, we function as partners in our working relationships with each other and we make our management decisions as partners.

Exhibit 1
(Continued)

Consolidated parcel delivery is our main business. Our long experience in this specialized field helps us provide better service and greater economy for our customers and fill a need that could not be satisfied in any other way.

We use our management and technical skills to help us develop other businesses. The aim of these diversification activities is to complement our efforts to maintain a financially strong company. Our entry into other businesses does not lessen our concentration on consolidated parcel delivery.

POLICY GROUP II

Our People
[The following are two of thirty-one policies in this policy group.]

We promote from within. Whenever possible, we fill managerial positions from our ranks. In doing so we take care to include for consideration and not overlook qualified people whose present job may make them less noticeable than other employees. We fill a vacancy from the outside only when we cannot locate one of our own people who has the capacity or the professional or technical skills which may be required by a particular assignment.

We strive to be considerate and understanding of our people. In supervision we try to lead, not drive; request, not command.

We believe that when this attitude prevails it helps us gain the cooperation of everyone to work more efficiently and attain higher standards in everything we do.

POLICY GROUP III

Our Service
[The following are two of twenty-two policies in this policy group.]

We provide a uniform service. This service is provided in each area for all our customers, large and small alike. We maintain the service standards of high quality and dependability and provide the features of service our experience shows shippers and receivers need and want.

We maintain a dependable delivery service. We make deliveries every delivery day in the entire service area, whether in a large city, small community, or rural area. Severe storms, floods, and other emergencies may occasionally make this impossible, but volume peaks or other operating problems do not excuse service failures.

The dependability of our delivery service is important to our customers and their customers. To assure on-schedule deliveries, we establish controls, conduct audits, and otherwise measure performance in all districts. We regard each service failure as a serious matter.

(Continued)

Exhibit 1
(Continued)

POLICY GROUP IV

Our Character and Reputation
[*The following are two of thirty-one policies in this policy group.*]

We insist upon integrity in our people. We present our company honestly to employees and in turn expect them to be honest with us.

We maintain our vehicles to look like new. We paint and service our vehicles frequently, wash or clean them daily, and repair dents and scratches promptly to prevent them from becoming unsightly.

   All vehicles should leave our buildings in a clean condition.

POLICY GROUP V

Our Economic Stability
[*The following is one of fourteen policies in this policy group.*]

We reinvest earnings to finance our growth. Earnings retained in the business, year after year, have provided the major part of the capital required to finance our continued growth and development.

UNITED PARCEL SERVICE (A)

Exhibit 2

1985–1986 Comparative Data, U.S. Transportation Companies
($ in thousands, except per share data)

Rank^a 1986	1985	Company	Operating Revenues	Rank^b	Assets	Net Income	Rank	Stockholders' Equity	Rank	Employees Number	Rank	Net Income as % of Sales %	Rank	Net Income as % of Stockholders' Equity %	Rank	Earnings per Share 1986/$	1985/$	1976/$
1	5	UAL (Elk Grove, Ill.)	$9,196,233	6	$8,716,517	$11,600	26	$2,292,610	8	87,000	2	0.1	35	0.5	34	0.25	(2.09)	0.75
2	2	United Parcel Service of America (Greenwich, Conn.)^b	8,619,703	9	4,801,133	668,966	1	2,469,798	7	168,200	1	7.8	6	27.1	2	3.96	3.36	N.A.
3	1	Burlington Northern (Seattle)	6,941,413	4	10,650,956	(860,485)	50	3,534,314	4	44,200	7					(12.07)	8.03	1.42
4	3	Union Pacific (New York)	6,688,000	3	10,863,000	(460,000)	48	3,408,000	5	32,700	12					(4.56)	4.18	2.09
5	3	CSX (Richmond)	6,345,000	1	12,661,000	418,000	3	4,873,000	3	48,000	6	6.6	7	8.3	25	2.73	(0.78)	1.44
6	6	AMR (Fort Worth)	6,018,175	8	7,527,969	279,132	4	2,484,896	6	54,300	4	4.6	11	11.0	15	4.63	5.94	1.97
7	4	Santa Fe Southern Pacific (Chicago)	5,801,600	2	11,601,800	(137,900)	45	5,040,300	2	53,423	5					(0.84)	2.67	1.27
8	8	Delta Air Lines (Atlanta)	4,460,062	11	3,785,462	47,286	16	1,301,946	9	38,901	8	1.1	29	3.6	30	1.18	6.50	1.76
9	14	Texas Air (Houston)	4,406,897	7	8,194,611	72,703	11	803,869	13	68,000	3	1.7	25	9.0	24	1.75	5.03	0.66
10	9	Norfolk Southern (Norfolk, Va.)	4,076,407	5	9,752,445	518,688	2	5,070,751	1	38,297	9	12.7	2	10.2	18	2.74	2.65	1.40
11	12	NWA (Eagan, Pa.)	3,589,174	10	4,322,854	76,941	9	1,105,916	10	33,427	11	2.1	23	7.0	26	3.26	3.18	2.39
12	10	Trans World Airlines (New York)	3,145,429	12	3,369,869	(106,328)	44	241,362	28	27,442	13					(3.87)	(6.10)	N.A.
13	11	Pan Am (New York)	3,038,995	15	2,107,539	(462,814)	49	8,763	48	21,500	17					(3.42)	0.45	2.24
14	13	Federal Express (Memphis)	2,606,210	13	2,276,362	131,839	5	1,091,714	11	33,988	10	5.1	10	12.1	12	2.64	1.61	N.A.
15	15	Consolidated Freightways (Palo Alto, Calif.)	2,124,467	20	1,275,440	89,109	8	655,048	16	24,600	14	4.2	14	13.6	10	2.31	3.10	1.56

(Continued)

UNITED PARCEL SERVICE (A)

Exhibit 2

(Continued)

Rank 1986	1985	Company	Operating Revenues	Assets	Rank[b]	Net Income	Rank	Stockholders' Equity	Rank	Employees Number	Rank	Net Income as % of				Earnings per Share		
												Sales %	Rank	Stockholders' Equity %	Rank	1986/$	1985/$	1976/$
16	21	Piedmont Aviation (Winston-Salem, N.C.)	1,865,473	1,717,650	16	72,363	12	783,888	14	20,798	18	3.9	16	9.2	23	3.48	3.89	1.22
17	16	USAir Group (Arlington, Va.)	1,835,199	2,147,081	14	98,352	6	1,057,953	12	14,976	21	5.4	9	9.3	22	3.34	4.05	2.19
18	20	Yellow Freight System (Overland Park, Kansas)	1,731,731	862,359	30	69,719	13	376,370	22	23,500	16	4.0	15	18.5	4	2.44	1.95	1.19
19	19	Roadway Services (Akron)	1,717,491	1,070,659	25	76,466	10	654,235	17	23,500	15	4.5	13	11.7	14	1.91	1.90	1.05
20	22	Leaseway Transportation (Beachwood, Ohio)	1,484,669	916,394	28	50,791	14	269,890	26	20,000	19	3.4	19	18.8	3	2.55	5.29	2.31
21	26	American President Cos. (Oakland)	1,466,714	1,343,304	19	17,956	22	640,562	18	3,970	38	1.2	28	2.8	32	0.71	1.86	2.61
22	27	Tiger International (Los Angeles)	1,110,948	883,457	29	45,063	42	(43,160)	50	6,200	27					(1.45)	(2.69)	1.61
23	32	CNW (Chicago)	959,490	1,691	50	43,040	17	397,275	21	9,500	24	4.5	12	10.8	16	2.31	(1.71)	0.62
24	25	McLean Industries (New York)	896,995	1,569,384	17	(248,773)	47	23,945	46	N.A.	46					N.A.	(1.89)	N.A.
25	35	PS Group (San Diego)	895,423	1,114,006	22	(13,930)	39	212,282	29	5,590	32					(2.25)	3.88	0.86
26	33	Emery Air Freight (Wilton, Conn.)	887,523	449,305	33	(5,440)	37	170,797	31	7,100	26					(0.28)	0.85	1.00
27	34	Purolator Courier (Basking Ridge, N.J.)	841,434	389,773	36	(57,643)	43	121,031	32	19,500	20					(7.54)	(3.86)	1.77
28	36	Southwest Airlines (Dallas)	768,790	1,078,190	24	50,035	15	511,580	20	5,819	31	6.5	8	9.8	21	1.55	1.54	0.37
29	28	Illinois Central Gulf Railroad (Chicago)	715,462	1,546,344	18	(171,674)	46	339,265	24	5,870	30					N.A.	N.A.	N.A.
30	38	Mayflower Group (Carmel, Ind.)	$705,796	$441,517	34	$3,527	31	$29,331	45	2,200	44	0.5	34	12.0	13	N.A.	N.A.	N.A.

SOURCE: "The Service 500," *Fortune*, June 8, 1987, pp. 212–213.

[a] All rankings shown in this exhibit are rankings among the 50 largest transportation firms.

[b] The firms with the largest operating revenues were UAL, Inc., in 1986 and Burlington Northern in 1985. Both, however, owned nontransport businesses.

Exhibit 3
Comparative Data from Three UPS Hubs, 1987

	Whites Creek (Nashville, Tennessee)	Meadowlands (New Jersey)	Chelmsford (Massachusetts)[a]
Capacity (packages per day)	360,000	700,000	800,000
Average daily volume	274,000	500,000	90,000
Number of management and hourly people[b]	643	1,700	350
Pre-seniority turnover[c]	32%	43%	9%
Seniority turnover[d]	22%	45%	13%

[a]The Chelmsford hub had been in operation only a few months.
[b]Full-time and part-time
[c]Proportion of new hires who do not complete the 30-day trial period
[d]Proportion of people (annualized) leaving the company after completing 30-day trial period

Exhibit 4
Selected Employment Information, February 1987

I. Analysis of Work Force by Job

Job	Number of Employees	Percentage of Total
Service workers	4,072	2.4%
Inside clerical	8,749	5.1
Inside manual	62,611	36.3
Package drivers	48,129	27.9
Driver helpers	256	0.0
Feeder drivers	9,861	5.7
Maintenance/mechanics	3,793	2.2
Clerical	11,199	6.5
Supervisors	18,660	10.8
Mid-managers	3,715	2.2
Staff	1,401	0.8
Total	172,446	100.0%

II. Analysis of Total Full-Time Hourly and Management Employees

Years of Service	Number of Employees	Percentage of Total
Up to 5	28,574	35.8%
5–9	20,431	25.0
10–14	13,787	17.0
15–19	12,434	15.0
20–29	4,200	5.0
25–29	1,300	1.6
30 and over	446	.6
Total	81,172	100.0%

UNITED PARCEL SERVICE (A)
Exhibit 5
UPS Corporate Organization Chart

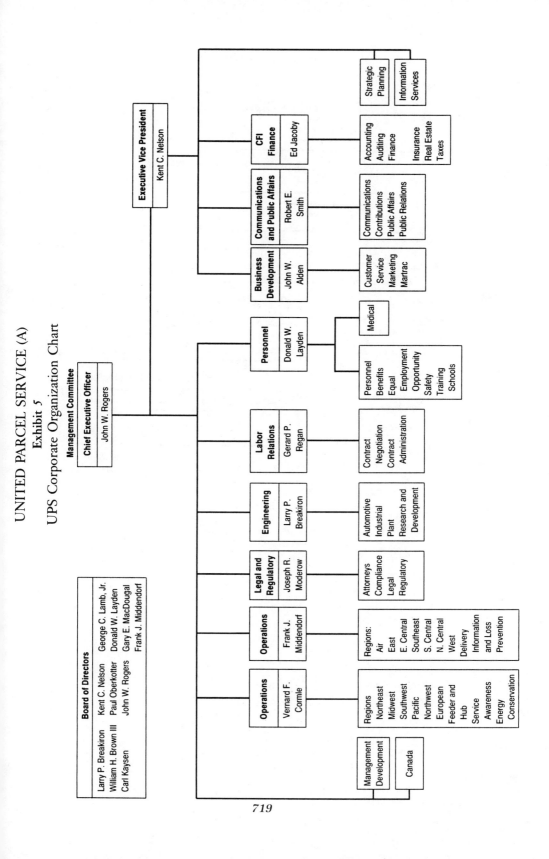

Exhibit 6
UPS Operations Organization Chart

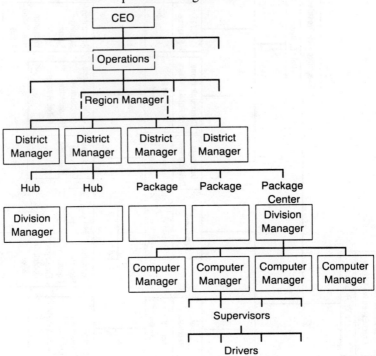

12

$\diamond$

Organizing Work

The way in which work is organized and people recruited, selected, trained, assigned, and rewarded to perform it will depend on the basic service concept of a firm or one of its departments. Decisions concerning these issues as well as the type of people and skills brought into the organization will be influenced heavily by the degree to which the service is to be customized and delivered in contact with customers. Once the degree of service customization and customer contact required in a service concept has been determined, a number of general questions often prove appropriate in analyzing opportunities. They include: What mix of human and technical skills is required in staffing front-line positions in this business? Can or should activities be organized into "front office" and "back office" (service factory) functions? What devices are needed to coordinate marketing and operations activities associated with a customer? Can "internal contracting" between the functions be employed? To what extent can jobs be expanded to keep outstanding service performers organizationally close to customers? To what extent can this same approach be used to "diet" the organization, eliminating both jobs and layers of management? Should front-line personnel be empowered to a greater extent? By what means can this be done while maintaining critical control over an operation? Have middle managers "bought in" to these efforts, perhaps through involvement in their planning? To what degree do structural decisions and the way they are implemented fit into a cohesive internal strategic service vision in which service concept, operating structure, and service delivery system are all aimed at a "target market" comprising employees rather than customers?

As you read David Maister's article, The One-Firm Firm: What Makes It Successful, ask yourself how it fits with the concept of an internal strategic service vision. Why are his examples only drawn from professional service firms? Can Maister's recipe for a strong culture (including loyalty, downplaying stardom, teamwork and conformity, long hours and hard work, a sense of mission, and an emphasis on client service) be extended to firms outside the professional service industries? Which ones? Why? What's the alternative to "the one-firm firm"? Are there any service industries in which your alternative could gain a competitive advantage?

The ServiceMaster Industries, Inc. case describes a company with many of the characteristics of the "one-firm firm." Will this company meet its growth goals? Why? Why is there such an emphasis on growth in this company? What must ServiceMaster Industries do to meet its growth plan? How, if at all, can a reorganization facilitate growth? By what criteria would you evaluate proposals by the planning task force on organization? If you were advising the task force, what proposals would you suggest it make for reorganization?

Next, as you read the Girl Scouts of the U.S.A. (A) case, keep some or all of these questions in mind: Do you agree with noted management observer, Peter Drucker, that the GSUSA is "the best-run organization in America"? Why? What are the most important accomplishments of Frances Hesselbein's administration at GSUSA? How were they achieved? To what extent is this a "one-firm firm"? As you turn to the (B) and (C) cases, what would you advise Laura Johnson (in the (B) case) and Frances Hesselbein (in the (C) case) to do? How does your proposed plan of action in each case fit with the character of the organization described in the (A) case?

The Club Med (B) case suggests the challenges of fostering change in a successful service organization with a strong culture. What are the causes of GO turnover here? What are the pros and cons of rotating GOs? What impact do GOs and the Club Med village teams have on customer satisfaction and patronage? What, if anything, would you recommend to Jacky Amzallag be done to remedy the situation?

The One-Firm Firm:
What Makes It Successful

DAVID H. MAISTER

What do investment bankers Goldman Sachs, management consultants Mc-Kinsey, accountants Arthur Andersen, compensation and benefits consultants Hewitt Associates, and lawyers Latham & Watkins have in common? Besides being among the most profitable firms (if not *the* most profitable) in their respective professions? Besides being considered by their peers among the best *managed* firms in their respective professions? The answer? They all share, to a greater or lesser extent, a common approach to management that I term the "one-firm firm" system.

In contrast to many of their competitors, one-firm firms have a remarkable degree of institutional loyalty and group effort that is clearly a critical ingredient in their success. The commonality of this organizational orientation and manage-,ment approach among each of these firms suggests that there is indeed a "model" whose basic elements are transferable to other professions. The purpose of this article is to identify the elements of this model of professional firm success, and to explore how these elements interact to form a successful management system.

Methodology

The information on specific firms contained in this article has been gleaned from a variety of "public domain" sources, as well as selected interviews (on and off the record) at a number of professional service firms, including but not restricted to those named herein. However, none of the information presented here represents "official" statements by the firms involved. As with most professional ser-

David H. Maister is President of Maister Associates, a Boston-based consulting firm specializing in the management of professional service organizations. Dr. Maister holds the B.S. degree from the University of Birmingham (England), the M.S. degree from the London School of Economics, and the Ph.D. degree from the Harvard Business School. He has been a consultant to numerous professional service firms and has served on the faculty of the Harvard Business School, the University of British Columbia, and the Polytechnic of the South Bank, London. Dr. Maister is the author of several books and has published articles in such journals as *Journal of Management Consulting, American Lawyer, Decision Sciences,* and *Sloan Management Review.*

Reprinted from "The One-Firm Firm: What Makes It Successful" by David H. Maister, *Sloan Management Review,* Fall 1985, pp. 121–131, by permission of the publisher. Copyright 1985 by the Sloan Management Review Association. All rights reserved.

vice organizations, the firms discussed here are private partnerships with no requirement, and with little incentive, to expose their inner workings. Consequently, public information on the management practices (and economic results) of such firms is difficult to obtain.

This situation is regrettable because the professional service firm represents the confluence of two major trends in the U.S. (and worldwide) economy: the growing importance of the service sector and the increasing numbers of "knowledge workers." As a result, any lessons that can be learned about successful management of such enterprises could potentially be of importance not only to the professions but also to other service entities and organizations grappling with the problems of managing large numbers of highly educated employees.

In an attempt to discover the principles of "good management" of professional service firms, I have worked very closely with a broad array of service firms in a variety of capacities. My research has been driven by two propositions: first, that professional service firms are sufficiently different from industrial corporations to warrant special study; and second, that the management issues faced by professional service firms are remarkably similar, regardless of the specific profession under consideration. I have chosen in this article to concentrate on the second proposition.

What Is Meant by "Well Managed"?

The firms chosen for discussion were identified in the following way. In the course of my research and consulting work, I have made it my practice to ask repeatedly the question, "Which do you consider the best-managed firm in your profession?" The question is, of course, ambiguous. In any business context, "well managed" can be taken to refer, alternatively, to profitability, member satisfaction, size, growth, innovativeness, quality of products or services, or any of a number of other criteria. The difficulty in identifying "successful" firms is particularly acute in the professions because many of the conventional indicators of business success do not necessarily apply. For example, since there are few economies of scale in the professions,[1] neither size nor rate of growth can be taken as unequivocal measures of success: many firms have chosen to limit both. Even if "per-partner" profit figures were available (which they are not), they would also be unreliable measures, since many professional firms are prepared to sacrifice a degree of profit maximization in the name of other goals such as professional satisfaction and/or quality of worklife. Finally, since "quality" of either service or work product is notoriously difficult to assess in professional work,[2] few reliable indicators of this aspect of success are obtainable.

In spite of these difficulties, it has been remarkable how frequently the same names appear on the list of "well-managed" firms in the professions, as judged by their peers and competitors. The firms discussed here were on virtually everyone's list of admired firms, often together with the comment, "I wish we could do what they do." It should be noted that other firms, not discussed here, were also mentioned frequently. However, as expressed earlier, what makes Arthur Andersen, Goldman Sachs, Hewitt Associates, and Latham & Watkins worthy of some special attention is not only that they are successful and well respected, but that, in spite of being in different professions, they appear to share a common approach to management (the one-firm firm system) that is readily distinguishable from many of their competitors. This approach is clearly not the only way to run a professional service firm, but it is certainly *a* way that is worthy of special study.

THE "ONE-FIRM FIRM" SYSTEM

Loyalty

The characteristics of the one-firm firm system are institutional loyalty and group effort. In contrast to many of their (often successful) competitors who emphasize individual entrepreneurialism, autonomous profit centers, internal competition and/or highly decentralized, independent activities, one-firm firms place great emphasis on firmwide coordination of decision making, group identity, cooperative teamwork, and institutional commitment.

Hewitt Associates (described along with Goldman Sachs in a recent popular book as one of "The 100 Best Companies in America to Work For")[3] says that, in its recruiting, it looks for "SWANs": people who are *S*mart, *W*ork hard, are *A*mbitious, and *N*ice. While emphasis on the first three attributes is common in all professional service firms, it is the emphasis on the last one that differentiates the one-firm firm from all the others. "If an individual has ego needs that are too high," notes Peter Friedes, Hewitt's managing partner, "they can be a very disruptive influence. Our work depends on internal cooperation and teamwork."

The same theme is sounded by Geoffrey Boisi, the partner in charge of mergers and acquisitions at Goldman Sachs: "You learn from day one around here that we gang-tackle problems. If your ego won't permit that, you won't be effective here."[4] By general repute, Goldman has achieved its eminence with a minimum of the infighting that afflicts most Wall Street firms. In contrast to many (if not most) of its competitors on the street, Goldman frowns upon anything resembling a star system.

Downplaying Stardom

The same studied avoidance of the star mentality is evidenced at Latham & Watkins. As Clinton Stevenson, the firm's managing partner, points out: "We want to encourage clients to retain the firm of Latham & Watkins, not Clint Stevenson."[5] Partner Jack Walker reinforces this point: "I don't mean to sound sentimental, but there's a bonding here. People care about the work of the firm."[6] The team philosophy at McKinsey, one senior partner explained to me, is illustrated by its approach to project work: "As a young individual consultant, you learn that your job is to hold your own: you can rest assured that the team will win. All you've got to do is do your part."

Above all else, the leaders and, more important, all the other members of these firms view themselves as belonging to an *institution* that has an identity and existence of its own, above and beyond the individuals who happen currently to belong to it. The one-firm firm, relative to its competitors, places great emphasis on its institutional history, broadly held values, and a reputation that all actively work to preserve. Loyalty to, and pride in, the firm and its accomplishments approaches religious fervor at such firms.

Teamwork and Conformity

The emphasis on teamwork and "fitting in" creates an identity not only for the firm but also for the individual members of the firm. This identity, for better or for worse, is readily identifiable to the outside world. References by others in the profession to members of one-firm firms are not always flattering. Members of other Big-8 firms, particularly those where individualism and individual contributions are highly valued, often make reference to "Arthur Androids." The term "A McKinsey-type" has substantive meaning in the consulting profession—sometimes even down to the style of dress. In the 1950s, I am told by a McKinsey-ite, a set of hats in the closet of a corporation's reception room was an unmistakable sign that the McKinsey consultants were in. The hats have disappeared, but the mentality has not. Goldman Sachs professionals are referred to by other investment bankers as the "IBM clones of Wall Street."

Long Hours and Hard Work

For all the emphasis on teamwork and interpersonal skills, one-firm firm members are no slouches. All of the firms discussed here have reputations for long hours and hard work, even above the norms for the all-absorbing professions in which they compete. Indeed, the way an individual illustrates his or her high involvement and commitment to the firm is through hard work and long hours. Latham & Watkins lawyers are reputed to bill an *average* of 2,200 hours apiece, with some heroic performers reaching the heights of 2,700 hours in some years: this contrasts with a professionwide average of approximately 1,750. At Goldman Sachs, sixteen-hour days are common. It has been said: "If you like the money game, here's [Goldman's] a good team to play on. If you like other games, you may not have time for them."[7] James Scott, a Columbia Business School professor, has commented: "At Goldman, the spirit is pervasive. They all work hard, have the same willingness to work all night to get the job done well, and yet remain in pretty good humor about it."[8] Similarly, McKinsey, Hewitt, and Arthur Andersen are all hard-working environments, above the norms for their respective professions.

Sense of Mission

In large part, the institutional commitment at one-firm firms is generated not only through a loyalty to the firm but also by the development of a sense of "mission," which is most frequently seen as client service. *All* professional service firms list in their mission statement what I call the "3 Ss": the goals of (client) Service, (financial) Success, and (professional) Satisfaction. What is recognizable about one-firm firms is that, in their internal communications, there is a clear priority among these.

Within McKinsey, a new consultant learns within a very short period of time that the firm believes that the *client comes first*, the firm second, and the individual last. Goldman Sachs has a reputation for being "ready to sacrifice anything—including its relations with other Wall Street firms—to further the client's interests."[9] At Hewitt Associates, firm ideology is that the 3 Ss must be carefully kept in balance at all times; however, client service is clearly number one. None of this is meant to suggest that one-firm firms necessarily render superior service to their clients compared with their competitors; nor that they always resolve inevitable day-to-day conflicts among the 3 Ss in the same way. The point is that there *is* a firm ideology which everyone understands and which no one is allowed to take lightly.

Client Service. The emphasis at one-firm firms is clearly one of significant attention to managing client relations. In these firms, client service is defined more broadly than technical excellence: it is taken to mean a more far-ranging attentiveness to client needs and the quality of interaction between the firm and its clients. Goldman Sachs pioneered the concept on Wall Street of forming a marketing and new business development group whose primary responsibility is to manage the interface between the client and the various other parts of the firm that provide the technical and professional services. In most other Wall Street firms, client relations are the responsibility of the individual professionals who do the work, resulting in numerous (and potentially conflicting) contacts between a single client and the various other parts of the firm. Hewitt Associates, alone in its profession, has also pioneered such an "account management" group.[10] At McKinsey, in the words of one partner, "Here everyone realizes that the [client] *relationship* is paramount, not the specific project we happen to be working on at the moment."

The high-commitment, hard-working, mission-oriented, team-intensive characteristics of one-firm firms are reminiscent of another type of organization: the Marine Corps. Indeed, one-firm firms have an elite, Marine Corps attitude about themselves. An atmosphere of a special, private club prevails, where members feel that "we do things differently around here, and most of us couldn't consider working anywhere else." While all professional firms will assert that they have the best *professionals* in town, one-firm firms claim they have the best *firm* in town, a subtle but important difference.[11]

SUSTAINING THE ONE-FIRM FIRM CULTURE

Up to this point, we discussed a type of firm culture, a topic much discussed in recent management literature.[12] Our task now is to try and identify the management practices that have created and sustained this culture. Not surprisingly, since human assets constitute the vast majority of the productive resources of the professional service firm, most of these management practices involve human resource management.

A good overview of the mechanisms by which an "elite group" culture, with emphasis on the *group*, can be created is provided by Dr. Chip Bell,[13] a training consultant, who suggests that the elements of any high-performance unit include the following:

— Entrance requirements into the group are extremely difficult.
— Acceptance into the group is followed by *intensive* job-related training, followed by team training.
— Challenging and high-risk team assignments are given early in the individual's career.
— Individuals are constantly tested to ensure that they measure up to the elite standards of the unit.
— Individuals and groups are given the autonomy to take risks normally not permissible at other firms.
— Training is viewed as continuous and related to assignments.
— Individual rewards are tied directly to collective results.
— Managers are seen as experts, pacesetters, and mentors (rather than as administrators).

As we shall see, all of these practices can be seen at work in the one-firm firms.

Recruiting

In contrast to many competing firms, one-firm firms invest a significant amount of *senior* professional time in their recruitment process, and they tend to be much more selective than their competition. At one-firm firms, recruiting is either heavily centralized or well coordinated centrally. At Hewitt Associates, over 1,000 students at sixty-five schools were interviewed in 1980. Of the seventy-two offers that were made, fifty accepted. Each of the 198 invited to the firm's offices spent a half-day with a psychologist (at a cost to the firm of $600 per person) for career counseling to find out if the person was suited for Hewitt's work and would fit within the firm's culture. At Goldman Sachs, 1,000 MBAs are interviewed each year; approximately thirty are chosen. Interviewing likely candidates is a major responsibility of the firm's seventy-three partners (the firm has over 1,600 professionals). Goldman partner James Gorter notes, "Recruiting responsibilities almost come before your business responsibilities."[14] At Latham & Watkins, all candidates get twenty-five to thirty interviews, compared to a norm in the legal profession of approximately five to ten interviews, As a McKinsey partner noted:

> In our business, the game is won or lost at the recruiting stage: we take it very seriously. And it's not a quantity game, it's a quality game. You've got to find the best people you can, and the trick is to understand what *best* means. It's not just brains, not just presentability: you have to try and detect the potentially fully developed professional in the person, and not just look at what they are *now*. Some firms hire in a superficial way, relying on the up-or-out system to screen out the losers. We do have an up-or-out system, but we don't use it as a substitute for good recruiting practices. To us, the costs of recruiting-mistake turnover are too high, in dollars, in morale, and in client service, to ignore.

Training

One-firm firms are notable for their investment in firmwide training, which serves both as a way to add to the substantive skills of juniors and as an important group socialization function.[15] The best examples of this practice are Arthur Andersen and McKinsey. The former is renowned among accounting students for its training center in St. Charles, Illinois (a fully equipped college campus that the firm acquired and converted to its own uses), to which young professionals are sent from around the world. In the words of one Andersen partner: "To this day, I have useful friendships, forged at St. Charles, with people across the firm in different offices and disciplines. If I need to get something done outside my own expertise, I have people I can call on who will do me a favor, even if it comes out of their hide. They know I'll return it."

Similarly, McKinsey's two-week training program for new professionals is renowned among business school students. The program is run by one or more of the firm's senior professionals, who spend a significant amount of time inculcating the firm's values by telling Marvin Bower stories—Bower, who ran the firm for many years, is largely credited with making McKinsey what it is today. The training program is not always held in the U.S. but rotates between the countries where McKinsey has offices. This not only reinforces the one-firm image (as opposed to a headquarters with branch offices) but also has a dramatic effect on the young professionals' view of the firm. As one of my ex-students told me: "Being sent to Europe for a two-week training program during your first few months with the firm impresses the hell out of you. It makes you think: 'This is a class outfit.' It also both frightens you and gives you confidence. You say, 'Boy, they must think I'm good if they're prepared to spend all this money on me.' But then you worry about whether you can live up to it: it's very motivating." All young professionals are given a copy of Marvin Bower's history of the firm, *Perspectives on McKinsey*, which, unlike many professional firm histories, is as full of philosophy and advice as it is dry on historical facts.

"Growing Their Own" Professionals

Unlike many of their competitors, all of the one-firm firms tend to "grow their own" professionals, rather than to make significant use of lateral hiring of senior professionals. In other words, in the acquisition of human capital, they tend to "make" rather than "buy." This is not to say that no lateral hires are made—just that they are done infrequently, and with extreme caution. "I had to meet with the associates (i.e., not only the partners) before the firm [Latham & Watkins] took me on," Carla Hills [former Secretary of Housing and Urban Development] recalls. "Lateral entry is a big trauma for this place. But that's how it should be."[16]

Avoiding Mergers. A related practice of one-firm firms is the deliberate avoidance of growth by merger. Arthur Andersen, unlike most of the Big-8 firms, did not join in the merger and acquisition boom of the 1950s and early 1960s, in an attempt to become part of a nationwide accounting profession network. Instead, it grew its own regional (and international) offices. Similarly, the decade-long merger mania in investment banking has left Goldman Sachs, which opted out of this trend, as one of the few independent partnerships on the street. In contrast to many other consulting firms, McKinsey's overseas offices were all launched on a grow-your-own basis, initially staffed with U.S. personnel, rather than on an acquisition basis. With one recent exception, all of Latham & Watkins's branch offices were grown internally.

It is clear that this avoidance of growth through laterals or mergers plays a critical role in both creating and preserving the sense of institutional identity, which is the cornerstone of the one-firm system.

Controlled Growth. As a high proportion of the professional staff shares an extensive, common work history with the one-firm firm, group loyalty is easier to foster. Of course, this staffing strategy has implications for the *rate* of growth pursued by the one-firm firm. At such firms (in contrast to many competitors), high growth is not a declared goal. Rather, such firms aim for *controlled* growth. The approach is one of, "We'll grow as fast as we can train our people." As Ron Daniel of McKinsey phrases it: "We neither shun growth nor idolize it. We view it as a by-product of achieving our other goals." All of the one-firm firms assert that the major constraint on their growth is not client demand, but the supply of qualified people they can find and train to their way of practicing.

Selective Business Pursuits. Related to this issue is the fact that one-firm firms tend to be more selective than their competitors in the type of business they pursue. It has been reported that an essential element of the Goldman culture is its calculated choosiness about the clients it takes on. The firm has let it be known, both internally and externally, that it "adheres to certain standards—and that it won't compromise them for the sake of a quick buck."[17] At McKinsey, the firm's long-standing strategy is that it will only work for "the top guy" (i.e., the chief executive officer) and, as illustrated internally with countless Marvin Bower stories, will only do those projects where the potential value delivered is demonstrably far in excess of the firm's charges. Junior staff at McKinsey quickly hears stories of projects the firm has turned down because the partner did not believe the firm could add sufficient value to cover its fees. Similarly, while Andersen has been an aggressive marketer (a property common to all the one-firm firms), Andersen appears to have taken a more studied, less "opportunistic" approach to business development than have their competitors.

Consequently, one-firm firms tend to have a less varied practice-mix and a more homogeneous client base than do their more explicitly individualistic competitors. Unlike, say, Booz, Allen, McKinsey's practice is relatively focused on three main areas: organization work, strategy consulting, and operations studies. In the late 1970s, the heyday of "strategy boutiques," many outsiders commented on the firm's reluctance to chase after fast-growing new specialties.[18] But McKinsey, like all of the other one-firm firms, enters new areas "big, or not at all." Andersen's strategy in its consulting work (the fastest growing area for all of the Big-8) has been more clearly focused on computer-based systems design and installation than have the variegated practices of most of its competitors. Goldman has been notably selective in which segments of the investment market it has entered, and has become a dominant player in virtually every sector it has entered.

Outplacement

One of the fortunate consequences of the controlled growth strategy at one-firm firms and the avoidance of laterals and mergers is that these firms, in contrast to many competitors, rarely lose valued people to competitors. At each of the firms named above, I have heard the claim that, "Many of our people have been approached by competitors offering more money to help them launch or bolster a part of the practice. But our people prefer to stay." On Wall Street, raiding of competing firms' top professionals has reached epidemic proportions; yet, this does not include Goldman Sachs. It is said that one of the rarest beasts on Wall Street is an ex-Goldman professional: very few leave the firm.

Turnover at one-firm firms is clearly more carefully managed than it is among competitors. Those one-firm firms that do enforce an up-or-out system (McKinsey and Andersen) work actively to place their alumni/ae in good positions preferably with favored clients. McKinsey's regular alumni/ae reunions, a vivid demonstration of its success in breeding loyalty to the firm, are held two or three times a year. In part, due to the "caring" approach taken to junior staff, one-firm firms are able to achieve a very profitable high-leverage strategy (i.e., high ratio of junior to senior staff) without *excessive* pressures for growth to provide promotion opportunities.[19]

Compensation

Internal management procedures at one-firm firms constantly reinforce the team concept. Most important, compensation systems (particularly for partners) are designed to encourage intra-firm cooperation. Whereas many other firms make heavy use of departmental or local-office profitability in setting compensation (i.e., take a *measurement*-oriented, profit-center approach), one-firm firms tend to set compensation (both for partners *and* juniors) through a *judgmental* process, assessing total contribution to the firm. Unique among the Big-8, Andersen has a single worldwide partnership cost-sharing pool (as opposed to separate country profit centers): individual partners share in the joint economics of the whole firm, not just their country (or local office). "The virtue of the 'one-pool' system, as opposed to heavy profit-centering, is that a superior individual in an otherwise poor-profit office can be rewarded apropriately," one Andersen partner pointed out. "Similarly, a weaker individual in a successful office does not get a windfall gain. Further, if you tie individual partner compensation too tightly to departmental or office profitability, it's hard to take into account the particular circumstances of that office. A guy that shows medium profitability in a tough market probably deserves more than one with higher profitability in an easy market where we already have a high market share."

Hewitt Associates sets its partner compensation levels only after all partners have been invited to comment on the contributions (qualitative *and* quantitative) made by other partners on "their" projects and other firmwide affairs. Vigorous efforts are made to assess contributions to the firm that do not show up in the measurable factors. Peter Friedes notes:

> We think that having no profit centers is a great advantage to us. Other organizations don't realize how much time they waste fighting over allocations of overhead, transfer charges, and other mechanisms caused by a profit-center mentality. Whenever there are profit centers, cooperation between groups suffers badly. Of course, we pay a price for not having them: specific accountability is hard to pin down. We often don't know precisely whose time we are writing off, or who precisely brought in that new account. But at least we don't fight over it: we get on with our work. Our people know that, over time, good performance will be recognized and rewarded.

Goldman Sachs also runs a judgment-based (rather than measurement-based) compensation system, including "a month-long evaluation process in which performance is reviewed not only by a person's superiors but by other partners as well, and finally by the management committee. During that review, 'how well you do when other parts of the firm ask for your help on some project' plays a big part."[20] At Latham & Watkins, "15 percent of the firm's income is set aside as a separate fund from which the executive committee, at its sole discretion, awards partners additional compensation based on their general contribution to the firm in terms of such factors as client relations, hours billed, and even the business office's 'scoring' of how promptly the partner has logged his or her own time, sent out and collected bills, and otherwise helped the place run well."[21]

Investments in Research and Development

In most professional service firms, particularly in those with a heavy emphasis on short-term results or year-by-year performance evaluations, any activity that takes an individual away from direct revenue-producing work is considered a detour off the professional success track within the firm and is therefore avoided. This is not the case with one-firm firms.

As the one-firm culture is based on a "team-player" judgment-system approach to evaluations and compensation (at both the partner and junior level), it is *relatively* easier (although it is never easy) for one-firm firms to get their best professionals to engage in nonbillable, stafflike activities such as research and development (R&D), market research, and other investments in the firm's future. For example, McKinsey is noted in the consulting profession for its internally funded R&D projects, of which the most famous example is the work that resulted in the best seller *In Search of Excellence.* This book, however, was only one of a large number of staff projects continually under way in the firm. An ex-student of mine noted that "at McKinsey, to be selected to do something for the firm is an honor: it's a quick way to get famous in the firm if you succeed. And, of course, you're expected to succeed. Firm projects are treated as seriously as client work, and your performance is closely examined. However, my friends at other firms tell me that firm projects are a high-risk thing to do: they worry about whether their low chargeable hours will be held against them later on."

Andersen likewise invests heavily in firmwide activities. For instance, it conducts extensive cross-office and cross-functional industry programs, which attempt to coordinate all of the firm's activities with respect to specific industries. In fact, it is rumored, although no one has the statistics, that Andersen invests a higher proportion of its gross revenues in firmwide investment activities than does any other firm.

Goldman's commitment to investing in its own future is illustrated by the firm's policy of forcing partners to keep their capital in the firm rather than to take extraordinarily high incomes. Hewitt's commitment to R&D is built into its organizational structure. Rather than scatter its professional experts throughout its multiple office system (staffed predominantly with account managers), it chose to concentrate its professional groups in three locations in order to promote the rapid cross-fertilization of professional ideas. Significant investments of professional time are made in nonbillable research work under the guidance of professional group managers who establish budgets for such work in negotiation with the managing partner.

Communication

Communication at a one-firm firm is remarkably open and is clearly used as a bonding technique to hold the firm together. All the firms described above make *heavy* use of memorandums to keep everyone informed of what is happening in other parts of the firm, above and beyond the token efforts frequently made at other firms. Frequent firmwide meetings are held, with an emphasis on cross-boundary (i.e., interoffice and interdepartmental) gatherings. Such meetings are valued (and clearly designed) as much as for the social interaction as for whatever the agenda happens to be: people *go* to the meetings. (At numerous other firms

I have observed, meetings are seen as distractions from the firm's, or the individual's business, and people bow out whenever they can.)

At most one-firm firms, open communication extends to financial matters as well. At Hewitt, they believe that "anyone has a right to know anything about the firm except the personal affairs of another individual." At an annual meeting with all junior personnel (including secretaries and other support staff), the managing partner discloses the firm's economic results and answers any and all questions from the audience. At Latham & Watkins, junior associates are significantly involved in all major firm committees, including recruiting, choosing new partners, awarding associate bonuses, and so on. All significant matters about the firm are well known to the associates.

Absence of Status Symbols. Working hard to involve nonpartners in firm affairs and winning their commitment to the firm's success is a hallmark of the one-firm firm and is reinforced by a widely common practice of sharing firm profits more deeply within the organization than is common at other firms. (The ratio between the highest paid and lowest paid partner tends to be markedly less at one-firm firms than it is among their competitors.) There is also a suppression of status differentials between senior and junior members of the firm: an important activity if the firm is attempting to make everyone, junior and senior alike, feel a part of the team. At Hewitt Associates, deemphasizing status extends to the physical surroundings: everyone, from the newest hire to the oldest partner, has the same size office.

The absence of status conflicts in one-firm firms is also noticeable across departments. In today's world of professional megafirms composed of departments specializing in vastly different areas, one of the most significant dangers is that professionals in one area may come to view *their* area as somehow more elite, more exciting, more profitable, or more important to the firm than another area. Their loyalty is to their department, or their local office, and not to the firm. Yet the success of the firm clearly depends upon doing well in all areas. On Wall Street, different psychological profiles of, and an antipathy between, say, traders and investment bankers is notorious: many attribute the recent turmoil at Lehman Brothers (now Shearson Lehman) to this syndrome. In some law firms, corporate lawyers and litigators are often considered distinct breeds of people who view the world in different ways. In some accounting firms, mutual suspicion among audit, tax, and consulting partners is rampant. In consulting firms, frequently there are status conflicts between the "front-room" client handlers and the "back-room" technical experts.

What strikes any visitor to a one-firm firm is the deeply held mutual respect across departmental, geographic, and functional boundaries. Members of one-firm firms clearly *like* (and respect) their counterparts in other areas, which makes for the successful cross-boundary coordination that is increasingly essential in today's marketplace. Jonathan Cohen of Goldman Sachs notes that out-of-office socialization among Goldman professionals appears to take place more frequently than it does at other Wall Street firms. Retired Marvin Bower of McKinsey asserts that one of the elements in creating the one-firm culture is mutual trust, both horizontally and vertically. This atmosphere is created primarily by the behavior of the firm's leadership, who must set the style for the firm. Unlike many other firms, leaders of one-firm firms work hard not to be identified with or labeled as being closer to one group than another. Cross-boundary respect is also achieved at most one-firm firms by the common practice of rotating senior professionals among the various offices and departments of the firm.

Governance: Consensus-building Style

How are one-firm firms governed? Are they democracies or autocracies? Without exception, one-firm firms are led (*not* managed) in a consensus-building style.[22] All have (or have had) strong leaders who engage in extensive consultation before major decisions are taken. It is important to note that all of these firms do indeed have leaders: they are not anarchic democracies, nor are they dictatorships. Whether one is reading about Goldman's two Johns (Weinberg and Whitehead), McKinsey's (retired) Marvin Bower and Ron Daniel, Latham & Watkins's Clinton Stevenson, or Hewitt's Peter Friedes, it is clear that one is learning about expert communicators who see their role as preserver of the "true religion." Above all else, they are cheerleaders who suppress their own egos in the name of the institution they head. Such firms also have continuity in leadership: while many of them have electoral systems of governance, leaders tend to stay in place for long periods of time. What is more, the firm's culture outlasts the tenure of any given individual.

Of course, the success of the consensus-building approach to firm governance and the continuity of leadership at one-firm firms is not fortuitous. Since their whole philosophy (and, as I have tried to show, their substantive managerial practices) is built upon cooperative teamwork, consensus is more readily achieved here than it is at other firms. The willingness to allow leaders the freedom to make decisions on behalf of the firm (the absence of which has stymied many other "democratic" firms) was "prewired" into the system long ago, since everyone shares the same values. The one-firm system *is* a system.

CONCLUSION: POTENTIAL WEAKNESSES

Clearly, the one-firm firm system is powerful. What are its weaknesses? The dangers of this approach are reasonably obvious. Above all else, there is the danger of self-congratulatory complacency: a firm that has an integrated system that *works* may, if it is not careful, become insensitive to shifts in its environment that demand changes in the system. The very commitment to "our firm's way of doing things," which is the one-firm firm's strengths, can also be its greatest weakness. This is particularly true because of the chance of "inbreeding" that comes from "growing-your-own" professionals. To deal with this, there is a final ingredient required in the formula: self-criticism. At McKinsey, Andersen, Goldman, and Hewitt, partners have asserted to me that "we have no harsher critics than ourselves: we're constantly looking for ways to improve what we do." However, it must be acknowledged that, without the diversity common at other professional service firms, one-firm firms with strong cultures run the danger of making even self-criticism a pro forma exercise.

Another potential weakness of the one-firm firm culture is that it runs the danger of being insufficiently entrepreneurial, at least in the short run. Other more individualistic firms, which promote and reward opportunistic behavior by individuals and separate profit centers, may be better at reorganizing and capitalizing on emerging trends early in their development. Although contrary examples can be cited, one-firm firms are rarely "pioneers": they try to be (and usually are) good at entering emerging markets as a late second or third. But because of the firmwide concentrated attack they are able to effect, they are frequently successful at this. (This similarity to IBM in this regard, as in much of what has been discussed above, is readily noticeable.)

The one-firm approach is *not* the only way to run a professional service firm. However, it clearly is a very successful way to run a firm. The "team spirit" of the firms described here is broadly admired by their competitors and is not easily copied. As I have attempted to show, the one-firm firm system is *internally* consistent: all of its practices, from recruiting through compensation, performance, appraisal, approaches to market, governance, control systems, and above all, culture and human resource strategy, make for a consistent whole.

REFERENCES

1. D. H. Maister, "Profitability: Beating the Downward Trend," *Journal of Management Consulting*, Fall 1984, pp. 39–44.
2. D. H. Maister, "Quality Work Doesn't Mean Quality Service," *American Lawyer*, April 1984.
3. R. Levering, M. Moskowitz, and M. Katz, *The 100 Best Companies to Work for in America* (Reading, MA: Addison-Wesley, 1984).
4. B. McGoldrick "Inside the Goldman Sachs Culture," *Institutional Investor*, January 1984.

5. S. Brill, "Is Latham & Watkins America's Best Run Firm?" *American Lawyer*, August 1981, pp. 12–14.

6. Ibid.

7. Levering et al. (1984).

8. McGoldrick (January 1984).

9. Ibid.

10. D. H. Maister, *Hewitt Associates* (Boston, MA: Harvard University, Graduate School of Business, HBS Case Services).

11. D. H. Maister, "What Kind of Excellence?" *American Lawyer*, January–February 1985, pp. 4–6.

12. See, for example, V. J. Sathe, *Culture and Related Corporate Realities* (Homewood, IL: Richard D. Irwin, Inc., 1985).

13. C. Bell, "How to Create a High Performance Training Unit," *Training*, October 1980, pp. 49–52.

14. McGoldrick (January 1984).

15. D. H. Maister, "How to Build Human Capital," *American Lawyer*, June 1984.

16. Brill (August 1981).

17. McGoldrick (January 1984).

18. See, for example, "The New Shape of Management Consulting," *Business Week*, 21 May 1979.

19. For a discussion of the role of turnover on professional service firm success, see D. H. Maister, "Balancing the Professional Service Firm," *Sloan Management Review*, Fall 1982, pp. 15–29.

20. McGoldrick (January 1984).

21. Brill (August 1981).

22. For a discussion of governance in professional firms, see D. H. Maister, "Partnership Politics," *American Lawyer*, October 1984.

ServiceMaster Industries Inc.

"**B**ecause this company is dedicated both to the development of the individual and our ministry to an increasing number of people, growth is an imperative. But given the size we have achieved, unless we find new ways of managing growth that are compatible with our basic objectives, we cannot achieve the goals we've set for ourselves." C. William Pollard, president and chief executive officer of ServiceMaster Industries Inc., reviewed his thoughts as he prepared to meet in June 1985 with five managers comprising the long-range planning group task force, charged several months earlier with the task of identifying needed changes in ServiceMaster's organizational structure.

BUSINESS AND MARKET DEVELOPMENT

ServiceMaster Industries employed 7,500 people in early 1985, of whom only 380 were housed at headquarters in the Chicago suburb of Downers Grove, Illinois. It contracted with hospitals, schools, and industrial firms for the management of the employees of these firms engaged in performing supporting functions such as housekeeping, laundry and linen distribution, food service, materials management, plant operations and maintenance, and clinical equipment maintenance. As a result, most of ServiceMaster's employees were managers. In addition, the company franchised individuals who provided a range of on-site carpet cleaning and lawn care services to residential and commercial customers.

Selected financial information for the years 1979 through 1985 (estimated) is shown in *Exhibit 1*. Nearly all of ServiceMaster's growth had occurred internally; recently its only acquisition was that of a hospital food service company, bought in 1981.

Health Care Services

Kenneth Hansen, chairman of ServiceMaster from 1973 to 1981, described how ServiceMaster had entered the hospital services business in 1962:

This case was prepared by Prof. James L. Heskett with the assistance of Mr. Andrew Segal as the basis for class discussion rather than to illustrate either effective or ineffective handling of an administrative situation. Copyright © 1987 by the President and Fellows of Harvard College; Harvard Business School case # 9-388-064 (Rev. 6/88).

We . . . founded [our hospital housekeeping management business] on the cornerstone of hard listening. . . . From 1957 to 1959 Ken Wessner [the company's current chairman] and I worked in tandem in a series of hearing sessions with individuals and groups of men and women who were a direct part of hospital managements.

As we listened, we thought we heard administrators saying that their time could be better used if they could have professional help for some of the more nonpatient-related functions of their hospital.

We seemed to hear administrators say that the hospital community was ready for the services of a specialist organization . . . one that would build itself on the hospital's objectives, and blend itself into their needs.

At the same time other companies heard there was going to be a lot of money spent by hospitals for contract housekeeping. They approached this job as some more buildings to clean. This is not what we heard at all.

In 1985 more than 1,000 of the roughly 7,000 hospitals in the U.S. contracted at least one service function with ServiceMaster. One company executive estimated that another 300 to 400 hospitals contracted management services with other contractors, and that the remaining hospitals provided their own support services internally. Fewer than 5% of ServiceMaster's hospital clients terminated their (typically three-year) contracts each year, a rate several times below the industry average. The primary reason for the loss of a contract was thought to be an annual turnover rate in hospital leadership of 10%; many incoming administrators seemed opposed to contracting out support services. Other reasons for termination included ServiceMaster's realization that some accounts proved unprofitable and that the firm was ineffective in its work in other accounts. A few terminations resulted from failure by ServiceMaster to perform up to customer expectations, a situation termed "heartbreaking" by a senior executive.

ServiceMaster Industries' revenue base reflected the increasing importance of hospital chains. It served 30 such chains, each of which previously had managed its nonmedical support services on a facility-by-facility basis.

Roughly 3% to 4% of the accounts lost each year went to competitors, while ServiceMaster displaced its competitors about 20% of the time in obtaining new accounts. Its largest competitors were ARA Services, the Marriott Corporation, and United Health Service, though in some functions local contractors provided the strongest competition.

By 1985 it was estimated that the total U.S. market for all health care support management services of the type offered by ServiceMaster was about $20 billion. This market had grown at the rate of about 23% per year in the 1970s, but had slowed to approximately a 10% growth rate by 1985 primarily because of governments' and insurers' efforts to contain health care costs.

These efforts created offsetting effects for ServiceMaster's business. On one hand, cutbacks would lead to the closing of medical facilities, thus reducing ServiceMaster's potential market. On the other hand, health care administrators were likely to perceive ServiceMaster's services as a vehicle for cost containment since the company's services were intended to be of low price. Nevertheless, potential constraints on the growth of hospital services had given urgency to efforts to develop alternative markets.

Education and Industrial Services

In 1980, ServiceMaster accrued $416 million in revenues, $405 million of which came from its hospital management services and $11 million of which was obtained from franchising fees and equipment and materials sales to residential and commercial cleaning franchises. In that year a long-range planning exercise named SMIXX (ServiceMaster Industries 20 years out) concluded that:

1. To satisfy its objective of fostering the growth of ServiceMaster people and their responsibilities, the company would have to continue to grow at a rate in excess of 20% per year.
2. To ensure the attainability of this growth objective, the company would need to develop new business opportunities such as management services for schools and industrial facilities.

William Pollard, the company's president and chief executive officer, described the difficulties of developing the school business:

At the outset of our effort, we only had a few managers who had experience with schools. . . . Most of our people didn't understand the new business. The development process languished until one of our younger managers came forward, told us he wanted to take on the responsibility, and sold about $6 million in agreements the first year. He also was involved in training and retraining managers to serve in this market.

The school service management market in the U.S. was approximately $14 billion in 1985, almost all of which was managed in-house by school administrators. Competition for educational services was predominantly local, except in food services where ARA and Marriott were important national competitors.

In 1982 ServiceMaster initiated similar management services for industrial firms. The total potential market for these services was thought to be larger than that for either hospitals or schools. Because of the market's size and variety, ServiceMaster targeted a limited segment of this market, concentrating on developing a small number of accounts among large industrial firms with several plants, such as General Motors. Targeted firms typically emphasized improved productivity, cleanliness, cost reduction, and employed about 3,000 to 5,000 people.

By 1985, the combined school and industrial services businesses had grown to represent 24% of total revenue, up from 17% in the previous year.

Franchising

Franchising at ServiceMaster had grown by 1985 to incorporate about 3,200 units realizing approximately $230 million in revenues. Roughly $11 million of these represented franchise fees and sales of specially designed equipment and supplies. Franchisees, often couples and families, typically provided carpet cleaning services as well as complete housecleaning and "disaster" cleanup services. Recently, ServiceMaster had begun franchising lawn care services, often to those franchisees already affiliated with its cleaning services.

Globalization

ServiceMaster began offering hospital management services internationally in 1975. By 1985, 30 Japanese hospitals and almost all of Jordan's hospital capacity was contracted to ServiceMaster. The company also had developed a number of contracts in Canada and Great Britain.

The first international franchise was awarded in 1958 in Great Britain. By 1985 the number of British franchises had increased to 175. In Japan, Service-Master was the leading franchiser, with 453 franchises in operation. The vice president of Corporate Education pointed out that its hospital and franchise operations quite possibly made the company the largest exporter in the world of management service to Japan.

BASIC GOALS

Four basic goals were posted in many ServiceMaster offices as well as displayed in its annual reports:

1. To honor God in all we do
2. To help people develop

3. To pursue excellence
4. To grow profitably.

William Pollard explained:

The first two are end objectives; the second two are means objectives. The first is meant to provide a common starting point for all of us, not to convey a religious point of view. In combination with the second, it guides us by suggesting ways in which we treat people. The last two objectives not only provide the means for achieving the first two; they keep us in balance and provide a kind of creative tension for the management. Securities analysts often ask me what the relation is between God and profits. I tell them that for us it's people. They provide the link between the two.

RESEARCH AND PRODUCT DEVELOPMENT

The company's research and development department was established in 1963 to study its employees' functions and to subsequently facilitate the work process by developing new products and equipment to support the work. By 1985 it had grown to a staff of 18 headed by two PhDs.

One of the department's studies resulted in the development of a new disinfectant mop dispenser which allowed the mop to be sanitized continually. In another study, a specially treated dry mop was designed that precluded the necessity of both wet mopping and dry mopping hallways. Other developed ideas included cordless vacuum cleaners, color-coded cleaning materials for illiterate employees, and hard-to-reach window scrubbers that cleaned more effectively as well as less laboriously.

Most of ServiceMaster's products had been developed in response to customer inquiries. The development process for the firm's materials management services was typical, according to the vice president of Corporate Development:

We were asked to look at certain transportation responsibilities within an institution. One institution wanted us to look at the transportation of food trays. Another asked us to look at the transportation of water carafes. . . . We began . . . analyzing the situation . . . as it involved receiving, storing, transporting, inventorying and control, collection, distribution, recycling . . . every process involving materials in the institution. . . . As a consequence, we drew in a number of departments that had been free-standing in the hospital and reconfigured them into what is essentially a new department, the materials management department.

Efforts were made to develop maximum value-added in each of the company's services. In 1985, for example, ServiceMaster invested in a large computer to aid in its plant operations services by inventorying its equipment and collecting maintenance data.

TRAINING AND PERSONAL DEVELOPMENT

ServiceMaster often developed a job-progression scheme through which its employees could move, as shown in *Exhibit 2*. The provision to employees of greater job variety and an expanded job progression was one incentive for ServiceMaster to obtain numerous service contracts with each of its clients. In addition, one of ServiceMaster's goals was to develop 20% of its new management trainees from the ranks of its customers' employees whom its managers supervised. Recently, the actual percentage ranged from 14% to 19% of its management trainees.

Kenneth Wessner, ServiceMaster's current chairman, explained, "We want to help people *be* something before we ask them to *do* something." The first page of a recent annual report stressed the importance of "providing opportunity for people to become all they were created to be." To support this philosophy, the company offered a number of educational opportunities ranging from basic literacy to college-level management courses both to its own managers and to employees of its clients.

ServiceMaster also developed extensive training techniques. An excerpt from one of the research development department's Technical Information Bulletins explains in *Exhibit 3* the correct procedure for damp mopping a corridor. It was intended for use by ServiceMaster supervisors in one-on-one training sessions, and was taught by the "quarter in the corner" challenge, in which a supervisor threw a quarter into one corner of a room and challenged the employee to mop the floor in a continuous 'S' stroke, moving the quarter out the door. Many employees were thought to still have their quarters as trophies.

To its own supervisors and resident managers, ServiceMaster offered a variety of personal development programs that ranged from operating-level seminars which emphasized management skills and introduced new equipment and materials, to a graduate executive development program in leadership management for upper-middle management candidates. Books on management and inspirational topics often were assigned for reading at all levels in the company's management. One division vice president responsible for health care and educational services sales and operations in the northeastern United States commented about the extent of training at ServiceMaster:

One of the four dimensions of my annual plan is training and development. This year, I've programmed eight days of training for each of my direct reports [functional division managers], eight days for area managers who report to them, ten days for each regional manager, and fifteen days for each facility manager who works "next to the customer." It's all built into my budget. This time includes planning meetings as well as more formal sessions on quality and financial control and "one-on-one" training by the area manager at the facility level.

In addition, Bill Pollard joins me once a year for a Management Review Process that prompts us to keep an eye on potential leaders. . . . The most important aspect of these reviews has to do with the ability of managers to encourage the development of people they supervise as well as secure measurable results on behalf of those they serve.

THE PLANNING PROCESS

On-the-job training for clients' personnel included classes in job performance as well as in self-esteem, communications, and personal health. In monthly meetings at which self-improvement programs were discussed, recognition was accorded to employees for a variety of work virtues, such as perfect attendance. Clients' employees also attended department meetings at which they learned from experts in the institutions in which they worked the value of their jobs to those institutions. Special ServiceMaster human development programs were designed to complement special clients' needs. One manager, for example, learned sign language in order to communicate more effectively with a client's deaf housekeeping employee. An extensive employee data base allowed ServiceMaster to keep track of over 120,000 health care, school, and industrial employees supervised by its managers.

The process for setting individual managers' goals was described by another division vice president:

The planning process starts with the Delta Plan in which we first state as individuals where we think we're going to be a year from now. This folds into Bill Pollard's statement of performance for the company, largely based on SMIXX long-range goals. In setting our financial goals, we take into account such things as market potential and trends in operating costs for our region, including training and development costs. We are also asked to state our personal goals, including the sponsorship of the development of other individuals in the organization as well as the amount of time I might want to spend, for example, with my division manager for sales contacting

CEOs of existing and potential customers; classes I might want to take; and community service activities in which I'll be involved. These are reviewed by the person I report to and then sent down to the people who report to me. For example, I get Bill Pollard's personal goal statement. Monthly reviews against our plans are conducted on the basis of a rolling quarter, including last month, this month, and next month.

THE SELLING PROCESS

One division vice president responsible for sales and operations in ServiceMaster's health care and educational markets explained the differences in the sales and service processes for hospitals and for schools:

> To sell a hospital, you have to sell the CEO. In schools, you have to sell to the entire school board as well as the superintendent; the atmosphere often is a lot more political. Schools put contracts out to bid more often. In the hospital where standards of cleanliness are keyed off the operating room there is a greater emphasis on quality as opposed to price. . . . In day-to-day operations, there is more visibility in the hospital; in many school systems, the superintendent is likely to be in another building.

Nearly all school contracts were guaranteed, that is, quoted on a fixed price typically over a multiyear period. ServiceMaster would pay charges in excess of the agreed price and keep or share cost savings. Many customers could not understand the guarantee feature of ServiceMaster's contracts. As a division vice president explained:

> In the customer's eyes, the arrangement often appears unfair either to ServiceMaster or the customer. Given that 77% of the costs on a typical project are payroll, and positions not filled accrue to ServiceMaster, customers are afraid we'll skimp on payroll. One customer insisted that we quote on a cost-plus basis and was flabbergasted when we gave them a $30,000 check at the end of one year with the message that we thought our charges were too high under the agreement. Generally, we think we're a lot sharper on a guaranteed contract basis.

In hospitals, most sales were made on the basis of taking away from administrators the charge of time-consuming and problematic service functions. Housekeeping, for example, was estimated to represent only 3% of a hospital's expenses but 25% of an administrator's time.

In industrial firms, the sales process generally involved presentations to union stewards, plant managers, and executive-level personnel, and required from six months' to two years' time to complete. Since the complexity of the process did not seem to vary proportionally with customer size, ServiceMaster's sales representatives concentrated on firms with the largest potential revenues.

The sales process often involved cold call, a survey of a potential customer's premises by ServiceMaster's sales representative, a review of union contracts in existence, a one-day tour of ServiceMaster's Downers Grove headquarters and laboratories, visits by a potential customer to existing customers' facilities, the introduction of the ServiceMaster operating manager to be assigned to the site, and the final negotiation of the contract.

At the conclusion of any contract it was assumed to be the responsibility of the on-site manager to obtain a contract renewal. Sales representatives typically located only new accounts.

OPERATING PERFORMANCE

An analysis of performance on one recently completed three-year contract indicated that in the third year the customer had incurred $1,830,000 in costs, about 1% less than what had been projected if the customer had continued to manage its own operations. Of this amount, roughly $1,520,000 was paid for 64 custodial and maintenance staff members, contracted service, and purchased maintenance supplies. The other $310,000 was paid to ServiceMaster for five supervisors, cleaning supplies, equipment, and gross profit. This comprised ServiceMaster payroll ($91,000); ServiceMaster supplies and contract labor ($34,000); engineering, training, and development support provided to the customer ($115,000); other expenses ($38,000); and ServiceMaster contribution ($32,000). Contribution was understated to the extent that ServiceMaster supplies, engineering, training, and development support also contained contribution margin. During the three-year period of time, quality measures had improved, the number of work orders performed had more than doubled, headcount had been reduced from 72 to 68, and the time and labor cost per work order had been cut nearly in half.

CUSTOMER REACTION

Some of ServiceMaster's customers, interviewed without the prior knowledge of the company, commented as follows:

> We selected ServiceMaster because they appeared to be well-organized and had well-developed policies, processes, and productivity standards as well

as an impressive laboratory. They thought we could reduce costs by 10% to 15% both by using fewer employees and better equipment and materials. . . . Their people are dedicated and purposeful. (Comments by a large hospital administrator)

The five-year contract with ServiceMaster was not renewed because a local building maintenance firm with a few hospital accounts came in with a lower bid at a time when we were looking for ways to save some money. It's true that ServiceMaster exceeded its goals for both improved quality and reduced costs. . . . They did repeatedly suggest better ways of doing things and brought in experts to prescribe a program for our slate floors. And they had good training programs with things like recognition, certificates, and events. But we had four different ServiceMaster housekeeping directors during the five years of the contract. They had all come up through the ranks. . . . For two, it was too big a promotion to our large, urban hospital. We had to work out their transfer with ServiceMaster's regional vice president after just a few months on the job for each. (Large hospital administrator)

We have had ServiceMaster housekeeping and laundry contracts for 16 years. I came close to kickin' 'em outta here a couple of times because of high manager turnover. Both times I checked costs in comparable hospitals around here and ours were 5% to 8% lower. And the quality was good. . . . [ServiceMaster was] responsive, but so many of their field people were here so often [that] they appeared to be overstaffed. Things got straightened out when they assigned an older [55-year-old] manager. They've tried to move him in the past seven years, but we've told them that if he goes, the contract goes. Now I couldn't tell you who the regional manager is; I haven't had any reason to be in contact with him. (Small hospital administrator)

ORGANIZATION

The organization of the company's senior ranks as well as that of a typical division is shown in *Exhibits 4* and *5*, respectively. It had evolved over time as divisions, areas, and regions were created to accommodate rapid growth in the number of accounts served, and simultaneously to make available new management opportunities to the company's managers.

Twelve divisions contracting services to health and educational institutions formed the heart of ServiceMaster's organization. Division managers (titled president or vice president) had sales and operations responsibility for all clients in their geographic areas. Reporting to each division manager were four to six area managers, each responsible for supervising operations producing between $20 million and $50 million of revenue. Most area managers were trained in sales as well, because, as one division manager explained. "A person couldn't perform the area manager's job without sales experience." Reporting to each area manager were four or five regional managers, each of which in turn supervised eight to sixteen facility managers. In sales, assignments transcended strict geographical boundaries. Each division employed between five and ten sales representatives.

Managerial training stressed experience in both sales and operations. This was deemed critical because operations personnel would have to obtain contract renewals in their own accounts and refer to salespeople opportunities for extending these contracts into different service functions. Moreover, the initial sale of a new account had to be carried out with a knowledge of possible operating problems that might develop.

POLICIES, VALUES, AND CULTURE

Company policy encouraged promotion from within, often from the ranks of hospital and school employees that its managers supervised. Recently, however, several entry-level managers had been recruited from regional undergraduate or MBA programs. Much emphasis was placed on the permanence of employment at ServiceMaster. The average age of senior management was 45 years, with 15 years of experience with the company. Few managers left ServiceMaster of their own volition. Total compensation for managers was considered highly competitive and higher than in organizations of comparable size. Benefits included profit sharing, incentive stock options, and performance bonuses. Compensation for higher ranking managers, for instance, was based both on base salary and on performance vis-à-vis goals. Up to 50% of a manager's earnings could result from the latter.

"Stretch" was a favored word at ServiceMaster headquarters, and implied the firm's drive for growth in business volume. For example, while the company was approaching the billion dollar mark in revenues in 1985, plans already were being made to place large "2's" in most offices to signify the goal of reaching $2 billion in revenues by 1990.

The most prominent values espoused by ServiceMaster were those connected to ethical business and personal conduct. These values were based on Judeo-Christian principles, family involvement in company affairs, employee participation and ownership, and conservative financial management. Frequent references to the Bible appeared in the company's annual reports as well as in senior executives' speeches. (The company name, in fact, was a shortened version of "Service to the Master.") As William Pollard put it,

God is the source for our values and as we live our values it is a way of life for us. It contributes directly to our concern for the dignity and development of all of the people associated with the company. For example, if you believe the Bible's teachings, it affects the way you treat people.

Although ServiceMaster kept no record of the number of employees actively practicing religion, all religions were represented in the company's ranks. Government reviews of the company's hiring practices had failed to disclose violations of Equal Employment Opportunity laws. The company's senior management encompassed a cross-section of religious beliefs; Pollard himself was not a member of any religious denomination.

Visitors to ServiceMaster's headquarters found portraits of Lillian and Marion Wade, Jean and Kenneth Hansen, and Norma and Kenneth Wessner in the lobby. This was intended to communicate the value the company placed on the family partnership as an important element in success; spouses were included in many company functions.

One employee's wife told an often-repeated story at ServiceMaster. Her husband, after leaving the firm for another job some years earlier, became seriously ill. Marion Wade, then ServiceMaster's chairman, flew some distance out of his way to visit his former associate and "announced that he had come to let my husband know he was praying for him." When asked about it later, Wade said, "It's what anyone would do." The man, remembering the gesture, returned to ServiceMaster after his recovery.

Just under 75% of the company's 7,500 full-time associates who had been with the company at least one year owned stock in the company. This had influenced dividend policies. In recent years, for example, the company had paid out approximately 75% of its earnings in dividends, and had increased the dividend 25 times in 15 years in addition to splitting the stock three-for-two in 1977, 1978, 1980, 1981, 1983, and 1985. Each share of stock purchased for the equivalent of $1.52 in 1971 was worth $22.50 at the end of 1985 and had yielded a total compounded annual return of 21%.

ServiceMaster carried little debt. Since the company's core businesses did not require extensive assets, its conservative policy toward debt had not restricted its growth.

COMMUNICATION PROBLEMS

The task of maintaining ServiceMaster's shared values fell heavily on the company's senior management. As the company grew, it became increasingly difficult to communicate these values throughout the organization. Several comments from division-level managers reflected increasing concerns:

> I know fewer and fewer people. I'm signing pay increases for people I haven't met.
>
> There is more and more stress on how to manage and control. We could lose our emphasis on people if we're not very careful.
>
> We need to stay close to the person who is closest to the customer. Given my responsibility for both operations and sales in hospitals and schools for my region, this is becoming harder to do.

It had been a long-standing custom at ServiceMaster for the chairman and president to meet with each incoming employee. Both, for example, taught in the management development program for new manager-trainees. By early 1985, new manager-trainees were arriving at the rate of about 1,000 per year.

In describing the way he divided his time, President William Pollard commented as follows:

> In a service organization, the touching of the operations by the president is very important. While I continue to spend 50% of my time out of the office, more of it is involved with investor or government relations. I'm far less involved in operations than I would like to be; it's a constant gnawing at me. Recently, as part of our next five-year strategic plan, I've become more involved with finding my successor, something that has become traditional with the CEO at a relatively early age in this company. As a result, I've spent more time identifying the poppies out there in the field. But I need to devote more time to teaching and dipping [relating to people in the field]. In all of this, my personal life has suffered; I just haven't had enough time for independent intellectual pursuit.

PROPOSALS FOR REORGANIZATION

Investment analysts and others had begun to question whether ServiceMaster could meet its goal of $2 billion in revenues by 1990 without resorting to one or more major acquisitions. It was becoming apparent that a doubling of size without some kind of reorganization would have a significant impact on the way the company was managed.

Concerns were being expressed within the company about the effectiveness of the existing organization. Senior management felt that it was becoming increasingly difficult to stay "close to the customer," something that had been highly valued since the founding of the company. With growth, levels had been added to the operating organization to provide adequate supervision and clear opportunities for advancement. One facility manager of a small hospital noted that due to ServiceMaster's rapid growth, "we were losing good managers because we were moving them around too much."

Several of the twelve division vice presidents (marked with asterisks in *Exhibit 4*) felt that the responsibilities of their area operations managers had outgrown the abilities of some of these individuals. By 1985 an area manager could be responsible for operations at as many as 80 sites. As a result, many area managers perceived that they were able to spend less time both with customers and in field education activities. Meanwhile, since upper management was reluctant to create more divisions or add levels of management, promotions for many of the better area managers were limited to transfers to larger areas.

Questions were being raised about the ability of area managers to maintain operating relationships with both school and hospital accounts, since the task of managing a hospital account was much different from that of managing an educational account. Area managers increasingly appeared to be better at managing one type of account.

Another problem was the increasing difficulty of dividing sales and operating responsibilities below the divisional level. One division vice president explained:

> We haven't had serious problems of coordination because many area managers have had both sales and operations experience. As the size of the operating group has grown in relation to sales, there are fewer opportunities for cross-functional training. If we don't substitute other coordinating devices for this, it may come back to haunt us in the future.

Increasing variability in the capabilities of regional managers and facility managers were being observed as well. Some were clearly overloaded, but could not be relieved of some responsibility without their thinking they had been demoted. The company had maintained a policy of assigning a full-time manager to each health care and educational facility, but it had become apparent that some smaller accounts did not warrant full-time facility managers.

As a result of these concerns, Bill Pollard appointed a task force of company managers to study alternative ways of organizing the company, both to accommodate its anticipated growth and to maintain its values.

At a meeting held in March 1985, set to launch the reorganization study, Pollard first suggested several criteria by which a reorganization proposal should be judged. Next, alternative organizational forms were discussed. These included arguments for creating separate business units for the hospital, school, and industrial/commercial markets; for changing the job of the divisional vice president to concentrate on one function (sales or operations) within a region; for maintaining the existing organization but creating more regions; and for eliminating levels of management. Since there was concern with the manner in which any change in organization might be implemented, a discussion ensued about whether an idea should be tested in one region or whether change should be made nationally as quickly as possible.

All of these alternatives had been discussed with a consultant. Pollard had asked both the consultant and members of the internal task force to "look beyond conventional organization solutions and search for the same kind of creative ideas on which this company was built."

Exhibit 1
Selected Financial Information, 1979–1985
(in millions of dollars unless otherwise noted)

	1985[a]	1983	1981	1979
Operating Results				
Operating revenue	$1,002	$701	$502	$339
Expenses:				
Cost of services rendered and				
products sold	871	597	420	282
Selling and administrative expenses	73	58	52	37
Non-operating expenses (income)	2	3	3	1
Federal and state income tax	24	17	9	8
Net income	33	26	18	11
Net income as:				
% of revenue	3.3%	3.7%	3.5%	3.3%
% of return on average equity	45.5%	45.2%	35.7%	34.6%
Financial Position				
Current assets	$ 83	$ 69	$ 55	$ 31
Current liabilities	42	34	19	11
Working capital	40	35	36	20
Current ratio	2.0–1	2.0–1	2.9–1	2.8–1
Non-current liabilities	15	2	1	1
Shareholders' equity	76	59	54	35
Total assets	133	95	74	47
Average net operating assets (total assets less cash, investments, accounts payable, and assets acquired as of December 31)	92	60	45	34
Per Share				
Net income ($)	1.00	.78	.53	.35
Cash dividends paid ($)	.77	.55	.35	.21
Price range of common stock				
High ($)	25.50	30.62	13.25	7.50
Low ($)	17.50	17.25	10.12	5.25
Shares used for computation (millions)	33	33	33	32

[a] Estimated.

SERVICEMASTER INDUSTRIES INC.
Exhibit 2
In-Company Career Development Education Programs

Career Path: EMPLOYEE — SUPERVISOR — NEW MANAGER — ASSISTANT MANAGER — RESIDENT COORDINATING MANAGER — MASTER COORDINATOR / SURVEY ENGINEER / DIVISION SPECIALISTS / DIVISION EDUCATION MANAGER / RECRUITING MANAGER / REGIONAL OPERATIONS MANAGER — DIVISION CONTROLLER / MANAGEMENT REPRESENTATIVE / AREA OPERATIONS MANAGER / DIVISION OPERATIONS MANAGER / DIVISION MANAGER / DIVISION V.P. / DIVISION PRESIDENT

	Employee	Supervisor	Assistant Manager	New Manager	Resident Coordinating Manager	Master Coordinator / Survey Engineer / Division Specialists / Division Education Manager / Recruiting Manager / Regional Operations Manager	Division Controller / Management Representative / Area Operations Manager / Division Operations Manager / Division Manager / Division V.P. / Division President
POSITION	Employee	Supervisor	Assistant Manager	New Manager	Resident Coordinating Manager	Master Coordinator; Survey Engineer; Division Specialists; Division Education Manager; Recruiting Manager; Regional Operations Manager	Division Controller; Management Representative; Area Operations Manager; Division Operations Manager; Division Manager; Division V.P.; Division President
PROGRAMS	Job Skill Training (JST) Housekeeping, Plant Operations & Maintenance; Job Skill Review (JSR) Housekeeping, Laundry POM. M.M.; Employee Special Programs; Facility Employee Programs; POM Skills Development; Succeed (Office In-Service); Safety Training	Basic Training Program; Supervisor Development Program (SDP); Leadership Human Relations Series (LHRS0) Teaching JSR; Supervisor Conferences; Leadership Development Program (LDP); POM Career Development	Orientation; Management Development Program (MOP); Management Development Seminar (MDS)	Management Review Program (MRP); Management Development Seminar #2 (Grid); POM Career Development Program; Leadership Development Program (LDP); Technical Workshops.	Regional Meetings; Area Team Program; Fall Mgmt. Conference; Award of Excellence Program; Development Coordinator Assignment; Development Coordinator Seminars; Financial Skills Seminars I and II; Teaching Human Relations Series (LHRS); Sponsoring Leadership Development Program (LDP)	ROP-Operational Procedures Manual, ROM Development Checklist; Area Team Development; ALERT Mgmt. Conferences; Management Skills Seminar; Engineering Managers Orientation; Division Education Manager G.L.U.E. Meetings	AOP-Operational Procedures Manual; Teaching Area Team Development Program; ALERT Mgmt. Conferences; GRAD Program; Management Representative Training Program
MEASUREMENT	Employee Training Schedules; Employee Appraisals	Supervisor Development Schedule; Supervisor Appraisal, 71109	Weekly Development Reviews of New Manager by Development Coordinator; Weekly Self-Appraisal	Management Review Progress Record; Manager's Appraisal Review (71005)	Quality Performance Quotient Inspections (QPQ); Facility Forced Ranking; Development Coordinator Rating (71054); Manager's Appraisal Review (71006)	Monthly Program Schedule Audits; Annual Program Review; ROM Appraisal (71072)	Monthly Program Schedule Audits

1. Appraisal and Review → 2. Annual Career Development Review → 3. Annual Personal Education Review → Continuing Education Coop. Program

Exhibit 3
Excerpt from a ServiceMaster Research Development Department
Technical Information Bulletin

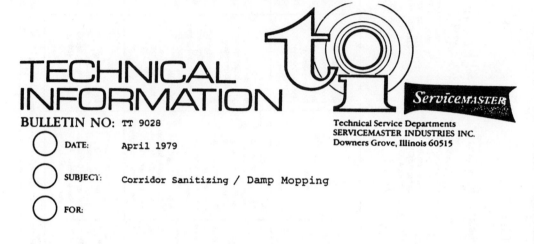

TECHNICAL
INFORMATION

BULLETIN NO: TT 9028

Technical Service Departments
SERVICEMASTER INDUSTRIES INC.
Downers Grove, Illinois 60515

 ◯ **DATE:** April 1979

 ◯ **SUBJECT:** Corridor Sanitizing / Damp Mopping

 ◯ **FOR:**

EQUIPMENT

 1 60 inch mop handle, 24 oz. mop head

 1 8 gallon stainless steel bucket and wringer

  Wet floor signs

  DuoClene <u>or</u> SaniMaster II

INITIAL PREPARATION

1. Mount mop head on handle and wringer on bucket.

2. Fill bucket with 5 gallons of cold water. Level should be 1 inch under wringer.

3. Dispense DuoClene at 1/2 oz. per gallon (2-1/2 oz. in bucket) <u>or</u> SaniMaster II at 1 oz. per gallon (5 oz. in bucket).

4. Place mop in bucket, hang wet floor signs on wringer handle and move to work area.

5. Floor must be dusted prior to sanitizing.

PROCEDURE

1. Place wet floor signs so as to section the corridor into 125' sections. By mopping 1/2 the corridor at a time, the 125' section will be about 4' wide. Traffic entering the area via stairwells, elevators, doorways, etc. should also be cautioned by the strategic placement of the signs.

2. Locate bucket in center of 4' x 125' section. Wring mop firmly. Mop along wall base as illustrated. Special attention should be given to corners and area where dust buildup may occur.

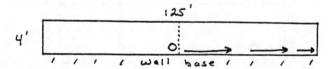

Exhibit 3
(Continued)

Bulletin #: TT 9028
Page 2

3. Return to bucket using "S" stroke as illustrated.

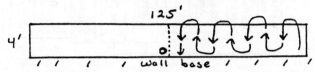

4. Sanitize other half of 4' x 125' section as illustrated. Use
    same procedure.

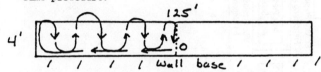

5. Move bucket to next 125' section (same side of corridor) and repeat
    operation. Wet floor signs from first section should be moved as
    each section dries.

6. Repeat steps 1-5 on opposite half of corridor. Refresh sanitizing
    mixture approximately every 5000 square feet. Replace mop head as
    necessary.

CLEANUP

1. Clean and store wet floor signs.

2. Empty sanitizing mixture, dry bucket and wringer and store.

3. Remove mop head, replace with clean mop head and transport soiled
    mop to collection site.

SERVICEMASTER INDUSTRIES INC.
Exhibit 4
Organization of Senior Ranks, June 1985

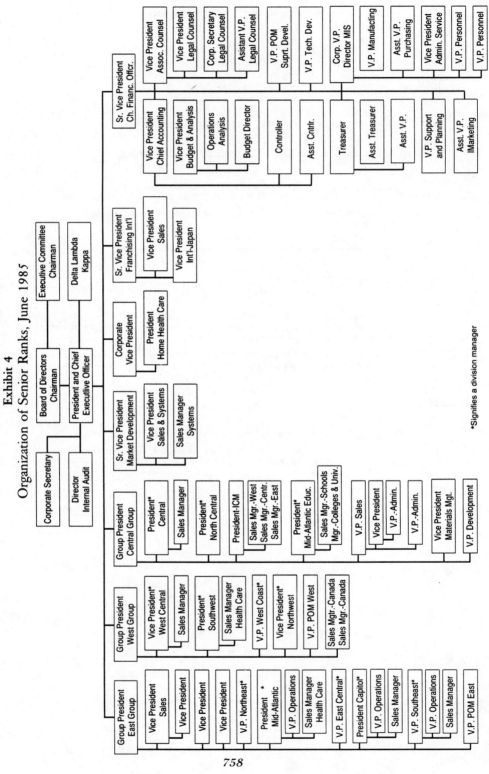

*Signifies a division manager

758

Exhibit 5
Typical Division Organization, June 1985

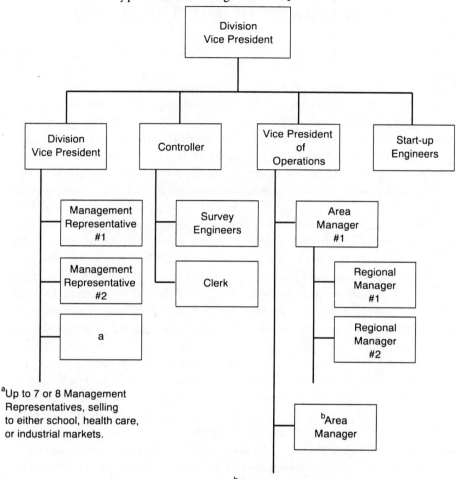

[a]Up to 7 or 8 Management
Representatives, selling
to either school, health care,
or industrial markets.

[b]Up to 7 or 8 Area Managers
divided by geographic market
into either school, health care,
or industrial accounts.

Girl Scouts of the U.S.A. (A)

Change was very much on Frances Hesselbein's mind as she came across a document prepared several years earlier summarizing a discussion she had held with a group of Girl Scout council leaders. Hesselbein, the National executive director of the Girl Scouts of the U.S.A., noted that the leaders, all executive directors of their own local Girl Scout councils, had emphasized the continuing need for a willingness to change on the part of the organization and its leadership. The document noted several challenges to the organization that would require continuing attention, including the declining viability of the traditional Girl Scout troop headed by a volunteer adult leader; the persisting image of the Girl Scouts as a white, middle-class organization; the waning interest of teenage girls in the Girl Scouts; and the large number of both paid staff and volunteers who did not welcome change. One challenge the document did not mention was the increasing interest among the leadership of the Boy Scouts of America (BSA) in extending its membership to girls. This had resulted, according to recent information received by Hesselbein, in the BSA's commissioning a feasibility study of the matter.

At the time, the discussion had confirmed some of Hesselbein's own experiences at the national level of the Girl Scouts of the USA (GSUSA), where from time to time issues had arisen about the degree to which local Girl Scout councils were encouraging diversity in ethnic and racial backgrounds of girl members, volunteers, and staff, as well as the importance of adult-generated income to support the Girl Scout program. She knew that how these issues were addressed could at times be nearly as important as the way they were resolved. Invariably, the process of resolution raised questions about the relative roles of national headquarters and local councils in fulfilling the organization's mission.

In reflecting on the work of the Girl Scouts in recent years, Hesselbein wondered whether the participants in that earlier discussion would reach quite the same conclusions today.

Professor James L. Heskett prepared this case as the basis for class discussion rather than to illustrate either effective or ineffective handling of an administrative situation. Copyright © 1989 by the President and Fellows of Harvard College; Harvard Business School case # 9-690-044 (Rev. 1/90).

BACKGROUND

"Come right over. I've got something for the girls of Savannah, and all America
. . . and we're going to start it tonight." Those words, spoken by Juliette Gordon
Low to her friend, Nina Pape, on March 12, 1912, signaled the start of a movement that would affect more girls than any other in the twentieth century in the
United States. The idea had begun in May 1910 with Sir Robert Baden-Powell
and his sister Agnes in England, where Juliette Low was living at the time with
her husband. The Baden-Powells had organized the Boy Scouts and Girl Guides,
respectively, there. Less than nine months after meeting the Baden-Powells in
England, Low registered 18 girls at the first meeting of the Girl Scout organization upon returning to her birthplace in Savannah, Georgia.

The U.S. organization, patterned after its British counterpart, was dedicated
to "inspiring girls with the highest ideals of character, conduct, patriotism, and
service that they may become happy and resourceful citizens."[1] Its mission was
based on "The Promise" (On my honor, I will try: To serve God and my country, to help people at all times, and to live by the Girl Scout law.) "The Law,"
which could be repeated by anyone who had ever been a Girl Scout, stated:

I will do my best:

- to be honest
- to be fair
- to help where I am needed
- to be cheerful
- to be friendly and considerate
- to be a sister to every Girl Scout
- to respect authority
- to use resources wisely
- to protect and improve the world around me
- to show respect for myself and others through my words and actions

The Promise and the Law were pursued through a program of skill- and
character-building activities, social events, camping, and the involvement of girl
members in the governance of their own troop.

A natural leader, Juliette Low threw herself into the task of creating a national
organization, traveling widely in the United States to introduce Girl Scouting,
form local councils, assist new leaders, and enlist support. The demand was im-

---

1. Constitution of the Girl Scouts of the United States of America.

mense from girls and young women whose lives were still relatively constrained, but who were attracted to the idea of becoming more self-sufficient, serving others, and earning proficiency badges reflecting contemporary challenges (such as one early in the organization's history for how to stop a runaway horse) and gaining skills in the process.

Unlike the development of most other nonprofit organizations, Juliette Low founded Girl Scouting as a national organization which later chartered local units, called councils. Within a year of its founding, the Girl Scouts' national headquarters was opened in Washington, D.C., with expenses and salaries financed by Low.

In its rapid growth, the organization marked many milestones. The first national training school for Girl Scout leaders was conducted in 1917, shortly after the first troop of physically disabled Girl Scouts was organized. In 1926, as the organization sought to achieve its goals of establishing a council in every city of 20,000 or more, Camp Edith Macy was opened as a national training center. Located on 404 acres of beautiful countryside just north of New York City, the camp was a gift of V. Everit Macy in memory of his wife, a dedicated Girl Scout volunteer who had envisioned a national training site for Girl Scout leaders. The gift set a pattern for many others that were to be made to local councils for camping purposes. In total, such gifts eventually would make Girl Scouting a very large landowner.

Local councils, each comprising a number of troops of girls with leaders, were formed as an effective means of delivering services and handling administrative duties at the community level. By 1920, there were nearly 100 councils comprising over 3,000 troops and 70,000 girl members in every state but one. From its beginning, the organization's membership was open to all girls.

In response to a need to help the Girl Scout program become better known and to aid troop financing, the Girl Scouts introduced their first cookie sale in 1936. This project, involving the sale by Girl Scouts of commercially baked cookies, replaced similar efforts by troops to home-bake and sell cookies. It was to make the cookie a Girl Scout hallmark. In 1988, councils reported the sale of 165 million boxes of cookies, making Girl Scout Cookies one of the most well-known products in the country.

By 1944, membership exceeded one million, with more than a quarter of the membership participating in camping experiences. By 1947, the need for camp expansion was made a national priority. International encampments for Girl Scouts and Girl Guides grew in importance. The 1940s and 1950s proved to be a golden age of recruitment for the organization as it reached two million members in 1953, three million in 1957 (three years ahead of plan), and 3.9 million in 1969, prior to declining in subsequent years.

Based on the findings of a study by the Survey Research Center of the University of Michigan, the Girl Scout program was reorganized into four age groupings in 1962. These comprised Brownie Girl Scouts, ages 7–9; Junior Girl Scouts, ages 10–12; Cadette Girl Scouts, ages 13–15; and Senior Girl Scouts, ages 15–17. In 1984, in response to the earlier involvement of children in educational and other activities, the Daisy Girl Scouts for five-year-old girls was formed. A membership decline starting in 1970 was halted in 1981, producing a membership of 3,166,000 by 1989.

In 1976, Frances Hesselbein became the latest in a line of national executive directors who served alongside volunteer national presidents at the head of the organization. She was the first national executive director in the history of the organization to be promoted with "field" experience as a troop leader, national board member, council president, and council executive director. Her familiarity with the organization was a real asset as she set about to institute a comprehensive corporate planning process, reorganize the staff, introduce corporate management training, and spearhead efforts to stimulate fund-raising projects such as the $10 million Edith Macy Conference Center, for use in leadership and management development activities, which opened in 1982.

Important program initiatives of the 1980s included a major study in conjunction with the National Urban League to gain insight into the impact of the Girl Scouts' outreach program on its membership, a study which generally found approval among both the general public and Girl Scout members for increased participation of minorities in the organization. In 1985, the national organization, in response to growing needs expressed by councils, created Safe at Home Alone, a national project that enabled councils to offer the Girl Scout program to "latch-key" girls who were at home alone after school.

Most recently, a National Center for Innovation had been created to encourage demonstration projects designed to increase racial-ethnic membership in Girl Scouting. Projects found to be successful could be replicated nationwide. Among the first of these projects, all of which were being tested in Southern California, were:

1. Daisy Girl Scouts—a Head Start on Literacy: Playing in the World of Words, a program to help five-year-olds graduating from Head Start programs learn to read and increase their self-esteem.
2. Winning Girls! Winning Women!, a program which attracted star athletes as well as college and high school athletes to become leaders for Junior Girl Scouts in schools where dropout rates were high.
3. Las Madrinas ("godmothers" in Spanish), involving business sponsors and mentors in providing support to new troop leaders in Hispanic communi-

ties, where increasing numbers of married couples were being recruited as leaders to overcome traditional beliefs that an adult married woman should devote all her time to her own family.

4. Valuing Differences: Camp staffing and training, intended to increase staff competence in working with girls to resolve tensions that arise from racism and classism.

5. Positive Futures: Discouraging Teen Pregnancy, in which Girl Scouts organized community forums and an after-school "Teen Talkline" to supplement existing crisis referral services.

ORGANIZATION

The foundation of Girl Scouting in 1989 was its 196,000 troops, 3,166,000 girl members, and 751,000 adult members, many of whom served as troop leaders. More than 99% of adult members were volunteers.

Troops

Membership activities and leadership of Girl Scout troops had changed as a reflection of social trends. Membership among minorities had increased from 5% in 1979 to 15% in 1989. The development of Daisy Girl Scout troops for five-year-olds had lowered the average age of troop members overall. The activities they engaged in long since had given less emphasis to cooking and household skills in preference to the growing interest of girls in science, the environment, and business, for example. Troop leadership had, in many cases, changed as a response to the difficulty of recruiting good leaders and the changing demographics of troop members. For example, greater emphasis was being placed on finding young women who were good role models, such as successful businesswomen, as troop leaders.

Councils

Troops in turn were organized into 334 councils, managed by paid staff and volunteers, and self-financed.

Councils were grouped by the national office, for purposes of organizing relevant support services, into four "service clusters," as follows:

Service Cluster	Girl Membership	Number of Councils[a]
Metro I	12,000 and above	55
Metro II	6,000–12,000	82
Midsize cities	3,000– 6,000	121
Small cities and rural	3,000 and below	76

[a]Based on girl membership as of September 30, 1988.

Each council was headed by a full-time, paid executive director who reported to a volunteer board of directors and led a staff of from five to 60 paid career associates. This staff, in turn, worked with volunteers to provide support to troops in recruiting, fund-raising, program development, and other activities. A sample organization chart for a Metro II Girl Scout Council is shown in *Exhibit 1.*

At one time there had been as many as 1,200 councils. Over a period of some 15 years in the 1960s and 1970s, a concentrated effort had been put forth to encourage councils to merge in the interest of providing more effective ways of marshalling resources to deliver services to troops. The consolidation accomplished its purpose, although in some councils it took several years to achieve a desired level of cohesion. By way of contrast, the Boy Scout organization operated with roughly four times as many councils as the Girl Scouts.

From September through June, much of the time of the council executive director was spent in preparing for and participating in board and committee meetings, developing tactical plans and supporting budget documents, supervising staff, preparing management reports, making fund development contacts, and working with the heads of other community agencies. In addition, from June through August was described as a "time of stress" for council staff members because such a large number of girl members were involved in outdoor activities requiring close attention to safety. Council staff members were on constant call in the event of such occurrences.

There were significant differences between councils. The contrast was perhaps the greatest between those located in rural or suburban areas and those whose territories included a large city center. The differences were illustrated by visits by the case writer to two adjacent councils, Spar and Spindle and Patriot's Trail.[2]

Spar and Spindle Council. The Spar and Spindle Council was headquartered in a modern, 50,000 square-foot building in North Andover, Massachusetts, just north of Boston. In 1989 it comprised 860 troops, about 10,400 girl members, 3,500 adult members, a paid staff of 30, and an operating budget of about $1.3 million. It served a geographic area comprising 53 towns and cities, many of

2. Names of council executive directors have been disguised.

them bedroom communities but some highly industrialized. A map of the council's jurisdiction in Eastern Massachusetts and Southern New Hampshire is shown in *Exhibit 2*.

Jane Ehrlich, executive director of the council, had previously occupied the same position in another council. There, she brought closure to a fragmenting capital campaign, laid a strong financial base, and instituted innovative outreach programs for membership growth. Prior to that job, she worked for a number of years at the national office. When she arrived at Spar and Spindle, its membership was declining. In the past year, it had registered an 11% increase in overall membership and a 26% increase in minority membership ("from a small base"). She credited the addition of an energetic director of field services and the upgrading of other jobs for the rapid turnaround.

According to Ehrlich, "money is not a problem in this council." Sources of council funding included product sales (33%); United Way (20%); program income, largely from camping (26%); investment income (13%); and contributions (8%). Like other councils, Spar and Spindle owned sizeable assets, the value of which was largely unknown. For example, while it listed the value of its assets at the end of 1987 as $1,489,000, this basically included only the depreciated value of its headquarters and its investments. In addition, the council owned six large pieces of property encompassing about 750 acres, all of them used for camping and nearly all situated on waterfronts, as well as a home on the ocean in Gloucester, Massachusetts, which was used frequently for meetings. The property had been obtained through gifts from Girl Scout alumnae through the years.

What did concern Ehrlich, however, was the need for greater outreach in her council, particularly through programs designed to reach Hispanic communities in Lawrence and Haverhill, the black population in Lynn, and a growing group of Asians in Lowell, an old mill town that was attracting people to its new high-technology factories. Also, she had to be constantly on the alert to deal with social issues, such as drugs and teenage pregnancy "without fracturing the council." According to Ehrlich, "Many people moved to this area to leave those problems behind. We use materials from National to legitimize our efforts. The Contemporary Issues series, even with its necessarily cautious approach to sensitive issues, has been a great help in this effort."

Ehrlich was in the process of organizing a more sophisticated fund development program to encourage giving by parents. This could help replace a 19% cutback in funding by the Merrimack Valley United Fund in 1989, a decision that irked her:

> They cut us back because they say we can earn our own funds. To some degree, United Fund giving is being dominated by crisis agencies whose problems are more immediate. But when they cut our funding, they actually

increased their funding to the Boy Scouts. When we figured it out, the United Fund allocations equaled $34 for every Boy Scout and $9 for every Girl Scout in the area. My board was furious. They considered withdrawal from that United Fund. But National has cautioned us not to run, because these are community funds. I'm ready to go another few rounds.

Contributions by the United Fund to the Girl Scouts carried with them certain restraints. For example, a recipient of funds had to agree not to approach corporations, foundations, or certain other sources of support.

One of Ehrlich's concerns was in attracting a more diverse racial and ethnic board of directors. She felt that this could lead to a greater interest in funding activities other than camping, which was the primary interest at present.

Ehrlich estimated that she worked on average 50 hours per week, including two nights per week away from home, much of it spent in meetings with volunteers and community leaders. Fridays, the weekday on which council offices were closed, afforded her the time to get caught up with administrative work. She described "burnout" as being a constant problem in the job, one of which all executive directors were especially conscious. As she put it, "The demands of balancing public and private roles are never-ending."

Patriots' Trail Council. Headed by executive director Judith Altobello, the Patriots' Trail Council was headquartered on the ninth floor of a large office building in downtown Boston. Responsible for a territory encompassing Boston and 64 surrounding communities, in 1989 the Council was the sixth largest in the United States, with 22,870 girl members, 4,900 adult members, and field offices in three outlying communities as well as Boston. Altobello presided over a staff of 55 paid people, 15 of them officed in outlying communities.

In her own words, Altobello was "as close to a career Girl Scout as you can get," having first become attracted to the organization as a young Girl Scout given an opportunity to work with a National Meeting. She had remained active in the organization through college and had pursued a career spanning more than 15 years with Girl Scouting, having held positions as executive director in Oklahoma City and Dayton before coming to Boston in 1989.

She explained that the Patriots' Trail Council had had a unique history. In the early 1970s, its predecessor council was the only council in recent years to have its charter revoked for failing to meet National's standards concerning financial management and progress toward a more diverse membership. This had required that it cease to operate as a corporate entity and come under the management of the national organization until the late 1970s when it became part of a four-council merger resulting in the formation of the Patriots' Trail Council. At the time, a fifth council resisted National's efforts to get it to participate in the merger, discounting arguments that the merger would create a broader-reaching program, expand children's horizons, and assist in developing Girl Scouting in Boston proper.

The merger produced a council that was "land rich and cash poor," with 22 camps and meeting sites, including a 26-acre tract on Martha's Vineyard, all requiring maintenance. Most of these were sold to environmentally sensitive buyers for about $1.2 million, allowing the Patriots' Trail Council to better maintain its remaining seven properties, which included a 90-acre camp on Cape Cod and a 90-acre camp on Lake Winnipesaukee in New Hampshire.

Altobello described how Girl Scouting had changed. Service projects for girls involving the preparation of tray favors for hospitals had been replaced by projects to promote literacy. The two most popular proficiency badges were now "Math Whiz" and "Computer Fun" instead of "Good Grooming" and "Hosting a Party." Where "gung-ho primitive camping" had once been preeminent as an activity, it was being replaced by camping as an opportunity to "have an intensive, interpersonal experience in teamwork and self-governance." In Altobello's words:

> A major challenge to the Council is that of helping troop leaders relate to girls. Troop leaders used to get involved in discussions about kissing and dating. Now we have to help them try to identify and deal with evidence of child abuse and tendencies toward suicide. In other generations, the entire society focused on raising children. Today, it is often seen as a burden. Therefore, leaders have to play a more supportive role with girls.

The biggest challenges for the council, in Altobello's opinion, were finding leaders, adapting the program to the inner-city, developing more collaborative efforts in the community, "communicating with people about who we are," and expanding the funding base away from cookie sales.

The need for new forms of leadership in serving girls in Boston had necessitated the council's hiring and training neighborhood "aides," often young women 18 or older and grandmothers, to look for and assist leaders of 10 to 20 troops in a particular area. According to Altobello, this was a departure from the National standards for volunteerism. But, in her words, "Standards are negotiable; policies are not. We have very few policies. Besides, volunteers are more reluctant to work in dangerous areas."

Ads produced by a local agency for the council had concentrated both on communicating a more current image for Girl Scouting and attracting a more diverse group of leaders. One such ad is shown in *Exhibit 3*. Another ad in the series, headlined, "Are you man enough to be a Girl Scout?" had provoked so much adverse comment from Girl Scouts that it was no longer used.

Camping represented a different concept for suburban and inner-city girls in the Council. It was still a highlight of the year's activities for suburban troops, who reserved the most desirable camping sites and times far in advance. By way of contrast, campers from the city had to be subsidized. The council reserved space for them to insure availability of camping capacity. In addition, a "Summer Evening Program" had been developed to get both families and 12- to 17-year-old girls from homeless shelters to a camp for an evening as a response to fears on the part of homeless mothers of parting with their daughters for even a few hours. Children from housing projects with little opportunity of joining a troop were bussed to camps for one-day programs focussed on building their self-esteem. This was all part of an effort to build trust with parents and children. According to Altobello, "Social workers help get them out the first time. The rest is easy."

The council had begun participating in collaborative community efforts to increase its outreach and stretch its funds. For example, at the Harbor Point low-income housing project, a group of agencies including the YMCA, YWCA, day-care agencies, the Girl Scouts, and others solicited funding for a comprehensive support program. The Boy Scouts were not represented in such efforts. According to Altobello, "Boy Scouting in this area has not been a highly collaborative agency." These kinds of efforts were very important in Boston where field services could cost five times what they did in the suburbs.

Efforts were being made to expand the council's funding base. Altobello was worried that 42% of the council's funding came from cookies sold by young girls, particularly since it was the organization's responsibility to insure their safety. More presentations of programs designed to attract contributions from business were being made. This was in response to the fact that only 2% of Girl Scout funding came from corporate contributions as opposed to 38% for the Boy Scouts. In addition, Altobello believed there was significant opportunity to develop "unrelated business income," including camp rentals to various groups for retreats. She was quite willing to see the council pay income tax on this income.

Altobello estimated that she worked 50 to 60 hours a week, including three evening meetings per week. In winter, her time was equally divided between board work designed to obtain consensus on various issues, staff supervision, and community development efforts. In summer, the council's attention turned to what she called "direct programming," involving more direct supervision of 200 people staffing three overnight and eight day camps. She felt that the benefits of managing a large council were that it was less dependent on National for specific expertise, there were more types of expert experience within the staff, and it was easier to call on the corporate "community" for services such as the design and preparation of advertising.

Altobello was reminded frequently of Boy Scout efforts to include girls in its programs. Her reaction was that, "As long as we do what we do well, we shouldn't worry about the potential competition of the Boy Scouts. Studies support the importance of single sex activities for young girls. And it's the girl delegates to our meetings who speak up for a single sex organization."

National

The National president of the Girl Scouts, Betty Pilsbury, was a volunteer elected by the National Council to be president of the corporation and of the National board of directors, comprising 52 volunteer members (down from 74). Members served on standing committees of the board responsible for communications, finance, human resources, membership and councils, planning and organization, and program. Pilsbury, described as a "down-to-earth person who understands the separation of policy and operations and who is very council-oriented," had served for a number of years in various volunteer positions and devoted a large portion of her time to duties such as presiding at meetings of the National Council and National board of directors, managing the selection process for the National executive director, representing the organization at numerous events around the world, and generally providing leadership for the corporate planning effort (described later). This required that she work closely with the senior salaried member of the organization, the National executive director. In addition, Pilsbury spent a significant amount of time visiting councils to provide visible leadership to the organization.

In addition to reviewing the performance of both the National president and National executive director annually, the board reviewed its own performance as well as that of the organization annually against preset operating objectives which were embedded in longer-term corporate goals. Corporate goals for 1985–1990 as well as the 1990 integrated operating objectives are shown in *Exhibit 4*. Prospective board members at both the national and local council levels were given a 48-page booklet describing the role, authority, major functions, requirements, management tasks, and legal liabilities of a Girl Scout corporate board of directors.

The paid staff of the National organization comprised 507 people, down from about 700 in the late 1960s. (For example, in one staff reduction in 1985, 70 positions had been eliminated when National realized a revenue shortfall.) Except for a small number located at the New Jersey product warehouse, the Edith Macy Conference Center, and Juliette Low's birthplace in Savannah, Georgia, all were officed in a 13-story building in mid-Manhattan owned by the organization.

Much of the effort in recent years had been on consolidating the organization in New York. Service centers, previously operated in Chicago and Dallas, as well as New York, were closed in early 1989 and the staff moved to New York. Reasons given for this decision were: (1) the need to achieve greater cohesion, coordination, and integration among all national staff members; (2) greater proximity to the national conference center where some members of the field center staff were instructors; and (3) more staff time in New York required to support planning and conducting meetings sponsored by GSUSA.

As a result of a major study, National Center West, a 15,000-acre site adjacent to the Big Horn National Forest in Wyoming, was being sold by GSUSA. As one staff member explained, only about 2,000 girls were using the camp each summer. The costs associated with transportation were high, and the organization's priorities had shifted somewhat. It was anticipated that the sale would be made to an organization that would agree to preserve the environment.

The National staff structure is shown in *Exhibit 5*. Headed by Frances Hesselbein, national executive director, the heart of the team comprised six assistant National executive directors (ANEDs) primarily responsible for field operations; fund-raising; human resources, program design, publications, and media services; legal; national and international relationships; and financial services, and a director of National Equipment Services (equipment sales).

Mary Rose Main was regarded by many in the GSUSA organization as chief operating officer. As one of the assistant National executive directors (ANEDs), she supervised all field services provided to councils, organizational development efforts, information systems, and in general the implementation of programs designed by the national office staff. Other assistant National executive directors included Florence Corsello, Dori Parker, Joel Becker, Patricia Smith, and Patricia Winterer. All ANEDs reported directly to Frances Hesselbein.

Aided by a staff of three people, Parker was responsible for capital fund-raising at the National level as well as the oversight function for fund-raising at the local level. According to Parker, GSUSA suffered from what she termed a "dual curse." In her words: "On the one hand we're seen as a goody two-shoes, traditional organization. On the other, we're seen as being well-managed, solvent, and not having severe financial needs. Both hurt us when we go to raise funding." Although councils were requested to clear requests to foundations through Parker's office, she was certain that it didn't always happen.

In addition to managing human resources in the National organization, Becker was responsible for the development of resources for councils as well as publications and advertising intended to foster internal and external communications. Sharon Hussey, who reported to Becker, was responsible for the design and publication of handbooks and booklets such as the Contemporary Issues Series. She dealt in large numbers and difficult issues. For example, a new edition of the Girl Scout Handbook might have a first printing of 1.5 million copies. On the other hand, in developing a Contemporary Issues booklet on teenage pregnancy, Hussey pointed out the need to be "values-rooted, not issues-rooted." As she put it, "For that reason, you won't find the word 'abortion' in that document."

John Sokolowski completed Frances Hesselbein's immediate management team. Corsello was the organization's controller and ANED for finance. Sokolowski headed up National Equipment Service (NES), the organization's merchandising arm. NES was responsible for the production and distribution of official Girl Scout uniforms, equipment, and handbooks through authorized Girl Scout agencies located in 1,400 retail stores and 135 council-operated shops, as well as a catalog which it prepared and distributed. Girl Scout merchandise was also retailed through J.C. Penney's and Sears' mail-order catalogs. More recently, $6.4 million in merchandise has been shipped to newly opened council shops. It was estimated that for every dollar's worth of merchandise sold at retail, National realized about 58 cents in revenues and incurred roughly 29 cents in cost of goods sold and 9 cents in other costs. This 20-cent differential had yielded about $12.8 million in net revenue to National in 1988. In addition, NES selected, licensed, and supervised commercial bakers authorized to produce Girl Scout cookies for sale by Girl Scout councils. Individual councils purchased from licensed bakers and negotiated specific prices.

Propelled by growth in Girl Scout membership, the performance of NES was achieving record levels, having exceeded goals for equipment sales for the past 36 straight months.

The effective working relationship between volunteers and paid staff members was reflected at the National level as well as each of the 334 local councils. It required that the presidents and executive directors at each level form a partnership relationship. Betty Pilsbury and Frances Hesselbein were described by one staff member as "mutually supportive working colleagues."

FINANCING

A basic tenet of Girl Scouting was that individual troops and councils as well as the national headquarters should all be self-supporting. As one executive put it, "Maybe because we are predominantly a female-oriented organization (with about 80% of the headquarters and council staff being female and a relatively small but growing number of male troop leaders, who served as co-leaders with women) we feel we have to manage ourselves a bit better. That means being self-supporting and achieving a balanced budget while delivering programs effectively."

Troops obtained their funding primarily through troop dues and the sale of cookies, from which they realized from 10 to 25 cents per box, depending on the council. In addition, troops earned money through activities such as car washing and Girl Scout calendar sales. They were prohibited from having more than two sales annually, including the cookie sale.

Council funding was obtained from United Way appeals, program services (camp fees, program service fees, and training fees), cookie sales, investment income, and contributions. Selected financial data for the Spar and Spindle and Patriots' Trail Councils are shown in *Exhibit 6*. A composite income statement for all councils for 1986 and 1987 is presented in *Exhibit 7*. Unlike troops, councils owned sizeable assets, most of which were recorded at historical costs on their balance sheets.

Funding for the national office was obtained largely through the collection of Girl Scout dues of $4 per girl per year and the sale of official equipment and publications. Together, they yielded about 75% of total funding. In addition, the national office solicited gifts from foundations and large corporations, especially for large capital expenditures such as those for the development of the Adult Learning Center at Edith Macy Conference Center. Financial statements for GSUSA are presented in *Exhibits 8* and *9*.

MANAGING FOR THE MISSION

In 1953, Frances Hesselbein reluctantly agreed to accept the job of Girl Scout troop leader of "thirty little ten-year-olds in a church basement" in Johnstown, Pennsylvania, for four weeks. In her words, "I was so impressed with the values of the organization, its worldwide orientation, and the diversity of membership I didn't find in my own neighborhood that I ended up making a career out of it." The mission of "helping every girl achieve her highest potential" proved irresistible. Few in the organization disagreed that Hesselbein brought boundless energy, an ingratiating manner, persistence in pursuing initiatives, and a sense of style to her work. It required that, as national executive director, she form a close partnership with the organization's volunteer president, Betty Pilsbury; preside over the entire national organization with about $32 million in revenues; insure that the organization monitor the needs of councils and deliver resources and services reflecting those needs; and carry out major fund-raising activities. In addition, she helped represent the organization to the outside world. Reflecting the diversity of her activities, the wall of her modest office at National Girl Scout Headquarters overlooking the intersection of Third Avenue and 51st Street in New York City was covered with photos of her either accepting awards from or making them to national figures, including Presidents of the United States, as well as turning over the first spadeful of earth (attired in the inevitable hard hat) to initiate the construction of the Edith Macy Conference Center.

In providing leadership to the organization, Hesselbein consciously used motto-like phrases to remind her colleagues of their tasks. For example, she frequently referred to the importance of "managing for the mission" of helping girls, and expected everyone else to do it. She described the organization as "mission-focused, values-based (as identified in the Promise and the Law), and demographics-driven (her code word for diversity of membership)." She described to the case writer a teeter-totter, writing "$24 million expense budget, millions of handbooks, 334 councils, and conference center" on one end; writing the words, "one 10-year-old girl," on the other; and announcing, "It balances." As she put it:

The power of language is so important in this job. People often refer to us as a traditional organization. I try to remind them that we're a contemporary organization with a great tradition. When people say Scouts, I point out that we're the Girl Scouts, not to be confused with (Boy) Scouts. When people, including those in our own organization, refer to cookie sales as a business activity, somebody has to remind them that it's a girl's program activity. All of us have to constantly remind ourselves that the bottom line in this organization is changed lives.

Hesselbein had made a conscious effort to encourage the GSUSA to develop a contemporary image. Among other things, she enlisted Halston and Bill Blass to redesign a line of uniforms for the Girl Scouts which preserved "keen green" as the central color but was also sufficiently fashionable to be worn for occasions other than scouting or GSUSA activities. She appeared on the cover of *Savvy* magazine in connection with an article on "Executive Excellence," to focus attention on the need for outstanding management in not-for-profit organizations.

In order to manage more effectively for the mission, a new corporate planning/management system was introduced in 1977.

THE CORPORATE PLANNING/MANAGEMENT SYSTEM

A product of a coordinated effort of representatives of councils and the national organization, the cooporate planning/management system was intended for use in both the Girl Scout national organization and in local councils of all sizes. Its underlying premise was that planning and management were synonymous. Under this sytem, corporate planning in Girl Scouting comprised strategic planning (with a six-year horizon, determined primarily because of its natural "fit" with the total Girl Scout organization's triennial cycle of national meetings), tactical planning (with a one-year horizon), and implementation, review, and performance appraisal (ongoing).

Strategic Planning

Strategic planning involved the review of the goals and mission of Girl Scouting and the establishment of corporate goals, utilizing internal and external data. The goals were established by the 52-member National board to give leadership to the Girl Scout movement during the six-year goal period.

Comprehensive data gathering, analysis, and study were conducted to prepare the National board for carrying out its role in this phase of corporate planning. This included examining and documenting information from Girl Scout council self-evaluations (conducted every three years) and from National meetings with council personnel; a survey of opinions and perceptions of key individuals and community groups; summaries of operational reports; and an analysis of demographic, membership, program, and financial statistics collected annually from councils. One important source of background information was the Environmental Scanning Report, an analysis of social and demographic trends affecting girls that was prepared semi-annually by the GSUSA staff.

With the use of this background data, members of the National board, officers, and National staff participated in a retreat to develop the first draft of the proposed organizational goals. Following the goal formulation retreat, the goals were tested for feasibility, edited, and refined into proposed goal statements for submission to the National board for adoption. Corporate goals for the 1985–1990 planning period are shown in *Exhibit 4*.

Tactical Planning

While the National board had the corporate responsibility for strategic planning, the National executive director had responsibility for tactical planning. This included setting operating objectives, specific measurable outcomes to be accomplished during one year of the six-year goal period; determining action steps, planned projects for achieving operating objectives; developing budgets; and costing out national services on a planned project basis.

Using suggestions from National board committees, operating objectives were developed by staff operating units and then integrated into a statement of the total organization's operating objectives designed to achieve corporate goals. The National board approved the annual operating objectives. Staff collaboration in developing and implementing action steps to achieve the operating objectives was equally important, with the expected outcome one tactical plan and supporting budget for the entire national organization. Operating objectives for the 1990 tactical plan are included in *Exhibit 4*.

Implementation, Review, and Performance Appraisal

Implementation included the communication of goals, provision of an extensive array of resources by the National organization to councils, and a comprehensive performance measurement and evaluation process carried out on an ongoing basis.

Goals were communicated through the cycle of national and regional meetings carried out during each three-year period. The cycle called for a National Meeting of presidents and executive directors of councils in the first year of the triennium. This was a forum allowing them to meet with National board and staff members to discuss the local and national trends affecting or expected to affect organizational progress. This meeting was an exercise in large-group strategic thinking involving more than 700 participants.

During the second year of each triennium, National Program Conferences were held in up to eleven locations across the country and involved approximately 5,000 girl members, troop leaders, council volunteers and executives, National program specialists, and many others who influenced both the delivery and development of Girl Scout program resources and systems. This gave the conferee an opportunity to react to current program content and materials, review new resources, discuss needs for future program direction, and share their experiences with each other.

In the third year of each three-year period, the same year in which the National board examined GSUSA's six-year goals to determine progress and make revisions, Girl Scouts met at the National Council Session. This meeting involved the governance of Girl Scouting. More than 2,000 delegates, elected in all Girl Scout councils, met to elect the officers and members of the National board, to vote on proposals related to future policy direction, and to discuss major issues. Members age 14 and over were eligible for delegate positions, and the National Council also attracted from 2,000 to 4,000 visitor-members from around the country.

The national organization provided a variety of supporting activities to help local councils achieve their objectives. Included among these were national departments organized to develop a full range of publications, including Girl Scout handbooks, monographs, and a Contemporary Issues series; design new programs, often centered around badges and recognitions; assist in the development of council fund-raising efforts; program new software for council computer systems, and others.

A new management services center was created in January 1989, occupying an entire floor at the New York GSUSA headquarters and employing 30 management consultants and a core of 100 national volunteers. Management consultants were responsible for providing direct services to councils in membership, program development, and funding. Consultants' problem-solving work was carried out at the request of councils. As Mary Rose Main, assistant National executive director, who was in charge of management consultants, said: "I tell them that your job is to find a way to get in there."

Six of the management consultants and 15 National volunteers were assigned to the task of helping councils with their periodic self-evaluations.

The Girl Scout Council Self-Evaluation was the heart of the performance evaluation process at the operating level. It was conducted every three years in all councils. In tandem with the initial chartering process, it provided not only the basis on which charters were renewed by the National organization, but also an important set of benchmarks against which a local council could check its progress. The Girl Scout Council Self-Evaluation manual was 112 pages in length, with 30 pages devoted to specific questions about progress in achieving some 21 standards, an example of which is shown in *Exhibit 10*. Standards were grouped under three "criteria": (1) membership and access to Girl Scout program, (2) maintaining organizational integrity, and (3) the development and stewardship of resources. Other portions of the manual were devoted to questions about the composition of the self-evaluation team, the make-up of a council's board of directors, profiles of every member of a council's staff, and instructions concerning the collection of data and perceptions from council board members, members of the communities served by the council, people delivering the council's services, scout leaders, girl members, and others in support of the self-evaluation. Following the preparation of the self-evaluation, an on-site visit by a team of executives from National headquarters was conducted to review questionnaire responses and visually inspect activities. On rare occasions, this process had resulted in the revocation of a council's charter.

The appraisal of individual job performance by supervisors and organizational performance by the National board was performed annually. The National executive director presented interim and annual management reports to the National board, relating the report content specifically to corporate goals and objectives. Based on this management report and information available through its standing committees and other sources, the National board conducted an evaluation of the organization's performance. It reviewed goals annually to determine if adjustments were called for either in performance or due to changes in internal or external data. At the midpoint of the six-year goal period, a comprehensive review was conducted to determine whether or not goals should be adjusted or changed.

Changes in goals often resulted in changes in the organization at the national level. For example, goal changes reflecting a greater need for local council management support resulted in a decision to create the management services center and staff it with management consultants. Because of both job rotation and the result of decisions such as this, employees at the national level often found themselves being reassigned to new tasks in new departments every two or three years. As one put it, "While there is strong job security here, you know you're not going to have the same reporting relationship for very long."

After several years of working within the process, Girl Scout personnel articulated the unique elements of the corporate planning/management system in a series of statements, including the following:

- It is comprehensive and involves all policy and operational groups within the organization.
- It is integrated with all plans previously developed by committees and departments into one GSUSA corporate plan.
- It has long-range dimensions.
- It maximizes collaboration by working with other community groups to gather trends and identify needs.
- It maximizes ownership by involving persons assigned the responsibility of carrying out plans in making them.
- It clarifies the role of the executive director, as the chief executive officer, in being accountable for the process of planning and the administrator of all operational work.
- It is basic to sound management, is result-oriented, and consistent with the guidelines and requirements of funding sources.
- It differentiates between policy-making/planning and operations responsibilities for both volunteers and staff and between making and influencing decisions.
- It provides congruence between personal and organizational goals.

By the end of the first decade since its initiation, the corporate planning/management system had been adopted by more than 80 percent of all councils.

LOOKING AHEAD

As Frances Hesselbein prepared to announce that she would step down from her post as National executive director in January 1990, she could take pride in the progress of the organization. Management expert Peter Drucker had called GSUSA the best-run organization in America.

On the other hand, Hesselbein knew that her successor would face significant challenges. She was certain that this would include keeping the organization's mission clearly in mind while sorting out continuing issues, many of which concerned the relative roles of local councils and the National organization.

She was confident that her managers were up to the task. She had frequently commented that "Our management has to be superior to for-profit businesses and government. We have no room for error."

GIRL SCOUTS OF THE U.S.A. (A)

Exhibit 1

Spar and Spindle Girl Scout Council, Inc., 1989

POLICY

OPERATIONS

CONSTITUENCIES
All members 14 and over who elect Delegates to the Council

ELECTS

THE GIRLS

GIRL SCOUT TROOP LEADERS GROUPED IN NEIGHBORHOODS

NEIGHBORHOOD SERVICE TEAM
NEIGHBORHOOD ADMINISTRATOR

FIELD DIRECTORS

ASSISTANT EXECUTIVE DIRECTOR

MEMBERSHIP SUPPORT DIRECTOR

OUTDOOR PROGRAM

CAMP DIRECTORS

PROGRAM

HUMAN RESOURCES

TRAINERS

CORPORATE DEVELOPMENT DIRECTOR

COMMUNITY DEVELOPMENT SPECIALIST

COMMUNICATION DIRECTOR

DIRECTOR FINANCE MANAGEMENT

ASSISTANT BOOKKEEPER

NEIGHBORHOOD COOKIE MGRS.

FEEDBACK INPUT

AREA DELEGATE CONGRESS

FEEDBACK INPUT

EMPLOYS

EXECUTIVE DIRECTOR

COUNCIL (Delegates)

NOMINATING COMMITTEE

ELECTS

BOARD OF DIRECTORS
Officers and Members-at-Large

ELECTS

ADMINISTRATIVE ASSISTANT

FACILITIES MANAGER

RANGERS

DIRECTOR BUSINESS OPERATIONS

BUSINESS STAFF

FINANCE MANAGEMENT

FUND DEVELOPMENT

KEY:
◯ POLICY
▢ VOLUNTEER OPERATIONS
▢ STAFF

780

GIRL SCOUTS OF THE U.S.A. (A)

Exhibit 2

A Map of the Region in Eastern Massachusetts and Southern New
Hampshire Served by the Spar and Spindle Girl Scout Council

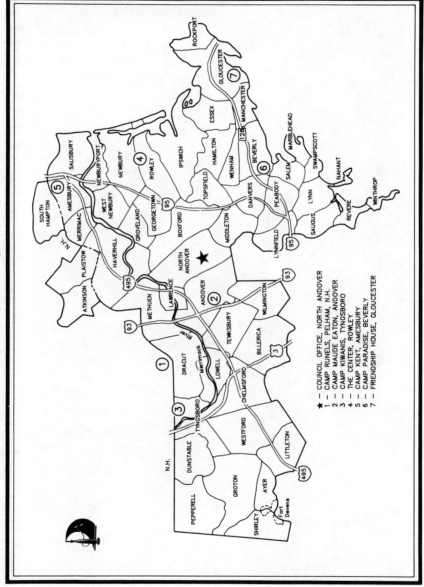

★ — COUNCIL OFFICE, NORTH ANDOVER
1 — CAMP RUNELS, PELHAM, N.H.
2 — CAMP MAUDE EATON, ANDOVER
3 — CAMP KIWANIS, TYNGSBORO
4 — THE CENTER, ROWLEY
5 — CAMP KENT, AMESBURY
6 — CAMP PARADISE, BEVERLY
7 — FRIENDSHIP HOUSE, GLOUCESTER

You don't have to be somebody's mother to be a Girl Scout Leader.

You can be an aunt, sister, neighbor, even a man.
So do something important with your spare time. Contact the Patriots'
Trail Council and join the Girl Scouts. Be a leader among girls.
Call 482-1078.

Exhibit 4
1985–1990 Corporate Goals and 1990 Integrated Operating Objectives

GOAL #1—MEMBERSHIP

GSUSA will work with councils to achieve membership growth and to develop a diverse leadership capable of delivering the Girl Scout program in varied ways.

Integrated Objective #1

By September 1990, overall membership will exceed that of September 1989 by at least 2%, with an increase in retention at all age levels, an increase at older girl age levels, and an increase in total girl and adult racial/ethnic membership of 4%.

Integrated Objective #2

By September 1990, GSUSA will have evaluated its standardized training system, produced new supporting training resources for Girl Scout councils, and expanded its career development program for national staff.

GOAL #2—PROGRAM

GSUSA will provide a program to help girls develop decision-making abilities and take action on personal, community, and global issues affecting their present and future well-being.

Integrated Objective #3

By September 1990, GSUSA will have developed resources and techniques for reaching 11- to 18-year-olds, especially in the areas of leadership development, global awareness, outdoor education, and wider opportunities, while continuing to meet the program needs of younger girls.

GOAL #3—ORGANIZATION DIVERSITY

GSUSA will increase pluralism and eliminate institutional racism throughout the Girl Scout Movement.

Integrated Objective #4

By September 1990, GSUSA will have developed and delivered new training curriculum and multimedia resources on recognizing and eliminating racist practices that bar equal access to Girl Scouting.

(*Continued*)

Exhibit 4
(Continued)

Integrated Objective #5

By September 1990, GSUSA will have enhanced collaboration between Girl Scout councils and local affiliates of national Asian, Black, Hispanic, Native American and Pacific Islander organizations, resulting in increased racial ethnic participation at all levels and in increased public recognition of pluralism efforts.

Integrated Objective #6

By September 1990, GSUSA will have given leadership and support to increase the number of racial and ethnic minorities filling national and council management positions.

GOAL #4—COMMUNICATIONS

GSUSA will communicate with its internal and external publics about the needs of girls and women and the significance of Girl Scouting's contribution to a changing and pluralistic society.

Integrated Objective #7

By September 1990, GSUSA will have communicated key messages about how Girl Scouting is meeting contemporary needs to targeted external audiences and provided resources and consultation to help Girl Scout councils communicate a more relevant image of Girl Scouting as a national and international movement.

GOAL #5—FINANCING THE ORGANIZATION

GSUSA will take the initiative to diversify funding sources and will emphasize adult responsibility for financing the total Girl Scout organization.

Integrated Objective #8

By September 1990, GSUSA will have prepared resources and delivered services to support Girl Scout councils' corporate officers and directors in developing contributed income and exercising fiduciary responsibilities.

Integrated Objective #9

By September 1990, GSUSA will have implemented new marketing strategies to attract funding and strengthen the financial position of Girl Scouts of the U.S.A.

Exhibit 4
(Continued)

GOAL #6—ORGANIZATION AND STRUCTURE

GSUSA will ensure that structures, relationships, and decision-making systems are flexible, productive, and responsive to the needs of members, councils, and the community.

Integrated Objective #10

By September 1990, GSUSA will have reviewed, revised, produced, and interpreted to Girl Scout councils and GSUSA, resources related to the Girl Scout corporate planning management system.

Integrated Objective #11

By September 1990, GSUSA will have completed all preparations for the 1990 National Council Session/Convention and the 27th World Conference of the World Associations of Girl Guides and Girl Scouts.

E OBJECTIVES

E-1   Throughout 1990, GSUSA will maintain facilities and services to support all Girl Scout councils in achieving a high level of performance and increased efficiency in carrying out their independent and interdependent accountabilities.

E-2   Throughout 1990, GSUSA will maintain the ongoing business and administrative responsibilities of the national organization at a high level of effectiveness and efficiency.

Approved by the
National Board of Directors,
January 31, 1989

GIRL SCOUTS OF THE U.S.A. (A)

Exhibit 5

Management Team, January 1988

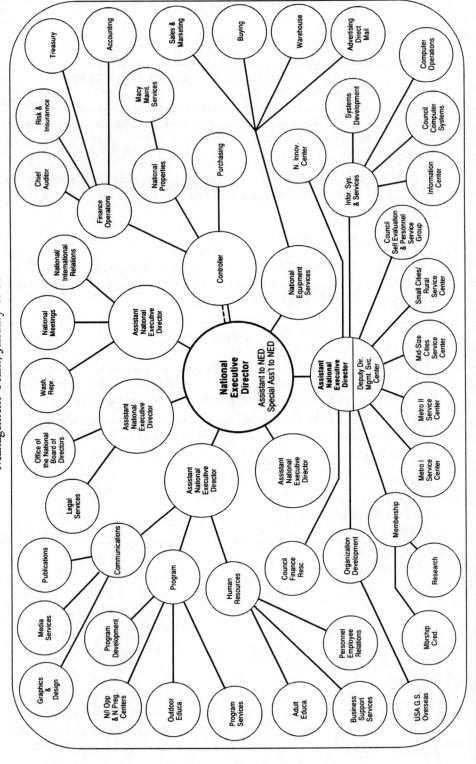

Exhibit 6
Selected Data, Spar and Spindle and Patriots' Trail
Girl Scout Councils, 1986 and 1987[a]

Items	Spar and Spindle		Patriots' Trail	
	1986	*1987*	*1986*	*1987*
Girl members	10,195	9,464	22,080	22,203
Adult members (volunteers)	2,823	2,890	5,736	5,839
Troops	839	820	1,678	1,650
Full-time staff:				
Exempt	14	16	40	36
Non-exempt	12	10	18	14
Current fund income (in thousands):				
United Way	$236	$240	$517	$548
Program income	155	188	809	847
Net product sale (net of costs and troop share of sales)	665	648	1,189	1,321
Investment income	136	153	90	83
Contributions	39	45	158	233
Capital campaign	0	0	370	40
Other income	33	33	230	230
Total income	$1,242	$1,308	$3,228	$3,302
Unrestricted general expenses (in thousands)	$1,033	$1,094	$2,791	$3,194
Net book value of land, buildings, and equipment (in thousands)	$1,354	$1,489	$2,584	$2,451

[a] For fiscal years ending September 30, 1986 and 1987.

Exhibit 7
Selected Cumulative Data, Girl Scout Councils, 1986 and 1987[a]

Items	1986	1987
Girl members	2,248,000	2,275,000
Adult members (volunteers)	669,000	673,000
Troops	174,000	179,000
Full-time staff:		
Exempt	3,645	3,759
Non-exempt	2,799	2,788
Current fund income (in thousands):		
United Way	$51,476	$51,382
Program income	29,186	32,249
Net product sale (net of costs and troop share of sales)	135,624	151,897
Investment income	18,099	17,738
Contributions	18,084	17,421
Capital campaign	4,217	3,686
Other income	11,755	14,942
Total income	$268,443	$289,314
Unrestricted general expense (in thousands)	$237,200	$263,258
Net book value of land, buildings, and equipment (in thousands)	$247,176	$259,327

[a]Based on reports and audited statements from 331 of 335 councils in 1986 and 330 of 335 councils in 1987 for fiscal years ending September 30 of each year.

Exhibit 8
Consolidated Statements of Revenue and Expenses, GSUSA, Years 1987 and 1988

	For the Year Ended September 30, 1988	For the Year Ended September 30, 1987
Revenue	Total	Total
Membership dues	$12,194,000	$11,776,000
National Equipment Service sales and other income, net of related costs[a]	12,770,000	14,030,000
Interest on inventory[a]	456,000	355,000
Gifts, grants, and bequests	1,362,000	1,202,000
Event revenue	2,107,000	1,787,000
Income from investments, including net gain on sale of securities of $824,000 in 1988 and $2,406,000 in 1987	2,877,000	4,083,000
Property operations, net	80,000	97,000
Other	72,000	39,000
Total Revenue	31,918,000	33,369,000
Expenses		
Program Services:		
Field services	6,292,000	6,490,000
Program and training development	2,775,000	2,366,000
Communications	2,788,000	2,937,000
Girl Scout activity accident insurance	610,000	577,000
International services	867,000	730,000
National centers administration	4,432,000	4,164,000
Total program services	17,764,000	17,264,000
Supporting Services		
Membership registration and credentials	1,598,000	1,805,000
Fund raising	342,000	338,000
Management and general	4,439,000	4,488,000
Total supporting services	6,379,000	6,631,000
Total expenses	24,143,000	23,895,000
Excess (deficiency) of revenue over expenses	7,775,000	9,474,000

Revenue and expenses relating to NES were:

	1988	1987
Sales and other income	$36,695,000	$39,050,000
Cost of sales and expenses	23,925,000	25,020,000
	$12,770,000	$14,030,000

[a] Included in cost of sales and expenses are interest charges from national headquarters of $456,000 in 1988 and $355,000 in 1987.

Exhibit 9
Consolidated Balance Sheets, GSUSA, as of September 30, 1987 and 1988

	September 30	
	1988	*1987*
Assets		
Cash and cash equivalents	$ 3,586,000	$ 3,757,000
Marketable securities, at cost	34,037,000	26,515,000
Accounts receivable (net of allowance for doubtful accounts of $57,000 in both 1988 and 1987)	6,027,000	6,281,000
Inventories	6,963,000	7,308,000
Prepaid expenses	2,009,000	1,221,000
Properties	20,124,000	20,448,000
	$72,746,000	$65,530,000
Liabilities and fund balances		
Accounts payable and accrued liabilities	$ 6,487,000	$ 7,145,000
Deferred revenue	1,617,000	1,518,000
Total liabilities	8,104,000	8,663,000
Fund balances		
Unrestricted:		
General fund	1,399,000	1,399,000
Capital fund	29,103,000	23,548,000
Properties funds	19,300,000	19,196,000
Special funds	8,765,000	6,621,000
Restricted funds	6,075,000	6,103,000
Total fund balances	64,642,000	56,867,000
	$72,746,000	$65,530,000

Exhibit 10
A Sample Page from the Girl Scout Council Self-Evaluation

Criterion III: The Development and Stewardship of Resources

An effective Girl Scout council develops sufficient resources and assumes the responsibility for managing them, in order to ensure the continuation and expansion of Girl Scouting in the council's jurisdiction.

---

[a]STANDARD 1   The council board ensures increasing racial/ethnic presence and
participation at all policy and operational levels.

1   2   3

Indicators of Effectiveness
1.1 The council continually monitors policies, procedures, and ways of work for institutional racism and takes corrective action.

Documentation: Review of policies and procedures, date of review, and action taken.

1   2   3

1.2 Representatives from different racial/ethnic groups participate in the monitoring process.

Documentation: Profile of monitoring groups.

1   2   3

1.3 Board leadership has resulted in increasing participation of members of minority groups at all policy-influencing levels.

a. elected delegates   e. committees/task groups
b. nominating committee   f. administrative volunteers
c. executive committee   g. executive staff
d. president's team

Documentation: Board minutes, correspondence, council communications, minority audit reports.

1   2   3

1.4 The board's leadership actively encourages continuous efforts to increase membership among racial/ethnic groups within the council's jurisdiction.

Documentation: Board minutes, correspondence, council internal publications.

1   2   3

[a]The key to the three-position scale used for evaluation was: (1) the council is meeting the standard of effectiveness at all times, (2) the council has taken significant action toward meeting the standard, or (3) the council is failing to meet the standard and has not taken sufficient corrective action.

Girl Scouts of the U.S.A. (B)

Laura Johnson, director of the Metro II Service Center at National headquarters of the Girl Scouts of the U.S.A. in September 1988 had just fielded a call from one of the management consultants on her staff concerning an incident that had occurred at the office of the South Texas Council. The management consultant had just been advised by a distraught member of the council's staff that the new executive director of the council, Evelyn Masters, had just fired the entire paid staff, indicating that "some will have the opportunity to reapply for their jobs." The firing occurred at the conclusion of a welcome coffee held by the staff for its new executive director. It was the latest in a series of incidents that led Johnson to ponder whether now was the time to take the serious step of initiating a Charter Compliance Audit, the first step in a process that could lead to revocation of the council's charter.

The South Texas Council had a history of problems, largely centered around financial stability and leadership. In 1982, the council's board had authorized the construction of a new office building by means of a large mortgage at a time when the council's finances already were weak. In 1984, the board had terminated its executive director for alleged alcoholism. In 1987, its executive director was dismissed for proven embezzlement. At that time, the council's board conducted a search process which was termed "atypical" by Johnson, in that it had failed to consider candidates from other Girl Scout councils. As a result, the new executive director was chosen from outside Girl Scouting, having served in a similar position with the National Children's League. On her first day on the job, she dismissed all 25 of the council's paid staff members.

Recently, Johnson had been alerted to the continuing problems in the South Texas Council by the receipt of a copy of a petition being circulated among volunteers in Brownsville, Texas, a community served by the council, calling for the possible secession of Brownsville from the council and the creation of a new council. The petition had been prepared by a lawyer who was a member of the council's board. According to the petition, it was prompted by the serious financial condition of the council, reflected by its sizeable bank loans and mortgage; an 80% annual rate of staff turnover (prior to the recent dismissal); serious com-

Professor James L. Heskett prepared this case as the basis for class discussion rather than to illustrate either effective or ineffective handling of an administrative situation. Certain of the names in this case have been disguised. Copyright © 1989 by the President and Fellows of Harvard College; Harvard Business School case # 9-690-046).

munication problems between the leadership team and its relatively weak board; and the unwillingness of the executive director to supply the board or the membership with accurate information. In contrast to more conventional methods of seeking change, this board member was described by Johnson as "having gone outside channels in organizing the community," apparently out of frustration.

Johnson's alternatives were limited. She could seek more information concerning the matter, begin an informal process to try to engineer the dismissal of the new executive director, or initiate with her superior a Charter Compliance Audit, the beginning of a careful, lengthy process.

One basic problem in developing additional information was the lack of communication between Johnson's staff of consultants at the National office and the leadership of the South Texas Council. According to Johnson, "It's hard to get hello and good-bye from them, let alone information." Thus, the information concerning the most recent incident was based on third-party conversations.

Engineering the dismissal of the new executive director at the very least would require the cooperation of the council's president and board. Johnson had no reason to believe that the president would cooperate in such a move; she could only assume that the president had agreed with the staff dismissal. If the local council board did elect to dismiss its executive director, the National office could offer to pay any additional salary required to hire an interim replacement.

The initiation of a Charter Compliance Audit could, with no corrective response, lead to the revocation of a council's charter. The grounds for such revocation are described in *Exhibit 1*. The process by which the National board might reach such a decision involved the filing of a request to the board for the audit. If the request was approved, it led to the following steps:

1. The National board of directors sends notice to the affected Girl Scout council, from one to three months prior to the scheduled date of the Charter Compliance Audit, citing specific examples of noncompliance.

2. Upon receiving notification of a Charter Compliance Audit, the Girl Scout council's board of directors appoints a local council documentation team of three to five members, including at least one officer, or other member of the local council board of directors, and the council executive director as a resource person.

3. The regional chairman and the director of the service cluster (and/or their appointees) comprise the national team that will conduct an on-site visit.

4. At least one month prior to the scheduled on-site visit, the local council documentation team collects data relevant to the identified problem areas and sends it to the national team.

5. During the on-site visit, the local council documentation team and the national team review all of the relevant data to validate expressed concerns

and problem issues. The national team gives an oral report on the teams' conclusions to the local council board of directors.

6. The regional chairman and the director of the service cluster prepare a written report of their findings and make recommendations regarding action to be taken to the Membership and Councils Committee. The Membership and Councils Committee reviews and acts upon the recommendation and submits its recommendation to the National board of directors.

7. The National board of directors receives a summary of the audit findings and takes the action required.

In total, the process could require six months in addition to any delay in the National board's action pending the receipt of information about corrective action. It relied heavily on volunteer participation and leadership.

Exhibit 1
Procedures for Non-Issuing or Revocation
of Term and Continuing Charters

When the National board of directors believes or is informed by the Membership and Councils Committee that a local council has been or might have been at fault through any of the following acts or omissions:

1. Violation of any term, condition, or requirement of its charter or its application therefor; or

2. Failure to comply with any policy, credential standard, or directive issued or established by or under the authority of the National board of directors; or

3. Deficiency in respect to its resources, finances, personnel, administrators, manner of supervising the program, effectiveness in its attempt to reach and serve all girls within its jurisdiction, or otherwise, such that in the opinion of the National board of directors it appears that such local council is unable adequately to develop, manage, and maintain Girl Scouting within its jurisdiction; or

4. Engaging in any act or omission, or any course of conduct, which in the opinion of the National board of directors is not in the best interests of Girl Scouting.

The National board may give notice to the local council involved, indicating generally the nature of the fault or failure.

The notice shall also state a reasonable time within which the local council shall respond in writing. The National board shall provide to such local council an opportunity to be heard by a committee named by the National board. That committee shall receive proof and information at such place and in such fair manner as the committee shall prescribe and shall then report its findings and recommendations to such local council and to the National board.

The National board shall thereupon determine, in its sole discretion, whether the charter shall be issued or revoked, or may take such action as it deems appropriate.

SOURCE: *Blue Book of Basic Documents 1988, Girl Scouts,* pp. 28–29.

Girl Scouts of the U.S.A. (C)

In preparing for a meeting of her management team in August 1988, Frances Hesselbein, National executive director of the Girl Scouts of the U.S.A., reviewed items that would be included on the agenda for the meeting. One of them concerned an ongoing effort by the national organization to encourage local Girl Scout councils to diversify their sources of income, placing less reliance on the sale of cookies and other items.

The latest in the efforts to encourage income diversification was a letter sent out over the names of Betty Pilsbury, National president, and Hesselbein clarifying the program standard on this matter which had been adopted by the National board of directors on January 26, 1986. A copy of the letter is shown in *Exhibit 1*. This letter had been sent to 17 of the 334 local Girl Scout councils that were known to be conducting two cookie sales each year.

One example of the extent to which some councils had come to rely on product sales for their income was the Monmouth Council, located on the north New Jersey shore, which was one of the recipients of the letter. The Monmouth Council, serving over 9,000 girls, received only 5.9% of its $840,000 annual budget from the United Way and 68% from the sale of cookies and calendars. In addition, it received approximately $25,000 from an annual giving campaign and other income from a fund-raising event honoring women of distinction in the community. The Monmouth Council agreed to give increased emphasis to efforts to increase contributions and to participate in a special GSUSA project to help it do so.

Five local councils gave little indication that any further action on their part was necessary. Reasons given for such reactions included:

1. "We have only one sale, carried out at two different times of the year. The younger Girl Scouts sell cookies in the fall and the older ones sell cookies in the spring."
2. "We have only one sale, involving the sale of cookies and calendars concurrently."
3. "We spend less time conducting our cookie sale in two parts than most councils spend conducting theirs in one."
4. "People would buy our cookies if we sold them 12 months of the year."

Professor James L. Heskett prepared this case as the basis for class discussion rather than to illustrate either effective or ineffective handling of an administrative situation. Copyright © 1989 by the President and Fellows of Harvard College; Harvard Business School case #9-690-047

5. "We are aware that we place a heavy emphasis on product sales, but we can't afford to drop our second cookie sale each year."

A letter typical of those received from this group of local councils is shown in *Exhibit 2.*

Among actions that Hesselbein's management team could take might be sending a follow-on letter to the recalcitrant local councils. Some effort might be made either directly or indirectly to bring peer pressure to bear on the councils by pointing out the unusual nature of their behavior. Apart from these possibilities, individuals ranging from the respective management consultants to the National president and executive director could begin an orchestrated campaign to encourage local council boards to place less emphasis on product sales. If nothing further were done, it was always possible that local councils would take corrective action on their own part.

Exhibit 1
Copy of Letter Sent to Local Councils

GIRL SCOUTS   690-047

June 21, 1988

Dear   :

In the new Girl Scout program standards, which were distributed with the May 1988 issue of <u>GSUSA News</u>, Standard #30 states that there may be only one cookie sale each year.

We understand that your council is conducting two cookie sales a year. We would like to make sure that you understand the thinking of the National Board of Directors, which adopted this standard at its meeting on January 26, 1986.

The National Board has two concerns. The first is that if girls participate in more than one cookie sale a year, too much of their time will be directed toward this one program activity, at the sacrifice of others. Involvement in a cookie sale offers an important opportunity for girls to develop a wide range of skills, but it must not become their major program activity.

A second concern is the protection of our tax-exempt status. We are not a business. To safeguard the cookie sale for all Girl Scout councils, it is important to limit the time devoted to selling cookies and to avoid any appearance of a year-round or continuing sale. Otherwise the specter of unrelated business income which is taxable may be raised and a council's tax-exempt status could be jeopardized as well as that of all councils and GSUSA.

The standard cited above was sent to councils with the President's Report of January 28, 1986, to become effective immediately. We trust you will now take the necessary steps to meet the standard. Please let us know if there is any way GSUSA can help you to move to one cookie sale a year.

Sincerely,

Betty Pilsbury   Frances Hesselbein
National President   National Executive Director

Exhibit 2
Copy of a Response Received from a Local Council

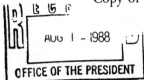

GIRL SCOUTS

Girl Scout Council, Inc.

Betty Pillsbury
GSUSA
830 Third Avenue
New York, NY 10022   July 28,1988

Re: Letter dated 6/21/88

Dear Mrs. Pillsbury;

    I am aware that Program Standard #30 states that troops/groups
may participate in no more than two council sponsored product sales
each year, and only one being a cookie sale. We do follow this guideline. The conception that   has two cookie sales is in
error. There is one cookie sale which has two divisions. Each troop
participates in only one division each year so that other program
activities do not suffer. The cookie sale has never been a major
program activity in a   troop.

    We do understand the concerns of GSUSA about girls program time
and protecting the tax exempt status of both Girl Scout Councils and
GSUSA. We also have those concerns and try to convey them to our internal and external publics. There is no appearance in this council of
a year-round or continuing cookie sale.

    I thank you for your concern.

Sincerely;

President

FILE:
ACTION: MRH-8/;
XC: FRH

A United Way Agency

Club Med (B)

Jacky Amzallag, director of Human Resources for Club Med's American zone, smiled warmly at his visitors and waved them in as he spoke rapidly over the telephone to Carlos, chief of the village at Playa Blanca, Mexico. "Another GO has quit?[1] That's two that you've fired and two who have quit so far this season . . . in just four weeks! Why did this one quit?" asked Jacky with a pained look. "Too many hours? No? Maybe he missed his sweetheart back home." Jacky winked at his visitors. "Bad *attitude*?" He looked astonished. "I don't understand! He had an excellent attitude. I interviewed him myself! What happened to him?" Jacky's head jerked back as he moved the handset a foot from his ear. A booming voice from several thousand miles away, obviously agitated, filled the room. Jacky's face took on a pained expression. "OK, OK. I'll get you a replacement windsurfing instructor. How soon? As soon as possible, of course. How soon? Impossible! I know, I know . . . I *have* been in your position! You were my chief of sports in Brazil . . . back in '82. Some friend. I teach you everything I know— all my tricks [another wink at his visitors]—and here you yell at me because your windsurfing instructor quits. Let me find out who is available."

Suddenly, Jacky leaned forward, listening intently with a smiling look of antici- pation. Howling with laughter, he asked "Where did you hear that one? Have you told it to anyone here? Good. I'll get good mileage out of that one! Salut, mon copain." Whirling around in his chair, Jacky pressed down on the intercom. "Debbie, would you pull the active resumes from the windsurfing instructor file?"

Jacky, smiling at his guests, leaned back in his chair and reflected. "Voltaire wrote, 'We cannot always oblige, but we can always speak obligingly.' " Then he sighed. "I have calls like that one almost every day. Despite our best efforts, there are problems in this business that just can't be avoided. It is, after all, a service business, and my department is fairly new . . . lots of bugs to iron out. It is vital to the Club's growth that we find these bugs and exterminate them.

This case was prepared by Assistant Professor Christopher W. L. Hart and Mr. Daniel Maher as the basis for class discussion rather than to illustrate either effective or ineffective handling of an administrative situation. Copyright © 1986 by the President and Fellows of Harvard College; Harvard Business School case #9-687-047 (Rev. 5/88).

1. The term "GO," pronounced "gee-oh," stands for "gentil organisateur" in French, "congenial host" in English. Each Club Med village employs a team of about 80 GOs who handle all jobs other than housekeeping and grounds-keeping. GOs organize the activities in a Club Med village and mingle freely with guests (called "GMs," pronounced "gee-ems": "gentils membres" in French, "congenial members" in English).

One of my biggest problems involves the turnover of newly recruited GOs, which is a responsibility of my department. Their turnover has been very high over the past several years, nearly 50%, and it is getting worse. What is the problem? Recruiting? Selection? Training? Maybe we have to learn more about the North American GOs and how to manage them. With the huge number of applications we get for GO positions, you would think that turnover would be much less than it is . . . about 25% per season, including all GOs—both old and new. This is almost twice as much as our GO turnover in Europe. Maybe 25% is not so bad, though, and we just have to learn to live with it." (See *Exhibit 1* for information on turnover.)

Jacky continued: "The Club is growing rapidly in the American zone, and my department is crucial to its success. My immediate objective is to get this GO turnover problem straightened out. I must provide my clients, the chiefs of the villages, with good service. I have some ideas about how to do this, but I'm not sure what my overall strategy should be. One thing is certain: I am committed to do whatever it takes . . . I love the Club. J'aime trop le Club."

COMPANY BACKGROUND AND HISTORY

Club Méditerranée (often referred to as "the Club"), the ninth-largest hotel company in the world, was founded by a group of friends in 1950 as a nonprofit sports association. The group was led by Gerard Blitz, a Belgian diamond cutter and water-polo champion, who, like the others in the group, loved sports and vacations in scenic seaside locations. Members slept in sleeping bags in tent villages and took turns cooking meals and washing dishes. As the size of the association grew, running it as an informal, loosely organized group became increasingly difficult. In 1954, Blitz invited his close friend, Gilbert Trigano, an active association member whose family business had been supplying the group with U.S. Army-surplus tents, to join the association on a full-time basis. Trigano, who saw commercial potential in the concept, became managing director and set out to turn the association into a business. In 1985, Club Méditerranée S.A., a publicly owned company traded on the Paris Stock Exchange, had 180 resort villages throughout the world and hosted 820,000 vacationers.

HISTORY OF THE AMERICAN ZONE

In 1972, Club Med, Inc. was formed as a U.S. subsidiary of Club Méditerranée. The subsidiary sold the company's vacation packages and operated its resorts in

North America, the Caribbean, South America, Asia, and the South Pacific. What was referred to in Club Med as the "American zone" comprised the 17 villages highlighted on the map in *Exhibit 2*.

Club Med's expansion into the western hemisphere was not without difficulty. The company's first village in the American zone, Buccaneer's Creek, located on the Caribbean island of Martinique, developed a "swinging-singles," sex-oriented reputation when it was first opened in the early 1970s. This image was in stark contrast to Club Méditerranée's family-oriented image in Europe. Management was so concerned that the village was temporarily closed; however, despite intensive company efforts to stamp out the "wild and crazy" reputation, the image persisted.

Gradually, however, the image was changing. The latest demographics on Club Med's clientele revealed the average age to be 37, with a median income of $39,000 and an average income of $54,000. More than 70% were aged 25 to 44, and half were married. More than 75% were college graduates and 28% held advanced degrees.

Another source of problems in the American zone had been cultural and language differences between Europeans and North Americans. Initially, almost all GOs in the American zone were French (or French-speaking). Misunderstandings frequently arose between European GOs and American GMs—and among European and North American GOs as well. In fact, a 1978 case study written on the company focused almost exclusively on problems between Europeans and North Americans. After examining the problem in depth, management decided, in the early 1980s, to dramatically increase the percentage of North American GOs, resulting in major recruiting drives in large U.S. and Canadian cities. Based on a substantial increase in guest-satisfaction ratings among American zone villages, this policy was judged to be a success. Jacky believed that this effort was meeting the need for North American GOs, while retaining the international flavor of the Club.

Some Club Med managers, however, voiced concern over continuing problems rooted in ethnic differences. Because the number of GOs recruited in Europe was much larger than the number of GOs recruited in North America, and the turnover rate for European GOs was roughly half that for American GOs, the number of European village chiefs and chiefs of service was disproportionately high.[2] (*Exhibit 3* shows the approximate ethnic composition of village chiefs in the American zone, and chiefs of service throughout the company.)

---

2. The term "chief of the village" is the equivalent of a general manager in American hotel parlance. Each village chief has seven assistants, called "chiefs of service," who manage specific functions such as sports, dining, entertainment, etc. The chiefs of service manage the GOs in their functional areas.

Finally, there had been problems at times with some of the company's personnel policies. In the 1970s, decisions concerning all GOs throughout the world were centralized in the personnel department at Paris headquarters. One of Club Méditerranée's long-established policies had been to rotate GOs to different villages every six months. A company tradition was to bring the GOs to the home base in Paris at the end of each season, so they could visit headquarters, reestablish old friendships, and find out where they would be assigned the next season. By 1977, the number of GOs had grown to more than 5,000 and this tradition had become a logistical nightmare. Consequently, it was stopped. To relieve the pressure on the personnel department created by the greater number of company villages and their wider geographic dispersion, a 1985 reorganization established four GO departments in Paris, each headed by a person known as "un parrain"—a "godfather."

Under the direction of Michel Perchet, director of Human Resources for Club Méditerranée, and his two assistants, the four "godfathers" served as functional area heads. Each "godfather" was responsible for those GOs (and chiefs of service) throughout the world who fell into one of four functional areas: sports, entertainment, maintenance, and administration. The new organizational setup improved the process of assigning GOs to new villages and gave GOs in each of the four functional areas the feeling that they had an ear in Paris.

Although the new structure was judged to be an improvement, rapid growth in the number of American GOs created new pressures on Paris, which ultimately led, in September 1985, to the formation of a New York-based, American zone "GO Village" at Club Med's headquarters on 57th Street in New York City. Jacky Amzallag, a French Moroccan who had joined the Club in 1966 and risen through the ranks, was chosen to head this new department, which was responsible for recruitment, hiring, orientation, placement, and performance appraisal of GOs in the American zone.

The Club wanted to increase the number of American chiefs of service, both in the American zone and in the rest of the world. Therefore, after three or four seasons, Jacky recommended promising American GOs to Michel Perchet and the functional "godfather" for promotion. These American GOs were given language goals, among others, as hurdles to jump before being promoted. Once promoted, a new American chief of service was eligible to be assigned to any Club Med village throughout the world.

VILLAGE ORGANIZATION

Each Club Med village was organized similarly. As shown in *Exhibit 4*, the chief of the village had overall responsibility for village operations. Reporting to the

village chief were seven chiefs of service, each of whom was in charge of a
different functional area. The eighty or so GOs in a village reported to their
respective chiefs of service. Such back-of-the-house activities as housekeeping and
groundskeeping were handled by non-GO workers who lived in the local area.

Chief of the Village. The title "chief of the village" accurately described
the position. Because of the remoteness of many villages and the Club's culture,
the chief of the village position had evolved as *the* key leadership position
in the organization. Although largely a formality, even the chairman of the board
requested permission from village chiefs before visiting their villages. Chiefs were
required to adhere to certain Club policies, but had wide latitude to set village
policies that affected GMs' vacation experiences.

The chiefs were a colorful and varied cast of characters; one American GO
described them as ". . . one part Napoleon, one part Santa Claus, one part Jerry
Lewis, and one part Long John Silver." Examples of the imaginative ways they
had dealt with impending disasters and major incidents were legion, creating an
almost reverential respect for the village chiefs throughout the organization.
(Most of Club Med's top-level managers had been village chiefs.)

For example, Sylvio de Bortoli, vice president of sales, who had been a village
chief for many years, recalled:

> When I was in Cancun one season, I received word that a charter from New
> York was experiencing horrible problems, and was going to arrive ten hours
> later than scheduled, at 4:30 *a.m.* I knew that the planeload of GMs would
> be miserable, probably angry, maybe even hostile.
>
> So I rounded up my GOs and we formulated a plan. We met the GMs
> at the airport, whisked them through customs, and had drinks waiting in
> the buses. On the ride to the village, our guests told us that they had experi-
> enced a horribly rough landing—so rough the oxygen masks descended!
> Then the pilot announced over the PA, "If you think *that* was bad, wait
> until you see how I taxi up to the gate!"
>
> When we arrived at the village, our chefs had laid out a lavish buffet,
> complete with champagne. The GOs put on an abbreviated, high-spirited
> show. A couple of hours after their arrival—with the sun coming up—our
> weary GMs wandered off to their rooms with *smiles* on their faces. It was
> the beginning of a *great* week—for our guests *and* for the GO team.

GOs. The Club sought individuals for GO positions who were young, person-
able, enthusiastic, and athletic. GOs were expected to put in long hours on the
job, although many in the Club felt strongly that being a GO was not a job, but
a way of life—and that the 80 or so a week that GOs interacted with
GMs was not "work" in the traditional sense. *Exhibit 5* shows the posted GO
schedule for a typical day. Not listed on the schedule were the six to seven hours

all GOs spent in their assigned jobs (e.g., restaurant hostess, tennis instructor, cook, bartender). These hours would be interspersed throughout the day, depending on the requirements of a particular GO position. Also not shown in the schedule is the casual contact time between GMs and GOs at such times as meals and sitting around the pool. The Club philosophy was for GOs to enjoy themselves and, in a sense, for them to be on vacation with GMs.

ROTATION

A Club Med practice that other hotel companies found incredible was the rotation of GOs to different villages every six months. Rotation included all village chiefs and chiefs of service. The only exceptions were the chiefs of maintenance and maintenance GOs; they stayed in a village for one to two years. Many questioned the efficiency of rotation, primarily on the grounds that it broke up groups that had become cohesive teams. Moreover, rotation often resulted in a temporary dip in guest-satisfaction ratings during the two four-week periods in the year when GOs from old teams were phased out and new GOs were phased in. Rotation of the over 1,300 GOs in the 17 villages located in the American zone also entailed substantial direct costs and logistical difficulties. Comments from company management tended to support rotation, however, although no figures pertaining to the direct costs of rotation had ever been calculated. Jacky stated that "After six months you need to break the routine. This is a motivator for the GOs. They can see different countries, and experience different cultures. They learn to adapt to many types of people." Comments from GOs are listed in *Exhibit 6*.

CLUB MED AMERICAN ZONE OFFICE, NEW YORK CITY

Jacky Amzallag's office, consisting of Jacky and five assistants, was charged with staffing the 17 American zone villages with all GOs except village chiefs and chiefs of service. Additionally, Jacky's office tracked GO development and made recommendations concerning which GOs should be promoted to chiefs of service. GOs who were promoted were no longer the responsibility of Jacky's office; Michel Perchet and the four "godfathers" at Paris worldwide headquarters handled all staffing decisions concerning village chiefs and chiefs of service.

According to Jacky, this had created difficulties. One major problem had been that more American chiefs of service were needed in, but were not being assigned to, American zone villages. Additionally, Jacky stated, "American GOs who are promoted to chief of service should stay in the American zone for at least a season or two, to ease their transition into management. That way, they have many American GOs reporting to them—and they can focus on learning to *manage*. If they have mostly European GOs under them, their job becomes much more complex—the language, customs, habits, etc. are so much different. For example, we had a windsurfing instructor; she was the world freestyle champion two years in a row . . . for both men and women! Different village chiefs watched her closely during her first few seasons as a GO to assess her potential to become a chief of service. When she was promoted, I argued with Paris that she should stay in the American zone for at least one season. But she was assigned to a village in Israel, where the GOs reporting to her were from many countries and she was in a foreign culture. This added great pressure to her job. But I understand Paris's reasons. They saw her as a great attraction for the village. 'The world champion from America!' The same is true of other Americans who become chiefs of service."

RECRUITING IN THE AMERICAN ZONE

In 1985, Club Med received about 10,000 resumes in response to ads for American GOs placed in major magazines. Each ad resulted in a flood of letters, often numbering 80 a day. Jacky's office was responsible for screening the resumes and notifying those who would be given interviews (1,300 candidates per season, 2,600 per year).

"It is harder for us to assess the resumes here in America," Jacky explained "because we cannot ask, for example, for a photo, or the person's age—because of the discrimination laws. In France, we don't have such laws, and recruitment is generally easier. Sometimes, we give interviews to people who really don't fit the ideal Club Med profile. For example," he laughed, "I interviewed one man who wanted to be an entertainer. The problem was, he had a horrible stutter. If I had hired him, it would have been a terrible experience for him and the guests. Luckily, he had ability in other areas and I was able to hire him to be a GO in another department. However, I usually cannot switch people around so easily." Jacky paused for a moment. "In that sense, we interview many more people here than we would in Europe, where we don't have discrimination laws."

Jacky continued, "On the other hand, I have seen so many resumes that I can usually tell the bad ones very quickly. It only takes five minutes to read a resume. And my assistants know what to look for," Jacky continued, "because it's really not so difficult once you do it for a while."

Comments from others indicated that accurate assessment of resumes was problematic because North Americans' resumes tended to be "creative." Many were designed to attract attention; others overstated applicants' qualifications. One GO, a veteran of five seasons, stated, "I wanted the job very badly, and knew the odds I was up against. So I wrote on my resume that I was an expert in all kinds of activities, figuring that if I was hired and sent to a village, I could learn whatever I needed to learn before anyone found out what I didn't know. I was hired and made a sailing instructor. In my first week on the job, I was asked if I could take out 50 or so GMs on the village's 46' schooner. What was I to do? I said, 'No problem.' Things went great the first day, but a major storm cropped up on my next voyage. I had visions of Gilligan's Island, but didn't panic and, luckily, we had plenty of wine and food on board. I guess I lost my bearings, because we ended up sailing into the cove of another hotel—on an island 30 miles away!"

After the initial screen of resumes by Jacky and his staff, those who were not invited to interview were sent rejection letters. The candidates who were granted interviews were notified by mail or by telephone with details about time and place. Interviews were conducted in major cities and on a few college campuses in the U.S. and Canada by Jacky and by the Club's regional sales managers. Arizona State and, to a lesser extent, UCLA and USC, had been fertile recruiting grounds for good GOs. A self-perpetuating grapevine had developed at Arizona State which was located close to the company's national reservations center in Scottsdale. The candidates, many of whom traveled fairly long distances, arrived up to four hours early for their interviews (9 a.m. for morning interviews, 2 p.m. for afternoon interviews). Jacky or the regional sales manager talked to all applicants, as a group, about the merits of the Club before the individual interviews began. Included in his 45-minute presentation was a short, glamorous movie on Club Med, filmed in several exotic locations, showing GOs at work and at play. (GOs were allowed to use the village's sports equipment when they had time.) Jacky said, "I do a good job when I give the presentation. I don't hear any complaints. I tell them the truth about the difficulties of being a GO, but in a funny way. I tell them they will get responsibility right away. When the new GOs land in the village they are immediately 'on stage', our term for GO interaction with the guests. We say 'the curtain goes up' when the GOs leave their rooms in the morning, and 'the curtain comes down' only when they go to sleep. I believe on-the-job training is the best way for new GOs to learn to interact with the guests—it is very difficult to simulate what goes on in a Club Med village. We can teach them to become 'technicians'—windsurfers, for example—but we cannot teach them to become human beings."

The candidates were interviewed by Jacky and two other Club Med personnel who had been GOs (and often had been village chiefs as well). Each interviewer conducted a 30-minute interview with each candidate and asked questions that sized up a candidate's talents, attitude, and potential. Ten days after the interviews, letters were sent to everyone interviewed. Jacky estimated that it took approximately two minutes for one of his staff members to prepare a notification letter to be sent to a GO applicant. If 300 new GOs were needed, 450 to 500 were told they would be hired to provide a reserve pool for GOs who quit or were fired during the season. The letters told those who were accepted to sign employment contracts (that were provisional upon the person actually being assigned to a village), and that they would be notified two weeks prior to departure to the village they were assigned to. This could be a few months later for those who departed during the regularly scheduled rotation period, but could easily become four to six months for the "extra hires" used to replace GOs who quit or were fired during a season.

Jacky was concerned about the time delay between recruitment and "shipment." "My staff spends 40% or more of their time on the phone with new recruits who want to know when and to which village they are going. They spend 15 minutes on each call. The problem is that *we* don't have the answers to their questions. My staff is too busy anyway—and this makes more work for everyone, especially me."

When the time for departure arrived, a member of Jacky's staff talked to the new GOs about flight information, their villages, clothes to bring, and their new bosses, the chiefs of the villages.

"I think the Navy has copied our philosophy," laughed Jacky. "You know how they say 'It's not just a job, it's an adventure'? When I interview around the country, it seems the people don't care so much about the pay [about 400 U.S. dollars per month] and benefits [room and board, bar allowance, medical plan], or the long hours I tell them they will have to work. They want to see the world, and they know they can with us."

"You don't earn a lot of money, but if you don't drink all your salary at the bar, at the end of the season you come back with a lot," said Patrice Prual, 34, this season's village chief at Cherating [Malaysia]. When he was a schoolteacher in Paris, Mr. Prual recalled, "at the end of the month I had zero."

The stress of paying bills, furnishing a home, owning a car, commuting to work—the average GO has none of this. "I prefer to work at Club Med with palm trees, coconuts, sun, sea," said 30-year-old Tazuko Shimamuda of Japan, who had been doing just that for six years. "It's not perfect, but it's better than taking the metro to work every day."[3]

After each recruiting season, the newly "hired" GO resumes were kept on

3. Barry Kalb, "Play Is Hard Work for Club Med Staff," *The New York Times*, September 24, 1986, p. A-33.

file in the New York office until Jacky and the chiefs of the village decided together which GOs would go to which villages. Jacky and his staff selected groups of new and old GOs for each village based on such factors as experience, personality, age, physical characteristics, special talents, and performance-appraisal reports already on file. Although the chiefs had the ultimate authority to pick their teams, the dossiers compiled by Jacky's office for each village were usually accepted after a round of haggling that, in some respects, was more cere-monial than substantive. "Naturally the chiefs all want the best team members," commented Jacky, "and they also might want a few of their favorite GOs from previous seasons. They are always allowed to keep a few chiefs of service whom they have worked with . . . some of them have worked together for years. But we obviously cannot give all the best GOs to certain chiefs. I would be killed by the other chiefs!"

Village chiefs had complete authority to dismiss GOs or chiefs of service, and request immediate replacements. The Club's offices in New York and Paris were often faced with the difficult task of locating qualified individuals who could depart to a particular village immediately.

"I was on the phone with Paris the other day, telling them I need more American chiefs of service." Jacky said with a sigh. "We have sometimes the miscommunication between the chiefs of service and their GOs. Let me give you an example. Suppose I am the chief of service, and see that a wall needs to be painted. If I see a French GO, I tell him 'Go paint the wall'; he finds the paint and the brush, and he paints the wall." He continued: "But, with an American GO, I must explain to him *why* I want him to paint the wall, what changes that will make, and why it is a change for the better. Then I must tell him where to find the paint and brush—he will not look for it himself. And he wants to finish what he is doing first. Finally, he wants feedback about the quality of his work." Jacky's face grew serious. "The European chiefs of service often don't under-stand how American GOs have to be managed, which can create serious morale problems. Additionally, the chiefs often have difficulties with the English lan-guage and accent, so they tend not to give as much training and feedback as they might. But we need the Europeans to keep the Club's international ambience. This is particularly true since the number of Europeans visiting our American zone villages is booming."

Since the American zone had 17 villages, each with about 80 GOs, the turn-over problem complicated the already complex village-assignment task. Assuming that suitable replacement GOs could be located in the files, the next step would be a flurry of telephone calls to determine availability. "For example," Jacky said, "halfway through last season I needed a tennis instructor for the village in Martinique. So Debbie, in my office, called the first person in the tennis instruc-tor file. No answer. The second one said she had been working somewhere else for two and a half months and was very happy with her job. The third one was very angry at not having been contacted earlier and told Debbie something that cannot be put in the case study.

"Finally, we found someone who wanted to go—but she wanted to give two weeks' notice to her current employer. Debbie asked her to please give shorter notice . . . that we needed her in Martinique *now.* She agreed after a while, but then she thought she was obligated to help her apartment mates find someone to take her place. They talked some more, and finally Debbie convinced her that her apartment mates could find someone without her help. I tell you . . ." Jacky shook his head, "that's a lot of work to replace a tennis instructor in Martinique."

Turnover occurred in four ways: a GO quit before the end of the season, a GO was fired before the end of the season, a GO quit at the end of a season, or a GO was given a poor evaluation by the village chief and was not asked back for the next season. Jacky's lead time to supply new GOs in the first two cases was zero.

In the third and fourth cases, the chiefs rated their GOs in mid-season in two categories: technical ability (i.e., in windsurfing) and attitude and comportment with GMs. The rating scale was 1, 2, or 3 points, in ascending order of excellence. Six was the highest possible score; GOs who were rated "3" were marginal—unless their performances improved, they would be allowed to continue the current season, but would not be invited back for another season. At the end of the season, a more complete performance appraisal was sent to Jacky. The evaluation forms had considerable space for "additional comments," but most chiefs were not inclined to elaborate on their GOs. (The space was often left blank.)

During the 1986 summer season, 66 GOs were fired by the 17 chiefs of the American zone villages. Another 74 quit. (See *Exhibit* 7 for GO comments on why they quit or were fired; *Exhibit* 8 shows comments from chiefs and GOs who did not leave.) Thus, Jacky's office had to replace 140 GOs from the reservoir of hired-but-not-assigned GOs. The GOs who quit or were fired usually were not given an exit interview.

OPTIONS

Jacky had several ideas about how to improve the system. First, some village chiefs fired two or three times as many GOs as other chiefs. "Why should that be?" he queried. "If they had to live with the aggravation it caused, perhaps they would try to work with their new GOs instead of executing them right away.

Why not have chiefs more involved in the recruiting process, maybe taking time off from their villages to visit cities and conduct interviews? Then they would have a greater appreciation of how difficult it is to find good GOs." In fact, one chief was said to have recruited a number of GMs who had stayed at his village and who ended up wanting to work for Club Med.

There was also talk about opening up a GO training school at the Club's new Sandpiper village in Florida. "I spoke with Marc Tombez, the director of training in Paris. He likes the idea of setting up a school where new GOs would be trained for a week or two before they go to their first assignment," said Jacky.

Jacky wanted to take a more personal approach in tracking the best GOs for advancement within the company. "I will make it a point to meet each GO who is identified as having excellent potential during my visits to the American zone villages. I believe my taking the time to talk to each of them individually will give them a better sense of our interest and commitment to them . . . leading to reduced turnover among the new GOs who are good. Maybe I will miss some, but, over time, this system will be an improvement. GOs who leave now because they are looking for advancement will see that the Club can be a career . . . and they will know that I know who they are."

Another of Jacky's ideas on how to better manage the recruiting process was to recruit and assign GOs to villages throughout the year, not on a seasonal basis. Approximately 10% of GOs would rotate (or have their contracts end) every month. A benefit would be less disruption in the villages at season's end. The reaction from chiefs of the village was that their teams would be disrupted constantly—that it would be hard to build their GOs into teams. A very practical concern of the chiefs was that they would have serious trouble putting on quality stage shows at night if GOs were constantly changing.

There had even been discussion in the Club about the effectiveness of rotation itself. Jacky pointed out, "We decided several years ago that the maintenance GOs should rotate every one or two years. Maybe it is time to consider rotating other GOs in a different pattern. Would it be so bad, for example, to have the chiefs stay in a village for a year at a time? Then a process of gradual GO rotation wouldn't be such a big deal."

Jacky stated, "I don't know exactly when I will have this turnover problem solved. I don't really think the way I recruit now is ideal. I know it can be done better, and I'm working on it. Maybe there are other approaches that I should consider." Then his face turned very serious. "However, there *is* one thing I'm convinced of—the North American GOs are a big part of the future success of the internationalization of the Club."

Exhibit 1
Information on GO Turnover

Number of GOs, by *nationality,* summer season 1986, American Zone

American/Canadian	738
French/European	454
Local	134
Other	15
Total	1,341

American/Canadian GO *turnover,* summer season 1986, American Zone (Quit or Fired or "Retired")

Quit during season	74
Fired during season	66
Quit after season	55
Fired after season, due to bad report	9
Total	204

Note: French/European GO turnover was approximately 50% of American/Canadian GO turnover during the same time period. (French/European GO turnover in the American Zone is essentially zero.)

American/Canadian GO turnover by *experience;* Historical Averages, 1980–1985, summer *and* winter seasons

Turnover during first season	46%
Turnover during second and third season	37
Turnover during fourth to tenth season	23
Turnover after tenth season	11

Exhibit 2
Location of Club Med Villages in the American Zone

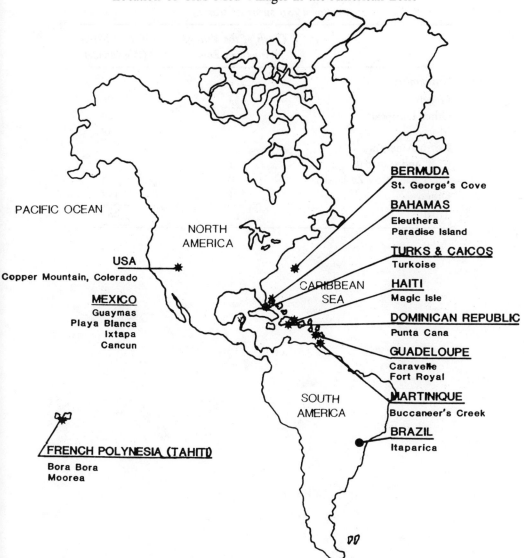

PACIFIC OCEAN

NORTH AMERICA

USA
Copper Mountain, Colorado

MEXICO
Guaymas
Playa Blanca
Ixtapa
Cancun

CARIBBEAN SEA

SOUTH AMERICA

BERMUDA
St. George's Cove

BAHAMAS
Eleuthera
Paradise Island

TURKS & CAICOS
Turkoise

HAITI
Magic Isle

DOMINICAN REPUBLIC
Punta Cana

GUADELOUPE
Caravelle
Fort Royal

MARTINIQUE
Buccaneer's Creek

BRAZIL
Itaparica

FRENCH POLYNESIA (TAHITI)
Bora Bora
Moorea

NOTE: A new village was due to open in Florida in 1987.

Exhibit 3
Ethnic Composition of Village Chiefs and Chiefs of Service
(for 1986 summer season)

Nationality:	Chiefs of the Village (American Zone)	Chiefs of Service (Worldwide)
French	13	1,006
Other European	1	224
Moroccan	1	39
North American (U.S. and Canada)	1	52
Australian/New Zealander	0	5
Other	1	143
Total	17	1,469

Exhibit 4
Organization of a Club Med Village

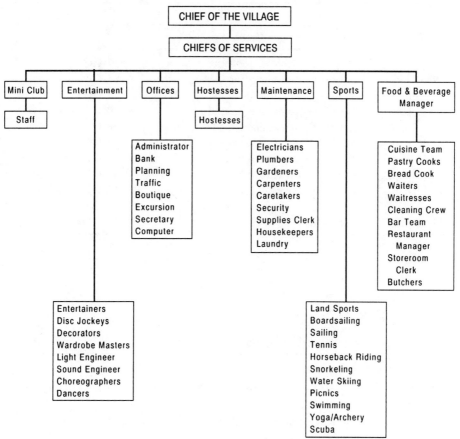

Exhibit 5
Typical Daily Schedule: GO Duties in Addition to Regular Job Tasks

	Sunday	
Time	*Event*	*# of GOs*
7:15 a.m.	Theatrical breakfast welcome	7 GOs
9:00 a.m.	Information meeting (for GMs)	5 GOs
12:00 noon	T-shirt presentation (for GMs)	5 GOs
12:15 p.m.	Sports demonstration around pool	30 GOs (sports GOs)
1:15 p.m.	Rehearsal for evening Broadway show	40 GOs
7:30 p.m.	Makeup for theatrical welcome at dinner	15 GOs
9:45 p.m.	Dancing around pool with GMs	10 GOs
10:15 p.m.	Evening show (Broadway)	40 GOs
11:15 p.m.	GO-GM basketball game	10 GOs (players)
		10 GOs (watching)
12:00 mid.	Initiate dancing at disco	20 GOs

Exhibit 6
GO Comments about Rotation

- "I like to move to different villages."
- "I've never been to Europe and would love to work at Corfu [in Greece] for a season."
- "I want to experience different cultures around the world."
- "I miss my Michel, my first chief of service; he was great!"
- "I need a change. I'm bored. There's no place to go around here except the Club."
- "I wish our entire team could be rotated together to a new village. This team works together better than any of the ones at the other five villages I have been."
- "The major reason for becoming a GO is to see the world."
- "I can't wait for my next village. The atmosphere in this village isn't too great."
- "My girlfriend and I . . . she is a GO . . . wish we could stay together."

Exhibit 7
Comments from GOs Who Quit or Were Fired[a]

- "They told me I could use the sports equipment, but who has time? All we do is work and sleep."
- "I met a GM from Connecticut who offered me a good job."
- "Some of the European GOs had a condescending attitude—they thought we had no idea of what the Club was all about. And we hardly got any positive feedback."
- "How many times can you tell GMs how to sign up for snorkeling before you go bonkers?"
- "No television, no radio, no magazines, no newspapers—I'm a college graduate, like most of the American GOs. My mind was going to waste down here on 'Gilligan's Island.'"
- "When I arrived they showed me my room and then told me 'go on stage.' What did that mean? No one showed me what to do. So I took advantage of the Club Med life and tried to live like a guest. Two weeks later, the chief canned me."
- "The life-style just wasn't for me, but I guess I had to experience it first-hand to know that."
- "I figured being an American in a French company wasn't going to do much for my career."
- "The European GOs have such a double standard—I think they're living in the eighteenth century."

---

[a] No exit interviews were conducted.

Exhibit 8
Comments from Village Chiefs and GOs
about GOs Who Quit or Were Fired

- "I had to fire those two GOs—they were drinking way too much."
- "That guy couldn't teach a fish to swim . . . he was useless."
- "She was really good; I wish she wouldn't have quit. But better that she should leave than stay and be unhappy."
- "That GO had plenty of enthusiasm—to *complain!* If she hadn't been fired, the other GOs would have drowned her, I think."
- "Two left today. They wouldn't have made it through the season. Two weeks was enough for them. They thought they were on vacation."
- "I know a guy who just quit after a few days. He was disillusioned . . . it wasn't at all what he expected."

13

◆

Conceiving Future
Breakthroughs

In recent years, trends in the development of new service concepts have generally fit a pattern of providing more things and services anywhere, any time.
Services ranging from medical to financial increasingly are available on a 24-hour
basis. Many of them, thanks to new technology, are made available many more
ways and in more locations than previously.

The demand for these new service concepts is fueled by such things as changing work habits, new life-styles, and the growth of global markets. New services
can now be developed in response to these demands, thanks to diverse developments such as improved information technology, global communication networks, deregulation, privatization, and reduced barriers to trade.

Because these trends will continue in some form, they force managers to rethink their current services if they are to remain competitive in the future. The
bases for future competitive service advantage are clear. The questions are how
fast and in what manner services will be offered any time, anywhere, not whether
it will happen. This will require that managers entertain unconventional ideas
and seek ways to break constraints and reject assumptions that often are built
up around conventional ways of doing things in various service industries.

These are the challenges facing managers in the two cases that follow. The
first, Citicorp Diners Club, describes a relatively young industry, credit card financing, in which accepted ways of doing things have developed rapidly. In
reviewing the case, the following questions may be useful to keep in mind: What
will this industry look like in the year 2000? Why? Who will the most important
competitors be? What does this suggest James Emshoff should begin doing now
to prepare for the future? In the near term, what are the most important problems facing Citicorp Diners Club? How should they be dealt with?

Turning to the Ford Motor Company: Dealer Sales and Service case, we are
confronted with a business involving many service complaints. As you read the

case, ask yourself: To what extent are auto service complaints explained by the way the industry is structured for service delivery? Is service a potential source of competitive advantage for a major auto manufacturer like Ford? Given trends documented in the case, assuming no major change in the industry, how will auto service be delivered in the year 2000? Who will do it? Based on your responses to these questions, should the management of the Ford Motor Company do anything about the delivery of service for autos? Keeping in mind the legal constraints of past dealer franchising agreements, what should Ford executives do? With what objectives in mind? Over what time frame?

Citicorp Diners Club

James Emshoff sighed and put down the copy of *Fortune* magazine. He had just finished an article in the latest issue entitled "The Great Plastic Card Fight Begins" (see Appendix) that particularly troubled him. Only six weeks earlier, Emshoff had left his position at the Campbell Soup Company to assume the presidency of Diners Club; at that time he'd been very excited at the prospect of using his knowledge of consumer products marketing to resuscitate the foundering organization. Now, in February 1985, he wasn't sure he could pull off that considerable task.

Diners Club, an international charge card business acquired by Citicorp in 1981, was experiencing tremendous growth: revenues from annual fees were pouring in, and since 1983 the company's credit card membership base had been increasing at an annual rate of 35%. A number of things concerned Emshoff, however. Losses from delinquent accounts were on the rise and Diners had internal problems as well: managerial turnover hovered at 40%—only three of the 200 managers who had been with the company in 1981 were still at Diners Club four years later. The head of marketing had resigned in mid-January, and the head of operations had just announced his decision to return to Citicorp in New York. Nevertheless, Citicorp CEO John Reed had made it clear to Emshoff that he expected Diners Club to make a profit in 1985, though it had not shown a profit for several years.

HISTORY

Diners Club was described in the industry as "the granddaddy of plastics." In 1950, Robert McNamara had introduced the original card, made of reinforced cardboard, and Alfred Bloomingdale had organized an international system of Diners Club franchised outlets operated by local entrepreneurs. Diners Club was the first multipurpose charge card to gain worldwide acceptance; eventually it even found markets in the USSR and Communist China.

In the early 1970s, the company was sold to Continental Insurance and

Research Associate Lucy N. Lytle prepared this case under the supervision of Professor W. Earl Sasser as the basis for class discussion rather than to illustrate either effective or ineffective handling of an administrative situation. Copyright © 1988 by the President and Fellows of Harvard College; Harvard Business School case #9-688-078 (Rev. 5/89).

entered a period of decline. The number of diners Club cardholders decreased as did the number of establishments that would accept the card. During the same period, Diners' chief rival, American Express, began a period of intense growth in the U.S. Market.

Diners Club was again sold in 1981, this time to Citicorp, which planned to use it to enter the travel and entertainment card market. Citicorp had made inroads into this market in 1979 with its acquisition of Carte Blanche, another proprietary branded card, which had a strong domestic market but no international presence. With its acquisition of Diners Club, Citicorp put Carte Blanche into a "maintenance mode"; by 1984, Carte Blanche had only 300,000 holders in the United States and less than 1 million worldwide, and its billings totalled $.4 billion. (The attrition rate of Carte Blanche cardholders at that time exceeded the acquisition rate of new members.)

Diners, although an acknowledged veteran in the card business, was by now considered by many to be on its last legs. As one insider noted: "They've got to make some broad changes to garner a bigger share of the market. People picture Diners as a restaurant card that's elite, but outdated."

How could the company come back? In 1983 Thomas Barnum, chairman of Citicorp Services, had decided Diners should adopt a market segmentation strategy and begin an aggressive domestic advertising campaign aimed at attracting the frequent business traveler through Diners' wide range of services. Citicorp thus pledged up to $80 million over the next three years to reverse the pattern of decline, and to establish the card in consumers' minds as a viable alternative to American Express. When American Express began to expand internationally in the early 1980s, Diners fought to maintain its global orientation by buying back its individual franchises and eventually regaining direct control of more than 70% of its business worldwide. (Japan was a major holdout.)

By 1985, operation of Diners Club had been organized into two divisions—domestic and international—and company headquarters had been moved three times: first to Los Angeles, where Carte Blanche was located; then to New York, where Citibank was based; and ultimately to Chicago.

Barnum's strategy seemed to be paying off. Charging an annual fee of $45 and requiring no preset spending limit, Diners Club now had 2.2 million cardholders in the United States, and approximately 5 million members worldwide. And billings in 1984 had reached $4.9 billion.

THE PLASTIC EXPLOSION

The use of credit cards had become a way of life in the United States by the mid-1980s, with the average consumer holding seven credit cards, such as MasterCard and Visa, travel and entertainment cards, and a variety of cards issued by retail stores. More than 700 million cards were in circulation nationwide. Although experts warned that this market was close to saturation, and that credit could not be extended indefinitely, consumers in 1985 were expected to charge 25% more goods and services than during the previous year, and to spend $331 billion using credit cards.

Credit card marketing expenditures skyrocketed as companies spent millions of dollars each year to persuade the public not only to sign up for new cards, but to increase the amount they charged on those they already held. Consumers were bombarded with messages everywhere they turned; splashy television ads promoting credit cards ran from early morning until late at night, print ads appeared in virtually every national periodical, and aggressive direct-mail pitches glutted mailboxes. Special features, known as "enhancements," that included a variety of services ranging from obtaining hotel rooms at a discount to insuring users against accidental death or dismemberment on public transportation, were a popular marketing tool. Enhancements not only differentiated one card from another but also enabled issuers of the cards to tie their members into a wide range of expensive financial and retail services, such as shopping by phone.

In order to increase their cardholder bases, credit card companies relaxed their credit review processes. This practice, coupled with direct mail efforts that often blanketed an area with applications or pre-approved cards, contributed to a dramatic increase in delinquent accounts. (Mailings, it was later discovered, had sometimes been addressed to unemployed teenagers, prison inmates, and even household pets.) On average, 30% of credit cardholders paid their bills immediately. But those who failed to pay after 12 to 18 months were written off as losses, amounting to nearly $2 billion a year.

BANK CARDS

The credit card business had a number of revenue streams. Bank cards, such as MasterCard and Visa, had revenue from revolving credit. Cardholders typically paid an annual fee of approximately $17 to use the card and made minimum monthly payments against the balance of their charge accounts, which had preset spending limits. Annual interest rates ranging from 13% to 22% were levied against unpaid balances (18.8% was the average), a very profitable arrangement for lenders, who borrowed money from the Federal Reserve at 8%. Lenders in 1985 were expected to collect $8 billion to $12 billion in interest on credit cards.

The charge to merchants for processing credit transactions was another important source of revenue for credit card companies. Visa and Mastercard charged 2% to 3.5% of each total sale to process the paperwork, passing along 1.5% of that charge to the bank that issued the card. The key marketing tool for bank card companies, thus, was their ability to manipulate annual fees and finance rates, in addition to card enhancements.

Visa

Visa, the most popular credit card in the world, had more than 77 million card-holders in the United States in 1984, and billings of $60.6 billion. (*Exhibit 1* presents data for each of the major credit card companies.) Visa was issued by banks, some of whom were linked into the company's automated teller network and allowed cardholders to get cash at 1,564 machines in 25 states. Visa was the payment method for 28% of sales by major retailers in the United States; it was accepted by 4.7 million merchants in the United States and abroad. Its wide target market consisted of those 25- to 54-year-olds who had incomes of at least $15,000. Visa hoped to grab a share of American Express's market, and was planning a major television and print campaign around the slogan "Bring your Visa card, 'cause they don't take American Express."

MasterCard

With 60 million cardholders in the United States, and billings in 1984 of almost $50 billion, Mastercard was the payment method for approximately 23% of all retail sales in the United States. Like Visa, MasterCard was issued by banks and enabled 9 million cardholders in the United States to get cash at 3,000 automatic teller machines in 28 states. MasterCard also was developing an electronic debiting card that would automatically deduct charges from the cardholder's bank account.

Whereas Visa and American Express cultivated a prestigious image, Master-Card positioned itself in the market as the practical Everyman's card through heavy advertising on late-night television and during major sports events.

RETAIL CREDIT CARDS

A minimal amount of competition for bank cards came from credit cards issued by retail stores. Generally, these cards, available to consumers for years, cost nothing and could be used in any of the chain's stores. Balances on charges were paid in regular or revolving monthly installments.

Potentially more threatening was a decision by Sears, Roebuck (already the issuer of a Sears credit card) to introduce its "Discover" card in early 1986, which would make it the first company to launch a major new credit card in 20 years. Sears hoped to use the new card to tap into a prospective market for its highly lucrative investment and insurance services.

T & E CARDS

Travel and entertainment (T & E) cards, such as Diners Club and American Express, were charge cards. Cardholders were obligated to pay their balances in full each month. Generally, there was not a preset spending limit. Sources of revenue for these cards included annual fees, which ranged two to three times higher than those for most bank cards; charges for processing credit transactions (3% to 5% of a merchant's total billings); and revenue generated by marketing a variety of services and merchandise to cardholders through gift catalogs.

American Express

American Express (AmEx) dominated the T & E market, with 15 million cardholders in the United States and an additional 5 million abroad. One observer hailed the company as "the marketer that made plastic seem classy," an image promoted in advertisements promising "Membership has its privileges."

American Express's "pay-as-you-go" policy attracted the consumer who wanted that particular card because of its convenience. The basic green card, established in 1958, was advertised in print and on national television, and cost the user $35 per year. Seventy-five percent of green cardholders were male, with annual incomes in excess of $25,000. For those with incomes in the $35,000 to $40,000 range, AmEx offered a gold card for $65 annually. The gold card was advertised primarily in print and on cable television because AmEx marketing executives deemed the major networks' television audience too broad for their card. In late 1984, a platinum card was introduced to target enterpreneurs and small business owners who traveled frequently (50 or more overnight trips a year) and/or had incomes in excess of $100,000. The price tag for this grey card was a fee of $250 per year.

In the late 1970s, faced with a stagnating membership base, American Express successfully marketed its cards to recent college graduates, a move that some felt tarnished the card's exclusive image. By 1984, with 2 million American Express corporate cardholders already in existence, the company also aggressively pursued the corporate card market, which was expected to grow by as much as 50% annually. During the same period, the company began to work for acceptance in many of the major retail chains, where it was used for 16% of all credit card sales.

American Express heavily advertised the services or "privileges" associated with card membership: a 24-hour customer-service hotline, 24-hour card replacement, and a global assist hotline that referred travelers to local doctors, lawyers, and interpreters. "Just your signature on the Card commands exceptional personal service," the application form promised. A large portion of the company's expenditures went to its Travel Related Services division, which ran 1,400 such offices worldwide to help cardholders with travel plans and provide access to emergency cash. In 1984, AmEx reportedly made $252 million on card-related revenues.

One industry analyst predicted that AmEx would spend more than $41 million to advertise its cards during the first nine months of 1985. (For projected media expenditures on bank and T & E cards, see *Exhibit 2*.) One marketing gambit centered around "causes"—such as The Special Olympics; AmEx would agree to donate a specific amount of money to such a cause each time a card was used within a certain period. During such periods, the volume of credit charges might increase by as much as 30%.

OIL COMPANY CARDS

Most of the major oil companies for years had issued cards that holders could use in place of cash to pay for gas and repair work on their cars. In 1985, Amoco and Shell planned to go one step further and offer "full-service" gas cards to provide services ranging from emergency cash to accident insurance to hotel and car rental discounts. Described in the industry as "modified T & E cards," they would be marketed to salespeople and others who traveled frequently by automobile.

DINERS CLUB

Jim Emshoff

In February 1985, Jim Emshoff reviewed his background over lunch. Prior to joining Diners Club, he had spent six years at the Campbell Soup Company, rising quickly from vice president, marketing and development, of the Swanson Foods Division to group general manager and head of the Soup Division. He held a Ph.D. in operations research from the University of Pennsylvania, where as an associate professor he had founded the Wharton Applied Research Center. He had also worked as a consultant for McKinsey & Company, a management consulting firm, in New York City.

Emshoff elaborated on his business philosophy in a memo to his senior managers:

The single most important principle to a successful service organization is a decentralized environment focused on the customer. You have to design a service delivery system that puts your best talent as close to the customer as possible, empowers them to deliver a solution to any problem or need that arises, and ensures that organization functions that do not have direct contact with customers are serving a role that supports the line people. You have to eliminate the layers of people who see their mission as managing the service delivery people instead of supporting them.

I also believe that a service organization needs to constantly monitor and re-examine its understanding of its customers' needs, and use this understanding as a basis for redefining its product or service offerings. Diners Club must strive to break new ground in its attempts to meet the needs and manage the expectations of our customers. No one should underestimate the benefits that can be accrued by making that extra effort in delivering a service. The power of positive word-of-mouth recommendations alone makes it worth the trouble.

Finally, I am convinced that no efforts to improve the quality of a service organization's offerings work well for very long unless the company's principles and priorities are clearly articulated by top management and the message is consistently and clearly communicated through their actions as well as words.

Strategy

Jim Emshoff was committed to developing strength from within Diners Club and to creating visible career paths for its employees. Currently, 70% to 80% of positions were filled by outside hires. One manager, who had been with Diners for about two years, noted, "People have been rolling through here who have no long-term commitment to this company." She went on to point out that before Emshoff accepted the position, Diners Club functioned for nine months without a president.

The core strategic issue facing Diners Club was the same one that other financial service companies were dealing with, the classic "chicken or the egg?" problem: in order to increase the number of establishments that accepted the Diners' card, it was necessary to increase the number of cardholders. But to increase the number of cardholders, it was necessary to prove that the card was widely accepted. This paradox lay at the root of Diners' no-holds-barred marketing campaign, which was increasing card membership by 35% annually.

"Segment the Market: Target the Frequent Business Traveler"

In an interview scheduled to appear in *The Bankers Magazine*[1] in the summer of 1985, Thomas Barnum, chairman of Citicorp Services, discussed Diners' 1983 decision to focus on a specific type of consumer:

> We didn't sit back and say, "We're going to go after the frequent business traveler, now let's see if they have any problems." In going through segments—the elderly, women, etc.—the biggest area of "problems" to be solved was with the frequent business travelers. Therefore, we said, "That is our segment."

Fortunately for Diners, this segment also spent more than the average consumer; its population often charged airfare, entertainment, and gifts. More important, it was willing and able to pay for a higher level of service. Barnum felt that there was less risk in offering specific services to a certain market segment than trying to "be all things to all people."

Building on Barnum's ideas, Emshoff predicted that as the financial service industry evolved, considerable segmentation would occur as the various card companies jockeyed for a share of the market. He pointed to the development of the packaged goods industries (products such as soap, beer, and cigarettes) to illustrate how the credit card industry might separate itself into a series of niches. Companies would differentiate themselves from one another through the products and services they developed to satisfy existing needs.

Barnum's article concluded:

> We're in a business of supplying a set of services and products for [the] frequent business traveler. The only reason we have a card is for identification so there's a way to bill the cardholder. We don't perceive ourselves in the card business per se . . .
>
> There will always be a market for quality products and services to the business person. You can look back pretty far and see that there has always been a business environment. Marco Polo would have been well-served to carry our card.

Of course, not everyone in the financial community shared this view, and a number of observers described Diners' narrow customer focus as a liability. Ray Pierce, formerly head of marketing at American Express, asserted:

> Diners has been a declining force for years because they allowed themselves to become too narrow, unlike American Express, which successfully went after a broader market.

1. "Changes at Diners Club," *The Bankers Magazine* (July–August 1985), pp. 30–34.

Incentive Program

Diners' strategy to attract big spenders centered on its incentive program. Certain special services and benefits were seen as incentives for owning a Diners' card. A monthly newsletter, called "In the Club," alerted cardholders to new and existing benefits and services. Typical services were: "Club Suites," which provided cardholders with a luxury suite for the price of a single room; "Club Chauffeur," which provided limousine service for only a few dollars more than the price of a taxi; "Club Business Offices," which provided access to private offices (with a full range of business services) in 46 major cities; "Club Workout Centers," which enabled users to exercise at private athletic clubs while on the road; "Club Gifts," a 24-hour phone line to a gift consultant who helped cardholders order anything from flower arrangements to rare antiques; and "Club Rewards," a program by which every dollar charged on a Diners Club card automatically earned a Club Rewards point, which could be redeemed for a variety of "rewards," from a ski weekend for two to a personal computer. "In the Club" also featured guest contributors, who wrote articles such as "Making the Most Out of Your Shopping Trip to Europe."

Retail Acceptance

Traditionally, Diners Club did not push as strongly for acceptance in retail establishments as American Express did, preferring instead to associate with an exclusive group of stores, such as Harrod's and Burberry's in London, Gucci in Rome, Baccarat in Paris, and Saks Fifth Avenue in the United States. And while the card generally was accepted at upscale restaurants and at American resorts such as The Breakers, it was seldom used at more affordable places. Emshoff agreed that focusing on upscale establishments helped to differentiate Diners from the competition but he also felt the company should begin to move down-market in order to make the card more widely accepted.

Retail acceptance of the card was increasing, largely because of the growth in the Diners' card member base. Emshoff planned to give it a further boost by linking the Diners Club and Carte Blanche cards with the establishment acceptance networks that supported Visa and Mastercard, which would process all transactions directly through Diners Club computers. He estimated that it would take two years to set up the system.

Corporate Card Market

In 1984, Diners signed an exclusive agreement to provide charge cards to the United States federal government and began to actively pursue corporate accounts. Emshoff foresaw more growth for the company in the corporate card market, but he wondered if this market's requirements of a charge card were the same as those of individual cardholders. Within a few years, he hoped to link Diners' monthly account statements for corporate card customers to a sophisticated MIS system that would automate expense report administration for travelers and provide corporations with new controls over travel costs. He knew this project would be a big investment for Diners Club.

CONCLUSION

It was obvious to Jim Emshoff that a major obstacle to his success centered around the turnover in Diners' management and the lack of continuity that it produced. Fewer than a handful of managers had survived the bumpy road the company had traveled in recent years. With 40% annual turnover, there was an almost palpable feeling of instability in the air. The recent departure of two key officers had been a major blow (see *Exhibit 3*); Emshoff worried that it could spark a rash of defections.

The company's marketing campaign was galloping ahead, but Emshoff wasn't sure that the increasing number of delinquent accounts was a reasonable price to pay for a dramatic increase in the size of the cardmember base. If not controlled, these delinquent accounts could cause Diners to begin to hemorrhage internally. Were such problems a normal consequence of rapid growth, or should he slow this thing down? Confessed Emshoff, "I feel like I'm on a merry-go-round. I'm running faster and faster just to stand still."

APPENDIX

THE GREAT PLASTIC CARD FIGHT BEGINS

MONCI JO WILLIAMS

> *A lot of corporations think the key to the financial future is made of plastic, and Citicorp is attacking fellow giants in a big-money battle to find it. Cards may not be as powerful as some think, but they sure can be profitable.*

Remember the fellow in *The Graduate* who whispered to Dustin Hoffman that plastic was the wave of the future? Corporate planners have bought the idea. Some giant American companies are betting that plastic, the kind people carry in their wallets, is about to become the ultimate strategic weapon. The biggest believer appears to be John Reed, 45, who became chief executive of Citicorp last September.

Reed has a full arsenal of cards at his disposal and, according to card-industry tracker Spencer Nilson, probably spent $150 million to $200 million last year to promote them. Some of the money went into nationwide marketing of MasterCard and Visa, both owned by bank cooperatives and also issued by thousands of other United States banks. But Citicorp really shelled it out for some of the proprietary cards in its silos. These include such familiar names as Diners Club and Carte Blanche—used mostly for travel and in restaurants—and a new advanced weapon, the Choice card, that is already held by a million Americans. Though little known outside states where the card is marketed—and Citi's home state of New York isn't one of them—Choice has the competition's radar blipping.

Reed's moves are part of his strategy to make Citi the first and foremost nationwide bank. Other card players have different goals, but all are trying to figure ways to reach the right consumers or investors, to persuade them to use their cards to do more things, or to cross-sell other products or services. Banks and nonbanks are doling out money for hardware and software so they can defend their positions, or advance them, as the nation moves to electronically based payment systems. The upshot is that plastic is about to become a battle-ground in a fight for turf.

Plastic may not prove as powerful as Reed and others hope, but it can be immensely profitable. At the moment, credit cards are a bright spot for belea-guered banks. Banks charge annual interest rates of anywhere from 13% to 22% for unpaid balances on Visa and MasterCards they issue—vs. 10.75% on loans made at the prime rate—plus an average annual fee of $17 per card. Banks also do a nice business processing credit transactions for merchants, traditionally those near their home turf, usually raking off 2% to 3.5% of total charges; they typically pass along 1.5 percentage points to the bank that issued the card.

American Express gets most of its card revenues by processing every single American Express receipt itself, a paperwork feat for which it charges merchants 3% to 5% of billings. Its annual card fees—$35 for the green card, $65 for the gold—comfortably exceed $650 million. Rodney Schwartz, a security analyst at Paine Webber, estimates that American Express netted $252 million from the card business in 1984, 42% of total corporate profits.

With 15 million United States cardholders, American Express virtually owns the so-called travel and entertainment market. But it frets about Citi, which is spending heavily to steal business for Diners Club, and about some other power-houses that are experimenting with card tricks. Among these is Sears, Roebuck, with 60 million cards. How long, the card watchers wonder, will Sears be con-tent to let its cards languish out there, underutilized, equipped only to make a Sears purchase? How long before Sears develops a multiple warhead?

Sears won't comment about its plans, nor will Citicorp. But it is a safe bet that none of the cardplayers feel secure. The sheer might of the competition is not the only worry. Deregulation of banking is sure to make doing business tougher; any company with lots of cardholders and processing power is a poten-tial threat; and technology could dramatically alter the way payments are made. Banks are promoters of debit cards, but they have mixed feelings about the trend toward electronic debiting in retail stores—paying for purchases with almost instantaneous withdrawals from bank accounts. As a system of payment, bankers prefer debit cards to checks, which are generally unprofitable to process. But what if debit cards begin to take the place of credit cards? This not only would threaten those profitable credit card loans, it would reduce what merchants pay banks for processing card purchases. In fact, a couple of pioneering retailers, Mobil Oil and Publix Super Markets in Florida, have invested in the hardware and software necessary to accept debit cards and, for providing the systems, are *charging some banks to make the transactions.*

With fast-moving technologies and deregulation blurring everybody's vision of the financial future, practically any articulate seer's scenarios seem plausible. Not to react seems unthinkable, so all the participants are doing something, often at great cost. It may be decades before the corporate winners are known, but in the meantime the battle should benefit every card-carrying consumer.

Reed is counting on his portfolio of plastic to establish a strong national consumer franchise for Citicorp. The plan is to place millions of cards bearing Citi's name in the hands of consumers all over the United States and then to cross-sell those cardholders mortgages, student loans, credit life insurance, and maybe even stocks and bonds. More important, Reed also aims to attract deposits this way, particularly CDs and money market accounts, by offering attractive rates or services. In short, Reed will use cards to help make him an end run around federal restrictions on interstate banking—by setting up a national banking network through the mail.

To attract rich customers, Citi has been spending much of its money lately promoting "prestige" cards. It has embarked on a huge campaign to issue Visa's Premier card, which Citibank calls Preferred Visa. And in the last two years Citi has poured at least $70 million into Diners Club, a weakling in the travel and entertainment (T & E) market when it was acquired in 1981 and probably still a money loser in the United States. The push to resuscitate the card began in earnest in 1983, directed by Richard S. Braddock, 43, Citicorp's top card executive. Until he joined the bank in the mid-1970s, Braddock had been a marketing man at General Foods, but Diners is not a piece of cake.

Citicorp's first task is to unsell consumers on the American Express card, which got its grip on the T & E market by convincing people that they can't leave home without it. Citi may have underestimated the difficulty of building up a base of cardholders and establishments willing to accept the card. It's a slow, expensive, brick-by-brick sort of task: consumers don't want a card if it isn't widely accepted by merchants, and merchants don't want to bother accepting a card that doesn't bring with it a lot of affluent card carriers. Though Diners is outnumbered two million to 15 million by American Express in the United States, the numbers look better abroad, where Diners has three million cardholders to American Express's five million. Until recently the Diners operations outside the United States were owned by franchisees, a different one in each country. For the last couple of years Citicorp has been busily buying those franchises. But almost nobody thinks Diners can catch American Express.

Citi's solution to the almost Sisyphean task at hand has been to buy its way in the market, using every marketing trick in the book. Last year Citi began a direct mail blitz for Diners, soliciting thousands of "preferred customers"—business travelers whose names Citi probably bought from the rosters of airline frequent-flier programs. "Frankly, Citicorp Diners Club wants your business, and we're willing to work for it!" the mailer began. But preferred customers who read on found that Citi wasn't just willing to work for their business, it was willing to pay for it. Citi offered all sorts of lavish incentives along with the card, among them a credit toward the first $25 in charges, free Citicorp's traveler's checks, and a round-trip ticket on American Airlines to anywhere in the United States, including Hawaii, or to the Virgin Islands, for a mere $175.

Those kinds of incentives have doubtless produced results, though one wonders what will happen if the incentives are no longer offered when the card comes up for renewal at $45 a year, $10 more than American Express's green. Citi hopes to pick up cardholders faster by going after corporate customers, who would furnish Diners cards to their executives in bulk. Citi kicked off its ad campaign last year using the tag line "Citicorp Diners Club . . . when you mean business." The ads and TV spots featured four companies that used Diners as their corporate T & E card. Top officers of two of them—United Technologies and Corning Glass Works—are directors of Citicorp.

The corporate market is also the segment that American Express has been planning to cultivate next, and the clash promises to be lively. American Express has surprised everyone, including American Express, with its success at expanding its cardholder base in other areas. The man who deserves most of the credit is Louis V. Gerstner, 42, chairman of the executive committee at American Express and head of the subsidiary that operates the card and travel services.

When Gerstner arrived in 1978 from McKinsey & Co., the management consulting firm, security analysts were saying that American Express's card business had reached maturity. The cards, they reasoned, were already in the hands of practically all the traveling executives who needed them, and they were accepted by most airlines, car-rental companies, hotels, and good restaurants. Since then, Gerstner has managed to keep earnings in the card business growing at an annual average rate of 25%, compounded. He discovered women, raising the proportion of female card members to 29% of the total from 16% four years ago, and he began adding graduating college students to the card-member base. He also went after retail stores, not previously hustled, and got merchants from Saks Fifth Avenue to the Gap to accept the card.

The trade-off for taking on new groups of cardholders was that the green card lost some of the cachet that went with a more exclusive approach. Gerstner, who believes that snob appeal sells, pushed the gold card hard to hold customers who otherwise might have been lured away by the Visa Premier card or MasterCard's gold model. Last year he introduced the platinum card, available only to people who have charged more than $10,000 on their American Express cards in the past year. So far it turns out that 50,000 of these big spenders are willing to fork over $250 to carry plastic platinum.

Gerstner is just beginning his push into the corporate market. The company has sold only about two million corporate cards, most of them to small businesses. Now American Express is aiming at large corporate accounts among the

Fortune 500. Gerstner thinks the corporate segment could grow by more than 50% a year, and he doesn't intend to share that growth with Citicorp or anyone else.

Jerry C. Welsh, a former head of card marketing and now in charge of worldwide marketing and communications for Gerstner's subsidiary, claims that American Express will "clean Citibank's clock" in the corporate card segment with a product called Travel Management Service, or TMS. The product is an integrated package of corporate services wrapped around the basic American Express card. The services include analyzing travel and entertainment costs by division, consulting with companies about travel policies, and actually operating as the travel department for companies that don't have their own. Gerstner's pitch is that TMS will help United States corporations control the $80 billion or so they spend on travel and entertainment for employees each year.

While Citicorp tangles with American Express in the corporate market, it is already well along in an experiment with the Choice card to find out whether it can collect deposits by mail. Back in 1977, when Reed was head of Citi's fledgling retail banking unit, Citicorp bought NAC, a small Baltimore-area charge card, and renamed it Choice. The bank did little with the card until 1980, when it reintroduced Choice in Baltimore. Now Choice is distributed mainly in the Baltimore-Washington area and in Colorado. The million cardholders have 60,000 places to use the card.

Last year Choice customers charged an estimated $700 million on their cards. Though it is small potatoes in the card game, Choice has performed impressively in the Baltimore-Washington area, where the test began. Ronald E. Geesey, president of the Citicorp subsidiary that markets the card, told a group of security analysts last year that in 1983 Choice accounted for more than 25% of sales by "major retailers" in that market—more than American Express (16%) and MasterCard (23%) and just a nose behind Visa (28%). As it has with Diners Club, Citi has equipped the card with all sorts of appealing features to get it into consumers' hands and to get them to use it. Cardholders receive Choice and an accompanying credit line of $750 to $5,000 without paying an annual fee, and are promised a rebate of 0.5% on all Choice purchases above the first $600 in any 12-month period. To find out whether consumers would hand over deposits through the mail, Citi has outfitted Choice with several interest-paying accounts. For deposits larger than $1,000, Choice was recently paying 10%, more than a point above prevailing money market rates. Cardholders who overpay their bills by less than $1,000 get 5.25%.

When Choice moved to Denver in 1983, it found an ideal test market. Colorado allows out-of-state bank holding companies to open limited-service banks that can collect consumer deposits, and it also requires banks in automated teller networks to share their terminals with other state banks. So in Colorado, through Citicorp Industrial Bank, Choice cardholders can get cash and make deposits at hundreds of ATMs around the state.

It's hard to get a fix on how much Citi has collected in deposits from Choice customers, since the bank isn't talking. But Citi must be encouraged by Choice's early returns. Last spring Geesey told the analysts that Choice had "a great future," adding that if the results of the Baltimore test could be duplicated nationwide, "we are talking about tens of millions of cardholders." Several months later, after it successfully petitioned Maryland legislators to pass a bill allowing out-of-state bank holding companies to set up shop in their state, Citicorp opened a Maryland banking subsidiary. Its purpose, Citi told shareholders last November, is to provide a launching pad from which "to market our Choice card nationwide . . . through mail and telephone marketing." Perhaps in anticipation of the rollout, Citi has recently signed up ATM networks in several states—including Florida, Texas, and California—at which Choice cardholders can get cash.

Citicorp was able to expand Choice's merchant base from Maryland and Washington, D.C., through Delaware, Virginia, North Carolina, and southern Pennsylvania by using the economies of scale in its huge credit card processing operations. To get into Virginia, Citi started a price war. Through what it called a "tri-card plan," it offered to process merchants' credit slips for Visa, Master-Card, and Choice for about half a percentage point below the approximately 3% charged by banks in the area. Randolph Wyckoff, a senior vice president in charge of credit cards at the Bank of Virginia, says he lost plenty of processing business to Citicorp. In fact, says Wyckoff, "they kicked our ass all over the block."

To protect the business he had left, Wyckoff went to Citicorp and offered to sell the Choice card to the merchants whose Visa and MasterCard slips he processed. Citi agreed, and the United Virginia Bank and Central Fidelity, two other Richmond-based banks, soon struck similar deals.

There was some growling from other banks in the state, since nobody in Virginia has much appreciation for Yankee invasions. "Sure they asked me, 'Why'd you let 'em in?'" drawls Wyckoff. "But what else are you gonna do? You can try to hold the door as long as you can—and then when it opens, it squashes you. Or you can try to find an advantage."

More companies may soon be trying to beat down the door. If Citi can make headway across the United States in spite of regulations that make it hard to leave the state, why can't big retailers with cross-country electronic networks for authorizing and processing credit purchases launch their own all-purpose credit cards? And for that matter, if the retailers happen to own banks or savings banks—as Sears does in California and both Sears and J.C. Penney do in Delaware—why can't they collect deposits the same way Citi hopes to?

Bankers say that Sears is testing the idea of an all-purpose credit/debit card like Choice that could be used at automated teller machines. And Sears is also looking for ways to link its card to its securities subsidiary, Dean Witter. In San Diego, Sears is experimenting with a card that gives some customers of Dean Witter and Sears Savings bank access to cash at automated teller machines throughout California.

Bankers and others take comfort from the thought that Sears would have trouble launching a nationwide credit card because other retailers would resist accepting a competitor's plastic. But Sears has been working on a deal with a noncompeting retailer, Phillips Petroleum. In a test, Phillips has been using Sears' sophisticated electronic network to check the credit of customers using cards and to process credit purchases. Penney has been marketing its electronic network through a subsidiary set up in 1983 called J.C. Penney Systems Services. Among its customers are Shell Oil and Gulf Oil, which pay Penney 10 cents to 13 cents per transaction to do what Sears is doing for Phillips. Late last year Penney even signed up a bank in Utah, which uses Penney's network to transmit data for its own bank-card operations. And just to scramble your senses, a 75%-owned subsidiary of American Express, called First Data Resources, thinks it is the largest nonbank processor for Visa and MasterCard transactions in the United States. The possible permutations suggested by all this, combined with the prospect of electronic debiting at the cash register, justify bankers' fears that nonbanks may wrest control of the payment systems.

Before the technology gets sorted out, and before Reed's great experiments prove anything, consumers must cast their votes. Do they really want a card that can zap their bank account to pay for things? Can deposits be coaxed from them, by mail or any other way, or will they coolly shop for the best rate? Do they like the idea of one-stop financial services, or is that just a planner's dream? Will corporations buy charge cards? Will people come to favor some new brand of card over the ones we already have? Strategists can only guess at the answers, but there will be winners among those who are willing to place their bets before all the answers are clear.

Exhibit 1
Credit Card Circulation

Card	1984 Billings (billions)	Issued in the U.S.
Visa	$60.6	77,200,000
MasterCard	49.7	60,000,000
American Express	36.6	15,000,000
Diners Club	4.9	2,200,000
Carte Blanche	.4	300,000

CITICORP DINERS CLUB
Exhibit 2
Projected Media Expenditures (January–September 1985)
(000)

Company	Total	Magazines	Network TV	Sports TV	Outdoors	Sunday Magazines	Network Radio	Cable TV
Bank Cards								
MasterCard	$16,232.6	$2,309.1	$11,754.9	$1,919.3	—	—	—	$249.3
Visa	15,600.4	5,454.2	7,369.8	176.7	79.7	—	2,466.4	53.6
Discover	401.1	197.9	—	203.2	—	—	—	—
Travel & Entertainment Cards								
American Express	41,740.4	17,401.4	16,031.0	7,493.2	13.3	583.6	—	217.9
Diners Club	6,643.6	3,765.3	—	2,496.4	49.5	—	—	332.4

SOURCE: Leading national advertisers/*Fortune* magazine (February 4, 1985), p. 21.

Exhibit 3
Diners Club Organization, 1985

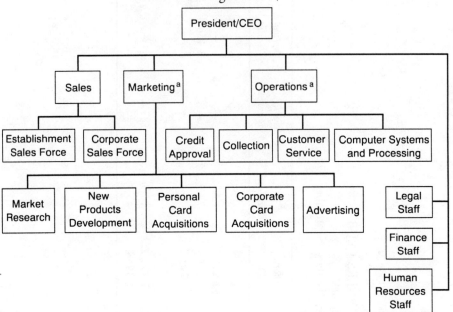

[a] Positions vacated in first quarter 1985.

Ford Motor Company: Dealer Sales and Service

I. INTRODUCTION

As the worldwide automotive globalization process accelerates and reaches maturity, automotive products will become more complex and technology intensive, the service marketing environment will be both more complex and more competitive, product quality will become less of a purchase motivation discriminator, and customer satisfaction requirements will intensify. A logical conclusion that can be drawn from this scenario is that automotive service and the capability to perform such services at best-in-class levels by a given brand's authorized outlets in concert with customer needs and value measures will play a dramatically more important role in the vehicle purchase motivation process than presently played.[1]

Many observers agreed with Ford's conclusions that the auto industry in the United States was changing. The difference between products and technology, several industry experts believed, would become less of a factor in customer decisions between makes. Differences in distribution and service would become more of a factor.

A report published by J.D. Power and Associates, an automotive research and consulting firm, entitled "Revolution in Automotive Retailing" agreed that product parity was approaching, putting increased pressure on the distribution networks. In addition, this report noted the number of dealers was decreasing and the sales per dealer increasing. Many dealers were opening second locations or were adding other makes to their existing facilities. Both of these changes necessitated higher levels of capital and increased management structure. The

Mr. Mark Pelofsky prepared this case under the supervision of Associate Professor Leonard A. Schlesinger as the basis for class discussion rather than to illustrate either effective or ineffective handling of an administrative situation. The names of Ford and dealer executives have been disguised. Copyright © 1989 by the President and Fellows of Harvard College; Harvard Business School case #9-690-030.

1. Ford Parts and Service Division, *Service Success Strategy: Customer-Driven Requirements* (internal document), 1989.

report concluded that "the dealership business may have become too big and too sophisticated to be considered entrepreneurial any more."[2]

Given these projected changes in the automotive marketplace, throughout 1988 and 1989 a hand-picked group of executives at the Ford Motor Company worked to rethink their distribution system. They knew that any changes would have to not only address the coming changes described above but also the realities and politics of the current 5,400 independent U.S. Ford and Lincoln-Mercury dealers.

To determine what a new distribution system should look like, the Ford executives first wanted to find out both what was wrong with the current system and what customers said they would like during the automobile sales and service process. In addition, allowances had to be made for the fact that there was not uniformity of customer opinions across all dealerships. In particular, often small dealerships did not face the same criticisms directed toward larger Ford dealers.

The Ford executives decided to focus on the problems of the larger dealers for several reasons. First, dealers with larger volume naturally had a larger impact upon the reputation and the success of Ford. Second, as mentioned above, larger dealerships were beginning to dominate the automobile sales landscape in the United States. Finally, the majority of customer complaints were aimed at larger dealers. Small dealerships, perhaps because of their size and personal relationships with their customers, seemed to do a better job of meeting customer needs both in sales and service.

II. SALES

The first significant contact between the dealership and the retail customer occurred during the sales process. Ford had commissioned several studies which focused on customer opinions of the automobile sales process at Ford and other dealerships. Overall these studies consistently found that, according to the American public, buying a car was among the most unpleasant consumer experiences in American life.

Customers

Customers had three major complaints about the car and truck purchase process:

- customers had to go through bargaining or "horse trading" to establish the price

2. J.D. Power and Associates, "Revolution in Automotive Retailing," June 1989, p. 19.

- salespeople were unresponsive to customers' stated needs
- dealer salespeople used high-pressure sales tactics.

Although they understood that salespeople were paid on a commission basis, customers felt that the manner in which salespeople tried to make their commissions made a difference in the customer's perception of the dealership.

The most significant cause of dissatisfaction among car and truck buyers was the fact that car prices were negotiable. Buyers felt that the dealer was playing a game and knew exactly what bottom line would be acceptable. Most customers stated that they would prefer to shop for cars the same way they do for other goods: look at the product, find out the fixed price, judge whether it is worth the price, and decide whether or not to purchase it. In addition, factory rebate programs confused the pricing situation further.

Another reported cause of dissatisfaction in the sales process was salespeople who did not listen to what a customer said. Many salespeople would try to sell a particular car rather than meet the stated needs of the customer.

Another complaint came from a salesperson's attempt to sell add-ons and options that the customer didn't want. Other unpleasant tactics included talking about a deal before the customer had decided to buy the car, splitting a husband and wife to work on each separately, and fast-talking without giving the customer time to think or ask questions. Women reported especially bad treatment; salespeople tended to direct their comments to a boyfriend or husband who accompanied the woman even if she was the one buying the car.

Customers understood the difficulty of establishing fixed prices, especially when a trade-in was involved. In addition, customers realized the temptation a dealer might have to undercut a competitor's fixed price. Despite their understanding of this pricing dilemma, customers still disliked the system.

Ford combined several pieces of research and constructed a list of do's and don'ts of customer service in the auto industry. (See *Exhibit 1*.) In addition, Ford commissioned a consultant to examine the new car buying process. The consultant reached several significant conclusions which are listed in *Exhibit 2*.

Finally, Ford visited companies outside the automotive business that were well-known examples of retailing excellence. From all of these sources, the Ford executives reached three conclusions about consumer behavior:

1. Customers were willing to travel relatively long distances to locate what they consider an acceptable deal.
2. Even when mistreated, customers would buy a new vehicle from a dealership if they could take immediate delivery.
3. Many customers would rather shop when a dealership was closed to avoid being hassled by high-pressure salespeople.

Dealers

New vehicle sales provided the engine that drove the dealership. New car and truck customers used dealerships for service, traded their used vehicles to dealers, and often financed new and used vehicles through the dealerships. In addition, sales was considered the more glamorous side of the business. Most dealers came from sales and some viewed service as a necessary evil rather than an important component of their dealership.

Dealers employed salespeople, and often a sales manager, all of whom typically sold both new and used cars and trucks. Most dealers paid their sales staff on a commission basis, though some paid a small salary plus commission. Paul Bennett, a general manager of a Ford dealership in Hartford, Connecticut, paid his salespeople a salary, the use of a car, and commission. His salespeople earned a total yearly compensation of $50,000 to $80,000.

Dan Johnson, a Ford dealer in a small town outside Springfield, Massachusetts, paid his salespeople $300 per week plus $25 per car sold. In addition, his salespeople shared a portion of the profit generated by the new and used car departments. Their total yearly compensation averaged between $25,000 and $35,000.

Johnson, who had won the Ford Motor Company President's Award for excellence in customer service, felt that the biggest problem with being a Ford dealer was the slow introduction of new lines and the company's desire to maximize short-term profits for shareholders:

> What we need is a new car like the Taurus every couple of years or so. But the company has been too worried about profits for the shareholder and unwilling to invest.
>
> The Taurus took too long to come out. If it hadn't worked out we would all be pushing up daisies. The Japanese can develop a new car in 36 months. Ford has to produce more models faster.
>
> The factory [Ford] has been making record profits while dealer profits have declined. One reason for the decrease in our profits has been the increase in floor plan costs—which are the interest carrying costs for the cars we have in inventory. Ford has encouraged the dealers to submit full orders and, unlike in the past, has been filling the entire order. In the past when a dealer marked an item "low priority," Ford would not send it or would send one or two of the ten ordered. This summer I had 300 cars on the lot and was selling about 60 per month, giving me a five months' supply. My goal is to have about three months' inventory on hand.
>
> Ford has been overly tight considering the low profits the dealers have been making. Dividends are too important.

Economics

Dealers bought new vehicles from Ford at a wholesale price and resold them for a price that gave the dealers a gross margin of about 12% (see section on Economic Model below). Ford established an allocation for dealer vehicle purchases each month by type of car and truck and encouraged, but could not force, the dealers to purchase that number of each type of vehicle. No vehicle was produced by Ford unless it had been ordered by a dealer; every vehicle produced was spoken for. Shortages in dealer orders could force temporary plant closures and result in tremendous losses to the manufacturer.

Dealers varied widely in size. The number of new vehicles sold by individual dealers ranged from 15 to 3,500 per year, with an average of about 700.

Dealers' new vehicle departments sold not only new cars and trucks but also financing and certain types of insurance. These financial products, called F&I, made a significant contribution to the profit of the new vehicle department. One import dealer, writing in *Automobile Executive*, estimated that the typical new vehicle department actually lost money before counting the profits from F&I. This dealer cited rising inventory carrying costs and advertising costs as the major causes of this profit squeeze.[3] While Dan Johnson and Paul Bennett agreed that their costs in the new vehicle department were rising, both felt that they could earn a profit on new vehicle sales.

III. SERVICE

Customers

Customers had four major complaints about dealer service:

- Dealer service was impersonal and uncaring
- Dealer service was incompetent
- Dealer service was not a good value for the price
- Dealer service was out of touch with customers' time constraints.

The image of dealer service as impersonal and uncaring pervaded most of Ford and other industry studies. Customers felt they were treated "like a number" by service departments that were so overloaded that they really did not want new

3. Renald Dembs, "The New-Car Department: A Profit Center in Decline," *Automotive Executive*, February 1989, p. 93.

business anyway. Many owners reported bringing their car in and just standing inside the door of the service area without knowing who to talk to. Other customers reported waiting needlessly:

> He [the service writer] was standing there talking to some other guy, shooting the bull, and I kept standing there and standing there. I was the only one standing there, and he just kept talking to this other guy for about 15 minutes. Then he said, "What can I do for you?" and I said, "Well, I need to get my car in here to get the oil changed and serviced." And he said, "We can't get to it for two or three hours."

In addition, service customers felt frustrated at not getting to meet the actual mechanic and explain the problem directly to the person who would be doing the work. This dissatisfaction was heightened by the contrast between treatment in the showroom and in the service area; customers buying a car reported much more personalized attention in the purchase process.

The quality of the work performed by the dealers' service departments also received criticism from customers. Having to take a car to a dealer more than once for the same problem caused the highest level of dissatisfaction. Many customers felt that low quality of work stemmed directly from their inability to explain the problem directly to the mechanic.

Customers also doubted the quality of the mechanics themselves. Many owners believed that turnover was high because mechanics worked at a dealership only as long as they needed to get enough experience to move on. In addition, customers thought that mechanics tried to maximize their earnings by spending as little time as possible on each problem.

In fact, during the warranty period, the automaker reimbursed a dealer a fixed fee for each type of repair. Therefore, there may have been an incentive for the dealer to attempt to complete a repair as quickly as possible and send it out without regard to the quality of the repair. If the dealership spent more time than allotted in trying to diagnose, fix, or test a particular problem, it could not bill more than the standard rate. If a vehicle came in a second time for the same warranty repair, the dealer could charge neither the customer nor the company for the work. In many cases the dealer would not pay the technician for a repeat repair either. However, if a repeat repair was diagnosed differently from the original service visit, Ford could be charged for the warranty work.

In addition, dealership service was perceived as expensive compared to other service outlets. Customers thought that the same hourly rate was charged whether a mechanic changed a light bulb or overhauled an engine. Therefore, most owners took their car or truck elsewhere for most small nonwarranty repairs, reserving the big jobs for the dealership service. The fact that discount outlets for oil changes and muffler existed further convinced customers that getting minor work done at the dealership was uneconomical.

Finally, service customers complained about the hours dealer service was open and the length of time necessary to get even a minor service job finished. The fact that dealer service was generally open only during daytime hours, conflicting with most customers' work schedule, contributed to the image that the dealers did not really want service business. Most dealerships were open early in the morning but stayed open only until 5 or 6 p.m. And most were closed on the weekend. Many customers felt that to get any repair done, the vehicle had to be dropped off early in the morning and left until at least the late afternoon before it could be picked up. This inconvenience prompted many owners to take their cars elsewhere for all but warranty or major repairs.

The Service Industry

Ford divided the service industry into six types of competitive channels. These six were:

- New car dealer
- Service station
- Independent garage
- Department/discount store
- Chain/specialty store
- Do-it-yourself.

Each year, Ford tracked industrywide customer use of each of these six as well as the satisfaction level with each. In the 1980s, two clear trends characterized the choice of service outlet for customer-paid work. First, new car dealers increased their share from 20% in 1980 to 30% by 1987. Second, the do-it-yourself share dropped from 23% in 1980 to 14% in 1987.

With automobiles becoming more technically sophisticated and including more computer chip components, the do-it-yourself share was projected to decrease in the future to nearly zero. Also because of this technology change, the share of the market, that captured by new car dealers, especially for complicated repairs, had risen and was predicted to increase. This share increase resulted from customer perception that dealers received technical support from the factory and had the computer diagnostics and high-tech machinery necessary to work on the new model cars.

Another reason for the increase in share for the dealers was the decrease in the number of service stations doing repair work. Because of their accessible real estate locations, many corner gas stations found it more profitable to sell food and drinks than to service automobiles. Paine Webber's automobile analysts estimated that the percentage of service stations performing repair had dropped from nearly 100% in 1970 to 55% by 1984. In addition, the absolute number of service stations had been decreasing over the same period. The net change in service stations performing repairs over that period then was a 70% decrease from over 200,000 in 1970 to just over 60,000 by 1984.

Ford and other domestic automotive companies had approximately a one-quarter share of the customer-paid service performed on their own makes. Imports had a moderately higher share at roughly 35% to 40%.[4] Similarly, customer satisfaction data from 1987 showed that domestic automobile companies received comparable customer satisfaction ratings and the imports scored higher. Satisfaction with dealer service across all makes had risen since 1978 but still lagged independent garages. Two-thirds of service customers of domestic dealerships and three-quarters of those at import dealerships reported that they were "very satisfied" with their service experience. In addition, the number of dealership service customers at the other extreme, somewhat or very dissatisfied, exceeded that of independent garages.[5]

The Dealers

Paul Bennett felt that customer expectations for service had become too high:

> We get customers in here who grew up on television and McDonald's. They expect the cars to be fixed instantly. We have improved but the customers want more. Sometimes we have to give them a little taste of reality and tell them they may have to wait.
>
> We are a high-volume dealer [over 1,500 new Fords sold per year] so the demand on the service department has increased. We have 20 mechanics working here but sometimes people still have to wait. We have about $1 million in parts inventory but that isn't even close to being every part that a customer might need.
>
> Some of the new dealerships such as the Acura also have an advantage with the physical layout of their buildings. Those buildings are designed to improve the traffic flow and cut down on customer waiting and inconvenience. If we are going to redo our building it would cost millions of dollars.

4. All market share data refer to customer-paid service only and ignore warranty work, paid by the manufacturer.

5. Ford North American Automotive Operations, "Attitudes Toward and Satisfaction with Various Service Outlets—1986 Study," March 31, 1987.

Bennett paid most of his service workers between $12 and $24 per hour. Some specialists made considerably more. Johnson paid his service people like his salespeople, giving them part of their compensation based on performance:

Unlike most dealers, I pay my service people as much as or more than my salespeople. They get between $275 and $350 per week for 45 hours of work. In addition, I give them 30% of their labor charge after the first $1,000 per month. If a worker generates $2,000 of labor billings in a month, he will get $300.

Johnson said that Ford Motor Company service field representatives were very interested in this compensation system and were trying to convince other Ford dealers to implement incentives for service technicians:

The manufacturer would like to see other dealers adopt a system like mine. However, I don't think many of them will change their compensation system. I wouldn't change mine either because people are scared of change. The only way I could make a change is to guarantee them that they wouldn't make less under the new system.

Economics

The service profit center (exclusive of profits generated from parts) generated an average loss of over 3.5% of sales. This loss came despite increasing manufacturers' warranty periods and service contracts that reimbursed the dealer at retail rates for service performed. In 1988, all major domestic dealers lost money while most imports made money in the service area.[6] Both Bennett and Johnson claimed to make profits from service but agreed that many dealers did not.

The high cost of technologically sophisticated diagnostic equipment (some cost over $100,000) necessary to service the increasingly complex products caused much of the loss in the service department. In addition, Ford had a fairly wide range of automotive products that required skilled technicians to repair. Paul Bennett, walking through his service area, stated:

We have many different models—Mustangs, Probes, Tauruses, Crown Victorias, Econoline Vans—and a whole series of trucks. My technicians have to know how to fix all of them and the different versions of each.

Dealers could not hope to overcome these service profitability problems by increasing volumes because of two constraints: service technician availability and

6. Jake Kelderman, "Dealership Profit Squeeze," *Automotive Executive*, July 1989, p. 23.

service stalls. By 1988, dealership service traffic had increased 51% since 1982.[7] This increase resulted from higher sales volume and units in operation (UIO). In addition, as outlined above, dealers were servicing a higher percentage of the market. Given the steady rise in UIO and no similar increase in service stalls or technicians, a service capacity problem appeared imminent. Paine Webber analysts estimated that the number of vehicles in operation per service bay had increased from 109 in 1978 to 138 in 1988. The shortage of qualified technicians already had driven wages up, further exacerbating the difficulty of making a profit from service.

Because dealers had little excess capacity, many were reluctant to do service work on same-make vehicles sold by other dealers. To do so would delay work for their own customers. Both Bennett and Johnson felt that certain dealers lured customers in with low car prices but couldn't properly service the vehicles after the sale. Dan Johnson said:

> I usually let customers of other dealerships get their warranty work done where they bought the car so they can see the problems of the other dealers. Then, maybe next time they will buy from me.

Walking through his service bays, Paul Bennett spotted a car bought from another dealer being serviced. He yelled at the technician and told him to get out of the car and stop servicing it. He asked if it was a warranty or pay job. Upon being told it was a paying customer he allowed the work to continue.

One area that generated consistent profits was the parts department. In 1988 the U.S. auto dealers earned over 8% pretax on parts sales.[8]

IV. FORD MOTOR COMPANY DEALERSHIPS

Since the 1950s two significant industry trends had occurred in the automobile dealer environment. First, the number of dealerships had declined. And second, the average size of the dealerships had increased. Closely associated with the latter was the emergence of mega-dealers, individuals who control numerous franchises of the same or competing makes.

Year	Number of Outlets	New Vehicle Sales per Outlet
1955	41,018	199
1988	25,105	625

SOURCES: *Automotive News*, R. L. Polk, Ford internal documents.

7. Ford Motor Company, "Long-term Strategy Report" (internal document), 1989.

8. Jake Kelderman, "Dealership Profit Squeeze," p. 27.

Likewise, Ford dealerships were decreasing in number but increasing in size.

Year	Number of Outlets[a]	New Vehicle Sales per Outlet
1955	8,933	255
1988	5,427	696

SOURCES: *Automotive News*, R. L. Polk, Ford internal documents.
[a] Includes Lincoln-Mercury dealers.

Tom Peters reported that a Ford executive claimed on the radio that U.S. auto manufacturers were nearly even on the product quality front but were being "done in" by poor dealer service. The implication, Peters concluded, was that giant Ford could not control its dealers. Peters reported that other U.S. executives had made similar statements about the inability of manufacturers to control customer service at the retail site.[9]

Therefore, no matter what changes Ford executives wanted to make to improve customer service, the realities of the current relationship between the company and the dealerships had to be considered. Ford Motor Company managers would have to consider what leverage they had with dealerships and how they could use that leverage to improve customer service delivery at the dealerships.

Ford dealerships were independently owned franchises. Ford sold no cars to end users directly; all end-user sales went through franchised dealerships. None of the dealerships were owned by Ford although the company did provide significant financing through Ford Credit, its subsidiary, including inventory, customer purchase, and capital improvement financing.

Unlike many other franchisors, Ford did not charge a franchise fee. And unlike those of other car manufacturers, Ford's franchises had no expiration or termination date. The franchises were granted to a specific individual or individuals for as long as the franchisee was alive, performed satisfactorily, and wanted to own the franchise. Typically, if a franchisee died, the heirs worked with Ford to either sell the dealership assets or continue to operate the dealership.

Over time, automobile dealers had acquired significant political strength and had formed organizations of dealers to increase their clout with the manufacturers and state and federal governments. Because automobile dealers in the United States were geographically dispersed and because many of them were wealthy and influential members of their communities, they often had substantially more power than Ford in regional politics. As a result, every state and the District of Columbia had enacted franchise laws particularly addressing the special case of automobile dealers. These special statutes protected dealers from

9. Tom Peters, "Bad Service, Worse Quality," *Skunks in Action*, (Berkeley, CA: TPG Communications, 1986), p. 17.

certain actions of the manufacturer. For example, Texas prohibited auto manufacturers from terminating a dealership for poor market performance alone.

In order to be granted a franchise, a person had to have sufficient financing as determined by the size of the dealer point or market area. Usually, at least $500,000 was required, of which half had to be unencumbered. Besides the financing, the applicant had to be judged by Ford to be capable of managing a dealership. The company preferred to grant franchises to people with vehicle sales experience.

Very few additional dealerships were added to the existing dealer body. Usually a newly appointed dealer would be granted a franchise to replace a previous owner who resigned for any one of a number of reasons. If Ford wanted to open an additional dealership in an area, it would have to satisfy existing dealers that the additional dealership wouldn't be encroaching on their market.

Once a dealer was appointed, he or she (most Ford dealers were men) had to make best efforts to sell and service Ford products. A franchise could be taken away from a dealer but only after a long and drawn-out process (which could end up in the courts). Ford granted any dealer threatened with removal the right of appeal to the Dealer Policy Board which was a committee that reported directly to the Ford board of directors. The decision of the Dealer Policy Board was binding on the company but not on the dealership.

In 1989 only 20 of the 5,400 Ford franchises were terminated. Some of them were voluntary and others were a case of the dealer essentially closing shop. Only a few were for significant failures to perform their responsibilities.

For the most part, however, Ford tried to treat its dealers as partners and influence them through incentives and participation in decision making. Ford's "Mission Values and Guiding Principles" published in 1987 described the dealer-company relationship:

> Dealers and suppliers are our partners. Why should we include dealers and suppliers in OUR Mission Statement? Because they play a major role in our competitive struggle. Our dealers and suppliers have a critical stake in the quality of our products and services—and we in theirs. They have a contribution to make to our mission and quest for continuous improvement, and they, too, must be involved.

The dealers elected a Dealer Council that represented all of the dealers. Ford approached the Dealer Council during the planning stage for most new policies and new products. The Dealer Council was often given proprietary information and asked to help make strategy decisions as well.

While many dealers believed most manufacturers had made progress toward this partnership, not everyone agreed. The extreme opposite view was held by Ron Tonkin, the 1989 president of the National Automobile Dealers Association

(NADA), a dealer of several makes of cars, and the organizer of a radical dealership group he called the "Rough Riders":

> Forget this crap that we have a partnership. It's not a partnership when one partner gets fat going to the bank and the other partner is having a difficult time. Dealers are much closer to the public, much closer to daily selling. Dealers buy cars from the automakers at set prices, the same price, by the way, if we buy one a month or 10,000 a month . . . but we have to sell those cars . . . at a negotiated price.
>
> Also, dealers have land, buildings. In many areas, their facilities are becoming more profitable for a use other than as an auto dealership. What's going to happen when these five- and six-acre dealerships suddenly become hotels or shopping centers?[10]

Some people in the company had a different characterization of the relationship between Ford and the dealers. "Ford's customer is the dealer and the dealer's customer is the car-buying public," James Broughton, a Ford executive involved in dealer relations, said.

Steve Wesson, a Ford executive in the Market Representation Department, agreed:

> The biggest influence on the dealer is the marketplace and we have no control over that. Most dealers that run into problems do themselves in. They often will try to make us the reason for their problem by saying we're not giving them the cars they need. But we can't vary the allocation. There is a specific formula that determines what the dealers can get. They can only get "hot" [popular] merchandise if they earn it by their sales record.

The formal basis of the company's relationship with the dealers derived from the "Ford Sales & Service Agreement" and Customer Service Bulletins issued from time to time.

The agreement, a 28-page document, contained many general obligations without corresponding specific criteria. For example, under the section on sales, dealers were charged with "promot[ing] vigorously and aggressively the sale at retail of CARS and TRUCKS to private and fleet customers within the DEALER'S LOCALITY, and shall develop energetically and satisfactorily the potentials for such sales and obtain a reasonable share thereof . . . "

Dealer sales performance determined the level of allocation available in the future but did not necessarily jeopardize the dealer's franchise. In the area of service, the agreement stated:

---

10. Bill Sharfman, "Ron Tonkin," *Automobile Magazine*, October 1989, p. 93.

The Dealer shall develop, maintain and direct a trained, quality service organization and render at the DEALERSHIP FACILITIES prompt, workmanlike, courteous and willing service to owners and users of COMPANY PRODUCTS, in accordance with the standards and procedures set forth in the applicable CUSTOMER SERVICE BULLETIN . . .

Customer Service Bulletins might introduce a new customer service program such as the one described in the September 1, 1982, bulletin. This "Owner Relations Plan for Customer Satisfaction" specified that the company would acknowledge promptly every customer assistance request received and normally refer the matter to the dealer. The company would review dealer performance based on the number of such requests received compared to the relative size of the dealership.

The QCP Program

While Chrysler's near collapse dominated the business headlines in the early 1980s, Ford, too, had significant financial problems. The company was losing money each year, product quality diminished, and internal and external studies indicated that the company had lost touch with the American consumers. One of the steps the company took to attack these problems was implementation in 1985 of the Quality Commitment Performance (QCP) program. To test the level of customer satisfaction, Ford sent each new vehicle purchaser a survey 30 days after the purchase and again nine months after the purchase.

Each month the company sent the dealer results from this survey for that dealership. The report compared dealers to others in the same size category and listed the results of the top dealer in the group.

Steve Wesson stated:

The goal is to show the dealer where to improve. We also show the dealer if he or she is a hero or a bum, which they would have had no way of knowing in the past, relative to the other dealers in the comparison group.

Our dealer scores now average about 7.5 out of 10 nationwide which we feel pretty proud about. But then J.D. Power comes out and punches our ego a little.

James Broughton discussed the use of the QCP ratings:

We give each dealer a rating from one to ten and we create this wonderful array of all of our dealers. Then the question becomes what do we do with it? Well, one idea is that we plan a trip to a resort and none of the dealers under a six rating can come.

Originally the idea was that no one could be terminated for a low QCP rating. The ratings were intended not as a punitive measure but as a device to measure dealers and show them where they can improve.

Well, we are getting away from that now and there is some talk about terminating some of the worst performing dealers for QCP. The dealers are not happy about that. They are saying that we are using the device as a sword. Well, I'm not so sure that we shouldn't stick to using it only as a way to provide feedback.

According to a Ford-sponsored focus group study, the QCP program was judged by many dealers to be too casual and closer to a public relations exercise than an agent of change. "Ford gives us a lot of pomp and glory but does not reward us monetarily for . . . QCP. I think Ford should pay me more for the prep work done on the car," said one Lincoln-Mercury dealer.[11]

Another problem cited in the focus group was slow turnaround time for the QCP reports. A Ford dealer in the Boston area commented that "the two-month lag between the survey and the report is too long. In order to correct problems and improve we need more immediate feedback."

"We see a direct relationship between QCP and profitability because 80% of our business is referrals or repeat purchases," another dealer commented. "The problem is that QCP feedback is slow."[12]

V. THE AUTOMOBILE INDUSTRY

Three Detroit-based manufacturers dominated the auto industry in the United States in the 1980s. General Motors (GM) owned a 36% share of the market in 1988, followed by Ford with 22% and Chrysler at 11%.[13] Imports, especially from Japan, began to take share from the Big Three in the late 1970s and by 1988 were selling nearly one-third of all automobiles in the United States.

The emergence of imports to the United States came largely due to higher oil prices which made small Japanese cars less costly to operate. In addition, poor quality of U.S. automobiles, lower Japanese production costs, favorable currency exchange rates, and customers' desire for better full economy all contributed to the success of Japanese automakers in the United States.

Meanwhile, the American producers tried to make inroads in foreign countries

11. "HBS Creative Marketing Strategy Field Study for Ford Motor Company," April 28, 1989.

12. Ibid.

13. *Auto News* 1989 Market Data Book, May 31, 1989, p. 40.

as well. Worldwide, GM led in sales due to its dominant share at home in the world's largest market. Ford, which generated approximately 25% of its sales in foreign countries,[14] was the second-largest producer worldwide. Chrysler trailed Toyota, Volkswagen, and Nissan in the world market.[15]

In many ways the world's largest industry, representing 2% of total world GNP, became, by the 1980s, one of its most global as well. These top six manufacturers accounted for 57% of the world's sales, although smaller companies produced cars in such diverse locations as India, Turkey, and Taiwan.[16]

With worldwide growth projected only at between 1% and 2%, industry experts predicted a glut in production capacity in the 1990s as well as constraint on growth in demand due to the inability of major cities to handle more traffic.[17] To be more competitive in this slowly growing market, many car manufacturers in the 1980s began creating strategic alliances with others in foreign countries to develop "new technologies, components, or even cars."[18] In addition, most of the larger automakers produced cars in plants scattered throughout the world.

Economic Model

Dealer pretax profits varied widely but averaged 2% of sales for Ford dealers (see *Exhibit 3*) and about 1.5% for the industry as a whole in 1988.[19] Even as new-vehicle sales per dealer increased to record levels, profits industrywide had dropped from a high of 2.4% of sales in 1984. Due to the high level of sales, manufacturers earned record profits. However, increasing dealership costs pushed dealer profits as a percentage of sales downward.

The primary reason for these shrinking margins, according to *Automotive Executive*, was the increase in advertising and inventory carrying costs. Other costs such as rent, equipment purchases, and salaries rose without a corresponding increase in gross margins.

According to a Ford executive who tracked dealership profitability, another measure, return on operating investment[20] (ROI), painted a different picture of

---

14. Alex Taylor III, "The U.S. Gets Back in Fighting Shape," *Fortune*, April 24, 1989, p. 45.

15. Alex Taylor III, "Who's Ahead in the World Auto War," *Fortune*, November 9, 1987, p. 76.

16. Ibid, p. 75.

17. Ibid., p. 75.

18. Ibid., p. 78.

19. Jake Kelderman, "Dealership Profit Squeeze," *Automotive Executive*, July 1989, p. 22.

20. Operating investment did not include land or buildings owned by the dealer.

the dealership profit situation. Earning less than 1% ROI in 1980, Ford dealerships averaged over 30% ROI in 1986. The average ROI declined slightly in 1987 and 1988 and was running at about 18% halfway through 1989. Although this trend matched that of the return on sales, which of the measures to use became something of a political struggle between the more militant dealer groups and the company. The dealer groups, trying to present a more dreary situation, argued for using return on sales. The company, in contrast, advocated ROI as the more relevant measure.

Overall, the average dealership in the United States made about 40% of its gross profit from parts and service. The new vehicle department generated nearly 38% of gross profit and the used vehicle profit center brought the remaining 22%.[21]

When Ford trained its new dealers, it gave them an income statement and balance sheet from an actual dealer, the identity of whom was disguised. The numbers were supposed to represent a typical dealership's financials. Part of that income statement is reproduced below:

Typical Dealer Income Statement—6 Months
($000)

	Total	New	Used	Parts	Service	Body
Sales	6,136	4,315	1,008	519	193	102
Cost of goods sold	5,313	3,886	884	367	108	69
Total gross	823	429	124	152	85	33
Selling expense	437	246	51	69	46	25
Fixed expense	245	81	50	35	50	29
Dealer salary	12	4	2	2	2	2
Operating profit	128	99	21	45	(14)	(22)
Dealer and employee bonus	73					
Other misc. operating income	14					
Estimate tax	6					
Net income	64					

Some balance sheet ratios for a typical automobile dealership in the United States are listed below:

21. *Automotive Executive*, "Trendline," July 1989, p. 12.

Balance Sheet Ratios

	Ratio
NET DEBT TO EQUITY	0.89
(Total liabilities less floor plan[a] to net worth)	
CURRENT RATIO	1.32
SERVICE & PARTS ABSORPTION	54.60
(Service and Parts departments' gross profit as a % of fixed overhead)	
RETURN ON ASSETS	4.22%[b]

[a] Inventory carrying costs.

[b] *Auto Executive*, "Trendline," July 1989, p. 12.

VI. SITUATION IN 1989

Each year, J.D. Power, an automobile industry consultant, performed a survey of customer satisfaction with automobiles and the sales and service process. Power converted the answers to the customer questionnaire into a score called the Customer Satisfaction Index (CSI). For most of the 1980s, Ford had done worse than either General Motors or Chrysler. Ford's Lincoln-Mercury division, a separate sales organization from the Ford division, was the only representative of Ford to break into the top 16 "nameplates" (major divisions of automobile companies) and its overall index score of 118 just matched the overall industry average and trailed Acura, the leader, by 29 points.

In 1988, Ford division ranked 28 overall out of 34 vehicle makes. The poor performance in 1988 ranked Ford below the industry average for the fourth straight year. The results of some of the key questions in the CSI survey are included as *Exhibit 4*.

In the summer of 1989 Ford got a reminder of the problems it might encounter in trying to bring about change. Ford held a focus group of consumers and presented some potential changes that were emphatically billed as hypothetical only. Nonetheless, some of the people in the focus group called their Ford dealer to report the changes the company was "planning" to make. The next day some Ford dealers called the company, angry about the changes and the fact that they weren't notified.

In sum, the Ford executives contemplating change in the distribution system realized the enormity of their challenge resulted from several factors. First, the automobile industry was changing, putting pressure on the distribution system to carry more of the burden for Ford's future success. Second, Ford had to navigate carefully through the precarious straits of the relationship with its powerful dealers. Third, Ford had not done well in the Power index and thus, at least by one standard, had further to improve than many other automakers. Finally, change came slowly in the automobile industry for no other reason than size alone. As the largest industry in the world, the automotive industry also was a target of government intervention because of the number of people employed by the industry and the dependence on it of many other industries such as steel, glass, and finance.

With these obstacles for change in mind, the Ford executives were ready to come up with some recommended changes that they hoped would dramatically improve the distribution and service of Ford vehicles in the United States into the next century.

Exhibit 1
12 Commandments of Customer Service

Six Do's
1. Perceived Good Prices (Good Value)
2. Immediate Delivery
3. Large Showroom Selection
4. Supermarket Hours
5. "Your Own Mechanic"
6. Owner Operated (Service)

Six Don'ts
1. Repeat Repairs
2. Inconvenient Hours
3. Unfriendly/Impersonal Treatment
4. "Surprise" Service Bills (Amount Higher Than Expected)
5. Negotiated Prices (Horse Trading)
6. High-pressure Salespeople

SOURCE: Ford internal document

Exhibit 2
The New Vehicle Shopping and Buying Process

1. New car buyers begin by looking at their "first choice" car.

2. By the time they are finished with their shopping and have purchased a car, 60% of new car buyers have visited one or more dealerships of makes other than the one they purchased.

3. People say the dealership where they buy is not really of that much importance to them. Many are willing to travel relatively long distances to locate what they consider to be an acceptable deal.

4. While some buyers start their shopping at the dealership where they bought their last car, this is the exception rather than the rule. Few showed any feelings of allegiance to the dealership or the salesperson where they bought their last car.

5. One exception to #4, older, domestic luxury car owners returned to the same dealership from which they bought their last car.

6. The product is the single most important factor, overshadowing all other considerations. Shoppers want to buy the car or truck off the lot.

7. Price is the second key criterion in selecting where to buy.

8. No one manufacturer, and very few dealers, have been able to set themselves apart in the area of sales or service. Shoppers' perception is that the experience they will have during the sale, and the after-sales service they will receive at the dealership, will be essentially the same and, generally, equally bad.

SOURCE: Goldfarb Consultants, "1982 Market Pulse I: Opportunities for Ford Motor Company Sales and Service Leadership: The Consumer's Perspective," (commissioned by Ford for internal use), July 1982.

Exhibit 3
Dealer Return on Sales

1980	.1%
1981	1.0
1982	1.1
1983	1.8
1984	2.2
1985	2.1
1986	2.2
1987	2.1
1988	1.9
1989	1.3 (through August 1989)

SOURCE: Ford Motor Company records

Exhibit 4
J.D. Power Customer Satisfaction Index
(*% Excellent unless otherwise noted*)

	Industry	*Ford Division*
Customer Handling Index		
Service Advisor Helpfulness	44	*
Service Personnel Helpfulness	38	*
Service Advisor Overall Performance	41	*
Service Advisor Understanding	40	*
Service Advisor Promptness	45	*
Performance of Warranty Repairs	20	
Number of Mechanics to Do Work	27	*
Availability of Proper Tools and Equipment to Do Work	32	*
Knowledge/Expertise of Service Personnel	32	
Helpfulness of Parts Department Personnel	29	*
Promptness in Handling Service or Repair Work	36	*
Ease of Obtaining Appointment for Service/Repair	43	*
Quality of Work Performed	30	*
Level of Training of Mechanics	26	*
Availability of Vehicle When Promised	40	*
Availability of Spare Parts for Home Vehicle Maintenance	22	
Reasonable Service Time (% Yes)	73	*
Vehicle Repair & Reliability		
Problems During Warranty Period (% Yes)	63	*
Problems at Delivery (% Yes)	42	*
Number of Repair Problems (% None)	26	*
Number of Repair Problems (Avg.)	1.4	
Times Returned Due to Unsatisfactory Service (% Never)	59	*
Times Returned Due to Unsatisfactory Service (Avg.)	0.9	
Ability to Fix Problem on First Visit	27	*
Availability of Parts for Service	25	*

SOURCE: J.D. Power and Associates CSI Follow-up Survey, Customer Research, NAAO (North American Automotive Operations) Marketing, October 1988.

*Indicates worse than industry average.

14

◆

Realizing Service
Breakthroughs

O utstanding service firms, those we regard as offering services that have broken the bounds of convention and artificially imposed constraints, are not
managed the same way as their merely-good competitors. In summarizing the
material in the rest of the book, it is important to reflect on how they are
different through a look at three firms, one (The Paul Revere Insurance Company) familiar to us through earlier cases and two (Nordstrom and Benetton)
possibly familiar to us through their stores. Reviewing this overarching question,
it is useful to ask: Do the managements of these businesses have a strategic service
vision? What is it? Have they built customer loyalty? By what means? For example, to what degree and how have they focused and positioned their services?
How, if at all, have they managed demand and supply? How do they manage
networks and information technologies important to their businesses? What kind
of efforts have they made to mobilize people and organize work? Is there any
indication of an appreciation on the part of management of the true value and
cost of quality? What, if any, devices are used to achieve total customer satisfaction? Are there any initiatives in place for managing for quality and productivity
gains?

The Paul Revere Insurance Co. (C): Competing for the Baldrige Award case
helps answer the questions: What is the Award, why is it important, and how
can it help a company competing for it? It may also suggest what it takes to win
one. As you review each of the four topics for which material is excerpted from
The Paul Revere's application, ask yourself: What score would I give The Paul
Revere, based on what I know about the company and the material in its application? Why? (Note: The "score" for each topic is actually a percentage, from 0
to 100 in increments of ten, of the points allocated to each item.) How well did
the company use the "approach, deployment, and results" cycle for the item?

Be prepared to compare scores you awarded with those of other members of the class and to defend your choices.

Nordstrom has perhaps been the source of as much lore and discussion as any U.S. retailer in recent years. The case describes various elements of the company's strategy. As you read it, ask yourself: What are the strengths and weaknesses of the way Nordstrom goes about empowering its store managers and paying its managers and salespeople for their performance? Can Nordstrom extend its strategic service vision to Eastern as well as Western U.S. markets? Why? Will Nordstrom be able to compete with rapidly growing specialty store chains (similar to Benetton)? Why?

The readings which follow the Nordstrom case raise significant questions about pay-for-performance policies and their administration. Among them are: What are the strengths and weaknesses of the Nordstrom approach to the management of its salespeople? What's the problem here? Could it have been avoided? How? What does this suggest about the future of pay-for-performance policies in retailing? In other customer contact service jobs? Based on what you know from the case and readings, is Nordstrom a breakthrough service organization? Why?

At Benetton, what are the most important elements of Benetton's marketing, logistics, manufacturing, and financial strategies? How does it gain advantage over its competition in Europe? Which of these important elements of strategy and sources of competitive advantage can it maintain in the U.S. market? Would you introduce Benetton to the U.S. at this time (1982)? Why? If so, how would you resolve questions posed in the case? What other questions might you suggest be addressed? Finally, why was a case involving a manufacturing company selected as the last case in this book?

Among leading corporations around the world, benchmarking has become a popular practice. It involves the identification of best practice by each of several outstanding firms on each of several dimensions of management interest, then setting all of them as standards to be attained by the firm doing the benchmarking. In a sense, material in this volume allows us to do the same thing. The result can be true service breakthroughs.

The Paul Revere Insurance Co. (C): Competing for the Baldrige Award

THE MALCOLM BALDRIGE
NATIONAL QUALITY AWARD EXERCISE

The Paul Revere Insurance Company (TPRIC) competed for the Malcolm Baldrige National Quality Award in 1988, having achieved progress through its quality teams (described in the case TPRIC (A)) and value analysis efforts (described in the TPRIC (B) case). (For a description of the Malcolm Baldrige National Quality Award, see The Malcolm Baldrige National Quality Award, HBS case #8-690-001 in Topic 7.)

Members of The Paul Revere's organization prepared an extensive application, using the "Examiner Application Scorebook," portions of which are shown in *Exhibit 1*. Selected passages from the resulting TPRIC application are shown in *Exhibits 2–5* for sections on the topics of leadership, strategic quality planning, employee quality involvement, and customer complaint handling, respectively. The Paul Revere's application was 73 pages in length.

Professor Christopher W. L. Hart, Christopher Bogan, and Dan Maher prepared this exercise as a basis for class discussion rather than to illustrate either effective or ineffective handling of an administrative situation. Copyright © 1989 by the President and Fellows of Harvard College; Harvard Business School case #9-690-002 (Rev. 1/90).

Exhibit 1

Application No. _____
☐ Basic Report
☐ Supplemental Report No. _____

Examiner Application Scorebook

Malcolm Baldrige
National
Quality
Award

Examiner Name _____

Applicant Name _____

Number of Hours Worked _____

Send to Senior Examiner by _____ *date*
Send via overnight mail to:

_____

_____

_____

_____

Sent to Examiner _____
                                   date

Received by
Senior Examiner _____
                                   date

Send copy of Summary Worksheet (#2)
via overnight mail to:

Malcolm Baldrige National Quality Award
American Society for Quality Control (ASQC)
310 West Wisconsin Avenue
Milwaukee, Wisconsin 53203

FOR OFFICE USE ONLY

Exhibit 1
(Continued)

In This Booklet

Introduction

Use of Scoring Worksheets

(Continued)

Exhibit 1

(Continued)

Introduction

This Scorebook is designed to provide Examiners with a concise, organized method to score Award Application Reports. The scoring procedures and turnaround times in the examination process are crucial to the success of the program; we ask that you please follow the instructions precisely.

The Examination Process is conducted in four parts: first-stage application review, second-stage application review, site visits, and Judges recommendations. The first-stage review was added in 1989 to accommodate an anticipated increase in the number of applications. The Scoring Process flow chart for the first- and second-stage application review is provided at the bottom of pages 4 and 5. Use this illustration for reference as you proceed through the scoring process.

In the first-stage application review, four Examiners and/or Senior Examiners score and write comments on 15 selected examination items (these items will be announced after May 5). In order to begin the second-stage application review, the Panel of Judges will select approximately 30 applications (Group I). The remaining applications (Group II) will be completely reviewed by either an Examiner or a Senior Examiner in order to draft a feedback report and to validate the results of the first-stage review.

The Scoring Process

First-Stage Application Review

• Read the Application Report and score 15 selected examination items.

• Complete Worksheets (#1) and (#2) for the scored items only. Comments on strengths and areas for improvement are required, but site visit issues are not needed in the first-stage review.

• Send the Scorebook containing the scores and comments to the Administrator.

Second-Stage Application Review

• Read the Application Report and score all items.

• Complete Worksheets (#1 and #2). Comment on significant strengths and areas for improvement. Provide site visit issues for Group I applications. Draft feedback reports for Group II applications.

The Scoring Process

For further information on the Award process, see Section III:
Examination Categories and Scorebook Use in the Examiners' Preparation Course Manual.

First-Stage: ## Second-Stage:

First-Stage	Second-Stage	
Application Reports are sent out for the first-stage application review. Examiners and Senior Examiners score 15 selected examination items. The Panel of Judges divides the applications into two groups: Group I, the top scoring applicants (approximately thirty), and Group II, the remaining applicants. When notified, Examiners return unassigned materials to the Administrator.	Group I applications will be assigned to a team of three Examiners and a Senior Examiner. Each Group II application will be assigned to one Examiner or Senior Examiner for a review of all of the items and preparation for the feedback report. When notified, Examiners return all material to the Administrator.	The assigned Examiners and Senior Examiner comment and score all items of the Group I Application Report. Upon completion, Examiners make two photocopies of the Scorebook. They send the original to the Administrator and a copy to the designated Senior Examiner. Examiners retain a copy.

Exhibit 1
(Continued)

- For Group I applications, send the original Examiner Scorebook to the Administrator. Send one photocopy of the Scorebook to the designated Senior Examiner and retain a copy for use in conferring with the Senior Examiner.
- The Senior Examiner will score the Group I application (using Worksheets #1 and #2) and then review all of the Scorebooks, comparing the scores and comments.

Immediately return application materials to the Administrator when notified to do so. This may occur at any time during the examination process.

Use of Scoring Worksheets

There are five primary scoring worksheets.

Both Examiners and Senior Examiners will use:
   #1: Examination and Scoring Worksheet
   #2: Summary of Examination Items Worksheet

Senior Examiners will use:
   #3: Category Summary Scoring Worksheet
   #4: Scoring Consensus Summary Worksheet
   #5: Resolution of Significant Differences by Item Worksheet

The scoring principles for Worksheets (#3) and (#4) are similar to those used in Worksheets (#1) and (#2).

Scoring

Scoring consists of evaluating each item in the application based on the Examiner's understanding of the item as stated in the Application Guidelines, of the Areas to Address required in the item, and of the importance of each area to the applicant's business. Comments are prepared reflecting the significant strengths and areas for improvement identified from the application. Using the scoring system described below, a numerical score is assigned that is consistent with the comments. A consensus process is used to arrive at an overall score for Group I applications.

Scoring is based on a set of guidelines referred to as the Scoring System (see Table A: *Scoring System* on page 6). These guidelines explain the scoring range and help the Examiner decide "how well" the applicant company is doing and what score should be given for the designated item.

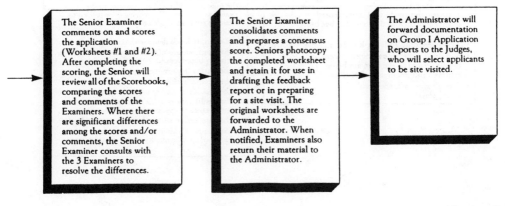

| The Senior Examiner comments on and scores the application (Worksheets #1 and #2). After completing the scoring, the Senior will review all of the Scorebooks, comparing the scores and comments of the Examiners. Where there are significant differences among the scores and/or comments, the Senior Examiner consults with the 3 Examiners to resolve the differences. | The Senior Examiner consolidates comments and prepares a consensus score. Seniors photocopy the completed worksheet and retain it for use in drafting the feedback report or in preparing for a site visit. The original worksheets are forwarded to the Administrator. When notified, Examiners also return their material to the Administrator. | The Administrator will forward documentation on Group I Application Reports to the Judges, who will select applicants to be site visited. |

(Continued)

Exhibit 1
(Continued)

The score assigned to an item is referred to as the **Percent Score**. Scores are to be assigned from 0-100% in increments of 10%, and will be placed in the Percent Score column of the scoring worksheets.

Identified in Table A are the scoring system characteristics associated with three points in the scoring range. The scoring characteristics represent three major dimensions (see panel):
- approach
- deployment
- results

The scoring system is designed to provide for a large degree of discrimination among the better performing companies. The variables of most significance in the upper scoring range (50% to 100%) are deployment and results. They include:
- how much improvement is shown
- how widespread the improvement is over all areas
- how sustained the results are
- where the company stands with respect to the best, e.g., world-class

TABLE A
Scoring System

Characteristics	Scoring
• Little or no evidence of a systematic or structured quality approach to the item? • Little or no evidence of results expected from the item.	0%
• A sound, thorough, well-documented quality approach to the item. Approach deployed in nearly all areas (i.e., technical, administrative, marketing, etc.), with appropriate early targets. • Improvement results that would be expected for the item being achieved and documented in most areas of coverage.	50%
• A sound, thorough, well-documented quality approach to the item that has been refined and honed. • Approach completely deployed in all areas. • Sustained, exceptional improvement results related to the item are being achieved and documented in all areas. • Overall approach and results are world-class.	100%

Approach

Approach refers to the methods the company uses to achieve the purposes addressed in the examination items. The scoring criteria used to evaluate approaches include one or more of the following:
- the degree to which the approach is prevention based
- the appropriateness of the tools, techniques, and methods to the application
- the effectiveness of the use of tools, techniques, and methods
- the degree to which the approach is systematic, integrated, and consistent
- the degree to which the approach embodies effective self-evaluation, feedback, and adaptation cycles to sustain continuous improvement
- the degree to which the approach is based upon quantitative information that is objective and reliable
- the indicators of unique and innovative approaches, including significant and effective new adaptations of tools and techniques used in other applications or types of businesses

Deployment

Deployment refers to the extent to which the approaches are applied to all relevant areas and activities addressed and implied in the examination items. The scoring criteria used to evaluate deployment include one or more of the following:
- the appropriate and effective application to all transactions and interactions with customers, providers of goods and services, and the public
- the appropriate and effective application to all internal processes, activities, facilities, and employees
- the appropriate and effective application to all product and service characteristics

Results

Results refers to outcomes and effects in achieving the purposes addressed and implied in the examination items. The scoring criteria used to evaluate results include one or more of the following:
- the quality levels demonstrated
- the contributions of the outcomes and effects to quality improvement
- the quality improvement gains
- the demonstration of sustained gains
- the breadth of quality improvement gains
- the significance of gains in terms of their importance to the company's business
- the comparison with industry and world leaders
- the company's ability to account for gains in terms of specific quality improvement actions

Exhibit 1
(Continued)

Examination and Scoring Worksheet (#1)

This is the primary scoring worksheet. Examiners and Senior Examiners will evaluate the applicants' quality efforts and record appropriate scores on these sheets. Worksheets progress item by item according to the seven CATEGORIES of examination.

1. Leadership

2. Information and Analysis

3. Strategic Quality Planning

4. Human Resource Utilization

5. Quality Assurance of Products and Services

6. Quality Results

7. Customer Satisfaction

CATEGORIES are indicated by whole numbers, e.g., 6.0 QUALITY RESULTS. The explanation of each category is provided on the scoring page of the Examination and Scoring Worksheet (#1). Each category is assigned points showing the maximum score an applicant can earn for that category.

Within each category are SUBCATEGORIES. Each subcategory is denoted by two integers, representing the category and the subcategory, e.g., 6.1 Quality of Products and Services.

Subcategories are further subdivided for scoring by ITEMS. Items are indicated by three integers, representing category, subcategory, and item number, e.g., 6.1.1. Item numbers and their descriptions are listed on the Examination and Scoring Worksheet (#1). The maximum number of points an applicant can receive for that item is also shown.

Key Dates

completed by May, 1989 — Examiner training

postmarked by May 5, 1989 — Award applications

First-Stage written application review May 5-June 14, 1989

Second-Stage written application review June 15-July 31, 1989

Site Visits August 1-September 30, 1989

Judges' Panel recommends Award recipients October, 1989

Award Ceremony Mid-November, 1989

(Continued)

Exhibit 1
(Continued)

Commenting on Strengths, Areas for Improvement, and Site Visit Issues

Worksheet (#1) also provides spaces to record comments on the applicant's strengths, areas for improvement, and site visit issues. Spaces are provided under the item description.

IMPORTANT: Preface all comments on strengths with a (+) sign. Use a (–) sign to indicate areas for improvement. Please make your comments item-specific and record them in the appropriate area provided.

Below is an example of the use of these signs and of typical comments:

6.1.1 Strengths and Areas for Improvement

\+ Major improvements in many measures of reliability — i.e., doubling of MTBF in the Enterprise product area.

\+ Response time to customer complaints considerably improved.

– No results of performance were provided for Columbia products.

– High defect rates reported for newly introduced products.

Examination and Scoring Worksheet

■ **6.0 QUALITY RESULTS** (150 points)

The *Quality Results* category examines quality levels and quality improvement based upon objective measures derived from analysis of customer requirements and expectations and from analysis of business operations. Also examined are current quality levels in relation to those of competing firms.

6.1 Quality of Products and Services

6.1.1 *(40 points)* Based upon key product and service quality measures derived from customers needs and expectations, summarize trends in improvement.
SITE VISIT ISSUES:

a) trends in key product and service quality measures
b) other objective measures of improved quality
c) connections between quality improvement results and improvement projects or initiatives

---

6.1.1 (+) STRENGTHS AND (–) AREAS FOR IMPROVEMENT

Check one:
☐ All Areas Addressed
☐ Areas Not Addressed _____

Site Visit Issues
• Clarify the status of the performance for Columbia products.
• Verify the results of reliability improvement testing for Enterprise products.

Exhibit 1
(Continued)

Summary of Examination Items Worksheet (#2)

The Summary Sheet (#2) contains all scores for each category, and item. Examiners and Senior Examiners are asked to transfer the scoring percents from Worksheet (#1) to this form, and to calculate the totals for each category and for the entire application.

Category Summary Scoring Worksheet (#3)

The Category Summary Scoring Worksheet (#3) is used by Senior Examiners only. It is used to compile consensus comments on strengths, areas for improvement, and site visit issues based on the evaluation of the Application Report by the three Examiners; it does not contain scores. The comments are summarized by item.

Examiner Name _____

Applicant Name _____ Applicant Number _____   *2*

SUMMARY OF EXAMINATION ITEMS	Total Points Possible A	Percent Score 0-100% (10% units) B	Score (A x B) C
6.0 QUALITY RESULTS *150* POSSIBLE POINTS			
6.1　Quality of Products and Services			
6.1.1	40	*100* %	*40*
6.1.2	30	*70* %	*21*
6.2　Operational and Business Process Quality Improvement			
6.2.1	30	*50* %	*15*
6.2.2	30	*90* %	*27*
6.3.1　Quality Improvement Applications	20	*80* %	*16*
Category Total	*150* SUM A		*119* SUM C

(Continued)

Exhibit 1
(Continued)

Scoring Consensus Summary Worksheet (#4)

The Scoring Consensus Summary Worksheet (#4) is also used only by Senior Examiners. It is used to compile consensus scores for Group I applications based on the Summary Worksheets (#2) prepared by the Examiners who originally scored the Application Report.

Resolution of Significant Differences by Item Worksheet (#5)

The Resolution of Significant Differences by Item Worksheet (#5) is used by Senior Examiners to document the resolution of discrepancies in scoring and comments among the Examiners. To achieve consistency, particularly for the resolution of significant differences, guidelines are provided.

Mailing Procedures

All mail for the Award Program related to scoring will utilize overnight mail service. Charges will be reimbursed (if required) through the Examiner Travel Expense Form. Reimbursement will be made on a timely basis.

Please note that when using overnight services a street address is required; packages will not be delivered to a post office box address.

The Administrator's street address is:
Malcolm Baldrige National Quality Award
American Society for Quality Control
310 West Wisconsin Avenue
Milwaukee, Wisconsin 53203
(414) 272-8575

Completing the Examination Process

The previous instructions refer to the written evaluation section of the examination process. There are still several steps that must be completed before Award recipients can be announced. These steps include selecting applicants to be site visited, conducting site visits and writing the site visit reports, analyzing the collected evaluation and site visit material a final time, and recommending Award recipients. At the conclusion of the Award process, the President of the United States will award medals to the recipients. Please refer to the illustration on the bottom of page 7 for time line information.

Guidelines for Assessing Written Applications

The evaluation of applications for the Malcolm Baldrige National Quality Award is dependent on the sound judgement of the Board of Examiners. Examiners need to apply their judgement in assessing how well a given applicant has met the examination items and Areas to Address. There will be some variation among scores given by different Examiners based upon differing interpretations and the relative importance of the Areas to Address. However, to help minimize the variation among scores, Examiners shall use the following guidelines:

1. Assess what is written and reasonably supported in the application. If something is vague, do not make assumptions that cannot be supported. However, note that these items should be checked during a site visit for clarifying information.

2. You should use *all* that is written in assessing an examination item. If material is cross-referenced between items, use the cross reference.

3. Keep the overall purpose of the category in mind when rating an item.

4. Check to be sure that *all* of the Areas to Address are responded to in the application. Remember that they can be included in any order within an item and that their importance varies from business to business.

5. Assign a score consistent with your comments and the importance of the Areas to Address to the applicant's business.

Exhibit 2
Examination and Scoring Worksheet

Item	Distributed Points	Criteria	Percent Score

1.0 Leadership (150 points)

How all levels of corporate management and staff provide leadership of quality improvement processes (QIP). Particular emphasis is placed on the sustained and visible role of top management including the Chief Executive Officer (CEO), the Chief Operating Officer (COO), and the Chief Quality Officer (CQO).

1.1 Senior Corporate Leadership (50 points)

1.1.1 Describe the major roles of the CEO, COO, CQO and other key executives in quality improvement processes (QIP). Include specific examples of sustained and visible executive involvement in the development of an effective corporate culture.
SITE VISIT ISSUES:

a) demonstration of continuous, meaningful leadership and involvement in addressing quality issues

b) direct interaction by these executives in many levels of the organization

c) involvement in external quality-related activities (i.e., speeches, professional societies, etc.)

d) evidence that executive leadership has resulted in improved product or service quality

1.1.1 (+) STRENGTHS AND
    (−) AREAS FOR IMPROVEMENT   Check one:
    ☐ All Areas Addressed
    ☐ Areas Not Addressed _____

Baldrige Award Application
Category One: Leadership

SUBCATEGORY 1.1: SENIOR CORPORATE LEADERSHIP
(50 POINTS)

Commitment from the top has been the hallmark of Paul Revere Insurance Group's Quality Has Value process from its beginning. Harvard Business School Case Study 9-687-013 describes how a Quality Steering Committee was formed in 1983. It was composed of the number-one or number-two executive from every division and major department in the company. Co-chaired by the vice president of the Operations Division and the vice president of Human Resources, it was given the assignment to create, structure, and staff a coherent approach to quality.

(Continued)

Exhibit 2
(Continued)

The Quality Steering Committee is still in existence with responsiblity for strategic and operational planning for Quality Has Value. Its membership has been opened to nonmanagement (see 3.2.1).

The Quality Has Value process, launched January 13, 1984, was the result of the Quality Steering Committee's deliberations. Emphasis was placed on the concept of process, rather than program. The company was informed from the outset that Quality Has Value was to be an ongoing effort, not a quick-fix approach.

Quality Has Value provides for a two-pronged approach to quality issues. Quality Teams address the question, "Are we doing things right?" Everybody at Paul Revere Insurance Group—from the president to the newest hire—is a member of a Quality Team. Value Analysis Workshops, conducted during the first two years of the process, asked "Are we doing the right things?" These management workshops were the precursor of action groups that address specific issues in the company today.

One of the major aims in the development of Quality Has Value was to stimulate change in the corporate culture. This change was expected to manifest itself in the increased ability of communications to flow from the bottom of the organizational ladder to the top and vice versa. Management's commitment to providing the environment for this change was not left to chance. Ample opportunity for direct interaction by executives with people at many levels of the organization was built into the process.

One explicit program for ensuring interaction is PEET, the Program for Ensuring that Everybody's Thanked. This requires (not suggests) that top management make informal visits to leaders of Quality Teams. Specific names are regularly given to the top 24 executives and each executive is required to fill out a PEET Sheet after a visit. Its importance as a leadership technique is emphasized by a training program consisting of a series of 15 videotapes, reading, evaluation, discussion and planning sessions.

In the last four years, Management By Wandering Around has taken root. PEET is supplemented by drop-in visits to team leaders on a less formal basis. Equally informal, the program of Quality Coins gives these same executives at Paul Revere an opportunity to say "thank you" to employees. Whenever one of these executives witnesses or hears of an action that merits recognition, they award a Quality Coin which entitles the bearer to a free lunch in the company cafeteria. It is a personal "thank you" to a particular employee for a particular action—an interaction which is usually followed by the employee keeping the coin rather than turning it in for a meal. (Only 15% of the coins are redeemed.) The number of these interactions varies, from five per executive per month (the minimum number of coins each executive distributes a month) on up (there is no limit on the number of coins given).

Top executives are also part of the Paul Revere Program of Recognition, Gratitude, and Celebration. Although the specifics of the program will be covered later, it should be noted that whenever a team earns an award, a corporate executive at the vice president level takes part in the presentation ceremony. Since the beginning of Quality Has Value, these executives have taken part in awards ceremonies on over 1,500 occasions.

Exhibit 2
(Continued)

These events are held in the Quality Team's home area and the team is encouraged to let the vice president know what improvements were made in quality to earn the award.

Senior management is always willing to communicate the methods and success of Quality Has Value. Written evidence of this activity includes two Harvard Business School Case Studies (9-687-013 and 0-687-033). The vice president of the Operations Division and Director—Quality Team Central were among the executives interviewed. The American Productivity Center Case Study 42 was based on information furnished by the first Director—Quality Team Central. His book on the Quality Has Value process, *Commit to Quality* published in 1986 by Wiley & Sons Press, is now in its fifth printing.

The vice president of the Operations Division made presentations at five AVCO Quality Quorums attended by AVCO and Textron divisions. During the last three years, he has made over a dozen presentations on quality before a variety of groups, including the Health Insurance Association of America (HIAA) and the Association of Health Underwriters (NAHU) organizations.

The Director—Quality Team Central took part in a number of local events, addressing the CMEA (Central Massachusetts Employers' Association), Worcester Sales Executives, Argonauts, local chapters of the American Business Women's Association, Rotary, International Association of Quality Circles, and the Hartford, Worcester, and Boston chapters of the American Society for Quality Control.

Beyond involvement in promoting awareness of the importance of quality, every executive at Paul Revere takes part in improving quality through Quality Team activity. There are 75 executives, second vice president and above. They currently represent membership on 28 Quality Teams, six are on two teams and four are team leaders. It is usually impossible to ascribe specific improvements to specific executives. Progress is deliberately recorded as team activity to avoid an I-can-produce-more-than-you-can competitiveness and to encourage teamwork.

Samples of ideas credited in 1984 to the "Big Guys," headed by the company president, included two morale boosters: discharge employees one hour early the day before July 4 and revitalize the Paul Revere mixed bowling league for better participation. A money-saving idea was personally negotiated by the company president in the form of a 25% discount from the company that handled relocations for Paul Revere. This saved the company at least $25,000 a year. The front page of *Quality News* chronicles the goals of "Big Guys" in 1986. An ambitious idea in 1987 by the "Soul Searchers," led by the vice president of the Operations Division, led to the Service Revolution, which will be discussed later.

Exhibit 3
Examination and Scoring Worksheet

Item	Distributed Points	Criteria	Percent Score

3.0 Strategic Quality Planning (75 points)

This category examines the extent to which quality considerations are taken into account in the planning process. Particular emphasis is placed on how and when information about customer requirements and satisfaction are identified and used for planning purposes.

3.2   Planning Function (20 points)

3.2.1 Describe the company's planning function and how the organization is structured to highlight quality improvement planning.

SITE VISIT ISSUES:

a) degree of integration of quality improvement planning into general business planning

b) adequacy of understanding by each organizational unit and management level of their planning responsiblities

c) effectiveness of methods used to identify and prioritize quality improvement issues

d) ability to translate quality improvement issues into defined projects with individuals assigned for responsiblity and accountability

e) establishment of periodic checks or critiques of the planning process to improve its effectiveness

f) evidence of customer, consumer, and employee input into the planning process

3.2.1 (+) STRENGTHS AND
    (−) AREAS FOR IMPROVEMENT

Check one:

☐ All Areas Addressed

☐ Areas Not Addressed _____

Exhibit 3
(Continued)

Baldrige Award Application
Category Three: Strategic Quality Planning

SUBCATEGORY 3.2: PLANNING FUNCTION
(20 POINTS)

The president and his direct reports comprise the company's central planning committee. They develop the corporate five-year strategic plan with input primarily from three sources:

- The heads of all operating departments, who are the people reporting to the president's staff. They provide insight into Paul Revere's delivery capabilities and financial position.
- A business assessment plan prepared by Market Research that describes the impact of external factors, and highlights trends in our major target markets.
- Product Management Teams that provide product line business plans outlining strategic initiatives to capitalize on strengths and to strengthen weaknesses. These PMTs are management action teams with representation from all key areas who meet to define products and service delivery systems based on input from customer focus groups, surveys and market research (see 5.1.1).

When the corporate strategic plan is completed, including product line business plans, each department develops a one-year operating plan to undertake projects in support of the strategic plan and the product business plans.

During this phase of planning, interdepartment and interdivision support requirements are addressed by plan coordinators. Plan coordinators are assigned at a division level (an organizational unit made up of a number of departments and headed by a member of the president's staff).

The Quality Has Value operating plan is one of the plans developed in this phase. From a strategic standpoint, this plan creates the best climate for successful realization of business goals through employee involvement and customer focus. Responsiblity for developing the Quality Has Value operating plan rests with the Quality Steering Committee and Quality Team Central. The current membership of the Quality Steering Committee include the president's direct reports, the second vice president—Quality Team Central, seven employees from all levels who are members for one year (replacements are selected from team leaders and members who are recognized as excellent achievers), and the staff of Quality Team Central.

Key components of the operating plan place emphasis on training in groupAction, open communications through sharing of information, team building and partnerships through cross-functional teams, a central theme based on overall strategic direction, monitoring participation, and assessing team results.

In addition to the corporate strategic plan, input for Quality Has Value operating

(Continued)

Exhibit 3
(Continued)

---

plan is gathered from feedback through direct contact with Quality Teams and their leaders. The feedback is provided both to members of the Quality Steering Committee and to members of the company's Management Committee via the PEET program and "drop in" visits (see 1.1.1). The Management Committee is a group of 21 high-level company officers who meet monthly to review the corporate position relative to the strategic plan. Quality Has Value is always first on the agenda. Feedback is also provided through the information loop described below.

Two changes to Quality Has Value were implemented in 1986 based on input from Quality Teams. These were:

- The change from an individual ideas orientation to a goals orientation (see 4.2.3).
- The move to flexible team organization that facilitated formation of cross-functional teams.

Support requirements arising from the Quality Has Value operating plan are coordinated as with other operating plans. The plan coordinator for the Human Resources Division is, by design, the second vice president—Quality Team Central, who is the head of Quality Team Central. This ensures that Quality Team Central has knowledge of all operating plans and helps other plan coordinators place quality initiatives in proper perspective for setting priorities.

When the operating plans are in final form, a circle of information begins:

- Quality Team Central reviews the Quality Has Value operating plan at a general meeting of team leaders highlighting changes. This meeting is process oriented.
- Division/Department managers review strategic plans and operating plans with their employees to highlight important opportunities, and changes.
- Quality Teams establish their goals which become, in effect, team operating plans. Teams have autonomy and remain free to set their own goals. Sources of input for team goals include strategic and operating plans; customers; and team knowlege of unit performance as measured against Quality, service, and productivity goals.
- Teams provide unit managers with copies of their goals, completing the loop of shared information.

Operating plans and Personal Objectives are monitored monthly, with formal reporting and review at top management levels quarterly. Teams assess progress against their own goals quarterly.

The emphasis placed on staff development and customer service within the strategic plan provides impetus for prioritizing key projects that support them. Two such projects resulted from the 1988 Operating Plan:

- Reorganize the Policyholder Services and Individual Underwriting departments to improve service capability. These Customer Service Teams address two issues:

  Job enrichment—by organizing workflow and job responsibilities on a team basis so employees understand and can perform the complete job.

Exhibit 3
(Continued)

Service capability—by establishing management responsiblity and accountability for the entire transaction.

- Establish an Office Skills training program to introduce new clerical level employees to current office system technology, customer service skills, telephone etiquette, etc.

Both projects are high on the list for 1988; their successful implementation is of strategic importance.

The planning process outlined above is the result of effort over two years (1986 to 1987) to define and implement a methodology that is both streamlined and effective. Plan coordinators meet to review and critique the process annually. Their recommendations are submitted to the Central Planning Committee and have resulted in significant planning effectiveness since 1985.

Exhibit 4
Examination and Scoring Worksheet

Item	Distributed Points	Criteria	Percent Score

4.0 Human Resource Utilization (150 points)

Examines the effectiveness and thoroughness of human resource utilization in quality management and QIP.

4.2   Employee Quality Awareness and Involvement

4.2.3   Describe employee involvement in the identification and resolution of quality problems and how corporation ensures involvement.
SITE VISIT ISSUES:

a) extent of explicit guidance for employees
b) number of employees involved at different levels   _____
c) change in employee involvement in last three years
d) evidence of resolution of specific quality problems because of employee initiative

4.2.3 (+) STRENGTHS AND
      (−) AREAS FOR IMPROVEMENT   **Check one:**
        ☐   All Areas Addressed
        ☐   Areas Not Addressed _____

(Continued)

Exhibit 4
(Continued)

Baldrige Award Application
Category Four: Human Resource Utilization

SUBCATEGORY 4.2.3: EMPLOYEE QUALITY INVOLVEMENT
(25 POINTS)

Quality Has Value had no difficulty in ensuring involvement. Every employee is on a Quality Team, and team leaders are trained in groupAction to stimulate team activity (4.3.1). Quality Team leaders are also provided a *Team Leader Manual* and meet regularly to talk about progress.

The trend in employee involvement in the last 3 years has been toward a more sophisticated understanding of what Quality Has Value represents. Several changes are evidence of this maturing process. The first is the shift in emphasis described by Pym's phases (see 4.1.1).

(From 4.1.1)

Participation in Quality Has Value is a condition of employment. One of the goals of the Quality Team Central department of Human Resources is to encourage employees to make the transition through the three stages of a quality process, as defined by Jeff Pym of Paul Revere of Canada. According to Mr. Pym, a process grows through three stages:

1. What can you do for me?
2. What can I do for me?
3. What can I do for you?

The second is the shift from correction and detection to prevention (see 2.1.2), and the third is the shift in focus from individual ideas to goals. This last might ultimately prove to be the most significant.

The process was redefined in response to a team leader meeting which requested more flexibility in setting long-term goals. Team leaders noted that counting ideas was an excellent first step and resulted in teams addressing problems of quality in fact. They felt, however, that it inhibited their ability to focus on customer perception—a much more difficult concept to tackle, requiring long-term effort. The change was explained in the January 1986 *Quality News*:

You know those BIG projects that you've been talking about for two years? The ones that will take several months to complete—yet may not save much money even though you know they will have a big impact on your customer? QHV '86 is the time!

Many Quality Teams have reported over the last two years that they had some ideas that they would love to concentrate on but were putting off until they

Exhibit 4
(Continued)

completed 10 . . . or 50 . . . smaller ideas. The ideas they did proceed with were good ones and did have a positive impact on their Quality, but it was that big one that they really wanted to pursue.

QHV '86 is structured to encourage teams to take on major ideas. As self-assessment points are reached every three months, it is possible that only intermediate goals will have been met, with final completion still months away. By previous rules, it would have been difficult to extend appropriate recognition for the effort expended, and for the preliminary results attained.

Now, through the self-assessment system, teams will be asked to judge their own efforts and accomplishments, making it possible to say "Thank you" for steady, or ahead-of-schedule, progress.

The use of various statistical tools—including surveys and tracking of individual actions over a period of time—also become even more appropriate in QHV '86.

QHV '86—an opportunity for personal and professional growth for the members of Quality Teams—and for continuing Paul Revere's drive to be the unquestioned Quality leader.

Quality News for December 1985 and December 1986 are provided in 7.5.1, both to document this shift and as evidence of resolution of specific quality problems because of employee initiative. There have been over 17,000 ideas from the Home Office and 9,400 ideas from the field implemented and certified since the beginning of Quality Has Value. Examples follow:

1984

Orv Miller and "Seven-Ups"

Removed some phrasing from Voluntary Accident Policy for AVCO Corporation. Phrasing had been cause of some expensive lawsuits in the past. The entire policy was reworded and resulted in $196,000 in new premiums and more than doubled the total coverage value. Both employees and company benefited.

Joan Hurley and "The Deadliners"

Two clerks left the company. The Quality Team decided they would like to try to handle the work without hiring replacements. They felt they could accomplish it because of the time saved from previous quality ideas. The result was both effective and efficient and saved the company over $30,000 salary expenses, plus benefits.

(Continued)

Exhibit 4
(Continued)

1985

Tony Martins and "Tech Services"—on the way to Septuple Gold

Rather than accept a dealer's "lowest offer" for a computer hardware upgrade package that the company needed, the team looked for alternatives. They located and bought a piece of equipment on the open market, married it to the existing leased equipment and saved $134,540. Options to upgrade further were made available sooner. The bottom line was more capability available sooner—at less cost.

Shirley Salah and "Shirl's Girls" in conjunction with Ken McNulty
and "Ken's Kost Kontrollers"

Two teams provided a fresh look at an old system. For years, there was a manual procedure for not relicensing nonproducing brokers. There is a cost of $10 to relicense a broker, and Paul Revere was relicensing many people who were not producing business for us. It was not an easy task to select the producers from the nonproducers because they were mingled on the lists. The idea involved asking whether computers could be used to sort the lists so these brokers could be separated. With a little programming, nonproducing brokers were automatically removed from the licensing list. This saved $65,000 the first year alone, saved time in the brokerage offices, and reduced errors.

1986

Becky Hyzer and "EC and the Retros" (Actuarial)

Updating a particular actuarial formula was a time-consuming, difficult, and labor-intensive procedure—a major project that had previously been done every four years. The improvements made by this Quality Team made the process much easier, making it possible to do on an annual basis. The benefit for the first year alone was $387,000.

Sue Donovan and David Russell and "The Navigators" (Financial Services)

This is the biggest dollar idea ($12,400,000) to come out of Quality Has Value. It didn't save Paul Revere anything, but it was a big help to one of our "corporate cousins."

The opportunity to help arose early in 1986 when tax debts were being computed for the various portions of Textron. Complicating the calculations was the merger of AVCO units the previous year into the Textron family. After making phone calls and researching tax laws, the Navigators found that by aligning Paul Revere statements, with no real loss or gain to the bottom line, they enabled AVCO to adjust

Exhibit 4
(Continued)

their bottom line. AVCO did not have to pay a $12,400,000 bill they were prepared to pay.

1987

Don Hopkin and "Systems"

Systems improved speed/performance and security of the Group Proposal Software for a savings of $72,629. This had a big impact on Paul Revere's field offices. This was a technical enhancement and compilation of the software system.

This team also provided a menu utility for all field offices to use on the hard disk computers. This had a big impact in the visibility of these computers and saved $44,181 in time spent going back and forth from the screen working to the menu.

(This team became so well-known outside the company that other insurance companies called for advice in solving field computer problems.)

Anne Jahnle and "Anna's Bananas"

Paul Revere was hiring help from temporary agencies in Worcester. After much research and discussion with Human Resources Management, Law Department, and the president, this team implemented a procedure to hire retirees back. This saves the company $24,000 per year (the difference between money paid to temporary agencies and the mid-point salaries for retirees), Paul Revere has the expertise of these valued former employees at its disposal, and everyone benefits.

Exhibit 5
Examination and Scoring Worksheet

Item	Distributed Points	Criteria	Percent Score

7.0 Customer Satisfaction (300 points)

This category examines the level of customer satisfaction with the corporation's products or services and trends in the level of customer satisfaction. A high level of customer satisfaction requires that a product or service meet advertised performance specifications, be reliable and safe to use, and be available on a timely basis and at a fair cost. Quantitative measurement of customer and consumer satisfaction is required as is linkage to product or service quality indicators such as performance, reliability, durability, or maintainability.

7.3. Customer Complaint Handling (75 points)

7.3.2 Describe customer complaint handling operation, and how information from the customer complaint system is used to improve quality.
SITE VISIT ISSUES:

a) adequacy of system for screening, logging, and classifying of complaints
b) evidence of timeliness and adequate response to complaints   _____
c) evidence that information from complaints is being used for quality management, quality control, and quality improvement purposes
d) adequacy of procedures used to assure public awareness of complaint handling procedures
e) evidence of positive customer opinions concerning complaint handling system

7.4. Customer Views of Guarantees and Warranties (50 points)

7.4.1 Describe product or service guarantees or warranties and data concerning customer views.
SITE VISIT ISSUES:

a) customer opinions on value of and appropriateness of guarantees or warranties
b) change in customer views during last three years   _____
c) comparison with guarantees or warranties of competitors
d) improvements during last three years
e) effectiveness and timeliness in resolving complaints
f) evidence of use of complaint information for product or service improvement

Exhibit 5
(Continued)

Item	Distributed Points	Criteria	Percent Score
7.4.2 Describe data collected from customers concerning quality of services under guarantees or warranties. SITE VISIT ISSUES:		a) world market views on quality of service b) change in customer views during last three years c) improvements in warranty service over last three years d) comparison of warranty service records with those of competitors	
7.3.2 (+) STRENGTHS AND (−) AREAS FOR IMPROVEMENT		Check one: ☐ All Areas Addressed ☐ Areas Not Addressed _____	
7.4.1 (+) STRENGTHS AND (−) AREAS FOR IMPROVEMENT		Check one: ☐ All Areas Addressed ☐ Areas Not Addressed _____	
7.4.2 (+) STRENGTHS AND (−) AREAS FOR IMPROVEMENT		Check one: ☐ All Areas Addressed ☐ Areas Not Addressed _____	

Baldrige Award Application
Category Seven: Customer Satisfaction

SUBCATEGORY 7.3.2: CUSTOMER COMPLAINT HANDLING
(75 POINTS)

Complaints can be received at the company through a number of sources, as outlined below. Complaints may be received by the specific department for which they are intended, or by the legal department, or by the president's office. The legal department maintains a formal complaint log where complaints are logged both chronologically for tracking and by state for purposes of recording disposition of the complaint.

The definition of a complaint is:

(Continued)

Exhibit 5
(Continued)

1. Any written communication from a current, past, or pending policyholder, especially one expressing a grievance.
2. A written communication from a person (broker or attorney) representing a policyholder in pursuit of an inquiry or grievance.
3. A written inquiry from a state insurance department regarding a complaint.

Upon receipt, complaints are then handled according to clear, well-defined procedure, and all complaints receive priority handling. Research and resolution generally begin the day a complaint is received. It is standard to resolve a complaint within 10 working days. If necessary, they are hand carried through the system.

Preliminary research is generally followed by a call to the policyholder or their representative to discuss resolution and to identify any additional problems. When a resolution is effected, a response letter is prepared, reviewed by the supervisor, and mailed to the policyholder or their representative. Original complaint, research material, and responses are reviewed by management. Copies are maintained on file in the legal department.

Opinions of customers help identify areas where procedures or training need attention. These adjustments can apply both to the Home Office and to the field. If a pattern of complaints or inquiries is noticed, a number of things can occur.

- Procedures are examined and updated.
- Training may be indicated and is addressed by the appropriate unit.
- A Quality Team takes on a problem-solving project.
- Communication and workflow are examined for change.

The number of complaints relative to the opportunity for complaint is very low (see 6.3.1). A brief evaluation survey card accompanies every complaint response. The number of cards returned to us are too few to support conclusions.

(From 6.3.1)

Paul Revere's relationship with policyholders is contractual in nature. Complaints and litigation arise when the policyholder perceives failure to fulfill the contract on our part. The formal complaint procedure will be outlined in Section 7.3.2. It provides for registration upon receipt and sets a 10-day time frame for resolution.

Complaints or litigation can occur either through claims experience or one of the numerous transactions involved in administering the policy. For purposes of comparison, Paul Revere looks at the number of complaints received compared to the opportunity for complaint—the size of the in-force block of business. To arrive at the in-force block of business, individual Disability Income, Life, Annuities, and the monthly average of Group certificates (insured individuals) for each year is used. See the following chart.

Exhibit 5
(Continued)

U.S. Complaints to U.S. In-force—DI, Life and Annuity				
	1984	*1985*	*1986*	*1987*
In-force Policies:				
Disability income	254,637	259,151	263,191	270,782
Life	170,463	158,087	144,820	135,389
Annuity	50,361	48,368	44,480	42,925
Group certificates	248,649	301,416	335,178	414,018
Total In-force	724,110	767,022	787,669	863,114
Complaints	320	237	300	257
Litigations	30	31	26	18
Legal fees per $1,000 of premium	1.59	1.54	1.52	1.39

Measured against the opportunity for complaint represented by 725,000 to 860,000 insureds, the number of formal complaints is almost insignificant. Even one lawsuit, however, can have a significant financial impact.

The legal staff's Quality Team has developed programs for a number of departments aimed at reducing the number of lawsuits arising from mishandled obligations. They have been proactive in pursuit of this goal, and the result has been a reduction in both the number of litigations (from 30 to 18, a 40% reduction) and the portion of premium income allocated to legal expenses ($1.59 per thousand to $1.39 per thousand, a reduction of over 12%). Paul Revere also has a staff of 20 Field Representatives with the dual responsiblity to investigate claims and to effect amicable resolution to any claim where a dispute arises. This assures Paul Revere tighter control on questionable claims, which keeps premium rates down and Disability Income insurance affordable to all applicants. Paul Revere is demonstrating an increased ability to reach an amicable resolution when complaints do arise.

SUBCATEGORIES 7.4.1/7.4.2: Customer Views of Guarantees/ Warranties (50 points)

Paul Revere Insurance Group does not deal in product or service warranties. There is an absolute guarantee, enforceable by law, to make every payment to which the insured is entitled.

Nordstrom

Bruce Nordstrom, age 45, cochairman of Nordstrom, and the eldest of the Nordstroms, typified the modest, unassuming attitude of the company's management. "There is nothing special or difficult about what we do," he said. "I mean, none of us has been to Harvard, Stanford, etc. We are all graduates of the University of Washington here." He almost painted a picture of being "just plain country boys."

However, there was nothing modest about Nordstrom's success. It had grown from sales of $67 million in 1970 to sales of $250 million in 1977 (January 31, 1978); 1978 sales were just under $300 million. Earnings too had increased from $2.8 million in 1970 to $13.7 million in 1978. From 1970 to date (April 1979) the company had built three Nordstrom stores and four Place Two stores in Washington State and three Nordstrom stores and one Place Two in Oregon. It had also expanded and remodeled existing stores. And in addition to its growth in its traditional trading areas, Nordstrom had acquired a department store company in Alaska in 1975 and had opened its first store in California in 1978. In May 1979 the company planned to open its first store in Utah. Nordstrom also operated leased shoe departments, but it was gradually phasing out this business. By the end of 1978, Nordstrom maintained only eight leased shoe departments, all in Hawaii. About 90% of its business came from its 16 Nordstrom stores, 6% from its 10 Place Two units, and the balance from its leased departments. *Exhibit 1* provides a five-year summary of financial results and other data.

All through their expansions, the Nordstroms had maintained their philosophy of offering a wide selection, exceptionally attractive shopping surroundings, good service, and competitive prices. At the same time, the organization offered its employees a decentralized management environment where initiative tended to be directly and strongly rewarded. If only one word could be used to describe the atmosphere within Nordstrom, it would have been "vitality." An extract from management's written statement of philosophy is shown in *Exhibit 2*.

The Nordstroms were confident that their philosophy and methods of operation could be transferred to their new locations. They recalled that a noted West Coast retailer had told them to "wait until you are a hundred million dollar

Associates Fellow Manu Parpia prepared this case under the supervision of Professor Walter J. Salmon as a basis for class discussion rather than to illustrate either effective or ineffective handling of an administrative situation. Copyright © 1979 by the President and Fellows of Harvard College; Harvard Business School case #9-579-218 (Rev. 12/89).

company," implying they could not maintain their philosophy in a larger organization. Yet the Nordstroms noted with pride that they were at $300 million and still going strong.

Could they continue to use this philosophy successfully? What should they be alert for? What changes should they expect, and what effect would they have on Nordstrom's performance? To answer these questions, it was important to identify why Nordstrom was successful.

NORDSTROM'S BACKGROUND

In the late 1880s, a 16-year-old boy left Sweden for the United States, arriving in the Midwest with five dollars in his pocket and a determination to succeed. His name was John W. Nordstrom. The young immigrant worked in the mines, in the logging camps, and at manual labor in Michigan, Colorado, California, and Washington before heading north to the Alaskan gold rush in 1896. He returned to Seattle two years later with a $13,000 stake, ready to settle down.

Carl F. Wallin, a Seattle shoemaker he had met in Alaska, offered Nordstrom a partnership in a shoe store, and in 1901 the store opened in downtown Seattle. The first day it made one sale and took in only $12.50, but the two men worked hard and lived thriftily, and gradually the business grew. In 1929 Wallin sold his interest to Nordstrom, and in 1930 John W. sold the company to his sons, Elmer, Everett, and Lloyd. Although the three had worked for Nordstrom earlier, they were not working for him in 1930. As Jim Nordstrom tells it, "Grandpa rang up Everett, who was working here in Seattle, and asked him if he and his brother would like to take over the business. Once they took over the store, Grandpa handed over the keys and just walked away."

The three brothers had built the single shoe store into a 27-unit operation with sales of $12 million by 1963. At this stage the next generation, Bruce and John Nordstrom, as well as their brother-in-law Jack McMillan, were working for the company, and Jim Nordstrom was about to join on a full-time basis. Each of the young Nordstroms had worked from stock boys on up in the shoe stores. They knew the fashion shoe business intimately. However, it was clear that to employ the young Nordstroms gainfully, the company would have either to expand the shoe business to other geographic regions or diversify into another business within the state. An expansion of the shoe business would mean, for at least some of the young Nordstroms, a permanent move to another region—the idea of establishing stores elsewhere without the presence of a Nordstrom was, at that time, unthinkable. But all the family enjoyed the outdoor life in Washington. They were very comfortable in Seattle and really didn't want to move. So Nordstrom had to diversify out of shoes.

In 1963 Nordstrom purchased Best's Apparel in downtown Seattle and in Lloyd Center in Portland, Oregon. Best's had an established reputation in fashion apparel and was considered one of Seattle's leading fashion stores. The Nordstroms reasoned that because they were familiar with shoes, a highly fashion-related business, fashion apparel would be relatively easy for them to retail successfully. It did not, however, turn out to be as easy as they had expected, and, in Bruce Nordstrom's words, "We took some tremendous markdowns." However, the family learned quickly, and profits soon recovered. In the late sixties, Nordstrom began to introduce men's clothing into some of its stores, and it found good customer acceptance. By 1971 there were seven Nordstrom-Best stores, with sales of nearly $80 million.

Nordstrom management again changed hands in 1970. Since 1963 the present generation of Nordstroms had been prominent in the management. Their fathers wanted to retire, and they faced three alternatives: sell to their sons as their father had done, sell out to an established company, or let their sons take over. They also wanted their estates to have an easily established market value. The first alternative was not feasible; it would have required more funds than the young Nordstroms had. The senior Nordstroms were inclined to sell out, but the younger Nordstroms prevailed on them to—as Bruce put it—"entrust their fortune to us." Once this decision was taken, the older Nordstroms quickly withdrew from day-to-day responsibilities—in fact, Elmer and Everett retired and Lloyd became chairman of the board. The company also went public, thus fulfilling the senior Nordstroms' desire for a market value to their estate. Thus, once again the transition between generations was accomplished smoothly, leaving the younger generation in full control.

The Nordstroms attributed their success in apparel to having applied the principles of the shoe business. Nordstrom shoe stores had offered an exceptionally wide selection of merchandise, attractive surroundings, a high level of service, and competitive prices. A broad selection of merchandise was a must for a successful, family shoe store. Operators had to ensure (within reason) that any customer who walked in could choose from a variety of appropriately styled shoes that would fit. As shoes were often branded merchandise, operators also had to ensure in catering to the mass market that they met competitors' prices. Finally, selling shoes is a service-intensive business. Store salespeople had to be willing to identify a customer's needs and tastes, locate appropriate shoes, and finally try them on the customer's feet.

The Nordstroms believed that they had effectively transferred these principles to apparel retailing. Nordstrom stores stocked a wide variety of depth of merchandise. Their inventory per square foot averaged almost twice that of comparable classifications in department stores. Nordstrom also had an established policy of meeting competitors on price. If a customer told a Nordstrom salesperson that he or she had seen the same item of apparel at a competitor's for $25 and the store was selling it for $26, the salesperson was authorized to sell the customer the merchandise for $25. After a suitable (but quick) check on the validity of the customer's claim, the entire stock would be marked down. Finally, Nordstrom management took pride in the fact that a customer would always find helpful and knowledgeable salespeople in their stores. Salespeople were encouraged to develop client lists and telephone their "regular" clients if new merchandise that would suit them had been delivered to the store. If merchandise to suit a customer's needs was not available, salespeople were encouraged to follow up with the buyers.

Even the Nordstrom policy of decentralized decision making was an offshoot of its shoe store origin. As a family shoe store operator, Nordstrom had believed that it had to allow the store manager flexibility in ordering, and particularly reordering, because Store A might have clientele with different tastes and different size needs than Store B. Initially the Nordstroms exercised control by having a "Nordstrom in every store," but soon this was not possible, so they had to delegate responsibilities to the store managers. As one Nordstrom put it, "Our objective is to transmit the entrepreneurial feeling to the store level—that's why we keep it decentralized." Another "transfer" from the shoe business was Nordstrom's policy of paying the majority of its salespeople commissions—common practice in shoe retailing.

The success of these transfers was apparent, and Nordstrom-Best continued to grow. In 1971 it substantially remodeled the headquarters store in downtown Seattle. Though it continued to expand, the company faced constraints, particularly in 1974. Concern about the environment resulted in a slowdown in building of new shopping centers and expansion of old ones. Money, too, became scarce. The Nordstroms found few opportunities to grow. They did note that many customers from smaller towns in the Northwest often asked why Nordstrom did not "come to their town." These towns could not support a full-fledged store, so Nordstrom examined what it could transfer, in its entirety, from its larger stores.

The examination culminated in the establishment of Place Two Stores. These were 15,000–20,000 sq. ft. stores to be located in towns with populations of 25,000–50,000. The stores stocked young men's and women's clothing. Ultimately they were placed under a separate general manager and given their own buying organization. The Nordstroms found this concept successful in locations with exceptionally high concentrations of young people, including college communities and locations in large standard metropolitan statistical areas where Nordstrom could not find a site for a full-scale store. Nonetheless, in the changed environment of the late 1970s, management felt that they should concentrate on the larger stores and that Place Two expansion should basically be limited to what the Place Two organization could itself finance.

In 1979 Nordstrom was recognized as Seattle's leading women's apparel store and a strong second choice in men's clothing. The store offered a wide variety of apparel, accessories, and, of course, shoes. It was Seattle's leading store for fashion shoes for both men and women. In fact, Nordstrom inevitably dominated the fashion shoe market once it was established in a location. The store did not offer major appliances, furniture, health and beauty aids, and the like, nor did it intend to.[1] In addition to its own charge cards, Nordstrom accepted Master Charge and VISA. Some idea of Nordstrom's market strengths can be gained from the results of a survey conducted by a marketing organization (*Exhibit 3*). The survey covered six counties around Seattle-Tacoma and consisted of 1,000 interviews over the telephone, lasting approximately 20 minutes each.

Nordstrom advertising strategy emphasized image advertising. Although the company used newspaper advertising to help achieve its goal, it did not aim to dominate newspaper advertising in its merchandise categories. Nordstrom also used direct mail advertising, sending catalogs and brochures to its active accounts about five to six times a year. And the company always inserted a few pamphlets advertising merchandise in its monthly customer statements. Nordstrom spent 2.1% of sales on advertising in 1978 and 2.2% in 1977—these figures excluded suppliers' promotional allowances.

Nordstrom had gone public in 1971; its stock was traded in the over-the-counter market. In 1976 and in 1978, the company had tapped the equity market, issuing 900,000 shares of common stock on each occasion.[2] As of January 31, 1979, the company believed it was in a strong financial condition with a long-term debt to capital ratio of 29%.[3] The company also believed that it could sustain a growth rate of two to three stores a year with internally generated funds. As its store base increased, the company believed it could accelerate its growth rate if it desired. As of April 1979, the Nordstrom family owned 57% of the common stock.

---

1. The Alaska division, which had been acquired in 1975, had sold a range of major appliances, but the Nordstroms had gradually phased out the appliances. The Alaska division stores still offered televisions and microwave ovens but did not sell refrigerators, cooking ranges, and so on. The company intended to move out of this category altogether. While stores did not offer a full line of health and beauty aids, they did sell cosmetics.

2. Adjusted for stock splits.

3. (Long-term debt + capitalized leases) ÷ (Long-term debt + capitalized leases + equity).

THE ORGANIZATION

The Nordstroms did not have an organization chart. As one of them put it, "It would be too confusing." However, all the managers knew that the top management consisted of "the five": the three Nordstroms—referred to widely in the company as "Mr. Bruce," "Mr. John," and "Mr. Jim"; John A. (Jack) McMillan, related to the Nordstroms by marriage; and Robert E. Bender, a close family friend. Each was responsible for a merchandise group (*Exhibit 4* gives their individual backgrounds and responsibilities).

The company was divided into four regions: Washington, Oregon, Alaska, and California. There were three regional managers; the Washington division reported to "the five." Except in Washington State, all the store managers reported to the regional manager. There Ray Johnson, the downtown store manager, was considered more equal than the others (mostly because he was Nordstrom's personal manager, too). However, if a store manager had any questions, he or she would ring up one of "the five," or, as Mr. Jim put it, "talk to any one of us who picks up the phone."

The regional managers were given a great deal of autonomy, including, in general, buying autonomy. There was, however, no hard and fast rule on the degree of buying autonomy delegated to the regions and, within each region, how much the buying was centralized.

Under each store manager were department managers and a personnel manager. Although department managers did report to the store managers, they also had to work with and work within guidelines given by their merchandise managers or buyers.

Nordstrom's buying organization was unusual if not unique in the industry. Four of "the five" had working for them general merchandise managers for each of the merchandise categories for which they were responsible. The organization within each category varied according to its needs. However, the guiding principle was to ensure the greatest extent of decentralization to allow initiative at the lower levels. The organization under John Nordstrom typified the variations that existed within the buying pyramid.

Mr. John was responsible for the men's clothing and the men's shoe divisions. In men's clothing, buying was completely centralized. One buyer bought for the whole company and was responsible for the inventory levels at each store. The company had tried to decentralize the buying function by delegating authority to regional buyers, but it had found that this did not work. The company kept experimenting, though, by giving buying authority to the regions. One of the possible reasons for this lack of success was that quality men's clothing still had a large handmade element. This meant that buyers had to be highly trained in the cuts and stitches used in the industry. Also, buyers had to decide on color and patterns on the basis of swatches of material, making buying a very specialized field. Possibly another reason was that very few vendors produced desirable merchandise, and thus vendor relations were more important than in most other merchandise lines.

The shoe department, however, was the very epitome of decentralization. There were a merchandise and four regional merchandise managers (because the California division was still small, the regional manager held the title of buyer). Each store had a department manager with the authority to purchase shoes for the store. The department managers' open-to-buy (OTB) was controlled by the regional merchandise manager, whose OTB was, in turn, controlled by the general merchandise manager.

The delegation of buying authority ranged between these two extremes. For instance, in women's sportswear (under Mr. Jim) in Washington State there were two buyers—one for the downtown store and three additional stores in the state, the other for the Tacoma store and the other three stores. In the other divisions (regions), there was only one buyer each. The department managers in every store had an OTB controlled by the buyers. Whenever sportswear vendors visited a region, all department managers attended a showing of the merchandise and made purchase decisions. If the department managers were unsure of their choices, the buyers would help. Only the buyers and the general merchandise managers would travel to out-of-town buying trips and make all the purchase decisions. The bulk of women's sportswear was purchased by the buyers.

Cosmetics, on the other hand, was more centralized. There were four regional merchandise managers, and the department managers at each store did not have the authority to reorder. *Exhibit 5* summarizes the organization and the delegation of responsibilities in the buying organization for key merchandise categories. This organization amplified the diversity in structure. One women's clothing buyer half-jokingly noted that her stiffest competition came from within—other women's departments in the company. Indeed, in recognition of this situation, the company enforced a rule that women's apparel buyers in different departments (as outlined in *Exhibit 5*) could not buy from the same vendor. One modification not noted in *Exhibit 5* was that the regional manager in Oregon felt he needed a merchandise manager for John McMillan's area, and he made one of the buyers into a regional merchandise manager, coordinating all the buyers of women's clothing in Oregon.

Despite its decentralized organization, Nordstrom's management believed that there was good coordination between buyers where necessary. For instance, there were two women's sportswear buyers for Washington State. If they were going to advertise and/or promote merchandise, they had to concur on which merchandise to advertise and which to mark down. Because it was in each one's best interest, the Nordstroms had found that they always reached an agreement. The difference was that if the buyers were on good terms, agreement was reached sooner; if they weren't it took longer. Thus, even though theoretically the buyers could advertise different merchandise in the same region or not carry advertised merchandise, this rarely happened.

When Nordstrom produced a catalog, all the buyers got together and agreed on which merchandise should go into it; they were then required to carry all the merchandise in the catalog.

KEY SUCCESS FACTORS

There appeared to be three key factors to Nordstrom's success in operating an unorthodox system—getting good people and paying them well, a good and up-to-date financial information flow, and its control system.

People

Nordstrom adhered strictly to a policy of promoting from within. Salespeople were hired at each store by the store manager or department manager. Except for certain stores in Washington (including the downtown store), Nordstrom's stores were not unionized. The company, except where restricted by union rules, met if it did not exceed hourly salaries paid by competition in the area of operation. Salaries within each of the four regions tended to be uniform. The company provided comprehensive health insurance coverage that included dental benefits. All employees who worked over 1,000 hours per year participated in the profit-sharing plan.

The amount paid under the profit-sharing plan depended on three factors—the total amount set aside by the board, length of service, and the employee's income during the year. Monies allocated to the employee were paid into a trust fund administered by a bank, which invested the funds in equities, bonds, and cash equivalents. Thus, an employee would share in any increase (or decrease) in the portfolio in proportion to the amount invested on the employee's behalf. The employee was entitled to the amount in the fund depending on his vesting percentage, which in turn was determined by duration of service. The vesting percentages ranged from 20% after 2 years' service to 100% after 10 years. The amount forfeited by employees who left the company before 10 years was reinvested in the portfolio. Management was proud of this plan, which had been instituted in 1951, and believed it to be an integral part of its philosophy of treating its employees well.

The hourly wages formed the base salary for most sales personnel, who were paid on a commission basis. The commissions varied by department, ranging from 5% to 10%; the median was 6¾%. A commission was not paid unless the amount due an individual exceeded the base salary on a semimonthly basis. Salespeople in departments such as women's accessories and children's apparel did not receive commissions because merchandise management (which included the concerned Nordstrom)[4] believed that, barring an unacceptably high percentage rate, these salespeople would not earn commissions given their relatively low-volume departments.

Generally, salespeople in the noncommission departments moved to commission departments as soon as there were openings. Nordstrom expected salespeople to reach their commission earning level fairly rapidly. The company maintained a daily record of sales per hour by individual. In fact, department managers, store managers, regional managers, and even the Nordstroms kept track of these data. If salespeople's performance lagged, the department manager would counsel them and point out their weaknesses. If they showed no improvement, then the department manager, after consultation with the store manager and the store personnel manager, would fire the employee. Employees' base wages were between $3.10 and $5.10 per hour. An employee with no previous retail selling experience earned the minimum. An employee with 700 hours of experience earned $3.50; 1,400 hours of experience earned $3.90, and everyone with over 2,100 hours of experience earned $5.10 per hour. Full-time salespeople on commission averaged annual earnings between $12,000 and $15,000.

Turnover at the salesperson level, although fairly high, was not considered a problem. The company estimated salesperson turnover at around 50–60%, most of which was accounted for by seasonal needs.[5] Turnover among permanent salespeople was estimated at around 15–20%, with family situations the primary reason for voluntary resignation. Termination by the company for poor performance or improper behavior accounted for up to 50% of the turnover of permanent employees.

Successful salespeople formed the basis of Nordstrom management. One had to achieve reasonable success as a salesperson to be promoted to department manager—the next step up the ladder. In keeping with the policy of hiring from within, all department managers had been salespeople. The store manager decided whom to promote after taking the advice of the department manager under whom the employee worked. In some instances, the store manager might also ask the advice of the department buyer. However, the decision was made by

4. Here Nordstrom means one of "the five" Nordstroms.

5. Excludes movement due to promotion.

the store manager. Often an employee would approach the store manager or department manager and express a desire to become a manager.

Department managers received a salary plus a commission on any sales they made. They were also eligible for a bonus, which was generally 1% of the sales increase over the previous year. Department managers' salaries ranged between $14,000 and $40,000; only $6,000 to $8,000 constituted base salary. The average department manager was estimated to earn around $18,000, of which $7,000 was base, $9,500 earned commission, and $1,500 bonus for increased sales. Store managers called on department managers to cover for them when they were not in the store.

The department managers had a dotted line relationship with their merchandise managers or buyers. Although they reported to the store manager, in many instances they had buying authority and had to work closely with the buyers. Store managers were responsible for recommendations on the promotion of department managers, but they always consulted the regional merchandise managers or buyers first.

A department manager could be promoted in two ways: to a larger department or to the position of buyer. The buyer, depending on the degree of autonomy in the department, bought for the region or just bought imports and merchandise not available locally (some merchandise categories had only department managers and regional merchandise managers). Buyers earned between $15,000 and $50,000 per year including bonuses. They earned one bonus on the percentage increase in sales over the previous year and another on gross margin performance. However, the latter bonus was not awarded for all merchandise categories. For instance, none of the buyers under Mr. Jim received it because he did not believe that this was appropriate for his merchandise categories. The regional manager was responsible for all the buyers in the region and decided on salary increases and, where necessary, the performance criteria for bonuses. However, the regional manager never decided on buyer remuneration without consulting the general merchandise manager. In addition, the regional manager generally informally discussed the buyer's salary increase with the Nordstrom in charge of the merchandise category.

A buyer could be promoted to either merchandise manager or store manager. Most store managers earned between $30,000 and $60,000 per year, with one or two earning more, of which up to 30% could be bonus based. The bonuses were paid on three criteria:

1. Sales increase—averaged 1% of the sales increase over the previous year. In some cases a lump sum was paid for achievement of a dollar increase target.

2. Expense goals as a percent of sales.

3. Shortage target—a relatively new target.

"The five" felt free to add to or subtract from the bonus criteria as the need arose. For example, if they felt personnel turnover was a problem, they might offer a manager a $5,000 bonus if he or she could achieve a lower specified rate. Regional managers were evaluated for regional performance on basically the same criteria as store managers.

Merchandise managers (general and regional) were evaluated using basically the same criteria as buyers, except they were responsible for inventory turns and in some cases for advertising expenses (net of vendors' promotion allowances) as a percent of sales. Even the general merchandise managers under Mr. Jim were responsible for gross margin and inventory turns. Thus, although the buyers in departments under Mr. Jim were not paid a bonus on gross margin, they were under pressure from their merchandise managers to ensure that gross margins did not get out of line.

Information Flow

"The five" received the following information in the form of printouts:

1. Sales by department by store (daily basis): This printout had daily sales this year; last year; this year as a percent of last year; and month to date this year, last year, and this year as a percent of last year. In summary, the printout gave the combined data for the department for all stores and also provided a comparison with the company as a whole (*Exhibit 6* amplifies).

2. Gross margin and inventory by department by store (monthly): The printout provided this year's and last year's figures for the month. The department data included beginning-of-the-month inventory, end-of-the-month inventory, percent change of end-of-the-month inventory, this year/last year, amount on order, sales by month and year to date, percent change in sales over previous year, markdowns, employee discount shown as a percent of sales, stock-to-sales ratio, and inventory turns (see *Exhibit 7*). The departmental data were also totaled by merchandise division.

3. Gross margin and inventory by department for the company (monthly): The printout listed the same data breakdown as that in Item 2 except for the company as a whole.

4. Sales per hour performance by employee (semimonthly): The printout gave employee name and number, store and department, hours worked, gross sales, returns, net sales, and sales per hour (*Exhibit 8*).

To ensure that the printouts were up to date, the company had installed a point-of-sale system. Each time a salesperson made a sale, he or she input the following information:

1. Salesperson employee number
2. Department number
3. Classification number
4. Charge account number (if any)
5. Price

Also, Kimball tickets were used at the merchandise manager's request. The following additional information was keypunched on these tickets: vendor, style, month merchandise arrived, color code, and size. However, the printout used by senior management was not dependent on Kimball ticket information. For the future, management was experimenting with a point-of-sale system that would provide information by stockkeeping unit. Here, too, the company expected that these details would not be given to top management and indeed would be provided to the merchandise manager only if he or she requested them.

Using the information on the printout, management could quickly pinpoint problem departments and keep track of their progress. However, "the five" rarely intervened directly in a problem. Rather, they waited to be contacted. Because the printouts were also sent to the respective merchandise managers, the "five knew" that the merchandise managers too must be aware of the problem. Store managers received similar printouts, giving them the sales breakdown by department within their stores as well as an overall sales comparison with other stores in their region and the company as a whole. This meant the store managers, too, would be aware of the data reaching corporate. Management reasoned that they would also react to correct a problem. The delegation of responsibilities ensured that top management managed through exception—and generally those exceptions were requests for help or clarification by regional managers, store managers, or merchandise managers.

"The five" met with their respective merchandise managers to work out planned sales and inventory figures for their department categories. They also met with store managers in the state on a monthly basis. Other meetings included regular visits to regions and stores. However, although important, these meetings were only a part of the information flow. The Nordstroms maintained a very informal atmosphere and were readily accessible to their employees. As one of them noted, they had their own offices, but the offices had no doors—this symbolized the openness of the company.

Employees had access to department performance data. For instance, in the downtown store any employee could view the daily sales performance printout for all departments for all stores on microfiche. These data were also made available in other stores, but with a lag for delivery of the fiche. Allowing employees access to sales information helped them feel a part of the team. As one employee put it, "In the company I used to work for, buyers used to get upset but we never knew why they were upset. Here we know if sales aren't doing well and we can do our best to improve sales."

Sales per hour by employee were posted semimonthly by each department manager for the department. Some store managers made available semimonthly sales per employee figures to all employees. In all stores the top sales per hour performances were publicly commended through a letter sent to all employees. In addition to the individuals' names, their sales per hour were shown.

The Control System

The diversity of the Nordstrom organization, the significant variation in responsibilities and duties for the same level of personnel in different merchandise departments, and the extent of decentralization were in the casewriter's opinion quite unusual, if not unique, for an organization of Nordstrom's size. To keep it all functioning smoothly and to ensure that the key management people kept in touch with significant events, the company relied on some equally unique control mechanisms.

Both buyers and store managers were paid bonuses on their percent increase in sales over the previous year. Achievement of a target increase as a prerequisite for the bonus was not a part of the system, but goal setting was achieved through peer pressure. Every year a meeting attended by all regional buyers and store managers was held at each region's headquarters. The regional manager, or in Washington State the Nordstroms, would call on each manager (or buyer), in turn to present his or her sales target for the year. As the figures were called out, the regional manager wrote them beside the individual's name on a large chart. Next to the figures was a space on which the regional manager had written his target for each manager. That figure was kept covered during the initial part of the meeting. Then, amid great suspense, the regional manager tore off the slip of paper that covered his or her target for each manager. If the manager's sales target was under that of the regional manager, the assembly would boo the unfortunate manager. However, if the manager's target was above that of the regional manager, the group would break out in cheers. One manager described the scene as being like a classroom before an exam, or perhaps during an exam, with all the store managers and buyers doing feverish calculations as they heard their peers' targets and were tempted to revise their own. The meeting held in Washington at Nordstrom's headquarters was the largest because, in addition to

the managers in Washington State, the regional managers attended. Any em- '
ployee was welcome at the meetings in each region.

To arrive at their targets, store managers consulted with their department managers. This process was similar to that of the larger meeting. Each department
manager read out the target figure for sales in his or her store. Then the store
manager revealed his or her figure for each department manager, accompanied
by boos or cheers. The store manager, however, did not use the department
manager's targets as the only basis for his own goals, but made adjustments
wherever he thought necessary. For instance, if the store manager considered a
particular department manager's target unrealistic, he/she would scale it down
in arriving at a total target for the store.

The buyer, too, would ask each store's department manager for a target. However, this was generally done over the telephone or in individual conversations.
This was because a department manager did not report directly to the buyer or
the merchandise manager. Once again, the merchandise manager or buyer would
use the department manager's target as a guide and adjust it as he/she thought
it necessary. Thus, if all the buying organization's targets were totaled, they
would give a different figure from the sum of all the store manager's targets.
This discrepancy was not important, however, because neither the buying organization nor the store managers or regional managers used these targets as their
criteria for planning. The buyers or merchandise managers had already agreed
or planned on certain open-to-buy figures for the next six months based on more
conservative planned sales figures, and the store managers used different and,
again, more conservative figures in their expense budgets.

In addition to the annual sales target meeting, there were monthly meetings in
each region attended by buyers, all store managers, and all department managers.
Various awards were distributed during these meetings. For instance, there was
a customer service award in each region. Every store had to enter the contest
for this award. Each store submitted an entry backed up by documentation.
There were no set criteria for the entry; selection was left to the store manager.
Among the documentation required were all complaint letters received by the
store during that month. Two or three stores won prizes, which ranged from
$300 to $1,500. These were collected by the store managers who in turn distributed them to outstanding customer service salespeople in their stores.

Also presented was the all-star award. For this each store manager brought a
salesperson who had done something to deserve this award. The store managers
then described their salespeople's activities to the meeting. A cash award of $100
was presented to the winning individual. A Nordstrom always attended these
monthly meetings; they shared attendance responsibilities on a rotating basis.

Buyers, too, were eligible for awards. Each division held a Make Nordstrom
Special contest every month, which awarded cash prizes of $200, $100, and

$50. The judges looked for good value, unique merchandise, good sales, good promotion, or some combination of the above.

Another award, the Pace Setters Club, recognized outstanding selling performance. Sales targets required to qualify for membership were posted early in the year. To help employees pace themselves, store managers often broke down goals into sales per hour terms. Some department managers asked salespeople to set sales targets and then helped them keep track of their progress. It is important to note that all salespeople had the same commission rate, whether or not they achieved targets and/or became a Pace Setter. Pace Setters were recognized through circulation of their names and a separate meeting over a meal with the Nordstroms.

The Nordstroms believed that these cash prizes, although not important in money terms, played an important role in keeping the organization vital and boosting employee morale.

NORDSTROM IN CALIFORNIA

To see how Nordstrom's philosophy worked when transplanted to a distant region where the Nordstrom name was not so well known, the casewriter visited Nordstrom's first (and only) store in California. The company had invested a great deal in the California store because it was their first move outside the Northwest. Management commented on the significance of their move in the 1979 annual report. "Never before had we devoted so much time and money in the planning of a new store because this was a totally new market area for us and it was vital that we get a strong start." The store was located in the South Coast Plaza Mall in Costa Mesa, in southern California. The casewriter interviewed Betsy Sanders, the regional manager for California.

Conversation with the Regional Manager

Sanders recalled with a twinkle in her eye her first interview with Nordstrom. She had returned to Seattle after a long spell in Europe, where she had obtained a degree in German in Munich and a graduate degree in Naples. In Seattle her husband had decided to return to college and Sanders had agreed to support them. However, because she could not get a teaching job she considered retailing. A friend gave her a letter of introduction to Mr. Bruce. She almost didn't go to the interview because she thought she wouldn't enjoy the work. Mr. Bruce almost didn't hire her because he thought she wouldn't be able to work in a department store given her, as he now recalls with a laugh, "dilettante" background. Until her husband completed his studies, Sanders was a salesperson and discovered that she enjoyed her work a great deal. When her husband got his degree, she decided to stay on at Nordstrom and make it a career. She recalled with pride that four years and two days after that decision she was a store manager. When she was offered her present position, her husband agreed to move to southern California.

Sanders exuded confidence and vitality. It appeared to the casewriter that the employees found working for her a joy and a challenge. She knew most of her employees by name. Because there was only one store, Sanders also filled the role of store manager. She discussed various aspects of her job:

— On selection of personnel for the California store Sanders said, "It was my decision on who to have as the buyers for this region. In keeping with our policy of hiring from within, all the buyers have worked for Nordstrom in one of the other three regions. I sent out a bulletin to various people in the divisions and then reviewed the responses. My criteria were basically that the people had to be successful in the positions they were in at that time. They had to prove to me they had knowledge and competence to buy. They also had to be able to manage constructively. By that I mean having the ability to get people to work together and not exercise their authority by fear. I looked for people who had a history of developing people because we will need people here to meet our growing needs. I also looked for a strong record of being customer oriented. Obviously I did not know all the people before and depended on regional managers and store managers to give me their recommendations. I think it worked and worked pretty well because a manager is interested in promoting his or her people, and they [managers] know that if they recommend someone who does not measure up to requirements, the next time I would regard their recommendations with a certain amount of skepticism. Of course, if this were to happen often, I just wouldn't ring them up.

— "We have strictly adhered to the policy of all managers must have been salespeople at Nordstrom. We don't hire from outside for two major reasons. On the one hand, we know they (in-house people) can perform because we have their record. On the other hand, they understand the company and the atmosphere within it and have obviously grown comfortable with that atmosphere. Just the other day two buyers from _____ came here to discuss a job at Nordstrom. I told them that I was very interested but that they would have to work on the floor and prove themselves before they could become buyers at Nordstrom. They were rather shocked and horrified. I think that many buyers in other stores regard selling as an operation they don't want to have anything to do with. In this store particularly, we have our buyers on the floor selling."

— Expanding on the previous statement, Sanders noted that the buyers in the Costa Mesa store spent a great deal of time on the floor. She felt this was particularly useful because it helped them to get to know the California customers better. Another unusual feature of the California region was that buyers, too, earned a commission on sales they made. Although Sanders had to present the case to corporate to institute that policy, corporate's agreement reflected the extent of decentralization and therefore diversity in Nordstrom's organization.

— Another difference in California was that all salespeople could earn commissions; even the accessories and children's apparel salespeople earned commissions if their percent of sales exceeded their base salary. In instituting this change, Sanders reasoned as follows: She believed that noncommissioned status reflected the union's concern that salespeople in certain departments would never really earn their commission and therefore should not be expected to work on a commission basis. However, because the California store was not unionized, Sanders did not believe it necessary to follow Seattle's policy. She also noted that sometimes a salesperson sold 80 handbags and put in creditable performance yet she would not feel rewarded when her paycheck came around unless she was allowed to earn a commission.

— Some of Sanders's other decisions also reflected the degree of freedom given to the regional manager. She determined the level of base pay for sales employees in California, and she decided to keep the union rates used in Seattle (these were much higher than those offered by the competition in California). When this became known to the competition, they expressed their unhappiness at Nordstrom's higher rates because most salespeople Nordstrom hired had substantial experience and therefore earned $5.10 an hour. Another change was Sanders's decision to advertise in magazines, such as *The New West* and *Los Angeles*. Nordstrom had always advertised in newspapers, but Sanders felt that this market required advertisement in magazines. Although corporate questioned her decision, it was her right, she noted, to control advertising within the region.

— On the budget process, Sanders commented that Nordstrom worked its budget forward and not backward. By this she meant that she decided on what raises to give various individuals, then worked out the total salaries to arrive at an expense figure for the year. She then looked at the sales target for the year and unless expenses as a percentage of sales were unacceptably high, that was the base she used for expenses. She noted that other stores often estimated their sales increase and then, using a target percentage, worked out the expense level in terms of dollars available for the year. After that they calculated the raises they could give to keep within that expense level. Sanders believed the difference in approach reflected Nordstrom's concept of treating and paying good people well.

— On goal setting, she recalled with obvious pleasure the scene at the previous February meeting (1978). She had set a goal of $15 million for the first nine months of operation. When she had given the figure, the Nordstroms had asked if she wished to revise it downward, because they felt it was very ambitious. Their own figure had been $10 million. (Note: for the first year or two of operations the manager of a new store earned a bonus based on a percentage of the amount by which sales exceeded the target.) Sanders noted, "Of course we achieved $15 million in sales last year. Incidentally, in our first full year of operation we achieved sales of $21 million. This year I set a target of $27 million, whereas their target was $25 million. Mine is the highest target for any branch store in the company."

— Sanders was asked to comment on the possible dichotomy between customer service and the measurement of employees by sales per hour and the fact that salespeople received a commission on sales. Might that make them less responsive to a customer's needs and more eager to make a sale? Sanders disagreed that a dichotomy existed because the employees' renumeration was dependent on satisfying customers and therefore they had to behave responsibly. She did agree that a few employees became too eager to generate sales and paid less attention to giving customers what they wanted. However, there were at least two means of controlling this. First, the department manager would notice the salespeople's behavior and counsel them to change their pattern; and second, customers would begin to avoid these salespeople and turn to others who were less pushy. Thus, such an aggressive stance was unlikely to pay off in the long run. Sanders added that it was the department manager's role to improve salespeople's customer service posture.

— Sanders noted with pride and perhaps a little regret that she had had 7 Pace Setters in the previous year. She had expected only 2 or 3 in the first year and therefore had promised them a breakfast in Seattle with the Nordstroms. Although she was pleasantly surprised that there were 7, she noted that next year she expected 30, and the division overhead would not support a visit to Seattle for breakfast.

Some miscellaneous reflections:

— Regional managers could influence the percentage markup for merchandise in their region. Sanders had decided to aim for the same markup as in Seattle, even though she believed that it was lower than that of competition in the area and that the merchandise might support a higher markup.

— Sanders noted that a big difference between Nordstrom and other stores in the shopping center was that once you walked into the store and were looking at merchandise, someone would ask if you needed help. That sort of inquiry, she believed, was almost a thing of the past with other stores.

— The key to Nordstrom's success, Sanders thought, was the Nordstroms' ability to put people in key positions who knew and understood the company's philosophy and were comfortable in the environment. The role of every manager was to ensure that the atmosphere of vitality and drive was maintained. This was a particularly important goal for store managers because each of them set the tone for a whole unit.

— Sanders noted that her store got responses from 1,500 people to its ad for help in the local newspaper (see *Exhibit 9*). Three people (including herself) did the initial interviewing. Selected applicants were called for a second round of interviews by department managers, who made the final decisions.

— Nordstrom did not have a formal training program; it believed in on-the-job training. "We hire what we consider good people and let them get on with their job. Of course the managers are there to help and provide guidance, but we encourage people to take initiative and reward them for doing so."

Other Interviews

The casewriter then talked with some of the buyers. Although at the time they bought only for one store, in a few years their responsibility would grow during Nordstrom's California expansion.

Jeff Cox, buyer of women's shoes, had left the military and joined Nordstrom in 1970 as a salesperson for shoes. He noted that the shoe business was tough. Unlike a buyer of dresses, a shoe buyer had to commit to purchases almost eight months in advance of delivery. This commitment consisted of decisions on style, color, size, and quantities. Cox noted that to order a shoe of one style and color in every size available would result in 72 pairs.

At the moment Cox was the only California buyer for shoes, but once the Brea store opened, each store would have a department manager who would buy the style, color, and size that he or she wanted for the store.[6] Cox would guide them and control their open-to-buy. Cox would buy direct imports, which constituted approximately 5% of total sales.

The shoe department took a weekly inventory by style and size. Stock time was paid for separately, and the hours used were not included in an individual's sales per hour computation. However, setting up displays and keeping them tidy was not paid for separately and had to be done on employees' time.[7] Cox agreed that some employees might avoid their share of this "maintenance" work in their desire to maintain their sales per hour. It was his job to see that the load was distributed equitably.

As a buyer, Cox would be evaluated and paid a bonus on (1) gross margin— the bonus on achievement of a gross margin above a certain percentage; and (2) sales increase—1% of the sales increase over the previous year. He also had to watch his expense ratio as a percent of sales, but this was an informal measure on which no bonus was paid. He noted that if the merchandise manager felt a particular department manager's expense ratio was too high, he or she might pay the department manager a lump sum bonus to reduce the percentage below a certain targeted figure.

Michelle Carrig, buyer for cosmetics, had been with Frederick & Nelson and had worked as a fine jewelry buyer. She believed she couldn't achieve growth in that company, and had joined Nordstrom five years before. She had been a buyer in Washington State before moving to California.

In discussing her operating procedures, she noted that she kept an open-to-buy line by vendor, for instance, Estée Lauder, and so on. Inventory by stock-keeping unit count was taken monthly. Every year case space and length were measured and sales per linear foot calculated for every store. If a supplier was not performing satisfactorily in terms of sales per linear foot, its space allocation tended to be reduced. Similarly, if a company did well, it might be granted more space.

Carrig noted that promotional allowances were a key factor in achieving profitability in her business. To encourage aggressive follow-up, the person who processed the invoices allowance was paid a bonus if able to keep promotional allowances above a certain percentage of sales. Such follow-up was necessary because some vendors did not pay promotional allowances unless prodded. Similarly, department managers, although not rewarded through a bonus on promotional

---

6. Brea would be Nordstrom's second store in California, scheduled for opening in October 1979.

7. All departments required salespeople to do "maintenance" work on their own time. Exceptions were made for substantial changes and stocktaking.

allowances, were evaluated informally on this percentage. Thus, they were encouraged to report accurately all sales by vendor. Department managers also supervised the monthly stocktaking.

Carrig noted that although a department manager did not have an open-to-buy for cosmetics, she as a buyer nevertheless expected good feedback from the department manager through notes and comments. She felt that department managers would be eager to provide good feedback because they would receive a bonus on sales and thus were anxious to ensure that the right products were available at their stores. She also noted that she often tailored needs to suit a department manager's taste. For instance, if a department manager felt more comfortable with pink and other lighter-colored lipsticks it was in Carrig's interest to ensure that she had a better variety of lighter shades.

Carrig herself was evaluated and received a bonus on sales increases, achievement of a gross margin target, and inventory turns. She also had to keep an eye on selling expenses as a percent of sales although she was not formally evaluated on that criterion.

E. N. Goodson, buyer of juniors' coats and dresses, had joined Nordstrom in 1974. There were only six or seven buyers for juniors in the company, and department managers did not have an open-to-buy. Goodson made frequent visits to New York along with the other buyers for U.S. purchases. All imports were bought by the general merchandise manager.

When asked about her buying philosophy, Goodson said she generally bought two to three months in advance. She believed this gave her a great deal of flexibility in timing. She and her merchandise manager mutually agreed every six months to an open-to-buy plan, but she could adjust this in line with sales by telephoning the merchandise manager. She had done this frequently as sales had outstripped all expectations in the first year of operation in California. Goodson characterized her method as buying a few items of each style, but purchasing a wide variety of styles. She compared this with other department stores, which bought a large quantity of items in a certain style. She believed her policy was more effective for juniors, because few juniors wished to wear the same thing as the person next door. If an item was hot Goodson did buy it in somewhat greater depth. Nonetheless, she believed it was worth being unable to reorder a hot item for the sake of providing a wide variety of fresh merchandise. She was not evaluated on gross margin and received a bonus on sales increases.

When asked to comment on working for Nordstrom, Goodson said that the main thing is "you are left to yourself. If you want help, you ask for it. If not, you are on your own. The sales goal is a personal commitment and not really a means of evaluation. It is really up to you what you make of it."

Salesperson Interviews

Person A. This employee was a fairly senior woman. She had worked for Bullock's for three and a half years before coming to Nordstrom. She expressed herself freely.

> The company [Nordstrom] has a very positive attitude. Everyone is working for the same excellent top management, and I have to say we are paid very well. I think the company takes pride in the people that work for them. For instance, it is a small thing, I know, but everyone was invited to the Christmas party, not just department managers and buyers.
>
> I also like the fact that the buyers are on the floor selling. I think the people like the feel of our store. I know there is a fine line between being helpful and being pushy, and we are very much aware of that.
>
> I keep a book of customers who shop regularly and who have expressed their tastes and desires to me. Whenever there is new merchandise which I feel will suit their needs, I call them up and tell them that it is available. I think there are very few other stores that offer this kind of service.
>
> In terms of rules, I feel there are only two hard and fast rules here: take good care of customers and do not steal. We are allowed a great deal of freedom within these constraints. Just the other day a lady came and bought a dress. Then she wanted a pair of shoes which would match the dress. I could go down and get those shoes for her, so that she had a complete shopping trip without having to move up and down. Besides, I knew that shoes matching her dress were available downstairs, something she may not have known.
>
> Comparing them [Nordstrom to Bullock's], without trying to run down Bullock's, I feel Bullock's almost felt that customer service was not important. They really weren't concerned about employees at the sales level. There was a great deal of emphasis on who was who and following the chain of command. There is no such constraint here, I feel.

Person B.

> I used to work in I. Magnin and May Company on a part-time basis. I really enjoy working for Nordstrom. They treat employees differently and treat them well. When I used to work for I. Magnin, I didn't know the people on the second floor. Here we get to meet everyone.
>
> Also, in both the [other] companies we didn't know any of the figures [financial data]. Therefore, we didn't know why managers got upset at certain

times. Here we get a good flow of information. We know how each line is doing and our opinions are often asked for. We are treated like people who can think, and I find this very encouraging.

Our buyer involves us in almost everything. She tells us about new fashions that are coming out, what is in, what we should expect in the future, and what will be moving out. Every month we meet on Sundays for breakfast. In the May Company we never even met on a yearly basis.

Nordstrom managers and employees stressed the fact there was no one organization structure method for doing things. Individuals were given responsibility and left to work things out for themselves in a manner they thought suitable—as long as it was not outrageous. The employees and managers appreciated this freedom and enjoyed working in such an environment.

Conversation with Jim Nordstrom

To conclude his interviews, the casewriter spoke with Mr. Jim, the youngest of the Nordstroms:

We [Nordstroms] have been moving away from the merchandising end of the business, even though we are the nominal merchandise managers. Yes, I guess I do feel a certain sense of loss, but I am really not that unhappy about it. After all, our business has improved since we have moved away, so maybe the people who have taken over are doing a better job than we were.

A great deal of our time now is spent looking for opportunities to locate new stores. However, our number one responsibility is our employees. In fact, normally an organization is depicted as a pyramid with the top management controlling the whole chain of command going down. We look at it the other way. We believe we are at the bottom of the pyramid here to ensure that our employees have everything that they need in order to do a good job, and not that the employees are here for us to supervise.

What Mr. Jim said tied in closely with the feelings expressed by the other Nordstroms. Mr. Jim also confirmed the view held by the other Nordstroms that store managers were more important than buyers, though of course both were valued. The Nordstroms viewed buyers as providing a service to the store managers, whose role was to service the customers and conclude the sale.

The casewriter asked if "delegation of responsibility" was the correct expression to use in describing Nordstrom's philosophy. Mr. Jim felt that it was not the best, because "delegation" implied that the Nordstroms retained a certain degree of control, which by and large they didn't have. He said quite candidly:

If I proclaim an edict, I don't know if it will get implemented. For instance, there have been signs in stores which said we don't take merchandise back unless accompanied by receipt. This is just not true. It is our policy to take back merchandise if the customer says they bought it from us, unless we had a valid reason to reject it. I have taken down the signs personally and told several people that this is not our policy. Yet time and again I see the signs. Well, that's life.

Mr. Jim also acknowledged that there was often a certain amount of conflict among buyers and sometimes among buyers and department managers, or others. But he felt very comfortable with the conflict. In fact, he said that "sometimes if there are no conflicts, particularly between buyers, I feel that they are being too kind to each other and not being critical. The conflict, as long as it is within reason, provides a means of competition."

Finally, Mr. Jim said that he didn't think the Nordstrom children would particularly enjoy working for the firm. "By the time they take over we'd be a large company and I think all the fun of growing and expanding will have gone."

CONCERNS FOR THE FUTURE

Summarizing Nordstrom's modus operandi, Mr. Bruce said:

We offer the customer great variety and depth of merchandise displayed in an attractive environment, with high levels of customer service. All these elements cost money and add to expense, so we compensate that by generating volume. We have to move the merchandise off the floor. We depend on good salespeople to help us do it and we take markdowns whenever we see that merchandise isn't moving as expected.

Nordstrom's sales per square foot figures reflected the emphasis on turnover. Sales per square foot of total space (excluding leased departments operated in other stores) rose from $127 in 1973 to $163 in 1977 and approximately $180 in 1978. This compared with a rise from $58 to $74 per square foot for department stores between 1973 and 1977.[8] Between 1973 and 1978 Nordstrom had more than doubled its space. Total sales had almost tripled in the same period.

Could Nordstrom maintain its pace of growth without detracting from the

8. Survey data for department stores and specialty stores, published by the National Retail Merchants Association. Figures relate to sales per gross square foot. The 1973 figure is for department stores with sales over $50 million, 1977 for department stores with sales over $100 million.

factors that contributed to its success? Growth would inevitably involve two components: number of stores and geographic dispersion.

Nordstrom had hitherto been identified with the Northwest, and even as late as the mid-sixties the Nordstroms had resisted growth outside the region. The casewriter asked Mr. Bruce, "Why grow?" "We have always had a fairly competitive nature," he said, "and growth is a yardstick of success. We've always had, you might call it, an instinct to do the best we can. Besides, we owe it to our employees to do the best we can for them. By growing we offer them opportunities and succeed in attracting good people."

Profitable growth had been essential to Nordstrom. The company had been able to maintain a conservative balance sheet by tapping the equity markets twice in the last three years in addition to generating funds through retained earnings. The southern California "experiment" had been a success, and the company planned to build four more Nordstrom stores there over the next two to three years. In addition it planned to open two stores in Oregon, one in Washington, and one in Utah and to expand some existing stores.

The board had set a long-term debt to capital ratio target of 35–40%. (Long-term debt included capitalized leases.) The company estimated that every 100,000 sq. ft. required an investment in land, building, fixtures, and inventory of approximately $10 million in 1978–79 dollars. Of this total, approximately $2–2.5 million consisted of inventory (at cost).[9] Accounts receivable were estimated at 15–18% of sales and working capital needs at 25–30% of sales. Thus, to maintain a conservative balance sheet and still take advantage of all the opportunities available, it was likely that Nordstrom would have to tap the equity markets again. To do this at reasonable cost, it had to continue to be successful.

Was continued emphasis on a decentralized organization, with maximum possible freedom to individual managers, the correct approach? Or would the company run into problems as it expanded?

9. If payables were taken into account, investment in inventory was estimated at $1.5 million at cost.

Exhibit 1
Operating Statement and Balance Sheet

Amounts in Thousands			Year Ended January 31,		
	1979	*1978*	*1977*	*1976*	*1975*
Operations					
Sales	$297,629	$249,690	$209,882	$179,229	$130,512
Cost of sales and related buying and occupancy costs	195,348	165,561	137,510	119,944	87,475
Selling, general and administrative expenses	72,626	59,099	50,597	43,115	31,510
Interest expense	3,343	2,893	2,641	2,845	2,116
Earnings before income taxes	26,312	22,137	19,134	13,325	9,411
Income taxes	12,645	10,440	9,288	6,375	4,343
Net earnings	13,667	11,697	9,846	6,950	5,068
Net earnings per average share of common stock	1.80	1.60	1.38	1.08	.79
Average shares outstanding	7,579,482	7,318,170	7,123,662	6,418,170	6,418,170
Dividends per share of common stock	.30	.24	.19	.15	.13
Net earnings as a percent of net sales	4.59%	4.68%	4.69%	3.88%	3.88%
Financial Position					
Accounts and notes receivable (net)	$ 56,599	$ 46,855	$ 36,927	$ 31,916	$ 22,269
Merchandise inventories	45,200	33,737	29,047	27,594	20,303
Property, buildings and equipment (net)	66,382	53,718	39,248	38,008	32,069
Total assets	180,950	138,896	116,688	98,864	77,579
Long-term debt	13,367	14,339	14,563	14,636	14,705

(Continued)

Exhibit 1
(Continued)
Operating Statement and Balance Sheet

Amounts in Thousands			Year Ended January 31,		
	1979	1978	1977	1976	1975
Working capital	70,589	51,699	49,256	32,268	28,623
Ratio of current assets to current liabilities	2.61	2.54	2.75	2.13	2.67
Shareholders' Equity					
Book value	$ 97,230	$ 67,618	$ 57,677	$ 39,620	$ 33,654
Per common share	11.83	9.24	7.88	6.17	5.25
Earnings per share of common stock as percentage of book value per share at beginning of year	19.5%	20.3%	20.5%	20.6%	17.2%
Stores and Facilities					
Company-operated stores	26	24	20	17	14
Total square footage	1,585,000	1,406,000	1,167,000	1,114,000	907,000

Consolidated Balance Sheets

Amounts in Thousands	January 31,	
Assets	1979	1978
Current Assets:		
Cash	$ 80	$ 1,216
Short-term investments, at cost (approximates market)	11,025	2,029
Accounts and notes receivable—Customers (net of allowance for doubtful accounts of $1,600 in 1979 and $1,227 in 1978)	53,724	40,798
Licensors and others	2,875	6,057
Merchandise inventories	45,200	33,737
Prepaid expenses and other assets	1,664	1,341
Total Current Assets	114,568	85,178
Property, Buildings and Equipment	66,382	53,718
	$180,950	$138,896

Exhibit 1
(Continued)
Consolidated Balance Sheets

Amounts in Thousands		January 31,	
Assets		1979	1978

Liabilities and Shareholders' Equity			
Current Liabilities:			
Accounts payable		$ 22,146	$ 15,732
Accrued salaries, wages and taxes		9,181	7,490
Accrued expenses		1,452	1,472
Accrued taxes on Income—			
Currently payable		2,276	1,341
Deferred		7,413	5,685
Current portion of long-term liabilities		1,511	1,759
Total Current Liabilities		43,979	33,479
Long-term Debt		13,367	14,339
Obligations under Capitalized Leases		26,374	23,460
Shareholders' Equity		97,230	67,618
		$180,950	$138,896

Financial Position

Amounts in Thousands	Year Ended January 31,	
	1979	1978
Working Capital was Provided by:		
Net earnings	$13,667	$11,697
Charge not affecting working capital—provision for depreciation and amortization	6,285	4,721
Working capital provided by operations	19,952	16,418
Proceeds from long-term borrowings	—	1,060
Obligations under capitalized leases	4,929	10,228
Proceeds from sale of stock	18,216	—
Disposition of property and equipment	1,643	2,636
	44,740	30,342

(Continued)

Exhibit 1
(Continued)
Financial Position

Amounts in Thousands	*Year Ended January 31,* 1979	1978
Working Capital was Used for:		
Additions to property, buildings and equipment	15,663	11,599
Property leased under capitalized leases	4,929	10,228
Cash dividends paid	2,268	1,756
Reduction of long-term debt	972	1,284
Reduction of obligations under capitalized leases	2,015	3,032
Fractional shares redeemed on share distribution	3	—
	25,850	27,899
Net Increase in Working Capital	$18,890	$ 2,443
Changes in Components of Working Capital:		
Cash	$ (1,136)	$939
Short-term investments	8,996	(8,628)
Accounts and notes receivable (net)	9,744	9,928
Merchandise inventories	11,463	4,690
Prepaid expenses and other assets	323	809
Accounts payable	(6,414)	(2,983)
Accrued salaries, wages and taxes	(1,691)	(1,468)
Accrued expenses	20	(301)
Accrued taxes on income	(2,663)	225
Current portion of long-term liabilities	248	(768)
Net Increase in Working Capital	$ 18,890	$ 2,443

Merchandise inventories are stated at lower of cost (first in/first out basis) or market using the retail method.

Exhibit 2
Extract from "The Nordstrom Philosophy"

Offering an in-depth selection of quality merchandise and exceptional customer service, Nordstrom has earned a reputation for value and reliability that is perhaps unsurpassed in the Northwest. So, too, has Nordstrom grown to become a fashion leader, gathering together in tasteful contemporary settings a spectacular array of the most sought-after fashions of the day.

Central to the Nordstrom philosophy is a strong belief in an *individualized* approach to fashion. Each Nordstrom store has been carefully tailored to reflect the lifestyles of customers in the surrounding area, showcasing a wide selection of shoes, apparel and accessories in a variety of distinctive "shops" that are rich in color, texture and design. Nordstrom buyers work closely with top-quality manufacturers from both here and abroad to obtain the best values, most unique items and widest selections for their customers; and salespeople, who keep notes on their personal customers' sizes and preferences, are quick to let their customers know when something that may be of interest arrives in the store. It is, in fact, this type of customer service which is perhaps the company's greatest strength—for Nordstrom is a place where friendliness, courtesy and a sincere desire to help are the rule rather than the exception.

An individualized approach is evident *within* the company, too—in a decentralized management structure where ideas and initiative are generated from the bottom up rather than filtered from top management down. Salespeople and department managers are encouraged to implement their own ideas; buyers, who have a great deal of autonomy, are encouraged to seek out and promote new fashion directions at all times. As a result of this distribution of responsibility, Nordstrom employees possess a remarkable amount of enthusiasm—both toward their company and their customers— and motivation is often quickly rewarded, as promotions are made almost exclusively from within.

There is little doubt that the Nordstrom philosophy of selection, value and service— begun in 1901 when John W. Nordstrom opened his first shoe store in Seattle—has contributed tremendously to the company's growth throughout the Northwest and Alaska. It is also the reason Nordstrom believes it can enter new market areas with confidence in the years to come.

Exhibit 3
Results of Marketing Organization Survey

Women's Apparel

When you think of fashion, what store comes to mind first?

Store	%
Nordstrom	29.3
Bon Marche	24.2
Frederick & Nelson	10.4
J.C. Penney	7.8
Jay Jacobs	3.3
Lamonts	3.3
Sears	3.1
K Mart	2.7
I. Magnin	1.6

Description of Competition

1. Bon Marche = Full line, middle of the road, department store—division of Allied Stores
2. Frederick & Nelson = Full line, better department store with middle to higher price points—division of Marshall Field's
3. Jay Jacobs = Specialty store catering to apparel for young men and women, juniors oriented. Promotional stance. Line includes shoes.
4. Lamonts = Middle of the road department store, similar to Bon Marche but more "bread and butter" oriented.
5. I. Magnin = Women's specialty store, with upper-middle price points—division of Federated Department Stores.

Women's Apparel
Location of Last Purchase

Active Sportswear	%	Denim Jeans	%
Bon Marche	18.2	Bon Marche	19.9
Nordstrom	17.2	Nordstrom	10.5
J.C. Penney	11.7	J.C. Penney	9.1
Frederick & Nelson	6.5	Sears	5.8
Sears	6.2	K Mart	5.8
Lamonts	4.5	Jay Jacobs	5.8
K Mart	4.1	Bernies & Bottoms	4.0
Sportswest	4.1	Lamonts	3.3

Exhibit 3
(Continued)

Women's Apparel
Location of Last Purchase

Tops & Blouses		*Pants*	
Bon Marche	24.0	Bon Marche	20.5
Nordstrom	14.4	J.C. Penney	14.2
J.C. Penney	11.8	Nordstrom	13.6
Frederick & Nelson	7.4	Lamonts	6.0
Lamonts	7.4	Sears	5.7
K Mart	6.0	K Mart	5.1
Sears	4.3	Frederick & Nelson	4.3
Lerner	1.9		
Dress		*Coat/Jacket*	
Bon Marche	20.5	Nordstrom	18.5
Nordstrom	15.5	J.C. Penney	12.0
Frederick & Nelson	11.5	Bon Marche	11.7
J.C. Penney	8.7	Frederick & Nelson	9.7
Lamonts	6.2	Sears	6.2
K Mart	6.0	K Mart	4.5
Sears	4.7	People's	2.3
		Jay Jacobs	2.3
Lingerie/Foundations		*Hosiery/Pantyhose*	
J.C. Penney	23.1	J.C. Penney	16.3
Bon Marche	21.9	Safeway	16.0
Nordstrom	11.8	Grocery Store	9.8
Sears	10.3	Bon Marche	8.3
Frederick & Nelson	9.0	Frederick & Nelson	6.0
Lamonts	6.3	Sears	5.3
Fred Meyer	3.3	K Mart	4.3
K Mart	2.8	Nordstrom	3.8
		Pay'n Save	3.8
Fashion Accessories		*Shoes/Boots*	
Bon Marche	20.3	Nordstrom	34.1
Nordstrom	18.2	J.C. Penney	7.7
J.C. Penney	12.7	Bon Marche	7.7
Frederick & Nelson	6.5	Sears	5.0
Lamonts	4.8	Frederick & Nelson	4.8
Fred Meyer	3.8	Kinney Shoes	4.1
K Mart	3.8	Leed's	3.6
Sears	2.7	K Mart	2.6
		Lamonts	2.6

(Continued)

Exhibit 3
(Continued)

Men's Clothing

When you think of fashion, what store comes to mind first?

Store	%
Bon Marche	21.7
Nordstrom	17.3
J.C. Penney	9.2
Sears	9.2
Frederick & Nelson	6.6
Klopfenstein's	4.0
Squire Shop	3.8
Lamonts	1.7
Finkelstein Goldberg & Feldman	1.4

Location of Last Purchase

Suits	%	*Top Coat/Rainwear*	%
J.C. Penney	13.6	Bon Marche	13.6
Bon Marche	13.3	Sears	10.0
Nordstrom	10.9	Frederick & Nelson	9.3
Frederick & Nelson	8.5	J.C. Penney	7.9
Sears	8.2	REI	7.1
Klopfenstein's	6.7	Nordstrom	6.4
		Klopfenstein's	5.0
Sport Coat		*Shoes*	
Bon Marche	16.4	Nordstrom	29.4
J.C. Penney	13.1	J.C. Penney	13.9
Nordstrom	11.3	Sears	10.5
Sears	6.9	Bon Marche	8.7
Klopfenstein's	5.8	Kinney Shoes	8.0
Frederick & Nelson	5.8	Florsheim	4.3
Fred Meyer	2.2	Thom McAn	3.4
		Fred Meyer	2.8
		Raff's	2.8

Exhibit 3
(Continued)

Location of Last Purchase

Dress Slacks

Bon Marche	20.7
J.C. Penney	13.8
Nordstrom	10.1
Sears	10.1
Frederick & Nelson	5.2
Squire Shop	3.7
Lamonts	3.2
People's	1.7
Fred Meyer	1.4

Exhibit 4
Brief Background Information on "The Five"

	Salaries[a]	Insurance benefits as reinvestments, profit sharing, and personal benefits
Bruce A. Nordstrom—Cochairman of the board of directors. Graduated from the University of Washington in 1955 with a degree in economics. Started as a shoe salesman; was then responsible for the shoe operation in Portland. Now merchandise manager for the Women's Shoe Division.	$135,500	$16,411
John N. Nordstrom—Cochairman of the board of directors. Graduated from the University of Washington in 1958 with a degree in accounting. Started as a shoe salesman and has since managed several departments and stores. Is now merchandise manager for Men's Clothing and Shoe Division.	$135,500	$15,859
James F. Nordstrom—Director and president. Graduated from the University of Washington in 1962 with a degree in business. Worked as a shoe salesman and manager of shoe stores. Is merchandise manager for Junior Apparel, Women's Sportswear, Children's Apparel, and Women's Shoe divisions.	$135,500	$17,133
John A. McMillan—Director and executive vice president. Graduated from the University of Washington in 1957 with a degree in economics. Started in Budget Shoe Department; now merchandise manager for the Women's Ready-to-Wear Division.	$135,500	$17,380

Exhibit 4
(Continued)

	Salaries[a]	Insurance benefits as reinvestments, profit sharing, and personal benefits
Robert E. Bender—Director and senior vice president. Graduated from the University of Washington in 1958 with a degree in marketing. Worked for J.C. Penney for six years. Was hired as manager of the Northgate store in 1964. Now merchandise manager for the Accessories and Cosmetics divisions.	$104,500	$10,430

[a]Proxy statement, April 20, 1979.

Exhibit 5
Buying Organization

Department	Member of "The Five" in Charge	Description of Department Organization
JUNIORS	Jim Nordstrom	A general merchandise manager, under Mr. Jim, two buyers in each region, one each for Sportswear and Ready-to-Wear (RTW). There were two department managers (Sports and RTW) in large stores and one department manager in smaller stores. The department managers had no buying authority.
CHILDREN'S CLOTHING	Jim Nordstorm	A general merchandise manager, one buyer in each state (division), except in Washington, where the department was broken down into Infants, Boys, and Girls with a buyer for each. Only one department manager per store, and they did not have buying authority.
COSMETICS	Robert Bender	A general merchandise manager, a regional merchandise manager for every division except Washington, where there were two buyers, who divided the buying responsibility by vendor. One department manager per store, who did not have the authority to buy. However, they had to take a monthly inventory.
SHOES (MEN'S) SHOES (WOMEN'S)	John Nordstrom Bruce Nordstrom	The organization for each, though separate, was similar. Each had a general merchandise manager, and each region had a merchandise manager who controlled the open-to-buys of the department managers in each division. Thus, department managers had full authority to buy for their stores except for imports, which were bought by the merchandise manager in each region.
MEN'S CLOTHING	John Nordstrom	Entirely centralized; one buyer bought for the whole company.

Exhibit 5
(Continued)

Department	Member of "The Five" in Charge	Description of Department Organization
WOMEN'S ACCESSORIES	Robert Bender	No general merchandise manager, but a buyer in each region. Department managers in each store had the responsibility and authority to reorder.
WOMEN'S READY-TO-WEAR[a]	Jack McMillan	No general merchandise managers. However, women's clothing was broken down into several departments by name: 1. Point of View: Three buyers in Washington State (broken down by coats, knits, and dresses). Two buyers in Oregon, and one each in California and Alaska. 2. Town Square: (Modern Missy) Same structure as in Point of View except in California, where there were two buyers—one for Sportswear and one for RTW. 3. Gallery: Two buyers in Washington (dresses and coats), two buyers in Oregon, one buyer each in California and Alaska. 4. Collectors: (Better Sportswear) One buyer in Washington (who also bought for Alaska), one buyer in Oregon, and one in California. 5. Savvy One buyer for whole company (a new department).

(Continued)

Exhibit 5
(Continued)

Department	Member of "The Five" in Charge	Description of Department Organization	
WOMEN'S SPORTSWEAR	Jim Nordstorm	A general merchandise manager, then broken down as follows:	
		1. Blouses:	Five buyers—two in Washington (divided by region), and one each in other divisions.
		2. Active:	Four buyers—one in California, one in Oregon, and two in Washington, the latter also buying for Alaska.
		3. Sportswear:	Same structure as in Blouses.
		4. Equipment: (skis, etc.)	One buyer in California, one in Washington, and one in Alaska.
		One department manager per store, who handled all four categories. Department managers in Washington had the authority to buy for their stores from local vendors.	

[a]There was a department manager in each store for each department; however, they did not have buying authority.

NORDSTROM
Exhibit 6
Daily Sales by Department Store

```
DAILY COMPARATIVE DATES      MONTH TO DATE INCLUSIVE DATES              DATES EXCLUDED FROM MONTH-TO DATE
THIS YEAR  04/02/79  MONDAY   THIS YEAR  04/01/79  THROUGH  04/02/79    THIS YEAR
LAST YEAR  04/03/78  MONDAY   LAST YEAR  04/02/78  THROUGH  04/03/78    LAST YEAR
```

| | • • • DAILY NET SALES • • • | | | | • • • MONTH-TO-DATE CUMULATIVE NET SALES • • • | | | |
| | | | DIFFERENCE | | | | DIFFERENCE | |
DEPT NO. / DEPARTMENT DESCRIPTION	THIS YEAR	LAST YEAR	AMOUNT	% OF LAST YR	THIS YEAR	LAST YEAR	AMOUNT	% OF LAST YR
STORE 0001 DOWNTOWN SEATTLE								
0045 MENS POLO SHOP								
0075 MENS BRASS RAIL								
0076 MENS CLOTHING								
0077 MENS SPORTSWEAR								
0078 MENS FURNISHINGS								
0080 LUGGAGE/WORK CLOTHES								
MENS WEAR TOTAL								
0024 MENS CASUAL SHOES								
0025 MENS DRESS SHOES								
MENS SHOES TOTAL								
MENS WEAR AND SHOES TOTAL								
STORE 0001 TOTAL								
STORE 0002 NORTHGATE								
0045 MENS POLO SHOP								
0075 MENS BRASS RAIL								
0076 MENS CLOTHING								
0077 MENS SPORTSWEAR								
0078 MENS FURNISHINGS								
0080 LUGGAGE/WORK CLOTHES								
MENS WEAR TOTAL								

(Continued)

929

NORDSTROM
Exhibit 6
(Continued)

REPORT NAME   DAILY DEPARTMENT/DIVISION COMPARATIVE NET SALES
REPORT RUN DATE AND TIME   04/03/79
DATE AUDITED THROUGH   03/25/79

REPORT NUMBER   SA000000
REPORT PAGE NUMBER   8R

DAILY COMPARATIVE DATES
THIS YEAR   04/02/79   MONDAY
LAST YEAR   04/03/78   MONDAY

MONTH TO DATE INCLUSIVE DATES
THIS YEAR   04/01/79   THROUGH   04/02/79
LAST YEAR   04/02/78   THROUGH   04/03/78

DATES EXCLUDED FROM MONTH-TO DATE
THIS YEAR
LAST YEAR

| | | DAILY NET SALES | | | | | | MONTH-TO-DATE CUMULATIVE NET SALES | | | |
| | | | | DIFFERENCE | | | | | DIFFERENCE | |
DEPT NO.	DEPARTMENT DESCRIPTION	THIS YEAR	LAST YEAR	AMOUNT	% OF LAST YR	THIS YEAR	LAST YEAR	AMOUNT	% OF LAST YR
	MENS WEAR AND SHOES TOTAL								
	PLACE 100 TOTAL								
	DIVISION ALL GROUPS								
0045	MENS POLO SHOP								
0075	MENS BRASS RAIL								
0076	MENS CLOTHING								
0077	MENS SPORTSWEAR								
0078	MENS FURNISHINGS								
0080	LUGGAGE/WORK CLOTHES								
	MENS WEAR TOTAL								
0024	MENS CASUAL SHOES								
0025	MENS DRESS SHOES								
	MENS SHOES TOTAL								
	MENS WEAR AND SHOES TOTAL								
	DIVISION ALL GROUPS TOTAL								

930

NORDSTROM

Exhibit 7

Monthly Gross Margin and Inventory by Department by Store

MERCHANDISE INVENTORY REPORT

	I N V E N T O R Y			M.T.U. NET SALES		Y.T.D. NET SALES		YTD AS % OF SALES	YTD MU SHRINK %	YTD EMPL DISC %	GROSS MARGIN OF SALES	STOCK TO SALES RATIO	INVEN TURN
BEGINNING OF MONTH	END OF PERIOD	% CHG END INV TY/LY	ON ORDER	AMOUNT	% CHANGE TY/LY	AMOUNT	% OF TOTAL TY/LY	% STORE CHANGE TY/LY						

STORE 01

DEPT
01 WOMENS SHOES
WOMENS SHOES

20

26

33

36

TOTALS WOMENS SHOES

DIV TOTALS WOMENS SHOES

COATS SUITS DRESSES
TOWN SQUARE

02

09

29

32

39

43

TOTALS TOWN SQUARE

POINT OF VIEW

10

46

47

TOTALS POINT OF VIEW

NORDSTROM

Exhibit 8

Semimonthly Sales Performance by Employee

PAY PERIOD ENDING 03/31/70

LADIES SHOES

EMPLOYEE NUMBER	EMPLOYEE NAME	STORE/DEPT	SELLING HOURS WORKED	GROSS SALES	RETURNS	NET SALES	SALES PER HOUR
17554		9026	9.00	1,780.20	152.80	1,631.40	181.26
6410		9320	83.03	15,431.18	1,337.13	15,524.23	176.99
1622		9020	-3.40	17,561.62	2,787.86	15,280.52	163.86
6703		0001	80.50	11,863.95	624.45	11,219.52	139.37
6518		9020	57.60	9,581.83	1,844.32	7,737.51	134.33
1194		9020	20.00	2,835.90	182.75	2,653.15	132.65
919		9020	15.50	5,035.33	342.45	4,692.88	132.25
22		9034	112.63	17,692.31	3,165.64	14,526.67	129.01
4830		9020	87.50	12,363.80	1,252.35	11,111.45	126.98
10036		9026	96.50	12,861.71	1,428.11	11,433.60	121.59
606		9020	26.80	3,731.17	237.60	3,411.58	117.55
4004		9020	35.03	3,731.18	254.10	3,077.277	114.82
608		9020	84.00	13,200.34	1,313.20	11,947.19	115.89
7408		0020	44.01	10,757.49	1,319.57	9,566.92	115.23
6176		3201	17.27	10,546.45	1,766.27	9,482.65	112.15
9578		9001	104.70	4,888.40	464.53	4,273.65	112.13
2152		9034	47.00	2,539.95	2,877.55	11,941.89	111.93
163		9020	85.70	3,734.97	282.55	5,257.45	111.85
2449		9026	10.10	10,334.90	1,113.36	3,761.87	106.76
8726		0026	91.53	11,775.16	473.15	5,924.59	106.51
611		9036	67.13	6,009.15	1,885.57	7,155.39	105.72
5666		0320	61.00	7,229.72	851.76	6,867.60	105.46
9240		9001	73.73	8,361.73	511.60	5,124.85	105.46
229		9036	48.50	5,738.05	611.20	9,665.76	104.76
7413		9020	92.03	11,025.03	2,255.97	4,159.52	104.91
2040		9026	35.63	4,179.73	24.95	8,152.52	104.78
631P		9025	82.03	9,565.11	976.61	8,952.38	104.68
2862		9020	80.83	9,422.11	969.72	7,125.07	104.48
1609		9020	68.23	8,103.12	977.15	451.60	104.15
10544		9020	4.33	513.00	62.00	4,996.17	102.45
4455		0320	65.10	7,865.53	855.36	8,433.99	102.19
47		9020	62.50	13,438.24	1,098.25	11,414.77	101.82
6296		0320	112.10	12,639.02	494.25	5,493.63	101.23
611		0336	54.50	6,674.78	1,131.15	7,491.96	100.60
9197		9020	34.70	4,517.81	1,164.41	6,110.77	99.74
6103		9034	74.83	6,832.72	713.95	4,617.18	59.81
627		9020	61.30	4,922.83	285.65	4,467.60	98.87
3290		9026	46.90	4,943.49	345.60	3,621.41	97.31
4661		9020	47.30	3,991.51	500.10	7,817.27	97.26
7463		9020	35.30	12,713.71	321.65	4,153.62	96.55
8352		9036	44.70	7,951.16	1,509.59	4,586.61	96.71
72		9020	64.60	8,365.25	1,254.15	6,811.10	95.70
1638		9020	71.15	4,156.63	491.25	3,664.15	95.66
97		0091	63	6,649.16	436.17	6,212.79	44.63

Exhibit 9
California Store Help Wanted Advertisement

WANTED:
people power

it's something nordstrom feels very strongly about. on
may 1 we will be opening our exciting new south coast
plaza store at costa mesa...and we are now taking
applications in our search for the best possible people
to staff it:
we are looking for experienced people who want to
learn, grow and expand with us. people who genuinely
like people; who find satisfaction in helping others, in
going out of their way to be of service.
we need people with an eye for detail, a brain for
figures, a will to succeed: experienced people to handle sales, to alter and wrap; to maintain the building
and keep it stocked. people to lead and people
to follow...
we need people to make things go smoothly. people
with ideas. all kinds of people with all kinds of potential.
people power, it's the difference at nordstrom. help us
make it happen at south coast plaza.
APPLY IN PERSON ONLY:

10:00-5:00 daily beginning march 20.
use n.e. entrance to store, follow signs in stairways.

an equal opportunity employer

nordstrom

Sales Job

At Nordstrom Stores, Service Comes First
—But at a Big Price

*Retail Clerks Work Overtime
For No Pay, Are Pressured
To Meet Selling Quotas*

Claim for Back Wages Upheld

BY SUSAN C. FALUDI[1]

SEATTLE—Recently, a too-thin woman walked into employment counselor Alice Snyder's office here, slumped in a chair and burst into tears. "I know this is going to sound strange," Ms. Snyder recalls the woman saying, "but I'm sure they're going to fire me." Never mind that she had worked for weeks without a day off, pulled 15-hour shifts without a break and stockpiled stacks of service awards and customer thank-you letters. None of this mattered. She missed her sales quota and now management was questioning her "commitment" to the company.

She knew her days were numbered.

Ordinarily, Alice Snyder might classify such thinking as paranoid. But not in this case: The woman is a salesclerk at Nordstrom.

"You're not alone," Ms. Snyder says she told the woman. "You're the fourth person from that store I've seen this week." Nervous "Nordies," as they call themselves, have limped through her office so regularly—suffering from ulcers, colitis, hives and hand tremors—that Ms. Snyder finally went to speak with Nordstrom Inc.'s personnel office at the company's headquarters here. She says a manager insisted the company was one happy "family," then briskly showed her the door.

1. Staff reporter, *The Wall Street Journal.*

PRESSURE TO PERFORM

But if this prospering retailer is a family, then reports from some of the "children" suggest it's a dysfunctional one. The retailer, renowned for pampering its customers, expects its salesclerks to work many hours without pay in an environment of constant pressure and harassment that incites employees to prey on each other, according to nearly 500 complaints filed with the workers' union and interviews with several dozen employees in stores from Seattle to Los Angeles.

Last Thursday, a three-month investigation by the Washington State Department of Labor & Industries reached similar conclusions: The agency found the company systematically violated state law by failing to pay employees for a variety of duties, from delivering merchandise to inventory work, and by short-changing employees on overtime pay. The agency ordered Nordstrom to pay back wages—which the union estimates at $30 million to $40 million—or face possible legal action. (State authorities wouldn't confirm the union's estimate.)

LARGE CLAIM

"We're looking at what is likely to be the highest wage claim in the history of the state," says Mark McDermott, the agency's assistant director for employment standards. "These are employment-practice patterns the company engaged in, not isolated incidents."

Nordstrom's working conditions are the flip side of the company's phenomenal success as a retailer. In the past decade, low labor costs and a system that compels employees to compete for their paychecks have generally helped generate big earnings, a soaring stock price and sales per square foot that are the envy of the industry. Though the company says it expects to report a drop in profit for its fiscal year ended Jan. 31, its overall success in recent years has spurred the retailer to undertake a big, national expansion.

Nordstrom's customers have been a major beneficiary of the exceptional service the department store chain demands. And, no doubt, thousands of salespeople have thrived in the Darwinian struggle on the sales floor. Pat McCarthy, a longtime salesman in the flagship store's men's clothing department, is one of them. He's turned two decades of cultivating customers into commissions that yield an $80,000-plus yearly salary. "It's really a people job, which I love," says Mr. McCarthy. "Every year my sales have gotten progressively better."

But for thousands of other Nordstrom employees, the working arrangements aren't so congenial. Just as retail chains of all kinds—from Bloomingdale's to

Nordstrom Employees
(Total number of employees at Nordstrom, by year in thousands)

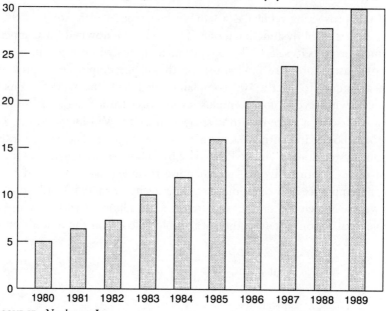

SOURCE: *Nordstrom Inc.*

Macy's—are rushing to duplicate the Nordstrom commission system, the stories of unhappiness at the company are spreading.

Salespeople were reluctant to tell their story until recently, when the union representing Nordstrom workers in the Seattle area began looking into complaints that employees are told to punch out on their timeclock before turning to the many "non-sell" duties—such as stock work and deliveries to customers. Otherwise, they were warned, the hours would dilute their critical sales-per-hour performance. A low "SPH" is grounds for dismissal.

The union, the United Food and Commercial Workers, is in the midst of contract negotiations with five Nordstrom stores in the Seattle area and has obviously been scouting for damaging data. Of Nordstrom's 30,000 employees nationwide, only 1,500 are unionized, and the union is eager to win more members and boost its influence. When union leaders began an informal inquiry into working conditions, they say they struck a mother lode of discontent, with possibly big ramifications for Nordstrom. "Unionization of other stores easily could happen as an offshoot of these developments," says Joe Peterson, president of local 1001 of the union.

Within two months, the union had received certified letters from hundreds of Nordstrom employees who have worked, on average, eight to 10 hours a week "off the clock." So many complaints came in, the union set up an 800 hotline to handle them all.

Nordstrom management says it will study the state's report and pay wage claims it considers legitimate. "We haven't seen any complaints" from the union, says Jim Nordstrom, co-chairman of the company with his brother John and cousin Bruce. He dismisses the labor board's findings as "simple record-keeping stuff" and the union's stack of claims as "a bargaining ploy." If employees are working without pay, breaks or days off, then it's "isolated" or by "choice," he says.

"A lot of them say, 'I want to work every day.' I have as many people thank us for letting them work all these hours as complain." In fact, Jim Nordstrom suspects employees aren't putting in as much time as they might. "I think people don't put in enough hours during the busy time," he says. "We need to work harder."

Nordstrom's incentives, some employees say, tend to be more stick than carrot. While good customer service is rewarded with cheers at company meetings, occasional $5, $10 and $100 bonuses, or "All-Star" honors, a steady flow of threatening management memos seems to be the preferred motivational tool. One Aug. 29, 1989 memo, issued by a Nordstrom cosmetics manager in a California store, is typical. It set a long list of goals for the cosmetics counters and made clear that, "In the next 60 days if any of these areas are not met to our expectations you will be terminated." Another manager's memo reminds employees that it is considered "a lot" to call in sick once every three months and will bring into "question your dedication."

STOKING THE VOLUME

"It reminds me of a cult the way they program you to devote your life to Nordstrom," says Cherie Validi, a salesperson in the women's clothing department who has spent her share of days off making home deliveries and attending Nordstrom's pep rallies, where blond bathing beauties prance on stage, chanting "Vol-ume! Vol-ume!" "Granted, the customer gets treated like a hundred bucks. And Nordstrom gets rich off it. So nobody loses—except the employee," she says.

Ms. Validi, one of the top saleswomen in her department, came out the loser herself recently when she received a $100 paycheck for two weeks of work. Why? The commission on a customer's $6,000 return was deducted from her wages, standard practice at Nordstrom. Ms. Validi complained that the sale wasn't hers, that it took place on a day she didn't work. But the company held firm.

Nordstrom insists the system works. It says that employees get one of the highest base pay rates in the industry—as much as $10 an hour—and especially industrious employees can make as much as $80,000 a year. The company also says it only promotes from within and, under its corporate policy of decentralization, managers have unusual freedom to make decisions. "A lot of what comes out makes it sound like we're slave drivers," says Jim Nordstrom, or "Mr. Jim," as he is called by his employees. "If we were that kind of company, they wouldn't smile, they wouldn't work that hard. Our people smile because they want to."

But employees say Nordstrom's high base pay isn't much comfort. Workers only receive base pay if they don't sell enough to qualify for commission—and if they miss that sales quota several times, they're fired. Moreover, of the 1,500 salespeople in the union, the company lists only seven as having made more than $40,000 last year. (Nordstrom won't reveal the number for its roughly 20,000 non-union salespeople, but says union and non-union employees make an average of $20,000 to $24,000 a year. The national average, for all retail salesclerks, is $12,000 a year.)

BE HAPPY

Even the smiles aren't necessarily a reliable gauge of employee sentiment. Nordstrom periodically dispatches "Secret Shoppers," people hired to dress up as customers, to check on workers' demeanor. A frown can wind up as a demerit in an employee file. The company also encourages Smile Contests. "They would go around and take pictures of whoever smiled the most" and then hang the photos in the lunchroom, recalls Andrea Barton, who worked for three years at a Nordstrom cosmetics counter in Seattle; she says she lost 20 pounds in the process. "I'd look at those pictures and go, 'Boy, some day I hope I'm up here.'" She groans. "I mean, the way I got when I was [working] there, it's just sickening."

She is only one of the more than 30 Nordstrom veterans, both current and former employees, who voiced such sentiments in interviews. Here are a few of their stories:

A divorced California homemaker who returned to the job market at 40, Patty Bemis joined Nordstrom in 1981, lured by the promise of a bigger income and the "status" of induction in the Nordie elite. She stayed for eight years.

"They came to me," she recalls of the Nordstrom recruiters. "I was working at The Broadway as Estee Lauder's counter manager and they said they had heard I had wonderful sales figures." Ms. Bemis was thrilled. "We'd all heard

Nordstrom was the place to work. They told me how I would double my wages. They painted a great picture and I fell right into it."

She soon found herself working progressively harder—for less money and amid more fear.

"The managers were these little tin gods, always grilling you about your sales," she recalls. "You felt like your job was constantly in jeopardy. They'd write you up for anything, being sick, the way you dressed." Once, she had to get a doctor's note so she wouldn't get in trouble for wearing low-heel shoes to work. Sufficiently cowed, she reported to work even when she had strep throat.

Worn down by the pressure, "the girls around me were dropping like flies," she says. "Everyone was always in tears. You feel like an absolute nothing working for them."

TAKING OUT THE TRASH

Ms. Bemis was consistently one of her department's top sellers, but some years she only made $18,000, far below what she had expected she would earn. She won a companywide sales contest, and received "a pair of PJs," she recalls. "Whoopie-doo!" And she logged many unpaid hours, delivering cosmetics to customers and unpacking hundreds of boxes of makeup. The department rarely had more than one stock person and, in some of the stores, the salesclerks are expected to empty the trash. Jim Nordstrom explains: "Yes, we're always cutting back on stock people." He adds: "It may have happened that some people were asked to pitch in" and carry out the trash. "That would be great if that happened. If people don't want to, then obviously some people don't want to work hard."

Ms. Bemis recalls that "working off the clock was just standard," crucial to elevating sales per hour. "In the end, really serving the customer, being an All-Star, meant nothing; if you had low sales per hour, you were forced out."

During a big Clinique sale, Ms. Bemis says she worked 12 and 15 hour shifts for a number of days without overtime pay or a day off. On the drive home at 10:30 on the tenth night, she passed out at the wheel and slammed into the freeway's center divider, she says. While she was at home recovering from head injuries, she recalls, "The manager kept calling me and saying, 'Patty, we can't hold your job any longer.'" Her doctor told her she should stay out a few more weeks but she didn't dare. "Now, I know I have all these rights. But at the time all I knew was I had to have that job."

She finally left last spring. "I just couldn't take it anymore—the constant demands, the grueling hours. I just said one day, life's too short." She took a sales post at Scandia Down Shops, where she says she makes $400 more a month than at Nordstrom. "And I can sleep at night."

A BROKEN CLOCK

The first time Lori Lucas came to one of the many "mandatory" Saturday morning department meetings and saw the sign—"Do Not Punch the Clock"— she assumed the managers were telling the truth when they said the clock was temporarily out of order. But as weeks went by, she discovered the clock was always "broken" or the timecards were just missing.

Finally, she and several other employees just marked the hours down on their timecard manually. She and another employee recall that their manager whited-out the hours and accused the two of not being "team players." The employees took the tampered timecards to the California labor board. In response to the state agency's inquiry, the company reimbursed four employees for the time, according to a notification the company filed with the labor board.

> **Cherie Validi:**
> *"It reminds me of a cult. . . . Granted, the customer gets treated like a hundred bucks. And Nordstrom gets rich off it. So nobody loses—except the employee."*

The department meetings "were unbelievable," Ms. Lucas recalls. "There you'd be at seven in the morning and they had all these security guards dressed up like the California Raisins, with plastic garbage bags stuffed with M&Ms around their midriffs. And all you can hear is people chanting, 'We're number one!' and 'You want to do it for Nordstrom.' Finally I went up to the store manager and said, 'What is this all about?' and she said, 'You are here to learn the Nordstrom Way.'"

The Nordstrom Way involved an endless round of contests ("Who Looks More Nordstrom" was a popular one, intended to encourage employees to shop at the stores) and the daily recital of "affirmations" ("I only sell multiples," was one chanted by salespeople). And the Nordstrom Way, Ms. Lucas discovered, meant working for free. "My manager would say, 'You go clock out and come down and we'll talk.' That was her little trick way of saying there's non-sell work to do." Ms. Lucas's manager declines to comment.

Like most salesclerks at Nordstrom, Ms. Lucas also had daily quotas of thank-you letters to write, and monthly customer-service "books" to generate—photo albums that are supposed to be filled with letters from grateful customers. ("People would get so desperate they would have their friends and relatives write fake letters for them," Petra Rousu, a 10-year salesclerk veteran, recalls.) Such duties, Ms. Lucas says, were supposed to be tackled only after hours. "I'd be up till 3 a.m., doing my letters, and doing my manager's books," she says. "Before you know it, your whole life is Nordstrom. But you couldn't complain, because then your manager would schedule you for the bad hours, your sales per hour would fall and next thing you know, you're out the door."

The pressure eventually gave Ms. Lucas an ulcer, she says. One day, after working 22 days without a day off, she demanded a lunch break. On her hour off, she applied for and got a new job elsewhere and gave notice as soon as she returned. "I remember thinking, I'm making less than $20,000 a year. Why am I killing myself? Nordstrom was the most unfair place I ever worked."

STAYING ON TOP

Every pay period, the Nordies gather around the bulletin board in the back room to view the chart. It ranks employees by sales per hour, and woe to anyone whose name falls below the red line.

Over the years, the need to stay above the line has inspired an ingenious set of scams and predatory maneuvers on the sales floor, some employees assert. "Sharking," as it's called, is so rampant that at one pep rally, the saleswomen did a skit to the music from "Jaws" and presented a shark mask to an employee they considered particularly conniving.

Some Nordies boost their sales per hour by hogging the register and taking all the "walk-ups," or customers who haven't been helped, workers say. Some have been known to cut a deal with the few non-commission cashiers on the floor, who then ring up sales on the employee's identification number. Others get their rival's number and use it when accepting returns.

When all else fails, there's one way to push your name up the list: Bump off the number-one seller.

For nearly two years, Cindy Nelson had stayed on top of the chart in one of the Bellevue, Wash., stores. She was on her way to making "Pacesetter" again— a prestigious title bestowed upon the employees with the top sales. A clique of salesclerks on the floor—led by numbers two and three on the charts—held a powwow one day, decided that Ms. Nelson must be stealing their sales and vowed to have her "watched," according to court depositions that later became part of a suit filed by Ms. Nelson against Nordstrom in Bellevue, Wash.

On September 29, 1986, Cindy Nelson reported for work and was immediately whisked into the personnel office. The department manager had before her five notes of complaint from the salesclerks, all unsigned, which claimed Ms. Nelson had been stealing sales.

DUE PROCESS

Ms. Nelson asked to inspect the sales receipts in question and confront her accusers, but the manager, Rhoda Eakes, refused. "I just didn't feel that it was any of her business," Ms. Eakes explained later in a deposition. Then she told Ms. Nelson that she was fired. (All of the managers and employees involved in Ms. Nelson's firing declined comment, referring queries to Mr. Nordstrom, who said, "That gal wasn't a good employee.")

"I was totally stunned," recalls Ms. Nelson, who had a stack of customer-service citations in her file and had been told she was about to make manager. She was also, up until then, "your 100-percent gung-ho Nordie. This whole time I thought I was going to be this great Nordstrom person and now I was nothing, a nobody. I became an emotional wreck."

She tried applying to other Nordstrom stores but was repeatedly rejected. Finally, she took a job in a small dress shop—and filed suit. Last October, a King County Superior Court jury awarded her $180,000 in damages. The company and Ms. Nelson later settled out of court for an undisclosed sum.

In Ms. Nelson's court case, Nordstrom's Achilles heel proved to be its employee handbook, which outlined the terms and procedures for warning and firing employees. The company has subsequently replaced the 20-page rulebook with a one-page sheet, and one rule: "Use your good judgment in all situations," it says.

Jim Nordstrom says management chose to rewrite the manual after receiving a raft of lawsuits from ex-employees. "Our wrongful termination problems have gone way down since we got rid of that darn handbook," he says.

THAT SPECIAL LOOK

Part of becoming a Nordie, employees say, involves acquiring a certain look. Lupe Sakagawa, a top saleswoman, recalls that on her first day on the job, her manager strong-armed her into buying $1,400 of the "right" clothes—all from the department. But that wasn't enough: The store manager then called her in and told her: "Correct your accent." Ms. Sakagawa is Mexican. "It was very hard for me to prove myself," she says, "because of that image of the Nordstrom Girl—blond hair, young and cute."

For years, moreover, minority leaders in Seattle have complained of the company's failure to hire and promote blacks. In 1987, after the company was hit with seven discrimination complaints filed with the Equal Employment Opportunity Commission, Nordstrom hired a consulting firm to rebut the charges. But the consultant's confidential report—subsequently leaked—turned out to be a stinging attack on Nordstrom's "band-aid approach" to affirmative action. "The current lack of definitive personnel policies and procedures . . . perpetuates a system of institutional racism," the report said, "and has had little utility in preventing previous overt racist acts."

Since then, Jim Nordstrom says, the company has hired a black human resources officer and "our minority numbers are outstanding." But he declines to reveal them. Charles Dudley, the human resource officer, won't supply the statistics either: "You'll have to talk to Mr. Jim about that," he says. He did confirm that no company vice presidents are black or Hispanic.

Patty Bemis:
"In the end, really serving the customer, being an All-Star, meant nothing; if you had low sales per hour, you were forced out."

Then there's the case of Sean Mulholland, a salesman who says he paid the price for failing to fit another aspect of the "Nordstrom image." He is gay.

In 1986, Mr. Mulholland started working in the men's clothing department in the Alderwood, Wash., store. He was careful to keep his private life a secret. A Nordie true believer, Mr. Mulholland accumulated a dozen company awards and a sales rating that never fell below No. 3 on the charts, according to records he has saved. "To me, Nordstrom was the Golden Fleece," he says. "I was so proud to work there. I strived to be what they wanted."

RAINING DOLLARS

His faith remained unshaken in spite of some of the company's more bizarre rituals, like the time employees were sent outside for a "surprise." On the roof, a Nordie tossed down $1 bills tied in yellow ribbons. Mr. Mulholland recalls watching, dumbfounded, as fellow clerks scrambled for the cash. "I got this picture in my head: peasants groveling for the loaves of bread from the castle," he says.

But Mr. Mulholland stuck by the company until soon after he discovered he had AIDS. He told no one at the store about his illness. He had heard the jokes around the store about "fag" customers—"don't shake their hands."

When Mr. Mulholland contracted a lung infection, he had to call in sick. His manager phoned him repeatedly at home and demanded an explanation. After four days, Mr. Mulholland reported to work. He was at once summoned to personnel.

"They just dug into me, 'Why were you sick?' 'Where's your doctor's excuse?'" He told them he had an upper respiratory infection, but still they pressed him, he says.

"Finally I broke down crying. As a last resort to save my job, I told them I had AIDS," he says. Honesty backfired. The manager sent him home and told him to stay there. When he tried to return, he says, she told him the company had filled his job and there were no openings.

Nordstrom spokeswoman Kellie Tormey maintains that Mr. Mulholland "asked to leave. It was entirely his choice." Nordstrom made "numerous attempts to find something else for him, but he never once followed up on these opportunities."

But Mr. Mulholland has saved copies of the rejection letters he received from Nordstrom managers as he attempted, 16 times in the course of the ensuing year and a half, to apply for job postings at four Nordstrom stores in the area. He was always turned away. "Finally I got the picture. They just cut the chain. One day I'm great, the next day I'm garbage."

VALUING TEAM SPIRIT

Nordstrom officials brush aside such stories as the gripes of a few bad seeds. "Our people development is probably the most significant advantage our company has," Ms. Tormey says. "If you speak to employees in the stores, you'll see that it's a company that really values the team spirit." But an attempt to walk in the stores and do that is resisted. Ms. Tormey explains: "If you want to interview someone, we need to know ahead of time. That's just one of the things we're sensitive to." Finally, the public relations office picks a slate of employees for interviews. Kathleen Sargent is one of them.

"It's a feeling, it's family," Ms. Sargent says enthusiastically, as she settles into a vinyl chair in the employee cafeteria. A public relations official sits at her side.

"Sure, during the busy seasons, you do work six to seven days a week," Ms. Sargent says. "But being in the store with the Christmas tree here, you create your own memories." Ms. Sargent, who has worked for Nordstrom in Seattle for seven years, says she doesn't mind working for free. "When I go home and do follow-ups or write thank-yous, I think it's inappropriate to be charging the company for that."

It turns out that Ms. Sargent is also the goddaughter of Anne Nordstrom, Bruce Nordstrom's sister. "I don't see what that has to do with anything," Ms. Sargent says, when she is asked about it later. "I'm sure the advertising people didn't even know that when they picked me to talk to the press."

At the San Francisco store, another set of company-approved employees testify to the company's virtues. "Here at Nordstrom, I feel I can be the best that I can be," says Doris Quiros, a salesperson in the women's sportswear department. While other retailers "give you a big book of rules, when I came here, Nordstrom gave me one with only one rule: Use your best judgment. That's because they want me to be my own boss."

In the women's shoes department, Tim Snow, a former waiter, says people are impressed now when they learn where he works. "You can be at the grocery store and you show them your ID card and they'll start right off on how much they love to shop there."

The reasons people do love to shop at Nordstrom are plainly evident one recent Saturday afternoon in Mr. Snow's department. Sitar and tabla players serenade shoppers with soothing music as salesclerks proffer Nordstrom's much-vaunted service. But the scene isn't nearly so genteel back in the stockroom, where harried employees clang up and down metal stairs, balancing towers of shoeboxes. Lining the walls are the ubiquitous performance charts and sales contests. "Make Your Goal," instructs one sign. "Don't Let Us Down!" says another. "Be a Top Dog Pacesetter! Go for the Golden Milkbones!!" says a third. One salesclerk stops for a second to eye a visitor taking notes. Finally she asks, only half-joking, "Are you with the Nordstrom Secret Service?"

Irate Nordstrom
Straining in Labor Fight
BY FRANCINE SCHWADEL[1]

Adversaries in the Nordstrom Union Battle:
Joe Peterson,
President, Local 1001, United Food & Commercial Workers
Union:
"As far as I'm concerned, we're having a strike without
having a strike."

Jim Nordstrom,
Co-Chairman, Nordstrom Inc.
"We got our brains beat out of us."

SEATTLE—A pensive Jim Nordstrom, his hands together as in prayer, is trying to fathom the firestorm of controversy that suddenly has marred the reputation for stellar service at the retail chain bearing his name.

"We were naive to think the product would speak for itself," says the Nordstrom Inc. co-chairman. "We got our brains beat out of us."

Mr. Nordstrom is smarting from the fallout of the fight his family picked last year with its weak clerks union, which has since retaliated with a barrage of accusations. There have been national press accounts of complaints that the retailer's vaunted service comes on the backs of the salespeople. There's been a ruling by Washington state regulators supporting that view. A union lawsuit. Shareholder litigation. Even union allegations that Nordstrom deceives shoppers by selling clothes its salespeople have worn—a charge Nordstrom denies.

It is impossible to predict whether the union spat will turn off Nordstrom customers or detract from the service they receive. The company is in the midst of a major national expansion. But whatever the outcome of the fight, the Nordstroms are taking the attack on their family-run business personally. They already pay some of the highest wages in retailing.

---

1. Staff reporter, *The Wall Street Journal.*

The company may have underestimated the abilities of a modern union. It is learning firsthand that organized labor is capable of tactics far more sophisticated than the traditional strike or boycott. The United Food & Commercial Workers Union, which represents about 2,000 of Nordstrom's 30,000 employees, is now attracting national attention to issues that Nordstrom had assumed last year were only of local interest.

"The tactics that were traditional in the past didn't work out well in the 1980s," says Daniel Mitchell, an industrial-relations professor at the University of California at Los Angeles. He says that the Nordstrom case is an example of a broad attempt by unions to try new strategies.

Nordstrom ignited the dispute last June when it angered labor leaders with an unusual contract proposal: Optional union membership for employees at its six stores in the Seattle and Tacoma areas. When the Seattle local put the proposal to a vote, only about 250 of its 1,500 members showed up. They overwhelmingly rejected the idea.

That's when the union, which has represented Nordstrom employees in hometown Seattle for more than 60 years, threatened to start a public-relations war. Nordstrom stood its ground.

"The company vastly underestimated our resolve to protect not only this contract but the other retail contracts" in the area, contends Joe Peterson, a former Nordstrom shoe salesman who heads Local 1001. "Optional union dues systems are meant to do one thing: to eliminate the contract."

Company officials insist they aren't trying to bust the union. Management proposed the contract change, Mr. Nordstrom says, because employees had complained over the years about mandatory union dues. "It's been a source of irritation for what we felt was the majority," he says.

President Jack McMillan, noting that union members in Seattle get the same wages and benefits as non-union Nordstrom salespeople elsewhere, calls the dues "a bad buy."

The union considered a strike against popular Nordstrom "suicidal," Mr. Peterson says. But it seized the opportunity to take on the company over what has come to be known as the "off-the-clock" issue.

Mr. Peterson says Nordstrom salespeople complained to the union that they were pressured to work without pay to attend store meetings and to perform other duties such as stock work, writing thank-you notes to customers and delivering merchandise to customers' homes and offices. Initially, Mr. Peterson says even he didn't believe that the practices were widespread.

Since then, a union inquiry uncovered 825 current and former salespeople who claim the company owes them more than $5.3 million in back wages. The state's Department of Labor and Industries, backing the union, ordered Nordstrom to change its practices and pay back wages. And the chain, after months of denying the charges, created a $15 million reserve for settling back-pay claims. It says it has already paid about $1 million to workers outside Washington state. It also changed its record-keeping procedures and vowed to pay salespeople for all time worked.

But Mr. Nordstrom insists "the off-the-clock issue is a nothing issue." He hints that Nordstrom may challenge the state ruling. "We don't think it will hold up under federal scrutiny," he says. "We think the law says if the bulk of their income is commissions, they're free to go to whatever lengths they want to sell more things. If it means doing things from home, we feel in most industries it means the time doesn't have to be accounted for."

The company also complains that it has been treated unfairly by the press, including this newspaper, which ran a page one story in February on working conditions at the company. Last week, Nordstrom announced a sharp cutback in advertising in Seattle's two daily newspapers. Company officials deny they were retaliating for unfavorable coverage. Mr. Nordstrom was quoted in the Seattle Times as saying "We think your coverage is horrible, the worst in the nation."

Nordstrom continues to believe the morale of most of its employees is good— but the union continues to fire a fusillade of complaints about the company to regulators, the courts and the press.

At Nordstrom stores, where Mr. Peterson acknowledges that union support "has always been the weakest" among the chains he has under contract, employees are choosing sides. Some have quit the union since its contract with Nordstrom expired August 1. The pro-company forces have attended rallies in Seattle and elsewhere along the West Coast.

Roughly half of the employees in Seattle and Tacoma have signed petitions seeking to decertify the union. "We're very angry about the way the union has slandered the company and the integrity of the people who work for the company," says John Rockwood, a shoe salesman in Seattle leading one of the anti-union drives.

"All the salespeople here operate as entrepreneurs," he says. As for the state's finding, he contends: "It's petty little time-keeping stuff. We make twice as much money as anybody else in the industry. We just haven't kept meticulous records as to the time we have actually spent working for the company."

But the National Labor Relations Board last week dismissed the Tacoma petition because of unresolved charges of unfair labor practices. And Mr. Rockwood's decertification drive met the same fate Monday. NLRB officials say they consider decertification efforts inappropriate when charges of unfair labor practices against an employer are pending.

In one charge, which the labor board has consolidated into its own complaint against the company, the union asserts that Nordstrom enhanced employees' vacation benefits without negotiating with the union. The labor board also is looking into a union complaint that Nordstrom sponsored the anti-union rallies.

The union's Mr. Peterson contends that the company is drumming up anti-union sentiment and aiding the anti-union forces in other ways. He claims that Mr. Rockwood's schedule was changed so he could lead the anti-union petition drive. Mr. Rockwood says he was able to take a week off to gather signatures because "business hasn't been great."

Still, even Mr. Rockwood can't explain how green pro-company buttons, proclaiming "No One Asked Us," suddenly showed up in the stores in February. "They just appeared in our department one morning," says Helen Thompson, who sells designer women's clothes in Tacoma.

Employees who support the union say the pressure from management isn't subtle. "The atmosphere here is, if you're pro-union, you're anti-Nordstrom," says Sherry Jacobson, who sold women's clothes at the store in Bellevue, Wash., until quitting this week. "Jim Nordstrom called me and said, 'I want to know why you have to hurt the company that way.'" She says he was referring to interviews she had done with a newspaper and a local TV station.

The company also produced a 22-minute videotape, shown recently to Nordstrom employees. In the video, Bruce Nordstrom, a cousin of Jim Nordstrom and one of three third-generation family members who share the title of co-chairman, explains the unfavorable press by saying: "Evidently, the union in Seattle feels so vehemently about the issue of union security that they're willing to attack us, even if it means dirty tricks and untruths that are being propagated in the press."

In the video, Bruce Nordstrom admits the company has been "sloppy" in some of its record keeping and is "taking every step possible to make sure that is cleared up." But he narrows his eyes for emphasis and says: "I view it as a personal attack. I would hope that . . . you folks feel it's a personal attack on you also."

Mr. Peterson, meanwhile, vows he won't give up the fight. "These issues are not going to go away," he says. "As far as I'm concerned, we're having a strike without having a strike."

Benetton (A)

In late 1982, Luciano Benetton was deciding how the Benetton Group should best carry out its plans to enter the U.S. and Japanese markets for casual-wear garments. In an office decorated with frescoes carefully restored to their original beauty in the splendid eighteenth-century Villa Minelli in Ponzano Veneto near Treviso, he spoke forcefully of the situation facing the company:

> When speaking of the "second-generation" Benetton, I am thinking of a new business reality which is extra-European in scope. But we have to take into account the diverse requirements of the markets we are planning to enter.

In addition to planning its product presentation for these markets, Benetton's management was reviewing alternative methods of providing production and logistical support for new markets. It hoped that some or all of the unique features of the company's marketing and operating strategies could be preserved to provide the company with the advantages it would need in these new, highly competitive markets.

COMPANY BACKGROUND

The Benetton[1] Group was part of the INVEP Group, an organization of business activities equally controlled by three brothers, Luciano, Gilberto, and Carlo Benetton, and their sister, Giuliana. By specializing in the production and retailing of casual-wear clothing items, particularly woolen sweaters, cotton T-shirts, and jeans, Benetton had, by 1982, become the world leader in the field of knitwear.

Professor Sergio Signorelli of the Istituto Studi Direzionali SpA and Professor James L. Heskett of the Harvard Graduate School of Business Administration prepared this case as the basis for class discussion rather than to illustrate either effective or ineffective handling of an administrative situation. Portions of it are based on a case, "Benetton," prepared by Professor Signorelli. Selected data in the case are based on estimates or are disguised. Copyright © 1984 by the Istituto Studi Direzionali SpA and the President and Fellows of Harvard College; Harvard Business School case #9-685-014 (Rev. 2/89).

1. Pronounced be-net-ón. Many people mistakenly pronounce the name as if it were spelled b-e-n-e-l-t-o-n. Names ending in consonants, while not typical of Italy in general, are quite common in the region in which Treviso is located.

In that year, it sold 26.9 million units of clothing, of which nearly half were for export from Italy. It supplied more than 1,900 shops, nearly all of which stocked only Benetton products. Benetton was the largest consumer of wool in the world, purchasing nearly nine million pounds in 1982. About 60% of all garments sold through Benetton stores were made of wool.

The Benettons had grown their business from rather meager beginnings. Their father, a truck driver in Treviso, a town situated north of Venice, had died just after World War II when the eldest child, Luciano, was 10 years old; he and his siblings thus had to find work at an early age. In 1965, Luciano and Giuliana, deciding that their complementary skills could provide the basis for a venture, formed Benetton. At the time, Giuliana was sewing woolen sweaters of traditional somber colors and scratchy wool for one of the region's many textile artisans; on her own, she developed more colorful and fashionable designs. Luciano, a wholesaler who sold the output of artisans to department stores, remarked: "I saw Giuliana's designs and I was sure I could sell them."[2]

Soon the pair had their first success with a violet pullover made of a soft blend of wool, angora, and cashmere. Other colorful sweaters achieved similar success, and the two younger Benetton brothers joined the partnership. Gilberto, formerly employed by the Crafts Association of Treviso, was put in charge of administration and Carlo, a draftsman in a small local engineering company, assumed responsibility for production.

The Benettons initially sold their products through leading Italian department stores. By 1968, their product line had expanded, and they opened their first shop in Belluno. It occupied only about 400 square feet, in part because the Benetton product line was still relatively limited at the time. But it set the pattern for the stores to follow. By 1975, the Benettons owned or franchised some 200 shops throughout Italy.

In 1978, the company achieved $78 million in sales, 98% of it in Italy. That same year, Benetton launched a major export program to the rest of Europe that provided the basis for even more significant growth. By 1982, Benetton's sales had grown to roughly $311 million,[3] or about two-thirds of INVEP Group sales. The latter included revenues of 20% from Benetton Cotone (cotton), as well as from three manufacturing operations. *Exhibits 1* and *2* present financial statements for the Benetton Group.

---

2. Kenneth Labich, "Benetton Takes on the World," *Fortune*, June 13, 1983, p. 114.

3. Actual sales figures for Benetton were 404 billion lire and for INVEP, 624 billion lire. An approximate average exchange rate of $1 = 1,300 lire has been assumed throughout the case for 1982.

THE KNITWEAR INDUSTRY

The knitwear industry comprised basic categories of knitted underwear, hosiery, and knitted overwear. Its development in Italy and the United States had followed distinctly different paths.

In Italy, knitted overwear represented about two-thirds of the industry production. In general, knitted overwear production involved more steps, more labor, less expensive equipment, and lower levels of technology than either underwear or hosiery production.

Starting with the low-level industrialization of knitting between 1870 and 1890, the industry extended from the Biella area across northern Italy. By the 1980s, it was concentrated among small subcontractors who specialized in one or more of the several production steps shown in *Exhibit 3*.

This so-called externally decentralized system of production had evolved from the original homework system. Through the 1950s, reliance on homework had offered companies significant labor cost savings, since it often meant low wages and no responsibility for fringe benefits. It limited investment in fixed assets to that required for simple knitting machines. It had allowed a company to smooth its work load while passing on fluctuations to individual homeworkers. And it had provided surprisingly high productivity.

In the 1950s, institutions called *groupers* began to appear. Groupers were owned by artisans who served as intermediaries between a company and homeworkers, collecting orders and in some cases material from contracting companies, distributing work to individuals paid directly by the grouper, and guaranteeing the final product. Relationships among companies, groupers, and homeworkers seldom were exclusive.

By the 1970s, small subcontractor companies had replaced many of the homeworkers. There were several reasons for this: growth in the sector requiring subcontractors with greater production capability; more complex products; the passage of a new law on homework introducing standards and making use of homework more expensive and less flexible; and the introduction in 1973 of tax reform to discourage hidden income. As a result, the importance of the grouper had declined.

Nevertheless, according to a 1981 estimate by Databank, the knitted overwear sector of Italy consisted of approximately 17,500 companies (consisting in turn of 27,000 local units) employing a total of 130,000 people other than homeworkers. There were perhaps only 17 companies with 250 employees or more. Benetton dominated these, with more than three times the sales volume of the next-largest manufacturer in the industry.

Italy had become the largest producer of knitted overwear in Europe, producing 60% of all European Economic Community output in 1977; the United Kingdom followed with 16%. Of Italy's production, 47% was for export, with Germany (38.5% of Italian exports) representing by far the largest market, followed by France and the Benelux countries. In total, EEC countries took 80% of Italy's exports. Unlike major exports from the Far East, most Italian exports of knitted overwear were marketed abroad under the trademarks of the producing companies.

Imports of knitted overwear garments in the EEC had been restricted by a series of Multifibre Agreements, which imposed strict limits on the growth of imports of such items from non-EEC countries. The current agreement extended such controls to 1986. By 1982, only 19% of the 810 million items of knitted overwear sold in the EEC originated from outside the community. Twenty-seven percent originated from EEC countries other than Italy, with Italian firms commanding a 54% share of total sales.

In the United States, the knitwear industry concentrated on the production of knitted underwear and hosiery. The need for high productivity in these sectors had resulted in high investments, factories employing hundreds of persons, and vertically integrated companies engaged in many stages between spinning yarn and producing finished garments. The largest of these companies was Burlington Industries, with 1982 sales of more than $2.5 billion. The strong promotion of, and preference for, garments of synthetic yarns had accentuated the trend toward investment and industry consolidation. Manufacturers of knitted overwear, in contrast, had steadily declined in importance. Of the nearly one billion knitted overwear garments sold in the United States in 1982, about 40% were imported, primarily from the Far East. This percentage was significantly higher in the lower-priced categories.

MANUFACTURING

The basic process for producing knitted overwear garments from wool and cotton is shown in *Exhibit 3*. Traditionally, it had involved spinning or purchasing and dyeing yarn, warehousing spun material in finished or unfinished form, finishing operations such as mercerizing (immersion in caustic soda to produce a shinier material), waxing (to improve gliding properties and reduce friction during manufacturing and cleaning), and removing residual oil.

For women's garments, for example, a prototype and sample collection were prepared. At Benetton, this was generally done four times per year under Giuliana Benetton's direction—twice for the major spring-summer and fall-winter collections and twice for "integrative" collections for Christmas and for sport. A major collection usually contained 450 items, and the "integrative" collection following it featured perhaps 50 fashion-oriented items. The same line was created for all countries. About half of the items contained in the two main collections represented about 90% of sales.

Once designed, garments were manufactured by machines that produced parts of garments in their correct shapes or woven materials that had to be shaped. The next stage, assembly, involved joining the basic parts of each garment, such as front, back, and sleeves for sweaters. This could be accomplished in a visible manner with the edges of two parts sewn together; for higher-quality garments, a remeshing process that produced an invisible seam was used. The latter process was used for most Benetton garments. Finishing operations included making buttonholes, sewing buttons, ironing, labeling, and final inspection prior to packaging for shipment.

Unlike knitted products made of natural materials, garments made from synthetic fibers, which dominated the U.S. market, could be shaped and assembled with highly machine-intensive operations. These products ranged from hosiery, which could be produced nearly totally by machine in several operations, to knitted underwear, for which finishing operations often were simple and inexpensive.

Putting Fashion on an Industrial Level

Benetton had, over the years, been an innovator in the production of knitted overwear products. For example, 10 years before the development of machinery for making hard and rough wool soft and pliable, Luciano Benetton had improved on a crude process that he had observed in Scotland for achieving this effect, which was produced by rudimentary machines with wooden arms that battered the raw knitwear in water. Similarly, to avoid the use of centrifugal dryers that shrank the wet knitwear, Benetton developed a process that placed the knitwear in a bag on a stick and rotated it vertically in the air.

When women's seamless stockings became popular in the 1960s, hosiery knitting machines that could only produce seamed stockings became obsolete. One of Benetton's employees had recommended buying and converting the equipment for the production of overwear. Machines that had provided 90% of Benetton's knitting capacity in its early years were thus purchased for approximately $1,000 per machine, were converted for an additional $4,000 each, and performed the work of machines valued at much more. They were eventually replaced by more modern knitting machines, some of them driven by magnetic tape programmed to provide intricate knitted designs.

Perhaps the most significant development in Benetton's operations occurred in 1972, when the company began dyeing assembled garments rather than yarn. This process required that garments first be treated in a strong chemical solution for about 20 minutes to soften them and increase their receptiveness to dye. Next, garments were "cooked" for 40 minutes and then stirred in dye-filled vats. The vat time required for the entire process, including time for softening, was about two hours.

The dyeing rooms at the Ponzano plant contained 10 smaller vats in which batches of about 300 garments were processed. Careful loading of batches and checking of dyes were required to ensure desired colors. The room also contained four newer dyeing machines with automatic dye control and water-extracting capability, each with a capacity of 530 garments per batch.

Dyeing represented a bottleneck at the Ponzano factory. As a result, for much of 1983 the dyeing machines were operated on a three-shift basis. Even though the process was critical to product quality, Benetton could dye only about 35% of its total production at the Ponzano factory and an additional 20% at other company plants. The remaining 45% was dyed by contractors, with more than half of it dyed by two large contractors owned by the Benetton family.

Labor and production overhead costs for garments dyed after manufacture were estimated to be 10% higher than those for garments knitted from dyed thread. Benetton was the only major manufacturer of woolen garments that dyed them from gray stock.

The garment-dyeing capability allowed more popular items in Benetton's line to be produced in response to requests for changes in preseason orders from agents serving retail outlets. As a result, it was estimated that Benetton's inventory turnover for cotton and woolen items at the factory and warehouse was no more than the typical industry figure of 4.5 times per year, in spite of the fact that its product line for knitted wear contained nearly 500 different color and style combinations.

As Luciano Benetton remarked in an interview with an American business journalist, "We have kept the same strategy all along—to put fashion on an industrial level. Most of the rest of Italian fashion is still on an artisan level."[4]

Manufacturing Organization

Benetton relied heavily on internally and externally decentralized operations. Its internal decentralization involved nine Benetton facilities: seven in Italy, one in France, and one in Scotland, employing about 1,700 people. Operations performed at the seven Italian locations, along with the associated flow of material,

4. Labich, "Benetton Takes on the World," p. 116.

are shown in *Exhibit 3*. All thread was received at the Cusignana warehouse (about 12 miles from Ponzano) and then shipped to various factories. Textile fabrics were shipped by suppliers directly to Benetton's plants, including those of two of its contractors.

Each factory in the group differed in size and functions performed. For example, some woolen knitwear was produced in Ponzano (all processes), some in Resana (chemical treatment and finishing), and some in Reggio Emilia and Monzambano (knitting and finishing). Some manufactured items (those in *tintura d' al greggio,* or undyed form) were then returned to Ponzano for dyeing and reshipment to the warehouse in Cusignana. Ready-made material for cotton garments was shipped to the Cusignana factory, assembled there, and stocked in the central warehouse. Summer cotton shirts, however, were produced in Fontane, where only a part of the manufacturing was done internally. Jeans were the only product category manufactured almost entirely outside Benetton's factories. However, final stages providing necessary controls were centralized in the Cusignana factory.

Functions performed and products made at Benetton's foreign factories differed as well. For example, the plant in Scotland manufactured only items knitted of cashmere for distribution through some 20 shops operated under the name Casa di Hogg, in Italy, with no association with Benetton's name. Another plant at Troyes, France, produced only woolen garments for distribution to a portion of the French retail stores. These garments accounted for only about 5% of Benetton's total sales, and none required dyeing. The construction of a company-owned wool-spinning mill that could supply about 20% of Benetton's needs was in the planning stage. *Exhibit 4* contains selected data on Benetton's factories.

In addition, Benetton utilized a network of about 220 production units, either subcontractors or groupers, that employed a total of about 10,000 people. Most were located near Benetton's production facilities in northeast Italy at Ponzano Veneto, Cusignana, and Fontane; some were being developed near other plants as well. Subcontractors and groupers performed about 40% of the company's knitting of wool, 60% of the work of assembling garments, and 20% of the finishing operations. Typically, the more complex garments were produced internally in Benetton's factories. Most of the wool was cut and dyed in Benetton's plants.

The contracting network on which Benetton relied represented a kind of "parallel empire" to the company itself. Many of the contractors were owned in whole or in part by managers of Benetton. According to one trade article:

> The system is now established, and one can say that there is no head or
> manager from Benetton who is not at the same time owner, president, or

director of a leading contracting company in the whole Lombardia-Veneto area (northern Italy).[5]

According to the head of the textile section of the trade union, the production rates among contractors were superior to those of Benetton's factories for comparable jobs. Subcontractors were a second tier in this system of external decentralization. One trade unionist alleged that trade union minimum wages and working hours were adhered to only at the first level of decentralization. There was no doubt that subcontractor costs included lower employment tax payments to the state than those incurred by Benetton. In addition to other benefits, the contracting network allowed Benetton a flexible production capacity that absorbed most of the fluctuations in demand. It also provided work for many relatives of the company's full-time employees.

The production processes required a constant shuttling of work in process from one location to another, a function performed largely by subcontractors. Although this reduced cost savings from external decentralization, it resulted in total production costs for woolen items that were perhaps 85% of those of European producers of garments of comparable quality, and were on a par with costs in the Far East. More important, it reduced Benetton's risk from business fluctuations.

Still other functions were centralized at the company's headquarters. Technical research and planning, for example, were carried out at Ponzano Veneto. Giuliana Benetton supervised product planning and design as well as the acquisition and exploitation of necessary patents and rights.

All purchasing was done at Ponzano Veneto. Wool was bought in spools from Italian producers. Material for newer items in the product line was acquired in more nearly finished form. Cotton was purchased already woven. Velvet arrived already dyed and ready for cutting. And the pre-dyed cloth for jeans, introduced by the company in 1972, was wholly imported from the United States. Cutting was done on the basis of layouts produced by computer at Ponzano.

The Supply Cycle

The large volume of business done by the company required that production planning for woven cotton and woolen items start far in advance of shipment to the stores. For example, for the spring-summer major line to be introduced in the stores in early January, final designs were prepared in February and early

---

5. Giuseppe Cosentino, "The Benetton Case—The Tip of the Iceberg," *Panorama*, December 15, 1982.

March, as shown in *Exhibit 5*. Samples of each of the 600 items in the total collection were assembled. In April, about a fourth of the items were eliminated in a "pre-presentation" meeting between Giuliana Benetton, Benetton's product and manufacturing managers, and several of the company's 70 agents. The remaining items were then produced in small quantities for presentation by area managers to agents and by agents to their individual clients (store owners) in a process that extended from mid-May to mid-July. Within two weeks after the agents collected the first orders from franchisees in early June, a rough production plan for the season, by fabrics and styles, was "exploded" from the first 5% to 10% of total orders. This allowed time for the placement of final orders for purchased threads and garments as well as negotiations with subcontractors for changes in subcontracted volumes. All this was done prior to the start of production of basic retail stocks early in July, in advance of the company's three- to four-week vacation in August.

As orders for basic stocks were received from agents, they were assigned reserved slots in the rough production plan by fabric, style, color, and individual store. These orders were produced for delivery to stores from early November through late May for a sales season beginning early in January in the stores. They were scheduled so that each store could present 80% to 90% of all items (fabrics, styles, and colors) in its basic collection at the start of the selling season. Other items and remaining quantities ordered arrived at the stores during the season.

Because Benetton required its clients to commit themselves to specific orders seven months before the start of the selling season, it provided several opportunities for franchisees to adjust the actual items presented to their customers. From August through early December, as they gathered more information about color preferences, clients and agents were allowed to specify colors for woven items held in *greggio* up to that point, with a limit of 30% of the total orders for woolen items on such orders. During this period, Benetton's product managers negotiated with agents to encourage them to concentrate their orders on the most popular items.

A second process, called the "flash collection," added about 50 items to each season's product line based on early customer requests for fabric-style-color combinations not found in the store. This occurred in January for the spring-summer collection. It required Benetton's product and manufacturing managers and a subset of agents to analyze requests prior to the presentation of the flash collection to the stores.

A third process, "reassortment," involved the acceptance of additional orders for rapid delivery later in the selling season, approximately March for the spring-summer collection. Fill-in reassortment orders were processed for store delivery roughly five weeks from the date of their receipt at Benetton. This process was made available for only a small number of items determined through negotiation between Benetton's product managers and agents. Because it dyed gray garments, Benetton's plant at Ponzano had the capability to fill an order within seven days of its receipt from an agent. This practice was discouraged because it often resulted in dye batches smaller than vat capacity and interfered with long-standing production plans.

Major collections were planned so that about 80% of a season's total sales volume was represented by the basic collection, less than 10% by the flash collection, and less than 10% by reassortment. The remaining sales were realized from a small "cruise" collection presented in the spring and a small "Christmas" collection presented in the fall. Sales of the fall-winter collection approximated 60% of a typical year's sales volume.

Production of the basic spring-summer collection ended in late April for final deliveries to stores by late May, by which time production for the following season's fall-winter collection was well under way.

Payments to subcontractors, a major cash outflow, were made 70 days after the end of the month in which production occurred or, in the case of the spring-summer collection, in October. Collections from retail franchisees were based on a season beginning date of March 30 for the spring-summer season, with one-third of payment due 30, 60, and 90 days after that date or the date of actual receipt of merchandise. This procedure was designed to minimize retailers' investment in inventories.

MARKETING

From the beginning, Benetton's marketing strategy had been based on the development of fashionable but casual knitted garments featuring bright colors, in contrast with much of what was then available in European stores. At that time, colors such as pink and turquoise were staples only in Benetton's product line and continued to be popular items.

Product Development

The basic philosophy behind the design of products had varied little over the years. According to one report:

> The company has no plans to vary the design philosophy behind its product line. Though Giuliana has hired designers from top firms all over the world and follows major fashion trends, she contends that she has merely enlarged

on her original insight that young, free-spending customers will always be attracted to brilliant reds and greens and a variety of pastels. "You never discover a new design," she says. "You merely make small changes in the old ones."[6]

The number of product lines had, however, been expanded in recent years in order to retail Benetton products under different labels and store names. Thus, a "012 Benetton" line of children's wear had been developed for presentation in shops decorated with stuffed animals and rainbows. "Jeans West" shops carried Benetton knitwear and trousers targeted to the youth market. Stores carrying Benetton knitwear and trousers with higher fashion content for men and women were named "My Market." A line of items was produced for the "Sisley" label, directed to sophisticated men and presented in stores with that name. Although there was no direct equivalent to Sisley for women, shops with the "Mercerie" name stocked some items aimed at a similar market segment, but bearing the Benetton label. Shops under all of these names were intended for central locations in European cities. In addition, a number of shops named "Tomato" had been opened in outlying urban areas to carry knitwear and trousers aimed at the youth market. They featured flashing lights and rock music.

In fact, for each trade name, the appropriate style of furniture and equipment, color of lighting, type of music, and appropriate sex, age, and dress style for salespeople was selected to attract the targeted clientele.

Overall, Benetton shops were identified by more than 10 different names, most of which were not known outside Italy. In spite of the multiplicity of names for stores, it was estimated that during 1982, 70% of total sales were made under the Benetton label and 25% under the 012 Benetton label. However, the company's product list contained more than 2,000 different item-label combinations.

Pricing

The median retail price of Benetton garments in 1982 was about $20. Prices ranged from under $10 for a pair of socks to $120 for a high-fashion denim jacket. While opinions differed, prices generally were considered lower than those of competitors for the quality of product, which was nearly always offered in natural wool or cotton. The price-quality combination, high-fashion content, and array of bright colors were at the core of the company's retailing strategy.

6. Labich, "Benetton Takes on the World," p. 115.

Distribution

As its product line developed, Benetton began searching for ways of gaining control over its channels of distribution.

Benetton had achieved its retail distribution through an unusual arrangement with agents in Italy and other European countries. According to one company marketing executive, the use of the term "franchising" in describing Benetton was a misnomer. Usually through verbal agreement, company agents were assigned large territories in which to encourage development of Benetton retail outlets. They would in turn establish partnerships with smaller investors and store operators who had the "Benetton mentality." An agent might supervise and hold an interest in a number of stores. Late in 1982, Benetton conducted its business with 70 such agents. Agents received a 4% commission on the factory sales of goods sold through their retail outlets, in addition to their share of profits from the stores in which they held ownership.

For their part, agents recruited and helped train individual store operators, displayed the Benetton collection to store operators in their regions, assembled orders for the initial stock and stock reordered during each season, and generally supervised the merchandising and pricing at the stores. Benetton's relationship with agents was based on trust. Agents rarely had to be replaced for failure to meet expectations.

Store owners were not required to pay Benetton a fee for use of its name, nor did they pay a royalty based on a percentage of sales or profits. But they were required to carry only Benetton merchandise, maintain a minimum sales level (equivalent to orders for about 3,500 garments per year), adhere to suggested markups of about 80% from cost, pay for their orders according to the preset schedule described earlier, and in the words of one Benetton manager, develop "an understanding of Benetton's way of doing business."

In a 1982 interview, Luciano Benetton had provided some insight into the company's strategy for developing shop owners:

> We have caused a [new] type of retailer to become important, who until the day before was perhaps a florist or a hairdresser. His prior career was of no importance, but he had to have the right spirit to work in a Benetton shop.

The ideal Benetton retailer was young and showed potential for "growing with Benetton."

All Benetton outlets were required to use Benetton fixtures and to follow basic merchandising concepts. The most important of these was that all merchandise was to be displayed on open shelves accessible to customers, who could touch it and try it on. The open displays in an otherwise undecorated space created an impression of great color and fashion to the window-shopping customer. This was considered especially effective with the 19- to 25-year-old market, toward which Benetton had directed its European marketing efforts.

Benetton clients were expected to maintain storage facilities that, in combination with their store shelves, could accommodate 30% to 40% of a season's sales in addition to merchandise still being sold from the preceding season. Typically, such storage consisted of small basement rooms under the retail outlets. (The company's written agreement with a client, when it existed, usually was limited to the use and protection of Benetton's trademark.)

Benetton had given a great deal of attention to store location, emphasizing areas of high traffic for young adults. Luciano Benetton and his assistants selected European locations according to a pattern of market development in which the first store in a given market often was sited in a high-prestige location. According to one legend in the company, it had taken Benetton six years to find the proper location for one shop in Turin. Once the site for a lead store had been selected and developed, the company tried to blanket the area around it with shops offering Benetton's merchandise.

As many as six different shops, of which no more than two might be called Benetton, could be located within several city blocks of one another. The company had 46 shops in Milan, Italy, alone. While their layout was adapted to fit desirable sites, all were much smaller and had several characteristics that set them apart from other young women's casual apparel shops, as suggested by the comparative profiles shown in *Exhibit 6*. The layout of a typical Benetton shop is shown in *Exhibit 7*.

By the end of 1982, shops were being opened in Europe at the rate of one every working day. Of the more than 1,800 shops in operation at the time in Europe, 1,165 were located in Italy alone. (See *Exhibit 8* for a list of shops by type and location.) According to one company executive, while many shops had been moved, "none had been closed."

While Benetton retail shops differed, depending on available real estate, they all carried only Benetton products, even though only 20 of Benetton's stores outside Italy were owned by the company.

Retailers were expected to follow guidelines for offering sale merchandise. These were established and managed by agents in each region, who also moved merchandise among shops as sales patterns developed. As a result, the typical level of markdowns as a percentage of sales for a Benetton retail outlet was low, approximating 7% of a retailer's prescribed initial margin. The "model" for Benetton retail store operations was that a store would have no more or less than 15% of a season's merchandise as it entered the last two weeks of a season.

This merchandise could then be sold at cost to allow the retailer to present a newly merchandised store to the customer at the start of the next season. Benetton did not accept merchandise returns from its agents or retailers.

Promotion

Benetton relied on location and bright, inviting store appearance for its promotional effort. Window displays often were spare and allowed a clear view of the open shelves of colorful merchandise. In addition, it advertised on European television and in the press, and sponsored sports events.

The company's television spots emphasized the "sport" and "youth" image of the Benetton name. Magazine advertising was used for institutional campaigns and emphasized color and the Benetton "life-style."

Benetton management had invested in sports events throughout much of the company's history, reflecting the Benettons' interests. The company sponsored a top Italian rugby team and a handball team. It had already committed an estimated $2 million to sponsor a race car for the 1983 season of World F-1 auto racing.

These efforts were put forth on behalf of the Benetton name, the only Benetton trade name with enough volume and outlets to support a multinational campaign, and were intended to support the image of a product line aimed at the active young adult or child. Benetton had spent more than twice as much for advertising in Italy as its nearest European competitor, Maglificio Piave, manufacturer of the Stefanel brand of clothing. More than two-thirds of Benetton's 1981 advertising budget for Italy, 955 million lire, was spent for magazine advertising.

LOGISTICS

Logistics played an important role in the Benetton strategy. Starting at the retail level, stores carrying Benetton products were designed with limited storage space for back-up stocks. Upon arrival at the store, merchandise usually was checked and placed directly on the display shelves. This required that shipments to stores be planned and executed according to a carefully planned schedule.

Agents managed the replenishment process by collecting and assembling orders from individual stores and relaying them electronically to Villorba, where directions were given for orders to be manufactured. In principle, Benetton did not manufacture anything without an order in hand. The company could have merchandise at the retail site in Europe no more than five weeks from the transmission of an agent's order. (This contrasted with the shipment of a season's initial assortment, for which production began 6 months and ended 40 days in advance of the display of merchandise in the stores.)

All merchandise was premarked in the currency of the country of destination, with tickets coded to be processed electronically at the time of the sale. To facilitate replenishment, Benetton had under design two major improvements in the logistics system. An elaborate new information network, relying on automatic cash registers in clusters of 10 shops (each hooked into Benetton's three large Siemens 7865 computing units in Italy and an Olivetti 5330 unit in Paris), had been proposed by Elio Aluffi, managing director of internal operations. It would be capable of instantly recording individual sales in Benetton's European shops. Its cost was estimated to be roughly $7.5 million. Although the network was proposed for implementation by the summer of 1983, several agents had indicated that the new system was not needed.

In addition, Luciano Benetton had on his desk a proposal for the construction of a new 200,000-square-foot central warehousing facility at Castrette, about 12 miles from the Ponzano headquarters, at a cost of about $20 million. The core of this facility would be 10 robot stacker cranes capable of stowing and picking cartons from its stocking capacity of nearly 250,000 boxes of merchandise. Its daily total handling capacity was estimated to be 15,000 boxes (either in or out of the warehouse). With the new warehouse operating by the end of 1984, plans called for a reduction from 40 to 35 days in the minimum lead time required for distribution of orders for each collection.

The number of items per box to be handled at Castrette would vary but would probably average 28. It depended on the size of the order directed to an individual factory where the items would be boxed and shipped to Castrette. No boxes would be opened while at the Castrette warehouse. All were labeled at the factory for use with optical scanners that routed the merchandise through the warehouse. Prices to retailers did not vary on the basis of the number of items per box.

In addition to service improvements, the new warehouse offered the possibility of savings of perhaps 20% on transport costs for finished products. Not only could orders for an individual store be consolidated at Castrette, but they could also be loaded in sequence for store delivery by truck. (All orders were sold at a "store-delivered" price. This price did not vary by destination.) While a detailed analysis of current transportation costs had not been completed, the casewriters estimated that they could be as high as 5% of sales.

With the opening of the Castrette facility, the current warehouse at Cusignana would be closed and all items produced in Italy moved through Castrette.

EUROPEAN COMPETITION

Benetton had experienced increasing competition in Italy and Europe, primarily from firms emulating elements of its strategy. For example, other Italian manufacturers had instituted programs of direct selling by franchising local retailers, but had to gradually abandon their wholesale customers and launch new trademarks.

One, Maglificio Torinese, had, since 1980, been opening shops for the exclusive sales of the Kappa Sport product line specializing in casual sportswear. It now had more than 100 outlets in Italy with plans to extend its sales network to other countries. Maglificio Piave, launching its "Stefanel" trademark in 1979 to replace the Sigma brand formerly sold to wholesalers, already sold through 150 exclusive outlets in Italy and some 30 others throughout Europe.

It was apparent to Benetton's management that its current product lines were reaching the saturation point in the Italian market. As a result of this as well as increasing competition, a growing amount of imported merchandise, and a stagnant economy, Benetton's billings in Italy had leveled out in real terms.

There had been some debate about the importance of other European markets in Benetton's future strategy. As Elio Aluffi, a long-time Benetton employee who was named head of internal operations, had said: "We haven't completed our work yet in Europe. We have to consolidate that market."[7]

But while there was still significant potential for Benetton in the rest of Europe, with expected annual increases in sales of 15% resulting from expanded efforts in England, Belgium, and the Netherlands, it appeared that potential margins to be obtained from incremental sales in Europe were lower than those that might be realized in new markets like Japan and the United States. As a result, the Benettons and their senior managers were studying alternatives for developing the U.S. market, where they felt they might open 1,000 or more retail outlets.

U.S. STRATEGY

Many issues had been raised at Benetton in the process of developing alternatives for serving the U.S. market. Company managers wondered whether the formula so successful in Italy could be applied in the United States, and if it couldn't, whether Benetton would enjoy the competitive advantage that was responsible for its success in Europe.

7. Labich, "Benetton Takes on the World," p. 118.

Several elements of the U.S. market were particularly worrisome. First, its sheer size could make it difficult for Benetton to accommodate the volume of potential sales it might enjoy. Second, the Benetton name and its associated labels were unknown except among those who had traveled in Europe. There was already formidable U.S. competition, primarily from well-established manufacturers and retailers of casual wear. Levi Strauss, with 1982 sales of about $2.3 billion, not only manufactured jeans and related items, but also operated retail stores, budgeting more than $100 million each year for advertising and promotion. In addition, several large retail chains carried a great deal of merchandise aimed at Benetton's prime markets, including The Limited (with approximately 750 retail stores), Charming Shops (260 stores), Petrie (nearly 800 stores), and Miller-Wohl (nearly 300 stores). While none of these competitors manufactured garments, many offered products produced with their labels. And several had used extensive media advertising to solidify their position; The Limited alone was thought to have an annual advertising budget of $20 million. All owned and controlled their own stores, mostly in modern shopping malls (largely non-existent in many parts of Europe), with a size and sales volume per store considerably larger than Benetton's.

Nevertheless, Benetton could potentially capitalize on the strong image of Italian design and the growing popularity of Italian fashion in the United States. And its nontraditional (for the United States) approach to retailing might enable it to find good store locations that competitors couldn't utilize.

Entry into the U.S. market prompted discussion about the product mix. For example, there was some support for upgrading the target market, average sales points, and dollar margins per item for a U.S. strategy. This could be centered around the Sisley and Mercerie merchandise lines for men and women. Consistent with this long-term target, the INVEP Group in 1981 had acquired a 50% interest in an Italian fashion house, Fiorucci. While the company was not highly profitable, the acquisition gave the Benettons entry into higher fashion markets, with potential benefits for the INVEP Group's other labels.

On the other hand, it was argued that the company could gain maximum penetration by maintaining its European price points, adjusted only for U.S. import tariffs of 35% of manufactured cost. If this were done, however, little or no additional budget could be used to develop designs especially for the U.S. market.

American preference for easy-to-care-for garments raised questions about the potential attraction of Benetton's natural fibers. Moreover, tastes seemed to be changing more rapidly than in the past. New products made of "plush" (velvet) and heavy knitted cotton had replaced wool among some consumers' preferences. As Luciano Benetton pointed out, however: "Heavy knitted cotton items have played an important part in all our recent collections. In cases such as this a company must be adaptable and ready to respond to the demands of the market."

In the process of developing an appropriate retailing strategy for the United States, several questions had been raised. Should Benetton develop markets as it had in Europe, relying on agents to build and control a retailing network? Twenty regions for U.S. development had been identified on the basis of population and per-capita clothing purchase data. Should Benetton rely on existing or new agents? Nearly all of its agents were from Europe or the Middle East. These agents knew the company and its policies and were trusted by Benetton's management. In addition, an opportunity to participate in the development of the U.S. market could increase their loyalty to the company. On the other hand, many of the existing agents did not know the U.S. market well, and several already had heavy work loads.

The company also had to decide whether to open "lead" stores displaying the Benetton name at prestigious addresses before blanketing a metropolitan area with numerous outlets. Alternatively, Benetton could rely on department stores to provide space for Benetton products until the name became better known in the United States. At least two leading U.S. department store organizations, Macy's and Associated Dry Goods, had approached Benetton with proposals to open small Benetton boutiques in their department stores, if necessary under the agent arrangement. However, both had desired an exclusive agreement with Benetton or its agents. Should a new type of retailing outlet be designed altogether? In addressing this last question, Luciano Benetton commented:

> The idea we are looking for would represent a new era in the point-of-sale development. For instance, instead of small structures, we would have larger retail areas in which we would present more diverse merchandise. . . . Small shops like our conventional points of sale cannot serve as points of reference where people meet or listen to music. Today the necessity is felt, abroad as in Italy, for large spaces where consumers can meet.

Even Benetton's small shops required an average investment of $70,000 each for the United States. This investment included $15,000 to $20,000 for pre-work to condition the space for Benetton's fixtures; about $40,000 for the fixtures; and $5,000 to $15,000 for transportation of the fixtures from Italy, depending on whether surface or air transport was used. Well-run stores required no investment in inventory and no "key money" to obtain desirable retail locations.

It was clear that Benetton could not launch a full-scale advertising program for the United States that was similar to its European campaign. But Benetton's retailers would expect some promotional effort. It was estimated that $2 million was the minimum annual advertising budget required just to achieve visibility in the United States. Questions remained, however, as to how to allocate a budget of that size to various media.

How would a new U.S. market be supported operationally? Alternatives under consideration were: (1) developing a new plant in the United States with dyeing facilities and a warehouse; (2) opening only a new warehouse to stock finished product shipped from the Ponzano factory; or (3) directly distributing to U.S. retail sites from Europe, using either conventional forms of communication or an extended computer linked up with product shipment by air.

The first of these options would require a capital investment of about $10 million and labor costs perhaps 50% higher than at the Ponzano plant. More important, it would be difficult to manage the crucial dyeing operation at a foreign site. Regardless of whether a new dyeing facility was opened in the United States, the company assumed that it could not afford to source "gray" garments in the United States at anywhere near the cost it experienced in Italy. Thus, added costs of shipping such garments by surface or air would be incurred anyway, with a difference of about three weeks in total transit time for the two methods. It was estimated that delivery by air to the United States in semifinished or finished form would add perhaps 50% to the current average of transportation costs for garments shipped in Europe or by surface means across the Atlantic Ocean.

The second alternative would make an investment in U.S. plant capacity unnecessary for the time being. But Benetton would lose inventory savings of the kind enjoyed in Europe, and its new warehouse at Castrette already could provide sufficient capacity to serve both the U.S. and European markets.

The third alternative would allow Benetton to delay significant commitments of capital to plant or inventory but would require increased transportation costs even if no computer link-up were attempted. The link-up might pay for itself in three years by providing more timely information.

Nor was entry into the U.S. market the only new venture confronting Benetton's management. Plans were under way to develop the Japanese market as well. And the family was reported to be considering a joint venture with a French perfume manufacturer to produce a new line of Benetton perfumes and cosmetics.

Benetton was reported to be having difficulties with its recent acquisition of an Italian shoe manufacturer, Calza Turificio di Varese, which manufactured one million pairs of shoes per year; it had 86 retail shops and 1982 sales of about $40 million. Benetton had bought a 70% interest in it for $12 million in June 1982. Although this had not dimmed management's enthusiasm for adding Benetton shoes to its retail lines, Luciano Benetton commented that "as an experience, it has been quite interesting. But the factory is old and there have been many problems."[8]

In response to an interviewer who had questioned the acquisition of the shoe manufacturer, Luciano Benetton replied:

I don't agree, because there are too many logical relationships. We are known for woolen knitwear. And when we started making trousers, we thought this already might be a different sector. Instead, it was coordinated exactly as we can coordinate the shoes. . . . If the common denominator is clothing, we will also have to produce evening dresses. But we don't because ours is the "casual" market segment comprising clothing without too much elegance for specific hours of the day.

By the end of 1982, Benetton had already taken action on a number of issues that concerned the development of the U.S. market. But other issues remained that could greatly affect the company's U.S. strategy.

8. Labich, "Benetton Takes on the World," p. 119.

Exhibit 1

Exhibit 1

Income Statements for the Benetton Group, 1981 and 1982

	1981[a]		1982	
	(in billions of lire)	(as % of adjusted billings)	(in billions of lire)	(as % of adjusted billings)
Net consolidated billings	373.7	92.9%	404.1	100.6%
= adjustments	+28.4	+7.1	−2.4	−.6
Adjusted billings	402.1	100.0	401.7	100.0
Expenses:				
Purchases	(157.4)	(39.1)	(134.5)	(33.5)
Labor costs	(21.1)	(5.2)	(26.4)	(6.6)
Other costs[b]	(148.0)	(36.7)	(175.4)	(43.7)
Balance	75.6	19.0	65.4	16.2
Less financial charges	(15.1)	(3.8)	(20.7)	(5.2)
Plus interest income	2.4	.6	3.5	.9
Less miscellaneous charges	(5.2)	(1.3)	(6.3)	(1.6)
Plus miscellaneous income	6.5	1.6	7.4	1.8
Less depreciation of multi-annual charges[c]	(9.1)	(2.3)	(6.3)	(1.6)
Less equipment and plant write-offs	(10.4)	(2.6)	(12.6)	(3.1)
Gross profit before reserves and transfers	44.7	11.2%	30.4	7.4%
Less various reserves	(9.8)[d]	(2.4)	(1.7)[e]	(.4)
Less losses on transfers of assets	(.1)	—	(.1)	—
Plus gains on transfers of assets	.7	.2	.3	.1
Plus capitalized financial charges	—	—	—	—
Gross profit before taxes	35.5	9.0%	28.9	7.1%
Less taxes	(16.3)	(4.1)	(12.6)	(3.1)
Net profit	19.2[f]	4.9%	16.3[f]	4.0%

[a]In evaluating 1981 data, please note that they cover 18 months for the main operating company (Benetton SpA).

[b]Of which royalties of 10.0 billion lire in 1981 and 13.0 billion lire in 1982 were paid to INVEP. Roughly 80% of these costs represented payments to Benetton's manufacturer-contractors.

[c]Including depreciation of start-up costs.

[d]Of which 4.0 billion lire was placed in reserves for future risks and 4.0 billion lire was placed in reserves for reinvestment funds (according to Law No. 675–1977).

[e]Of which 1.4 billion lire of exchange fluctuation reserves were increased by Benetton and Benetton Lana.

[f]For purposes of rough calculations, the average exchange rate for the dollar against the lira was about $1 = 1,150 lire in 1981 and $1 = 1,300 lire in 1982.

Exhibit 2

Consolidated Balance Sheets of the Benetton Group, at December 31, 1981, and December 31, 1982 (in billions of lire)[a]

Account	1981	1982
Cash	12.8	3.4
Net commercial credits	85.5	140.1
Remainders of the period	52.0	49.6
Financial credits to the Holding Society	9.7	6.7
Other current active accounts	11.5	25.6
Gross current assets (1)	171.5	225.4
Suppliers (accounts payable)	65.3	72.6
Negative balances with banks	23.2	47.3
Financial debits to the Holding Society	1.7	—
Other current debits	18.8	16.9
Current debits (2)	109.0	136.8
Current net assets (1 − 2) = (3)	62.5	88.6
Gross technical investments	57.8	71.9
Less depreciation	(10.4)	(22.6)
Net technical investments	47.4	49.3
Preemptions for investments	.4	8.4
Financing for third parties	—	—
Net investments (4)	47.8	57.7
Multiannual charges (5)	1.2	2.5
Start-up charges (6)	16.3	10.5
Medium- and long-term passive funds:		
Guaranteed loans	5.1	4.6
Nonguaranteed loans	.1	47.7
Employees' pension fund	2.8	3.7
Tax fund	16.2	.3
Currency fluctuation fund	1.1	2.0
Total, medium- and long-term passive funds (7)	25.3	58.3
Net capital (3)+(4)+(5)+(6)−(7)	102.5	101.0

[a]Exchange rates were $1 = 1,212 lire on December 31, 1981, and $1 = 1,382 lire on December 31, 1982.

BENETTON (A)
Exhibit 3
Work Flow through Benetton's Factories and Subcontractors

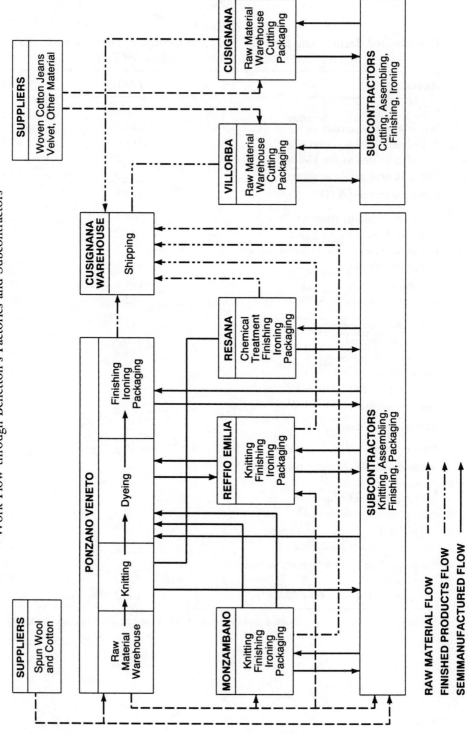

RAW MATERIAL FLOW -------

FINISHED PRODUCTS FLOW -·-·-·-

SEMIMANUFACTURED FLOW ———

Exhibit 4
Selected Data for Benetton's Facilities, December 1982

Company Name	Location	Land and Building Surface in Square Meters[a]		Number of Employees	Product (Processes)
Benetton Lana	Ponzano Veneto	39,720[b]	(19,901)[b]	346	Wool knitwear
Benetton Lana	Rosana	20,440	(3,233)	138	Wool knitwear
Benetton Lana	Mozambino	6,500	(4,751)	180	Wool knitwear
Benetton Lana	Quattro Castella	23,542	(3,523)	77	Wool knitwear
Benetton Cotone	Fontane	16,852	(5,794)	94	Cotton overwear
Benetton Cotone	Villorba	13,865	(14,100)	130	Cotton overwear
Benetton Jeans	Cusignana	65,665[c]	(40,417)[c]	274	Trousers, jeans
Benetton[d]	Castrette	—[c]	—[c]	—	
Benetton	Ponzano Veneto	—	—	247[f]	Control, management
Benetton	Cusignana	—	—	51	Control, management
Totals		186,584	(91,719)	1,537	

[a]One square meter equals approximately 10 square feet. Land surface is indicated in the left-hand column. The portion of land surface devoted to buildings is indicated in parentheses in the right-hand column.

[b]Includes the area of the technical offices in Ponzano Veneto rented by Benetton.

[c]Includes the area of the factory rented by Benetton.

[d]The company also owned the Villa Minelli, located in Ponzano Veneto. This was an historical building used for management offices situated on 37,935 square meters of land with a floor space of 5,049 square meters.

[e]Construction of an industrial complex on this piece of land was started in 1982. Warehousing for finished products, now located at Cusignana in the factory owned by Benetton Jeans, was to be moved here.

[f]Including the employees at Villa Minelli.

Exhibit 5
Operating Cycle, Benetton Group

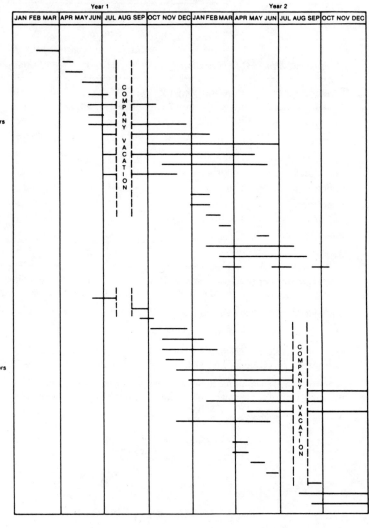

Exhibit 6
Comparative Profiles for Typical Benetton Store, European Young Women's
Apparel Store, and American Specialty Chain Store for Young Women's Apparel

Item	Typical Benetton Store[a]	Store of European Competition	American Specialty Chain Store[a]
Annual sales ($)	$305,000	$150,000	$400,000
Selling space (sq. ft.)	500	1,200	2,700
Storage space (sq. ft.)	200	300	300
Type of location	Downtown Street	Downtown Street	Suburban Shopping Mall
Initial margins, as % of sales price	44%	50%	57%
Realized margins, as % of sales price	37%	45%	45%
Median sales price per unit ($)	$18	$40	$23[b]
Average size per transaction ($)	$26	$50	$35[b]
Employee hours per week	90	200	230
Selling hours per week	45	45	76
Average store inventory, at cost[c]	$40,000	$30,000	$50,000
Expense categories, as a % of sales:			
Cost of goods sold	61%	55%	55%
Labor	7	29	13
Occupancy (rent and utilities)	5	7	10
Other (including overhead)	8	6	10
Total	81%	97%	88%
Net profit before tax	19%	3%	12%

[a]Based on casewriters' estimates.

[b]These figures had risen with the introduction of designers' clothing for casual wear. Stores not carrying such clothing realized average prices of perhaps $18 per garment. Stores featuring such clothing averaged as much as $55 per item for lines of clothing comparable to those sold by Benetton.

[c]Estimated on the basis of a store capacity of 2,000 pieces plus a back-up stock varying between 500 pieces toward the end of one season and 2,500 pieces at the beginning of the next.

Exhibit 7
Typical Layout of a Benetton Retail Store

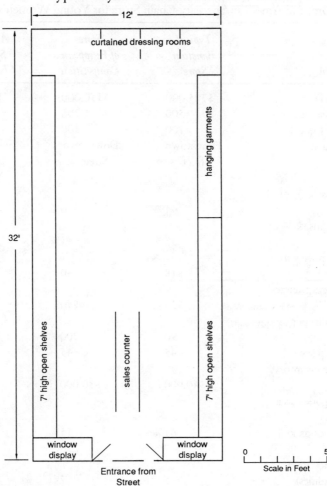

NOTE: If a Benetton and Benetton 012 store were located next to one another, they might be connected by an interior doorway.

Exhibit 8
Location of Benetton Stores by Country and Product Line, December 1982

Country	Benetton[a]	Number of Stores, by Product Line		
		012[b]	Sisley[c]	Total
Italy[d]	659	380	126	1,165
France	198	80	5	283
Germany	138	30	—	168
Switzerland	53	10	3	66
United Kingdom	35	8	1	44
Austria	28	8	—	36
Belgium	12	2	—	14
Ireland	8	5	1	14
Sweden	9	4	—	13
Holland	8	3	—	11
Spain	9	—	—	9
Other	79	15	—	94
	1,236	545	136	1,917

[a] Figures for Benetton in Italy included stores operated under the names of Tomato, Mercerie, My Market, Fantomex, Jeans West, Puloveria, and several others.

[b] The 012 stores carried children's clothing.

[c] The Sisley stores specialized in fashion-oriented casual wear for men.

[d] Figures for Italy included "franchised affiliates," store sites developed and supervised by agents in the manner described in the case, and "third-party shops," which, although not bound by agreements, adopted the same sales formula as that of the affiliates. Many of the latter had been converted to franchised affiliates, leaving only about 400 third-party shops by the end of 1982. At its peak in 1978, the number of company-owned shops reached 58; by 1982, there were none in Italy.